KT-473-411

Introduction to Criminology

Introduction to Criminology

Theories, Methods, and Criminal Behavior

Fifth Edition

Frank E. Hagan
Mercyhurst College

WADSWORTH
THOMSON LEARNING™

Australia • Canada • Mexico • Singapore
Spain • United Kingdom • United States

Executive Editor, Criminal Justice: Sabra Horne
Acquisitions Editor: Shelley Murphy
Development Editor: Terri Edwards
Assistant Editor: Dawn Mesa
Editorial Assistant: Lee McCracken
Marketing Manager: Jennifer Somerville
Marketing Assistant: Karyl Davis
Advertising Project Manager: Bryan Vann
Technology Project Manager: Susan Devanna
Project Manager: Teri Hyde
Print Buyer: Tandra Jorgensen
Permissions Editor: Joohee Lee
Production Service: Shepherd, Inc.
Photo Researcher: Mary Reeg
Copy Editor: Colleen Yonda
Cover Designer: Laurie Anderson
Cover Image: Dohemy Dance by Peter Foley. Mixed Media, © Peter Foley. Courtesy the artist
Cover Printer: R. R. Donnelley, Willard
Compositor: Shepherd, Inc.
Printer: R.R. Donnelley, Willard

Printed in the United States of America
3 4 5 6 7 05 04

Library of Congress Cataloging-in-Publication Data

Hagan, Frank E.
Introduction to criminology : theories, methods, and criminal behavior / Frank E. Hagan.-- 5th ed.
p.cm.
Includes bibliographical references and indexes.
ISBN 0-534-53444-9
1. Criminology. 2. Criminology--United States. 1. Title

HV605. H26 2002
364--dc21 2001026168

Wadsworth/Thomson Learning
10 Davis Drive
Belmont, CA 94002-3098
USA

For more information about our products, contact us:
Thomson Learning Academic Resource Center
1-800-423-0563
http://www.wadsworth.com

International Headquarters
Thomson Learning
International Division
290 Harbor Drive, 2nd Floor
Stamford, CT 06902-7477
USA

UK/Europe/Middle East/South Africa
Thomson Learning
Berkshire House
168-173 High Holborn
London WC1V 7AA
United Kingdom

Asia
Thomson Learning
60 Albert Street, #15-01
Albert Complex
Singapore 189969

Canada
Nelson Thomson Learning
1120 Birchmount Road
Toronto, Ontario M1K 5G4
Canada

Contents in Brief

Contents

Preface

This fifth edition maintains the purpose of the original text: to serve the needs of instructors in criminology who wish to avoid the excessively legal and crime-control orientation of many recent textbooks. Certainly, some familiarity with the legal and criminal-justice systems is both necessary and desirable, but in emphasizing these elements some introductory texts give short shrift to the real and vital core of criminology—theory, method, and criminal behavior. To overstress detailed analyses of social control agencies while neglecting to provide adequate descriptions of criminal activity produces a text that would more accurately be called an *Introduction to Criminal Justice Systems.* An *Introduction to Criminology,* by contrast, should offer thorough descriptions and explanations of criminal behavior, because that is the basis on which effective social policy and social agencies must be developed.

No social science inquiry is entirely unbiased or value-free, but in this text the author has attempted to present an eclectic theoretical view. If a bias remains, however, it is best described as liberal/conflict. The chapter sequence has been amended according to suggestions from reviewers and users, but most instructors have their own organizational preferences and will adapt the book to their own needs.

Chapter 1 presents a general introduction to the study of criminology, and Chapter 2 follows with an examination of research methods. This identifies and evaluates the sources of data on crime and criminals. Chapter 3 then describes general patterns and variations in crime.

Chapters 4 through 6 present theoretical explanations of crime and criminality. Chapter 6 represents an expansion of the treatment of theories in response to reviewer suggestions. In Chapters 7–14, the text offers a closer look at specific forms of criminal behavior, using a greatly expanded and modified version of Marshall Clinard and Richard Quinney's criminal behavior systems typology.

Chapter 7 considers violent criminal behavior—murder, assault, rape, robbery, domestic violence, and drunk driving—crimes that do physical, psychological, and economic harm to their victims and threaten the social fabric by creating a climate of fear.

Chapter 9 compares and contrasts occasional and conventional property crime. Occasional crime, committed sporadically and irregularly, is opportunistic; conventional crime (e.g., burglary, larceny), committed on an ongoing and regular basis, constitutes serious commitment to criminal life.

In Chapter 10 professional crime and criminals are presented. These are committed, sophisticated criminals—for example, con artists, "cannons" (pickpockets), and "boosters" (shoplifters). Emerging patterns in professional crime are discussed, including art theft, boiler room fraud, oil and gas lease lottery scams, and franchise fraud. Chapters 10 and 11 cover "white collar" crime, dividing it into "occupational crime" and "organization/corporate crime." These crimes are the most costly to society, but the laws against them are the least strictly enforced. Political crime, committed by or against a government for ideological reasons, is the subject of Chapter 12. Chapter 13 delves into the changing world of organized (syndicate) crime. Chapter 14 explores public order crime—vice-related or "victimless" crime as well as speculates on the future of crime and on possible social policy responses.

Besides updating theories and crime data, there are a variety of new materials that have been added to this edition that are too numerous to mention. These include: The FBI Top Ten Fugitive List, Crimes of the Century, What Works in Criminal Justice, The Crime Dip, The Nacirema Revisited, American Indians and Crime, Racial Profiling, Shopping Mall Crime, High Risk Colleges, the latest international crime statistics, cyber-crime, Operation Casablanca, and expanded treatment of money laundering. Also included in this edition are: the Taliban War against Women, Presidential Scandals, Human Rights and Terrorism Reports, the Worst Corporations of the 1990s, International Bribery and Corruption, and the Ford Explorer-Firestone Scandal.

An Instructor's Resource Manual is available to assist instructors in using the fifth edition successfully. For each text chapter the manual includes a list of key concepts, a chapter outline, a lecture outline, and discussion questions, as well as a list of recommended readings. In addition, the manual concludes with suggestions for a criminology term paper. A Test Bank of over 1,000 items is available in both a printed format and on IBM-compatible disks. The Test Bank contains true-false and multiple-choice questions, discussion/essay questions, and short answer questions. This edition also features a student study guide authored by Clayton Steenberg of Arkansas State University, Mountain Home as well as a large number of supportive resources available through Wadsworth Publishing.

I want to thank the many people who assisted in this answer endeavor. For their help with the earlier editions, I again thank Jonathan H. Turner (University of California--Riverside); Lawrence F. Travis III (University of Cincinnati); George E. Evans (William Rainy Harper College); John Burian (Moraine Valley Community College); E. Ernest Wood (Edinboro University); and Sylvia Hill (University of the District of Columbia). I would also like to thank the reviewers for this edition who included: the indisputable Stanley Shernock (Norwick University), Peter Kratcowski (Kent State University), Susan Williams (Kansas State University) and Nanette Davis (Western Washington University), and Barbara Perry (Northern Arizona University).

I would like to thank my very first criminology professor Dan Koenig of the University of Victoria. As always, I thank Steve Ferrara for his help in guiding previous editions. For assistance in providing international statistics, I want particularly to thank my former student Phillipe LeJeune, research analyst at the Interpol Secretariat, Lyons, France who was extraordinary in providing the most recent statistics; Carol Kalish of the Bureau of Justice Statistics, for steering me to the latest U.N. figures; and Dr. Odile Frank of the

World Health Organization in Geneva, Switzerland. This edition has benefited from the guidance and support of the criminal justice team at Wadsworth Publishing Company. The author would like express his gratitude to Sabra Horne (Executive Editor), Shelley Murphy (Acquisitions Editor), Teri Hyde (Senior Project Manager), and Peggy Francomb of Shepherd Inc. for their help.

Finally, I would like to express my greatest appreciation to my wife, Mary Ann, whose tireless and patient efforts in typing and editing and whose moral support made completion of this project possible. I dedicate this edition to Mary Ann and to our daughter Shannon and son-in-law Mark Glennon.

Frank E. Hagan

1 INTRODUCTION

VANTAGE POINTS

IN THE NEWS

> Imagine a society of saints, a perfect cloister of exemplary individuals. Crimes, properly so-called, will there be unknown; but faults which appear venial to the layman will create there the same scandal that the ordinary offense does in ordinary consciousness.
>
> —Émile Durkheim, *The Rules of Sociological Method* (1950 [1895]), pp. 68–69

> Crime is a sociopolitical artifact, not a natural phenomenon. . . . We can have as much or as little crime as we please, depending on what we choose to count as criminal.
>
> —Herbert Packer, *The Limits of Criminal Sanction* (1968), p. 364

Criminology

Women are attacked by post-parade crowds in Central Park; terrorists' bombs kill innocent civilians at the World Trade Center and Oklahoma City federal building; two students massacre their fellow students at Columbine High School in Colorado; hackers tap into high security facilities to perform unauthorized functions; and major corporate officials are accused of stealing billions from consumers.

What all of these events have in common is that they refer to various forms of criminal behavior; as we enter the dawn of the twenty-first century, we can only guess what new, unforeseen horrors await us. The field that addresses this issue of crime and criminal behavior and attempts to define, explain, and predict it is criminology.

While criminologists sometimes disagree regarding a proper definition of the field, **criminology** is generally defined as the *science or discipline that studies crime and criminal behavior.* Specifically, the field of criminology concentrates on forms of criminal behavior, the causes of crime, the definition of criminality, and the societal reaction to criminal activity; related areas of inquiry may include juvenile delinquency and victimology (the study of victims). Applied criminology also claims what is labeled as the field of criminal justice: the police, the courts, and corrections. Criminological investigation may probe any or all of these areas. While there is considerable overlap between criminology and criminal justice, criminology shows a greater interest in the causal explanations of crime, and criminal justice is more occupied with practical, applied concerns, such as technical aspects of policing and corrections. In reality, the fields are highly complementary and interrelated, as indicated by overlapping membership in the two professional organizations representative of the fields: the American Society of Criminology and the Academy of Criminal Justice Sciences.

If you tell your friends that you are taking a course in criminology, many will assume that you are a budding Sherlock Holmes, on your way to becoming a master detective trained in investigating crime scenes. That describes the field of *criminalistics* (the scientific evaluation of physical evidence), which is sometimes confused in the media and public mind with criminology. Criminology is more concerned with analyzing the phenomena of crime and criminality, in performing scientifically accurate studies, and in developing sound theoretical explanations of crime and criminal behavior. It is hoped that such criminological knowledge and scientific research can inform and direct public policies to solve some crime problems. The major concentration in this text will be on the central areas of criminal behavior, research methodology, and criminological theory. Other areas will be included only to the degree that they impact on these critical concerns.

Fads and Fashions in Crime

A variety of crimes were of major concern in the past, but appear in modern societies only in old movies on the late show. Train robbery, piracy, stagecoach robbery, cattle rustling, gunfights such as that at the OK Corral, and grave robbery have some modern remnants, but for the most part have disappeared. Some of these practices have reappeared in different forms. In the seventies, South Vietnamese "boat people" attempting to escape from their homeland were robbed, raped, and murdered by Thai pirates. Brinks trucks have replaced stagecoaches, and semitrailer trucks full of prepared beef are hijacked instead of herds of live cattle. Post-Civil War gangs of Wild West robbers such as those of Doc Holliday, Jesse James, the Daltons, Black Bart, the Younger brothers, and Butch Cassidy disappeared with the settlement of the frontier only to reappear on wheels during the Depression of the thirties in the persons of such infamous characters as Dillinger, "Pretty Boy" Floyd, the Barrows, Bonnie Parker, and the Ma Barker gang. Mobile, organized gangs of bank robbers have largely faded into a quaint, unsavory history; they are now replaced by cybercriminals who can commit global electronic robbery.

Skyjacking, a very big problem in the sixties, was virtually eliminated as a result of better security measures, only to reappear in the United States in the early eighties as Cuban refugees attempted to use this method as a means of returning home. Kidnapping, a major concern in the United States in the thirties (as illustrated by the famous Lindbergh case), is less of a concern today despite highly publicized cases such as the Patty Hearst kidnapping and the rash of child kidnappings by noncustodial parents. On the other hand, since the seventies kidnapping has become a major crime in Italy, as best illustrated by the highly publicized kidnapping of billionaire John Paul Getty's grandson; the kidnappers mailed one of the young man's ears to police to impress upon them the seriousness of their intentions. In 1995 in Colombia, a kidnapping was reported every six hours. This was believed to have been precipitated by huge income disparities and inefficient police. The United States, by contrast, has experienced fewer than 12 kidnappings for ransom every year (Brooke, 1995, p. A7). Nostalgic views of the past tend to romanticize bygone violence or suppress its memory. Most apt to be forgotten are conditions of the past that more than match any chronicle of horrors of the present.

IN THE NEWS 1.1 examines the FBI's "*Ten Most Wanted Fugitives*" list.

Scientific Research in Criminology

Many, including practitioners in criminal justice, question the need and usefulness of much criminology research. They wonder why, for instance, after all the myriad research efforts, criminologists are still unable to answer the fundamental question, "What causes crime?" Many research results strike the layperson as irrelevant academic jargon, as intimidating and indecipherable statistics, or as confusing elaborations of what any person with common sense knows anyway. This view exists despite the fact that these research activities are usually conducted at great cost to the taxpayer, and at a time when needed operational programs are being eliminated. Some recent research findings are illustrative:

1. The elderly and females fear crime because they are the most heavily victimized groups.
2. Victims of crime seldom know or recognize their offenders.
3. The typical criminal offender is either unemployed or on welfare.
4. In general, residents of large cities believe that their police are doing a poor job.
5. Blacks and Hispanics are less likely than the population as a whole to report personal crimes to police.
6. Most residents of large cities think that their neighborhoods are not safe.
7. Blacks are overrepresented on death rows across the nation; this overrepresentation is more pronounced in the South than in other regions.
8. Crime is an inevitable accompaniment of complex, populous, and industrialized societies.
9. White collar crime is nonviolent.
10. Regulatory agencies prevent white collar crime.
11. The insanity defense allows many dangerous offenders to escape conviction.

IN THE NEWS 1.1

THE FBI's TEN MOST WANTED FUGITIVES

The year 2000 marked the 50th anniversary of the FBI's "Ten Most Wanted Fugitives" program. Much of the public image of the crime problem is stirred by the media via celebrated cases as well as vehicles such as the Federal Bureau of Investigation's "Ten Most Wanted Fugitives" list.

Figure 1.1 depicts the wanted poster for international terrorist Usama Bin Laden, who is on the FBI's Ten Most Wanted list for planning and supporting terrorist acts against Americans and American facilities. The official list is maintained on the FBI's World Wide Web site (*www.fbi.gov*).

In 1950 a news reporter asked the FBI for the ten worst "tough guys" that they were hunting. The resulting publicity was so good that the list became an official FBI program. It satisfied the public's hunger for details about notorious criminals and served as a means of exposing fugitives and encouraging citizen participation (Glasser, 2000a).

The FBI claims that 134 "Ten Most Wanted Fugitives" have been apprehended as a result of citizen recognition. Perhaps the most memorable case was the arrest of bank robber Willy Sutton when a clothing salesman recognized him on the New York City subway. After the citizen's story was run in the New York Times, mobster Albert Anastasia had the salesman killed because, as he stated, "I hate squealers" (Ibid.).

The list very well reflected the social climate of the time in America. The 1950s list consisted primarily of bank robbers, burglars, and car thieves, while the 1960s featured revolutionaries and radicals. The 1970s list featured organized criminals and terrorists and, while this emphasis continues, serial murderers and drug-related offenders abound in later lists. A recent "Top Ten List," shown in Figure 1.2, features:

Usama Bin Laden—international terrorist

Ramon Eduardo Arellano-Felix—a leader of the Tijuana drug cartel

James Bulger—a Boston organized crime figure wanted for extortion and Racketeer Influence in Corrupt Organization charges

Victor Manuel Gerena—a bank robber who robbed a security company netting $7 million

Glen Stewart Godwin—a murderer and escaped prisoner

James Charles Kopp—a killer of an abortion doctor

Eric Robert Rudolph—killed a police officer and injured over 150 people in a series of bombings including one during the Olympic Games in Atlanta

Hopeton Eric Brown—murder, drug conspiracy, attempted murder of witness

Eric Franklin Rosser—producer, transporter and distributor of child pornography

Donald Eugene Webb—murder of a Pennsylvania police chief

While this list does not feature any women, they have been on the list in the past beginning with Ruth Eisemann-Schier for kidnapping and extortion in 1968. Inclusion of anti-war activists such as Angela Davis and Bernardine Dohrn was greeted with public scorn engendered by growing disenchantment with the Vietnam War.

Now succeeded by television programs such as "America's Most Wanted," the list serves as an interesting chronicle of Americana.

Research Project

Visit the FBI web site and examine the latest "Ten Most Wanted Fugitives" list. Are any of the people the same as in our IN THE NEWS section? If yes, do they differ in any way from the IN THE NEWS list? Are any of them women or white collar criminals?

InfoTrac® College Edition Research

Search the "FBI's Most Wanted List" and discuss either a current fugitive or the history of this list.

FIGURE 1.1 FBI Ten Most Wanted Fugitives—Osama Bin Laden

FBI TEN MOST WANTED FUGITIVE

MURDER OF U.S. NATIONALS OUTSIDE THE UNITED STATES; CONSPIRACY TO MURDER U.S. NATIONALS OUTSIDE THE UNITED STATES; ATTACK ON A FEDERAL FACILITY RESULTING IN DEATH

USAMA BIN LADEN

Date of Photograph Unknown

Aliases: Usama Bin Muhammad Bin Ladin, Shaykh Usama Bin Ladin, the Prince, the Emir, Abu Abdallah, Mujahid Shaykh, Hajj, the Director

DESCRIPTION

Date of Birth:	1957	**Hair:**	Brown
Place of Birth:	Saudi Arabia	**Eyes:**	Brown
Height:	6' 4" to 6' 6"	**Complexion:**	Olive
Weight:	Approximately 160 pounds	**Sex:**	Male
Build:	Thin	**Nationality:**	Saudi Arabian
Occupations:	Unknown		
Remarks:	Leader of a terrorist organization known as Al-Qaeda "The Base". He walks with a cane.		
Scars and Marks:	None		

CAUTION

USAMA BIN LADEN IS WANTED IN CONNECTION WITH THE AUGUST 7, 1998, BOMBINGS OF THE UNITED STATES EMBASSIES IN DAR ES SALAAM, TANZANIA AND NAIROBI, KENYA. THESE ATTACKS KILLED OVER 200 PEOPLE.

CONSIDERED ARMED AND EXTREMELY DANGEROUS

IF YOU HAVE ANY INFORMATION CONCERNING THIS PERSON, PLEASE CONTACT YOUR LOCAL FBI OFFICE OR THE NEAREST U.S. EMBASSY OR CONSULATE.

REWARD

The United States Government is offering a reward of up to $5 million for information leading directly to the apprehension or conviction of Usama Bin Laden.

June 1999

FIGURE 1.2 The FBI's Ten Most Wanted Fugitives

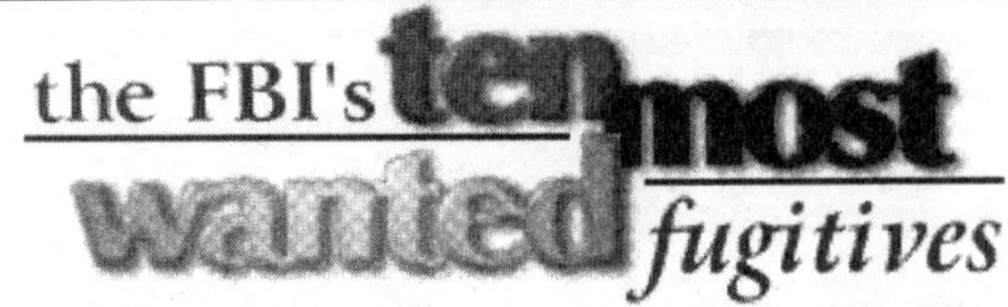

Hopeton Eric Brown

Usama Bin Laden

James J. Bulger
En Espanol

Ramon Eduardo Arellano-Felix

Victor Manuel Gerena

Glen Stewart Godwin

James Charles Kopp

Eric Franklin Rosser

Eric Robert Rudolph

Donald Eugene Webb

The FBI is offering rewards for information leading to the apprehension of Top Ten Most Wanted Fugitives. Check each fugitive page for the specific amount.

Notice: The official FBI Ten Most Wanted Fugitives list is maintained on the FBI World Wide Web Site. This information may be copied and distributed, however, any unauthorized alteration of any portion of the FBI's Ten Most Wanted Fugitives posters is a violation of federal law (18 U.S.C., Section 709). Persons who make or reproduce these alterations are subject to prosecution and, if convicted, shall be fined or imprisoned for not more than one year, or both.

One might respond to all of this by noting that common sense could have told us the same thing, however, sometimes common sense is nonsense. The above statements represent myths regarding crime (Bohm, 1987; Pepinsky and Jesilow, 1984; Walker, 1989; Wright, 1985; and U.S. Department of Justice, 1978), as we discover in subsequent chapters.

Unfortunately, those who criticize the need for scientific crime research tend to follow a convoluted line of argument; if the findings are agreeable to them and if after the fact they appear obvious, those findings are dismissed as simply examples of common sense. On the other hand, if the findings are disagreeable to these critics, they are condemned as unscientific or due to faulty research methods—and common sense tells the critics so. In following a scientific approach and seeking to isolate, define, and explain the critical features of crime and criminal behavior, it is one of the express purposes of this book to question such conventional wisdom or such common sense views. A major purpose of criminology is to supply, through the sound application of research methods, accurate and objective data regarding crime and criminal behavior. Despite the need for accurate criminological data, the per capita investment in justice research as late as the late 1980s in the United States was eight cents, versus thirty-six dollars for health care research (Stewart, 1988, p. v).

The Emergence of Criminology

French sociologist Auguste Comte (1798–1857) viewed the **progression of knowledge** as consisting of *three stages,* from the predominantly *theological* explanations to *metaphysical* (philosophical) approaches to *scientific* explanations (Comte, D. 1857). Prior to the emergence of modern criminal law in the eighteenth century, religion was the primary basis of social control beyond kinship organization. Theological explanations (to be explored more fully in Chapter 4) used supernatural or other-worldly reasons for understanding reality. Recall, for instance, the papal condemnation of Galileo for heretically questioning biblical descriptions of the earth and of astronomy. In the metaphysical stage, philosophy sought secular (worldly) events to provide understanding through a new spirit of inquiry—rationality and logical argument. The **two features of the scientific stage** *combined this rational spirit of investigation with the scientific method,* emphasizing empiricism or experimentation. The scientific orientation emphasized measurement, observation, proof, replication (repetition of observation), and verification (analyzing the validity of observations).

Systematic application of the scientific method enabled humankind to unlock many of the mysteries of the ages. At first, breakthroughs in knowledge took place in the physical sciences; more recently, changes have also begun to occur in the social sciences, such as sociology and criminology. Since the scientific method provided major understanding and ability to predict and control physical reality, the hope is that these same methods are applicable to and will prove useful in the social sciences. While many view criminology as a science, others, such as Sutherland and Cressey, view it as an art similar to medicine, a field based on many sciences and disciplines (Sutherland and Cressey, 1974, pp. 20–21).

Criminology as a field of inquiry had its beginnings in Europe in the late 1700s in the writings of various philosophers, physicians, physical scientists, sociologists, and social scientists. Much of the early theory was heavily couched in biological frameworks that have largely been abandoned by modern American criminology (Gibbons, 1982, p. 16). As will be described in greater detail in Chapter 4, criminology emerged along with eighteenth-century criminal law. In fact, it was the early writings of Cesare Beccaria (1738–1794), especially his famous *Essay on Crimes and Punishment* (1963), which was first published in 1764, that led to the reform of criminal law in Western Europe.

Despite its European roots, most of the major developments in modern criminology took place in the United States. Criminology was closely linked with the development of sociology, gaining its place on the U.S. academic scene between 1920 and 1940. Criminology has been largely a subdiscipline of sociology; even though criminoloy is interdisciplinary in focus, sociologists have devoted the most attention to the issue of criminality. Once regarded by sociology as a prodigal child, criminology has contributed a surprising depth of theory and research. The earliest U.S. textbooks in the field were by Maurice Parmelee, John Gillin, Philip Parsons, and Fred Hayes; but it was the text and later writings of Edwin H. Sutherland, the acknowledged "dean of criminology," that received the most deserved recognition.

Crime and Deviance

Deviance or *deviant behavior* may refer to a broad range of activities that the majority in society may view as eccentric, dangerous, annoying, bizarre, outlandish, gross, abhorrent, and the like. It refers to *behavior that is outside the range of normal societal toleration.* One sociologist questioned a cross section of the public and asked them to list types of people they thought were deviant:

> The sheer range of response predictably included homosexuals, prostitutes, drug addicts, radicals and criminals. But it also included liars, career women, Democrats, reckless drivers, atheists, Christians, suburbanites, the retired, young folks, card players, bearded men, artists, pacifists, priests, prudes, hippies, straights, girls who wear makeup, the president, conservatives, integrationists, executives, divorcées, perverts, motorcycle gangs, smart-aleck students, know-it-all professors, modern people, and Americans (Simmons, 1969, p. 3).

Definitions of deviance are relative to the time, the place, and the person(s) making the evaluation; and some acts are more universally defined than others. For instance, in the mid-nineteenth century in the United States, bathing in a tub was considered immoral as well as unhealthy.

All societies have **cultural values**—*practices and beliefs that are prized or believed to be of benefit to the group.* For instance, despite cultural relativity in defining deviance, anthropologists have identified a number of cultural universals, practices or customs that in general form exist in all known cultures. All cultures that have been studied look dimly on indiscriminate lying, cheating, stealing, and killing. Societies protect their values by creating norms, which are basically rules or prescribed modes of conduct.

Sumner's Types of Norms

Early American sociologist William Graham Sumner, in his classic work *Folkways* (1906), identified three types of **norms: folkways, mores,** and **laws.** These norms reflect the values of a given culture; some norms are regarded by its members as more important than others. *Folkways are the least serious norms and refer to usages, traditions, customs, or niceties that are preferred, but are not subject to serious sanctions:* manners, etiquette, and dress styles, for example. The character Reb Tevye in the musical *Fiddler on the Roof,* when learning that his daughter has rejected the marriage mate chosen by the matchmaker, wails, "Tradition—without our traditions life would be as precarious as a fiddler on the roof." Recognizing changing times or folkways, however, he shrugs and accepts his daughter's decision to choose her own mate. *Mores refer to more serious customs that involve moral judgments as well as sanctions* (rewards or punishments). The mores cover prohibitions against behaviors that are felt to be seriously threatening to a group's way of life. Our previous examples of lying, cheating, stealing, and killing are most certainly included in the mores. Both folkways and mores are examples of informal modes of social control and are characteristic of small, homogeneous cultures that feature simple technology and wide-scale consensus.

The evolution of normative controls to laws is described well by Thomas and Hepburn (1983, pp. 46–47): "Everywhere we find that the increasing complexity of social, economic, and political relationships erodes the ability of less formal methods of social control to ensure a reasonable level of stability, to mediate conflict and to protect the weak from exploitation." *Laws represent formal modes of control, codified rules of behavior.* If one accepts the consensus model of law (to be discussed shortly), laws represent an institutionalization or "crystallization" of the mores.

Mala in Se and *Mala Prohibita*

We already identified deviant acts as those that violate group expectations and crime as any act that violates criminal law. Crime and its definition are social products. Society (human groups) decides what is a crime and what is not.

Criminologists make the distinction between ***acts mala prohibita*** and ***acts mala in se.*** Acts that are defined as *mala prohibita* refer to those that are "bad because they have been prohibited." That is, such acts are *not viewed as bad in themselves but are violations because the law defines them as such.* Traffic violations, gambling, and infractions of various municipal ordinances might serve as examples. Such laws are viewed as assisting human groups in making life more predictable and orderly, but disobedience carries little stigma other than (usually) fines. The criminalization of such acts might be viewed as institutionalization of folkways. On the other hand, acts *mala in se* are "acts bad in themselves," *forbidden behaviors for which there is wide-scale consensus in the mores for prohibition.* The universality of laws against murder, rape, assault, and the like, irrespective of political or economic systems, bears witness to the lack of societal conflict in institutionalizing such laws.

(© Library of Congress)

During Prohibition, scenes like this were not uncommon. These prohibition officers are raiding a lunchroom on Pennsylvania Avenue in Washington. D.C.

One can note that not all deviant acts are criminal, nor are all criminal acts necessarily deviant, assuming that laws against many acts *mala prohibita* are commonly violated.

Definitions of criminal activity may exhibit both undercriminalization and overcriminalization (to be explored more fully in Chapter 14). **Undercriminalization** refers to the fact that the *criminal law fails to prohibit acts that many feel are mala in se.* Elements of corporate violence, racism, structured inequality, and systematic wrongdoing by political officials are examples. **Overcriminalization** involves the *over-extension of criminal law to cover acts that are inappropriately or not responsibly enforced by such measures.* Examples are the legislation of morality and attempts to regulate personal conduct that does not involve a clear victim (drug abuse, sexual conduct, and the like). Morris and Hawkins (1970) claim that the United States has one of the most moralistic systems of criminal law in history although one might suspect that ecclesiastical regimes such as Iran would more than give it a run for the money. They further state (p. 2): "Man has an inalienable right to go to hell in his own fashion, provided he does not directly injure the person or property of another on the way. The criminal law is an inefficient instrument for imposing the good life on others. In short, the law has become too much of a moral busybody."

Social Change and the Emergence of Law

Western societies have undergone a long-term evolutionary development from sacred or **Gemeinschaft-type** societies to secular or **Gesellschaft-type** societies (Becker, 1950; Toennies, 1957). *Gemeinschaft societies are simple, communal, relatively homogeneous societies that lack an extensive division of labor and are also characterized by normative consensus.* Social control is assured by the family, extended kinship groups, and the community through informal modes of control: the folkways and mores. Such societies lack and do not need formally codified laws since sacred tradition, the lack of change, and cultural similarity and isolation assure a degree of understanding and control. *Gesellschaft societies are complex, associational, more individualistic, and heterogeneous (pluralistic);* they are characterized by secularity, an extensive division of labor, and, in free societies, by a variety of moral views and political pressure groups. The assurance of social control is attempted by means of formal controls; codified laws administered by bureaucratic agencies of the state. Utilizing Sumner's notions of norms, as a society industrializes, urbanizes, and becomes more bureaucratic, complex, and pluralistic, clear consensus with respect to the mores as a means of social control becomes less likely. Complex societies must rely more and more on formal controls—laws. As the mores or informal modes of control become weaker, the need for laws becomes greater. For example, as the family as an agent of social control becomes weaker, much of its responsibility is passed on to the state (see Shelley, 1981).

In a modern pluralistic society that has many conflicting values and norms, laws may reflect the values of only one particular group, usually one that has the power and resources to pressure the state to put its interests first on the social agenda. This conflict perspective of law, to be discussed in more detail shortly, points out that laws may not have the full support or consensus of all members of society and may, in fact, be detrimental to the interests of some.

Sumner (1906) suggested a general maxim: in general, if laws do not have the support of, or are not in agreement with, the mores of a particular culture, they will be ineffective. The story is often told of the Christian missionaries in the South Sea Islands who, having been shocked by the unabashed nudity of the natives, ordered that all females must henceforth wear blouses. They were dismayed the next day to discover that, though all of the females abided by this new rule, they had strategically cut openings in their new clothing so as to display their breasts.

The introduction of changes or new laws in society can be explored by Merton's concepts of manifest and latent functions (Merton, 1961, p. 710). The classic example is what has been described as "the noble experiment," the Prohibition Era in the United States. **Manifest functions** are *intended, planned, or anticipated consequences of introduced changes or of existing social arrangements.* In perhaps the last gasp of rural Protestant religious power in the United States, one group managed to pressure Congress into passing the Prohibition Amendment. Alcohol abuse was (and still is) a major problem, and the well-intended goal was for it to be stamped out by totally forbidding alcohol consumption by law. **Latent functions** *entail unintended or unanticipated consequences, ones that may have either positive or negative outcomes.* The latent functions of Prohibition included increased corruption, disobedience, and public disrespect for the law. By eliminating legitimate suppliers of a commodity in high public demand, the state in effect created a monopoly for illegitimate entrepreneurs. It was Prohibition that converted small, localized gangs into large, powerful, and wealthy regional and even national organized criminal syndicates.

Laws are by no means the most efficient means of social control; the passage of more and more laws may indicate that social solidarity and more effective informal modes of control in the society are weakening. The police and the criminal justice system become the agents or agencies of last resort. Many people view crime as an evil intrusion into an otherwise healthy society, whereas increased crime levels may be latent functions of increased freedom, affluence, competition, and other desirable manifest functions in society. Sociologist Durkheim (1950) suggested that crime may be a normality, a positive product, a functional necessity in a healthy society. To present once again the quotation from Durkheim with which we began this chapter:

> Imagine a society of saints, a perfect cloister of exemplary individuals. Crimes, properly so called, will there be unknown; but faults which appear venial to the layman will create there the same scandal that the ordinary offense does in ordinary consciousness. If then, this society has the power to judge and punish, it will define these acts as criminal and will treat them as such (pp. 68–69).

Thus **Durkheim's "Crime as a Functional Necessity"** proposes that *wrongdoing or crime serves to force societal members to react, condemn, and thus establish the borders of and reconfirm societal values.* It is this organized resentment that upholds social solidarity.

Viewing crime as a normality is not to say that criminologists perceive it as a desirable prospect. Gibbons (1982, pp. 10–11) puts it succinctly: "When sociologists speak of the normality of crime, they often have in mind the broad claim that lawbreaking arises out of root causes or criminogenic conditions that are part and parcel of the social structure of societies." It is indeed a possibility that rising crime rates in a society may serve as an indicator of modernization, growing affluence, and rising standards and expectations of morality. Crime itself, in being a violation of criminal law, is socially defined and is affected by social change. Abortion and drug laws are just two examples.

The term *Crime of the Century* seems to be perennially used to refer to the latest dramatic crime. VANTAGE POINT 1.1 explores crimes to which this label was attached this past century.

Consensus vs. Conflict Model of Law

The **consensus model** of the origin of criminal law envisions it as *arising from agreement among the members of a society as to what constitutes wrongdoing.* Reflecting the "social contract theory" of Locke, Hobbes, and Rousseau, criminal law is viewed, as in our previous discussion of Sumner, as a "crystallization of the mores," reflecting social values that are commonly held within the society. The **conflict model,** on the other hand, sees the

VANTAGE POINT 1.1

The Crimes of the Century

Every year it seems some particularly notorious or atrocious crime occurs that is described by the media as the "crime of the century." Now that the twentieth century is over we might take stock of some that have been candidates. APBnews.com (*www.apbnews.com*), an internet service specializing in crime news chose their "Ten Crimes of the Century" based on input from their editors, historians, criminal justice experts, and users who voted in their poll, as well as those answering their telephone survey. The "Ten Crimes of the Century" in the APBnews.com survey listed chronologically were:

President McKinley's Assassination
The St. Valentine's Day Massacre
The Lindbergh Baby Kidnapping
The Rosenberg Spy Trial
President Kennedy's Assassination
Martin Luther King, Jr.'s, Assassination
Watergate Break-In
Ted Bundy Serial Killings
O.J. Simpson Trial
Oklahoma City Bombing

The assassination of President William McKinley in 1904 by Leon Czolgosz was a political crime in support of a hoped-for class revolt, while the St. Valentine's Day Massacre by the Capone mob in the twenties illustrated the ascendancy of ruthless organized crime groups during Prohibition. The tragic kidnapping of the Lindbergh baby led to legislation designating kidnapping as a federal offense. The trial and subsequent execution of Julius and Ethel Rosenberg, native Americans who betrayed their country by giving the Soviets America's atomic secrets, solidified the Cold War. The assassinations of President John Kennedy and five years later of civil rights leader the Reverend Dr. Martin Luther King, Jr., gave rise to numerous conspiracy theories that secret, sinister forces were responsible.

The Watergate affair would lead to the first forced resignation of an elected president in disgrace in American history, and it remains the benchmark against which all political scandals are compared. Ted Bundy, the serial killer, represents just one of a number of bizarre multiple killers who seemed to proliferate in post World War II America. The O.J. Simpson murder trial, in which a former National Football League star was found not guilty of murdering his ex-wife and her friend, despite considerable evidence to the contrary, illustrates a number of celebrity cases that attracted public attention over the years. Finally the Oklahoma City terrorist bombing (and the World Trade Center bombing, which is not listed) demonstrated the growing vulnerability to terrorism in modern society. The Oklahoma City bombing repre-

criminal law as *originating in the conflict of interests of different groups.* In this view, the definition of crime is assumed to reflect the wishes of the most powerful interest groups who gain the assistance of the state in opposing rival groups. The criminal law then is used primarily to control the behavior of the "defective, dependent and delinquent," the dangerous classes (Skolnick and Currie, 1988, p. 2); the crimes of the wealthy are very often not even covered. While the consensus model views criminal law as a mechanism of social control, the conflict approach sees the law as a means of preserving the status quo on behalf of the powerful.

While both of these models will be explored in greater scope in Chapter 6, the criminal law appears to reflect both patterns. As Thomas and Hepburn (1983, p. 51) indicate, " . . . nobody would be too elated at the prospect of being murdered, raped or assaulted;" such prohibitions clearly reflect the consensus model. And Schafer (1976, p. 25) describes the conflict view dramatically: "While ordinary criminals use a gun or knife to make the victim an ever-silent witness, the white-collar criminals substitute for the gun or the knife their political or economic power to avoid appearing in the crime statistics."

A third model of law is the interactionist approach, which takes its name from the symbolic interactionist school of criminology. This school of thought views humans as responding to abstract meanings and symbols as well as to concrete meanings. According

VANTAGE POINT 1.1—*Continued*

sented the worst terrorist attack, in terms of casualties, on American soil in history. It also punctuated for a complacent America that "it can happen here."

In its "Crime Stories of the Century," *U.S. News and World Report* (Cannon, 1999) included:

The Stanford White Murder
The Execution of IWW Leader Joe Hill
St. Valentine's Day Massacre
Lindbergh Kidnapping
Rosenberg Spy Case
Lynching of Emmett Till
Charles Manson Murders
"Son of Sam" Killings
Jeffrey Dahmer, Cannibal

While the *U.S. News* list includes many of the same entries as APNews, it also includes less-known events such as the high society murder of Stanford White, a well known architect, due to a romantic dispute. The execution of labor leader Joe Hill, of the radical union International Workers of the World, for allegedly killing company owners exemplifies the labor unrest early in the twentieth century. Other additions are more serial murderers: Manson; "Son of Sam" Berkowicz; and Jeffrey Dahmer, the personification of our own worst nightmares. Many of these acts changed the country, inspired new laws, mesmerized a nation waiting for a verdict, or tore at the American collective conscience. While we might not agree with the specific selection of "crimes of the century," most candidates share either a celebrity quality, bizarre violent characteristics, or political implications. In fact, of those listed on the APB list, six of the ten involved political crime, that is, crime for ideological purposes by those supporting a cause. The remainder illustrated organized crime, celebrity involvement (Lindbergh and Simpson), or bizarre violence (Bundy). Bundy seems to be a stand-in for any number of monsters of multiple murder in the twentieth century. Note also that the list is of crimes in the U.S. and does not include crimes such as Hitler and the Holocaust, for example.

While the fascinating and mesmerizing quality of these crimes gives them a timeless quality that still enthralls the public, a dance macabre that appalls yet entices, it is the very rare, atypical quality of these crimes that gives them notoriety. The typical picture of crime in most societies is far less dramatic, but often just as deadly, traumatic, or fear-inspiring. Domestic violence, rape, robbery, murder, burglary, theft, and other crimes bring crime up close and personal to its victims and will be more the subject of this text.

InfoTrac College Edition Research
What do you think was the "Crime of the Century?" Visit InfoTrac and see if you can find other nominees for a "Top Ten Crimes of the Century" list.

to George Herbert Mead, even the mind and self-consciousness are social creations (Mead, 1934). Reflected in labeling theory (see Chapter 6), criminality is viewed as a label or stigma attached by a societal reaction that is subject to shifting standards. Laws are viewed as reflecting moral entrepreneurship on the part of labelers.

Crime and Criminal Law

A *purist legal view of crime* would define it as violation of criminal law. No matter how morally outrageous or unacceptable an act, it is not a crime unless defined as such by criminal law. Fox (1976, p. 28) indicates: "Crime is a sociopolitical event rather than a clinical condition. . . . It is not a clinical or medical condition which can be diagnosed and specifically treated." In this view, which is technically correct, unless an act is specifically prohibited by criminal law, it is not a crime. There are four **characteristics of criminal law:**

1. It is assumed by political authority. The state assumes the role of plaintiff or the party bringing charges. Murder, for example, is no longer just an offense against a person, but is also a crime against the state. In fact, the state prohibits individual revenge in such matters; perpetrators must pay their debt to society, not to the individual wronged.

2. It must be specific, defining both the offense and the prescribed punishment.
3. The law is uniformly applied. That is, equal punishment and fairness for all, irrespective of social position, is intended.
4. The law contains penal sanctions enforced by punishments administered by the state (Sutherland and Cressey, 1974, pp. 4–7).

Criminal law has very specific criteria: "Crime is an intentional act or omission in violation of criminal law (statutory and case law), committed without defense or justification, and sanctioned by the state as a felony or misdemeanor" (Tappan, 1960, p. 10). *Felonies* generally refer to offenses punishable by a year or more in a state or federal prison, whereas *misdemeanors* are less serious offenses punished by less than a year in jail. Some specific criteria that must be met in the U.S. criminal law in order for an act to be considered a crime include:

1. The act is prohibited by law and contains legally prescribed punishments. "Nullum crimen sine lege" ("no crime without law") is the Latin expression, which can be expanded to include the notion that "ex post facto" (after-the-fact) laws are also inappropriate. The act must be forbidden by law in advance of the act.
2. *A criminal act, "actus reus"* (the act itself, or the physical element), *must take place.*
3. *Social harm of a conscious, voluntary nature is required.* There must be injury to the state or people.
4. The act is *performed intentionally* (although cases of negligence and omission may be exceptions). *Mens rea* (criminal intent or "guilty mind") is important in establishing guilt. A person who may have committed a criminal act (for example, John Hinckley, who shot former President Reagan) may be found not guilty under certain conditions.

5.The voluntary misconduct must be *causally related* to the harm. It must be shown that the decision or act did directly or indirectly cause harm.

(© Reproduced with permission of Criminals Hall of Fame, Niagara Falls, Ontario, Canada)

The "Criminals Hall of Fame" might be better titled "Criminals Hall of Shame." The notoriety and public fascination with such criminals borders on glamorizing such criminals.

Crimes were originally considered simply private matters: the offended party had to seek private compensation or revenge. Later, only offenses committed against the king and, still later, the king's subjects were considered crimes. When compensation developed, fines were levied on behalf of the king (the state), thus making the state the wronged party. In addition to being defined by *legislative statute* **(statutory law),** criminality may also be interpreted by means of case law (common law). In contrast to laws enacted by legislatures, common law is based on judicial decision, with its roots in precedence or previous decisions. In addition, administrative law, as enforced by federal regulatory agencies, may carry criminal penalties for offenders. Thus criminal law provisions may be contained in statutory law, common law, and administrative law.

VANTAGE POINT 1.2 describes some typical legal definitions of crimes in the United States.

Who Defines Crime? Sociological Definitions of Crime

Since crime was previously defined as any violation of criminal law, should criminologists restrict their inquiry solely to acts so defined? Should the subject matter of criminology be decided by lawyers and politicians? This would relegate the field of criminology to a position as status quo handmaiden of political systems. Hitler's genocide or Stalin's purges were accepted conduct within their political ideological systems. Criminologists must study the deviants, the criminals, as well as the social structural contexts that define them. Skolnick and Currie (1988, p. 11), in examining the analysis of social problems, state:

> In spite of its claim to political neutrality, the social science of the 1960s typically focused on the symptoms of social ills, rather than their sources: criminals, rather than the laws; the mentally ill, rather than the quality of life; the culture of the poor, rather than the decisions of the rich; the "pathology" of the ghetto, rather than problems of the economy.

A *sociological view* of crime does not restrict its concept of criminality only to those convicted of crime in a legal sense. Allen et al. (1981, pp. 19–20) indicate:

> In a simplistic way, one can say that a criminal is one who commits a crime. Such a definition, however, makes no distinction between the one-time and the habitual offender, and thus makes no provision for the temporary application of the label of criminal. It does not take into account the difference between the convicted criminal, the fugitive, and the individual whose crime is known only to himself. Nor does it provide a guideline for the classification of someone believed by prosecutors, police and researchers to be guilty but found not guilty by a court of law (for example, Lizzie Borden, well-known defendant widely believed guilty in a case in which she was accused and exonerated of murdering her father and stepmother).

Many "white collar crimes" that we will discuss differ from other crimes only in the implementation of the law, which segregates white collar criminals administratively from other criminals. Reiman indicates that many acts that are not treated as criminal acts are as great or more a danger to society than acts that are. "Thus, the disproportionality between our heavy-handed response to crime and our kid-glove response to noncriminal dangers continues to need explanation" (Reiman, 1998, p. viii). Were we to restrict analysis of crime solely to the legal definition in most countries, we would discuss primarily "crime in the streets" and ignore "crime in the suites." We would study the poor, dumb, slow criminal and conclude that low IQs and inferior genetics cause crime; we'd ignore the fast, smart, slick violator, and ignore the possibility that maybe Ivy League educations and working on Wall Street or for the defense industry cause crime. Hyperbole (exaggeration) is useful at times for effect and obviously we must not loosely throw around the label *criminal,* but neither should we ignore dangerous acts that do great harm, simply because the criminal justice system chooses to ignore them.

The Crime Problem

Radzinowicz and King (1977, pp. 3–5), in commenting on the relentless international upsurge in crime in the later decades of the twentieth century, indicate: "No national characteristics, no political regime, no system of law, police punishment, treatment, or

VANTAGE POINT 1.2

What Is Crime?

Crimes are defined by law.

In this report we define crime as all behaviors and acts for which a society provides formally sanctioned punishment. In the United States what is criminal is specified in the written law, primarily state statutes. What is included in the definition of crime varies among federal, state, and local jurisdictions.

Criminologists devote a great deal of attention to defining crime in both general and specific terms. This definitional process is the first step toward the goal of obtaining accurate crime statistics.

To provide additional perspectives on crime it is sometimes viewed in ways other than those suggested by the standard legal definitions. Such alternatives define crime in terms of the type of victim (child abuse), the type of offender (white collar crime), the object of the crime (property crime), or the method of criminal activity (organized crime). Such definitions usually cover one or more of the standard legal definitions. For example, organized crime may include fraud, extortion, assault, or homicide.

What is considered criminal by society changes over time.

Some types of events such as murder, robbery, and burglary have been defined as crimes for centuries. Such crimes are part of the common law definition of crime. Other types of conduct traditionally have not been viewed as crimes. As social values and mores change, society has codified some conduct as criminal while decriminalizing other conduct. The recent movement toward increased "criminalization" of drunk driving is an example of such change.

New technology also results in new types of conduct not anticipated by the law. Changes in the law may be needed to define and sanction these types of conduct. For example, the introduction of computers has added to the criminal codes in many states so that acts such as the destruction of programs or data could be defined as crimes.

What are some other common crimes in the United States?

Drug abuse violations Offenses relating to growing, manufacturing, making, possessing, using, selling, or distributing narcotic and dangerous non-narcotic drugs. A distinction is made between possession and sale/manufacturing.

Sex offenses In current statistical usage, the name of a broad category of varying content, usually consisting of all offenses having a sexual element except for forcible rape and commercial sex offenses, which are defined separately.

Fraud offenses The crime type comprising offenses sharing the elements of practice of deceit or intentional misrepresentation of fact, with the intent of unlawfully depriving a person of his or her property or legal rights.

Drunkenness Public intoxication, except "driving under the influence."

Disturbing the peace Unlawful interruption of the peace, quiet, or order of a community, including offenses called "disorderly conduct," "vagrancy," "loitering," "unlawful assembly," and "riot."

Driving under the influence Driving or operating any vehicle or common carrier while drunk or under the influence of liquor or drugs.

Liquor law offenses State or local liquor law violations, except drunkenness and driving under the influence. Federal violations are excluded.

Gambling Unlawful staking or wagering of money or other thing of value on a game of chance or on an uncertain event.

Kidnapping Transportation or confinement of a person without authority of law and without his or her consent, or of a minor without the consent of his or her guardian.

Vandalism Destroying or damaging, or attempting to destroy or damage, the property of another without his or her consent, or public property—except by burning, which is arson.

Public order offenses Violations of the peace or order of the community or threats to the public health through unacceptable public conduct, interference with governmental authority, or violation of civil rights or liberties. Weapons offenses, bribery, escape, and tax law violations, for example, are included in this category.

How do violent crimes differ from property crimes?

The outcome of a criminal event determines whether it is a property crime or a violent crime. Violent crime refers to events such as homicide, rape, and assault that may result in injury to a person. Robbery is also considered a violent crime because it involves the use or threat of force against a person.

Property crimes are unlawful acts with the intent of gaining property not involving the use or threat of force against an individual. Larceny and motor vehicle theft are examples of property crimes.

In the National Crime Survey (NCS) a distinction is also made between crimes against persons (violent crimes and personal larceny) and crimes against households (property crimes, including household larceny).

VANTAGE POINT 1.2—*Continued*

How do felonies differ from misdemeanors?

Criminal offenses are also classified according to how they are handled by the criminal justice system. Most jurisdictions recognize two classes of offenses: felonies and misdemeanors.

Felonies are not distinguished from misdemeanors in the same way in all jurisdictions, but most states define felonies as offenses punishable by a year or more in a state prison. The most serious crimes are never "misdemeanors" and the most minor offenses are never "felonies."

What are the characteristics of some serious crimes?

Crime/Definition	*Facts*
Homicide: Causing the death of another person without legal justification or excuse, including UCR (FBI Uniform Crime Reports) crimes of murder, non-negligent manslaughter, and negligent manslaughter.	• Murder and non-negligent manslaughter occur less often than other violent UCR Index crimes. • 58 percent of the known murderers were relatives or acquaintances of the victim.
Rape: Unlawful sexual intercourse with a female, by force or without legal or factual consent.	• Most rapes involve a lone offender and a lone victim. • About a third of the rapes recorded by National Crime Victimization Survey (NCVS) were committed in or near the victim's home. • Most of the rapes occurred at night, between 6 P.M. and 6 A.M.
Robbery: The unlawful taking or attempted taking of property that is in the immediate possession of another, by force or threat of force.	• Robbery is the violent crime that most often involves more than one offender. • About half of all robberies involve the use of a weapon.
Assault: Unlawful intentional inflicting, or attempted inflicting, of injury upon the person of another. Aggravated assault is the unlawful intentional inflicting of serious bodily injury or unlawful threat or attempt to inflict bodily injury or death by means of a deadly or dangerous weapon with or without actual infliction of injury. Simple assault is the unlawful intentional inflicting of less than serious bodily injury without a deadly or dangerous weapon or an attempt or threat to inflict bodily injury without a deadly or dangerous weapon.	• Simple assault occurs more frequently than aggravated assault. • Most assaults involve one victim and one offender.
Burglary: Unlawful entry of any fixed structure, vehicle, or vessel used for regular residence, industry, or business, with or without force, with the intent to commit a felony or larceny.	• Residential property was the target in 2 out of every 3 reported burglaries; nonresidential property accounted for the remaining third. • Over a third of all residential burglaries occurred without forced entry. • Over a third of the no-force burglaries were known to have occurred during the day between 6 A.M. and 6 P.M.
Larceny/theft: Unlawful taking or attempted taking of property other than a motor vehicle from the possession of another, by stealth, without force and without deceit, with intent to permanently deprive the owner of the property.	• Fewer than 5 percent of all personal larcenies involve contact between the victim and the offender. • Pocket picking and purse snatching most frequently occur inside nonresidential buildings or on street locations. • Unlike most other crimes, pocket picking and purse snatching affect the elderly about as much as other age groups.

VANTAGE POINT 1.2—*Continued*

Motor vehicle theft: Unlawful taking or attempted taking of a self-propelled road vehicle owned by another, with the intent of depriving him or her of it, permanently or temporarily.

- Motor vehicle theft is relatively well reported to the police.
- The stolen property is more likely to be recovered in this crime than in other property crimes.

Arson: The intentional damaging or destruction or attempted damaging or destruction by means of fire or explosion of property without the consent of the owner, or of one's own property or that of another by fire or explosives with or without the intent to defraud.

- Single-family residences were the most frequent targets of arson.

Sources: Bureau of Justice Statistics, *BJS Dictionary of Criminal Justice Data Terminology,* 2nd edition, 1981; Bureau of Justice Statistics, *BJS Criminal Victimization in the U.S.* 1985; FBI, *Crime in the United States 1985;* Bureau of Justice Statistics, 1988b, *Report to the Nation on Crime and Justice,* 2nd edition, Washington, D.C.: Government Printing Office, March, pp. 2–3.

InfoTrac College Edition Research
Using InfoTrac, search laws, regulations, and criminal law. Read and discuss any article related to the Imperial Criminal Code, criminal law reform, self-defense, or mens rea.

even terror, has rendered a country exempt from crime. . . . What is indisputable is that new and much higher levels of crime become established as a reflex of affluence." Despite rival explanations such as problems with statistics (to be discussed in Chapter 2), there has been an obvious increase in crime internationally since World War II.

It is difficult, if not impossible, to measure the economic costs of crime. Estimates of the actual financial operation take us into the "megabucks" range where notions such as "give or take a few billion dollars" stagger the imagination and numb us to the reality of the amounts we are really talking about.

In 1992 in Los Angeles, riots broke out in response to a jury verdict of not guilty for police officers accused of the brutal videotaped beating of Rodney King. Those riots resulted in one of the bloodiest series of civil unrest in the United States in recent history. Fifty-three people were killed, over 2,000 were injured, 15,000 were arrested, and property damage was estimated at nearly $800 million. Although far less dramatic, losses at the nation's savings and loans in the eighties and early nineties are estimated to have cost the American taxpayer $500 billion, or 625 Los Angeles riots. VANTAGE POINT 1.3 provides some estimates of the cost of crime.

While recent estimates rank the sale of illegal narcotics as the criminal world's greatest source of income, there is a problem with such assessments. These estimates do not even begin to measure the full impact of corporate price-fixing and other criminal activities. Added to these costs are economic costs incurred by victims of crime and the costs of running the criminal justice system. Not considered at all in these economic estimates are the social and psychological costs to society and to crime victims. Fear, mistrust, a curtailing of public activity, and a decline in the quality of life are but a few of the inestimable impacts of crime on society. Horror stories abound of the impact of crime on the forgotten figure in the criminal justice equation—the crime victim.

Summary

Criminology is the *science or discipline that studies crime and criminal behavior.* Major areas of investigation include criminal behavior, etiology (theories of crime causation), the sociology of law and societal reaction; related areas include juvenile delinquency and vic-

(© Ellis Herwig / MGA / Photri)

(© David Young Wolff / Tony Stone Images)

Losses at the nation's savings institutions in the eighties and nineties cost the American taxpayer an estimates $500 billion, or 625 L.A. riots.

timology. Criminology also shares with the field of criminal justice the areas of policing, the courts, and corrections. Debunkers of the relevance of the scientific approach to criminology often recommends substituting common sense, but they should beware of this approach, since it often becomes nonsense.

Knowledge is defined as one's understanding of reality. This understanding is made possible through the creation of symbols or abstractions. Comte identified three stages in the progression of knowledge: the theological, metaphysical (philosophical), and scientific. *Science* combines the spirit of rationality of philosophy with the scientific method, which is characterized by the search for empirical proof. Criminology and sociology are more recent applicants for the scientific credentials already enjoyed by the physical sciences. Having its origins in the eighteenth century in Europe, particularly in the writing of Beccaria who was influential in codifying modern continental law, criminology has largely become a twentieth-century U.S. discipline. This is particularly reflected in the work of Sutherland, who has been identified as "the dean of criminology."

Deviant behavior refers to activities that fall outside the range of normal societal toleration. Definitions of such activities are relative to time, place, and persons. *Values* are practices or beliefs that are prized in society and that are protected by *norms,* which are rules or prescribed modes of conduct. Sumner in his classic work *Folkways* identifies three types of norms: *folkways, mores,* and *laws.* While *folkways* are less serious customs or traditions, *mores* are serious norms that contain moral evaluations as well as penal sanctions. Both folkways and mores are examples of informal modes of control. *Laws,* codified rules of behavior, represent formal methods of attempting to assure social control.

Acts *mala in se* refer to acts that are "bad in themselves," such as murder, rape, and the like; acts *mala prohibita* are ones that are "bad because they are prohibited," such as

VANTAGE POINT 1.3

The Cost of Crime in the United States

A full assessment of the cost of crime is perhaps inestimable. It includes not only economic costs, but psychological and social ones as well. It also includes the costs of running a criminal justice system consisting of police, courts, and various correctional facilities. A variety of efforts have been made to tally these costs. In 1994, using a number of sources, *U.S. News & World Report* (1995, pp. 40–41) presented crime costs as $674 billion. This included:

Federal, state, and local policing	=	$39 billion
Prison system	=	$29 billion
Legal/judicial costs	=	$10 billion
Total criminal justice	=	$78 billion
Private police protection	=	$64 billion
Medical/mental health		
Due to violent crimes	=	$11 billion *(direct cost)*
Victims' lost wages/ pain/suffering	=	$191 billion *(indirect cost)*
Total medical	=	$202 billion *(total cost)*
Crimes against business (includes retail pilferage, shoplifting, bribery, kickbacks, and embezzlement schemes)	=	$120 billion
Stolen goods and fraud		
Robbery and burglary	=	$20 billion
Noncorporate fraud	=	$40 billion
Total stolen goods and fraud	=	$60 billion
Drug abuse	=	$40 billion
Driving while intoxicated	=	$110 billion
Total crime	=	$674 billion

(*U.S. News & World Report*, 1994, pp. 40–41)

The indeterminate nature of such estimates can be noted by the fact that the National Institute of Justice (NIJ) estimated the costs at $450 billion a year in 1996 (National Institute of Justice, 1996). The NIJ report indicates (National Institute of Justice, 1996, p. 1–2):

Crime exacts a heavy toll—on governments, on society at large, and especially on its victims. The cost of crime has two dimensions: a dollar amount calculated by adding up property losses, productivity losses, and medical bills; and an amount less easily quantifiable because it takes the forms of pain, emotional trauma, and risk of death from victimization. Just how much of our social resources are drained has been uncertain; previous studies have been able to estimate some of the short-term costs attendant on victimization, but long-term estimates have been incomplete. The research summarized here adds the long-term costs and the intangibles of pain, suffering, and risk of death.

The researchers found that victimizations generate $105 billion annually in property and productivity losses and outlays for medical expenses. This amounts to an annual "crime tax" of roughly $425 per man, woman, and child in the United States. When the values of pain, long-term emotional trauma, disability, and risk of death are put in dollar terms, the costs rise to $450 billion annually (or $1,800 per person).

Number of Victimizations

For counts of crime, the researchers used the FBI's Uniform Crime Reports and the National Criminal Victimization Survey (NCVS), supplemented by data from other representative national surveys. For the most part, only street crime and domestic crime were counted and their costs calculated. This study diverges from most other victimization figures by: (1) including crimes against people under age 12; (2) using estimates of domestic violence and sexual assault from surveys that focus specifically on these topics and ask more explicitly about these crimes; (3) more fully accounting for repeat victimizations; and (4) including child abuse and drunk driving. Certain categories were excluded, among them crimes against business and government, personal fraud, white-collar crime, child neglect, and most "victimless" crime.

The new calculations produced an estimate of more than 49 million victimizations and attempted victimizations annually for the period 1987 to 1990. More specific categories are as follows:

- *Fatal crimes:* These crimes, which include criminal and vehicular homicide, arson, and child abuse, claimed some 31,000 lives in 1990.
- *Child abuse:* A conservative estimate of the number of children sexually, physically, or emotionally abused was 794,000 in 1990.
- *Rape:* The number of rape and sexual assault victims in 1992 was estimated at 1.1 million (figure based on data from a recent national survey). The definition of rape and sexual assault used here is slightly broader and the age range is broader, than in the NCVS redesigned survey.
- *Assault:* The number of nonfatal assaults against children under 12 comes to about 450,000 annually (estimated from health care data). (To avoid double-counting, this figure excludes 194,000 child physical

VANTAGE POINT 1.3—*Continued*

abuse incidents.) The study estimated the number of domestic assaults at 2 million, a figure reasonably consistent with data from the redesigned NCVS.

- *Drunk driving:* Tentative estimates put the number of physical injuries from drunk driving at about half a million, with another 2.4 million people estimated to be involved in sometimes psychologically devastating crashes.
- *Arson:* The study estimated 137,000 arson victimizations, including 15,000 that resulted in injuries.

Costs and Other Consequences

Both intangible and tangible costs were calculated. Although the study involved extensive data collection and cost imputations, the basic logic was straightforward: (1) count the number of crimes of various types; (2) estimate from a variety of sources the average costs of each type; and (3) multiply costs by the number of crime incidents to obtain aggregate figures. Not all costs were included. This study focused on victim-related costs, not the costs of operating the criminal justice system.

The following examples of costs per victimization (for the period 1987–90) show that quality-of-life losses generally exceed all tangible losses *combined:*

Crime	*Tangible Costs*	*Intangible Costs*	*Total Costs*
Murder	$1,030,000	$1,910,000	$2,940,000
Rape/Sexual Assault	5,100	81,400	86,500
Robbery/Attempt with Injury	5,200	13,800	19,000
Assault or Attempt	1,550	7,800	9,350
Burglary or Attempt	1,100	300	1,400

In the aggregate, tangible losses amounted to $105 billion annually, but intangibles were much higher at $345 billion. Overall, rape is the costliest crime. With annual victim costs at $127 billion, it exacts a higher price than murder.

The calculations shed new light on domestic violence against adults, revealing the aggregate costs of crimes in this category to be $67 billion per year. Losses due to violence against children, some 40 percent of which is domestic violence, exceed $164 billion.

The Aggregate Burden of Crime

Perhaps the most ambitious comprehensive attempt to assess the total cost of crime was by David Anderson (1999) in an article entitled "The Aggregate Burden of Crime." Anderson includes the costs of the legal system; victim losses; and criminal justice agencies; as well as opportunity costs of victims', criminals', and prisoners' time; the fear of crime; and cost of private policing. His basic theme is "How much could the U.S. save if we had a crime-free environment?" His answer: $1.7 trillion. The *aggregate burden of crime* for 1998 consists of (Ibid., p. 47):

- Crime induced production = $397 billion
- Opportunity (time) costs = $130 billion
- Risks to life and health = $574 billion
- Transfers = $603 billion

Aggregate Burden = $1,705 billion
–Net Transfers = $1,102 billion

Crime induced production refers to costs in resources to fight crime. This includes police ($47.1 billion), corrections (35.9 billion), locks and safes ($4 billion), surveillance cameras ($1.4 billion), computer security ($8 billion), federal agencies to fight crime ($23 billion), and drug trafficking (the highest cost at $160 billion).

Opportunity costs refer to lost time by potential victims and perpetrators who could have spent their lost time doing something more productive. Anderson (1999, p. 44) estimates these opportunity costs as:

- Time spent securing assets = $89.6 billion
- Lost work days in prison and planning crime = $40 billion
- Victim lost work days = $0.8 billion
- Neighborhood Watch time = $0.7 billion

Approximate Total $130 billion

For *life and health costs* Anderson estimates roughly 72,000 crime-related deaths per year and 2.5 million crime-related injuries per year at $6.1 million per death and $52,637 per injury for a total of $574 billion. While these figures strike the author as somewhat high, Anderson is using accepted court, medical, and insurance estimates.

Transfers refers to money obtained through fraud and theft. It is called a transfer since the money (or property) is transferred from one person to the next. Estimated at $603.1 billion, this figure includes items such as fraud at work ($203 billion), unpaid taxes ($123 billion), health insurance fraud ($108 billion), telemarketing fraud ($16.8 billion), and motor vehicle theft ($8.9 billion).

The aggregate burden of crime in 1999 using Anderson's figures was $4,118 per person.

Sources: U.S. News & World Report, "Cost of Crime: $674 billion," January 17, 1994, pp. 40–41; National Institute of Justice, "The Extent and Costs of Crime Victimization: A New Look," *National Institute of Justice Research Reviews,* January 1996; David Anderson, "The Aggregate Burden of Crime," *Journal of Law and Economics,* 42(2) October, 1999.

InfoTrac College Edition Research

Locate an article on a specific type of crime, for example, burglary or embelzzlement, and report on the estimated cost of the crime.

laws regulating vagrancy and gambling. While not all criminal acts are viewed as deviant, neither are all deviant acts criminal. *Undercriminalization* involves the failure of the law to cover acts mala in se, while *overcriminalization* entails overextension of the law to cover acts that may more effectively be enforced through the mores. As societies undergo transition from *Gemeinschaft* (communal, sacred societies) to *Gesellschaft* (associational, secular societies), they must rely more on formal agencies of control. In order to be effective, laws require the support of the mores.

Manifest functions are intended or planned consequences of social arrangements, whereas *latent functions* refer to unintended or unanticipated consequences. While the manifest function of Prohibition was to eliminate alcohol abuse, its latent functions were to encourage corruption, organized crime, and public disrespect. Durkheim viewed crime as a normal condition in society that served a positive function, by the reactions it developed to encourage reaffirmation of values. *Crime,* a violation of criminal law, is characterized by politicality, specificity, uniformity, and sanctions. In explaining the origin of criminal law, the *consensus model* views the criminal law as reflecting agreement or public will, while the *conflict model* claims that it represents the interest of the most powerful group(s) in society. In reality, criminal law reflects elements of both models.

For official purposes crimes are identified as felonies, misdemeanors, and, in some states, summary offenses. Although there is variation by state in the actual assignment to categories, a *felony* refers to more serious crime that bears a penalty of at least one year in a state prison, a *misdemeanor* is a less serious offense subject to a small fine or short imprisonment.

The issue of "Who defines crime?" should not be answered simply by accepting current definitions, since to do so would permit others to define criminology's subject matter. The crime problem is a growing international problem; the costs of crime are economic (which can only be estimated), psychological, and social in nature. The full social costs are inestimable.

KEY CONCEPTS

Administrative Law
Characteristics of Criminal Law
Common Law
Consensus vs. Conflict Model of Law
Costs of Crime
Crime
Criminal Law
Criminology
Cultural Values
Deviance
Durkheim's "Crime as Functional Necessity"
Felony
Folkways
Gemeinschaft
Gesellschaft
Latent Functions
Laws
Mala in Se
Mala Prohibita
Manifest Functions
Misdemeanor
Mores
Norms
Overcriminalization
Stages of Progression of Knowledge
Statutory Law
Two Features of Science
Undercriminalization

REVIEW QUESTIONS

1. In addition to the myths regarding crime supplied in this chapter, can you think of and document any others?
2. What are some crimes that were not much regarded as problems in the past but now are regarded as problems; conversely, what are some that were problems in the past and no longer loom as a major concern? Do you have any predictions of emerging, future crimes?
3. Besides "Prohibition," what are some other social policies that have contained latent functions?

4. Do you think the American criminal justice system reflects a *consensus* or *conflict* model of law? Explain and defend your judgments.
5. Why don't criminologists simply use the legal classifications of criminals in their studies of crime and criminal behavior?
6. The early European settlers in the U.S. sometimes referred to indigenous people as savages. Why were they wrong in this belief?
7. What is the purpose of scientific research in criminology?
8. What are some characteristics of the criminal law that you believe the common person on the street may be unaware of?
9. What is the difference between criminal law, statutory law, case law, civil law, and administrative law?
10. What are some elements that must be taken into account in the effort to count the cost of crime?

INFOTRAC COLLEGE EDITION RESEARCH

Vantage Point 1.1 InfoTrac College Edition Research
What do you think was the "Crime of the Century?" Visit InfoTrac and see if you can find other nominees for a "Top Ten Crimes of the Century" list.

Vantage Point 1.2 InfoTrac College Edition Research
Using InfoTrac, search laws, regulations, and criminal law. Read and discuss any article related to: the Imperial Criminal Code, criminal law reform, self-defense, or mens rea.

Vantage Point 1.3 InfoTrac College Edition Research
Locate an article on a specific type of crime, for example, burglary or embezzlement, and report on the estimated cost of the crime.

In the News 1.1 InfoTrac College Edition Research
Search the "FBI's Most Wanted List" and discuss either a current fugitive or the history of this list.

SELECTED READINGS

Robert Bohm. 1987. "The Myths About Criminology and Criminal Justice: A Review," *Justice Quarterly* 4: 631–42.
This classic article reviews the many works on, and claims about, myths in criminology and criminal justice. A review such as this of misconceptions in criminology is an excellent means by which to assess the state of current knowledge in the field.

Elliott Currie. 1985. *Confronting Crime: Why There is So Much Crime in America and What We Can Do About It.* New York: Pantheon.
Elliott Currie has remained a consistent voice of liberal thought in the area of crime policy. He challenges conservative thought of crime, which tends to be defeatist, and tends to ignore the role of structural conditions such as inequality and discrimination in crime causation.

John R. Fuller and Eric W. Hickey, editors. 1999. *Controversial Issues in Criminology.* Boston: Allyn and Bacon.
Fuller and Hickey provide an excellent collection of fourteen articles featuring a debate between two criminologists on each subject.

Don Gibbons. 1979. *The Criminological Enterprise: Theories and Perspectives.* Englewood Cliffs, N.J.: Prentice Hall.
In this slim volume, Don Gibbons provides a very readable history of criminological thought that provides undergraduates with an excellent overview of the history on development of criminology and criminological theory.

Philip Jenkins. 1984. *Crime and Justice: Issues and Ideas.* Monterey, California: Brooks/Cole.
This book by one of the most lucid writers in criminology provides a very readable, original, and scholarly discussion of a number of criminological controversies such as serial murders and moral panics.

Steven F. Messner and Richard Rosenfeld. 1994. *Crime and the American Dream.* Belmont, California: Wadsworth.
In this small volume, the authors build on Robert Merton's anomie or strain theory by speaking to the development of an institutionalization of deviant means in American society. According to this theory, legitimate institutions begin to adopt illegal means of achieving their competitive objectives.

Carl E. Pope, Rick Lovell and Steven G. Brandl, editors. 2001. *Voices From the Field: Readings in Criminal Justice Research.* Belmont, California: Wadsworth.
This collection features eighteen articles on research on a variety of criminological issues. It particularly underlines the point that research in criminology stresses scientific analysis over mere opinion.

Jeffrey Reiman. 1995. *The Rich Get Rich and the Poor Get Prison.* 4th edition. New York: Macmillan.
Reiman's work is an acknowledged classic in the field that documents the continuing inequality in the U.S. criminal justice system. His analysis serves as an

excellent illustration of the conflict model in criminology.

Frank R. Scarpitti and Amie Nielson, editors. 1998. *Crime and Criminals: Contemporary and Classic Readings in Criminology.* Los Angeles: Roxbury. Surprisingly there is a shortage of good general readers in criminology. Scarpitti and Nielson more than fill the gap with a fine selection of 41 readings that serves to complement texts in criminology, including this one.

Sam Walker. 1989. *Sense and Nonsense About Crime.* 2nd edition. Monterey, California: Brooks/Cole. In this short book, Sam Walker provides a very succinct and readable coverage of critical issues in criminology using as an organizational gimmick the theme of myths in criminology.

Research Methods in Criminology

Vantage Points

In the News

> We measure the extent of crime with elastic rulers whose units of measurement are not defined.
>
> —Edwin H. Sutherland and Donald Cressey (1984)

Theory and Methodology

Two critical features of any discipline are its theory and its methodology. **Theory,** which will be the subject of Chapters 4, 5 and 6, *addresses the questions of "Why?" and "How?"* **Methodology (methods),** on the other hand, *is concerned with "What is?"*

Theories involve attempts to develop reasonable explanations of reality. They are efforts to structure, summarize, or explain the essential elements of the subject in question. What causes crime? Why do some individuals become criminals? Why are some nations or areas more criminogenic than others? Theories represent the intellectual leaps of faith that provide fundamental insights into how things operate; they attempt to illuminate or shed light upon the darkness of reality. Without the generation of useful theoretical explanations, a field is intellectually bankrupt; it becomes merely a collection of "war stories" and carefully documented encyclopedic accounts. It fails to explain, summarize, or capture the essential nature of its subject matter. Studying a field devoid of theory would be akin to a mystery novel in which the author neither told us "whodunit" nor how and why they did it.

Methodology involves the collection and analysis of accurate data or facts. With respect to criminology, this would comprise information regarding: How much crime is there? Who commits crime? How do commissions of crime or definitions of crime vary? and the like. If the facts regarding crime are provided by defective models they will be in error, and then theories or attempted explanations of this incorrectly described reality will most certainly be misdirected.

In the social sciences there at times exists a chasm between those who are primarily interested in theory or broad conceptual analysis analogous to philosophy and those who are methodologists. Theory devoid of method, explanation without accurate supportive data, is just as much a dead end as method devoid of interpretive theory. The former resembles armchair theorizing, the latter a fruitless bookkeeping operation. In reality, in order to realize mature development, criminology needs both incisive theory and sound, accurate methodology.

The purpose of this chapter is to alert and sensitize the reader to the variety of research methods that are employed in criminological research. Many readers of lengthy prose in textbooks are relatively oblivious to sources that are cited by authors. But writers cite supportive references so the reader may consult them for further information on any given issue. Thus, a textbook, rather than representing a compendium of unsupported opinion, attempts to convey the latest thinking and research. Such a presentation, particularly in social science disciplines such as criminology, is of necessity tentative and can represent only our current state of understanding of reality. The purpose of this chapter on methodology is to identify the research base on which the findings presented in this book rest, and to point out their relative strengths and shortcomings.

The Research Enterprise of Criminology

Objectivity

A basic canon of scientific research is that researchers attempt to maintain **objectivity.** This requires that the *investigators strive to be "value free" in their inquiry* (Weber, 1949) *and, in a sense, to permit the findings to speak for themselves.* A researcher may occasionally find the attitudes, behavior, or beliefs of a group he or she is studying repugnant or immoral, however, the researcher is trained not to judge but rather to objectively record and to determine what meaning these findings have for the field of criminology and to the development of its knowledge base.

Ethics in Criminological Research

Because it is part of the social sciences, the subject matter of criminology is different in kind from that of the physical sciences. While the latter concentrates on physical facts, criminology's subject matter—crime, criminal behavior, victims, and the criminal justice system—is concerned with human behavior, attitudes, groups, and organizations. Like physical science investigations, criminological inquiry must be concerned with its potentially adverse impacts on human subjects.

The researcher in criminology of necessity often wears many hats: a researcher, a practitioner, a citizen, and a humanitarian. These roles obviously conflict at times, raising potential moral dilemmas. To mediate these potentially conflicting roles, the researcher must enter the investigation with eyes wide open. Important decisions, such as one's commitment to the research undertaking and clarifications of possible role conflicts, must be considered beforehand. While there are no hard and fast rules and each research endeavor has its own unique qualities, the researcher's primary role is that of scientist. This does not mean that the scientist's role should in all cases take total precedence over the agenda, however, the investigator should address these issues of subject accountability and limits and priorities prior to embarking on a study.

Ultimately, **ethical conduct in research** is an *individual responsibility tied into deep moral judgments;* a blind adherence to any checklist grossly oversimplifies a very complex decision. Until recently the fields of criminology and criminal justice relied on the codes of ethics of parent fields such as sociology or psychology for guidance. Beginning in 1998, however, both the Academy of Criminal Justice Sciences and the American Society of Criminology began compiling and later adopting **codes of ethics.** While space does not permit full discussion of each, some of the *guidelines of both of these codes of ethics include* (ACJS, 1998 and ASC, 1998):

- Researchers should strive for the highest technical standards in research.
- Acknowledge limitations of research.
- Fully report findings.
- Disclose financial support and other sponsorship.
- Honor commitments.
- Make data available to future researchers.
- Not misuse their positions as fraudulent pretext for gathering intelligence.
- Human subjects have the right to full disclosure of the purposes of the research.
- Subjects have the right to confidentiality.
- Research should not expose subjects to more than minimal risk. If risks are greater than the risks of everyday life then informed consent must be obtained.
- Avoid privacy invasion and protect vulnerable populations.
- All research should meet with human subject protection requirements imposed by educational institutions and funding sources.
- Researchers should properly acknowledge the work of others.
- Criminologists have an obligation not to create social injustice such as discrimination, oppression or harassment in their work.

In the name of research, criminologists should have no interest in behaving as "mad scientists" who inhumanely pursue science for its own sake. In most research, informed consent of participants based on knowledge of the experiment is essential. If some form of deception is necessary, it is even more incumbent on the researcher to prevent harm and, where possible, to debrief, reassure, and explain the purposes of the project afterwards. Obviously, criminology cannot afford to limit its inquiry to volunteers. **Reciprocity** involves a system of *mutual trust and obligation between the researcher and subject.* Subjects are asked to share themselves in the belief that this baring of information will not be used in an inappropriate, harmful, or embarrassing manner. A basic tenet of any scholarly research is the dictum that the investigator maintains objectivity and professional integrity in both the performance and the reporting of research. The researcher, first and foremost, is an investigator and not a hustler, huck-

FIGURE 2.1 Preventing Crime: What Works, What Doesn't, What's Promising

In 1996 Congress required that the Attorney General and the National Institute of Justice evaluate the effectiveness of 500 funded programs in a manner that would be "independent in nature" and "employ rigorous and scientifically recognized standards and methodologies." The Institute on Criminology and Criminal Justice at the University of Maryland was contacted to undertake this task and to serve as a clearinghouse. It issued its report entitled *Preventing Crime: What Works, What Doesn't, What's Promising* (Sherman et al., 1997). These evaluations are regularly updated (www.preventingcrime.org), where full reports or research in brief summaries can be downloaded. They can also be obtained from the Bureau of Justice Statistics website (www.ojp.usdoj.gov/bjs/). A few of the programs included in the list are:

What Doesn't Work

- Gun "buyback " programs
- Drug Abuse Resistance Education (DARE)
- Arrest of unemployed suspects for domestic assault
- Storefront police offices
- Correctional boot camps using traditional military basic training
- "Scared Straight" programs whereby minor juvenile offenders visit adult prisons
- Shock probation, shock parole
- Home detention with electronic monitoring
- Intensive supervision on parole or probation
- Residential programs for juvenile offenders using challenging experiences in rural settings

What Works:

- For infants—frequent home visits by nurses and other professionals
- For delinquents and at-risk preadolescent—family therapy and parent training
- For schools
  - —organizational development for innovation
  - —communication and reinforcement of consistent norms
  - —teaching of social competency skills
  - —coaching in "thinking skills" for high risk youth
- For older male ex-offenders—vocational training
- Extra police patrols for high-crime "hot spots"
- For high risk offenders—Monitoring by specialized police units —incarceration
- For employed, domestic abusers—arrest
- For convicted offenders—rehabilitation programs with risk-focused treatments
- For drug-using offenders in prison—therapeutic community treatment programs

What's Promising?

- Proactive drunk driving arrests with breath testing
- Police showing greater respect to arrested offenders (may reduce repeat offending)
- Higher number of police officers in cities (may reduce crime generally)
- Gang monitoring by community workers and probation and police officers
- Community monitoring by Big Brothers/Big Sisters of America (may prevent drug abuse)
- Community-based after school recreation programs
- Battered women's shelters
- Job Corps residential training for at-risk youth
- Prison-based vocational education programs
- Two clerks on duty in already-robbed convenience stores
- Metal detectors
- Proactive arrest for carrying concealed weapons (may reduce gun crime)
- Drug courts
- Drug treatment in jails followed by urine testing
- Intensive supervision and aftercare of juvenile offenders

None of these evaluations as "working" or "not working" is final; constant replication (repeated experiments) and reevaluation is required, but a persistent, independent, scientific program of evaluation will go a long way in replacing what we think works or what doesn't with what actually does work.

Sources: Irvin Waller and Brandon Welsh. "Reducing Crime in Harnessing International Best Practice." *NIJ Journal.* October, 1998: 26–32; and Lawrence Sherman et al. "Preventing Crime: What Works, What Doesn't, What's Promising?" *NIJ Research in Brief.* July, 1998.
Web Sources: National Institute of Justice: *www.ojp.gov/nij;* Justice Information Center: *www.ncjrs.org;* University of Maryland preventing crime project: *www.preventingcrime.org;* International data on what works: *www.crime-prevention-intl.org.*

InfoTrac College Edition Research

Using one of the titles of the programs described above (e.g., boot camps or drug courts) find an article that describes one of these programs and whether the program worked or not.

Visit *www.preventingcrime.org* and examine a specific program. Does this program work, show promise of working, or not work?

ster, salesperson, or politician. Researchers should avoid purposely choosing and reporting only those techniques that tend to shed the best light on their data, or "lying with statistics" (Huff, 1966). Related to these issues is the fact that the researcher should take steps to protect the confidentiality and privacy of respondents. One procedure for attempting to protect the identity of subjects, organizations, or communities is the use of pseudonyms, aliases, or false names. Names such as "Doc," "Chic," "The Lupollo Family," "Vince Swaggi," "Deep Throat," and "Wincanton," to mention just a few, have become legend in criminology.

Pure vs. Applied Research

Many disciplines in the social sciences have experienced academic guerrilla warfare between two camps: those primarily interested in pure research and those who espouse applied research. **Pure research** is concerned with *the discovery of knowledge, even that which may have no present applicability, in order to contribute to the development of a science or discipline.* **Applied research** deals with *finding answers in order to direct policy analysis of present problems.* In reality, the division between pure and applied research is somewhat hazy, since there is in fact much overlap between the two types (Rabow, 1964). Often the most obscure and abstract research, that which critics might call "ivory tower" research, will in the long run produce the critical breakthroughs that may pay off more directly than many premature applied projects: Pasteur, Einstein, and Galileo were not applied researchers. On the other hand, even though critics of applied researchers may describe them at times as shamans or quacks attempting to provide advice or guide policy without adequate theoretical or methodological support, many existing projects require immediate policy decisions that cannot wait and must represent the best we have to offer at the present time.

Those who are impatient with or question the need for research in criminology or criminal justice often raise the questions of "So What?" or "Of what practical use are all of these research projects?" Perhaps in answer to such questions, in 1996 the U.S. Congress required the Attorney General to provide "a comprehensive evaluation of the effectiveness" of over $3 billion spent annually in Department of Justice grants that had been designed to assist state and local law enforcement and communities in preventing crime (Sherman et al. 1997). See Figure 2.1.

Who Is Criminal?

To illustrate the importance of methodological precision, let us examine the basic, but deceptively complex questions, "Who is criminal?" and "How much crime is there?" While an initial response to these questions might be, "Why, of course, we know," the answers are not as obvious as they seem.

Taking what would appear to be the easiest question—"Who is criminal?"—Most would agree that long-term recidivists (repeaters) who have repeatedly been found guilty are criminals. Yet some ideologues (those committed to a strict adherence to a distinctive political belief system) might even on this point maintain that some of these "career criminals" are in fact not criminals, but are, from the conflict perspective, political prisoners. They are viewed as victims of an unfair class system or of a politically oppressive system (Quinney and Wildeman, 1977; Turk, 1982). Additionally, not all apprehended individuals or persons accused of crime are guilty; and what about those who commit crimes but who are not arrested?

It becomes apparent that the manner in which the variable "criminal" is operationalized will have a major influence on the definition of the concept of criminal. A **variable** is *a concept that has been operationalized or measured in a specific manner and that can vary or take on different values, usually of a quantitative nature.* **Operationalization** involves *the process of defining concepts by describing how they are being measured;* the notion of operationalization can be practically explained by completing the statement "I measured it by __________." In Chapters 4, 5 and 6, we will describe many theories that assume excess criminality among lower class groups based on official statistics; however, what methodological problems and biases in addressing this issue are introduced by relying solely on one measure of crime?

Official Police Statistics—The Uniform Crime Reports (UCR)

Internationally, until relatively recently the major source of information regarding crime statistics was official police statistics. Gathered for government administrative purposes with only secondary attention paid to their usefulness for social science research, these data tended to be uneven in quality and were not gathered or recorded in any systematic manner. Basically, criminologists had no efficient statistics to consult in order to answer even basic questions such as whether crime was increasing or decreasing.

Since 1930 the *U.S. Department of Justice has compiled national crime statistics,* the **Uniform Crime Report (UCR),** *with the Federal Bureau of Investigation (FBI) assuming responsibility as the clearinghouse and publisher.* Although participation in the UCR program by local police departments is purely voluntary, the number of departments reporting and the comprehensiveness of the information have steadily improved over the years, with police departments from large metropolitan areas historically the best participants (Banas and Trojanowicz, 1985).

Sources of Crime Statistics

Returning to our question "How much crime is there?" an examination of the UCR and its relationship to sources of data on crime and criminals is useful. Figure 2.2 illustrates the relationship between crime committed and the sources of crime statistics, including the UCR. It is unclear whether an accurate estimate of the amount of crime committed is possible, for several reasons. Not all crimes that are committed are discovered. Some crimes may be known only to the perpetrators, in which case the victim is unaware of loss. Perhaps there is no identifiable victim, as in the case of a gambling violation. The further a source of statistics is from the "crimes committed" category, the less useful it is as a measure of the extent of crime. Not all crimes that are discovered are reported to the police. Similarly, not all reported crimes are recorded by police.

In addition, some law enforcement agencies may purposely conceal recorded crimes; a number of purported crimes may be **unfounded** or defined by investigating officers as *not constituting a criminal matter.* For instance, when a complainant reports an attempted burglary, investigating officers may conclude that there is not enough evidence to support that a crime took place.

Despite this problematic relationship between crimes recorded and crimes committed, the UCR until recently represented the best statistics available on crime commission and, as will be discussed later in this chapter, still represents one of the best sources. Again in Figure 2.2, once we move beyond crimes recorded as a measure of crime commission, we are getting further removed from the accurate measurement of crime commission. Thus arrest statistics, indictments, convictions, incarcerations, and other dispositions such as probation and parole are not as useful. Such statistics have much more to do with police

FIGURE 2.2 Sources of Crime Statistics: The Flow of Offenders through the Criminal Justice System

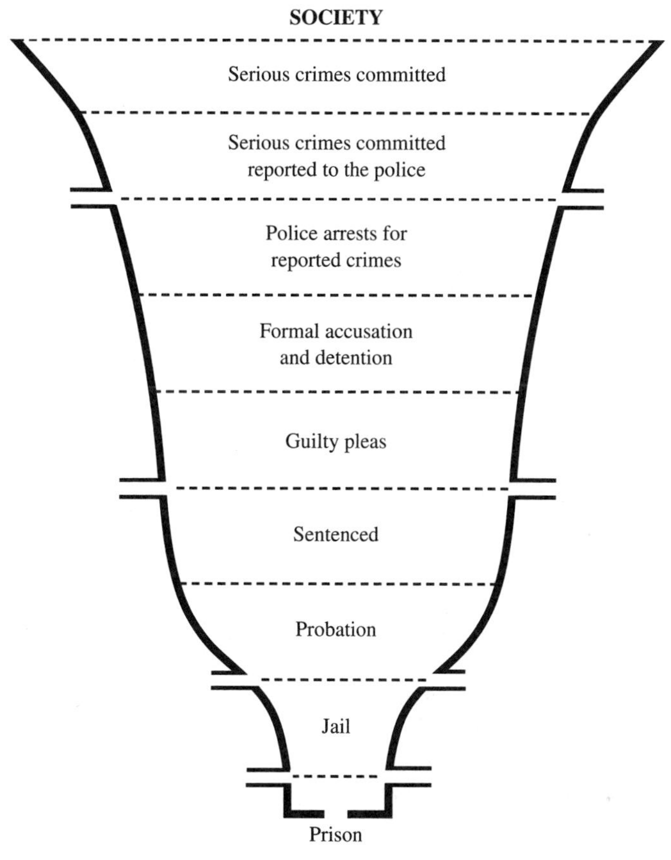

Source: Adapted from the President's Commission on Law Enforcement and the Administration of Justice. 1967a. *The Challenge of Crime in a Free Society,* Washington D.C.: Government Printing Office, pp. 262–63.

efficiency or allocations to the criminal justice system and general societal policies toward crime control policy than they do with measuring the extent of the crime problem.

Most media accounts of changes in the crime rate are based on the annual summary presented in the UCR. While the UCR contains many qualifying remarks regarding the meaning of these statistics, in most instances the press tends to report these data uncritically and often in an alarmist manner. Obviously, the researcher who chooses to utilize UCR data must become as familiar as possible with any shortcomings or sources of bias in these statistics. The FBI receives its information for the UCR from local police departments. Considerable variation exists in state penal codes regarding criminal offenses and their definitions, although participating departments receive instruction in uniform crime recording in order to standardize their reports for use in compiling nationwide figures. In the majority of states, UCR systems require that all local departments report their statistics to the state. These data are then shared with the FBI. The Census Bureau estimates that about 97 percent of the total national population were covered by the report.

The Crime Index

Historically, the UCR has been divided into two parts: **Part I crimes** consist of the **index crimes,** *major felonies that are believed to be serious, to occur frequently, and to have a greater likelihood of being reported to the police.* The index offenses are:

1. Murder and nonnegligent manslaughter
2. Forcible rape
3. Robbery
4. Aggravated assault
5. Burglary
6. Larceny/theft
7. Motor vehicle theft
8. Arson

The original index and the one used for historical comparison consist of the first seven offenses. Arson was added as a result of a law passed by the U.S. Congress in October 1978. As we will see shortly, the crime rate is calculated with the index offenses. Figure 2.3 defines the various offenses in uniform crime reporting.

Part II crimes are nonindex offenses and are not used in the calculation of the crime rate. This includes:

- Simple assault
- Forgery and counterfeiting
- Fraud
- Embezzlement
- Receiving stolen property
- Vandalism
- Illegal carrying of weapons
- Prostitution and related offenses
- Sex offenses (statutory rape, etc.)
- Drug law violations
- Liquor law violations
- Public drunkenness
- Disorderly conduct
- Vagrancy
- Curfew violations/loitering
- Runaways
- All other violations of state and local laws (except traffic violations)

Issues and Cautions in Studying UCR Data

An extensive literature has accumulated regarding shortcomings of UCR statistics. While the UCR has steadily improved and been refined since its inception in 1930, researchers utilizing these data should exercise **caution** and be aware of certain limitations. *Some primary shortcomings of the UCR* include the following:

1. The recorded statistics represent only a portion of the true crime rate of a community. Victim surveys suggest that there is possibly twice as much crime committed as appears in official statistics.
2. The big increase in the crime rate beginning in the mid-sixties may be explained in part by better communications, more professional and more efficient police departments, and better recording and reporting of crime. Larger, improved, and professionalized police departments appear to be positively related to rising crime rates. This

FIGURE 2.3 Offenses in Uniform Crime Reporting

Offenses in Uniform Crime Reporting are divided into two groupings, Part I and Part II. Information on the volume of Part I offenses known to law enforcement, those cleared by arrest or exceptional means, and the number of persons arrested is reported monthly. Only arrest data are reported for Part II offenses.

The Part I offenses are:

Criminal homicide: a. Murder and nonnegligent manslaughter: the willful (nonnegligent) killing of one human being by another. Deaths caused by negligence, attempts to kill, assaults to kill, suicides, accidental deaths, and justifiable homicides are excluded. Justifiable homicides are limited to: (1) the killing of a felon by a law enforcement officer in the line of duty; and (2) the killing of a felon, during the commission of a felony, by a private citizen. b. Manslaughter by negligence: the killing of another person through gross negligence. Traffic fatalities are excluded. While manslaughter by negligence is a Part I crime, it is not included in the Crime Index.

Forcible rape: The carnal knowledge of a female forcibly and against her will. Included are rapes by force and attempts or assaults to rape. Statutory offenses (no force used—victim under age of consent) are excluded.

Robbery: The taking or attempting to take anything of value from the care, custody, or control of a person or persons by force or threat of force or violence, and/or by putting the victim in fear.

Aggravated assault: An unlawful attack by one person upon another for the purpose of inflicting severe or aggravated bodily injury. This type of assault is usually accompanied by the use of a weapon or by a means likely to produce death or great bodily harm. Simple assaults are excluded.

Burglary/breaking or entering: The unlawful entry of a structure to commit a felony or theft. Attempted forcible entry is included.

Larceny/theft (except motor vehicle theft): The unlawful taking, carrying, leading, or riding away of property from the possession or constructive possession of another. Examples are thefts of bicycles or automobile accessories, shoplifting, pocket-picking, or the stealing of any property or article which is not taken by force and violence or by fraud. Attempted larcenies are included. Embezzlement, "con" games, forgery, worthless checks, etc., are excluded.

Motor vehicle theft: The theft or attempted theft of a motor vehicle. A motor vehicle is self-propelled and runs on the surface and not on rails. Specifically excluded from this category are motorboats, construction equipment, airplanes, and farming equipment.

Arson: Any willful or malicious burning or attempt to burn, with or without intent to defraud, a dwelling house, public building, motor vehicle or aircraft, personal property of another, etc.

The Part II offenses are:

Other assaults (simple): Assaults and attempted assaults where no weapon is used and which do not result in serious or aggravated injury to the victim.

Forgery and counterfeiting: Making, altering, uttering, or possessing, with intent to defraud, anything false in the semblance of that which is true. Attempts are included.

Fraud: Fraudulent conversion and obtaining money or property by false pretenses. Included are confidence games and bad checks, except forgeries and counterfeiting.

Embezzlement: Misappropriation or misapplication of money or property entrusted to one's care, custody, or control.

Stolen property; buying, receiving, possessing: Buying, receiving, and possessing stolen property, including attempts.

Vandalism: Willful or malicious destruction, injury, disfigurement, or defacement of any public or private property, real or personal, without consent of the owner or persons having custody or control.

Weapons-carrying, possessing, etc.: All violations of regulations or statutes controlling the carrying, using, possessing, furnishing, and manufacturing of deadly weapons or silencers. Attempts are included.

Prostitution and commercialized vice: Sex offenses of a commercialized nature, such as prostitution, keeping a bawdy house, procuring, or transporting women for immoral purposes. Attempts are included.

Sex offenses (except forcible rape, prostitution, and commercialized vice): Statutory rape and offenses against chastity, common decency, morals, and the like. Attempts are included.

Drug abuse violations: State and/or local offenses relating to the unlawful possession, sale, use, growing, and manufacturing of narcotic drugs. The following drug categories are specified: opium or cocaine and their derivatives (morphine, heroin, codeine); marijuana; synthetic narcotics—manufactured narcotics that can cause true addiction (demerol, methadone); and dangerous nonnarcotic drugs (barbiturates, benzedrine).

Gambling: Promoting, permitting, or engaging in illegal gambling.

Offenses against the family and children: Nonsupport, neglect, desertion, or abuse of family and children.

Driving under the influence: Driving or operating any vehicle or common carrier while drunk or under the influence of liquor or narcotics.

Liquor laws violations: State and/or local liquor law violations, except "drunkenness" and "driving under the influence." Federal violations are excluded.

Drunkenness: Offenses relating to drunkenness or intoxication. "Driving under the influence" is not included.

Disorderly conduct: Break of the peace.

Vagrancy: Vagabondage, begging, loitering, etc.

All other offenses: All violations of state and/or local laws, except those listed above and traffic offenses.

Suspicion: No specific offense; suspect released without formal charges being placed.

Curfew and loitering laws (persons under age 18): Offenses relating to violations of local curfew or loitering ordinances where such laws exist.

Runaways (persons under age 18): Limited to juveniles taken into protective custody under provisions of local statutes.

Source: Federal Bureau of Investigation. 1995. *Crime in the United States, 1994, Uniform Crime Reports.* Washington, D.C.: Government Printing Office, pp. 383–84.

(© Jim Pickerell / Tony Stone Images)

Modern urban police departments depend on high-tech methods of communication and on computer-assisted recording and reporting of crimes.

was particularly the case in larger urban areas. In the seventies, while the official crime rate increased dramatically, victim surveys and self-report surveys showed a fairly stable crime rate.

3. Increased citizen concern and awareness of crime, higher standards of expected public morality, and greater reporting of and response to ghetto crime might all have had impacts on increasing the recorded crime rate.
4. Most federal offenses, "victimless" crimes, and white collar crimes do not appear in the UCR. Analysis of age, racial, and sexual characteristics of those arrested shows that the UCR concentrates on "crime in the streets," the crimes of the inept and poor, and fails to include "crime in the suites," or crimes of the elite.
5. Changes in record-keeping procedures (such as computerization), transition in police administrations, and political shenanigans can have a major impact on crime recording. The FBI attempts to monitor and control abuses. In 1949 it refused to publish New York City Police Department data. With "improved" recording, the robbery rate jumped 800 percent the next year. Changes in police practices showed similar leaps elsewhere: 61 percent in Chicago in 1961 when a new chief took over, 202 percent in Kansas City in 1959 due to departmental reform, and 95 percent in Buffalo in the early sixties (President's Commission, 1967a, p. 25). Similar dramatic drops in the crime rate have taken place when required for political purposes. Nixon's targeting of the District of Columbia for a crime-busting program showed such a decline, which was more likely simply a matter of reclassifying crimes to keep them out of the index. Until 1973, grand larceny of $50 or more could be classified as under $50 and thus unrecorded in the index from which the crime rate is calculated.
6. In interpreting UCR statistics, keep in mind what arrest statistics do and do not mean:
   a. Arrests do not equal crimes solved or suspects found guilty.
   b. Many reported crimes are declared unfounded by police.

c. In the situation involving multiple offenses, only the most serious offense is recorded for UCR purposes.
d. The majority of crimes committed are not index offenses.

7. The crime index is made up primarily of property crimes. Auto theft, a less serious and highly reported and cleared offense, artificially inflates this index and perhaps should be dropped from Part 1 designation (Savitz, 1978). Inflation causes bicycle thefts to become larceny, an index offense; while after 1973, all larcenies were included in the index, thus increasing the crime rate (Rhodes, 1977, p. 168). Greater insurance coverage further encourages reporting of property loss.
8. The crime index is an unweighted index; it is a simple summated scale in which a murder counts the same as a bicycle theft. Surprisingly, most bodily injury crimes are "nonindex" offenses (Savitz, 1978).
9. The existence of the "crime index" may encourage concentration by police agencies on these offenses at the expense of others.
10. The crime rate is calculated on the basis of decennial census population figures. Rapidly growing cities of the Southwest would, under this system, have worse appearing rates since, for example, 1979 crimes would be divided by a 1970 population base.
11. Demographic shifts may provide partial explanations for changing crime rates. Some criminologists had prophesied the crime dip (a decline in the crime rate trend) in the 1980s based on a general aging of the baby boom generation (children born in the post-World War II era, from 1946 through the mid-fifties). This larger-than-normal population cohort overwhelmed hospital nursery wards, elementary and secondary schools, and later colleges. These establishments now have extra space. Similarly, the criminal justice system was overwhelmed by a larger-than-normal proportion in the maximal crime-committing ages (15–24), as the job market and housing industry inherit this now "middle-age boom." Barring other factors, as this group ages, the criminal justice system should find itself with a more manageable situation, although Blumstein and Cohen (1987) had predicted an expected "echo boom" in the 1990s. This did not happen. Also countering this downward trend are high violent crime rates, particularly by juveniles. This involves higher crime rates by the children of the baby boomers. The researcher who decides to make use of official statistics such as the UCR must become familiar with such inadequacies in order to avoid drawing inappropriate conclusions or analyses. Despite the shortcomings that have been identified, the UCR remains an excellent source of information on police operations. Treatment of actual UCR data and trends using the crime index offenses and the crime rate will be deferred until the next chapter and the discussion of variations in crime.

The Crime Rate. The **crime rate** is *a calculation that expresses the total number of index crimes per 100,000 population.*

$$\frac{\text{Number of crimes}}{\text{Population}} \times 100{,}000 = \text{Crime Rate}$$

The purpose of an index (like the Dow-Jones Industrial Average or the Consumer Price Index) is to provide a composite measure, one that does not rely too heavily on any one factor. An index also allows controlling for population size, thus permitting fair comparisons of different-sized units. As previously indicated, it is this UCR crime rate that one reads about in the newspaper, with accounts of crime either rising or falling by a given percent. A principal difficulty with the UCR crime rate as an index of crime in the United States is that it is an unweighted index. That is, each crime, whether murder or bicycle theft, is added into the total index with no weight given to the relative seriousness of the offense. Thus no monetary or psychological value is assigned. For instance, a city with

(© Patrick Frilet / Sipa Press)

Young men with guns embody the public perception of crime in the streets. Their rate of violent crime runs counter to the general trend.

100 burglaries per 100,000 population and one with 100 homicides per 100,000 population would have the same crime rate.

One alternative that has been proposed is the calculation of a weighted index using crime-seriousness scales (Sellin and Wolfgang, 1964; Rossi et al., 1974). In a weighted crime index, criminal incidents are assigned weights on the basis of variables such as amount stolen, method of intimidation, degree of harm inflicted, and similar salient factors.

Redesign of the UCR Program: NIBRS. The redesigned UCR Program is called **NIBRS (National Incident-Based Reporting System).** In 1982, in response to the criticisms and limitations of the UCR program, the Bureau of Justice Statistics and the FBI formed a joint task force and contracted with a private research firm (Abt Associates, Inc.) to undertake revisions in the UCR program. This was the first in the program's then more than fifty years of existence (Poggio et al., 1985; Rovetch, Poggio, and Rossman, 1984). On the basis of recommendations of a steering committee made up of police practitioners, academicians, and the media, the *NIBRS suggestions for changes in the UCR included:*

- A new two-level reporting system in which most agencies continue to report basic offense and arrest data much as they do at present (Level I), while a small sample of agencies report more extensive information (Level II).
- The entire UCR system is to be converted into unit-record reporting in which police agencies report on the characteristics of each criminal incident (for example, location, time, presence of weapon) and on the characteristics of each individual arrest.
- Distinguish attempted from completed offenses.
- Distinguish among crimes against businesses, individuals or households, and against other entities.
- Institute ongoing audits of samples of participating UCR agencies to check for error in the new program.
- Support better user services particularly in making databases more available to outside researchers.
- NIBRS will collect data on each single incident and arrest in 22 crime categories. (U.S. Department of Justice, 1988, p. 82)

FIGURE 2.4 Crime Clock 1998

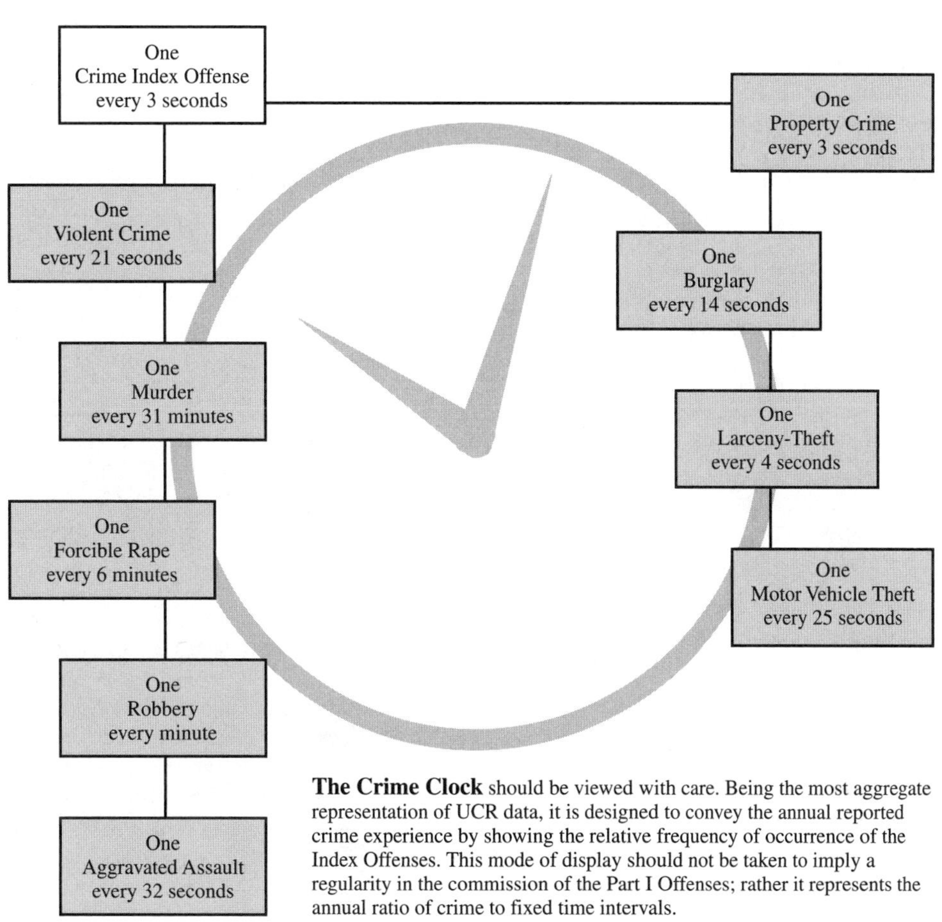

Source: Federal Bureau of Investigation. 1999. *Crime in the United States,* 1998. FBI web site: www.fbi.gov

It is believed that these revisions in the program, which are taking longer to implement than anticipated, will overcome a number of past criticisms as well as provide a database that will be more useful both for researchers and policy-makers.

Crime Clocks. Figure 2.4 presents a summary device that is displayed in the UCR with proper cautionary statements—an illustration called a crime clock. Despite UCR warnings to readers, the media and others tend to either misunderstand or misuse this graphic device in summarizing trends in crime. The **crime clock** device is *the poorest graphic device for analyzing crime change because it fails to control for population growth and uses a constant fixed unit of comparison—time.* Relative to population growth, a community could be experiencing a per capita decline in crime and the crime clock would still show an increase. Suppose, for example, that a community in 1960 had a population of 1 million and 100 serious crimes and in 1990 had a population of 2 million and 200 serious crimes. The crime rate would be ten in each period, but the crime clock would have shown an increase. The crime clock graphic device serves little function with growing populations other than

IN THE NEWS 2.1

THE CRIME DIP OF THE NINETIES

From the first compilation of crime statistics by the Federal Bureau of Investigation in the early 1930s until the early 1960s, the crime rate in the United States had been declining. Some experts had even unwisely predicted that, given existing trends and growing affluence, crime might become a rarity by the twenty-first century. By the mid-sixties, however, recorded crime made a reversal and rose to unprecedented levels, producing in its wake yet new predictions of unrepentant explosions in the crime rate. A brief levelling off in the early eighties was followed by an epidemic of youth violence beginning in the mid-eighties with the advent of crack cocaine and widespread use of weapons to defend disputed drug trafficking turf. By the 1990s an assumed inevitability of rising crime rates was greeted by unexpected declines, beginning in large cities such as New York. Between 1993 and 2000, index crimes had declined over 30 percent.

The causes of this crime dip are a subject of dispute. Factors associated with the crime dip that began in the 1990s include:

- A healthy economy
- Crime prevention programs
- Decline in domestic violence
- An incarceration binge
- Compstat and community policing
- A decline in the crack cocaine epidemic
- Legalized abortion

The most prosperous American economy in over thirty years highlighted by low unemployment and low inflation may be the major reason for falling crime rates. Such an explanation may not be the case, however. During the 1960s crime rates rose sharply at a time of low unemployment. More recently, Sunbelt cities with low unemployment have had higher crime rates than older cities with high unemployment. New York City's murder rate in the 1990s fell over 66 percent despite high unemployment (Witkin, 1998a, p. 30).

Crime prevention, which shows much promise for early prevention programs with high risk juveniles, has shown only modest impacts on crime rates.

Domestic murders (among intimates) demonstrated a 40 percent decline between 1976 and 1996. Part of the explanation for this was a decline in marriages among 20–24 year olds, as well as greater opportunities for abused women to escape such relationships.

America's incarceration binge has been phenomenal, increasing from 744,000 in 1985 to approximately 1.8 million in 1998. This is the largest imprisoned population of any country in the world outside Russia. While locking up an extra million prisoners must have some impact, New York City showed the most dramatic drop in crime, while the state of New York (with 70 percent of its prison population from New York City) increased its prison population by only 8 percent between 1993 and 1996. Utah on the other hand

to misleadingly alarm the public. In fact, companies peddling burglar alarms and security devices are particularly fond of reproducing these figures in their advertising.

The nineteenth-century British Prime Minister Benjamin Disraeli has often been cited as having remarked, "There are three types of lies: lies, damn lies and statistics." Obviously, caution must be exercised in examining graphic devices and statistical reports (Huff, 1966; and Zeisel, 1957). In the 1980s and early 1990s, rising juvenile violent crime led conservative commentators such as Robert Bennett and John Dilulio to forecast grim prophecies of exploding juvenile crime among violent criminal predators raised in mean minority ghettoes and in maternal, single-parent households—a foreboding inevitability born of moral rot. In the 1990s these very "hopeless areas" showed the greatest decline in crime, one which few had predicted. IN THE NEWS 2.1 assesses this "Crime Dip of the Nineties."

Alternative Data-Gathering Strategies

Official crime statistics published by national governments have their uses, however, criminologists would be remiss in their duty as scholars and scientists if they were to restrict their inquiries and sources of statistics to data gathered for administrative purposes by gov-

IN THE NEWS 2.1—*Continued*

raised its incarceration rate by 19 percent between 1993 and 1996, but its violent crime rate went up (Ibid., p. 31).

Another candidate for explanation has been better and more effective policing. "Compstats" (computer statistics) was used to computer map and identify "hot spots" (high crime areas) by the New York City police to assign target patrols. Kelling and Wilson's "Broken Windows" (1982) theory emphasized focusing on small, nuisance crimes under the assumption that such crimes left unpunished breed more serious crimes. The fact that many cities that did not employ community policing strategies also experienced major declines in recorded crime—and some innovative departments experienced increases—leaves the more effective policing explanation in question.

A rival explanation is that the police departments are manipulating statistics to show lower crime rates. While this may occur in individual cases, such a simultaneous mass conspiracy by most departments seems unlikely. In 1998 the Philadelphia Police Department was accused of systematically underreporting crime for years. *The Philadelphia Inquirer* reported routine downgrading of the seriousness of crimes in which stabbings and beatings were redefined as "hospital cases" and burglaries became "lost property" (Associated Press, 1998).

Blumstein and colleagues (Blumstein and Rosenfeld, 1998) point out that all of the increase in homicide in the late 1980s to early 1990s was among younger people (under 21), and this was primarily due to a crack cocaine epidemic in American cities beginning in 1986 that peaked in 1993. This epidemic was accompanied by a great increase in the carrying of firearms to settle turf wars.

A final intriguing explanation in an article by Levitt and Donohue (1999) argues that legalized abortion is responsible for falling crime rates. They claim that half of the drop in crime since 1991 might reflect the Supreme Court's 1973 *Roe v. Wade* decision legalizing abortion. Some unwanted, potential criminals were not born because their potential mothers had abortions. The decline in crime began in 1992 just when those youths that would have been born in the mid-1970s would have hit their peak crime years (18–24). Even Levitt and Donohue admit, however, that other factors may be more explanatory of the crime dip than abortion. Just as criminologists debated the causes of the rise of crime, there is no consensus regarding explanations for the decline in crime or even prognostications as to when crime might rise again.

Sources: Associated Press. 1998. "Philadelphia Crime Statistics Questioned." November 2; Alfred Blumstein and Richard Rosenfeld. 1998. "Assessing the Recent Ups and Downs in U.S. Homicide Rates." *National Institute of Justice Journal.* October, 9–11.; Steven Levitt and John Donohue. 1999. "Legalized Abortion and Crime." *Chicago Tribune.* August 8: Gordon Witkin. 1998. "The Crime Bust: What's Behind the Dramatic Drug Bust?" *U.S. News and World Report.* May 25, pp. 28–37.

InfoTrac College Edition Research

Using InfoTrac College Edition find an article that attempts to explain the reasons why the crime rate fell. Do you agree with this article? Explain.

ernment bodies. In some totalitarian regimes, for instance, there would be nothing to study, since the official government ideology might simply hold that there is no crime in the people's paradise. Even in open societies, official statistics seldom cover crimes of the elite. Fortunately, criminologists have at their disposal a veritable arsenal of techniques whose application is limited only by the researcher's imagination and skill.

Figure 2.5 offers a model or paradigm (schema) with which to consider and compare the alternative data-gathering strategies that can be employed in criminal justice and criminological research. As an illustrative device, Figure 2.5 is an attempt to broadly describe the relative advantages and disadvantages of the different data-gathering strategies. The model suggests that, as we move up the list of techniques or vertical arrows to experiments, we tend to obtain: quantitative measurement (which lends itself to sophisticated statistical treatment), greater control over other factors that may interfere with one's findings, and increased internal validity (or accuracy in being certain that the variable[s] assumed to be responsible for one's findings are indeed the causal agent[s])—but at the expense of artificiality. The latter point suggests that, as a result of controlling for error, the researcher may have created an antiseptic or atypical group or situation that no longer resembles the "real world" that one is attempting to describe.

FIGURE 2.5 Alternative Data-Gathering Strategies

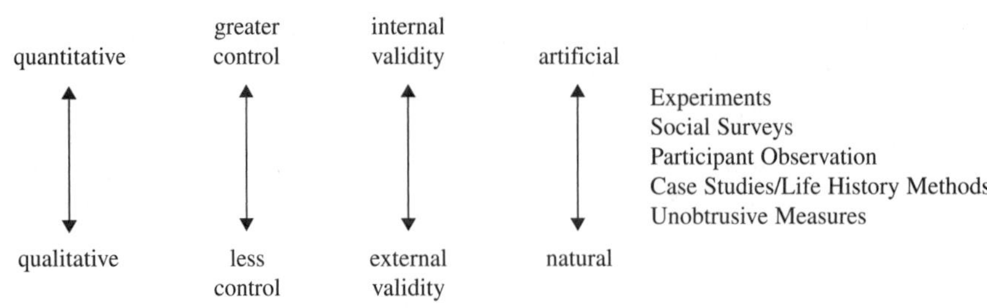

Source: Frank E. Hagan, 1993. *Research Methods in Criminal Justice and Criminology.* 3rd edition. New York: Macmillan p. 101. Reprinted by permission of Allyn & Bacon.

Generally, as one proceeds down the vertical arrows or list of techniques, the methodology employed becomes more qualitative. Qualitative techniques involve less commitment to quantitative measurement on the part of the researcher, more engagement with field and observational strategies, and less direct means of obtaining information. Generally, as one moves down the list, one has less control over manipulating the research setting and rival causal factors. Such procedures, however, increase external validity (the ability to generalize to larger populations) as well as present the opportunity to study subjects in more natural settings. Such qualitative research permits the researcher to utilize a more craftsmanlike process in which he or she can alter or shift data-collection processes as the research progresses (Haar, 1992, p. 6). Implicit in this model is the fact that each method has its own relative strengths and weaknesses, and often the very strength of one technique is the weakness of another and vice versa. No one technique has an a priori superiority over any other means of obtaining data.

Criminologists, like other researchers, tend to favor their own particular methods of data gathering; this is to be expected. At times, however, academic battles break out among those who claim that their preferred method contains some inherent superiority over other procedures. Such **methodological narcissism** (or methodologism) is *a fanatical adherence to a particular research method, often at the expense of a concern for substance* ("Martinson Attacks His Own Earlier Work," 1978, p. 4; Martinson, 1979; and Bayley, 1978). This "methods for methods' sake" orientation ignores the fact that methodology is not an end in itself but a means to an end—the development of criminological knowledge. It is more useful to permit the subject to dictate the proper methodology than to assert that, unless a subject lends itself to deployment of one's favorite method, it is not worthy of study.

Experiments in Criminology

The experiment is the lodestone or benchmark for comparison with all other research methods. It is the most effective means of controlling for error or rival factors before the fact through the very design of the study (Campbell and Stanley, 1963). While there are myriad variations of the experiment, the point of departure or prototype is the classic experimental design. **The Classic Experimental Design** *contains three key elements:*

- *Equivalence*
- *Pretests and posttests*
- *Experimental and control groups*

Basically, equivalence means the assignment of subjects to experimental and control groups in such a manner that they are assumed to be alike in all major respects. This can be done either through random assignment (where each subject has an equal probability of appearing in either group) or through matching (a procedure in which subjects with similar age, sex, and other characteristics exhibited by the experimental group are recruited for the control group). The *experimental group* is to receive the treatment (*X*), while the *control group* will receive no treatment but will be observed in order to compare it with the experimental group. Both groups are given pretests (pre-observations in order to note conditions that exist prior to treatment) designated as 01, or observation time one, and posttests or observations after the experimental treatment (*X*) has taken place. The logic of the experiment assumes that, since both groups were equivalent in the pretest period, any differences in the posttest observation must be due to the fact that one group received a particular treatment and the other did not. Increasingly, such experiments are being utilized in order to inform public policy decision making. Such experiments are seen as giving answers that enable fairly clear policy direction (Kelling, 1988a; Garner and Visher, 1988).

Some Examples of Experiments in Criminology

Candid Camera. In an attempt to increase both the apprehension and the conviction rates of robbers of commercial establishments, the Seattle Police Department created a field experiment using high-risk establishments, some of which were designated as the experimental group, others as the control group. The treatment for the experimental group involved installation of special hidden cameras that could be triggered during a holdup by a clerk's pulling a "trip" bill from the cash drawer; prints of the photograph of the robber would be made available immediately. A posttest of the two types of sites found 55 percent of robberies in the experimental group cleared by arrest compared to 25 percent for control locations. (Clearance indicates that suspects have been arrested, charged, and turned over to the court for prosecution or that the police consider further investigation unnecessary.) While 48 percent of the robbers at camera sites were convicted, only 19 percent of the control group brigands were found guilty ("Hidden Cameras Project," 1978).

Scared Straight. Much fanfare was raised in the United States in the late seventies over a novel program intended to deter wayward juveniles from progression to more serious criminal activity by means of blunt, "heart-to-heart" talks in prison with specially selected inmates. Portrayed in a film, Scared Straight, the initial Rahway, New Jersey, prison project was intended to counteract the glamorized image associated with criminal life. Although many jurisdictions rushed to imitate what appeared to be the latest panacea in corrections, further research suggested that this optimism was premature (Finckenauer, 1982). Yarborough evaluated the JOLT (Juvenile Offenders Learn Truth) program at the Jackson State Prison, Michigan, by randomly assigning youths to experimental and control groups. He then measured their delinquency rates three and six months afterwards and found no significant differences between those who had attended the JOLT sessions (experimentals) and those who had not (controls) ("Scared Straight Found Ineffective Again," 1979).

Obedience to Authority. Milgram's experiments, reported in *Obedience to Authority* (1974), raised many ethical problems like those we discussed at the beginning of the chapter. The experiments dealt with conditions under which people would commit immoral acts when instructed to do so by what they perceived as competent authorities. Volunteers were told they were participating in a learning experiment; they were to administer electric shocks to pupils (actually confederates who were in on the experiment) each time they gave an incorrect answer. Switches on a fake shock-generating machine ranged from small voltage to "XXX-Unknown." All of Milgram's subjects administered the mildest shocks, and a large proportion threw the most lethally labeled switches, despite screams and pleas from the pupils. They apparently did so because they were assured by officials running the study that it was appropriate to do so.

While these experiments have been criticized with respect to artificiality and demand characteristics (participants willing to do the bidding of researchers because they wish to be good subjects), Milgram claims that the situation was real to the participants. While some of the subjects experienced temporary psychological distress, follow-up studies demonstrated no lasting adverse impacts.

Mock Prison. Haney, Banks, and Zimbardo 1973) conducted a "simulated prison study" by creating a mock prison in which undergraduate volunteers were assigned roles as either guards or prisoners. The experiment had to be prematurely canceled when the guards, carried away by their roles, became increasingly brutal and aggressive, and the prisoners displayed progressive hostility and passivity.

Evaluation of Experiments

Experiments are an excellent *means of controlling for factors that may affect the internal validity of studies.* Before the fact, through the very design of the study, the researcher is able to control for rival factors that may tend to invalidate a study. In most instances, experiments are also a relatively quick and inexpensive means of data gathering. The researcher can control the stimulus, the environment, the treatment time, and the degree of exposure.

As discussed previously, the chief disadvantage of experiments is their potential artificiality. The very controls imposed in order to exclude rival causal factors often create atypical groups and conditions, thus impeding the ability to generalize to large populations. Other difficulties relate to problems in obtaining proper subjects or conditions. Ethical issues are raised, particularly since human subjects are involved. Random assignment in prison research might, for instance, constitute a violation of the right of due process or equal treatment under the law (Glaser, 1978, p. 775). Experimenter effects may also occur, in which researchers unwittingly give cues to subjects as to desired results (Rosenthal, 1966). Although the research design features of the experiment are second to none, the experiment as a data-gathering procedure is by no means the most effective or best strategy; and, depending on one's research problem, some alternative research strategy may be desirable.

A particularly thorny issue affecting experimental work in criminology has been given the name "**the dualistic fallacy**" by Sue Titus Reid (1982, p. 657). She defines this as "*the assumption that a population has two mutually exclusive subclasses, such as criminals and noncriminals.*" This problem presents itself in many studies that compare incarcerated populations, which are assumed to represent the criminal class, with the population at large, which is assumed to be purely noncriminal.

Surveys

Most readers are familiar with the use of **surveys** in public opinion polls, in voting-prediction studies, and in marketing research. Surveys are also used in criminology, particularly in analyzing victimization, self-reported crime, public ratings of crime seriousness, measurements of fear of crime, and attitudes toward the police and the criminal justice system. The *principal methods employed in gathering data for surveys are variations of questionnaires, interviews, or telephone surveys.* Just as experiments control for error and rival causal factors before-the-fact by the very design of the study, survey researchers attempt to control for these factors after-the-fact through the use of statistical procedures.

A key issue that is often ignored when discussing the results of surveys is the fact that surveys measure expressed attitude or claimed behavior rather than the attitude or behavior itself. Another issue is that while some surveys, such as the decennial U.S. Census, involve a complete enumeration of the population, for reasons of economy, most surveys entail some type of sampling. **Sampling** involves *choosing a portion of the population, usually in such a manner that the sample represents a microcosm of the population.* The logic of probability sampling methods assumes that, if a careful selection method (EPSEM or equal probability of selection method) is employed, there is a very high likelihood that the sample will contain characteristics similar to those of the population at large. Using such a sample will result in a great savings in time and cost (Babbie, 1975).

Victim Surveys

One of the major shortcomings of such official police statistics as the UCR is that they fail to account for undiscovered or unreported crime; the "**dark figure of crime**" is the *phrase early European criminologists used to refer to offenses that escape official notice.* The assumption was that for every crime that came to the attention of authorities, there were an unspecified number of undiscovered crimes—"the dark figure."

Victim surveys are specifically *designed to record an estimate of claimed victimizations by a representative sample of the population.* One major finding, beginning with the U.S. surveys of the late 1960s, was that overall about twice as much crime was reported to interviewers as appeared in official police records (Biderman et al., 1967; Ennis, 1967; Reiss, 1967). Although now many countries conduct such surveys, the most ambitious and continuing victim survey program has been carried out since the early seventies by the Law Enforcement Assistance Administration (LEAA) of the U.S. Department of Justice. This effort is now under the auspices of the U.S. Bureau of the Census. We will now briefly describe the National Crime Victimization Survey, some problems with such surveys, and some means that have been devised to attempt to control for errors in such surveys.

National Crime Victimization Surveys (NCVS)

Beginning in 1972, the **National Crime Surveys** were conducted. The NCS (now called the National Crime Victimization Survey) *consisted of the Central City Surveys and the National Crime Panel Surveys.*

The Central City Surveys were essentially *cross-sectional studies of households and commercial establishments in selected cities.* Initially, probability samples of approximately 10,000 households and 1,000 to 5,000 commercial establishments were surveyed in 26 central cities. The great expense of such surveys in each city led to their discontinuance (U.S. Department of Justice, 1974, 1975a, 1975b, 1976, and 1979). The National Crime Panels employed *a sophisticated probability sample of housing units and businesses throughout the United States.* In contrast to the central city surveys, which were cross-sectional or studies of one time only, *the panels were longitudinal in nature, that is, studies over time of a particular group.* This enabled bounding of victim reports or the use of pretests in order to have a reference point for the survey reporting period. The initial interview acted as a boundary or time period benchmark with which to compare future reported victimizations. Consisting of about 50,000 households to be interviewed every six months and 15,000 (later upped to 50,000) businesses, the national panels repeated the interviews twice a year in order to achieve the bounding feature previously described. Each housing unit remained in the sample for three years, while every six months a subsample of 10,000 was rotated out of the sample and replaced by a new group. While the initial findings were heralded at the time as the first accurate statistics on crime, further analysis suggests that this conclusion may have been prematurely optimistic. Just as the UCR was found to have shortcomings, so any measure of crime, including victim surveys, can be found wanting in some respects. VANTAGE POINT 2.1 provides examples of the types of questions asked in the NCVS.

Issues and Cautions in Studying Victim Data

Some possible problems in victim surveys include, but are not limited to: the expense of compiling large samples, false or mistaken reports, memory failure or decay, telescoping of events, sampling bias, over- and/or underreporting, interviewer effects, and coding and mechanical errors.

1. While large-scale public opinion polls such as those by Gallup or Roper can be conducted with sample sizes of fewer than 1,000, the rarity of some types of victimization such as rape requires large samples in order to turn up a few victims. Hundreds may need to be surveyed in order to find one victim (Glaser, 1978, p. 63).

   A parallel could be drawn with attempting to survey lottery winners on the basis of a sample of the general population. Many would have to be canvassed before turning up only a few winners. If the chances of winning the lottery were one in a million, in order to discover one winner by chance the researcher would have to interview one million players.
2. False or mistaken reports can result in error. Levine, for example, found inaccuracies in respondent reports regarding their voting behavior, finances, academic performance, business practices, and even sexual activity (Levine, 1976, p. 98). Should we assume greater precision in victim reports? Many respondents may also be relatively ignorant of the law, reporting as criminal acts incidents that the police would declare "unfounded" or not criminal matters.
3. Memory failure or decay tends to increase with the distance between the actual time of the event and the interview concerning the event (Panel for Evaluation, 1976, p. 21; Gottfredson and Hindelang, 1977).
4. Telescoping of events, a type of memory misfire, involves the moving of events that took place in a different time period (for example, before the reference period) into the time studied. A victimization of two years ago is mistakenly assumed to have occurred this past year. Subjects may even unconsciously telescope events in order to please interviewers (Biderman et al., 1967). Such demand characteristics or overagreeability on the part of respondents can certainly bias victim studies.
5. Sampling bias may produce an underenumeration of the young, males, and minorities. These very groups that tend to be undercounted by the U.S. Census are also more heavily victimized.
6. Overreporting in victim surveys generally involves subjects' reporting incidents to interviewers that they normally would view as too trivial or unimportant to call for police involvement. Much of the dark figure of crime consists of minor property crime, much of which could be considered unfounded by police (Black, 1970). Underreporting is particularly prevalent if the perpetrator is a friend, relative, or family member. Also, like the UCR, victim surveys fail to account for occupational, corporate, professional, political, and victimless crimes. Moreover, most victim studies are restricted to central city residents, thus underestimating tourist and commuter victims. In addition, police statistics are based on the crime incident, while victim surveys look at individual victims: one robbery involving ten victims would result in two different measurements—ten incidents in victim counts, but only one in official incident counts (Glaser, 1978, p. 64).

VANTAGE POINT 2.1

Were You a Victim of Crime?

Household Screen Questions

38. Now I'd like to ask some questions about crime. They refer only to the last 6 months: between ____ 1, 19__ and ____, 19__. During the last 6 months, did anyone break into or somehow illegally get into your (apartment/home), garage, or another building on your property?	☐ Yes: How many times? ________ ☐ No
39. Other than the incident(s) just mentioned did you find a door jimmied, a lock forced, or any other signs of an ATTEMPTED break in?	☐ Yes: How many times? ________ ☐ No
40. Was anything at all stolen that is kept outside your home or happened to be left out, such as a bicycle, a garden hose, or lawn furniture (other than any incidents already mentioned)?	☐ Yes: How many times? ________ ☐ No
41. Did anyone take something belonging to you or to any member of this household, from a place where you or they were temporarily staying, such as a friend's or relative's home, a hotel or motel, or a vacation home?	☐ Yes: How many times? ________ ☐ No
42. How many DIFFERENT motor vehicles (cars, trucks, motorcycles, etc.) were owned by you or any other member of this household during the last 6 months?	☐ None: Skip to 45 ☐ 1 ☐ 2 ☐ 3 ☐ 4 or more
43. Did anyone steal, TRY to steal, or use (it/any of them) without permission?	☐ Yes: How many times? ________ ☐ No
44. Did anyone steal or TRY to steal parts attached to (it/any of them), such as a battery, hubcaps, tape-deck, etc.?	☐ Yes: How many times? ________ ☐ No

Source: National Crime Victimization Survey screening instrument. Bureau of Justice Statistics, 1987.

InfoTrac College Edition Research

Search the term "Victims." What issues exist in the current literature regarding victims of crime?

7. Interviewer effects or bias can range from deception and exaggeration to the simple production of demand characteristics or agreeability in which respondents, wanting to appear helpful, may report incidents they otherwise would consider unimportant.
8. Coding and mechanical errors relate to human or machine errors in coding (assigning numbers to responses), keypunching, or analysis. Sussman and Haug (1967) have noted serious levels of such unchecked errors in large surveys.

Controlling for Error in Victim Surveys. Some ways of controlling for error in victim surveys include, but are not limited to: the use of panels and bounding of target groups, evaluations of coding and other sources of human or mechanical error in data processing, reverse record checks of known groups, reinterviews of the same group, and interviews with significant others. Panels (longitudinal studies of the same group) were discussed previously as a means of bounding (establishing the time period during which events were recalled as having taken place), thus controlling for forward telescoping (the tendency to move prior incidents into the time frame being studied). Quality controls on coding, keypunching, and data management—such as rechecking calculations and double coding and verification in order to control for coding errors—can provide more accurate data (Crittenden and Hill, 1971; Ennis, 1967, p. 93; Sussman and Haug, 1967). Reverse record checking of known groups involves studying a group whose behavior is already known, for example, known crime victims (Panel for the Evaluation, 1976; National Advisory Committee, 1976b, p. 146). Reinterviews of the same group in the National Crime Panel enables a tracking of reported crime incidents, and the checking of responses with significant others (those who know the respondent well) provides yet another measure of accuracy.

The primary benefit of victim surveys is that they provide us with another independent measure of crime, separate from official statistics. Neither official statistics nor victim surveys begin to tap the extent of occupational, corporate, and public order crime; in that regard both measures seriously underestimate the extent of crime. For "garden variety" or traditional crimes, the true rate is most likely somewhere between victim surveys, which overestimate by including minor property offenses, and official estimates, which underestimate crime. Victim studies provide us with a clearer picture of victims, their characteristics, and attitudes, as well as a better description of criminals and their operations. Such surveys can also be used to explore the fear of crime, reasons for not reporting crime, satisfaction with the criminal justice system, and the like. The National Crime Victimization Survey has undergone and continues to undergo revamping and redesign (Taylor, 1989). In addition to official statistics and victim surveys, the third major primary source of information regarding crime commission comes from self-report surveys.

Redesign of the National Crime Victimization Survey. Criticisms of the NCVS, particularly of its inability to gather accurate information regarding sexual assaults and domestic violence, prompted development of improved methodology that enhanced the ability of respondents to recall events. The survey changes increased the number of rapes and aggravated and simple assaults reported. The redesigned instrument also gathered information on other victimizations, such as nonrape sexual assault and unwanted or coerced sexual contact, for the first time. Improvements in technology and survey methodology were incorporated in the new design (Bureau of Justice Statistics, 1994).

An analysis of available data indicates that we have only a limited idea of the proportion of crime that is committed by any category of individuals or groups in a particular society. This is certainly the case if we rely entirely on official statistics for our discussions. Two primary sources of crime information that have been discussed are the Uniform Crime Reports (UCR) and the National Crime Victimization Survey (NCVS). VANTAGE POINT 2.2, "Measuring Crime," compares the definitions of crimes utilized in these measures.

Self-Report Measures of Crime

As with victim surveys, **self-report measures** attempt to provide an alternative to official statistics in measuring the extent of crime in a society (Menard, 1987). *Criminologists ask individuals,* as in the illustration in VANTAGE POINT 2.3, *to admit to various crimes and/or delinquent acts.* This may be achieved through anonymous questionnaires or surveys in which the respondent is identifiable that can be validated by later interviews or police records. Additionally, signed instruments that can be checked against official records, validation through later interviews or threats of polygraph (lie-detector) test, and interviews alone, as well as interviews that are then checked against official records may be used (Nettler, 1978, pp. 97–113).

Most self-report surveys that have been conducted in the United States have been of "captive audiences," such as school or college populations (Hood and Sparks, 1971, p. 19; Glaser, 1978, p. 72). Few studies have been done of the adult population. One of the earliest, by Wallerstein and Wyle (1947), found that 99 percent of their adult sample had committed at least one offense. Some of the percentages of admission for males and females, respectively, were: larceny—89 and 83 percent; indecency—77 and 74 percent; assault—49 and 5 percent; grand larceny (except auto)—13 and 11 percent; and tax evasion—57 and 40 percent. These figures suggest a remarkable level of criminality on the part of an assumed noncriminal population.

Controlling for Error in Self-Report Surveys. Reliance on self-reported data as a measure of crime commission poses a major question with respect to the relationship between claimed behavior and actual behavior. Nettler states that "asking people questions about their behavior is a poor way of observing it" (Nettler, 1978, p. 107). If people are inaccurate in reporting other aspects of their behavior, such as voting, medical treatment, and the like, it may be questionable to assume any greater accuracy in admitting deviant behavior. Some problems with self-report studies include: possibly inaccurate reports, the use of poor or inconsistent instruments, deficient research design, and poor choice of subjects. While mistaken or inaccurate reports may impinge on such surveys, Hood and Sparks (1971, p. 65) question the number of trivial offenses that are labeled delinquent in the United States and are included in such studies. They point out that in Europe delinquency is a synonym for crime committed by the young. While small and unrepresentative samples are problematic, self-report surveys are also affected by possible lying, poor memory, and telescoping (Elliott and Ageton, 1980, p. 96).

A large body of literature has accumulated suggesting that, despite these criticisms, the self-report approach is a viable method of obtaining data on crime or delinquency commission (Elliott and Ageton, 1980; Farrington, 1973; Hardt and Hardt, 1977; Hirschi, 1969; Gold, 1966; Clark and Tifft, 1966; Erickson and Empey, 1963; Dentler and Monroe, 1961; Nye and Short, 1956). Some means of checking for errors in self-report surveys include: comparison with official or other data, checking with other observers or peers, the use or threat of polygraph (lie detector), studies of known groups, the use of "lie scales" (measures of internal consistency), and the rechecking of reports using interviews.

A number of studies have been conducted that check self-report data with official reports such as police records, school records, and the like (Hardt and Hardt, 1977; Farrington, 1973; Erickson and Empey, 1963; Voss, 1963). These studies, for the most part, have found agreement between self-report and official data. But Nettler (1978, p. 11) points out the paradox of critics of official statistics using these same data to validate what they claim is a superior self-report instrument. Hirschi (1969) and McCandless, Persons, and Roberts (1972) found underreporting in their samples, while researchers such as Gold (1966) interviewed associates of the respondents to check their claims. Short and Strodtbeck (1965) used confirming reports of detached workers. Threatening the use of a polygraph, Clark and Tifft (1966) found that fewer than 20 percent altered their response. Other researchers such as Voss (1963) and Short and Nye (1958) studied groups whose official transgressions were already known. While some discrepancies were found, Hardt and Hardt (1977) concluded that these might have appeared because of a problem with the instruments used rather than because of any inadequacy in the self-report method itself.

Another means of checking the validity or accuracy of the self-report survey includes the use of "lie scales" or "truth scales." These consist of a series of questions woven among the others that ask the respondent to admit to certain outrageous behaviors or similarly to

VANTAGE POINT 2.2

Measuring Crime: A Comparison of Definitions in the UCR and the NCVS

National crime statistics focus on selected crimes.

The two sources, UCR and NCVS, concentrate on measuring a limited number of well-defined crimes. They do not cover all possible criminal events. Both sources use commonly understood definitions rather than legal definitions of crime.

"Crime" covers a wide range of events. It isn't always possible to tell whether an event is a crime. For example, if your personal property is missing, you may not know for certain whether it was stolen or simply misplaced.

The UCR Index shows trends in eight major crimes.

In 1927 the International Association of Chiefs of Police (IACP) formed a committee to create a uniform system for gathering police statistics. The goal was to develop a national system of statistics that would overcome variations in the way crimes were defined in different parts of the country.

Because of their seriousness, frequency of occurrence, and likelihood of being reported to the police, seven crimes were selected as the basis for the UCR Index to allow for evaluating changes in the volume of crime. Arson was added as the eighth UCR Index offense in 1978.

The NCVS adds information about victims and crimes not reported to police.

In 1973, to learn more about the statistics of crimes and the victims of crime, including arson (which is difficult to measure), the National Crime Victimization Survey began to measure crimes not reported to police as well as those that are reported. Except for homicide (which is well reported in police using survey techniques), the NCVS measures the same crimes as the UCR. Both the UCR and NCVS count attempted crimes as well as completed crimes.

The portraits of crime from NCVS and UCR differ because they serve different purposes and are based on different sources.

These are some of the more important differences in the programs, thought to account for a good deal of the differences in resulting statistics:

- The UCR counts only crimes coming to the attention of the police. The NCVS obtains information on both reported and unreported crime.
- The UCR counts crimes committed against all people and all businesses, organizations, government agencies, and other victims. NCVS counts only crimes against persons age 12 or older and against their households.
- The two programs, because they serve different purposes, count crimes differently in some instances. For example, a criminal robs a victim and steals someone else's car to escape. UCR counts only the robbery, the more serious crime. NCVS counts both; one as a personal crime and one as a household crime.
- Each program is subject to the kinds of errors and problems typical of its method of data collection, which may serve to widen or narrow the differences in the counts produced by the two programs. For example, it is widely believed that the rise in the number of rapes reported to police stems largely from the special programs established by many police departments to treat victims of rape more sympathetically.

deny extremely ordinary behaviors. A related procedure measures internal consistency of response by means of interlocking or contradictory questions; if some respondents are judged to be inconsistent in their responses, their reports may be discarded for analysis purposes (Edwards, 1957). Finally, subsequent interviewing of subjects may give an opportunity to double-check the reliability or consistency of responses.

A particularly innovative program for checking self-reports is ADAM (Arrestee Drug Abuse Monitoring Program), formerly the Drug Use Forecasting (DUF) Program sponsored by the National Institute of Justice. Groups of arrestees are asked questions regarding their drug-use behavior and then are asked to voluntarily provide urine specimens that can be tested for drug use. Besides providing an ingenious way of estimating drug use

VANTAGE POINT 2.2—*Continued*

How Do UCR and NCVS compare?

Uniform Crime Reports	*National Crime Victimization Survey*
Offenses Measured:	
Homicide Rape Robbery (personal and commercial) Assault (aggravated) Burglary (commercial and household) Larceny (commercial and household) Arson	Rape Robbery (personal) Assault (aggravated and simple) Household burglary Larceny (personal and household)
Scope:	
Crimes reported to the police in most jurisdictions; considerable flexibility in developing small-area data.	Crimes both reported and not reported to police; all data are for the nation as a whole; some specific data are available for a few large geographic areas.
Collection Method:	
Police department reports to FBI	Survey interviews; periodically measures the total number of crimes committed by asking a national sample of 50,000 households representing over 100,000 persons over the age of 12 about their experiences as victims of crime during a specified period.
Kinds of Information:	
In addition to offense counts, provides information on crime clearances, persons arrested, persons charged, law enforcement officers killed and assaulted, and characteristics of homicide victims	Provides details about victims (such as age, race, sex, education, income, and whether the victim and offender were related to each other) and about crimes (such as time and place of occurrence, whether or not reported to police, use of weapons, occurrence of injury, and economic consequences)
Sponsor:	
Department of Justice Federal Bureau of Investigation	Department of Justice Bureau of Justice Statistics

Source: Bureau of Justice Statistics. 1983 b. *Report to the Nation on Crime and Justice: The Data,* Washington. D.C.: Government Printing Office, p. 6.

InfoTrac College Edition Research

Searching under the labels of either "Uniform Crime Reports" or "National Crime Victimization Survey," locate the Whie House Press Secretary's press releases on the UCR and NCVS and compare them.

among criminal populations, the program provides a barometer on the impact of various policies on drug usage (National Institute of Justice, 1991). ADAM provides state and local drug policymakers, courts, law enforcement agencies, treatment providers, and prevention specialists with information that can be used to conduct local research and evaluation and to inform local policy decisions (National Institute of Justice, 1998). In 1998, NIJ launched International ADAM, which involves a partnership among criminal justice agencies in many countries providing a global assessment of drug use. In conclusion, while self-report surveys have certain problems, they—like victim studies—provide us with an independent measure of crime commission. We no longer have to rely on just one measure of crime.

VANTAGE POINT 2.3

Self-Reported Delinquency Items

Please indicate if you have ever done the following:

1. Stolen items of little value (less than $50).
2. Stolen items of great value ($50 or more).
3. Destroyed the property of others.
4. Used someone's vehicle without his or her permission.
5. Hit or physically attacked someone.
6. Been truant from school.
7. Consumed alcoholic beverages.
8. Used illegal drugs such as marijuana, heroin, or cocaine.
9. Indecently sexually exposed yourself in public.
10. Been paid for having sexual relations.

InfoTrac College Edition Research
What are some past problems and future prospects of the Arrestee Drug Abuse Monitoring Program (ADAM)? This program was formerly known as DUF (Drug Use Forcasting).

Participant Observation

Participant observation involves a *variety of strategies in which the researcher studies or observes a group through varying degrees of participation in the activities of that group.* Ned Polsky's classic *Hustlers, Beats and Others* (1967) presents both a moving statement on the need for deployment of this strategy and sound advice in this regard.

Participant Observation of Criminals. Contrary to the advice given at one time in most criminology textbooks (Sutherland and Cressey, 1960, p. 69), uncaught criminals can be studied in the field. Biologists have long noted that gorillas in a zoo act differently than gorillas in their natural habitat. It is imperative that criminologists break their habit of studying the confined, slower, less intelligent, lower class criminal. Polsky (1967, p. 147), in advocating field studies of criminals, states:

> Until the criminologist learns to suspend his personal distaste for the values and life-styles of the untamed savages, until he goes out in the field to the cannibals and headhunters and observes them without trying either to civilize them or turn them over to colonial officials, he will be only a veranda anthropologist. That is, he will be only a jailhouse or courthouse sociologist, unable to produce anything like a genuinely scientific picture of crime.

One of the reasons often given for discouraging such research is the belief that the researcher must pretend to be part of the criminal world. In fact, such a strategy would be highly inadvisable, not to mention unworkable and dangerous. Polsky suggests that the distance between criminal and conventional types is not as wide as many would suggest and that the difficulty in gaining access to such subjects is highly exaggerated.

There are, of course, problems in studying criminals *au naturel.* The researcher must realize that he or she is more of an intruder than would be the case in a prison setting. Unincarcerated criminals have more to lose than those already in jail do. And on their own turf, criminals are freer to put the researcher down or to refuse to be observed. Having successfully employed participant observation in studying uncaught pool hustlers, organized criminals, and drug addicts, Polsky (1967, pp. 117–49) offers some sage advice regarding procedures to employ in studying criminals in the field:

- Avoid using gadgets such as tape recorders, questionnaires, and the like. Construct field notes later, after leaving the scene for the day.
- Keep your eyes and ears open, but keep your mouth shut.
- Learn the argot, the specialized language or jargon of a group, but don't overuse it.

(Courtsey of Columbus B. Hopper)

Beginning in the mid-1970s, Columbus B. Hopper and others at the University of Mississippi Sociology and Anthropology Department conducted field research on outlaw motorcyclists and their female associates. Bikers would not fill out questionnaires, allow tape recordings, or note taking, but researchers interviewed and corresponded with several hundred outlaw motorcyclists both in open society and in state and federal prisons. Initial contact was primarily through former biker and outlaw club president Johnny Moore who gained them admittance and acceptance at biker clubhouses and "blow-outs" such as the one pictured here at Gulfport, Mississippi.

According to Hooper's thesis of the changing role of women in outlaw motorcycle gangs, this tattooed female, although an intriguing oddity, probably has lower status than many of her non-tattooed peers. Because gangs are increasingly involved in crime and other money-making activities, the women are valued for the money they bring in as strippers or prostitutes, whose marketability decreases if their bodies are tattooed.

- You can often gain entry into the setting through common recreational interests, for example, card games, the track, or poolrooms.
- Do not pretend to be one of them. As soon as practicable, make them aware of your purposes.
- Be open to permitting the criminal(s) to study you as well, and be prepared to be defined as "a right square," "a vicarious junkie," or "too scared to steal."
- Draw the line between yourself and the criminal. For instance, Polsky indicated that he did not wish to actually witness certain criminal acts. Use pseudonyms (fake names or aliases) in order to protect the identities of informants.
- Have a firm notion as to who you are, in order to avoid being maneuvered into an accomplice role. Polsky, for instance, was told he would make a fine "steerhorse"(someone who "fingers" the "mark") or "wheelman" (driver of a getaway car).
- While it is important not to pretend to be one of them, don't "stick out like a sore thumb." In studying heroin use and distribution, Polsky, while fitting into the scene, also wore a short-sleeved shirt and an expensive watch in order to advertise the fact that he was not a heroin addict.
- Be flexible; have few unbreakable rules.
- If you choose such field studies, be prepared for a very demanding, time-consuming, and at times very boring routine. Even criminals spend the bulk of their time in mundane activities.

Finally, Polsky raises a number of related issues to be considered in field studies of criminals. In some ways, researchers may be breaking the law or be considered accessories to the fact. Honoring reciprocity with respondents, observers must be prepared to be "stand-up guys" under police questioning. Although their actual legal status is unclear, social researchers in many cases have no guaranteed right to confidentiality or privileged information and are vulnerable to subpoena. Some field researchers such as Lewis Yablonsky (1965a, p. 72) feel that strict moral limits must be set in mediating the roles of scientist and citizen and that researchers should avoid nonmoralistic stances. Polsky, on the contrary, argues that the scientist's role is preeminent and that a few social scientists must take this stance in order to get a true picture of little-understood subject matters.

Evaluation of the Method of Participant Observation. A researcher's decision to use participant observation as the primary means of gathering data represents an orientation toward a more qualitative and "sensitizing" approach. This represents a commitment toward in-depth field studies in which the investigator attempts to obtain the "big picture" of a group by temporarily viewing the world through its eyes (Glaser and Strauss, 1967). In some instances, participant observation may represent the only viable means of data gathering (imagine, for instance, attempting a survey or experiment with volunteers from the ranks of organized crime). Participant observation is an excellent procedure for studying little-understood groups. Some examples of participant observation studies with criminological ramifications have been Whyte's *Streetcorner Society* (1955); Polsky's *Hustlers, Beats and Others* (1967); Yablonsky's *Synanon* (1965b) and *The Violent Gang* (1962); Ianni's *A Family Business* (1972); Albini's (1986) study of the Guardian Angels; and Humphreys's *Tearoom Trade* (1970). Eleanor Miller (1986) did field research interviewing 64 prostitutes in Milwaukee; Marquart (1986) worked as a prison guard; Hopper (1991) studied outlaw motorcycle gangs; and Sanchez-Jankowski (1991) spent ten years living with and studying street gangs in Los Angeles, Boston, and New York.

The usefulness of such field studies in exploring settings that would not readily lend themselves to quantitative analysis is illustrated by some recent studies. Philipe Bourgois, author of *In Search of Respect: Selling Crack in El Barrio* (1995) spent the five years from 1985 to 1990 in East Harlem studying young Puerto Rican men on street corners, in crack houses, bars, and homes. Elijah Anderson's *A Place on the Corner* (1981) took place in the 1970s and reported on Chicago ghetto life from Jelly's, a bar and liquor store that he studied for over three years. Anderson's *Streetwise* (1990) describes two other Philadelphia neighborhoods. Mark Hamm's *American Skinheads* (1993) reports on his field study of neo-Nazi hate groups, which included communications with skinheads via the WAR (White Aryan Resistance) web site on the Internet. Jim Aho in *This Thing of Darkness* (1994) conducted a participant observation study of Idaho Christian Patriots until he defined such involvement as increasingly too dangerous. Miller and Tewksbury in *Extreme Methods: Innovative Approaches to Social Science Research* (2000) and Ferrell, Hamm, and Adler in *Ethnography at the Edge: Crime, Deviance and Field Research* (1998) provide very interesting collections of articles on difficult-to-access deviant groups that require more innovative, and sometimes controversial, means of investigation.

The major advantages of a participant observation relate to the qualitative detail that it can produce. Using this sensitizing or *verstehen* strategy, the researcher is less influenced by prejudgments. The technique is very flexible and less artificial, and enables the investigator to observe subjects in their natural environment. Such ethnographic methods provide insider accounts and acquaint students with the perspectives of the subjects (Cromwell, 1996). This technique has produced some of the most exciting and enthralling literature in the field, rivaling even some of the best of modern fiction. Examples from this genre will be presented in subsequent chapters. Some potential disadvantages of partici-

This white Aryan Resistance (WAR) Web site page, downloaded from the Internet, is a chilling reminder that modern technology can be made to serve antisocial purposes.

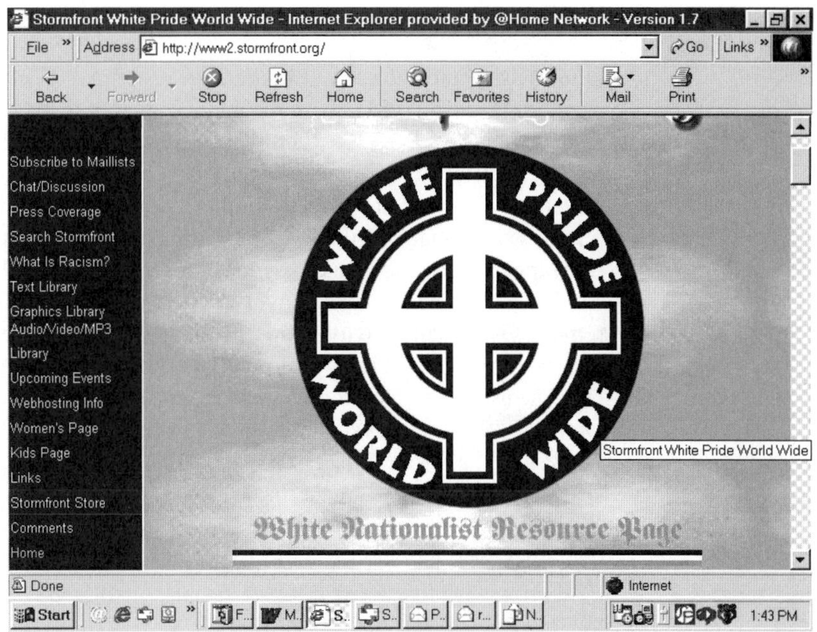

pant observation include the very time-consuming nature of the technique; it may exact high demands on the personal life of the observer (for example, see Carey, 1972). The observer faces the dual dangers of overidentification with, or aversion to, the group being studied, often testing to the limits the researcher's commitment to objectivity. In addition to possible observer bias and the challenge of making sense of a mass of nonquantitative data, participant observation can pose major ethical dilemmas.

Life History and Case Studies

A classic illustration of the use of **case study** and **life history** in criminology was Edwin Sutherland's *The Professional Thief* (1937), based on his interviews with an incarcerated professional thief given the pseudonym "Chic" Conwell. Like participant observation, case studies/life histories represent an *interest in an in-depth close-up of only one or a few subjects in order to obtain a greater understanding or verstehen* (Weber, 1949) that a more aggregate analysis might obscure. This method may employ diaries, letters, biographies, and autobiographies in order to attempt to capture a detailed view of either a unique or a representative subject. Some more recent examples of the life history approach have been Chambliss's *Box Man* (1975a); Klockars's *The Professional Fence* (1974); Steffensmeier's *The Fence* (1986); Shaw's *The Jackroller* (1930); and Snodgrass's *The Jack-Roller at Seventy* (1982).

Travis (1983, p. 46) notes an unfortunate decline in the coverage of case studies in criminology and criminal justice texts and their eclipse by more quantitative methods. The former involve oral and life histories, "recounts of events by participants" (Laub, 1983, p. 226). In *Criminology in the Making: An Oral History,* Laub (1983) conducts in-depth interviews with major criminologists in order to construct a history of the field. Since many subjects may not be subject to analysis through quantitative research, case studies can provide a view of the subjective elements of institutions (Kobrin, 1982; Bennett, 1981; Bertaux, 1981; Hagan, 1989).

Unobtrusive Measures

Unobtrusive measures are *clandestine, secretive, or nonreactive methods of gathering data* (Webb et al., 1981). Such techniques attempt to avoid reactivity, the tendency of subjects to behave differently when they are aware that they are being studied. This certainly has been a problem in much prison research, where the question might be asked whether research volunteers are indeed volunteers. *Major types of unobtrusive methods* include: physical trace analysis; the use of existing records like archives, available data, and autobiographies; and simple and disguised observation, as well as simulation.

Physical trace analysis involves studying deposits, accretion of matter, and other remains of human activity, while archival and existing records contain information that may be useful in providing historical overviews of criminological issues.

The uses of *available data* include procedures such as *content analysis* and *secondary analysis.* Content analysis refers to the systematic classification and study of the content of mass media, for example, newspapers, magazines, and the like. Secondary analysis consists of the reanalysis of data that was previously gathered for other purposes. The use of all of these types of data-gathering procedures is an excellent, cost-effective means of obtaining data, particularly in a period of growing respondent hostility to studies. In an interesting example of the imaginative use of existing data, criminologist John Laub discovered more than 60 boxes of dusty files in the sub-basement of the Harvard Law School Library (Associated Press, 1994). These turned out to be the research files of Eleanor and Sheldon Glueck, who had been at Harvard from the 1920s to the 1970s. They had conducted one of the first longitudinal studies in criminology in which male juveniles were followed from age 14 until age 32, attempting to predict the cause of criminal behavior. In an example of secondary analysis, Laub computerized their data and analyzed it. VANTAGE POINT 2.4 presents lists of useful sources for criminological research.

Observation requires the researcher to keep participation with subjects to a minimum while carefully recording their activities; in disguised observation the investigator secretly studies groups by temporarily deceiving them as to his or her real purpose. For example, in order to study difficult subjects in the field, researchers have posed as "thieves and victims" (Stewart and Cannon, 1977), a "watch queen" (Humphreys, 1970), a "mental patient" (Caudill, 1958), "black panther supporters" (Heussenstamm, 1971), "a naíve international tourist" (Feldman, 1968), and "a caretaker" (Sherif and Sherif, 1966), among other roles.

Simulation entails *research strategies that attempt to mimic or imitate a more complex social reality.* For example, since actual research into jury deliberations is prohibited, researchers may set up simulated juries by reenacting actual trial conditions in order to investigate the decision-making process.

While the obvious advantage of unobtrusive measures is that they are nonreactive—that is, they prevent subject awareness of being observed and ideally escape reactivity—such techniques also have the strength of being more natural and of evading the overreliance upon attitudinal data. By making use of data that have already been gathered, researchers are able to exercise great economies of time and expense. Too many researchers assume that doing a study must necessarily involve the expense and time of gathering new data when, in fact, vast storehouses of potential information exist right under their noses, as close as the nearest library and scattered throughout the records of public and private organizations. On the debit side of the ledger, unobtrusive methods raise potential problems of privacy invasion. Does a researcher have the right to observe the private behavior of individuals without their permission? Compounding this ethical issue is that criminological researchers have no state-recognized right to confidentiality or claim to privileged communication comparable to that in a doctor-patient relationship. In addition, nonreactive measures may yield atypical subjects, be time consuming, and be prone to observer bias.

VANTAGE POINT 2.4

Useful Sources for Criminological Research

Selected Journals
American Journal of Criminal Justice
American Journal of Sociology
American Sociological Review
Crime and Delinquency
Criminal Justice Policy Review
Criminal Justice Review
Criminology
Federal Probation
Journal of Criminal Justice
Journal of Research in Crime and Delinquency
Justice Quarterly
Law and Society Review
NIJ Reports
Social Forces
Social Problems
Sociology and Social Research
Victimology

Abstracts/Indexes
Crime and Delinquency Abstracts
C J Abstracts (online)
InfoTrac® College Edition (online)
National Criminal Justice Reference Service
New York Times Index
Police Science Abstracts
Psychological Abstracts
Reader's Guide to Periodical Literature
Social Science Index
Sociological Abstracts

Internet Sources
Cecil Greek *www.stpt.usf.edu/-greek/cj.html*
National Institute of Justice *www.ojp.usdoj.gov/nij/*
Bureau of Justice Statistics *www.ojp.usdoj.gov/bjs/*
National Criminal Justice Reference Service *www.ncjrs.org*
Federal Bureau of Investigation *www.fbi.gov/*
Library of Congress *www.loc.gov/*
U. S. Department of Justice *www.usdoj.gov/*
Central Intelligence Agency *www.cia.gov/index.html*
Department of Justice Career Opportunities *www.usdoj.gov/careers.html*
General Accounting Office *www.gao.gov/*
Justinfo Online *www.ncjrs.org/justinfo/*
Wadsworth Criminal Justice Resource Center *http://cj.wadsworth.com*

This is only a small selection of available sources. Check the periodicals and reference sections of your college library for more.

InfoTrac College Edition Research
Using InfoTrac College Edition, locate and review an article involving the use of criminological research. (Hint: Search using titles such as "crime research".) What types of methods were used and what were the findings of the article? Do a general search of "crime." What are some useful or interesting items that you discovered?

Validity, Reliability, and Triangulation

In the past a number of researchers have been critical of the accuracy of much criminological research. Bailey (1971), in a review of 100 correctional research studies, pointed out that much of the research was invalid, unreliable, and based on poor research design. In an analysis of the quality of publications in criminology, Wolfgang, Figlio, and Thornberry (1978) judged that the methodological sophistication was very poor and that a greater display of concern was needed for adequate research design and execution. Although later modifying his view and admitting methodological narcissism, Martinson (1974, 1978) blasted correctional research, claiming that in his review of the evidence of programs in corrections and their impact on recidivism, he found that "nothing works." What is to be said of this sad state of affairs? If the data regarding "what is?" with respect to crime are defective, then what might we expect of the theories that are based upon these data? Fortunately, criminologists have plenty of methodological company with economists, psychiatrists, and meteorologists, to mention just a few. The problem of imprecise measurement is not unique to the field of criminology and, furthermore, is not an insoluble one.

Validity concerns *accuracy of measurement.* It asks the questions, "Does my measuring instrument in fact measure what it claims to measure?", "Is it a true and accurate measure of the subject in question?" **Reliability,** on the other hand, involves the *consistency and/or stability of measurement.* If repeated measures were made of the same entity, would stable and uniform measures ensue? Obviously, validity is a more crucial issue than reliability; if a measurement is inaccurate, the consistency of inaccuracy becomes a moot question.

The problem of inadequate methods in criminology arises not because of the inherent shortcomings of any particular method, but because a given method is used alone. It is foolhardy to concentrate on the insufficiencies, the reliability, and/or the validity of any one concept, measured at one time using one measure. **Triangulation** involves *the use of multiple methods in measuring the same entity.* It is similar to the notion of corroborating evidence in law; if different measures of the same concept produce convergence or similar results, then we have greater confidence in the validity of an observation or finding.

Sanders in *The Sociologist as Detective* (1976) makes very clever use of Arthur Conan Doyle's fictional sleuth Sherlock Holmes as a means of illustrating the notion of triangulation. Holmes, in attempting to answer the question "Whodunit?", employed multiple methods (triangulation) like those a social scientist might employ. In attempting to discover "who killed the lord of the manor," Holmes observed carefully, attempted reenactment of the crime (simulation), questioned suspects and witnesses, and carefully collected and evaluated the physical evidence at the crime scene. He collected some data through direct questioning, other data through astute observation. "Did the family dog bark the evening of the suspected murder?" If not, perhaps the murderer was a family member or friend. "Did any of the questioned suspects develop a nervous tic?" "Were there footprints or clues?" By combining these various methods, Holmes was able to make a reasonable guess as to which hypotheses to reject or accept (see also Truzzi, 1976).

This chapter has exposed the reader to a variety of methods that criminologists use in obtaining information on the nature of crime and criminals. The outcomes or findings that result from the application of these methods will be presented in forthcoming chapters. It is hoped that the reader has been alerted to viewing this material with a critical methodological eye, carefully weighing the sources of evidence for the materials presented. For more detail on research methods, see Hagan (1993).

Summary

Theory and methodology are the two critical features of any discipline, including criminology. Theory is an attempt to provide plausible explanations of reality and addresses the question "Why?" Method (methodology) involves procedures for the collection and analysis of accurate data or facts and is concerned with the issue "What is?"

The research enterprise of criminology involves certain basic procedures. Objectivity, a commitment to a "value-free," nonbiased approach to the subject matter, is an essential canon of research. Despite conflicting roles, the criminologist's primary role is that of scientist. Some general principles of ethical conduct in criminology include that the researcher should avoid harmful procedures, honor commitments and reciprocity, exercise objectivity and integrity, and protect the privacy of subjects, as well as maintain confidentiality.

Pure research is concerned with expansion of the knowledge base of a discipline regardless of immediate societal concerns or problems. In contrast, applied research addresses present policy issues and represents an attempt to provide answers to present-day problems. Criminology incorporates both approaches.

The process of methodological thinking was illustrated by means of the research question "Who is criminal?" Until recently the primary source of information regarding crime statistics has been official police statistics, which represent crimes recorded by police. The Uniform Crime Reports (UCR) presents such statistics for the United States. Such statistics fail to account for unrecorded crime, "the dark figure of crime."

The UCR "crime index" from which the crime rate is calculated consists of Part I crimes: murder and nonnegligent manslaughter, forcible rape, robbery, aggravated assault, burglary, larceny/theft, motor vehicle theft, and arson. Researchers should be cognizant of shortcomings of official data such as the UCR. The redesigned UCR (NIBRS/National Incident-Based Reporting System) is an attempt to improve the system. Crime clocks are the poorest graphic devices for describing crime trends, since they fail to control for population growth and use a constant (time) as their base for comparison.

Other alternative measures of crime and criminal activity include crime seriousness measures, which attempt to provide a weighted index of crime. Alternative data-gathering strategies include: experiments, social surveys, participant observation, case studies/life history methods, and unobtrusive methods. Each possesses relative strengths and weaknesses, vis-à-vis the others with respect to quantitative/qualitative control, internal/external validity, and degrees of artificiality/naturalness.

A key point is that, contrary to methodological narcissism (fanatical adherence to one's favorite method), no one method has any inherent superiority over any other. Methodology is a tool and not an end in itself. For each method, the text provides descriptions as well as examples of the method's application in criminological research. For instance, victim surveys are a critical alternative measure of criminality. Similarly, self-report surveys are a useful means of tapping hidden criminality. The basic strategy of participant observation (field studies), life histories, and case studies in criminology is delineated. A particularly moving pitch for the need for such studies emerges from Ned Polsky's research. Unobtrusive (nonreactive) methods are a very cost-effective and neglected means of obtaining data. These include techniques such as physical trace analysis, use of archives/existing data (including content and secondary analysis), and autobiographies. Other procedures include simple and disguised observation and simulation.

Much of the criticism of criminological research is really questioning the validity (accuracy) and reliability (consistency/stability) of the methodology that has been employed. Triangulation (the use of multiple methods) is proposed as the logical path to resolve this issue.

KEY CONCEPTS

Cautions in the UCR
Classic Experimental Design
Code of Ethics for Research
Confidentiality
Crime Clocks
Crime Index
Crime Rate
Dark Figure of Crime
Dualistic Fallacy
Ethics in Research
Experiments
Life History/Case Study
Methodological Narcissism
Methodology (Methods)
National Crime Survey (NCS)
National Incident-Based Recording System (NIBRS)
Objectivity
Operationalization
Part I Crimes
Participant Observation
Pure vs. Applied Research
Reciprocity
Reliability
Sampling
Self-Reports of Crime
Simulation
Sources of Crime Statistics
Surveys
Theory
Triangulation
Unfounded Crimes
Uniform Crime Reports (UCR)
Unobtrusive Measures
Validity
Variables
Victim Surveys

REVIEW QUESTIONS

1. Reviewing IN THE NEWS 2.1 The Crime Dip of the Nineties, which factor/s do you find to be most plausible in explaining the crime dip? Using these same factors, do you predict that crime will continue to decrease or do you foresee an increase in the near future? Explain your reasoning.
2. Examining the Codes of Ethics of the Academy of Criminal Justice Sciences and the American Society of Criminology, what stipulations do you regard as most important and which of least importance? Are you familiar with any additional studies that have raised ethical concerns? Search the web, InfoTrac® College Edition, C J Abstracts, and NCJRS under titles such as research ethics or codes of ethics and see if you can turn up any recent controversies.
3. What are some sources of information used by criminologists to examine the extent of crime in the United States?
4. Compare the UCR with the NCVS. Which of these is the better measure of crime?
5. How does the FBI compile and calculate the crime rate? What types of crime does this include?
6. What are some problems or shortcomings of the UCR?
7. What are some other ways of gathering data in criminology besides reliance on official police statistics? Give an example of each.
8. Why are crime clocks considered a misleading graphic device?
9. How accurate is the NCVS? Is it a better measure of crime than the UCR?
10. What is ADAM and what does it measure? Is there any way of checking on its accuracy?

INFOTRAC COLLEGE EDITION RESEARCH

Vantage Point 2.1 InfoTrac College Edition Research Search the term "Victims." What issues exist in the current literature regarding victims of crime?

Vantage Point 2.2 InfoTrac College Edition Research Searching under the labels of either "Uniform Crime Reports" or "National Crime Victimization Survey," locate the White House Press Secretary's press releases on the UCR and NCVS and compare them.

Vantage Point 2.3 InfoTrac Research What are some past problems and future prospects of the Arrestee Drug Abuse Monitoring Program (ADAM)? This program was formerly known as DUF (Drug Use Forecasting).

Vantage Point 2.4 InfoTrac College Edition Research Using InfoTrac College Edition, locate and review an article involving the use of criminological research. (Hint: Search using titles such as "crime research".) What types of methods were used and what were the findings of the article? Do a general search of "crime." What are some useful or interesting items that you discovered?

In the News 2.1 InfoTrac College Edition Research Using InfoTrac College Edition find an article that attempts to explain the reasons why the crime rate fell. Do you agree with this article? Explain.

SELECTED READINGS

Jim Aho. 1994. *This Thing of Darkness: The Sociology of the Enemy.* Seattle: University of Washington Press. The author conducts a participant observational study of right wing Patriot groups in Idaho.

Bruce Berg. 1998. *Qualitative Research Methods in the Social Sciences.* 3rd edition. Boston: Allyn and Bacon. This is a text devoted exclusively to qualitative methods in the social sciences, a subject which is sometimes neglected in standard methods texts.

Paul Cromwell. Editor. 1996. *In Their Own Words: Field Research on Crime and Criminals—An Anthology.* Los Angeles, California: Roxbury Press. This is an excellent anthology of articles involving field research of uncaught criminals on their own turf.

Jeffery Ferrell and Mark S. Hamm. Editors. 1998. *Ethnography at the Edge: Crime and Deviance in Field Research.* Boston: Northeastern University Press.

The authors describe their articles as unorthodox invitations to heresy. Research among uncaught criminals often put researchers in compromising positions on the edge of illegality.

Frank E. Hagan. 2000. *Research Methods in Criminal Justice and Criminology.* 5th edition. Boston: Allyn and Bacon.
This is the author's own text on criminological and criminal justice research and features detailed coverage of issues only introduced in our account in this chapter.

John M. Hagedorn. 1994. "Homeboys, Dope Fiends, Legits and New Jacks." *Criminology.* 32 (May): 197–219.
This field study of gang turf and drug use utilizes people from the neighborhood as co-researchers.

Mark S. Hamm. 1993. *American Skinheads: The Criminology and Control of Hate Crime.* Westport, Connecticutt: Praeger.
Author Mark Hamm uses imaginative, triangulated methods in order to study skinheads.

Martin Sanchez Jankowski. 1991. *Islands in the Streets: Gangs and American Urban Society.* Berkeley, California: University of California Press.
Forty-four youth gangs are studied in the field over a ten year period by Sanchez Jankowski.

Pamela Tontodonato, and Frank E. Hagan. Editors. 1998. *The Language of Research in Criminal Justice.* Boston: Allyn and Bacon.
Thirty-four articles are featured, illustrating research in criminology and criminal justice. These are articles that are often cited in texts.

Richard T. Wright and Scott Decker. 1994. *Burglars on the Job: Streetlife and Residential Break-Ins.* Boston: Northeastern University Press.
The authors interview uncaught burglars in the field asking questions such as how they choose targets and avoid being arrested.

General Characteristics of Crime and Criminals

3

Vantage Points

In the News

> This is our basic conclusion: Our nation is moving toward two societies, one black, one white—separate and unequal . . . . White racism is essentially responsible for the explosive mixture which has been accumulating in our cities since the end of World War II.
>
> —*U.S. Riot Commission Report* (Kerner 1968), pp. 1, 10

> From the wild Irish slums of the nineteenth century eastern seaboard to the riot-torn suburbs of Los Angeles, there is one unmistakable lesson in American history: a community that allows a large number of young men to grow up in broken families, dominated by women, never acquiring any stable relationship to male authority . . . asks for and gets chaos, crime, violence, unrest, disorder—most particularly the furious, unrestrained lashing out at the whole social structure that is not only to be expected; it is very near to inevitable. And it is richly deserved.
>
> —Daniel P. Moynihan, *Family and Nation* (1986), p. 9

Caution in Interpreting Crime Data

In Chapter 2 we treated at length the necessity of carefully examining the data base or sources of criminological research findings and conclusions. This advice is especially applicable to the material presented in this chapter. Descriptions of characteristics of crime and criminals can vary immensely, depending on the sources of information—for example, official statistics, victim surveys, self-reports—as well as on the type of crime or criminality that is being addressed, whether traditional crimes or crimes by the elite. The particular method chosen for analysis provides data that flavor the types of theories developed; likewise the theoretical framework for analysis may subjectively influence the methods of analysis. While the process of inquiry is seldom entirely value-free, triangulation assists in providing multiple assessments of the subject matter. As previously indicated, statistics regarding crime and delinquency are not easily measured. Realizing the limitations of these statistics, we will attempt to avoid misleading and incorrect inferences.

International Variations in Crime

International or cross-cultural comparisons of crime statistics are hazardous given the different definitions of criminal activity, the quality of data, ideological considerations, and the sheer logistical problems of compilation (see Terrill, 1999; Rounds, 2000; Fairchild and Dammer, 2000). In a pioneering effort Archer and Gartner (1980 and 1984) constructed a "Comparative Crime Data File" based on data they had collected from 110 nations and 44 major cities. Analysis of cross-cultural crime rates can produce some interesting conclusions. For instance, the inexorable rise in crime in the United States and other industrialized countries in the sixties was contradicted by a declining crime rate in Japan, which discredited the assumption that modernization inevitably produces increased criminality. Adler's *Nations Not Obsessed by Crime* (1983) and Clinard's *Cities with Little Crime* (1978) also indicate that crime is not a major concern in such countries as Switzerland. In a contrary view others indicate that the Swiss police omit crime statistics and the media ignore criminality, not to mention that Switzerland is a haven for white collar crime (Balrig, 1988; Gerber, 1991). The low crime rate in Japan is achieved by a strong *Gemeinschaft* (communal) orientation and group conformity, a high level of unchallenged police power, and a tendency to ignore violations of human and individual rights that would be found unacceptable in the Western democracies (Williams, 1991a). Utilizing data from The International Police Organization (Interpol) and the World Health Organization (WHO), Brantingham and Brantingham (1984, p. 295) point out:

> At the world level of resolution, clearly different patterns emerge for crimes of violence against the person and for crimes against property. The highest overall crime rates were experienced by the nations of the Caribbean region during the mid-1970s, followed by the nations of Western Europe, North America, and Oceania. The highest levels of violent crimes against the person were experienced in the Caribbean, in North Africa and the Middle East, in sub-Saharan Africa, and in Latin America. Property crimes were highest in Western Europe, North America, and Oceania. Crime patterns appear to be closely associated with high economic development and with income inequality; and high levels of violent crimes against the person are associated with lack of economic development and with high income inequality. Modernization and urbanization are both associated with higher levels of property crime and lower levels of violent crime.

Similar patterns with respect to the impact of income inequality and the lack of economic development and high crime rates have been noted by others (Clinard and Abbott, 1973; Krahn, Hartnagel, and Gartrell, 1986). At the beginning of the twenty-first century we find that the breakdown of political order, lack of police training, and growing urbanization—particularly in developing countries—produce higher global crime. The Overseas Security Advisory Council of the U.S. State Department issues timely travel advisories to tourists warning of special dangers. Nonviolent theft and pickpocketing are the most common crimes that business travelers endure. In 1999 attacks in unregulated taxicabs in Mexico City were of concern, while pickpockets and thieves were more prevalent in eastern Europe. Particularly dangerous were capital cities of West and East Africa, where the breakdown of tribal authority and poor police training cultivated high crime. The former Soviet Union in general had experienced high levels of violence, organized crime, and corruption (Nicolova, 1999). In Thailand, a favorite tourist destination, economic collapse and an increase in drug-related crime had increased violence against foreigners and weak law enforcement had attracted foreign criminal gangs (Cheesman, 1999).

Particularly interesting is concern among Americans about being potential victims in some foreign lands, when in fact the murder and rape rates in general are higher in the U.S. than in other developed countries. By the year 2000, however, seven years of declining official crime rates in the United States found that for assault, burglary, robbery, and motor vehicle thefts the U.S. rates were actually lower than rising rates in some other developed countries such as England and Wales (Langan and Farrington, 1998).

Cross-national crime statistics have steadily improved over the years with Interpol, the United Nations, and the World Health Organization publishing such data. In addition the United Nations has sponsored the International Crime Victimization Survey (ICVS), as well as the United Nations' Surveys on Crime Trends and Operations and International ADAM (Arrestee Drug Abuse Monitoring), a self report survey of arrests modeled after the U.S. ADAM.

Van Dijk and Kangaspunta (2000) indicate the following difficulties in analyzing crime data across countries:

- Varying definitions—legal codes define crimes in different ways.
- Recording practices—different police departments record things differently (e.g., bicycle thefts are vehicle thefts in some countries).
- Operating practices—in some countries, only crimes reaching court are recorded.
- Factual inequalities—hidden factors may affect crime rates such as age, urbanism, and the like.
- Problems especially associated with recorded crime—governments may regard such statistics as indicators of criminal justice system workloads rather than accurate indicators of crime prevalence.

Table 3.1 presents Interpol crime rates for 1998. Given our previous discussion, the reader should interpret these official police statistics with caution.

A comparison of U.S. crime rates with those of other countries using Interpol data found (see Table 3.1):

- For 1998 the U.S. homicide rate was 6.3 using UCR data; the rate in Europe was generally between 1 and 2 using Interpol data. Colombia (56.3), Jamaica (37.2), Russia (18), Mongolia (24.6), and other, mostly Latin American and African countries had higher rates than the U.S. Not shown in the table is South Africa's murder rate of 56.9.
- The U.S. rape rate was 34.4 using UCR data. This rate was virtually tied with Jamaica, Namibia, and Zimbabwe, although rape statistics tend to be notoriously underestimated in many countries. Rates in most developed countries were under 10.
- The U.S. robbery rate was 165.2. Others with high rates were: Australia (127.6), France (144.1), Guyana (168.8), Jamaica (116.9), Russia (106.1), Spain (162.9), and Trinidad (193.8). Japan was lowest with 2.1.
- The U.S. burglary rate of 862 was exceeded by other developed countries. Australia (2338.4), Belgium (2031.3), Denmark (1925.2), Finland (1757), Germany (1183.1), Israel (1122.3), and Switzerland (1172.5) were all higher.
- The U.S. rate of 459 for auto theft was also exceeded by Belgium (530.2), Canada (1155.7), Australia (706.2), Denmark (709.5), Finland (482.2), Israel (694.1), Norway (487.5), and Switzerland (1129.9).

In addition to traditional criminal activity, the multinational nature of organized, white collar, and more sophisticated crimes is a growing phenomenon. In November 1995 a 138-nation United Nations-sponsored conference was held in Naples, Italy, on international crime. The end of the Cold War has opened borders and provided an opportunity for collaboration among organized crime groups. Transnational crime poisons business climates, corrupts political leaders, undermines banking and finance, and represents a global challenge of immense proportions.

As an illustration of ideological influences on crime statistics, one need only look at Russia in the late eighties and the influence of Gorbachev's *glasnost* (openness) on crime statistics. In the first publication of crime statistics in more than half a century, the Soviet Interior Ministry reported a sharp rise in crime of 18 percent for 1988 over 1987 ("Soviet Crime Rate Up," 1989) and 32 percent in 1989 (Bogert, 1990). In 1991 the number of robberies, muggings, burglaries, and thefts had jumped by 90 percent over 1990 (Shapiro, 1992). Instrumental in this increase was the collapse of an authoritarian regime (whose police were omnipresent) combined with declining economic conditions and general political confusion.

Organized crime groups often filled the power void. Having previously controlled the black market, such groups were well trained for the new, legal capitalism. Such increased levels of crime have also been experienced throughout former Eastern European satellite countries of the former Soviet Union and throughout the world—in the People's Republic of China, South Africa, the Baltic states, and even Vietnam (Larimer, 1996, p. A7).

There does appear to be a relationship between heterogeneity (pluralism or diversity) of a nation's population and higher crime rates, although not a direct one, as demonstrated by Switzerland's relatively low rates. The United States, a nation of immigrants, is one of the most heterogeneous countries in the world. Indeed New York City is one of the largest Irish, Jewish, Puerto Rican, or black cities in the world; Chicago is one of the largest Polish cities, and Miami is the second largest Cuban city. One might point out that one of the cities showing great decreases in crime in the late 1990s was New York City, one of the nation's most heterogeneous.

In 1994, at the American Society of Criminology (ASC) Meetings, Attorney General Janet Reno appealed to those assembled for assistance in resolving some specific policy issues. The ASC appointed task forces to address each of these, and the results are reported in this text as Vantage Points.

TABLE 3.1 Crime Rate in Selected Countries, 1998: Interpol Data (Incidents per 100,000)

Country	*Homicide*[a]	*Rape*	*Robbery*	*Burglary*	*Auto Theft*
UnitedStates[b]	6.3	34.4	165.2	862	459
Albania	(17.3) 30.3	1.5	16.4	9.5	14
Australia	3.6		127.6	2,338.40	706.2
Austria	(1.9) 2.0	(4.5) 6.4	(54.5) 59.2	(878) 1008.9	(25.4) 35.8
Bahamas	(15.8) 21.9	(66.1) 76.1	(538.2) 566.2	(2055.2) 2229.1	(346.4) 393.2
Belarus	(8.2) 10.2	(3.1) 4.5	64.2	173.9	17.5
Belgium	(2.2) 5.3	(5.3) 16.8	(160.7) 189	(1503.2) 2031.3	(530.3) 535.8
Bolivia	(28.6) 13.6	(17.5) 20.7	102.4	0.9	
Brazil	(6.6) 21.2	8.1	0.5	5.2	61.2
Bulgaria	(4.7) 7.5	(7.9) 9.4	(53.5) 54.6	(525.6) 532.5	(94.3) 97.3
Canada	(1.8) 4.3		95.6	1155.7	547.2
Chile	3.5	10.6	77.6	464.6	12.9
Colombia	56.3	1.4	66.9	57.9	75.3
Denmark	(.9) 3.9	7.9	49.2	1925.2	709.5
Ecuador	(12.1) 22	(6.4) 7.8	(53.3) 71.1	(117.1) 125.2	(53.8) 61.2
Ethiopia	(11.4) 13.3	1.5	(7.7) 8.3	2.2	1.9
Finland	0.4	9	43.5	1757	482.2
France	(1.7) 3.7	13.4	144.1	676.9	546.1
Germany	(8.5) 10.7	(7.2) 9.6	(63.2) 78.5	(1183.1) 1507	(125.5) 134.9
Greece	(1.7) 3.3	(1.5) 2.1	(20.9) 21.9	(414.9) 418.7	(163.1) 163.9
Guyana	(14.3) 17.9	(5.0) 13.4	168.8	426.5	
Ireland	(1.7) 1.8	8.1	74.7	709.6	28.6
Israel	2.4	14.3	28.5	1122.3	694.1
Jamaica	37.2	34.5	116.9	135.7	7.2
Japan	(.6) 1.1	(1.1) 1.5	(2.4) 2.7	(159.2) 187.9	28.4
South Korea	2.1	4.4	11.7	6.8	
Mongolia	24.6	16.5	15.2	425.7	1.3
Namibia	(16.7) 45.2	(26.8) 34.4	(79.2) 80.8	(551.3) 562.6	(51.4) 57.7
Norway	(1.0) 1.9	(10.3) 12.7	37.9		487.5
Paraguay	(14.4) 16.5	(3.7) 5	(13.1) 15	(17.3) 20.4	48.4

(continued)

TABLE 3.1 Continued

Country	*Homicide*[a]	*Rape*	*Robbery*	*Burglary*	*Auto Theft*
Russia	(18) 20.1	(5.2) 6.1	(106.1) 109.6	519.7	24.5
Saudi Arabia	0.5	1.5			45.4
Spain	(1.1) 2.6	3.2	(162.9) 169.9	(538.8) 570.2	(341.4) 343.1
Switzerland[c]	(1.1) 2.6	(4.2) 5.4	(31.3) 36.2	1172.5	
Trinidad/Tobago	(7.2) 9.7	(19.4) 20.4	(193.8) 205.9	(449.1) 452.7	80.6
Zimbabwe	(5.9) 9.0	(28.5) 31.2	94	384	13.7

[a] Some homicide statistics included attempts. These are presented in parentheses. The author recalculated these to obtain actual rates. Those without parentheses are actual rates.
[b] U.S. statistics were not included in the Interpol report and were from the Uniform Crime Reports for 1998.
[c] Swiss data for auto theft include stolen bicycles and were therefore excluded. Similarly Finnish data include unauthorized use.
Source: Interpol. *International Crime Statistics,* 1998. Lyons, France: Interpol Secretariat, 1999.

Table 3.2 presents data from the U.N. International Crime Victimization Survey. There have been four International Crime Victimization Surveys, with surveys begun in 1989, 1992, 1996, and 2000. The last involved 92 surveys in 56 countries and was expanding to over 100 surveys, involving cities as well as countries. The data in Table 3.2 are from the 1996 survey, which presents selected findings from 49 countries in three regions: Central and Eastern Europe, Western Europe, and North America.

Examining the full version of the victimization data in Table 3.2 finds that the United States, Canada, and the Czech Republic rank among the highest for burglary, motor vehicle theft, and petty crime. Other countries with higher levels of these crimes were Bulgaria, Estonia, and Slovakia. Low property crime victimization rates were found in Belarus, Norway, Switzerland, and Macedonia. High violence rates were to be found in countries of the former Soviet Union such as Estonia, Kazakhstan, Kyrgyzstan, and Russia. The U.S. has high violence scores compared to lower levels in Canada and Western European nations. Low violence levels were to be found in Western Europe, Hungary, and Macedonia (van Dijk and Kangaspunta, 2000, p. 39). For more information on international crime and surveys see Newman (1999) and www.vn.fi/om/suomi/heuni/.

The reader is reminded that, due to unreliability in such statistics, international comparisons are risky; however, Bennett and Lynch (1990) found similar results when they compared four widely used data sets.

The Prevalence of Crime

Estimates of the extent of crime commission depend upon how far or wide one may wish to cast the net. Estimates of official statistics (UCR), victim surveys (NCVS), and self-report surveys increase the estimate. Inclusion of other forms of nontraditional criminality, such as corporate crime or tax avoidance, would make crime seem even more pervasive.

Table 3.3 presents the UCR index of serious crimes, sometimes referred to as Part I offenses. Examination of crimes known to police in Table 3.3 underlines the point that the bulk of crime is made up of property crimes.

Table 3.4 reports the crimes that most frequently result in arrest. These data refer to persons arrested and not, as in the case of the index offenses, simply crimes known to police. Examination of these primarily Part II offenses indicates the extent to which policing is occupied with drunk driving, drunkenness, and disorderly conduct.

TABLE 3.2 International Crime Victimization, 1995 (percent of population per year)

	All Crimes	**Car Theft*	*Burglary*	*Robbery*	*Sexual Assault*
Western Countries					
Austria	18.8	0.1	0.9	0.2	3.8
Canada	25.2	1.5	3.4	1.2	2.7
England/Wales	30.9	2.5	3.0	1.4	2.0
Finland	18.9	0.4	0.6	0.5	3.2
France	25.3	1.6	2.3	1.0	0.9
Netherlands	31.5	0.4	2.6	0.5	3.5
Scotland	25.6	1.7	1.5	0.8	1.3
Sweden	24.0	1.2	1.3	0.9	4.6
Switzerland	26.7	1.9	2.6	1.3	2.5
Centr./East Europe					
Estonia		4.2	7.2	4.9	2.2
Slovak Republic		2.9	6.5	1.2	0.2
Russia		6.3	2.5	3.8	2.5
Latvia		5.2	2.9	3.4	0.4
Hungary		3.0	2.5	0.7	—
Croatia		1.4	0.9	0.8	1.0
Ukraine		4.1	3.6	5.7	1.7
Bulgaria		1.9	5.8	3.1	1.0
Mongolia		0.7	9.0	3.6	1.1
Kyrgyzstan		1.7	4.0	1.6	1.9
Developing Countries (city surveys)					
Kampala		6.6	14.1	6.8	[a]6.7
Dar Es Salaam		7.0	21.2	8.3	10.8
Johannesburg		7.4	7.2	5.4	2.4
Cairo		3.4	3.0	5.6	5.5
Tunis		3.8	7.5	5.6	5.5
Rio de Janiero		3.4	1.5	9.0	4.6
Buenos Aires		6.6	2.9	4.6	4.6
Manila		2.0	2.9	2.7	1.2
Bombay		4.0	1.3	0.6	0.5
Jakarta		1.3	3.0	1.4	4.5
Beijing		1.1	1.5	0.5	2.4

*owners only
[a]sexual incidents

Source: 1996 International Crime Victimization Survey, Unicri, Rome: *International Crime Victimization Survey,* Leiden University: P. Mayhew and J.J.M. van Dijk. 1997. *Criminal Victimization in Eleven Industrialized Countries,* The Hague: Ministry of Justice.

Trends in Crime

As discussed in the previous chapter, official crime statistics represented by the UCR have risen dramatically since the first study in the early 1930s. Figures 3.1 and 3.2 present trends in these index crimes.

Although, as we learned in Chapter 2, caution should be exercised in interpreting these statistics, these trend lines certainly dramatically depict an inexorable rise in official recorded crime since the mid-sixties, declining in the nineties. Despite this rise in official rates, victim surveys since the seventies reported relatively stable or falling rates, perhaps

TABLE 3.3 Index of Crime in the United States, 1998

Offense	*Number*	*Rate per 100,000*
Crime Index Total	12,475,634	4,615.5
Violent Crime	1,531,044	566.4
Property Crime	10,944,590	4,049.1
Murder	16,914	6.3
Forcible Rape	93,103	34.4
Robbery	446,625	165.2
Aggravated Assault	974,402	360.5
Burglary	2,329,950	862.0
Larceny Theft	7,373,886	2,728.1
Motor Vehicle Theft	1,240,754	459.0
Arson*	—	—

*Sufficient data are not available to estimate this offense.

Source: Modified from Federal Bureau of Investigation. 1999. *Crime in the United States, 1998.* Washington, D.C.: Government Printing Office, pp. 66–67.

TABLE 3.4 Number of Persons Arrested for the Ten Most Frequent Offenses, 1998

Offense	*Number Arrested*
1. Drug Abuse Violations	1,559,100
2. Driving Under the Influence	1,402,800
3. Other Assaults	1,338,800
4. Larceny/Theft*	1,307,100
5. Drunkenness	710,300
6. Disorderly Conduct	696,100
7. Liquor Laws	630,400
8. Aggravated Assault*	506,630
9. Fraud	394,600
10. Burglary*	330,700

*Denotes index crimes.

Source: Compiled from Federal Bureau of Investigation, 1999, *Crime in the United States, 1998.* Washington, D.C.: Government Printing Office, p. 210.

reinforcing the point that better recording and reporting may have in part accounted for some of the rise in official statistics.

The public alarm concerning the rapid rise in UCR crime statistics beginning in the mid-sixties was abetted by the fact that the decades of the 1940s and 1950s with their post-war prosperity demonstrated relative stability in many categories of crime. The new "crime wave" appeared particularly out of place. Historians of crime and violence in the United States remind us of our myopia in this regard and that waves of crime and violence, however difficult to measure, were characteristic of this land since colonial times, particularly in the post-Civil War era. (This subject will be given greater scope in Chapter 7). VANTAGE POINT 3.1 views the American crime problem from a global perspective. In 1968 the President's Commission on Law Enforcement and the Administration of Justice (1967a, p. 101) addressed this historical issue:

> There has always been too much crime. Virtually every generation since the founding of the Nation and before has felt itself threatened by the specter of

FIGURE 3.1 Trends in Crimes Against Persons, Rates per 100,000 People since 1933

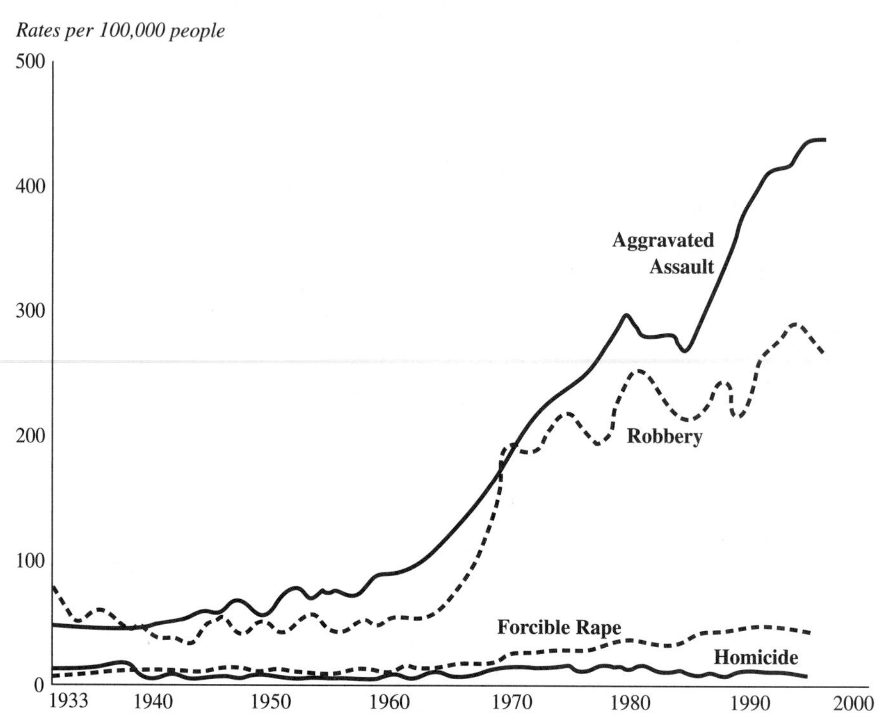

Source: President's Commission on Law Enforcement and the Admistration of Justice, 1967a, *The Challenge of Crime in a Free Society,* Washington D.C.: Government Printing Office, p. 23, updated with yearly Uniform Crime Reports data.

> rising crime and violence. A hundred years ago contemporary accounts of San Francisco told of extensive areas where "no decent man was in safety to walk the street after dark, while at all hours, both night and day, his property was jeopardized by incendiarism and burglary." Teenage gangs gave rise to the word "hoodlum;" while in one central New York City area, near Broadway, the police entered "only in pairs, and never unarmed." A noted chronicler of the period declared that "municipal law is a failure . . . we must soon fall back on the law of self preservation." And in 1910 one author declared that "crime, especially its more violent forms, and among the young is increasing steadily and is threatening to bankrupt the Nation."

However violent crime is in large cities today, both urban and rural areas of Sweden, Holland, and England were more violent during the Middle Ages (Johnson and Monkkonen, 1996). In *Hooligans* Pearson (1982) remarks on the historical myth of a crime-free past in England and attributes it to the abundance as well as sophistication of modern statistics, a nostalgia for the past, and cultural amnesia. The relationship of crime to the early history of many countries can be illustrated by Australia, a country that was settled as a penal colony for England. Gangs of "bushrangers" (horse rustlers) achieved notoriety, particularly the group led by Ned Kelly, whose reputation reached mythic proportions. This Robin Hood-like figure received support in opposing authority from small farmers who were nicknamed "cockatoos" or "cockys" because, like the bird, they scratched out a living from the ground. The cocky spirit was one of independence

FIGURE 3.2 During Trends in Crime Against Property, Rates per 100,000 People since 1933

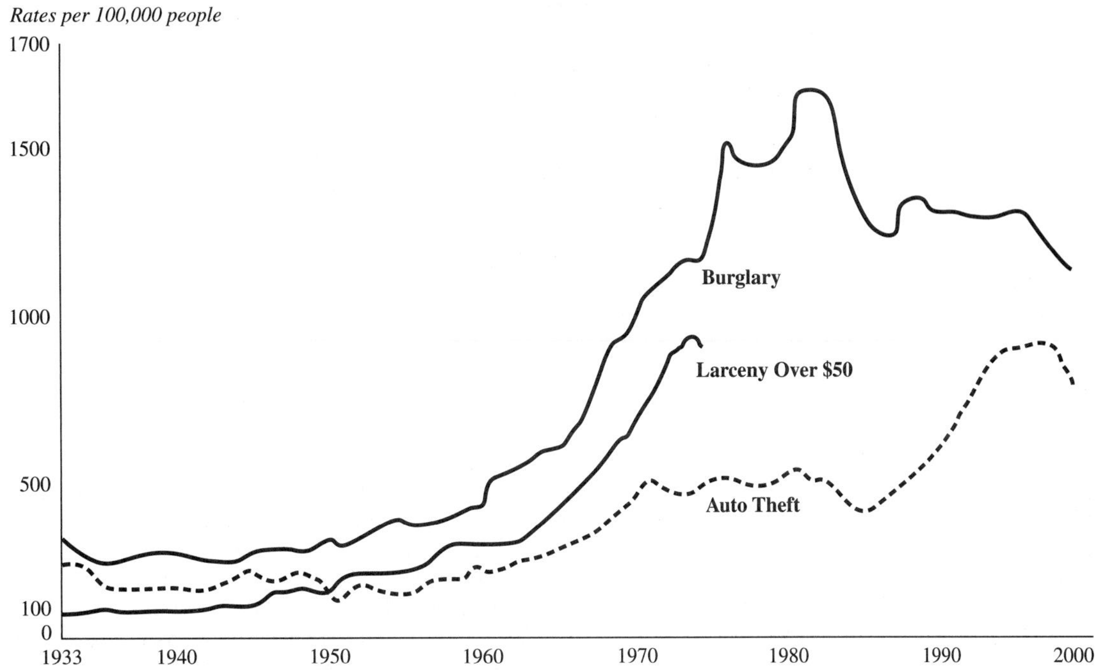

Source: President's Commission on Law Enforcement and the Adminstration of Justice, 1967a, *The Challenge of Crime in a Free Society,* Washington D.C: Government Printing Office, p. 23 updated with yearly Uniform Crime Reports data.

and defiance of authority as illustrated by Ned Kelly, who was obstinate to the end and was hanged at age twenty-five. This spirit is illustrated in Australia's most beloved song about a vagabond who steals a sheep and commits suicide rather than be caught (Levathes, 1985, p. 261):

> Up jumped the swagman
> Sprang into the billabong
> "You'll never catch me alive," said he.
> And his ghost may be heard
> as you pass by that billabong
> "Who'll come a-waltzing Matilda with me?"

Because systematic victim data have been available only since the early seventies, a relative comparison with UCR data before 1973 is not possible. Figure 3.3 and Table 3.5 present information from the National Crime Victimization Survey.

Comparison of these trend lines with those from the UCR for the same period suggests similarities as well as differences. While most of the crimes in both measures are predominantly against property rather than against persons, the NCVS did not demonstrate the same steep rise in offenses in the seventies that the UCR reported.

In considering these figures it is important to realize that, if we were to consider the full range of economic crimes such as the impact of corporate price fixing, then in fact every household has been touched by crime. Casting a wider net, were we to consider self-report data, particularly of minor offenses, we would conclude that the rate of criminality is pervasive. Despite problems in instruments used and in samples drawn, self-report studies provide much-needed evidence of the extensiveness of hidden

VANTAGE POINT 3.1

American Crime Problems from a Global Perspective

Issues

Transnational crime (i.e., crime that violates the laws of several international sovereignties or impacts another sovereignty) has grown incrementally over the past two decades, at a rate roughly corresponding to both the increase in international trade import-export figures and the developments in transportation and communications. Several events demonstrate the stark reality of transnational crimes: the destruction by a terrorist bomb of Pan American Flight 103 over Lockerbie, Scotland in 1988; the 1993 terrorist bombing of the World Trade Center; the more recent conspiracy in New York City to destroy all Hudson River crossings and both FBI and United Nations headquarters; and the Bank of Credit and Commerce (BCCI) scam, with its estimated cost to U.S. taxpayers of between $200 billion and $1.4 trillion by the year 2021.

In each of these cases, U.S. law enforcement authorities responded vigorously, but with limited overall success. Our system has been developed to deal with criminality at the city/county level and, in some cases, at the national level. With respect to global crime, however, we lack readiness—in terms of education, research sponsorship, interagency cooperation (between the Departments of Justice and State), and a full commitment to a centralized and coordinated international effort.

Crime is not a strictly local or even national problem; although its impact is felt at the local level, much crime is internationally conditioned and coordinated. For instance, the connection between street crime and the importation and dissemination of drugs is well established. Similarly, an increase in fraud is commensurate with growth in the operational reach of commercial transactions. Profits from the international drug trade, "laundered" overseas and reinvested in American real estate, commercial, or entertainment enterprises, significantly affect U.S. citizens, who must pick up the burden for uncollected taxes on these transactions.

In addition, the impact of ethnic gang criminality on our "local" crime scene is readily apparent, e.g., the wholesale trade in cocaine, controlled by illegal immigrants from Colombia; the importation of Chinese slave labor into the U.S. and exploitation of Chinese-American businesses by Chinese gangs (triad-based); trade in arms and drugs by Jamaican gangs; burglaries by Albanian gangs; and involvement in the fuel distribution market and the international trade of weapons and nuclear materials by Russian gangs. These new ethnic gangs maintain intra-ethnic contacts, as well as relations with their countries of origin, and local law enforcement professionals are powerless to stop or control them.

Policy Recommendations

- *U.N. Convention:* Section 32098 of the 1994 Crime Act (dealing with the development of a United Nations Convention on Organized Crime) should be retained and further implemented.

criminality and law violation; moreover, they support the notion of the "dualistic fallacy" discussed in the previous chapter, which points out that one must exercise great care in comparing "criminals" and "noncriminals." One may control misunderstanding or overgeneralizations in referring to "criminals" by using operational definitions such as "those arrested" or "those identified by victims" or "those admitting to certain offenses."

Age and Crime

Most of those arrested are young. VANTAGE POINT 3.2 presents data on ages of those arrested for particular crimes. The peak arrest age for property crime is sixteen, while age eighteen is the highest for violent crime. Overall, crime commission declines with age.

VANTAGE POINT 3.1—*Continued*

- *Overseas deployment:* The achievements of the federal government in dealing with the complex problems of transnational crime, including deployment of U.S. law enforcement personnel in overseas stations, should be publicly highlighted and strengthened.
- *Training:* Strategies to deal with transnational crime should require that schools of criminal justice provide more focused training in areas such as geography, geopolitics, foreign criminal justice systems, comparative criminological methods, and global approaches to crime control.
- *Data bases and strategies:* The capacity of the Bureau of Justice Statistics and the National Institute of Justice to develop international data bases and strategies for dealing with transnational crime—in collaboration with the U.N. Crime Prevention and Criminal Justice Branch and groups of American scholars—should be strengthened.
- *Interagency cooperation:* The Departments of Justice and State should strengthen their cooperative efforts to deal with organized crime.
- *Counter-terrorism:* The Omnibus Counter-Terrorism Act of 1995 deserves vigorous implementation and constant evaluation/monitoring of its impact.
- *Global perspective:* Every effort should be made to move the crime control debate out of the current gridlock of national versus local approaches; most local crime is the result of worldwide developments and, thus, falls under the foreign policy clause of the U.S. Constitution.
- *Local perspective:* The effort to deal with "local" crime as the product of worldwide events should focus on criminality pertaining to drugs, fraud, and ethnic gangs.
- *Ethnic recruitment:* To deal with ethnic gang criminality, a vigorous recruitment drive should be initiated to enlist candidates from "new" ethnic minorities who can understand or infiltrate such gangs in affected communities; this recruitment could be part of the community policing program initiative to deploy 100,000 new police officers, or it could be part of the block grant program.

Source: "American Society of Criminology Task Force Report to Attorney General Janet Reno," *The Criminologist* (Special Issue), 20, 6, November/December 1995. Task force members were Gerhard O.W. Mueller (Chair), Paul Friday, Robert McCormack, Graeme Newman, and Richard H. Ward.

InfoTrac College Edition Research

Examine the issue of international crime. What is an additional, emergent crime problem not mentioned in VANTAGE POINT 3.1? What strategies are needed for coping with this?

Particularly glaring is the involvement of younger groups in serious property crimes. It is important to note that, while most persons arrested and convicted as adult criminals were first arrested as juveniles, most juvenile delinquents do not become adult criminals. Youthful offenders in urban areas are probably overrepresented in arrest statistics. Such areas have more efficient, formalized policing, while youth generally have less power than their elders to shield themselves from arrest. Juveniles also commit the types of crimes on which municipal police departments tend to concentrate. Excluding common youth offenses, such as curfew and runaway violations, and assuming juvenile offenders are often handled and recorded differently depending on police jurisdictions, the median age for arrested robbers, burglars, thieves, auto thieves, arsonists, and vandals is under twenty in all categories. Estimates of the average age of embezzlers, price-fixers, bribers, and the like considerably alter this age profile, however, since these crimes are committed by older criminals. The "graying of America," with a large

(© Chang W. Lee / NYT Pictures)

FBI officers arrest Yaponchik (Vyacheslav Kirillovich Ivankov), an alleged leader of Russian organized crime in North America. The FBI's "Russian squad" was formed to combat and contain the activities of Russians gangsters in the United States.

proportion of the population becoming elderly, has led to forecasts of an increase in the number of older criminals (Wilbanks and Kim, 1984).

Criminologists had predicted a possible demographic time bomb as the number of people in the maximum crime committing ages of 15–24 expanded at the end of the century. From 1996 to 2000 there were 500,000 more males in this age group than there were a decade earlier—about a 20 percent increase. The homicide rate among 15-to-19 year olds increased 154 percent between 1985 and 1991. This increase began with the advent of crack in the mid-1980s, along with a proliferation of guns to protect crack markets (Blumstein, 1995). The rate decreased beginning in 1992, in part due to an end in this "crack epidemic."

VANTAGE POINT 3.3 reports on the policy suggestions of the American Society of Criminology task force on delinquency to former Attorney General Janet Reno.

Age/Crime Debate. An intramural academic war of sorts has broken out in criminology. It could be described as the "age/crime debate." On the one side of the debate are Gottfredson and Hirschi (1986, 1987, 1988), who view the "maturing out of" crime or desistance from crime as individuals age as a constant. They indicate (1986, p. 219):

> Further, this distribution is characteristic of the age-crime relation regardless of sex, race, country, time or offense. Indeed, the persistence of this relation across time and culture is phenomenal. As long as records have been kept, in all societies in which such records are available, it appears that crime is an activity highly concentrated among the young.

They question the emphasis on career criminal research, incapacitation, and the recent fetish for longitudinal research that justifies a search for groups of offenders (career criminals) whose criminality does not decline with age (Blumstein, Cohen, and Farrington, 1988a, 1988b; Cohen and Land, 1987; and Farrington, 1986). Blumstein and Cohen

(© Susan Mails / MGA / Photri)

The city of Amsterdam, where bicycle traffic is heavy, has a high rate of bicycle theft.

FIGURE 3.3A Property Crime Rates, United States, 1973–98

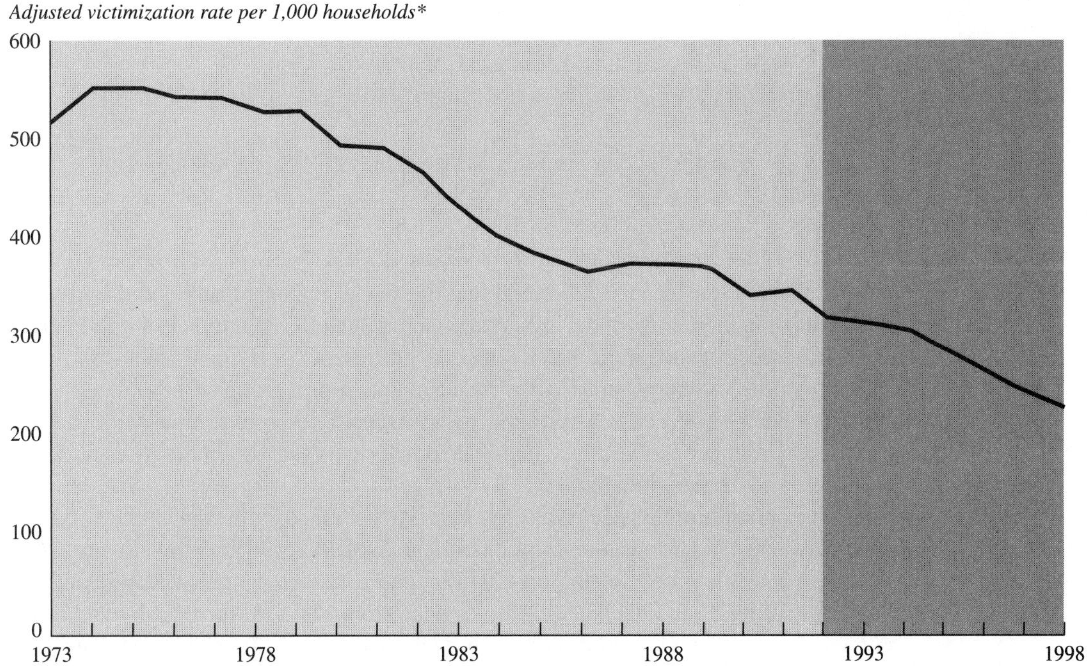

Note: The property crimes included are burglary, theft, and motor vehicle theft.

*The National Crime Victimization Survey redesign was implemented in 1993; the area with the lighter shading is before the redesign and the darker area after the redesign. The data before 1993 are adjusted to make them comparable with the data collected since the redesign.

Source: Bureau of Justice Statistics, *National Crime Victimization Survey.*

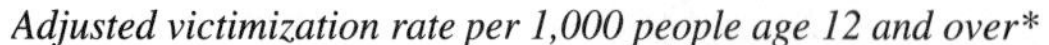

FIGURE 3.3B Violent Crime Rates by Gender of Victim, United States, 1973–98

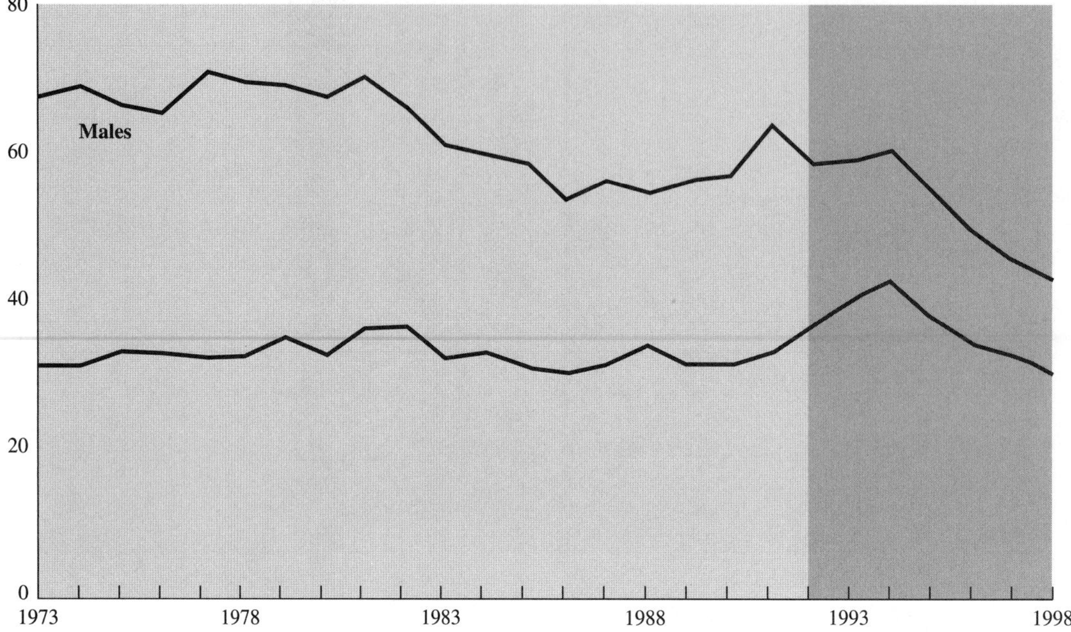

Note: The violent crimes included are rape, robbery, aggravated and simple assault, and homicide.

*The National Crime Victimization Survey redesign was implemented in 1993; the area with the lighter shading is before the redesign and the darker area after the redesign. The data before 1993 are adjusted to make them comparable with the data collected since the redesign.

Sources: Bureau of Justice Statistics, *National Crime Victimization Survey;* and FBI *Uniform Crime Reports.*

(1987), in a longitudinal study of those arrested for more serious crimes in the District of Columbia and Detroit in 1973, found that those who remained active in their twenties did not age out in their thirties, but only after age forty-five. Farrington (1986, p. 189) suggests that offenses of different types peak at different times and that this represents " . . . crime switching rather than replacement of one group of offenders by another." Steffensmeier (1989a) finds variation by age-specific type over time with the offenders becoming younger and younger, and that some crimes such as embezzlement or fraud are less likely to decline with age.

The outcome of this age/crime controversy is claimed by the disputants to have important consequences for career criminal research (Tittle, 1988). Why do most criminals "mature out of" crime? Farrington (1986) suggests factors such as the influence of wives and/or girlfriends, the decline of gang or peer group support, increased penalties, as well as increased legitimate opportunities as individuals reach their twenties. The decline in crime involvement is not explained by the physiology of aging since substantial decline in fitness does not occur until the late fifties or older. Social changes are more important than physiological changes in explaining this decrease. Steffensmeier and Allan (1990) identify a number of social changes that encourage conformity, including: more legitimate access to material goods and excitement, changes in age-graded norms and anticipatory socialization, changes in lifestyle and peer groups, stronger social bonds, higher legal and social costs, and fewer illegitimate opportunities.

TABLE 3.5 Criminal Victimization Experienced in the United States, 1998

	Number in Millions	*Rate per 1,000*[a]
All Crimes	31.3	—
Violent Crime	8.1	36.6
Simple Assault	5.2	23.5
Aggravated Assault	1.7	7.5
Robbery	.9	4.0
Rape/Sexual Assault	.3	1.5
Personal Theft[b]	.3	1.3
Property Crime	22.9	217.0
Property Thefts	17.7	168.1
Household Burglary	4.1	38.5
Motor Vehicle Theft	1.1	10.8

- National Crime Victimization Survey violent crime rates declined 7%, and property crime rates fell 13% from 1997 to 1998. The 1998 rates are the lowest recorded since survey's inception in 1973.*
- Based on preliminary FBI data, the number of murders dropped about 8% between 1997 and 1998.
- The overall 1-year decline in violent crime resulted from a slight yet significant decline in aggravated assault rates. From 1997 to 1998 no significant changes in rates of rape or sexual assault, robbery, or simple assault occurred.
- Every major type of crime measured—rape or sexual assault, robbery, aggravated assault, simple assault, burglary, theft, and motor vehicle theft—increased significantly between 1993 and 1998.
- For virtually every demographic category considered, violent victimization decreased between 1993 and 1998. Male violent victimization rates fell 39 %, and black violent victimization rates fell 38 %.
- Property crime rate declines occurred across all demographic groups between 1993 and 1998. Property crime rates declined 31% for white, black, urban, and suburban households.
- In 1998 males were victimized at significantly higher rates than females, and blacks were victimized at somewhat higher rates than whites. Non-Hispanics and Hispanics were victimized at about the same rate.
- About half the violent crime victims knew the offender(s) in 1998. Over 7 in 10 rape or sexual assault victims knew the attacker(s), and 5 in 10 aggravated assault victims knew the offender(s).
- Offenders used a weapon in about one-fourth of violent victimizations in 1998. About 4 in 10 robbery victims faced a weapon, as did fewer than 1 in 10 rape or sexual assault victims.
- From 1993 to 1998, almost half of all violent victimizations were reported to the police. Females and blacks reported violent victimizations in higher percentages than males and whites, while no reporting differences emerged between non-Hispanics and Hispanics during the same period.

—Not applicable
[a]Per 1,000 persons age 12 or older, or per 1,000 households
[b]Includes pocket picking and purse snatching
*After adjusting rates following the 1992 NCVS redesign

Source: Bureau of Justice Statistics, 1999, "Criminal Victimization 1998: National Crime Victimization Survey," Bureau of Justice Statistics Bulletin, August 25 (revised).

Perhaps one of the best kept secrets in criminology is the existence of the "Bible of Juvenile Justice Research"—*Juvenile Offenders and Victims,* an annual report by Howard Snyder and Melissa Sickmund (1999) produced annually by the National Center for Juvenile Justice in Pittsburgh. This documents, with tables and figures, the latest trends in juvenile justice.

Gender Differences in Criminality

Table 3.6 presents some recent statistics on "women offenders" in the United States (Greenfeld and Snell, 1999).

Of all demographic variables, gender is the best predictor of criminality; most persons arrested are males. In the United States, in the nineties, males represented about 83 percent of those arrested; and, with the exception of primarily female offenses such as

VANTAGE POINT 3.2

What Is the Relationship between Age and Crime?

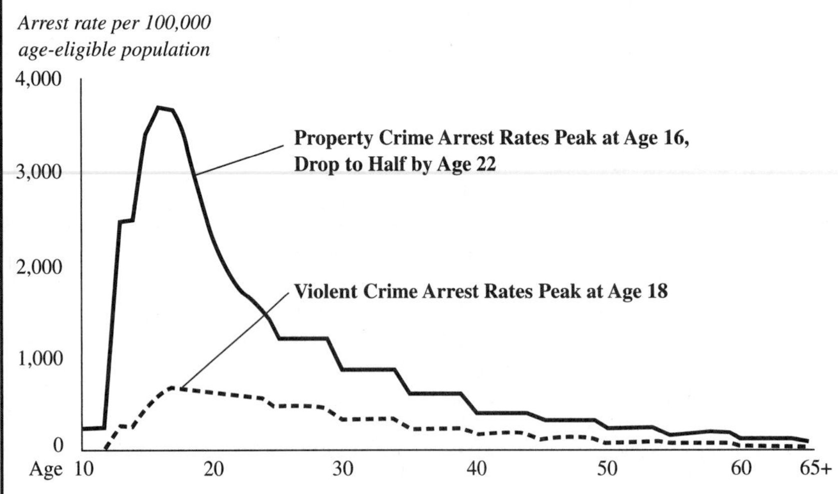

Sources: FBI *Uniform Crime Reports* 3-year averages, 1983–85.

Participation in crime declines with age.

Arrest data show that the intensity of criminal behavior slackens after the teens, and it continues to decline with age. Arrests, however, are only a general indicator of criminal activity. The greater likelihood of arrests for young people may result partly from their lack of experience in offending and also from their involvement in the types of crimes for which apprehension is more likely (for example, purse snatching vs. fraud). Moreover, because youths often commit crime in groups, the resolution of a single crime may lead to several arrests.

The decline in crime participation with age may also result from the incapacitation of many offenders. When repeat offenders are apprehended, they serve increasingly longer sentences, thus incapacitating them for long periods as they grow older. Moreover, a RAND Corporation study of habitual offenders shows that the success of habitual offenders in avoiding apprehension declines as their criminal careers progress. Even though offense rates declined over time, the probabilities of arrest, conviction, and incarceration per offense all tended to increase. Recidivism

prostitution (in which "Johns," or customers, are seldom arrested), this difference holds for all criminal offenses. The male crime rate exceeds that of females universally, in all nations, in all communities, among all age groups, and in all periods of history for which statistics are available. Whereas in some more traditional countries the crime-gender arrest ratio may range from 200-to-1 to 1,000-to-1, in modernized societies the gap in gender variation in crime has been closing. Why such variation? Gender per se is not the key variable so much as a particular culture's conception of gender. The female crime rate appears to be closer to the male level in countries in which females enjoy more equality and freedom and thus an increased opportunity to commit crime.

This universality of disproportionate male criminality can best be explained by the differential treatment of males and females. Traditionally, males are socialized to be

VANTAGE POINT 3.2—*Continued*

data also show that the rates of return to prison tend to be lower for older than for younger prisoners. Older prisoners who do return do so after a longer period of freedom than younger prisoners.

Different age groups are arrested and incarcerated for different types of crimes.

- Juveniles under age 18 have a higher likelihood of being arrested for robbery and UCR index property crimes than do members of any other age group.
- Persons between ages 18 and 34 are the most likely to be arrested for violent crimes.
- Among jail and prison inmates, property crimes, particularly burglary and public order crimes, are more common among younger inmates.
- Violent crimes were more prevalent among older inmates admitted to prison in 1982 but showed little variation among jail inmates of different ages.
- Drug crimes were more prevalent among inmates age 25-to-44 in both prisons and jails.

Percentage of Arrestees under 18 Years of Age, by Type of Crime

Most Serious Offense Charged		*Juvenile Arrests as a Percent of Total Arrests*	
Total	19%	Stolen property (buying, receiving, possessing)	25
Violent Crime Index	17	Vandalism	43
Murder and nonnegligent manslaughter	14	Weapons (carrying, possessing, etc.)	24
Forcible rape	17	Prostitution and commercialized vice	1
Robbery	30	Sex offenses (except forcible rape and prostitution)	18
Aggravated assault	14	Drug abuse violations	14
Property Crime Index	35	Gambling	17
Burglary	37	Offenses against family and children	7
Larceny-theft	34	Driving under the influence	1
Motor vehicle theft	40	Liquor laws	25
Arson	50	Drunkenness	3
Other assaults	17	Disorderly conduct	27
Forgery and counterfeiting	7	Vagrancy	11
Fraud	3	All other offenses (except traffic)	12
Embezzlement	8		

Source: Howard Snyder and Melissa Sickmund. 1999. *Juvenile Offenders and Victims: 1999 National Report.* Pittsburgh: National Center for Juvenile Justice, p. 116.

Source: Bureau of Justice Statistics. 1988b. *Report to the Nation on Crime and Justice,* 2nd edition, Washington, D.C.: Government Printing Office, March, pp. 32–33.

InfoTrac College Edition Research
Search "age and crime" and locate the "age-crime debate." What is it and what is its importance?

dominant, active, and aggressive. In fact, chivalry and the law often require that the male take responsibility for what occurs. In many traditional societies it is the husband who is punished for his wife's transgressions. Similarly, customary gender role socialization of females emphasizes passivity and subordination.

Merlo (1995, p. 119) indicates:

> Female criminality in the 1990s is, in some respects, as misunderstood as it was in the 1970s. The typical female offender is not a corporate or computer criminal, a terrorist, a burglar, or a murderer. Instead, she is likely to engage in theft, fraud, drug offenses, forgery, embezzlement, and prostitution. Despite the reality of female offense patterns, the media and the public prefer to focus on the

VANTAGE POINT 3.3

Early Prevention of and Intervention for Delinquency and Related Problem Behavior

Issues

Strong evidence links early problem behavior to later adolescent delinquency and serious adult criminality. Many children in the United States are lacking fundamental elements essential for human development. These children are legally entitled, but have no access, to safe shelter, adequate food, basic health care, and sufficient preparation to become economically viable adults. The absence of these resources has been linked to abnormal development, economically and socially marginal existence, and persistent criminality.

Children whose parents are criminals have a high probability of becoming delinquents. Those identified in court as abused or neglected by their parents are more likely than other children to become delinquent. Offenders whose parents were also criminals have a high probability of becoming high-rate predatory criminals. However, whether or not their parents have criminal histories, children raised by mothers or fathers with good parenting skills are less likely to become delinquents or serious offenders. Inmates who assume responsible family roles after they are released are less likely to recidivate than offenders without family ties. The vast majority of delinquents and criminals eventually "mature out" of crime; assumption of family responsibilities can be a key factor in this process.

Research documents the effectiveness of early prevention and intervention in forestalling these outcomes. Waiting until the mid-to-late teenage years to intervene in persistent delinquency ensures that winning the battle will be difficult, if not impossible. The current focus on older juveniles is at best a stopgap measure; it ignores younger children, who, in the absence of early prevention/intervention, will soon follow the same nonproductive path as their teenage role models. Research also suggests that early childhood programs cost relatively little compared to the costs associated with the problems they prevent later, such as drug and alcohol abuse, teen pregnancy, special education requirements, or institutionalization.

Successful early childhood programs when compared to less successful ones most often have these characteristics:

- They attempt to ameliorate more than one or two factors associated with delinquency and focus on multiple problem behaviors.
- They are designed to be appropriate for children of specific ages and at specific stages of development.
- They involve long-term efforts of more than a few months, often lasting several years.

Based on the above and other current research, the task force policy recommendations focus on how the U.S. Department of Justice can assist with early prevention and intervention.

Policy Recommendations

- **Early prevention.** The U.S. Department of Justice should take a leading role in the interagency development of early prevention efforts that have shown evidence of being effective, in particular:

"glitzy exceptions" suggesting that women's involvement in crimes of violence (like serial murder) and property crimes (like industrial espionage) is increasing.

In explaining some of the social, psychological, and physical reasons for these differences, Steffensmeier (Blaum, 1991, p. 1) notes that "there is no female equivalent to the 'romanticized' rogue male." For some males crime is macho and enhances status, while female crime is usually stigmatizing. Despite social change, social expectations of women still center on nurturing, beauty, virtue, and stereotypes of femininity that are incompatible with qualities valued in the criminal underworld. Steffensmeier (Blaum, 1991) also sees female criminals as more likely to be drug-dependent or to come from deprived family backgrounds. They are more likely to engage in crime because of intimate or romantic

VANTAGE POINT 3.3—*Continued*

Establishment of home visitation programs for mothers at high risk for abusing, neglecting, or inadequately providing for the needs of their children.

Establishment of educational daycare programs with a home visitation component for at-risk infants and children. Such programs provide assistance to parents, teach parenting skills, and involve marital and family therapy.

De facto as well as *de jure* provision of services to which children and adolescents are legally entitled, especially services essential to their safety and wholesome development (e.g., development of neighborhood-based collaborative community development and youth development programs that emphasize provision of basic needs for infants and preschool children and actively recruit and sustain participation of older children in the nonschool hours).

- **Criminal parents.** Early prevention and intervention efforts should be targeted to parents who are under supervision of the criminal and juvenile justice systems and the family courts. In the short term, these efforts can produce crimes committed by parents; in the long term, they can reduce future crimes that might otherwise be committed by the children of offenders and interrupt the cycle of criminal behavior in sequential generations. Promising approaches include:

Prenatal counseling, perinatal care (including substance abuse treatment) for pregnant offenders, and hands-on parenting classes for offenders with babies and young children.

Therapeutic communities or similar residential programs, especially those that help inmates in assessing and improving their interactions with children and spouses, for prison or jail inmates who are within a year of release or who have just been released.

Family focus/parenting programs with active door-to-door outreach in communities in which many children have fathers in jail or prison. Referral and advocacy for health, nutrition, and related services for children of parents under juvenile/criminal justice system supervision or conditional release.

Recruitment of more stable extended family members to care for the children of offenders, especially in cultural groups in which the extended family has traditionally played a key role in childrearing.

- **Juvenile offenders.** Programs should be developed to assist families of youths 10-to-12 years old who are coming to the attention of the juvenile justice system. For older, more persistent juvenile offenders, community-based programs that focus on behavioral skills should be developed.
- **Research needs.** The Department of Justice should design and support high quality evaluations of major prevention and intervention programs, including those described above as promising, for pre- and post-natal children, preschool-age children, school-age children, and school-age youth.

Source: "American Society of Criminology Task Force Report to Attorney General Janet Reno," *The Criminologist* (Special Issue), 20, 6, November/December 1995. Task Force members on delinquency were Marcia Chaiken and David Huizinga.

InfoTrac College Edition Research
Visit the Bureau of Justice Statistics web site and review a new program for dealing with delinquency not mentioned in this VANTAGE POINT.

relationships and are often introduced to crime by a significant other. Male physical strength and agility also favor males' greater participation in certain crimes such as robbery and burglary. The threat of potential sexual victimization also limits females' mobility and access to criminal haunts.

Females tend to concentrate on less rewarding types of crime, such as shoplifting and employee theft, rather than on more lucrative, organized activities, such as burglary rings, drug cartels, and fencing networks. Even prostitution is usually controlled by males. Racketeering and corporate fraud are almost overwhelmingly male-dominated (Blaum, 1991). Girls exposed to a variety of familial risk factors are found to be far less likely to deviate than boys raised in similar circumstances (Dornfeld and Kruttschnitt, 1991).

TABLE 3.6 Women Offenders

Women Offenders	*Violent Offenders*	*All Arrestees*	*Convicted Felony Defendants*	*Correctional Populations*
Number	2,135,000	3,171,000	160,500	951,900
as a Percent of Each Category	14%	22%	16%	16%

- Based on the self-reports of victims of violence, women account for about 14% of violent offenders—an annual average of about 2.1 million violent offenders.
- Male offending equals about 1 violent offender for every 9 males age 10 or older, a per capita rate 6 times that of women.
- Three out of four violent female offenders committed simple assault.
- An estimated 28% of violent female offenders are juveniles.
- Three out of four victims of violent female offenders were women.
- Nearly 2 out of 3 victims had a prior relationship with the female offender.
- An estimated 4 in 10 women committing violence were perceived by the victim as being under the influence of alcohol and/or drugs at the time of the crime.
- The per capita rate of murder offending by women in 1998 was the lowest recorded since 1976; the rate at which women commit murder has been declining since 1980.
- In 1998 there were an estimated 3.2 million arrests of women—accounting for about 22% of all arrests that year. The per capita rate of arrest among juvenile females was nearly twice the adult female rate.
- Since 1990 the number of female defendants convicted of felonies in state courts has grown at more than 2 times the rate of increase in male defendants.
- In 1998 an estimated 950,000 women were under the care, custody, or control of correctional agencies—probation or parole agencies supervising 85% of these offenders in the community. The total equals a rate of about 1 woman involved with the criminal justice system for every 109 adult women in the U.S. population.
- Women under supervision by justice system agencies were mothers of an estimated 1.3 million minor children.
- Nearly 6 in 10 women in state prisons had experienced physical or sexual abuse in the past; just over a third of imprisoned women had been abused by an intimate in the past; and just under a quarter reported prior abuse by a family member.
- About 84,000 women were confined in prisons in 1998. In 1996 the average sentence and time served for women were shorter than for males with equivalent offenses.

Source: Lawrence A. Greenfeld and Tracy L. Snell. 1999. "Women Offenders." *Bureau of Justice Statistics Special Report.* December, NCJ175688.

The traditional handmaiden of sexism has been paternalism, a sort of sexual *noblesse oblige* in which males felt that they were responsible for protecting the dependent female. This policy is reflected in the law and its administration, since females generally receive much lighter sentences for the same offense, are viewed more favorably by judges and juries, and seldom receive the death penalty.

Recent literature on the subject of gender and crime note the **androcentric** (*male-centered*) **bias** in many delinquency and crime theories (Chesney-Lind, 1989). Burnett (1986) also notes that women have been left out of criminological scholarship and that a new era began with publications such as Adler's *Sisters in Crime* (1975), Simon's *Women and Crime* (1975), and Adler and Simon's *The Criminology of Deviant Women* (1979).

Using UCR data Simon (1990) notes increases in female crime particularly in property offenses, especially white collar offenses involving small-to-medium amounts of money. While writers such as Adler (1975) were arguing that a gender convergence or closing of the gap between male and female crime rates was taking place, others such as Steffensmeier (1978) and Steffensmeier and Allan (1988) found no such closing of the crime-gender ratio.

Self-report data on admitted offenses by gender show mixed results, with some demonstrating less of a gap between male and female criminality (Jensen and Eve, 1976;

Hindelang, 1979; Short and Nye, 1958). Other researchers indicate that the differences are similar to those that exist in official arrest statistics (Hindelang, Hirschi, and Weis, 1979; Williams and Gold, 1972).

A major literature is developing regarding gender and crime. One example is a "power-control theory" of delinquency and gender (Hagan, Gillis, and Simpson, 1985 and 1987), which proposes that male and female children react differently to parental power sharing. They hypothesized that " . . . balanced family structure [shared power by spouses] reduces the disparities in delinquency between genders and that unbalanced family structures perpetuate those differences" (Singer and Levine,1988, p. 643). Both Singer and Levine (1988) and Morash and Chesney-Lind (1991) found little support for this theory. For further review of this literature the reader is referred to Nagel and Hagan (1983), Mann (1984), Moyer (1990), and Rosenbaum (1989b).

Social Class and Crime

Social class is not a category included in the Uniform Crime Reports, yet the vast majority of those arrested or labeled as criminal are from lower social classes. Criminality for traditional crimes is higher among lower class individuals, totally apart from bias in statistics or the administration of justice. Part of the excess rate is likely to be due to their lack of power and sophistication in shielding themselves from formal litigation proceedings. Traditional explanations of crime and social class view the relationship as an inverse one; that is, as social class becomes higher, the volume of crime commission decreases proportionately. Figure 3.4(a) attempts to depict this relationship schematically. Reckless (1967) proposes a bimodal theory of the distribution of crime commission in which the criminality curve has two modes (most frequently appearing cases) among the lower class and the upper class, though crimes of the latter are seldom reflected in national crime statistics. Figure 3.4(b) illustrates this relationship.

The relationship between social class and criminality remains a subject of debate. The early self-report surveys (Short and Nye, 1958; Nye, Short, and Olson, 1958) found no relationship other than that lower class offenders were more likely to be officially processed. Tittle, Villemez, and Smith (1978), in a literature review of major self-report studies, found no relationship between class and criminality. More recent research and reviews of self-report surveys suggest that much of this lack of difference by class may have been due to the measuring instruments, which tended to concentrate on rather trivial offenses. Lower class youth were found to commit more serious crimes more often; and their offense profile was found to more closely follow that presented by official statistics (Hardt and Hardt, 1977; Elliott and Ageton, 1980; and Hindelang, Hirschi, and Weis, 1979). Examining "calls to police" Warner and Pierce (1991) found that poverty of area consistently increased the rate of assault, robbery, and burglary, although in examining delinquency Larzelere and Patterson (1990) found that parental monitoring and discipline were more predictive than social class. It is important to caution, however, that official statistics undercount the typical crimes of upper socioeconomic groups so that, even though the lower class has higher official crime rates, this does not indicate that individuals in this class are necessarily more criminal.

Race and Crime

In the Watergate scandal, twenty-one of Nixon's aides were sent to prison for their crimes. G. Gordon Liddy, who was uncooperative with investigators, served fifty-two months. The others served prison terms ranging from four to twelve months. Nixon himself received a pardon.

FIGURE 3.4 Models of the Relationship between Social Class and Criminality

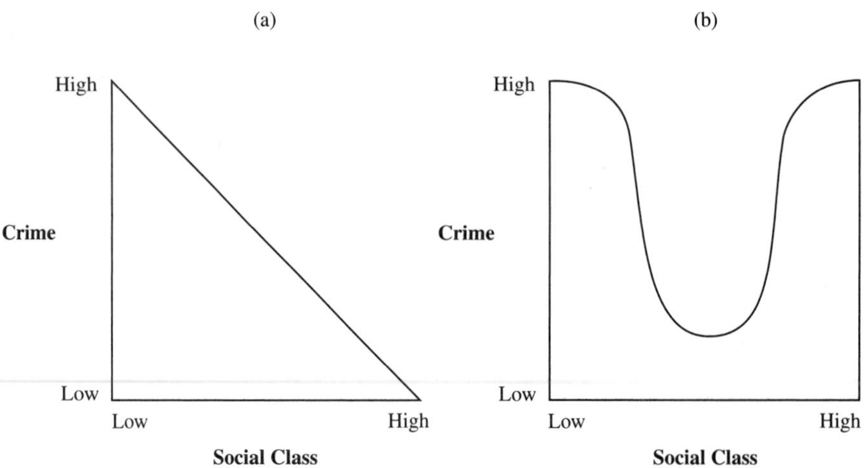

> Nine years after Nixon's resignation, Frank Wills—the security guard who discovered the Watergate break-in—was arrested for shoplifting in Augusta, Georgia. Unemployed at the time, he had stolen a pair of shoes for his son. Unlike "the president's men," Mr. Wills received the maximum sentence: twelve months in prison for stealing a $12 pair of shoes.—Joseph Melusky, *The American Political System: An Owner's Manual,* 2000, p. 256.

Just as an androcentric bias was identified earlier, a Eurocentric bias may also exist in criminology because African American criminologists have not played a significant role in the field (Young and Sulton, 1991). Eurocentric bias refers to the belief that the field of criminology is dominated by views reflecting those of European (white) descent and that such a bias may tend not to fully appreciate the interaction between racism, inequality, and the experiences of African Americans in the criminal justice system.

Race is a relatively arbitrary, socially defined status. For example, in an early study, Herskovits (1930, p. 177) estimated that of the total number of black persons classified as "Negro" in the United States, 15 percent were more "white" than Negroid, 25 percent were equally "white" and Negroid, and 22 percent were unmixed Negroid. Thus, the concept of "race" is more a socially defined category than a taxonomically simple biological classification. As Sutherland and Cressey (1974, p. 132) point out: "There is no avoiding the fact that at least 80 percent of the offenders contributing to the 'black' crime rate are part 'white.' "

Given the increasing ethnic diversity of the United States, a racial and ethnic classification system that pigeonholes entire segments of the population obfuscates true understanding. Scientists have proven there is no biological basis for such traditional racial classifications. Students need to be aware of the inherent problems in this currently accepted system. The validity of this shorthand method of identifying different groups in an increasingly diverse society needs to be questioned by more criminologists (Mellow, 1996, p. 7).

The foregoing facts become important in light of cryptoracist theories rediscovered and received with some respectability in the 1970s. These regenerated long-discredited hereditary theories of racial inferiority to explain why blacks, or African Americans, despite social changes in the 1960s, had failed to succeed (Skolnick and Currie, 1988, p. 12). Such theories obviously ignore the black experience in a nation that until relatively recently practiced institutionalized racism against blacks.

To paraphrase one writer (Dr. Charles King), we have a society that crippled a people—then blamed them for limping (Ross and McMurray, 1996, p. 3). The long legacy of slavery, followed by "Jim Crow" laws (legalized or *de jure* segregation and discrimination) and then succeeded by *de facto* (in fact) discrimination placed a generational burden on black Americans that far exceeded the milder forms endured temporarily by other ethnic groups. Much of the discrepancy between black and white crime rates can perhaps be explained by the fact that African Americans until relatively recently have been locked disproportionately into the lower class through a pseudo caste system.

In the late sixties through early nineties, roughly 27 percent of those arrested in the United States were black, while blacks made up only about 12 percent of the population. In the early nineties roughly one in four young black males in the United States was behind bars, on parole, or on probation. This was more than the number of black men in college. While 23 percent of black men in their twenties were under supervision, only 10 percent of Latinos and about 6 percent of whites were being similarly sanctioned (Marshall, 1992). In Washington, D.C., estimates have been made that 70 percent of all black men have been arrested and served time in jail before the age of 35. The disparity of rates between blacks and nonblacks was much greater for offenses of violence than for property offenses. This difference in arrest rates is generally taken to indicate equally disproportionate rates of crime commission. Most studies indicate that these differences are not a result of police discrimination.

In a book entitled *The Myth of a Racist Criminal Justice System,* Wilbanks (1987) claims that although the criminal justice system was racist in the past, there is little racism or systematic discrimination in the criminal justice system today. One of his primary themes is that any disproportion in black arrest and incarceration rates reflect actual higher offense rates among blacks. In critiquing this, Mann (1989 and 1993) argues that racism in criminal justice is institutionalized in the same way that it is in other institutions in the United States such as education, politics, religion, and the economic structure. If our society is racist, do we not expect the criminal justice system to reflect this? Mann claims that Wilbanks ignores the informal aspects of the criminal justice system, or what Georges-Abeyie (1989) calls "petit apartheid realities," namely, stop-and-question and stop-and-frisk police practices that cause the police to be viewed by blacks as rude, insulting, and sometimes brutal. Claims of a nonracist system would have to be justified or supplemented with qualitative, observational research and actual accounts of minority experience.

In the News 3.1 "Racial Profiling" describes a practice by some police departments of discriminatory practices in stopping and searching a disproportionate number of blacks and minorities particularly in traffic stops.

Spohn and Cederblom (1991, p. 305) summarize much of the literature on race and sentence disparity:

> The issue of racial discrimination in sentencing continues to evoke controversy and spark debate. Some researchers (J. Hagan, 1974; Wilbanks, 1987) assert that racial discrimination has declined over time and contend that the predictive power of race, once legal factors are taken into account, is quite low. Others (Klepper, Nagin, and Tierney, 1983; Zatz, 1987) claim that discrimination has not declined or disappeared but simply has become more subtle and difficult to detect. Still others (Humphrey and Fogarty, 1987; Kleck, 1981; and Myers and Talarico, 1986) argue that pockets of discrimination remain for particular types of crime (i.e., capital crimes and politically sensitive crimes such as rape) or in particular settings (i.e., southern and rural court systems).

Spohn and Cederblom's (1991) study found support for Kalven and Zeisel's (1966) "liberation hypothesis," which holds that racial discrimination in sentencing is significant primarily in less serious cases. While race was found to play no role in judicial decision making in Pennsylvania (Steffensmeier and Kramer, 1990), black on white murders were

IN THE NEWS 3.1

RACIAL PROFILING

Crime Profiling

Crime profiling refers to attempts to construct typical characteristics of types of criminals (Holmes, 1989). It has been found particularly useful in programs such as the FBI's Behavioral Science Unit and its tracking down serial killers. It has been highly controversial when applied to traffic stops of those fitting the general profile. Phrases such as DWB (driving while black) or BWB (breathing while black) have been developed by black citizens who feel that they have been unfairly singled out for police attention for fitting the suspicious profile of being black.

Charges of racial bias in the criminal justice system are certainly given support in cases such as the New York City Police Department's incidents involving Abner Louima and Amadou Diallo. Louima was sodomized and brutalized while in police detention, while Diallo was killed by many volleys from police revolvers when reaching for his identification. David Cole in his *No Equal Justice: Race and Class in the American Criminal Justice System* (1999) indicates that, between 1995 and 1997, 70 percent of those stopped on Interstate 95 in New Jersey and Maryland were blacks and Hispanics, even though they constituted only 17.5 percent of speeders. Similar findings were noted for Illinois (Cole, 1999).

While blacks are only 12 percent of the population, they represent over one-half of the nation's prison population. In fact, one out of every three black men in their 20s is either in prison, in jail, on probation, or on parole. Much of this disparity in arrest rates is due to the "war on drugs." While the U.S. Public Health Service estimates that blacks represent 14 percent of U.S. illegal drug users, they are 35 percent of those arrested, 55 percent of those convicted, and 74 percent of those sentenced to prison for drug possession—a rate six times their representation in the population.

Racial profiling has what sociologists call a "self-fulfilling" prophecy quality about it. According to the developer of the concept, W.I. Thomas (1928), "If men define situations as real, they are real in their consequences." Blacks are perceived as more criminal. They are arrested and incarcerated more than other groups. Studies of incarcerated populations show that a disproportion of prisoners are black, therefore, when authorities are profiling or looking for criminals, they concentrate on blacks. Cole concludes by stating:

> *Finally, and fundamentally, we need to think beyond policing. It sometimes appears that the only public resources that the majority is eager to supply to the inner cities are more (and more aggressive) police officers. But if similar levels of crime were occurring in white neighborhoods, and large numbers of white children were under criminal-justice supervision, isn't it likely that we would be hearing calls for different kinds of social investments, such as better schools, more job training, better after-care programs, and drug treatment? To restore legitimacy the majority needs to show that it is willing to invest in something other than the strong arm of the law.*

Source: David Cole, 1999. *No Equal Justice: Race and Class in the American Criminal Justice System.* New York: New Press; and Kathryn K. Russell. 1999. "Is There a Witness" (Book Review of Cole's work). *The Washington Post National Weekly Edition.* February 22: 32; and Kathryn K. Russell. 1998. *The Color of Crime.* New York: New York University Press.

InfoTrac College Edition Research

What are some later developments in the issue of crime (racial) profiling? Have there been any new public policies for dealing with this issue?

found more likely to result in the death penalty in Kentucky (Keil and Vito, 1989). In the 1990s federal drug laws featured more severe penalties for crack cocaine (favored by black dealers) than for powder cocaine (favored by whites). As a result, a disproportion of those given longer prison sentences were black.

Crime has in the past been primarily intraracial in nature; that is, in most cases, whites victimize whites and blacks victimize blacks. According to UCR arrest data, blacks represent 62 percent of robbers and exhibit particularly disproportionate rates for murder, rape, and assault (Bureau of Justice Statistics, 1988b, p. 47). All of these crimes are relatively unsophisticated and command a great deal of police attention.

Statistics on crime by race are subject to countervailing pressures that may on the one hand overestimate and on the other underestimate the actual black crime rate. Blacks are more

(© Associated Press)

In the highly controversial practice of "racial profiling" police have been criticized for disproportionate stops of black and minority motorists who described the offense as DWB—"driving while black."

likely to be arrested, indicted, convicted, and imprisoned than are whites. If convicted, they are less likely to receive probation, parole, or pardon. These factors may tend to exaggerate the black crime rate. In the past especially, many crimes by blacks against other blacks were ignored by the criminal justice system. A certain proportion of the rising crime rate beginning in the sixties reflected a greater willingness on the part of the police to respond to ghetto crime, which had previously been overlooked (see Walker, Spohn, and DeLone, 1995).

Despite these offsetting trends, the crime rate of blacks is disturbingly disproportionate to that of the general population. Wolfgang's (1958) analysis of homicide in Philadelphia found the crime rate for nonwhite, twenty- to twenty-four-year-old males to be about twenty-five times the Caucasian rate for the same age group (see also Wolfgang, 1987). The few early self-report surveys suggested no significant differences by race with respect to admitted offenses (Gould, 1969; Hirschi, 1969; Voss, 1963). However, more recent research (Elliott and Ageton, 1980) again points to the tendency of many early measurement instruments to concentrate on trivial offenses. For more serious offenses, such as assault, robbery, and the like, black youths were significantly more persistent offenders, their rates in self-report surveys being similar to those in official studies.

Review of studies argue that there is no discrimination in the administration of justice (J. Hagan, 1987; Myers and Talarico, 1987; Petersilia, 1983; Klein, Turner, and Petersilia, 1988); however, the relationship is a subtle one as identified by other writers (Georges-Abeyie, 1984; Sampson, 1985). Hawkins (1986a, 1986b, and 1987) found that racial differences between rates of arrest and imprisonment vary with the type of offense. The level of arrest failed to account for overincarceration of blacks for drug offenses, forgery, and driving under the influence, and an unexpected underincarceration for rape and robbery. Hawkins concludes that we must avoid the simplistic assumptions that blacks will be treated more severely than whites for all types of crime—the system of criminal justice is oppressive, but not without contradictions. A report by the National Council on Crime and Delinquency entitled *And Justice for Some* (2000) found that black and Hispanic youth were treated more severely than white teenagers at each step of the juvenile justice system. Minorities were more likely than their white counterparts to be arrested, referred to juvenile court, detained prior to trial, formally processed by juvenile courts, found guilty in juvenile court, waived to adult criminal court, placed in juvenile prisons, and admitted to adult state prisons. Blacks charged with drug offenses are 48 times more likely than whites to be sentenced to juvenile probation. On a final note it should be pointed out that the African American crime rate for insider-trading, price-fixing, defense procurement rip-offs, and other white collar crimes is minimal.

Native Americans. The indigenous peoples in the United States are members of about 550 federally recognized tribes including: Cherokee (16.4 percent), Navajo (11.7 percent), Chippewa (5.5 percent), Sioux (5.5 percent), Choctaw (4.4 percent), Pueblo (2.8 percent), Apache (2.7 percent), and all others (51 percent) (Greenfield and Smith, 1999, p. 1). Figure 3.5 illustrates the annual victimization rate for Native Americans.

In 1999 the Bureau of Justice Statistics (BJS) issued a special report entitled *American Indians and Crime* (Greenfeld and Smith, 1999). The data were based on over five years of National Crime Victimization Survey data and reported that the rate of violent victimization among the nation's 2.3 million Native Americans is well above that of other American racial and ethnic groups and twice as high as the national average. Astoundingly, the rate of violent crime experienced by Native American women was nearly 50 percent higher than that reported by black males.

The BJS study indicated that the rate of Native American victimization was 124 violent crimes per 1,000 Native Americans which was twice the rate of the nation (50 per 1,000). The average for whites was 49, for blacks 61, and for Asians 29 per 1,000. Native Americans, unlike other racial/ethnic groups, are more likely to be victims of interracial violence

FIGURE 3.5 Native Americans

Average annual number of violent victimizations per 1,000 persons age 12 or older, 1992–96

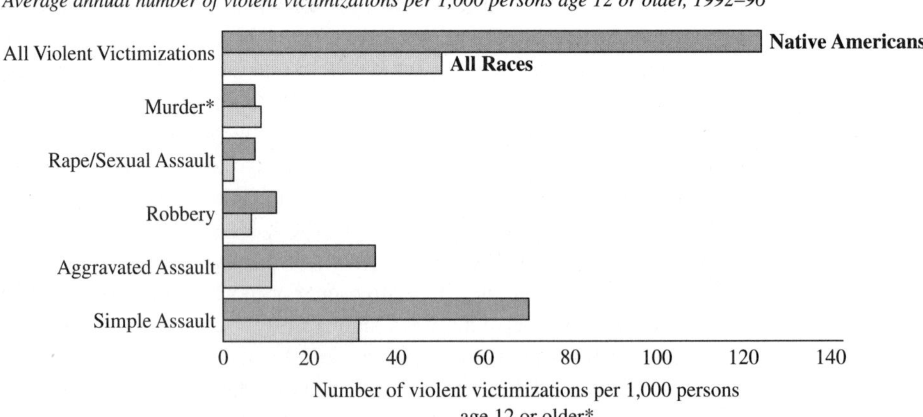

The rate for Native Americans (124 violent crimes per 1,000 Native Americans) was more than twice the rate for the nation (50 per 1,000 persons)

*The annual average murder rate is per 100,000 residents of all ages.

Source: Bureau of Justice Statistics, 1999. "American Indians and Crime." *Bureau of Justice Statistics Report*, February.

(that is, between races). Sixty percent of those committing crimes against Native Americans were whites; most offenses were attributed to racism and alcohol. The rate of murders committed by Native Americans (1996) was 4 per 100,000, well below the then national average of 7.9 and the white rate of 4.9. Native Americans are, however, twice as likely as blacks and three times more likely than whites to be victims of rape or aggravated assault.

Native Americans are one of the smallest minority groups, yet they represent one of the largest percentages of prison inmates. There are 555 recognized Native American tribes in the United States and, despite the well-publicized success of gambling facilities on some reservations, a third of the country's two million Native Americans live below the poverty line. This figure is higher than for all other minority groups (Blackman and Simmons, 1995). In 800 or more treaties, native tribes were guaranteed a reasonable level of education, health, and resources. Such promises were not honored and, instead, these people—who experienced near cultural and physical genocide—have also experienced high levels of unemployment, social disorganization, alienation, alcoholism, and crime. "Most Indians are incarcerated because of crimes they have committed while intoxicated" (Price, 1994, p. 5).

Native American youth are the largest category of youth incarcerated under federal jurisdiction, about 65 percent (75) of the 124 confined in 1994 (Greenfeld and Smith, 1999: 30). Similar to other indigenous peoples in other colonized countries, Native Americans were marginalized from the dominant society (Nielson, Fulton and Tsosie, 2000, p. 5). Nielson, et al. (1998: 143) indicate:

> Native Americans have endured a century and more of government policies that ranged from genocidal to assimilative to supportive of limited sovereignty. The assimilative policies in general were, and still are (to the extent that they can still be found in American Indian law), important contributors to the development of social and economic conditions conductive to the development of Native American gangs.

Minority Groups and Crime. Race per se is not as crucial an explanatory variable in traditional crime commission as is social class. Until recently, a large percentage of blacks were concentrated in lower socioeconomic class ghettos that have traditionally exhibited high rates of breakdown. African Americans are disproportionately represented in the very largest cities. Early research by the "Chicago school" of sociology, most notably that of Shaw and McKay (1942) and their utilization of Burgess's "concentric zone theory" (1925), serves as an illustration of this relationship (see Figure 3.6).

In examining certain areas for delinquency, Shaw and McKay report similar rates of delinquency in the same area of transition (zone II) despite changeover in racial and nationality groups. Despite this assumption, Nettler (1982, vol. 2, p. 58) points out that Dutch, German, and Scandinavian settlers in the United States have had low crime rates in general, particularly for violent crimes. In addition, the low rates for Jews and Asians challenge the assumption that racial visibility, prejudice, and discrimination are sufficient explanations of criminality. It should be pointed out, however, that many of these groups were not lower-class immigrants, but instead had migrated during a period in which their craft, mercantile, and other skills were economically in demand (Flowers, 1988).

The excessive violent crime rate for blacks in the United States stands in contrast to that of Latinos who are poorer, less educated, and have more menial jobs, but who also have lower rates of violent crime. Silberman (1978) in analyzing New York City crime rates found the rate of black violent crime to be three times higher than the Latino rate—twice as high for homicide.

Since other minority groups who at one time were discriminated against were able to overcome difficulties and "rise from the ashes," so to speak, many ask the question: "Why haven't blacks been able to achieve the same success?" In 1968 in the aftermath of the worst series of urban riots in modern U.S. history, the Kerner Commission, the National

FIGURE 3.6 Burgess's Concentric Zone Theory

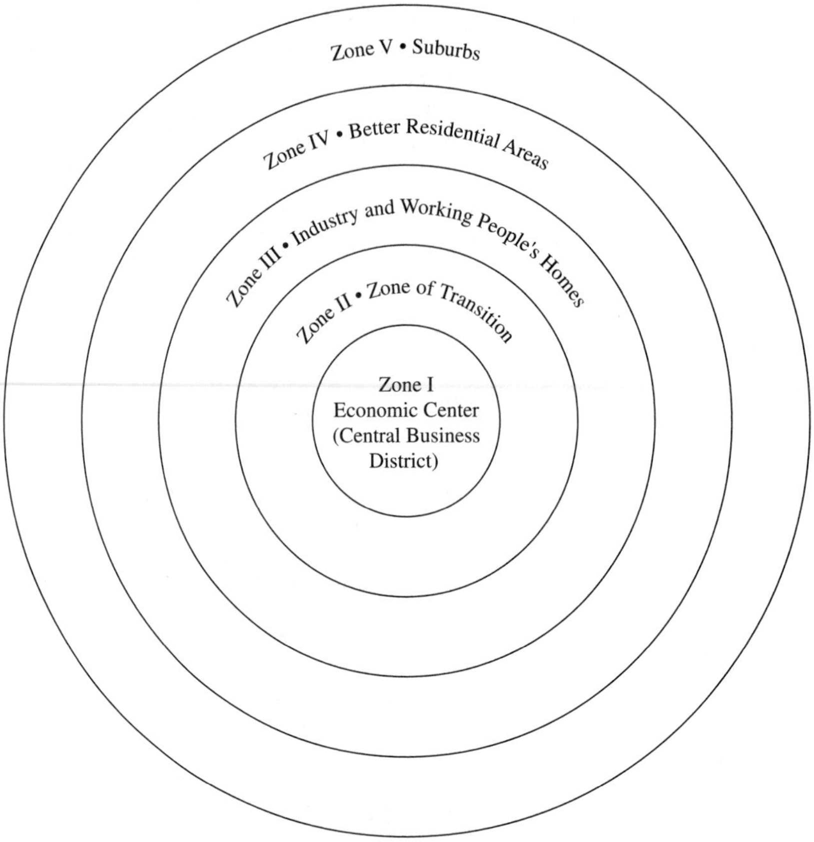

Source: Figure is based upon theoretical presentations in Ernest W. Burgess, 1925, "The Growth of the City," in *The City,* edited by Robert E. Park, Ernest W. Burgess, and Robert D. McKenzie, Chicago; Chicago University Press, pp. 47–62.

Advisory Commission on Civil Disorders, addressed this issue by suggesting four reasons for differences between the immigrant and black experiences:

1. *The Maturing Economy:* When the European immigrants arrived they gained an economic foothold by providing the unskilled labor needed by industry. Unlike the immigrant, the Negro migrant found little opportunity in the city. The economy, by then matured, had little use for the unskilled labor he had to offer.
2. *The Disability of Race:* The structure of discrimination has stringently narrowed opportunities for the Negro and restricted his prospects. European immigrants suffered from discrimination, but never so pervasively.
3. *Entry into the Political System:* The immigrants usually settled in rapidly growing cities with powerful and expanding political machines, which traded economic advantages for political support. Ward-level grievance machinery, as well as personal representation, enabled the immigrant to make his voice heard and his power felt.

   By the time the Negro arrived, these political machines were no longer so powerful or so well equipped to provide jobs or other favors, and in many cases were unwilling to share their influence with Negroes.

4. *Cultural Factors:* Coming from societies with a low standard of living and at a time when job aspirations were low, the immigrants sensed little deprivation in being forced to take the less desirable and poorer-paying jobs. Their large and cohesive families contributed to the total income. Their vision of the future—one that led to life outside of the ghetto—provided the incentive necessary to endure the present.

Although Negro men worked as hard as the immigrants, they were unable to support their families. The entrepreneurial opportunities had vanished. As a result of slavery and long periods of unemployment, the Negro family structure had become matriarchal; the males played a secondary and marginal family role—one which offered little compensation for their hard and unrewarding labor. Above all, segregation denied Negroes access to good jobs and the opportunity to leave the ghetto. For them, the future seemed to lead only to a dead end (Kerner, 1968, p. 15).

William Julius Wilson in *The Truly Disadvantaged* (1987) points out how the deindustrialization (loss of blue collar factory jobs) of the inner cities combined with racism, segregation, and poverty to condemn the black, inner-city poor to chronic unemployment and hopelessness. In 1989 an astonishing 35 percent of black males between sixteen and thirty-five were arrested at some point, and much of this was because of an aggressive nationwide crackdown on drugs that affected blacks much more than whites. Even though blacks represent about 12 percent of users, their visibility and greater involvement in trafficking in targeted urban areas has had a devastating effect. Particularly problematic was the fact that much heavier sentences were levied against those using crack (a form of rock cocaine preferred by blacks) than against those abusing the same amount of powder cocaine (preferred by whites). Morley (1995, p. 21) explains:

> What is indisputable is the effect of the 1986 law. Imagine two drug dealers, one a supplier and one a street dealer. The supplier sells the street dealer three grams of cocaine. The street dealer mixes the drug with baking soda, cooks it in his microwave oven, producing six grams of crystalline smokeable crack cocaine. If he gets arrested and sent to federal court, he faces a mandatory minimum of five years in jail. The supplier has to get caught with 500 grams of powder cocaine—about 1.7 pounds—to face that much time in federal prison. One curious effect of "get tough" laws is to punish cocaine retailers while extending relative leniency to cocaine wholesalers.

Decreasing job prospects in such areas has created a vicious cycle in which:

- Discrimination holds blacks back in the job market.
- The loss of blue collar jobs, erosion of real wages for low-skilled work, and weakened unions make unskilled work less available and attractive.
- Drug dealing becomes a fairly lucrative alternative employment option.
- Once caught, dismal job prospects for ex-cons make them less desirable marriage partners.
- This creates more female-headed households, a major cause of poverty (Marshall, 1992).

Hawkins et al.(2000) point out that more attention has to be paid to within-group differences, for example, between poor and middle class blacks. One study of firearm death rates between 1979 and 1989 found deaths varying among fifteen-to-nineteen year olds from 143.9 per 100,000 in core areas of large cities to 48.2 in nonmetropolitan locations (Fingerhut, Ingram and Feldman, 1992).

Does minority group status itself produce higher crime rates? In general, the answer to this question is no. Much depends upon the particular minority group and its specific values and cultural traditions. In the United States, for instance, the crime rate among Japanese-Americans and Asians in general is lower than that of the general population. Many newer immigrant groups in the United States such as Cambodians, Koreans, and

(© 1993 Aneal Vohra / Unicorn Stock Photos)

These men, unable to find work, may become trapped in the vicious circle of unemployment, crime, alienation, and alcoholism that besets many Native Americans.

Vietnamese have low crime rates in part because of close extended family ties, a strong work ethic, and merchant skills (Launer and Palenski, 1988; Light and Bonacich, 1988). On the other hand the crime rates for Algerians in France or Finns in Sweden or Latinos in the United States are higher than those of the general population.

Most immigrants to the United States have come from close-knit peasant societies; and the crime rate for this first-generational group is usually lower, with the exception of crimes peculiar to the area from which they migrated. For instance, for the first-generation Italian immigrant crime rates were lower, with the exception of murders and assaults. Since the areas of southern Italy and Sicily from which they came were experiencing at that time a wave of vendetta and violence, this pattern was carried over into the new world. Similarly, Irish immigrants experienced higher rates for alcohol-related offenses, since in the nineteenth century Ireland reputedly had the highest alcoholism rate in the Western world.

It is not the parental group of immigrants that exhibits excess criminality; for many groups, it is the second generation that exhibits a marked upsurge in crime. Living in a strange, new land and often the victims of discrimination, the first generation often clings to old values. Moreover, this group may fear deportation. Wishing to be Americanized, the second generation often rejects many of these ways and attempts to assimilate the general values of U.S. culture. Unfortunately, in the milieu or area in which these individuals live (zone II, for instance), they also assimilate the criminal values of a high crime area. Not being placed in such environments or possessing a higher parental social class explains the relative success of Vietnamese immigrants in the United States.

Nettler (1982, vol. 2, pp. 48–62) in a four-volume work, *Criminal Careers,* does an excellent job of summarizing much of the international research on ethnic migrants and crime. Care must be exercised in examining these data, since many of the studies refer to *Gastarbeiter* (guest workers), who are not immigrants as such, but rather temporary workers in the host community. Studies in Switzerland found the crime rate higher for foreign-

TABLE 3.7 Crime by Region, 1998 (rates per 100,000)*

Offense	*Northeast*	*Midwest*	*South*	*West*	*U.S. Total*
Crime Index Total	3473.5	4379.4	5223.5	4879.4	4615.5
Violent Crime	500.5	494.1	633.0	593.1	566.4
Property Crime	2973.1	3885.3	4590.5	4286.3	4049.1
Murder	4.3	5.7	7.8	6.1	6.3
Forcible Rape	23.7	36.8	38.1	35.4	34.4
Robbery	184.8	141.4	169.1	167.1	165.2
Aggravated Assault	287.7	310.2	418.0	384.5	360.5
Burglary	589.2	775.7	1,045.4	895.7	862.0
Larceny/Theft	2011.0	2713.4	3079.7	2810.0	2728.1
Motor Vehicle Theft	372.8	396.2	470.4	580.6	459.0

* Arson not included
Source: FBI *Uniform Crime Reports,* 1999, pp. 66–73.

ers than natives, particularly for violent crime. Ferracuti (1968) claimed that the crime rate of foreign workers increased as their numbers increased, although many of their crimes went unreported. Nettler (1982, vol. 2, pp. 48–49) cites similar findings that suggest higher rates among Hungarians and Yugoslavs in Sweden; for Turks, Italians, Africans, and Mediterraneans in West Germany and Belgium; for Algerians in France; and for Irish, Asians, and West Indians in England. However, one chief problem in many of these studies is their failure to control for age and sex differentials, since many immigrant groups consist of a heavier population of young, single males, a group with a higher crime commission potential.

Regional Variation in Crime

Not only do crime rates, however difficult to measure, vary between nations, they also vary by region within a country (see Brantingham and Brantingham, 1984). Table 3.7 shows that in 1998 the rates for murder, rape, aggravated assault, larceny, and burglary were highest in the South, which also had the highest overall crime rate. The Northeast had the lowest overall crime rate. Those for aggravated assault, vehicle theft, and larceny-theft were highest in the West; and those for robbery were highest in the Northeast.

Urban/Rural Differences

Internationally, urban recorded crime rates are generally higher than rural crime rates; and, with few exceptions, this difference appears to have been the case since cities began. Although crime rates tend to increase with the size of the community, there are some important exceptions. UCR statistics in general show a positive relationship in which, as size of community increases, the crime rate increases (see Table 3.8). This same relationship with size of community also holds in the NCVS. Even if one assumes less reporting and recording of rural crime, the difference between rural and urban rates persists; in the 1998 data, however, the rates for property crime were actually higher for smaller than for larger cities. Yet rural and suburban crime rates have actually been increasing faster than those of central cities since the sixties. Urbanism and its "way of life" is no longer confined just to cities. The advent of modern communications and transportation has effectively erased many of the distinctions between rural and urban lifestyles, creating a truly urban society. The relatively high rates of violent crime in rural areas may be explained by certain criminalistic

TABLE 3.8 Crime Rates by Size of Community

	UCR Index Crime Rates per 100,000 Population	
	Violent Crime	*Property Crime*
Metropolitan Statistical Areas (MSAs) are urbanized areas that include at least one city with 50,000 or more inhabitants, or a Census Bureau-defined urbanized area of at least 50,000 inhabitants and a total population of at least 100,000.	630.5	4,344.6
Non-MSA cities do not qualify as MSA central cities and are not otherwise included in an MSA.	444.3	4,543.0
Rural Areas.	226.6	1,771.4

Source: Federal Bureau of Investigation, 1999. *Crime in the United States, 1998.* Washington, D.C.: Government Printing Office, p. 65.

traditions in some areas that are much closer to frontier values and by a possible "subculture of violence," (to be explored in Chapter 7) may explain high rural rates in the South as well as southern Appalachia. In contrast to the U.S. pattern, Canadian murder rates are higher in rural than in urban settings (Schloss and Giesbrecht, 1972, p. 22).

Ferdinand (1991), in what he calls the "theft/violence ratio," notes that historical studies show a relationship between social structure and levels of property or violent crime. Theft was more prevalent in older, established cities with a preindustrial history, whereas violent crime was more common in rural, agricultural regions and in rapidly and newly industrializing cities.

Using their "Comparative Crime Data File," Archer and Gartner (1984, pp. 115–16) found that homicide rates were higher the larger the city between 1966–1970 in twenty-four societies, but found no support for the proposition that city size and homicide rates increase together. The city's size relative to its society is more important in determining homicide rates than its absolute size. " . . . [A]ny jurisdiction more urban than its national environment will have a homicide rate higher than the national average" (p. 116).

Institutions and Crime

Sociologists define social institutions as relatively stable social patterns that serve a broad range of crucial functions in society; examples are economy, family, church, state, and schools. In contrast, associations are special-purpose organizations that serve a narrow range of interests; examples are corporations, unions, and professional societies.

The Family and Crime

The family is the primary or most important agent of socialization, particularly during childhood. The family has exclusive contact with the child during the period of greatest dependency and plasticity. Despite considerable popular literature on the subject, there is little, if any, scientific evidence on the subject of child rearing. Advocates of permissive or restrictive socialization to the contrary, the key appears to be firm but consistent discipline that is reinforced as well as understood by the child. The most important variables correlated with delinquency are probably poor home discipline, neglect, and indifference (Rosenbaum, 1989a).

Many U.S. studies of delinquency include under that label a significant number of activities, such as truancy, incorrigibility, and the like, that would not be criminal had they been committed by an adult. In a review of family factors associated with delinquency, Sutherland and Cressey (1974, pp. 203–18) as well as Hirschi (1983, pp. 53–68) point to moderate-to-high correlations between delinquency and immorality or criminality or alcoholism of parents, absence of one or both parents, a lack of parental control, unhappy home life, subcultural differences in the home, and economic pressures. The general process of family influence relates to the fact that the parental social class determines the residence, school, and associates of their offspring. Parental transmission of criminogenic attitudes or failure to train the child may influence delinquency. Similarly, a poor home environment may force the youth into the streets seeking peer primary group support.

Statistics on broken homes, ordinal positions (birth order) of siblings, and number of siblings, and their influence on crime and delinquency appear inconclusive (Rosen and Neilson, 1978; Sutherland and Cressey, 1974, pp. 216–17). It would appear that the quality of family interaction instead of the family structure per se is important.

More sophisticated family studies of delinquents appear in early research by Sheldon and Eleanor Glueck (1950), who examined 500 delinquents and 500 nondelinquents and found roughly 50 percent of the delinquents were from broken homes compared with about 29 percent of nondelinquents. Delinquents were more likely to have families characterized by physical illness, mental retardation, mental disturbance, alcoholism, and parental criminality. Such parents employed poor child-rearing practices, being either overly strict or overly permissive and exercising discipline inconsistently. Thus defective family relations were perceived as a key causal variable in deliquency (Hagan and Sussman, 1988a and b). Cathy Spatz Widom (1992) found that childhood abuse increased the odds of delinquency and future adult criminality by about 40 percent. Neglect alone, not just physical abuse, was significantly related to later violent behavior.

In the longest longitudinal study of delinquents—the "Cambridge-Somerville study"—begun in 1937, William and Joan McCord (1958) found delinquents to be products of poor or weak parental discipline as well as a quarrelsome home environment. Family structure, that is whether the home was broken or intact, was less salient than the nature of family interaction. All of the boys from quarrelsome environments had been convicted of crime (Wilson and Herrnstein, 1985, p. 232). West and Farrington's (1977) longitudinal study of London working class boys found the following associated with delinquency: low IQ, poor child-rearing practices, criminality of father, large family size, and low family income. Similar findings with respect to defective parental supervision and socialization have been suggested by Hirschi (1969), Baumrind (1978), Patterson (1982), Van Voorhis et al. (1988), and Wright and Wright (1995).

Loeber and Stouthamer-Loeber (1986), in an exhaustive analysis of the literature, summarize the relationship between family and delinquency as exhibiting: (1) the most powerful predictors—lack of parental supervision, parental rejection, and lack of parent-child involvement; (2) medium predictors—background variables such as parents' marital relations and parental criminality; and (3) weaker predictors—lack of parental discipline, parental health, and parental absence. Research by other scholars confirm these findings (Patterson and Dishion, 1985; Johnson, 1986; Farrington, Ohlin, and Wilson, 1986; Laub and Sampson, 1988). Wright and Wright (1995, pp. 199–200) point out:

> In the lives of the children most at risk of becoming delinquent, however, some or all of the following circumstances may be operating: (1) they receive little love, affection or warmth, and are physically or emotionally rejected and/or

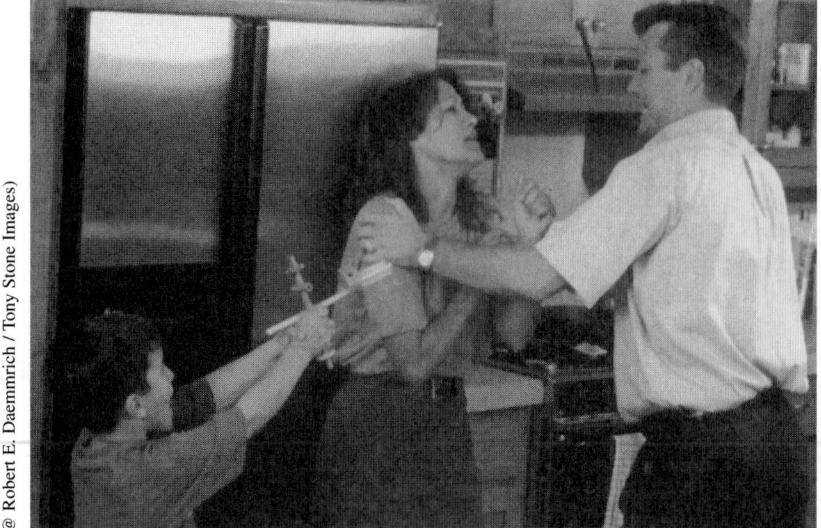

(@ Robert E. Daemmrich / Tony Stone Images)

Children exposed to severe"—perhaps even violent"—conflict between adults in their homes often vent their anger, confusion, and frustration in delinquent behavior. Is this boy imitating what he sees?

> abandoned by their parents; (2) they are inadequately supervised by parents who fail to teach them right and wrong, who do not monitor their whereabouts, friends, or activities, and who discipline them erratically and harshly; and (3) they grow up in homes with considerable conflict, marital discord, and perhaps even violence (Farrington, 1990, p. 94; Leitenberg, 1987). Families at greatest risk of delinquency are those suffering from limited coping resources, social isolation, and (among parents) poor child-rearing skills (Loeber and Stouthamer-Loeber, 1986, p. 97). The presence of any of these family circumstances increases the chances of raising a delinquent child. The presence of more than one factor increases the odds further (Farrington, 1990; Farrington et al., 1988; Kruttschnitt, et al., 1987; Loeber and Stouthamer-Loeber, 1986; Lytton, 1990; McCord, 1990; Minty, 1988).

The proportion of children living in American households with both parents has declined since 1970. In 1970, 90 percent of white children lived in intact households and 74 percent in 1997. For black children the figures were 64 percent (1970) and 35 percent (1997) (Thornberry, et al., 1990). An estimated 40 percent of white children and 75 percent of African American children will experience parental separation or divorce by age 16, many of them multiple family transitions. Longitudinal studies of youth in Rochester, Denver, and Pittsburgh found substantial changes in family transition: Rochester—64.5 percent, Denver—49 percent, and Pittsburgh—30 percent. They found a consistent relationship between higher numbers of family transitions and higher delinquency.

Conservative writers who have more recently dominated the literature, such as Hirschi (1983) and Wilson and Herrnstein (1985), seem to view material disadvantage and quality of family life as mutually exclusive explanations. Currie calls this belief that what goes on in the family is somehow separate from outside social forces that affect the family the "**fallacy of autonomy**" (Currie, 1985, p. 185). Those who commit this fallacy fail to view the family in a larger social context, have an obsessive concern with control rather than supportive social policies, and lend the impression of intractability of family problems, unresponsive to enlightened social policy.

Two influential works that challenge our criminological conception of family and crime are Daniel Moynihan's *Family and Nation* (1986) and Elliott Currie's *Confronting Crime* (1985). Moynihan reiterates his theme of the disintegration and siege of the American family, an issue that he claims should have concerned us in the sixties. He indicates that the individual has been the center of public policy in the United States rather than families. "This was a pattern almost uniquely American. Most of the industrial democracies of the world had adopted a wide range of social programs designed specifically to support the stability and viability of the family" (Moynihan, 1986, p. 5). While growth in federal entitlement programs since the sixties led to a major achievement—the virtual elimination of poverty among the elderly—by the 1980s the United States had achieved another unique distinction: it had become the first society in history in which people are more likely to be poor if they are young than if they are old.

The age bias of poverty is pronounced, affecting 24 percent of school age children. The principal correlate has been this change in family structure—the rise of female-headed households and the **feminization of poverty.** In 1984 nearly half of the poor in the United States lived in female-headed households (Moynihan, p. 96). The percentage of such households nearly doubled from the 10 percent of all families in 1960. A flattening of the tax system and federal reduction in income maintenance programs constituted a federal family policy in reverse. While three-fourths of median family income in 1948 was exempt from federal tax (a powerful national family policy), by 1983 less than one-third of such income was exempt, although the new tax law promises to remove many low-income groups from the tax rolls. Of particular concern in fueling single parenthood are rising illegitimacy rates in the United States. Studies by the Alan Guttmacher Institute point out that 39 percent of 15-year-old mothers indicate that the fathers of their babies are 20 years old or older (Shapiro and Wright, 1995, p. 51). Under statutory rape laws such sexual activity constitutes "unlawful sex with a minor."

While broken homes per se are an uncertain predictor of delinquency and crime, the stresses and lack of support systems that result in changed family functioning for the more impoverished and growing numbers of single mothers and children are of concern. Currie (1985, p. 219) states:

> The real issue is whether we regard the evidence on the persistence of family problems and the continuity of troubling behavior from childhood to adult life as indicative of predispositions that are largely unrelated to their social context and that we are virtually powerless to alter.

Education and Crime

The relationship between education (formal schools/schooling) and crime and delinquency is at least twofold. First, for adolescents in modern societies, schools, particularly high schools, represent a major factor in their self-esteem at a very important stage in their lives. Secondly, there is an inverse (negative) relationship between the amount of formal schooling individuals possess and arrest rates for traditional crimes.

The fact that traditional crime commission decreases with the amount of formal education simply reflects the fact that legitimate opportunities increase with formal education, as do occupational and corporate criminal opportunities, which are less likely to be criminally stigmatizing. It is not formal education per se that causes or prevents crime; rather, educational status reflects one's social class, location of residence, and exposure to criminal and/or delinquent opportunity.

Research on crime and delinquency has come to focus most heavily on family and education as critical variables (Hawkins and Lishner, 1987; Wilson and Lowry, 1987). Moynihan (1986, p. 92) cites a study commissioned by the National Association of Elementary School Principals (1980) entitled *The Most Significant Minority: One-Parent Children in the Schools,* which found that one-parent kids were twice as likely to drop out and showed significantly lower achievement in school.

Fagan and Wexler (1987) argue that social influences outside the family, such as schools, peers, and community, are very strong, and that the role of the family alone should not be overstated. Fagan, Piper, and Moore (1986) note that violent delinquents in inner cities differ from nondelinquents in their attachment to school, their peers, and weak maternal authority, among other variables. They indicate (p. 463):

> Complex social, economic and political factors are contributing to the creation of a vast new class of poor persons who are younger, more poorly educated and more likely to give birth sooner. One of the predictable consequences of this phenomenon is the continuing isolation of inner-city communities and a hardening of the processes observed among these samples . . . . These findings suggest that delinquency policy should be linked with economic development policy. The infusion of material and social resources into inner-city neighborhoods may strengthen social institutions including schools and families and alter the familiar correlates of serious delinquency by providing for the natural controls which characterize lower-crime neighborhoods.

Strong school bonding decreases the likelihood of delinquency. Denno (1985) indicates that a major predictor of delinquency is misconduct in school. An example of a highly successful program is Head Start, a program for preschool enrichment. Schweinhart and Weikart (1980) in evaluating such a program for disadvantaged black children found better later elementary school performance, higher rates of graduation from high school, employment, and less crime and delinquency. Adler (1983) in a previously cited study of low crime nations analyzed 47 variables and found the only factor common to all low crime countries was strong social controls outside the formal system of justice. This well illustrates the fact that crime and justice matters are not to be treated in isolation from general societal conditions. VANTAGE POINT 3.4 describes a successful school based program—FAST—Families and Schools Together.

Religion and Crime

Ellis (1996), in a review of criminology texts, found that only two of eighteen even mentioned religion as a variable in crime causation despite the fact that a significant one-third of the public believes it plays a significant role. Of major religions in the U.S., Jews have the lowest official crime rate, followed by Protestants; Catholics have the highest rates. "Why?" There is a hidden variable: social class. Catholics in the U.S. include a significant proportion of low income minorities, particularly in the Southwest. Of Protestant denominations, Presbyterians and Episcopalians have lower crime rates, while Baptists have the highest. Social class rather than denominational affiliation is the explanation. Ellis (1985) reviews over sixty studies in the research literature on this religion-crime connection. The majority of the studies confirm, as might be expected, that attendance at religious services reduced crime commission. This is a stronger relationship than religious denomination and crime.

War and Crime

War has an impact upon crime. Although it is an example of institutionalized violence, elements of war itself may be considered violations of international law. Social conflict theorists such as Simmel (1955) and Coser (1956) tell us that conflict with an outside group tends to increase the internal solidarity within groups; that is, as conflict with outside enemies increases, conflict within groups decreases.

During major wars, the domestic crime rate as a whole tends to decline. This probably reflects increased social solidarity, group cohesion against an outside enemy, and high employment. Juvenile delinquency tends to increase during such periods because of displace-

VANTAGE POINT 3.4

FAST—Families and Schools Together

FAST (Families and Schools Together) is a program that is concerned with youth violence and chronic delinquency by enhancing youths' relationships with their families, peers, teachers, school staff, and community. Such relationships form a social safety net that can help at-risk children avoid delinquency, addiction, and violence. This safety net helps prevent:

- Juvenile violence and crime by increasing multiple levels of social bonding.
- Family alcohol and drug abuse by increasing connections, shared routines and resilience.
- Reducing isolation and promoting strong families in order to reduce child abuse and neglect.
- School failure by promoting parental involvement for school success.

The FAST Process is aimed to help youth succeed as adolescents and later as adults. FAST works to:

- Enhance family functioning by strengthening the parent-child relationship and empowering parents to become primary prevention agents for their children.
- Prevent school failure by improving the child's behavior and performance in school, empowering parents as partners in the educational process, and strengthening the child's and family's affiliation with the school.
- Prevent alcohol and other drug abuse in the family.
- Reduce the stress that families experience from daily life.

The program begins with outreach, in which parent-professional partnerships visit homes of isolated, stressed families who are invited to FAST meetings at the schools. Social events, play therapy, and other programs assist them in working with their children. Bonding with other families in the program, the families strengthen their relationships with their children and school.

Assessments of the program show dramatic improvement in classroom and home behavior, family closeness, parental involvement in school, and reduced social isolation. Such children showed reduced conduct disorder. FAST was the only family program featured at the White House Conference on School Safety in October 1998 and is currently being implemented in Australia, Austria, Canada, and Germany.

Source: Lynn McDonald and Deborah Howard. 1998. "Families and Schools Together." *OJJDP Fact Sheet.* December, #88. Also available from OJJDP's web page, www.ncjrs.org/ojjhome.htm.

InfoTrac College Edition Research
Besides the FAST program, locate another program that links families and schools.

ment of families and increased mobility. As noted earlier, female crime rates increase because of increased opportunity. A major form of crime that tends to increase during wartime is "white collar crime" such as black marketeering, profiteering, wartime trade violations, violations of wage-price freezes, and the like (Sutherland and Cressey, 1974, pp. 240–41).

Archer and Gartner (1984, pp. 79–81), using their "Comparative Crime Data File," found that nations participating in World Wars I and II were more likely to experience postwar increases in homicide than control nations (those who had not participated). The differences are similar, but less pronounced, after smaller wars. They found their data supporting a "legitimation of violence model" (p. 92) in which wars tend to legitimate the general use of violence in domestic society.

Economy and Crime

In summarizing the diverse literature on the relationship between economic trends and crime, Sutherland and Cressey (1974, pp. 225–26) draw the following conclusions:

- Serious crimes have a slight and inconsistent tendency to rise in periods of economic depression and to fall in periods of prosperity.
- The general crime rate does not increase significantly in periods of economic depression.

- Property crimes involving violence tend to increase in periods of depression; but property crimes involving no violence, such as larceny, show only a slight and inconsistent tendency to increase in depression periods.
- Juvenile delinquency tends to increase in periods of prosperity and to decrease during periods of depression.

Using data from the United States, Canada, England, Scotland, and Wales, Brenner (1978) examined historical data for all major crimes since 1900 and their relationship to employment/unemployment, per capita income, inflation, and other economic indices. He found in all five political areas that the rate of unemployment showed strong and significant relationships to increases in all major categories of crime (p. 562). There is a significant difference in these statistics for before and after World War II. There is a speeded up or a quicker reaction to unemployment since World War II, particularly an increase in violent crimes. The United States in particular demonstrated inverse (negative) correlations between employment and incarceration rates (see also Cantor and Land, 1985).

Currie (Skolnick and Currie, 1988, p. 471) argues that conservative criminologists tend to underemphasize the impact of economic forces on crime. He points out that, while little crime increase took place during the Depression, crime rose during the more prosperous sixties. Currie feels there is a strong, although subtle, relationship and that those who underemphasize the economy ignore three factors:

> First, subgroups with high crime rates—such as young black men—do have high unemployment rates, even when overall unemployment is low. Second, unemployment has a different impact when it portends a lifetime of diminished opportunity. And finally, unemployment statistics do not reflect the quality of available work.

John Hagan (1993) points out that, while unemployment increases crime, the reverse also occurs; that is, individuals with criminal records become less employable.

Mass Media and Crime

A subject of continual heated debate is the role of the mass media in encouraging crime, particularly crimes of violence. Do comic books, music, newspapers, magazines, movies, and/or television cause an increase of crime? This protracted debate is periodically fueled by crimes, particularly brutal ones, that appear to have some link with the media coverage or fictionalization of criminal events.

Two rival hypotheses exist with respect to media and violence: the **catharsis hypothesis** and the **precipitation hypothesis.** The former claims that *exposure to media violence enables a vicarious letting-off-of-steam and thus has a calming effect.* This notion comes to us from the Greek tragedies, in which it was assumed that audiences, as a result of identification with the terrible travail and violent experiences of the characters, would feel an emotional purging of their own frustration, anger, or desire. The precipitation hypothesis *assumes that exposure to media coverage of violence, fact or fiction, will produce greater propensities to aggression and violence.*

In a report entitled *Television and Behavior,* the Department of Health and Human Services (1982) concluded on the basis of a review of the research literature that there is an association between the viewing of television violence and aggression. One finding that seems continually to present itself concerns the image of society that television creates. In an American Broadcasting Company poll of viewers (ABC, 1983b), 51 percent of respondents (1) thought television news gives too much coverage to crime and violence and that this distorts the public view of what is really going on in the streets; (2) leads to the perception that crime is more rampant and a person more likely to be victimized than is, in fact, the case; and (3) brainwashes us into fear, suspicion, and feelings of vulnerability.

Glaser (1978, p. 236) indicates that television networks exert pressure against federal sponsorship of research on the impact of television on violence and for the suppression of reports on such research for fear of public boycotts (Cater and Strickland, 1975). The National Institute of Mental Health, in its review of the literature, concluded that violence on television was one factor in children's aggressiveness, although not necessarily in their violent behavior (ABC, 20/20, 1983b).

One key to explaining media precipitation of violence is that portrayals of violence appear to have different effects on different viewers. Individuals vary in their vulnerability to suggestion (Belson, 1978), with physically aggressive boys both watching televised violence and practicing it (McCarthy et al., 1975; Bandura, 1973; Leftkowitz et al., 1977). Nettler (1982, p. 265), in a review of such studies, concluded that "evidence points to the possibility that persons in 'poor psychological and social health' are more vulnerable to lethal suggestions" (see also Liebert and Baron, 1972; Comstock, 1975).

In the U.S., the Surgeon General's Scientific Advisory Committee on Television and Social Behavior (1972) sponsored 23 independent research projects to examine the impact of television on violence. They claimed:

> By the time the average American child graduates from high school he had seen on television some 18,000 murders and countless highly detailed incidents of robbery, arson, bombing, forgery and torture. One hundred forty-six research articles based on 50 studies involving 10,000 children had all shown that viewing violence increased aggressive behavior in the young. A review of the literature on the subject did not reveal a single study which showed that violence did not have such an effect (Haskell and Yablonsky, 1983, p 199).

In support of the precipitation hypothesis, Glaser (1978, p. 235) states: "The $30 billion spent annually in the United States on advertising—about $5 billion of it on television—suggests that many people have faith in the impact of mass communication on conduct."

In 1996 President Bill Clinton signed the TeleCommunications Act, which called for the development of a "V-chip" (Violence Chip), a device that can block the transmission of violent television programs. In addition he called on the television industry to exercise self-censorship and to devise a ratings code for the content of programs. That same year a study sponsored by the National Cable Television Association concluded that children were at risk due to watching so many programs in which violence goes unpunished (Schorr, 1996).

A contrary view is presented by a fourteen-nation international study of television violence, which found that Japan has the most violent programming and is relatively free of violent crime ("Japanese TV," 1992). This low crime rate appears unaffected by graphically violent comic books, tabloids, videos, and a thriving market in pornography. The limits of free speech are tested by groups such as 2 Live Crew, who sold almost 2 million records featuring a song about graphic, offensive degradation of women. Such degradation and abuse of women are presented under the guise of entertainment. Armstrong (1991) analyzed popular themes in both country music and rap music, finding that both deal heavily with traditional crimes of violence involving the focal concerns (see Miller, 1958) of trouble, toughness, smartness, excitement, fate, and autonomy. "Gangsta" rap had its counterpart in "outlaw" country music. Sociologist Elijah Anderson (1990) calls much gangsta rap an example of "oppositional culture" of the streets, a subculture with its own gangsta values, attitudes, and codes of street behavior. Rejecting values of civility and decency, it romanticizes violence and glorifies having a violent reputation. While clearly rap is a legitimate urban music form—and most of it is probably not bad—many releases feature violence, obscene lyrics, and graphic videos celebrating guns, gangs, and drugs, and denigrating women.

Nathan McCall, author of *Makes Me Wanna Holler: A Young Black Man in America* (1994), points out that never before have young people been bombarded nonstop by such violent language and imagery. In response to criticism, MTV (Music Television) and BET (Black Entertainment Television) began refusing to play videos featuring guns and gratuitous violence. Considerable debate continues regarding censorship versus freedom of expression with respect to rap music (Hamm and Ferrell, 1994; Krzycki, 1994). In 1992 Time Warner, Inc. finally pulled its "Body Count" album by Ice-T, which included the song "Cop Killer," which some felt encouraged ghetto youth to kill police officers. Groups such as 2 Live Crew, or Niggas with Attitudes, are not characteristic of the genre, however; and many rap songs feature nonviolent themes.

Copycat Crimes. The issue of differential impacts of the media on different subgroups can be illustrated by means of the notion of "copycat crimes." The term copycat is a slang expression for imitation; thus **copycat crimes** *are fads in crime and are often stimulated by media coverage or portrayals.*

In the early days of television there was tremendous concern about children imitating Superman by jumping from the tops of buildings. In the 1990s, when a 5-year-old girl in Norway was stoned and kicked by playmates and left to freeze to death in the snow, the Scandinavian network TV-3 dropped the "Mighty Morphin Power Rangers" from its broadcasts in Norway, Sweden, and Denmark (Mellgren, 1994). Other examples include the film "Money Train" which portrays a man dousing a subway token booth with a flammable liquid and burning the attendant. This gruesome act was imitated in three similar incidents within one week in New York. In 1993 an episode of "Beavis and Butthead" was blamed by a mother for her five-year-old starting a fire that killed his little sister. The episode featured a character setting fire to others' hair by using a match to ignite spray from an aerosol can. The 1976 film "Taxi Driver," in which a character played by Robert DeNiro attempts to kill the President, inspired Reagan's attempted assassin, John Hinckley, Jr. The film "The Program" inspired two teenagers to copy a scene in which drunken football players play "chicken" by lying in the middle of a highway. The boys were killed. The film "Natural Born Killers" was banned in Great Britain and Ireland because of copycat murders in the United States and France (Murr and Rogers, 1995, p. 47). The film "Child's Play" and its sequels featured a demonic, animated character called Chucky, and may have inspired two boys from Liverpool to lure a 2-year-old boy from a Liverpool shopping mall and subsequently to murder him (Kolbert, 1994, p. A13). The horrible dragging death of black man, James Byrd, Jr., behind a pickup truck in Jasper, Texas, in 1998 by three white men was followed by two similar crimes in Illinois and Louisiana. Similar patterns with school shootings and workplace violence have also been noted.

Much like the tobacco industry, the purveyors of such violent themes claim no direct causal relationship between their product and harmful outcomes, yet the scientific studies are overwhelming in predicting harmful effects, even though in any particular case not all individuals are adversely affected.

On July 26, 2000, the American Medical Association, the American Academy of Pediatrics, the American Psychological Association, and the American Academy of Child and Adolescent Psychiatry issued a joint declaration stating (www.ama-assn.org/ama/pub/article/1617-2887.html):

> Viewing violence may lead to real life violence . . . Children exposed to violent programming at a young age have a higher tendency for violent and aggressive behavior later in life than children who are not so exposed.

Noting that before he or she reaches age 18, the average child will witness more than 200,000 acts of violence on television including 16,000 murders, they indicated that the link between media violence and real violence has been quite clearly demonstrated by research primarily in its role of leading to emotional desensitization.

Criminal Typologies

One limitation of many discussions of crime and of theories of crime causation is the global manner in which the concept of crime is employed. To expect criminologists to address the question, "What causes crime?" is comparable to asking medical pathologists to answer the query "What causes sickness?" Asking "What *type* of sickness?" or "What *type* of crime?" is the next logical step in approaching these questions. While the only thing most sicknesses have in common is that they have produced an unhealthy biological state, the only thing most crimes have in common is that they are—in a given place, at a given time—a violation of criminal law. Thus cancer, polio, and the common cold probably have about as much in common as shoplifting, embezzlement, and murder.

While it is important that the field of criminology continue the theoretical work of explaining crime and criminal behavior as a whole, it is also important and perhaps more expeditious in the short run to explain particular criminal behaviors. Until an acceptable general theory is developed, it is desirable to delimit the specific areas to which a theory is applicable, to coordinate these theories, and to try to build a general theory. We need both general and specific theories and must avoid confusing the two.

Criminal typologies are *attempts to classify types of crimes and criminals.* These attempts may represent one of the oldest theoretical and practical approaches to crime. Although the work of Lombroso (to be discussed in greater detail in Chapter 4) is often pointed to as the beginning of criminal typologies, the tradition of attempting to classify lawbreakers precedes him (Schafer, 1976, p. 104; 1969, pp. 140–82). Criminal typologies are based on various criteria. VANTAGE POINT 3.5 outlines a few of the better-known efforts to develop typologies of criminals or criminal behavior. These typologies are not intended to be memorized; they merely serve as exhibits of the many different attempts to classify criminal behavior.

A Critique of Typologies

Typologies can have two purposes: (1) to be used as a scientific classificatory system, or (2) to be utilized as a heuristic scheme (an educational tool). The former effort is exemplified by taxonomical classifications in biology where life forms are sorted into categories such as phylum, species, and the like on the basis of physical characteristics. Related to this tradition are prison classification systems (Fox, 1976, pp. 345–61) that attempt to line up criminal offense records with treatment regimens. This effort has obviously been limited by inadequacies of offense records themselves for the purposes of classifying individuals. Many critics of the typological approach expect typologies to meet rigorous taxonomical refinement. Their critiques of typologies include:

- Specific offenses vary according to time and place.
- Some offenders exhibit great diversity, participating in more than one behavior system, or may in fact change their offense profiles.
- No typology can contain purely homogeneous types.
- The number of career criminals specializing in one type of offense is smaller than has been suggested by the typologies developed thus far (p. 354).
- Some typologies attempt to make types of crimes and criminals more distinct from each other than they really are, thus oversimplifying reality (Conklin, 1982, Ibid., p. 16).
- No single typology is useful to group all offenders (Thomas and Hepburn, 1983, p. 262).
- Typologies overemphasize unique aspects and minimize similarities among types (p. 262).

VANTAGE POINT 3.5

Some Sociological Typologies of Criminal Behavior

Gibbons's "Criminal Role Careers"

1. Professional thieves
2. Professional "heavy" criminals
3. Semiprofessional property offenders
4. Naïve check forgers
5. Automobile thieves, "joyriders"
6. Property offenders, "one-time losers"
7. Embezzlers
8. White collar criminals
9. Professional "fringe violators"
10. Personal offenders, "one-time losers"
11. Psychopathic assaultists
12. Statutory rapists
13. Aggressive rapists
14. Violent sex offenders
15. Nonviolent sex offenders
16. Incest offenders
17. Male homosexuals
18. Opiate addicts
19. Skid Row alcoholics
20. Amateur shoplifters

Schafer's "Life Trend" Typology of Criminals

1. Occasional criminals
2. Professional criminals
3. Abnormal criminals
4. Habitual criminals
5. Convictional criminals

Lombroso's Types of Criminals

1. Born criminals
2. Criminaloids
3. Occasional criminals
4. Criminals by passion

Abrahamsen's Types of Criminals

1. Acute criminals
   a. Situational
   b. Associational
   c. Accidental
2. Chronic offenders
   a. Neurotic
   b. Psychopathic
   c. Psychotic

Glaser's Types of Crime

1. Predatory crime
2. Illegal performance offenses
3. Illegal selling offenses
4. Illegal consumption offenses
5. Disloyalty offenses
6. Illegal status offenses

Sources: Don C. Gibbons, 1982, *Society, Crime and Criminal Behavior,* 4th edition, Englewood Cliffs, N.J.: Prentice-Hall, p. 225; Stephen Schafer, 1976, *Introduction to Criminology,* Reston, Va.: Reston, pp. 107–108; Gina Lombroso-Ferrero, 1972, *Criminal Man According to the Classification of Cesare Lombroso,* Montclair, N.J.: Patterson Smith, p. 100; David Abrahamsen, 1960, *The Psychology of Crime,* New York: Columbia University Press, p. 14; Daniel Glaser, 1978, *Crime in Our Changing Society,* New York: Holt, Rinehart and Winston, p. 15

InfoTrac College Edition Research
Search under "Gender and Crime" and locate an article that discusses the relationship between gender and some specific area of crime.

Feeling that the use of typologies as a taxonomical system is trivial, Gibbons, who has grown more skeptical of the typological approach, admits that many criminals "defy pigeonholing" (Gibbons, 1982, p. 263) and further states:

> Typological systems that sort offenders into relatively homogeneous types do have *heuristic values* [italics mine], alerting us to broad categories of lawbreak-

> ers that make up the criminal population. However, they put forth an oversimplified characterization of the real world of criminality and criminals. Many criminals are "situational casual" criminals who are involved in various forms of short-run criminality, such that they do not fall into any clear-cut type, syndrome, or role-career (p. 232).

A Defense of Typologies

The real value of criminal typologies is their educational benefit in providing a useful, illustrative scheme, a practical device that, although subject to abstraction and overgeneralization, enables us to simplify and make sense of complex realities. Any ideal types are prone to oversimplification, but without them the categorical equivocations in discussing reality become overwhelming. Although critics of typologies make many good points, it would be interesting to have any of them attempt an extensive discussion of crime or criminal behavior at any length without using the implicit typologies that often consist of the very labels they have rejected.

The first purpose of typologies as classificatory systems requires empirical verification using actual quantitative research, while the second purpose recognizes that concepts or typologies as ideal types have qualitative, heuristic value. They sensitize or alert us to and are useful in explaining critical features of reality even though as ideal or constructed types they obviously oversimplify that same reality.

Criminal Behavior Systems

As an organizing, heuristic scheme, this text will make use of a variation of a typology of **criminal behavior systems** originally developed by McKinney (1966) and elaborated by Clinard and Quinney (1986) in their now classic work, *Criminal Behavior Systems: A Typology.* This typology is based on constructed types "that serve as a means by which concrete occurrences can be compared and understood within a system of characteristics that underlie the types." Clinard and Quinney (1986, p. 15) identify nine types of criminal behavior:

1. Violent personal crime
2. Occasional property crime
3. Occupational crime
4. Corporate crime [added to the typology later]
5. Political crime
6. Public-order crime
7. Conventional crime
8. Organized crime
9. Professional crime

These types are based on four characteristics:

1. The criminal career of the offender
2. Group support of the criminal behavior
3. Correspondence between criminal and legitimate behavior
4. Societal reaction and legal processing of offenders

Clinard and Quinney admit that there are undoubtedly other ways of delineating crime into types, taking into account these four characteristics; however, the typology serves useful purposes that permit the ordering of presentation of research on various forms of crime. Rather than using legal categories for the organization of materials, the purpose is to derive as few categories of crime, based on behavior similarities, as possible, in order to simplify analysis. Chapters 7 through 14 will concentrate on crime and criminal activity making use of a variety of elements of this typology.

Summary

In examining descriptions and statistical accounts of crime and criminals it is important to examine the data base or sources of findings and conclusions. Official statistics, victim surveys, self-reports, and other sources all provide different pictures. Similarly, the type of criminal activity being addressed, whether traditional or elite, will provide different findings. Although they differ slightly in definitions of crime, concentrating on incidents in the UCR and on victims in the NCVS, the two measures are viewed as converging, with each providing certain information that the other lacks.

Estimates of the prevalence of crime depend on the measure used, with the extent of crime increasing as we move from UCR to NCVS to self-reports to estimates of corporate crime and other forms of criminality. The bulk of UCR Part I or *index* crimes consists of property crimes; the most frequent arrests among Part II crimes are for service functions. Trends in crime as measured by the UCR demonstrate a major crime wave in the United States since the mid-sixties. Comparison of trends using the NCVS since the early seventies shows only a small increase, if not a stable pattern in criminal victimization. Despite the lack of good, representative self-report surveys of the general population, existing studies certainly suggest that crime is even more pervasive than is reported in the UCR and NCVS.

Official statistics on crime indicate that most of those arrested are young (fifteen-to-nineteen years of age). This is particularly the case with serious property crimes. *Age* profiles obviously would be altered upward were we to have accurate estimates for corporate and "upperworld" violators. Of all demographic variables, *gender* is the best universal predictor of criminality; with the exception of prostitution, the male crime rate exceeds the female rate for all crimes, although the gap has been closing, particularly in developed societies. This difference in criminality by gender can best be explained by cultural and socialization differences rather than by innate genetic ones. While some self-report studies demonstrate less of a gap, others indicate patterns like those in official data.

Official statistics show an inverse relationship between *social class* and criminality (as measured by arrests); that is, as social class rises, criminality decreases. This relationship remains a subject of debate. Most recent self-report surveys indicate that patterns of lower class admissions match those of official statistics. Such findings still do not belie the possibility of high upper class criminality, since the most typical upper class offenses are not tapped by such sources.

In examining *race* and crime, the reader was informed of the precariousness of the scientific concept of *race* and that a goodly proportion of the "black" population in the United States might better be described as of "mixed" race. UCR arrest statistics indicate a black crime rate, particularly for violent crimes, that greatly exceeds their proportion of the U.S. population. Despite countervailing biases in these statistics, it would appear that they are accurate descriptions of excess commission of these offenses. Most crime is intraracial in nature; that is, most whites victimize whites and most blacks victimize blacks. While self-report surveys show mixed results, more recent studies confirm higher rates among blacks for serious offenses.

Minority group status itself does not result in higher crime rates. Early research demonstrated high rates in the area of transition (zone II) despite turnover in the minority in residence. Some groups—Dutch and Japanese, for example—never appear to have had higher crime rates. The first generation of immigrants generally has lower crime rates than the native population. It is their offspring, becoming Americanized into the lower class, who experience higher rates. Blacks have had higher rates than other minorities in part because of a maturing economy, the disability of race, late entry into the political system, and cultural factors. Crime patterns of European immigrants are similar to U.S. patterns, although many immigrants are really temporary guest workers.

Official U.S. crime rates vary by *region,* with the South highest for murder, rape, and burglary; the West highest for assault, vehicle theft, and larceny; and the Northeast highest for robbery. International variations are difficult to determine because of inadequacies in crime statistics. Urban crime rates are generally higher than suburban and rural ones, particularly for property crimes. Recently, suburban and rural rates have been increasing more rapidly than urban rates.

While much has been written regarding the impact of the *family* on crime, with variables such as poor home discipline, neglect, indifference, parental criminality, and others identified as correlates, the key appears to be the quality of the family interaction rather than its structure as such. The impact of *education* and crime is highly intercorrelated with social class.

Major external conflicts (*wars*) appear to decrease internal conflicts (crime), with the exceptions of female crime, juvenile delinquency, and certain "white collar crimes." Studies of economic trends and crime show inconsistent results; however, since the end of World War II there has been a quicker crime increase, particularly in violent crimes, with dips in the economy.

The nature of the impact of *media* upon crime is unresolved. While some propose a *catharsis hypothesis* (media violence as a vicarious tension-relieving function), others support a *precipitation hypothesis* (media violence as an encouragement of the acting out of fictional themes). Television portrayals of violence appear to create increased feelings of potential vulnerability on the part of the public. Surveys of the literature by the Department of Health and Human Services, the Surgeon General's Committee, and the National Institute of Mental Health all concluded that violence on television tends to increase aggressiveness in children. Media violence appears to have particular, although unpredictable, impacts on certain subpopulations of viewers. This point was illustrated by *copycat crimes,* imitation crimes based on media portrayals.

Criminal typologies (attempts to classify criminals or criminal behavior) have two purposes: (1) a scientific classification system, and (2) a heuristic (practical) scheme. While many criticisms have been levied against such typologies as pure scientific classes, the heuristic benefit of using criminal typologies as organizing schemes for presentation or discussion purposes remains. After a brief review of other typologies, Clinard and Quinney's typology of "criminal behavior systems" was presented. This examines nine criminal behavior systems: violent personal, occasional property, occupational, corporate, political, public-order, conventional, organized, and professional crime from the standpoints of criminal career, group support, correspondence with legitimate behavior, societal reaction, and legal processing.

KEY CONCEPTS

Age/Crime Debate
Androcentric Bias
Catharsis Hypothesis
Copycat Crimes
Crime Trends
Criminal Behavior Systems
Criminal Typologies
Fallacy of Autonomy
Feminization of Poverty
Precipitation Hypothesis

Variations in Crime
- **Age**
- **Gender**
- **Social Class**
- **Race**
- **Minority Status**
- **Region**
- **International**
- **Urban/Rural**

Institutions
Family
Education
Religion
War
Economy
Mass Media

REVIEW QUESTIONS

1. How does crime vary internationally? Where does the U.S. stand with respect to crime compared with other countries of the world?
2. What is the androcentric bias in criminology and what trends are taking place in the field to counteract it?
3. What is the issue of racial profiling? What impact has this had on rates of arrest and incarceration, and what is being done to remedy the problem?
4. How are Native Americans affected by crime both as perpetrators and victims? What explanations are there for this?
5. What is William Julius Wilson's major point in *The Truly Disadvantaged*? What are some steps that have been proposed to remedy this problem?
6. What is the role of the media in crime? What are some proposals for controlling media precipitation of crime?
7. What is the importance of crime typologies? How would you begin to answer the following question: "What causes crime?"
8. What role does age play in explaining crime rates?
9. What is transnational crime? What are some policy recommendations for dealing with this phenomenon?
10. What are some problems/limitaitons in using and interpreting international measures of crime?

INFOTRAC COLLEGE EDITION RESEARCH

Vantage Point 3.1 InfoTrac College Edition Research
Examine the issue of international crime. What is an additional, emergent crime problem not mentioned in VANTAGE POINT 3.1? What strategies are needed for coping with this?

Vantage Point 3.2 InfoTrac College Edition Research
Search "age and crime" and locate the "age-crime debate." What is it and what is its importance?

Vantage Point 3.3 InfoTrac College Edition Research
Visit the Bureau of Justice Statistics web site and review a new program for dealing with delinquency not mentioned in this VANTAGE POINT.

Vantage Point 3.4 InfoTrac College Edition Research
Besides the FAST program, loacte another program that links families and schools.

Vantage Point 3.5 InfoTrac College Edition Research
Search under "Gender and Crime" and locate an article that discusses the relationship between gender and some specific area of crime.

In The News 3.1 InfoTrac College Edition Research
What are some later developments in the issue of crime (racial) profiling? Have there been any new public policies for dealing with this issue?

SELECTED READINGS

Joanne Belknap. 1996. *The Invisible Woman: Gender, Crime and Justice.* Belmont, California: Wadsworth.
This book provides an excellent review and assessment of critical issues related to the issue of gender in criminology and criminal justice.

David Cole. 1999. *No Equal Justice: Race and Class in the American Criminal Justice System.* New York: New Press.
Cole makes a strong case that inequality exists in the American Criminal Justice System primarily due to uneven enforcement as part of the war on drugs.

Erika Fairchild and Harry Dammer. 2000. *Comparative Criminal Justice Systems.* Belmont, California: Wadsworth.
This update of a classic provides an outstanding review of world criminal justice systems and issues related to international criminology.

Coramae Richey Mann. 1993. *Unequal Justice: A Question of Color.* Bloomington, Indiana: Indiana University Press.
As the title suggests, Mann makes strong arguments for the existence of racism within the criminal justice system in the U.S.

Alida Merlo and Peter Benekos, editors. 1999. *What's Wrong with the Criminal Justice System: Ideology, Politics and the Media.*
This book reviews what is "wrong" with the criminal justice system and what can be done to make it "less wrong." It reviews three themes: the impact of ideology, the role of the media, and the politicization of crime and criminal justice.

Kathryn K. Russell. 1999. *The Color of Crime.* New York: New York University Press.
Russell examines the role of race in the operations of the American justice system.

Howard Snyder and Melissa Sickmund. 1999. *Juvenile Offenders and Victims, 1999 National Report.* Washington, D.C.: Office of Juvenile Justice and Delinquency Prevention.
This annual report on the state of the U.S. Juvenile Justice System might better be entitled "Everything You Always Wanted to Know About the American Juvenile Justice System, But Were Afraid to Ask." This "bible" of juvenile justice features excellent, multicolored graphics and is also available in a CD version. Contact the Office of Juvenile Justice.

Richard Terrill. 1999. *World Criminal Justice Systems: A Survey.* 4th Edition. Cincinnati: Anderson.
Terrill provides a very incisive review of criminal justice systems in countries throughout the world including updates on China and Russia.

William Julius Wilson. 1987. *The Truly Disadvantaged: The Inner City, the Underclass and Public Policy.* Chicago: University of Chicago Press.
In what has become a modern day sociological classic, Wilson describes the "deindustrialization" and abandonment of areas of our inner cities and the accompanying social disorganization and crime.

4

Criminological Theory I: Early, Classical, and Positivistic Theories

Vantage Points

> My object all sublime I shall achieve in time—To let the punishment fit the crime.
>
> —Gilbert and Sullivan, *The Mikado*

> The increasing popularity of the idea that much if not most crime and delinquency reflect innate and intractable predispositions has more to do, I think, with the larger social and economic trends in America in the last quarter of the twentieth century than it does with the meager and contradictory empirical evidence invoked to support it.
>
> —Elliott Currie, *Confronting Crime* (1985)

In Chapter 1 *theory* was discussed as referring to a plausible explanation of reality, a reasonable and informed guess as to why things are as they appear. Theorizing represents a leap of faith, an *élan vital* (vital force) with which to shed light on the darkness of reality. The term *theory* is derived from the Greek *theoros, to observe and reflect upon the meaning of an event.* Representatives from the city-states of ancient Greece were sent to observe celebrations in honor of the gods and were asked to attempt to separate themselves from their personal views and try to conceive of what the gods wished. Without incisive theories, a field or discipline becomes a hopeless catalog of random and seemingly unrelated facts. However, theories are not laws or facts, though this is sometimes forgotten by those who become convinced of the correctness of a particular theory that they come to espouse. Thus, as powerful and persuasive as they may be, Freudian and Marxist theories, for example, are just that—theories: general or systemic models of how human personalities or societies function.

According to Turner (1974, p. 2):

> Theorizing can be viewed as the means by which the intellectual activity known as "science" realizes three principal goals: (1) to classify and organize events in the world so that they can be placed into perspective, (2) to explain the causes of past events and predict when, where, and how future events will occur, and (3) to offer an intuitively pleasing sense of "understanding" why and how events should occur.

Pure and Applied Theory

In Chapter 2 we distinguished between pure research, which is concerned with advancing the knowledge base of a discipline, and applied research, which is concerned with finding or prescribing solutions to immediate problems or needs. Similarly **pure theory** is concerned with *the search for cause and basic principles underlying phenomena,* while **applied theory** attempts to *provide practical explanations with which to guide existing policy.* The rift that often exists between pure and applied researchers may also be evident between pure and applied theorists.

Pure theorists' efforts to explain or understand crime causation—which account for most theories to be presented in this and the next chapter—are often viewed as attempts to justify and excuse crime and/or as being wholly inadequate in guiding practical, existing social policy. Explaining why or how things happen should not be confused with justifying or defending them. If we ignore this obvious fact, we risk killing the messenger bearing bad (though possibly important) news. The uninitiated find review and critique of these theories a futile exercise in self-flagellation in which criminologists parade their dirty laundry in bitter debates between warring camps of theorists. High hopes are raised for the discovery of a "key" to explaining all crime and criminality, though no such breakthroughs have occurred in the parent social sciences—sociology, psychology, political science, and economics—themselves, and many of the same competing schools do battle in these fields. Those who are uncomfortable with such a theoretical morass might best be advised to

Heretics were burned at the stake under the Spanish Inquisition. Under Iran's fundamentalist regime symbolized by the Ayatollah Khomeini, criminals or opponents of the state are subject to torture, death, or other forms of the "wrath of Allah."

(© The Bettmann Archive)

(© UPI / Bettmann Newsphotos)

study chemistry or biology or auto mechanics—fields in which the theoretical and empirical turf is tidier; the subject matter of the social sciences is infinitely more complex and not likely to yield to a general and universally accepted theory in the near future.

In the meantime, what of the demands of applied theorists and practitioners for explanations with which to guide immediate policy? Some have abandoned pure theory as fruitless in providing guidelines for existing policy needs, yet they then propose therapies, treatments, and policies that surprisingly are based on one or the other of the pure theories they have rejected. In reality, criminology as an interdisciplinary field requires both pure and applied theory. The search for basic, underlying cause is important in itself for the mature development of the discipline, while obviously applied theories need not and cannot wait until ultimate laws are discovered before attempting to advocate existing policy programs. Many fields of learning utilize workable applied theory without having resolved the issue of ultimate causal theory.

VANTAGE POINT 4.1 discusses the sociological classic, *The Body Ritual of the Nacirema.* Read it and then, when reading our theory chapters, ask not only, "Do these theories explain the behavior of criminals?" but also ask, "Do they explain the behavior of Nacirema undergraduates?" Many Nacirema reject having their picture taken; but if you would like to see one, locate a "Rorrim" and look into it.

Major Theoretical Approaches

This chapter begins with an exploration of many early theories that represent the historical legacy of the field and finishes with a sketch of modern biological and psychological theories; the next chapter explores more current sociological theories of crime. While many of the early theories have been discredited, their examination is warranted not only from the standpoint of gaining a sense of continuity of the discipline, but also because many expressions of these theories are resurrected in new forms in modern thinking. Sometimes these theories will be accepted or rejected on the basis of ideology rather than on the basis of empirical evidence (Blankenship and Brown, 1993, p. 171).

Figure 4.1 presents an outline of the *major theoretical approaches in criminology.* The last type, sociological theory, is subdivided and described in more detail in the following chapter. This division of criminological theories into types or schools of thought is primarily for purposes of convenient presentation since, in fact, some theorists demonstrate evolution in their views and may in fact exhibit theoretical conceptions that meld different types or schools of thought. The primary theoretical approaches in criminology (Figure 4.1) are: the demonological, classical (neoclassical), ecological (geographic), economic, positivistic (biological and psychological), and sociological (whose many subtypes will be discussed in Chapters 5 and 6). Discussion will begin with the demonological or supernatural approach to explaining crime causation, which is based in a superstitious and tradition-oriented past in which wrongdoers were perceived as controlled by otherworldly forces.

Demonological Theory

Demonological or *supernatural explanations of criminality* dominated thinking from early history well into the eighteenth century; modern remnants still survive (see Huff, 1990). In a system of knowledge in which theological explanations of reality were predominant, the criminal was viewed as a sinner who was possessed by demons or damned by otherworldly forces. Humankind was viewed as at the mercy of the supernatural: fates, ghosts, furies, and/or spirits. Felonies (mortal sins) were viewed as manifestations of basically evil human nature reflecting either allegiance to the "prince of darkness" or an expression of divine wrath. The Salem Witch Trials in Puritan New England and the Spanish Inquisition serve as examples of the torture, hanging, burning at the stake, and other grim executions awaiting heretics, witches, and criminals. Such a world view perceived the violator's actions as deterministically controlled by forces beyond the individual's mastery. In Genesis (22:1–12) Abraham was ordered by God to sacrifice his son Isaac, although he was

VANTAGE POINT 4.1

The Nacirema Undergraduate as Criminal: A Criminological "Whydoit?"

It was anthropologist Horace Miner who first brought the strange customs of the Nacirema to public attention nearly half a century ago. He prefaced his description of this tribe by explaining that anthropologists are trained in avoiding ethnocentric bias so that they are able to present objectively and without shock such extreme, exotic customs as exhibited by the ***Nacirema.*** *In his classic "The Body Ritual of the Nacirema," Miner (1956) describes a group whose land,* ***Asu,*** *lies between the Canadian Cree, the Carib of the Antilles, and the Yaqui Indians of Mexico. Miner indicates (1956, p. 503):*

> **Little is known of the origin, although tradition states that they came from the east. According to Nacirema mythology, their nation was originated by a cultural hero Notgnihsaw, who is otherwise known for two great feats of strength—the throwing of a piece of wampum across the river Pa-To-Mac and the chopping down of a cherry tree in which the spirit of truth resided.**

If you have not figured it out by now, Nacirema is American spelled backwards and Notgnihsaw is Washington. The entire piece is a clever pun that pokes fun at American culture as it might be viewed by someone who is wholly unfamiliar with the real reasons for certain American customs and beliefs. After a brief presentation of Miner's Nacirema, Hagan and Benekos (1999) tease some updates examining Nacirema undergraduates and invite you to apply the theories you are about to explore to analyze not criminals, but Nacirema undergraduates who are deviant or not performing as expected.

Nacirema Customs and Rituals

The Nacirema have an obsession with the human body and its care and adornment, without which they believe that their friends and lovers would desert them. Despite this they believe that their bodies are naturally ugly and condemned to disease and decay. Only by using powerful rituals and visiting specialized witchdoctors do the Nacirema believe they can escape this corporeal destiny. Daily, secretive rituals in a room called the **moorthab** involve what Miner assumed was "worshipping" before a shrine box within which were stored various magical charms and solutions that the natives felt were necessary for living. Such potions were obtained from special shamans in return for very rich gifts. When ill, the Nacirema visit the witchdoctor, who would often put magical wands in their mouth and inject them with supernatural needles.

Since Miner's analysis a major trend has been the large number of Nacirema youth who now attend college rather than work after their initial rite of passage. In the past only the children of the top leaders attended college, while now the majority of youth do so. In colleges large gifts are given to older members of the tribe known as Talkers or **Forp.** The Nacirema undergraduates work very hard at their assigned task, transcribing and later reciting or recounting shared tribal knowledge. New Nacirema inventions such as little boxes with brains called a **spotpal** can store and record information as well as access the **tenretni,** a magical stream of words, pictures and ideas that has accelerated even further changes in the land of Asu.

Theories of Nacirema Undergraduate Deviance

The ability of criminological theory to explain criminal/deviant behavior awaits theoretical developments in sociology, psychology, and the other social sciences that adequately explain normal behavior. Let us pretend for a moment that, instead of attempting to explain criminal behavior in society, we could apply these same theories to aberrant behavior by undergraduates in Nacirema colleges and universities. While space does not permit detailed coverage, a cursory visit should suffice.

What explains the poorly performing Nacirema undergraduate whose parents could purchase a new **rac** every year for the price they pay for their child to listen to a Forp? Despite the high prices, some students attend few classes, sleep, daydream, perform at terrible levels and even eventually are asked to leave. Early theories might suggest that such students were possessed by demons, while later ones pursued more secular explanations. Some Nacirema undergraduates cheat on examinations or steal ideas from others for papers that they claim are their own work. Classical theories of criminology would explain that such deviants are rational and that the penalties for such behavior (flunking or expulsion) do not exceed the rewards (passing or graduating without doing the work).

Other theories would suggest that the students' social background or lower social class adversely impacts on them and explains their poor performance, while positivistic theories seek explanation in biological and psychological shortcomings. Are poor or deviant students atavistic "throwbacks to the ape," born deviants whose biological inheritance dooms their chances of conformity and success? Perhaps mental deficiency, feeblemindedness, physical inferiority, mesomorphic body types, or brain disorders explain their zombie-like behavior and inadequate preparation, interest, and performance compared to their more accomplished peers. Many do a noncannibalistic imitation of the classic film, "Night of the Living Dead."

Most likely, the problem is not biologic at all, but psychological. Do they possess born, uneducable personalities; are they unconsciously repressing their sexual instincts; or are they victims of extroversion, inadequate behavioral conditioning (namely anti-intellectualism) or low I.Q.s? A long neglected explanation may be found in the work of the then-26-year-old genius and president of the University of Chicago, Robert Maynard Hutchins, who in *Zuckercandl!* (1968) discusses the theories of the all but forgotten philosopher, Alexander Zuckercandl, who, instead of trying to explain how people should behave, developed explanations for how people (in this case students) do behave. Zuckercandl's genius was to reverse Freudian theory. The latter enjoined us to "become conscious of our unconscious," while Zuckercandl indicates "we must become unconscious of our conscious," a motto to which many undergraduates might relate.

Modern sociological theories of crime view society and social groups as far more likely explanations of human (student) misconduct than those that have been mentioned. Edwin Sutherland's "theory of differential association" explains that individuals learn to become "poor students" due to an excess of contacts that advocate not taking seriously academic work and, as a result, students are predisposed to regard intellectual activity in a negative manner (Sutherland and Cressey, 1960). If students have a frequency and duration of such negative views (e.g., anti-intellectual background) and do not prefer or find meaningful academic pursuits, then such persons will tend to perform poorly. Nacirema society preaches that all members of the tribe should be able to become successful (own many gadgets) if they perform well as undergraduates, thus obtaining high ranking tribal positions such as shamans, talkers, and listeners.

Robert Merton (1957, 1968), in his theory of "anomie and modes of personality adaptation," explains that such high tribal positions and rewards are preached as available to all Nacirema if they pursue the legitimate means of being successful in college. Anomie (normlessness) ensues when a gap exists between the goal of success (high position and rewards) and adequate means for their achievement (undergraduate academic success). While most students demonstrate "conformist" personalities in that they accept this goal and adequate means exist for them to be successful in college, others find that they lack the adequate means in order to be successful. These students can become "innovators" and lie, cheat, and steal in order to graduate. Others are "retreatists." They reject the goal of success and spend their time rejecting the means (going to classes and getting good grades) as well. Alcohol and drugs may replace books as a primary orientation. "Ritualistic" students show up for class, but forget the purpose of doing so—getting good grades. They daydream and sleep in class and assume somehow they will learn what they consider irrelevant academic information through a process of osmosis. Finally, the "rebel" may use legitimate or illegitimate means to challenge the values and goals presented by the college.

Student as Renosirp

Another dimension of this analogy is that some students also display behaviors which incorporate norms that are characteristic of offenders in captivity. Rather than identifying with Forps, some Nacirema students cultivate anti intellectual attitudes and values which enforce a code of silence and impose sanctions on those who violate what is described as the "**Renosirp** rules." Similar to inmate codes such as "don't talk to the screws," "don't trust the guards," and "don't snitch" (Sykes, 1958), Nacirema undergraduates affect disinterest and ascholarly views. The student code may include the following: "don't be smart, don't ask questions, don't answer questions, do your own time, and be cool." For example, one report found that 90 percent of college students say they would not turn in someone for cheating; that is, "don't snitch" (Kleiner and Lord, 1999, p. 57). As prisoners do their time by developing a prisoner subculture, students also develop a subculture which fosters their identity and legitimizes their roles as nonacademics and provides rationalizations for their deviant behaviors. Kleiner and Lord report that "plagiarism, copying, and similar deceits devalue learning" but that "the pressure to succeed . . . can drive students to consider extreme measures" (1999, p. 57). This suggests the "innovation" that Merton (1957, 1968) typologized as a adaptive mode to blocked means.

Students also use their dress to symbolize some of their codes. For example, part of the student uniform at the turn of the century was a well-worn piece of head gear called a **pac llab,** sometimes pulled down low over

VANTAGE POINT 4.1—*Continued*

the forehead to conceal the eyes, thus avoiding eye contact with Forps and the dreaded possibility of being asked a quesiton. When a pac is worn in reverse, it is done so to pay homage to Yogi Berra, a philosopher students have grown to admire and one who represents their worship of sports heroes.

By disdaining books, global events, and politics, students instead form identification with heroes of sporting events. These athletic stars represent models for success, fame, and wealth that surpass the financial achievement and professional status based on traditional adaptations that emphasize education, intellectual growth, and deferred gratification. By worshipping the athlete as a godlike figure, students seek vicarious success by adorning themselves with the colors and emblems of their favored sports gangs. This identification with these gladiator gangs represents another salient custom of the Nacirema undergraduate.

As prisoners do their own time, reject the rejecters, and try to avoid the guards, students also demonstrate behaviors that avoid socialization to college norms and values, i.e., "collegization." The students as criminals distance themselves from Forps by sitting in the back of the classroom, by avoiding note-taking, by not participating in discussion, and generally by adhering to the Renosirp norms: "don't get involved, don't ask questions, don't show emotion" (i.e., interest). Instead of engaging in intellectual growth and scholarship, these students have precipitated a cooptation of college values with an importation of working-class street values. Historically, college has reflected a middle class orientation, and students assimilated appropriate norms and values. With the increasing number of high school graduates who would not have gone to college in the past now entering such institutions, a critical mass of students has facilitated a subculture that deflects socialization and assimilation of middle class values and establishes norms to support alternative student behaviors (Miller, 1958).

One might ask, "Why don't all students behave in this manner?" Here again, criminological theory would say they would if they dared; but their attachments to parental units and Forps, belief in the academic model, commitment to accomplishing normative goals, and involvement in classes and intellectual exercises "bonds" (Hirschi, 1969) them to conformity. In contrast, those students who enter college as a default often manifest ritualistic behaviors (Merton, 1957, 1968) and lack commitment, involvement, beliefs, or attachments to ensure their bond to the scholarly community. In fact, as noted above, as a critical mass of nonscholar undergraduates is attained, the culture of the college becomes transformed. As with penal institutions, the question is often asked, "Who rules the joint?"

Criminological theory offers one approach to explaining this curious paradox in which students resist/reject pro-intellectual elements of college while drifting toward deviant norms that demonstrate the student as criminal. Theories of subculture, strain, social control, and differential association provide useful concepts in understanding how "normal" Nacirema students become "criminals" in academe.

Sources

Frank Hagan and Peter Benekos. 2000. "The Nacirema Undergraduate as Criminal: A Theoretical Analogy." Paper presented at the Academy of Criminal Justice Sciences Meetings, New Orleans, Louisiana, March.
Travis Hirschi. 1969. *Causes of Delinquency.* Berkeley, California: University of California Press.
Robert M. Hutchins. 1968. *Zuckercandl!* New York, NY: Grove Press.
Carolyn Kleiner and Mary Lord. 1999. "The Cheating Game." *U.S. News & World Report.* (November):55–57; 61–66.
Robert K. Merton. 1957, 1968. *Social Theory and Social Structure.* Revised edition. New York, NY: The Free Press.
Walter Miller. 1958. "Lower Class Culture as a Generating Milieu of Gang Delinquency." *Journal of Social Issues* 14(May):5–19.
Horace Miner. 1956. "Body Ritual Among the Nacirema." *The American Anthropologist.* 58:503–507.
Edwin H. Sutherland and Donald C. Cressey. 1960. *Criminology.* Philadelphia, PA: Lippincott.
Gresham M. Sykes. 1958. *The Society of Captives: A Study of a Maximum Security Prison.* Princeton, NJ: Princeton University Press.

InfoTrac College Edition Research

What are some recent cases of actual campus crime among Nacirema college students? Search "campus crime."

FIGURE 4.1 Major Theoretical Approaches in Criminology*

Theoretical School	*Major Themes/Concepts*	*Major Theorists*
Demonological	criminal as "evil," "sinner," "supernatural pawn"	traditional authority
Classical (Neoclassical)	criminal as "rational, hedonistic, free actor"	Beccaria, Bentham
	"incapacitation, punishment, deterrence"	Wilson G. Becker
Ecological (Geographic)	"group characteristics, physical and social ecological impacts on criminality"	Quetelet and Guerry Lieber and Sherin
	"geographical and climatic impacts on criminality"	
Economic	"capitalism, social class inequality, and economic conditions cause crime"	Marx, Bonger
Positivistic Biological	"physical stigmata, atavism, biological inheritance cause criminality"	Lombroso, Ferri, Garofalo Goring
	"mental deficiency"	Goddard
	"feeblemindedness"	Hooton
	"physical inferiority"	Sheldon
	"somatotypes—mesomorphs"	
	"brain disorders, twin studies, XYY syndrome, physiological disorders"	Moniz, Christiansen, Jacobs
Psychological	"unconscious repression of sexual instincts," "criminal personality," "extroversion," "inadequate behavioral conditioning," "IQ"	Freud, Eysenck, Skinner, Hirschi, Hindelang
Sociological	"anomie, subcultural learning, elite dominance cause crime"	Durkheim, Sutherland, Quinney

*See Figures 5.1 and 6.1 for greater detail regarding "sociological theory" in criminology.

later released from this injunction. Appeasement of God or the gods, a world beyond human cognition and interpretable only by the clergy, the shaman, and other emissaries to the supernatural, was supported by a traditional world view that looked to the "wisdom" of the past rather than attempt a rational interpretation of the present for guidance (see Fox, 1976, pp. 7–12).

Application of the theological approach to crime control is not confined to the past but can be illustrated in the modern era by the ecclesiarchy (state-church fusion) in Iran under the Ayatollah Khomeini, in which criminals or opponents of the state were summarily subject to torture, death, or the "wrath of Allah." The primary challenges to theological approaches to explaining reality were philosophical arguments that sought worldly, rational, secular explanations for human fate. The reasons for crime and criminality were to be found not in the supernatural, but the natural world. Figure 4.2 provides a chronology of major developments in criminological theory.

Classical Theory

Classical theory in Criminology refers to an approach that emphasizes free will and rationality on the part of the criminal actor.

Prior to the formulation and acceptance of **classical theory,** the administration of criminal justice in Europe was cruel, uncertain, and unpredictable. In England alone in the early nineteenth century there were over one hundred crimes punishable by the death penalty (Heath, 1963, p. 98). Penal policy was designed to control the "dangerous classes," the mass of propertyless peasants, workers, and unemployed. Emerging liberal philosophies espoused by such writers as Locke, Hobbes, and Rousseau advocated the "natural rights of man" and reason as a guide to regulating human conduct. This Enlightenment of

FIGURE 4.2 Chronology of Selected Important Events in Criminology

1750 B.C.	Hammurabi's Code	1950	Glueck and Glueck, *Unravelling Juvenile Delinquency*
1766	Beccaria, *On Crime and Punishment*	1951	Lemert, *Social Pathology*
1776	American Revolution	1951	Cohen, *Delinquent Boys*
1787	French Revolution	1958	Vold, *Theoretical Criminology*
1788	Bentham, *Moral Calculus*	1958	Miller, "Lower Class Culture and Delinquency"
1833	Guerry, *An Essay on Moral Statistics*	1964	Eysenck, *Crime and Personality*
1835	Quetelet, *Treatise on Man and the Development of His Faculties*	1967	Reckless, "Containment Theory"
1848	Marx, *Communist Manifesto*	1967	Clinard and Quinney, *Criminal Behavior Systems*
1859	Darwin, *Origin of Species*	1969	Hirschi, *Causes of Delinquency*
1863	Lombroso, *Criminal Man*	1970	Quinney, *The Problem of Crime*
1897	Durkheim, *Suicide*	1971	Chambliss and Seidman, *Law, Order and Power*
1910	Dugdale, *The Jukes*	1973	Bandura, *Aggression*
1913	Goring, *The English Convict*	1973	Taylor, Walton and Young, *The New Criminology*
1916	Bonger, *Criminality and Economic Conditions*	1975	Adler, *Sisters in Crime*
1920	Freud, *General Introduction to Psychoanalysis*	1979	Cohen and Felson, *Routine Activities*
1925	Park, Burgess, and McKenzie, *The City*	1980	Clinard and Yeager, *Corporate Crime*
1937	Tannenbaum, "Dramatization of Evil"	1984	Lea and Young, *Left Realism*
1937	Sutherland, *The Professional Thief*	1988	Daly and Chesney-Lind, *Feminist Theory*
1938	Merton, *Social Theory and Social Structure*	1991	Quinney and Pepinsky, *Peacemaking*
1939	Hooton, *The American Criminal*	1992	Clarke, Situational *Crime Prevention*
1939	Sutherland, "Differential Association"	1993	Messner and Rosenfeld, *Crime and the American Dream*
1940	Sheldon, "Somatotypes"		

the seventeenth and eighteenth centuries questioned the power of the clergy and aristocracy and gave birth to the American and French revolutions.

Cesare Beccaria. Italian Cesare Beccaria (1738–1794), actually Cesare Bonesana, the Marquis of Beccaria, was, along with British philosopher Jeremy Bentham (1748–1832), the principal advocate of the classical school of criminological theory. Beccaria's (1963) essay entitled *On Crimes and Punishments,* originally published in 1764, had a profound impact on continental European as well as on Anglo-American jurisprudence. His essential point is expressed in the concluding paragraph of this work (Beccaria, p. 99):

> From what has thus far been demonstrated, one may deduce a general theorem of considerable utility, though hardly conformable with custom, the usual legislator of nations; it is this: In order for punishment not to be, in every instance, an act of violence of one or of many against a private citizen, it must be essentially public, prompt, necessary, the least possible in the given circumstances, proportionate to the crimes, dictated by the laws.

Beccaria was appalled by the arbitrary nature of the European judicial and penal systems of his time, which were unpredictably harsh, exacted confessions by means of torture, and were completely subject to the whim of authorities. Since potential criminals had no way of anticipating the nature of the criminal law and its accompanying penalty if violated, punishment had little deterrent value. Beccaria was primarily interested in reforming the cruel, unnecessary, and unpredictable nature of punishment, feeling that it made little sense to punish lawbreakers with unjust laws (Vold and Bernard, 1986, p. 29). Beccaria was responsible for the abolition of torture as a legitimate means of exacting confessions. "Let the punishment fit the crime" is a succinct summation of Beccaria's argument.

Jeremy Bentham. Beccaria's British counterpart, Jeremy Bentham (1823), borrowed from Beccaria the notion that laws should provide "the greatest happiness shared by the greatest number" (Beccaria, 1963, p. 8). Bentham has been called an advocate of "utilitarian hedonism" or "felicific calculus" or "penal pharmacy." *Utilitarianism* is a practical philosophical view that claims "we should always act so as to produce the greatest possible ratio of good to evil for all concerned" (Barry, 1983, p. 106). One of Bentham's best known contributions to criminology was his invention of the "panopticon" (from the Greek, meaning "all seeing"). The panopticon, or "inspection house," was envisioned as a circular prison with a glass roof, featuring a central grand tower from which inspectors could observe all cells located around the perimeter. While prisons incorporating this design were built in both England and the United States, the plans were later found impractical and modified (Hagan, 1996a).

The classical theorists viewed individuals as acting as a result of "free will" and as being motivated by **hedonism.** The latter refers to a "pleasure principle"—*the assumption that the main purpose of life is to maximize pleasure while minimizing pain.* Individuals are viewed as entirely rational in this decision-making process in which they will attempt to increase pleasure, even illicit desires, until the anticipated pain to be derived from a particular activity appears to outweigh the expected enjoyment. In a work entitled *Seductions of Crime: Moral and Sensual Attractions in Doing Evil,* Jack Katz's (1988) research based on interviews with career criminals supports Beccaria's notion of the pleasure or thrill of evil outweighing the fear of punishment. Image, danger, glamour, the excitement of crime overshadow any desire for a successful life in straight society. In assessing Katz's theory, McCarthy (1995) noted that such thrill-related property crime is influenced by age, gender, and strain associated with inadequate economic opportunities.

Critique of Classical Theory. The *classical school* and the writing of Beccaria in particular were to lay the cornerstone of modern Western criminal law as it became formulated from 1770 to 1812. The characteristics of modern Western criminal law—politicality, uniformity, specificity, and described penal sanctions—are in essence called for in Beccaria's essay. The *French Declaration of the Rights of Man* (Jacoby, 1979, p. 215), which was passed by the revolutionary National Assembly of France in 1789, included the statement: "The law ought to impose no other penalties but such as are absolutely and evidently necessary; and no one ought to be punished, but in virtue of a law promulgated before the offense, and legally applied." The Eighth Amendment to the U.S. Constitution, prohibiting "cruel and unusual punishment," was also a Beccarian legacy.

Some recent analysis suggests that the importance of Beccaria's works may have been exaggerated and that he was actually less important than other social reformers of the eighteenth century such as Voltaire and Bentham (Newman and Marongiu, 1990). Beirne (1991) claims that Beccaria's famous treatise *Dei Delitti e Delle Pene* (*On Crimes and Punishments*) was the application to crime policy, not of rationality and humanism, but of the Scottish-inspired "science of man," which emphasized utilitarianism and determinism. He felt that Beccaria was less of an advocate of free will than has been supposed and that his writings exhibited much determinism (Beirne, p. 812).

The revolutionary and liberating impact of the ascendancy of classical theory in reforming Western jurisprudence is now taken for granted; but without the fundamental changes classical theory introduced, the remaining criticisms and subsequent modifications would not have been possible. However, classical theory contained the seeds of its own demise. While Justitia, the blind goddess of justice carefully weighing the evidence irrespective of the violator, is an appealing symbol, classical theory by its very insistence

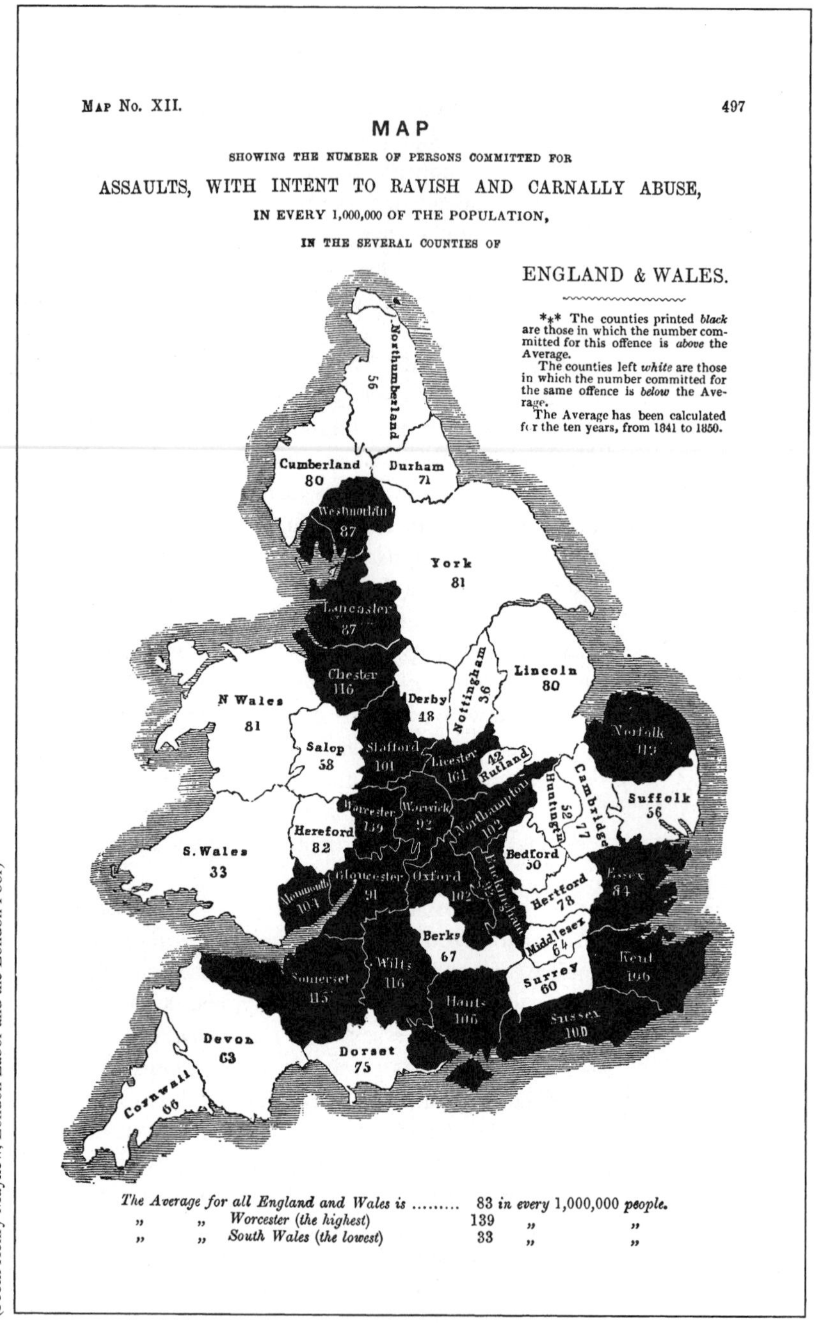

(From Henry Mayhew, London Labor and the London Poor)

An aerial map from Mayhew's London Labour and the London Poor depicts the crime rate in the countries of England and Wales from 1841 to 1850.

on equality of punishment proposes inequality. Should minors or the insane be treated in the same manner as others? Should repeat offenders be accorded the same sanctions as first offenders for an equivalent act? Thomas and Hepburn (1983, p. 137) state:

> Contemporary criminologists tend to assign little importance to [classical theory's] concepts and ideas. Perhaps the two major reasons are that it focuses our attention on criminal law rather than criminal behavior and that it is based on a speculative set of philosophical premises rather than a sound theory that could be verified or refuted by the collection of systematic empirical evidence.

Application of the pure classical theory would rob judges of discretionary power, and seems to rest on a simplistic assumption of the ability to exactly measure individual conceptions of pain and pleasure. Recent revivals in the United States of determinate sentencing and mandatory punishments for specific offenses are remnants of classical theory. Although theoretically appealing because of the essential cookbook application of graduated punishment reflecting the seriousness of crime, implementation becomes problematic for reasons already described: the quantification of such acts and their perpetrators defies such a simplistic scheme.

Neoclassical Theory

The **neoclassical** school basically *admitted environmental, psychological, and other mitigating circumstances as modifying conditions to classic doctrine.* The beginnings of this approach can be found in the later writings of Cesare Lombroso (1835–1909) and in those of his students, Ferri and Garofalo, to be discussed shortly. Beginning in the late 1960s—particularly in the writings of economist Gary Becker (1968), James Q. Wilson (1983a and 1983b), and Ernest Van den Haag (1966)—a resurgence in neoclassical doctrine can be noted. Becker advocated a "cost/benefit" analysis of crime, reminiscent of hedonistic doctrine. Becker argues that individuals freely choose crime based on their estimate of their likelihood of being caught. Disappointed with criminology's overconcern with the search for basic causes of crime, Wilson (1975) proposed a *policy analysis approach,* applied research that is less concerned with finding "causes" and more concerned with "what works." These writers have sparked an interest in the abandonment of treatment and rehabilitation and in a return to the classical punishment model. Often ignored by devotees of such theories are the very limited categories of crime such theorists, in fact, address. Wilson (1975), for instance, quite clearly indicates that this call for incapacitation of offenders (criminals in jail can no longer victimize) is applicable to what we have described as conventional property offenders or common burglars and thieves. Although a more practical, policy-oriented approach is needed, what is disturbing in such theories is the relatively conservative ignorance of criminogenic, social structural conditions, as well as an often cavalier disregard for theoretical approaches to crime causation. While the neoclassicists argue that less theory and more action is needed, they at times ignore the fact that the basic theoretical underpinnings of their own theories are rooted in assumptions of eighteenth-century hedonism, utilitarianism, and free will. On balance, however, they make a key point: that one need not have a basic explanation of cause or wait for one in order to meet pressing policy needs that cannot wait for final explanation.

In another neoclassical theory, Cornish and Clarke's (1986) "rational choice theory" proposes that offenders weigh the opportunities, costs, and benefits of particular crimes. The argument by rational choice theorists is not that individuals are purely rational in their decision making, but rather that they do consider the costs and benefits. A number of factors may constrain choice, such as social factors, individual traits, and attitudes toward crime. Rational choice theorists also argue for a "crime-specific approach" to crime; that is, the circumstances involved in the typical burglary may differ from robbery or domestic assault. Research support has been mixed for rational choice theory. While consideration is given for the cost and benefit of crime, many criminals do not carefully plan their crimes. Changing such opportunity structures (e.g., creating defensible space and target hardening) may discourage potential offenders. Analyses of offenders' motivations, however, have shown that many act impulsively and fail to fully consider negative possibilities (Piliavin et al., 1986; Tunnell, 1991). VANTAGE POINT 4.2 presents an application of rational choice theory to controlling gang violence in Los Angeles.

VANTAGE POINT 4.2

"Designing Out" Gang Homicides and Street Assaults

Situational Crime Prevention

One of the leading theories of criminal opportunity is "situational crime prevention." Developed by criminologist Ronald V. Clarke, the theory is based on the assumption that crime can be reduced by pin pointing and blocking the forces that facilitate would-be offenders' criminal acts. Would-be offenders, the theory proposes, make rational choices in planning their criminal acts. For example, gangs may choose a particular street to commit a crime because they rationally determine that the way the street is situated provides them with ready access and exit, thereby creating an opportunity to more easily elude arrest.

Applying the model to gangs, the LAPD (Los Angeles Police Dept.) assumed that they did in fact make a "rational choice" about whether to engage in a particular act of criminal violence and whether to do so in a particular neighborhood setting. Evidence to support the theory has come from studies of residential burglary, shoplifting, and other crimes, but OCDS was an initial attempt to apply situational crime prevention to gang violence.

Issues and Findings

Discussed in this Brief. The use of a deceptively simple tactic, traffic barriers, to block automobile access to streets as a way of reducing gang violence. The tactic was used in a crime-plagued area of Los Angeles that had experienced the city's highest level of drive-by shootings, gang homicides, and street assaults. The National Institute of Justice (NIJ)-sponsored evaluation of Operation Cul de Sac (OCDS), as the program was called, examined whether the tactic could reduce gang crime.

Key Issues. OCDS was based on the theory of situational crime prevention, which postulates that crime occurs partly as the result of opportunity and can be reduced by first identifying and then blocking these opportunities rather than attempting to eliminate "root causes." The Los Angeles Police Department noted that in the OCDS target area gang crime clustered on the periphery of neighborhoods linked to major roadways; police set up traffic barriers as a way to block the opportunities for crime the roadways created. The evaluation sought to determine whether these street closures could help to "design out" gang crime.

Key Findings. In its 2 years of operation, 1990 and 1991, OCDS appeared to reduce violent crime.

- The number of homicides and street assaults fell significantly in both years and rose after the program ended.
- Property crime decreased substantially during the first year of the program, but it also decreased in the comparison area where was no OCDS, indicating that some factor or factors other than the traffic barriers were responsible for the reduction in the OCDS site.
- In the second year of the program, property crime rose, suggesting the street closures affected only violent crime.
- Crime was not displaced to other areas. Violent crime fell, not only in the OCDS area, but also in contiguous areas. This may be because the areas of potential displacement are the turf of rival gangs. As such they would be off-limits to gangs that might want to enter new territory when the traffic barriers reduced their opportunities to commit crime on their own turf.
- Traffic barriers can be used as part of an approach to maximize neighborhood residents' defensible space by increasing their span of control. Zones configured with the barriers heighten the visibility of suspect activities. They can be particularly effective when combined with "natural guardians"—people who serve as informal sources of surveillance and social control.

Although these findings indicate traffic barriers may work to reduce violent crime, it should be kept in mind that the experiment was conducted at only one site. Replications of OCDS and further evaluations are needed to fully test the effectiveness of the tactic.

Target Audience. Police chiefs, sheriffs, urban designers and planners, crime prevention organizers.

Source: James Lasley. 1998. " 'Designing Out' Gang Homicides and Street Assaults." *National Institute of Justice Research in Brief.* November.

InfoTrac College Edition Research

Find and discuss a recent article on "environmental design and crime."

Ecological Theory

While some would point to Cesare Beccaria and his writing as the beginning point of criminology, his primary interest was not so much in the analysis of crime and criminals as in the reform of criminal law and punishment. Others point to the writings of Cesare Lombroso, to be discussed shortly, and view the century between the works of the two Cesares as a criminological Dark Age. On the contrary, the writings and research of A. M. Guerry (1802–1866) of France and Adolphe Quetelet (1796–1874) of Belgium qualify them as the "fathers of modern criminology" (Vold and Bernard, 1986, p. 39; Gibbons, 1982, p. 17). Thomas and Hepburn (1983, p. 138) best reflect this writer's view:

> It is hard to understand why so many criminologists persist in their apparent conviction that scientific criminology was not to be found until Lombroso. . . . Nevertheless, the wealth of scientific analyses published by those we can classify as members of the statistical [ecological] school are commonly ignored while the often absurd and poorly executed work of Lombroso is considered to be the first true criminological analysis.

Another explanation for the popularity and widespread acceptance of the Lombrosians and the relative obscurity of the early ecological theorists might be the fact that the latter were not translated into English until much later (p. 152).

The **ecological school of criminological theory** is also referred to as the statistical, geographic, or cartographic school. *Ecology* is that branch of biology that deals with the interrelationships between organisms and their environment. **Human ecology** deals with the interrelationship between human organisms and the physical environment. This school was called *statistical* because it was the first to attempt to apply official data and statistics to the problem of explaining criminality. The labels *geographical* and *cartographic* have been assigned because writers in this group tended to rely on maps and aerial data in their investigations.

A. M. Guerry and Adolphe Quetelet. Sometime after 1825, A. M. Guerry published what many regard as the first book in "scientific criminology," *An Essay on Moral Statistics* (Guerry, 1833) (Vold, 1979, p. 167). Guerry was more cartographic in his approach, relying exclusively on shaded areas of maps in order to describe and analyze variations in French official crime statistics. Since he employed these sections of maps and used them as his principal units of analysis, he is often viewed as the founder of the ecological or cartographic school of criminology (Thomas and Hepburn, 1983, p. 139). Comparing poverty with crime, Guerry found that the wealthier areas of France had higher property crime. Urban, industrial, northern regions had more property crime than rural, southern regions (Courtright and Mutchnick, 1999). He concluded that the higher rates were due to greater opportunity. Thus, burglary and theft occurred where more goods were available. Violent and personal crimes were higher in rural areas and southern regions. These rates were consistent annually.

Guerry was also credited with being a pioneer in comparative crime statistics in comparing English and French rates. Schafer (1969, p. 76) indicated that Guerry was the first to use "moral statistics" in that he applied cartographic methods to the state of morals in terms of crime (Courtright and Mutchnick, 1999, p. 3). Another adherent of this school was Henry Mayhew (1862a), who in his *London Labour and the London Poor* made extensive use of official statistics and aerial maps.

Quetelet (Lambert Adolphe Jacques Quetelet) was the first to take advantage of the criminal statistics that were beginning to become available in the 1820s (Radzinowicz and King, 1977, p. 64; Beirne, 1987). He was the first scientific criminologist, employing an approach to his subject matter that was very similar to that of modern criminologists, and is the "father" (parent) of modern sociological and psychological statistics (Thomas and Hepburn, 1983, pp. 140, 145; Schafer, 1969, pp. 118–20; Mannheim, 1965, pp. 96–98). Challenging the classical school's view that individuals exercise free will in deciding on their actions, Quetelet insisted on the impact of group factors and characteristics. In his *Treatise on Man and the Development of His Faculties* ([1835] 1969), which was translated into English in 1842, Quetelet noted that there was a "remarkable consistency" with which crimes appeared annually and varied with respect to age, sex, economic conditions, and other sociological variables. This consistency in group behavior, in crime rates, and the like, speaks against crime being solely a matter of individual choice. He argues (Quetelet, 1969, pp. 299–308):

> We can count in advance how many individuals will soil their hands with the blood of their fellows, how many will be swindlers, how many prisoners, almost as we can number in advance the births and deaths that will take place. . . . Society carries within itself, in some sense, the seeds of all the crimes which are going to be committed, together with the facilities necessary for their development.

He described this constancy of crime as the annual "budget" of crime which must be paid by society with remarkable consistency. In a sense, the stage and script are provided by society and only the faces playing the individual characters change.

In his *Research on the Propensity of Crime at Different Ages* (1984) he viewed age as the greatest predictor of crime, with crime peaking at age 25. Courtright and Mutchnick (1999, p. 4) point out that, in examining poverty, relative economic inequality was the critical variable. Crime increases when an individual "passes in an abrupt way from a state of ease to misery and to insufficiency in satisfying all the needs which he has created" (Quetelet, 1984, p. 67). Schafer (1969, p. 76) even claims that, due to his extensive use of crime statistics and statistical predictions, Quetelet was recognized by some as the "father of statistics."

Some of Quetelet's findings included the propensity for crime among younger adults and males, and the tendency of crimes against persons to increase in summer and property crimes to predominate in winter. In what is called his **"thermic law" of crime,** he claimed that *crimes against persons increase in equatorial climates while property crimes are most prevalent in colder climates* (Fox, 1976, p. 64). Social conditions such as heterogeneity of population tended to be associated with increased crime, as did poverty—although the latter not in the manner usually supposed. Noting that some of the poorest provinces of France also had very low crime rates, Quetelet anticipated the concept of "relative deprivation" by suggesting, not absolute poverty, but a gap between status and expectation as a variable in crime causation (Quetelet, 1969, pp. 82–96).

Critique of Ecological Theory. The work of Guerry and Quetelet was done nearly half a century prior to the writings of Lombroso, to be discussed shortly, who is often viewed ("the Lombrosian myth") as "the father of criminology" (Lindesmith and Levin, 1937). Lombroso's principal work *L'Uomo Delinquente* (*The Criminal Man*), first published in 1876, emphasized the notion of "born criminality." Rather than representing progress in criminological investigation, the dominance of the early positivists such as Lombroso may have set the field on a half-century (plus) journey guided by arcane and ultimately useless concepts. The superordination of the early positivists may have represented an ideological coup d'etat in which medical concepts and *psychologism* (a reduction of analysis solely to the individual level) temporarily retarded the early mainstream sociological efforts of the ecologists. Pointing the finger at the individual, rather than social conditions, as had Guerry and Quetelet, was intellectually acceptable to the wealthy, who preferred to view criminality as an individual failing of the dangerous classes rather than as a societal shortcoming (Vold and Bernard, 1986, p. 40; Lindesmith and Levin, 1937; Radzinowicz, 1966).

On this point, Radzinowicz (pp. 38–39) states:

> This way of looking at crime [the ecological school's approach] as the product of society was hardly likely to be welcome, however, at a time when a major concern was to hold down the "dangerous classes" . . . who had so miserable a share in the accumulating wealth of the industrial revolution that they might at any time break out in revolt in France. . . .
>
> It served the interests and relieved the conscience of those at the top to look upon the dangerous classes as an independent category, detached from the prevailing social conditions . . . a race apart, morally depraved and vicious. . . .

The social statisticians with their emphasis on social facts, statistics, the use of official data, and external social factors were perhaps ahead of their time. Shortcomings in their analysis, such as lack of full awareness of the inadequacies of official statistics and appropriate use of statistics themselves, are excusable given their pioneering efforts and the state of knowledge of the time. The ecological school represented a critical transition from the philosophical and purely theoretical approach of Beccaria to the more scientific criminological approaches of the twentieth century.

Other Geographical Theories. The ancient origin of human interest in astrology and the assumed role of astrological bodies on human behavior represent just one of many attempts to predict human emotion and activity on the basis of outside physical forces—the moon, the weather, climate, and the like. The word "lunatic," from the Latin word *luna,* or moon, indicates the belief that human minds can be affected by phases of the moon. This is illustrated by legends and myths such as those about *les lupins* (werewolves) in French folklore. These creatures supposedly appeared on moonlit nights (Cohen, 1979, p. 87) and were dramatically presented in fiction in the introduction to the popular 1943 Universal Pictures film, *The Wolf Man:*

> Even a man who is pure in heart
> And says his prayers by night
> Can become a wolf when the wolf bane blooms
> And the moon is full and bright.

Cohen (pp. 84–89) cites studies of mental hospital records that claim more admissions of mental patients during new and full moons, as well as a study by a suicide prevention center and one by a coroner's office, both indicating more successful attempts at suicides around the full-moon period. The most frequently cited recent study of this type is Lieber and Sherin's (1972) research on lunar cycles and homicides. They note that synodic cycles (phases of the moon) influence physical variables such as gravitation and atmospheric pressure, which, in turn, influence human behavior. For instance, tidal periodicity is greatest during the new and full moon because of stronger gravitational influences. Assuming such forces may also affect human behavior, Lieber and Sherin analyzed homicide statistics for Dade County (Miami), Florida, and Cuyahoga County (Cleveland), Ohio, and found a statistically significant difference at full and new moon periods for the Dade County figures and a high, but not statistically significant, relationship for Cuyahoga County. Indicating that a lunar influence may exist, they explain that the differences could be due to the fact that Florida is closer to the equator and would be more influenced by the gravitational pull of the moon. Other analyses of these same correlations, however, fail to support their hypothesis (Nettler, 1982, vol. 1, p. 31; Pokorny, 1964; Pokorny and Jachimczyk, 1974). Most such studies do not show a relationship and, although more replications are needed, criminological interest in this line of investigation has waned. Criminologists interested in geographical and ecological impacts on criminality have focused their attention instead on the social as well as artificial environment. "The Chicago school" of sociology and its contribution to U.S. criminology will be detailed in the next chapter as an illustration of such an approach.

In examining a related line of inquiry, Fox (1976, p. 64) tells us that Quetelet's "thermic law" of crime was actually borrowed from Montesquieu, who claimed that criminality increases as one nears the equator, while drunkenness increases in proximity to the poles. Examination of official statistics both internationally and within the United States, France, Great Britain, and Canada seems to generally support this hypothesis (see Brantingham and Brantingham, 1984, pp. 251–96). While statistical analysis of official crime reports such as the UCR indicates that rapes and other violent crimes are more prevalent in warmer months and that property crimes such as shoplifting are heaviest in December (Christmas season), these increases are more likely due to cultural rather than climatic effects (Cheatwood, 1988; LeBeau, 1988). Brantingham and Brantingham (1984, p. 296), in analyzing spatial patterns in crime, indicate:

> Different crime patterns are associated with different demographic, economic, and social profiles. Homicide and assault are associated with high proportions of minority population, with poverty and low income, with low-status jobs and low education, and with income inequality. Robbery is highest in large, dense cities that rely on public transit and have high levels of pedestrian traffic. Burglary and theft rates are highest in cities with growing populations, with growing suburbs, and with low density.

In a related manner one can find that combinations of hot weather and foul air (polluted with airborne toxins such as ozone) may provoke violence, particularly family disputes.

> . . . the findings which link high levels of both pollution and crime do fit into the growing knowledge that, in the long run, many chemicals can cause nerve damage and behavioral changes.
>
> For example, scientists have known for years that mercury causes brain damage: the 19th century "mad hatters" stammered, twitched and trembled from inhaling mercury vapors in London hat factories. Today, many factories use masks and protective hoods to shield workers from the worst effects of chemicals (Londer, 1987, p. 6).

While increased social interaction during warmer months in part explains increased violent crime, the most pronounced effect appears during heat waves, which might suggest that heat itself promotes aggression (Gladwell, 1990). Block and Block (1988) found that the rate of violent crime in the Uniform Crime Reports showed a stronger seasonal variation than that in the National Crime Victimization Survey. This may be because such incidents are less private and more likely to come to police attention in warmer months. Cohn (1990) found that assaults, burglary, collective violence, and rape increased along with a temperature up to about 85 degrees Fahrenheit. The relationship with homicide was uncertain, while there was no relationship between temperature and robbery, larceny, or motor vehicle theft.

While recognizing that climate itself is not a major factor but rather a precipitating or mitigating circumstance in deviant behavior, Lab and Hirschel (1988a and 1988b) emphasize studying the impact of the actual weather rather than seasonal or monthly data. After examining precipitation, humidity, temperature, and barometric pressure, they indicate that "not a single text or journal article substantiates the lack of a relationship between weather and crime" (1988a, p. 282). They conclude that the potential for weather conditions playing a part in criminal activity is related to the perspective of "routine activities" (LeBeau and Langworthy, 1986), in which criminal behavior is viewed as part of normal, everyday behavior. These social-ecological impacts on criminal behavior will be discussed as well as critiqued in greater scope in the discussion of the "Chicago school" in the next chapter.

Forerunners of Modern Criminological Thought

The three thinkers who would have a critical impact upon the shaping of social ideas, as well as criminological inquiry, in the twentieth century did not even specifically address the issue of crime. Their ideas, however, would influence criminological theorists in a profound manner. The first figure was *Karl Marx* (1818–1883), whose *Communist Manifesto* (1848) and *Das Kapital* (*Capital*) (1867)—the former coauthored with Friedrich Engels—emphasized the economic basis of societal conflict and would give birth to the economic school of criminology. The second was *Charles Darwin* (1809–1882), whose *Origin of Species* (1859) and *Descent of Man* (1871) contained theories of *evolution,* natural selection, and survival of the fittest that would heavily inspire the biological positivists, to be discussed shortly. The third was *Sigmund Freud* (1856–1939), whose many volumes dealing with *unconscious sexual motivation* would influence not only psychiatry but also the psychological positivists. These themes of economics, biology, and sex underlie a large number of the criminological theories to be discussed.

Economic Theory

Karl Marx. Karl Marx, the inspirational figure behind most economic criminological theories, was an economic determinist. He insisted that the economic substructure determines the nature of all other institutions and social relationships in society. In his view, the emergence of capitalism produces economic inequality in which the **proletariat** (*workers*) are exploited by the **bourgeoisie** (*owners or capitalist class*). This exploitation creates poverty and also is at the root of other social problems. Since Marx did not specifically address the issue of crime, Marxist criminologists draw on his economic and philosophic writings and apply them to the crime issue.

Marx viewed the history of all existing societies as one of class struggle. Influenced by the writings of the German philosopher Hegel, Marx described this conflict as a dialectical process in which theses (existing ideas or institutions) spawn their opposites, or antitheses, until a final synthesis (new idea or social order) emerges. Thus for Marx, capitalism (thesis) breeds its own destruction by giving birth to a proletarian revolution (antithesis) and finally a new world order of socialism (synthesis). Since Marx applied Hegel's theory to the material world, this is often described as Marx's theory of dialectical materialism. For Marx the resolution of social problems such as crime would be achieved through the creation of a socialist society characterized by communal ownership of the means of production and an equal distribution of the fruits of these labors.

Willem Bonger. The foremost early Marxist criminologist was the Dutch philosopher Willem Bonger (1876–1940), whose most noted work was *Criminality and Economic Conditions* (1969), which first appeared in 1910. Bonger viewed the criminal law as primarily protecting the interests of the propertied class. In contrast to precapitalistic societies, which he claimed were characterized by consensus and altruism, capitalistic societies emphasized egoism (selfishness). Capitalism was viewed as precipitating crime by creating unequal access to the necessities of life as well as by viewing success in economic competition as a sign of status (Turk, 1969b). Bonger's work provides a very detailed review of a large number of works of the time that examined the impact of economic conditions on crime, a persistent theme since early times. In referring to the early Marxist orientation, Schafer (1969, p. 76) indicates:

> Napolean Colajanni, Enrico Ferri and Willem Bonger and a number of others in the last 150 years represented the same "new" trends that our radicals seem to claim as their invention. The classical authors presented these proposals in a scholarly fashion quite often superior to that of our modern radicals; in fact

Left: Cesare Lombroso. Right: Actor Kevin Pollak playing a "criminal type"—"hardware specialist" Tod Hockney in the movie The Usual Suspects.

> almost nothing is said today in this line that was not already written in criminology a century ago.

Greenberg (1981, p. 11) points out that a large number of early Marxist thinkers did not seriously consider the crime issue, viewing it with typical "Marxian contempt for the lumpen proletariat—the beggars, pimps and criminals" in capitalist society. Many writers with a distinctive Marxian and/or economic view of criminality are cited in the Bonger work (1969), although as Greenberg correctly indicates, Bonger is often mistakenly viewed as the only early Marxist criminologist.

Some of the basic claims made by Bonger regarding criminality included (Turk, 1969b, pp. 7–12):

- Notions of what constitutes crime vary among societies and reflect existing notions of morality.
- Criminal law serves the interest of the ruling class in capitalist systems and is enforced by force rather than by consensus.
- Hedonism (pleasure seeking) is natural among people, but capitalism encourages egoism (selfish individualism) to an extreme and to the disadvantage of the society and the poor.
- All groups are prone to crime in capitalist society, but seldom are the crimes of the wealthy punished.
- Poverty resulting from capitalism encourages crime. The unequal distribution of rewards and encouragement of egoistic material accumulation encourage crime.
- Most crimes (other than those due to mental problems) would be eliminated in a socialist system in which the goods and wealth of a society would be equally distributed.

The writings of the early Marxist criminologists were more historical, analytic-inductive, and descriptive than empirical. The early Marxist theorists had the luxury of making theoretical predictions without empirical referents at the time. Marx and Bonger predicted the hypothetical benefits of a socialist state, comparing these with the evils of early capitalism, which were a grim reality. Shortcomings of socialism could not be observed. Modern radical and Marxist criminologists no longer have this luxury, as we will show later in discussing the conflict and radical schools of criminology.

Positivist Theory

Positivism is a philosophical approach proposed by French sociologist Auguste Comte (1798–1857) and stated in the title of his work *A System of Positive Polity* (1877), originally published in 1851. Comte proposed the use of empirical (quantitative) or scientific investigation for the improvement of society. Taylor et al. (1973, p. 22) indicate that the **basic premises of positivism** are: **measurement** (*quantification*), **objectivity** (*neutrality*), and **causality** (*determinism*). In applying Comte's approach, criminological positivists emphasize a consensus world view, a focus on the criminal actor rather than the criminal act, a deterministic model (usually biological or psychological in nature), a strong faith in the scientific expert, and a belief in rehabilitation of "sick" offenders rather than punishment of "rational" actors. There are three elements to the *positivistic approach,* which stresses a scientific rather than a philosophical orientation:

1. application of the scientific method
2. discovery and diagnosis of pathology (sickness)
3. treatment (therapy or corrections)

Through the systematic application of the scientific method, the positivists seek to uncover the basic cause of crime and then to prescribe appropriate treatments in order to cure the individual deviant. This section will examine precursors to positivism as well as the major types of positivism: early biological positivism, recent biological positivism, and psychological positivism.

Precursors of Positivism. Prior to and competing with emergent positivism were various popular pseudosciences, some of which had existed since ancient times. **Astrology** had been used to predict human behavior by *studying the alignment of the stars.* The Copernican revolution and the realization that the earth did not occupy a fixed place in the universe discredited the basic premises of astrology leaving it as a "hokum device" for fortune tellers and their superstitious clients.

Similar ideas whose time was rapidly passing were phrenology, physiognomy, and palmistry. **Phrenology** attempted to determine intelligence and personality on the basis of the size and shape of the skull and posited that certain areas of the brain corresponded to various psychological and intellectual characteristics. Writers such as Franz Gall (1758–1828) measured bumps on the head in order to identify brain development. Since sections of the brain do not completely govern specific personality characteristics and could hardly be analyzed by measuring configurations of skulls, phrenology was rapidly replaced by the more scientific methods of emergent positivism.

Physiognomy involved measuring facial and other body characteristics as indicative of human personality, while **palmistry** was concerned with "palm reading," analyzing a person's character and future by examining the lines on the palm. The fact that palmistry is not dead is illustrated by a brochure this writer received advertising a book by Paul Gabriel Tesla entitled *Crime and Mental Disease in the Hand: A Proven Guide for the Identification and Pre-Identification of Criminality, Psychosis and Mental Defectiveness* (1990). These theories have been discredited simply because their proponents were unable to provide any proof of accuracy in their forecasts and were rapidly overtaken by developments in modern biology and the social sciences.

Biological Positivism. As previously indicated, the works of Charles Darwin, beginning in the mid-nineteenth century, had a profound impact on theory in the social sciences as well as on criminology. Concepts such as evolution, natural selection, survival of the fittest, and human genetic connections to a savage past captured the imaginations of theorists in the young social sciences, including criminology.

Cesare Lombroso. *Cesare Lombroso* (1835–1909) is sometimes called "the father of criminology." In this writer's and others' opinions (Thomas and Hepburn, 1983; Mannheim, 1965, pp. 96–98; Lindesmith and Levin, 1937), this is inaccurate, but he was certainly the most influential figure in biological positivism. Although he is best known for his early work—which gives an overly simplistic picture compared with his later, more sophisticated writing—Lombroso's ideas are important because of the large number of adherents and subsequent research he inspired. His most important work was *L'uomo Delinquente* (*The Criminal Man*) (Lombroso, 1911), first published in 1876. Lombroso was highly influenced by Darwin's theory of evolution, and this led him to the development of his theory of **atavism**—that criminals were "throwbacks" to an earlier and more primitive evolutionary period. Such born criminals could be identified by certain **physical stigmata,** outward appearances, particularly facial, which tended to distinguish them from noncriminals. He claimed to have made his discovery almost by serendipity during an autopsy of a criminal that he was performing in the course of his duties as a prison physician (Lombroso, 1911, p. xiv, in Wolfgang, 1960, p. 184):

> This was not merely an idea, but a revelation. At the sight of that skull, I seemed to see all of a sudden, lighted up as a vast plain under a flaming sky, the problem of the nature of the criminal—an atavistic being who reproduces in his person the ferocious instincts of primitive humanity and the inferior animals. Thus were explained anatomically the enormous jaws, high cheek-bones, prominent superciliary arches, solitary lines in the palms, extreme size of the orbits, handle-shaped or sessile ears found in criminals, savages, and apes, insensibility to pain, extremely acute sight, tattooing, excessive idleness, love of orgies, and the irresistible craving for evil for its own sake, the desire not only to extinguish life in the victim, but to mutilate the corpse, tear its flesh, and drink its blood.

Some examples of *physical stigmata* provided by Lombroso sound similar to characteristics Hollywood directors would search for in casting the villain on the silver screen: heavy jaw and cheekbones, eye defects, large or small ears, strange nose shape, protruding lips, sloped forehead, and the like.

While Lombroso's early work was well received at the time, it is not seriously regarded today. What remains, however, is his emphasis on observation, data collection, and the need to obtain positive facts to support theory. When his theories of atavism came under attack from mounting evidence to the contrary, Lombroso modified his theories, although still maintaining that atavism existed in about a third of all criminals. His other categories were the insane criminal, the epileptic criminal, and the occasional criminal, hardly an exhaustive, comprehensive list of criminal types.

Lombroso's notions of *biological determinism* of criminality were very compatible with the ideological climate of the late nineteenth century, in which the philosophy of social Darwinism provided intellectual backing to the harsh realities of emergent industrial capitalism. **Social Darwinism** claimed that there is a *"survival of the fittest" among human beings and social institutions.* The success or failure of individuals competing in society was not to be interfered with, since success or failure was all part of a natural system of societal evolution. The Lombrosian model, which minimized the importance of social conditions such as inequality and ignored the extensive literature of the ecological school, blamed criminality on the individual rather than the society. This triumph of Lombrosian theory represented a "seizure of power of the medical profession who viewed criminology as a branch of medicine" (Lindesmith and Levin, 1937, p. 669; Bottomley, 1979, p. 44). Criminal behavior was viewed as the actions of "defective" individuals who were unable to adjust to an otherwise healthy society, the unfit in the struggle for survival.

The other two important figures in the Italian or continental school of positivists were Lombroso's students, Enrico Ferri (1856–1929) and Raffaelo Garofalo (1852–1934).

Ferri's *Criminal Sociology* (1917) was first published in 1878, and Garofalo's *Criminology* (1914) was originally published in 1884. Lombroso, Ferri, and Garofalo have been called "the holy three of criminology" by Stephen Schafer (1969, p. 123).

Enrico Ferri proposed four types of criminals: insane, born, occasional, and criminal by passion. He proposed a multiple-factor approach to crime causation, admitting both individual and environmental factors. Often ignored in considering the diversity of Ferri's views was the fact that long before twentieth century criminologists began to consider the shortcomings of official statistics, Ferri (1917, p. 77, cited in Vold, 1979, p. 173) proposed his **"law of criminal saturation".** Like Parkinson, Ferri suggested that *crime expands to fit the amount of control machinery assigned to it.* Traveling widely as a visiting professor throughout Europe and South America and spreading the evangelism of the new positivism, he later became a supporter of Mussolini. Vold (1979, p. 42) indicates: "The end of Ferri's career, ascent to Fascism, highlights one of the problems of positivistic theory, namely, the ease with which it fits into totalitarian patterns of government." Raffaelo Garofalo strongly advocated social Darwinism, the physical elimination of the "unfit" and their offspring, and also became a supporter of Mussolini's fascist regime.

Early positivism contributed theoretically to a scientific approach to criminology and inspired others to study the subject, but otherwise little remains of it in current criminological theory. Lombroso and his colleagues used poor sampling techniques, their findings were statistically insignificant, and they ignored the fact that physical stigmata were most likely environmental defects (due to poverty and malnutrition). Moreover, modern genetics negates their atavism theory. Their findings have been refuted by later investigators, particularly by their earliest and most vehement critic, Charles Goring.

Charles Goring. *Charles Goring* (1870–1919) in 1913 published *The English Convict,* the results of a study begun in 1902 of 3,000 English convicts and comparison groups of college students, hospital patients, and soldiers. He compared these "criminals" and "noncriminals" with respect to physical characteristics, personal histories, and mental qualities. The only differences he was able to discover were that the criminals in general were shorter and weighed less and, most important, were "mentally defective." While refuting Lombroso's theory of distinctive physical characteristics, he launched yet another search for hereditary mental deficiency as the cause of crime.

While Goring refuted Lombroso's notion of physical differences, his own methodology was critically flawed. Eschewing the then available Simon-Binet tests of mental ability, he used his own impressions in order to operationalize the mental ability of his subjects (Reid, 1982, p. 96). The nail in the coffin of Goring's theory was the advent of wide-scale mental testing of U.S. military conscriptees during World War I. Using Goring's definitions of **feeblemindedness,** nearly one-third of the draftees would have been so classified; the standards for such tests were modified as a result. Other studies comparing mental age found no difference in performance between prisoners and the draft army, and one even found that the former performed better. As a result, the notion of feeblemindedness as a cause of criminal behavior was interred in the graveyard of outmoded criminological concepts (Vold, 1979, pp. 85–87). However, later we will examine modern psychometric approaches to crime and current efforts to identify and measure the "criminal personality" that represent more sophisticated revivals of this line of inquiry.

The Jukes and Kallikaks. Other attempts to stress heredity as a source of criminality appeared in two case studies of generations of criminals who were claimed to be examples of degeneracy and depravity. Published only a year after Lombroso's *The Criminal Man,* Robert Dugdale's (1841–1883) *The Jukes* (1877) was a case study of generations of an American family. Tracing more than 1,000 descendants of Ada Jukes (a pseudonym), he found 280 paupers, 60 thieves, 7 murderers, 140 criminals, 40 venereal disease victims, 50 prostitutes, as well as various other deviants—proof positive, he claimed, of inherited criminality.

A similar case study was conducted by Henry Goddard in his *Kallikak Family* (1912), which dealt with the offspring of one Martin Kallikak, a militiaman during the American Revolutionary War. Kallikak fathered a child out of wedlock to a "feebleminded barwench," a large number of whose descendants were feebleminded or deviant. The offspring of his marriage to a "respectable" woman were, on the other hand, all of the highest moral and mental standards. Goddard took these findings as proof positive of the real cause of crime—feeblemindedness, or low mentality. He also was the first to use the term *moron.*

Smith (1985) took a close look at Goddard's Kallikak research and reported that the photographs included in Goddard's book of the "bad" Kallikaks were retouched to make the Kallikaks appear more evil, that the methodology was unscientific, and that the historical data were simply not true (Haas, 1985). Rafter in *White Trash: The Eugenic Family Studies, 1887–1919* (1988), as well as Gould in *The Mismeasure of Man* (1981), document Goddard's deceptions. Gould went to New Jersey and found some of the "bad" Kallikaks, who turned out not to be so bad after all.

The popularity of this type of research can be explained by the fact that ". . . it makes society's so-called superiors feel better about themselves" (Haas, 1985, p. 74). Fancher (1985) indicates ". . . the science of intelligence and its measurement has from the start been dominated by men who have been eager to show that the disenfranchised of society are at the bottom rung of the ladder because they are inherently inferior" (Haas, 1985, p. 74). A more detailed critique of biological positivism will follow shortly.

Earnest Hooton. Goddard attracted a major critic in the form of a neo-Lombrosian, Earnest Hooton (1887–1954), a Harvard anthropologist who in *Crime and the Man* (1939) claimed that, on the basis of a very detailed and extensive study of physical differences between criminals and noncriminals, he had discovered the cause of criminality: *physical inferiority.* His twelve-year study of 14,000 prisoners and 3,200 college students, firemen, and others led him to conclude (1939, p. 309):

> Criminals are organically inferior. Crime is the resultant of the impact of environment upon low grade human organisms. It follows that the elimination of crime can be effected only by the extirpation [eradication] of the physically, mentally, and morally unfit, or by their complete segregation in a socially aseptic environment.

Some physically distinguishing characteristics of Hooton's damned included: tattooing; thin beard and body hair, but thick head hair; straight hair; red-brown hair; blue-gray and mixed eye color; thin eyebrows; low and sloping foreheads; thin lips; pointed and small ears; and long, thin necks with sloping shoulders. These findings and their interpretations could be regarded with a tolerant, mild curiosity if they had appeared in Lombroso's 1876 work, but these were released in 1939 by a professor from one of America's finest universities. Positivism's compatibility with totalitarianism was again illustrated. In the same year that Hooton's work appeared, Hitler had already built experimental gas chambers in mental hospitals and in a two-year period "extirpated" (murdered) 50,000 non-Jewish Germans, a grim prophecy of what was in store for millions of Jews, Eastern Europeans, and groups the Nazis considered to be *Unter menschen* ("subhumans"). Since many criticisms of biological positivism apply in general to all such theories, a detailed critique will be presented at the conclusion of this section.

Body Types. Imagine if, as part of your college freshman orientation, you were asked to report to the college infirmary and have nude photographs taken as part of a research project. From the 1940s through the 1960s, all freshmen at many Ivy League and other prestigious universities complied with just such a request as part of a study on body shape and intelligence. The Smithsonian Institution as late as 1995 was in possession of such photographs, which most likely included Senator Hillary Rodham Clinton, ABC's Diane Sawyer, New York Governor George Pataki, and former President George Bush.

Advocates of attempts to discover distinctive body types and relate them to crime include Ernst Kretschmer (1926), William Sheldon (1940), and Sheldon and Eleanor Glueck (1950). In the best-known of these efforts Sheldon (1940) proposed three **somatotypes**—*body builds that relate to personality characteristics (temperaments).* Endomorphs have soft, round, plump physiques and tend to be relaxed, easygoing, and extroverted; mesomorphs are hard and muscularly built, and are aggressive, assertive, extroverted, and action-seekers; and ectomorphs are thin and fragile of form as well as introverted, sensitive, and subject to worrying. Comparing judgmental samples of "problem" youths with college males, Sheldon claimed that the problem youths tended to be mesomorphic.

Similar studies by the Gluecks (1956) found delinquents to be more mesomorphic than nondelinquents and suggested that this body type may be more suited to the delinquent role, while endomorphs were too slow and ectomorphs too frail to occupy it. In similar research Cortés (1972) found 57 percent of his delinquent sample mesomorphic while only 19 percent of nondelinquents had such body builds. McCandless, Persons, and Roberts (1972) were unable to find any relationship between body type and self-reported delinquency.

Describing much of biocriminology as a "frightening slice of historical criminology," McCaghy (1976b, p. 11) points out:

> Today scarcely a year goes by without some revelation concerning the possible connection between a biological characteristic and human behavior. In fairness to the scientists of today they are generally far less sweeping in their claims than were the researchers of a few decades ago. But the probing of every nook and cranny of the human system goes on. One can only sense the public's anticipation that someday a pill or a swipe of a scalpel will put an end to thievery, homosexuality, and all sorts of behavior.

G. K. Chesterton (1935) felt that such early positivism gave draconian powers to control agents who could use such theories as weapons against the poor (Jenkins, 1982, p. 13). Jenkins quotes Chesterton and offers a summary of his position (1935, pp. 171–77):

> Eugenics, psychology and criminology were pseudo-sciences, and were class ideologies which obviously ignored the interests of the poor. "Crime is not a disease," he wrote. "It is criminology that is a disease." The methodological foundations of the new penology were especially shoddy. Criminal anthropology meant "that very poor men, and especially poor men more or less in the hands of police, can safely have their ears pulled, their skulls measured, their teeth counted, tested or pulled out, so as to establish by scientific methods a sort of composite photograph of all criminals, which was really a composite photograph of all very poor men." He imagines what might happen if a criminologist attempted to apply the same methods to a corrupt American millionaire. The "galleries of criminal types" therefore lacked something vital; "the defect being the entire absence of any types of anti-social activity [among those] who had ever [earned] more than £ 200 a year." This class bias made criminology and sociology no more valid than astrology or alchemy.

The fact that the search goes on can be illustrated by means of a brief treatment of more recent examples of biological positivism. But first a critique of early biological positivism from Lombroso to the Gluecks is in order.

A Critique of Early Biological Positivism. Here are some common problems that nearly all of the early biological positivistic theories share:

- They suggest that one can genetically inherit a trait or propensity (to violate criminal laws) that is socially defined and culturally relative.
- Any biological differences that are found are likely to explain only a minor proportion of criminal behavior compared with social and cultural factors.
- The biopositivists seem to share a conservative consensus world view, an unquestioned acceptance of official definitions of criminality, and the social class bias that crime is primarily to be found among "the dangerous class."
- Most of these studies reflect Reid's "dualistic fallacy" notion, which assumes the mutual exclusivity of criminals (defined as prisoners) and noncriminals (defined as nonprisoners).
- Most of their analyses are plagued by weak operationalization of key concepts such as "feebleminded," "inferior," and "crime."
- Not all biological differences are inherited; many may be due to prenatal environment, injury, and inadequate diet (Vold, 1979, p. 99).
- Modern genetics has simply bypassed many of these simplistic theories. Most modern biologists speak against notions of the inheritance of acquired characteristics, emphasizing instead selective adaptation and mutation (p. 100).
- Many of these studies are based on small and/or inappropriate samples.
- As a result of the dominance of this approach, criminological theory was very likely led down the wrong path. The popularity of many of these theories related to their conservative and individualistic emphasis and to their compatibility with authoritarian and simplistic solutions to the crime problem.

Biology applied to human behavior has a disturbing legacy of misuse. "Social Darwinism" borrowed portions of evolutionary theory and twisted them into justifying class differences (Goode, 2000, p. D9). Social Darwinists argued that the struggle for power and wealth was, to use the words of sociologist Herbert Spencer, "a survival of the fittest." Associations of such theories with Nazi genocide and racist propaganda also led to disrepute.

On balance, however, it should be pointed out that the early biological positivists made some important contributions:

- The commitment of the early positivists to testing their theories by means of experiments, the collection of empirical data, and the employment of statistics are continuing features of modern criminology.
- As the following discussion of neobiopositivism illustrates, one cannot rule out the biomedical approach simply because of this school of thought's association in the past with simplistic theories or the political abuse of such theories by fascist regimes. In *Taboos in Criminology* Sagarin (1980) views the exploration of many of these subject areas as unfortunately representing topics that have recently been declared "untouchable," fruitless, or "mined-out."
- The early positivist approach did influence Western criminal codes and led to modifications in the classical model. Special treatment of juvenile offenders, indeterminate sentences for career criminals, extension of the insanity ruling, probation, corrections, and rehabilitation were all positivist contributions (Radzinowicz and King, 1977, p. 62).

Pierre Van den Berghe in an article entitled "*Bringing Beasts Back In*" (1974) argues that modern criminology, in rejecting early positivism, had swung the other way and was ignoring the biological basis of human behavior. A brief examination of some of the research of modern biological positivists may provide some support for his point. Modern biological positivism replaces simplistic biological determinism with biological approaches that take into account the interplay of biological and socio-environmental factors (Shah and Roth, 1974). Whether criminality can be explained by human nature (genetics, inherited characteristics) or nurture (environment, learning, socialization) is a continuing debate among criminological thinkers.

More Recent Biological Positivism. Shah and Roth (1974) in their review of criminology's **nature versus nurture controversy** (*whether criminality is explained by genetics or environment*) detail a variety of research including biochemical effects, brain disorders, endocrine and hormonal problems, nerve disorders, and other factors that can hardly be ignored in explaining at least a restricted number of individual cases of criminality (Marsh and Katz, 1985).

The newest biological theories (some advocates prefer the name *biosocial theories*) focus on a broad range of biological factors including genetic and environmental. Factors such as head injuries, diets, exposure to toxins such as lead, and birth complications are viewed as affecting the nervous system. "No one argues that there is a gene leading directly to crime" (Cullen and Agnew, 1999, p. 3). Most of these theories recognize that interaction exists between biological factors and the environment and suggest that some biological factors partially account for some crime in some types of offenders.

Brain Disorders. While the early phrenologists were convinced of their ability to map areas of the brain that controlled aspects of personality, modern attempts to probe the brain were begun by the Portuguese physician Antonio Moniz, who beginning in 1935 performed prefrontal **lobotomies** (*destruction of portions of the frontal lobes of the brain*) as a last resort for nonresponsive mental patients. McCaghy (1976b, p. 28) reports:

> His subjects were twenty mental patients who had been unaffected by other treatments; according to Moniz fifteen showed some degree of improvement as a result of the operation. One lobotomized patient was later to pump five bullets into Dr. Moniz, but the operation and variations of it were widely hailed as the answer to many behavioral problems.

An American version used ice picks inserted through eye sockets to destroy brain tissue.

Psychosurgery, surgical alterations of brain tissue in order to alter personality or behavior, became quite popular. Roughly 50,000 such operations were performed in the United States alone from the mid-thirties to the mid-fifties (McCaghy, 1976b). Lobotomized patients were indeed more controllable with respect to behavior, but were often described as resembling hollow shells of human beings, zombies, or human vegetables, devoid of a full range of normal emotions. The impact of lobotomies was illustrated by the fate of the hero in Ken Kesey's novel *One Flew Over the Cuckoo's Nest.*

Consider an illustrative case of the misapplication of such a drastic procedure. In the forties actress Frances Farmer was forced into psychiatric treatment, allegedly for alcoholism and other related problems. Her real "problem" was radicalism, which was "treated" with psychosurgery (Jenkins, 1984, p. 180).

Vernon Mark and Frank Ervin (1970) in *Violence and the Brain* proposed the use of psychosurgical procedures in order to control brain malfunctions, particularly those that may trigger aggressive behavior. Although they have been known to produce some positive results (Brown et al., 1973), biomedical and surgical approaches to criminality represent a last resort, a "quick fix" that, although applicable in rare, special cases, has little to offer as a general solution to the crime problem.

By the 1950s drug therapy began to replace lobotomies. A more sophisticated form of psychosurgery called *cingulotomy* was used on a selected basis with consenting patients after other treatments were exhausted.

> The procedure involves passing an electrode needle through two small holes in the skull and searing a tiny lesion in the cingulum, a bundle of nerve fibers linking the emotional centers of the brain with the thought centers in the cortex (Beck and Cowley, 1990).

Twin Studies. Studies of twins and adoptees are ingenious ways of attempting to address the "nature vs. nurture debate," that is, whether criminality is inherited or learned. Such studies are *ex post facto* in nature. They begin with criminals who have a twin and then attempt to find the other twin in order to discover whether he or she is also criminal (Lange, 1931; Rosanoff, Handy, and Plesset, 1934; Christiansen, 1968; Dalgard and Kringlen, 1975). Such studies often compare monozygotic (MZ) with dizygotic (DZ) twins. *Monozygotic (identical) twins* are produced by a single egg and therefore exhibit the same hereditary environment, while *dizygotic (fraternal) twins* are produced by separate eggs and reveal less biological similarity.

Although findings have been mixed, Dalgard and Kringlen's (1975) study of all twins born in Norway between 1900 and 1935 concluded that the significance of hereditary factors in registered crime is nonexistent. They examined 33,000 twins in order to turn up 139 pairs in which one or the other committed crime as measured by a national crime registry. Their study and others found greater **concordance** (*similar patterns with respect to criminality*) among **monozygotic** than among dizygotic pairs. A review of studies conducted from 1929 to 1961 by Mednick and Volavka (1980) found roughly 60 percent concordance among MZ twins and about 30 percent among DZ pairs. Christiansen's (1968) study of 3,586 male twins found 52 percent MZ concordance and 22 percent among DZs.

Adoption Studies. Related in design and execution to twin studies are adoption studies. The assumption underlying such studies is that, if the behavior of children more closely matches that of their biological parents than that of their adoptive parents, this finding would support the argument for a biological base of human behavior. Schulsinger (1972), for instance, found criminality in adopted boys to be higher when biological fathers had criminal records. Hutchings and Mednick (1977) studied 1,145 male adoptees born in Copenhagen between 1927 and 1941; they found 185 adoptees with criminal records and determined that the criminality of the biological father was a major predictor of the child's behavior. Crowe (1974), however, discovered no differences between adoptees and a control group, except that the former demonstrated a higher proportion of psychopathic personalities. However, he admits problems with small samples as well as the fact that other environmental influences may have been responsible for the higher psychopathy among adoptees.

Problems with Twin/Adoption Studies. There are a number of methodological problems associated with twin and adoption studies, despite painstaking research and admirable scholarship on the part of those who have conducted them:

- Most studies involve a small number of cases, since they attempt to combine two phenomena: twins/adoptees and crime.
- Some studies are subject to unsystematic and uncontrolled samples (Dalgard and Kringlen, 1975, p. 230).
- Often the operationalization of DZ and MZ relies on official records rather than on blood-serum group samplings. The latter is a far more accurate means of distinguishing between identical and fraternal twin patterns.
- Official records are the major source of data on the dependent variable-crime commission.
- A shift of only a few cases (which may have been misdiagnosed) can erase the DZ-MZ differences.

(© Phtotfest)

Frances Farmer in her "problem" days.

- Higher concordance among MZs (identical twins) may still be due to more similar environmental treatment—identical twins are likely to be treated the same.

XYY Syndrome. In the late fifties in England, speculation began regarding males who possessed an XYY chromosome pattern—an extra male chromosome. Of the forty-six chromosomes most humans possess, males receive an X chromosome from their mothers and a Y chromosome from their fathers, while females receive two X chromosomes, one from each parent. Beginning with papers by Patricia Jacobs et al. (1965), in which a large number of the 197 Scottish inmates they studied were found to be "double Ys," the hypothesis was proposed of a "double male" or "supermale syndrome." This theory held that the possession of an extra Y chromosome caused males to be unusually tall, to suffer severe acne as adolescents, and to be *predisposed to aggressive and violent behavior.* During the late sixties, defense attorneys for brutal murderers in France and in Australia and for Richard Speck, the murderer of eight Chicago nurses, employed as part of their defense the claim that their clients were XYYs. Only in the Australian case was the accused acquitted (Sarbin and Miller, 1970).

While early research suggested that a larger proportion of XYYs could be found in prisons than among the general public (less than one double Y per 1,000 live male births) further research has found no difference (Shah and Roth, 1974, p. 137; Witkin et al., 1976). Because of the relative rarity of the syndrome, studies demonstrating a large number of cases are difficult. A Danish study by Witkin et al. (1976) did not support the aggression hypothesis and even found that incarcerated XYYs showed less aggression while in prison than did the other inmates. Earlier reviews of the research by Fox (1971) and Sarbin and Miller (1970) essentially agreed with these findings and found XYYs when institutionalized to have less serious offense records than others. While more research is required in this area, the negative findings have considerably lessened interest in the XYY syndrome as a cause of criminality.

Other Biological Factors. Further theoretical and empirical work in the tradition of biological positivism in criminology continues to raise interesting hypotheses and some explanations of individual cases of criminality (see Fishbein, 1990; Walters and White, 1989).

In the 1970s ideas proposed by Edward Wilson (1975) in his book *Sociobiology* attracted adherents. Basically, the sociobiological perspective insists on the genetic base of human behavioral differences. Individuals are born with different potentialities; their reactions to the social environment are modified by biochemistry and the cellular reactions of the brain. Each individual's unique genetic code and nervous system react differently to the same environmental stimuli (Jeffrey, 1978, p. 162). One study suggested that birth trauma-induced brain injury among high risk children may contribute to violent criminality (Kandel and Mednick, 1991). White et al. (1991) found that children with Attention Deficit Disorder with Hyperactivity (ADDH) are at high risk for delinquency. A variety of other biological factors have been explored, primarily by means of the limited case-study approach, and require more study before definitive conclusions can be drawn.

Variables such as diet, environmental pollution, endocrine imbalance, and allergies have been claimed to have criminogenic influence. In our discussion of the "Twinkie defense" in Chapter 6, we see claims that sugar consumption (too little or too much) is a causal agent in crime. Hypoglycemia (low blood sugar) also has been claimed to be linked to impaired brain function and violent crime.

Explorations of endocrine imbalance have found an obvious connection with sexual functioning, but no clear relationship with crime. Theories of relationship between male hormones (testosterone levels) and criminality have been found inconclusive, although injection of the female hormone (estrogen) has been found to decrease male sexual potency (Mednick and Volavka, 1980). Dalton's (1961) study "Menstruation and Crime" found that nearly half of the crimes of her sample of female inmates had occurred during menstruation or premenstruation. The PMS (Premenstrual Syndrome) defense emerged in the early eighties when two women had their murder charges reduced to manslaughter on the basis that severe PMS reduced their mental capacity (Rittenhouse, 1991).

Cerebral and neuroallergies to food substances have also been suggested as potential criminogenic factors (Wunderlich, 1978; Schauss, 1980). In Schauss's study comparing nutritional differences between delinquents and nondelinquents, the surprising major difference was that delinquents drank more milk. Similar investigations of the effects of environmental pollution on aberrant behavior indicate that substances such as lead, mercury, and other poisonous substances can adversely affect human behavior and life itself.

Neurological studies have suggested that criminals are more likely to exhibit abnormal electroencephalogram (EEG) patterns (a measurement of brain waves), although studies of association of such patterns with criminality have presented mixed findings (Moyer, 1976). Denno (1985, p. 713) reports:

> Considerable evidence indicates that many biological and developmental disorders associated with delinquency (for example, learning and reading disabilities) may be attributable, in part, to minor central nervous system (CNS) dysfunction which is linked, most predominantly, to complications occurring before and after birth.

She also points out that biological factors are more predictive of female behavior and environmental factors more predictive of male behavior. While female behavior is more subject to cultural and social constraint, male behavior is more susceptible to environmental forces (Denno, 1990).

It is important that criminologists keep an open mind on this matter and not view such studies as a taboo area (Sagarin, 1980) nor mistake more modern biological studies for their more primitive Lombrosian ancestors. Ellis (1982, pp. 57–58), in his review of the genetics and criminal behavior literature of the seventies, offers prudent conclusions:

> Sensing the weight of this accumulating evidence, especially throughout the past decade, along with several other types of less direct evidence not treated in this article (e.g., the discovery of a growing number of neurological and neurochemical correlates of criminal and psychopathic behavior), many scientists have concluded since the start of the 1970s that some significant genetic factors are probably, or at least very possibly, causally involved in criminal behavior variability. . . . However, it seems important to quickly insert and underscore the point that none of these scientists in any way excluded the possibility of environmental factors also being involved.
>
> In fact, nearly all of them specifically entertained hypotheses about what one or more of those environmental factors might be within the very same reports in which they acknowledge possible or probable genetic influences.

In the last twenty years, new developments in genetics and molecular science have further argued that biology has some impact on the way people behave. Evolutionary psychology might involve laboratory experiments, crosscultural studies, and other approaches. Such researchers approach the mind as an ancient engineering project, developing and testing out hypotheses about what "design problems" needed solving and what universal mental structures might have been designed, by the pressures to survive and reproduce, to solve them (Goode, 2000, D9).

Ellis and Walsh (1997) review *five evolutionary (or gene-based) theories of criminality.* These all believe that genetic factors predispose people to various criminal behavior and natural selection has operated on humans to favor certain tendencies toward criminal and antisocial behavior.

- Evolutionary theory of rape argues that a substantial proportion of males in most populations would employ rape, especially when the prospects of being punished are low.
- Evolutionary theory of spousal and dating assault is associated with mainstay copulatory access.
- Another evolutionary theory attempts to explain child abuse and neglect.
- A "cheater theory" that claims that some males have been naturally selected to make lower parental investment than women by seeking numerous partners.
- The r/K continuum theory of crime which indicates that criminals and psychopaths are at one end of a continuum of reproduction. The K end (qualitative end) has persons who proliferate their genes by major investment in a small number of offspring, while the r end (quantitative end) proliferate offspring and neglect them. The latter propagates criminals and psychopaths.

Ellis and Walsh (1997, p. 229) indicate that the theories are too new to have been fully tested. They have, however, received much play in the media. They note: "Decades of careful empirical testing will be required to assess the merit of many of these hypotheses." Ellis and Walsh (2000, pp. 302–303) summarize "perinatal, health, morphologic and internal biological correlates of crime that they maintain are well established or established variables correlated with crime commission." These are: low birth rate and shorter gestation, minor physical anomalies, maternal smoking during pregnancy, accidental injuries, hypoglycemia, premenstrual syndrome, body type, physical attractiveness (lack of) and skin conductivity (less perspiration under threatening conditions).

They also (Ibid.) summarize well established and established hormonal, neurotransmitter and miscellaneous biochemical correlates, and neurological correlates of crime. These include: serotonin levels (lower neurotransmitter activity), cholesterol (lower for criminals), monoamine oxidase (MAO) (an enzyme that is lower among criminals), abnormal brain patterns, slow brain response to external stimuli, and greater pain tolerance.

A literature review examining the link between learning disabilities and criminality commissioned by the Law Enforcement Assistance Administration concluded that no such connection had been proven (Murray, 1976). Some studies have claimed that brain dysfunction (damage) is associated with violence, suicide, and the likelihood of being processed by criminal justice authorities (Monroe, 1978).

Critique of Neobiological Positivism. While recent biological positivistic research is more sophisticated and less grandiose than the early theories discussed previously, most examples given are of limited case studies. Illustrative cases can be found that show connections with criminality, but often just as many cases can be brought forth of individuals with the same "claimed causative agent" whose behavior is normal. Much of this research is limited by small samples, is prone to the dualistic fallacy, is overreliant on incarcerated subjects, and often employs poor sampling procedures. While undoubtedly biological factors have impact on particular individuals and their commission of certain crimes, biological explanations tend to be limited and appear to offer less exposition than social and cultural factors. Goldkamp (1987, p. 129) notes that once-taboo biological explanations have enjoyed a resurgence of respectability and that "the long frustrated ghost of Lombroso must be smiling at last."

Neobiological research that continues attempts to draw such literature into the criminological mainstream, such as Wilson and Herrnstein's *Crime and Human Nature* (1985), has not received the same laudatory reviews in criminology and criminal justice as it has in the popular press (Austin, 1986; Gibbs, 1985).

In 1992 a National Institute of Mental Health-sponsored conference on genetics and crime scheduled to take place at the University of Maryland was cancelled when protestors threatened to disrupt the proceedings. The conference later took place at a rural conference center on Maryland's eastern shore, despite being disrupted by protesters who accused the conference of being racist and of condoning genetic research on criminal behavior (Wheeler, 1995). This concern regarding such theories is that they attempt to provide scientific justification for conservative ideological policies current at a given time. Such findings of a biological cause of violence supports a political climate in which the blame for crime, poverty, and other social ills is placed solely on the individual and not on national social policies. Nelkin (1995, p. A17) indicates:

> The idea of a criminal gene also implies a hope of controlling crime, not through the uncertain route of social reform, but through biological manipulation. . . . But, at its core, the debate over crime has more to do with social than biological causes; we must deal with the real sources of crime: social conditions that are so strongly associated with violence. Biological predisposition is not necessary to explain why a child who suffers racism and violence, without much hope of escape, might become indifferent to human life.

It should be quickly said that an appreciation of these biosocial theories is necessary if we are to understand all factors having an impact on crime. Explanation of crime requires a consideration of biological, psychological, and sociological factors. It is clear that biological and psychological factors play a role in some crime, especially in understanding the behavior of chronic offenders.

Psychological Positivism. Various psychological, psychiatric, and psychoanalytic theories of criminality share in common the *search for criminal pathology in the human personality.* Although the approaches overlap, psychology is the study of the individual human mind, personality, and behavior, while psychiatry is a branch of medicine that deals with the diagnosis and treatment of mental disorders. *Psychoanalysis,* originally based on the writings of Sigmund Freud, is an applied branch of psychological theory that employs techniques such as free mental association and dream therapy in order to diagnose and treat mental problems; the therapist assists the patient in probing the unconscious in search of sources of mental pathology. Most such theories tend conservatively to take for granted the existing social order and to scrutinize the human psyche for explanations of individual deviation. Much of this approach can be illustrated with the continual quest for "the criminal personality," measurable traits that enable the distinguishing of criminals from noncriminals. Many adherents of this approach also concentrate more on applied therapy and rehabilitation of identified criminals and less on pure theoretical explanations of crime causation (see Bartol and Bartol, 1986; Hollin, 1989).

Freudian Theory. While Charles Darwin was the intellectual forefather of many biological positivistic theories, other early psychological and psychoanalytic approaches were based on the writings of Sigmund Freud (1856–1939). While Freud did not address his writings specifically to the crime issue, his theories of personality as well as psychopathology have been applied to explanations of criminal behavior. He emphasized the instinctual and unconscious bases of human behavior.

Freud viewed the human personality as being made up of three parts: id, ego, and superego. The *id* is the instinctive, natural, or animalistic self. It is totally selfish and seeks to maximize pleasure. Expressions of this pleasure principle (or libido) are the life or love instinct (eros) as well as the death instinct (thanatos). The *superego* is the socialized component of the personality, the part developed in order to function and gain acceptance in human society. Repressing the pleasure-seeking instincts, the superego is in constant conflict with the id. The *ego* is the mediator or "referee" in this contest (Freud, 1930).

Psychoanalytic adherents of Freudian theory view much criminality as unconsciously motivated and often due to repression (hiding or sublimation into the unconscious) of personality conflicts and unresolved problems experienced in early childhood. Hostility to male authority symbols (the Oedipus complex) originates when the male child's id, desiring sexual relations with the mother, is blocked by the father. Overly harsh toilet training, premature weaning, or other unpleasant sex-related episodes contain the seeds of unconscious motivation for later adult criminality. Some hold that the inability to control instincts due to inadequate ego and superego development causes criminality (Friedlander, 1947). Crime represents a substitute response (displacement reaction); that is, when original goals are blocked, they are sublimated (displaced) and replaced by substitute goals. Crime may be committed because of the unconscious desire to be caught and punished (an expression of the thanatos complex, or death wish).

Relying extensively on case studies, Freudians document examples of the operation of the Oedipus or Electra complex, the death wish, inferiority complex, frustration-aggression, birth trauma, castration fears, and penis envy, in which crime is a substitute for forbidden acts (Vold and Bernard, 1986, p. 113). While it has had a profound impact on Western thought, Freudian theory, dealing as it does with abstract notions of the human psyche, has not lent itself well to empirical analysis. Most of his hypotheses have been neither verified nor refuted.

Cullen and Agnew (1999, p. 5) indicate that there are two general types of psychological theory in criminology: those that focus on traits and those that focus on learning theory. The former searches for individuals with certain traits which cause them to be more prone to crime, while the latter examines crime as a learning process.

Psychometry. Psychometry is the *field that seeks to measure psychological and mental differences between criminals and noncriminals.* This search for the distinctive criminal mind or personality could also be described as taking the form of a criminological "wild goose chase." While it originates in the work of Goddard, described earlier, modern and more sophisticated tests have been employed in the attempt to discern basic mental and psychological differences. In an early literature review, Schuessler and Cressey's (1953) examination over a twenty-five-year period of such studies was unable to find conclusive evidence of specific personality characteristics related to criminality. Later reviews by Waldo and Dinitz (1967) of the literature from 1950 to 1965 confirmed Schuessler and Cressey's conclusion, as does a later survey by Tennebaum (1977).

In this tradition of mental testings, or searching for traits in criminals, the Gluecks (1950) conducted a survey of 500 delinquent boys and 500 nondelinquent boys, and found the former to be more assertive, defiant, destructive, hostile, and ambivalent toward authority. Even these differences were small and may have been an illustration of *post hoc* error, where differences observed after the fact (the official labeling of delinquency) are assumed to be the cause of behavior. Similarly, some research suggests that incarcerated criminals suffer greater emotional disorders than the general population, a likely reaction to confinement, as illustrated by the "simulated prison" study discussed in Chapter 2. Other studies attempting to link "psychopathology" and crime have also been inconclusive.

Hans Eysenck. Hans Eysenck (1977) in *Crime and Personality* merges a number of streams in social scientific thought in proposing a theory of criminality. Borrowing from psychologist B. F. Skinner (1971), as well as from the classical school of criminology, he views human conscience and guilt as merely conditioned reflexes, simple reactions to the apprehension of pleasure and pain. Eysenck claims the extroverted (outgoing) personality is more delinquent or criminal than the introverted (inhibited) personality. His disciple, Gordon Trasler (1962), feels that conditioned anxiety reaction (fear of punishment) inhibits individuals from crime. Extroverts, however, are less responsive to this conditioning. Viewing the labeling of deviant acts as nonproblematic, Eysenck feels that society is too permissive in its child-rearing practices and is unwilling to rationally apply the knowledge of modern psychology in the area of behavioral modification which attempts to encourage positive behavior through the application of pleasure and pain (Taylor et al., 1973, p. 49). Kraska (1989, p. 2) explains:

> Eysenck's theory could best be termed as a "biologically rooted conditioning theory" (Eysenck, 1980). He maintains that individuals refrain from law breaking to the extent that they are adequately socially conditioned and acquire an internalized conscience. This conditioning takes place in early childhood when one learns moral habits and develops a conscience governing his or her conduct. Thus, the undersocialization of the conscience is the key to antisocial and criminal behavior.

Hindelang's (1971) self-report survey of 234 high school boys supported Eysenck's theory that extroverts are more delinquent, particularly among the most normal or middle-neurotic group.

B. F. Skinner. Perhaps the most influential proponent of the branch of applied theory called behavioral psychology is B. F. Skinner (1953), who in his *Science and Human Behavior* views behavior as primarily a response to consistent conditioning or learning reinforced through expected rewards and punishments. Through **behavioral modification** (sometimes in laboratory settings, called operant conditioning), which is widely used in juvenile corrections, *unacceptable behavior can theoretically be engineered toward acceptable behavior.* While an apparently effective therapeutic strategy, Skinner's approach is a pure behaviorist approach: that is, it says "behavior causes behavior;" it is less concerned with addressing the issue of the underlying origin of crime, criminal law, or conditions in the social order that act as prior conditions to the transmission of behavior. As an applied theory or therapeutic strategy, it is attractive, despite its shortcomings as pure theory.

Albert Bandura. Bandura's (1973) *social learning theory* looks at the thought processes of the person and external sanctions. By observing others, individuals "learn" how to engage in aggression. This might include exposure to such models, aversive treatment by others, or positively anticipating participating in such actions. The reinforcement or punishment of such actions is important (Cullen and Agnew, 1999, p. 4).

Samuel Yochelson and Stanton Samenow. More recent advocates of the existence of a distinctive *criminal personality* are psychiatrist Samuel Yochelson and clinical psychologist Stanton Samenow (1976), who on the basis of their fourteen-year therapeutic work with 240 hard-core criminal and delinquent subjects at St. Elizabeth's Hospital for the criminally insane in Washington, D.C., claim to have challenged prevailing sociological and economic theories of crime causation. In a revival of early biological and psychological positivism, they argue that socio-environmental constraints on individual criminality are irrelevant, that there is a "criminal personality," and that such individuals freely choose to become criminal (1976, p. 199). Feeling that their criminal patients were conning them by using current theories in the social sciences to rationalize their criminality, they claim that criminals were victimizers of society rather than its victims (Vold and Bernard, 1986, p. 253).

Proposing a therapeutic treatment technique rather than a theory of crime causation, they make some of the following points:

- The criminal personality is imprinted at birth and is relatively unaffected by the family.
- Criminal personalities seek the excitement of crime.
- They are exploitative and selfish in interpersonal relationships.
- They are amoral, untrustworthy, intolerant of others, manipulative, lack empathy, and are in a pervasive state of anger.
- They lack trust and refuse to be dependent.
- In all, Yochelson and Samenow claim to have discovered fifty-two criminal thinking patterns (Yochelson and Samenow, 1976).

Yochelson and Samenow propose a treatment program similar to programs like Alcoholics Anonymous (AA), Synanon, the Delancey Street Foundation (Fox, 1985, p. 255), and the program proposed in Glasser's (1965) Reality Therapy, in which criminals must confront their antisocial thoughts. AA calls this a rejection of "stinkin' thinkin'," in which the subjects abandon past excuses and rationalizations. Criminals are expected to totally reject their former criminal personalities and assume personal responsibility for their wrongdoing.

Despite its promise as a behavioral therapy, Yochelson and Samenow's theory has a naive "old-wine-in-new-bottles" flavor about it; it seems a revival of the biological "grunts and bumps" theories of the past. They cite little convincing empirical evidence of success for their treatment. They fail to refute evidence regarding environmental and social influences. Among their methodological problems, their operationalization of basic terms is unclear. In response to their claim that they have refuted criminological theory of environmental influences on crime, Vold (1979, p. 159) retorts:

> It does not appear, however, that the study demonstrates that point. It is certainly possible that providing a criminal with insight into the root causes of his behavior does not change that behavior. That is very different than saying crime does not have root causes.

Rather than restricting its focus to specific types of offenders, the search for "the criminal personality" of which Yochelson and Samenow's theory is the most recent example is too globally ambitious in trying to explain all types of criminals.

Intelligence and Crime. Hirschi and Hindelang (1977) charge that, because of the discrediting of much of the early work on intelligence and crime by Goddard and Goring and others, the field of criminology has ignored the strong evidence of a link between **intelligence quotient (IQ) and crime.** On the basis of an extensive literature review, they argue that the textbooks have been wrong on this subject and that:

- IQ is more important in predicting official delinquency among white boys than is social class.
- IQ is a better predictor of delinquency than is the father's social class, especially among black boys.
- All other things being equal, the lower the IQ, the higher the recidivism.
- There is a roughly nine-point deficit in the IQs of delinquents compared to nondelinquents.

Unable to find contrary conclusions in current research, Hirschi and Hindelang (1977) conclude that IQ is at least as good a predictor of delinquency as race and social class. Wolfgang, Figlio, and Sellin's (1978) study found arrested juveniles in their Philadelphia cohort to have lower IQs, but also found that race was a more important predictor, while the contribution of IQ to criminality, independent of race and class, was also indicated in a literature review of such studies by Herrnstein (1983). Research by Gordon (1987) similarly claims to have demonstrated that black-white differences in juvenile delinquency rates were best predicted by IQ rather than by socio-economic variables.

Richard Herrnstein and Charles Murray in *The Bell Curve* (1994) once again resurrected this theme of IQ. They see blacks as performing more poorly on IQ tests than whites, thus demonstrating less intelligence. They view this poor performance as predominantly genetically-caused and contend that it is relatively unaffected by social programs or public policy. This school of psychometry has a long tradition of discovering that Jews are not very smart, that Mediterranean people are genetically inferior to Nordic ones, and that the average mental age of white military enlistees in World War I was 13 (Holt, 1994, p. A15). Vold and Bernard (1986, p. 82) cite the rather seamy history of the IQ controversy, indicating that blaming low IQ for delinquency has a long tradition. In the 1820s the high delinquency of the Irish was attributed to their inferior racial stock (Finestone, 1976, pp. 12–36), and at the turn of the century early IQ tests were utilized to show the inferiority of Southern and Eastern European immigrants. The IQs of Italian-American children, with a median of 84, were 16 points below the national norm (Pinter, 1923), about the same as those of black children today.

Modern advocates of a relationship between IQ and delinquency and crime do not, as did earlier writers, insist that intelligence potential is entirely inherited, viewing it as an acquired as well as inherited entity. Given criticisms of cultural bias in intelligence testing, they insist that, although no test is culture-free, one obtains similar results from a variety of measures. IQ remains a critical variable in explaining traditional crime and delinquency and may even shed light on white collar crimes whose perpetrators are likely to have higher IQs. Little research, however, has taken place with respect to the latter.

A full and detailed account of modern psychological and psychiatric approaches to crime exceeds the intentions of this volume. Much of this literature, which has often been given short shrift by criminological theorists, is important, but it also has been of an applied theoretical or clinical nature, proposing treatment rather than postulating causes (see Kutchins, 1988). Schafer (1976, chapters 8 and 9) provides excellent coverage of such work by Erik Erikson (1950) on identity crisis, family therapy, reality therapy (Glasser, 1965), gestalt therapy (Perls, 1970), and other important therapeutic approaches. Similarly Jacks and Cox (1984) provide an excellent anthology of psychocriminology. On this point Fox (1976, p. 416) states:

> Crime is so complex that a single theory or small constellation of theories is difficult to operationalize and evaluate through controlled research. There is disagreement between the research and the clinical viewpoints, most graphically demonstrated by the demand for solid research by (pure research) sociologists and experimental psychologists, on the one hand, and the more pragmatic clinical viewpoint (applied research) held by psychiatrists, clinical psychologists, and social workers on the other. . . . These disparate viewpoints will probably never become congruent. It is apparent that both are needed.

A Critique of Psychological Positivism. Some of the same shortcomings that plague biological positivism also impinge on the psychological theories:

- Many of these theories focus almost exclusively on the individual personality, ignoring social conditions and life situations. This appears to commit the error that Ryan (1971) calls "blaming the victim" (see Vold, 1979, p. 156; Cohen, 1955, p. 55).
- Being more concerned with therapy than with measurement, many psychiatric theories in particular tend to be speculative rather than scientific.
- Many of these theories overemphasize the case study approach and are prone to observer bias.
- They often fail to use useful control groups, and the experimental groups are usually institutionalized populations.
- A number of studies have used inadequate, unrepresentative samples and unclear operationalization of concepts.
- Many of these theories fail to recognize crime as a socially or legally defined act, considering it almost a physical or clinical condition.

Vold and Bernard (1986, p. 107) best sum up the state of such theories by indicating that many of these theories may be correct with respect to particular types of criminals, but they ignore the conflict basis of criminal law.

It is important that, in explaining the forest (environmental and sociological influences, to be discussed in the next chapter), we do not ignore the individual trees (biological and psychological differences among individuals). Monahan and Splane (1980, p. 42) indicate: "What the field of criminology needs, it appears to us, are sociologists who use psychological intervening variables without embarrassment and psychologists who are aware of the social roots of the individual processes they study." Psychological theories are very important in explaining micro-criminology. Why do some individuals respond to the same environment differently than do others?

Summary

A *theory* is a plausible explanation of a given reality. While *pure theory* attempts to search for basic causes or underlying principles, *applied theory* is concerned with finding explanations with which to guide practical social policy. Criminology as an interdisciplinary field requires both. The *major theoretical approaches in criminology* are: the demonological, classical, ecological, economic, positivistic (biological and psychological), and sociological approaches.

The earliest theories of crime causation were *demonological* in nature, seeking supernatural explanations for criminality. The criminal was viewed as possessed, sinful, or evil. The *classical school* of criminological theory, which developed in the eighteenth century, was reflected in the writings of Beccaria, Bentham, and later Garofalo and Ferri. Seeking rational explanations, classical theorists viewed the criminal as exercising *free will,* as motivated by *hedonism* (pleasure-seeking), and as carefully weighing potential pleasure vs. pain to be derived from an activity. Attacking the cruel and unpredictable penal methods of the time, classical theory inspired the reform of Western criminal law. *Neoclassical theory* admits extenuating circumstances (insanity, age, and the like) to the equal treatment for equivalent-offense notions of the classical school.

Ecological theory (sometimes called statistical, geographic, or cartographic) is concerned with the impact of groups and social and environmental influences on criminality. The earliest writers, Guerry and Quetelet, could be regarded as the "fathers of modern criminology" in that they employed statistics and scientific analysis in the investigation of their theories. Quetelet's "thermic law" hypothesized that violent crimes predominate in warmer climates, while property crimes increase in colder zones. Since he and Guerry extensively employed maps in their analyses, they are sometimes called the *cartographic school.* The work of this school was interrupted and for a time forgotten as a result of the popularity of the Darwin-inspired biological positivism of Lombroso. Other *geographic theories* relating to moon cycles, climate, weather, and the like have attracted considerable interest, but research verification has been inconclusive.

Three major thinkers who have inspired much criminological theory have been *Marx* (*economics*), *Darwin* (*evolution*), and *Freud* (*unconscious sexual motivation*). Early *economic theories,* based on Marx's writings, view crime as determined by the economic system in which capitalism creates inequalities that produce crime. Socialism is viewed as the solution to the crime problem. Bonger, a Marxist criminologist, suggests that egoism (selfishness), developed as a result of capitalism, causes criminality.

Positivistic theory was based on three elements: (1) use of the scientific method in order to (2) diagnose individual pathology and thus enable (3) the prescribing of treatment. The criminal is viewed as sick. Precursors to positivism included astrology, phrenology, physiognomy, and palmistry, none of which criminologists take very seriously today.

Biological positivism proposed the notion of "the born criminal." Lombroso viewed criminals as atavistic beings (savage "throwbacks" to earlier human ancestors); he proposed the identification of physical stigmata as a means of identifying such persons. *Social Darwinism* is a philosophy that posits "a survival of the fittest in society" among human groups and their institutions. Ferri and Garofalo extended and modified the biopositivist tradition, which was well accepted by conservative and totalitarian political structures, since the blame for crime rested on the individual and not society. The text presents a critique of early positivism. Goring's research, which was highly critical of Lombrosian theory, proposing instead "inherited mental deficiency"—*feeblemindedness*—as the explanation of crime, has been discredited by more sophisticated mental tests. Other biopositivist theories include: case studies of the Jukes and the Kallikaks, Hooton's notion of "physical and mental inferiority" of criminals, and Sheldon's "somatotypes" (body types). The text also presents a more detailed critique of early biological positivism.

More recent biological positivism is more sophisticated in addressing the "nature vs. nurture" argument; it generally views criminality as produced by a combination of genetics and environment. Such research includes variables such as brain disorders, biochemical effects, endocrine and hormonal abnormalities, and nerve disorders. *Twin and adoption studies* have produced mixed findings, but suggest that monozygotic (identical) twins are more similar (concordant) in their criminal behavior than are dizygotic (fraternal) twins. A critique of such studies includes the point that many twins experience similar environmental influences. The XYY syndrome, the supermale phenomenon, has been largely discredited. Other areas of inquiry in this tradition include sociobiology (which insists on the genetic base of human behavior). A further critique is presented.

Psychological positivism reflects psychological, psychiatric, and psychoanalytic theory; much of the early work was based upon Freud's writings. The latter includes a tripartite personality system consisting of the id (instinctual self), ego (mediator), and superego (socialized self). According to *Freudian theory* as applied to criminology, the basis of deviance can be found in repressed sexual motivations deeply hidden in the individual's subconscious.

Psychometry (mental testing) attempts to discover personality characteristics of criminals. Various literature reviews of these efforts find the evidence inconclusive. Research by the Gluecks suggests that differences do exist between delinquents and nondelinquents, as does Eysenck's research, the latter attributing crime to extroverted personalities who lack adequate societal conditioning (training).

Skinner's theory of *behavioral modification* (modeling behavior by means of rewards and punishments) has had a major impact on clinical programs in corrections. The continual search for a distinctive "criminal personality" is illustrated in the work of Yochelson and Samenow, who on the basis of their clinical studies identify specific traits and propose a therapeutic technique similar to that of Alcoholics Anonymous in which criminals are challenged to take personal responsibility for their actions and to reject rationalizations. Although perhaps clinically useful, as a theory of crime causation the theory leaves much to be desired.

Hirschi and Hindelang revive the IQ controversy by insisting that on the basis of their literature review criminologists have been too unappreciative of the role of IQ in crime and delinquency.

The text provides a critique of psychological positivism, along with a rejoinder that criminologists, while concerned with sociological forces in crime causation, cannot afford to ignore individual factors.

KEY CONCEPTS

Applied Theory
Astrology
Atavism
Basic Premises of Positivism
Behavioral Modification
Biological Positivism
Bourgeoisie
Classical Theory
Critiques of Each Theoretical School
Demonological Theory
Ecological Theory
Economic Theory
Feeblemindedness
Freudian Personality Theory
Hedonism
Human Ecology
IQ and Crime
"Law of Criminal Saturation"
Lobotomy
Monozygotic Concordance
"Nature-Nurture" Controversy
Neoclassical Theory
Palmistry
Phrenology
Physical Stigmata
Physiognomy
Positivism
Proletariat
Psychological Positivism
Psychometry
Pure theory
Social Darwinism
Somatotypes
"Thermic Law" of Crime
XYY Syndrome

REVIEW QUESTIONS

1. You have been exposed to a brief historical account of early theories in criminology. What do you consider to be the beginnings of criminology and who the parent(s) of criminology: Beccaria, Quetelet and Guerry, or Lombroso?
2. Some feel that modern socio-biology is a far cry from the primitive early biological positivism. Do you agree or disagree? Defend your answer.
3. What are some of the basic concepts of the classical school of criminological theory? What is your opinion of the pros and cons of this theory?
4. What theories do you feel were influenced by the forerunners of modern criminological thought?
5. What are the basic elements of the positivist approach? How does this differ from classical theory?
6. Positivism, particularly early biological positivism, has been described as a "frightening slice of American criminology." G.K. Chesterton felt so strongly that he described early criminology as a pseudo science. Explain why there has been such a strong reaction to biological positivism

by such critics. What do you think about these criticisms?

7. What is the "nature vs. nurture" controversy and how are twin and adoption studies designed to address this issue? What has been resolved by research?
8. What is the claimed relationship between intelligence and crime according to Hirschi and Hindelang? What are some criticisms of this claimed relationship?
9. What are some primary ideas of the Marxist approach to criminology?
10. What are some basic findings of Quetelet and Guerry and their ecological approach to criminology?

INFOTRAC COLLEGE EDITION RESEARCH

Vantage Point 4.1 InfoTrac College Edition Research
What are some recent cases of actual campus crime among Nacirema college students? Search "campus crime."

Vantage Point 4.2 InfoTrac College Edition Research
Find and discuss a recent article on "environmental design and crime."

SELECTED READINGS

Ronald L. Akers. 1994. *Criminological Theories: Introduction and Evaluation.* Los Angeles: Roxbury Press.
Akers provides a succinct overview of major criminological theories in a very clear, concise manner. This book is very readable for undergraduates.

Robert M. Bohm. 1997. *A Primer on Crime and Delinquency.* Boston: Allyn and Bacon.
This brief (140 page) overview of major theories serves the purpose of giving a succinct picture of criminological theories. An excellent introduction for undergraduates.

Francis Cullen and Robert Agnew, editors. 1999. *Criminological Theory: Past to Present.* Los Angeles: Roxbury.
This selection of 38 featured articles is in this writer's opinion one of the most informative anthologies available. The authors' clear, succinct introductions to the readings are superb and simplify some very complex theories.

Don C. Gibbons. 1994. *Talking About Crime and Criminals: Problems and Issues in Theory Development.* Englewood Cliffs, N.J.: Prentice-Hall.
The strength of this work is its historical development of major theoretical views in criminology. This provides a context from which to view each theory.

J. Robert Lilly, Francis T. Cullen, and Richard A. Ball. 1995. *Criminological Theory: Context and Consequences.* 2nd edition. Thousand Oaks, California: Sage.
The authors provide a useful overview of major criminological theories both of a classical and contemporary variety.

Randy R. Martin, Robert Mutchnick, and Tim Austin. 1990. *Criminological Thought: Pioneers Past and Present.* New York: Macmillan.
The authors provide detailed chapters on fifteen pioneers in criminology who they feel have shaped the discipline into what it is today. These theorists are Beccaria, Lombroso, Durkheim, Freud, Park, Sheldon, Sutherland, Reckless, Merton, Albert Cohen, Ohlin, Sykes, Goffman, Becker, and Quinney.

George Vold, Thomas Bernard, and Jeffrey Snipes. 1998. *Theoretical Criminology.* 4th edition. New York: Oxford University Press.
This classic work by George Vold has been updated for two editions by Thomas Bernard, and now Jeffrey Snipes has been added. It does a sound, readable job of reviewing criminological theory.

Frank P. Williams III and Marilyn D. McShane. 1999. *Criminological Theory.* 3rd edition. Upper Saddle River, N.J.: Prentice-Hall.
This succinct review of theory provides an excellent overview for undergraduates of the critical contributions made by each criminological theory.

Thomas Winfree, Jr. and Howard Abadinsky. 1996. *Understanding Crime: Theory and Practice.* Chicago: Nelson-Hall.
Winfree and Abadinsky detail major classical and contemporary theories in American criminology.

5 Criminological Theory II: Sociological Mainstream Theories

Vantage Points

In the News

> Positive criminology accounts for too much delinquency. Taken at their terms, delinquency [crime] theories seem to predict far more delinquency than actually occurs. If delinquents were in fact radically different from the rest of conventional youth . . . then involvement in delinquency would be more permanent and less transient, more pervasive and less intermittent than is apparently the case. Theories of delinquency yield an embarrassment of riches, which seemingly go unmatched in the real world.
>
> —David Matza, *Delinquency and Drift* (1964)

The early classical, biological, and psychological traditions in criminology theory were similar in their relatively conservative view of society (the consensus model) as well as in their search for the cause of crime in either lack of fear of deterrence, defective individual genetics, or the psyche. The individual criminal was the unit of analysis. The only departures from this deviant behavior approach to criminality were found in the writings of the economic theorists (Marx and Bonger) and the ecologists (Quetelet and Guerry). Economic and ecological theories constitute the groundwork for the preeminence of sociological approaches to criminological theory beginning in the 1930s in the United States. Societal conditions, groups, social disorganization, and conflict have become additional units of analysis. Crime is perceived as a status (definition) as well as behavior (pathology), and sociological criminology in general takes a more critical stance toward the society itself as generator of criminal conduct.

Major Sociological Theoretical Approaches in Criminology

Figure 5.1 is a more detailed outline of the sociological theories that were briefly presented in Figure 4.1, Major Theoretical Approaches in Criminology. These include *mainstream sociological theories:* anomie, social process, and social control.

Discussion will begin with the mainstream tradition and the views of late nineteenth-century sociologist, Émile Durkheim, and the "anomie theories" that he inspired. Other representatives of this approach are Robert Merton, Richard Cloward and Lloyd Ohlin, and Albert Cohen.

Anomie Theories

Émile Durkheim and "Anomie." The writings of French sociologist Émile Durkheim (1858–1917) were in sharp contrast to the Social Darwinist, individualist, and psychological and biological positivist theories dominant in the late nineteenth century. The works of Durkheim represented a return to the thinking and orientation of the statistical/ecological theories advocated by Quetelet and Guerry, an approach that had been preempted by the popularity of Lombroso and the early biological positivists.

In his works—which included *The Division of Labor in Society* (1964), originally published in 1893, and *Suicide* (1951), first released in 1897—Durkheim insisted on the primacy of groups and social organizations as explanatory factors of human misconduct. As we said in Chapter 1, he viewed crime as a normal phenomenon in society because group reactions to deviant actions assist human groups in defining their moral boundaries. In his doctoral dissertation, *The Rules of Sociological Method* (1950), which was completed in 1893, Durkheim defined the sociologists' role as that of systematic observers of "social facts," empirically observable group characteristics that impact on human behavior. Durkheim's analysis of suicide clearly demonstrated his hypothesis of group influences on individual propensity to suicide. In *Suicide* (1951) he identified several types, which included: altruistic ("selfless" suicide), egoistic (self-centered suicide), and anomic (suicide due to "anomie" or a state of normlessness in society). The latter concept is Durkheim's principal contribution to the field of criminology.

FIGURE 5.1 Major Theoretical Approaches in Mainstream Criminology (Sociological)*

Theoretical School	Major Themes/Concepts	Major Theorists
Sociological Mainstream	"crime reflects consensus mode"	
Anomie Theory	"anomie (normlessness) lessens social control"	Durkheim
	"anomie (gap between goals and means) creates deviance"	Merton
	"differential social opportunity"	Cloward and Ohlin
	"lower class reaction to middle class values"	Cohen
Social Process	"social disorganization and social conditions"	Shaw and McKay
	"routine activities"	Cohen and Felson
	"crime is learned behavior, culturally/subculturally transmitted	Sutherland
	"local concerns of lower class	Miller
	"subterranean values, drift techniques of neutralization"	Matza
Social Control	"containment theory"	Reckless
	"social bonds weakened reducing individual stakes in conformity"	Hirschi
	"low self-control and self-interest"	Gottfredson and Hirschi

*See Figures 4.1 and 6.1 for other theoretical approaches in criminology.

The term *anomie* appeared in the English language as early as 1591 and generally referred to a disregard for law (Fox, 1976, p. 115). **Anomie** as used by Durkheim involves *a moral malaise; a lack of clear-cut norms with which to guide human conduct (normlessness).* It may occur as a pervasive condition in society because of a failure of individuals to internalize the norms of society, an inability to adjust to changing norms, or even conflict within the norms themselves.

Social trends in modern urban-industrial societies result in changing norms, confusion, and lessened social control over the individual. Individualism increases and new lifestyles emerge, perhaps yielding even greater freedom but also increasing the possibility for deviant behavior. The close ties of the individual to the family, village, and tradition (what Durkheim calls "mechanical solidarity"), though confining to the individual, maintained social control. In modern societies (characterized by "organic solidarity") constraints on the individual weaken. In a theme that would influence many later criminological theories, Durkheim viewed anomie in modern societies as produced by individual aspirations and ambitions and the search for new pleasures and sensations that are beyond achievement even in times of prosperity (Durkheim, 1951, p. 256).

This notion of anomie would influence a number of criminological theories, constituting a theoretical school of thought within mainstream or conventional criminology that began with the work of Robert Merton in the late thirties and continued with Richard Cloward and Lloyd Ohlin and Albert Cohen in the post-World War II period. Chronologically preceding these later developments in the anomie tradition was the work of "the Chicago school" of sociology and another major approach—the social process school of thought. These theories were less concerned with the origin of crime in society and concentrated instead on the social process (learning, socialization, subcultural transmission) by which criminal values were transmitted to individuals by groups with which they were affiliated.

Merton's Theory of "Anomie." Robert Merton's theory of "anomie" first appeared in 1938. Modifying Durkheim's original concept, Merton (1957, pp. 131–94) viewed anomie as a condition that occurs when discrepancies exist between societal goals and the means available for their achievement. This discrepancy or strain between aspirations and achievement has resulted in Merton's conception being referred to as "strain theory." According to this theory, U.S. society is firm in judging people's social worth on the basis of their apparent material success and in preaching that success is available to all who work hard and take advantage of available opportunities. In reality the opportunities or means of achieving success "the American dream" are not available to all. Merton (1938, p. 78) states:

> It is only when a system of cultural values extols, virtually above all else, certain common symbols of success for the population at large while its social structure rigorously restricts or completely eliminates access to approved modes of acquiring these symbols for a considerable part of the same population, that antisocial behavior ensues on a considerable scale.

Thus according to Merton's theory of anomie, antisocial behavior (crime) is produced by the very values of the society itself in encouraging high material aspirations as a sign of individual success without adequately providing approved means for all to reach these goals. This discrepancy between goals and means (strain) produces various "modes of personality adaptation," different combinations of behavior in accepting or rejecting the means and goals. Given this high premium placed on individual success without concomitant provision of adequate means for its achievement, individuals may seek alternate (nonapproved) means of accomplishing this goal. American fiction, the Horatio Alger stories of "rags to riches," the media, and literature constantly pound home the theme of success. "Social Darwinism" (the theme that the capable or fit will succeed) and the "Protestant ethic" (the attachment of religious value to work) have been persistent philosophies. These values are generally accepted by persons of all social classes.

One of the essential premises of this approach is that organization and disorganization in society are not mutually exclusive, but rather that many of the cultural values that have desirable consequences ("manifest functions") often contain within them or produce undesirable consequences ("latent functions") (Merton, 1961).

Modes of Personality Adaptation. Merton describes five possible **modes of personality adaptation** that represent types of adjustments to societal means and goals: the conformist, the innovator, the ritualist, the retreatist, and the rebel. All except the conformist are deviant responses. The *conformist* accepts the goal of success in society and also the societally approved means of achieving this status, such as through hard work, education, deferred gratification, and the like. Acceptance of the goals does not indicate that all actually achieve such satisfactory ends, but that they have faith in the system.

The *innovator* accepts the goal of success, but rejects or seeks illegitimate alternatives to the means of achieving these aims. Criminal activities such as theft and organized crime could serve as examples, although societally encouraged activities such as inventing could also provide illustrations. An interesting example is the case of Fred Demara, Jr., well known through the book *The Great Imposter* (Crichton, 1959). A high school graduate, Demara was disappointed that people had to spend much of their lives preparing—usually for only one occupation. Forging credentials and identities he launched into careers as a college professor, Trappist monk, penitentiary warden, and surgeon in the Canadian Navy, to mention just a few.

The *ritualist* is illustrated by the "mindless bureaucrat" who becomes so caught up in rules and means to an end that he or she tends to forget or fails to place proper significance on the goal. This individual will compulsively persist in going through the motions with little hope of successful achievement of goals.

The *retreatist* represents a rejection of both societally approved means and ends. This adaptation might be illustrated by the advice of Timothy Leary, the prophet of psychedelic drugs in the sixties, who preached, "tune in, turn on, and drop out." Chronic alcoholics and drug addicts may eventually reject societal standards of jobs and success and choose the goal of "getting high" by means of begging, borrowing, or stealing.

The *rebel* rejects both means and goals and seeks to substitute alternative ones that would represent new societal goals as well as new methods of achieving them, such as through revolutionary activities aimed at introducing change in the existing order outside normal, societally approved channels.

A Critique of Merton's Theory. Merton's theory, very well received in sociology and in criminology, became the basis of a number of subcultural theories of delinquency to be discussed shortly. Criticisms of the theory include that:

- His assumption of uniform commitment to materialistic goals ignores the pluralistic and heterogeneous nature of U.S. cultural values.
- The theory appears to dwell on lower class criminality, thus failing to consider law breaking among the elite. Taylor et al. (1973, p. 107) express this point: "Anomie theory stands accused of predicting too little bourgeois criminality and too much proletarian criminality."
- The theory is primarily oriented toward explaining monetary or materialistically oriented crime and does not address violent criminal activity.
- If Merton is correct, why does the United States now have lower property crime rates than many other developed countries?

While many writers (Hirschi, 1969; Johnson, 1979; Kornhauser, 1978) have concluded that Merton's theory does not hold up empirically, more recent research by Farnworth and Lieber (1989) argues in favor of its durability. They indicate that strain (anomie) theory combines psychological and structural explanations for crime and thus avoids purely individualistic explanations, and that the research of the critics failed to examine the gap or strain between economic goals and educational means. Farnworth and Lieber found this a significant educational predictor of delinquency in their sample of juveniles, and concluded that the theory is ". . . a viable and promising theory of delinquency and crime" (1989, p. 273).

Classic strain theory (as it is sometimes called given the strain or discrepancy between goals and means) has had additional conflicting support. Research did not find higher delinquency among those with the greatest gap between aspirations and expectations. Those with low aspirations and low expectations had the highest offense rates. Other studies, however, have shown support (Agnew et al., 1996; and Cullen and Agnew, 1999, p. 119).

There have been a variety of efforts to revise strain theory. One revision involves using the concept of "relative deprivation," one's felt sense of deprivation relative to others, such a reference group. Another alteration is to view adolescents as pursuing a number of goals besides monetary and status ones. These might include popularity with peers and romantic partners, good grades, athletic prowess, and even positive relationships with parents (*Ibid.*)

Robert Agnew's General Strain Theory. A persistent writer in the strain tradition has been Robert Agnew (1992, 1995, and 1997). He views *strain* as due to negative relationships in which individuals feel that they are being mistreated. These negative relationships may take a variety of forms: others preventing the achievement of goals such as monetary success; activities that threaten to remove valued relationships such as the loss or death of a significant other; finally, the threat of negatively valued stimuli such as insults or physical assault. For some, such activities increase the likelihood for anger and frustration, as well as the likelihood that crime becomes a means of resolving this. Agnew and White (1992) claim that delinquency was higher among those experiencing negative life events, for example, parental divorce or financial problems. It was also higher for those with interactional problems with teachers, parents, and others. Why some react to the strain by committing crime and others not needs to be specified.

An extension of Merton's theory has been offered by Steven Messner and Richard Rosenfeld in their *Crime and the American Dream* (1994) and their "institutional anomie theory." The hunger for wealth is viewed as insatiable, and all social institutions become subservient to the economic structure. Culturally induced pressure to accumulate material rewards combined with weak controls by noneconomic institutions produces an institutionalization of anomie (Chamlin and Cochran, 1995) and an institutionalization of the use of deviant means for success. The unimpeded pursuit of monetary success is the "American Dream." Economic institutions predominate subordinating all other institutions such as the family, church, or school, reducing their power particularly in the socialization of children.

Subcultural Theories. Merton's modification of Durkheim's notion of anomie began the "anomie tradition" in U.S. criminology, with further influential theoretical work by writers such as Richard Cloward and Lloyd Ohlin and Albert Cohen, which directed itself toward subcultural theories of delinquency.

Merton's theory had a major impact on many of the more sociologically oriented theories of crime and delinquency. A major area of theoretical focus from the thirties through the sixties in U.S. criminology related to juvenile gangs, as studies of citations in recent criminology textbooks (Schichor, 1982) and frequently cited books and journal articles (Wolfgang, 1980b) show.

Cohen's "Lower Class Reaction" Theory. Albert Cohen's (1955) *Delinquent Boys* presents a theory about lower class subcultural delinquency. According to his theory, delinquency is a *lower class* reaction to *middle class values.* Lower class youth use delinquent subcultures as a means of reacting against a middle-class-dominated value system in a society that unintentionally discriminates against them because of their lower class lifestyles and values. Unable to live up to or accept middle class values and judgments, they seek self-esteem by rejecting these values. Cohen (1955, p. 25) carefully qualifies his remarks by indicating that this theory is not intended to describe all juvenile crime.

He views much lower class delinquency as nonutilitarian, malicious, and negativistic. Much theft, for instance, is nonutilitarian, performed for status purposes within the gang rather than out of need. Maliciousness is expressed in a general disdain for middle class values or objects and a negative reaction to such values. The delinquent gang substitutes its own values and sources of self-esteem for the middle class values it rejects. Some examples of middle class values include: ambition, individual responsibility, verbal skills, academic achievement, deferred gratification (postponement of rewards), middle class manners, nonviolence, wholesome recreation, and the like. The gang subculture offers a means of protection and of striking back against values and behavioral expectations the lower class youth is unable to fulfill.

A Critique of Cohen's Theory. Major criticisms of Cohen's theory relate to:

- His overconcentration on lower (working) class delinquency.
- His assumption that lower class boys are interested in middle class values (Kitsuse and Dietrick, 1970).
- Cohen, like other subcultural theorists, fails to address ethnic, family and other sources of stress as well as the recreational ("fun") aspects of gang membership (Bordua, 1962).
- By emphasizing the nonutilitarian nature of many delinquent activities, Cohen tends to underplay the rational, for-profit nature of some juvenile criminal activities.

Cohen's theory fits into the "anomie tradition" in that he views lower class delinquency and gang membership as a result of strain or a reaction to unfulfilled aspirations.

A related subcultural theory by Walter Miller disagrees with this strain hypothesis and argues instead—in the social process tradition of Shaw, McKay, and Sutherland—that lower class delinquency represents a process of learning and expressing values of one's membership group. Miller's theory will be discussed in detail shortly.

Cloward and Ohlin's "Differential Opportunity" Theory. An extension of the works of both Merton and Sutherland (to be discussed) appeared in Richard Cloward and Lloyd Ohlin's (1960) *Delinquency and Opportunity. A Theory of Delinquent Gangs.* According to their theory of **differential opportunity,** *working class juveniles will choose one or another type of subcultural (gang) adjustment to their anomic situation depending on the availability of illegitimate opportunity structures in their neighborhood.* Borrowing from Merton's theme, Cloward and Ohlin view the pressure for joining delinquent subcultures as originating from discrepancies between culturally induced aspirations among lower class youths and available means of achieving them through legitimate channels. In addition to legitimate channels, Cloward and Ohlin stress the importance of available illegitimate opportunities, which may also be limited, depending on the neighborhood. Neighborhoods with highly organized rackets provide upward mobility in the illegal opportunity structure. Individuals occupy positions in both legitimate and illegitimate opportunity structures, both of which may be limited. Illegitimate opportunities are dependent on locally available criminal traditions.

Delinquent Subcultures. Cloward and Ohlin identified *three types of illegitimate juvenile subcultures:* criminal, conflict, and retreatist. The criminal subculture occurs in stable slum neighborhoods in which a hierarchy of available criminal opportunities exist. Such a means of adaptation substitutes theft, extortion, and property offenses as the means of achieving success. Disorganized slums (ones undergoing invasion-succession or turnover of ethnic groups) are characterized by a conflict subculture. Such groups, denied both legitimate and illegitimate sources of access to status, resort to violence, "defense of turf," "bopping," and/or "the rumble," as a means of gaining a "bad rep" or prestige. The retreatist subculture is viewed by Cloward and Ohlin as made up of "double failures." Unable to succeed either in the legitimate or illegitimate opportunity structures, such individuals reject both the legitimate means and ends and simply drop out; lacking criminal opportunity, they seek status through "kicks" and "highs" of drug abuse. These subcultures become the individual's reference group and primary source of self-esteem. According to this theory, delinquent gang members do not generally reject the societal goal of success, but lacking proper means to achieve it, seek other opportunities.

A Critique of "Differential Opportunity" Theory. Cloward and Ohlin's theory, building as it had on other respected theories, was well received in the field of criminology. Criticisms of the theory have generally involved:

- This theory focused exclusively on delinquent gangs and youths from lower and working class backgrounds, ignoring, for instance, middle class delinquent subcultures.
- It is doubtful that delinquent subcultures fall into only the three categories they identified. In fact, much shifting of membership and activities among members appears common (Bordua, 1961; Schrag, 1962).
- The orientation and specialization of delinquent gangs, even if the analysis is restricted to the United States, appear far more complex and varied than their theory accounts for.

Despite criticism, Cloward and Ohlin's ideas were very influential in the field and comprised a broader theory than that of Albert Cohen (1955). Where Cloward and Ohlin viewed delinquency as an anomic reaction to goals, means discrepancy, and the particular form of adaptation dependent on available illegitimate opportunities, Cohen perceived delinquency as a reaction of lower class youth to unobtainable middle class values.

Social Process Theories

Social process theories emphasize criminality as a learned or culturally transmitted process and are presented as an outgrowth of the "Chicago school of sociology" in the works of Henry Shaw and David McKay, Edwin Sutherland, Walter Miller, and David Matza.

The Chicago School. In 1892 the first American academic program in sociology was begun at the University of Chicago, marking the inception of sociology's **Chicago school.** Names associated with this school would constitute a virtual Camelot of sociology: Park, Burgess, Wirth, Shaw, McKay, Thrasher, Zorbaugh, Anderson, Mead, Faris, Dunham, Thomas, Znaniecki, Cressey, and Sutherland, to mention just a few. Originally begun by sociologist Albion Small, the school would have a primary influence on the development of sociology as a distinctive American discipline in the twenties and thirties with Robert Park, Ernest Burgess, and Louis Wirth as the primary mentors. This group would develop a comprehensive theoretical system—urban ecology—that would generate a remarkable number of urban life studies (Stein, 1964, pp. 13–46).

Human Ecology. Like Durkheim, Park (1952) saw that freedom from group constraints often also entailed freedom from group supports. While Durkheim referred to this as anomie, Park used the notion of "individualization due to mobility." Ecology is a *field that examines the interrelationship between human organisms and environment.* Park's theory was based on **human ecology,** looking at humans and the environment and, more specifically, at urban ecology, viewing the city as a growing organism, heavily employing analogies from plant ecology. According to Park, the heterogeneous contact of racial and ethnic groups in the city often leads to competition for status and space, as well as conflict, accommodation, acculturation, assimilation, or amalgamation—terms all quite similar to concepts in botany (plant biology), such as segregation, invasion, succession, and dispersion. One of Park's key notions was that of **natural areas,** *subcommunities that emerge to serve specific, specialized functions.* They are called "natural" since they are unplanned and serve to order the functions and needs of diverse populations within the city. Natural areas provide institutions and organizations to socialize its inhabitants and to provide for social control. Such natural areas include: ports of embarkation, Burgess's "zone of transition" (discussed in Chapter 3), ghettos, bohemias, hobohemias, and the like. Burgess's (1925) "concentric zone theory," which views cities as growing outward in concentric rings, served as the graphic model for the Chicago school's theory of human ecology. Wirth's (1938) theory of "Urbanism as a Way of Life" viewed the transition from the rural to the urban way of life as producing social disorganization, marginality, anonymity, anomie, and alienation because of the heterogeneity, freedom, and loneliness of urban life. The "Chicago school" expressed an antiurban bias in its analysis and a nostalgia for the small Midwestern towns in which most of its theorists had originated.

Using Park's concept of natural areas as a building block, Chicago school students were enjoined to perform case studies of these areas in order to generate hypotheses as well as, it was hoped, generalizations. Park (1952, p. 198) expressed the hope:

> The natural areas of the city, it appears from what has been said, may be made to serve an important methodological function. They constitute, taken together, what Hobson has described as "a frame of reference," a conceptual order within which statistical facts gain a new and more general significance. They not only

> tell us what the facts are in regard to conditions in any given region, but insofar as they characterize an area that is natural and typical, they establish a working hypothesis in regard to other areas of the same kind.

This empirical orientation, as opposed to armchair theorizing, was the chief contribution of the Chicago school. Among the students inspired to perform field research were Clifford Shaw and David McKay, and Edwin Sutherland.

Shaw and McKay's "Social Disorganization" Theory. Ironically, although Clifford Shaw and David McKay are pointed to as members of the Chicago school, they never enjoyed faculty status at the University of Chicago, but performed their research while employed by the Illinois Institute for Juvenile Research in Chicago. Snodgrass (1972) indicates that neither Shaw nor McKay received his doctorate because of foreign language requirements, but worked closely with many faculty and students from the University (Carey, 1975, pp. 84–92). The lasting contribution of Shaw and McKay's ecological studies in the thirties was their basic premise that crime is due more to social disorganization in pathological environments than the deviant behavior of abnormal individuals (Gibbons, 1979, p. 45).

In the tradition of the statistical school of criminological theory, Shaw and McKay made extensive use of maps and official statistics to plot the ecological distribution of forms of social disorganization such as juvenile delinquency (Shaw, 1929; Shaw and McKay, 1942). Using Burgess's concentric zone theory as a schema, as well as Park's notion of natural areas, they were able to document the ecological impact on human behavior. For instance, one transitional area (an area undergoing invasion/succession) was shown to exhibit very high crime rates despite considerable change in its ethnic makeup. Such areas breed criminogenic influences that predispose occupants to crime and social disorganization. In other research, Shaw utilized ethnographic and autobiographical field methods in order to provide case studies of criminals and delinquents (Shaw, 1930; Shaw, McKay, and MacDonald, 1938). Imposing concentric circles on mapped areas of Chicago on which rates of social disorganization had been plotted, Shaw (1930, pp. 198–204) was able to demonstrate the highest rates of truancy, crime, delinquency, and recidivism in Zone II (area of transition), while such rates declined as one moved further out from the rings. Criminal attitudes and social pathology were viewed as culturally transmitted within the social environment.

A Critique of "Social Disorganization" Theory. The human ecologists' insistence on ecological and social conditions having criminogenic impacts on otherwise normal individuals would inspire later criminologists such as Sutherland. Their stress on field studies and an empirical orientation would provide credibility to the fledgling disciplines of sociology and criminology and win them greater academic acceptance. A number of shortcomings, however, have been identified:

- Their theories at times border on ecological determinism: that an area or physical environment causes social pathology. Concentration on the geophysical environment tends to make the social structure and institutions secondary.
- The attempt to borrow an organic analogy and adapt biological concepts, such as competition, invasion, succession, and the like to criminology, saddled the field with unnecessarily primitive concepts.
- Some of the studies tend to commit the **ecological fallacy** (Robinson, 1950), in which group rates are used in order to describe individual behavior. Aggregate statistics do not yield accurate estimates if the intended unit of analysis is the behavior of individuals.
- Although Shaw and McKay studied other cities, the theories and conceptions of the Chicago school (such as the concentric growth of cities) were perhaps applicable to

Chicago, a city undergoing fantastic urbanization during the twenties and thirties, but may not apply to other urban communities, particularly since the post-World War II period.

- These theories assume stable ecological areas, which in fact do not exist. Such areas disappeared in the post-World War II decentralization of urban areas (Bursik, 1988, pp. 523–24; Schuerman and Kobrin, 1986).
- Problems in operationalizing (measuring) key concepts, such as delinquency rate and disorganization, arise when there is a heavy reliance on official statistics (Pfohl, 1985, p. 167).
- There is an overemphasis on consensus in community and a lack of appreciation of political conflict (Bursik, 1988, p. 524).

In defense of Shaw and McKay, Brantingham and Brantingham (1984, p. 312) point out that they were not as guilty of falling into the ecological fallacy trap as many of their followers, since they supplemented many of their statistical studies with case studies. This was illustrated by ethnographic works such as Shaw, McKay, and MacDonald's (1938) *Brothers in Crime* and Shaw's (1930) *The Jack Roller.* Focusing on group or social process, the urban ecologists—Shaw and McKay in particular—were influential in shifting criminological analysis from an overconcentration on the individual deviant and instead toward the criminogenic influences of social environments.

Routine Activities Approach. A resurgence and rediscovery of interest in the ecological and social disorganization theories of crime have been rekindled by formulations such as Cohen and Felson's (1979) and Felson's (1983) "routine activities approach" to crime causation. This approach says, "the volume of criminal offenses will be related to the nature of normal everyday patterns of interaction. . . . There is a symbiotic relationship between legal and illegal activities" (Messner and Tardiff, 1985, pp. 241–42). In summarizing the routine activities approach, Felson (1987, p. 911) indicates that:

> (1) It specifies three earthy elements of crime: a likely offender, a suitable target, and the absence of a capable guardian against crime. (2) It considers how everyday life assembles these three elements in space and time. (3) It shows that a proliferation of lightweight durable goods and a dispersion of activities away from family and household could account quite well for the crime wave in the U. S. in the 1960s and 1970s without fancier explanations. Indeed modern society invites high crime rates by offering a multitude of illegal opportunities.

Koenig (1991) explains that one of the origins of this theory was the Hindelang et al. (1977) "lifestyle exposure" theory, which proposes that the probability of crime varies by time, place, and social setting. An individual's lifestyle places him or her in social settings with higher or lower probabilities of crime.

Other works that illustrate the reaffirmation of social disorganization theory are by Simcha-Fagan and Schwartz (1986), who include social disorganization and subcultural approaches in explaining urban delinquency. Similarly Byrne and Sampson (1986) indicate that the social-ecological model is based on the premise that community has independent impacts on crime that are not able to be separated from the individual level. White (1990) found that neighborhood burglary rates varied by highway accessibility; ease of entry increases both familiarity with escape routes and vulnerability. In "Deviant Places," Stark (1987) argues that "kinds of places" explanations are needed in criminology in addition to the "kinds of people" explanations. He codifies thirty propositions from over a century of ecological explanations of both the Chicago school and the moral statisticians of the nineteenth century.

Stark identifies five aspects of high deviance areas: density, poverty, mixed use, transience, and dilapidation. These elements create criminogenic conditions for crime. His

(© Jeroboam)

The three earthy elements of crime are caught in this photograph: The likely offender (young, male, aggressive) is approaching his suitable target (female, appears frightened, may have something worth stealing) in the absence of a capable guardian (deserted street, darkness).

propositions include that density is associated with interaction between least- and most-deviant populations, higher moral cynicism, overcrowding, outdoor gatherings, lower levels of supervision of children, poorer school achievement, lower stakes in conformity, and increased deviant behavior. Crowding will increase family conflict, decrease the ability to shield wrongdoing, and thus increase moral cynicism. While Stark's hypotheses are too numerous to cover here, his systematic extraction of propositions from over a century of social disorganization/ecological research represents a reaffirmation and resurgence of such literature (see also Taylor and Harrell, 1996). VANTAGE POINT 5.1 reports on the ASC Task Force on "Designing Out Crime." VANTAGE POINT 5.2 also discusses the application of environmental design strategies to parking facilities.

IN THE NEWS 5.1 presents the APB/Neighborhood Crime Check ratings developed for APBnews.com by CAP Index, Inc. Use your home ZIP code to do a crime vulnerability assessment of your neighborhood.

Sutherland's Theory of "Differential Association." Perhaps the most influential general theory of criminality was that proposed initially in 1934 by Edwin Sutherland (1883–1950) in his **theory of differential association.** Simply stated, the theory indicates that *individuals become predisposed toward criminality because of an excess of contacts that advocate criminal behavior.* Due to these contacts a person will tend to learn and accept values and attitudes that look more favorably on criminality.

VANTAGE POINT 5.1

Designing Out Crime

Issues

Our failure to bring crime under control through a wide range of modifications to the criminal justice system has blinded us to the successful efforts continuously being made by a host of private and public entities—municipalities, schools, hospitals, parks, malls, bus companies, banks, department stores, taverns, offices, factories, parking lots—to bring a wide range of troublesome and costly crimes under control. In most cases these successes are achieved by identifying ways to reduce opportunities for highly specific kinds of crime, the approach advocated by environmental crime prevention.

The essential tenets of environmental crime prevention, of which Crime Prevention through Environmental Design (CPTED) and Situational Crime Prevention are the best known examples, are to:

- Increase the difficulty of committing crime (e.g., credit card photos).
- Increase the perceived risks (e.g., burglar alarms).
- Reduce the rewards associated with criminal acts (e.g., PIN for car radios).
- Reduce the rationalizations that facilitate crime (e.g., simplify tax forms).

While the federal government gave some support to CPTED in the 1970s, interest in environmental crime prevention has languished in our country. One reason for this loss of support was the concern that blocking opportunities for crime would result in its displacement to some other target, time, or place (i.e., the net amount of crime would remain the same, although its manifestations would be different). This belief was bolstered by criminological theories that generally failed to recognize important situational determinants of crime, such as the availability of tempting goods to steal and the absence of adequate guardianship of vulnerable property and persons.

In recent years, however, new criminological theories have emphasized the role of opportunities in crime causation. These theories, which include routine-activity theory and rational-choice theory, argue that as the number of opportunities for crime increases, more crimes will be committed; conversely, as opportunities are reduced, so crime will decline. Whether or not displacement takes place depends on the ease with which offenders can obtain the same criminal rewards without greatly increased effort or risks. Somebody who has developed the habit of shoplifting from the supermarket will not inevitably turn to some other form of crime, involving greater risk of detection and more severe penalties, if the store takes effective preventive action. In fact, particular crimes serve special purposes for the offender. A thwarted rapist will not turn to mugging or drug dealing.

Policy Recommendations

- **Federal Crime Prevention Department:** A crime prevention department should be established in the Department of Justice along the lines of similar units now functioning in a number of European countries. This unit would have a research and dissemination role and would also initiate action to "design out crime" that more naturally falls to central government than to state or local agencies. For example, the department could ensure the security of the phone system, of credit cards, or of ATM cards through federal influence on manufacturers and service providers at an industry level. Important preventive initiatives that currently need federal government sponsorship include development of effective personal alarms for repeat victims of domestic violence and the use of PIN numbers for VCRs and other electronic devices that are targets for burglary.
- **Crime Prevention Extension Service:** A Crime Prevention Extension Service, linked to local universities, along the lines of the successful agricultural model, should be developed within the Department of Justice. Its mandate should be to deliver expert crime prevention advice to small businesses and local communities. Such a service would complement rather than compete with the work of the police, especially as community policing ideas take hold.

Sources: "American Society of Criminology Task Force Report to Attorney General Janet Reno," *The Criminologist* (Special Issue), 20, 6, November/December 1995. Task Force members on "Designing Out Crime" included: Ronald V. Clarke, chair; Patricia Brantingham, Paul Brantingham, John Eck, and Marcus Felson.

InfoTrac College Edition Research

Search the name; "Oscar Newman." What is his main thesis regarding the impact of defensible space on crime?

Sutherland's theory was strongly influenced by Charles Horton Cooley's (1902) theory of personality—"the **looking-glass self.**" Cooley viewed the human personality as a "social self," one that is learned in the process of socialization and interaction with others. The personality as a social product is the sum total of an individual's internalization of the impressions he or she receives of the evaluation of others—"mirror of alters." "Significant others," people who are most important to the individual, are particularly important in this socialization process. Thus in Cooley's perception, *the human personality is a social self, a product of social learning and interaction with others.* Sutherland was also influenced by Shaw and McKay's (1942) notion of social disorganization and cultural transmission of crime, as well as by French sociologist Gabriel Tarde's (1912 [1890]) concept of imitation as the transmitter of criminal values. Similarly, in Sutherland's explanation of criminality, crime is a learned social phenomenon, transmitted in the same manner that more conventional behavior and attitudes are passed on.

In explaining how he developed the theory, Sutherland indicated that he was not even aware that he had done so until, in 1935, Henry McKay referred to "Sutherland's theory": "I asked him what my theory was. He referred me to pages 51–52 of my book" (Sutherland, 1956b, p. 14). The first edition of Sutherland's text was published in 1924; while the 1934 edition to which McKay referred contained the nexus of a theory, it was in the 1939 edition that Sutherland outlined its major propositions. These were slightly modified in the 1947 edition and have remained essentially the same in subsequent editions, which have been coauthored or (since Sutherland's death in 1950) authored by Donald Cressey.

The nine propositions of the differential association theory are these (Sutherland, 1947, pp. 6–7):

- Criminal behavior is learned.
- Criminal behavior is learned in interaction with other persons in a process of communication.
- The principal part of the learning of criminal behavior occurs within intimate personal groups.
- When criminal behavior is learned, the learning includes: (a) techniques of committing the crime, which are sometimes very simple; and (b) the specific direction of motives, drives, rationalizations, and attitudes.
- The specific direction of motives and drives is learned from definitions of the legal codes as favorable or unfavorable.
- A person becomes delinquent because of an excess of definitions favorable to violation of law over definitions unfavorable to violation of law.
- Differential association may vary in frequency, duration, priority, and intensity.
- The process of learning criminal behavior by association with criminal and anticriminal patterns involves all of the mechanisms that are involved in any other learning.
- While criminal behavior is an explanation of general needs and values, it is not explained by those general needs and values since noncriminal behavior is an expression of the same needs and values.

Differential association theory is not directed at the issue of the origin of crime in society, but concentrates instead on the transmission of criminal attitudes and behavior. It is a behavioristic theory—"previous behavior causes subsequent behavior"—and contains elements of a "soft social determinism," that is, exposure to groups does not cause but predisposes individuals to criminal activity or causes them to view it more favorably. Why, then, do not all with similar exposure become similarly criminal? Sutherland's notion of variations in contacts provides for individual reaction to social groups and exposures.

Contacts in differential association vary according to frequency, duration, priority, and intensity. *Frequency* deals with the number of contacts, *duration* with the length of time over which an individual is exposed to such contacts. The sheer length and volume of association

VANTAGE POINT 5.2

Crime Prevention through Environmental Design in Parking Facilities

Because parking facilities are more likely settings for crime—both violent and property—than all other real estate except residential, security is one of the most critical issues facing the owners and operators of parking facilities today. Local government officials are also concerned about the security of these facilities, some of which are city owned or operated, because parking affects the economic viability of a community.

Crime Prevention Through Environmental Design (CPTED), which emphasizes the proper design and effective use of a created environment to reduce crime and enhance the quality of life, is particularly applicable to parking facilities. Incorporating CPTED can significantly reduce the fear and risk of crime, as well as the considerable costs associated with hiring security personnel.

This Research-in-Brief offers an overview of up-to-date design concepts for parking facility securing measures and other possible security and existing parking facility ordinances. The framework and rationale for a flexible plan to improve parking lot security is described.

Crime in Parking Facilities

Because parking facilities comprise a large area with relatively low levels of activity, violent crime is more likely to occur in a parking facility than in other commercial facilities. A typical suburban shopping center requires 1.5 square feet of parking space for every square foot of leasable retail space; office buildings generally need at least 1 square foot of parking space for every 1 square foot of office space.

Therefore, a shopping center that consists of 1 million square feet will probably have 1.5 million square feet of parking. More than 10,000 people may be at a mall during the peak hours of a busy shopping day; however, only a small fraction will be in the parking lot, which is 1.5 times as large as the mall. This fact increases the likelihood that an individual can be isolated in a parking area and targeted for an attack, which, in turn, attracts people with criminal intent.

Other features that make security difficult are simply inherent to parking facilities:

- Parked cars provide hiding places and impede the distribution of lighting.
- Most parking facilities are open to the public.
- An offender's car is not likely to be noted as strange or memorable in a public parking facility.

Passive security refers to physical design features such as lighting. All passive security measures essentially incorporate CPTED concepts. Active security refers to human activities that may or may not involve specialized equipment, such as security patrols, intercoms, and monitored closed circuit television (CCTV) systems.

Even though consultants who specialize in parking design have espoused the use of CPTED for almost 20 years, it has not yet taken hold in the industry. In 1979 the first edition of *The Dimensions of Parking,* published by the Urban Land Institute and authored by the Parking Consultants Council (PCC) of the National Parking Association (NPA), devoted an entire chapter to security design, most of which conforms to today's concept of CPTED.

Why then are so many parking facilities designed with little or no attention to security? Basically because most property owners and architects are not familiar with the basic principles of CPTED. Very lit-

with criminogenic influences impact on different people in different ways. Humans are not robots responding in a predictable manner to a given number of influences. *Priority* refers to the preference individuals express toward the values and attitudes to which they are exposed, while *intensity* entails the degree of meaning the human actor attaches to such exposure. While Sutherland (1947) admits an inability to reach a quantitative or exact measurement of these modalities, a very general example should illustrate their operation. What explains the good child in the bad environment? Despite a great frequency and long duration of exposure to criminal attitudes, such individuals fail to prefer such values and attach greater meaning to noncriminal attitudes that, although less frequently available, may be found in "significant others," perhaps role models such as teachers, coaches, peers, and the like.

VANTAGE POINT 5.2—*Continued*

tle time is devoted to parking designs in typical architectural education programs, and assignments for such projects are often relegated to the most inexperienced members of architectural teams. As a result, active security systems are often needed to correct problems created by architectural designs that failed to incorporate CPTED.

Issues and Findings
Crime Prevention Through Environmental Design (CPTED) concepts can be applied to parking facilities along with active security measures such as guards and emergency communication systems.

Key Issues
Because parking facilities comprise a large volume of space with relatively low levels of activity, violent crime is more likely to occur in a parking facility than in other commercial facilities.

- Many parking facilities lack CPTED design features because most property owners and architects are not familiar with basic principles of design concepts for crime prevention.
- Zoning ordinances and building codes can sometimes hinder effective use of CPTED principles. Examples include requiring landscaping to screen parking facilities, placing height limits on light poles, and mandating enclosure of exit stairs.
- Although CPTED principles can be readily incorporated into parking facilities at design and construction stages, it is often difficult and expensive to upgrade security at a later date.

Key Findings
Municipal governments can have a major influence on building design, and local officials can play a much stronger role in fostering security planning.

- The single most important CPTED security feature is lighting. Lighting codes should meet the standards of the illuminating Engineering Society of North America.
- Elevator lobbies and stairs in open parking garages should be open to the parking areas except at roof levels where glass enclosures may be provided for weather protection.
- Where possible, elevators and stairs should be located on the perimeter to permit natural surveillance from exterior public areas via glass-back elevators and glass at stairs and elevator lobbies.
- Access control and perimeter security should always be considered in the initial design stage. Even if the potential site for the parking facility is low risk, the risk level could change in the future.
- Emergency communications such as panic buttons and closed circuit television cannot compensate for a lack of CPTED; however, they can enhance CPTED in high-risk facilities, and all facilities should be designed so such enhancements can be easily installed.

Officials framing a municipal ordinance to mandate security features in parking facilities should consider requiring facilities to regularly submit an updated management plan that responds to the particular needs of a facility. The plan should include a risk audit and proposed CPTED and active security measures, such as emergency communications.

Source: Mary S. Smith. 1996. "Crime Prevention Through Environmental Design in Parking Facilities." *National Institute of Justice Research in Brief.* April.

InfoTrac College Edition Research
Search the term "Routine activities" and locate an article by Bjarnason and Thorolfur. How do capable guardians and structural restraints have an impact on violent victimization?

A Critique of "Differential Association." Because it is a general theory of criminality and is relatively compatible with many other criminological explanations of crime, differential association theory enjoyed widespread acceptance in the field. It was not, however, without critics. Donald Cressey, Sutherland's coauthor, explains that since Sutherland's principal propositions are presented in only two pages in his textbook, the theory is often misinterpreted by some critics, most notably Vold (1958, p. 194). Among these claimed errors of interpretation, Cressey (Sutherland and Cressey, 1974, pp. 78–80) mentions the following:

- The theory is concerned only with contacts or associations with criminal or delinquent behavior patterns. (It actually refers to both criminal and noncriminal behavior, as demonstrated by the use of terms such as "differential" and "excess" of contacts.)

IN THE NEWS 5.1

CAP INDEX, INC. CRIME VULNERABILITY ASSESSMENT

The CAP (Crimes Against Persons and Property) Index was developed by criminologists Robert Figlio and Steven Aurand. CAP Index, Inc. claims to be the leading provider of crime risk assessment to corporate America and Canada. It can be accessed at: www.apbnews.com/resourcecenter/datacenter/crimecheck/result.html. CAP Index, Inc. has used demographic data to assess the average crime risk in a given area. Enter a ZIP code for local crime maps; a risk rating of one indicates that the risk of violent crime for that area is less than one-fifth the national average, while a rating of ten indicates the risk is ten times the national average. The rating is a weighted statistical average for the entire ZIP code. Such crime risk for residents is different than that for businesses.

The CAP Index is compiled using 21 demographic variables including: population data, housing data, population mobility, economic data, and educational information. These data are more detailed and predictive than standard Uniform Crime Report (UCR) data. A crimecast model is constructed using these data as an indicator of "social disorder."

Source: http://capindex.com/ZIPcode.htm or www.APB.com.

Research Project

Visit the CAP Index, Inc. site: www.apbnews.com/resourcenter/datcenter/crimecheck/result.html, and search your home ZIP code. Does this rating fit your view of the crime risk in your neighborhood?

- The theory says persons become criminals because of an excess of associations with criminals. (It actually says that criminal attitudes can be learned from the unintentional transmission of such values by noncriminals.)
- Using the 1939 version of the theory, critics believe the theory refers to "systematic criminals." (This has been modified since the 1947 version to refer to all criminal behavior.)
- The theory fails to explain why persons have the associations they have. (It does not pretend to do so.)

Cressey (1960) also addresses other criticisms that he feels are misinterpretations, however, a number of shortcomings have been identified:

- While Sutherland traces the roots of criminality to culture conflict and social disorganization, a comprehensive theory of criminality should provide more explanation of the origin of crime.
- Since it is a general theory, it is difficult to either empirically prove or disprove it by means of research, and reformulations are necessary in order to permit testing (see Burgess and Akers, 1966; DeFleur and Quinney, 1966).
- The theory fails to account for all forms of criminality.
- The theory fails to acknowledge the importance of non-face-to-face contacts such as media influences (Radzinowicz and King, 1977, p. 82).

Despite these and other criticisms, differential association remains important as a useful general theory of criminality even though it may fail to specify the process for each individual case of criminality. The theory of differential association remains one of the most cited theories in modern criminology and will probably remain so until a more acceptable general theory of criminality appears. It has also received support in recent research (Matsueda, 1988; Orcutt, 1987), although Warr and Stafford (1991)

(© Marc PoKempner / Tony Stone Images)

Caught by the camera against a backdrop of gang graffiti, these teenagers make "gang signs" with their hands. Gangs transmit their own social values through peer-group interaction.

indicate that attitude is not as important as actual peer behavior and group pressures to conform.

A variation of differential association can be found in Ronald Akers and Robert Burgess's (Burgess and Akers, 1966) "differential reinforcement" (social learning) theory.

> "Differential reinforcement" refers to the balance of anticipated or actual rewards or punishments that follow or are consequences of behavior. Whether individuals will refrain from or commit a crime at any given time . . . depends on the past, present, and anticipated future rewards and punishments for their action (Akers, 1994, p. 98).

Akers' theory combines Sutherland's concept with behavioral conditioning and even classical concepts of rewards and punishments and has found considerable empirical support (Ibid., pp. 102–104).

Miller's "Focal Concerns." Walter Miller's (1958) ideas appeared in an article entitled "Lower Class Culture as a Generating Milieu of Gang Delinquency." Miller limits the applicability of his theory to ". . . members of adolescent street corner groups in lower class communities" (1958, p. 5). Unlike Cohen, who viewed such delinquency as a lower class reaction to middle class values, Miller views such activity as a reflection of the **focal concerns** of dominant themes in lower class culture. These are ". . . areas or issues which command widespread and persistent attention and a high degree of emotional involvement" (p. 7). Faced with a chasm between aspirations and the likelihood of their achievement, lower class youth seek status and prestige within one-sex peer units (gangs) in which they exaggerate focal concerns already in existence in lower class culture. Thus gang delinquency, rather than representing an anomic reaction to unobtainable middle class goals, represents, in the tradition of social process theory, a pattern of subcultural transmission or learning of values prevalent in the local environment.

The **focal concerns of lower class culture** emphasize: *trouble, toughness, smartness, excitement, fate, and autonomy.* Getting into *trouble* often confers prestige and a means of obtaining attention. The "class clown" and the "bad dude" become attention-getting roles. *Toughness,* "machismo," having physical prowess, or being able to handle oneself are highly prized characteristics among lower class males. The "hard guy" is preferable to the "chump," "wimp," or "sissy." *Smartness* ". . . involves the capacity to outsmart, outfox, outwit, dupe, 'take,' or 'con' another . . ." (p. 7). This is illustrated by the "streetwise" game of "playin' the dozens" (Berdie, 1947), a highly ritualistic game of razzing, "ranking," or "cappin' on someone's Mom" practiced by lower class black males in particular. Extremely foul insults are traded by two antagonists, the themes usually relating to sexual matters and female relatives of one's opponent. Such insults are rhythmically presented one-liners whose object is to leave the opponent speechless or "humbled out." "Playin' the dozens" is also known as *signification.* A young man engaging in such activities, creating poetry of the streets, would be regarded in conventional society as having a "bad mouth."

The theme of *excitement* emphasizes the quest for skill, danger, risk, change, activity. Rather than a subject of control and planning, the future is perceived as a matter of *fate,* luck, or good fortune. Gambling's popularity in lower class culture makes it the "poor person's stock exchange." *Autonomy* (independence) looms as a dominant concern in lower class culture, particularly among males, even though it is less likely to be achieved given their narrow occupational and life options. "Being one's own man"—that is, being free from authority, "the man," and external constraint—is a strong value.

A Critique of Miller's Theory.

- Like the other subcultural theories, Miller's theory also ignores middle and upper class delinquent/criminal activity.
- By focusing exclusively on the lower class, Miller and others in this tradition are perhaps most responsible for the criticism that mainstream sociology ignores deviance of the powerful.
- Miller's theory rests very heavily on the assumption of the existence of a distinctive lower class culture that holds values and attitudes distinct from, if not at odds with, dominant middle class values. The pluralistic nature of U.S. society makes it quite uncertain that such a distinctive value system, solely based on class, indeed exists.

Miller's theory views criminogenic influences as learned or transmitted as part of subcultural values. Similarly, the writings of David Matza present delinquency as part of a general social process of learned cultural values rather than as an anomic reaction to unobtainable goals.

Matza's "Delinquency and Drift." The theories of David Matza are presented in his book, *Delinquency and Drift* (1964), and in a coauthored article with Gresham Sykes (Sykes and Matza, 1957), entitled "Techniques of Neutralization." Matza's theories are an example of **soft determinism,** which holds that, *although human behavior is determined to some extent by outside forces, there still exists an element of free will or individual responsibility* (Matza, 1964, pp. 5–7). Humans are neither entirely constrained nor entirely free, nor is the individual entirely committed to delinquent or nondelinquent behavior. Matza (p. 28) explains the drift theory of delinquency:

> The delinquent exists in a limbo between convention and crime responding in turn to the demands of each, flirting now with one, now the other, but postponing commitment, evading decision. Thus he drifts between criminal and conventional action.

Subterranean Values. Rather than being wholly committed to delinquency, most delinquents are dabbling in it and are acting out **subterranean values** of society (pp. 63–64) that exist alongside more conventional values in a pluralistic society such as the United States. Conventional society attempts to control the expression of these values and reserve it for the proper time and place; in a sense, it is the practice of "morality with a wink." The delinquent, rather than being committed to goals that are alien to society, exaggerates society's subterranean values and acts them out in caricature. Sykes and Matza explain (1957, p. 717):

> The delinquent may not stand as an alien in the body of society but may represent instead a disturbing reflection or caricature. His vocabulary is different, to be sure, but kicks, big time spending and rep have immediate counterparts in the value system of the law abiding. The delinquent has picked up and emphasized one part of the subterranean values that coexist with other, publicly proclaimed values possessing a more respectable air.

Thus, while conventional mores disapprove of subterranean values, they often represent "hidden" patterns or themes in the culture. Illicit sexual behavior, slick business practices, a dislike of work, substance abuse, and media violence as a popular form of entertainment are examples. Delinquents simply have poor training and timing in the expression of subterranean values. The pervasiveness of subterranean values might be illustrated by the attempt of conventional members of "straight" society to appear "hip," "with it," and "streetwise." "Can you dig it?"

Techniques of Neutralization. Sykes and Matza's (1957) term **techniques of neutralization** refers to *rationalizations or excuses that juveniles use to neutralize responsibility for deviant actions.* In drift situations, offenders can lessen their responsibility by exaggerating normal legal defenses (for example, self-defense or insanity) or by pointing to the subterranean values prevalent in society. They identify *five techniques of neutralization:*

1. *Denial of responsibility,* such as appeals based on one's homelife, lack of affection, and social class.
2. *Denial of harm to anyone,* such as defining stealing as "borrowing" or drug abuse as harming no one but the offender.
3. *Denial of harm to victim,* in which the assault is justified since the person harmed was also a criminal.
4. *Condemning the condemners,* reversing the labeling process by claiming that authorities are more corrupt than the offender, and are hypocritical as well.
5. *Appeal to higher authority,* which claims that the offense was necessary in order to defend one's neighborhood or gang.

As an illustration of the techniques of neutralization, the song "Gee, Officer Krupke" from the musical *West Side Story* has members of the Jets arguing that they are victims of "a social disease."

Sykes and Matza (p. 668) explain:

> The delinquent both has his cake and eats it too, for he remains committed to the dominant normative system and yet so qualifies its imperatives that violations are "acceptable" if not "right." Thus the delinquent represents not a radical opposition to law abiding society but something more like an apologetic failure, often more sinned against than sinning in his own eyes. We call these justifications of deviant behavior techniques of neutralization; and we believe these techniques make up a crucial component of Sutherland's "definitions favorable to the violation of the law." It is by learning these techniques that the juveniles become delinquent, rather than by learning moral imperatives, values or attitudes standing in direct contradiction to those of the dominant society.

A Critique of Matza's Theory. Matza provides a transition between Sutherland's social process theories and the social control theories to be discussed next. By combining deterministic models with the notion of free will, he avoids the overly deterministic nature of many earlier theories and explains why the majority of individuals who find themselves in criminogenic settings do not commit crime. His concept of neutralization enables him to escape the problem inherent in previous subcultural theories of delinquency, which rested on the premise that delinquent values were at variance with conventional values. Some possible shortcomings of Matza's views include the following:

- While some research has shown offenders to be prone to rationalizing their behavior (Regoli and Poole, 1978; Ball, 1980), Hindelang (1970) found different value systems among delinquents. Obviously more research is needed.
- In order for his theory to be correct, empirical evidence must demonstrate that Matza's neutralization takes place during the period of drift preceding the act, a concept that may be difficult to operationalize.

Hamlin (1988) argues that the notion of rational choice in neutralization theory has been misplaced and that such rationalizations are utilized after the fact only when behavior is called into question (see Minor, 1981 and 1984, for additional analysis).

The transitional nature of Matza's theories with social control approaches can be found in his notion of drift, in which individuals become temporarily detached from social control mechanisms. This release from group bonds is the basic unit of analysis in social control theories.

Social Control Theories

The final grouping of mainstream socio-criminological theories to be discussed is referred to as **social control theories** and is represented by the work of Walter Reckless and Travis Hirschi.

Social control theories address the issue of how society maintains or elicits social control and the manner in which it obtains conformity or fails to obtain it in the form of deviance. As Gibbons (1979, p. 113) points out, this once-major area of sociological investigation is still viable. While one aspect of the concept dealt with penology or corrections, another aspect, the subject of this discussion, was concerned with socialization and learning processes, the internalization of societal norms (inner controls), and external influences (outer controls) (Clark and Gibbs, 1965). Although a number of writers have contributed to social control theories, this presentation will concentrate primarily on the formulations of Walter Reckless and his associates (1956, 1961; Reckless and Dinitz, 1957, 1967) and Travis Hirschi (1969).

Reckless's "Containment" Theory. One of the earliest and best-known examples of social control theory was Walter Reckless's (1961) containment theory. Like his contemporary Sutherland, Reckless was a product of the Chicago school of sociology and one of the mainstream pioneers in U.S. criminology (Gibbons, 1979, p. 115). Reckless wrote an early textbook called *The Crime Problem* in 1940, and in a much later edition began to state his theories. **Containment theory** basically holds that *individuals have various social controls (containments) that assist them in resisting pressures that draw them toward criminality.* This theory attempts to account for social forces that may predispose individuals to crime as well as for individual characteristics that may insulate them from or further propel them toward criminality. Various social pressures, treated in previously discussed deterministic theories, exert pushes and pulls on the individual; these pressures interact with containments (protective barriers), both internal and external to the individual, and these containments add the element of free will in resisting criminality. Thus the presence or absence of social pressures interacts with the presence or absence of containments to produce or not produce individual criminality.

The basic elements of Reckless's containment theory (Reckless, Dinitz, and Kay, 1957; Reckless and Dinitz, 1967) can be summarized:

- *Layers of Social Pressures:*
  External pressures push an individual toward criminality. Variables impinging on an individual include: poor living conditions, adverse economic conditions, minority group membership, and the lack of legitimate opportunities.
  External pulls draw individuals away from social norms and are exerted from without by bad companions, deviant subcultures, and media influences.
  Internal pressures push an individual toward criminality; they include personality contingencies such as inner tensions, feelings of inferiority or inadequacy, mental conflict, organic defects, and the like.
- *Containments:*
  Inner containments refer to the internalization of conventional behavioral values and the development of personality characteristics that enable one to resist pressures. Strong self-concept, identity, and strong resistance to frustration serve as examples.
  Outer containments are represented by effective family and near support systems that assist in reinforcing conventionality and insulating the individual from the assault of outside pressures.

Reckless and his colleagues (Reckless, Dinitz and Kay, 1957) felt that the theory was helpful in explaining both delinquency and nondelinquency, as indicated by the title of one article, "The 'Good Boy' in a High Delinquency Area." Individuals may become predisposed toward criminality because of strong external pressures and pulls and weak inner and outer containments, while others with these same pressures may resist because of a strong family or through a strong sense of self. Weak containments plus strong external pressures provide the conditions for individual criminality. The attractiveness of containment theory is its general ability to subsume variables discussed in other more specific theories as well as its attempt to link the deterministic and free will models and to intersect socioeconomic factors, as well as biological and psychological factors, with individual biography.

A Critique of "Containment" Theory. Reckless and associates (Reckless, Dinitz, and Murray, 1957; Reckless, Dinitz, and Kay, 1957; Scarpitti et al., 1960) have attempted to verify his theory. In one study, they had teachers in a high delinquency area nominate "good boys;" they found strong self-images as well as more conventional behavior among this group four years later. But critics call for more research, indicating that poor operationalization and weak methodology have plagued these studies (Schwartz and Tangri, 1965; Schrag, 1971). As a very general sensitizing theory that attempts to account for both criminogenic forces and individual responses, the containment theory is a useful descriptive model; but actual empirical specification of the process is problematic.

Hirschi's "Social Bond" Theory. Travis Hirschi (1969) in *Causes of Delinquency* presented his **social bond theory,** which basically states that *delinquency takes place when a person's bonds to society are weakened or broken, thus reducing personal stakes in conformity.* Individuals maintain conformity for fear that violations will rupture their relationships (cause them to "lose face") with family, friends, neighbors, jobs, school, and the like. In essence, individuals conform not for fear of prescribed punishments in the criminal law, but rather from concern with violating their groups' mores and the personal image of them held by those groups. *These bonds to society consist of four components: attachment, commitment, involvement, and belief.*

Attachment refers to a bond to others (such as family and peers) and important institutions (such as churches and schools). Weak attachment to parents and family may impair personality development, while poor relationships with the school are viewed as particularly instrumental in delinquency. *Commitment* involves the degree to which an individual maintains a vested interest in the social and economic system. If an individual has much to lose in terms of status, job, and community standing, he or she is less likely to violate the law. Adults, for instance, have many more such commitments than do juveniles. *Involvement* entails engagement in legitimate social and recreational activities that either leaves too little time to get into trouble or binds one's status to yet other important groups whose esteem one wishes to maintain. Finally, *belief* in the conventional norms and value system and the law acts as a bond to society. Like Reckless's containment theory and Matza's delinquency and drift, Hirschi's social bond theory combines elements of determinism and free will; individual choice still enters the equation.

A Critique of "Social Bond" Theory. Social bond theory has been relatively well received because as a general theory it subsumes and is supported by many more specific findings with respect to relationships between crime/delinquency and particular variables. School performance, family relationships, peer group attachments, and community involvement as predictors of norm violation have been stock items in criminological research. Research by Hirschi (1969), a partial replication by Hindelang (1973), and review of studies by Bernard (1987) provide some strong support for control theory. Strong parental attachments, commitment to conventional values, and involvement in conventional activities and with conventional peers were found to be predictive of nondelinquent activity. While Agnew (1985) found that social control variables explained only 1-to-2 percent of future delinquency and that cross-sectional studies exaggerated the importance of Hirschi's theory, Rosenbaum (1987) found that the theory explained some types of delinquency better than others. The theory accounted for more female than male crime and for more drug use than violence or property offenses. Variations of social control theory have been offered by Briar and Piliavin (1965), who theorize that individuals evaluate the risk of being caught and punished once bonds are weakened, and Glaser (1978, p. 126), who combines elements of differential association, control, and classical theory. While Hirschi's social control appears to be quite useful in explaining the general process of commitment/noncommitment to delinquency, more research is certainly needed in order to specify and modify it. Hirschi's theory is not concerned with societal origins of crime but with individual deviation from given societal norms.

Gottfredson and Hirschi's "General Theory of Crime." As a successor to his "social bond" theory, Hirschi joined with Michael Gottfredson in proposing another theory. Combining elements of classical, positivistic, and social control theories, Gottfredson and Hirschi (1990; Hirschi and Gottfredson, 1990) claim to have developed a "general theory of crime." This general theory is that "low self-control" in the pursuit of "self-interest" causes crime. Deficiencies in parenting distinguish those who express this trait from those who do not, who express themselves in greater deviance and criminality. Those with high self-control would be less likely to become involved in such activity. Surprisingly, Hirschi and Gottfredson also claim that this same "self-control" theory explains "white collar crime" (Hirschi and Gottfredson, 1987) and that the causes of white collar crime are not distinct from the causes of other crimes (see Cullen et al., 1991; Daly, 1989).

Glaser (1990, p. 2) notes that Gottfredson and Hirschi's "general theory of crime" is "usefully complemented, and not contradicted, by differential association, deviant subculture, and social learning theories. These theories explain why socially disorganized neighborhoods provide the greatest opportunities, social support, and learned rationalizations for persons to express low self control in street felonies."

While Gottfredson and Hirschi's "general theory of crime" is a very ambitious effort, it is regarded as severely flawed in relation to what later in this chapter is described as the "global fallacy," the tendency to make a useful specific theory of crime explain all crime. Is this theory intended to explain corporate price fixing, insider trading on Wall Street, international terrorism? Hirschi and Gottfredson also rely upon the Uniform Crime Reports (UCR) for their measurement of white collar crime. This is a "baffling" (Reed and Yeager, 1991) error since, as any student of criminology is aware, the UCR measures only "the white collar crimes" of fraud, forgery, and embezzlement, and even these tend to be less serious cases (Steffensmeier, 1989b). The UCR is a worthless measure of white collar crime. Reed and Yeager (1996) further point out that Hirschi and Gottfredson test their theory by focusing on white collar crimes that most resemble conventional crimes. When Reed and Yeager examined the theory using organizational (corporate) offenders, they found it inadequate.

Finally, as discussed in Chapter 3 in the section on the family, there is a tendency in this theory to commit what Currie (1985, p. 185) calls the "fallacy of autonomy," to assume that what happens in the family (poor parenting creating low self control) is somehow separate from other social policies, inequality, racism, unemployment, and social neglect.

John Hagan's "Power-Control" Theory. John Hagan (1989) in his **power control theory** of crime, attempts to rectify a major shortcoming in delinquency theory—its almost total ignoring of female offenders. *Viewing much delinquency as risk taking or fun, children who are exposed to strong parental controls will avoid risk, which lessens delinquency.* According to John Hagan, power relationships between father and mother influence the control exercised over sons and daughters.

In traditional patriarchal households, boys are exposed to fewer controls than girls and are, therefore, greater risk takers and more delinquent than girls. In more equalitarian family structures, both sexes are subject to similar social controls and have more similar delinquency levels. Cullen and Agnew (1999, p. 165) indicate that the empirical validity of Hagan's thesis is still in doubt. The theory does not appear to address single parent families or more serious, violent crime.

Summary

Theory is necessary for capturing the essence of criminology. The *major sociological theoretical approaches in criminology* are: mainstream theories (anomie, social process, and social control approaches) and critical theories (labeling, conflict, and radical [Marxist] theories).

Émile Durkheim is the father of the "anomie tradition," which also includes Merton's notion of "anomie and personality adaptations," Cloward and Ohlin's "differential social organization," and Cohen's theory that delinquency is a "lower class reaction" to middle class values. While Durkheim viewed anomie as a state of normlessness, a moral malaise experienced by individuals when they lack clear-cut guidelines, later theorists such as Merton adapted the theory to refer to a situation that results from a gap between societal goals and the means provided to achieve them. This results, according to Merton, in "modes of personality adaptation": conformity, innovation, retreatism, ritualism, or rebellion. Cloward and Ohlin argue that the juvenile-subculture gang response to anomie depends on the "differential social organization" (legal and illegal opportunity structures) in the neighborhood. Depending on the type, one of three juvenile delinquent subcultures may emerge: the criminal, conflict, or retreatist. Cohen's theory of delinquency presents it as "lower class reactions to unobtainable or rejected middle class values" such as ambition, verbal skills, nonviolence, and the like. He views much delinquency as nonutilitarian, malicious, and negativistic.

The *social process tradition* concentrates on learning, socialization, and subcultural transmission of criminal values. Originating in the work of the "Chicago school" of sociology in the twenties and thirties, and in particular with the works/ideas of Burgess ("concentric zone model"), Park ("natural areas"), and Wirth ("urbanism as a way of life"), *human ecology* was seen, at least initially, as an organizing perspective. This approach examines the interrelationship between humans and their physical/social environment. Included among better-known Chicago school criminologists are Clifford Shaw and David McKay, and Edwin Sutherland.

Making extensive use of maps and official statistics, Shaw and McKay viewed delinquency as reflecting the "social disorganization" of areas in which individuals lived, so delinquency was less a matter of individual abnormality and more a matter of "cultural transmission" or social learning. Concern that Shaw and McKay committed the "ecological fallacy" (attributed group characteristics to individuals) may be alleviated by the fact that they performed a number of case studies of criminals. Cohen and Felson's (1979) "routine activities approach" views crime as related to everyday, normal activities such as the proliferation of consumer goods and the lack of guardians. Sutherland's "differential association theory," the most popular theory in U.S. criminology, states that individuals become predisposed toward criminality because of an excess of contacts that advocate criminal behavior, *contacts that vary according to frequency, priority, intensity, and duration.* Differential association aims at describing the process by which crime is transmitted but does not address itself to origins of crime. Miller's theory of delinquency views it as reflecting "the focal concerns of the lower class," such as an emphasis on trouble, toughness, smartness, excitement, fate, and autonomy.

David Matza's "delinquency and drift" theory claims that individuals are often in a limbo or uncommitted status between delinquent and nondelinquent behavior. He and Gresham Sykes view delinquents as acting out "subterranean values" (underground values that exist along with more conventionally approved values) and utilizing "techniques of neutralization" (rationalizations) in order to justify their behavior.

Social control theories argue that individuals deviate when removed or weakened. Reckless's "containment theory" views *containments* (Walter Reckless) or *social bonds* (Travis Hirschi) as individuals resisting or giving in to various pressures based on social controls (self-concept or close support systems). Hirschi's "social bond theory" states that delinquency arises when bonds to society are reduced and the individual has fewer stakes in conformity. These bonds consist of: *attachment, commitment involvement, and belief.*

KEY CONCEPTS

Anomie
"Chicago School"
Cohen's Lower-Class Reaction Theory
"Containment" Theory
Delinquency and Drift
Differential Association Theory
"Differential Opportunity"
Ecological Fallacy
Human Ecology
"Looking-Glass Self"
Merton's "Anomie" Theory
Miller's Focal Concerns
Modes of Personality Adaptation
Natural Areas
"Power Control" Theory
"Social Bond" Theory
"Social Control" Theory
Social Disorganization Theory
Soft Determinism
Subcultural Theories
Subterranean Values
Techniques of Neutralization

REVIEW QUESTIONS

1. How does Merton's concept of anomie differ from that of Durkheim? What is your assessment of the usefulness of Merton's anomie/strain theory in explaining crime in the United States?
2. What contribution did the Chicago School of Sociology make to the study of criminology?
3. What are Sutherland's "Differential Association" theory's assumptions regarding crime causation?

4. What is Miller's notion of delinquency reflecting the focal concerns of the lower class? How does this differ from Albert Cohen's notion of delinquency being a "lower class reaction to middle class society?"
5. David Matza had three important concepts: "delinquency and drift," "subterranean values," and "techniques of neutralization." Discuss each of these and explain how they explain delinquency/crime.
6. Discuss Reckless's "Containment Theory." What are some containments that enable individuals to overcome the various layers of social pressures?
7. What is the major premise of "social bond theory?" How do these bonds vary for each individual? What have been some criticisms of this theory?
8. What is your assessment of Gottfredson and Hirschi's "General Theory of Crime?"
9. How do mainstream sociological theories differ from the earlier classical, economic, ecological, and positivistic theories?
10. What is "routine activities" theory? Give an example of the practical application of this theory.

INFOTRAC COLLEGE EDITION RESEARCH

Vantage Point 5.1 InfoTrac College Edition Research
Search the name: "Oscar Newman." What is his main thesis regarding the impact of defensible space on crime?

Vantage Point 5.2 InfoTrac College Edition Research
Search the term "Routine activities" and locate an article by Bjarnason and Thorolfur. How do capable guardians and structural restraints have an impact on violent victimization?

SELECTED READINGS

Cesare Beccaria. 1963. *On Crimes and Punishments.* Translated by Henry Paolucci. Indianapolis: Bobbs-Merrill.
This slim volume is Beccaria's major statement on crime and punishment—the thoughts that had a profound impact on the reformation of Anglo-American and continental criminal justice.

Francis Cullen and Robert Agnew, editors. 1999. *Criminological Theory: Past to Present.* Los Angeles: Roxbury.
This anthology has a selection of 38 classic and contemporary articles and features excellent introductory essays to each section.

Lee Ellis and Anthony Walsh. 2000. *Criminology: A Global Perspective.* Boston: Allyn and Bacon.
This criminological textbook features three chapters providing one of the best contemporary presentations of biologically-related crime theories.

Stephen Gould. 1981. *The Mismeasure of Man.* New York: Norton.
A persistent critic of biological positivism, Gould even went to New Jersey to document the misrepresentation of the Kallikaks and other discussions of early genetic studies and criminality.

Jack Katz. 1988. *Seductions of Crime: Moral and Sensual Attractions in Doing Evil.* New York: Basic Books.
In an update of classical theory, Katz proposes the theory that the major motivation for crime is the sheer fun and dangerous excitement of crime.

Robert K. Merton. 1961. *Social Theory and Social Structure.* Revised edition. New York: The Free Press.
This work contains many of the seminal ideas of a giant in American criminology—Robert Merton.

Steven F. Messner and Richard Rosenfeld. 1994. *Crime and the American Dream.* Belmont, California: Wadsworth.
In a well-received update of Merton's strain theory, Messner and Rosenfeld discuss an institutionalization of deviant means to economic success as pervasive in American society. This theory can be used to explain white collar crime.

B. F. Skinner. 1971. *Beyond Freedom and Dignity.* New York: Knopf.
Skinner's concept of "behavioral modification" has had a major theoretical and practical impact on rehabilitation programs, particularly in the area of juvenile delinquency in the U.S.

George B. Vold, Thomas J. Bernard, and Jeffrey B. Snipes. 1998. *Theoretical Criminology.* Fourth edition. New York: Oxford University Press.
This remains the standard reference on past and current developments in criminological theory.

Frank Williams III and Marilyn McShane. 1994. *Criminological Theory.* Second edition. Englewood Cliffs, N.J.: Prentice-Hall.
This is an excellent general reference work that covers the entire range of criminological theory.

CRIMINOLOGICAL THEORY III: SOCIOLOGICAL CRITICAL THEORIES

> The whole political process of law making, law breaking, and law enforcement becomes a direct reflection of deep-seated and fundamental conflicts between interest groups and their more general struggles for the control of the police power of the state.
>
> —George Vold, *Theoretical Criminology* (1958; 208–209.)

Mainstream vs. Critical Criminology

The general characteristics of mainstream criminology, although subject to variation in individual anomie, social process, or social control theories, include the following (Gibbons, 1979, pp. 77–79; Gibbons and Garabedian, 1974):

- An emphasis on criminal behavior rather than on the criminalization of behavior. Emphasis had been on the criminal rather than on the social control machinery.
- A consensus world view in which the existing society and its operations are perceived as relatively viable or unquestioned.
- A critical, sometimes cynical, stance with respect to societal institutions, combined with a liberal optimism on reform measures.
- A mild pessimism regarding the perfectibility of the criminal justice system, but willingness to work within the established social order.
- Advocating the rehabilitation of offenders and their adjustment to the status quo.
- A positivistic orientation that stresses objectivity and empirical analysis.

Much contemporary criminological theory fails to address the full range of criminal behavior and confines its theorizing to the measurable, official crime and delinquency and lower level white collar crimes. It is unclear whether John Gotti, Charles Keating, Oliver North, or Ramzi Yousef lack self-control, have no bonds to society, or have IQ deficits; and it is unclear whether executives at General Electric, North American Rockwell, General Motors, or Ford fit traditional "lambda" profiles (rates of offending), have IQ or genetic deficits, or should be the subjects of "three strikes and you're out" provisions.

Critical criminology consists of a variety of perspectives that challenge basic assumptions of mainstream criminology. It is espoused by a group of U.S. thinkers who emerged in the sixties and seventies and who have been variously labeled as representatives of "conflict," "radical," "new," "critical," or "Marxist" criminology. Inciardi (1980, p. 7) explains:

> The perspective is new and radical in that it departs somewhat from the mainstream or traditional criminological emphases on the nature and etiology of criminal behavior; it is conflict oriented and critical in that it focuses more fully on value and cultural differences, social conflicts, racism, and sexism as sources of crime and deviance in contemporary society; and it is Marxist in that a number of its representatives argue that law—and, by extension, crime—and the structure of individual and group interactions which support legal codes flow from the manner in which the relations of economic production are organized.

Critical Criminology

Critical criminology consists of *five major types of theoretical approach: the labeling (societal reaction) perspective, conflict theory, feminist, new critical, and radical (Marxist) viewpoint.* While each of these approaches will be detailed shortly, here are *some common characteristics of critical criminology:*

- Crime is a label attached to behavior, usually that of the less powerful in society.
- More powerful groups in society control this labeling process in order to protect their vested interests.

- The conflict model rather than consensus model explains the criminalization process.
- Crime is often a rational response to inequitable conditions in capitalistic societies.

More extreme statements advocate a critical philosophy and practical revolutionary action (*praxis*) as opposed to value-free scientific inquiry.

While views of critical criminologists diverge, making it difficult to identify unitary themes, critical criminologists perceive themselves as making a radical break with a consensus, ameliorative, and essentially conservative world view. Critical criminologists view their mainstream counterparts as handmaidens or social technicians for the status quo and see themselves as champions of the underdog and sometimes as prophets of a new social order. They feel that mainstream theories seemed to ignore economic, racial, and sexual inequality. Milovanovic (1996) sees more recent critical criminology as an outgrowth of radical and feminist criminology of the 1970s and 1980s.

The discussion of critical criminology will begin first with the labeling (societal reaction) theory, followed by conflict, feminist, new critical, and radical criminological theory.

Labeling Theory

> "If men define situations as real, they are real in their consequences."
>
> —W. I. Thomas, *The Child in America* (1928)

Although there were earlier precedents, *labeling theory* (sometimes called "*the societal reaction perspective*") became a major criminological approach in the sixties, primarily in the United States. Labeling theorists base their point of view on symbolic interactionism, a school of thought that emphasizes the subjective and interactional nature of human experiences. Derived from the writings of George Herbert Mead and Charles Horton Cooley and expressed later in the work of Herbert Blumer, George Homans, and Harold Garfinckel, with variations called exchange theory, ethnomethodology, and role theory, the emphasis in symbolic interactionism is on analysis of subjective meanings of social interaction as perceived from the standpoint of the actor. Individuals perceive the meaning of their activity through the reaction of others.

Labeling theory says that *individuals are deviant mainly because they have been labeled as deviant by social control agencies and others.* The notion of deviance is not inherent in the act itself, but rather in the reaction and label attached to the actor; that is, crime is a label and not an act. Frank Tannenbaum called the process of attaching a label to deviants "the dramatization of evil" (1938). He (pp. 19–20) viewed this criminalization process as:

> . . . a process of tagging, defining, identifying, segregating, describing, emphasizing, making conscious and self-conscious; it becomes a way of stimulating, suggesting, emphasizing, and evoking the very traits complained of. . . .

Along with Edwin Lemert (1951), Howard Becker (1963, 1964), Edwin Schur (1969, 1971), and others, Tannenbaum and the labeling theorists attempted to shift criminological inquiry from the deviant act to the machinery of social control and societal reaction. In a sense, this reverses the usual process of analysis; rather than assuming that criminal behavior causes societal reaction, it posits that societal reaction causes criminal behavior.

Schrag (1971, pp. 89–91) summarizes some of the basic assumptions of labeling theory:

- No act is intrinsically criminal.
- Criminal definitions are enforced in the interests of the powerful.
- A person does not become a criminal by violation of the law, but only by the designation of criminality by authorities.
- Due to the fact that everyone both conforms and deviates, people should not be dichotomized into criminal and noncriminal categories.

- The act of "getting caught" begins the labeling process.
- "Getting caught" and decision making in the criminal justice system are a function of the offender as opposed to offense characteristics.
- Age, socioeconomic class, and race are the major offender characteristics that establish patterns of differential criminal justice decision making.
- Labeling is a process that eventually produces identification with a deviant image and subculture and a resulting "rejection of the rejectors."

Lemert's "Secondary Deviance." Two important concepts in labeling theory are Edwin Lemert's (1967, p. 17) notions of primary deviance and secondary deviance. **Primary deviance** refers to *the initial deviant act itself,* while **secondary deviance** is concerned with *the psychological reorganization the individual experiences as a result of being caught and labeled as a deviant.* Once this stigma or discrediting mark or status is attached, the individual may find it very difficult to escape the label and may come to identify with this new deviant role.

Deviant behavior, then, is viewed as having been created in society by control agencies representing the interest of dominant groups (Piven, 1981, p. 490). For Lemert the usual approach to analyzing deviance is reversed. He states (Lemert, 1967, p. v):

> This is a large turn away from the older sociology which tended to rest heavily upon the idea that deviance leads to social control. I have come to believe that the reverse idea, i.e., social control leads to deviance, is equally tenable and the potentially richer premise for studying deviance in modern society.

Cullen and Agnew (1999, p, 271) give the example of sexual assault on women. In the past designation of rape was reserved for victimizations by strangers in which physical injuries have occurred—what Estrich (1987) said the criminal justice system at the time considered to be "real rape." The women's rights groups challenged this and broadened the label to include "date rape," or sexual assaults committed in intimate relationships. A new reality was constructed, and rape was broadened to include a wider range of victimizations.

Sociologist Howard Becker (1963) has coined the term *moral entrepreneurs* to describe agents or officials who are concerned with creating and labeling new categories of deviance in order to expand the social control function of their organization. In Becker's view, deviance, rather than being inherent in the quality of the act, is so designated only by societal reaction and the subsequent labeling or stigmatization process.

A Critique of Labeling Theory. Some of the criticisms of the labeling perspective include the following:

- Labeling theory is overly deterministic and denies individual responsibility. Akers (1967, p. 46) very dramatically states:

  > Those of this school come dangerously close to saying that the actual behavior is unimportant. . . . One sometimes gets the impression from reading this literature that people go about minding their own business, and then—"wham"—bad society comes along and slaps them with a stigmatized label. Forced into the role of deviant the individual has little choice, but to be deviant. This is an exaggeration of course, but such an image can be gained easily from an overemphasis on the impact of labeling.

  Violators of societal rules are not passive robots of societal reaction.
- Some acts are universally regarded as intrinsically "wrong" (Wellford, 1975, p. 334). While labeling theorists have concentrated on public order crimes where the model may be more appropriate, they tend to generalize to all forms of deviance. Murder,

forcible rape, aggravated assault, and robbery are more universally regarded as *mala in se.* Schur (1971, p. 14) observes: ". . . borderline forms of deviance seem to be especially good candidates for labeling analysis and those deviations on which widespread consensus exists less promising candidates."

- The societal reaction approach pays inadequate attention to the causes of the initial deviant act, almost as if to say that the social control agencies cause crime.
- While labeling theorists citing self-report surveys argue that nearly everyone commits crime, their argument seems to suggest that labels are attached capriciously, almost randomly. In fact offenders involved in serious crimes are more likely to be labeled.
- Wellford (1975, p. 343), on the basis of a review of Schrag's assumptions and the existing empirical evidence in criminology and the social sciences, concluded, ". . . the assumptions underlying the theory are at significant variance with the data as we now understand it, or are not crucial to the labeling perspective."

Robert Bohm (1997, pp. 116–118) offers some additional criticisms of labeling theory:

- In siding with the "underdog," labeling theorists tend to romanticize the offender as someone reacting to an unjust society. Most of these offenders are victimizing others from the same social group and are committing real harm and suffering.
- Labeling is not a theory, but a "sensitizing concept."
- It does not explain primary deviance. The label does not create the initial act. In some instances people develop criminal self images without ever being labeled. Bohm (1997, p. 117) indicates: "Furthermore, if the delinquent label is so stigmatizing, why do most delinquents not engage in adult criminality . . . why do most criminals stop their illegal activities when they reach middle age?"
- Labeling theory ignores individual differences among criminals, for example, low risk versus high risk criminals.
- The theory has a simplistic view of the criminalization process and the differential power of label makers.
- Does the process of labeling create more crime than it prevents? The answer is unknown.

By focusing primarily on the social control machinery, labeling theory has obvious inadequacies as a general theory of criminality; but this focus on societal reaction corrected an overly conservative, positivistic approach to criminological theory—a tradition to be even further challenged by conflict criminology. While critics are correct that studies of the enforcement laws and administration of justice for traditional crimes (murder, rape, and the like) do not indicate bias (Wellford, 1975), this does not therefore repudiate the labeling point of view since it still does not speak to the conflict perspective that acts committed by the poor are more likely to be labeled criminal than acts committed by the wealthy. Labeling theory appears to have some validity with respect to areas of deviant behavior, such as mental illness, and in highlighting the lack of stigmatization in many areas of organizational and occupational crime, but it has clearly been repudiated when attempts have been made to apply it to traditional and universally condemned crimes such as murder.

John Braithwaite's Shaming Theory. John Braithwaite's (1989a) **shaming theory** argues that *stigmatizing shaming of offenders makes matters worse and increases crime.* Such a process makes the offender an irredeemable outlaw, irreconcilable with the community. In a sense the person is made into a permanent *persona non grata* and has little choice but to associate with similarly stigmatized persons. Braithwaite calls for "reintegrative shaming," efforts to reintegrate the offender back into the community of respectables. He claims that this is practiced in Japan and is one of the reasons for that country's low crime rate. Significantly, Braithwaite (1989b) applies his theory to organizational offenders, an admirable effort given criminological theory's obsession with juvenile delinquency. Acceptance back into the conventional society reinforces conventional social bonds and reduces recidivism.

Conflict Criminology

Conflict theory in sociology has a long tradition, beginning with Georg Simmel (1955) in his *Conflict and the Web of Group Affiliations,* originally published in English in 1908. Criminological expressions of this tradition can be traced to Marx and Bonger, discussed in Chapter 4, and more recently to Ralf Dahrendorf (1959) and George Vold (1958). In Chapter 1 we made a distinction between the consensus model, which views criminal law as originating in agreement of the majority, and the conflict model, which points to a conflict of interest among groups in which the dominant group controls the legal machinery of the state. The initial edition of Vold's *Theoretical Criminology* was the first to be extensively based on the conflict approach. Thorsten Sellin's (1938) notion of "culture conflict" as an explanation of crime is also part of this tradition. Sellin viewed criminal law as originating in cultural or normative conflict in which more powerful groups in society are able to make laws that reflect their norms and values.

Ralf Dahrendorf (1959) reformulated Marxian theory in *Class and Class Conflict in Industrial Society,* proposing a more pluralistic conflict theory that depicts numerous groups competing for power, influence, and dominance. While Dahrendorf did not specifically speak to the crime issue, his theoretical work influenced much of the conflict tradition in criminology.

George Vold's (1958) *Theoretical Criminology,* subsequent editions of which were posthumously updated by Thomas Bernard (Vold, 1979; Vold and Bernard, 1986), builds on the work of Dahrendorf. Vold proposed that society is made up of a variety of continually competing interest groups and that conflict is one of its essential elements (Vold, 1979, p. 204), with more powerful groups able to have the state formulate laws in their interests. In Vold's view, many criminal acts represent challenges by subordinate groups to the existing dominant group's control, although he seems to restrict this explanation to issues related to political-ideological conflicts such as political reform movements, union conflicts, civil rights disputes, and the like. Crime, then, can be explained as a product of intergroup conflict that expresses the political struggle of these groups. While Vold's theory does not adequately explain irrational, personal, violent acts, his emphasis on the conflict basis of criminal law had a profound impact on later theories.

As indicated previously, a number of tags are used to refer to the "new" or emergent conflict criminology in the seventies. It is at times difficult to distinguish between "conflict" criminology (which, as expressed by Vold and Dahrendorf, proposes a pluralistic model with a variety of competing groups) and "radical" criminology (which generally espouses an orthodox, neoMarxian, ideological view). Austin Turk has been one of the more persistent advocates of conflict criminology. Many figures to be discussed, particularly William Chambliss and Richard Quinney, demonstrate theoretical evolution from early conflict-orientation to later, more Marxian conceptions. The pluralistic conflict approach assumes that different class, racial, ethnic, and subculturally distinct interest groups vie for political dominance and the assistance of the legal machinery of the state in order to protect their interests (Hills, 1971). Unlike the situation with the Marxian model, no one group dominates completely.

Austin Turk. Austin Turk (1969a, 1972, and 1980) has been a prolific writer in the conflict perspective. His basic position can be summarized in the following propositions (Turk, 1980, pp. 82–83):

- Individuals are different in their understandings and commitments.

- Divergence leads to conflict.
- Each conflicting party tries to promote his or her own views.
- This leads to a conscious struggle over the distribution of resources.
- People with similar beliefs tend to join forces and develop similar understandings and commitments.
- Continuing conflicts tend to become routine and develop into stratification systems.
- Such systems exhibit economic exploitation, sustained by political domination in all forms.
- The relative power of conflicting parties determines their hierarchical position as well as changes in the distribution of power.
- Human understandings and commitments are dialectical, characterized by continual conflict.

Turk's theory, while abstract, alerts us to the political nature of criminal law as well as to the pluralistic conflict basis of such norms.

William Chambliss and Richard Quinney—Conflict Theory. Other statements of conflict theory are in the early works of William Chambliss (with Robert Seidman, 1971) and Richard Quinney (1970); their later writings would evolve into more radical perspectives. Chambliss and Seidman viewed criminal law as representing the interests of the most powerful forces in society and deviance as a political rather than moral question (Chambliss and Seidman, 1971, p. 4). Richard Quinney (1970, pp. 15–23) in *The Social Reality of Crime* presented six propositions describing the relationship between crime and the social order:

- Crime is a definition of human conduct created by authorized agents in a politically organized society.
- Criminal definitions describe behaviors that conflict with the interests of segments of society that have power to shape public policy.
- Criminal definitions are applied by segments of society that have power to shape the enforcement and administration of criminal law.
- Behavior patterns are structured in segmentally organized society in relation to criminal definitions, and within this context persons engage in actions that have relative probabilities of being defined as criminal.
- Conceptions of crime are constructed and diffused in the segments of society by various means of communication.
- The social reality of crime is constructed by the formulation and application of criminal definitions, the development of behavior patterns related to criminal definitions, and the construction of criminal conceptions.

Critics of Quinney's formulations argue that his propositions oversimplify reality and that many represent statements rather than necessarily empirically supported propositions (Manning, 1975). A more detailed critique will be provided at the conclusion of this chapter.

W.E.B. Du Bois. Chambliss, in a classic study in conflict criminology, examined the vagrancy laws in fourteenth-century England that made it illegal to give alms to anyone who was able, but unemployed. Due to the plague, there was a vast need for labor. W.E.B. Du Bois did a similar analysis and, as pointed out by Gabiddon (1999), he represents a neglected conflict criminologist. While most of his activities were associated with civil rights activity, Du Bois' academic publications included his book *The Philadelphia Negro* (Du Bois, 1899 [1973]). As Gabiddon indicates, his most important work concerning conflict theory was "The Spawn of Slavery: The Conflict Lease System in the South" (Du Bois, 1901). According to Russell (1992), Du Bois may also be considered the "Founder of Black Criminology". Similar to Chambliss' study of vagrancy laws, Du Bois discussed the enactment of the Black Codes and convict lease system by the Southern oligarchy as a means to compensate for lost labor and profits as a result of Emancipation. The courts meted out two forms of justice—different sentences for whites and blacks. As Gabiddon (1999, p. 4) indicates: "African-Americans were criminalized to secure the necessary labor for aristocracy." The fact that his work may have represented one of the earliest, scientific works on crime, but was ignored by early American criminology, illustrates the "Eurocentric bias". The latter refers to the dominance of criminological discourse by writers of European descent and the ignoring of works by those of African descent (Greene, 1979; Ross and Edwards, 1998; and Young and Sulton, 1991).

Jeffrey Reiman. In *The Rich Get Richer and the Poor Get Prison,* Jeffrey Reiman (1998) argues a conflict perspective that includes the following propositions:

- Acts that are not treated as crimes pose at least as great a danger to the public as those that have been criminalized.
- Acts that aré criminalized are generally those of the poor.
- The system often fails to treat as criminal the dangerous acts of the wealthy and powerful.
- The failure of the criminal justice system in fighting street crime conveys an important ideological message—the greatest danger to the average citizen is from below him or her on the economic ladder.
- Crime in the suites should be prosecuted in the same manner as crime in the streets, and all acts should be prosecuted in proportion to the actual harm they produce.

Reiman (1984, p. 162) concludes: ". . . every step toward economic and social justice is a step that moves us from a system of *criminal* justice to a system of *criminal justice.*"

Feminist Criminology

Feminist criminology comes in a variety of forms, but shares in common the general theme that *"malestream" (male-mainstream)* (McDermott, 1992; Renzetti, 1993) *approaches to criminology express an androcentric bias and exclude women from their analysis.* Emphasizing various perspectives including Marxist, interactionist, and critical theory, feminist writers view dominant empirical positivism as failing to include gender as a central force, as blind to its ideological bias, and ignoring females. Their view is that much nonfeminist research is sexist due to cultural beliefs and to a preponderance of perspectives that assume traditional gender roles. This bias expressed itself in the past, particularly on topics such as rape and domestic violence.

A huge literature now exists on feminist theory in criminology (see Belknap, 1996; Chesney-Lind and Shelden, 1998; Simpson and Elis, 1995; Rafter and Maher, 1995; Daly and Tonry, 1997; Bowker, 1998; Dobash, Dobash and Noaks, 1995; Miller, 1998; Muraskin, 2000; and Messerschmidt, 1997). Three general areas of crime have received the most attention in feminist theories: the victimization of women, gender differences in crime, and gendered justice (the differential treatment of females in the justice system) (Bohm, 1997, p. 133). Crime is examined as it is related to gender-based inequality. There are actually a variety of approaches under the rubric of feminist criminology.

A basic distinction can be made between "liberal feminists" and "critical" or "radical feminists." The "liberal feminists" are represented by pioneering works in the 1970s such as Rita Simon's *Women and Crime* (1975) and Freda Adler's *Sisters in Crime* (1975). Simon predicted an increase in female crime as opportunities increased. Adler also foresaw an increase in female criminality. She assumed that, as women assumed more assertive positions in society, they would participate in more previously "masculine" activities including crime. While the relationship appears logical, little support for this thesis was found. This liberation thesis was additionally not supported in that the greatest increase in female offenders were among those not achieving greater occupational equality. Radical feminists argued that the liberal feminists understated the role of patriarchy (male dominance) and its ability to continue to control and victimize women (Cullen and Agnew, 1999, p. 343).

Radical feminism is the dominant approach today in feminist criminology. Its major theme is patriarchy (male power and domination in society). "Patriarchy defines women as subjects, with men having the right of control. Sexism defines the value of women in terms of the family (unpaid housework as natural) and gives men control over reproduction" (Williams and McShane, 1994, p. 236). Male violence against women—especially domestic violence and rape—was traditionally ignored and helped bolster the patriarchal system (Danner. 1989). To overcome the androcentric bias in criminological theory it was viewed as necessary to develop gender-specific theories.

In what is called the "generalizability problem" the question is raised as to whether theories of men's behavior apply to women (Daly and Chesney-Lind, 1988). Reviews of the criminological literature suggest that the answer is in the affirmative. This does not mean that gender-specific theories are not needed (Cullen and Agnew, 1999, p. 344). A "gendering" of traditional crime theories with larger structural (patriarchal) conditions holds promise.

James Messerschmidt in *Masculinities and Crime* (1993) claims that, even though feminists brought gender to the center of criminological theory, their vision of men is stereotypical. He views crime for some males as a way of "doing gender," exerting their manliness when other means are unavailable. This exertion of masculinity varies by age, class, race, and the like. Critics ask, "How does this relate to female crime?" While certainly a long overdue development, feminist criminology has been criticized for overfocusing on gender as its central theme. What about differences between white and black women? More research is needed, but feminist criminology will remain an active subject of inquiry and a permanent fixture in the field of criminology.

Encouraging women to examine crime through their own experiences with sexism, feminist research is at times in opposition to the scientific method (Simpson, 1989). While liberal feminism emphasizes affirmative action, it is viewed as not challenging "white, male, capitalist privilege" (Daly and Chesney-Lind, 1988). Socialist feminism sees capitalism and patriarchy as creating inequality and crime (Messerschmidt, 1986). Radical feminism views male aggression and control of female sexuality as the basis of patriarchy and the subordination of women. Rape, for example, is defined as a crime of male power and the use of violence to control and dominate women.

New Critical Criminology

New critical criminology includes emerging perspectives such as left realism (DeKeseredy, 1988), peacemaking, and postmodernism (Schwartz and Friedrichs, 1994). Such perspectives view the causes of crime as due to class, ethnic, and patriarchal (male-dominant) relations endemic in society (DeKeseredy and Maclean, 1993, p. 362).

Left Realism. **Left realism** questions the conservative approaches to crime control that emphasize prisons, more police, and longer sentences and argues instead for greater public access to, and involvement with, the police (DeKeseredy, 1988; Kinsey, Lea, and Young, 1986). Unlike Marxists, the left realists accept the reality of street crime and do not view it as a sort of revolutionary activity of the oppressed. With its primary expression in Britain (Jock Young) and Canada (Walter DeKeseredy), left realism attempts to translate

The passive and friendly presence of police at a large metropolitan ethnic festival demonstrate the peacemaking approach to crime prevention.

radical ideas into realistic social policy (Williams and McShane, 1994, p. 166). Realists recognize that crime is a real problem that exists in socialist as well as capitalist societies, but insist on social justice as an important policy objective.

The term "realism" comes from the attempt to translate radical ideas into realistic social policy. Williams and McShane (1994) indicate that work by Tony Platt (1985) in the U.S. also reflected the attempt to make the perspective of practical use to policymakers without losing a critical perspective. Realists also believe that crime control is something to be taken seriously since it affects all social classes including the poor and working class. Proposals for police initiatives have included democratic forms of control over the police and community participation in the formulation of crime prevention schemes. Finally, left realists have one major goal: to emphasize "social justice as a way of achieving a fair and orderly society" (Matthews and Young, 1986: p. 6; and Williams and McShane, 1994, p. 167).

Some of the proposals of Lea and Young (1984) contain some of the basic elements of left realism:

- Demarginalize offenders and instead of prisons, emphasize community service and restitution.
- Preemptive deterrence (before-the-fact) through citizen groups.
- Minimal use of prisons.
- Transform the "police force" into a "police service."
- Criminologists should be realistic about crimes (Beirne and Messerschmidt, 2000, p. 231).

Peacemaking. A traditional role of policing has always been "peacekeeping." Advocates of what we will call "peacemaking" theory go beyond this and propose that crime can be eliminated once we establish peace and justice. **Peacemaking theory** or the "peacemaking movement" has its origins in the writings of Richard Quinney (1980 and 1988) and Harold Pepinsky (Pepinsky and Quinney, 1991) and combines criminology with a transcendental or religious approach (Martin, Mutchnick, and Austin, 1990, p. 399). In *Providence* (1980) Quinney's thinking moved to a theological level. For example, he states: "Our historical struggle is thus for the creation of a social and moral order that prepares us for the ultimate of divine grace—the kingdom of God fulfilled. Peace and justice through the Kingdom of God" (Quinney, 1980, p. 114).

In *Peacemaking* (Quinney, 1988, p. 67) he states: "Crime can be ended only with the ending of suffering (only when there is peace)—through the love and compassion found in awareness." Peace can end suffering, which can end crime. Peacemaking is also a nonviolent approach to criminal justice. It assumes that violence cannot be overcome with more violence. Pepinsky (Pepinsky and Quinney, 1991, p. ix) calls for an " 'expressive criminology' of compassion, forgiveness and love . . . a continuing movement for a world of peace and social justice."

Quinney's (1991) progression to spiritualism as an approach to crime views social justice as the solution to the crime problem. Individuals must transcend their selves and understand that there is suffering in the world and that crime is suffering. Crime will cease when social justice is accomplished and suffering ended. Programs such as "restorative justice" fits with the peacemaking theme very well. Such an approach seeks to mediate conflict, assist victims, and reintegrate offenders into the community (Cullen and Agnew, 1999, p. 273). VANTAGE POINT 6.1 describes some restorative justice programs.

It is as difficult to critique "peacemaking theory" as it is to criticize the religious beliefs of others. In a way, the field of criminological theory has come full circle from theological to philosophical to scientific and now back to a less demonological, humanistic theological approach. The message is the same message of prophets of old—love one another and do God's work. But it is a theme that underlies much sociological thinking regarding crime and deviance; a more just social order (justice) is necessary before one can achieve law and order. In this writer's opinion, peacemaking in the final analysis is an admirable social movement, a utopian *Weltanschauung* (world view) more than it is an attempt to explain specific types of crime.

Postmodernism. **Postmodernism** is a movement that attacks modernity. Bohm (1997, pp. 134–135) tells us that postmodernism began in the late 1960s as a rejection of "modern" or Enlightenment scientific rationality as the predominant philosophy for gaining knowledge and achieving progress. Unconscious, free-floating signs and images, and the rejection of knowledge and languages' ability to create hierarchy and domination were viewed as critical. Postmodernists argue for a *plurality of interpretations of the law and an abandonment of standard theories of crime causation* (Ibid.). The latter assumes that people can control objects, nature, and reality whereas the former assumes that objects now have more and more control over us (Schwartz and Friedrichs, 1994, p. 223). Having originated in the field of literary and linguistic analysis, postmodernists examine how knowledge is constituted, the significance of language and signs, and how metaphors and concepts capture reality and set the context and conditions in which crime occurs. Media and technology create a "hyperreality" in which simulations and reality become confused. Modernity has become a force not for liberation, but subjugation, oppression, and repression.

Criminologists who have been identified with postmodernism are Dragan Milovanovic (1992), Stuart Henry (Henry and Milovanovic, 1993), and Stephen Pfohl (1993). Stuart Henry and Dragan Milovanovic (1996) describe a three elements of post modernism in criminology:

- Crime is the ability to impose one's will on others.
- Some persons construct harms to others in the expression of power and control in which others are objectified as "separate, dehumanized entities" (Ibid., p. 175).
- Law definers must be provided with "liberating life narratives" (Ibid., p. 224).

While postmodernism has generated controversy and empirical research, its literature has been described as "gratuitously obscure, incoherent, and undisciplined" (Schwartz and Friedrichs, 1994, p. 228; see also Michalowski, 1993).

Radical "Marxist" Criminology

Richard Quinney—Radical Criminology. Perhaps the foremost spokesperson for radical criminology is the same Richard Quinney who was at one time a more moderate conflict theorist and is now a peacemaker. For Quinney—then an orthodox Marxist—crime was the result of capitalism, and the crime problem could be resolved only by the establishment of a socialist state (Quinney, 1974a, 1974b, 1974c, 1977). In his critical theory of crime control in the United States, he provides the following propositions:

- U.S. society is based on an advanced capitalist economy.
- The state is organized to serve the interests of the dominant economic class, the capitalist ruling class.
- Criminal law is an instrument of the state and the ruling class to maintain and perpetuate the existing social and economic order.
- Crime control in capitalist society is accomplished through a variety of institutions and agencies established and administered by a governmental elite, representing ruling class interests, for the purpose of establishing domestic order.
- The contradictions of advanced capitalism—the disjunction between existence and essence—require that the subordinate classes remain oppressed by whatever means necessary, especially through the coercion and violence of the legal system.
- Only with the collapse of capitalist society and the creation of a new society based on socialist principles will there be a solution to the crime problem.

For Quinney and other Marxist criminologists, crime is a necessary outcome of inequality in capitalistic societies. Criminal law originates in conflict of interest in which the most powerful ruling class (capitalists or *bourgeoisie*) makes the laws and controls the criminal justice machinery. Marxist criminologists often reject the positivistic tradition of analyzing crime causation through objective and empirical analysis. Instead, they advocate an ideological commitment to Marxist philosophy wherein their task is to provide descriptive and analytical examples to serve as evidence for a preconfirmed social reality—that capitalism causes crime.

William Chambliss. Radical criminologists argue that, by concentrating on the crimes of the poor rather than on racism, imperialism, and inequality, criminologists become conservative handmaidens of state repression (Platt, 1974). Advanced industrial capitalism creates "surplus people" (Spitzer, 1975), an underclass that is unneeded in the system of production. Among William Chambliss's (1975b) later views regarding capitalism and crime are these:

- As capitalist societies industrialize and the gap between the bourgeoisie and the proletariat widens, penal law will expand in an effort to coerce the proletariat into submission.
- Crime diverts the lower classes' attention from the exploitation they experience and directs it toward other members of their own class rather than toward the capitalist class or the economic system.
- Crime is a reality that exists only as it is created by those in the society whose interests are served by its presence.
- Crime is a reaction to the life conditions of a person's social class.
- Socialist societies should have much lower rates of crime because the less intense class struggle should reduce the forces leading to the functions of crime.

Similar perspectives have been enunciated by many others, including Gordon (1973), Krisberg (1975), and Taylor et al. (1973, 1975). In their *Critical Criminology,* Taylor and associates (1975, p. 49) called for the use of Marxism as the method of analysis in a

VANTAGE POINT 6.1

Incorporating Restorative and Community Justice into American Sentencing and Corrections

Programs based on restorative and community justice principles have proliferated in the United States over the past decade simultaneously with tough-on-crime initiatives like three-strikes, truth-in-sentencing, and mandatory minimum laws. Restorative justice and community justice represent new ways of thinking about crime. The theories underlying restorative justice suggest that government should surrender its monopoly over responses to crime to those most directly affected—the victim, the offender, and the community. Community justice redefines the roles and goals of criminal justice agencies to include a broader mission—to prevent crime, address local social problems and conflicts, and involve neighborhood residents in planning and decision making. Both restorative and community justice are based on the premise that communities will be strengthened if local citizens participate in responding to crime, and both envision responses tailored to the preferences and needs of victims, communities, and offenders.

In contrast to this bottom-up approach, recent changes in sentencing law are premised on retributive ideas about punishing wrongdoers and on the desirability of controlling risk, increasing public safety, and reducing sentencing disparities. Restorative and community justice goals of achieving appropriate, individualized dispositions often conflict with the retributive goal of imposing certain, consistent, proportionate sentences.

What Is Restorative Justice?

Restorative justice has evolved from a little-known concept into a term used widely but in divergent ways. There is no doubt about its appeal, although the varied uses of the term cause some confusion. The umbrella term "restorative justice" has been applied to initiatives identified as restorative by some but not by others. Examples are sex-offender notification laws, victim impact statements, and murder victim survivors' "right" to be present at executions. Most advocates of restorative justice agree that it involves five basic principles:

- Crime consists of more than violation of the criminal law and defiance of government authority.
- Crime involves disruptions in a three-dimensional relationship of victim, community, and offender.
- Because the crime harms the victim and the community, the primary goals should be to repair the harm and heal the victim and the community.
- The victim, the community, and the offender should all participate in determining the response to crime; government should surrender its monopoly over that process.
- Case disposition should be based primarily on the victim's and the community's needs—not solely on the offender's needs or culpability, the dangers he presents, or his criminal history.

The original goal of restorative justice was to restore harmony between victims and offenders. For victims, this meant restitution for tangible losses and emotional losses. For offenders, it meant taking responsibility, confronting shame, and regaining dignity.

This notion has evolved, with the major recent conceptual development the incorporation of a role for the community. Many people still associate restorative justice primarily with victim–offender mediation or, more broadly (but mistakenly), with any victim-oriented services. The more recent conceptualization—that offenses occur within a three-dimensional relationship—may change the movement.

All three parties should be able to participate in rebuilding the relationship and in deciding on responses to the crime. The distinctive characteristic is direct, face-to-face dialogue among victim, offender, and increasingly, the community.

What Is Community Justice?

The concept of community justice is less clear. It can be portrayed as a set of new organizational strategies that change the focus of criminal justice from a narrow, case processing orientation; operations are moved to neighborhood locations that offer flexible working hours and services, neighborhoods are assigned their own officers and are provided with more information than is standard practice, and residents may identify crime problems and define priorities for neighborhood revitalization. Most experience with community justice is in the context of community policing, but prosecutors, judges, and correctional officers are increasingly rethinking their roles and goals.

VANTAGE POINT 6.1—*Continued*

Restorative Justice Practices

Although something akin to restorative justice has long been observed in premodern and indigenous societies, restorative justice principles, in the form of victim-offender reconciliation programs, appeared in Western industrialized countries only in the 1970s. The first program was established in 1974 in Kitchener, Ontario. By the 1990s, such programs had spread to all Western countries—at least 700 in Europe and 300 in the United States.

Victim-Offender Mediation. Victim-offender mediation is the most widespread and evaluated type of restorative program. Offenders and victims meet with volunteer mediators to discuss the effects of the crime on their lives, express their concerns and feelings, and work out a restitution agreement. The agreement is often seen as secondary to emotional healing and growth. Victims consistently report that the most important element of mediation is being able to talk with the offender and express their feelings, and offenders also emphasize the importance of face-to-face communication. Advocates believe that developing an offender's empathy for the victim has preventive effects.

In many countries, victim-offender mediation is widely used. In Austria, for example, it became an official part of the juvenile justice system as early as 1989. Public prosecutors refer juveniles to mediation, probation officers coordinate cases, and social workers serve as mediators. If an agreement is reached and completed, the case is dismissed.[1] In the United States, most programs are operated by private, nonprofit organizations; handle largely juvenile cases; and function as diversion programs established and operated (or at least initiated) by corrections departments, police, or prosecutors; and are used as a condition of either probation or dropping charges. Most studies of mediation programs report high rates of success.[2]

Advocates are beginning to challenge the assumption that mediation is not suitable for violent or sexual crimes. Increasingly, in the United States and Canada, for example, victims and offenders meet in prisons. These meetings are not oriented to a tangible goal such as a restitution agreement, nor does the offender obtain benefits like early release or parole consideration. Usually the meetings are held because the victim wants to meet the offender and learn more about what happened to reach beyond fear and anger and facilitate healing. The results of a Canadian survey indicated that 89 percent of victims of serious, violent crimes wanted to meet the offender.[3]

Serious violent crimes are usually mediated on a case-by-case basis, but the need for permanent programs is growing. Such progras are offered, for example, by the Correctional Service of Canada in British Columbia and the Yukon Territory and by the Texas Department of Criminal Justice.

Family Group Conferencing. Family group conferencing is based on the same rationales as victim-offender mediation, with two main differences. Conferencing involves a broader range of people (family, friends, coworkers, and teachers), and family members and other supporters tend to take collective responsibility for the offender and for carrying out his or her agreement. The other difference is that conferencing often relies on police, probation, or social service agencies for organization and facilitation.

Family group conferences originated in New Zealand, where they became part of the juvenile justice system in 1989. There, the new juvenile justice model, which incorporates Maori traditions of involving the family and the community in addressing wrongdoing, has four dispositional options:

- An immediate warning by the police
- "Youth Aid Section" dispositions in which a special police unit may require, for example, an apology to the victim or community service
- Family group conferencing
- Traditional youth court sentencing

About 60 percent of juvenile offenders receive a warning or go the Youth Aid Section, 30 percent go to conferencing, and 10 percent go to youth court.[4]

By the mid-1990s, family group conferencing had been adopted in every state and territory of Australia. In South Australia, it is used statewide as a component of the juvenile justice system and resembles the New Zealand approach. In Wagga Wagga, New South Wales, conferences (originally part of a police diversion program) were organized and facilitated by police officers who were often in uniform.[5] Responsibility was transferred to juvenile justice agencies in 1998, and trained community members now facilitate conferences. In Canberra, the Federal Police set up a program called the Reintegrative Shaming Experiment, which involved more than 100 trained police officers.

There is evidence that conferencing can be successful. A recent evaluation of the Bethlehem, Pennsylvania, Police Family Group Conferencing program revealed that typical police officers were able to conduct conferences in conformity with restorative justice and due process principles if adequately trained and supervised, and that very high percentages of offenders, victims, and other participants were pleased with the process.[6] Evaluation of Canberra's Reintegrative Shaming Experiment showed similar results.[7]

VANTAGE POINT 6.1—*Continued*

Sentencing Circles. Sentencing circles originated in traditional Native Canadian and Native American peacemaking. They involve the victim and the offender, their supporters, and key community members, and they are open to everyone in the community. They attempt to address the underlying causes of crime, seek responses, and agree on offenders' responsibilities. The process is based on peacemaking, negotiation, and consensus, and each circle member must agree on the outcomes.

Sentencing circles are so named because participants sit in a circle, and a "talking piece" (a feather, for example) is passed from person to person. When participants take the talking piece, they explain their feelings about the crime and express support for the victim and the offender. Separate circles often are held for the offender and the victim before they join in a shared circle.

In Minnesota, sentencing circles are used not only in Native American communities but also in rural white, suburban, and inner-city black communities. Community Justice Committees, established by citizen volunteers, handle organizational and administrative tasks and provide "keepers" who lead the discussions. Judges refer cases, and the committees make the final decision on acceptance. The agreements reached are presented to the judge as sentencing recommendations. In some cases, the judge, prosecutor, and defense attorney participate in the circle, and then the agreement becomes the final sentence.

Reparative Probation and Other Citizen Boards. Reparative probation in Vermont involves a probation sentence ordered by a judge, followed by a meeting between the offender and volunteer citizen members of a Reparative Citizen Board. Together they draw up a contract, based on restorative principles, which the offender agrees to carry out. Fulfilling the contract is the only condition of probation.

Vermont's program is different from most other restorative justice initiatives in the United States. Designed by the State's Department of Corrections, it operates statewide, handles adult cases, and involves a sizable number of citizen volunteers. Compared with family group conferencing or sentencing circles, the Reparative Citizen Boards work faster, require less preparation, and can process more cases; however, they involve fewer community members. For example, offenders' and victims' families and supporters usually are not present.

Citizen boards also may be established to adjudicate minor crimes. For example, a Merchant Accountability board in Deschutes County, Oregon, consists of local business owners who adjudicate thefts of property valued at $50 or less and some more serious cases involving property valued at between $51 and $750. Under an agreement with the district attorney, the police refer all minor shoplifting cases directly to the program. If offenders decide to participate, they are typically ordered by the board to pay fines, make restitution, or both.

Manitoba's Restorative Resolutions Project offers an alternative to custodial sentences for offenders who otherwise are likely to face a minimum prison sentence of 6 months. Offenders and project staff develop sentencing plans, and victims are encouraged to participate. The plans are presented to judges as nonbinding recommendations. Most plans require restitution, community service, and counseling or therapy. A recent evaluation revealed that offenders who participate have significantly fewer supervision violations and slightly fewer new convictions than those in comparison groups.[8]

The Future of Restorative and Community Justice. How deeply restorative and community justice ideas will penetrate the traditional justice system remains to be seen.

"materialistic criminology" whose purpose is to expose the basis of social control in capitalistic societies. The tenets of Marxist theory, rather than representing subjects for empirical analysis, now become foregone conclusions, ideological dictates requiring illustration rather than proof.

Radical or Marxist criminologists view **praxis** (*practical critical action*) as more important than the objective analysis of their theoretical formulations. "They view 'intellectualism' as a negative quality due to the 'academic repression' and 'elitism' associated with intellectuals. Praxis is then the most important factor in the struggle to replace capitalism with socialism" (Pelfrey, 1980, p. 96).

Cullen and Agnew (1999, pp. 299–300) do a nice job of reviewing other writers who, although they are not Marxists, support the general theme of the harmful impacts of economic structure on youth opportunities. David Greenberg (1993), for example, indicates that an economic system that is unable to provide full-time jobs for teenagers consigns them to schools

VANTAGE POINT 6.1—*Continued*

So far, restorative justice approaches are used much more for juveniles than for adults, and for minor offenses rather than for serious crime. Experience with community justice has consistently shown that generating citizen involvement and building relationships with the community is a challenge. Both movements have spread rapidly, however, and both are increasingly reaching out to encompass adult offenders, more serious crime, and disadvantaged urban communities where, arguably, the need is greatest.

Notes

1. Lösching-Gspandl, Marianne, and Michael Kilchling, "Victim/Offender Mediation and Victim Compensation in Austria and Germany-Stock-Taking and Perspectives for Future Research," *European Journal of Crime, Criminal Law and Criminal Justice* 5 (1997): 58–78.
2. Umbreit, Mark, *Victim Meets the Offender. The Impact of Restorative Justice and Mediation,* Monsey, NY: Criminal Justice Press, 1994. It should be noted that evaluations of restorative justice conducted in the United States are usually not based on experimental and control groups, do not often measure recidivism rates, and seldom use sophisticated research designs.
3. Gustafson, Dave, "Facilitating Communication between Victims and Offenders in Cases of Serious and Violent Crime," *The International Community Corrections Association Journal on Community Corrections* 8 (1997): 44–49.
4. Maxwell, Gabrielle, and Allison Morris, *Family, Victims, and Culture: Youth Justice in New Zealand,* Wellington, New Zealand: Social Policy Agency and Institute of Criminology, Victoria University of Wellington, 1993.
5. Wundersitz, Joy, and Sue Hetzel, "Family Conferencing for Young Offenders: The South Australian Experience," in *Family Group Conferences: Perspectives on Policy and Practice,* ed. John Hudson et al., Monsey, NY: Criminal Justice Press, 1996.
6. McCold, Paul, and Benjamin Wachtel, *Restorative Policing Experiment: The Bethlehem Pennsylvania Police Family Group Conferencing Project,* Pipersville, PA: Community Service Foundation, 1998. This evaluation was sponsored by the National Institute of Justice.
7. Sherman, Lawrence, Heather Strang, Geoffrey Barnes, John Braithwaite, Nova Ipken, and Min-Mee, *The Experiments in Restorative Policing: A Progress Report to the National Police Research Unit in the Canberra Reintegrative Shaming Experiments (RISE),* Canberra: Australian Federal Police and Australian National University, 1998.
8. Bonta, James, Jennifer Rooney, and Suzanne Wallace-Capretta, *Restorative Justice: An Evaluation of the Restorative Resolutions Project,* Ottawa: Solicitor General of Canada, 1998.

Source: Leena Kurki. 1999. "Incorporating Restorative and Community Justice Into American Sentencing and Corrections." (Sentencing and Corrections Issues for the 21st Century). National Institute of Justice *Research in Brief,* Papers from the Executive Sessions on Sentencing and Corrections No. 3, September.

InfoTrac College Edition Research

Locate an article on "restorative justice." How does this article view the role of restorative justice in rehabilitating offenders?

and prolonged adolescence. Peer group activities requiring consumption increases adolescent theft. "Masculine status anxiety" strikes those who are unable to gain employment and assume traditional male roles. Structural conditions of the economy may block the American dream (Cullen and Agnew, 1999, p. 299). Colvin and Pauly (1983) argue that parents' class position influences how they discipline their children. Those in "dead end jobs" are more coercive in socialization, often alienating their children and reducing parental bonds.

John Hagan in *Crime and Disrepute* (1994) views the capital disinvestment in inner city minority neighborhoods as creating what William Julius Wilson (1987) calls "the truly disadvantaged." Such neighborhoods rob their youth of opportunities for legitimate advancement and push them toward criminal subcultural adaptations such as drug markets. Inequality and racism in post-industrial capitalism presents no solution to the crime problem unless there is large scale investment in such inner city neighborhoods (Cullen and Agnew, 1999, p. 300).

Conflict vs. Marxist Criminology

While the two are often confused, conflict criminology posits a pluralistic conflict model (a diversity of conflicting parties), places less emphasis on capitalism alone as the source of crime, favors objective research, does not reject the legal order, and advocates reform rather than revolution (Friedrichs, 1980b, p. 39; Bohm, 1982). Marxist or radical criminology, on the other hand, advocates a singularistic conflict model (capitalistic class control), names capitalism and inequality as the sources of crime, holds Marxist theory as a fact to be illustrated rather than a subject for empirical investigation, rejects the legitimacy of the existing legal order, and advocates revolutionary overthrow of the system.

Critiques of Conflict and Radical Criminology

While conflict criminology has done much to reverse overconcentration on criminal actors and unquestioned acceptance of the consensus model of criminal law and to point to the criminal justice system as a possible transgressor, it has been criticized for ignoring the consensual basis of much criminal law and for assuming rather than demonstrating discrimination in traditional law enforcement.

Radical (Marxist) criminology has attracted a barrage of critics. In Geis and Meier's (1979) survey of leading criminologists, nearly 40 percent of the respondents indicated the emergence of Marxist ideology in criminology as a "less healthy development" in the field. Comments such as "ideology whether in theory or method is pretentiously seen as 'new paradigms,' 'theories,' 'methods' "; "the substitution of ideology for science"; "nonscientific voices"; "Marxist rhetoric and ideological narrowness" (Geis and Meier, 1979, p. 180–81) were offered. In the previous chapter we cited Toby's (1980) statement that much of "the New Criminology is the Old Baloney," that this tradition ". . . far from being new, is the explicit assertion of a relativism and a sentimentality that is as old as sympathy for members of the oldest profession." Sparks (1980) criticizes radical criminologists for the lack of attention to solid research that would critically test their theoretical assumptions.

Klockars's Critique. The definitive though most controversial critique of Marxist criminology appears in Carl Klockars's (1979) "The Contemporary Crisis of Marxist Criminology," which in turn has stirred considerable commentary (Akers, 1980; Mankoff, 1980; Friedrichs, 1980a). Klockars's critique can be paraphrased in the following way:

- Marxist criminology resembles an untrustworthy social movement, since it ignores Russian gulags (Solzhenitsyn, 1975), Cuban domestic repression, and other abuses within socialist states. By giving a social movement a higher priority than academic inquiry, they abandon science for ideology and are untrustworthy as objective scholars.
- Marxist criminology as a social movement operates on predictable, orthodox lines. After class, the legal order and capitalism are blamed for everything; these themes are reiterated ad nauseam.
- In their subjective zeal for advocating social revolution, Marxist criminologists find evil in everything associated with the American state, legal, and economic system, ignoring good laws. In their mystical transcendence of reality, they destroy their academic credibility. They dramatize and stress issues—e.g., that politicians are corrupt or businesses dishonest—as if these were startling revelations, insulting the intelligence of the general public.
- All of the problems of justice are collapsed into the economic interest of classes.
- American Marxist criminologists criticize society from ". . . a moral ground set so high and so far removed from any extant social reality that it loses all perspective" (Klockars, 1979, p. 484).

- They elevate Marx from a social philosopher to the status of prophet or saint. By describing the ideal of Marxism, they avoid responsibility for the present depredations of existing Marxist states.
- Marxist criminology resembles a new religion in which its "true believers" are unwilling to test, evaluate, or objectively examine their theories or beliefs.

While the Klockars critique pulls no punches, it is difficult to apply these points to all writers within the Marxist tradition, although his criticisms appear on target on the whole. As Akers (1980, p. 138) states:

> Compared to a socialist ideal system, the real American system looks unjust, repressive, and controlled by a tiny capitalist elite. Compared to the Soviet Union, China, Vietnam, North Korea, East Germany or Cambodia, to name some socialist alternatives, or to Iran, South Korea or Chile, to name some nonsocialist alternatives, American society looks pretty good.

The collapse of Soviet communism may have in part reduced interest in Marxism.

Integrated Theories of Crime

Multifactor Approach. A primary criticism of most theories that have been discussed is their tendency to associate crime with a single cause, for example, some biological or psychological defect. Critics of these approaches merely had to demonstrate the presence of these conditions in equal proportions among noncriminals in order to refute these assumptions. This single-factor deficiency has led some writers (Healy, 1915; the Gluecks, 1950) to propose a *multifactor approach* in which crime is assumed to be produced by multiple factors—biological, psychological, and sociological—with different combinations of variables coming into play, depending on the type of crime being examined. This approach is appealing in that multiple factors are indeed involved in any causal explanation of criminality, however, the identification of factors associated with a process does not constitute a causal theory. In that sense, the multifactor approach is atheoretical (without theoretical content).

Albert Cohen (1951) has provided a succinct critique of the multifactor approach, which may be paraphrased:

- Advocates of this approach confuse causal theories that employ a single variable with those that propose a single theory. Simply listing correlations of factors associated with crime does not represent a theory, while a single theory may utilize multiple factors.
- Due to the emergence of easily available, sophisticated statistical programs that enable the calculation of multiple correlations, researchers forget that correlation does not equal causation. Since variables account for a certain proportion of variance in crime, this does not mean that they substantively cause that amount of crime.
- This approach falls into the "evil causes evil" fallacy: evil outcomes require evil causes, which represents a conservative, consensus view of crime as an evil intrusion into an otherwise healthy society.

Integrated Theories. Integrated theories attempt to combine various theoretical traditions into one theory. Such integrated theories are more than the identification of factors involved in crime, but attempt to theoretically link these factors into theories that explain crime. Messner, Krohn and Liska in *Theoretical Integration in the Study of Deviance and Crime* (1989) were very influential in identifying this genre of theories. Cullen and Agnew (1999, p. 207) tell us that the most common strategy for formulating integrated theories is to temporally order theories "end to end." That is, a theorist might

FIGURE 6.1 Critical and Integrated Criminological Theories

Theoretical School	Major Themes/Concepts	Major Theorists
Critical	"crime reflects the conflict model"	
Labeling	"societal reaction"	
	"dramatization of evil"	Tannenbaum
	"secondary deviance"	Lemert
	"crime as label, status"	
Conflict	"imperatively coordinated associations"	Dahrendorf
	"pluralistic model"	Vold
	"more powerful groups define criminal law"	Turk
Feminist	"feminist criminology"	Daly
	"androcentric bias"	Chesney-Lind
	"patriarchy"	Messerschmidt
New Critical	"left realism"	Young
	"realistic social policy"	DeKeseredy
	"peacemaking"	Quinney and Peplinsky
	"postmodernism"	Milovanovic
		Henry
		Pfohl
Radical	"capitalism causes crime"	Quinney and Chambliss
Integrated	"attempts to link theories"	
	"integrated theory of juvenile delinquency"	Elliott
	"interactional theory of delinquency"	Thornberry

Note: See Figures 4.1 and 5.1 for other theoretical approaches in criminology.

link theories by showing how a high level of strain might lead individuals to join subcultures, which then leads to crime. This can be illustrated by Figure 6.1.

In order to illustrate the usefulness of theories, Figure 6.2 presents an intensive aftercare model used in research sponsored by the Office of Juvenile Justice and Delinquency Prevention for guiding serious, chronic juvenile offenders. This particular model links strain (anomie)theory, social learning theory, and social control theory.

They also point out that many theories, although not specifically identified as "integrated theories" possess that quality in attempting to link different theories (Ibid., p. 208). Shaw and McKay of the Chicago School attempted to bring together elements of strain, learning, and social control theory. Cohen's "lower class reaction" theory tried to tie together strain and differential association as did Cloward and Ohlin. While most of the integrated theories have been at the micro level attempting to explain individual deviance, some have also been at the macro level looking at the impact of cultural and social structural forces. While a number of theories have been identified as being examples of integrated theories (see Akers, 1994), two examples that are on nearly every list are Delbert Elliott et al.'s (1979) "integrative theory of juvenile delinquency" and Terence Thornberry's (1987) "interactional theory of delinquency."

Delbert Elliott's Integrative Theory. Delbert Elliott and associates (1985) combine strain (anomie), social control, and learning theory. Delinquency (as measured by self-reports in the National Youth Survey) is due to:

1. Strain due to the gap between aspirations and achievements as well as other sources of strain such as the family and school (strain theory).
2. Attachment and commitment to family and school (social control or bonding theory).
3. Exposure to, preference for, and identification with deviant peers (learning theory).

Elliott has found support for his theory using the National Youth Survey. In this he found that bonding and strain variables had little effect themselves on delinquency. Bonding to delinquent peers had the major effect. Thus social learning appeared most signifi-

FIGURE 6.2A Intervention Model for Juvenile Intensive Aftercare

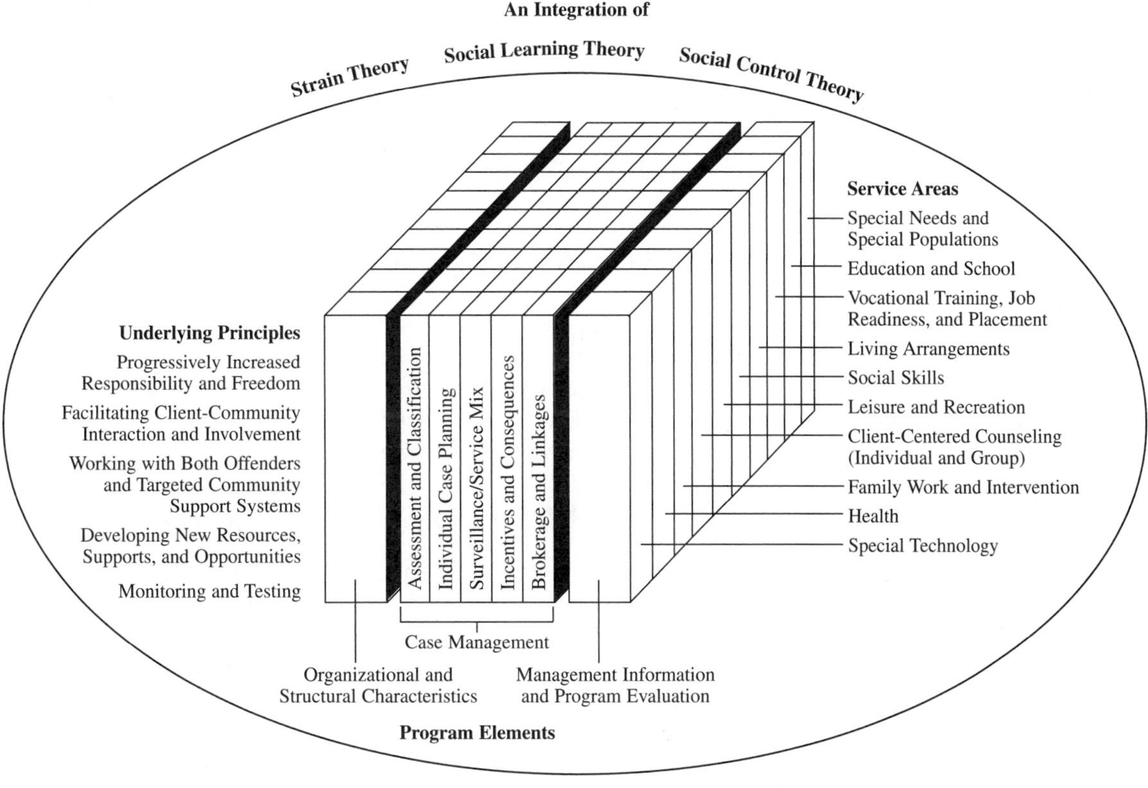

Source: David Altschuler and Troy L. Armstrong, 1994, *Intensive Aftercare for High-Risk Juveniles: Policies, Procedures,* Office of Juvenile Justice and Delinquency Prevention, September, pp. 3–4.

FIGURE 6.2B Integrated Control/Strain/Social Learning Model

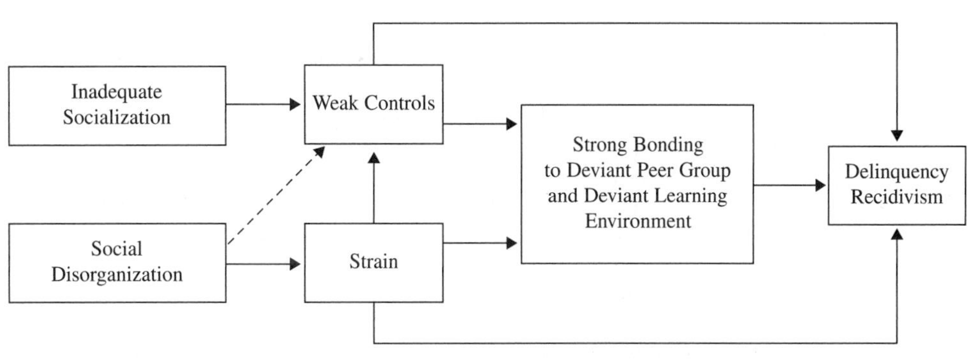

Source: David Altschuler and Troy L. Armstrong, 1994, *Intensive Aftercare for High-Risk Juveniles: Policies, Procedures,* Office of Juvenile Justice and Delinquency Prevention, September, pp. 3–4.

cant (Akers, 1994, p. 189). Social learning rather than social bond theory was most predictive. "The social bonding proposition that strong attachment to others prevents delinquent behavior, even when that attachment is to unconventional peers, is not supported" (Ibid., p. 190). Thus, in an attempt to integrate social control with social learning theory, only the latter survives. More research, of course, is still needed.

Terence Thornberry's Interactional Theory. Thornberry's (1987) interactional theory attempts to combine social structure, social control, and social learning theories. Social structure, such as race, social class, and community, affect social control and learning. The weakening of bonds to society predisposes adolescents to delinquency. Now the learning factor occurs, in which identification and association with delinquent peers happens. These relationships are reciprocal and not unilinear (one way), that is, family attachment may affect school commitment, but the opposite is also true (Cullen and Agnew, 1999, p. 191). Thornberry also adds a life course dimension to his theory indicating that the importance of different variables changes over the life course. Akers (1994), p. 192) tells us that Thornberry et al. (1991) did not find support for their hypothesis about reciprocal relationships between parental attachment and school commitment.

Theoretical Range and Criminological Explanation

This presentation of theories in criminology can only introduce major themes and schools of thought, leaving more formalized and sophisticated exposition to upper-level theory texts (see Vold and Bernard, 1986); detailed explication of the general theories' applications to types of criminal behavior would require far more space than is possible in this volume. However, to summarize the interrelationship between descriptions, criminal behavior typologies, and general theory, some final points may prove fruitful.

Theoretical range, or scope in this writer's view, refers to *the unit(s) of analysis and levels of explanation that may be sought in a particular theory.* In their *New Criminology,* Taylor et al. (1973, pp. 270–78) provide an example of theoretical range when they describe the formal requirements or scope of a general theory in criminology. Such a model must describe:

1. The wider origins of the deviant act.
2. Immediate origins of the deviant act.
3. The actual act.
4. Immediate origins of the societal reaction.
5. Wider origins of the deviant reaction.
6. The outcome of the societal reaction on the deviant's further action.
7. The nature of the deviant process as a whole.

Harry Allen et al. (1981, p. 39) address this issue of theoretical range:

> . . . what has been, and is, remiss in theoretical criminology in the opinion of many, is the spurious attempt to explicate all crime on the basis of one unitary, universal theory. Any theory that attempts to explain all crime, it is charged, cannot escape being a general theory of all human behavior, because criminal behavior encompasses a wide and divergent body of conduct. A general theory of crime would have to explain too much and therefore would explain too little. The essential questions are: what kinds of criminals and what kinds of circumstances, result in the commission of what kinds of crime? In short, the development of criminal typologies, in this view offers the most plausible approach to the etiology of crime.

The Global Fallacy. Williams and McShane (1988, p. 134) point out:

> The sheer variety of behavior defined as criminal also presents a problem. When we use the term "crime," the reference is often to a wide range of illegal behav-

> ior. . . . Thus, theories of crime and criminal behavior must encompass a wide range of human activity. This is the reason that some criminologists advocate the limiting of theories to a very specific behavior.

A long-recognized limitation of many discussions of crime as well as theories of crime causation, particularly early ones, relates to the global (or broad) manner in which the concept of crime is employed. The only thing most crimes hold in common is the fact that they are at a given point in time defined or viewed as violations of criminal law. The **global fallacy** refers to *the tendency to attempt to generalize relatively specific explanations to all types of crimes* (Hagan, 1987c). Many individual theories are not invalid in themselves, but are either too globally ambitious or are interpreted as such. A perfectly appropriate theory for explaining burglary may not apply at all to inside trading nor should it be expected to do so.

Ferdinand (1987, p. 855) calls this the domain of theory or the area of crime or delinquency that a theory intends to explain. An excellent illustration of the global fallacy is the neoclassical "general theory of crime" proposed by Gottfredson and Hirschi (1990; Hirschi and Gottfredson, 1987, 1989). They maintain that all crime is due to an individual's lack of self-control and that white collar crime (defined solely as the Uniform Crime Reports' inadequate measures of only embezzlement, fraud, and forgery) does not require any different explanation than street crime. This is a "baffling" (Reed and Yeager, 1991) disregard of elementary research findings on white collar crime, which will be discussed in Chapters 10 and 11. Do corporations, state terrorists, the Mafia, or Iran-Contra conspirators all lack self-control?

The range of theories may be at the general (macroscopic) level, addressing a broad issue such as "How does crime originate in society?" or at the specific (microscopic) level, addressing a question such as "What causes specific individuals to commit specific crimes?" Merton (1968, p. 45) advocates development of "theories of the middle range," proposing explanations aimed at describing specific activity between macroscopic and microscopic levels. Gibbons (1992, p. 8) also argues that "progress lies in the direction of theories focused on specific forms of lawbreaking." All of the major theoretical views in criminology in these last two chapters were seen as subject to certain shortcomings; in many instances, the criticisms were as much based on what the theories failed to cover as they were on what they did address.

Figure 6.3 presents a summary schema that compares the major theoretical views in criminology in terms of whether they address the following range of activities:

1. Origin of crime in society.
2. Immediate factors of transmission of criminal values.
3. Individual criminality.
4. Prevention of individual criminality.
5. Prevention of crime in society.

In addition, Figure 6.3 indicates types of criminal behavior addressed by each theory discussed in this book. While the author's analysis of presence or absence of features of each theory may be debated, and you can judge for yourself as we examine each type of criminal behavior, none of the general theories applies to all of the types of criminal behavior. Many specific theories discussed, such as Wolfgang and Ferracutti's "subculture of violence" and Cressey's "theory of embezzlers," represent "theories of the middle range," more of which are needed to build more crime-specific explanations. Until more all-encompassing, all-purpose theories concerned with all types of crimes are developed, the middle range, crime-specific theories appear to be taking a fruitful direction. In the discussion of typologies it was suggested that the first response to "What causes crime?" is "What type of crime?" Perhaps a criminological Einstein or Galileo will yet arrive to provide an acceptable general theory. Until then more Sutherlands, Mertons, and Hirschis will hopefully provide needed "middle range" theoretical explanations.

FIGURE 6.3 Range of Major Theoretical Views in Criminology

Range	Demonological	Classical	Ecological	Economic	Positivist Biological/Psychological	Anomie	Social Process	Social Control	Labeling	Conflict	New Critical and Feminist	Radical
(1) Origin of Crime in Society				X		X				X	X	X
(2) Immediate Factors of Transmission			X		X	X	X	X	X			
(3) Individual Criminality	X	X	X		X	X	X	X	X			
(4) Prevention of Individual Criminality	X	X			X		X	X				
(5) Prevention of Crime in Society				X		X				X	X	X

Types of Criminal Behavior Addressed	Demonological	Classical	Ecological	Economic	Positivist Biological/Psychological	Anomie	Social Process	Social Control	Labeling	Conflict	New Critical and Feminist	Radical
Organizational/Occupational							X			X		X
Violent	X		X		X	X					X	
Conventional Property	X	X	X	X	X	X	X	X		X	X	X
Occasional Property	X	X	X	X	X	X	X	X		X		X
Public Order	X					X			X			
Political	X					X				X		X
Organized						X						
Professional							X					

Note: An X indicates that a particular theory addresses a particular explanatory range as well as a particular type of criminal behavior.

Source: Frank E. Hagan, *Theoretical Range in Criminological Theory,* paper presented at the Academy of Criminal Justice Sciences Meetings, Las Vegas, Nevada, April, 1995.

The purpose of the three theory chapters in this text is a modest one, and that is to acquaint the beginning student with criminological theory. More detailed exposition would require too much space here and would be appropriate in a course on theory. The reader is referred to some excellent works on this subject by Akers (1994); Curran and Renzetti (1994); Lilly, Cullen, and Ball (1995); Vold and Bernard (1986); Williams and McShane (1994); and Cullen and Agnew (1999).

Summary

Mainstream criminology (anomie, social process, and social control theories) has been viewed as emphasizing the study of the criminal rather than of social control agencies—thus stressing positivism, a consensus world view, and liberal reformism. In response to this, in the sixties and seventies in the United States, *critical criminology* emerged, *which consists of the labeling, conflict, and radical perspectives.* Critical criminology stresses the conflict model, inequality, the process of assigning criminal labels, and, in some cases, ideology.

Labeling theory (societal reaction approach) is derived from symbolic interactionism (a stress on subjective meanings of social interaction). Labeling theory assumes that individuals are criminal because they have been labeled as such by social control agencies: i.e., societal reaction causes criminality. Schrag's summary of the basic assumptions of this school of thought was presented along with Lemert's concept of "secondary deviance;" the latter refers to continued deviance once an individual has been caught and labeled.

Conflict theory advocates a "pluralistic conflict model" of criminal law. It is represented in the writings of Dahrendorf and Vold and, in conflict criminology, in the works of Austin Turk and the early work of Richard Quinney and William Chambliss, as well as that of Jeffrey Reiman. According to conflict criminology, a variety of groups compete for control of the law-making and enforcement machinery in order to protect their vested interests. *New critical theories* include left realism, peacemaking, and postmodernism. *Feminist theory* represents a large and growing theoretical perspective in criminology.

Radical "Marxist" criminology, as presented in the later writings of Quinney and Chambliss, views crime as a result of capitalism, with the criminal law representing the interests of the capitalist class. The Marxist prescription for solving the crime problem is the collapse of capitalism and the creation of a socialist state. Major critiques of radical criminology, as well as of each of the other theoretical approaches, were presented in this chapter.

Theoretical range refers to the units of analysis and level of explanation that may be sought in a particular theory. This range may focus on the macroscopic level—for example, general theories of the origin of crime—or on the microscopic—explanations of individual criminality. Merton's concept of "theories of the middle range" argues for explanations aimed at describing specific activity between the macro- and microscopic.

The "range of major theoretical views" (Figure 6.3) attempts to summarize the theoretical range (origins, immediate factors, individual criminality, individual prevention, and societal prevention) of each theory and its ability to address different types of criminal behavior. This illustrates the view that the question "What causes crime?" must first be met with the question "What type of crime?" The answer to the first question awaits the development of an acceptable general theory of criminology.

KEY CONCEPTS

Conflict Criminology
Critical Theory
Feminist Criminology
Global Fallacy
Labeling Theory
Left Realism
Peacemaking
Postmodernism
Praxis
Radical "Marxist" Criminology
Secondary Deviance
Shaming
Theoretical Range

REVIEW QUESTIONS

1. How do critical criminological theories differ from mainstream criminological theories? What do you see as the strengths and weaknesses of each?
2. How does labeling theory reverse the usual approach to crime and criminality? What are some pros and cons of this "societal reaction" approach to crime?
3. Compare conflict criminology with radical criminology. What is the major difference between the two?
4. Discuss feminist criminology. What is the difference between liberal and more radical feminist criminology?
5. How do the concepts of "malestream" and "androcentric bias" and "patriarchy" influence traditional criminology according to feminist criminologists?
6. What is the basic assumption of "left realism?"
7. Discuss the notions of "peacemaking" and "restorative justice." How do these approaches differ from "just deserts," "retributive justice" and "three strikes and you're out" approaches?
8. What is postmodernism and postmodernist criminology?
9. What is the goal of integrated theories in criminology? Give an example.
10. What is the "global fallacy" in criminological theory?

INFOTRAC COLLEGE EDITION RESEARCH

Vantage Point 6.1 InfoTrac College Edition Research
Locate an article on "restorative justice." How does this article view the role of restorative justice in rehabilitating offenders?

SELECTED READINGS

Joanne Belknap. 1996. *The Invisible Woman: Gender Crime and Justice.* Belmont, California: Wadsworth. This work presents an excellent example of feminist criminology.

John Braithwaite. 1989. *Crime, Shame and Reintegration.* Cambridge, England: Cambridge University Press. Braithwaite outlines his shaming and reintegration of offenders conceptualizations.

Meda Chesney-Lind and Randall G. Shelden. 1998. *Girls, Delinquency and Juvenile Justice.* 2nd edition. Belmont, California: Wadsworth. The authors present a more radical feminist perspective in examining gender and delinquency.

Stuart Henry and Dragan Milovanovic. 1996. *Constitutive Criminology: Beyond Postmodernism.* London: Sage. This work provides an example of postmodernist thinking in criminology.

James Inciardi, editor. 1980. *Radical Criminology: The Coming Crisis.* Beverly Hills, California: Sage. Author Inciardi puts together a very readable anthology that represents some of the earlier thinking on radical criminology.

Harold Pepinsky and Richard Quinney, editors. 1991. *Criminology as Peacemaking.* Bloomington, Indiana: University of Indiana Press. The emergent "peacemaking" perspective is presented in a series of articles.

Jeffrey Reiman. 1998. *The Rich Get Rich and the Poor Get Prison.* 5th edition. Boston: Allyn and Bacon. Reiman's highly cited work examines inequalities in the criminal justice system.

Martin D. Schwartz and David O. Friedrichs. 1994. "Postmodern Thought and Criminological Discontent: New Metaphors for Understanding Violence." *Criminology.* 32(May): 221–246. One of the few, understandable attempts to appraise the postmodernist criminological perspective.

Ian Taylor, et al. 1973. *The New Criminology: For a Social Theory of Deviance.* New York: Harper and Row. British writers present one of the earliest views of radical (critical) criminology.

VIOLENT CRIME

> Violence is as American as cherry pie.
>
> —H. Rap Brown, black militant of the sixties

Violence by human beings against other human beings has scarred history from earliest times. In addition to hundreds of smaller conflicts, the twentieth century has witnessed two major world wars with casualties in the millions and devastation, such as that at Hiroshima and Nagasaki, that is unparalleled in human history. Mass genocide of populations by the Nazis, human purges in which millions disappeared as in Stalin's Russia, and continuing torture of political opponents in many countries throughout the world have made it a frightening century indeed.

While writers such as Konrad Lorenz (1966) and Robert Ardrey (1963) argue that humans have a "killer instinct," a natural predisposition toward violence and aggression, most social scientists reject this view, arguing instead that individuals learn violence, like nonviolence, through socialization. Anthropological studies have discovered wide variations in the degree of violence prevalent in human cultures, with a few cultures in which violence is unknown. Japan's transition from a violent, warlike society before and during World War II to a pacifist society in the postwar period suggests that violence is not an inevitability. Just as violence can be learned and assumed to be a natural part of a culture, it probably also can be unlearned.

History of Violence in the United States

In their report to the National Commission on the Causes and Prevention of Violence entitled *Violence in America: Historical and Comparative Perspectives,* Hugh Davis and Tedd Gurr (1969) indicate that we ignore history when we view our present levels of violence as unusual. They claim that violence in the United States is rooted in *six historical events* that are deeply imbedded in our national character (pp. 770–74):

1. Revolutionary doctrine expounded in the Declaration of Independence.
2. A prolonged frontier experience, which tended to legitimize violence and vigilante justice.
3. A competitive hierarchy of immigrants that has been highly conducive to violence.
4. A pervasive fear of governmental power, which "has reinforced a tendency to define freedom negatively as freedom from" (p. 772).
5. The Industrial Revolution and the great internal migration from countryside to city, which has produced widespread social dislocation.
6. Unmatched prosperity combined with unequal distribution and unequal opportunity, which has produced a "revolution of rising expectations" in which improved economic rewards can coincide with relative deprivation that generates frustration and violence.

Glaringly absent from this list is the bitter legacy of slavery and subsequent racially motivated violence against blacks. The burning cross of the KKK (Ku Klux Klan) symbolized the bombings, lynchings, murders, shootings, arsons, mutilations, and other violent tactics used against African Americans as well as others. In the fifties and sixties the bombing of churches and murders of civil rights workers, often in collusion with local police officers, aroused a nation to oppose racism (Wade, 1987; Revell, 1988, p. 10). While item two above mentions frontier violence, elaboration of this theme would note that the almost eternal war by white settlers against Native American tribes was of genocidal proportions, a holocaust that wiped out entire tribes as part of stealing their land.

Historian Richard Brown (1969, pp. 69–70) sums up much of this:

> Violence has formed a seamless web with some of the noblest and most constructive chapters of American history: the birth of the nation (Revolutionary violence), the occupation of the land (Indian wars), the stabilization of frontier society (vigilante violence), the elevation of the farmer and the laborer (agrarian and labor violence), and the preservation of law and order (police violence). The

Four people were killed and a dozen others injured when a bomb exploded in this Birmingham, Alabama, Baptist church in September of 1963. Police officers inspect the damage done by the blast to a car parked outside the church. In May, 2001 (38 years later) Thomas Blanton was convicted for his role in the killings of four young black girls in the blast.

(© UPI - Cobis - Bettmann)

> patriot, the humanitarian, the nationalist, the pioneer, the landholder, the farmer, and the laborer (and the capitalist) have used violence as a means to a higher end.

Violence may indeed reflect a society's values. For example, Americans value "life, liberty, and the pursuit of happiness," while their less violent next-door neighbors, the Canadians, reflect a less revolutionary view of society and applaud "peace, order, and good government." The United States has inherited a violent cultural tradition, but as a relatively young country, its tradition may not be that much different from the early histories of older civilizations of Europe and Asia. It has been just over 100 years since 1890, the date that historian Frederick Jackson Turner (1975) earmarked as signifying the closing of the American frontier. Moreover, as discussed in Chapter 3, the assimilation of culturally divergent populations has not been a smooth process, as Canada and England are beginning to realize firsthand. Racial violence and a history of institutionalized racism until just a generation ago have made this the very first generation of Americans to attempt to provide justice to the nation's oldest immigrant minority—African Americans.

The U.S. is not alone in being plagued by violent crime. IN THE NEWS 7.1 describes international experience in this regard.

IN THE NEWS 7.1

INTERNATIONAL VIOLENT CRIME

The United States, while it has higher rates than other developed countries with respect to murder and rape, does not stand alone with respect to violent crime (Rounds, 2000). Some recent examples serve as illustrations:

- Schools in France closed their doors to protest rising levels of school violence. Teachers and students joined in a strike to protest conditions.
- Eight London youths in a racially motivated gang rape brutally raped and attacked an Austrian tourist before throwing her into a canal. She survived the attack.
- At 110 per 100,000 (1995) Johannesburg, South Africa, has a higher murder rate than Washington, D.C.

Homicides in Cities
(per 100,000 population, average, 1995–1997)

Vienna	*1.8*
Ottawa	*1.9*
London	*2.2*
Paris	*3.3*
Berlin	*3.8*
Stockholm	*4.1*
Copenhagen	*4.6*
Rotterdam	*5.0*
Amsterdam	*7.9*
New York	*16.8*
Washington, D.C.	*64.1*

- In 1996 Rio de Janeiro recorded 53.3 murders per 100,000 compared with 20 for Los Angeles. A garrison state existence is becoming more common as the wealthy retreat behind their own private fortresses.
- Avid soccer fan and fan of the film series "Nightmare on Elm Street" movies, 19-year-old Italian Pietro Marso, along with friends, murdered his parents in hopes of receiving his inheritance. His explained motive was to obtain a brilliant life, with expensive cars and good quality clothes (Cowell, 1994). This lust for material success was dubbed "the Verona syndrome."
- At least 103 people were beheaded in Saudi Arabia in 1999, one more executed than in the United States, which uses mostly lethal injections.
- Overall, five people are kidnapped per day in Colombia, mostly children and teenagers. This is the highest rate in the world (Faiola, 1999).
- In India parents of two lovers kill them for breaking a marriage taboo. This is called an "honor killing" (to preserve the honor of the clan). They had broken the taboo of marrying another from the same village (Bearak, 1999).

Source: British Home Office, 1998. Frans van Dijk and Jaap de Waard. 2000. *Legal Infrastructure of the Netherlands in International Perspective: Crime Control.* Amsterdam: Ministry of Justice, the Netherlands, p. 7.

InfoTrac College Edition Research

Search the term "murder" and locate some intersting international examples. How do these examples compare with our discussion of U.S. homicides?

Murder and Mayhem

In 1966, former Eagle Scout leader and engineering honor student Charles Whitman murdered his wife and mother and then, with a small arsenal of weapons and ammunition, climbed to the top of a tower at the University of Texas. Taking aim with deadly accuracy he randomly killed sixteen persons and wounded another thirty before being killed himself by police.

On August 8, 1969, devotees of a cult mesmerized and run by Charles Manson brutally murdered pregnant actress Sharon Tate and four other guests at her home and two days later murdered two members of the La Bianca family in an apparent attempt to foment a race war. Particularly frightening in the incident was Manson's Rasputin-like ability to inspire undying devotion in his followers, most of them young female drifters.

After the dismembered remains of eleven victims were found in his apartment in July 1991, Jeffrey Dahmer admitted killing seventeen boys and young men, primarily in the Milwaukee area, over a thirteen-year period. After luring victims to his apartment to take nude pictures, watch videos, and have sex, he drugged, killed, and dismembered them. He often took pictures of his victims and boiled some of their skulls in order to preserve them.

Each of these cases is an example of multiple murders. While cases such as these attract much public attention, they are relatively rare and make up only a very small proportion of the incidents of violent crime. Media, fictional, and popular accounts of violent crime tend to focus on the dramatic tales of murder and mayhem that make our blood curdle as much as the latest Stephen King novel. The post-World War II period has had no shortage of material for such chronicles.

Types of Multiple Murders: Multicide

Holmes and DeBurger (1988, p. 19) estimate that between 3,500 and 5,000 persons may be slain per year in the United States by multiple murderers, and that even though such killings are not new, they appear to have increased since the sixties. Much of the gap in our academic knowledge of multiple murder is being addressed by more recent scholarship (Egger, 1984; Fox and Levin, 1985; Hickey, 1986; Jenkins, 1988, Leyton, 1986). Criminologists agree that at least *three different types of multiple murders* (multicide) exist: serial murder, mass murder, and spree murder (Bureau of Justice Statistics, 1988b).

Serial Murder. **Serial murder** is *the killing of several victims in three or more separate incidents over weeks, months, or even years.* Herman Mudgett, Juan Corona, Wayne Henley, John Wayne Gacy, Ted Bundy, and David "Son of Sam" Berkowitz are just a few of the "Jack the Rippers" who have shocked us in modern times. In April 1989, the thirteenth victim of cult slayings was discovered in Matamoros, Mexico, the work of cult "godfather" Adolpho de Jesus Costanzo and cult "witch" Sara Aldrete, who allegedly ritualistically sacrificed victims in order to "provide a 'magical shield' for members of a drug-smuggling ring" ("13th Victim," 1989, p. A1.) In a case reminiscent of the classic movie *Arsenic and Old Lace* directed by Frank Capra, in 1988 Dorothea Puente, a boardinghouse landlady in Sacramento, California, was charged with poisoning at least eight of her elderly boarders and collecting their social security checks. Finally, in Philadelphia in 1987, police arrested Gary Heidnik and an accomplice, charging them with running a "Little Shop of Horrors" (Johnson, 1987, p. 29). Heidnik, who had a history of psychiatric problems, attracted women to his house and imprisoned, tortured, sexually abused, murdered, and cannibalized them. Police have accounted for at least six victims.

Between 1982 and 1984, 48 bodies of women, mostly prostitutes, were found along the banks of the Green River near Seattle. No one has ever been prosecuted. Similarly, it is estimated that from 1955 to 1966 the "Zodiac killer" in San Francisco killed over 50 people in the bay area. He scribbled Zodiac signs around their bodies. No one was ever prosecuted in these cases. The Green River and Zodiac killers terrify the public, which seems transfixed with Hollywood movies such as *Silence of the Lambs* and characters such as Hannibal Lector.

A variety of typologies (taxonomies) of serial killers have been proposed. One of the most accepted typologies of serial killers is that of Holmes and DeBurger who identify (1988, pp. 55–60):

1. Visionaries: Believed to be suffering from some sort of psychosis, they kill in response to voices or visions.
2. Mission-oriented: Their mission in life is to rid society of "undesirables," for example, prostitutes.
3. Hedonists: These are "thrill seekers" who murder for creature comforts, profit, or pleasures in life, as well as lust murderers.
4. Power/control: These enjoy power and control over helpless victims and enjoy watching them suffer and beg for mercy.

After ex-Boy Scout leader Thomas Hamilton took four rifles into a Scottish primary school and slaughtered 16 children and their teacher, laws were passed that effectively prohibited the private ownership of handguns.

Serial killing is always sexual in nature (Ressler and Shachtman, 1992, p. 4). Such killers fantasize extensively before their murders. The FBI Behavioral Science Unit, which has conducted extensive investigations and crime profiling of such murders, indicates that the victims often represent someone in the killer's adolescence who inflicted some perceived pain on them (Douglas and Olshaker, 1995, 1997).

Organized serial killers usually plan their offenses, transport their victims, and keep "trophies" (victim belongings); they are normal in appearance and socially competent. Disorganized serial killers are usually socially and sexually incompetent. Both types often return to the gravesite or dumpsite, often to satisfy their sexual fantasy through masturbation.

Many serial killers display what is called "the terrible triad" as children: bedwetting, firestarting, and cruelty to animals. Most were products of dysfunctional families.

Mass Murder. **Mass murder** is *the killing of four or more victims at one location on a single occasion.* Thomas Hamilton (who in 1996 slaughtered 16 kindergartners and their teacher in Scotland), Richard Speck (who murdered eight Chicago nurses), James Huberty, Charles Whitman (see p. 270), and George Hennard are examples of mass murderers. In 1984 Huberty killed twenty-one and wounded a dozen others at a McDonald's restaurant in San Ysidro, California. In 1991 Hennard drove his pickup truck through the windows of Luby's Cafeteria in Killeen, Texas, and at point-blank range shot and killed twenty-two and wounded twenty-three, making the Killeen massacre the worst in U.S. history (although eighty-seven died in an arson fire at the Happy Land nightclub in New York City in 1990).

In 1999 Mark Barton, a day trader (internet stock speculator) in Atlanta, distraught over heavy stock losses, killed nine people and wounded thirteen others before killing himself. Saying things such as "It's a bad trading day and it's about to get worse." Barton had also killed his wife and two small children. In 1993 a Brooklyn man, Colen Ferguson, opened fire in a crowded commuter train on Long Island, killing six people and wounding seventeen.

Spree Murder. The **spree murderer** *kills at two or more locations with almost no time break between murders* (Bureau of Justice Statistics, 1988b, p. 4; Crockett, 1991).

One of the most celebrated cases of "spree murder" was the case of Andrew Cunanan, the murderer of Italian fashion designer Gianni Versace in Miami Beach, Florida, in 1997. Cunanan, who was HIV-positive, left San Diego on April 24, 1997, and five days later murdered his ex-lover David Madson and friend Jeffrey Trail. The largest unsuccessful manhunt in U.S. history ended on July 15 with Cunanan's suicide. After the first two killings, he also killed Lee Miglin, a wealthy Chicago developer; William Reese, a cemetery worker in New Jersey; and Versace.

African Americans and Serial Murder. Wayne Williams, age twenty-three and himself black, terrorized the African-American community of Atlanta, murdering an estimated twenty-eight young blacks over a two-year period ending in 1981. Hating poor young blacks, whom he regarded as racially inferior, Williams lured them into his company with promises of fame in the entertainment business and then murdered them when they agreed to perform homosexual acts (see Detlinger, 1983).

As a black serial murderer, Williams appears to be an anomaly since most media portrayals feature white killers. In a thorough analysis of this issue, Jenkins (1992a) concludes that blacks are proportionately as likely as whites to be serial murderers. He indicates (1992a, pp. 16–17):

> For centuries, the lives of African-Americans have often been blighted by stereotypes, usually negative, and frequently associating them with crime and violence (Lynch and Patterson, eds., 1992; Rose and McClain, 1990). This paper has considered an area where stereotypes imply a diametrically opposite image, and Blacks appear disproportionately free of involvement in the most serious of violent crimes. However, this image is false; and this apparently favorable stereotype is both as inaccurate and as pernicious as any of the more familiar racial slurs. Significantly, the very failure to draw attention to Black serial killers might in itself arise from a form of bias within the media and law enforcement.
>
> African-Americans make up a sizeable proportion of serial killers, and this has practical consequences for the fate of those Blacks and other minorities who are most likely to fall victim to this type of predator. Underestimating minority involvement in serial homicide can thus lead to neglecting the protection of minority individuals and communities who stand in greatest peril of victimization.

As previously indicated, while bizarre and mass murders attract media and public attention, they represent the rare and dramatic rather than the typical violent crime.

Victim Precipitation

Victimology is the study of victims of crime, a group that in the past has been neglected by the criminal justice system. In examining violent crime, Lombroso was one of the first to note that passionate criminals often acted under the provocation of victims. In many violent crimes such as assault and voluntary manslaughter, a flip of the coin separates the victim from the offender, with both parties active participants. In many violent crimes, victims contribute to their own harm (Von Hentig, 1948). Benjamin Mendelson (1963), one of the pioneers of victimology, developed a *typology of victims* in terms of their degree of guilt in the perpetration of crime:

- The completely innocent victim, such as a child or an unconscious person
- The victim with minor guilt, such as a woman who provokes a miscarriage and dies as a result
- The victim as guilty as offender, such as in cases of suicide and euthanasia
- The victim as more guilty than the offender, such as those who provoke someone to commit a crime
- The victim as most guilty, such as the aggressive victim who was killed in self-defense
- The simulating or imaginary victim, such as paranoids, hysterics, or senile persons

Wolfgang (1958, p. 252), in his study of criminal homicide in Philadelphia, viewed victim precipitation as present in incidents in which the victim initiated the altercation by being the first to use and/or threaten violence. Victim precipitation is common in murder and assault: it may also be common in other crimes.

Typology of Violent Offenders

John Conrad (Spencer, 1966; Vetter and Silverman, 1978, p. 65) has proposed a very useful *typology of violent offenders:*

- culturally violent offenders
- criminally violent offenders
- pathologically violent offenders
- situationally violent offenders

Culturally violent offenders are individuals who live in subcultures (cultures within a culture) in which violence is an acceptable problem-solving mechanism. The "subculture of violence" thesis, to be explored shortly, is used as a means of explaining the greater prevalence of violent crime among low income minorities from slum environments of large central cities.

Criminally violent offenders use violence as a means of accomplishing a criminal act, such as robbery. Mental illness or brain damage characterize *pathologically violent offenders.* (Discussions later in this chapter focusing on psychiatry and the law and on psychopathy will further elaborate on the mentally disturbed violent criminal.)

Finally, *situationally violent offenders* commit acts of violence on rare occasions, often under provocation, such as in domestic disputes that get out of hand. These incidents are often described as "crimes of passion," in which the individual temporarily loses control and often expresses regret for the actions later.

Legal Aspects

VANTAGE POINT 7.1 provides a brief outline of the key legal features of violent crimes. Although violent crimes were at one time treated under tort law as a matter of private wrong to be settled by the parties involved, today the state has assumed authority and jurisdiction in cases of harmful, violent personal behavior. Private revenge is forbidden and is replaced with retribution. The violent act is viewed as a threat to the well-being of the society, and the culprit must pay his or her debt to society.

Psychiatry and the Law

In order for an individual to be held guilty or responsible for violating the criminal law, he or she must exercise *mens rea* or proper criminal intent. Exceptions to this rule are cases of negligence or strict liability, such as the felony murder doctrine. Anglo-American common law is based on the classical theory of criminology that assumes that individuals are rational actors and thus will respond in kind to threats of punishment. Individuals are to be held responsible for their conduct, but what if the individual is insane?

Basic Decisions. The **M'Naghten rule** is named after an 1843 English decision regarding Daniel M'Naghten, an individual who, suffering from severe delusions of persecution (paranoia), attempted to shoot Sir Robert Peel (the famous founder of the London police, who were nicknamed "Bobbies" in his honor). M'Naghten missed and killed Peel's secretary. This decision held that individuals who are insane, unable to distinguish between right and wrong, cannot be held responsible for their actions. The M'Naghten rule became the basis of psychiatric justice in Anglo-American criminal law, such individuals being held "not guilty due to insanity." It is sometimes referred to as the "right-wrong test" or the **NGRI defense** (not guilty by reason of insanity). Individuals who are successfully defended under this rule are usually institutionalized for long-term psychiatric treatment. In 1897 the federal courts as well as many states added a modification called the "irresistible impulse" test to the "right-wrong" test. Accused persons could not be found guilty if they had a mental disease that prevented them from controlling their conduct (Morris, 1987, p. 1).

The Durham decision was a 1954 decision in the U.S. Court of Appeals, District of Columbia, regarding Monte Durham, a burglar who had been found guilty in a lower court when psychiatrists indicated that there was no clear evidence that Durham could not tell right from wrong, even though he had a long history of psychotic and deranged behavior. The appeals court overturned the previous decision and ruled that individuals are not guilty due to insanity if their acts are the *product* of mental disease or defect. This rule was valid in the federal system from 1954 to 1972.

The Brawner Test. In 1972 the federal system rejected Durham and adopted a standard suggested by the Model Penal Code. This is used by half of the states, although it is subject to increasing restriction in the wake of the Hinckley trial. John Hinckley, the attempted assassin of former president Reagan, had been tried under what is called the Brawner test (*United States v. Brawner*), which holds:

> A person is not responsible for criminal conduct if at the time of such conduct as a result of mental disease or defect he lacks *substantial capacity* [italics mine] either to appreciate the wrongfulness of his conduct or to conform his conduct to the requirements of the law (Morris, 1987, p. 2).

Although the Brawner test dominated federal and state practice until the Hinckley trial, after the adverse reaction to this trial, a new standard resembling the original M'Naghten rule was adopted, which placed the burden of proof of insanity on the defendant. Figure 7.1 summarizes these insanity defense standards.

Guilty but Mentally Ill. By the early eighties a number of states (Morris, 1987, p. 2) had abolished the NGRI defense and substituted the "guilty, but mentally ill" rule in which convicted individuals undergo civil commitment until cured and then serve out their time in jail. Other states such as Oregon have established psychiatric review boards both to determine release and to monitor continuous follow-up counseling. Over half of the states have joined the federal government in tightening insanity defense standards.

The Twinkie Defense. "You are what you eat!" "Be careful not to eat too many Twinkies, or you might become a killer!" In San Francisco a gay riot resulted when under a "diminished responsibility" argument a jury found Dan White not guilty of first-degree murder in the 1978 killing of that city's mayor William Mosconi and Harvey Milk (a gay city supervisor). Despite the fact that White gave a full confession, psychiatrists convinced

VANTAGE POINT 7.1

Legal Aspects and Definitions of Violent Crime

Assault: Threatening to do bodily harm to a person or placing him or her in fear of such harm. Assault is attempted, but uncompleted, battery.

Battery—(Aggravated Assault): "An offensive, unconsented to, unprivileged and unjustified offensive bodily contact." Battery includes *mens rea,* meaning that the contact was intentional or resulted from wanton misconduct, and indicates that bodily harm takes place.

Forcible Rape: Forcible and unlawful sexual relations with a person against her or his will. Rape is defined in common law as "carnal knowledge of a female forcibly and against her will."

Statutory Rape: Sexual relations with a victim under the age of consent.

Murder: Killing that is "calculated, in cold blood" or with "malice aforethought."

First Degree includes the following:

1. intent to effect death with "malice aforethought"
2. deliberate act
3. premeditated act

Second Degree includes:

1. intent to effect death with "malice aforethought"
2. without deliberation or premeditation. In essence, in most states second degree murder is any murder that is not defined as first degree.

Felony Murder Doctrine: If in the act of committing a felony the death of one of the victims is brought about, this is murder though it does not necessarily result from intent, deliberation, or premeditation.

Manslaughter: Homicide without malice aforethought.

Voluntary: (nonnegligent) intentional killing without "malice aforethought:" often described as homicide "in hot blood" and often results from provocation.

Involuntary: (negligent) unintentional killing without "malice aforethought," for example, vehicular homicides.

For additional details on legal definitions and the nature of the criminal law, see Katkin (1982) *The Nature of Criminal Law* or any text on criminal law.

Sources: Adapted from Bureau of Justice Statistics 1983b, *Report to the Nation on Crime and Justice: The Data,* Washington, D.C.: Government Printing Office, pp. 2–3; and Federal Bureau of Investigation, 1992, *Crime in the United States, 1991,* Washington, D.C.: Government Printing Office, p. 340 and Henry C. Black, 1991 *Black's Law Dictionary,* St. Paul, MN: West.

InfoTrac College Edition Research
Review the concept of "criminal law." What are some current issues in this field?

the jury that his overindulgence in junk food (Twinkies and Cokes) diminished his ability to premeditate (NBC, 1983).

Growing steroid (synthetic growth hormone) abuse by athletes and bodybuilders in order to "bulk up" has led to the increasing documentation of adverse side effects including "bodybuilder's psychosis," which involves bizarre and violent behavior. It has led some to speculate on yet another tool for defense attorneys— "the dumbbell defense" (Monmaney and Robins, 1988, p 75).

In 1988 a New York jury ruled that Reuben Pratts, a Vietnam veteran, was not guilty of a murder he confessed to because he suffered from chronic post-traumatic stress disorder (PTSD) resulting from traumatic experiences in Vietnam. Pratt had experienced flashbacks to his wartime experiences (French, 1989; Palmer, 1990). In 1990 lawyers first began using the "Prozac defense" to argue that their clients were not legally responsible for their crimes. Prozac, an antidepressant drug, was blamed for, among other things, a mass murder-suicide in Louisville, Kentucky. The first trial resulted in reduced charges because the jury believed that the accused was suffering from side effects of Prozac. So far, the success in other cases has been mixed (Marcus, 1991; "Eli Lilly," 1990). Similar

FIGURE 7.1 Insanity Defense Standards (Tests)

Test	Legal Standard Because of Mental Illness	Final Burden of Proof	Who Bears Burden of Proof
M'Naghten	"didn't know what he or she was doing or didn't know it was wrong"	Varies: Balance of probability	Defense
Irresistible Impulse	"could not control his or her conduct"	Beyond reasonable doubt	Prosecutor
Durham	"the criminal act was caused by his or her mental illness"	Beyond reasonable doubt	Prosecutor
Brawner Test	"lacks substantial capacity to appreciate the wrongfulness of his or her conduct or to control it"	Beyond reasonable doubt	Prosecutor
Present Federal Law	"lacks capacity to appreciate the wrongfulness of his or her conduct"	Clear and convincing evidence	Defense

Source: Norval Morris, 1987, "Insanity Defense," *Crime File,* National Institute of Justice, p. 3.

defenses arguing that drugs such as Halcion, a widely used sleep remedy, were responsible for violence and murder have been unsuccessful (Cowley, 1992).

A related defense strategy has been called the "abuse excuse" (Dershowitz, 1994). In the celebrated case of Lorena Bobbit, a physically abused wife who cut off her husband's penis, the defendant was found not guilty by reason of insanity because of her history of abuse. "Roid rage" (due to steroids), "black rage" (due to racism), "fetal trimethadione syndrome" (due to a mother's use of a drug during pregnancy), "adopted child syndrome," and "abused child syndrome" (used in the Menendez trial) have all become part of the "I am a victim of ______ excuse" (Slade, 1994, p. B12). In a claimed "cultural insanity defense," a black bank robber standing trial claimed that he was the victim of long-term exposure to white racism that drove him insane. He claimed he was a victim of "post traumatic stress disorder" due to unwarranted exposure, victimization, and repetitive confrontation with white racism. The first use of this defense was by two black men on trial for the beating of white truck driver Reginald Denny during the 1992 Los Angeles riots. The men claimed that pent-up rage due to racism caused them to attack Denny (Forsthoffer, 1999).

Despite the bizarre nature of these and similar cases and the media attention they arouse, the reader should be aware that such cases are rarities and attract interest for that very reason. Morris (1987, p. 1) points out that another reason for the rare use of the insanity defense is that a person found not guilty by reason of insanity may be held in a mental hospital longer than he or she would be imprisoned if convicted. The insanity defense is raised in only one percent of all felony cases, and in only about a quarter of these is it successful. For additional information on the insanity defense, the reader is referred to Hermann, 1983; Moran, 1985; Morris, 1987; Simon and Aaronsen, 1988; Toch and Adams, 1991.

The Psychopath

Psychopath, sociopath, and antisocial personality are all terms referring to the same phenomenon—the inadequately socialized personality. While at one time such persons were viewed as having innate psychological defects, the concepts of psychopath, sociopath, and antisocial personality imply that such personalities are learned through socialization. Harrington (1972, p. 15) describes the roots of psychopathy in the following manner:

> Persons diagnosed as psychopathic begin as rejected, cruelly or indifferently treated children, or may possibly have suffered early brain damage, detected or not. They strike back at the world with aggressive, unrestrained, attention-drawing

> behavior. (Why one person emerges from a disordered childhood inhibited and neurotic and another, the psychopath, with the opposite tendencies remains unclear.) Since conscience is instilled by early love, faith in the adults close by, and desire to hold their affection by being good, the child unrewarded with love grows up experiencing no conscience. Uncared for, he doesn't care, can't really love, feels no anxiety to speak of (having experienced little or no love to lose), does not worry about whether he's good or bad, and literally has no idea of guilt.

A psychopath never really develops the full range of human emotions. Some general characteristics linked with the phenomenon include the lack of inhibition, guilt, fear, conscience, or superego. Such individuals' lack of empathy is illustrated by mass killers such as Charles Manson, who was described as viewing other people as furniture or objects in the world around him.

Hervey Cleckley (1976), in *The Mask of Sanity,* identifies the following traits as characteristic of psychopathy: unreliability, insincerity, superficial charm, inability to learn from mistakes, impersonal sexual behavior, and an incapacity to love. The background of Charles Manson is instructive. Manson was born to a sixteen-year-old prostitute who did not know the identity of the father. She was sent to prison when he was four, and he spent the next four years with relatives who gave little love or affection. His mother finally returned and took up her old ways. At the age of either nine or twelve, he was sent to a reform school; by age thirty-two he had spent nearly his entire life in correctional institutions in which he had been exposed to a considerable amount of violence. He had become totally institutionalized to prison. When he was finally eligible for release on parole, he pleaded with officials to permit him to remain in prison (Scheflin and Opton, 1978, pp. 28–29). Manson attracted a small, devoted following, but imagine a sociopath operating in a larger arena.

The following description of Adolf Hitler by Albert Speer, his armaments minister, illustrates both the shallowness and the inexplicable charm of the psychopath:

> . . . Hitler could fascinate, he wallowed in his own charisma, but he could not respond to friendship. Instinctively, he repelled it. The normal sympathies that normal males and females enjoy were just not in him. At the core, in the place where the heart should be, Hitler was a hollow man. He was empty . . . the man's drive—his iron will, his demonism—fascinated even while it repelled . . . I was enthralled (Harrington, 1972, p. 32).

In October 1999, Luis Garavito confessed to killing 140 children over a five-year period in Colombia. Donald Black in *Bad Boys, Bad Men: Confronting Antisocial Personality Disorder* (1999) describes Columbine killers Eric Harris and Dylan Klebold as "antisocial personalities," cold and calculating with no regard for the consequences. Others who have been described as fitting the mold have been Ted Bundy, who murdered 50 women, and Andrew Cunanan, who killed five including designer Gianni Versace (Barovick, 1999).

The actual definition and diagnosis of psychopathy are elusive; there is considerable disagreement and confusion within the psychiatric profession itself regarding the concept. Many critics view it as a "wastebasket concept," a catchall, a diagnosis of convenience or of last resort. If some inexplicably horrible crime defies our sensibilities, the person who commits it is labeled a psychopath.

Homicide and Assault Statistics

Nearly all murders arise from some form of aggravated assault and, although the latter generally is not taken as seriously as murder, in fact there is a thin line separating the two. Both offenses entail the use of violence as a means of resolving some grievance; in the case of murder, the victim dies. In our previous discussions of the shortcomings of crime statistics, it was pointed out that official police statistics such as the UCR underestimate the actual rate of crime commission. While this is true, the accuracy of these statistics varies according to the type of crime, and homicide statistics are one of the most accurate (see Reidel and Zahn, 1985).

Generally, homicide is regarded as the most serious crime. A body is present; there may be witnesses; and, as a result, such a crime is very likely to be reported to the police. In addition, homicide is the type of crime that the public, the media, and the police place a high priority on solving. Because of all of these factors, homicide has the highest "clearance by arrest" proportion of all UCR offenses. Clearance means that, as far as the police are concerned, the person responsible for the crime has been accounted for through arrest and/or incarceration.

Assault statistics are less accurate, and figures on rape have been notoriously poor until relatively recently. In fact, police and criminal justice professionals have applauded the recent rise in the rape rate, not because more rapes are occurring but because there is a greater willingness on the part of victims to report the crime to the police. The least accurate violent crime statistics relate to intrafamily violence such as spouse abuse, child abuse, and incest. Such offenses, which will be described in detail shortly, have been regarded as family secrets until relatively recently.

Figure 7.2 shows the overall trend with respect to homicide statistics in the United States, while Table 7.1 provides comparative international figures on the rate of homicide in selected countries. While the willful homicide rate declined from its peak in 1933 only to be surpassed again in the seventies, this dip may be misleading. Faster ambulances, better communications, transportation, and emergency room service meant better treatment for seriously injured persons, so that many who previously would have been homicide statistics

FIGURE 7.2 Homicide Trends in the United States

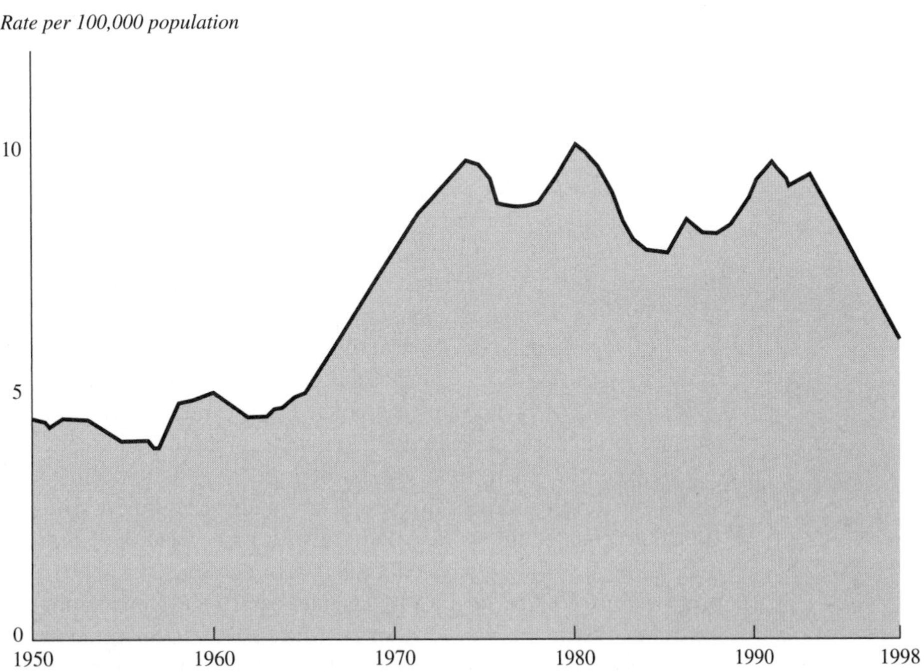

Source: Bureau of Justice Statistics, www.ojp.usdoj.gov/bjs/.

TABLE 7.1 Interpol Homicide Statistics, 1998 (per 100,000)

Country	Homicide (attempts)/actual	
United States		6.3
Australia		3.6
Austria	(2.0)	.9
Brazil	(21.2)	6.4
Bulgaria	(7.5)	4.7
Canada	(4.3)	1.8
Chile		3.5
Colombia		56.3
Denmark	(3.9)	.9
Dominican Republic		15.8
Estonia	(17.1)	13.7
El Salvador		38.8
England/Wales	(2.8)	1.5
Finland		0.4
France	(3.7)	1.7
Germany	(3.5)	1.2
Greece	(3.4)	1.7
Ireland	(1.8)	1.7
Israel		2.4
Italy	(4.4)	1.5
Jamaica	37.2	
Japan	(1.1)	.6
Mongolia		24.6
Namibia	(45.7)	16.7
Netherlands	(10.9)	1.2
Norway	(1.9)	1.0
Russia	(20.1)	18
Paraguay		16.5
Spain	(2.6)	1.1
Switzerland	(2.6)	1.1

Source: Interpol. International Crime Statistics, 1998. Lyons, France: Interpol Secretariat, 1999.

were surviving. By the seventies, however, the sheer volume of violence had surpassed these extraordinary means of patching up the victims. It is also important to note that, although prior to the thirties the United States had no national statistics, fragmentary information suggests that at the turn of the century we had violent crime rates equal to present levels. In 1916 Memphis had a homicide rate seven times greater than its rate in 1969, and Boston, Chicago, and New York during and after World War I had higher rates than they did in 1933, when the first national statistics were published (National Commission, 1969, p. 20). Despite problems of measurement, there is little denying that there was a precipitous increase in violence, particularly in homicide, in the United States beginning in the sixties.

Between 1989 and 1998, the murder rate in the U.S. declined 21 percent. There were a total of 16,914 murders in 1998. The South was highest with a murder rate of 8 per 100,000 compared to the West and Midwest with 6 and the Northeast with 4 per 100,000 (FBI, 1999, p. 14). Aggravated assault also decreased in 1998 for the fifth consecutive year. There were 360 aggravated assaults per 100,000 population. The rates were 418 in the South, 384 in the West, 310 in the Midwest, and 288 in the Northeast.

By 1998 the U.S. homicide rate had fallen to its lowest level in three decades (Fox, 2000). The homicide rate doubled from the mid 1960s to the late 1980s. It peaked at

10.2 per 100,000 (1980) and fell to 7.9 in 1985. It rose again in the late 1980s and peaked at 9.8 in 1991. Since then it has declined, reaching 6.3 by 1998.

Table 7.1 presents Interpol homicide statistics for 1998. These statistics do not include those for many Third World countries that have notoriously poor statistics. Countries with the highest homicide rates were: Colombia (56.3), El Salvador (38.8), Jamaica (37.2), Mongolia (24.6), and Russia (18). It is also not clear whether these rates excluded war-related activities in Colombia and El Salvador or whether the rates included attempts in all countries but Russia. The U.S. rate of 6.3 was higher than any other developed country with comparative rates of 3.6 (Australia), 1.8 (Canada), 1.7 (France), and lowest rates in Austria and Denmark (.9), Japan (.6), and Finland (.4).

Although rates have declined since then, in the mid-eighties a particularly disturbing increase in homicide rates among young black males began. Between 1984 and 1988 it increased 68 percent for black men fifteen-to-twenty-four years of age and nearly doubled for those aged fifteen-to-nineteen. One of every 1,000 young black men died a violent death each year—ten times the rate for whites the same age. In some cities young black males between fifteen and twenty-four were more at risk than were U.S. soldiers in Vietnam. The causes are poverty, discrimination, and unemployment, combining lethally with rising drug trafficking, gangs, and possession of increasingly deadly weapons.

Patterns and Trends in Violent Crime

Despite the association of crime with urbanization, crime was basically a rural rather than an urban problem during ancient times and the Middle Ages. Walled cities were built to provide protection from marauding highwaymen (Fox, 1976, p. 41). In the United States it was not until the sixties that urban rates for homicide exceeded those of rural areas (Glaser, 1978, p. 210), and in Canada the rural homicide rate still exceeds the urban rate (Schloss and Giesbrecht, 1972, p. 22). VANTAGE POINT 7.2 contains policy suggestions of the Youth Violence Task Force to Attorney General Janet Reno.

Racial disparity in arrest rates is highest for crimes of violence. The black arrest rate for homicide is about eight times the white rate. Wolfgang's (1958, pp. 33, 66) classic study *Patterns in Criminal Homicide* found that the overall murder rate for white males in Philadelphia was 1.8 per 100,000 and, for white males age 20–24, 8.2 per 100,000. These same rates for black males were 24.6 and 92.5, respectively. In the Northeast and Midwest, the highest rates are for recent black migrants from the South to large cities. Internationally, lower class slum backgrounds are significantly associated with high rates of violence.

Nettler (1982, vol. 2, pp. 32–39) found that a number of studies indicate that countries with greater inequalities in income distribution have higher murder rates. International homicide statistics are questionable, however, since totalitarian regimes do not report statistics for government murder of citizens. Studies by Messner (1980) and Atkinson (1975) found moderate relationships between inequality in income distribution and homicide rate ($r = .40$ to $.59$).

Suppose you have been tipped off that you are likely to be the victim of a violent crime. Whom would you avoid? When? Where? Surprisingly, you are most likely to be stabbed, shot, beaten, or abused in your own home or in the home of one of your friends, relatives, or acquaintances. Saturday nights are lethal, as is the month of December, when friends and relatives get together and drink; summer months are even more lethal. Alcohol is a contributing factor in the majority of homicides, assaults, and rapes; it serves as a deinhibitor, causing individuals to have less rational control over their emotions as well as less awareness of the consequences of their actions (see Collins, 1981; Fagan, 1990). In the United States more people are killed by drunk drivers every year than by all other types of killers.

VANTAGE POINT 7.2

Youth Violence

Issues

Sharp increases in juvenile violence have heightened the sense of personal risk experienced by those who live and work in urban areas and contributed strongly to the widespread fear of crime in general. This fear derives from the randomness (the victims of juvenile homicides are strangers about 30 percent of the time), the early onset, and the seriousness of violence perpetrated by youths. Between 1985 and 1992, the juvenile homicide arrest rate, the juvenile homicide victimization rate, the number of juvenile homicides involving guns, and the rates of murder committed by 15- and 16-year-olds increased by more than 100 percent. In addition, the arrest rate of nonwhite juveniles for drug offenses doubled. Public anxiety extends beyond fears for personal safety to include concern about an irreparable breach of the social contract.

Consider this working hypothesis about the growth in juvenile violence:

- When crack cocaine hit the streets in 1985, it changed illegal drug buying habits and distribution patterns. The number of transactions increased markedly, as people bought one "hit" at a time, rather than larger quantities that could be stored for later use.
- To accommodate the higher number of transactions, youths (primarily African Americans in center-city areas) were recruited into the drug market.
- Since they could not easily ask the police for protection, the new recruits needed guns to protect themselves and their valuable wares.
- Their tight networking through schools and the streets led to a broader diffusion of guns into the larger youth community, primarily for self-defense but also, perhaps, for status.
- Because of the presence of guns, the fights that routinely occur among youths can rapidly turn from fistfights to shootings. Adult gun carriers, even those in the drug market, seem better able to exercise restraint.
- As more young people carried guns, they provided an incentive for other youths to arm themselves, resulting in an escalating process of gun-carrying (the familiar "arms race") which, in turn, has led to a greater propensity in any dispute for either party to use his gun before the other person does.

The key here is the "diffusion hypothesis," which suggests that the growth in juvenile homicides is a consequence of the larger community's adoption of behavior

Homicide rates began to decline in the early nineties, however, the rate of homicide by juveniles—particularly black, urban juveniles—exploded. From 1990 to 1993 the murder rate for Americans age 25 and older dropped 10 percent while the rate for 18–24 year olds increased by 14 percent and the rate for juveniles overall increased 26 percent. Blumstein (1994) explains that juvenile involvement in crack cocaine distribution in the mid-eighties led to an arms race on the streets in which fist fights became shootings. Further exacerbating the situation were high levels of poverty, single-parent households, educational failures, and economic hopelessness. By 1993 the crack cocaine epidemic had peaked and crime rates began to decline.

Recent UCR data display a disturbing trend: growth in the number of homicides in which the relationship between victim and offender is "unknown." The popular press present this as murder among strangers, but that is not true. Most of the "unknown" murder victims were involved in drugs and/or gangs. In 1993 for instance, 47 percent of victims were killed by family members, friends, neighbors, or acquaintances and 39 percent involved "unknown" relationships. Gun-related homicides are on the rise, particularly among juveniles (Glick, 1994). Female murder rates have remained constant or declined. Women perpetrate a small proportion of murders and, when they do murder, they generally do so in self-defense and in marital/intimate relationships. "The availability of shelters and other supportive services may be providing some women avenues to escape self-defensive homicide as well as lethal victimization by their partners" (Benekos, 1995, p. 234).

VANTAGE POINT 7.2—*Continued*

endemic to the drug industry—carrying guns and using them to settle disputes. The diffusion hypothesis is supported by the fact that, since 1985, the homicide arrest rates of both white and nonwhite juveniles have grown, respectively, by 80 percent and 120 percent, although there has been no evident growth in the involvement of white youths in the drug market.

Policy Recommendations

- *Guns on the street:* Because carrying a handgun is illegal almost everywhere, the task of getting guns out of the hands of juveniles requires stronger and more focused enforcement of existing legislation. The federal government's main role should be to offer technical assistance to localities that would like to pursue this strategy but need help in doing so. For example, the recent NIJ project in Kansas City came out with some important findings with regard to approaches for capturing illegal guns. Even if we stop the flow of guns to and from drug markets, we still have to worry about the guns that are already on the streets.
- *Guns in the market:* Illicit gun markets (especially those that sell to juveniles, and especially in urban areas) must be more tightly controlled. Law enforcement has focused on the drug market while largely ignoring the market for illegal firearms. The challenge is a clear federal responsibility because so much of the traffic in guns is interstate.
- *Treatment and prevention:* Consideration should be given to shrinking the size of drug markets by siphoning off some of the demand for drugs. Measures should include increasing the resources and effort put into treatment and prevention. It also calls for finding ways to bring certified addicts into treatment programs, such as those supported under the SSI program.
- *Socialization of youth:* In the long run, we must face the widespread problem of socializing the growing number of young people who see no hope for their economic future and are willing, therefore, to take whatever risks are necessary to gain respect and earn an income. These disenfranchised youth represent ready recruits for any illicit markets that present themselves.

Source: "American Society of Criminology Task Force Report to Attorney General Janet Reno," *The Criminologist* (Special Issue), 20, 6, November/December 1995. The Youth Violence Task Force was chaired by Alfred Blumstein.

InfoTrac College Edition Research
Find an interesting article on "youth violence." How does this article contribute to our understanding of this issue?

The American cultural tradition of violence, combined with certain subcultures in which resort to aggression is legitimized, presents a strong predisposition to violence in the United States. These are the raw materials of typical interpersonal homicides. The spark that sets off this kindling could be any number of interpersonal conflict situations, such as arguments over money, love triangles, threats to masculinity, and the like. While such disputes do not ordinarily lead to violence, the addition of two other fuels to the fire can spell danger: alcohol and guns.

Workplace Violence. **Workplace violence** is the number two factor in on-the-job deaths and number one among women. Women were more than three times as likely to be murdered on the job than men. Since about 1980 the violent victimization rates of women and men have converged. By 1994 the rate of female violent victimization was 43 per 1,000 women, about two-thirds the 60 victimizations per 1,000 men. The rate for men was decreasing while that for females remained stable, if not increasing. Nine of ten female murder victims were killed by males (Craven, 1996; for online resources on violence against women: www.ojp.usdoj.gov/vawgo.)

The National Crime Victimization Surveys (NCVS) for 1992–96 indicate that on average about two million violent victimizations occur annually while people are at work or on duty. Simple assault was the most common (about 1.5 million victimizations), followed by 396,000 aggravated assaults, 51,000 rapes and sexual assaults, 84,000 robberies, and 1,000 homicides (Warchol, 1998). Of the occupations examined, law enforcement had the highest rate of workplace victimization followed by corrections officers, taxi drivers, private security, and workers in bars. The majority of workplace violent crime was committed by a stranger. Intimate perpetrators were identified as less than one percent, while 35 percent of the offenders were acquaintances.

Between 1993 and 1996 most workplace homicides were the result of robbery (average of 760 per year), coworkers or customers (100), and personal acquaintances (50). The most dangerous occupation for murder was sales (327 per year), taxi drivers and chauffeurs (74), and police (70). Workplace homicides have been declining, from 1,074 in 1993 to 709 in 1998. Convenience store robberies have particularly declined. Better security in the workplace has been effective. Among the security measures suggested to control workplace violence were: pre-employment screening to identify "high risk" applicants; 24-hour employee hotlines for confidential reporting of concerns; and access controls such as card keys, photo badges, and video surveillance (Pinkerton Inc., 1999).

A survey by the National Institute for Occupational Safety and Health (Grimsley, 1996, p. 34) in 1995 reported that homicide had become the second leading cause of occupational fatalities, exceeded only by motor-vehicle-related deaths. The most dangerous occupations were those related to taxicabs, law enforcement, and gasoline service stations. Retail proprietors (179), cashiers (105), taxicab drivers (86), hotel and restaurant managers (46), security guards (76), and police officers (70) were among the fatalities in 1995. While men make up 80 percent of the victims, murder on the job is the leading cause of workplace death for women. The survey also indicated that, despite public perceptions, worker-to-worker violence (such as the highly publicized U.S. Postal Service slayings) is relatively rare—4 percent of all workplace homicides. Particularly vulnerable to assault (but not homicide) are health-care workers and government workers. A survey by the Society for Human Resource Management of 500 human resource professionals in 1993 found 75 percent of violent incidents in the workplace were fistfights, 17 percent were shootings, 7.5 percent were stabbings, 6 percent were rapes or other sexual assaults, and fewer than 1 percent were explosions (Swisher, 1994, p. 11S). Protective measures to discourage victimization have included bulletproof glass in taxicabs and at hospital admission desks, escort services for evening workers, better illumination, more careful screening of employees, and limits on the amount of cash on hand.

School Violence. The U.S. is not unique in having school violence, but it leads the world in this type of violence. Some U.S. school shootings have included (Lawrence, 1998):

- February, 2000. A six-year-old boy shot and killed a six-year-old classmate at Buell Elementary School in Mount Morris Township, Michigan.
- May 1999. A 15-year-old opened fire at Heritage High School in Conyers, Georgia, with a .357-caliber handgun and a rifle, wounding six students.
- April 20,1999. Two students at Columbine High School in Littleton, Colorado, killed twelve students.
- May 21, 1998. Two students killed and injured more than twenty by opening fire at a high school in Springfield, Oregon.
- April 24, 1998. A teacher was killed at an eighth-grade dance in Edinboro, Pennsylvania.
- March 24, 1998. Four students and a teacher were killed and ten wounded in Jonesboro, Arkansas, when two boys, aged 11 and 13, opened fire from nearby woods.
- December 1, 1997. Three students were killed and five others wounded at Heath High School in West Paducah, Kentucky.

It is critical that a balanced picture of school violence be drawn. Fewer than one percent of school-age homicides occur in or around schools. Despite the highly visible, horrific cases such as Columbine, school-related violence has actually been decreasing during the 1990s. Richard Lawrence (2000, p. 1) speculates that the relative infrequency of school violence is the very reason it is frequently covered in the media. He also adds that, while such media coverage has distorted the actual risk of violent death at school, it has had a positive effect on enhancing safety and preventing bullying and other threatening behavior (Ibid., p. 5).

Some elements of a solution to school shootings that have been suggested include:

- Better control over the access to guns. This is countered by one of the most powerful lobbies in the U.S.—the National Rifle Association.
- Identify and help troubled youths before they attack. The "goths," black trenchcoat mafia at Columbine, had been identified as potentially dangerous.
- Involvement of parents is critical.
- More and earlier intervention and prevention programs.
- Anti-bullying programs.

Guns

In 1996 handguns were used to murder two people in New Zealand, 15 in Japan, 30 in Great Britain, and 9,390 in the United States. In the nineties the Brady bill finally became law despite opposition by the NRA. This law required a waiting period plus a record check before purchase of a firearm. Much emotion surrounds the gun-control debate, with opponents of control arguing that regulation would hurt only the law-abiding, who would be unable to protect themselves from the criminal. The law-abiding, however are also of concern. The very weapon purchased to protect the family against outside intruders all too often causes the death of a loved one. Morris and Hawkins (1970, p. 72) describe the issue quite succinctly. A major precipitating condition of murder in the United States is the possession of a gun. They state, "Easy access to weapons of this kind may not merely facilitate violence, but may also stimulate, inspire, and provoke it."

Why such continuing opposition to handgun control, despite clear public support for such measures? The National Rifle Association is probably the single most powerful lobby in Washington, representing a $2 billion per year business with a generous campaign donation policy and a strategic direct mail effort. Yet more Americans have been killed with guns by their fellow citizens in this century than have been killed in all of the wars this nation has ever fought, from the Revolutionary War through the Vietnam War.

A popular defense of the pro gun lobby in the United States is: "Guns don't kill people, people kill people." In fact, people with guns (particularly handguns) do kill people, and it is no coincidence that the United States has both the highest homicide rate by far of any developed nation and the largest armed civilian population in the world. This widespread ownership of firearms combined with a culture and subculture of violence foments lethal combinations. VANTAGE POINT 7.3 presents a succinct summary of some major arguments both for and against gun control.

In February 1998, Great Britain instituted a total ban on private ownership of handguns in response to public outcry over the 1996 massacre of 16 school children and their teacher in Dunblane, Scotland. At the same time there remains an estimated 50–70 million firearms in the United States in private hands. On Mothers Day, May 14, 2000, a Million Mom March on Washington took place, calling for stronger background checks, licensing of handgun owners, comprehensive gun registration, safety child locks, limits on handgun purchases, and reasonable cooling off periods before newly purchased firearms could be taken into possession.

In light of success in suing tobacco companies for causing a public health menace, public bodies, particularly cities, have filed suit against gun manufacturers. In a typical action the city of Chicago filed a $433 million law suit against 38 gun retailers, distributors, and

VANTAGE POINT 7.3

Pros and Cons of Gun Control

Pro

Some arguments in favor of gun control include:

- No federal court has ever ruled that the Constitution (Second Amendment) guarantees Americans the right to own guns. The widespread legal and judicial view is that the Second Amendment guarantees states the right to be armed—for example, the right to have National Guards.
- In states with new laws authorizing carrying concealed weapons for self-defense, crime has not decreased. Florida passed such a law in 1986, and between 1987 and 1992 violent crime increased roughly 18 percent. In 1993 homicides dropped, but Florida had the nation's highest rate of violent crime. In three states that passed such laws, gun homicides increased. In some Florida cities, homicides went up after the law was passed, and many criminals were able to get permits for guns.
- Guns in homes are far more likely to be used against family members than against outside intruders.
- Other developed countries with strict gun control laws have much lower homicide rates than the United States.
- A six-year study of firearm deaths in the home in Seattle showed 9 instances of self-defense, 12 accidental deaths, 41 criminal homicides, and 333 firearm suicides. Greater gun availability in an area is associated with greater gun availability for criminals. Guns in the home are especially tempting burglary targets (Spitzer, 1995, p. 83).
- Most gun homicides occur among family members, friends, and acquaintances during a heated dispute. If a gun is involved, death is more likely to occur.
- The Brady bill, waiting periods, and background checks have worked in some states to block felons and undesirables from purchasing firearms. In the first year after the Brady bill passed, up to 45,000 convicted felons were prevented from purchasing firearms (Butterfield, 1995).
- Given current trends, by the year 2003 firearms will surpass auto accidents as the number one cause of injury-related deaths in the United States.

Con

Some arguments against gun control include:

- Gun control restricts legitimate use of weapons, but has little impact on illicit markets. Restrictions on firearm ownership violate the Second Amendment, a Constitutional guarantee, and invade freedom and privacy.
- ". . . most modern scholarship affirms that so far as drafters of the Constitution were concerned, the right to bear arms was to be enjoyed by everyone, not just a militia" (Polsby, 1994).
- People who are armed make unattractive victims. "When guns are outlawed, only outlaws will have guns" (NRA slogan). People can always obtain guns on the streets.
- "Guns don't kill people, people kill people" (NRA slogan).
- If all firearms were outlawed, how could the government confiscate the nation's nearly 200 million privately owned firearms?
- "People are less likely to be robbed and are less likely to be injured when they use a gun to resist," claims Gary Kleck (1992, p. 3). He suggests that escalating gun ownership may act as a deterrent against crime.
- Repeat violent offenders account for most cases of domestic violence and practically all homicides. According to Kleck, there are few crimes of passion in which a normally nonviolent person simply loses control and kills someone. That is a myth perpetrated by the media (Witkin, 1994, p. 28).
- There is no evidence that guns precipitate higher suicide rates (Kleck, in Witkin, 1994, p 30).

InfoTrac College Edition Research

What has been the impact of the "Brady Law" on handgun violence?

manufacturers, alleging they had created a public nuisance by knowingly saturating the city with illegal firearms. The city of New Orleans charged the manufacturers had created "unreasonably dangerous" products (Witkin, 1988b). In February 1999 a Brooklyn jury awarded Steven Fox $500,000 for injuries suffered in a shooting. The jury found fifteen companies guilty of "negligent distribution" of guns and ordered three to pay Fox for his injuries.

While heated arguments continue between opponents and proponents of gun control, more research is needed on the potential impacts of various policy options (Zimring, 1987). As an example, a large survey of convicted felons by Wright and Rossi (1986) suggested the following:

- Rather than reducing crime in violent urban neighborhoods through gun control, the violence endemic to such impoverished areas must be reduced, thus reducing the need for carrying weapons.
- The theft of firearms must be reduced.
- The informal market for guns must be interdicted.
- Mandatory sentences for crimes with guns are ineffective and do not serve as a deterrent.
- The control of "*Saturday night specials*" (cheap handguns) would simply encourage criminals to switch to more lethal weapons (Bonn, 1987).

It is quite difficult to target public policy objectives when there is no consensus regarding the essential nature of the problem of firearms and high violent crime rates in the United States. A promising intermediate strategy has tested positive in the "Kansas City Gun Experiment." Police directed patrols at gun crime "hot spots" and were able to reduce gun crimes by seizing illegally carried weapons (Sherman, Shaw, and Rogan, 1995). The project is being replicated in Indianapolis. Sheley and Wright (1995) in interviews with juvenile inmates and students in inner city high schools found that the primary motivation for gun possession by these groups was fear, not criminal activity, gang membership, or drug trafficking.

For more information on gun control see Freedman, 1989; Kleck, 1984; Robin, 1991; Spitzer, 1995.

Sexual Assault

> On the night of July 10, 1991, at St. Kizito's coed boarding school in Meru Kenya, 71 teenage girls were raped by their classmates and 19 others died when the boys attacked the girls for refusing to join them in a strike against the school's headmaster. A report on the front page of the Kenya Times called the rape of the St. Kizito coeds a "common occurrence" sanctioned by the principal and his staff. The paper quoted the deputy principal as saying, "The boys never meant any harm against the girls. They just wanted to rape" (Heise, 1991).

This attitude is not uncommon. In some countries rape is viewed as a man's right or as a crime against the honor of the woman's family or husband—not an offense against the woman. The word itself is derived from the Latin for "theft." A large percentage of rapes are perpetrated against children. In fact, more than half of rape victims are under 18, and the younger the victim the more likely the attacker is to be a relative or acquaintance and the less likely the rape is to be reported. In some countries women are often blamed and punished for the rape (Heise, 1991). Susan Estrich, a rape victim herself, maintains in her book, *Real Rape: How the Legal System Victimizes Women Who Say No* (1987), that little has changed in the way most rape cases are handled by the courts and that judges still use their personal views to decide the victim's claim (Berger, 1988). This all depends on whether the rape is viewed as "real rape" or "simple rape." [These terms are put in quotes to indicate that such distinctions are made by ill-informed persons.]

Real rape is *aggravated rape involving violence, weapons, attackers, and is recognized as rape by the courts.* **Simple rape** *is everything else, including date rape, and is dismissed as not "real rape."* Victims of simple rape are viewed with suspicion, as not really victims, particularly if the victim did not physically resist. "The reasonable woman, it seems, is not a school boy 'sissy'; she is a real man" (Berger 1988, p. 65). VANTAGE POINT 7.4 illustrates some international comparisons with respect to rape, although caution must be exercised because of unreliability of measurement.

VANTAGE POINT 7.4

International Rape Rates

Rape

International rape statistics appear notoriously poor and suspect. Most of the countries reported below had "exactly" the same rates in 1998 that they had in 1994—an astounding statistical coincidence indeed.

Interpol defines a sex-offense category that includes rape as follows: "Each country should use the definitions in its own laws to determine whether or not an act is a sex offense; rape shall always be included in this category." It then asks countries also to report rape separately, but it does not define the term. Interpol leaves the matter of statutory rape to each country. The U.N. defines rape as "sexual intercourse without valid consent," which includes statutory rape.

Few individual countries provided explanatory notes for rape. None provided any to Interpol. Egypt reported sexual offenses, including rape, but did not provide separate figures for rape. Norway and the United States reported to the U.N. that their figures did not include statutory rape; Belize noted that rape included indecent assault; and Greece reported that the rape category included "lewdness, sodomy, seduction of a child, incest, prostitution, and procuring."

Nine European countries and the United States reported identical rates for rape in 1980 to both the U.N. and to Interpol. It appears that in both cases they simply reported their official rape statistic for that year. If the official number corresponds to the U.N. definition, it includes statutory rape.

The eight other countries that reported to both the U.N. and Interpol tended to report higher rates to the U.N., suggesting that they did not include statutory rape in the number they reported to Interpol. Most 1998 rates were exactly the same as 1994. This curiously suggested that the 1994 rates were simply re-reported.

In any comparison of rape rates, two underlying factors must be noted, even though they cannot be quantified. One is the degree of freedom and independence women have within a society and, consequently, the degree of exposure they have to the possibility of rape. Another is the extent to which stigma still attaches to a rape and the consequent reluctance of victims to report the crime to authorities. The first factor may actually affect the volume of rape from one country to another. The second will not affect the total volume of rape but will affect the proportion of rape cases reported to the police. Both of these factors will tend to raise the reported rape in developed countries, compared to some less developed nations.

Source: Carol B. Kalish, 1988, *International Crime Rates,* Bureau of Justice Statistics Special Report, May, pp. 4–5.

InfoTrac College Edition Research

Locate an article on rape in another country. How was rape viewed there and were there any proposed solutions?

The women's movement has been largely instrumental in altering public and official views of rape and rape victims. Susan Brownmiller (1975) in *Against Our Will: Men, Women and Rape* claims, correctly or incorrectly, that the criminalization of rape took place with the emergence of a money economy in which violation of virginity posed potential economic loss for the family since the future bride was now tainted goods. Statistics regarding the extent of rape have been notoriously poor. Women have been reluctant in the past to report rapes for a variety of reasons, including:

- The stigma attached to rape, which alleges that the victim either invited the attack or cooperated in it
- Sexist treatment of many rape victims, who are in effect mentally raped a second time by the criminal justice system (the police, defense attorneys, and judges)
- Legal procedures that have permitted defense attorneys to probe the victim's sexual past in potentially humiliating ways
- The burden of proof, which has been shifted to the victim so she must show that the attack was against her will and that she resisted the assault

VANTAGE POINT 7.4—*Continued*

Table A International Rape Statistics, 1998. Interpol Data (per 100,000)

Country	*Rape (attempt) actual*	
United States[a]		34.4
Austria	(6.4)	4.5
Belgium	(16.8)	12.3
Chile		10.6
Denmark		7.9
Ecuador		8.2
Estonia		8.3
Finland		7.6
France		11.3
Germany	(9.6)	7.2
Greece		2.5
Hungary		4.2
Ireland		5.2
Israel		9.4
Jamaica		24.4
Japan		1.3
Paraguay		4.1
Russia		9.4
Saudi Arabia		1.5
Spain		4.1
Switzerland		3.9
Zimbabwe		23.7

Source: Interpol. International Crime Statistics, 1998. Lyons, France: Interpol Secretariat, 1999.
[a]U.S. statistics were not included in the Interpol report for 1998 and were taken from the Uniform Crime Reports for 1998.
Special Note: These rape statistics should be viewed with caution. In addition to being very low estimates, many were the exact same numbers reported for 1994 which is somewhat amazing unless 1994 data were simply substituted for 1998 ones that were not reported.

VANTAGE POINT 7.4 presents rape rates in selected countries using Interpol statistics. Caution should be exercised in interpreting these statistics given their historically questionable nature as well as cultural reluctance to record such data. Given those limitations, the highest rape rates were for: the U.S. (34.4), Jamaica (24.4), Zimbabwe (23.7), and Belgium (12.3). The U.S. rape rate was much higher than other developed countries, with the lowest rates in Greece (2.5), Saudi Arabia (1.5), and Japan (1.3).

Only recently have a significant proportion of rape victims been willing to report rapes and undertake prosecution of their attackers. The growth of rape crisis centers, featuring counseling and support services for victims, has been instrumental in this greater willingness to prosecute. Other factors that account for an increase in the tendency to report rape include:

- More women police officers
- Better training of police in sensitive handling of rape cases
- Changes in rape laws in many states, which, for instance, prevent defense attorneys from probing into the victim's prior sexual behavior

Rape was the fastest growing of all UCR index crimes in the seventies, increasing 85 percent from 1970 to 1979. However, the NCVS victim data available for part of this same period show virtually no change in the rape rate. The increase in the seventies rape rate was primarily due not to an increase in the number of rapes, but rather to a growth in the willingness to report such crimes.

Figure 7.3 presents rape rates for the U.S. since 1973 using National Crime Victimization Survey data. Data prior to 1992 were adjusted to make them more similar to data collected after that using redesigned methodology.

The Department of Health and Human Services (Associated Press, 1998) reported that half of all rape victims were assaulted before their 17th birthday and that an estimated 17.7 million women in the United States—nearly 18 percent—have been victims of rape or attempted rape.

The Uniform Crime Reports for 1998 reported 93,103 forcible rapes nationwide. This was the sixth consecutive annual decrease. The South had the highest rate at 75 victims per 100,000 females followed by the Midwest at 72, the West at 69, and the Northeast with 46. Convicted and arrested rapists generally present the same demographic profile as other violent and conventional property criminals; that is, for the most part they are fifteen-to-twenty-four years old, unmarried, from lower-class and minority backgrounds (particularly black), and they choose victims of the same race. Amir (1971) in his Philadelphia study of forcible rape found that most rapists had backgrounds in property offenses rather than in violent criminal activity. He examined 646 cases in 1958 and 1960 and found rape twelve times higher among blacks than among whites. Amir's research was based solely

FIGURE 7.3 Rape Rates for the United States

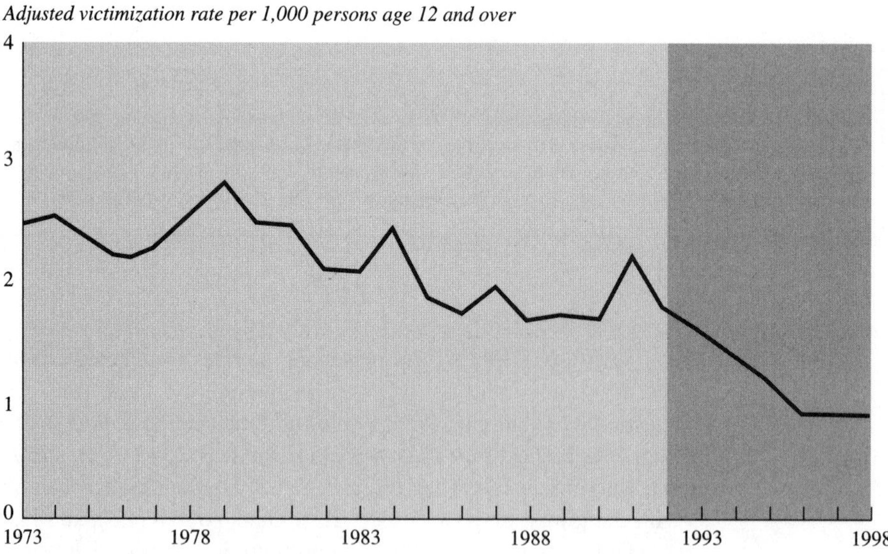

Note: Includes both attempted and completed rapes.

The light area indicates that because of changes made to the victimization survey, data prior to 1992 are adjusted to make them comparable to data collected under the redesigned methodology. The adjustment methods are described in *Criminal Victimization 1973–95*. Estimates for 1993 and beyond are based on collection year while earlier estimates are based on data year. For additional information about the methods used, see *Criminal Victimization 1998*.

Source: Bureau of Justice Statistics, www.ojp.usdoj.gov/bjs//

on official police reports, however, and for that reason has been subject to dispute. VANTAGE POINT 7.5 presents the ASC Task Force Report on Rape.

Acquaintance Rape

Highly publicized rape trials such as those of Mike Tyson and William Kennedy Smith have intensified interest and awareness of date rape, the most common type of sexual assault. Many of these attacks take place within established dating relationships, and the vast majority are never reported. Victims often fear the publicity, notoriety, and family reaction that pressing charges would entail.

While official data suggest that about half of all rapes involve strangers, this is partially offset by the victims' greater willingness to report stranger-precipitated incidents. Victimization surveys suggest that over 80 percent of rapes and attempted rapes are by strangers (McDermott, 1979). Amir (1971, p. 143) found that 58 percent of single-offender and 90 percent of group rapes were planned rather than spontaneous events and that rape by more than one attacker took place in over 40 percent of the cases. But studies of attempted rapes reported in anonymous surveys by high school and college women indicate that many of these incidents are unlikely to be reported even to other household members, let alone to victim-survey interviewers. Such potential "date rapes" do not meet the stereotype of the attacker as a stranger on a dark street. Contrary to Amir's research, these findings suggest that attacks by intimates and acquaintances make up the majority of rapes (Kirkpatrick and Kanin, 1957; Christensen and Gregg, 1970).

Many of these rapes constitute acquaintance rapes, in which false expectations on the part of some males in the dating game in U.S. society create situations in which males assume they are expected to press for greater degrees of sexual intimacy and females to set the limits. The presence of alcohol as a disinhibitor is a further predisposing factor in anywhere from one-third to one-half of the cases (Amir, 1971, p. 98). As if things were not bad enough, the advent of "rape drugs" further complicates the ability of women to protect themselves. Drugs such as GHB, an odorless, colorless drug, is slipped into a woman's drink and she is knocked out by depression of her central nervous system. In some cases the woman dies. In 2000, three Detroit men were convicted of involuntary manslaughter and poisoning charges for slipping GHB into the soft drink of Samantha Reid, a 15-year-old who died. Her 16-year-old friend who also ingested the drug, was in a brief coma, but survived. GHB has been linked to at least 58 deaths and 5,700 recorded overdoses since 1990 (Irwin, 2000).

Gang rape is usually perceived as something that occurs across the tracks among the underclass, but Ehrhart and Sandler's *Campus Gang Rape* (1985) and Sanday's *Fraternity Gang Rape* (1990) tell us of the close-to-home nature of such activity. Belknap (1990, pp. 285–86) notes:

> There exists a strong misogynistic, sexist, racist rape culture at most universities which appears to be particularly virulent among fraternities . . . . The male entitlement acquired through fraternity or male athletic team membership helps these young men believe that they are special and superior not only to women, but also to other men.

The practice of campus gang rape is called "playing train" or "pulling train" (one man follows another). A common pattern is described by Ehrhart and Sandler (1985, pp. 1–2):

> A vulnerable young woman, one who is seeking acceptance or who is high on drugs or alcohol, is taken to a room. She may or may not agree to have sex with one man. She then passes out, or is too weak or scared to protest and a train of men have sex with her. Sometimes the young woman's drinks are spiked without her knowledge and when she is approached by several men in a locked room, she reacts with confusion and panic. Whether [she is] too weak to protest,

VANTAGE POINT 7.5

Rape and the Criminal Justice System

Issues

As a result of a nationwide, grassroots effort during the past 20 years to reform rape laws in this country, each of the 50 states has in some way modified its traditional rape statutes. These reforms encompassed three goals: (1) to treat rape like any other crime by concentrating on the unlawful acts of the offender, (2) to encourage victims to come forward about rape, and (3) to facilitate the successful prosecution and conviction of rapists. However, research has shown that reforms have fallen far short of achieving their goals: the incidence and prevalence of rape have not significantly declined, reporting has not dramatically risen, and the rates of arrest, prosecution, and conviction of rapists have not appreciably improved.

Similarly, findings show that corroboration requirements persist in a *de facto* manner, resistance standards continue to provide the basis for decisionmaking, and past sexual activity evidence still influences the treatment of rape cases—in spite of enactment of shield legislation. Moreover, victim credibility remains at issue for courtroom participants (as well as for the public) and all too often accompanies beliefs about victim culpability. Attributions that blame victims perpetuate the persecution of rape victims, rather than the successful prosecution of rape offenders.

Policy Considerations and Recommendations

- *Marital rape:* Some states still do not legally recognize marital rape, while others have extended this exemption to cohabitors. Legal initiatives are needed on this issue.
- *Victim anonymity:* One particularly difficult issue that demands redress is protection of the anonymity of victims who pursue prosecution. Laws and policies that forbid disclosure of victims' names and addresses are important for victim privacy; however, First Amendment considerations, as well as concerns that perpetuation of the rape stigma results from anonymity protection, have both arisen.
- *Accountability:* Discretionary decisionmaking must be made more visible and criminal justice officials held more accountable for the decisions that shape the implementation of reforms. Implementation should be monitored, incentives should be created, and public pressure should be used to achieve compliance.
- *Victim compensation:* Recourse for victims (for the costs and pains of victimization, such as lost work days, medical bills, etc.) should be expanded through the development of new programs (that do not exclude large categories of victims, such as violent crime victims). Compensation programs need to be funded and extended at all levels of government.
- *Victim advocacy:* For victim advocacy to begin to meet the overwhelming need for services, financial support for rape crisis centers and victim-witness units must grow. Local programs could productively network with national PACs and organizations, such as the National Organization for Women or the League of Women Voters, to mobilize resources.

> frightened, or unconscious, as has been the case in quite a number of instances, anywhere from two to eleven or more men have sex with her. In some party invitations the possibility of such an occurrence is mentioned with playful allusions to "gang bang" or "pulling train."

As if being raped itself is not degrading enough, consider the additional and final victimization of also being a victim of AIDS. Unfortunately, most schools do not formally punish either date rapists or gang rapists, choosing to keep such activity quiet. Parents of a Lehigh University freshman who was raped and murdered in 1986 forced the passage of the "Cleary Law" that requires the publication of campus crime rates in order to inform parents and students of potential danger. Adopted in 1992, the Crime Awareness and Campus Security Act requires colleges and universities to disclose their crime statistics or risk losing federal aid.

There was a time in this country that, when Americans thought of possible victimization, the last places they would fear were colleges and universities and shopping centers; but universities have become major workplaces and employers and shopping malls the new retail downtowns. Accurate mall crime statistics are hard to obtain. Often the surrounding

VANTAGE POINT 7.5—*Continued*

- *Outreach to minorities:* Racial and ethnic minorities are underserved. Outreach efforts, such as providing multilingual services, hiring minority staff, forging links with existing community services, and providing community education should be expanded.
- *Training for information providers:* In order to make the criminal justice system as nonthreatening to victims as possible, it is important to continue providing special training for criminal justice personnel, including police, prosecutors, and judges. Multi-disciplinary teams consisting of criminal justice, professionals and sexual assault counselors should provide such training. Similarly, dedicated units/personnel to deal with "sex crimes" should continue to be trained.
- *Public awareness:* Media campaigns are needed to help make rape a national priority and place it on an agenda for change. Mediated slogans have been effective in combating other social problems and could be developed for rape issues. Similarly, films could be rated for degrees of sexism and the derogation of women, with particular emphasis on how violence against women is portrayed. Another possible model for intervention is the town meeting; town meetings with criminal justice personnel, educators, academicians, and social services providers could be coordinated as part of a national plan to prioritize the problems of rape and violence against women.
- *Cultural change:* Systematic education, starting with young people, is needed to challenge the traditional cultural beliefs and values that lead to sexual violence. The approbation of sexist notions, inequalities, and violence contribute to our "rape culture." A vision, plan, or program that ignores sex and power differences addresses only symptoms, not root causes, of violence against women.
- *Research needs:* Statistics on the incidence and prevalence of rape and sexual assaults need to be improved for accurate measurement of these problems nationwide. Some definitions should be changed to reflect new legal categories, and new data (e.g., on the discretionary decisions rendered in rape cases) should be collected. More extensive research on the implementation of reforms should be funded to point the way for new efforts. More recent reforms, such as Federal Rules 413–415 that make admissible the sexual history of offenders, also need to be examined for their impact on the treatment of rape cases.

Source: "American Society of Criminology Task Force Report to Attorney General Janet Reno," *The Criminologist* (Special Issue), 20, 6, November/December 1995. The Violence Against Women Task Force (which included rape as a topic) members included: Edna Erez, chair; Joanne Belknap; Susan Caringella McDonald; Meda Chesney-Lind; Kathleen Ferraro; David Ford; Julie Horney; Susan Miller; and Elizabeth Stanko.

InfoTrac College Edition Research
Search the concept of "acquaintance rape." What are some current issues in this area?

area is a good tip-off of a criminogenic environment. APBnews.com and CAP Index Inc. have ranked the nation's 1765 shopping malls in terms of danger of violent crime such as murder, rape, and robbery. Southgate Shopping Center in Memphis, Tennessee, was the highest risk mall for 1999, while Great Lakes Mall in Mentor, Ohio (Cleveland area), was the lowest. The top ten high crime risk shopping centers were (Port, 1999):

1. Southgate Shopping Center (Memphis)
2. Pecanland Mall (Monroe, Louisiana)
3. Omni International Mall (Miami)
4. Saint Louis Centre (St. Louis)
5. New Orleans Centre (New Orleans)
6. Concourse Plaza Shopping Center (New York)
7. Mondawmin/Metro Plaza (Baltimore)
8. Greenbriar Mall (Atlanta)
9. Westland Mall (Hialeah, Florida)
10. Long Beach Plaza (Long Beach, California)

(© Craig Porter, Detroit Free Press)

In 1999, teens (two in ties, one in stripped shirt) were convicted of slipping a fatal dose of GHB into 15-year-old Samantha Reid's soda. The man at right was charged with delivery of marijuana.

APBnews.com also used the CAP Index to rate college communities. The ten most high risk colleges for 1999 were (APBnews, 1999b):

1. Morris Brown College (Atlanta)
2. LeMoyne-Owen College (Memphis)
3. Spelman College (Atlanta)
4. Clark Atlanta University (Atlanta)
5. Morehouse College (Atlanta)
6. VanderCook College of Music (Chicago)
7. City University of New York/City College (New York City)
8. Edward Waters College (Jacksonville, Florida)
9. Southern University and A&M College (Baton Rouge, Louisiana)
10. Illinois Institute of Technology (Chicago)

It should be pointed out that these ratings are based on ZIP code demographics and may reflect high crime rates in the surrounding neighborhood rather than the campuses themselves. Penn, Columbia, and Yale led the Ivy League in high risk.

Amir vs. Brownmiller

Chappell and Fogarty (1978) in the literature review *Forcible Rape* indicate that two major landmark works preempt the field: Menachem Amir's (1971) *Patterns in Forcible Rape* and Susan Brownmiller's (1975) *Against Our Will: Men, Women and Rape.* Amir's work, the most widely cited source in rape literature, espouses a now controversial *theory of victim precipitation,* in which the victim's behavior is seen as contributing to the incident. This theory was viewed as perpetuating many of the common myths regarding rape. Brownmiller's work espouses a theory that rape is "nothing more or less than a conscious process of intimidation by which all men keep all women in a state of fear" (1975, p. 15). Chappell and Fogarty indicate that much of the pre-1972 literature such as MacDonald's (1971) *Rapists and Their Victims* suffered from male chauvinist biases prevalent at that time.

Rape as a Violent Act

Rape is often perceived primarily as a sexually motivated act, but most authorities on rape identify it as *primarily a violent act* in which sexual relations are merely a means of expressing violence, aggression, and domination. While our discussion will give consideration to arguments as to whether rapists are sexually or violently motivated or both, the classification of rape as a crime of violence looks not at the motivation of the offender but at the perception of the act by victims. Similar to the argument that robbery is really a property crime, sex (rape) or money (robbery) may be the motivation, but the tool employed and perceived by victims is violence or threats of violence and intimidation. For this reason the author views rape as a crime of violence. On the basis of their study of over 500 convicted rapists, Groth and Birnbaum (1979) in *Men Who Rape* identify three types of rape:

- The *anger rape,* in which sexual attack becomes a means of expressing rage or anger, involves far more physical assault on the victim than is necessary. Groth and Birnbaum claimed that 40 percent of their subjects were anger rapists.
- The *power rape,* in which the assailant primarily wishes to express his domination over the victim, is viewed as an expression of power rather than a means of sexual gratification. Thus, the rapist generally uses only the amount of force necessary to exert his superordinant position. The majority, about 55 percent, of Groth and Birnbaum's offenders were of this type.
- The *sadistic rape,* in which the perpetrator combines the sexuality and aggression aims in psychotic desires to torment, torture, or otherwise abuse his victim. About 5 percent were of this type.

Glaser (1978, p. 364) proposes *four categories of rapists:* naive graspers, meaning stretchers, sex looters, and group conformers. *Naive graspers* are usually sexually inexperienced youths with an unrealistic conception of female erotic arousal. Awkward in relating to the opposite sex, they hold high expectations that their crude advances will be met with affection by their victims. They possess a strong desire for affection but little respect for their victim's autonomy in resisting such advances. *Meaning stretchers* are the most typical rapists, the date rapists. They stretch the meaning of, or misinterpret, a woman or date's expressions of friendliness and affection as indicating that the female desires coitus even when she says no. *Sex looters* have little desire for affection and/or little respect for the victim's autonomy and callously use women as sex objects. This type figures in the stranger-precipitated rape that is most likely to be reported to the police. *Group conformers* participate in group rapes or gang bangs, often following the leader—a sex looter—out of a sense of conformity and a perverted notion of demonstrating masculinity. The 1989 "wilding" rape of a female jogger in Central Park by a gang of youths may serve as an example.

In an examination and criminal profiling of forty-one convicted "serial rapists" (defined in the project as those who had committed ten or more rapes), Hazelwood, Burgess, and associates (Hazelwood and Warren, 1989; Hazelwood and Burgess, 1987; Burgess et al., 1987) found that 76 percent had been sexually abused as children. The majority of the serial rapes had not been reported to authorities.

Such typologies may not accurately reflect the motivations of typical rapists at the time of the offense. They are based on *ex post facto* case studies of incarcerated offenders and interviews with offenders, which makes them prone to *post hoc* error. They are also unnecessarily steeped in psychiatric assumptions regarding offender motivations. In addition, incarcerated rapists are more likely to be of the "stranger" variety and perhaps either more violence-prone or more willing to use violence than the nonstranger rapists.

Advice on victim resistance appears to be mixed. While resistance as Sanders proposes (particularly screaming rather than physical defense) increases the likelihood of escape, it also increases the possibility of injury.

The Criminalization of Forced Marital Intercourse (Sigler and Haygood, 1988), or "marital rape," underscores the view of rape as a violent rather than sexual crime. In *State v. Rideout* (1978) an Oregon court challenged the marital immunity defense—that is, the husband's right to force involuntary intercourse. This is now recognized as rape in many states.

Finally, an examination of prison inmates is telling.

One in five violent offenders serving time in state prison report having victimized a child. Two-thirds of prisoners convicted of rape or sexual assault had committed their crime against a child. Inmates who victimized children were less likely to have a prior criminal record. Three in ten child victimizers had multiple victims, and in the vast majority of cases they knew the victim prior to the incident. In fact, one-third committed their crime against their own child (Greenfeld, 1996).

Sexual Harassment

Even though Anita Hill's charges of sexual harassment against then-Supreme Court nominee Clarence Thomas before an all-male Senate committee were unsuccessful in blocking his confirmation, they were successful in raising national consciousness of sexual harassment. In 1992, while attending a naval aviators' Tailhook Association convention, twenty-six women, fourteen of them officers, were sexually assaulted by retired and active-duty Naval officers in the hallway of a Las Vegas hotel. The women were pushed down a gauntlet of molesters who grabbed and pawed at them. The Navy at first treated the incidents as if they were part of a giant fraternity party. Only after one of the victims, Lieutenant Paula Coughlin, publicly spoke out was action taken.

In 1996, in the biggest federal sexual harassment lawsuit in history, the Equal Employment Opportunities Commission charged that Mitsubishi Motor Manufacturing of America (at its Normal, Illinois plant) was guilty of tolerating a work environment of extreme sexual harassment of female employees (Jaroff, 1996). Such activities may constitute a prelude to workplace violence and can foster a sinister work environment. The Paula Jones sexual harassment lawsuit against then-Governor Bill Clinton nearly toppled a Presidency. It was settled out of court, but her allegations and Clinton's cover-up were used in the subsequent grand jury and impeachment trial.

Sexual harassment is unwelcome, uninvited, coercive, or threatening sexual attention, often in a nonreciprocal relationship. This may include unwanted sexual or suggestive comments, attempts to coerce a sexual relationship, punishment or threats of punishment for refusal to comply, a demand for sexual favors in return for jobs or grades, or the creation of a hostile, intimidating, and offensive work environment. While offensive in itself, much sexual harassment is only one step removed from sexual assault and can do psychological and other damage to its victims.

Sexual Predators. Another category of sexual offenders are the violent sexual predators who prey upon children. In 1994 Megan Kanka, a seven-year-old New Jersey girl, was kidnapped, raped, and murdered by a convicted sex offender who lived across the street from her. Unbeknownst to the family the man had a long record of sexual attacks on children. In response to this incident, New Jersey and later other states and the U.S. Congress, passed "Megan's Law," requiring states to inform local communities when known high-risk sex offenders are being released into the community. A related offense, stalking, is deliberately—and without justification—following or surveilling (or both) another person. It also includes threatening another person with immediate or future bodily harm, sexual assault, or confinement.

Stalking. *Stalkers* may include spurned lovers, ex spouses, admirers, obsessive fans, and the like. California passed the first anti-stalking law in 1990, and at least 20 other states have followed suit with laws prohibiting the willful, malicious, and repeated following, threatening, and/or harassing of another person.

The National Violence Against Women Survey funded by the National Institute of Justice and Centers for Disease Control (Tjaden, 1997, p. 1) defined stalking as "a course of

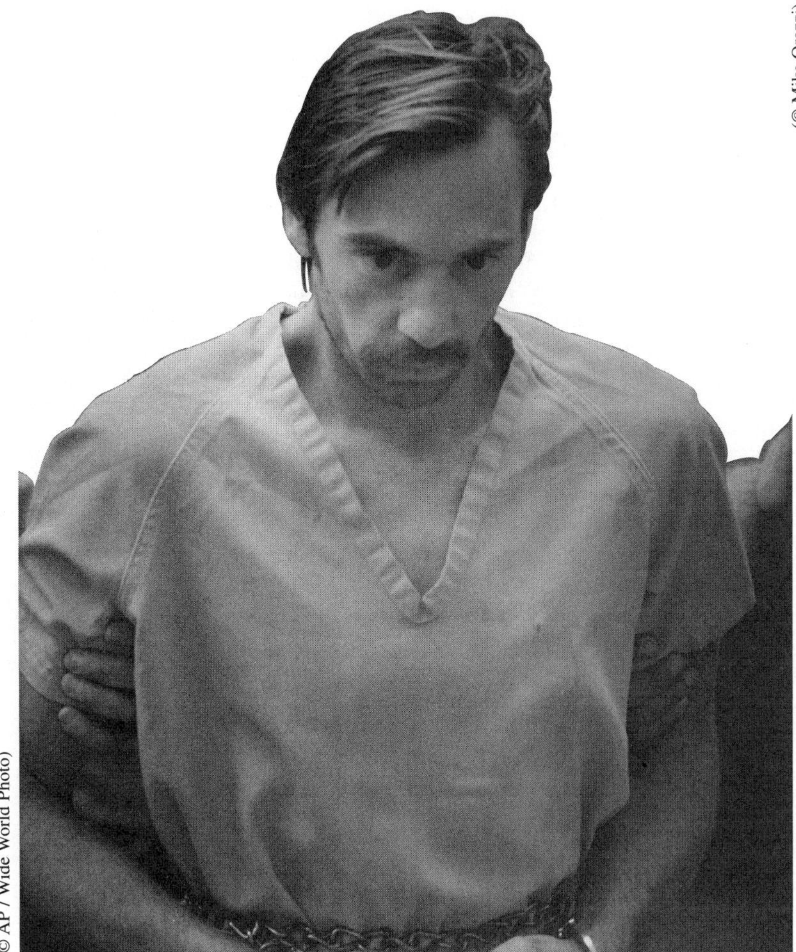
(© AP / Wide World Photo)

(© Mike Orazzi)

Jesse Timmendequas and his rape-and-murder victim Megan Kanka—the faces behind "Megan's Law."

conduct directed at a specific person that involves repeated physical or visual proximity, nonconsensual communication, or verbal, written, or implied threats" sufficient to evoke fear in a reasonable person. The survey discovered that stalking was a much bigger problem than previously believed with about 1.4 million victims annually. Controlling behavior and physical, psychological, and sexual abuse by a woman's former intimate partners was the major mode of conduct. Nearly half of the incidents were reported to the police, and about 25 percent resulted in a restraining order. The former partners wanted to keep the victim in a relationship.

Robbery

Robbery involves theft through violence or the threat of violence. Cook (1983, pp. 1–2) describes robbery as the "quintessential urban crime:"

> The six largest cities (with 8 percent of the population) experienced 33 percent of the robberies in 1980. New York City alone had more than 18 percent. Robbery is more highly concentrated in large cities than any other of the major crimes. The 56 cities with populations exceeding 250,000 in 1980 (which contained 19 percent of the U.S. population) reported 60 percent of all robberies, as

VANTAGE POINT 7.6

International Robbery Rates

Robbery

The Interpol definition of robbery is "robbery and violent theft." The UN definition is "the taking away of property from a person, overcoming resistance by force or threat of force."

The United States defines robbery as "the taking or attempting to take anything of value from the care, custody, or control of a person or persons by force or threat of force or violence and/or putting the victim in fear."

England and Wales reported to Interpol that their definition of aggravated theft, which is the sum of robbery and burglary, includes the crime of "going equipped for stealing." It is not clear if this crime is included in robbery or in burglary or is divided between the two.

Table A International Robbery Statistics, 1998 Interpol Data (per 100,000)

Country	*Robbery (attempts)*	*actual*
United States[a]		165.2
Australia		127.6
Austria	(59.2)	54.5
Belgium	(189)	160.7
Canada		95.6
Chile		77.6
Colombia		66.9
Denmark		49.6
Ecuador		65.1
England/Wales		128.5
Finland		43.5
France		144.1
Germany	(78.5)	63.2
Greece	(21.9)	20.9
Ireland		74.7
Italy		19.1
Japan	(2.7)	2.4
Netherlands		92.3
New Zealand		48.8
Norway		37.9
Spain		169.9

Source: Interpol. International Crime Statistics, 1998. Lyons, France: Interpol Secretariat, 1999.

[a]U.S. Statistics were not included in the 1998 Interpol report and were taken from the Uniform Crime Reports data for 1998.

InfoTrac College Edition Research

Search for the term "robbery" and report on some recent cases.

> compared with 46 percent of all criminal homicides and 30 percent of all burglaries . . . . Controlling for population density, there is no pronounced regional pattern to urban robbery.

In 1998 the estimated 446,625 robberies was the lowest since 1978 and was a ten percent decline from 1997. Robberies were down 23 percent from 1989 levels. Bank robberies averaged $4,516, while gas station robberies were $546 (FBI, 1999, p. 27). The FBI's violent crime and major offenders' section hypothesizes that serial robbers commit many of the heists. The cost of bank robberies has increased in the United States from an estimated

FIGURE 7.4 Robbery Rates in the United States

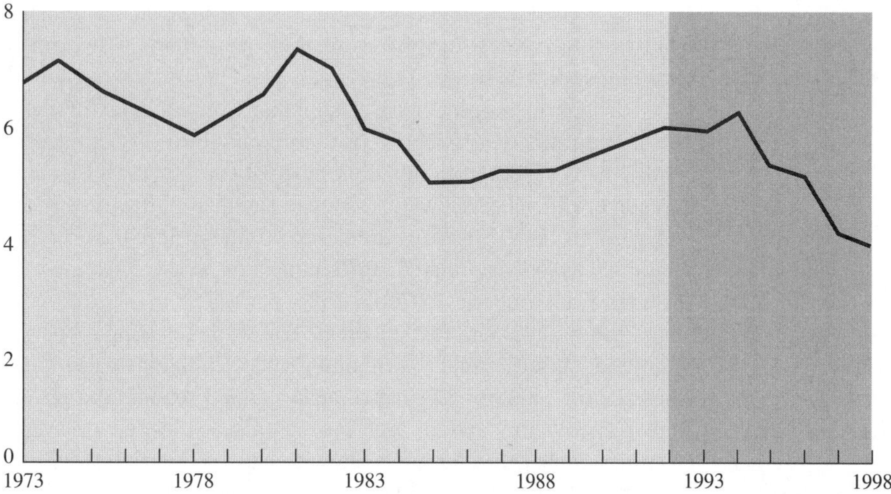

Note: The light area indicates that because of changes made to the victimization survey, data prior to 1992 are adjusted to make them comparable to data collected under the redesigned methodology. The adjustment methods are described in *Criminal Victimization 1973–95*. Estimates for 1993 and beyond are based on collection year while earlier estimates are based on data year. For additional information about the methods used, see *Criminal Victimization 1998*.

Source: Bureau of Justice Statistics, www.ojp.usdoj.gov/bjs/

loss of $20 million in 1993 to over $446 million in 1998. For a number of years Los Angeles has led all cities in the United States in bank robberies, accounting for one-fifth of the national total (Florida and New York are runners-up). It has a lot of new branch banks that are not built like many of the older fortresslike banks back East, and there are many convenient freeways for quick escape. Despite relatively low takes (the average heist in 1998 was $998), poor odds for success (85 percent of bank robbers are caught), stiff sentences (armed robbery carries a twenty-five-year maximum), and easy detection because of witnesses, pictures, and police attention, many robbers are still not deterred. A new variation of bank robbery is the stealing of entire ATMs with a forklift and truck (Suskind, 1991). Bank robbers are not always the craftiest. One opened a bank account in his real name and then robbed the same bank. Another was mugged outside the bank he had just robbed and called the police to complain.

VANTAGE POINT 7.6 reports international robbery statistics. Using Interpol statistics, countries with the highest robbery rates in 1998 were Spain (169.9), U.S. (165.2), Belgium (160.7), and England/Wales (128.5). The lowest rates were exhibited by Denmark (49.6), Finland (43.5), Norway (37.9), and Greece (20.9).

Figure 7.4 presents trends in the U.S. in robbery rates using the National Crime Victimization Survey.

The typical robbery is rather minor. Most robberies are of individuals rather than of commercial establishments and for amounts considerably less than the millions mentioned in our examples. A disproportionate number of robbers are young black males, while a large proportion of victims are white males over twenty-one. The unusual interracial nature of robbery, unlike other violent crimes, can be explained by the fact that robbers are primarily interested in money and adult white males are perceived as good targets. Haran's

(1982) examination of armed robberies in New York City found that, in the sixties, 60 percent of the robbers were older white males, but that, in the seventies, 61 percent were black males—58 percent of them under age twenty-six. But Glaser (1978, p. 254) points out that official statistics overlook both juvenile offenders and victims. More people are serving time in U.S. prisons for robbery than for any other single crime category (Bureau of Justice Statistics, 1983b, p. 31).

Perhaps the biggest cause of apprehensiveness in victims of robbery is the fear of personal harm in street robberies. Roughly one-third of victims are harmed to some degree, with 2 percent requiring inpatient hospital care. In 1988 FBI statistics claimed that about 20 percent of murders were associated with robbery, arson, or other felonious circumstances. "In New York City for example, 24 percent of the criminal homicides in 1980 were classified as robbery-related; amazingly, a majority of slayings of whites in New York City resulted from robberies" (Cook, 1983, p. 4).

Feeney and Weir (1975) indicate that while resisting robbery greatly increases the possibility of suffering injury, screaming and yelling may cause the robber to quit and do not increase the likelihood of harm. Many armed robbers are primarily interested in intimidating the victim and in fact may employ unloaded or even fake weapons, whereas unarmed robbers are far more likely to attack their victims (Conklin, 1972, pp. 113–16).

In September 1992 a Maryland woman was dragged to her death by thieves stealing her car. They forced the woman from behind the steering wheel and threw her two-year-old child, car seat and all, from the moving vehicle. In a new variation of robbery called carjacking, armed car thieves approach occupied vehicles and commandeer them. *Carjacking* (robbery auto theft) is defined as completed or attempted robbery of a motor vehicle by a stranger to the victim. It differs from other vehicle theft because the victim is present and the thief uses or threatens force. Between 1992 and 1996 the NCVS estimates an average of 49,000 attempted or completed carjackings in the U.S. Half of these were successful (Klaus, 1999). Carjacking has been a federal crime since 1992. Some experts speculate that carjacking has increased in response to new anti-theft devices, particularly on expensive automobiles.

Conklin's Typology of Robbers

Conklin (1972) developed a **typology of robbers** based on interviews with sixty-seven convicted robbers in Massachusetts prisons, as well as ninety victims. He classified them as:

1. The professional robbers
2. The opportunist robbers
3. The addict robbers
4. The alcoholic robbers

Professional robbers have a long-term commitment to crime, their major source of livelihood. They are very rational about crime and plan their operations carefully. (This type of criminal will be discussed in detail in Chapter 9 on professional crime.) The most common type of bandits are the *opportunist robbers.* Having little commitment to, or specialization in, robbery, they are all-purpose property offenders. Their engagement in robbery is infrequent and relatively unplanned. Often young and from lower class, minority backgrounds, such offenders often operate in groups. Gabor and Normandeau (1989, pp. 273–82) in studying armed robbers in Montreal found that most did not fit the stereotype of the meticulous professional. Most were under twenty-two years of age, wore no disguise, and usually stole less than $100. Nearly half of the robbers either did not plan ahead at all or planned their robbery far less than an hour in advance. The robbers indicated that they viewed armed robbery as the fastest and most direct means of getting money compared with burglary and fraud. Younger robbers in particular claimed that they enjoyed the thrill, excitement, status, and feeling of power associated with the crime.

Addict robbers are addicted to substances such as heroin or other drugs and commit robbery to support their expensive habits. Most drug abusers are interested in safe and quick criminal gain, and are less likely to be involved in robbery than in burglary and sneak thievery. Such offenders are less likely to use weapons and therefore more likely to use physical force as a means of intimidation. *Alcoholic robbers* have little commitment to robbery; they engage in unplanned robberies on occasion in order to support their habit. Many claim to be intoxicated at the time of their offense.

Perhaps the most feared type of robber—though not a separate type—is the *mugger,* a "strong-arm" robber who generally does not use a weapon. Many muggers are semiprofessional; they do some planning and specialization, though not to the extent of the professional robber. *Mugging,* an American slang term for robbery, may refer to everything from purse-snatching to brutalization or murder of the victims. Working in groups, muggers may start by carefully surveying the scene and the mark (victim). The actual techniques employed vary from the "yoke," a method of grabbing the victim from behind around the neck, to the use of knives or guns to scare the victim. Young black offenders are more likely to commit purse snatches and street robberies, netting small amounts, while adult white offenders are more likely to participate in commercial robberies (Dunn, 1976, p. 12).

Wright and Decker in *Armed Robbers in Action: Stickups and Street Culture* (1997) conducted field research on 86 uncaught robbers in St. Louis. They indicate (Ibid., p. 128):

> The offenders in our study typically compel the cooperation of intended victims through the creation of a convincing illusion of impending death. They create this illusion by catching would-be victims off guard and then using tough talk, a fierce demeanor and the display of a deadly weapon to scare them into unquestioning compliance.

High robbery rates are not an inevitable product of urbanization in advanced capitalistic societies, as can be illustrated by Japan. In the late seventies, New York City had eleven thousand robberies per million residents while Tokyo had about forty robberies per million population (Nettler, 1982, vol. 2, p. 34).

Domestic Violence

In our previous discussion, we indicated that one stands the greatest chance of being kicked, stabbed, shot, or otherwise brutalized within the refuge of one's own home. Child abuse may include excessive physical assault, neglect, and/or sexual molestation. (The last topic will be discussed in Chapter 14.) Spouse abuse usually involves physical assaults by husbands against their wives, although the reverse is not unheard of.

Child Abuse

While corporal punishment is an approved-of disciplinary practice in many societies, **child abuse** is defined as *excessive mistreatment, either physical or emotional, of children beyond any reasonable explanation* (Kempe and Kempe, 1978). In 1996 another sad case of child abuse and death caught the public eye—the death of 6-year-old Elisa Ezquierdo. Of particular concern was the failure of New York City's child protection system. Rescuers who pulled little Elisa from her bed found deep red blotches, welts, and cigarette burns over her entire body; bruises near her kidney, face, and temples; and ghastly wounds around her genitals. Despite repeated expressions of concern in reports to child care workers by other family members, Elisa had been put in the care of her deranged mother. The mother believed the child was possessed by the devil.

In a nationwide survey of 2,143 families, Gelles (1978) discovered that during the previous year over 20 percent of children had been assaulted by their parents by having objects thrown at them or by being kicked, bitten, or hit with fists. A 1995 Gallup poll of 1,000 parents estimated that 5 percent of parents punish their children by punching, kicking, or throwing the child down or hitting with a hard object on some part of the body other than the bottom. The poll also found that 1.3 million children were sexually abused. These figures are much higher than those cited by the National Center on Child Abuse and Neglect, which estimated over 200,000 victims of physical abuse and 130,000 victims of sexual abuse. The federal statistics are based on reported cases (Lewin, 1995, p. A17).

The child batterer strikes the defenseless. Historically, he or she is exercising a traditional prerogative of parents. Infanticide was a parental privilege in many ancient societies, and childhood was simply not regarded as a particularly important stage in life. Ironically it was not until 1866 that state protection of abused children was begun, using SPCA (Society for the Prevention of Cruelty to Animals) authority for the removal of a child from an abusing household.

The extent of homicide and brutal assault and torture vented upon child victims was illustrated by a study by Raffali (1970). Following up on 302 battered children reported by some New York City hospitals, he discovered that one year later 35 had died and 55 suffered permanent brain damage from their injuries. A study by Gil (1971) estimated serious physical abuse of children under 18 at about 9 per 100,000, comparable to the homicide rate at that time. The fact that most instances are never reported to police or come to the attention of authorities would suggest a large "dark figure" of child abuse. Gelles and Straus (1979) put this statistic as high as 1.9 million per year who are physically abused. Abusive activities seem to take place more often in families that have a foster or stepparent present (Zalba, 1971), with boys more frequently the targets than girls until age twelve, after which girls are more subject to attack.

A virtual statistical epidemic in reports of child abuse has occurred since the sixties, primarily because of increased efforts at detection and reporting. Emergency room personnel, for instance, receive special training in spotting the "battered child syndrome," which includes a variety of symptoms including lethargy, fear of parents, subdural hematoma (blood and swelling next to bones or skull), multiple broken bones demonstrating various stages of healing (thus multiple incidents), and suspicious bites, bruises, and the like that cannot be reasonably explained by parents (Fontana, 1973, pp. 28—29). Between 1976 and 1985 reports of child abuse grew from 669,000 reports per year to 1.9 million. It is important to note that more than half of the latter figure were unfounded; that is, determined not to have taken place (Whitman, 1987, p. 39). In a reversal of previous rulings, the U.S. Supreme Court in *Coy v. Iowa* ruled that children in sexual abuse cases must confront their alleged abusers "face-to-face" (Lauter, 1988, p. 6A). Such a ruling may discourage prosecutions of real batterers.

Studies of spouse and child batterers suggest a frightening although not inevitable link in which former child-abuse victims grow up to become child or spouse abusers themselves. Not all abused children become scarred irreparably or turn into future abusers; but, not surprisingly, many do (see Koski, 1988). Researchers have found that the abused and neglected, particularly males, exhibit a higher frequency of arrest for adult violent offenses (Widom, 1989; Miller, 1989). Widom (1992) found that childhood abuse or neglect increased the odds of future delinquency or adult criminality by about 40 percent.

In addition to a history of abuse, some other characteristics of child abusers include family isolation from helping resources in periods of crisis, disappointment with the child, and some crisis that precipitates maltreatment (Kempe and Kempe, 1978, p. 24).

According to Bakan (1975, p. 100), hostility toward children is generally associated with two age-maturity distortions. First, the adult may ascribe to him- or herself the role of a younger person. Second, he or she may ascribe to the child a maturity beyond the child's years. Studies of child abusers and their personality characteristics, however, are often plagued by **post hoc error,** the *assumption that since one variable is observed after another, it must be the cause of that outcome.* Gelles (1977) indicates that often psychological conditions that are identified as being present after an abuse incident tend to be viewed as the cause of the incident. Abusers are often described as being depressed and paranoid, but these conditions could be results of the incident rather than its cause.

Child battering may constitute assault or even homicide, but most cases in the United States are handled in family or juvenile courts as categories of child neglect or abuse. Such courts have an orientation toward rehabilitation rather than toward imposing penalties or imprisonment (Glaser, 1978, p. 246). Often children are removed from the home for their own protection and temporarily placed in foster homes until their parents are adjudged fit, but a major objective in the past has been to maintain the family unit. This could account for the one-third of abused children who later suffered death and brain damage in Raffali's (1970, p. 301) study.

Austria, Croatia, Cyprus, Denmark, Finland, Italy, Latvia, Norway, and Sweden bar parents from spanking their children (Straus, 1999). Germany and Great Britain in 2000 were also considering placing limits on corporal punishment. Murray Straus in his book *Beating the Devil Out of Them: Corporal Punishment in American Families* (1994) indicates that, while working as a sanction in the short run, corporal punishment increases the probability of violence and future crime.

Spouse Abuse

Despite the fact that ex-football star O. J. Simpson won his criminal case and was found not guilty of the murders of his ex-wife Nicole Brown Simpson and Ron Goldman, tape recordings of a 911 call for assistance by Nicole, as well as pictures and police testimony, documented Simpson's history of battering Nicole. This history was also a factor in the civil action brought against him by the Brown and Goldman families. That "wrongful death" suit was successful, and Simpson was ordered to pay several million dollars in damages. This called public attention to the widespread nature of an all-too-common form of violence—spouse battering.

Straus, Gelles, and Steinmetz (1980) claim a "sexual symmetry" in spouse abuse: that husbands and wives are equally likely to batter each other. Most others, however, find the male the major aggressor. In a 1975 survey and again in a 1985 national survey Straus and Gelles (1986) found men and women about equally likely to be the assailant. In a more extreme view Thibault (1992) even claims that anti-male sexist stereotypes tend to ignore female-initiated violence, giving women a license to batter their children and male partners in the home. Even if this is the case, violence by men tends to cause more serious injury to victims than does violence by women. Studies such as "The Marriage License as a Hitting License" (Straus, Gelles and Steinmetz, 1982) and "The Family as a Cradle of Violence" (Steinmetz and Straus, 1978) illustrate the intimate nature of intrafamily violence, particularly with respect to spouse abuse.

While family conflict studies show equal rates of domestic assault by men and women, victimization and clinical studies show much higher rates of assault by men (Johnson, 1995). Other studies have shown that much of women's violence really consists of "self defense" or "fighting back" (DeKeseredy et al. 1998). The National Crime Victimization Survey estimates that in 1998 about one million "intimate partner crimes" were committed by current or former spouses, boyfriends, or girlfriends. About 85 percent of such crimes were committed against women. The rate of intimate partner crimes have been declining at a rate of four percent per year for males and one percent per year for females. In 1998 women represented almost three out of four victims of the 1,830 murders by intimate partners (Rennison and Welchans, 2000). While men are killed by women in self defense, the greatest danger to women is when they decide to leave an abusive relationship. The men are the pursuers, not defenders.

Some of the reasons for the decline in intimate partner homicide may be: better police and prosecution procedures, greater female participation in the work force, better services for victims, and better legal advocacy including protection from abuse orders (Dugan, Nagin, and Rosenfeld, 2000). Later age at marriage could be added to this list.

In their self-report survey of 2,143 husbands and wives, Straus, Gelles, and Steinmetz (1982, pp. 274–75) indicate that one out of every six couples admitted one of the following in the past year: threw something at spouse, pushed, grabbed, shoved, slapped, kicked, bit, hit with fist or other object, beat up, and/or threatened with or used a knife or gun against the spouse. In line with our earlier discussion of victim-precipitation of many assaults, they found the most common situation was one in which both spouses used violence, although husbands employed the most dangerous and injurious forms of violence and were greater repeaters. Often family members—such as women and older persons, who are generally thought of as victims—become assailants and spontaneously strike back, sometimes with lethal consequences (Kratcoski, 1988; Kuhl, 1985).

Traditionally in Western society "a man's home is his castle," and wife-beating has been the prerogative of the "master of the house" as was abuse of children. In codifying common law in the eighteenth century, Blackstone determined "a rule of thumb" for wife abuse. While Somers (1994) claims it is a fable, under this rule a husband had the right to physically discipline an errant wife as long as the stick used was no thicker than his thumb (Straus and Gelles, 1986, p. 465). Many traditional societies approved of husbands murdering their wives for serious transgressions such as adultery, although the "double standard" did not permit reverse action.

Although the list is subject to post hoc error, Newman (1979, pp. 145–46) identifies the following as characteristic of wife abusers:

- alcohol abuse
- hostility
- dependence on their wives
- excessive brooding over trivial events
- belief in societal approval of battering
- economic problems
- a sudden burst of anger
- present military service
- having been a battered child

A study by the Police Foundation (1977) found that, in the two years preceding a domestic assault or homicide, the police had been at the address of the incident five times or more in half of the cases. In the Minneapolis Domestic Violence Experiment (Sherman and Berk, 1984), a randomized field experiment demonstrated that arrested domestic offenders were about half as likely to commit repeat violence as nonarrested offenders. While care must be taken in replications that specify this policy, the experiment certainly illustrated that there are things police can do to intervene in and prevent family violence (Berk and Newton, 1985; Binder and Meeker, 1988). Of the six completed replications of the Minneapolis study, three showed positive correlations and three did not. One finding, for example, was that mandatory arrest worked better with employed than unemployed offenders. The effects of the criminal sanctions depend upon the strength of the family bonds (Sherman, 1992; Buzawa and Buzawa, 1990). Another welcome sign is that the domestic murder rate in the United States has been declining since 1976, perhaps in response to various efforts to fight domestic violence during that period. VANTAGE POINT 7.7 presents the ASC Task Force Report on Violence Against Women.

Elisa Ezquierdo was only one of the many children assaulted and abused by a parent. Her death at her mother's hands made Elisa one of the best-known victims in 1996.

Elder Abuse

With longer life expectancies and, consequently, larger populations of elderly in modern societies, a growing problem of abuse of elderly has presented itself. Koenig (1991) notes that our knowledge of elder abuse is probably where our knowledge of child and spouse abuse was two or three decades ago. Elder abuse may take place both inside and outside of institutional care and may involve actual physical harm, which is a criminal matter, as well as more subtle neglect and psychological and material abuse.

Kidnapping

Kidnapping, the holding of individuals hostage for ransom purposes, is most noted in the United States by the famous 1932 Lindbergh case, when the 20-month-old son of Charles Lindbergh was kidnapped for ransom and murdered. This led to the passage of the Lindbergh law making kidnapping a federal offense. Kidnapping is relatively rare in the United States, while world figures by region show for 1995 through 1998: South America—6,755 kidnapped, Asia/Far East—617, Europe—271, Africa—211, Middle East—118, and North America—80. Only one in ten kidnappings worldwide ends in the death of the person abducted (Whitelaw, 1999; Auerbach, 1998). The Philippines, Colombia, Pakistan, Brazil, and Mexico top the international list for kidnap-for-ransom (Kohut, 1997). Foreign business people are favorite targets, while ransoms vary from $50,000 to $100,000 in the Philippines to much larger sums (sometimes $1 million or more) in Latin America.

VANTAGE POINT 7.7

Violence Against Women

Issues

The number of women in U.S. prisons has tripled over the past decade. This may be correlated to the fact that many women who serve prison terms for violent crimes are incarcerated because they used violence to avert an attack or defend themselves against repeated violence by family members or intimates. Efforts to reduce violence against women, including rape and sexual abuse, should consider the following:

- Twenty years after legislative reforms on rape swept the nation, research shows that although there has been some progress, reforms related to rape have fallen far short of goals. Overall, rape has not significantly declined, reports of rape have not dramatically risen, and the process of arrest, prosecution, and conviction of rapists has not significantly improved. In addition, "marital rape" by husbands or cohabitators must be clarified and recognized as a crime.
- Rapists have very high rates of recidivism, indicating that imprisonment is not an effective deterrent.
- Victims of violence against women suffer not only physically and emotionally, but lose time from work and are a burden on the medical community.
- Stereotyping of victims persists. The legal system and the public continue to believe that rape victims are somehow to blame and that their sexual history and the degree of their resistance during the crime can be mitigating factors. Battered women are also stigmatized for not leaving abusive relationships.

Research suggests that relying solely on the criminal justice system to stop violence against women is a mistake, because it often does not serve all their needs. Rather, violence against women must be understood as embedded in wider issues, such as shortcomings in the law and social service agencies, and male dominance, sexism, racism, and poverty.

Many people feel that violence against women can be reduced only through legislative change, improved monitoring of the criminal justice system, more and better-funded victim compensation programs, community education, increased victim services such as crisis centers and counseling, minority outreach, inservice training for criminal justice practitioners on victims' rights and services and the legal process, and counseling and treatment programs for rapists and batterers.

Drunk Driving

In May 1988, a drunken driver in Kentucky drove his pickup truck the wrong way on an interstate highway. He crashed head-on into a school bus carrying sixty-seven passengers, killing 24 teenagers and three adults when the bus's gas tank ruptured, engulfing the interior in flames (Highway Safety, 1988). In March 1989 the oil tanker Exxon Valdez ran aground and ruptured, releasing ten million gallons of oil and creating the worst oil spill in North America. The captain was alleged to have been (but not convicted of being) drunk, and to have left the ship in the hands of an untrained third mate. Rhetoric regarding the war on drugs tends to overlook the fact that alcohol abuse remains the Western world's number one drug problem. More Americans are killed or injured every year by drunk drivers than are murdered or assaulted in standard violent criminal behavior. Between 1990 and 1997 the number of arrests for driving under the influence declined 18 percent, even though the number of licensed drivers had increased 15 percent (Maruschak, 1999). With 1.5 million arrests in 1997, the decline in arrests may be explained in part by the aging of licensed drivers. DUI offenders in general are more often older, better educated, white, and male than the average offender. Despite this fact, the likelihood that a drunk driver, on any given evening, will be stopped by police is small. Even chronic abusers slip through the cracks, often until it is too late and they maim or kill someone. In the past, drunk driving was simply not taken very seriously. Then political pressure groups (such as MADD, Mothers Against Drunk Drivers), particularly those

VANTAGE POINT 7.7—Continued

Policy Recommendations

- The Violence Against Women Act is essential to the safety of women, and it should continue to be funded.
- To address violence against women at the national level, the Attorney General should issue and disseminate short papers to police, prosecutors, judges, and other court personnel on the experiences of victims and model law enforcement responses. Ongoing feedback, discussions, and training with local shelters should follow.
- Shelters for battered women and their children should be treated as key components in multiagency, community-based strategies. Shelters and their advice lines offer crucial services, particularly to victims of repeated violence who are most in need because they require continuous assistance from the police, courts, and hospitals. Shelters should receive more funds, and political action committees should be used to mobilize support and financial resources.
- Public education on violence, including violence in the home, should become part of all school curriculums, and the Attorney General should work with other federal agencies to improve public education and to develop public service announcements modeled on successful programs elsewhere.
- The Attorney General should reconvene a task force on family violence, such as the one that met in 1984, to assess progress and address new issues for research. Data collection on issues surrounding rape, sexual abuse, and other violence against women must be improved and expanded.
- A federal task force on women in prison should be established to provide national leadership to determine what factors lead to incarceration of women and how women can be helped before they, in turn, resort to violence.

Source: "American Society of Criminology Task Force Report to Attorney General Janet Reno," *The Criminologist* (Special Issue), 20, 6, November/December 1995. Edna Erez, chair (see Rape Task Force for other committee members).

InfoTrac College Edition Research
What are some recent developments in the United States to prevent "violence against women"?

made up of the families and other survivors of such victimization, began to apply pressure to legislatures for stricter laws.

Beginning in the seventies, many states passed more stringent laws in an effort to cut down the carnage on U.S. streets and highways. These laws included mandatory jail sentences for offenders and temporary suspension of licenses, as well as **DWI** (Driving While Intoxicated) or DUI schools that the offender had to pay to attend. Policies such as the immediate seizure of licenses, longer suspensions, and the impounding of vehicles of habitual offenders promise success in reducing fatalities. In addition, civil and criminal suits against negligent bartenders and public service work for offenders, offer some additional hope. While some researchers have not been very impressed with the impact DUI laws have had in deterring drunk drivers (Kingsworth and Jungsten, 1988; Wheeler and Hissong, 1988), others point out the need for continuing research on this matter (Jacobs, 1988). The Centers for Disease Control (CDC) reports that the number of alcohol-related traffic deaths, even during holidays, has been decreasing every year since 1982.

Criminal Careers of Violent Offenders

Conservative writers in the early 1990s predicted a massive wave of violent superpredators. IN THE NEWS 7.2 reviews this prediction.

IN THE NEWS 7.2

BODY COUNT: THE CASE FOR VIOLENT SUPERPREDATORS

William Bennett, John DiIulio, Jr., and John Walters' *Body Count: Moral Poverty and How to Win America's War Against Crime and Drugs* (1996) sparked the conservative conscience in this country with their prediction that: *America's beleaguered cities are about to be victimized by a paradigm shattering wave of ultraviolent, morally vacuous young people some call 'the superpredators.' A new generation of street criminals is upon us—the youngest, biggest and baddest generation any society has every known.*

This "moral poverty" rather than underlying social and economic causes calls for an expanded war on drugs, tougher policing, longer sentences, more imprisonment and religion according to Bennett, DiIulio, and Walters (Skolnick, 1997). This "moral poverty" ignores such factors as racism, joblessness inequality, and poverty. Such language as "superpredator" or James Q. Wilson's "feral, pre-social beings" pander to racism (Ibid.).

The main problem with the superpredator prediction is that this forecasted wave never took place. In fact the crime rate declined (as of this writing) by seven straight years, primarily due to big declines among the very groups that were supposed to have been the superpredators. In reviewing the book *Body Count,* Jerome Skolnick (1997, p. 91) concludes: *Certainly we need to revitalize community groups—not only churches but also schools, civic associations, and other neighborhood resources. We also need to reduce chronic joblessness in communities where crime and victimization are most pronounced. The remorselessness of some youthful offenders is all to real and, in some cases tragically irreversible. But, such underlying causes of juvenile crime as poverty, racism, and inequality cannot be addressed mainly by a summons to virtue. If we ignore those problems and look only to prisons and the politics of rectitude to pull us out of criminality, then I agree: Crime will be on the rise and look out.*

Source: William J. Bennett, John J. DiIulio, and John P. Walters. 1996. *Body Count: Moral Poverty and How to Win America's War Against Crime and Drugs.* New York: Simon and Schuster; and Jerome K. Skolnick. 1997. "Tough Guys." *The American Prospect* 30 (January): 86–91.

Research Question

Why do you think that the prediction of a wave of superpredators never took place?

InfoTrac College Edition Research

In examining the issue of "violent crime," what role do communities play in violent crime according to the article by Matthew R. Lee?

Most violent offenders, such as murderers, assaulters, and forcible rapists, do not have criminal careers or extensive backgrounds in and commitment to violent crime as a major component of their lives. Most do not view themselves as criminals nor associate with other criminals. The major exceptions to this are people incarcerated for robbery, whose crimes, except for their violence, resemble those of conventional property criminals (to be discussed in Chapter 8).

As seen in Chapter 3, various cultural and subcultural values and attitudes regarding violence have an impact on the relative frequency of violent crimes and their prevalence in various countries, regions within countries, urban/rural areas, social classes, races and ethnic groups, ages, and sexes.

Culture of Violence

Entire cultures can have a predisposition to the use of violence to resolve grievances. Given a lack of centralized law enforcement in the last century, areas such as Sardinia and Sicily were characterized by vendettas, which required personal revenge for wrongs against oneself or one's kin. In some cases, whole families killed each other off, responding in kind to the need to avenge past harm to relatives. Additionally, in the 1950s the nation of Colombia experienced what has been called "violencia Colombiana," in which during a ten-year period two hundred thousand persons were killed in a nation of only ten million, a fantastic rate of one out of every fifty Colombians. In the 1980s Colombia had a homicide rate estimated at an unbelievable eight times the U.S. rate (Rosenberg, 1991). Moreover, Wolfgang and Ferracuti (1967, p. 280) claim that in the 1960s in Mexico City the risk of death from homicide was greater than the risk of death from bombing during the London blitz in World War II. With the collapse of communism in Albania, vendettas have returned, most of them involving family feuds over land reform. Local blood feuds going back as far as the fifteenth-century Ottoman Empire have been rekindled. In the past such violence was officially approved and avengers received light sentences (Post and Field, 1992).

Subculture of Violence

Marvin Wolfgang and Franco Ferracuti (1967) in their now-classic *The Subculture of Violence* refer to the "culture within a culture" that exists among some ethnic and lower-class groups and demonstrates favorable attitudes toward the use of violence as a means of resolving interpersonal grievances. In such subcultures, violence is viewed as a necessary means of upholding one's masculinity. "Quick resort to physical combat as a measure of daring, courage, or defense of status appears to be a cultural expectation, especially for lower socioeconomic class males of both races" (p. 189). The southern United States has traditionally had higher rates of homicide than other regions of the country. This has led some to view the region as imbued with a subculture of violence. Not coincidentally, the South also has the highest rates of firearm ownership. A rival explanation for the higher murder rates in the South may relate to the fact that poorer emergency medical services exist there than in other regions of the country (Doerner and Speir, 1986; Doerner, 1988).

A basic tenet of the "subculture of violence" thesis is that, in such subcultures violence is not viewed as undesirable conduct, and little guilt or disapproval is experienced when aggression is used. Erlanger (1974), in an empirical assessment of this concept, indicated the surprising lack of examples in the ethnographic literature, citing Liebow's (1967) *Tally's Corner* and Whyte's (1955) *Streetcorner Society* as examples. Other such literature, which he does not cite, certainly does lend credibility to the theory: for example, Allen's (1977) *Assault with a Deadly Weapon* and Brown's (1964) *Manchild in the Promised Land.* In a reanalysis of data originally gathered for the President's Commission on Violence, Erlanger (1974) concluded that on attitudinal measures of approval/disapproval of violence, lower class and minority groups were no different from the general society. He concludes that the social and economic deprivation experienced by these groups is primarily a result of social structural factors—for example, poverty and racism—rather than the product of group pathology. In essence, while there is no greater attitudinal approval of violence, the lack of sophistication with respect to other means of resolving grievances results in higher rates of violent behavior. Other researchers have indicated that blacks and Latinos had lower tolerance of violence than the general population. "Demographic and residential variables explained more of the variance in violence tolerance and experiences with violence than did ethnic background" (Shoemaker and Williams, 1987, p. 464).

Luckenbill (1991) and Best and Luckenbill (1982) proposed a model of murders as "character contests" in which the parties involved attempt to save face and demonstrate character at each other's expense. The stages of this "character contest" involve (Savitz et al, 1991, pp. 20–21):

- A *personal offense* (statement or gesture) in which a person feels that he or she has lost face (self-image)
- An *assessment* that interprets the action as offensive
- *Retaliation* or demonstration of strength of character ("face") by showing anger or contempt

Colombian soccer star Andrés Escobar was appalled when his effort to block the ball sent it into the Colombian goal, giving the U.S. team the victory in a June 1994 game. Less than two weeks later, on July 2, he was shot to death in a confrontation with angry fans.

(© Jeff Vinnick / Reuters / Corbis - Bettmann)

- A *working agreement* that violence is an appropriate means of settling the matter
- A battle in which the offender has or obtains a weapon and attacks the victim
- *Termination,* when the target falls and the contest is over

In examining a sample of murders, Savitz, Kumar, and Zahn (1991) concluded that over half of the killings fit Luckenbill's model, although many cases lacked sufficient detail to establish whether they fit the model.

Luckenbill and Doyle (1989), as an addendum to this model, proposed the hypothesis that "disputatiousness" (likelihood of being offended or seeking reparation through protest) increases if a person is attacked by an equal in a public place.

Machismo, the code of conduct requiring that males defend their sense of honor, is particularly virulent in Latin American cultures. In Brazil, for instance, some courts until recently refused to convict husbands of killing unfaithful wives, although the reverse did not apply. The view is that a man should not be punished for defending his honor. Bourgois (1988) described a "culture of terror" in the underground drug economies of U.S. central cities in which regular displays of violence are necessary for success in the street-level drug-dealing world. What outsiders view as senseless violence may be viewed as public relations, "a curriculum vita (resumé) that proves their capacity for effective violence and terror" (Bourgois, 1988).

Career Criminals/Violent Predators

Petersilia, Greenwood, and Lavin (1977), basing their research on interviews with forty-nine incarcerated robbers, found that such individuals committed roughly 214 offenses apiece, although these crimes were nonspecialized and were as likely to involve conventional, nonviolent property crime. They divided *career criminals* into *two types:* the *intensives* and the *intermittents.* Intensives have continuing criminal involvement from an early age and commit on the average fifty-one crimes per year. Intermittents are irregular in their offense patterns, committing five crimes per year, generally with lower takes from their victims. In a previously discussed longitudinal study of Philadelphia delinquents by Wolfgang,

Figlio, and Sellin (1972), it was indicated that roughly 6 percent of the 1945 male birth cohort were "chronic offenders," accounting for 52 percent of all the crimes committed by this group. Chaiken and Chaiken (1982) in *Varieties of Criminal Behavior* used self-reports and official records in a survey of 2,200 inmates in California, Michigan, and Texas, in which they identified "violent predators" who commit a highly disproportionate amount of crime, consisting of a combination of robbery, assault, and drug dealing. These criminals began taking drugs as juveniles, committed violent crimes before age sixteen, were addicted to multiple drugs, and perpetrated an exceptionally high level of robberies, property crimes, and assaults in order to support their addictions. Most were unmarried, had few other family obligations, and were irregularly employed. Their distinctive characteristic was multiple drug use—for example, heroin with barbiturates or alcohol, or amphetamines with alcohol. The California inmates who had been addicted admitted, on the average, thirty-four robberies, sixty-eight burglaries, and seventy-two thefts per year, while the same figures for those not using drugs were two, three, and eight per year.

Societal Reaction

As our discussion has suggested, most violent crime is intimate; a large proportion of violent offenders are not career criminals and reflect situational or subcultural reactions to interpersonal disputes. Studies indicate that a high proportion of crimes are committed by a small portion of the criminal population, the chronic or career offenders, so social policies to identify and specially process these career criminals hold much promise. The creation of special career criminal bureaus by police departments and district attorney offices, using computerized information on up-to-date offense records that are shared with the courts, can assist in preventing such career felons from slipping through the cracks in the system.

As previously cited, a Police Foundation (1977) survey in Kansas City found that in the two years preceding an assault or homicide, police had answered calls about domestic disturbances in 85 percent of the cases and at least five times in half of the cases. Thus, early use of crisis intervention teams could help reduce the high rates of domestic violence. Social programs related to substance abuse and family crisis intervention address two key components of the violence equation.

In 1985 the FBI began the Violent Criminal Apprehension Program (VICAP). VICAP is a nationwide data information center designed to collect and analyze data submitted by police departments regarding special crimes of violence. Local police departments fill out a separate data form in circumstances involving unsolved or solved homicides involving abduction, series victimizations, or random, motiveless, or sexually-oriented themes. It is also used for missing person reports where foul play is suspected and to indicate unidentified dead bodies. VICAP can analyze such cases for possible linkages—for example, in the case of serial murderers (Howlett, Hanfland, and Ressler, 1986).

A key explanatory variable in explaining the very high interpersonal violence rates in the United States compared to other developed countries is the widespread availability and ownership of handguns. Although the majority of the population favors stricter legislation and control, the public has remained relatively passive in this regard. Until strong, active public pressure is felt, Americans will continue to murder one another at a rate that bewilders most of the civilized world.

Justifications for Punishment

The punishment of criminals has at least four justifications: *retribution, deterrence (including incapacitation), rehabilitation, and protection and upholding the solidarity of society* (Sutherland and Cressey, 1974, pp. 325–30). *Retribution* is the societal counterpart of individual revenge. When criminal laws were formulated, the state assumed responsibility for punishing offenders and forbade victimized parties from taking the law into their own hands. Criminals must pay their debt to society, not to the harmed party. Beginning as early as *lex talionis,* "an eye for an eye and a tooth for a tooth," criminals have been viewed as having to suffer in some way for justice to be served. Retribution is a moral motive for punishment, not simply a utilitarian one. Nazi hunters who are still searching for war criminals decades after World War II, when asked, "What good does it do?" reply, "It does justice." So public sentiment and outrage are the guideposts for enforcement, rather than any direct effect on future crime commission.

Deterrence refers to the belief that perceived punishment will serve as a warning and inhibit individuals (*specific deterrence*) and groups (*general deterrence*) from involvement in criminal activity. Based on the classical school of criminology and the writings of Cesare Beccaria (discussed in Chapter 4), the deterrence model assumes that if the pain (clear, swift, and certain punishment) outweighs any pleasure to be derived from the criminal act, then crime will be prevented. *Incapacitation,* the prevention of crime by keeping criminals behind bars for longer periods, is an additional example of special deterrence. In a revival of classical criminology, large and impressive bodies of literature have begun to accumulate on the issue of specific deterrence. Although inconclusive at this point, the research suggests the potentially positive impact of selective incapacitation of career criminals on lowering crime rates (Clarke, 1974, and Greenberg, 1975).

Rehabilitation, which has been the watchword in the United States in the post-World War II period, assumes that the purpose of punishing criminals is to reform or resocialize them to conventional, law-abiding values. Even name changes indicate this philosophical shift: The field of penology is now called corrections and prisons are correctional facilities. Nevertheless, there appears to be more talk about rehabilitation than programs to facilitate it. Martinson (1974), in "What Works?—Questions and Answers about Prison Reform," examined a large number of correctional programs and their claims of success in rehabilitation as well as their recidivism (repeating of crime) rates; he felt that there was little evidence that any significant programs in corrections had an important impact on reducing recidivism. Only later ("Martinson Attacks His Own Earlier Work," 1978; Martinson, 1979) did he retract this devastating critique by admitting that he may have suffered from "methodological fanaticism," in which substance was overlooked in the name of method and that some of the programs did have positive outcomes. With estimates of recidivism and reincarceration rates as high as 65 percent (Greenberg, 1975, p. 551), there seemed to be a decline in liberal optimism about the success of the rehabilitation model (Bayer, 1981). However, in defense of rehabilitation, some feel that it has never been given a decent chance. Badillo and Haynes (1972) indicate that in the early seventies only about 5 percent of correctional budgets was used for rehabilitation programs and that rehabilitation has often been more a matter of talk than action (see Cullen and Gilbert, 1982). Glaser (1994) identifies a variety of programs that utilize penalties, fines, community services, restitution, and intermediate punishments that do indeed work.

Protection and the upholding of social solidarity as a goal of punishment reflect Durkheim's (1950) point made in Chapter 1, that a society reaffirms its values in reacting to and punishing wrongdoers. In this justification the purpose of punishment is not to obtain revenge or deter or change the criminal; rather it is an attempt to protect society from criminals and in so doing to reinforce group solidarity.

The Death Penalty Debate

Support for the death penalty in the United States appears to follow the crime rate; that is, higher crime rates bring greater support for the death penalty. During the low-crime period of the early 1960s support dropped to a low of 42 percent in 1966. It steadily increased thereafter, the Gallup poll of 1988 showing 79 percent of Americans in favor. Retribution and vengeance appeared the major reasons for favoring the death penalty, since many were aware that such executions were not a deterrent (Dionne, 1990).

The subject of capital punishment has fueled heated debate among criminologists and the public at-large.

Arguments in favor of the death penalty include:

- It is sanctioned in the Bible as well as by historical tradition as a culturally approved manner of dealing with heinous offenders.
- It is an effective deterrent in preventing cold-blooded murder.
- It is more economical than the permanent, lifelong warehousing of the most dangerous criminals.
- It is the ultimate specific deterrence.
- In terms of retribution, those who kill innocent persons in cold blood deserve similar punishment; just deserts.
- Enactment of the death penalty where appropriate discourages private revenge and vigilantism.

Arguments against capital punishment include:

- The death penalty is irreversible; thus the rare execution of an innocent party cannot be undone.
- No matter what the reason for execution, the state becomes a murderer, a cold-blooded killer.
- The death penalty is savage and has no place in civilized society. The society becomes as inhumane as the condemned.
- It has not been proven that the death penalty is a deterrent to crime.
- The adjudication of cases involving the death penalty is far more costly and raises difficulties in finding juries willing to find defendants guilty.
- Capital punishment has always been discriminatory. In the United States, the majority of those executed have been black (Bowers, 1974), and in 1982 blacks still represented over half of the death row population.
- All countries whose values resemble those of the United States have eliminated the death penalty.
- New scientific developments using DNA evidence have cleared a number of death row inmates.

In 1999 Governor George Ryan of Illinois put all executions on hold in Illinois. "Until I can be sure that everyone sentenced to death in Illinois is truly guilty—until I can be sure with moral certainty that no innocent man or woman is facing a lethal injection—no one will meet that fate" (Irvine, 2000, p. 5A). In Los Angeles, a police scandal revealed that 99 people were framed and convicted. Relying on DNA testing, at least 63 men convicted of murder or rape have been freed in the U.S. False confessions, bungled forensics, self-serving informants, and eyewitnesses identifying the wrong person have also taken place.

The research on capital punishment has indicated that the death penalty is no more of a deterrent than life imprisonment (Schuessler, 1952; Sellin, 1959; Reckless, 1967; Bowers and Pierce, 1975). Ultimately the capital punishment debate is a moral one that is likely to continue to be heated (Van den Haag and Conrad, 1983; Schmalleger, 1990; Bohm, 1990).

In the next chapters, we will explore other types of criminal activity, but violent crime, particularly by strangers, has had a profound impact on urban life in the United States. In many respects urban wastelands—including some downtown areas in the evening—are grim reminders of an erosion of the urban vitality that is the hallmark of civilized societies. Until society can control violent crime, our culture will fail to realize its full potential.

Summary

Violence is an ignominious blot on the history of civilization, particularly in the twentieth century. Some writers claim that violence is instinctual in humans, but most social scientists view it as a *culturally learned* phenomenon. The Violence Commission identified *six factors that may explain the high level of violence in the United States:* the Declaration of Independence, the frontier experience, immigrant competition, fear of government power, movement from rural to urban/industrial centers, and relative deprivation amidst affluence. Violence has also been intimately tied to major historical changes throughout U.S. history, although other young countries have had similar experiences.

Social and technological changes have impact on various *fads and fashions* in crime, many of which, such as train robbery, cattle rustling, and grave robbing, have now largely disappeared. Brief accounts of murder and mayhem of the past, such as Five Points, Mudgett's "murder castle," and the Jeffrey Dahmer case, indicate that horrible, violent criminals of the present such as Whitman, Williams, and Manson are not mere modern aberrations. Multiple murders may take the form of *serial murder, mass murder,* or *spree murder.*

Victim-precipitation is quite common in many violent crimes. Mendelson's types of victims include the completely innocent victim, one with minor guilt, one that is as guilty as the offender, the guilty victim, and the imaginary victim. *Conrad's typology of violent offenders* includes: culturally violent offenders, criminally violent offenders, pathologically violent offenders, and situationally violent offenders. Haskell and Yablonsky's types include violence by the state as well as by syndicates, both of which will be discussed in later chapters. VANTAGE POINT 7.1 provides general legal definitions of violent crimes.

The discussion of *psychiatry and the law* details the M'Naghten rule (NGRI—not guilty by reason of insanity, or the "right-wrong test"), the Durham decision (innocent because of mental defect), as well as the "irresistible impulse test" (mental disease at time of act) and the "substantial capacity test" (lack of capacity to appreciate criminality of the act). Many states, in reaction to cases such as Hinckley, are passing *guilty but mentally ill* laws and abolishing NGRI. The "Twinkie defense" (poor nutrition obviates guilt) was briefly discussed as yet another bizarre defense. The concept of *psychopath-sociopath-antisocial personality* is used as a catch-all constructed to describe individuals who exhibit a variety of characteristics including the lack of empathy, guilt, fear, conscience, and superego. Actual diagnosis of psychopathy has been unreliable and of questionable validity.

The *close relationship between homicide and assault* was described; in the case of the former, the victim dies. Homicides have the highest clearance rate by police because of their serious nature, the presence of witnesses, and the high priority they are given. Rape statistics have been notoriously underreported, but have improved as a result of better support for victims.

The *overall trend in homicide* in the United States has been a decline from a peak in 1933, a rise in the sixties, and new highs from the seventies to the present. The dip in the forties and fifties may actually have been due to better medical treatment procedures which masked a rise in potentially lethal violent assaults. Fragmentary historical evidence suggests even higher rates prior to 1933. The United States possesses by far the highest homicide rate among economically developed countries, although this rate is lower than those of many developing countries. Domestic homicide in the United States in this century exceeds the combined fatalities of every war the country has ever fought.

Patterns of violent crime indicate perpetration and victimization associated with large cities, males, youths, the lower class, and ghetto blacks. Unlike robbery, most violent crime occurs between intimates. A large proportion of violent crimes are committed by repeaters. Some relationship between social inequality and homicide rates is suggested. Surprisingly, one's own home is the most likely setting for one's murder, and intimates/acquaintances are the most likely perpetrators. *Alcohol consumption* has a high association with violent crimes such as homicide, assault, and rape—and particularly with vehicular homicide. *Factors associated with the typical homicide* include a backdrop of cultural/subcultural traditions of violence, personal dispute, alcohol, and guns—the last being the most telling.

Workplace violence is now the second leading cause of occupational fatalities. The United States has the *largest armed civilian population* in the world, and a relationship between firearm possession and homicide rate is strongly suggested.

Estrich distinguishes between "real rape" (aggravated, involving violence) and "simple rape" (all other types). The latter is still not recognized in the courts.

The *reluctance to report rape* has been due to stigma, sexist treatment by the criminal justice system, prosecutorial invasion of privacy, and shifting the burden of proof onto the victim. *Increased reporting* has been spurred by victim centers, female officers, better trained police, and changes in the law. While UCR data show a precipitous rise in rape in the seventies, victim data show no such increase. Rapists are generally young, lower-class, unmarried, and disproportionately black. Other analysis suggests that victims *underreport rapes* by offenders whom they know, in which case rape may more closely resemble most other violent crimes. Factors involved in most rapes are violent values, machismo, sexist views of women as legitimate victims, conducive dating-game circumstances, and alcohol. While Amir views rape as a sexual and sometimes *victim-precipitated act,* Brownmiller views it as entirely a method of male intimidation and *violence against women.* While both authors take extreme positions, there is little argument that *rape is a violent crime,* regardless of offender motivation. Many typologies of rapists suffer from after-the-fact analysis and post hoc error. More research is needed.

Robbery rates show great recent increases according to the UCR, but stability according to victim surveys. Robbery is more likely to be interracial and to involve strangers than other violent crimes, although official statistics overlook large numbers of juvenile offenders and victims.

The majority of robberies do not involve direct physical harm, although "strong-arm" robbery (mugging) and victim resistance (other than screaming) increases its likelihood. *Conklin's typology of robbers* includes professional, opportunist (the most common), addicted, and alcoholic robbers. Other research and types by McClintock and Gibson were presented.

Recent research has suggested that arrest of domestic assaulters can deter repeat offenses, at least for certain types of assaulters.

Drunk drivers kill more Americans yearly than are killed in homicides; only recently have stricter laws attempted to address this problem. Such laws may not be enforced as vigorously as had been intended. *The largest "dark figure" of violent crime has been spouse and child abuse;* there has been a virtual statistical epidemic of such crimes since the sixties. Although post hoc error also operates in this area, it appears that many of those abused as children are likely to become future abusers.

Most violent offenders do not make a career of such violations and have little commitment to crime. *Cultures/subcultures of violence* may serve to reinforce predispositions to use violence in resolving grievances. Wolfgang and Ferracuti's *subculture of violence* thesis is used to explain the disproportion of such crimes among certain lower-class minorities and the high rates in the South. Violent predators who are persistent offenders are labeled career criminals; they are responsible for a disproportionate number of crimes of violence. Programs to identify, isolate, and expedite incarceration of such offenders are viewed as a promising strategy to decrease the rate of violent crime. Recent research suggests a variety of types and patterns of *career criminality.* Better programs in family crisis intervention, alcohol treatment, and career offender rehabilitation are viewed as trends in societal reaction.

The *four justifications for punishment* are: retribution, deterrence (including incapacitation), rehabilitation, and protection and maintenance of social solidarity. Arguments in favor of and against implementation of the death penalty were briefly presented.

KEY CONCEPTS

Assault
Battery
Child Abuse
Culture of Violence
Death Penalty, Pros and Cons
DUI
Durham Decision
Factors in Rape
Felony Murder Doctrine
Forcible Rape
Gun Control
Justifications for Punishment
Manslaughter
Mass Murder
Minneapolis Domestic Violence Experiment
M'Naghten Rule
Murder, 1st Degree
Murder, 2nd Degree
NGRI
Patterns/Trends in Violent Crime
Post Hoc Error
Psychopath-Sociopath-Antisocial Personality
Rape as Violent Act
Real Rape
Serial Murder
Spouse Abuse
Statutory Rape
Subculture of Violence
Twinkie Defense
Types of Assassins
Types of Career Criminals
Types of Robbers
Types of Violent Offenders
Victim-Precipitation
Workplace Violence

REVIEW QUESTIONS

1. One of the explanations for the United States having higher violent crime rates than other developed countries is that we have had an extensive history of violence, some would say a culture of violence. Discuss this theory.
2. Discuss the three types of multiple murder and give examples of each.
3. Discuss the insanity defense standards in U.S. criminal law. What are some common misconceptions regarding the insanity defense?
4. Discuss the pros and cons of gun control. What side of this issue do you tend to favor? Defend your choice.
5. What explains the greater willingness of women to report rape in the United States? What explains the growing recognition of "acquaintance rape?"
6. What is the claimed "sexual symmetry" of interpersonal violence? Do you agree with this notion? Explain.
7. Discuss the "subculture of violence" thesis. Give some examples of countries, regions, and places where this is found.
8. What are the justifications for punishment? Give examples of the application of each.
9. Discuss some pros and cons of the death penalty debate. Which arguments do you find most persuasive? Defend your view.
10. What patterns do you see in our international comparisons of murder, robbery, and rape? What do you think explains these differences?

INFOTRAC COLLEGE EDITION RESEARCH

Vantage Point 7.1 InfoTrac College Edition Research
Review the concept of "criminal law." What are some current issues in this field?

Vantage Point 7.2 InfoTrac College Edition Research
Find an interesting article on "youth violence." How does this article contribute to our understanding of this issue?

Vantage Point 7.3 InfoTrac College Edition Research What has been the impact of the "Brady Law" on handgun violence?

Vantage Point 7.4 InfoTrac College Edition Research Locate an article on rape in another country. How was rape viewed there and were there any proposed solutions?

Vantage Point 7.5 InfoTrac College Edition Research Search the concept of "acquaintance rape." What are some current issues in this area?

Vantage Point 7.6 InfoTrac College Edition Research Search for the term "robbery" and report on some recent cases.

Vantage Point 7.7 InfoTrac College Edition Research What are some recent developments in the United States to prevent "violence against women"?

In the News 7.1 InfoTrac College Edition Research Search the term "murder" and locate some intersting international examples. How do these examples compare with our discussion of U.S. homicides?

In the News 7.2 InfoTrac College Edition Research In examining the issue of "violent crime," what role do communities play in violent crime according to the article by Matthew R. Lee?

SELECTED READINGS

Ann Auerbach. 1998. *Ransom: The Untold Story of International Kidnapping.* New York: Henry Holt and Company.
This is one of the few books to explore the neglected topic of international kidnapping. While there is little kidnapping in the U.S., it is quite common in some other countries.

Donald Black. 1999. *Bad Boys, Bad Men: Confronting Anti-Social Personality.* New York: Oxford University Press.
The psychopath, sociopath, anti-social personality remains a little understood complex. Black explores this concept and provides interesting examples.

Hugh Davis and Ted Gurr. 1969. *Violence in America: Historical and Comparative Perspectives.* New York: The New American Library.
This work brings together many of the materials provided to the *Violence Commission* (1968) regarding the history of violence in America.

Jack Douglas and Mark Olshaker. 1997. *Journey Into Darkness.* New York: Scribners.
Douglas, a retired member of the FBI's Behavioral Science Unit, gives accounts of crime profiling and investigation of serial murderers.

Egger, Steven A. 1984. "A Working Definition of Serial Murder." *Journal of Police Science and Administration.* 12: 348–57.

James Alan Fox and Jack Levin. 1985. *Mass Murder: America's Growing Menace.* New York: Plenum Press.
The world of serial murder is explored by two criminologists.

Nicholas Groth and H. Jean Birnbaum. 1979. *Men Who Rape: The Psychology of the Offender.* New York: Plenum Press.
This highly cited classic features their typology of rapists as well as excellent examples.

Peggy R. Sanday. 1990. *Fraternity Gang Rape.* New York: New York University Press.
Sanday explores the all too neglected misogynist world of college fraternities and the hidden rapes that occur on campus.

Murray A. Straus. 1994. *Beating the Devil Out of Them: Corporal Punishment in American Families.* San Francisco: Lexington.
One of America's best known family sociologists reports on a survey of spanking and concludes that it has negative impacts for future criminality and other anti-social conduct.

Marvin Wolfgang and Franco Ferracuti. 1967. *The Subculture of Violence.* London: Tavistock.
This is the classic work on the concept of "subculture of violence."

Richard T. Wright and Scott H. Decker. 1997. *Armed Robberies in Action: Stickups and Street Culture.* Boston: Northeastern University Press.
Wright and Decker report on their field study of uncaught robbers in the field.

PROPERTY CRIME: OCCASIONAL AND CONVENTIONAL

8

VANTAGE POINTS

> The more things available for theft and the lower the probability of penalty, the more larceny.
>
> —Gwynn Nettler, Criminal Careers (1982)

Introduction

Offenses against property were among the first to be punished under formal legal systems. The basic offense, theft, was referred to under English common law as *larceny,* defined simply as the taking of the property of another without the owner's consent. Although the specific legal definition varies by country and state, the various forms of larceny include: embezzlement, the receipt of stolen goods, shoplifting, employee theft, burglary (breaking and entering with intent to steal), robbery (stealing by means of force or threat of force), forgery (the fraudulent use of commercial instruments), auto theft, vandalism, and arson (the willful burning of a dwelling or property). More specific legal definitions of property crimes are presented in VANTAGE POINT 8.1.

Larceny can be committed by a variety of criminal types, ranging from the most amateur to the most highly organized or professional criminal. Figure 8.1 depicts the range of criminals involved in property offenses (though actual placement on the continuum is obviously more problematic than is suggested by a simple schema).

At the far end of the continuum is the career criminal. The notion of **career criminality** is explained by Clinard and Quinney (1973, p. 57):

> The characteristics of a fully developed criminal career include identification with crime and a conception of the self as a criminal. There is group support for criminal activity in the form of extensive association with other criminals and with criminal norms and activities. Criminality progresses to the use of more complex techniques and frequent offenses, and ultimately crime may become a sole means of livelihood. Those who have careers in crime generally engage in some type of theft of property or money.

White collar property offenses will be covered in Chapters 10 and 11, and professional criminality and organized (syndicate) criminality will be detailed in Chapters 9 and 13. This chapter will concern itself with comparing and discussing *two different types of criminal behavior systems: occasional property criminals and conventional property offenders.*

Occasional offenders are the opposite of career criminals; conventional criminals are usually unsuccessful aspirants to careers in crime (Clinard and Quinney, 1973, pp. 57, 132). **Occasional property criminals** steal or damage property on an infrequent basis. They account for most, but not all, auto theft, shoplifting, check forgery, and vandalism (see Hepburn, 1984). These offenses are committed relatively irregularly and rather crudely, with little skill or planning. In contrast, **conventional criminals** tend to commit crimes of theft-larceny and burglary on a more regular basis and, although they are at the bottom rung of the ladder or continuum of career criminality, they exhibit elements of career criminality.

In Figure 8.1, occasional property criminals represent the noncareer end of the continuum; organized and professional criminals generally exhibit characteristics of career criminality; conventional offenders exhibit the rudiments of such characteristics; and white collar and occupational offenders, because of their commitment to the conventional world, fall closer to the noncareer criminality pole of the continuum. UCR index offenses statistics show that property crimes outnumbered violent crimes nine to one.

VANTAGE POINT 8.1

Definitions of Common Property Offenses

Burglary:
The unlawful entry of a structure to commit a felony or theft. The use of force to gain entry is not required to classify an offense as burglary. Burglary in this program [UCR] is categorized into three subclassifications: forcible entry, unlawful entry where no force is used, and attempted forcible entry.

Larceny/Theft:
The unlawful taking, carrying, leading, or riding away of property from the possession or constructive possession of another. It includes crimes such as shoplifting, pocket-picking, purse-snatching, thefts from motor vehicles, theft of motor vehicle parts and accessories, bicycle thefts, etc., in which no use of force, violence, or fraud occurs. In the Uniform Crime Reports, this crime category does not include embezzlement, 'con' games, forgery, and worthless checks. Motor vehicle theft is also excluded from this category inasmuch as it is a separate crime index offense.

Motor Vehicle Theft:
The theft or attempted theft of a motor vehicle. This definition excludes the taking of a motor vehicle for temporary use by those persons having lawful access.

Arson:
Any willful or malicious burning or attempt to burn, with or without intent to defraud, a dwelling house, public building, motor vehicle or aircraft, personal property of another, etc. Only fires determined through investigation to have been willfully or maliciously set are classified as arsons. Fires of suspicious or unknown origins are excluded.

Forgery and Counterfeiting:
Making, altering, uttering or possessing, with intent to defraud, anything false which is made to appear true. Attempts are included.

Fraud:
Fraudulent conversion and obtaining money or property by false pretenses. Included are larceny by bailee and bad checks, except forgeries and counterfeiting.

Vandalism:
Willful or malicious destruction, injury, disfigurement, or defacement of any public or private property, real or personal, without consent of the owner or persons having custody or control.

Source: Federal Bureau of Investigation, 1984. *Crime in the United States, 1983,* Washington, D.C.: Government Printing Office, pp. 342–43.

InfoTrac College Edition Research
What is the "couch potato factor" in explaining rates of property crime?

FIGURE 8.1 Range of Career Criminal Involvement in Property Crime

Noncareer (Amateur) Criminality		*Career Criminality*	
Occasional Property Crime	White Collar (Occupational and Corporate)	Conventional Property Crime	Organized and Professional Crime

Occasional Property Crimes

Most occasional property criminals lack a past official history of criminality. They exhibit little progressive knowledge of criminal techniques or of crime in general. In contrast to career criminals or even conventional criminals, crime is not their sole or major means of livelihood, and they do not view themselves as criminal. Not identifying with criminal behavior, they have little of the vocabulary or "street sense" of the conventional criminal.

Under the category of occasional property offenses, discussion will center on most shoplifting, vandalism, motor vehicle theft, and check forgery. (Professional crimes of these types will be discussed later.) Surprisingly, there have not been many studies that focus on occasional and ordinary property offenders (Hepburn, 1984; Shover, 1983).

Shoplifting

The polite term for **shoplifting** used by the retail trade industry is "inventory shrinkage"—quite literally, goods have disappeared or shrunk from the total of accountable inventory. The slang term "five-finger discount" is a less polite term for this same process. While shoplifting is perhaps as ancient as trade, the post-World War II emergence of a consumer society and of large retail chains has created both a greater desire and a greater opportunity for retail theft. Inventory shortage costs in the United States for 1991 were estimated at $12.6 billion, accounting for about 2 percent of retail sales; the actual proportion may be considerably higher, depending on location, product, and clientele (Bremer, 1980; Rupe, 1980; Cherrington and Cherrington, 1982; Thompson, Hage, and Black, 1992).

The classic study on shoplifting is Mary Owen Cameron's (1964) *The Booster and the Snitch: Department Store Shoplifting,* which was based on store records and arrest data in the late 1940s; more recent research by Cohen and Stark (1974) supports her findings (see also Klemke, 1992). Cameron distinguished between "boosters" (or "heels")—professional shoplifters—and "snitches," amateur shoplifters. **Boosters** (to be discussed in detail in Chapter 9), are like other professional criminals in carefully planning and skillfully executing their thefts and in concentrating on expensive items that can be quickly converted to cash by prearrangement with a "fence" (dealer in stolen goods). On a continuum of shoplifters, between the booster and the snitch are "shadow" professionals (Stirling, 1974, p. 120; Hellman, 1970), individuals who in an avocational manner supplement their legitimate incomes by stealing. The majority of shoplifters are **snitches,** amateurs or individuals who do not view themselves as criminals. According to Cameron most are females and the vast majority have no official history of previous recorded criminal involvement.

Sensormatic Electronics Corporation, the largest maker of electronic antitheft devices, conducted a review of 166,000 theft reports from 101 retailers that showed that sneakers, earrings, and compact discs were among the most common items stolen (Huang, 1999). The male rate was only slightly larger than the female rate. While there were more adult shoplifters than juveniles, the latter were more frequently caught. Shoplifting increases during the Christmas shopping season, while shoplifting arrest rates increase in March (spring break holidays). The National Retail Federation estimates that $11 billion in losses were due to employee theft and nearly $9 billion to shoplifters (Ibid.).

Most snitches steal small, inexpensive items for their own personal use. In most instances they have on their person sufficient funds to cover the stolen items. Such snitches come from all walks of life. Nettler (1982, vol. 3, p. 106) indicates, for instance, that "theories of poverty and low education and shoplifting would surprise store owners in university towns who experience three times the amount of theft as stores in other neighborhoods."

Most snitches simply do not anticipate being caught. In the past when snitches were apprehended, most stores avoided lawsuits or possible adverse publicity by releasing the offenders after brief admonishment. When apprehended, most snitches attempt to rationalize or excuse their behavior. For the middle class offender with a psychological bent, "kleptomania," a compulsion to steal, becomes a handy rationalization.

Adventure, excitement, need, greed, or simply available opportunity or inadequate security may prove more likely reasons. Cameron claims that most snitches, when caught and faced with an unacceptable criminal self-image, cease shoplifting.

Sensormatic Electronics assumes that shoplifting tends to increase during recessions— "when the going gets tough, some of the tough go shoplifting" (Newman, 1990).

Inventory shortage costs due to shoplifting are estimated at 2 percent of retail sales.

(© Robert E. Daemmrich / Tony Stone Images

Sensormatic produces a variety of equipment, including tags attached to articles that will set off alarms if the article is taken from the store without the tag having been removed by a salesperson. Recently a number of states have passed antishoplifting statutes that enable retailers to stick shoplifters with some of the cost of security. "Civil demand" letters are sent to the accused shoplifters or their parents asking for payment of a $100 to $200 penalty in addition to the returned merchandise in return for the retailer not suing for civil damages (Schellhardt, 1990).

Most retail thefts involve employees pilfering goods. Sixty percent of inventory shrinkage is thought by retail experts to be due to employee theft, 30 percent to outside shoplifters, and 10 percent to paper errors (Rupe, 1980). Far more research on shoplifting is required to gain a definitive picture of its varieties. A mail survey of 850 employees at fifty different grocery companies by the Food Marketing Institute in 1994 found 44 percent admitted to some form of theft, although only 1 percent said they stole money from their employers (Boccella, 1994). Of those admitting theft, 32 percent ate food, 20 percent stole merchandise, 3 percent shortchanged customers, 2 percent gave refunds for unpurchased items, and 1 percent stole money. Those who were about to quit stole seven times as much as others. Males ages 16–30 on the night shift had the highest rates, while females over thirty were the most honest. A rather interesting case is one of a shoplifting ring that involved a head football coach, two teachers, and two students at Green Run High School, Virginia Beach, Virginia. In 1999, a 17-year-old honor student who was employed at Big K Mart gave away merchandise or undercharged her co-conspirators who brought goods to her checkout line (Brush, 1999).

Vandalism

Vandalism involves the willful destruction of property without the consent of the owner or agent of the owner. The term is derived from the Vandals, a barbaric Teutonic tribe that sacked Rome in the fifth century, senselessly destroying many priceless works of art. Clinard and Quinney (1973, p. 59) explain:

> Vandalism or the willful destruction of property is widespread in American society. It constitutes one of the largest categories of juvenile delinquency but occurs at all ages. It is associated with affluence for it virtually never occurs in less developed countries (except as a part of rioting) where the destruction of goods in limited supply is inconceivable. Vandalism in the United States is widespread against schools, parks, libraries, public transportation facilities, telephone and electric company facilities, traffic department equipment and housing. In one year, the public school system of Washington, D.C., reported a loss of 28,500 window panes, replaced at a cost of $118,000.

Wade (1967) identifies **three basic types of vandalism:** *wanton, predatory, and vindictive. Wanton vandalism* consists of destructive acts that have no purpose and produce no monetary gain. These are the most common acts of vandalism, "senseless" destruction practiced by juveniles "just for the hell of it" or for fun. *Predatory vandalism* comprises destructive acts for gain, such as "trashing" or destroying vending machines in order to steal their contents. *Vindictive vandalism* is undertaken as an expression of hatred, such as of a particular racial or ethnic group; examples are swastikas painted on synagogues, Ku Klux Klan attacks on black churches, or antibusing groups' assaults on school buses.

Most acts of wanton vandalism are committed by juveniles, who regard their activities as an extension of play activity, "goofing off," or "raising hell." In some U.S. communities, the evening before Halloween is called "devil's night" when juveniles play tricks that may not be restricted to throwing eggs at houses or soaping windows. Wade (1967) describes the typical pattern of wanton vandalism as consisting of:

- hanging around waiting for something to happen
- an initial exploratory gesture of vandalism by one member
- mutual conversion of others to participate
- an escalation of destructive behavior from minor to major property damage
- after-the-fact feelings of guilt and remorse combined with pleasure at having done something "naughty"

Such vandalism is rationalized by the offenders as not really criminal, since they did not plan or intend it, and realized no monetary gain. Often urban public facilities—for example, some large city subway systems—are "graced" with the unrequested graffiti of freelance "artists" or anyone who can afford a can of spray paint. New York City had great success in eliminating such graffiti through a program begun in 1984 that involved more patrolling of trains, targeting known offenders, developing logo intelligence files, special protection for clean trains in "lay-up" yards, and undercover operations in train storage areas (Kelling, 1988a).

In 1994 at Millersville State University (in Pennsylvania), students gathered for the annual "Naked Coed Relays" in which naked students raced around a stadium track, then went on a vandalism rampage when they discovered the stadium locked ("Naked Vandalism," 1994). In July 1998 more than 1500 people attending a State College, Pennsylvania, arts festival (many of them Penn State students and alumni) went on a rampage after the bars were closed. They tore down street lights, smashed storefronts, set bonfires, and even stripped naked and burned their underwear (Kinney, 1998). A bit more sinister, more organized example of wanton vandalism was "Chaos Days 95" in Hanover, Germany ("Germany's Punks," 1995) in which thousands of self-described punks converged on the city, drinking, fighting, and generally trashing the place. In some cities "tagging" is practiced; gangs tag or mark their territory with their colors, nicknames, club names, and symbols. This type of vandalism, in most instances, is an extension of wanton vandalism. Such senseless vandalism is not restricted to juveniles. Drunken fans of a team winning a Superbowl, World Series, or NCAA championship sometimes "trash" downtown areas as part of the celebration. Recent football (soccer) "hooliganism" in England has cost not only property, but human lives. The United Kingdom's National Criminal Intelligence Service carried the following advertisement on their web site in 1999 (www.ncis.co.uk/web/Help/Hotline.html):

> Are You a Fan with Intelligence?
> Do You Know Anyone Planning Trouble?
> Do You Know Where They Will Be Meeting Before or After the Game?
> Do You Know How They Will Get There?
> Do You Know Who their Mates Are?
> Anyone with information, please call our 24 hour confidential Football Hooligan Hotline on Freephone 0800-515495

One variation of predatory vandalism and theft is "bibliotheft" and destruction, in which students intentionally steal and destroy library reference materials. Rather than take notes or make copies of materials, students tear out the needed information, thus raising the cost of library materials and denying others the opportunity to use such references.

Motor Vehicle Theft

Harris and Clarke (1991) note a serious lack of scholarly attention devoted to auto theft compared to that devoted to other crimes. In 1998 there were 459 motor vehicle thefts per 100,000 population in the U.S. This was 27 percent lower than the 1989 rate. The West was highest with 581 vehicle thefts per 100,000, with 470 for the South, 396 in the Midwest, and 373 for the Northeast (FBI, 1999, p. 50). In 1998, the 1989 Toyota Camry was the most frequently stolen vehicle in the U.S. followed by the 1988 and 1990 Toyota Camry. Fourth most frequently stolen was the 1994 Honda Accord. The top 13 were all Japanese-made vehicles, with the 14th being the first American—the 1997 Ford XL pickup. The reason for the popularity of Japanese cars as targets is simply that many had been sold and their parts were in high demand. The cars are very durable and have many interchangeable parts.

Figure 8.2 presents trends in motor vehicle theft in the U.S. using the National Crime Victimization survey. The rates have declined from 19.1 per 1,000 households being victimized in 1973 to 10.8 in 1998. The National Insurance Crime Bureau assigns its highest theft risk to six- to eight-year-old models, which are stolen for their parts (Perin, 1997).

Car theft rates in the nineties began dropping, particularly in large cities in the United States, due to better vehicle security design and more precautions by owners. The highest UCR vehicle-theft rates in 1998 were in the West (580.6 per 100,000) and South (470.4), and the lowest were in the East (370.2). The Midwest was third with a rate of 396.2. The overall motor vehicle theft rate has been declining in the U.S. VANTAGE POINT 8.2 presents Interpol auto theft rates for 1998. The highest vehicle theft rates were to be found in Denmark (709.5), Australia (706.2), Norway (487.5), and Canada (547.2). The U.S. rate was 459, while the lowest rates were Russia (24.5), Austria (26.7), Japan (28.4), and Ireland (28.6).

McCaghy, Giordano, and Henson (1977) have proposed a *typology of auto thefts* which includes:

- *Joyriding:* the temporary "borrowing" of an automobile, usually by juveniles, not for theft purposes, but for temporary adventure and enjoyment.

FIGURE 8.2 Motor Vehicle Theft Rates 1973–1995

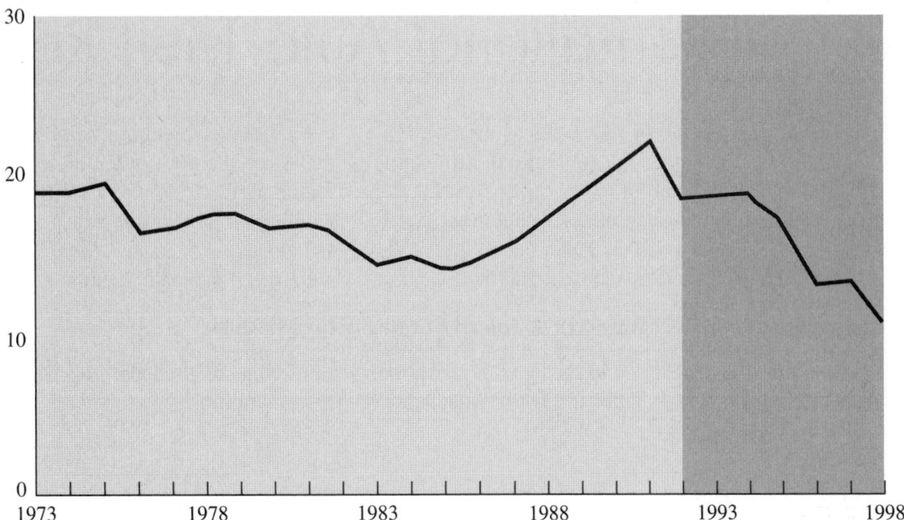

Note: The light area indicates that because of changes made to the victimization survey, data prior to 1992 are adjusted to make them comparable to data collected under the redesigned methodology.

Source: Bureau of Justice Statistics. Motor Vehicle Theft Trends www.ojp.usdoj.gov/bjs/

- *Short-term transportation:* the vehicle is stolen as a temporary means of transportation and then abandoned.
- *Long-term transportation:* the car is stolen for the purpose of providing a relatively permanent means of transportation for the thief.
- *Profit-motivated:* highly organized auto theft rings permanently alter the vehicle's identity; "chop shops" cannibalize the auto for parts; and "auto strippers" abandon the hulk after removing the valuable parts.

Because of state laws requiring auto insurance, as well as insurance regulations requiring police reports for reimbursement, auto theft is the most regularly reported of larcenies (about 90 percent reported to police). *Joyriding* is occasional property crime committed almost exclusively by juveniles on an unplanned, unskilled, and sporadic basis. A car is stolen, either by "hot wiring" (jumping the ignition) or by finding keys left in the ignition. The car is then temporarily used for cruising and abandoned when it runs out of gasoline. The intent is not to strip the vehicle of parts or to permanently possess it. Most offenders view their activity as a prank and rationalize that, since they had not intended to actually steal the car and were simply borrowing it, their behavior was not really criminal. In contrast to the occasional property criminal, profit-motivated offenders are for the most part either conventional criminals or professionals. Such profit-oriented auto thieves may range from sporadic amateur thieves (the hubcap crooks) to full-time professionals in auto theft rings.

Check Forgery

As defined in the UCR, *forgery* is "making, altering, uttering or possessing, with intent to defraud, anything false which is made to appear true." *Fraud* involves the conversion or obtaining of money or property under false pretenses. Both fraud and forgery may vary

VANTAGE POINT 8.2

International Auto Theft Rates

Auto Theft

Since the UN groups all of its crimes of theft into one category, it has no statistics for auto theft. Interpol defines auto theft as "theft of motor cars." The U.S. definition includes theft of any motor vehicle that is self-propelled and runs on a surface rather than on rails. This includes motorcycles, motor scooters, and the like; however, the overwhelming number of U.S. motor vehicle thefts are thefts of autos or trucks. Probably the most important factor in the rate of motor vehicle theft is the number of motor vehicles per capita in the country. Developed nations in which automobile ownership is widespread generally had the highest rates of auto theft.

International Auto Theft Rates, 1998, Interpol Statistics (per 100,000)

Country	*Auto Thefts (attempts)*	*actual*
United States[a]		459
Australia		706.2
Austria	(35.8)	26.7
Belgium	(376.5)	252.1
Canada		547.2
Chile		104.3
Colombia		75.3
Denmark		709.5
Ecuador		61.2
France		546.1
Germany	(137.4)	93.3
Greece		169.9
Ireland		28.6
Italy		79.6
Japan		28.4
Netherlands		239
Norway		487.5
Russia		24.5
Spain		341.4
United Kingdom		753

[a]U.S. statistics were taken from the *Uniform Crime Reports for 1998* (Federal Bureau of Investigation, 1999).
Source: International Crime Statistics, 1998. Lyons, France: Interpol Secretariat, 1999.

InfoTrac College Edition Research

Search the concept of "car theft" and examine how Palm III (handheld organizers) may pose a new threat to break-ins to cars.

from the simple actions, to be discussed in this section, to elaborate professional "con" games, to be examined in Chapter 9.

The classic study on check forgery was that of Edwin Lemert (1953), "An Isolation and Closure Theory of Naïve Check Forgery," in which he makes the distinction between "naïve check forgers" and "systematic check forgers." The majority of check forgers, those passing bad checks, are **naïve check forgers.** Faced with a financial crisis, such as an alcoholic binge, gambling debts, or creditors demanding immediate payment, they resolve this crisis by writing checks for which there are no covering funds. "Closure" is what Lemert calls this use of bad checks to solve personal problems, since it is a last resort for solving a financial crisis. In his study of naïve check forgers, Lemert found that such offenders did

FIGURE 8.3 Property Crime Rates 1973–1995

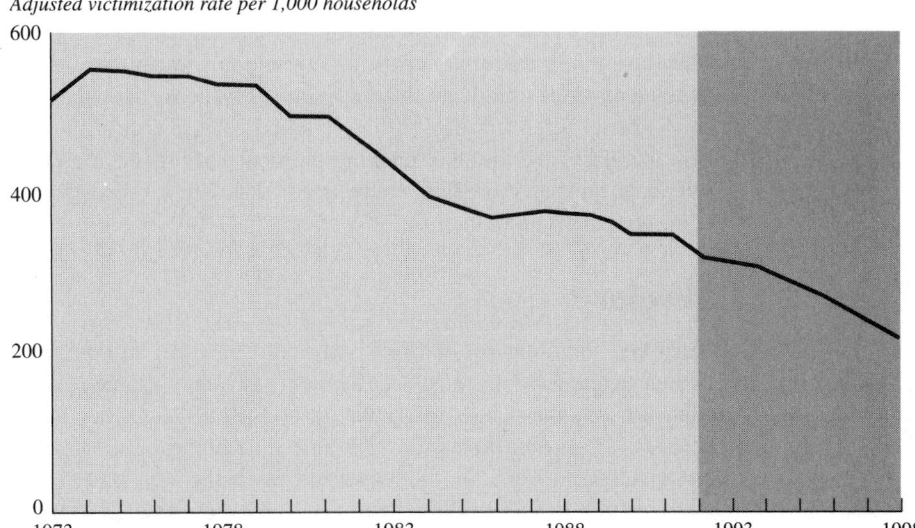

Note: Property crimes include burglary, theft, and motor vehicle theft.
The light area indicates that because of changes made to the victimization survey, data prior to 1992 are adjusted to make them comparable to data collected under the redesigned methodology.

Source: Bureau of Justice Statistics Property Crime Trends www.ojp.usodj.gov/bjs/

not identify themselves as criminals nor associate with criminals. While most amateur forgers were from middle-class backgrounds, many were also unemployed, divorced, or alcohol abusers, conditions that tended to isolate them and bring about closure.

In contrast to the amateur, the **systematic check forger** or "paper hanger" is a professional, making a good portion of his or her living passing bad checks. Most check artists work alone and associate very little with other criminals.

While there are different types of vandals, auto thieves, check forgers, and shoplifters, the majority of these offenders are described as occasional property offenders because, in contrast to conventional property offenders (to be discussed next), most commit their crimes sporadically, infrequently, and crudely. They also lack identity with criminal lifestyles.

Conventional Property Crimes

Figure 8.3 illustrates the decline in property crime in the U.S. using the NCVS since 1973. This includes burglary, theft, and motor vehicle theft.

U.S. property crimes continue to plummet since 1974, and the United States now has lower burglary and motor vehicle theft than countries such as England, Denmark, and Sweden. Why? Some point to a growing "couch potato" factor wherein more people stay home due to VCRs and cable TV. Two-car garages, which have increased in the last twenty years, protect cars and bicycles. A more affluent society has reduced demand for many stolen items, since most people already have them. The use of credit cards and less cash carrying has caused pocket picking and purse snatching to drop 53 percent from 1991–1997. Private security measures have added additional protections. More improvement is needed in that property crime rates are still about five times greater than in the 1950s (Cohen, 1998).

Conventional property criminals commit crimes of theft/larceny and burglary on a fairly persistent basis. Their activities constitute rudimentary forms of career criminality. Most such offenders identify with criminal behavior and associate with other criminals. They are often described as "semiprofessionals" or "minor leaguers" in the world of crime. They begin their careers in crime as juvenile delinquents and, even though most juvenile delinquents do not graduate to adult criminality, conventional property criminals do. Most conventional offenders exhibit a diversified offense record including theft, larceny, robbery, burglary, and the like. Lacking the skill and organization of more successful career criminals, they are more likely to be arrested and imprisoned. The majority will retire from conventional crime in their mid-twenties.

Burglary

Burglary, the unlawful entry of a structure in order to commit a felony or theft, may include actual forcible entry, unlawful entry where no force is used, or attempted forcible entry. In 1998 the U.S. burglary rate of 862 per 100,000 was the lowest in more than two decades, 32 percent below the 1989 rate. The highest rate was in the South (1045), with 896 in the West, 776 in the Midwest, and 589 in the Northeast. The estimated losses to burglary in 1998 was $3.1 billion, with the average loss of $1299 for residential burglaries and nonresidential losses at $1432 (FBI, 1999, p. 39). As a general rule, burglars are nonviolent and choose this particular brand of thievery as a relatively safe, nonconformist means of obtaining booty. VANTAGE POINT 8.3 presents international burglary comparisons for 1998. The highest burglary rates were to be found in the Netherlands (3100.4), Australia (2338.4), Denmark (1925.2), and England/Wales (1832.7). The U.S. rate was 862, while the lowest rates were Ecuador (125.2), Japan (159.2), Greece (414.9), and Norway (487.5).

Types of Burglars. Marilyn Walsh (1977), in *The Fence,* provides an interesting *typology of burglars,* a continuum from most organized to least organized. The types of burglars are: professionals, known burglars, young burglars, juvenile burglars, and junkies. The *professional,* "skilled," or "master" burglar exhibits the characteristics of professional criminal behavior. Such offenders are highly-skilled, undertake extensive planning, and concentrate on "big jobs," since burglary is often their sole livelihood. *Known burglars* are far less sophisticated, professional, or successful, even though burglary may represent a major source of their livelihood. Their operations are generally much more crude, and they rely less upon organization than do more professional burglars. Being older and more experienced than other amateur burglars, the known burglars are so-called because they are known to the police, which suggests that they are less successful than professionals. They are an excellent illustration that "practice does not always make perfect" (see Shover, 1973; Rengert and Wasilchick, 1985).

Young burglars are usually in their late teens or early twenties, have less planning or organization in their operations than professionals, and are well on their way to becoming professional or known burglars. *Juvenile burglars* are under 16 years of age and prey on local neighborhood targets chosen by chance or occasion; such juveniles often operate under the supervision of older fences and burglars. Finally, *junkies* are simply opportunist burglars and are the least skilled of such thieves.

Other analyses of burglars have basically supported Walsh's distinctions (Scarr, 1973; Repetto, 1974; Pope, 1980). Although not constituting a distinct typology as such, Repetto's case study of ninety-seven burglars provides some interesting profiles. Juvenile offenders were generally unskilled, concentrated on local easy targets of small gain, and viewed crime more as a game than as a commitment to a way of life. The 18- to 25-year-old offenders, despite previous convictions, continued to burglarize because they found low risk targets. Many in this group were drug users. Their targets were more likely to be outside their neighborhoods and produced higher gains; they made more extensive use of

VANTAGE POINT 8.3

International Burglary Rates

Burglary

For most crimes U.S. rates are much higher than European rates. Burglary is the only crime explained in the Bureau of Justice Statistics' comparison for which U.S. rates are less than double those of European countries. In 1998 a number of European countries had higher rates than the United States. Since the United Nations groups all theft into one category, it has no statistics for burglary. The Interpol definition of burglary is "breaking and entering." The U.S. definition is "the unlawful entry of a structure to commit a felony or theft. The use of force to gain entry is not required to classify an offense as a burglary."

International Burglary Rates, 1998, Interpol Data (per 100,000)

Country	*Burglaries (attempts) actual*
United States[a]	862
Australia	2336.4
Austria	1008.9
Belgium	2031.3
Canada	1155.7
Denmark	1925.2
Ecuador	125.2
England/Wales	1832.7
Finland	1757
France	676.9
Germany	1507.1
Greece	414.9
Ireland	709.6
Japan	159.2
Netherlands	3100.4
Norway	487.5
Russia	549.7
Spain	538.8
Switzerland	1172.5

[a]U.S. statistics were taken from the Uniform Crime Reports for 1998.

Source: Interpol. *International Burglary Rates, 1998.* (per 100,000) (Interpol, 1999).

InfoTrac College Edition Research

Read Lyman Rosselini's article "The High Life of Crime" and the exploits of Blane Nordahl, the "cat burglar." How typical of burglars is Nordahl?

fences. Older offenders (over 25) had extensive incarceration histories, continued at burglary because of its low risk, exercised better planning, and had fewer but higher quality targets. Such individuals were more highly committed to criminal careers. Drug users were likely to perform more burglaries than nonusers, but were more likely to work near their own neighborhoods and to be more reckless or unplanned in their operation. In contrast, the non-drug-user performed fewer but better planned burglaries. In a statistical analysis of burglaries in California, Pope (1980) found that those with no criminal records concentrated on nonresidential targets while those with records preferred residential sites. He concluded that "unlike violent crimes in which there is an interactive pattern [between type of burglar and type of burglary], burglary and other property crimes as well, may reflect more opportunity than choice" (Pope, 1980 p. 50; see also Wright and Decker, 1996).

Characteristics of Burglary. In the United States in 1998, burglary rates were highest in the South and West and lowest in the Northeast. The most popular months for burglary were July and August. Some statistics on burglary indicate that:

- In 1998, 65 percent of all burglaries involved forced entry.
- About 53 percent of burglaries took place during daylight hours.
- Two-thirds of burglaries were residential.

Figure 8.4 depicts the decline of burglary rates using the NCVS since 1973.

Litton (1990) poses the interesting contention that without insurance there would be far less property crime. Insurance companies themselves do not do enough research or use their data to discourage such crime. Hard insurance data are closely guarded rather than available for research. Insurance companies do not keep their data in a useful format and lack basic information on risks of burglary, methods of entry, and the use of protective measures.

The biggest news on burglary in the United States is its decline from 3.8 million reported cases in 1981 to 2.7 million in 1994, a nearly 30 percent drop. In New York City during this period burglary decreased more than 50 percent (Krauss, 1995). While other crimes also declined during this period, the decrease in burglaries was the most persistent. Explanations have included changes in tax write-off laws for burglary losses, better security awareness, proliferation of guns (which favors robbery), replacement of heroin with crack (the latter requiring more and quicker money), and better police investigations.

Fencing Operations

Of great importance in the crime of burglary as well as other property crime is the burglar's connections with **fences,** dealers in stolen property. "Professional or master fences," full-

FIGURE 8.4 Burglary Rates 1973–1995

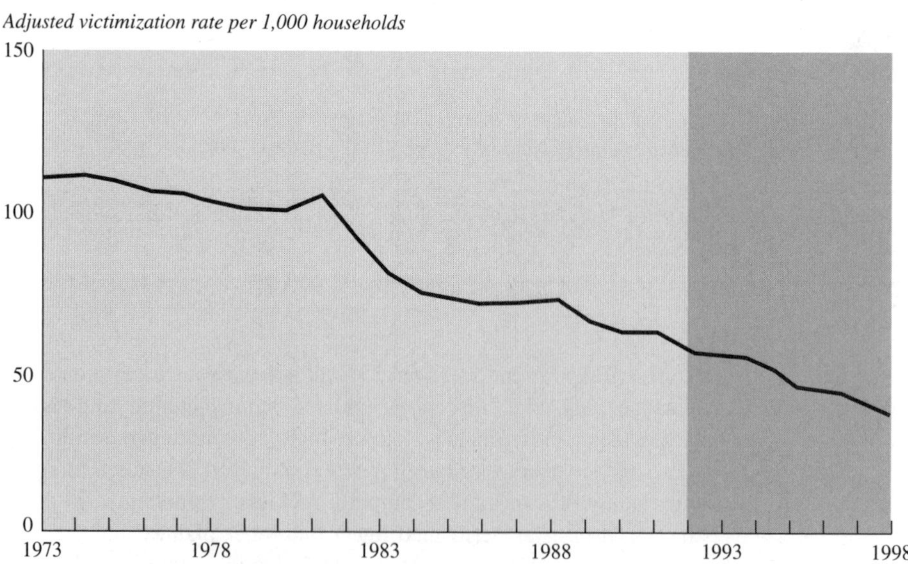

Note: The light area indicates that because of changes made to the victimization survey, data prior to 1992 are adjusted to make them comparable to data collected under the redesigned methodology.

Source: Bureau of Justice Statistics, Burglary Trends, www.ojp.usdoj.gob/bjs/

time specialists in stolen property, are essential to the operation of professional burglars and are detailed later in Chapter 9. Amateur burglars and less professional burglars are more likely to deal with a "neighborhood fence" or an "outlet fence" (Blakey and Goldsmith, 1976, pp. 1530–35). The Neighborhood Watch Program, featuring community involvement and the engraving of valuables to make them more traceable and more difficult to fence, is one strategy that has met with some success (Gilham, 1992).

Related to fencing are pawnshops, which purchase or give loans for items placed as collateral. These are often used for fencing hot goods. Recent database software designed for pawnshops, which permits monitoring of inventory and downloading periodic reports for police, may be closing one avenue of unloading hot goods (Krane, 2000).

Stings

Because conventional burglars shop around for fences, "sting operations" (police antifencing programs) have been relatively successful. In these efforts, the police pose as dealers in stolen goods. These operations, first introduced at the federal level in 1974, have obtained a 98 percent conviction rate and produced a subsequent decline in property crimes in the areas in which they have operated.

An interesting early sting operation was PFF, Inc., which ran for five months in Washington, D.C., in 1975 ("The Sting," 1976). PFF, Inc., stood for Police-FBI Fencing, Incognito, and was headquartered in an abandoned warehouse. Undercover agents hung Playboy centerfolds at the entrance; behind them a camera photographed entering customers and videotaped each transaction. Their customers assumed the proprietors were mafiosi, and one subject filled out an application for a "hit man" job in which he supplied information on a hitherto unsolved murder. Running out of "buy money"—funds with which to purchase the stolen property—PFF announced a formal party to which they invited their good customers. The customers checked their guns at the door and on entering were arrested and escorted out the back door to jail.

"Operation Road Spill" was an FBI sting operation of auto thieves conducted in South Kearney, N.J., until it was closed down in September 1994. Posing as an auto leasing agency whose shady dealers were willing to buy "hot" cars, agents purchased 120 cars, valued at $4 million, for $140,000 before arresting 30 men and seeking another 15. Half of the thieves were members of a loosely knit Brooklyn car-theft ring known as the Flatbush Pulley Gang for the device they used to pull out ignition locks. The gang had about one hundred members (McFadden, 1994).

Larceny/Theft

Most conventional property offenders tend to hustle or to be generalists in theft. Some may concentrate on burglary, but they are also opportunists, taking advantage of a given occasion to commit any variety of larceny/theft.

Larceny/theft makes up the largest category of the UCR index. With an estimated 7.4 million offenses, larceny/theft represents 59 percent of the 1998 UCR crime index total and 67 percent of all property crime. The 1998 larceny/theft rate was 2728, about 14 percent below 1989 levels. The rate was highest in the South (3075), followed by the West (2810), Midwest (2713), and the Northeast (2011) per 100,000 population. Estimates of the value of losses are conservative since many cases of small value are not reported to the police. The categories of larceny/theft and estimated average losses (1998) were: total, $650; pocket-picking, $407; purse-snatching, $362; shoplifting, $142; thefts from buildings, $1,028; from motor vehicles, $675; and from coin-operated machines, $328 (FBI, 1999, p. 44).

Larceny/theft as a category in the UCR has been correctly described as a "garbage can" (McCaghy, 1980, p. 164), a "wastebasket concept," a catch-all for miscellaneous property crime. It covers a large variety of offenses and lumps together relatively minor offenses with major professional operations.

Arson—A Special-Category Offense

It is an irresistible although admittedly bad joke to say that arson is a hot topic or a burning issue, but only since the late seventies have U.S. law enforcement officials devoted attention to this matter to a degree proportional to its seriousness. Defined by the UCR as "any willful or attempted malicious burning of a structure, vehicle, aircraft, or property of another," **arson** was added to the crime index (Part I crimes) in 1979 by congressional statute. Since arson differs from other crimes, statistics are acquired from fire services and the insurance industry as well as from law enforcement agencies. Since fires of suspicious or unknown origin are not included in the statistics and only those determined through investigation are included, the actual number of arsons is probably higher than indicated by the UCR. For 1998, 78,094 arson offenses were reported in the U.S. (FBI, 1999, p. 54).

One fire department official calls arson "the cheapest crime in the world to commit. All you need is a box of matches" ("Arson," 1977, p. 22). While the actual annual cost of arson in the United States can only be estimated, such guesses have ranged from $1 billion to $15 billion. The full cost of arson increases when we include (National Criminal Justice Reference Service, 1979):

- Death and injury to innocent citizens and firefighters
- Increased insurance premiums
- Increased taxes to support fire, police, and court services
- Inferior education facilities during reconstruction of burned-out schools
- Erosion of tax base as property values fall
- Loss of jobs at burned-out factories and businesses
- Lost revenue to damaged stores and shops

In the early nineties about 16 percent of arsons were cleared by arrest, with roughly 40 percent of those arrested under age 18, a higher percentage of juvenile involvement than for any other index crime. Arson is viewed as a special category offense because of the varying motives of its perpetrators. Based on these motives of arsonists described by Boudreau et al. (1977) and Inciardi (1970), McCaghy (1980) proposes a typology of arson that includes: profit-motivated arson, revenge arson, vandalism arson, crime concealment arson, sabotage arson, and excitement arson.

Profit-motivated arson is illustrated by insurance fraud, in which structures are purposely torched in order to collect on their insured value. Insurance companies themselves have in the past encouraged such practices by insuring questionable properties for large amounts as well as by not performing sufficient investigation before honoring claims. Arson often serves as an index of urban decay as owners unload their deteriorating properties on the companies that insure them. Profit-motivated arson is most often committed by "white collar criminals," occupational and corporate offenders, often in conjunction with professional "torches." This crime may also be committed, as in New York City, by welfare recipients seeking city assistance in gaining better accommodations, by drug addicts, or even by conventional criminals called "mango hunters" by New York City police. These offenders burn structures in order to expose and facilitate the stealing of fire resistant plumbing and fixtures (Arson, 1977, p. 22).

Revenge arson may take place out of spite or jealousy, as a means of getting even. The burn-for-hate category includes fired employees who seek revenge against employers or the jealous suitor who burned down a nightclub in which his girlfriend was socializing with someone else. This category could also serve as an example of vindictive *vandalism arson,* in which arson is an expression of hatred toward a particular group or individual. Vandalism accounts for most arsons in deteriorating urban areas. Any structure may be torched in an extension of play activity, but abandoned properties are particular targets. *Crime concealment* arson is a way to dispose of murder victims or physical evidence or to draw attention away from a crime being committed elsewhere. *Sabotage arson* covers fires set during labor or racial strife, prison riots, or other civil disturbances.

Excitement arson is often carried out by pyromaniacs, individuals who have a morbid fascination with setting and observing fires. Freudians would assign a sexual basis to pyromania, in which such individuals experience erotic satisfaction by means of arson.

Revenge arsonists resemble violent personal criminals, but arson for crime concealment may involve conventional property offenders or corporate or organized offenders. Arson as sabotage resembles political criminality, and vandalism-inspired arson is associated with the occasional property offender. Finally, pyromania is the area of the psychotic or psychopathic offender.

Criminal Careers of Occasional and Conventional Property Criminals

The distinction between occasional and conventional offenders does not lie in the legal categories of the offenses that they commit but in the way they commit crimes and the degree of their identification with the criminal world. Most snitches, amateur shoplifters, wanton vandals, joyriders, and naïve check forgers do not view their activities as criminal, have short or no official criminal records, do not commit crime as a means of livelihood, and are not "streetwise" or "crimewise," in the language of the criminal life. On the other hand, most conventional property offenders exhibit minor levels of career criminality. Many have early histories of truancy, vandalism, street fighting, delinquent gang membership, and contact with the law (Clinard and Quinney, 1973, p. 149).

The criminal careers of most conventional criminals peak in their late teens and rapidly decline after they reach their mid-twenties. Reaching ages where the full weight of criminal penalties falls on them as adult offenders and not being skilled enough to make a living at crime, most simply curtail their level of criminal involvement. Middle age and maturity, rather than any specific rehabilitation regimen, eventually reform the conventional criminal. Werthman (1967, p. 170) indicates:

> After a few years of this existence [street hustling], these boys are really at the end of their "delinquent" careers. Some get jobs, some go to jail, some get killed, and some simply fade into an older underground of pool rooms and petty thefts. Most cannot avoid ending up with conventional jobs, however, largely because the "illegitimate opportunities" available simply are not that good.

Occasional property offenders do not require criminal associations in order to commit their crimes. Their crimes are fairly easy to commit, requiring little training or skill. In contrast, conventional property offenders often operate in groups or gangs in which they learn many of the techniques of crime from their peers. While most occasional offenders maintain their commitment to conventional society and reject criminal identities, conventional offenders are only partially committed to legitimate society.

Societal Reaction

The societal reaction to occasional property offenders is relatively mild. Since most offenders lack a previous criminal record, charges are usually dismissed, or the individual is given immediate probation or a suspended sentence. In contrast, societal reaction toward conventional property offenders is relatively strong and, until recently, even stronger than that against professional, organized, and corporate criminals (Cullen et al., 1982b). Conventional offenders are of a different social class than those who make and enforce the law. This may in part explain the stronger legal processing of such offenders when compared with that of corporate offenders.

Occasional property offenders strongly identify with middle class societal values and reject criminal identification. Because of this, most offenders are deterred from future activity once they are confronted with legal action or arrest. Relative leniency with offenders is often justified, since few have previous criminal records of any substance and most are unlikely to progress into a career of crime. Since many such offenders come from the same social class as those who make and enforce the laws, they fail to fit popular public stereotypes of criminals. Diversion of such offenders into restitution programs or accelerated rehabilitation dispositions also relieves the caseload burden of the courts.

Most conventional criminal offenders tend to identify with criminal behavior and are less likely to be deterred by the threat of arrest or the stigmatization of the label of criminal. For some, criminal processing enhances their "bad" reputation on the street. The attachment of the criminal label and record may also begin a criminalization process that isolates the individual from more conventional associates and reinforces a criminal identity. Because of their relative lack of skill and organization, most conventional criminals are eventually arrested and a large proportion are imprisoned. About half of all prison inmates in the United States are conventional criminals. It is to this population that the term "revolving door of justice" has been applied because some end up doing the equivalent of "life" on the installment plan; conventional rehabilitation plans are relatively unsuccessful with this group of offenders (Martinson, 1974). Most of these offenses are outgrowths of deprived lower class environments and subcultures, and legal processing appears to have only minimal effects.

Tunnell (1991), in a study of property offenders, found most were motivated by the need for quick cash for drugs, alcohol, and living expenses. They also expressed a sense of accomplishment and of winning a game. While they feared being caught and jailed, most overcame this, and basic deterrence policy had little effect. Conservatives such as James Q. Wilson (1975 and 1983b) call for incapacitating through imprisonment larger proportions of serious conventional offenders, while liberals suggest that preventive social programs aimed particularly at reducing inequality are necessary to erase the family and social conditions that breed the next generation of losers—semiprofessional criminals.

The predatory street crime pattern is typical of juveniles, who commit such offenses for years, then cease such activity because of the threat of jail, the availability of conventional job opportunities, the development of simple maturity, or some combination of these factors. One researcher, Mercer Sullivan, claims that solutions calling for employment programs and/or of "getting tougher" with such offenders are too simplistic and that the campaign for selective incapacitation particularly misses the mark: most offenders are not identified as serious offenders until they are at least twenty years old—"over the hill in terms of street crime" (Press, 1983, p. 68). A strategy to treat such individuals as hard-core, career criminals earlier and to incapacitate them through imprisonment, assuming that 5 to 8 percent account for over 50 percent of juvenile crime (OJJDP, 1983, p. 1), ignores the fact that most teen crime careers are short; thus, such policies risk incarcerating juveniles at the very time when most would be ending their criminal careers.

Comparing white, African-American, and Latino juveniles, Sullivan says that they begin in conflict-oriented gangs that prey only on each other. Growing older, white teenagers are able to obtain part-time jobs through their parents' contacts. These jobs occupy their time and supply money, and street robberies would not be tolerated by the neighbors. African Americans and Latinos lack such employment contacts, and many become the self-employed of the streets, experimenting with muggings and burglaries, sometimes at the expense of their neighbors. Local muggers, since they tend to operate close to home, are not tolerated, and most are eventually arrested.

While the crimes of occasional property offenders point out the pervasiveness of violations among those in otherwise respectable society, offenses of conventional property offenders and the relative lack of success of correctional efforts with such offenders continue to disappoint crime control policy planners. Conventional property offenders fail to respond to the very policies, such as threat of jail and stigmatization, that appear to work very well in discouraging occasional property offenders. Conservative approaches that aim to reform individuals without concomitant efforts at social reform are likely to continue to fail.

Summary

Offenses against property, among the first to be punished under formal legal systems, include a wide variety of violations usually labeled larceny (theft). These offenses can be committed by a variety of criminal types, two of which are discussed and contrasted in this chapter: *occasional property criminals* and *conventional property criminals. Career criminality* is characterized by identification with crime, criminal self-concept, group support, association with other criminals, progression in criminality, and crime as a sole means of livelihood. While occasional property offenders are the antithesis of career criminals, conventional property violators are on the bottom rung of the ladder or continuum of career criminality. Occasional property offenders commit their crimes relatively infrequently, irregularly, crudely, and without identifying themselves as criminals. Conventional criminals commit their offenses more regularly and tend to aspire to career criminality.

Occasional property criminal behavior includes most, but not all shoplifting, vandalism, motor vehicle theft, and check forgery. Cameron distinguishes between two types of shoplifters: boosters (professionals) and snitches (amateurs). The majority of snitches have no previous criminal history, do not identify with criminality, and are deterred from future activity when threatened with formal legal processing. *Vandalism,* the willful destruction of the property of others, has been identified by Andrew Wade as consisting of three types: wanton (senseless), predatory (criminal), and vindictive (hateful). Wanton vandalism by juveniles is the most common type and usually represents an extension of play activity. Motor vehicle theft also consists of a variety of types: joyriding, short-term transportation, long-term transportation, and profit. Joyriders, who borrow a car for temporary adventure, illustrate well the occasional property criminal.

Check forgers have been distinguished by Lemert as consisting of two types: naïve check forgers and systematic check forgers. The former, who are occasional property criminals, write bad checks as a means of resolving a temporary crisis. The bad check writing is a result of closure or limited possibilities by which to solve this problem.

Conventional property criminals are those who commit larceny/theft and burglary on a fairly persistent basis, constituting a rudimentary form of career criminality. Such offenders are less skilled and organized than their professional counterparts and represent about half of the prison inmates in the United States. Most will eventually reduce or cease their "careers" by their mid-twenties. *Burglary* involves the unlawful entry of a structure in order to commit a felony or theft. This may include actual forcible entry, unlawful entry without force, or attempted entry. As a rule, burglars attempt to avoid violence. Walsh (1977) identifies types of burglars. These include: professionals, known burglars, young burglars, juvenile burglars, and junkies, in decreasing order of sophistication and organization. Other characteristics of burglars and burglary were described by Scarr (1973), Repetto (1974), and Pope (1980). Indispensable to property criminals and particularly burglars is the fence, a dealer in stolen property. Successful police "stings" or antifencing operations were described. Most conventional offenders are nonspecialists; they "hustle" or take advantage of various criminal opportunities.

Larceny/theft, which includes a broad category of property crimes, makes up over half of the index offense total and as a category constitutes a "wastebasket concept," a catchall. Property offenses are more characteristic of youthful offenders, who tend to commit crimes in groups. Criminological research on youth gangs, a problematic concept, was described as very much reflecting ideological climate. Arson, which has since 1979 been included as a UCR index offense, involves any willful or attempted malicious burning of another's property. Arson is described as a special category property offense because of the variety of motivations involved, including profit, revenge, vandalism, crime concealment, sabotage, and excitement.

Comparisons of criminal careers of occasional vs. conventional property criminals demonstrate that only the latter exhibit any level of commitment to criminality, and even they are often youthful offenders whose property criminality peaks at age sixteen, halves by age twenty, and continues to decline thereafter. *Societal reaction* to occasional offenders is relatively mild, but it is relatively strong against conventional property offenders. Anthropological field research suggests that programs aimed at identifying and getting tough with "career criminals" must be careful to examine the interplay between employment, threatened incarceration, and aging of offenders lest they get tough at the very time that most will mature out of crime (Shover, 1983).

KEY CONCEPTS

Arson
Booster
Burglary
Career Criminality
Conventional Criminality
Fences
Larceny/Theft
Motor Vehicle Theft
Naïve Check Forgers
Occasional Property Criminality
Shoplifting
Snitch
Systematic Check Forgers
Types of Arson
Types of Vandalism

REVIEW QUESTIONS

1. Compare and contrast occasional property criminals with conventional property criminals.
2. What are some different types of and trends in shoplifting?
3. What are the three types of vandals and how do they differ in their motivations?
4. What are some trends and patterns in auto theft both nationally and internationally?
5. Discuss international patterns in burglary. Why do you think property crimes are declining in the U.S.?
6. Why is arson described as a "special-category" offense?
7. How do the criminal careers of occasional and conventional property criminals differ?
8. Discuss how the societal reaction differs for conventional property criminals from occasional property criminals.
9. Why do occasional property offenders not fit our public conceptions of criminals?
10. Discuss fencing operations and their importance to burglars. What are stings and how have they been effective weapons against burglars?

INFOTRAC COLLEGE EDITION RESEARCH

Vantage Point 8.1 InfoTrac College Edition Research
What is the "couch potato factor" in explaining rates of property crime?

Vantage Point 8.2 InfoTrac College Edition Research
Search the concept of "car theft" and examine how Palm III (handheld organizers) may pose a new threat to break-ins to cars.

Vantage Point 8.3 InfoTrac College Edition Research
Read Lyman Rosselini's article "The High Life of Crime" and the exploits of Blane Nordahl, the "cat burglar." How typical of burglars is Nordahl?

SELECTED READINGS

Elijah Anderson. 1990. *Streetwise: Race, Class and Change in an Urban Community.* Chicago: University of Chicago Press.
Black sociologist Elijah Anderson presents a field study of inner city crime and social change. A very readable, sensitizing study.

Mary Owen Cameron. 1964. *The Booster and the Snitch.* New York: The Free Press.
This is the classic study of shoplifters using a secondary analysis of the records of retail theft of private department stores.

Marshall B. Clinard and Richard C. Quinney. 1994. *Criminal Behavior Systems: A Typology.* 3rd edition. Cincinnati: Anderson.
This is an update of the classic work that presented one of the most widely used typologies of criminal behavior.

James Inciardi. 1970. "The Adult Firestarter: A Typology," in *Criminology.* 8, August, pp. 145–155.
An excellent typology and analysis of arsonists.

Carl Klockars. 1974. *The Professional Fence.* New York: The Free Press.
This is a very readable example of a case study of the world of "Vince Swaggi," a professional fence in Philadelphia.

Frank Scarpitti and Amie L. Nielsen, editors. 1999. *Crime and Criminals.* Los Angeles: Roxbury.
An excellent selection of readings that illuminate many of the issues discussed in the text.

Darrell Steffensmeier. 1986. *The Fence: In the Shadow of Two Worlds.* Totowa, NJ: Rowman and Littlefield.
Sociologist Darrell Steffensmeier's case study of the world of professional fence "Sam Goodman."

Kenneth Tunnell. 2000. *Living Off Crime.* Chicago: Burnham.
Kenneth Tunnell's in-depth interviews of jailed property criminals opens the door to a little explored world.

Richard Wright and Scott Decker. 1994. *Burglars on the Job.* Boston: Northeastern University Press.
Wright and Decker interview burglars in the field to gain information on their careers, modus operandi, and motivations.

Professional Crime

Vantage Points

> There's a sucker born every minute.
> —P.T. Barnum

> . . . because that's where the money is.
> —Willie Sutton
> (when asked why he robbed banks)

In 1996 a rebellion broke out in formerly Communist Albania. Citizens blew up bridges, attacked police stations, and looted military arsenals. Armed with military weapons including tanks and patrol boats, they took over areas of the country. The reason for the revolt: anger on behalf of thousands of Albanians who had been swindled in a huge Ponzi scheme. Many of those involved in organizing the scam were high government officials. Reports claim that nearly every Albanian was victimized by the scheme (Nelan, 1997; Simon and Hagan, 1999, p. 88). The Albanian government collapsed as a result of a professional crime, the Ponzi scheme, to be discussed in this chapter.

On the rainy night of October 29, 1964, Roger Clark dropped off Jack Murphy and Allan Kuhn at the American Museum of Natural History in Manhattan. Jack "Murph the Surf" Murphy and his accomplice scaled an eight-foot fence, climbed a ladder from a courtyard to a fourth-floor ledge, opened a window, lowered themselves into the museum's Morgan Hall of Minerals and Gems, and proceeded to steal twenty-four precious stones. These included the Midnight Star Sapphire, the DeLong Star Ruby, and the celebrated sapphire, Star of India. The latter was a most extraordinary gem. Weighing more than 563 carats, it was the largest such stone in the world and was estimated to be worth more than $1 million in 1986 (Preston, 1986, 210–11).

The "Star of India" burglary bore an uncanny resemblance to the plot of the then-current film *Topkapi,* which was about a jewel theft at the Topkapi Palace Museum in Istanbul. Murphy and his accomplices claimed to have been inspired by the film ("Museum Jewel Robbery," 1964, p. 23). Prior to the "Star of India" burglary they had cased the Guggenheim Museum and the Metropolitan Museum of Art before settling on the American Museum of Natural History as their target. Ten days of reconnaissance at the museum included a dry-run nighttime burglary. But despite their elaborate plans and successful heist, the trio were shortly arrested and convicted. Of the three thieves, Murphy attracted the most press attention because of his glamorous Miami beachboy lifestyle. This same "charmer" would later carry out other jewel thefts, including the strong-arm robbery of a $25,000 diamond ring from actress Eva Gabor, and would eventually be convicted of the double murder of two women, for which he served prison time until 1984. Murphy was even the object of a made-for-television movie starring Robert Conrad in 1975. "Murph the Surf" and his accomplices represent the more glamorized, romanticized view of professional criminals. But what, in fact, are professional criminals (Hagan and Benekos, 1992, p. 3)?

The Concept of "Professional Crime"

In sociology, the **concept of profession** refers to occupations that require (a) esoteric, useful *knowledge* acquired after lengthy training, and (b) a claimed *service* orientation and code of ethics that permit occupations to attempt to obtain (c) *autonomy* or independence of operation and various concomitants such as high prestige and remuneration (Hagan, 1975). This knowledge-service-autonomy dimension of the professions is inapplicable to criminals and criminal activity. Mack (1972) prefers the term *able criminal,* while Klein (1974) suggests the concept "grifter" (one who acquires money illicitly) as a more appropriate construct. Some field studies of criminal subjects indicate that they do not use the category of "professional criminal" (Letkemann, 1973; Prus and Sharper, 1977; Steffensmeier, 1986). However, labeling certain types of criminals as "professionals" is widespread in the literature, which justifies treating professional crime as a separate category,

Jack (Murph the Surf) Murphy wearing dark glasses, is taken by a detective from a police station where he was held overnight on a hotel-robbery charge.

(© UPI / Bettmann Newsphotos)

though we will consider other constructs. Cressey (1969, p. 45) warns that many skilled criminals are simply slightly better than other crooks at lying, cheating, and stealing and that we should be careful about calling them "professionals." Studies of career criminals by Petersilia and associates (1977) suggest the term *intensives* for those who commit more sophisticated crimes and face lesser chances of arrest or conviction. Therefore, while the professional criminal is not truly a professional in the sociological sense, the term is appropriate in reference to those who earn a considerable portion of their livelihood in criminal pursuits.

Characteristics of Professional Crime

The benchmark in the United States for analysis of professional criminal behavior was Edwin Sutherland's (1937) *The Professional Thief,* a work based on interviews and a detailed case study of a professional thief/confidence man with the pseudonym "Chic Conwell." In his original formulation Sutherland saw the professional thief as characterized by crime as a sole means of livelihood, careful planning, reliance on technical skills and methods, and a migratory lifestyle. Professional thieves have a shared sense of belonging, rules, codes of behavior, and a specialized language (Sutherland, 1937, pp. 3–4).

Professional crime is a sociological rather than a legal construct. What distinguishes professional crime from other crimes is not the legal definition of the behavior, but the way the crimes are performed. Clinard and Quinney (1973, p. 246) identify the following features of professional crime:

1. Crime is the criminal's sole livelihood and is engaged in for economic gain.
2. The criminal career is highly developed.
3. Considerable skill is involved.
4. High status in the criminal world is bestowed on professional criminals.
5. Professional criminals are more successful than others at avoiding detection and imprisonment.

Argot

Acts of professional criminals differ from those of less professional criminals only in the distinctive manner in which they are committed. Professional crime primarily involves the relatively safe and consistent stealing of large sums of money on a systematic, rational, planned, skillful, and nonviolent basis. Professional criminals attempt to avoid "heat," or the daring and bravado characteristic of many amateur criminals, which tends to attract public attention and often subsequent police action. Distinctive **argot** or *specialized language* is also characteristic of the world of professional crime. Arthur Judge's *The Elizabethan Underworld* (1930), Henry Mayhew's *London's Underworld* (1862b), and McMullan's *The Canting Crew: London's Criminal Underworld 1550–1700* (1984) provide some of the argot of seventeenth-century Elizabethan professional criminals (see also Taylor, 1984). Sutherland's informant, "Chic Conwell," provides us with the criminal argot of the United States in the early twentieth century (Sutherland, 1937).

Early Twentieth-Century U.S. Argot.

Cannons: professional pickpockets
Heels: sneak thieves who operate in stores and offices
Boosters: professional shoplifters
Pennyweighting: stealing from jewelry stores by substituting fake lookalikes
Hotel prowling: stealing from hotel rooms
The con: confidence games
Hanging paper: passing bad checks, money orders, and other commercial paper
The shake: extorting money from others who are criminally involved

Maurer (1964, p. 55) quotes a professional pickpocket who was asked to explain in court what he had done:

> Well, Judge, your honor I was out gandering around for a soft mark and made a tip that was going to cop a short. I eased myself into the tip and just topped a leather in Mr. Bates' left prat when I blowed I was getting a jacket from these two honest bulls. So I kick the okus back in his kick and I'm clean. Just then this flatfoot nails me, so here I am on a bum rap. All I crave is justice, I hope she ain't blind.

A Model of Professional Crime

Figure 9.1 depicts a continuum **model of professional crime.** Like that of the "organized crime continuum" in Chapter 13, the purpose of this model is to underline the fact that there are no hard-and-fast divisions between professional and amateur crime; the professionalism of criminal activity is a matter of degree rather than of kind. Thus, the greater the extent to which an individual's criminal activity involves key factors—crime as a sole livelihood, an extensive criminal career, skill, high status in the criminal world, the successful avoidance of detection and/or immunity from prosecution, and a criminal subculture and organization—the greater the likelihood that such activity can be labeled "professional crime." The concept, however, is an "ideal type," a heuristically useful overgeneralization that is unlikely to exist in pure form.

Professional crime is similar to legitimate occupations such as entertainment and professional sports in that it is a "skyrocket profession." For those who succeed, it can be a glamorous life of fast living; however, it shares another characteristic with these fields, and that is that "many are called, but few are chosen." Many semiprofessional criminals who might occupy a middle ground on the continuum are unable to survive with crime as their sole livelihood—they are not good enough. Most eventually leave the world of crime because they simply cannot make a living at it; they are less skillful, enjoy less status in

FIGURE 9.1 A Model of Professional Crime

Amateur Crime		*Professional Crime*
Occasional	(Source of Income)	Full-time
Short Duration	(Extent of Career)	Lifelong
Little	(Level of Skill)	Extensive
Low	(Status)	High
Unsuccessful	(Avoidance of Detection)	Successful
None	(Association with Criminal Subculture)	Extensive
None	(Level of Planning)	Extensive
No	(Employment of "the Fix")	Yes

the criminal world, and are less successful at avoiding detection. Although they belong to criminal subcultures to a degree, these subcultures lack the network of talent and successful contacts that the more professional criminal enjoys. Finally, such less professional offenders generally commit crimes that require or involve less planning and have less success in avoiding prosecution and incarceration.

In Chapter 8, career criminality was said to include characteristics such as identification with crime, extensive association with other criminals, progression and specialization in crime, as well as crime as a sole means of livelihood. Professional and organized criminals best fit this model, though differences between these types are often a matter of degree rather than kind. Similarly, criminal pursuits such as videotape/motion picture pirating, drug sales, prostitution, and pimping are pursued by criminals of various degrees of sophistication, with career criminals generally more persistent and successful in their activities. Professionals tend to "freelance" or be less tied to relatively permanent criminal organizations than their organized crime counterparts. In the last analysis, however, criminologists have not arrived at a consensus in categorizing these activities.

Edelhertz's Typology

Edelhertz (1970) has developed a typology of white collar crime. Figure 9.2 presents one of Edelhertz's categories of white collar crime, which is more professional than occupational or corporate in nature. The main distinction between professional crime and occupational/corporate crime is that in the former the sole purpose of the business is to perform criminal activity, while in the latter crime is incidental to a legitimate business or professional service. Some offenses listed in Figure 9.2 are not simply professional crimes but, following the model, become so to the degree that they involve the characteristics of professional criminal activity.

Scams

Scam is a criminal slang term used to refer to *various criminal techniques, "hustles," or operations.* Many criminal operations that may be described as examples of professional crime or sometimes even as white collar crime (since they are committed by stealth, nonviolently, and by persons of apparent respectability) are in fact semiprofessional in nature.

FIGURE 9.2 Edelhertz's Categories of White Collar Crime (Professional Crime)

White collar crime as a business, or as the central activity.

1. Medical or health frauds
2. Advance fee swindles
3. Phony contests
4. Bankruptcy fraud, including schemes devised as salvage operations after insolvency of otherwise legitimate business
5. Securities fraud and commodities fraud
6. Chain referral schemes
7. Home improvement schemes
8. Debt consolidation schemes
9. Mortgage milking
10. Merchandise swindles:
    a. Guns and coins
    b. General merchandise
    c. Buying or pyramid clubs
11. Land fraud
12. Directory advertising schemes
13. Charity and religious frauds
14. Personal improvement schemes:
    a. Diploma mills
    b. Correspondence schools
    c. Modeling schools
15. Fraudulent application for, use, and/or sale of credit cards, airline tickets, etc.
16. Insurance fraud:
    a. Phony accident rings
    b. Looting of companies by purchase of overvalued assets, phony management contracts, self-dealing with agents, intercompany transfers, etc.
    c. Fraud by agents writing policies to obtain advance commissions
    d. Issuance of annuities or paid-up life insurance, with no consideration, so that they can be used as collateral for loans
    e. Sales by misrepresentation to military personnel or those otherwise uninsurable
17. Vanity book and song publishing schemes
18. Ponzi schemes
19. False security fraud, i.e., Billy Sol Estes or De Angelis types of schemes
20. Purchase of banks, or control thereof, with deliberate intention to loot them
21. Fraudulent establishing and operation of banks or savings and loan associations
22. Fraud against the government:
    a. Organized income tax refund swindles, sometimes operated by income tax "counselors"
    b. AID frauds: i.e., totally worthless goods shipped
    c. F.H.A. frauds:
       (1) Obtaining guarantees of mortgages on multiple family housing far in excess of value of property with foreseeable inevitable foreclosure
       (2) Home improvement funds
23. Executive placement and employment agency frauds
24. Coupon redemption frauds
25. Money-order swindles

Source: Herbert Edelhertz, 1970, *The Nature and Prosecution of White-Collar Crime,* National Institute of Law Enforcement and Criminal Justice, Washington, D.C.: Government Printing Office, pp. 73–75.

They involve little skill, and they prey on gullible victims. **Confidence (con)** games meet this definition. These may be called "confidence" because they rely on winning the confidence of the victim in order to steal from him or her. Another possible origin of the term *con* is "cony," meaning dupe or victim. Sometimes called "flim flam" or "bunko" or "short cons," such scams come in an infinite variety, although some of the more common ones are disturbingly familiar and successful. It is surprising to many that most short con artists at the present time are women, as are most of their victims.

The **pigeon drop** is one of the best known simple confidence swindles. Here is a description of an actual pigeon drop that has been repeated hundreds of times with remarkable success:

> A 61-year-old widow (the "mark" or victim) gave her $3,596 in life savings to two con artists in a downtown five-and-dime with the assumption that she would receive this back and $6,000 besides. A woman (one of the con artists—the "catch woman") approached the widow while she was shopping in a department store, began talking to her and a few seconds later a third woman (accomplice) appeared. The third woman said she had found a wallet with $20,000 in cash and a note saying that the money should be delivered to Castro in Cuba. She showed them some loose twenties (the rest of the roll of money actually consists of a "Michigan bankroll" of phony money), and the three women discussed the situation for a while. Then the woman with the wallet convinced them that she would phone "Attorney Burger," a fictitious man, who she said worked in City Hall.
>
> After a fake phone conversation with him, she reported that he asked all three to put up some money to show good faith ("good faith deposit") until the money could be divided three ways, with $2,000 for the lawyer. The woman who had first spoken to the victim said she could come up with $4,000 from a recent insurance claim, and she supposedly went to get it. Then the other woman took the victim to a bank for her life savings, which she turned over to them in the ladies' room of a five-and-dime. She was told to report to "Attorney Burger at City Hall" at 4:30 p.m. She arrived at the appointed time and came to the grim realization that she had been duped. "I've read about that one in the papers, but I never thought it could happen to me," she told police ('Con Game,' 1972, p. 11A).

Many victims are so humiliated that they do not even report their victimization to the police. Short cons such as the pigeon drop usually prey not upon the affluent, but on middle-aged, retired, and widowed working-class types, particularly females.

The **badger scam** also preys on the naïveté of victims.

> An alert teller at a savings and loan association alerted police when an obviously distressed 81-year-old man withdrew his life savings of $10,622—in cash. He had been visited on a number of occasions by a 19-year-old girl who had indicated that she represented a Bible Institute. During the last visit, a man feigning the role of an outraged father burst into the apartment and accused the victim of having illicit relations with his daughter. His paternal rage could, however, be forgotten for the right price (Langway and Smith, 1975, p. 67).

In the **bank examiner's scam,** swindlers pretend to be government investigators who are seeking the cooperation of the victim in order to catch a dishonest bank teller. The mark (victim) is asked to withdraw money and turn it over to the investigators, who will mark it in order to apprehend the dishonest employee. Obviously, government agencies are not so hard up that they have to use the money of private citizens in order to conduct their undercover operations.

"Too-good-to-be-true" opportunities for easy money, and "get-rich-quick" schemes lure victims. The following examples are illustrative:

- *Postal fraud* is widespread. It includes skipping town with payments for orders, precollecting fees for fake franchises, and offering to arrange a "guaranteed" business loan or employment for an "advance fee"—then failing to deliver as promised. Beware of paying advance fees for estates that have been left to you by unknown people, chain letters, work-at-home schemes, and sales of far-off land.

- Hundreds of companies are sending out millions of postcards guaranteeing rewards for "prize winners" if the recipients send money for shipping and postage. The prizes are either nonexistent or virtually worthless.
- *Circus grifting* (dishonest carnival games) is another example of a short con. Grifters will often work with a "shill," or plant, who pretends to be a winning customer. Such "con games" were quite common in traveling carnival shows that worked midwestern county fairs. Hidden pedals for gambling wheels, switched rings for the ring toss, loaded dice for the "crap" game, fake "two-headed" ladies or men purported to be half-human, half-ape, and willing customers ever eager to part with their money embody P.T. Barnum's slogan, "There's a sucker born every minute."
- In this same vein of "short cons," readers should beware of *snake oil* salespersons or offers to increase breast size or sexual prowess or to sell diplomas (Stewart and Spille, 1988). In one home-repair scam that targeted the elderly, the swindler would short out electric wires, start fires near furnaces, or release bugs or mice in order to create problems in need of solution. Claiming to be waterproofing the customer's roof with a clear silicone-based liquid, he would spray water on the roof ("Home Repair Scam," 1986).
- By 1992 the Federal Communications Commission finally began cracking down on the abuse of "900" telephone numbers, which charge the unwary exorbitant fees per minute for "phone sex," "advice," "astrology," anything to keep "suckers" on the line. Needless to say, when telephone solicitors call claiming to be checking credit card numbers, one should never reveal one's account number.
- *Toll call fraud,* the unauthorized use of others' calling card numbers, is facilitated by con artists who stake out airports with binoculars and sell telephone numbers.
- The *three-card monte* is the floating card sharp's equivalent of the shell game and is common in Times Square, New York. Monte dealers deftly shuffle three bent cards atop a cardboard box while palming a bettor's selection (whose chance of winning is zero). They often have six to eight confederates (shills) in the crowd who fake winning (see McNamara, 1995).

Peter Maas (1975) in *King of the Gypsies* describes the elaborate gypsy con game of **boojo,** in which superstitious victims, usually visitors to fortune-telling parlors, are conned into turning over their life savings in cash in order to have a "curse" removed. The gypsy con artist removes the cash instead. In one boojo operation a Warren, Missouri, farm couple was warned that the darkness or hex had been placed on them by their family and not to talk to them. A long string of evil omens and misfortunes were forecast, including fatal cancer and gangrene. Each could be removed by paying the gypsy woman money. The family lost over $150,000 in the scam before they finally wised up (O'Connor, 1987, p. 41).

A recurring scam for the past couple of decades has been the "Nigerian fee fraud scam" or 419 scam (named for the section of Nigerian criminal law applicable to the scam). The victim is contacted via mail or e-mail by someone claiming to be a "Nigerian official" with an offer to share millions of dollars if the victim would provide an account in which funds can be hidden, after which the victim is promised a share in the payoff. Once the victim's account number is obtained, the con artists drain the account. The victims pay processing fees, travel costs, and bribes in anticipation of rewards. The scam artists ask for more and more money to assist in the transfer of funds.

Many scams are on the edge of slick business practices. Used car dealers have been known to leave spouses alone to talk over the deal in a "bugged" office. Or after the agreement seems to be made and the papers are almost filled out, they use "the close and bump." Pretending to take the papers with the agreed-upon price to the boss in the back room, the salesperson then says that the boss wants $100 more. Some may even roll back odometers.

In old cars, if the one-tenth-mile digit vibrates while the car is moving, the odometer has probably been rolled back (Bennett and Clagett, 1977, p. 142).

Big Cons

Maurer's *The Big Con*

David Maurer in *Whiz Mob* (1964) and *The Big Con* (1940) describes the following steps in the big con (Maurer, 1964, pp. 15–16):

1. Putting up the mark (investigating and locating likely victims)
2. Playing the con (gaining the confidence of the victim)
3. Roping the mark (steering the victim to meet the inside man or woman)
4. Telling the tale (showing the victim how he or she can make big money dishonestly)
5. Giving the convincer (permitting the victim to make a profit)
6. Having the victim invest further
7. Sending the victim after more money
8. Playing the victim against the big store and fleecing him or her
9. Getting the victim out of the way
10. Cooling out the mark (having the victim realize that he or she cannot turn to the law), and
11. Putting in the fix (bribing or influencing action by the law).

While not all big confidence games involve all the steps Maurer describes, each example to be discussed demonstrates variations of these steps. Wealthy marks, such as business executives, entertainment personalities, and, recently, wealthy professionals (such as doctors and dentists who are hunting for "tax shelters" or even greater affluence), are ideal targets for those on the lookout for "fingering the score."

"Yellow Kid" Weil—Master Swindler

One of the most famous American swindlers of all time was Joseph "Yellow Kid" Weil, who was given the nickname from a popular cartoon strip character of the 1890s. Elaborately attired and exuding success in his lavish lifestyle, Weil made an estimated eight million dollars in nearly forty years of the big con. Weil made his money peddling worthless oil stocks to bankers (Nash, 1975, vol. 2, pp. 410–14). Just one example of "Yellow Kid's" ingenious frauds was based on his belief that people would trust anything in print. He located an article concerning an investor who had made a fortune from purchasing an abandoned gold mine. Next he had a friend who was a printer reproduce facsimiles of the article, with Weil's own picture in place of the investor's. Weil's first stop in each town was the local library, where he switched the fake copy for the original. He later assured doubting victims that they could check out his credentials in the local library. After fleecing his victims, he was always careful to replace the original article in the library before moving on to the next town (Nash, 1975, pp. 411–12).

VANTAGE POINT 9.1 describes the insidious crime of "identity theft."

Ponzi Schemes

Perhaps the most legendary swindler of all times was Charles "Get Rich Quick" Ponzi, whose *modus operandi* has now inherited his name—Ponzi schemes. A **Ponzi scheme** *pays off early investors with money obtained from later investors in a doomed enterprise.* In 1919 Ponzi discovered that postal return coupons could be purchased overseas and redeemed in the United States at anywhere from 100 to 300 percent profit. He offered investors 40 per-

Charles "Get Rich Quick" Ponzi gave his name to the Ponzi scheme. Ponzi swindled $15 million from 40,000 people shortly after World War I.

(© Bettmann / Corbis)

cent profit in ninety days. He then paid off his first investors sooner and with larger dividends than promised. Once the word got around, investors were beating down his door. Many preferred to reinvest rather than to withdraw their money. As investors multiplied, he ran out of the product (coupons) and simply operated a **pyramid scheme** in which *early customers were paid off with money obtained from later ones.* Ponzi lived like a king and was rumored to have taken in over $15 million. When it was discovered that Ponzi had a criminal record that included forgery, the house of cards fell. Investors demanded their money; but of course he had spent it all. After serving various sentences, he eventually died in 1971 in a Brazilian charity ward, but the legacy of Ponzi's technique lives on. Ponzi schemes prey on greedy victims, who want something for nothing (Nash, 1975, vol. 2, pp. 337–41).

In a Ponzi scheme of immense proportions, the Foundation for New Era Philanthropy, which declared bankruptcy in 1995 and was run by John G. Bennett, Jr., scammed about three hundred churches, museums, universities, and philanthropists—including former Treasury Secretary William Simon and venture capitalist Laurance Rockefeller—of as much as $500 million. Paying off early investors with money from later investors, Bennett convinced organizations such as Drexel University and the Philadelphia Orchestra to invest millions. The money would be held for a period of six months, at which time it would be matched by an anonymous donor, thus doubling the gift. No such anonymous donors existed (Stecklow, 1996).

Also in 1995, Steven Hoffenberg of Towers Financial Corporation of New York City, pleaded guilty in a $460 million Ponzi scheme, which consisted largely of a phony financial empire with inflated profits and fictitious revenue that created the impression of a major health-care financing company (Henriques, 1995).

The explosion of financial services, deregulation, and the bewildering number of new investments available to the public all contribute to the resurgence of Ponzi schemes in the 1990s. Many of the new Ponzi schemes rely on "the herd instinct" for new investors.

VANTAGE POINT 9.1

Identity Theft

What Is Identity Theft?

Identity theft involves acquiring key pieces of someone's identifying information, such as name, address, date of birth, social security number, and mother's maiden name, in order to impersonate them. This information enables the identity thief to commit numerous forms of fraud that include, but are not limited to, taking over the victim's financial accounts, opening new bank accounts, purchasing automobiles, applying for loans, credit cards, and social security benefits, renting apartments, and establishing services with utility and phone companies.

The following information provides the actions recommended by the U.S. Postal Inspection Service and the financial industry to help reduce the likelihood of becoming a victim of identity theft. The last section provides names and phone numbers of the agencies referred to throughout this pamphlet.

Preventive Actions

- Promptly remove mail from your mailbox after delivery.
- Deposit outgoing mail in post office collection mailboxes or at your local post office. Do not leave in unsecured mail receptacles.
- Never give personal information over the telephone, such as your social security number, date of birth, mother's maiden name, credit card number, or bank PIN code, unless you initiated the phone call. Protect this information and release it only when absolutely necessary.
- Shred preapproved credit applications, credit card receipts, bills and other financial information you don't want before discarding them in the trash or recycling bin.
- Empty your wallet of extra credit cards and IDs, or better yet, cancel the ones you do not use and maintain a list of the ones you do.
- Order your credit report from the three credit bureaus once a year to check for fraudulent activity or other discrepancies.
- Never leave receipts at bank machines, bank counters, trash receptacles, or unattended gasoline pumps. Keep track of all your paperwork. When you no longer need it, destroy it.
- Memorize your social security number and all of your passwords. Do not record them on any cards or on anything in your wallet or purse.
- Sign all new credit cards upon receipt.
- Save all credit card receipts and match them against your monthly bills.
- Be conscious of normal receipt of routine financial statements. Contact the sender if they are not received in the mail.
- Notify your credit card companies and financial institutions in advance of any change of address or phone number.
- Never loan your credit cards to anyone else.
- Never put your credit card or any other financial account number on a postcard or on the outside of an envelope.
- If you applied for a new credit card and it hasn't arrived in a timely manner, call the bank or credit card company involved.
- Report all lost or stolen credit cards immediately.
- Closely monitor expiration dates on your credit cards. Contact the credit card issuer if replacement cards are not received prior to the expiration dates.
- Beware of mail or telephone solicitations disguised as promotions offering instant prizes or awards designed

During its initial stages the scheme may zero in on members of a specific pro football team, a law office, or a military base and then rely on initial victims to enthusiastically recruit new customers.

In 2000, Ponzi schemer Patrick Bennett was sentenced to 30 years in prison for swindling thousands of small investors out of $700 million. He sold phony "lease-backed securities," investments in leases for photocopying fax machines and other office equipment. Many of these were sold to duplicate sets of investors or the contracts did not even exist ($700 Million Ponzi Schemer, 2000).

As of this writing the FBI is still seeking Shalom Weiss, who vanished rather than face his sentence of 845 years in February 2000. His Ponzi scheme is believed to have siphoned

VANTAGE POINT 9.1—*Continued*

solely to obtain your personal information or credit card numbers.

Internet and On-Line Services

- Use caution when disclosing checking account numbers, credit card numbers or other personal financial data at any Web site or on-line service location unless you receive a secured authentication key from your provider.
- When you subscribe to an on-line service, you may be asked to give credit card information. When you enter any interactive service site, beware of con artists who may ask you to "confirm" your enrollment service by disclosing passwords or the credit card account number used to subscribe. Don't give them out!

Who to Contact for Copies of Your Credit Report

- Equifax
  P.O. Box 105873
  Atlanta, GA 30348-5873
  Telephone: 1-800-997-2493
- Experian Information Solutions
  (formerly TRW)
  P.O. Box 949
  Allen, TX 75013-0949
  Telephone: 1-888-397-3742
- TransUnion
  P.O. Box 390
  Springfield, PA 19064-0390
  Telephone: 1-800-916-8800

Action Steps for Identity Theft Victims

- Contact all creditors, by phone and in writing, to inform them of the problem.
- Call your nearest U.S. Postal Inspection Service office and your local police.
- Contact the Federal Trade Commission to report the problem.
- Call each of the three credit bureaus' fraud units to report identity theft. Ask to have a "Fraud Alert/Victim Impact" statement placed in your credit file asking that creditors call you before opening any new accounts.
- Alert your banks to flag your accounts and contact you to confirm any unusual activity. Request a change of PIN and a new password.
- Keep a log of all your contacts and make copies of all documents. You may also wish to contact a privacy or consumer advocacy group regarding illegal activity.
- Contact the Social Security Administration's Fraud Hotline.
- Contact the state office of the Department of Motor Vehicles to see if another license was issued in your name. If so, request a new license number and fill out the DMV's complaint form to begin the fraud investigation process.

Report Identity Theft to:

- Equifax Credit Bureau, Fraud
  1-800-525-6285
- Experian Information Solutions
  (formerly TRW)
  1-888-397-3742
- TransUnion Credit Bureau, Fraud
  1-800-680-7289
- Federal Trade Commission
  1-877-FTC-HELP
- Local Police Department
- U.S. Postal Inspection Service *(local post office)* *(See federal government phone list)*
- Social Security Administration, Fraud Hotline
  1-800-269-0271

Source: U.S. Postal Inspection Service. www.usps.gov/postalinspectors

InfoTrac College Edition Research
What steps are being taken to reduce "identity theft"?

$450 million from an insurance company that went bankrupt. Weiss and accomplices bought the company with a check and then loaned themselves the money to cover the purchase price. Once in charge, they bought worthless stocks and mortgages in deals that lost the insurer millions. Most of this money ended up in Weiss bank accounts.

Pyramid Schemes

A **pyramid scheme** resembles the familiar chain letter that asks you to send a dollar to the first name on the list, add your name to the bottom, duplicate four copies of the new list, and recruit four new members to continue the chain. Assuming that the chain is not broken, you could reap, for example, $256 in return for your original dollar investment—*if* the four people you recruit obtain four others each (16) and they secure four each (64), and they in turn find four others (256), who all mail a dollar to you (the name at the top of the list). The problem with such schemes is that they generally break down before reaching the bottom of the pyramid, and thus usually provide rewards only to the initial organizers.

In 1994 the Friends' Network, a massive pyramid game, was closed down in at least thirteen states. The con was spread by word of mouth among friends and relatives. Players gave a $1,500 "unconditional gift" (which they believed was tax free) to the person who recruited them. Then they each recruited one more new player. The money was passed up the chain to the name at the top of the pyramid.

In 1991 the Securities and Exchange Commission charged Melvin Ford and his International Loan Network based in Washington, D.C., with operating a pyramid scheme that defrauded more than 40,000 investors. Promising investors returns of 500–1,000 percent in as little as 180 days, the organizers charged clients $125 to $1,000 for initiation fees and promised them bonuses for anyone they recruited, setting up a pyramid. Later members could join additional income-opportunity programs. International Loan Network had not been paying promised returns, and its only source of income was the continued recruitment of new investors (Salwen, 1991, p. B8).

Also in 1991 the Federal Trade Commission and the Securities and Exchange Commission began an investigation of Nu Skin International, which encourages pyramidal distributorships (over 100,000 in 1991), for possible "pyramid scheme" violations. If signing on new distributors becomes more lucrative and important than selling a product, a violation exists (Springer, 1991).

In 1999 William Koop ran a multi-million-dollar pyramid scheme that ripped off at least 80 investors in 28 states. One investor gave him $2.5 million and was promised an 800 percent return, or $20 million, in 45 days. Koop claimed that he had knowledge of super-secret bank trades and that the investments were guaranteed (Lefer, 1999). The only problem was that no such trades existed and prime bank notes were fictitious financial instruments.

Religious Cons

Today, a new source of big money in professional crime appears to be burgeoning religious cults. Although most are probably sincere operations, a number appear to be interested in capturing the minds, bodies, and assets of their members. The son of L. Ron Hubbard (author of *Dianetics* [1973] and founder of Scientology, a pseudoreligious movement), claimed that the organization was simply a front or con for the private aggrandizement of Hubbard, who used most of the organization's money to buy drugs ("Scientology Fraud," 1983). An IRS audit in the early 1970s proved that Hubbard had skimmed millions of dollars from the church, laundering the money through dummy corporations in Panama and then hiding it in Swiss banks. Hubbard employed his own private police force, the "guardians organization," to attack and harass enemies and defectors from the organization. His son also claimed that the guardians on one occasion broke into an IRS office in an attempt to steal income tax records.

Televangelists such as W. V. Grant, Larry Lea, and Robert Tilton can hide behind the constitutional right to religious freedom in their pocketing of immense amounts of tax-free funds. Grant raised $350,000 per month for an orphanage in Haiti but actually gave it between $2,000 and $4,000. Lea solicited funds for, and claimed to be building, a church at Auschwitz that was actually being built by another group. Tilton, the self-proclaimed "Apple of God's Eye," had run "preacher scams" since his days as a college prankster and was an associate of Savings and Loan scammer Herman Beebe ("Men of God," 1991).

In this era of Elmer Gantry evangelism, mystic cults, charlatans, channelers, spoonbenders, and faith healers, psychics are:

> . . . joined by people whose honesty is difficult to assess because they appeal to messages from supernatural sources to justify their asking for our money. . . . [One] evangelist . . . told Americans that God would "take" him to another world if he did not receive $4.5 million in donations by April, 1987 (Nettler, 1989, p. 73).

In 1986 magician James Randi exposed psychic spoon-bender Uri Geller as a faker and also debunked faith healer Peter Popoff as using the old trick of "calling out" to people in an audience and listing their names, occupations, ailments, and other surprising personal information. Randi showed an audience on the Johnny Carson show how Popoff simply used confederates beforehand to garner information and transmit it to him through a tiny earpiece (Randi, 1988). Randi (in Jaroff, 1988, p. 72) reports:

> Popoff says that God speaks directly to him because he's an anointed minister. Three things amaze me about that. First of all, it turns out that God's frequency—I didn't know that he used a radio—is 39.170 MHz, and that God is a woman and sounds exactly like Popoff's wife Elizabeth.

Affinity group fraud involves individuals claiming to be fellow members of the victim's religion, ethnic group, or professional group and claiming to want to help one of their fellow members. The victim is more likely to trust a person who is from the same group. In 1999 a trial of Tampa-based Greater Ministries International Church charged conspiracy, money laundering, and mail fraud in a massive Ponzi scheme that allegedly defrauded more than 17,000 investors of as much as $200 million. Many of the victims were fundamentalist Christians, including Mennonites. They were promised their money would double in installment payments made over 17 months or less. Investors were quoted Luke 6:38: "Give and it shall be given unto you." They were told their investments were "gifts" and payments to investors were "blessings" and not subject to taxes (Department of Corporations, 1999).

The PTL Scandal. In 1987 a major scandal broke, toppling the PTL (Praise the Lord) Ministry empire of televangelist Jim Bakker and his wife, Tammy Faye. The Bakkers were charged by the IRS with drawing $9.3 million in excess pay and by others (ABC, 1987) with perpetrating the biggest religious fraud in history, with as much as $100 million of the church's funds siphoned off for their personal use. Their posh lifestyle came complete with an air-conditioned dog house. The last straw in the collapse of the Bakker operation was a sex scandal. Bakker was removed from the ministry and defrocked (Carey, 1988).

Boosters

While con artists represent the "aristocracy of the professional criminal world," "boosters" (professional shoplifters) or "heels" represent the lowest class. Among professional criminals, boosting is viewed as requiring less skill or talent and thus enjoys less status. One confidence man said of a booster, "While he is undoubtedly a professional thief, I should have been ashamed to be seen on the street with him. . . . My reputation would have suffered in the eyes of my friends to be seen in the company of a booster" (Adams, 1976, p. 76). Mary Owen Cameron's (1964) classic, *The Booster and the Snitch,* distinguishes between the booster (professional) and snitch (amateur) shoplifter. Boosters carefully plan their operations for big "scores" in order to minimize risks and to make sure they will be able to sell their booty to a fence (dealer in stolen property). Snitches, on the other hand, often commit their crimes on the spur of the moment, with little planning, and take enormous risks in order to "five-finger discount" relatively inexpensive items for their own personal use.

Boosters often rely on a variety of equipment and special paraphernalia such as "booster boxes" (boxes with slots or removable sections), special scissors or razor blades for removing labels, and special booster bags, coats, pants, and skirts with hidden compartments. Fat

VANTAGE POINT 9.2

Emerging Patterns of Professional Crime

Boiler rooms, slammers, taps, mile busters, and *dirt pile swindles* are all part of the jargon of contemporary professional crime. Some of these activities include phony accident claims, art theft, boiler room frauds, the investigator scam, abusive tax shelters, oil and gas investment and lease lottery frauds, gold and silver investment frauds, business opportunity and franchise frauds, commodity and penny stock frauds, vacation time-sharing scams, precious metals financing programs, and "dirt pile" gold swindles (Hagan, 1991).

- *Phony accident claims* (insurance fraud) persist. SEPTA (Southeastern Pennsylvania Transportation Authority) paid out $47 million in injury claims in 1990 (about 18 percent of fare collection). In one publicized bus crash eleven "passengers" filed suit, even though the bus was unoccupied (Stieg, 1990b, p. 16A). In 1989 the estimated loss to insurance companies due to fraudulent claims was estimated at $17 billion ("Super Sleuths," 1991, pp. 3–4).

  Calling it "Showtime" or "Let's Go Make a Movie," "crashers" or "cappers" fake car accidents in California to the tune of an estimated $500 million a year in bogus insurance claims. Crashers use "hammers" (crash cars that will hit other cars). They plan the script, stage the actual accident, and collect the insurance ("Crashers," 1992). Some rings use Hollywood stunt drivers, as well as crooked doctors and "ambulance-chasing" lawyers. The doctors, lawyers, and cappers split the settlement three ways. In a recent and more deadly insurance scam, truckers on California freeways are set up for rear-end collisions by criminals seeking large insurance settlements (Hall, 1992).
- *Art theft* is now estimated by Interpol as the second largest international trafficking crime after drugs, and only 10 percent of such cases are ever solved (Plagens, Starr, and Robins, 1990, p. 50). Art theft internationally is estimated at $860 million to $2.6 billion (Del Piano, 1993). The International Foundation for Art Research began keeping track of art theft in 1976. By 1979 there were 1,300 recorded thefts, and by 1989 this number had risen to over 30,000 cases on file. Various groups, many of them made up of professional criminals, are involved. French police speculate that the Japanese Yakuza participated in recent French and U.S. thefts, as well as in networks organized by French and Italian antique dealers. They also claim that the international art, narcotics, and arms underworlds overlap (Dickey, 1989, pp. 65–66). Periodic explosions in art prices contribute to the increase in thefts as do the willingness of insurance companies to negotiate with thieves. Thieves have long looted archeological sites and sold their booty to a waiting international art market (Carley, 1991). Extortion and bribery are part of the world of art forgery. Even the sloppiest imitations find their way into auction houses (Carlisle, 1998). In one auction, the forged works were dated four years after the artist's death.
- On March 18, 1990, the biggest art theft in history took place at the Isabella Stewart Gardner Museum in Boston. A team of robbers stole treasures valued in excess of $300 million. At 1:24 am, two men in uniform convinced a security guard to open the museum's side door and tricked him into summoning his partner. Both guards were handcuffed and duct taped. Then the thieves roamed the museum stealing masterpieces (Blumenthal, 1994). The crew used police-band radios, lookouts, transfer vehicles, and other signs of planning. A provision to the 1994 crime bill makes art theft a federal felony.
- *Boiler room frauds* are the basis of many schemes. Boiler rooms are rented offices with banks of telephones operated by high-pressure operators or salespersons (called slammers in the trade) who solicit funds or tout products with outrageous promises. Such telemarketing fraud can catch the unwary by surprise (Hagan and Benekos, 1992, p. 6). These phone solicitors often use "sound-alike charities" or names for their organizations that sound very similar to known legitimate organizations. They use lists of suckers, or "taps" as they are called in the fundraising game, since they can be tapped again and again.

  Selling bogus products and services via 900 phone numbers is a major new scam that began in the late 1980s. The primary aim is to keep the victim on the line for expensive charges for each minute of service. Phone sweepstakes, in which "winners" are encouraged to call a 900 number for details, and employment scams are current favorites. In the latter, customers are given information they could have obtained for free in the local newspaper. It turns out that, with few exceptions, 900 numbers are havens for rip-off artists.

VANTAGE POINT 9.2—*Continued*

- *The investigator scam* is a variation of the old "bank examiners' scam" in which "marks" (victims) are asked to put up their money to help investigators catch dishonest tellers. Con artists now use the telephone in an attempt to get credit card numbers. Such operators may pose as investigators for the credit card company or long-distance service and claim to need the person's card number and expiration date in order to check whether it has been used fraudulently. They may even give the victim a toll-free 800 number to call the following day to verify the call. When called, that number turns out to be out of service.
- *Abusive tax shelters* are defined by the Internal Revenue Service as any "that involve transactions with no economic foundation, inflated appraisals, and where claimed tax benefits are disproportionate to any economic ones. Abusive tax shelters are entered into with no expectation of a positive financial outcome, but rather with the sole expectation of evading taxes." Such tax shelters often involve movies, master recording tapes, real estate ventures, lithographs, books, and gold and precious metal mining ventures (Pennsylvania Securities Commission, 1983b, p. 1).

  When the IRS challenges abusive tax shelter schemes, it is the investors who lose deductions, pay penalties or interest, and may also be stuck with large loan repayments.
- *Oil and gas lease lottery frauds* are used by boiler rooms to get consumers to invest in oil and gas lease lotteries run by the U.S. government and the state of Wyoming. Many of the firms involved in recent frauds charged exorbitant fees, used high-pressure sales techniques, and misrepresented their services and the government leasing system. Individuals were not made aware that they could enter these leasing systems directly without contacting a leasing service. Although they were offered the hope of a "sleeper lease" (a valuable lease with few filing on it), some parcels had 10,000 filings, and only one could be granted. Although "cease and desist orders" had been filed by security administrations in various states, over 250 companies charged as much a $300 per filing, with some investors putting as much as $20,000 (Pennsylvania Securities Commission, 1983a). Related to these frauds were oil and gas investment frauds.
- *Oil and gas investment frauds* involve scams in which investors are talked into buying securities in oil/gas wells that are fake or are never drilled. Wells are often claimed to exist in inaccessible areas in order to discourage investor inspections.
- *Gold and silver investment frauds* are popular during recessions, when interest in investments such as precious metals and coins increases. Many of the firms offering such investments, however, are relatively unregulated and also use misrepresentation and high-pressure sales tactics. A recent operation involved a deferred delivery agreement scam. Some unscrupulous firms do not actually buy the ordered materials, hoping the market will go down. A "red flag" is the dealer's refusal to deliver purchased gold after it is requested. Many coin and bullion dealers are not subject to regulatory oversight.
- *Business opportunity and franchise frauds* take advantage of the American dream of being a self-employed entrepreneur. Business opportunity swindles that cater to this desire are estimated to cost $500 million per year. Such scams include: "raise them in your guest room" worm farms; distributorships for worthless gas-saving devices for cars; and requests for a few hundred dollars for a "start-up" inventory of industrial-strength cleanser or for $12,000 for an "equity investment" in a car wash in a nonexistent franchise. Many phony franchise dealers are recidivists with extensive careers involving fraud, embezzlement, and deceptive practices (Pennsylvania Securities Commission, 1984a).
- *Commodity frauds* involve commodity future contracts, which are fast-paced, volatile investments in the future prices of everything from soybeans and pork bellies to precious metals and treasury bonds. Unscrupulous dealers rely heavily on unsolicited, high-pressure phone calls, claims of inside information, "you must act at once!" pitches, and claims of no-risk, large, "get rich quick" profits. The National Futures Association (the commodity industry's self-regulatory organization) warns that many firms are unlicensed and unregulated. They often use impressive "sound-alike" names such as "Dunn and Bradford" and "Forbes and Lloyds" as well as impressive addresses such as "Wall Street" or "One Corporate Plaza." These dealers usually prey on individuals who can least afford to lose in the risky area of commodity investing (Pennsylvania Securities Commission, 1984b).
- *Penny stock frauds* involve "penny stocks" that are traded at very low prices to promote new, untested products. They are highly speculative, but are sometimes a fixed, inside game. State security regulators

have taken a variety of actions against crooked promotions.

Forty-five percent of seventy-eight new penny stock issues surveyed by Venture magazine had participants who were convicted felons, securities violators, targets of securities investigations, reputed crime figures, or principals who faced serious charges of insider financial misdealing (Pennsylvania Securities Commission, 1984c, p. 1).

- *Vacation time-sharing scams* take advantage of the popularity of time-sharing programs, which offer weeks (intervals) at vacation resorts for a fee that can be financed through installment payments. Additional fees are charged for maintenance and other costs. Some time-shares involve a "right-to-use (lease) agreement" only, in which case if the project fails, the entire investment is lost. Timeshares are often sold through "free vacation" promotions or other incentives and are accompanied by high-pressure sales tactics. Many time-sharing programs are unregulated and do not produce as promised (Pennsylvania Securities Commission, 1984d).

  One state closed a time-share company that did not own some of the property it was selling and another that oversold property it did own. Some time-shares are offered without adequate financing or before construction has begun. When companies go bankrupt, the investors are often left out in the cold.

- *Precious metals bank financing programs* became quite popular in the late 1980s. Notice was taken of the large growth in off-exchange commodity futures. Particularly of concern was the increase in sales of gold, silver, and platinum in conjunction with bank financing. In these transactions the typical soliciting dealer is unlicensed and unregulated.

  To make a precious metal purchase pursuant to a bank financing program, the customer places an order for bullion with the soliciting dealer. The customer must put down 20–30 percent of the purchase price and pay an additional "buy charge." The difference between the down payment and the total purchase price is financed from the proceeds of a loan obtained from a bank that the dealer will suggest to the customer.

  A major problem with these purchasing programs is whether the metal supposedly sold to each investor is in fact being held for the investor by a reliable institution. Many of the operators are boiler room scam artists. Legitimate precious metal investing is highly volatile and risky, a high-stakes game that is compounded if the investments involve leverage, margin, high commissions, hidden costs, and unregistered, possibly crooked, sellers. The hazards of a leverage purchase (buying on margin) can be illustrated in the area of coin purchasing. Some coin brokers advertise coins at a fraction of the sale price through a deferred payment or leverage contract program. The balance of the price is financed by a bank loan. This increases the potential for profits as well as losses. If coins lose value, it is possible to lose substantially more money than the initial investment (Pennsylvania Securities Commission, 1987, p. 5).

- "Dirt pile" gold swindles are also a popular scam. The fools' gold rush of 1988 found tens of thousands of Americans losing roughly $250 million to at least fifty-two known phony gold mine operations promoted by boiler room operators.

  At the heart of the "dirt pile" swindle is the promise of gold at bargain basement prices. The catch is that the gold, if there is any at all, is still in the ground. A typical "dirt pile" investment involves a payment of $5,000 for unprocessed dirt guaranteed by the promoters to contain twenty ounces of gold, which works out to a price of $250 an ounce, well under the prevailing world spot market price. Delivery of gold is deferred for fifteen months to three years (Pennsylvania Securities Commission, 1988, p. 1).

  A California entrepreneur named Murray Brooks sold dirt from the Comstock mines in Nevada for $16,000 a ton. Brooks said his purported bonanza relied on new technology that could extract gold left behind by miners in the 1870s. "Our inspector took a backhoe, dug the dirt himself, did an analysis and showed there wasn't a speck of gold to be found." That wasn't surprising. The Comstock Lode was a famous silver strike (Neff, 1991, p. 11A).

  Many victims, hoping against hope, keep their faith in their promoters. The latter take advantage of this when facing legal action. In what sounds like a familiar litany used by savings and loan thief Charles Keating, promoters insist that they would be producing the promised gold were it not for all the legal and governmental red tape and harassment. Shifting blame is a typical tactic in almost every swindle that unravels (Neff, 1991, p. 11A). Many professional swindlers simply change the name of their firm and open up shop in a different state.

Source: Frank E. Hagan, "The Professional Criminal in the Nineties." Paper presented at the Academy of Criminal Justice Sciences Meetings, Nashville, Tennessee, March, 1991.

InfoTrac College Edition Research

What are some new "scams" or new examples of scams that may not have been discussed in this chapter?

shoplifters may employ the "crotch walk," in which goods are actually held between their legs and hidden by long coats or dresses.

Professional shoplifters usually work in groups, with each individual having an assigned role. The "stall" "throws a hump" or creates a commotion in order to attract the attention of the store personnel, while the "clout" steals the goods and possibly turns them over to a "cover," who may actually carry the booty out of the store.

In what sounds like Charles Dickens' *Oliver Twist,* a school for shoplifters, complete with a "how-to-do-it" manual, was discovered by police in New York City. About seventy-five boys ages 11 to 14 were believed to be involved. They were trained in avoiding security at suburban shopping malls and sent on expeditions with shopping lists in hand (Hamilton, 1987). Since statistics on shoplifting are poor, it would be hazardous to estimate the proportion perpetrated by professionals. However, it is clear that professionals account for only a small proportion.

Cannons

Professional *pickpockets* (sometimes called "cannons," "dips," or "picks") require exceptional dexterity and an awareness of the art of misdirection. Most pickpockets work with a "stall" who "puts up" (sets up) the mark. This is usually accomplished by tripping against, bumping, or otherwise distracting the subject, while the "tool" or "claw" or "mechanic" actually hooks or steals. According to Stirling (1974, p. 105), authorities on the subject claim that South Americans are the world's most skillful pickpockets. In the late eighties some large airports in the United States were plagued by gangs of thieves who specialized in pickpocketing and stealing from luggage-laden travelers. Speculation was that the gangs were graduates of the infamous "School of the Seven Bells," a shoplifting school in Colombia. In order to graduate, students must steal items from the instructor's coat, to which seven bells are attached. If a bell rings, the student flunks (Fry, 1986, p. 7D). Since ancient times pickpockets have worked crowds at parades, carnivals, sporting events, and the like. In medieval Europe, even during public executions of pickpockets, cannons "worked the crowds." Today, Derby day, Super Bowl week, and world's fairs all attract a large influx of cannons.

The next time you attend a large sporting event, see if, with the practiced eye of a bunko squad detective, you can spot the cannons in the crowd. Look for the people who are continually watching the crowd rather than the event. Unless they are security personnel, they may very likely be cannons attempting to "set a mark."

Pickpockets usually work in groups of two, three, or four, with a specific role for each. One may select *marks,* another may locate the valuables or money on the person ("fanning") and maneuver him or her into position, and another pickpockets the item and passes it off to yet another (Inciardi, 1977, 1983, 1984).

Related to, but less skillful than, pickpockets are "cutpurses," those who attempt to surreptitiously steal women's purses by cutting the purse straps. If such a theft involves rough stuff, such as shoving or physical force, the "cutpurse" has crossed the boundary from pickpocket to strong-arm robber or mugger. A related sneak thief is a "moll buzzer," who attempts to steal unattended purses in public places. The number of expert or class cannons has considerably declined from the thousands during the pre-World War II period to fewer than a thousand today (Inciardi, 1977, p. 21).

Professional Burglars

An example of professional burglary crews in operation was revealed when 22 were arrested in burglaries of Kennedy Airport cargo in 1994. Three major rings were stealing merchandise whose value was estimated in the tens of millions of dollars from air-cargo warehouses. Although they were not members of organized crime "families," the thieves paid tax or tribute to local organized crime groups (Firestone, 1994). Shover (1973) interviewed 143 successful career burglars, some of whom were professionals. Such burglars typically work in groups, although there might be constant turnover in the members from job-to-job. Critical connections for a professional burglar's success are tipsters, fixers, and fences. Tipsters provide information on likely targets in return for a portion of the take, while fixers are attorneys and bondsmen who use bribery to fix or ward off prosecution. Fences or criminal receivers readily convert the burglar's booty into more portable cash. Many burglars rationalize their activity by claiming that most people are insured anyhow and that, when they read reports of their burglaries, the amount lost often is inflated by the victim in order to cheat the insurance company.

One of the more flamboyant professional burglars was a former paratrooper dubbed "Spiderman" (Derrick James), whose exploits resemble Hitchcock's 1950s classic, *To Catch a Thief,* starring Cary Grant. Without any equipment, he scaled luxury high rises in South Florida and very selectively stole expensive jewelry. He seldom left the scene in disarray, and often the victims did not even know they had been burglarized until months later when they tried to find a particular item to wear. While ten floors up was standard, he once broke in on a 30th floor (Pressley, 1998). He rated his own police task force involving 25 police agencies. Upon his arrest in 1998, police contend he was responsible for over 100 burglaries worth over $8 million.

Picking a lock is just one of the many skills of an able burglar. The best lock pickers may practice daily and are the first to buy and master the latest "burglar-proof" locks when they become available. Some take locksmith correspondence courses advertised in magazines, and some are even licensed locksmiths. On entering premises, the skilled burglar will often stick a small object such as a matchstick into the lock so that it will jam if the occupants unexpectedly return and insert their key.

Plate (1975, p. 20) describes some burglaries of jewelry firms in Manhattan in the seventies that involved such feats as breaking through two concrete walls and opening two huge safes without leaving even a fingerprint. In one job, the front windows were sprayed with black paint, and in another the main cable serving a protection-service alarm system was cut, affecting thousands of Manhattan customers.

"Chic Conwell," the professional thief in Sutherland's 1937 book, used the term "hotel prowler" to refer to burglars who specialize in stealing from hotel rooms. Such sneak thieves are particularly active in convention towns; they may pay off hotel employees, who act as accomplices. One hotel prowler told Plate (1975, p. 50) that, after first obtaining a master key from an accomplice, he would wait until 2:00 a.m., maintaining that at that hour few conventioneers were in their rooms sleeping and, if they were, they were so "bombed" they would not notice his presence. The only town he had problems in was Philadelphia, where he claimed the town was so dead at night that conventioneers stayed in their rooms and drank.

The Box Man

At the top of the hierarchy of burglars are safecrackers or "box men." Chambliss's (1975a) edition of professional safecracker Harry King's autobiography, *Box Man* (reissued as *Harry King: A Professional Thief's Journal* [King and Chambliss, 1984]), reveals that King ranks professional safecrackers, although a dying breed, with the big con artists as high status criminals within the professional criminal hierarchy.

Safecracking has engendered a constant escalation of technology, first to secure safes and second, in reaction, to develop better ways to open them. **Box men** are really *professional burglars who specialize in breaking into safes.* Between 1890 and 1940 professional burglary gangs flourished, hampered only by the newly developed burglar alarm. Telephones and automobiles were also beginning to narrow the apprehension gap (Rosberg, 1980, pp. 44, 52). As more and more sophisticated safes were developed, the methods employed to break into them improved. Since dynamite often damaged the safe contents, a core drill (a diamond-tipped construction device) provided more sophisticated means of entry, as did burning bars (oxygen lances that burn at temperatures up to 7,000 degrees Fahrenheit).

The Professional Fence

The dilemma of a thief who makes a "big score," but who lacks connections needed to dispose of the goods, was brought home to the author one evening in Cleveland while I was walking across a parking lot of a neighborhood shopping center. Two shady-looking characters blocked my path with their car, and the driver said, "Hey, sport, I have a bunch of cashmere sport coats in the back; and if we can find one that fits ya, I'll give you one helluva deal." Sure enough, glancing into the back seat I could see at least twenty boxes with a recognizable name in men's clothing on them. When I indicated a lack of interest, they shrugged, saying, "Suit yourself, sport," and drove off. Such amateurs without connections are not only in the business of stealing, but also in the even riskier business of soliciting unscreened customers in order to dispose of "hot" goods. More experienced and professional thieves would have quickly disposed of the property with a reliable fence or receiver of stolen property.

A **fence** is *an individual who buys and sells stolen property.* Legitimate operators of pawnshops, second-hand and antique shops, junkyards, and other general merchandisers may knowingly add stolen goods to their inventory; but a professional fence does this on a regular basis. Hall (1952) distinguishes between the "lay receiver" (customer), the "occasional receiver" (a rare buyer), and the "professional receiver" (a specialist in stolen property). Professional burglars could not operate on a long-term basis without reliable relationships with fences willing to buy large quantities of stolen property on short notice. Klockars (1974) describes how "Vince Swaggi," the professional fence he studied, was able to sell a lot of factory seconds and other legitimate merchandise to customers who assumed the goods were "hot" (stolen) and thus a bargain. Similar findings caused Steffensmeier (1986) to entitle his case study *The Fence: In the Shadow of Two Worlds.* Fences and other professional criminals may also obtain a certain degree of immunity by acting as informants to the police. The importance of the fence to property criminals and sneak thieves is well illustrated by the relative success of police fencing sting operations that, after being in operation for only a short time, are able to arrest large numbers of thieves.

The classic professional fence was an Englishman by the name of Jonathan Wild, who operated in the early eighteenth century (Klockars, 1974). Wild placed advertisements in the newspaper and claimed that he was a "thief-taker," that he could recover stolen goods. He paid thieves higher-than-usual prices for their booty and then sold the goods to the victims at considerable profit. Wild was a "double dealer," building quite a reputation for turning in thieves as well as for fencing their goods. Finally, when some thieves accused him of being a fence, he was tried, found guilty, and hanged in 1725.

Blakey and Goldsmith (1976, pp. 1530–35) identify four types of fences: the *neighborhood fence,* the *outlet fence,* the *professional fence,* and the *master fence,* in rising order of sophistication. The *neighborhood fence* is usually a small merchant who occasionally deals in stolen goods, while the *outlet fence* regularly sells "hot" merchandise along with legitimate stock. Using a legitimate company as a front, the *professional fence* is a major distributor of stolen articles. The *master fence* is involved at all levels, from organizing the theft to contacting customers in advance to distributing the goods; theft of art and museum masterpieces and their sale to wealthy private collectors may serve as one example. Plate

(1975, p. 65) tells us that most fences determine the price for items they buy and sell by using the Sears wholesale catalog or, if pressed, by calling the manufacturer directly, pretending to be an interested customer.

Paper Hangers

Paper hanging (*passing bad checks and other documents*) is a persistent form of professional crime. In the United States, cash is becoming the poor man's credit card. A larger proportion of transactions are conducted by means of checks and credit cards, which create a ripe situation for the forger. Lemert (1958) distinguishes between *naïve check forgers* and professionals, or *systematic forgers;* the former are amateurs and only occasional offenders (as discussed in Chapter 8), while the latter make an illegal business of forging checks (see Klein and Montague, 1977). Lemert also found that forgers often operate independently and are less a part of the world of professional criminals than some other offenders (Lemert, 1958). Sutherland (1937) also claimed that forgers and counterfeiters are considered marginal in professional crime, perhaps because such operators are often loners or *technicians* and thus do not share the professional criminal subculture (see Bloom, 1957).

Old-fashioned counterfeiting of money has not disappeared and may even be proliferating with recent technology—so much so that the U.S. government is considering changing the currency by, for instance, printing bills of different denominations in different colors. Many developed countries have based the design of their paper currency on that of U.S. currency. Color copiers, bleaching dollar bills and using the paper to print bills of higher denominations, and other ingenious methods have been used to make counterfeit money (Gladwell, 1990). In 1992 C-notes ($100 bills) began popping up around the globe, notes so authentic looking that they fooled currency-handling equipment at the federal reserve. Speculation has it that an unfriendly foreign government or a terrorist organization may have been the culprit (Wartzman, 1992).

Color copiers have accelerated the number of counterfeit bills in circulation. The amount has doubled every year and was estimated at $1.6 to $2 billion by the end of the nineties. In order to fight counterfeiting, particularly superbills (near-perfect fake $100 bills), the U.S. Mint changed the $100 bill, the favorite of counterfeiters, first. Figure 9.3 describes some of the security features of the new $100 bill. These security features have since been incorporated into lower denomination bills as well.

Secret Service and CIA officials have speculated that a possible source of the "Superdollar" may be the government of Iran, which was sold the same intaglio printing presses used at the U.S. Mint before the fall of the Shah.

A growing area of professional fraud and counterfeiting relates to phony credit cards, records, tapes, and spare parts. The latter are produced in foreign factories and are reasonable facsimiles of the real thing. These pose some minor problems for those who purchase phony, inexpensive, "hot" watches from "Duke the Goniff" at the Greyhound station. They present major problems if they happen to be unsafe parts for airplanes, elevators, and manufacturing machinery.

Credit card counterfeiting was relatively unknown before 1990, and by 1998 was estimated to cost $1.5 billion per year (Wallace, 1998). Counterfeiters thwart each technological security advance in credit cards. Holograms were simply made by counterfeiters themselves, and embedded magnetic strips were defeated by "skimming" to read the information and then using laptop computers for duplication. Chinese organized crime groups dominate the trade in California. Groups such as the Wo Hop To Triad, Wah Ching, and United Bamboo are active (Ibid.)

Law enforcement of the future is faced with increasing sophistication in this area. For example, how do businesses control checks that an hour or two after being cashed decom-

FIGURE 9.3 Security Features of the New $100 Bill

1. **Smaller Letter Size** that is difficult to duplicate without blurring.
2. **Federal Reserve Seal**, replacing the Federal Reserve District seal.
3. **Serial Numbers** with 11 numbers and letters, instead of the current 10 numbers and letters.
4. **Security Threads** visible only when exposed to ultraviolet light.
5. **Larger, Off-Center Portrait** that is easier to recognize and has more detail.
6. **Fine-Line Printing** that traditional copying methods cannot reproduce.
7. **New Ink** that changes color when viewed from different angles.
8. **Watermark** of portrait visible only under light.

Source: U.S. Treasury Department.

pose and disappear? Advanced laser printers and color copiers make counterfeit documents such as checks, letterheads, and business cards more difficult to detect. In 1998 Canadian Mounties and the U.S. Secret Service busted a group with believed links to Russian and Asian organized crime groups that used scanners and ink-jet printers to create over $2 million in Canadian $100 and $50 bills. They also used thermal, silkscreen printers to produce exact replicas of credit cards from six banks. Police were surprised that Canadian currency was being produced, since most false notes are usually American (Mounties, 1998). Gordon (1991) indicates that there is little or no international law dealing with international financial crimes. Many countries have bank secrecy laws. Most counterfeit credit cards are produced in Hong Kong, where it is not a crime to manufacture them. In other countries it is illegal to use, but not to possess, such cards. The need for multilateral agreements to fight such transnational crime is obvious (Gordon, 1991). Malaysia, Thailand, and Hong Kong account for 44 percent of global credit-card counterfeiting and are known as the "plastic triangle" (Duckworth, 1991). Although they are very costly, enforcement officials are calling for the adoption of "smart cards," which have a small semiconductor memory circuit; but even these would only buy time until counterfeiters cracked the technology. In "Fraud Masters: Professional Credit Card Offenders and Crime," Jerome Jackson (1994) examined the working habits of a gang of credit card thieves. Part of their reason for choosing this form of offending was the knowledge that there was little risk of being caught, reported, or prosecuted.

A growing racket is that of "credit doctors" who sell clean credit references to people with bad credit (Reibstein and Drew, 1988). Using computers, credit thieves can steal your good credit and sell it, along with your social security number and credit references, to someone who has a similar name. Needless to say, your credit will not remain good for long.

"Video piracy," the massive production of fake videotapes, became a burgeoning industry during the late eighties. We are not talking here about people making tapes for their own personal use, but about well-organized syndicates that can often get "knock-off copies" to the market before the originals, causing the manufacturers to lose about $1 billion a year as a result. An estimated 15 percent of the movie videos on display in U.S. stores are illegal (Pauly, Friday, and Foote, 1987). Theft of cable services was estimated to cost U.S. cable companies $3 billion annually in the early 1990s.

Another example of the dangers of counterfeit products was the accusation in 1987 (Anderson and Van Atta, 1987) that bogus bolts made of cheaper alloys have either been found in, or are believed to be in, the nation's airplanes, buildings, bridges, nuclear power plants, and military hardware.

In 1873 archaeologist Heinrich Schliemann discovered the ancient remains of the fabled City of Troy. Many of the "treasures" found at the site were later determined to be hoaxes, bought from dealers or brought from other sites. Art is now a major item of investment, but "art forgery" is not clearly defined in the law (Haywood, 1987, p. 7). Interpol, the U.S. Treasury Department, and the New York Police Department's Fine Arts Squad estimate that some ten thousand stolen works of art are on the market. The identification of forgeries has found even major art museums deceived (Dutton, 1983; Savage, 1976).

Professional Robbers

Professional robbers differ from most other professional criminals in that they threaten, and are willing to use, force if necessary. Also, in contrast to others, they need little specific training or skill to be "stickup artists." Professional "heavy" criminals (Gibbons, 1977, p. 2), such as robbers, tend to band together for particular jobs, but only on a short-term basis. This is in sharp contrast to the Jesse James-type gangs of the Wild West or the Depression-era Bonnie-and-Clyde type groups.

In 1994 the clock finally ran out for Patrick Mitchell, head of a bank robbery ring known as the "Stopwatch Gang" or "the presidential robbers." The former name was given them because the gang tried to complete their jobs in two minutes; the latter name came from the masks of presidents they wore during robberies. This gang is estimated to have pulled more than one hundred bank jobs since 1980 (Harrist, 1995). Also arrested that same year was Johnny Madison Williams, Jr., one of the most successful bank robbers in U.S. history. Responsible for 56 bank robberies, which he carefully documented in a handwritten log, Williams was known as "the Shootist" because he always fired shots in the air at the start of his robberies. The eight years before his arrest constituted the longest unsolved string of bank robberies ever investigated by the FBI ("A Confession," 1994). The most successful type of robbery today is probably the hijacking of trucks (Glaser, 1978, p. 446). Writers such as Abadinsky (1983a), Teresa (1973b), and Walsh (1977) have all found increasing cooperation between professional and organized criminals, particularly in the area of truck hijacking.

One major difference between amateur robbers and professional robbers is that the former tend to rob individuals while the latter tend to concentrate on commercial establishments. Letkemann (1973), based on his interviews with bank robbers, describes how many, in planning their jobs ("casing the joint" in gangster English), were aided by the fact that many branch banks were architectural clones of each other. Such similar layouts plus practiced impression management—a persona that robbers utilize to verbally intimidate bank personnel and customers—made many stick-ups routine. Robbers try to show they mean business in order to enhance cooperation. In short, no one gets hurt. Professional robbers, in contrast to most other criminals, do not require as much subcultural support from other professional criminals to acquire skill and technique or to plan and execute their operations.

Gangs of professional jewelry thieves called "The Colombians" stalk, set up, and rob members of America's jewelry industry. Many are from Colombia and five other Latin American nations, and they consist of 2,000 thieves organized in teams of 10 to 20 individuals. They particularly target salespeople on the road. The gangs are especially violent and survey and trail likely victims for days before attacking (Annin and Rhine, 1999).

Professional Arsonists

Most arson is committed by amateurs, individuals who do not make a career out of burning down structures. However, there are professional arsonists. In the late seventies, Morris Klein, a member of a ring of torch artists, boasted, "I can make concrete burn" (Karchmer, 1977). Klein's ring, which sold a complete package of arson services to businesses, was responsible for hundreds of fires in several states. For a percentage of the insurance settlement, he could mobilize a team of engineers, torches, and insurance experts. He was

> . . . a fire broker who scouted around for troubled firms to sell. . . . If the business kept fumbling, Klein would approach the owner with an arson scam proposal. . . . He informed clients that their buildings were burning with the code message "The sky is red" (Karchmer, 1978).

Professional Auto Theft Rings

While most of us carefully guard and secure our valuables, one of our most expensive investments, an automobile, is often left unguarded on the streets or in a parking lot. While most automobiles are stolen by amateur juveniles for joyriding purposes, a significant number are stolen by auto theft rings and either chopped up for parts or refinished, complete with new papers and serial numbers, and sold to a waiting market. While professionals organize such rings, the job with the greatest risk—actually stealing the cars—is done by young car thieves who may even be given shopping lists for specific makes or models (Savitz, 1959).

Some car thieves are professionals who possess standard burglary tools and master keys. Plate (1975, p. 28) indicates that Porsche master keys go for several thousand dollars. Master keys may be duplicated from those bought from showroom employees, for instance. Another tool is a "slam hammer" or "bam-bam" instrument, which is usually used to take dents out of cars. Thieves can use this tool to heist a car by inserting one end of the small hammer over the door lock of a car, which enables the entire door lock to be removed in seconds. Looking at the code number on the lock and using an auto code key book and key cutter, the thief can prepare the exact key for the auto in less than two minutes (Plate, 1975, pp. 29–30).

The thief's job ends when the car is left at the drop-off spot, usually a local shopping center. Runners or "gophers" transport the car to the shop. New plates can easily be obtained from states with lax inspection laws. Using a die tool, new numbers can be etched into the VIN number (vehicle identification number), which can be found die-cast on various parts of the car. Dishonest junkyard owners can also furnish registration cards to serve as false ownership credentials. Other auto theft rings operate "chop shops," where the stolen auto is immediately cannibalized for parts and sold to legitimate repair shops, which can now, because of low overhead, underbid competitors on repair work. Obviously, professional auto thieves vary in their operations, sophistication, and organization.

In 1992 auto thieves in Dade County, Florida, claimed to be earning $15,000 per week stealing vehicles. Many of the vehicles not on their way to "chop shops" were driven onto container ships and sold for millions of dollars in Latin American countries such as the Dominican Republic, which is awash in luxury automobiles from the United States. Jail overcrowding often means that, when car thieves are caught, few get jail time ("Auto Thieves," 1992). A stolen vehicle will often net double its price overseas, and auto theft is often viewed as victimless since it is usually covered by insurance. "The low apprehension, prosecution, and conviction rate of auto thieves makes this crime a booming industry, with high profits and low risks" (Beekman and Daly, 1990, p. 16). When federal authorities were able to successfully bust these container ship operations, the thieves shifted gears. They exported legitimate cars, removed their VIN numbers when they arrived at the foreign port, and sent these back to the United States to be placed on "born again" stolen vehicles (Beekman and Daly, 1990, p. 17).

International auto theft rings are estimated to operate an $8 billion industry increasingly associated with crime syndicates (Ragava and Kaplan, 1999). Of the 1.4 million stolen vehicles in 1997, at least 200,000 ended up overseas. Vehicle theft is one of the lowest crimes on the law enforcement priority list. There is only a 14 percent arrest rate for auto theft, the lowest of any crime category. Mexico is the principal port of destination for stolen U.S. autos. In 1997 the cities with the highest auto theft rates were Miami, Jersey City, Fresno, Memphis, and New York. European experts document similar activity in Europe and even claim that it is now as big an international problem as drug smuggling (August, 1997). Russian and Chechen syndicates transport stolen vehicles to the former Soviet Union. In some cases owners of the vehicles sell them to the thieves and then report them as stolen in order to collect the insurance.

Professional Killers

Professional assassins, "hit men," are popular subjects of fiction and, undoubtedly, a few do in fact exist, for instance, in the shady world of international espionage. Most organized crime executions appear to be assigned to members in addition to their ordinary tasks. Even members of *Murder Inc.* did not spend most of their time performing executions. The literature is either scant or unreliable in providing an accurate picture of professional killers.

Criminal Careers of Professionals

Reviews of the use of the term *professional criminal* in the field of criminology (Staats, 1977; Winslow, 1970) point out the heavy reliance on case studies and popular sources. Anthologies such as Bruce Jackson's (1972) *In the Life* and Duane Denfield's (1974) *Streetwise Criminology* are illustrative. These provide firsthand accounts, primarily by incarcerated criminals, of their lives in crime. While these are revealing, it is unclear how typical such accounts may be. Given this methodological limitation, much of the description of criminal careers of professional criminals is limited and certainly requires more investigation.

Indicating that professional criminals may not be specialists in any one area of crime, Plate (1975, pp. 7–10) identifies ten characteristics of professional criminals:

1. They seek anonymity.
2. They are often on speaking terms with police as informants, bribers, or simply as those who work in a related area.

3. They are not necessarily members of organized crime, although they cooperate in some cities.
4. They are usually not drug addicts.
5. They take arrest and imprisonment in stride, often putting money away for a rainy day.
6. They do not leave fingerprints.
7. When possible, they will run through a crime (practice it) beforehand.
8. They are well aware of the law and police clearance rates.
9. Most avoid gaudy display or conspicuous consumption.
10. Many are stable, family members.

When some professional criminals, such as hired killers or professional robbers, are into "heavy" crimes, most attempt to avoid rough stuff, to avoid "heat," to operate through wit, guile, cunning, technical skill, and "grifting." Most professional criminals look with disdain on the tactics and senseless violence of amateur criminals. Professionals plan and carefully choose their victims in order to maximize the score and minimize risks.

A criminal does not usually simply decide one day that he or she is going to be a professional criminal. Recognition, skill, and contact with other hustlers and professionals are prerequisites; without this contact, the required knowledge and experience for a successful move into professional crime is less likely. Recruits into the world of professional crime may come from the ranks of hotel workers, waitresses, and cab drivers, as well as of pimps, fences, and promising conventional property criminals. While in earlier times, professional training schools such as Fagin's in *Oliver Twist* did in fact exist, today the training appears to be much more informal, although the nation's prisons seem to be a major training ground for some.

A leading explanation of professional criminality is Sutherland's (Sutherland and Cressey, 1978, pp. 80–83) "differential association" theory. In explaining patterns of professional criminality, the theory points to criminal contacts (values and attitudes) as essential to the learning process. Some professional criminals, particularly cannons, con artists, and professional burglars, participate in an informal apprenticeship of jobs, learning very specific skills and making the indispensable contacts with fixers and fences without which they would have great difficulty in operating. Letkemann (1973) sees this "crime as work" orientation among professional criminals as involving not only the learning of technical skills, but, just as importantly, social and organizational skills such as victim management. An important component of professional criminality is the shared subculture that requires frequenting common haunts (bars, restaurants, and the like) in order to discover "what's going down" or "what's happening."

Compared with other categories of criminal activity, professional crime is rare and perhaps becoming rarer. Generally, most professional criminals come from better economic backgrounds than conventional or organized criminals. Many begin their careers at a later age. This varies, however, with the area of criminality. Safecrackers and bank robbers, for instance, appear to require early juvenile crime experience (Conklin, 1981, p. 265). Maurer (1964) describes the professional criminal as one who approaches crime in a businesslike manner, expecting to earn his or her living from it. Professional criminals know and are known to other professional criminals. Such criminals highly identify with criminal activity and are proud that they are good at their work. Many professional criminals rationalize their activity, feeling that all people are crooked or involved in what Al Capone called "the legitimate rackets." As Mel Weinberg, the ABSCAM consultant, put it: "I'm a swindler . . . the only difference between me and the congressmen I met on this case is that the public pays them a salary for stealing" ("The Man Behind ABSCAM," 1980, p. 1A). Con artists justify their behavior on the basis of the dishonest behavior of many of their victims, who may be trying to avoid taxes or buy stolen goods.

Informants from the ranks of professional crime as early as the time of Sutherland's (1937, pp. 2–42) "Chic Conwell" have indicated that, while cannons tend to restrict their criminal activities to their specialty of pickpocketing, most others "hustle" or engage in a variety of offenses, even though they may prefer their specialties. Boosters and paper hangers appear to be more similar to cannons in attempting to stick to their specialties.

Societal Reaction

Most experts on the subject see professional criminality as declining since its heyday during the Depression (Inciardi, 1975; Klein, 1974; Shover, 1973). This decline may simply represent an increase in semilegal enterprises (Roebuck and Windham, 1983). Bank robbery for the most part has passed into the hands of amateurs. There appear to be fewer bigtime con artists around than previously. Pickpockets, although still around, have been replaced by muggers. Female involvement in bunko operations has increased considerably in the post-World War II period. Inciardi (1975) suggests that the decline of professional crime began in the 1940s with the application of modern communication and scientific methods to the field of criminal investigation. Computerized information, fingerprints, regional cooperation in law enforcement, and greater professionalization of criminal justice "raised the ante" for a career in crime.

Other observers (Staats, 1977; Chambliss, 1975a; Hagan, 1991) see professional crime, not as declining, but as shifting into other areas of operation. The "professional street crime" characteristic of an industrial society has given way to "white collar professional crime." While professional burglars and pickpockets have declined in numbers, there has been an increase in the number of sophisticated con artists. In a paper entitled "The Ghost of Chic Conwell: Professional Crime and Fraud in the Twenty-first Century" (Hagan, 2000), this writer feels that Chic Conwell (professional crime) is not dead but has moved into cyberspace.

As previously described, most professional criminals attempt to commit crimes that are difficult to track, and their operations are often characterized by use of specialists for each element of the job. Since most criminals, even the best, are eventually caught, the more sophisticated professionals will attempt to forestall action by victims or the criminal justice system by "putting in **the fix**"—*gaining the cooperation of corrupt officials: crooked judges, court administrators, lawyers, or police officers.* The latter, for instance, could convince victims of the futility of attempting to proceed with a case and offer immediate compensation. According to the President's Commission on Law and the Administration of Justice (1967a, p. 154), two essential elements that explain the success of professional crime are "the fix" and "the fence." Yet another element should be added—a steady demand for stolen goods. Without a ready market, much professional theft would dry up.

The traditional public view of burglary and thievery is that the perpetrators of these crimes are unorganized and are reduced to crime to support a drug or gambling habit. However, 90 percent of the dollar value of objects taken is stolen by crime rings, although those rings are responsible for only 10 percent of the incidents of burglary (Pennsylvania Crime Commission, 1980, p. 167).

While the very nature of post-industrial society and its reliance on banking, international trade, computers, and instantaneous communications has created fertile ground for fraud and professional crime, efforts in public and private investigation have begun to meet the challenge. Most noteworthy in this regard are beefed-up efforts by the Federal Bureau of Investigation, the National White Collar Crime Center, and the Association of Certified Fraud Examiners.

Most discussions of white collar crime by organizations, such as the U.S. Chamber of Commerce, or federal law enforcement agencies, such as the FBI, concentrate on areas we have discussed in this chapter as professional crime, particularly the work of confidence artists. This would suggest that the most serious white collar crimes are committed by "hustlers," "fast buck artists,"—actors who are clearly unacquainted with standard business practices. In fact, such operations, although a serious concern, are relatively minor compared with pervasive and economically more costly operations that are incidental sidelines of legitimate business enterprise, where many of the same tactics are employed.

Summary

In sociology, *professions* are occupations that possess useful knowledge and claim a service orientation for which they are granted autonomy. In this light the term "professional" may be an inappropriate tag with which to designate skilled, able grifters or intensive career criminals. It is so widely used in the literature, however, that not to use the concept would be more confusing than to employ it. Sutherland's classic work on the subject, *The Professional Thief* (1937), describes some characteristics of professional criminals as including: crime as sole livelihood, planning, technical skills, codes of behavior, high status, and an ability to avoid detection. Professional crime is a sociological rather than a legal entity.

The argot (specialized jargon) of the professional world uses Depression-era U.S. terms. Some examples of the latter included: cannons (pickpockets), heels (sneak thieves), boosters (shoplifters), the con (confidence games). A continuum *model of professional crime* presents crime as being professional to the degree that it possesses the following characteristics: sole livelihood, extensive career, skill, high status, avoidance of detection, criminal subculture, planning, and "the fix." *The fix* refers to the ability to avoid prosecution by compromising the criminal justice process. *Scam* refers to various criminal techniques or hustles. Professional crime differs from occupational/corporate crime in that, in the former, crime is the sole purpose of a business. Some examples of professional crime from Edelhertz's typology were presented, most of which are examples of fraud.

Some professional crime might be described as *semiprofessional* in that it involves less skill and planning. Sometimes called *bunko* or *flim flam* or *short con* operations, these scams include: the pigeon drop, the badger scam, the bank examiner's scam, postal frauds, circus grifting, *boojo* (a gypsy con game), and various home-improvement frauds.

The *big con* involves far more skill, more elaborate planning, higher-status victims, and much larger rewards for the criminal. *Ponzi schemes* are frauds in which early investors in a nonexistent product are paid high dividends on the basis of money obtained from later investors. *Pyramid schemes* require investors to seek a chain of other investors in order to reap a promised high return. Examples of big con operations also included religious cons.

Various professional criminal trades include boosters, cannons, professional burglars, box men, fences, paper hangers, robbers, arsonists, and auto thieves.

Descriptions of criminal careers of professional criminals are methodologically limited by the need to rely on case studies and popular sources for many accounts. Most professional criminals seek anonymity, know the police and members of organized crime, are very deliberate in plying their trade, and avoid conspicuous consumption. They avoid rough stuff and "heat" and attempt to minimize risks. Requiring skill and contact with others, most seek subcultural support as suggested in Sutherland's "differential association" theory.

The professionalization of criminal justice has appeared to reduce many of the previous opportunities available in professional crime. The President's Commission on Law

Enforcement and the Administration of Justice (1967a) points to the importance of two essential elements that explain the success of professional crime: "the fence" and "the fix." The high cost of legal defense also may be responsible for a portion of the decline of such crime.

KEY CONCEPTS

Argot
Badger Game
Bank Examiner's Scam
Boojo
Booster
Box Man
Cannon
Characteristics of Professional Crime
Confidence Games
Fence
Heel
Model of Professional Crime
Paper Hanging
Pennyweighting
Pigeon Drop
Ponzi Schemes
Profession
Professional Crime
Pyramid Schemes
Scams
The Fix

REVIEW QUESTIONS

1. What are some characteristics of professional crime? Using "the model of professional crime" explain how this type of crime differs from non-professional crime.
2. How does a "big con" differ from "short cons?" Discuss some of the argot for the steps in a big con.
3. What is a "Ponzi scheme?" Give some examples.
4. What is a "pyramid scheme?" Give some examples.
5. Discuss some new and emerging patterns of professional crime.
6. What are some trends and new wrinkles in the field of "paper hanging?"
7. How do the operations of professional robbers differ from those of amateurs?
8. What are "affinity frauds" and how do they operate?
9. Distinguish between boosters and snitches.
10. Discuss the operations of professional burglars. What are some of their critical connections and typical operations?

INFOTRAC COLLEGE EDITION RESEARCH

Vantage Point 9.1 InfoTrac College Edition Research
What steps are being taken to reduce "identity theft"?

Vantage Point 9.2 InfoTrac College Edition Research
What are some new "scams" or new examples of scams that may not have been discussed in this chapter?

SELECTED READINGS

Mary Owen Cameron. 1964. *The Booster and the Snitch: Department Store Shoplifting.* New York: The Free Press.
This is the classic study by Cameron using the records of private security to analyze the operations of professional and amateur shoplifters.

Harry King and William Chambliss. 1984. *Harry King: A Professional Thief's Journal.* New York: Wiley.
This update of *Box Man* is a case study of a safecracker, Harry King.

Carl Klockars. 1974. *The Professional Fence.* New York: The Free Press.
The world of professional fence "Vince Swaggi" is explored in a case study by Klockars.

David W. Maurer. 1964. *Whiz Mob.* New Haven: College and University Press.
Linguist Maurer examines the argot, roles, and lifestyles of professional con artists.

Stephen Pizzo, Mary Fricker, and Paul Muolo. 1989. *Inside Job: The Looting of America's Savings and Loans.* New York: McGraw-Hill.
This is an account of the biggest series of white collar crimes in American history with losses of $500 billion. One-third of these losses were due to fraud.

David Simon and Frank Hagan. 1999. *White Collar Deviance.* Boston: Allyn and Bacon.
Chapter 5 looks at the world of professional crime, defined as professional white collar deviance.

Darrell Steffensmeier. 1986. *The Fence: In the Shadow of Two Worlds.* Totowa, NJ: Rowman and Littlefield.
This is Steffensmeier's classic on "Sam Goodman," a professional fence.

Edwin H. Sutherland. 1937. *The Professional Thief.* Chicago: University of Chicago.
Sutherland's account of the professional criminal world of "Chic Conwell" is the beginning point in the analysis of professional crime.

Richard T. Wright and Scott H. Decker. 1994. *Burglars on the Job: Streetlife and Residential Break-ins.* Boston: Northeastern University Press.
This is an excellent field study of unincarcerated burglars. The authors' interviews provide an inside look at the world of burglars.

Richard T. Wright and Scott H. Decker. 1997. *Armed Robbers in Action: Stickups and Street Culture.* Boston: Northeastern University Press.
This is one of the few studies of unincarcerated robbers.

10 Occupational Crime

All great fortunes begin with great crimes.

—Quote attributed to Honore de Balzac

Seldom do members of a profession meet, even be it for trade or merriment that it does not end up in some conspiracy against the public or some contrivance to raise prices.

—Adam Smith, The Wealth of Nations [1776] (1953), p. 137

White Collar Crime—The Classic Statement

Although previously discussed in the popular literature, the concept of *white collar crime* was first introduced in the social sciences by Edwin Sutherland in a 1939 presidential address to the American Sociological Association. Defining white collar crime as "a crime committed by a person of respectability and high social status in the course of his occupation" (Sutherland, 1940), Sutherland's address was important in that it was the first major statement on white collar crime in academic criminology. Volk (1977, p. 13) describes Sutherland's pioneering effort as "the sign of a Copernican revolution in Anglo-Saxon criminology," a radical reorientation in theoretical views of the nature of criminality. Mannheim (1965, p. 470) felt that if there were a Nobel Prize in criminology, Sutherland would deserve one for his effort. It certainly represented, to use Kuhn's (1962) notion, "a paradigm revolution," a new model that served to radically reorient future theoretical and empirical work in the field.

Sutherland's (1949) investigation using records of regulatory agencies, courts, and commissions found that of the seventy largest industrial and mercantile corporations studied over a forty-year period, every one violated at least one law and had an adverse decision made against it for false advertising, patent abuse, wartime trade violations, pricefixing, fraud, and/or intended manufacturing and sale of faulty goods. Many of these corporations were recidivists with an average of roughly eight adverse decisions issued for each. On the basis of his analysis, it becomes obvious that, although he used the general label *white collar crime,* Sutherland was in fact primarily interested in organizational or corporate crime.

Sutherland maintained that while "crime in the streets" attracts headlines and police attention, the extensive and far more costly "crime in the suites" proceeds relatively unnoticed. Despite the fact that white collar crimes cost several times more than other crimes put together, most cases are not treated under the criminal law. White collar crime differs from lower class criminality only in the implementation of criminal law that segregates white collar criminals administratively from other criminals (Sutherland, 1949). Furthermore, white collar crime is a sociological rather than a legal entity. It is the status of the offender rather than the legal uniqueness of the crime that is important.

The hazard of identifying white collar crime simply by official definitions is demonstrated by Hirschi and Gottfredson (1987 and 1989). They (erroneously) dispute the usefulness of the label "white collar crime," because the four UCR measures of white collar crime (fraud, embezzlement, forgery, and counterfeiting) show that most offenders are middle-class and differ little from traditional offenders. Steffensmeier (1989b) correctly responds that UCR offense categories are not appropriate indicators of white collar crime.

Related Concepts

One of the earliest scholars to discuss types of behaviors that later would be described as "white collar crime" was Edward Ross (1907) in an article that appeared in the *Atlantic Monthly.* Borrowing a term used by Lombroso (Lombroso-Ferrero, 1972), Ross referred to "**criminaloids**" as "those who prospered by flagitious [grossly wicked] practices which may not yet come under the ban of public opinion" (Ross, 1907, p. 46). Describing the criminaloid as "secure in his quilted armor of lawyer-spun sophistries" (Ross, 1907, p. 32), Ross viewed such offenders as morally insensible and concerned with success, but not with the proper means of achieving it. C. Wright Mills used a similar notion, "the higher immorality," to characterize this moral insensibility of the power elite. Mills felt this was a continuing, institutionalized component of modern U.S. society, involving corrupt, unethical, and illegal practices of the wealthy and powerful (Mills, 1952).

A variety of other terms have been proposed as substitutes, synonyms, variations, or related terms for white collar crime, including "avocational crime" (Geis, 1974a), "corporate crime" (Clinard and Quinney, 1986), "economic crime" (American Bar Association, 1976), "elite deviance" (Simon, 1996), "the criminal elite" (Coleman, 1994), "occupational crime" (Clinard and Quinney, 1986; Green, 1990), "organizations crime" (Schrager and Short, 1978), "professional crime" (Clinard and Quinney, 1986), and "upperworld crime" (Geis, 1974b). (See also Schlegel and Weisburd, 1994; Albanese, 1995; Blankenship, 1995; Jamieson, 1995; Friedrichs, 1995).

Sutherland's (1949, p. 9) initial concept of white collar crime, defined as "a crime committed by a person of respectability and high social status in the course of his occupation," has been criticized on a number of points, mainly relating to: the uncertain importance attached to the status of the offender, the exact meaning of the status of the offender, and the fact that such "crime" includes deviant behaviors that are not necessarily illegal (Quinney, 1964, p. 285). All of these criticisms are on target; however, the importance of Sutherland's concept lies not in its scientific utility but rather in its sensitizing quality. It alerted us to a phenomenon and, as a result, the field of criminology will never be the same.

In July 1996 at an academic workshop sponsored by the National White Collar Crime Center (1996), a number of white collar crime writers and experts tentatively agreed on the following definition:

> **White collar crime** refers to "illegal or unethical acts that violate fiduciary responsibility or public trust, committed by an individual or organization, usually during the course of legitimate occupational activity by persons of high or respectable social status for personal or organizational gain."

This chapter, as well as the next, will concentrate on two key types of criminal activity: occupational criminal behavior and corporate (organizational) criminal behavior. **Occupational crime** refers to personal violations that take place for self-benefit during the course of a legitimate occupation, while **corporate (organizational) criminal behavior** refers to crimes by business or officials, committed on behalf of the employing organizations. Though organizational crime refers to crime on behalf of the organization, it becomes corporate (business) crime when it is done for the benefit of a private business. Thus much of what ordinarily would be branded as corporate (business) crime in a free enterprise economy is labeled organizational crime when committed by state bureaucrats in socialist systems. The organizational, economic crimes discussed in this chapter are also distinct from political crimes by government, which will be discussed in Chapter 12; the latter have more to do with efforts to maintain power, ideology, and social control than with economic advantage.

Figures 10.1a and 10.1b depict the relationship between the many definitions of white collar crime. Figure 10.1a is an attempt by this author to address the debate among writers as to whether the best term for this subject of study is elite deviance (Simon, 1996), white collar crime (Coleman, 1994), or economic crime (various writers). This author views elite deviance as the broadest term, while white collar crime focuses on elite "crimes" but also includes non-elite activities—for example, employee theft and lower-level occupational crime. When observers ignore the status of the offender, economic

FIGURE 10.1A Interrelationship Between Elite Deviance, White Collar Crime, and Economic Crime

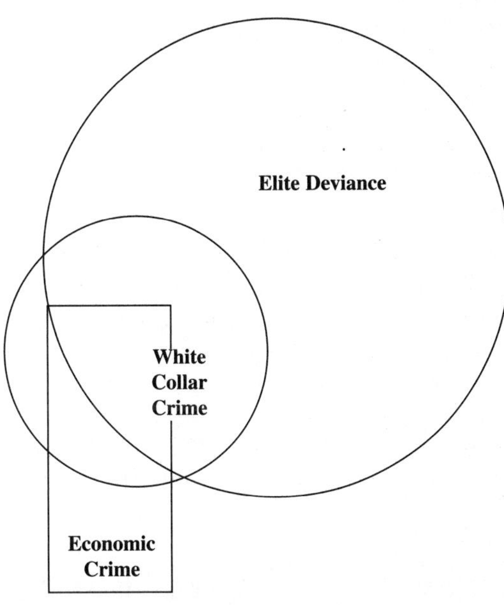

FIGURE 10.1B Types of White Collar Crime

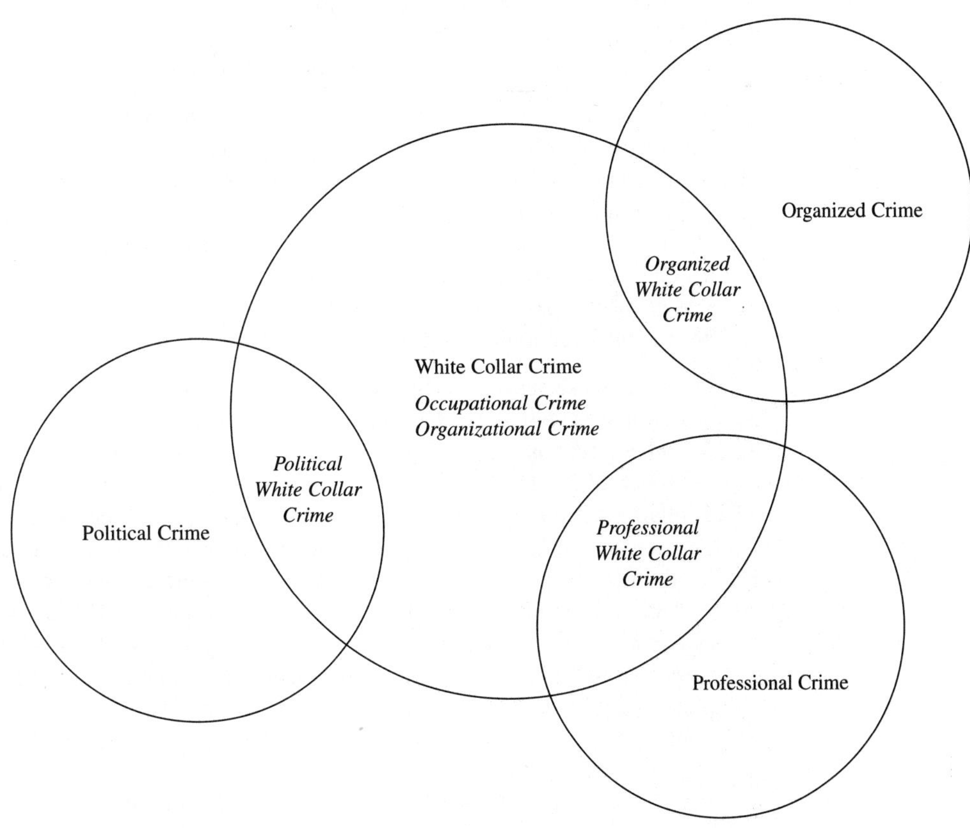

crime can include minor fraud, embezzlement, and the like, even when it is not committed by individuals of high status. The issue is not which of these concepts is best, but rather how each taps a different dimension of "white collar crime."

Figure 10.1b illustrates the author's notion that there are five types of white collar crime:

1. Occupational Crime
2. Organizational Crime
3. Professional White Collar Crime
4. Organized White Collar Crime
5. Political White Collar Crime (Hagan, 1996b)

While occupational and organizational (corporate) white collar crime are accepted by most scholars as the core of white collar crime, new hybrid forms of white collar crime are emerging. Professional white collar crime is illustrated by the Savings and Loan scandal, the PTL scandal, or Sears' cheating on automobile repairs (to be discussed shortly). Organized white collar crime is spotlighted by prosecutions of legitimate businesses under federal RICO (Racketeer-Influenced and Corrupt Organizations) provisions. Finally, political white collar crime is illustrated by the BCCI (Bank of Credit and Commerce International) affair and Iran-Contra, all to be discussed in this and the next chapter.

The Measurement and Cost of Occupational Crime

Even in societies that permit a measure of freedom of information, the collection of accurate data on most occupational and corporate crimes is difficult. Our primary sources of data (discussed in Chapters 2 and 3), such as official statistics (the UCR), victim surveys (the NCVS), and self-reports, generally do not include much information on corporate or upper-level occupational crimes.

Problems faced by researchers who attempt to examine occupational crime include:

1. The higher professions are self-regulating, and very often codes of silence and protectionism rather than sanctions greet wrongdoers.
2. Many employers simply ask for resignations from errant workers in order to avoid scandal and recrimination.
3. Occupational crime statistics are not kept on a systematic basis by criminal justice agencies or by professional associations.
4. Probes of occupational wrongdoing by outsiders are usually greeted by secrecy or a professional version of "honor among thieves."

For all of these reasons, estimates of the cost of white collar crime (which includes corporate crime as well as much occupational crime) are difficult to arrive at. This remains an area where criminologists still rely on anecdotes and secondary sources, primarily because much of the hard data simply are not readily available. Estimates of the cost of white collar crime do not appear in standard official reports such as the UCR.

The Senate Subcommittee on Investigations (Senate Permanent Subcommittee, 1979) estimated that cost at roughly $36 billion in 1976. Estimates for the early 1980s place the figure at upwards of $50 billion, a costly sum considering that FBI estimates for all UCR property crimes such as burglary, larceny, and robbery were in the $10 billion range in the early 1980s. Much higher estimates of revenues from white collar crime have been made by the Judiciary Subcommittee on Antitrust and Monopoly, which put the figure between $174 billion and $231 billion annually in the late seventies (Clinard and Yeager, 1980, p. 8). By the nineties, the estimated cost of $500 billion for bailing out savings and loan companies alone, with 5 to 40 percent of the losses due to fraud, justifies even higher estimates. The cost of white collar crimes far exceeds the cost of traditional crimes as recorded in official police statistics and as previously discussed in Chapter 1.

The History of Corporate, Organizational, and Occupational Crime

Current publicity and concern with corporate, organizational, and occupational crime sometimes creates the false impression that such activities did not exist in the past. Nothing could be further from the truth. In fact, history is replete with examples of past corporate wrongdoing; the current business climates probably set higher moral expectations than ever before.

In the early history of capitalism and the Industrial Revolution fortunes were made by unscrupulous "robber barons," who viewed the state and laws as negotiable nuisances. Cornelius Vanderbilt, the railroad magnate, when asked whether he was concerned with the legality of one of his operations, was quoted as having stated: "Law! What do I care about Law. Hain't I got the power?" (cited in Browning and Gerassi, 1980, p. 201).

Journalistic "muckrakers" or specialists in exposing what Becker calls "sex, sin and sewage" (Becker, 1954, p. 145) preceded criminologists in analyzing abuses in high places. Works such as Lincoln Steffens' *The Shame of the Cities* (1904) and Upton Sinclair's *The Jungle* (1906) dramatically focused on and aroused public interest in corruption and abuse in public and private organizations. John Kenneth Galbraith tells the story of John D. Rockefeller, the founder of the family fortune, and a lecture he was fond of giving to Sunday school classes: "The growth of a large business is merely the survival of the fittest . . . . The American Beauty rose can be produced in the splendor and fragrance which bring cheer to its beholder only by sacrificing the early buds which grow up around it" (Peter, 1977, p. 87). Browning and Gerassi (1980) in *The American Way of Crime* claim that the period between the Civil War and World War I was probably the most corrupt in U.S. history and describe this time as a "dictatorship of the rich." No one valued private property more than the industrial magnates who were stealing it (Browning and Gerassi, 1980, p. 210). Jay Gould, a captain of industry, gobbled up railroads through stock manipulation, rate wars, the falsifying of profit records, and the intimidation of competitors by means of hired thugs such as the Hell's Kitchen mob (pp. 133–36). Myers (1936, pp. 13, 17) in his *History of Great American Fortunes* reports an episode in which Russel Sage and his business associates masterminded a swindle against their creditors; after it succeeded, Sage conned his own partners out of their proceeds from the caper.

Political corruption, bribery, kickbacks, and influence-peddling among political officeholders—federal, state and local—have been rife since the very beginnings of the republic. The widespread acceptance of such corruption has given rise to a number of humorous comments, for example, the description of Mayor Curley of Boston as having been so crooked that when they buried him, they had to screw him into the ground. Another cynical remark claims that it was so cold the other day that the politicians had their hands in their own pockets.

In the post-Civil War period in the United States, political machines were epitomized by "Boss" Tweed's Tammany Hall (New York City's Democratic party), in which widespread vice and corruption were combined with political favoritism and vote fraud. More than one political election was won with stuffed ballot boxes or the graveyard vote. Ross (1988) in *Fall from Grace: Sex, Scandal and Corruption in American Politics from 1702 to the Present* documents the fact that political scandals have struck in nearly every decade since before the American Revolution.

Such political corruption and scandal is hardly limited to the United States. Places such as Italy, Japan, and the Latin American countries have been wracked by high-level scandals. In the nineties, for instance, former President Raul Salinas of Mexico was in prison on charges of illegally amassing $120 million by selling favors to industrialists. Former Venezuelan President Carlos Perez was found guilty of misusing a $417-million secret fund. A dozen Argentinean officials were convicted of a multimillion dollar fraud involving IBM, and Ecuador's vice president fled to Costa Rica to escape charges of embezzlement (Moffett and Friedland, 1996).

Typologies of White Collar Crime

One useful typology of occupational and organizational crime is suggested by Bloch and Geis (1970, p. 301), who distinguish between offenses committed:

1. by individuals as individuals (for example, lawyers, doctors, and so forth);
2. by employees against their employers (for example, embezzlers);
3. by policy-making officials for the employers (for example, antitrust cases);
4. by agents of the corporation against the general public (for example, in false advertising); and
5. by merchants against customers (for example, in consumer frauds).

Another widely cited typology of white collar crime is proposed by Edelhertz (1970, pp. 19–20). He identifies:

1. crimes by persons operating on an individual ad hoc basis (for example, income tax violations, credit card frauds, bankruptcy frauds, and so on);
2. crimes committed in the course of the occupations of those operating inside business, government, or other establishments, in violation of their duty of loyalty and fidelity to employers or clients (for example, embezzlement, employee larceny, payroll padding, and the like);
3. crimes incidental to, and in furtherance of, business operations, but not central to the purpose of the business (for example, antitrust violations, commercial bribery, food and drug violations, and so forth);
4. white collar crime as a business, or as the central activity. [This is covered in this text under the label "professional crime;" it refers to activities such as medical and health frauds, advance fee swindles, and phony contests.]

Eliminating Edelhertz's item four as more appropriately an example of professional crime and combining elements of both Bloch and Geis and Edelhertz, Figure 10.2 proposes an **Occupational/Organizational Crime Grid,** which classifies the crimes in terms of both perpetrators and victims. Goff and Reasons (1986) have proposed a similar model for organizational crime.

While many crimes in fact defy placement in mutually exclusive, homogenous categories, these types offer a useful scheme for organizing the presentation of occupational crime in this chapter and organizational/corporate crime in the next chapter.

Legal Regulation

Occupations and the Law

In Western societies, the legal regulation of occupations is often "self-regulation." Although laws and codes of ethics purportedly exist to protect the public from harmful occupational activity, much self-governance has been used instead to protect the interests of members of the occupation. The more developed *professions* attempt to convince legislatures that they possess highly sophisticated, useful, esoteric knowledge; that they are

FIGURE 10.2 The Occupational/Organizational Crime Grid

		Crime Committed by:		
		Individual (Public, Consumer)	*Employee*	*Organization (Corporation, State)*
Crime Committed Against (Victim):	*Individual (Public, Consumer)*	(1) Merchant vs. Consumer Professional vs. Client	(2) Individual Corruption, Payoffs	(3) Production of Unsafe Products Deceptive Advertising
	Employee	(4)	(5) Sweetheart Contracts	(6) Occupational Health and Safety Violations Environmental Hazards on Job
	Organization (Corporation, State)	(7) Insurance Fraud Tax Fraud	(8) Embezzlement Inside Trading	(9) Industrial Espionage Unfair Competition Patent Violations

Type	*Description*
(1)	Individual vs. Individual (Public)
(2)*	Employee vs. Individual (Public)
(3)	Organization vs. Individual (Public)
(4)*	Individual vs. Employer
(5)*	Employee vs. Employee
(6)	Organization vs. Employee
(7)*	Individual vs. Organization
(8)	Employee vs. Organization
(9)	Organization vs. Organization

*These crimes may not have direct corporate or occupational ramifications.

committed to serving societal needs through a formal code of ethics; and that they therefore should be granted autonomy, since they and only they are in a position to evaluate the quality of their service. In fact, the actual legal codes that control occupational practice tend to be formulated by the occupations themselves in order to dominate or monopolize a line of work. Playwright George Bernard Shaw (1941, p. 9) in *The Doctor's Dilemma,* has one of his characters state that "all professions are a conspiracy against the laity." The original source for Shaw's statement was the eighteenth-century conservative economist Adam Smith (1953, p. 137), who claimed, "Seldom do members of a profession meet, even be it for trade or merriment, that it does not end up in some conspiracy against the public or some contrivance to raise prices."

More developed occupations (professions) virtually control the law-making machinery affecting their work. Professional organizations and their political action committees are quite effective in blocking legislation that may be detrimental to their interests. An excellent case in point was the effective lobbying campaign orchestrated by the American Bankers Association in 1983 to block proposed legislation that would have required banks to withhold interest paid on accounts for federal income tax purposes. Although this would have represented more work for banks, the Internal Revenue Service lost an effective weapon with which to collect unpaid taxes; it could have increased federal revenues an estimated $8 billion.

Another example of professional power is the AMA (American Medical Association), which Friedson (1970) describes as "professional dominance" and Harmer (1975) as American Medical Avarice. The AMA as a lobbying organization appears more concerned with guarding profit, competition, and private enterprise in the business of medicine than in supporting legislation that would improve the equality of medical care delivery. According to the *Report of the National Advisory Commission on Health Manpower* (1968, p. 268), the health statistics of certain groups in the United States, particularly the poor, resemble the health statistics in a developing country.

Occupational crime may be controlled by professional associations themselves, by traditional criminal law, by civil law, and by administrative law. Actions by professional ethics boards may include suspensions, censure, temporary or permanent removal of license and membership, and the like. Traditional criminal prosecution also may occur, such as for larceny, burglary, and criminal fraud; civil actions by the government may include damage and license suspension suits. Administrative proceedings may call for taking away licenses, seizing illegal goods, and fines.

The FBI in its early history was involved primarily in investigating and enforcing white collar crimes, such as false purchases, security sales violations, bankruptcy fraud, and antitrust violations; only later did it become preoccupied with its gangbuster image (Lowenthal, 1950, p. 12). As late as 1977, however, the House Judiciary Subcommittee charged that the FBI was soft on white collar crime and that its idea of white collar crime was small-scale fraud (Simon and Swart, 1984).

This issue of legal processing of corporate and occupational offenders will be further explored at the end of this chapter. But first we will explore the nature and types of such crime.

Occupational Crime

Crimes by Employees

Although there are cases of overlap, both "crimes by employees" and "crimes by individuals" are examples of occupational crime—crime committed in the course of a legitimate occupation for one's own benefit. While the types of activities to be discussed in this section are executed by employees (those who work for someone else), those to be examined in "crimes by individuals" will primarily be crimes by professionals.

Edelhertz's Typology. One attempt to delineate white collar crime is the widely cited typology and examples provided by Edelhertz (1970, pp. 73–75; see VANTAGE POINT 10.1). While Edelhertz had two other types in his classification, many of those listed in his "crimes by persons operating on an individual basis" are not necessarily occupational in nature, except that the victims often happen to be organizations (business or the state). Some examples that he gives include bankruptcy frauds and violations of Federal Reserve regulations by pledging stock for further purchases, flouting margin requirements. His category of "white-collar crime as business, or as the central activity" better fits the definition of professional crime as defined in the preceding chapter. Edelhertz's category A fits our discussion of "occupational crime," while category B better fits our definition of "corporate crime."

Crimes by Employees Against Individuals (the Public)

Self-aggrandizing *crimes by employees against the public* (type 2 in Figure 10.2), take the form of political corruption by public servants or office-holders (public employees), or commercial corruption by employees in the private sector. These activities are distinguished from corporate or organizational criminal activities of the same type by the fact that in this case the employee personally benefits from the violation.

VANTAGE POINT 10.1

Edelhertz's Typology of White Collar Crime

Edelhertz's typology of white collar crime details a variety of offenses:

A. Crimes committed in the course of their occupations by those operating inside business, government, or other establishments in violation of their duty of loyalty and fidelity to employer or client.
   1. Commercial bribery and kickbacks, i.e., by and to buyers, insurance adjusters, contracting officers, quality inspectors, government inspectors and auditors, etc.
   2. Bank violations by bank officers, employees, and directors
   3. Embezzlement or self-dealing by business or union officers and employees
   4. Securities fraud by insiders trading to their advantage by the use of special knowledge
   5. Employee petty larceny and expense account fraud
   6. Frauds by computer, causing unauthorized payments
   7. "Sweetheart contracts" entered into by union officers
   8. Embezzlement or self-dealing by attorneys, trustees, and fiduciaries
   9. Fraud against the government:
      a. Padding of payrolls
      b. Conflict of interest
      c. False travel, expense, or per diem claims

B. Crimes incidental to and in furtherance of business operations, but not the central purpose of the business
   1. Tax violations
   2. Antitrust violations
   3. Commercial bribery of another's employee, officer or fiduciary (including union officers)
   4. Food and drug violations
   5. False weights and measures by retailers
   6. Violations of Truth-in-Lending Act by misrepresentation of credit terms and prices
   7. Submission or publication of false financial statements to obtain credit
   8. Use of fictitious or overvalued collateral
   9. Check-kiting to obtain operating capital on short-term financing
   10. Securities Act violations, i.e., sale of non-registered securities to obtain operating capital, false proxy statements, manipulation of market to support corporate credit or access to capital markets, etc.
   11. Collusion between physicians and pharmacists to cause the writing of unnecessary prescriptions
   12. Dispensing by pharmacists in violation of law, excluding narcotics traffic
   13. Immigration fraud in support of employment agency operations to provide domestics
   14. Housing code violations by landlords
   15. Deceptive advertising
   16. Fraud against the government:
       a. False claims
       b. False statements:
          1) to induce contracts
          2) AID fraud
          3) housing fraud
          4) Small Business Administration fraud, such as bootstrapping, self-dealing, crossdealing, etc., or obtaining direct loans by use of false financial statements
       c. Moving contracts in urban renewal
   17. Labor violations (Davis Bacon Act)
   18. Commercial espionage

Source: Herbert Edelhertz, 1970, *The Nature, Impact and Prosecution of White-Collar Crime,* National Institute of Law Enforcement and Criminal Justice, Washington, D.C.: Government Printing Office, pp. 73–75.

InfoTrac College Edition Research

Using the "keyword search," examine "white collar crime." What are some types discussed in the articles?

Public Corruption.

There is no distinctly American criminal class except Congress.

—Mark Twain, 1899, p. 98

"Cigar smoke, booze, and money delivered in brown paper bags"—This is how Hedrick Smith envisions the backroom world of politics in *The Power Game* (1989). The list of occupation-related crime on the part of political employees or office-holders may include furnishing favors to private businesses such as illegal commissions on public contracts, fraudulent licenses, tax exemptions, and lower tax evaluations (Clinard and Quinney, 1973, p. 189). As an example, health inspectors in New York City ("City Inspectors," 1988) turned the Department of Health into the Department of Wealth and doubled or tripled their salaries by extorting payments from restaurants, threatening to cite them for health code violations if they did not pay up.

In 1999 eight federal food inspectors were arrested in a bribery and kickback scheme that permitted wholesalers to cheat their suppliers. The scheme involved the inspectors grading fruit and vegetables as low quality, gaining lower prices for the wholesalers who then turned around and sold the items as Grade A produce. Some of the inspectors earned over $100,000 a year in payoffs (Weiser, 1999).

The use of public office for private gain defines political corruption. Such behavior is widespread internationally. The Transparency International Corruption Perception Index (CIP), developed by Berlin headquartered Transparency International Incorporated, rates countries on the basis of seven surveys of business people, political analysts, and the general public. The Corruption Perception Index for the year 2000 (www.gwdg.de/~uwvw/2000Data.html) ranged from a high of 10 (highly clean) to 0 (highly corrupt). Some selected country ranks and scores included:

Rank		*CPI Score*
1	Finland	10
2	Denmark	9.8
3.5	New Zealand	9.4
3.5	Sweden	9.4
5	Canada	9.2
10	United Kingdom	8.7
14	USA	7.8
25	Belgium	6.1
39	Italy	4.6
49	Brazil	3.9
59	Mexico	3.3
71	Venezuela	2.7
82	Russia	2.1
85	Indonesia	1.7
87	Ukraine	1.5
89	Yugoslavia	1.3
90	Nigeria	1.2

Another survey of expatriate business people by Political and Economic Risk Consultancy Ltd. had 450 respondents grade twelve Asian countries on a scale of 0–10, where zero was an ideal situation (www.theaustralian.com.au:80/finance/43827778.htm). Singapore ranked best at 1.55 for low corruption, followed by Hong Kong (4.06) and Japan (4.25). In descending order they were followed by Taiwan, Malaysia, Thailand, and South Korea. The worst countries were: Vietnam (8.5), Indonesia (9.91), India (9.17), and China (9.0). In 2000, in a show of seriousness in China's war on corruption, China executed a senior official after he was convicted of bribe taking.

After a 1999 report commissioned by the European Parliament indicated that 2–10 percent of the value of business transactions involves bribery, twenty European commissioners resigned en masse after criticism of their failure to do anything about it (Partridge, 1999). Dolive (1999), in examining systematic corruption in Italy, Japan, and Russia, claims that the corrupt politicians in those countries were the initiators and perpetuators of systematic corruption. Rather than the system being dependent on particular individuals who are at times exposed or removed, successors continue the system of corruption, which is the driving force of both the economy and politics.

- In France, in the Elf scandal (named for state-owned oil company Elf Acquitane), slush funds and corruption were traced to former foreign minister Roland Dumas and, in 2000, to former interior minister Charles Pasqua. Also implicated was former German Chancellor Helmut Kohl's political party (Ignatius, 2000).
- In Russia, a group of gangster-capitalists called the "oligarchs" looted the assets of the state during the 1990s.
- In the U.S., officials at Citibank operated as the "private bank" for unsavory figures such as Raul Salinas, brother of the former president of Mexico, who is now in prison for murder; Asif Zardari, former husband of former Pakistani prime minister Benazir Bhutto, who is in prison for kickbacks; and two daughters of former president Suharto, who allegedly stole billions of dollars from that country.
- A Swiss investigation in 1999 uncovered evidence that Mabetex, a construction company, paid $10–$15 million to Russian officials including then-president Boris Yeltsin in order to obtain contracts (LaFraniere, 1999).

In 1999 fugitive financier and embezzler Martin Frankel was extradited to the United States from Germany after an international manhunt and indicted on 36 counts of fraud, money laundering, and racketeering in an embezzlement scheme that cost southern insurance companies $200 million. Frankel used a Swiss bank account and converted, stole, and embezzled funds by acquiring stakes in insurance companies, withdrawing assets for investments, and simply pocketing the money. He covered his theft with false profit and loss statements. He also lived a lavish lifestyle in a mansion on four acres in Greenwich, Connecticut (Wayne, 1999).

Joel Henderson and David Simon in their book *Crimes of the Criminal Justice System* (1994) document widespread and persistent corruption and wrongdoing throughout the criminal justice system.

Police Corruption—The Mollen Commission. Between 1992 and 1993 the Mollen Commission, named after a former New York City Deputy Mayor for Public Safety, conducted an investigation of corruption in that city's police department and focused attention on police wrongdoing the likes of which had not existed for twenty years (since the Knapp Commission of the 1970s revealed widespread corruption, particularly associated with narcotics enforcement). Called because five New York City officers were arrested by Suffolk County police for selling cocaine, the hearings featured informants from within the ranks who revealed police extortion practices, theft and reselling of drugs, rolling of drunks, robbing of dead people, snorting cocaine while on duty, and indulging in brutality—particularly in poor sections of the city. Often higher-ups in the department had blocked investigations ("NYC's Mollen Commission," 1993). A blue wall of silence and loyalty to peers can take precedence over concerns about graft and violation of oath of office (see also Kappeler, Sluder, and Alpert, 1994).

Certainly police wrongdoing was not limited to the nation's largest department:

- In 1995 racist and brutal statements made on tape by Los Angeles Police Detective Mark Fuhrman were primary factors in a jury's decision to find O.J. Simpson not guilty of murdering his wife and her friend.

- In New Orleans in 1993, over fifty officers were convicted on charges including murder, rape, assault, and drug trafficking. One was convicted of killing another police officer while robbing a convenience store.
- In Philadelphia six officers pleaded guilty to framing people in court and stealing money (Witkin, 1995).
- In Jersey City, N.J., police officers were accused, among other things, of participating in what police investigators called "Operation Boneyard:" stolen and illegally parked cars were towed to the city car pound and converted to city property without the owners being notified.
- In 1995 in Atlanta, six officers were arrested for shaking down drug dealers and extorting money from citizens.
- In 1987 nearly 100 Miami police officers (1 in 18 on the force) were believed involved in serious corruption primarily related to drug trafficking ("Miami Police," 1987).
- In Cleveland an FBI sting operation resulted in the arrest of 23 police officers who served as security guards for illegal gambling dens and warned them of impending raids ("FBI Gambling Sting," 1991).
- In Detroit, former Police Chief William Hart was convicted of helping embezzle $2.6 million from a special police fund to give his girlfriend lavish gifts ("Detroit's Former Chief," 1992).

In 1999 at Rampart Community Police Station in Los Angeles, twenty police officers were involved in systematic corruption. Some planted illegal drugs on innocent people, planted guns on suspects who had been shot by police, burglarized the homes of petty criminals, and framed roughly 100 people. In a plea bargain, one officer testified that prisoners were routinely railroaded by fabricated evidence and police lies. As a result, a large number of convictions have been overturned. In 2000 a jury acquitted four New York officers who mistakenly gunned down innocent citizen Amadou Diallo with 41 rounds, killing him instantly. In 2000 New York City police officer Justin Volpe was sentenced to 30 years in prison for torturing Abner Louima in the bathroom of a Brooklyn stationhouse by sticking a broom handle up his rectum, doing considerable damage. As a result of cover-ups by police during the initial stages of these incidents, juries have become more skeptical of testimony by police officers and other witnesses.

While public preoccupation with police corruption is viewed defensively by police, for most people the police officer symbolizes the law and engenders higher public expectations of proper conduct (Barker and Carter, 1986). Coleman (1994, p. 45) explains that "police officers simply have more opportunities to receive illegal payments than other public employees" because they are asked to enforce inadequate vice laws that try to control very profitable black markets.

Police corruption is mirrored in other agencies of government, in industry, in labor, and in the professions. In Pennsylvania, a large scale police raid of Graterford Prison by the state police, correctional officers, and U.S. Customs officers closed down wide-scale drug trafficking in the prison. Thirteen guards were arrested because they were believed to have been instrumental in the drug overdose deaths of 11 inmates ("Drug Raid," 1995). In 1988 an undercover investigation in Philadelphia city jails (Jacoby, 1988) found over 30 guards involved in, among other offenses, smuggling drugs, money, and weapons into the prison; helping inmates escape; and taking bribes from reputed mobsters.

Judgescam—"Operation Greylord." In 1983 Federal Bureau of Investigation agents revealed that for three years they had posed as lawyers and criminals to run a "sting" operation on the Cook County, Illinois, criminal justice system. The "sting" was code-named "Operation Greylord" (referring to the powdered wigs historically worn by judges). This was the largest and most successful investigation into judicial misconduct in

U.S. history, and by the fall of 1987 it had resulted in convictions of 61 persons, including 11 judges, police officers, lawyers, and court officials, with additional trials and indictments ongoing (Bensinger, 1987).

In 1998 the *Pittsburgh Post Gazette* published a ten-part series that alleged that federal agents and prosecutors repeatedly broke the law in the pursuit of convictions (Moushey, 1998). Investigators claimed to have found examples of prosecutors lying, hiding evidence, distorting facts, engaging in cover-ups, paying for perjury, and setting up innocent people in order to obtain indictments, guilty pleas, and convictions. Some criminals walked free as a reward for conspiring with the government.

Watergate. Perhaps no one event evokes images of official corruption, deceit, and subterfuge as does Watergate. This story began with the discovery of an illegal break-in at the Democratic National Committee Headquarters located in the Watergate complex in Washington, D.C. The burglary was carried out by agents in the employ of President Nixon.

Richard Nixon certainly was not the first U.S. president to be involved in crooked practices (see Chambliss, 1988a). He was, however, the first to be driven from office in disgrace because of the extent of his activities and the first to be saved from certain criminal prosecution through a full pardon before-the-fact (issued by his successor, President Gerald Ford). At the time, President Nixon's attitude toward the probe appeared in one of the later-to-be-released "missing tapes": "I don't give a shit what happens. I want you to stonewall it. Let them plead the Fifth Amendment, cover up, or anything else if it'll save the plan" (cited in Peter, 1977, p. 317).

Among the offenses of the Watergate team were: burglary, illegal surveillance, attempted bribery of a judge (Ellsberg case), selling ambassadorships in return for illegal campaign donations, maintenance of an illegal "slush fund;" destruction of evidence; use of "dirty tricks" in political campaigns planned by the FBI director and the president; requests by U.S. Attorney General John Mitchell (the nation's top law enforcement officer) for IRS audits on opponents; use of the CIA and FBI to attempt to halt the investigation; perjury; withholding information; altering evidence; and deliberate lying to the American public by the nation's top officeholder (Simon, 1996, p. 3).

ABSCAM. ABSCAM (Arab or Abdul Scam) was an FBI sting operation in which agents posing as rich oil sheiks bribed a number of members of the U.S. Congress. Whether we call it *baksheesh* (Middle East), *bustarelle* (Italy), *pot de vin* (France), *mordida* (Latin America), or just plain bribes (North America), kickbacks and corruption are apparently both widespread and international in scope. Individuals in their occupational roles may give or receive bribes for their own personal benefit (occupational crime) or for the benefit of the organization/corporation (organizational/corporate crime). Bribery, influence peddling, and corruption are acceptable patterns of international commerce and are not even illegal in many countries.

Particularly revealing in the ABSCAM operation was the relative ease with which foreign agents were able to bribe members of the U.S. Congress. Though many regard such federal sting operations as entrapment (causing a crime to happen that would not have occurred if the stimulus had not been put there by the government), others perceive such "aggressive tactics" as the only means of ferreting out "upper-world crime." VANTAGE POINT 10.2 details official wrongdoing of the Reagan administration, during which more officials were indicted or resigned than ever before in U.S. history.

Private Corruption. *Commercial bribery and kickbacks* (in which the individual personally benefits) can take place in a variety of ways. Buyers for large retail chains may accept gifts or cash in return for placing orders. At the expense of the general public in

VANTAGE POINT 10.2

Crimes of the Reagan Era

Both alleged and actual crime and wrongdoing during the Reagan administration far exceeded those during any previous administration, including that of Nixon, Harding, Grant, and Buchanan. Between 1980 and 1988 over 200 Reaganites came under either ethical or criminal investigation, the greatest number of scandals in any administration in U.S. history (Ross, 1988, p. 1). Paralleling public fiascos of the eighties were a variety of private sector financial scandals such as the savings and loan scandal and insider trading on Wall Street. While neither of these is directly linked to then-President Reagan, the deregulatory, laissez-faire enforcement environment created by his administration certainly played a hand.

The major public scandals of the Reagan era were:

- Corruption at the Environmental Protection Agency
- The Wedtech Scandal
- The Pentagon Procurement Scandal
- Abuses at the Department of Housing and Urban Development
- The Iran-Contra Affair

The latter will be covered in Chapter 12, "Political Crime."

Environmental Protection Agency (EPA) Scandal

In 1983 the EPA became embroiled in charges of mismanagement, conflicts of interest, and sweetheart deals with polluting companies. When Congress began an investigation, then-President Reagan instructed the EPA administrator, Anne Gorsuch Burford, to refuse to release documents. She later resigned amid charges of unethical conduct, political manipulation, and sweetheart deals. Her assistant, Rita Lavelle, was also fired and later found guilty of perjury and obstructing a congressional investigation (Kohn, 1989).

In all, over twenty senior EPA employees were removed from office and others resigned under pressure for having been influenced by lobbyists for the chemical industry. Similar regulatory neglect of nuclear safety is estimated to have racked up a $200 billion deferred bill for cleanup after Reagan left office (Johnson, 1991).

Wedtech

Wedtech was a former machine shop in the South Bronx, which in five years (1980–85) would be parlayed into a multimillion-dollar defense contractor through bribery and corruption. In investigating influence peddling and kickbacks at Wedtech, federal prosecutors would eventually dispatch 25 persons to prison, but were placed in the curious position of investigating their own boss, Attorney General Edwin Meese (Thompson, 1990).

Wedtech also illustrated a pattern to be repeated in the abuses at the Department of Housing and Urban Development (HUD); that is, how greedy, well-connected opportunists pillaged programs designed to assist the poor and, in this case, minorities. Among those caught up in the Wedtech saga were Representative Mario Biaggi, Robert Garcia, and Bronx borough president Stanley Simon (all non-Reaganites); Lynn Nofziger (a Reagan staffer whose conviction was reversed); and E. Robert Wallach, counselor to Meese, who was sentenced to six years in jail but who also protected Meese and Reagan. Wallach's conviction was overturned in 1992. Meese, when questioned before a congressional committee, would have "amnesia" similar to that experienced by Reagan in his appearance during an Iran-Contra probe. Meese's memory failed 37 times before the committee (Traub, 1990).

Operation Ill Wind and the Pentagon Procurement Scandal

"Operation Ill Wind" was the name of a secret FBI undercover probe begun during the summer of 1986 to uncover corruption in the awarding of procurement con-

the form of higher prices, insurance adjusters, contracting officers, and quality control inspectors may all be willing to accept bribes in return for overlooking their duties to employers.

Auto dealers are both perpetrators and victims of *sharp practices.* In analyzing what they call "coerced crime," Leonard and Weber (1970) describe how the four major domestic auto producers pressure their roughly thirty thousand dealers (who are technically independent proprietors) into bilking their customers. These dealers commit "coerced crime" because in order to retain their franchises they must meet minimum sales quotas, and in order to meet these, they must often employ "shady practices." The latter include: forcing

VANTAGE POINT 10.2—*Continued*

tracts by the Department of Defense. The Pentagon Procurement Scandal illustrates insider trading, Washington-style (Duffy et al., 1988, p. 16). By September 1991 Operation Ill Wind had resulted in the conviction of 45 defense contractors, executives, and Pentagon officials, as well as five corporations. Melvyn Paisley, a former assistant secretary of the Navy, was the highest Defense Department official to plead guilty to charges of conspiracy to defraud the government, bribery, and theft of government property (Skorneck, 1991, p. 3A). One charge against Paisley included rigging a $100-million contract for reconnaissance drones. In 1991 Paisley pleaded guilty to accepting bribes from Unisys Corporation and Martin Marietta Corporation on four separate weapons systems. Prosecutions continued in 1992 (Pasztor, 1991).

The HUD Scandals

Ethical and criminal violations by government officials of the Department of Housing and Urban Development may have represented the biggest set of executive-branch violations during the Reagan administration. By 1989, 28 of 48 agency programs were found to have fraud or other significant problems amounting to losses of over $4 billion (Roberts, Shapiro, and Taylor, 1989, p. 29). The scandals at HUD would not be fully disclosed until May 1989 (after Reagan's term), when the House Government Operations Committee began a 14-month investigation. In November 1990 the committee issued a scathing report that the Reagan administration's HUD was "enveloped by influence-peddling, favoritism, abuse, greed, fraud, embezzlement, and theft" (Pound, 1990, p. B8); and this went to the highest levels and included charges against HUD secretary Pierce and top aids.

Pierce was accused of approving grants and subsidies for friends and helping the politically well-connected obtain contracts, including members of his old law firm (Roberts, Shapiro, and Taylor, 1989). In 1983 assistant HUD secretary Emanuel Savas resigned before he could be fired for "abuse of office." Johnson (1991, p. 180) explains:

> **Long before the investigations were concluded, the public was given an inside look at the way the Reagan HUD officials and former officeholders operated for their mutual self-interest through the awarding and receiving of government contracts. They knowingly profited from poverty. Dozens of former officials, many from HUD and others with close ties to the Reagan White House, earned millions of dollars in consulting fees in return for their efforts in winning HUD housing subsidies and grants for their clients.**

HUD was a dumping ground for unqualified political appointees and became rampant with fraud and favoritism. High consulting fees were granted for little or no work by the politically well-connected.

Many of the instances of graft and corruption, particularly in the EPA, HUD, and Wedtech Affairs, were symptomatic of a general lack of concern with conflict of interests or ethical rules characteristic of the Reagan years. Of particular note were antigovernment officials appointed to public office, who then "cashed in" and personally profited from these positions.

Source: Frank E. Hagan, 1992a, *Crimes of the Reagan Era,* paper presented at the Academy of Criminal Justice Sciences Meetings, Pittsburgh, Pennsylvania, March.

InfoTrac College Edition Research

Search on the crimes of the Reagan era, for example, "Iran contra." What happened to him since his initial convictions for "insider trading"?

accessories on the customer, service gouging, high finance charges (at times even employing loan sharks), overcharging for parts, misuse of "book time" (preset and inflated charges for labor time on repairs), and odometer (mileage meter) tampering.

Crimes by Employees Against Employees

While a variety of crimes like theft may be committed by an employee against another employee for personal benefit (type 5 in Figure 10.2), many such violations would not necessarily be occupationally related and, therefore, would not be appropriate examples for the "Occupational/Organizational Crime Grid." But one type of violation that certainly fits is the *sweetheart contract* in labor-management negotiations, which involves labor officials and negotiators secretly making a deal with management to the disadvantage of the workers whom the labor officials represent. For example, the union president and representatives might make a deal with management to take a bribe of $50,000. They then might indicate to the workers that they have examined the company books and found that management can only afford a twenty cent per hour raise rather than the fifty cents originally promised. Depending on the size of the work force, management could save millions of dollars.

Another example is workplace violence perpetrated by a fellow employee. Such perpetrators take out their frustrations—usually associated with loss of job—on their fellow workers and supervisors. While murder is the most highly publicized form of workplace violence, other forms include assaults, rapes, suicides, as well as psychological and mental health episodes. Drug and alcohol abuse may create hazardous work conditions. Hostile, intimidating, and offensive sexual work environments may also foster sexual harassment, sexual assault, and other psychological and emotional damage.

Crimes by Employees Against Organizations

Organizations are vulnerable to a variety of offenses that employees can commit against them (type 8 in Figure 10.2). In this section we will briefly focus on employee pilferage, computer crime, and embezzlement; but employee crimes obviously include many types of offenses discussed under crimes against the individual (public), corporate bribery, and the like.

Embezzlement. One form of stealing from one's employer is through embezzlement, which is theft from an employer by an individual who has reached a position of financial trust. The classic work on the subject is Donald Cressey's *Other People's Money* (1953), which contains interviews with 133 incarcerated embezzlers. He proposes the following explanation of why trust-violators steal:

1. Individuals who have achieved a position of trust are faced with what they conceive of as a non-shareable financial problem.
2. They feel they can resolve this problem by violating their position of trust, that is, by "temporarily borrowing" from their employer.
3. This rationalization of "borrowing" eventually breaks down as embezzlers realize they have been discovered and cannot make repayment in time (Cressey, 1953, p. 30).

Gambling, sexual affairs, and high living are often the factors behind the unshareable nature of the financial problem.

The typical embezzler does not fit the stereotype of the criminal. Most are middle-aged, middle class males who have lived relatively respectable lives and lack a history of criminal or delinquent activity, however, in *Women Who Embezzle or Defraud,* Zeitz (1991) notes increased embezzlement by women as managerial and executive positions open up for females. One example is the case of Dorothy Hutson, a Merrill Lynch stockbroker, who systematically cheated investors out of $1.4 million and used the money to finance Las Vegas and Lake Tahoe gambling junkets (Siconolfi and Johnson, 1991).

In one of the larger recent embezzlements, Phar-Mor, Inc., a discount drug store chain, disclosed that two executives had allegedly embezzled more than half of the company's net worth. The company estimated its losses at $350 million (Phar-Mor, 1992). In December 1995 Michael Modus, former president of Phar-Mor, Inc., was sentenced to nearly 20 years for fraud, tax evasion, and embezzlement. In 2000 Merrill Lynch discovered a $40 million embezzlement was perpetrated by a former employee who stole from elite, private banking clients by using the name of a dead person to transfer the securities from Arab International Bank to Swiss bank accounts (Huang, 2000).

Cressey's analysis of embezzlers has been criticized by Schuessler (1954, p. 604), who claimed that it was limited to an ex post facto (after the fact) study of only caught embezzlers and that his descriptions may not be characteristic of most embezzlers. Nettler's (1974) study found embezzlers to be motivated by greed and temptation as well as by the opportunity to commit the crime. Unlike Cressey, Nettler did not find a non-shareable problem that was a necessary component of embezzlement.

Smigel and Ross (1970) in *Crimes against Bureaucracy* indicate that individuals, particularly employees, feel less guilt the bigger the victim organization. Many individuals who would consider themselves criminals were they to steal from other persons rationalize their theft from large, impersonal organizations by saying that "they can afford the loss." According to Smigel and Ross, the very size, wealth, and impersonality of large bureaucracies, whether governmental or business, provide a rationalization for those who wish to steal from such organizations. The "Robin Hood myth" holds that theft from such organizations really hurts no one, since the victim is a large, wealthy organization. Combined with this is a certain public antipathy toward the large corporation or big government. Obviously, the Robin Hood rationalization breaks down when we consider the higher cost-of-goods consumers must pay because of "inventory shrinkage."

In a survey sponsored by the National Institute of Justice ("Satisfied Workers," 1983, pp. 6–7) and conducted in three metropolitan areas, one-third of the employees of the 47 corporations studied admitted stealing company property. Almost two-thirds indicated "counterproductive workmanship" practices (such as abuse of sick leave and substance abuse on the job) and other misconduct (such as extra-long lunch and work breaks). The estimated $5–$10 billion price tag on employee pilferage, while controllable through better security controls, was found to be strongly affected by the workers' perception of job satisfaction and feelings about employers' concern for their interests. Unhappy workers engaged in more counterproductive behavior and were also more likely to be involved in pilferage.

A 1997 study of crimes by 1,324 employees by the Ethics Officer Association and the American Society of Chartered Life Underwriters and Chartered Financial Consultants found that 48 percent of U.S. workers admitted to ethical or illegal activities in the previous year. This included cheating on expense accounts, discriminating against co-workers, participating in kickbacks, forging signatures, trading sex for sales, and violation of environmental laws. Over half (57 percent) indicated that they felt more pressure to be unethical than five years ago, and 40 percent believed that it had gotten worse over the past year (Jones, 1997).

Cameron (1964) in her classic work on retail theft, *The Booster and the Snitch,* suggested that "inventory shrinkage" (loss of goods) in retail establishments was primarily caused by employee theft rather than shoplifting. Store security personnel concur, estimating that as much as 75 percent of such loss is due to employee theft. A familiar story relates to security personnel who suspected that an employee was "ripping off" the company because every day he left work with a wheelbarrow full of packages. Every day they carefully checked the packages to no avail. When finally discovered, the employee had stolen over a thousand wheelbarrows. Employees are quite ingenious in illegally supplementing their wages at the expense of their employer.

Some common techniques in employee retail theft include:

1. Cashiers who ring up a lower price on single-item purchases and pocket the difference, or who ring up lower prices for "needy" friends going through the checkout.
2. Clerks who do not tag some sale merchandise, sell it at the original price, and pocket the difference.

3. Receiving clerks who duplicate keys to storage facilities and return to the store after hours.
4. Truck drivers who make fictitious purchases of fuel and repairs, and split the gains with truck stops.
5. Employees who simply hide items in garbage pails, incinerators, or under trash heaps until they can be retrieved later (McCaghy, 1976b, p. 179).

Abuse of expense accounts, travel allowances, and company cars are additional means by which employers are robbed of organizational income.

Computer Crime. Beginning in the sixties, computers became essential elements of modern society. Major concern about criminal acts committed with computers has led to the passage of much "computer crime" legislation. Hollinger and Lanza-Kaduce (1990) point out that both the experts (particularly Parker, 1976, 1979, 1983; Bequai, 1978, 1987) and legislatures relied very heavily on media accounts to encourage more laws. During the early 1980s extensive accounts of the "414 hackers," a group named for the Milwaukee area code, who had electronically broken into eighty computer installations, such as those at the Sloan Kettering Cancer Institute, Security Pacific Bank, and Los Alamos National Laboratory, raised public concern regarding the vulnerability of sensitive computer information (Marbach, Conant, and Rogers, 1983). The 1983 movie *War Games,* in which a fictitious young hacker uses his computer to crack the North American Air Defense Command (NORAD) computer in Wyoming, almost triggering a nuclear war, caused the media to "fixate" (Hollinger and Lanza-Kaduce, 1990, p. 33) on computer crime.

While many traditional crimes such as embezzlement, robbery, and burglary are now facilitated by a new tool—computers—other crimes are more specifically computer related. The illegal production of computer software is very big business in Southeast Asian countries and particularly in Hong Kong, where illegal copies of popular software such as Lotus 1–2–3 are sold for a fraction of their normal cost ("Taking a Byte," 1990). "Software pirates," those who illegally reproduce and use software, cost software manufacturers billions of dollars a year in lost revenue. U.S. manufacturers have found hundreds of illegal copies of their software in legitimate firms such as Britain's General Electric or Atari Taiwan Manufacturing Company. When illegal software is discovered, manufacturers attempt to bring both civil and criminal charges against the offenders and their companies. Part of the problem is the ease of making duplicate copies of floppy disks containing the computer software. This is comparable to the technological ease of illegally reproducing television movies on a videocassette recorder. Some examples of computer crimes include (Spernow, 1995): insider crime, malicious hacking, activities in support of criminal enterprises, telecommunications fraud, on-line pedophilia, and high tech espionage.

While not inclusive of all computer crime nor mutually exclusive, these types demonstrate the variety of current computer crime. It is estimated that about 80 percent of computer crimes are committed by "insiders" or employees. Most of this, however, is not reported to police. Thirty-five percent of the theft of proprietary information is perpetrated by discontented employees; outside hackers steal 28 percent, U.S. companies 18 percent, foreign corporations 11 percent, and foreign governments eight percent, according to a 1999 survey by Kessler and Associates, a New York security firm (Noack, 2000). "Malicious hackers" desire forbidden knowledge. Many have an anti-establishment attitude or exhibit a "hackers' ethic" that there should be no restrictions on their right to surf the net and test systems. Computers can be used to "support criminal enterprises." This could entail planning crimes or record keeping, and many such criminal operations are better equipped than law enforcement agencies.

Computers can also be used for gambling, child pornography, security fraud, production of phony documents, counterfeiting, and the like. In 1993 it is estimated that U.S. banks lost $5 billion in fraud and $815 million to fraudulent checks created on personal computers (PCs). A California Vietnamese triad gang duplicated payroll checks on PCs, for example. There is even an underground publication called "2600" in which hackers share their findings on compromised numbers. As an example, Kevin Mitnick (code name "Condor") messed with computer expert Tsutomu Shimomura's home computer files, and Shimomura and others tracked him down. Mitnick at the time was being hunted by the FBI for various violations, including theft of about 20,000 credit card numbers from computer systems. He was captured in February 1995 after nearly destroying a computer service by reading its internet subscribers' mail and using their accounts as a way of attacking computers across the net.

Telecommunications fraud can take a variety of forms. A common type is the stealing of telephone access codes over the user's shoulder or by using scanners. Those stealing cellular phone numbers then use equipment to make cellular phones operate with these stolen codes (Levy, 1995). "On line pedophiles" capitalize on the fact that young "wannabe" hackers have characteristics similar to those of many pedophile victims. They share gender, age, intellectual interests, and interpersonal skills. Those involved in "high tech espionage" are usually industrial spies who sell such knowledge to rivals or foreign bidders. The FBI has established a computer analysis and recovery team to attempt to keep up with the burgeoning use of cyber-sleuthing (see also Icove, Seger, and VonStorch, 1995).

Crackers. Coined by hackers in 1985 in order to defend against journalists misusing the term hacker, *crackers* are ill-intended hackers who attempt to crack (break into) computer systems often in order to do damage. They might be thought of as cybervandals. The National White Collar Crime Center, NW3C (2000) identifies the following **types of attacks on computer systems:**

Denial of Service Attacks
E-Mail Bombs
Dictionary Attacks
Trojan Horses
Password Phishing
Web Spoofing
Worm
Sniffer
Social Engineering

Denial of service attacks involve programming a computer to continuously send fake authentication messages to a targeted server, keeping it constantly busy and forcing out legitimate users. On February 9, 2000, an orchestrated attack of bogus traffic shut down Amazon, eBay, CNN, Buy.Com, Inc., and Yahoo. Such a denial of service or synchronized (SYN-flood) attack floods the computer with requests; when the computer attempts to reply, it is unable to connect to the phony addresses. Such attacks are now routine, and many site operators claim fending off nine or ten similar attacks per week. The suspected culprits of the February 9th attacks were two teenage boys (NW3C, 2000).

E-mail bombs involve overwhelming an e-mail system with an enormous amount of mail. A Monmouth University (New Jersey) student crashed the university's e-mail system by sending e-mail bombs to two university administrators, consisting of 24,000 random-text messages that damaged the system (NW3C, 2000). In a related "ping flood" attack, a "smurf" (malicious internet user) fooled hundreds of computer systems into sending traffic into one location, flooding the location with "pings."

A **dictionary attack** consists of guessing numerous common passwords in order to log on to a computer system. Software programs such as "cracker" are used to run through potential passwords until the correct one is found.

Trojan horses are subprograms (hidden in a program) that contain a virus, bomb, or other harmful feature. These often masquerade as inviting attachments that offer harmless

Computer hacker Kevin "Condor" Mitnick was arrested for violations including credit card fraud, but his downfall was his decision to invade computer expert Tsumo Shimomura's home computer files.

(© Jim Bounds / Raleigh News Observer / Sygma)

software upgrades, help files, screen savers, or pornography. When users open the attachment, a secret program steals their password and mails it back to the cracker. The outgoing message is deleted from the victim's e-mail outbox (NW3C, 2000).

Password phishing entails a cracker stealing passwords, account, or credit card information. An America Online (AOL) subscriber could not understand why his dial screen told him he was inactive. AOL had canceled his account because 500 people had received a Trojan Horse from his e-mail account. Crackers had stolen his password and used his account to spread a Trojan Horse designed to steal more numbers.

Web spoofing creates a false (shadow) version of a Web site controlled by the attacker. All network traffic between the victim's browser and the shadow web are funneled through the attacker's machine. This enables interception and alteration of information and the acquisition of passwords, credit card numbers, and account numbers. In 1999 clients of the second largest bank in Holland attempted to log on to the bank's Web site to access their accounts and received an error message the first time they entered their password and user name, but were able to get on the second time. The first attempt was actually on a shadow site set up by a cracker who used the stolen information to take five guilders (about $2.35) from each account (a "salami slice"), a sum not immediately noticed (Regan, 1999).

Worm is similar to a virus that reproduces itself and subverts computer systems. While a virus must be carried from system-to-system, worms can spread with no assistance. The term "worm" originated in a science fiction story, The Shockwave Rider by John Brunner (1976), where freedom fighters attack a totalitarian government's computer with a program called tapeworm which shuts down the network (NW3C, 2000).

Sniffer programs display the contents of all packets passing through a network and are used to gain passwords to access accounts. This can be used to access software, impersonate the owner, or gain access to other accounts.

Social engineering is the manipulation of people in order to obtain critical information about a computer/network system. A typical example involves the target receiving a telephone call from someone identifying himself as being with tech support and claiming the server is being reset with new passwords and that s/he needs the old password to get your account running again. Users of AOL might receive fake messages stating there is an account billing problem and requesting that you enter your name and password. An old, low-tech standby is "dumpster diving" in which crackers seek out old manuals, memos, program printouts, internal phone books, and other items.

Some Additional Argot of Computer Crime. The world of computer offenses has produced its own argot, a fraction of which is defined below.

Cyberpunks are computer hackers who develop harmful programs.
Salami techniques are used to steal small amounts (slices) from assets of many sources and transfer them to the thief's account. For example, a fraction of a percent of thousands of savings accounts could be retained for the thief's account.
Time bombs (logic bombs) are computer programs that perform a task, such as printing a message or destroying data, on a certain date. *Vaccines* are computer programs that seek out and destroy viruses.
Viruses are rogue programs that copy themselves onto other programs or disks (Markhoff, 1988).

Computer crimes come in a wide variety:

- Volkswagen lost nearly $260 million because of an insider computer scam involving fake currency exchanges.
- In Fort Worth, Texas, a former insurance company employee deleted more than 160,000 records from the company's computer.
- A bank employee sneaked into a computer and placed an order for Brinks to deliver 44 kilograms of gold to a remote site, collected it, and vanished.
- "Demon dialers," automatic speed dialers used by computer hackers, were used to dial 800 numbers until the codes were broken. The hackers then used the ID codes to steal $12 million in phone service from NASA (Rogers, 1992).
- Robert Sutton, a computer hacker, used a home-grown computer chip to alter cellular phones so that they would dial for free (Keller, 1991). Such free calls were costing the industry about $200 million a year.
- A group calling itself "The Legion of Doom" has broken into business, university, and military computers. They have altered credit reports, stolen telephone long-distance access codes, and tampered with AT&T software that could have disrupted 911 emergency services (Schwartz, 1990a).
- In 1988 Robert T. Morris, Jr., a Cornell graduate student, was convicted of unleashing a virus or worm that clogged thousands of computers nationwide, particularly those used by universities, industries, and government. He was found guilty in May of 1990 but given no jail time.
- In August of 1995 the managers at the Naval Command, Control, and Ocean Surveillance Center in San Diego discovered in their computer system several innocuous-looking,

unauthorized files with names like "sni 256" and "test." When they opened them up, they found a "sniffer" program. This is a program that secretly copies vital information such as the passwords given by legitimate users when they log into the system. Investigators tracked the intruder to Telecom Argentina and Julio Ardita ("Hacker Traced," 1996).

- In 2000 a computer intruder tried to extort $100,000 from an Internet music retailer after claiming to possess over 300,000 customer credit card files. When the company refused to be blackmailed, some of the files were released. The electronic extortionist was traced to somewhere in Eastern Europe (Markoff, 2000, p. A1).
- Online stock traders and day traders utilize "pump and dump" techniques to personal advantage. Traders pump their stocks in newsgroups and chatrooms to boost sales, then dump the stocks at a profit, causing the value of stock to plummet.
- Of critical concern is information warfare by foreign intelligence services and terrorists.
- World Wide Web (one of the largest zones in the Internet) has a flaw, a "hole" in the software that runs Web sites, that permits intruders to do anything the site owner can do. Better security is needed (Quittner, 1995).

Part of the problem with attempting to crack down on juvenile computer hackers is "hacker's ethic," a view that such illegal and potentially dangerous experimentation is a necessary part of the computer training for a creative next generation of hackers. Apple cofounder Steve Wozniak claims that a little mischief is essential in the quest for knowledge. He points out that his experience in building illegal "blue boxes" for "phone-phreaking" (devices for making free phone calls) helped him develop his later computer hardware skills (Schwartz, 1990b, p. 37).

Crimes by Individuals (or Members of Occupations)

Crime in the Professions.

Medicine. Medical quackery and unnecessary operations may very well kill more people every year in the United States than crimes of violence. A House subcommittee estimated that the American public was the victim of 2.4 million unnecessary surgical procedures per year, which resulted in a loss of $4 billion and in 11,900 deaths (Coleman, 1994, p. 37). A Harvard study (Gerlin, 1999) estimates that one million American patients are injured yearly by hospital errors and 120,000 die as a result. This is equivalent to a jumbo jet crash every day and three times the 43,000 people killed each year in U.S. automobile accidents. Americans may be becoming overdoctored, having twice the per capita number of surgeons, anesthesiologists, and operations as England and Wales, yet higher mortality rates. Jesilow, Pontell, and Geis (1985) estimate that U.S. physicians defraud federal and state medical assistance programs of up to 40 percent of all program monies. Charges have been levied that Medicare (a medical program for the elderly) is beginning to resemble a welfare program for doctors. Until recently, weak monitoring of medical claims has invited cheating. The medical industry in the United States makes up one-seventh of the economy and is the nation's largest business with nearly $1 trillion in annual revenue. About $100 billion of this is lost to insurance fraud alone (Davis, 1995).

In 2000 then-President Clinton ordered all hospitals in the United States to take steps recommended by the National Academy of Sciences to reduce medical errors and urged states to require the reporting of such errors. The American Medical Association and American Hospital Association strongly opposed such a reporting system claiming that it would encourage lawsuits. In the early 1990s the federal government finally began to take seriously health-care fraud estimated to cost between $50 and $80 billion per year (Witkin, Friedman, and Guttman, 1992). Some of the medical pilfering of Medicare funds includes:

nursing home purchases of boats and trips to Hawaii; laboratory kickbacks for new accounts; charges for fake services; unnecessary or unadministered treatments, laboratory tests, and operations.

Some other violations that physicians may become involved in include practices such as *fee splitting* (in which doctors refer patients to other doctors for further treatment and split the fee with them). "Ping-ponging" doctors refer patients to other doctors in the same office; "steering" entails directing patients to particular pharmacies; and "gang visits" involve billing for unnecessary multiple services ("White-Collar Crime," 1981). In 1988 the Department of Health and Human Services established a nationwide computer bank to monitor malpractice suits and disciplinary actions against doctors and dentists in order to keep track of incompetent practitioners (Estill, 1988). Quinney's (1963) analysis, "Prescription Violations by Pharmacists," reveals higher numbers of violations among pharmacists who see themselves as business persons rather than as professionals. If clients (whom the professional views with concern for their health and the provision of ethical service) are seen as customers (whose greater consumption equals greater profit), then more frequent occupational violations are likely to ensue.

With the end of the Cold War in the nineties the FBI reassigned agents from counterespionage activity to the investigation of health-care fraud, and this began to show dividends. In a 1992 undercover operation, FBI agents arrested 82 pharmacists and physicians for cheating private insurance companies and Medicaid. Some of the schemes involved pharmacists filling prescriptions with generic drugs, billing for brand-name products, and charging payers (insurance or Medicaid) multiple times for the same prescription or for prescriptions that were never written or filled. Dabney (2000), using survey data on over 1,000 practicing pharmacists, found 41 percent reported at least one lifetime incident of illicit prescription drug use. The vast majority of those began using drugs in pharmacy school and obtained their drugs by pilfering them from pharmacy stock.

In 1994 the Public Citizen's Health Group claimed that some 420,000 Caesarean baby deliveries are performed unnecessarily each year in the United States. It is currently the most common surgery performed in the country. In 1970 C-sections accounted for only 5.5 percent of births, but were nearly 25 percent by 1988. The most Caesareans are performed in for-profit hospitals (Neergaard, 1994). Another survey of 449 programs in adult and pediatric critical care found that 39 percent used the bodies of people who had just died to teach medical procedures, but only 10 percent required that the patient's family give consent (Kolata, 1994).

In 1993 National Medical Enterprises, the operator of psychiatric and acute care hospitals, agreed to pay $125 million to settle charges by three major insurers for filing fraudulent claims. The company also faced charges by 130 former psychiatric patients who claimed that the company held them against their will, misdiagnosed patients, physically abused them, and administered unnecessary medications and treatments in order to run up bills (Kerr, 1993). In 1998 Allstate Insurance Company sued 45 doctors, lawyers, chiropractors, and others for alleged involvement in systematically staging fake auto accidents and filing phony insurance claims (Abram, 1998).

Finance. Wrongdoing has certainly not been limited to the health and medical professions. "The Great Savings and Loan Scandal," to be discussed in the next chapter, was the biggest financial public policy failure in U.S. history, with estimated costs of $500 billion. In *The Greatest-Ever Bank Robbery: The Collapse of the Savings and Loan Industry,* Mayer (1990, p. 298) indicates:

> What makes the S&L outrage so important a piece of American history is not the hundreds of billions of dollars, but the demonstration of how low our standards

> for professional performance have fallen in law, accounting, appraising, banking and politics—all of them.

The federal government is suing many of these professionals and their firms for collusion in many S&L collapses. In *The Big Six: The Selling Out of America's Top Accounting Firms,* Mark Stevens (1991) asks: if CPA firms are truly independent of the clients they audit (who foot the bill), "how can accountants be truly independent of the cash register that pays their bills?" Berton (1991, p. A12) notes, "Many legislators and the General Accounting Office, an arm of Congress, are rapidly losing confidence in accountants because their independence seems tarnished and they still duck the job given them by government of protecting the public against financial fraud."

Law. Illegal and unprofessional activities by lawyers may include "ambulance chasing," i.e., soliciting and encouraging unnecessary law suits (such as fraudulent damage claims) in order to collect commissions (Freedman, 1976; Reichstein, 1965). Describing the practice of law as sometimes constituting a "con game" against clients, Blumberg (1967) mentions activities in which the lawyer collects fees for defending a client and then simply "plea-bargains" to expedite the case, with little concern for the client's well-being.

Carlin (1962), Ladinsky (1963), and Wood (1967) have all pointed to the fact that lawyers who attended less prestigious law schools (often because of poor and/or ethnic backgrounds) and who were in "solo" practice were more likely to be stuck with the dirty work of the profession—fixing cases, bribing officials, and other "occupational fringe violations" (Gibbons, 1982, pp. 328, 333). On the other hand, graduates of more prestigious institutions spend much of their time, not in tasks portrayed by television stereotype Perry Mason, but in defending corporate criminals and violators. Other legal rackets include home closings (in which regular fees are collected for very little work) as well as the collection of contingency fees on liability cases (in which lawyers receive a percentage of anything won) (Merry, 1975, p. 1).

Concern has been raised that, with nearly one million lawyers, the United States is becoming an overlitigious society; that is, one in which too many resources are expended on legal actions. Olson (1991) notes that the United States has three times as many lawyers per capita as Great Britain, ten times per capita the number of lawsuits, thirty-to-forty times the number of malpractice suits, and nearly one hundred times the number of product claims. The United States is the only society that encourages such lawsuits through our way of financing litigation. Only in the United States must the winning party pay his or her lawyer (Crovitz, 1991, p. A17). Such conduct was even illegal under English law and called "champerty" (lawyers receiving fruits of the successful action) and "barratry" (instigating and maintaining suits and quarrels in courts) (Ibid.).

In 1990 three members of a personal injury law firm in Manhattan were indicted for bribing witnesses to perjure themselves in court and for falsifying evidence in nineteen accident cases dating from 1979 (Hevesi, 1990). Fireman's Fund, an insurance company, hired an auditor to examine how their defense attorneys were spending their funds and exposed twenty lawyers, representing plaintiffs and defendants, who cooperated in manipulating lawsuits and billing up to $100 million in dubious fees to insurance companies (Schmitt, 1992, p. Al). In explaining rising thievery by lawyers, bar association officials, while noting that only a minority are involved, point to tough economic times, the high cost of practicing law, substance abuse, and even glamorized images of lawyers on television (Marcus, 1990).

Until recently, bar associations published minimum fees and sanctioned attorneys who charged less, even though the Sherman Anti-Trust Act made no exceptions for professional associations in prohibiting price-fixing (Coleman, 1994, p. 61). The concentration of legal talent in the defense of wealthy and corporate violators and the underconcentration in representing their victims (the state and the public) raise questions regarding the ethics of the legal profession itself.

Other Occupations. Examples of crimes against consumers by professionals, merchants, and members of other legitimate occupations are numerous:

- The "greasy thumb on the scale," or short-weighting customers and overcharging for products.
- "Bait 'n' switch" techniques by small merchants, in which the product advertised is unavailable and a more expensive product is pushed on the customer.
- Phony or unnecessary repair work.
- Security violations by stockbrokers, such as misleading clients or **insider trading** (making use of inside information for personal benefit).
- Abuses in the nursing home industry in which private owners often place profit ahead of the health and safety of elderly residents. Such practices are described by Mendelson (1975) as *Tender Loving Greed.*
- While not a blanket indictment of the profession as a whole, Mitford's (1963, p. 8) *The American Way of Death* describes illegal or unethical activities of funeral directors, including: misuse of the coroner's office in order to secure business, bribery of hospital personnel to "steer" cases, the reuse of coffins, and duplicate billings in welfare cases.
- "Churning" by stockbrokers collecting high commissions by running up sales with unnecessary buy-and-sell orders.

In "pump and dump" stock scams, online brokers (day traders) buy an inexpensive stock and then hype it while driving up the price, enticing others to buy the stock. Then the stock is sold at the high price after which the stock dives, costing unaware investors plenty. In 1991 the New York Stock Exchange kicked Peter Ryan out of the securities business after he had cheated numerous customers. In one example:

> A customer with "virtually no prior experience" in investing opened an account with Mr. Ryan in March 1985 listing the investment objective as "appreciation with safety." The customer's $114,000 dwindled to $8,800 after Mr. Ryan made numerous trades "without [the customer's] knowledge or authorization," the Big Board said. Mr. Ryan allegedly made about $47,000 in commissions on these transactions (Power, 1991, p. C17).

In the illegal practice of "loss-dumping" another broker:

> allegedly would buy the options [high-risk stock index options] without attaching the customer account number to the order. Then he would dump the trades that declined in value into the family trust's account without telling the trustees about the losses or even the purchases. The broker put profits into his account or those of two other brokers (Hagedorn and Barrett, 1991).

In 1991 a price-rigging scam caused $10 million in losses to thousands of customers. Fraud charges were brought by the Manhattan district attorney against three securities firms and 21 brokers. This group manipulated the prices of over-the-counter stocks in certain companies by buying and selling over and over again among themselves (21 Brokers, 1991).

"Insider trading" occurs when agents, brokers, and company officials who are aware of pending developments make use of this privileged information to buy and/or sell stocks before the public becomes aware of these events. Revelations of such wrongdoing (see IN THE NEWS 10.1) led to the collapse and declared bankruptcy of Drexel Burnham Lambert. However, in 1989, two months before declaring bankruptcy, the company gave out over $260 million in bonuses to employees, twice the amount of the debt on which Drexel

IN THE NEWS 10.1

DEN OF THIEVES: INSIDER TRADING ON WALL STREET

Other financial scandals abounded during the eighties, but none had the impact of the revelations of major "insider trading" on Wall Street and the kingpins of these deals, Ivan Boesky and Michael Milken. "Insider trading" involves agents or brokers making use of confidential market information for their trading advantage and often to the disadvantage of clients and other traders. James Stewart in *Den of Thieves* (1991a) reports that, since many of the principals in these episodes were permitted to strike deals with the government in return for testimony, the full extent of their misdeeds may not fully be realized.

In the eighties the Reagan administration cut back regulations at the very time that financial markets became much bigger and more complex. Stewart's den of thieves consisted of four Wall Street operators: Dennis Levine, Martin Siegel, Ivan Boesky, and Michael Milken. This insider-trading ring made millions as they rigged stock market trading.

The Milken-Boesky conspiracy story broke in May 1996, when the Securities and Exchange Commission and federal prosecutors accused Drexel Burnham Lambert broker Dennis Levine of making $12.6 million in insider-trading profits. He agreed to be a government witness in return for a two-year jail sentence. Former investment banker with Kidder, Peabody and later with Drexel, Martin Siegel also agreed to cooperate in return for a two-month jail sentence. This cooperation served up Ivan Boesky, a major stock speculator and insider trader, who also made a deal to cooperate in return for which he would serve two years of a three-year prison term and pay $100 million in fines and restitution.

Boesky delivered Milken and the firm of Drexel Burnham Lambert. Milken, a broker at Drexel, used junk bonds to supply financing for Boesky's leveraged buyouts of companies. Milken agreed to plead guilty to six felonies and to pay off a record $650 million in fines for offenses including stock manipulation and insider trading. Milken was charged with robbing clients by trading on confidential information for his own gain, manipulating securities prices to force deals and make huge fees, gouging clients on junk-bond trades, and stealing his clients' securities (Stewart, 1991b). Milken, who is believed to have earned over $1.1 billion from Drexel alone for selling junk bonds and funding takeovers, was given what is regarded as a stiff ten-year jail sentence in November 1990.

To illustrate the interconnections between insider trading and the collapse of the nation's savings and loans, on August 16, 1991, former Drexel chief executive officer Frederick Joseph agreed to pay $3–$3.5 million to settle charges that Drexel had rigged the junk-bond market and defrauded savings and loan associations. Milken's high-priced legal talent, such as Arthur Liman and Alan Dershowitz, continue to appeal his case, and he still denies having been involved in insider trading. For fixing the stock market, Boesky served just over two years, Levine less than two years, Siegel six weeks, and Milken had a ten-year sentence reduced to two years time served in return for his cooperation in other prosecutions.

Source: Frank E. Hagan, 1992, Crimes of the Reagan Era, paper presented at the Academy of Criminal Justice Sciences Meetings, Pittsburgh, Pennsylvania, March.

InfoTrac College Edition Research

One of the principal figures in the "Den of Thieves" was Michael Milken. What happened to him since his initial conviction for "insider trading?

defaulted. A few executives received $10 million each while Drexel, on paper, lost $40 million. While not illegal, such activity certainly fits Mills' theme of the "higher immorality."

In 1995 the Securities and Exchange Commission, in the largest settlement of its kind, had Merrill Lynch and Company and Lazard Frères and Company each agree to pay about $24 million to settle charges that they were involved in a secret fee-splitting scheme with municipal bond underwriters and officers and municipalities ("There's a New Sheriff," 1995, pp. C1 and C7).

Scandals in education are yet another growth industry. The "Coded-Pencil-Caper" which took place in 1996 took advantage of the U.S. time zone difference to assist people in cheating on the Graduate Record Exam, Test of English as a Foreign Language, and Graduate Management Admission Test. Those taking the test on the East Coast would phone the questions and answers to collaborators on the West Coast, who prepared coded pencils with the answers written on them to be used during the tests. Hundreds of prospective test takers paid the American Test Center $6,000 each. The company had advertised a "unique method" for preparing for the exams. The test takers were flown to the West Coast to take the tests and receive the promised "uniquely" high scores before the whole scheme was busted (Simon and Hagan, 1999, p. 83).

In 1999, 52 educators from 32 New York City public schools were charged with helping students cheat on the standardized reading and math tests. In some cases teachers actually erased and corrected answers. Many teachers felt pressured by their principals to cheat (Kelly, 1999). In 1995 Steinmetz High School (Chicago) won a statewide academic contest, the Academic Decathlon, by memorizing the answers to a stolen copy of the test. Sponsors of the event became suspicious when they noticed that only twelve students in the country had scored 900 or better on the math quiz and six of them were from Steinmetz, a working class high school. The title was revoked when the students refused to take a validation test. At a five-year reunion some of the students indicated they would do it again, with no guilt, because that is the way the world works (Johnson, 2000, p. A6).

Criminal Careers of Occupational and Organizational Offenders

Occupational and corporate offenders generally do not view their activities as criminal; their violations are usually part of their occupational environment. Such offenders maintain a commitment to conventional society while violating some of its laws because their activities often are supported and informally approved of by occupational or corporate subcultures or environments (see Frank and Lombness, 1988).

Sutherland (1956a, pp. 93–95) sees many parallels between the behavior of corporate criminals and that of professional and organized criminals:

1. They are recidivists, committing their crimes on a continual and frequent basis.
2. Violations are widespread, and only a relatively few are ever prosecuted.
3. Offenders do not lose status among their peers or associates as a result of their illegal behavior.
4. Like professional thieves, business people reveal contempt for government regulators, officials, and laws that they view as unnecessarily interfering with their behavior.

The corporate or executive offenders involved in what gangster Al Capone used to call "the legitimate rackets" differ from professional criminals in that they do not view themselves, and are not usually perceived by others, as criminals. Since occupational offenders and corporate/organizational offenders share much in common, examination of societal reaction to occupational criminals will be deferred until the end of the next chapter.

Summary

The formative statement on white collar crime was made by Sutherland in 1939. He defined it as "crime committed by a person of respectability and high social status in the course of his occupation." Despite the much greater cost of widespread corporate violations, the criminal justice system finds it more politically expedient to concentrate on traditional crimes. Related to Sutherland's notion is Ross's (1907, p. 44) notion of criminaloids as "those who prospered by flagitious practices which may not yet come under the ban of public opinion" and Mills' concept of the higher immorality or moral insensibility of the power elite. The concept of white collar crime has been criticized as too global in nature, and a variety of other terms have been suggested. Particularly important are the concepts of "occupational," "organizational," and "corporate" crime. *Occupational crime* refers to violations that are committed for self-benefit during the course of a legitimate occupation, while *organizational crime* refers to crimes by businesses or officials on behalf of the employing organization. Organizational crime becomes *corporate crime* when undertaken on behalf of a private business or organization.

The reasons for the lack of research on occupational and corporate crime were detailed, indicating that criminologists, because of the lack of readily available data, still rely on many secondary sources. Data and figures from various sources were presented in an attempt to measure the cost of white collar crime. While conservative estimates place the figure at $36 billion, more liberal estimates place the cost for monopolistic practices at over $230 billion. Any of the cost estimates far exceed those for traditional crimes.

Myopia must be avoided when viewing current white collar crime, since historical analysis suggests that similar activities may have been even more prevalent in the past. Analysis of legal regulation of occupational practice points out that the more developed professions have been granted a mandate for self-governance even though such self-policing has been less than impressive.

While different typologies of white collar crime have been offered (Bloch and Geis; Edelhertz), the author suggests an "Occupational/Organizational Crime Grid" as a heuristic device for presentation purposes in this chapter. This results in nine theoretical types based on the criminal (individual, employee, or organization) and the victim (individual, employee, or organization).

Crimes by employees may include a variety of offenses as detailed in Edelhertz's typological examples. *Crimes by employees against individuals/the public* were portrayed by means of public corruption (the Knapp Commission, Judgescam, Watergate, and ABSCAM), as well as private corruption and sharp practices by auto dealers. *Employee vs. employee crime* was examined by means of "sweetheart contracts" while *crimes by employees against organizations* were depicted with descriptions of embezzlement, employee fraud, pilferage, and computer crimes (including the argot of electronic "hackers"). *Crimes by individuals* (or members of occupations) were delineated by describing crooked practices in medicine, law, and pharmacy as well as in business-related trades and occupations. The *criminal careers* of occupational and corporate criminals entail little identification with crime; these offenders enjoy subcultural support and employ rationalizations to explain away responsibility for wrong-doing.

KEY CONCEPTS

ABSCAM
Argot of Computer Crime
Churning
"Coerced Crime"
Computer Crime
Computer Virus
Corporate Crime
Costs of White Collar Crime
Criminaloid
Embezzlement
Higher Immorality
Insider Trading
Judgescam
Logic Bombs
Occupational Crime
Occupational/Organizational Crime Grid
Organizational Crime
Reasons for Lack of Occupational Crime Research
Salami Techniques
Sweetheart Contracts
Trojan Horse
Types of Computer Crime
Watergate
White Collar Crime

REVIEW QUESTIONS

1. Discuss Edwin Sutherland's concept of white collar crime. Why was this considered a Copernican revolution or paradigm shift in criminology?
2. Discuss Cressey's theory of embezzlement. Does research support his hypothesis?

3. What were some major public scandals of the Reagan era? What happened as a result of these scandals?
4. What are some different types of computer crime? Give an example of each.
5. Discuss and give examples of crime or unethical practices in the field of medicine.
6. What are some crimes or unsavory practices in the legal profession?
7. What is insider trading? How did the den of thieves commit their crimes?
8. Discuss occupational crime in other professions besides medicine and law.
9. Do most occupational criminals view their activities as criminal? Discuss.
10. Is white collar crime worse today than in the past? Give examples.

INFOTRAC COLLEGE EDITION RESEARCH

Vantage Point 10.1 InfoTrac College Edition Research
Using the "keyword search," examine "white collar crime." What are some types discussed in the articles?
Vantage Point 10.2 InfoTrac College Edition Research
Search on the crimes of the Reagan era, for example, "Iran contra." What happened to him since his initial convictions for "insider trading"?

In the News 10.1 InfoTrac College Edition Research
One of the principal figures in the "Den of Thieves" was Michael Milken. What happened to him since his initial conviction for "insider trading?

SELECTED READINGS

Jay Albanese. 1995. *White Collar Crime in America.* New York: Prentice Hall.
One of America's leading experts on white collar crime examines the motivations and control of organizational offenders.

James Coleman. 1998. *The Criminal Elite.* 4th edition. New York: St. Martin's Press.
Coleman's text provides in-depth coverage of both occupational and corporate crime. He also explores theoretical explanations for white collar criminality.

Donald Cressey. 1953. *Other People's Money.* New York: The Free Press.
This is the classic case study on embezzlers, which proposes the hypothesis that embezzlers have a "non-shareable problem" that serves to motivate them to embezzle.

M. David Ermann and Richard J. Lundman, editors. 1982. *Corporate and Governmental Deviance.* 3rd edition. New York: Oxford University Press.
This reader in white collar crime contains an excellent selection of articles both classic and contemporary.

David O. Friedrichs. 1995. *Trusted Criminals: White Collar Crime in Contemporary Society.* Belmont, California: Wadsworth.
This text on white collar crime by one of America's most incisive thinkers on the topic contains a wealth of leads to needed research on the topic in the twenty-first century.

Stephen Pizzo, Mary Fricker, and Paul Muolo. 1989. *Inside Job: The Looting of America's Savings and Loans.* New York: McGraw-Hill.
This is an account by three California journalists of the biggest series of white collar crimes in American history, the "Great Savings and Loan scandal" of the eighties.

David Simon. 1999. *Elite Deviance.* 6th edition. Boston: Allyn and Bacon.
In this book, author David Simon insists that "elite deviance" is a better name for the phenomena of "white collar crime" since it concentrates on harm rather than legal definitions. It also permits the inclusion of unethical behavior.

David Simon and Frank Hagan. 1999. *White Collar Deviance.* Boston: Allyn and Bacon.
In this work David Simon and the author attempt to reconcile the elite deviance tradition (Simon) with that of white collar crime (Hagan), thus the new concept: "white collar deviance."

James Stewart. 1991. *Den of Thieves.* New York: Simon and Shuster.
Journalist James Stewart examines the world of Wall Street "inside traders" such as Ivan Boesky and Michael Milken.

Edwin H. Sutherland and Donald Cressey. 1978. *Criminology.* 10th edition. Philadelphia: Lippincott.
In this classic text originally authored by Edwin Sutherland, he presents his "Differential Association Theory" as well as standard textbook coverage by a pioneer in American criminology.

ORGANIZATIONAL/ CORPORATE CRIME

11

VANTAGE POINTS

IN THE NEWS

> We have no reason to assume that General Motors has an inferiority complex or Alcoa Aluminum Company a frustration-aggression complex or U.S. Steel an Oedipus complex or Armour Company a death wish, or that Dupont wants to return to the womb.
>
> —Edwin H. Sutherland, "Crime of Corporations," in White Collar Crime (1956a)

> The best way to rob a bank is to own one.
>
> —Statement by William Crawford, California Savings and Loan Commissioner (Pizzo, Fricker, and Muolo, 1989, p. 318)

> One question among many others raised in recent weeks had to do with whether my financial support in any way influenced several political figures to take up my cause. I want to say in the most forceful way I can, I certainly hope so.
>
> —Savings and Loan Swindler, Charles Keating (Babcock, 1989, p. 10)

Corporate Crime

Organizational crime refers to crime committed on behalf of and for the benefit of a legitimate organization. *Corporate (business) crime* is a type of organizational crime committed in free enterprise economies and thus involves criminal activity on behalf of and for the benefit of a private business or corporation.

Corporate crime takes many forms, including price fixing, kickbacks, commercial bribery, tax violations, fraud against government, and crimes against consumers, to mention a few (see Hochstedler, 1984; and Blankenship, 1995). Sutherland's studies of white collar criminality in the 1940s set a tone and sparked other studies during that initial period. Surprisingly, however, with the exception of a few scholarly works, investigative journalistic pieces, and consumer studies (particularly by Ralph Nader and associates), there was a considerable hiatus of research activity in this area until the middle to late seventies. In 1977 Geis and Meier (1977, p. 1), in revising their classic reader on white collar crime originally published nine years previously, found that they were able to add less than a third new material. With the exception, then, of works by Sutherland (1940, 1941, 1945, 1949, and 1956a), Clinard (1946 and 1969), Hartung (1950), and Nader and associates (Nader 1965, 1970, 1973), white collar crime was ripe for the research picking. Friedrichs (2000) adds that it is remarkable that criminology has a "bottomless well of analysis applicable to the delinquency of inner city youths and relatively little to contribute to the crimes of the most powerful adults [crime in high society] in our own society."

A new renaissance in studies of white collar crime took place in the late seventies with publications by Clinard and Yeager and associates: *Illegal Corporate Behavior* (1979) and later *Corporate Crime* (1980). Other than Sutherland's pioneering effort, which was modest by comparison, the research conducted by Clinard and Yeager and their colleagues represents a landmark: the first large-scale, comprehensive investigation of corporate crime. With a large grant from the Law Enforcement Assistance Administration, they conducted a systematic analysis of administrative, civil, and criminal actions either filed or completed by 25 federal agencies against 477 of the largest manufacturing corporations in the United States during 1975–1976. In addition, they performed a less comprehensive survey of 105 of the largest wholesale, retail, and service corporations (Clinard and Yeager, 1980, p. 110). Among their findings:

- Sixty percent of the large corporations had at least one action initiated against them during the period.
- The most deviant firms (multiple violators) accounted for 13 percent of those charged (8 percent of all corporations studied) and for 52 percent of all offenses. The average

for these corporations was 23.5 violations per firm, while the average for all corporations was 4.2.
- Large corporations were the chief violators, with oil, pharmaceutical, and automobile industries the biggest offenders and the most often cited. These three groups alone accounted for almost half of all the violations.
- The general leniency with which corporate violators are treated, noted over forty years previously by Sutherland, appears to persist.

The Measurement of Corporate Crime

Among others, Clinard and Yeager (1978, pp. 255–72) and Geis and Meier (1977, pp. 3–4) suggest that there are a number of reasons for the **lack of research on corporate crime** in the past:

1. Many social scientists are inexperienced in studying corporate crime, which often requires some sophistication in areas of law, finance, and economics.
2. Corporate violations often involve administrative and civil sanctions to which criminologists have limited exposure.
3. Enforcement is often carried out by state and federal regulatory agencies rather than by the usual criminal justice agencies.
4. Funds for such studies have not been generally available in the past.
5. Corporate crime is complicated by the very complexity of corporations.
6. Research data are not readily available because of the imperviousness of the corporate board room.
7. Corporate crime raises special problems of analysis and research objectivity.

Despite these obstacles, rising public concern about corporate wrongdoing has encouraged increased research into corporate crime.

Legal Regulation

Organizations and the Law

A corporation is a legal entity that permits a business to make use of capital provided by stockholders. Although the federal government has had the power to charter corporations since the 1791 *McCulloch v. Maryland* decision, it rarely uses it; most chartering is done by the states. Corporations have been considered legal "persons" since a Supreme Court decision of 1886 (Clinard and Yeager, 1980, pp. 25–28).

In the United States, beginning in the nineteenth century, certain business activities were defined as illegal. These included: restraint of trade, deceptive advertisements, bank fraud, sale of phony securities, faulty manufacturing of foods and drugs, environmental pollution, as well as the misuse of patents and trademarks (Clinard and Quinney, 1986, p. 207). In the late nineteenth century, concern grew about the development of monopolies, which threatened to control economies and stifle competition and thereby jeopardized the very philosophy of free-market enterprise.

The *Sherman Antitrust Act* (1890) was the first of many regulatory laws passed to control corporate behavior. This law forbids restraint of trade and the formation of monopolies; it currently makes price fixing a felony, with a maximum corporate fine of $1 million, and authorizes private treble (triple) damage suits by victims of price fixing. For the most part, the policing of corporate violations is done by federal regulatory agencies, for example, the Federal Trade Commission (FTC), which was set up in 1914 at the same time as the Clayton Antitrust Act and the Federal Trade Act. There are over fifty *federal regulatory agencies* with semipolicing functions with respect to corporate violations. Among these agencies are: the Civil Aeronautics Board (CAB), the Environmental Protection Agency (EPA), the Federal Communications Commission (FCC), the Food and Drug Administration (FDA), the Federal Power Commission (FPC), the Interstate Commerce Commission (ICC), the National Labor Relations Board (NLRB), the Nuclear Regulatory Commission (NRC), the Occupational Safety and Health Administration (OSHA), and the Securities and Exchange Commission (SEC). Some areas regulated by these agencies and discussed in this chapter are: air safety, air and water pollution, unfair advertising, safe drugs and healthy food, public utility services, interstate trucking and commerce, labor-management practices, nuclear power plants, health and safety in the workplace, and the sale and negotiation of bonds and securities.

Regulatory agencies have a number of sanctions they can use to force compliance with their orders: warnings, recalls, orders (unilateral orders, consent agreements, and decrees), injunctions, monetary penalties, and criminal penalties (Clinard and Yeager, 1980, p. 83). In addition to criminal proceedings, acts such as the Clayton Act (Section 4) permit "treble damage suits" by harmed parties. Guilty companies, with their batteries of lawyers and accountants, generally have more expertise, time, and staff to devote to defense than the Justice Department, under its Anti-Trust Division, has for prosecution. Indefinite delays and appeals are not uncommon.

If the government appears to have a solid case, corporations are permitted to plead **nolo contendere** "no contest" to charges. This is not an admission of guilt, and thus enables corporations to avoid the label of criminal. Consent decrees amount to a "hand slap"; that is, the corporation agrees to quit violating the particular regulation for which it was charged.

A number of *criticisms have been levied against federal regulatory agencies* and their efforts against corporate crime:

1. Lacking sufficient investigative staff, the agencies often rely on the records of the very corporations they are regulating to reveal wrongdoing.
2. The criminal fines authorized by law are insignificant compared with the economic costs of corporate crime and become, in effect, a minor nuisance, "a crime tax," "a license to steal," but certainly not a strong deterrent.
3. Other criminal penalties such as imprisonment are rarely used and, when they are, tend to reflect a dual system of justice: offenders are incarcerated in "country club" prisons or are treated in a far more lenient manner than traditional offenders.
4. The enforcement divisions of many regulatory agencies have been critically understaffed and cut back, as in the Reagan administration's EPA and other agencies, to inoperable levels.
5. The top echelons of agency commissions are often filled with leaders from the very corporations or industries to be regulated, creating potential conflict of interest.
6. Relationships between regulators and regulated are often too compatible, with some agency employees more interested in representing the interests of the corporations they are supposed to be regulating than in guaranteeing the public well-being. The fact that many retiring agency employees are hired by the formerly regulated companies lends support to this argument.

In reviewing the state of regulation of illegal corporate activity, Clinard and Yeager (1980, p. 96) state:

> One may well wonder why such small budgets and professional staffs are established to deal with business and corporate crime when billions of dollars are willingly spent on ordinary crime control, including 500,000 policemen, along with tens of thousands of government prosecutors and officials.

Gross (1980) in his book *Friendly Fascism* answers their question by letting us in on what he calls "the dirty secrets:"

> We are not letting the public in on our era's dirty little secret: that those who commit the crime which worries citizens most—violent street crime—are, for the most part, products of poverty, unemployment, broken homes, rotten education, drug addiction, alcoholism, and other social and economic ills about which the police can do little if anything . . . . But, all the *dirty little secrets* fade into insignificance in comparison with one **dirty big secret:** Law enforcement officials, judges as well as prosecutors and investigators, are soft on corporate crime . . . . The corporation's "mouthpieces" and "fixers" include lawyers, accountants, public relations experts and public officials who negotiate loopholes and special procedures in the laws, prevent most illegal activities from ever being disclosed and undermine or sidetrack "overzealous" law enforcers. In the few cases ever brought to court, they usually negotiate penalties amounting to "gentle taps on the wrist" (Gross, 1980, pp. 110, 113–15).

The Clinton administration and Congress, in order to downsize and reinvent government and decrease the annual budget deficit, may have participated in "deregulation by default" (Skrzycki, 1996). By cutting regulation agency personnel and resources, they made such agencies increasingly vulnerable to Congress and to corporate lobbyists.

While every year the FBI publishes its *Uniform Crime Reports* to give an annual account of primarily street crime, no such annual exists to measure the far more costly corporate crime. Robert Mokhiber, editor of the Washington-based *Corporate Crime Reporter,* ranked the "top 100 corporate crimes" of the 1990s. These were only the tip of the iceberg in that the majority of corporate wrongdoing is handled under civil law. This list includes only those who were caught and criminally fined. The 100 corporate criminals fell into 14 categories of crime (www.corporatepredators.org/top100.html): environmental (38), antitrust (20), fraud (13), campaign finance (7), food and drug (6), financial crimes (4), false statements (3), illegal exports (3), illegal boycott (1), worker death (1), bribery (1), obstruction of justice (1), public corruption (1), and tax evasion (1). The top ten of the 100 identified by Mokhiber were:

1. **F. Hoffman-LaRoche Ltd.** The Swiss pharmaceutical company pled guilty and paid a record $500 million criminal fine for fixing prices on vitamins.
2. **Daiwa Bank Ltd.** The bank pled guilty to 16 federal felonies and paid a $340 million criminal fine. They pled guilty to two counts of conspiracy to defraud the United States and the Federal Reserve Bank, misprision (concealment) of felony, ten counts of falsifying bank records, two counts of wire fraud, and one count of obstructing a bank examination.
3. **BASF Aktiengesellschaft.** This German pharmaceutical pled guilty and agreed to a $225 million criminal fine for fixing prices on vitamins.
4. **SGL Carbon Aktiengesellschaft.** The world's largest producer of graphite and carbon products pled guilty to price-fixing and paid a $135 million fine for price fixing.
5. **Exxon Corporation.** Exxon pled guilty to criminal charges related to the 1989 Exxon Valdez oil spill and paid a $125 million fine. This was the largest criminal recovery obtained in an environmental case.
6. **UCAR International Inc.** The largest producer of graphite electrodes in the U.S. pled guilty to fixing prices and paid a $110 million criminal fine.
7. **Archer Daniels Midland.** Pleading guilty and paying a $100 million fine, the company was involved in price fixing of lysine and citric acid markets.

8. (tie) **Banker's Trust.** Fined $60 million for making false reports of financial performance, the bank had made false entries in books and records.
9. (tie) **Sears Bankruptcy Recovery Management Services.** Sears pled guilty to bankruptcy fraud and agreed to pay a $60 million fine. The company had already paid over $180 million in restitution to 188,000 debtors and $40 million in civil fines to 50 state attorneys general. Sears systematically misled those in bankruptcy into believing they had to pay certain debts.
10. **Haarman and Reimer Corporation.** A subsidiary of the German Bayer AG, the corporation pled guilty and agreed to pay a $50 million fine for fixing prices on the citric acid worldwide market.

Crimes by Organizations/Corporations Against Individuals (the Public)

Included in the discussion of *crimes by organizations against individuals (the public)* are multinational bribery, corporate fraud, price fixing, manufacturing and sale of faulty or unsafe products, inequitable taxes, and environmental crimes, to mention just a few.

Multinational Bribery. Embarrassed by the public disclosure and international scandal of American-based multinational corporations' expending millions of dollars to bribe foreign officials, the U.S. Congress passed the *Foreign Corrupt Practices Act* (1977). This law forbids the payment of bribes in order to obtain business contracts.

In 1996 the United States convinced 26 other member countries in the Organization for Economic Cooperation and Development to change their laws so that bribes abroad will no longer be tax deductible. Some specific incidents that prompted the passage of this legislation included the following:

- In the early seventies, multimillion dollar bribes by Lockheed to Japanese prime minister Kakuei Tanaka caused his resignation, toppled his government, and threatened Japanese-American relations. Similar payments by Lockheed caused scandal in the Netherlands and Italy. Ironically, in 1989 Japanese prime minister Noboru Takeshita was also forced to resign in an "influence peddling" scandal, although this time the corrupters were Japanese.
- The Communist party in Italy won impressive electoral support as a result of campaigning on a corruption issue involving Exxon's disbursing of over $50 million to Italian politicians.
- The same laundered funds from secret "slush funds" in offshore accounts that are used to bribe foreign officials are used domestically for illegal political campaign donations. About three hundred corporations admitted making such "donations" to Richard Nixon's campaigns in 1968 and 1972, using the same "laundered" money from which bribes of foreign officials were made (Anderson, 1983, p. 7A).
- In 1996 heavy financial donations to Bill Clinton's presidential race by Indonesian banker James Riady and others raised concern regarding undue foreign influence in U.S. politics.

In the previous chapter the Transparency International "Corruption Perceptions Index" (CPI) was discussed. In 1999 this same organization produced a Bribe Payers Index (BPI). The questions used in the construction of the index related to leading exporters having to pay bribes to senior public officials. Only 19 countries were analyzed. A ten on the index represents negligible bribery, while a zero indicates high levels of bribery. Some select countries and their scores were (www.transparency.de/documents/cpi/indix.html):

Sweden	*8.3*
Australia	*8.1*
Canada	*8.1*
United Kingdom	*7.2*
Germany	*6.2*
USA	*6.2*
Japan	*5.1*
Italy	*3.7*
South Korea	*3.4*
China (including Hong Kong)	*3.1*

Corporate Fraud. In 1989 an FBI undercover sting operation of commodities traders at the Chicago Board of Trade uncovered traders who overcharged customers, did not pay customers the full proceeds of sales, used their knowledge of customer orders to "inside trade" for their own benefit, and executed orders for fictitious practices (Berg, 1989).

Perhaps one of the biggest computer swindles in history, amounting to an estimated $2 billion, came to light in 1973 with the bankruptcy of the Equity Funding Corporation of America.

Executives at Equity Funding's life insurance subsidiary used the company computer to create roughly 56,000 phony or "ghost" policies (about 58 percent of all policies the company held). Reinsurers who bought the rights to the dummy policies were out millions of dollars; stockholders alone lost over $100 million. Using computer records rather than hard copy records, the Equity Funding executives mixed genuine and phony policies in the master tape files; thus, printouts showed that the company had nearly 100,000 policies. When auditors took samples to check against hard copies, they were held off for a day or two during which phony hard-copy records were produced ("Conning by Computer," 1973). The president and twenty-four other employees and officers were indicted. While the former received an eight-year sentence, the others received shorter terms (Blundell, 1978). Convicted of complicity in the case, outside auditing firms were ordered to pay $39 million to former equity shareholders (Ermann and Lundman, 1982, pp. 43–48).

Corporate fraud can be found in a variety of enterprises. Anspach (1990) explored the borderline of white collar crime by examining the questionable sales practices of some firms selling mutual funds, which he views as often "the legal taking of other people's money" or "collective corporate theft." In one case, the average commission rate for such salespersons was 43 percent, the risky junk bond nature of the fund was misrepresented, and the majority of clients either lost money or dropped out of the plan.

In 1990 the Chrysler Corporation pleaded guilty to selling previously wrecked vehicles as new and disconnecting the odometers on about 60,000 vehicles. Chrysler pleaded no contest and was fined $7.6 million ("Chrysler Fined," 1990). Other examples of corporate fraud include a 1985 plea bargain by E. F. Hutton to 2,000 counts of defrauding hundreds of U.S. banks through a check-kiting scheme. Hutton agreed to a record $2 million fine and other settlements (Taylor, 1985). In 1992 Sears was accused of overcharging and making unnecessary repairs to customers' vehicles at their auto service centers in California and New Jersey. Undercover investigators documented a systematic fraud in California involving overselling 90 percent of the time (Yin, 1992). Stanford University was accused in 1991 of overcharging the federal government for contracted research. One overcharge was for $7,000 for bed sheets for the president of the University (Stout, 1991).

General Electric was fined $10 million and two executives were sentenced to prison for cheating the government on a contract for battlefield computers in 1990. In 1985 G.E.

paid a fine of roughly $1 million for illegally claiming cost overruns on Minuteman missiles (Stieg, 1990a, p. 2A). An example of "serial fraud," in 1992 G.E. pleaded guilty to defrauding the federal government in the sale of military engines to Israel and agreed to pay $69 million in a settlement of criminal charges and a civil lawsuit ("G.E. Pleads Guilty," 1992).

The Big Four superbrokers of the Japanese stockmarket admitted reimbursing 231 big investors to the tune of $933 million for losses suffered in the 1987 stockmarket crash. While their actions were not technically illegal, smaller and foreign investors felt on the outside of an insiders' game (Ohmar, 1991).

In 1999 Cendant Corporation, which owns Days Inn and Ramada hotels, agreed to pay $2.8 billion to stockholders. The company admitted irregular accounting practices which were used to inflate earnings and permit insiders to sell at a profit ("Cendant to Pay," 1999).

In 1994 Prudential Securities, a division of the Prudential Insurance Company of America, paid out over $1 billion in settlements and regulatory fines levied by the Securities and Exchange Commission and state securities regulators. This is a record, the costliest fraud scandal for any investment in Wall Street's history, exceeding the previous record by Drexel Burnham Lambert Inc. of $650 million in 1989 (Eichenwald, 1994). Clients were fraudulently sold risky investments and were lied to and deceived with sales materials. In 1996 Prudential agreed to pay a record fine of more than $20 million and repay policyholders millions more for having "churned" (causing unnecessary sales to gain commissions) customers' accounts. Agents talked customers into trading in paid-up policies in order to finance new, more expensive ones. Some estimate that Prudential may have to pay between $280 million and $1 billion in order to reimburse cheated customers ("Prudential Fined Millions," 1996).

In 1998 Hertz, the rental car company, admitted overcharging customers and insurance companies $13 million for accident repairs in which employees forged repair bids ("Hertz," 1988). This was minor fraud compared with the operations of defense firms. In 1989 the FBI launched a major investigation into massive fraud, bribery, and bid rigging in defense industry bids on Pentagon contracts. Particularly under attack was "the revolving door," a system in which defense company executives serve stints as Pentagon officials and then return to the industries they previously oversaw as contract officers. Such obvious conflict of interest might be viewed as "deferred bribes" in which cooperative defense contract officers will be later rewarded with defense industry jobs. The losers, of course, are the nation's armed forces and the nation's taxpayers (Waldman, 1989).

IN THE NEWS 11.1 describes the collapse in the 1990s of one of France's largest banks, Crédit Lyonnaise, due to fraud and corruption.

The medical and insurance business has been a particular area of fraud. The United States is the only developed country in the world without national health insurance. It pays 50 percent more to run its system, and special interests effectively block any attempt to extend guaranteed health care to all as is the case in other developed countries. Big profits attract big fraud. In 1997 Blue Shield of California paid $12 million to settle charges for submitting false Medicare claims (Howe, 1997). In 1993 Metropolitan Life was fined $20 million for cheating its customers, and in 1996 Mutual of New York was fined $12.5 million for deceptive sales tactics.

Systematic fraud by Medicare providers is estimated to cost about 10 percent of total Medicare costs in the United States. Some examples of such fraud include (Sparrow, 1998, p. 2):

- In March 1995 the FBI director stated that intelligence had indicated that cocaine traffickers in Florida and California were switching from drug dealing to the safer and more lucrative health care fraud business.

IN THE NEWS 11.1

THE CRÉDIT LYONNAISE SCANDAL: THE DIRTIEST BANK IN THE WORLD

In the late 1990s the collapse of Crédit Lyonnaise, one of France's biggest banks, was described as an "octopus of fraud" with losses estimated as high as $20 billion, exceeding those of the infamous BCCI (Bank of Credit and Commerce International) failure with a $7 billion loss (McClintock, 1999). Described as the "dirtiest bank in the world," the Crédit Lyonnaise affair represents the biggest bank debacle in history. The government-owned bank was investigated for over 100 cases of fraud, embezzlement, bribery, perjury, forgery, money laundering, blackmail, and arson. While today the bank has been largely privatized and is again profitable, the specter of past wrongdoing still haunts it. Some continuing investigations include:

- U.S. investigators examined charges of securities fraud, mail fraud, and lying to the Federal Reserve in a purchase of California insurance company Executive Life (Ibid.). Crédit Lyonnaise hid its purchase since California law forbids such ownership by foreign entities.
- Probes of connections with former clients Robert Maxwell, the British publisher who died under mysterious circumstances, and Bernard Tapie, Adidas owner who went to prison in a separate bribery case.
- Money was loaned to business investors with no collateral or documentation.
- Bank officers accepted gratuities and "consulting payments."
- Loans to Italian criminals/businessmen Giancarlo Parreti and Florio Fiorini of $2 billion were obtained through bribes. The loans were used to purchase Metro-Goldwyn-Mayer studios in 1990, the biggest financial scandal in the history of Hollywood.
- In a Caribbean subsidiary in the Netherlands Antilles, millions of dollars disappeared in crooked real estate deals. Buildings were sold for more than they were worth and huge kickbacks were pocketed by the bankers.

Similar to the U.S. Savings and Loan scandal in the 1980s, the ultimate victims of the Crédit Lyonnaise treachery were the taxpayers of France, who had to pay for the bank's losses.

Source: David McClintock, 1999, "The Dirtiest Bank in the World," Forbes, December 13.

InfoTrac College Edition Research

Using both the Internet and InfoTrak, locate some other examples of bank fraud. How are these "financiopaths" able to get away with such illegal activities involving such large amounts of money?

- A Medicare contractor in 1998 agreed to pay $144 million in civil and criminal penalties for concealing poor performance in reviewing and paying claims of Medicare beneficiaries.
- In an early 1998 scheme, more than $1 billion in phony medical bills using names of unsuspecting patients and doctors had been submitted to private insurers.

In 1995 Caremark International pled guilty to paying kickbacks to doctors for steering patients its way. The company agreed to pay $159 million (Burton, 1995). In the largest health care settlement in U.S. history, National Medical Care, Inc., agreed to pay $500 million in civil fines penalties, and restitution including $101 million in criminal fines for requiring needless tests of Medicare recipients and paying kickbacks for referrals (APBnews.com, 2000a).

Price Fixing. Collusion and price fixing to set artificially high prices had become the norm in the electrical industry, with the firms taking turns (rotational bidding) submitting the lowest bid. This cost the American public untold millions, perhaps billions, of dollars in higher prices.

The Great Electrical Industry Conspiracy. The "Great Electrical Conspiracy" involved price fixing on Tennessee Valley Authority equipment. In February 1961 seven of the highest executives in the electrical industry, from firms such as General Electric and Westinghouse, were given jail sentences of thirty days, an unprecedented benchmark decision that sent a warning to corporate price fixers, bid riggers, and market slicers. In addition, General Electric was fined $437,500 and Westinghouse $372,500. In all, twenty-nine companies and forty-five executives were convicted of bid rigging and price fixing estimated at approximately $2 billion (Herling, 1962). The conspirators were well aware of the illegality of their activities: they met under fictitious names in hotel rooms, called their meetings "choir practice," and referred to the list of participants as "the Christmas card list."

Plumbers Fix More Than Leaks. In 1975 the U.S. Department of Justice filed an antitrust suit against three plumbing manufacturers (American Standard, Borg Warner, and Kohler) and three executives for conspiring to fix prices on $1 billion worth of bathroom fixtures. The case actually began in 1966 with seventeen corporate and individual coconspirators named. The others pleaded no contest to the charges, got short jail terms, and were fined a total of $370,000 ("U.S. Begins Price-Fixing Prosecution," 1975). The $1 billion stolen by these organizations from the public dwarfs by far the more "mundane" criminal activity that gains so much media attention. For instance, the Boston Brinks robbery netted only $2 million and the largest robbery in U.S. history as of 1980—that of the Lufthansa airport warehouse in New York City—scored only $4 million (Clinard and Yeager, 1980, p. 8). This was superseded in 1983 by the $11 million robbery of a Sentry Armored Car warehouse in New York City ("Wells Fargo," 1983). Thus the "great plumbing equipment rip-off," which is far less dramatic and well-known, cost the American public the equivalent of five hundred "great Brinks robberies."

Panasonic Price-Fixing Scheme. In 1989 the Japanese electronics giant, Panasonic, settled out of court and agreed to pay $16 million in rebates to over 665,000 U.S. consumers for overcharges as a result of an aborted price-fixing scheme. Although such price setting is legal in Japan, the firm had illegally threatened to cut off supplies of their VCR camcorders and cordless telephones unless retailers agreed to sell these items at prices dictated by Panasonic. Such a scheme would have cost consumers hundreds of millions of dollars ("Panasonic," 1989).

The U.S. Justice Department filed suit in 1994 against General Electric Company for fixing prices on industrial diamonds in consort with DeBeers Centenary A.G., which controls 90 percent of the $1-billion market for synthetic diamonds. This trial constituted the first antitrust case to go to trial in about two decades.

In 1980 the Energy Department filed suit against fifteen major refining companies and charged them with more than $10 billion in possible pricing violations. As part of some out-of-court settlements, several of the corporations agreed to reimburse overcharged customers, pay the government, give rebates on past charges, cut prices, and accelerate investment in refining, exploration, and production (Lyons, 1980).

The most expensive series of white collar frauds in U.S. history is "The Great Savings and Loan Scandal." VANTAGE POINT 11.1 defines some of the jargon used by S&L scam artists. (This jargon is presented to give the reader an example of S&L scams, but is not intended for memorization.) VANTAGE POINT 11.2 provides a brief account of the scandal.

Imagine crooks being so low-down that they would steal milk from children. In 1990 the Southland Corporation and Borden, Inc., agreed to plead guilty to rigging bids on school milk contracts in Florida and to pay fines totaling $3.5 million ("Companies Fined," 1990). Concern has been expressed that Japanese automakers in the United States, by

VANTAGE POINT 11.1

Can You Speak S&L-ese? Argot of Savings and Loan Scam Artists

In Chapter 9, "Professional Crime," the argot of professional criminals was examined. In the 1980s financial thieves ("financiopaths") developed a whole new jargon—"S&L-ese"—which would give the "hip, slick, and cool" language of streetwise professional criminals described in Chapter 9 a run for its money. Using RAP accounting and beards and straw borrowers, go-go thrifts busted out many S&Ls as well as FIZZLIC itself. With "cash-for-trash" and "dead horses for dead cows" land flips and paper parking, they managed to Ponzi the American public ("the weak, the meek, and the ignorant") as well as the feds. With daisy chains and inflated appraisals, paper was kissed, loans scraped, and walking money was produced from brokered deposits and invested in junk bonds. If revolving doors or fees could not buy off the professionalism of accountants, lawyers, and members of Congress, white knights could be used to rescue zombie thrifts.

In the 1980s white collar financial criminals not only began to "talk the talk" of professional criminals but also began to "walk the walk" (imitate their operations). Some selected idioms of financial jargon in the S&L scandal include:

Alligators (which take bites out of the taxpayer) are properties that are losing money and which federal agencies such as the Federal Savings and Loan Insurance Company (FSLIC) were stuck with when they closed defunct thrifts.

*Beards (*straw borrowers) are individuals with clean records who front for mobsters.

Bust-outs are scams in which dishonest operators purchase a legitimate firm and systematically loot it from within.

Cash-for-trash is a policy of requiring borrowers to purchase "bad" property in order to make a thrift appear solvent.

Daisy chains (linked financing) are phony paper transactions such as "land flips" in which intermediaries buy and sell a commodity in order to artificially raise its price.

Dead horses for dead cows ("If you buy my dead horses, I'll buy your dead cows.") refers to a practice in which bad assets (dead horses) could be swapped with other S&Ls (for their dead cows) in order to hide them from thrift examiners.

FIZZLIC (FSLIC) refers to the now-defunct Federal Savings and Loan Insurance Corporation, the federal agency that guaranteed thrift deposits.

Go-Go thrifts are savings and loans that took the most risks or were on the fast track.

Inflated appraisals involve overestimating the value of property.

Kissing the paper is a scam in which a person with a good credit history receives a loan and then sells it to a weak borrower (i.e., kisses the paper).

Land flips are deals that artificially raise the price of an item by buying and selling it back and forth.

Lender participation is the issuance of loans on the condition that the lender (S&L) gets a portion of the project.

RAP accounting (Regulatory Accounting Principles) is a looser accounting system established specifically for thrift institutions.

Revolving doors refers to the practice of offering federal inspectors future positions if they are cooperative in their evaluations.

Scraping is stealing some of the proceeds of a loan through "double invoicing" or keeping two sets of books.

Straw borrowers (beards) are people who front for mobsters or S&L crooks in obtaining loans.

Walking money is money borrowed in excess of what is needed for the project.

White knights are phony "bail-out" borrowers who suddenly appeared to rescue thrifts when a regulatory crackdown threatened.

Zombie thrifts are hopelessly insolvent thrifts that stay alive only through federal insurance and guarantees.

For more details on these and additional terms, see Stephen Pizzo, Mary Fricker, and Paul Muolo, *Inside Job: The Looting of America's Savings and Loans,* New York: McGraw-Hill, 1989.

Source: Frank E. Hagan and Peter J. Benekos, 1991, "The Great Savings and Loan Scandal: An Analysis of the Biggest Financial Fraud in American History," *Journal of Security Administration,* 14, June, pp. 62–64.

InfoTrac College Edition Research

Search the "Savings and Loan Associations Bailout Crisis." Read the article by Calavita, Tillman, and Pontell. Which terms from our discussion of "S and L ese" were used?

VANTAGE POINT 11.2

The Great Savings and Loan Scandal: The Biggest White Collar Crime in U.S. History

The Great Savings and Loan Scandal, with an estimated cost of $500 billion, represents the biggest, costliest series of white collar crimes in U.S. history, far exceeding the Teapot Dome Affair of the 1920s or the Oil Scam of the 1970s. It represents about forty years of all other property crime combined, and it also represents the most costly public policy failure in U.S. history. Five hundred billion dollars is more than the cost of all of the bank robberies in this country since its founding. The U.S. attorney general, the FBI, and the General Accounting Office estimate that at least one-third of these losses was due to either regulatory neglect or criminal fraud. The savings and loan (S&L) scandal reflected increased criminal opportunity resulting from an economic crisis and deregulation taken advantage of by greedy insiders who collectively looted financial institutions and sent the bill to the U.S. taxpayers. It represented a criminal justice failure of record-breaking proportions.

A succinct account of the S&L crisis may tend to oversimplify a complex history, but let it suffice to say that the federal government, in order to protect against bank collapses, decided to guarantee bank and savings-and-loan deposits in the 1930s. This $10,000 per deposit would eventually be raised to $100,000 per deposit. In return for this, S&Ls were strictly limited to home mortgages and interest loans/payments. By the 1970s double-digit inflation wreaked havoc on the industry, which was stuck with 6 percent, thirty-year mortgages when inflation was 14 to 16 percent. S&Ls began to collapse and, as a rescue attempt, the federal government in 1982 decided to deregulate them. This included permitting them to charge more competitive interest rates and to invest in other commercial activities and banking services. Despite these measures, over three hundred federally insured S&Ls collapsed between 1980 and 1986, and many others were "zombies," technically insolvent with negative net worth (Kane, 1989; Cranford, 1989). The thrift industry persuaded Congress to continue to postpone inevitable closings, thus raising the final costs. Ignored by Congress and the president, who had their eyes on the next election, S&Ls became unregulated and victimized by congressional incompetence and regulatory ineptitude (Pilzer and Deitz, 1989, p. 126). "Heads I win, tails FSLIC (Federal Savings and Loan Insurance Corporation) loses" became a common phrase in the industry.

Deregulation created a climate of criminal opportunity, a backing of a "junk bond [high-risk] speculative environment" with federal deposit insurance. Wealthy criminals, such as Charles Keating robbed the S&Ls, and they were aided and abetted by the "best and brightest" professional talent the United States had to offer. More than eighty law firms represented Charles Keating to the tune of $70 million in legal fees. Six of the "Big Eight" accounting firms were charged by federal authorities with illegal conduct. Wall Street brokerage firms unethically took advantage of unsophisticated thrift managers (Mayer, 1990). Pizzo, Fricker, and Muolo (1989, p. 289) claim:

> **A financial mafia of swindlers, mobsters, greedy Savings and Loan executives, and con men capitalized on regulatory weaknesses created by deregulation and thoroughly fleeced the thrift industry. While it was certainly true that economic factors (like plummeting oil prices in Texas and surrounding states) contributed to the crises, the Savings and Loans would not be in the mess they are today, but for rampant fraud.**

Charles Keating bought Lincoln S&L with $50 million in junk bonds purchased from Michael Milken, and then used the S&L's money almost exclusively to buy more junk bonds from Milken. Millions in campaign donations and a mistaken overemphasis on constituent service led members of Congress to ignore their oversight function and left the S&Ls as a playground for professional scam artists with the taxpayer as the hapless victim.

Sources: Frank E. Hagan and Peter J. Benekos, 1991, "The Great Savings and Loan Scandal," *Journal of Security Administration,* 14, July, pp. 41–64; Peter J. Benekos and Frank E. Hagan, 1991, "Fixing the Thrifts," *Journal of Security Administration,* 14, July, pp. 65–104; and Frank Hagan and Peter Benekos, 1992, "What Charles Keating and 'Murph the Surf' Have in Common: A Symbiosis of Professional and Occupational and Corporate Crime," *Criminal Organizations,* 7, Spring, pp. 3–26.

InfoTrac College Edition Research
Locate the article "Will Charlie Keating Ride Again? By L.J. Davis. What fears does Davis express?

exporting their "Keiretsu" supply system (lifelong, exclusive contracts with parts suppliers), are freezing out U.S. parts companies and violating antitrust laws. The Bush administration took a stricter stance than the Reagan administration on "vertical restraints on distributors," in which manufacturers (Mitsubishi and Nintendo, to name two) have been accused of setting minimum retail prices for their products, thus discouraging competition (Barrett, 1991). In 2000, federal investigators claimed that two of the largest auction houses, Sotheby's and Christie's, fixed prices by fixing commissions. The decision was made in secret meetings by the chairpersons of both companies (Frantz, Blumenthal, and Vogel, 2000). While at times it may appear that antitrust enforcement is fruitless, Scott (1989) notes that public exposure of trade conspiracies serves as a deterrent despite weak penalties.

Sale of Unsafe Products.

Pinto leaves you with that warm feeling.

—(Advertisement for Ford Pinto, 1973)

The Ford Pinto Case. In the early sixties, in order to compete with compact foreign imports, the Ford Motor Company rushed the compact Pinto model into production. Since retooling for the assembly line was already a costly investment, the company chose to proceed with production despite the results of its own crash tests, which indicated that the gas tank exploded in rear-end collisions. Choosing profit over human lives, the company continued to avoid and to lobby even eight years later against federal safety standards that would have forced modification of the gas tank (Dowie, 1977; Cullen, 1984).

An estimated five hundred persons were burned to death because of the firetrap engineering of the tanks. Once the word spread, Ford withdrew the commercial that the car gave one a "warm feeling." *Mother Jones* (an investigative magazine) collected documents and called to public attention Ford's wrongdoing (Dowie, 1977; Cullen, Makestad, and Cavender, 1987). While the company estimated that it could have made the necessary modifications for about $11 per car, *Mother Jones* estimated the cost at half that. Using the National Highway Traffic Safety Administration estimate of the cost per fatality (assuming lawsuits) of roughly $200,000, Ford had, according to a company memorandum, performed a cost/benefit analysis of the problem. Paying for deaths, injuries, and damages without changing the tanks was guessed to cost about $49.5 million, while the cost of modifying the 12.5 million vehicles would run $137 million. It was "cheaper" to ignore the problem and face the lawsuits.

In May of 1978 the Department of Transportation finally recalled all 1971 to 1976 Pintos and, although it was the biggest auto recall until that time, the decision amounted to too little too late for the conservatively estimated five hundred dead, maimed, and scarred victims (Ermann and Lundman, 1982, p. 18). The Ford Pinto case was also a landmark, representing the first time in U.S. history that a corporation was indicted for murder. In 1978 Indiana prosecutors charged Ford with homicide after three people were burned alive in a Pinto (Browning and Gerassi, 1980, p. 406). Even though Ford was acquitted, the trial of a corporation for murder may have served as a signal that the public reaction to corporate crime was changing (Swigert and Farrell, 1980). When asked what fate Lee Iacocca, then president of Ford, deserved, one person sarcastically suggested that someone buy him a Ford Pinto complete with Firestone 500 tires (yet another dangerous product whose manufacturer hid its defects until an unacceptable number of human sacrifices sparked federal action).

X–Cars = Brand X. Brand X has never been a favored label for a product. It perhaps was prophetic that GM chose this name for what appears to have been a real brand X product. The National Highway Traffic Safety Administration (NHTSA) filed suit on August 3,

In 1994 American tobacco executives lied under oath before a Congressional Committee regarding the addictive nature of their product. In 1998 the new CEOs admitted to the health risks.

1983, against General Motors, alleging that the corporation with full knowledge had sold 1.1 million X-model cars with faulty brakes that later killed fifteen and injured seventy-one persons. The government charged that the company knew of these problems and purposely withheld information that the rear brakes, because of a defect, tended to lock. To lend further complexity to the case, the congressional General Accounting Office (GAO) accused the NHTSA of a cover-up and of failing to follow usual procedures in alerting the public to a known danger.

The suit sought a recall on all 1980 X-cars and $4 million in civil penalties. The former alone would be expected to cost GM about $300 million. At congressional hearings on the issue, Representative Timothy Wirth charged, "They [the NHTSA] have been trying to protect GM all the way down the line" ("Washington *vs.* GM," 1983, p. 9). On March 30, 1983, 240,000 X-cars were recalled (Coleman, 1985, p. 41).

The Ford Explorer-Firestone Tires Recall. In 2000 executives of the Ford Motor Company and Bridgestone/Firestone Incorporated both appeared before the U.S. Congress to answer questions regarding possible cover-ups of defects in the Ford Explorer (sport utility vehicle), particularly when equipped with Firestone tires. The tread on Firestone ATX and Wilderness tires would peel off forcing the Ford Explorer to roll over. By 2000 it became apparent that numerous accidents had taken place due to defects that compounded when the two products were combined. By February 2000, tires were recalled in Thailand and Malaysia. In May a National Highway Traffic Safety Association (NHTSA) study was begun and Ford recalled 30,000 tires in Venezuela, Ecuador, and Colombia. In August Firestone recalled 6.5 million tires; Ford CEO Jacques Nasser apologized on television, and Bridgestone/Firestone CEO Masatoshi Ono apologized to the U.S. Congress. Half of the property damage and injury claims received from 1997 to 1999 were for ATX tires. By August 31, 2000, NHTSA labeled 1.4 million more tires defective and estimated fatalities at 88 and injuries at 250. Ford had recalled the tires in 16 countries, but had not

(© Associated Press)

Ford executives including CEO Jacques Nasser, center, listen to testimony on Capitol Hill regarding tire problems.

issued a U.S. recall until later. While both companies pointed the finger at the other for the defects and crashes, in fact neither were as forthcoming as they could have been in identifying problems; it took congressional pressure to force them to act as good corporate citizens.

Reminiscent of Mills' (1952) "higher immorality" notion, Heilbroner et al. (1973) in their book *In the Name of Profit: Profiles in Corporate Irresponsibility* maintain that the people who run our supercorporations are not merely amoral, but positively immoral. They and other authors cite examples like these:

- B. F. Goodrich plotted to sell defective air brakes to the U.S. Air Force by faking test records and falsifying laboratory reports. National security and the lives of fighter pilots appeared to be of little concern.
- In the early 1970s a General Dynamics engineer warned his superiors of dangerous defects in DC-10 cargo doors. They ignored this warning. Two years later a DC-10 crashed in France when the cargo doors opened in flight, killing all 346 passengers (Nader, Green, and Seligman, 1976).
- Theo Colburn in *Our Stolen Future* (1996) claims that toxic chemicals released in the last fifty years mimic natural hormones and may be responsible for human male sperm counts decreasing 50 percent since 1938 and growing infertility, genital deformities, breast and prostate cancer, and neurological disorders.
- With a rollover accident rate for rear-wheel drive, Bronco IIs double the sport vehicle average. In 1992 Ford had spent $113.4 million to settle 334 lawsuits for rollovers. In 1995 a jury ordered Ford to pay $22.5 million in punitive damages to parents of a Texas A&M University student who died when her Bronco blew a tire and overturned.
- In 1994 Secretary of Transportation Federico Pena made a deal with General Motors not to order recall of its pickup trucks, whose defects cost 150 lives, in return for a payment of $51 million to support safety programs. The latter were calculated to have

the benefit of saving more lives than the calculated 32 more people who would die due to faulty design of the trucks (Bennett, 1994).

- In the largest product liability settlement in U.S. history, a federal judge in 1994 granted $4.25 billion in a class action suit against 60 silicone breast implant manufacturers. Dow Corning Corporation agreed to pay the largest share—$2 billion. The largest previous settlement had been by asbestos manufacturer Manville Corporation for $3 billion. One study showed that Dow knew of the dangers as early as 1975 (Blakeslee, 1994).
- In 1994 the FBI employed a General Electric engineer to infiltrate a General Electric jet engine plant to spy on managers who were later charged with compromising the safety of military and commercial aircraft by covering up engine flaws. General Electric had been involved in more cases of contractor fraud against the Pentagon than any other manufacturer (Frantz and Nasar, 1994). This included 16 criminal convictions and civil judgments.
- In 1995 top executives of seven tobacco companies told a Congressional committee under oath that they did not know for certain that tobacco was addictive or caused disease. Attorney General Janet Reno asked the U.S. Justice Department if the companies were guilty of fraud and perjury when it was revealed that Brown and Williamson Tobacco Corporation documents revealed that their own research had shown for years that cigarettes were addictive and harmful, and the company had covered up such knowledge (Hilts, 1995). A record $368 billion deal was agreed to by the tobacco companies with 40 states, affecting everything from how cigarettes are advertised and sold to punitive damage awards of $50 billion.

The National Consumer Product Safety Commission estimates that 20 million serious injuries and thirty thousand deaths a year are caused by unsafe consumer products (Coleman, 1994, p. 9). When Richardson-Merrell's MER/29, a cholesterol inhibitor, was tested, all the rats died; nevertheless, the company falsified the data and marketed the product. When over five thousand users suffered serious side effects, it was withdrawn from the market and the company received a minor fine (Coleman, 1994, p. 84). In 1988 the Cordis Corporation pleaded guilty in federal court to concealing defects in thousands of pacemakers (these are implanted in heart patients to regulate the heartbeat). The company agreed to a fine of $264,000 plus court costs. Executives were charged separately ("4 Indicted," 1988).

Defective products continue to plague consumers. More recent examples are defective breast implants that maim, deform, and destroy immune systems; flawed heart valves (Ingersoll, 1991); and unsafe pacemakers (Burton, 1991).

Environmental Crime. In 1962 the publication of Rachel Carson's *Silent Spring* signaled the beginning of the age of environmental awareness. Specifically attacking toxic chemicals and pesticides, Carson's work very dramatically called attention to the irreversible and final genetic and biological harm the poisoning of the environment could bring about. According to Regenstein (1982, p. 132), "The accuracy and validity of *Silent Spring* was no inhibition to the chemical industry's attacking and attempting to discredit it, a vicious campaign which started even before the work was published and continues today."

Three Mile Island. Ironically, in the film *The China Syndrome* (so-named because of the false belief that a nuclear meltdown in the United States would bore through the earth to the other side—China) a character indicates that a nuclear mishap could render an area the size of Pennsylvania uninhabitable. Almost prophetically, after the release of the film, the worst potential nuclear plant disaster in history occurred at Three Mile Island, Pennsylvania. The accident released radioactivity into the surrounding area and required the temporary evacuation of young children and pregnant women from the immediate vicinity.

On November 7, 1983, a federal grand jury indicted Metropolitan Edison, the owners of the TMI facility, on criminal charges of faking safety test records before the accident. The indictment alleged that the company attempted to conceal from the Nuclear Regulatory Commission the rate of leakage in the main cooling system, in which water passes over the reactor's radioactive core ("Feds Indict," 1983). Allegations had been made that the corporation was anxious to have the reactor on line by a certain date in order to take advantage of tax benefits.

In April 1984 Metropolitan Edison pleaded guilty to knowingly using inaccurate and meaningless testing methods and agreed to pay a $1 million fine. The company also pleaded no contest to six other criminal counts, including manipulating test results, destroying records, and not filing proper notice of cooling system leaks ("Judge Agrees to TMI Plea Bargain," 1984).

Toxic Criminals. Potential environmental hazards created by new technologies require that corporations and businesses exercise a higher level of ethical behavior than that exhibited in the Ford Pinto incident or other cover-ups and deceptions of the public and of government regulatory agencies. Bhopal (India), Love Canal, Times Beach, Seveso (Italy), and Chernobyl are well-known environmental disasters. Each year about three hundred health-care workers die from hepatitis B after exposure on the job (Anderson and Van Atta, 1988a). Toxic wastes also expose the public to possible harm. In 1979 the EPA estimated there were 109 very hazardous dumpsites and 32,254 sites where hazardous wastes were buried. That latter figure was subsequently raised to 51,000, with "significant problems" existing at between 1,200 and 34,000 (Brown, 1982, p. 305). In the late 1980s beaches in various parts of the United States had to be closed because illegally dumped medical wastes were washing ashore. Blood gushing out of trash compactors and body parts found in trash piles illustrate the ghoulish proportions of such hazards.

VANTAGE POINT 11.3 reports on the deadliest air pollution disaster in American history, the Donora Fluoride Death Fog.

Alcoa agreed to pay criminal penalties of $7.5 million to the State of New York for illegally holding thirty-three rail cars full of PCB-tainted soil at a Massena, New York, facility over several months while preparing fake documents to dispose of the material as nonhazardous (Milbank and Allen, 1991).

U.S. v. Allied Chemical. In 1976 Judge Robert Merhige (Richmond, Virginia) fined Allied Chemical $13.2 million after it pleaded nolo contendere to 153 charges of conspiracy to defraud the EPA and Army Corps of Engineers. Allied had polluted the James River and had deceptively blocked the efforts of these agencies to enforce water pollution control laws. In justifying the largest fine ever imposed in a single environmental case, the judge stated, "I don't think that commercial products or the making of profits are as important as the God-given resources of our country" (Beauchamp, 1983, p. 97).

Much of the work social scientists or federal agencies should have been doing in investigating corporate crime has until relatively recently been shouldered by investigative journalists and consumer advocates, such as Ralph Nader and his associates. A partial list of such studies and their subject matter includes:

Cox, Fellmuth, and Schulz (1969), a report on the Federal Trade Commission.
Esposito and Silverman (1970), Vanishing Air, *on air pollution regulation.*
Turner (1970), The Chemical Feast, *on the Food and Drug Administration.*
Wellford (1972), Sowing the Wind, *on health and environmental hazards.*
Green et al. (1973), The Monopoly Makers, *on antitrust activity.*
Page and O'Brien (1973), Bitter Wages, *on occupational safety and health.*

VANTAGE POINT 11.3

The Donora Fluoride Death Fog: A Secret History of America's Worst Air Pollution Disaster

An environmental horror story similar to works by Michael Crichton visited Donora, Pennsylvania (near Pittsburgh), on Halloween night, 1948. History tells us that a temperature inversion trapped smog in the narrow industrial valley and produced the worst single air pollution disaster in American history, with twenty dead and hundreds injured and dying. This incident resulted in the passage of the 1955 Clean Air Act. Bryson (1998) and Snyder (1994) relate the Donora cover-up.

Fluoride emissions from the Donora Zinc works and steel plants owned by U.S. Steel caused these injuries. Philip Sadtler, a chemical consultant who conducted research at the scene of the disaster, concluded that U.S. Steel conspired with U.S. Public Health Service (PHS) officials to cover up the role that fluoride played in the disaster (Bryson, 1998). One-third of the town's 14,000 residents were affected by the smog, with hundreds evacuated or hospitalized.

While the official PHS report stated "no single substance" was responsible and laid blame on the temperature inversion, Sadtler charged that the PHS report was designed to assist U.S. Steel in escaping liability for the deaths and prevent controls of toxic fluoride emissions. The national fluoride clean-up would have cost billions.

The Public Health Service was then part of the Federal Security Agency headed by Oscar Ewing, a former top lawyer for Alcoa. The latter was facing lawsuits at the time for wartime airborne fluoride emissions. Sadtler, in the December 13, 1948, issue of *Chemical and Engineering News,* reported fluorine blood levels of the dead and ill patients to be 12-to-25 times above normal. Afterwards, pressure was brought to bear by manufacturers to prevent the journal from publishing any more articles by Sadtler (Ibid.)

Researching the disaster 50 years later, investigators discovered that important records were missing from the PHS archives and U.S. Steel records were not open to researchers. Despite the fact that, at the time, the Donora disaster was the largest government environmental investigation ever conducted, almost all the records mysteriously vanished when Dr. Lynne Page Snyder was doing research for her dissertation from the University of Pennsylvania. Snyder's dissertation was entitled "The Death-Dealing Smog Over Donora, Pennsylvania: Industrial Air Pollution, Public Health Policy and the Politics of Expertise, 1948–1949" (Snyder, 1994). She suspects the archives were determined to be too hot to handle and were gotten rid of.

As a sequel to the "Fluoride Death Fog in Donora," Bryson (2000) describes "Fluoride and the Mohawks" between 1960–1975:

> **Cows crawled around the pasture on their bellies, inching along like giant snails. So crippled by bone disease they could not stand up, this was the only way they could graze. Some died kneeling, after giving birth to stunted calves. Others kept on crawling until, no longer able to chew because their teeth had crumbled down to their nerves, they began to starve.**

The cattle belonged to Mohawk Indians on their reservation that straddled the New York-Canadian border when fluoride emissions from nearby aluminum plants devastated their herds and way of life. Crops and trees, birds and bees withered and died. Today, fish caught in the St. Lawrence River by the Mohawks have ulcers and spinal deformities, and Mohawk children also exhibit signs of bone and teeth damage.

In 1980 the Mohawks filed a $150 million lawsuit against two aluminum companies; but after five years of legal costs, the bankrupt tribe settled for $650,000 in damages to their cows.

Source: Chris Bryson, 1998, "The Donora Fluoride Fog," *Earth Island Journal,* Fall; also Chris Bryson, 2000, "The Donora Fluoride Fog," www.fluoridation.com/donora.htm; Lynne Page Snyder, 1994, "The Death-Dealing Smog Over Donora, Pennsylvania: Industrial Air Pollution, Public Health Policy and the Politics of Expertise, 1948–1949," Doctoral dissertation, University of Pennsylvania.

InfoTrac College Edition Research

Read "A Darkness in Donora" by Edwin Keister Jr. Does the article shed any further light on the Donora disaster?

(© Vanessa Vick, Photo Researchers, Inc.)

When the Exxon Valdez spilled 11 million gallons of crude oil on Alaska's North Slope, a court ordered cleanup was undertaken, which cost over $3 billion. Additional payments to local fishermen cost $300 million.

In addition to these, Nader and his associates have generated numerous other investigations and reports (Nader, 1965; Nader, Petkas, and Blackwell, 1972; Nader and Green, 1973; Nader, Green, and Seligman, 1976).

On the subject of environmental and health assaults on consumers, Simon (1996, pp. 177–78) describes some cases of "corporate dumping," a practice whereby corporations sell overseas products that have been deemed unsafe in this country by the EPA, FDA, or other federal agencies (see VANTAGE POINT 11.4).

Toxic crime may indeed be the ultimate and most insidious of crimes. Birth defects, long-term genetic damage and mutation, congenital heart defects and disorders in children—many of these effects may turn up twenty-to-thirty years later and be difficult to link to the original causative agents or toxic criminals. In that sense, those who commit environmental crimes may represent the first "intergenerational criminals:" the victimized may not have been born at the time the crime was perpetrated, and the criminal may be deceased by the time the victimization takes place.

Radiation Leaks. In 1988 in the wake of the Chernobyl disaster in the Soviet Union, investigations began to reveal a massive cover-up by the U.S. federal government of the dangers and harm its nuclear facilities and testing program had posed to unwarned workers and neighbors. Fallout from atomic tests in the 1950s and 60s resulted in little warning by the Atomic Energy Commission of exposure hazards such as birth deformities, cancer, and early death (McGrory, 1988). The Department of Energy runs federally owned nuclear plants that produce the fuel for the nation's nuclear weapons. These obsolete plants have worse safety features than most privately owned plants. The radioactive waste problem at the Energy Department's Hanford nuclear weapons reservation in Washington is unbelievable. It is described as (Lippman, 1991):

> the most polluted and dangerous nuclear compound in the United States and perhaps the world—the submarine hulks [21 buried radioactive reactor vessels] are

VANTAGE POINT 11.4

Corporate Dumping

- When *Dalkon Shield IUDs* (intrauterine contraceptive devices) killed seventeen women in the United States, the product was withdrawn from the U.S. market, but continued to be advertised and sold overseas (Mintz, 1987).
- Children's garments containing *Tris* fire retardant (a known carcinogen) were pulled off the domestic market by the Consumer Products Safety Commission (CPSC). These garments were then shipped overseas and sold.
- *Lomotil* is an antidiarrheal medicine that is sold only by prescription in the United States because it can cause death when consumed in amounts exceeding those recommended. It is sold off the shelf in countries such as Sudan and advertised with the slogan "used by astronauts." In such countries it is recommended for children as young as twelve.
- *Depo Provera,* a contraceptive produced by Upjohn, is known to cause malignant tumors, but is sold in seventy other countries and even used in U.S.-sponsored population control programs.
- Many U.S. *asbestos* manufacturers, faced with stricter safety regulations, have simply moved to Mexico.
- The lack of effective international standards found the Nestlé Corporation marketing *baby formula* in Third World countries. Their advertising encouraged mothers to use such mixes rather than nurse their own infants. Many infants died when their mothers could no longer afford the formula or dangerously stretched the limited supply of formula by adding water, tea, or chocolate drink (Lappé and Collins, 1977). The sad part of all of this is that had the mothers not been influenced to let their own milk dry up, the infants would have received the best possible nutrition from their mother's milk. Because of public pressure, Nestlé discontinued this marketing practice in 1984, but in 1988 resumed such practices (Griffin, 1989).
- *Lethal pesticides* that are prohibited in this country are exported overseas. Products sprayed with such poisons are nevertheless imported into the United States and consumed by an unknowing public (Simon, 1996, p. 178).
- In 1983 it was revealed that Eli Lilly Company had continued to sell the drug *Oraflex* even though it was aware that the drug had deadly side effects. FDA investigators found in Lilly's possession reports of deaths that they had purposely hidden from the agency. Although the drug was finally withdrawn from the market, there was no prosecution (ABC, 1983b).

Dowie (1987, pp. 49–50) explains a number of ways of circumventing regulatory agencies at home and importers abroad, including:

- *The Name Change* If bad publicity arises in the U.S. market, change the name of the product.
- *Last Minute Pullout* If the EPA threatens not to pass a chemical, the manufacturer pulls the application for approval and labels it "for export only." The manufacturer is not required to notify the importing country that the chemical is banned in the U.S.
- *Dump the Whole Factory* Move overseas where regulations are easier.
- *Change the Formula* by simply adding or subtracting inert ingredients.
- *The Skip* If the target country says the drug or product must be approved in the exporting country, export first to a country with looser laws, then export to the target country.
- *The Ingredient Dump* If the product is banned, export the ingredients separately, reassemble, and dump.

InfoTrac College Edition Research

Read Coro Strandberg's "Corporations as Good Citizens." Could social audits reduce practices such as corporate dumping?

little more than a novelty. In fact, they are a stable controllable form of waste in a nightmare world of volatile, explosive, toxic and radioactive junk.

So great is the mess, so diverse the streams of waste—solids and liquids, above ground and beneath, in the water and in the soil, stationary and migrating—that the most optimistic forecasts say it will take at least 30 years and $30 billion

Then lawyer John Foster Dulles brokered a deal for Bosch. His firm drafted papers enabling the Nazis to use a Swedish dummy owner to mask for German control during the war.

(© Peter Cuerlis / Black Star)

> to clean it up. And that's if all goes well, if none of the tanks of lethal liquids explodes and if scientists can figure out what to do with material for which no disposal technology exists. That's if all the waste can be contained before any more of it seeps into the Columbia River.

More and more of our food is processed and packaged by large corporations and, if recent investigations are to be believed, the food processors have not improved much since Upton Sinclair's (1906) exposés in *The Jungle.* Despite a 1906 federal Meat Inspection Act and a 1967 Wholesome Meat Act, abuses continue. In a Hormel plant in 1969, a Department of Agriculture inspector was bribed $6,000 annually for overlooking the production of "Number 2" meat (McCaghy, 1976b, p. 216):

> When the original customers returned the meat to Hormel, they used the following terms to describe it: "moldy liverloaf, sour party hams, leaking bologna, discolored bacon, off-condition hams, and slick and slimy spareribs." Hormel renewed these products with cosmetic measures (reconditioning, trimming, and washing). Spareribs returned for sliminess, discoloration, and stickiness were rejuvenated through curing and smoking, renamed Windsor Loins and sold in ghetto stores for more than fresh pork chops.

Corporate Violence. From what has been said so far it should be clear that, while the general public tends to view corporate crime as nonviolent, we might be more persuaded by Hills, who in *Corporate Violence* (1987, p. vii) describes " . . . 'respectable' business executives who impersonally kill and maim many more Americans than street muggers and assailants." He notes that the tools of such violence include:

> . . . exploding autos, defective medical devices, inadequately treated drugs and other hazardous products that are manufactured and marketed despite knowledge by corporate officials that such products can injure and kill consumers. There are reports of toxic chemical dumps that have poisoned drinking supplies, caused leukemia in children and destroyed entire communities; of cover-ups of asbestos-induced cancer, and the gradual suffocation of workers from inhaling

> cotton dust; of radioactive water leaking from improperly maintained nuclear reactors; of mangled bodies and lives snuffed out in unsafe coal mines and steel mills—and other dangers to our health and safety.

Crimes by Organizations Against Employees

Organizational (corporate) crime against employees (type 6 in Figure 10.1) may take many forms; the most insidious relates to purposive violation of health and safety laws that may not only threaten workers' lives, but may genetically damage their offspring.

During World War II, I. G. Farben, a large German manufacturing corporation, worked captive workers (slave labor) to death in its factories. According to Harry Wu, a former Chinese political prisoner, many Chinese exports sold in the United States have been produced in the harsh conditions of Chinese labor camps (Southerland, 1991). While most modern manufacturers do not directly kill their workers, health and safety violations by corporations and organizations against their employees can take many forms (see Frank, 1985). Some occupational exposure to injury and disease may be a necessary part of employment, but unnecessary, preventable hazards and their disregard by employers are regulated by the Occupational Safety and Health Administration (OSHA) and can incur criminal penalties. Terms such as black lung (due to coal exposure), brown lung (due to cotton mill exposure), and white lung (due to asbestos exposure) have become familiar to U.S. workers. The sheer number of new chemicals to which workers are exposed and their long-term impact are enormous. Occupational hazards are not new. In 1812 in Lawrence, Massachusetts, sweatshop conditions in the textile mills produced death in one-third of the workers by the age of 25 (Browning and Gerassi, 1980, p. 237).

Just to cite one example of corporate negligence and cover-up, an examination of the asbestos industry is enlightening. Carlson, appearing before a Congressional Subcommittee on Compensation, Health, and Safety (Carlson, 1979, pp. 25–52) indicated:

- Examination of corporate memos, letters, and other documents from as early as 1934 showed that senior executives at Johns-Manville and Raybestos-Manhattan (two of the biggest asbestos producers) knew of and covered up company-sponsored research findings that described asbestos-caused diseases.
- Asbestos industry-sponsored research in the 1930s and 1940s also showed asbestos dangers, and researchers were prevented from publishing their results.
- One company, Philip Carey Company, fired its medical consultant when he warned of possible lawsuits from workers exposed to asbestos.
- Years before the companies acknowledged any awareness of asbestos dangers, documents demonstrated that they had quietly settled injury and death claims from workers who had handled asbestos.
- Johns-Manville purposely did not notify employees of the results of their medical examinations that showed asbestosis, despite executives' knowledge that the disease was progressive and fatal unless treated in an early stage.

In 1988 OSHA fined meatpacker John Morrell and Company $4.33 million for having forced hundreds of injured workers in its Sioux Falls, S.D., plant to keep working even right after surgery. This was the largest fine against a single employer in the agency's history. Workers in this industry chronically suffer from carpal-tunnel syndrome and tendinitis, in which joints stiffen because of the erosion of soft tissue ("Meatpackers," 1988).

In 1990 USX agreed to pay $3.25 million for hundreds of alleged worker safety violations, including what OSHA called fatal, uncorrected hazards (Ball, 1990). That same year a federal jury awarded damages of $26.3 million to a retired insulation worker. Materials once made by Owens Corning Fiberglas Corporation had not been properly labeled as dangerous, causing the worker to develop asbestosis (Green and Geyelin, 1990).

Larry Agran (1982) in "Getting Cancer on the Job" documents that the cancer epidemic has been primarily fed by many industries' systematic unconcern for workers' health, in which company physicians cover up evidence of unsafe exposure to carcinogenic substances. He concludes that the government regulatory agencies are either too timid to enforce the law or lack staff or resources with which to protect workers.

In 1999 apparel workers and human rights groups filed the largest legal challenge ever against sweatshops on American soil. The suit alleged that major American retailers conspired to place thousands of workers in involuntary servitude and horrible work conditions (Greenhouse, 1999). Poor, young women from China, the Philippines, Bangladesh, and Thailand are led to believe that they are going to the United States to work; instead they are taken to Saipan (Mariana Islands), a U.S. possession where many work 12 hours a day, 7 days a week, sometimes without pay if they fall behind in their quotas. Sometimes exits are locked, pregnant workers are forced to have abortions, and workers are housed in barracks surrounded by barbed wire. On top of all of this, the clothing labels can read "Made in U.S.A."

Such activity taps only the tip of the iceberg in economic globalization, which often represents a "race to the bottom" in search for the cheapest labor possible, including child labor or, as in China, labor by prisoners. These activities are all in violation of the United Nation's "Universal Declaration of Human Rights."

If there are any heroes or heroines in the world of corporate crime, they can be found among the ranks of **whistleblowers** employees who are willing to step forward, usually at great personal sacrifice, to reveal wrongdoing on the part of their employers (see Westin, 1981). "You don't bite the hand that feeds you," states the old adage. The decision to inform on organizational violations has often meant firing, family disruption, ostracism from friends and former co-workers, as well as the end of one's career, as employers retaliate against the "squealer" or "stool pigeon."

In 1990 jurors ordered Lockheed Corporation to pay $45.3 million in damages to three former employees who had been fired for being whistleblowers regarding safety problems of C-5B military cargo planes. According to the workers, some of these planes with defective mainframes had been used to transport troops to Saudi Arabia ("Lockheed Ordered," 1990).

Some examples of well-known whistleblowers include:

- Frank Serpico, former New York Police Department officer, who informed on fellow officers during the Knapp Commission investigation in the 1960s
- John Dean, former legal counsel for President Nixon, who cooperated with the government in the Watergate investigation
- Bertrand Berube, a General Services Administration employee, who revealed that the Reagan administration used funds previously scheduled for the Pentagon for White House entertaining
- Daniel Ellsberg, who revealed *The Pentagon Papers* to the press, alleging the government was misleading the public regarding the Vietnam War
- Casey Ruud, who was fired in 1987 for revealing plutonium safety problems at a weapons facility
- Engineers at Morton Thiokol, who testified before Congress regarding unsafe O rings in the Challenger space shuttle disaster
- Ernie Fitzgerald, a Defense Department employee, who testified regarding a $2 billion cost overrun in the product of C-5A transports

In extreme cases an employer may even threaten an employee's life. While the following horror story is by no means typical, it profiles a true hero in the fight against corporate crime (see Mokhiber, 1988).

The Karen Silkwood Case. Congressional hearings (U.S. Congress, 1976) and Rashke's (1981) *The Killing of Karen Silkwood* describe the Silkwood episode. She was

Occupational hazards: Boys working in coal mines in the early 1900s suffered from black lung. A 1940s welder wearing asbestos gloves was subject to asbestos poisoning.

(© MGA / Photri)

(© Frederick Lewis / Archive Photos)

an employee of the Kerr-McGee nuclear plant in Guthrie, Oklahoma. The company used plutonium, one of the most lethal of substances, in its plant. A union activist for stricter safety standards at the company, Silkwood had gathered considerable information documenting the firm's negligence of health and safety measures for employees, as well as dangerous defects in the plutonium compounds being used.

On the evening of November 13, 1974, Silkwood was enroute with documents to a meeting with a union official and a reporter from the New York Times when her auto crashed into a ditch, killing her. The documents, which had been observed at the scene by state troopers, disappeared. In a subsequent trial investigating her death, Kerr-McGee was found guilty of negligence in health and safety practices, as well as criminally liable in Silkwood's contamination by radiation leaks during her employment. The Atomic Energy Commission found the company in violation of the majority of the union complaints, including the contamination of seventy-three employees in seventeen safety lapses over a five-year period (Rose, Glazer, and Glazer, 1982, p. 407). The jury also ordered the company to pay Silkwood's estate $10.5 million in damages ("Silkwood Vindicated," 1979, p. 40). The company appealed the case, and in January 1984, the decision was upheld by the U.S. Supreme Court.

In 1986 U.S. Congress passed additional legislation to protect whistleblowers' jobs, as well as reward them for whistleblowing. They are entitled to as much as 15 percent of what the government collects. Some have collected millions.

Environmentally dangerous occupations include those of chemical and insecticide workers, miners and shipyard workers who deal with asbestos, petrochemical and refinery workers, coal miners, coke-oven workers, textile and lead workers, medical radiation technicians, and those employed in the plastics industry. The exposures and risks are enormous; since most workers cannot easily switch jobs, they are even more dependent on federal regulatory agencies to protect their health and safety. Occupational hazards may be a necessary evil in modern industrial societies, but corporate subterfuge in unnecessarily exposing workers to such threats is not. Weak enforcement of OSHA regulations has resulted in the United States having five times as many work-related deaths per capita as Sweden and three times as many as Japan (Kinney, 1990).

In the mid-eighties, five executives from Film Recovery Systems, Inc., were charged with murder and two with manslaughter in the death due to cyanide poisoning of Stefan Golab, a Polish immigrant and employee of their company. They knowingly failed to advise him of the extreme hazards and necessary precautions in working with dangerous chemicals. In the *first recorded case of employers charged with murder for the work-related death of an employee,* each defendant was sentenced to twenty-five years in prison and the corporation was fined $25,000 (Frank, 1987). The verdicts were later overturned on technical grounds.

Crimes by Organizations (Corporations) Against Organizations

Criminal activity by organizations against other organizations (type 9 in Figure 10.1) may take many forms, including crimes by private corporations against the state (e.g., wartime trade violations, cheating on government contracts, or income tax violations) and crimes by corporations against corporations (e.g., industrial espionage and illegal competitive practices).

Wartime Trade Violations. Because of their international structure, multinational corporations can sometimes play both sides of the fence in wartime. In *Trading with the Enemy,* Higham (1982) raises eyebrows with the following accusations:

- While gasoline was being rationed in the United States, managers of Standard Oil of New Jersey were shipping fuel through Switzerland to the Nazis.
- Ford trucks were produced for German occupation troops in France with authorization from Ford executives in the United States.
- Chase Manhattan Bank did business with the Nazis during the war.

An early, classic study of "white collar crime" by Marshall Clinard (1969), originally published in 1952, was entitled *The Black Market.* Using records of federal regulatory agencies during World War II, Clinard examined wartime trade violations on the part of businesses. He found extensive violations of rationing, price-ceiling offenses, tie-in sales, and lack of quality control. In a study conducted about the same period, Hartung (1950) found many violations of wartime economic regulations in the Detroit wholesale meat industry.

While it is not uncommon for victors to demand that losing countries pay reparations or war debts for damages, it is surprising that the United States paid for damages to U.S. multinational plants that were ruined during Allied bombing of Nazi-occupied Europe.

Parenti (1980, p. 76) describes such postwar payments to General Motors (GM) and International Telephone and Telegraph (ITT). ITT had produced Nazi bombers and received $27 million in damages, while GM had produced Nazi trucks and obtained $33 million in compensation. Public furor arose after World War II when it was revealed that many oil companies had collaborated with the Nazis during the war. Although President Truman ordered that the Justice Department investigate and prosecute, the case was finally settled after fifteen years of litigation with a minor consent decree (Coleman, 1985, p. 178).

In the 1990s a renewed effort was undertaken internationally to recover the money of holocaust victims held in Swiss banks. In addition, survivors of the holocaust sued German and Japanese companies for damages for slave labor during World War II. Charges were also made that subsidiaries of U.S. auto manufacturers were key elements of Hitler's war machine. Chase National Bank is also being investigated, along with law firms, for collaboration (Hirsh, 1998).

Industrial Espionage. Until recently, **industrial espionage** has been a relatively neglected area of investigation by criminologists. Much of the work in this area has either appeared in trade magazines or has been done by journalists (see Barlay, 1973; Engberg, 1967; Hamilton, 1967). Such espionage (literally spying, or the acquiring of information through deceptive or illegal forms) is performed by three different groups: (1) intelligence agencies, (2) competing firms, and (3) disloyal employees. While espionage by intelligence agencies will be discussed later (under political crime, in Chapter 11), commercial espionage by foreign powers can be illustrated by the former Soviet KGB Directorate T, the scientific and technological bureau whose primary task was to steal information and commercial secrets. This section of the text will concentrate on commercial espionage by competing firms, although disloyal employees often steal ideas for sales to competing firms (Bottom, 1989).

Bergier's (1975, p. 51) highly readable *Secret Armies* tells the story of an industrial-espionage agent who traveled from office to office of a corporate headquarters with a pushcart telling everyone that he was doing a check on secret documents, which he then proceeded to wheel away. The documents and their collector were never seen again.

Industrial spying goes back at least as far as 3000 B.C., when industrial and commercial secrets relating to silkworms and porcelain were stolen from China. In the Middle Ages it was so widespread that it led to patent laws. Bergier (1975, p. 15) claims that piracy by industrialists and governments was a significant factor in the spreading of the Industrial Revolution. From 1875 to World War I, Japan had the best industrial spies, after which Nazi Germany and the U.S.S.R. dominated European spying. In the recent Hitachi case, a Japanese corporation attempted to steal state-of-the-art computer secrets from International Business Machines (IBM). Some examples provided by Bergier include:

- One large Detroit company found nine television transmitters hidden in the air vents of the main drafting room; these were probably transmitting the company's latest drawings to the competition.
- A telephone tap discovered in Manhattan covered 60,000 phone lines, presumably to pick up useful market tips, blackmail information, and the like.
- Several cases in England involved spies posing as typewriter repairmen and removing typewriters for "repair" in order to peruse used ribbons.
- Cars of important figures are stolen only to be quickly recovered—the aim is to bug them.

In free societies, about 95 percent of industrial information is available in the trade and popular publications. In fact a growing area of investigation is called "competitive intelligence," which involves the use of open sources (unclassified documents) to gather information on one's competition. Sources of information on U.S. industry range from legitimate to illegal, as described by the *Wade System of Sources of Information on American Industry* (Hamilton, 1967, pp. 222–23) (VANTAGE POINT 11.5). The first seven

VANTAGE POINT 11.5

The Wade System of Sources of Information on American Industry

1. Published material and public documents
2. Disclosures made by competitors' employees that are obtained without subterfuge
3. Market surveys and consultant reports
4. Financial reports and brokers' research surveys
5. Trade fairs, exhibits, and competitors' brochures
6. Analysis of competitors' products
7. Reports of salesmen and purchasing agents
8. Legitimate employment interviews with people who worked for a competitor
9. Camouflaged questioning and "drawing out" of competitor's employees
10. Direct observation under secret conditions
11. False job interviews with competitor's employee (i.e., when there is no real intent to hire)
12. False negotiations with competitor for license
13. Hiring a professional investigator to obtain a specific piece of information
14. Hiring an employee away from the competitor to get specific information
15. Trespassing on competitor's property
16. Bribing competitor's supplier or employee
17. "Planting" your agent on competitor's payroll
18. Eavesdropping on competitors (e.g., via wiretapping)
19. Theft of drawings, samples, documents, and similar property
20. Blackmail and extortion

Source: Peter Hamilton, 1967, *Espionage and Subversion in an Industrial Society,* London: Hutchinson, pp. 222–23.

InfoTrac College Edition Research
What are some recent developments in "business intelligence" and "corporate espionage."

sources are usually legal and ethical, while the remainder, as one descends the list, become less so, depending on the particular means employed.

There has been an unexpected wave of foreign espionage with the end of the Cold War. Some examples of such activity include:

- A South Korean rival plants a radio transmitter on the target company's fax machine.
- IBM claims to have lost $1 billion because of French and Japanese espionage.
- The French Intelligence Service, the Direction Generale de la Sécurité Exterieure (DGSE), has been most brazen, even bugging seats of businesspeople on flights and ransacking their hotel rooms for documents.
- Many companies are canceling plant tours. Americans used to be amused by the number of pictures Japanese business tourists would take when touring their plants. Many of these photographs proved very useful (Hamit, 1991).

In 2000 countries of the European Union alleged that U.S. Intelligence agencies (specifically, the Central Intelligence Agency and the National Security Agency) were using secret "Echelon," a worldwide electronic spy network to benefit U.S. companies in gaining a competitive edge. In effect the agency had redirected some of its Cold War assets towards economic intelligence. Despite denials, the information is believed to have helped Boeing sell 747s to Saudi Arabia, Raytheon sell a surveillance system to Brazil, and the Hughes Network in contracts for a telecommunications system in Indonesia (Windrem, 2000). The European parliament alleges that all e-mail and worldwide telephone and fax communications in Europe are intercepted. Whether this is true or not, the NSA appears to have that capability.

A National Institute of Justice survey of the American Society of Industrial Security's list of directors of security in major industries found that 48 percent had experienced the theft of trade secrets (proprietary information) within the past year, and over 90 percent had some theft within the past ten years (Mock and Rosenbaum, 1988, p. 18). The major targets were research and development data, new technology, customer lists, program plans, and financial data. Misuse of authority/position was the principal method employed, followed by physical theft, computer penetration, subversion of employees, and false documents/authorization (Mock and Rosenbaum, 1988, p. 22).

In 1998 textile manufacturer Milliken and Company was charged with hiring consultants to steal customer, supplier, and manufacturing information from nine competitors. They hired a private firm for $500,000 to conduct illegal spying operations (Peterson, 1998a). Figure 11.1 presents a brief account of the U.S. Economic Espionage Act (EEA) of 1996, which criminalizes the theft of trade secrets.

Two of the earliest cases prosecuted under the act were the Avery Dennison case and the PPG case. In the first example, the Avery Dennison Corporation near Cleveland, two Taiwanese citizens were charged with stealing millions of dollars worth of trade secrets by bribing an Avery Dennison employee. In the PPG case, they were informed by a competitor that they were approached with an offer to sell PPG trade secrets. The suspect (a former PPG employee) had carried secrets out of PPG headquarters in a gym bag. Cooperation of the competitor may have been gained by the fact that under the EEA they could have been prosecuted as a co-conspirator had they not (Nasheri, Hedieh, and O'Hearn, 1998).

While crimes by private organizations against other private organizations raise problematic areas in jurisprudence, what if the perpetrator is a country? In the 1990s China and countries in Asia tolerated widespread patent and trademark violations within which fake name-brand products were copied and sold at a fraction of their cost. While the United States and other countries continue to threaten trade sanctions over such violations, China seems to make only halfhearted attempts to comply.

Criminal Careers of Organizational Offenders

Corporate Environment and Crime. Corporate crime does not occur in a vacuum, but is affected by characteristics of an organization and its market structure. For instance, in an analysis of auto makers, Leonard and Weber (1970) found that price fixing requires two market forces: a few suppliers and inelastic demand (i.e., a steady need or demand for a product irrespective of a rise or fall in cost). Summarizing these forces, Conklin (1977, pp. 51–52) lists six environmental situations that are conducive to corporate crime:

1. *Seller concentration:* If a few producers hold a large share of the market, this leads to possible monopolization of markets or antitrust violations.
2. *Buyer concentration:* A small number of buyers or wealth concentrated in a few buyers may lead to bribes and kickbacks from sellers.
3. *Price elasticity of demand:* When price increases do not affect the demand for goods or services, price fixing is likely.
4. *False product differentiation:* When there are few differences in the product, false advertising may be used to create fraudulent distinctions.

FIGURE 11.1 The Economic Espionage Act of 1996 A Brief Guide

Territorial Limits

Outlaws economic espionage where:

1. The conduct occurs in the U.S., or
2. The conduct occurs outside the U.S. and either:
   a. *an Act in furtherance of the offense was committed in the U.S., or*
   b. *the offender is a U.S. person or organization.*

Guards Confidentiality

The court must issue orders necessary to protect the confidentiality of trade secrets consistent with Federal Rules of Procedure and the Constitution. Also, the prosecution is permitted to immediately appeal any order authorizing or directing disclosure of a trade secret.

Criminal Provisions

1. Imposes up to a 15 year prison term and/or a maximum $500,000.00 fine on any person and a $10 million fine on any organization who steals or destroys a trade secret of value with intent to benefit any foreign power.
   (Title 18 USC § 1831)
2. Imposes up to a 10 year prison term and/or a maximum $250,000.00 fine on any person and a $5 million fine on any organization who knowingly steals or destroys any trade secret with intent to:
   a. *Economically benefit anyone other than the owner; and*
   b. *Injure the owner of the trade secret*
   (Title 18 USC § 1832)

Forfeiture

Requires the forfeiture to the U.S. Government of proceeds or property derived from economic espionage and may require forfeiture of property used to commit economic espionage. The victim can apply to the U.S. for restitution.

Civil Relief

The Government can apply for injunctive relief to prevent trade secret crimes.

Owner Defined

The term 'owner,' with respect to a trade secret, means the person or entity in whom or in which rightful legal or equitable title to, or license in, the trade secret is reposed.

Trade Secret Defined

The term "Trade Secret" means all forms and types of financial, business, scientific, technical, engineering or economic information, including patterns, plans, compilations, program devices, prototypes, formulas, designs, procedures, methods, techniques, codes, processes, or programs, whether tangible or intangible and whether or how stored, compiled or memorialized physically, electronically, graphically, photographically, or in writing if:

(A) the owner thereof has taken reasonable measures to keep such information secret; and
(B) the information derives independent economic value, actual or potential, from not being generally known to, and not being readily ascertainable through proper means by, the public.

Company Responsibility

To take reasonable measures to keep trade secret information secret.

How to Contact the FBI

To report violations or to obtain additional information about the Economic Espionage Act or other national security matters, contact the local FBI Awareness of National Security Issues and Response (ANSIR) Coordinator. Telephone numbers for FBI field offices are listed in most telephone directories and on the FBI home page on the Internet:

http://www.fbi.gov

National Security Begins With You!

Source: Prepared by the Community Training Branch, National Counterintelligence Center.

5. *Entry barriers:* These may be created by discriminatory pricing or dumping in order to eliminate competitors.
6. *Slow growth rate of demand:* This may encourage deceptive advertising.

Corporate Concentration. The marketplace in postindustrial or advanced capitalistic societies has moved from competitive capitalism of companies to shared monopolies controlled by huge corporations and conglomerates. The growing concentration of markets can be demonstrated by the fact that, in 1960, 450 U.S. firms controlled about 50 percent of all manufacturing assets and made 59 percent of all profits. By 1979, 79 percent of the assets and 72 percent of the profits were controlled by these firms (Simon, 1996, p. 15).

Overpricing of products is more likely to occur when four or fewer companies control a market. As a result of such shared monopolies, the FTC estimates that prices are 25 percent higher than they should be and that such concentrated market firms enjoy profits that are 50 percent higher than those of less concentrated industries (Simon, 1996, p. 19). In size, complexity, assets, and power, these large corporations dwarf most states and most national governments. Their wealth and their power in elections, in private foreign policy, and in the international economy make public sector regulation increasingly difficult.

Rationalizations. Having little or no criminal self-concept, offenders view violations as part of their work. Among the rationalizations, or ways of explaining away responsibility, for white collar criminality are (Clinard and Yeager, 1980, pp. 69–72):

- Legal regulations of business are government interference with the free enterprise system.
- Such regulations are unnecessary and reduce profits.
- Such laws are too complex, create too much paperwork, and are incomprehensible.
- Regulatory laws are not needed and govern unnecessary matters.
- There is little deliberate criminal intent (mens rea) in corporate violations.
- "Everybody is doing it," and I have to keep up with competitors.
- The damage and loss are spread out among large numbers of consumers, thus little individual loss is suffered.
- If corporate profits do not increase as a result of the violation, there is no wrong.
- Violations are necessary in order to protect consumers.

Ethics and Subcultures. Beauchamp (1983) and Beauchamp and Bowie (1983) provide examples that show that while there are books on business ethics, this type of literature has obviously not been on the business best seller list. In a 1975 survey, Silk and Vogel (1976) found that the majority of the fifty-seven top corporate executives they interviewed felt that unethical conduct was prevalent throughout industry and an expected part of everyday business.

Societal Reaction

The UCR for the mid 1990s estimated that property crimes such as robbery, burglary, and larceny cost U.S. society nearly $16 billion. Federal investigators estimate that the federal government is being ripped off by at least $50 billion a year, primarily through fraud. In terms of threat and damage to property, health, theft, and corruption of law enforcement agencies, corporate crime, therefore, is the "big leagues." The cost of the savings and loan scandal of the 1980s was estimated at $500 billion, while the celebrated "Great Brinks Robbery" netted only $2 million. The latter is much better known and has received more publicity than the former, even though 250,000 Brinks robberies would be required to equal the cost of bailing out the S&Ls.

Despite growing public pressure for more severe treatment of higher occupational and corporate offenders, the likelihood of prosecution and conviction remains rare. When offenders are convicted, the penalties remain rather minuscule, considering particularly the economic loss to society. High recidivism rates among such criminals continue. Many are even "deadbeats" in paying assessed fines. The "big, dirty secret" remains true: judges and government agencies are "soft" on corporate crime.

Returning to the previous example of the "Great Savings and Loan Scandal," the costliest series of white collar crimes in American history, by 1994 the average sentence given for major thrift cases was 36 months compared to 38 months for car thieves and 56 months for burglars. It should be noted that most of the sentences were handed down before more strict federal sentencing guidelines were instituted in 1989 (Pontell, Calavita, and Tillman, 1994).

Why the Leniency in Punishment?

If white collar crimes are economically the most costly crimes to society, why are such acts seldom punished? A number of reasons have been suggested:

- Many acts were not made illegal until recently. For example, many environmental and occupational health and safety regulations are of post-World War II vintage, and not until the twentieth century were false advertising, fraud, misuse of trademarks and patents, and restraint of trade considered criminal matters.

- American business philosophy has been dominated by beliefs in laissez-faire economics (government noninterference in business) as well as by caveat emptor ("let the buyer beware").
- Public concern with corporate crime is of recent vintage. Once this resentment becomes organized, public pressure against white collar crime and pressure for legislation and enforcement can be expected. A recent national survey suggests the general public regards white collar crimes as even more serious than conventional crimes such as burglary, robbery, and the like (Wolfgang, 1980a, p. E.21). Thus, lenient treatment of elite offenders is not supported by the public.
- In the past, white collar crimes were given less publicity; sometimes the media were owned by businesses that themselves were violators (Snider, 1978). Fear of loss of major advertising revenue may also have an impact.
- White collar criminals and those who make and enforce the laws share the same socioeconomic class and values. They fail to match the public stereotype of the criminal. Vilhelm (1968) also suggests that citizens don't oppose such crime because they themselves often violate many of these same laws on a modest scale.
- Political pressure groups often block effective regulation or enforcement. Some of the biggest campaign contributors are also the biggest violators. Funding for such groups may come from previous tax avoidance, laundering, and other shady practices. Since such criminals are seldom prosecuted, many are first offenders and thus are treated with leniency.
- It is easier for politicians and public officials to concentrate on the crimes of the young and lower class, groups that lack political clout.
- The long-term nature of corporate violations and court delays make sanctions difficult.

We have indicated that asbestos manufacturers had full knowledge that they were killing their workers, as Johns-Manville did, for instance, when they estimated dust control equipment installation and operation at $17 million and only $1 million for workers compensation payments, and judged that it was cheaper to infect workers (Brodeur, 1974, p. 128). But those responsible are hard to punish. Ermann and Lundman (1982, pp. 71–72) point out an often overlooked problem:

> The reason why executives are not sanctioned is quite straightforward. As was true of asbestos decisions, there frequently is such a gap between decision and consequence that corporations find it difficult, if not impossible, to sanction executives responsible for long-term blunders. Executives who make these decisions are promoted, retired, or dead which makes them invulnerable to corporate penalties. Others, therefore, pick up the pieces left in the wake of serious mistakes.

In analyzing public reactions Cullen et al. (1982a, pp. 19–20) concluded:

- While traditional crimes resulted in longer sentences, respondents also were quite punitive toward violent white collar crime and embezzlement.
- There was a call for harsher penalties against violent white collar crime and violations of financial trust and more leniency expressed for property crimes by or against corporations.
- There was little support for coddling "respectable" offenders. The sample favored prison sentences in the majority of white collar crimes.

This pattern has been further documented in studies by Schrager and Short (1980) as well as by Cullen et al. (1982b), Sinden (1980), Braithwaite (1981), and Rossi et al. (1974).

A 1999 National Public Survey of White Collar Crime conducted by the National White Collar Crime Center (Rebovich and Layne, 1999) revealed that the public regarded many types of white collar crime as serious or more serious than traditional street crime. For instance, in answering which was more serious:

- Someone steals $100 on the street or a contractor cheats someone out of $100: Robbery, 41 percent; Fraud, 40 percent; Equal, 20 percent.
- Someone steals $100 on the street or a bank teller embezzles $100 from his employer: Robbery, 27 percent; Embezzlement, 54 percent; Equal, 18 percent.
- Person robs someone at gunpoint or auto maker fails to recall a vehicle with a known defective part: Armed Robbery, 46 percent; Defective Product, 40 percent; Equal, 14 percent.
- Person robs someone at gunpoint or a store owner sells a shipment of meat he knows is bad: Armed Robbery, 39 percent; Tainted Product, 42 percent; Equal, 19 percent.

Sentencing

In white collar offenses, the low risk of apprehension and negligible penalties appear to negate the deterrence model (Orland, 1980, McCormick, 1977; Hagan and Palloni, 1986; Cullen, Makestaad, and Cavender, 1987). Simpson and Koper (1991) found some evidence that past guilty verdicts combined with labeling previous misdemeanors as felonies may inhibit recidivism. The label of criminal and harsh penalties may have impact. Lofquist (1992) suggests that heavier use of organizational probation may serve as a stronger deterrent than fines alone, in that it would give regulatory agencies more oversight.

Research continues to document relative laxity and leniency in corporate and higher level occupational crime enforcement (Benekos, 1983; Clinard et al., 1979; Hagan et al., 1980; Snider, 1982). Hagan et al. (1980, p. 818) point out the overlooked fact that much white collar prosecution requires defendant cooperation, which is likely to lead to more lenient sentences. Pleas of nolo contendere, consent decrees, warnings, and cease-and-desist orders continue to remind us of the separate status accorded such offenders.

These crimes tend also to be more complex and long-term; malicious intent is often easy to cover up; and pursuing criminal prosecutions may be economically unfeasible. Perhaps this last point was missed in the Yale White Collar Crime studies of sentencing in federal district courts. Stanton Wheeler and associates (Weisburd et al., 1990, 1991) found, using 1,090 presentence investigations prepared by federal probation officers, that those of higher status were more likely to be imprisoned and, when sentenced to prison, received longer sentences than comparable offenders. Since most cases of serious white collar crime are not prosecuted criminally, such a conclusion seems unwarranted.

The major reason for the use of consent decrees (in which the corporation promises not to violate the same regulation again) is the simple fact that understaffed and underfinanced legal staffs of the regulatory agencies cannot litigate most cases (Clinard and Yeager, 1980, p. 97). Deregulation and cuts in staffing of regulatory agencies during the Reagan era led to things such as higher injury rates in mining (Curran, 1991). The antitrust division of the Department of Justice has filed relatively few criminal cases; and, even when convictions are won, they typically result in weak penalties that lack deterrent effect. Since December 1974, increased authorized penalties in the law and upgrading of violations to felony stature opened the door for more strict reactions (Clinard and Yeager, 1980, pp. 144, 150).

McCormick's (1977) study of sentencing and convictions in antitrust cases by the Department of Justice from 1890 to 1969 shows that the 2 percent of corporate violators who served prison sentences did so for labor violations.

In November 1991 new federal guidelines for corporate criminal sentences were introduced, which would require that much higher minimum fines—based on a variety of factors—be assessed by federal judges. A particularly controversial and powerful law against organizational crime is the RICO feature of the 1970 Organized Crime Control Act. The Racketeer-Influence and Corrupt Organizations (RICO) title of this act permits the Justice Department to criminally prosecute as racketeers or civilly sue companies that have committed two or more crimes within a ten-year period. Drexel Burnham Lambert settled out of court for $650 million in 1989 and pleaded guilty to fraud rather than risk an indictment that would have labeled them racketeers and possibly destroyed the entire firm. (RICO is discussed in greater detail in Chapter 13.) Corporate and white collar offenders cry foul when it appears that they might be treated as just another group of criminals. Braithwaite (1989a) proposes that "shaming" corporate offenders might serve as a deterrent.

White Collar Criminal "Deadbeats"

The "higher immorality" of criminaloid corporations and "upperworld crime" create greater inequalities and an underclass in society, and they indirectly foster "crime in the streets." Indifference to prosecution of society's most expensive forms of criminal activity supports the "dual system of justice" in the conflict model of criminal law, which argues that there are two systems of justice—one for the wealthy and one for the poor. This is a serious indictment of the fundamental equity of law on which our system of criminal justice is morally and philosophically based. Any attempt at law and order that leaves untouched the pervasive criminality of respectable society is a travesty of justice.

Finally, in reading the remaining chapters of this text, keep in mind that if we ended our discussion of crime with this chapter we would have covered the largest, most costly category of crime. All the other forms of criminal behavior together do not equal the costs of occupational and organizational (corporate) crime.

Summary

Reasons for the dearth of studies of corporate crime were detailed. In the United States the legal governance of business organizations began in the nineteenth century, particularly with the Sherman Antitrust Act (1890). Much regulation of corporate activity takes place through federal regulatory agencies such as the FCC, ICC, and SEC. These agencies can utilize civil and criminal as well as administrative means of assuring compliance, but they seldom do. Most agencies are "outgunned" by the industries they are supposed to control, and, in fact, they are sometimes controlled by these industries. Gross characterizes this nonenforcement and kid-glove treatment of elite criminals as "the big dirty secret."

Studies by Clinard and Yeager and associates signaled a new renaissance in studies of corporate criminality—the first large-scale, comprehensive study of corporate crime. In an examination of *crimes by organizations against individuals/the public,* detailed examples were provided, such as multinational bribery, and case examples such as the Equity Funding Scandal, the Great Electrical Industry Conspiracy, and the Great Oil Scam. Other important illustrations presented included the Ford Pinto case, toxic criminals, environmental violations, and corporate dumping of unsafe products.

Crimes by organizations against employees primarily relate to threats to the health and safety of workers, as dramatically illustrated by the tragic Karen Silkwood case. *Crimes by organizations against organizations* were illustrated by examples of wartime trade violations, industrial espionage (such as the Hitachi Case), and corporate fraud against government, particularly on the part of defense contractors.

Characteristics of the corporate environment, such as supply and demand, and corporate concentration, such as the number of producers of a product, are predisposing factors in corporate criminality. *Societal reaction* to higher-level occupational and corporate crime has in the past been characterized by leniency. A number of reasons were provided for such indulgence, including policies of laissez-faire economics and a caveat emptor philosophy prevalent in the past. Recently, public reaction to such crimes has hardened and now rivals or exceeds that for traditional crimes. Recent research suggests some improvement in punishing elite offenders but still not in concomitance with the quantity, prevalence, and cost of such activities. Some retrenchment in regulatory activities may be occurring in response to a more conservative, pro-business political climate. The *toleration of white collar criminals and deadbeats* raises a major challenge to claims of equitable standards of justice and indirectly fosters crime in the streets through the perpetration of inequality.

KEY CONCEPTS

Big Dirty Secret
Corporate Dumping
Corporate Environment and Crime
"Daisy Chain" Scam
Equity Funding Scandal
Ford Pinto Case
Great Oil Scam
Industrial Espionage
Karen Silkwood Case
Nolo Contendere
Reasons for Lack of Corporate Crime Research
Reasons for Leniency with White Collar Offenders
Revolving Door
The Power Elite
Whistleblowers
White Collar "Deadbeats"

REVIEW QUESTIONS

1. Why, despite its cost, has there been so little research on corporate crime?
2. Who polices corporate crime? Name some of these agencies and their jurisdictions.
3. What have been some criticisms of federal regulatory agencies? Do you see any improvements in these activities?
4. How serious are anti-trust violations in the United States? Give some examples.
5. Discuss the "Great Savings and Loan Scandal." How was it possible for what has been described as the "greatest series of white collar crimes in American history" to take place, and why was the American public unaware of this?
6. Do you see any parallels between the Ford Pinto case and the Ford Explorer/Firestone case?
7. Discuss some examples of crimes by organizations against their employees. What recourse do employees have in such circumstances?
8. Give some examples of whistleblowing. What are some hazards as well as benefits of such activity?
9. Discuss the problem of industrial espionage, and give some examples. What are some measures that you think could be taken to protect company secrets?
10. Why is there continuing leniency in the punishment of corporate offenders?

INFOTRAC COLLEGE EDITION RESEARCH

Vantage Point 11.1 InfoTrac College Edition Research
Search the "Savings and Loan Associations Bailout Crisis." Read the article by Calavita, Tillman, and Pontell. Which terms from our discussion of "S and L ese" were used?

Vantage Point 11.2 InfoTrac College Edition Research
Locate the article "Will Charlie Keating Ride Again? By L.J. Davis. What fears does Davis express?

Vantage Point 11.3 InfoTrac College Edition Research
Read "A Darkness in Donora" by Edwin Keister Jr. Does the article shed any further light on the Donora disaster?

Vantage Point 11.4 InfoTrac College Edition Research
Read Coro Strandberg's "Corporations as Good Citizens." Could social audits reduce practices such as corporate dumping?

Vantage Point 11.5 InfoTrac College Edition Research
What are some recent developments in "business intelligence" and "corporate espionage."

In the News 11.1 InfoTrac College Edition Research
Using both the Internet and InfoTrak, locate some other examples of bank fraud. How are these "financiopaths" able to get away with such illegal activities involving such large amounts of money?

SELECTED READINGS

Jay Albanese. 1995. *White Collar Crime in America.* New York: Prentice Hall.
A very readable presentation on the issue of organizational offenders by one of America's leading authorities on the subject.

Marshall B. Clinard and Peter Yeager. 1980. *Corporate Crime.* New York: Macmillan.
This is the largest study of corporate crime ever conducted and an excellent update of Sutherland's original investigation.

James Coleman. 1994. *The Criminal Elite.* 3rd edition. New York: St. Martin's Press.
Coleman has carried the torch for studies of white collar crime since the 1980s by producing a very lucid text that updates and formulates the literature in the field.

Daniel O. Friedrichs. 1995. *Trusted Criminals: White Collar Crime in Contemporary Society.* Belmont, California: Wadsworth.
Friedrich's text might very well be the most scholarly and thorough contemporary account of white collar crime. It weaves together a mass of literature and is a must-read for anyone who claims to be informed on this subject.

Gilbert Geis and Robert Meier, editors. 1977. *White Collar Crime: Offenses in Business, Politics and the Professions.* Revised edition. New York: The Free Press.
This collection contains many of the classic studies in the field. The lead author is one of the most respected writers in the field and president of the Association of Certified Fraud Examiners.

Michael Levi. 1987. *Regulating Fraud: White-Collar Crime and the Criminal Process.* London: Routledge.
There is an entire tradition of practitioners and academics who investigate fraud, not white collar crime. British scholar Levi portrays that tradition.

Stephen Pizzo, Mary Fricker, and Paul Muolo. 1989. *Inside Job: The Looting of America's Savings and Loans.* New York: McGraw-Hill.
This book by three California journalists was the first to call attention to the biggest series of white collar crimes in American history. The appendix, which reflects secret notes taken by regulators of their meeting with "the Keating Five," is particularly interesting.

Neal Shover and John Paul Wright, editors. 2001. *Crimes of Privilege: Readings in White Collar Crime.* New York: Oxford University Press.
The authors supply an excellent selection of 31 articles on the issue of white collar crime. These include classic as well as very contemporary selections.

David R. Simon and Frank E. Hagan. 1999. *White Collar Deviance.* Boston: Allyn and Bacon.
David Simon and the author combine the traditions of elite deviance and white collar crime and explore new hybrids of white collar deviance, such as political white collar deviance, professional white collar deviance, and organized white collar deviance.

Edwin H. Sutherland. 1949. *White Collar Crime.* New York: Holt, Rinehart and Winston.
Sutherland's classic text is the beginning point for any discussion or analysis of white collar crime.

Political Crime

12

Vantage Points

In the News

King, there is only one thing left for you to do. You know what it is. You have just 34 days in which to do it. (This exact number has been selected for a specific reason.) It has definite practical significance. You are done. There is but one way out for you.

—Note sent to Dr. Martin Luther King, Jr., by the FBI 34 days before he was to receive the Nobel Peace Prize. The note allegedly suggested that he should commit suicide. (Nelson Blackstock, *Cointelpro: The FBI's Secret War on Political Freedom, 1976*)

The tree of liberty must be refreshed from time to time with the blood of patriots and tyrants.

—Thomas Jefferson, "Letter to William Stevens Smith," 1787, in *The Shorter Bartlett's Familiar Quotations*

Ideology

An **ideology** is a distinctive belief system, idea, or abstract ideal. Communism, capitalism, fascism, Islam, Judaism, Christianity, fundamentalism, and the like can serve as ideologies, or can combine to supply their adherents with a guide to societal and individual behavior. "True believers," extremists, or ideologues often are zealots and are absolutely certain of the righteousness of their cause—so much so that they feel justified in forcing their beliefs on others.

Schafer (1971, 1974) uses the term *convictional criminals* when referring to politically motivated criminals. Such a criminal is "convinced of the truth and justification of his own beliefs" (Schafer, 1976, p. 138). The actual crimes committed by political criminals may be traditional crimes, such as kidnapping, assassination, blackmail, robbery and the like. It is not the crimes themselves that distinguish political criminals, but their motivations, their views of crime as a necessary means to a higher ideological goal. Some political criminals, particularly human rights advocates, have committed no crime, but have expressed their political views in authoritarian or totalitarian societies that forbid individual expression or criticism of the states, or in free societies where civil disobedience may be viewed with suspicion and considered criminal.

Political Crime: A Definition

Political crime refers to criminal acts committed for ideological purposes. Rather than being motivated by private greed or benefit, these offenders sincerely believe they are following a higher morality that supersedes present society and its laws. Such political criminals may act for social-political reasons (Robin Hood), out of moral-ethical motivations (antiabortion activists), to advance religious causes (Martin Luther), to disseminate scientific beliefs (Copernicus, Galileo), or to publicize political concerns (Nathan Hale, Benedict Arnold) (Schafer, 1976). *Such crime may take one of two forms: crime by government or crime against government.*

Crimes by government include violations of human rights, civil liberties, and constitutional privileges, as well as illegal behavior that occurs in the process of enforcing the law or maintaining the status quo. Secret police violations, human rights abuses, genocide, and crimes by police, as well as illegal surveillance, disruption, and experiments are just some of the examples of governmental crime to be discussed in this chapter.

Crimes against the government may range from protests, illegal demonstrations, and strikes to espionage, political whistleblowing, assassination, and terrorism. "One person's terrorist is another's patriot" is a common expression that suggests the relative nature of such political crime. In revolutions, the victors' beliefs become the status quo, and the victors inherit the power and privilege by which to brand the acts of their enemies as criminal.

There is a surprising paucity of literature on political crime in criminology (Hagan, 1986; Martin, Haran, and Romano, 1988). Fewer than ten works in the field have specifically addressed this issue (see Ingraham, 1979; Kelman and Hamilton, 1988; Kittrie and Wedlock, 1986; Proal, 1973; Roebuck and Weeber, 1978; Schafer, 1974; Schur, 1980; Turk, 1982). In his classic *Political Crime,* which was originally published in 1898, Louis Proal (1973, p. 28) indicates:

> Political passions have bathed the earth in blood; kings, emperors, aristocracies, democracies, republics, all governments have resorted to murder out of political considerations, these from love of power, those from hatred of royalty and aristocracy, in one case from fear, in another from fanaticism.

While political crimes may be committed by or against the government, seldom do governments or government officials choose to acknowledge their own lawlessness. Sagarin (1973, p. xiv) very aptly points out that political crime includes the tyrant as well as the assassin.

Legal Aspects

In the United States, various laws are, or have been, intended to protect the government from the clear and present or probable danger of disruption or overthrow. Laws such as the Alien and Sedition Act, Espionage Act, Voorhis Act, Smith Act, Internal Security Act, and McCarran-Walter Act are examples. The 1940 Voorhis Act requires registration of agents of foreign powers while the Smith Act (1940), which was later struck down by the Supreme Court, outlaws advocating the overthrow of the government. The Internal Security Act (McCarran Act) calls for registration of Communists and Communist-front organizations, while the McCarran-Walter Act (1952) provides for deportation of aliens who espouse or have associates who espouse disloyal beliefs (Clinard and Quinney, 1973, p. 155).

Cuba and other authoritarian countries enact criminal laws forbidding propaganda against the state, complaining about social conditions to foreigners, and attempting to publish works not authorized by the state. Many of these laws and their enforcement bear an uncanny resemblance to those in George Orwell's *1984* and to his descriptions of the Minitrue (Ministry of Truth) in which thought criminals become political criminals or enemies of the state.

Under Anglo-American legal traditions, political crime and political criminals are not recognized as such, and these types of offenders are dealt with under traditional or nonpolitical laws. Anglo-American criminal law considers intent, but not motive. The motive, whether good or bad, has no bearing on guilt. Sagarin (1973, p. ix) points out: "At one time it was against the law in some parts of this country to preach freedom and abolition of slavery to slaves, or even to free men; it was often against the law to organize into trade unions; at various times political parties have been driven underground and their leaders jailed."

Kittrie and Wedlock in *The Tree of Liberty* (1986) provide historical documents related to elements of political criminality either by the state or by persons accused of such offenses:

- The important Peter Zenger trial of 1735 for false, scandalous, and seditious libel, which established the "freedom of the press" doctrine
- The "crime of being black or Indian," which led to the "Trail of Tears" of the Cherokee Nation and to the outlawing of Abolitionism, the underground railroad, and harboring fugitive slaves

- Subjugation of blacks through private conspiracies and terrorism
- Genocide against Indians
- Voter registration drives and Freedom Rides during the Civil Rights struggle
- Imprisonment of Japanese-Americans in internment camps during World War II
- Antiwar protest, burning draft cards and records
- Arson, bombing, and other violations against abortion clinics
- "Sanctuary activists" hiding Central Americans, whom they consider to be political refugees

The Nuremberg Principle

After World War II, the victorious Allies held a tribunal and convicted Nazi war criminals. The Nuremberg trials were the first occasion on which defeated war leaders were held responsible in an international legal area for activities that were legal, even encouraged, by their governments at the time they were committed. Defenses such as "I was just following orders" were rejected and held to be unjustifiable explanations for Nazi atrocities. Kelman and Hamilton (1988) refer to this as an example of a "crime of obedience." Offenses defined by the international tribunal included war crimes and crimes against humanity (Smith, 1977; Maser, 1979; "Nuremberg Principle," 1970, p. 78).

War Crimes. Violations of law or customs of war include, but are not limited to, murder, ill treatment, or deportation for slave labor—or for any other purpose—of civilian population of or in occupied territory; murder or ill treatment of prisoners of war or persons on the high seas; killings of hostages, plunder of public or private property, wanton destruction of villages, towns, or cities, or devastation not justified by military necessity.

Crimes Against Humanity. These include murder, extermination, enslavement, deportation, and other inhumane acts committed against any civilian population, before or during the war, or persecutions on political, racial, or religious grounds, whether or not in violation of the domestic law of the country where perpetrated.

The Universal Declaration of Human Rights

The concept of human rights is an outgrowth of the period of Enlightenment in Western society and is expressed in such documents as the Magna Carta, the English Bill of Rights, the American Declaration of Independence, the French Declaration of the Rights of Man and of the Citizen, and the United Nations **Universal Declaration of Human Rights.** All of these documents support the notion of *inalienable rights and freedoms that supersede those of government* (VANTAGE POINT 12.1).

International Law

Since much political criminality is international in scope, it theoretically falls under the jurisdiction of international law, the power of which is limited. This covers fairly nonproblematic diplomatic and commercial customs between nations; agreements such as treaties that are drafted in international conventions; as well as international courts such as the International Court of Justice, sponsored by the United Nations. Using precedents (past decisions), customs, and general principles of law, international law is theoretically binding on any signatories to international treaties, although it may also through custom be held to be binding on those who have not ratified the treaties. Stipulations of the Geneva Convention of 1929 regulating wartime conduct serve as an example.

VANTAGE POINT 12.1

The Universal Declaration of Human Rights

The Universal Declaration of Human Rights, which was adopted unanimously by the UN General Assembly on December 10, 1948, is a proclamation, but not a treaty or an international agreement. The basic elements of these human rights, which were the cornerstone of the Carter administration's foreign policy, *consist of three principles: integrity of persons, basic human needs, and civil and political liberties. Integrity of persons* is addressed in the following articles of the Universal Declaration (1948):

Article 3: Everyone has the right to life, liberty, and security of persons.

Article 5: No one shall be subjected to torture or to cruel, inhuman, or degrading treatment or punishment.

Article 9: No one shall be subjected to arbitrary arrest, detection, or exile.

Article 10: Everyone is entitled in full equality to a fair and public hearing by an independent and impartial tribunal, in the determination of his rights and obligations and of any criminal charges against him.

Basic human needs are addressed specifically in the following articles:

Article 25: (1) Everyone has the right to a standard of living adequate for the health and well-being of himself and of his family, including food, clothing, housing, and medical care and necessary social services, and the right to security in the event of unemployment, sickness, disability, widowhood, old age, or other lack of livelihood in circumstances beyond his control.
(2) Motherhood and childhood are entitled to special care and assistance. All children, whether born in or out of wedlock, shall enjoy the same social protection.

Article 26: Everyone has the right to education. Education shall be free, at least in the elementary and fundamental stages. Elementary education shall be compulsory. Technical and professional education shall be made generally available and higher education shall be equally accessible to all on the basis of merit.

Some articles of the Universal Declaration dealing with *civil and political liberties* include:

Article 13: (1) Everyone has the right to freedom of movement and residence within the borders of each state. (2) Everyone has the right to leave any country, including his own, and to return to his country.

Article 19: Everyone has the right to freedom of opinion and expression; this right includes freedom to hold opinions without interference and to seek, receive, and impart information and ideas through any media and regardless of frontiers.

Article 20: (1) Everyone has the right to freedom of peaceful assembly and association. (2) No one may be compelled to belong to an association.

Article 21: (1) Everyone has the right to take part in the government of his country, directly through freely chosen representatives. (2) Everyone has the right of equal access to public service in his country. (3) The will of the people shall be the basis of the authority of government; this will be expressed in periodic and genuine elections which shall be by universal and equal suffrage and shall be held by secret vote or by equivalent free voting procedures.

Source: Congressional Research Service, 1978, *Human Rights Conditions in Selected Countries and the U.S. Response.* Report prepared for the House Committee on International Relations, 95th Congress, 2nd Session, Washington, D.C.: Government Printing Office, July 25, pp. 10–14.

InfoTrac College Edition Research
Search the issue of "human rights." What are some recent human rights issues throughout the world?

While international bodies past or present, such as the World Court, the League of Nations, and the United Nations, have the facade of law, they lack the crucial power to enforce their decisions, ultimately through force if necessary (Kidder, 1983, p. 34). The closest entities to international police organizations are specially created UN police units, which are intended to temporarily block hostile armies, or Interpol, which is a criminal intelligence-sharing organization with membership primarily made up of the Western democracies and former British Commonwealth nations.

Essentially, international law lacks teeth—the authority and power to assure compliance. The end of the Cold War has considerably improved the prospect for international cooperation in enforcing international law and sanctions. UN actions in forcing Iraq to withdraw from Kuwait in 1991 are one such example.

Crimes by Government

The first major category of political crime to be discussed is crimes by government. These are crimes or violations of human rights committed for ideological reasons by government officials or their agents. The government political criminal is motivated not by self-interest so much as by a commitment to a particular belief system, a conviction that he or she is defending the status quo or preserving the existing system. Since many such violations are not formally recognized or enforced by the criminal law in most states, the concept of political crime by government is more *a sociological than a political entity.* Friedrichs (1992, pp. 26–27) prefers the term "governmental crime," which he defines as:

> the broad, all-encompassing term for a range of illegal and demonstrably harmful activities carried out from within or in association with, governmental status . . . . They [governmental crimes] are committed within a governmental context, and facilitated by governmental power.

Secret Police

All countries require some type of **secret police** for *clandestine intelligence gathering and internal security.* Plate and Darvi (1981, p. 8) define secret police as

> official or semi-official organs of government. They are units of the internal security police of the state, with the mandate to suppress all serious, threatening political opposition to the government in power and with the mission to control all political activity within (and sometimes even beyond) the borders of the nation-state.

Secret police are often involved in extraordinary illegal surveillance, searches, detention, and arrest; as a matter of practice, they may violate or border on violating human rights.

In totalitarian societies the effectiveness of secret police in deterring illegitimate violence (crime in the streets) occurs through legitimate violence (crime by the state). The specter and practices of such infamous secret police as Hitler's Gestapo, Stalin's OGPU (later KGB), and Haiti's Tonton Macoutes—midnight raids, tortures, and disappearances—are frightening indeed.

Austin Turk (1981) prefers the term *political policing* to refer to secret police operations. In "Organizational Deviance and Political Policing," Turk (1981, pp. 238–39) provides a number of illustrations:

- Assassination or maiming of political figures
- "Geneva Offenses" such as germ warfare, letter bombs, or use of cattle prods to torture political prisoners. The Geneva Convention originally forbade the mistreatment of sick or wounded soldiers.
- The torture of political detainees, such as those listed by Amnesty International
- Character assassination
- Intervention in conventional politics, such as the FBI campaign against Martin Luther King, Jr.
- Violations of civil or human rights, for example, from illegal surveillance to mental institutionalization of political dissidents in the former USSR

- Economic or political harassment of dissident groups
- Use of "agents provocateurs," informants, and spies in order to manipulate public institutions
- Subversion of economic or other institutions, e.g., the overthrow of the Chilean government of Salvador Allende by the Central Intelligence Agency

If state agents of social control wish to suppress a social movement, the agents have an entire repertoire of actions to choose from (Baylor, 1990). Marx (1979, cited in Baylor, 1990, p. 2) identifies a number of tactics including:

- Litigation against the movement or leaders
- Administrative harassment
- Disinformation campaigns
- Wiretaps and other electronic surveillance methods
- The use of informants and agents provocateurs
- Support of counter or alternative groups
- Bad jacketing or snitch jacketing
- Police response, including force

In many of these the state officially encourages its agents to commit crime (Marx, 1990). The criminological study of such crimes by government has been far less a topic of research than similar crimes against the government because of a lack of funding for the former (Longmire, 1988). Chambliss (1988b) calls many of these activities, such as state-sponsored piracy, smuggling, assassinations, murder, and experiments, examples of "state-organized crime," while Barak (1991) simply calls it "state crime."

In 1999 President Clinton issued an apology to the people of Guatemala on behalf of the United States for helping support major atrocities in that country in the past. An independent truth commission had issued a 3,500 page report accounting the Guatemalan government's campaign of terror against its own people during its 36-year civil war (McGrory, 1999). Over 200,000 mainly Mayan Indians were massacred, executed, tortured, or disappeared due to U.S. support for security forces. These poor, uneducated, and voiceless majority native peoples were the hardest hit. Cold war fear of communism had been the motivation.

Human Rights Violations

Perhaps the most dramatic illustration of crimes by government is the pervasive international violation of **human rights.** Thousands of "political prisoners"—individuals who have committed no crimes other than their espousal of political ideas—are tortured, murdered, or abandoned throughout the world. It is difficult, because of governmental secrecy, to gain an accurate count of such prisoners, although human rights organizations such as Amnesty International provide rough figures. Authoritarian and totalitarian regimes of the left and right are the least tolerant of dissent and are thus the biggest violators. These countries most resemble what George Orwell described in *1984,* in which the state is preeminent. VANTAGE POINT 12.2 presents elements of the annual State Department Report on Human Rights.

While Savak (the Iranian secret police) under the shah was recognized as a brutal force, in the subsequent theocracy created by Khomeini in Iran, as many as 60,000 political prisoners have been held and over 25,000 executed as of 1984. In 1990 members of the People's Mojahedin claimed that over 90,000 had been executed and 150,000 tortured (Anderson and Van Atta, 1990). According to a report by Amnesty International (Lippman, 1987), torture is routinely practiced on detainees in order to extract confessions. Beatings, floggings, suspension by limbs, and mock executions are common. Thefts are punished by

VANTAGE POINT 12.2

The State Department's Human Rights Report, 1999

A. Developments in Human Rights

1. The Right to Democratic Dissent.

Article One of the United Nations Declaration on Human Rights Defenders states that "everyone has the right to promote and to strive for the protection and realization of human rights and fundamental freedoms." All too often, we take this principle for granted. Yet each year, dedicated human rights activists and democratic dissidents around the world lose their lives defending this remarkable, transforming idea. In a large number of the countries covered in this report, human rights defenders and democratic dissidents face harassment, imprisonment, disappearances, or torture; in some cases, the risk comes from government sources. In many others, however, the risk is from nongovernmental insurgent, terrorist, or criminal elements.

Certain countries seem to take particular pleasure in restricting the right to democratic dissent. Take Serbia, where the government of Federal Republic of Yugoslavia President Slobodan Milosevic initiated a brutal and indiscriminate police and military crackdown against ethnic Albanian opponents in Kosovo and sought to limit and suppress dissent closer to home. The Kosovo campaign ended only after the international community intervened militarily. Before and during the conflict, Kosovar Albanians known to oppose the regime were murdered, raped, expelled, or detained in Serbian prisons.

Similarly in Cuba, the regime of Fidel Castro continued to suppress opposition and criticism. Cuban authorities routinely harass, threaten, arbitrarily arrest, detain, imprison, and defame human rights advocates and members of independent professional associations, including journalists, economists, doctors, and lawyers—often with the goal of coercing them into leaving the country.

In Asia, dissidents and defenders face a range of challenges. In China authorities broadened and intensified their efforts to suppress those perceived to threaten government power or national stability. Citizens who sought to express openly dissenting political and religious views faced widespread repression.

In North Korea, government repression is so severe that no organized opposition to the regime is known to exist. The Government regards almost any independent activity—including listening to foreign broadcasts, writing letters, and possessing "reactionary" printed matter—crimes against the state.

In the Middle East, dissidents and defenders had to contend with similar difficulties. In Iraq the regime of Saddam Hussein continued to commit widespread, serious, and systematic human rights abuses, summarily executing actual and perceived political opponents. In Syria the government uses its vast powers to quash all organized political opposition.

Defenders and dissidents in Africa also faced severe challenges. In Sudan, despite the adoption of a new Constitution through a referendum in June 1998, the government continues to restrict most civil liberties, including freedom of assembly, association, religion, and movement.

A growing trend around the world is the threat posed to democratic dissent by nongovernmental insurgent, terrorist, or criminal forces. In Colombia, for example, paramilitary forces, some with links to the armed forces, were responsible for the murder of numerous human rights activists, as well as threats against many others. Guerrillas of the Revolutionary Armed Forces of Colombia (FARC) murdered three American indigenous rights activists who had traveled to that country to work with local indigenous leaders. In Sri Lanka human rights defender and Tamil parliamentarian Neelan Tiruchelvam was killed by a suicide bomber believed to be linked with the separatist Liberation Tigers of Tamil Eelam (LTTE).

2. Human Rights in Countries in Conflict.

Civilians continue to endure human rights abuses, war crimes, and violations of humanitarian law in those countries facing internal insurgencies or civil war. Throughout the world, insurgents, paramilitary forces, government security, military, and police forces used murder, rape, and inhumane tactics to assert control over territory to secure the cooperation of civilians and to silence opposition voices.

Africa continues to be the locus of many of the world's worst conflicts. In Sierra Leone rebel forces committed numerous egregious abuses, including murder, abduction, deliberate mutilations, and rape. Progovernment militias also committed abuses, albeit on a lesser scale. The rebels continued their particularly vicious practice of cutting off the ears, noses, hands, arms, and legs of noncombatants—including small children and elderly women. Rebel forces abducted missionaries, aid workers, UN personnel, and journalists; ambushed humanitarian relief convoys; raided refugee sites; and extorted and stole food. They abducted children to use as

VANTAGE POINT 12.2—*Continued*

soldiers and other civilians to serve as forced laborers, sex slaves, and human shields. After the May cease-fire, insurgents continued to commit abuses, although significantly fewer were reported.

Other parts of the world were not immune to conflict. In Serbia, government military and security forces forcibly expelled over 850,000 Kosovar Albanians from their homes. Many women were raped in the process.

As this report was going to press, there were credible reports that Russian forces were rounding up Chechen men of military age and sending them to "filtration" camps, where they allegedly were tortured.

Afghanistan suffered its 20th consecutive year of civil war and political instability. Both the ultraconservative movement known as the Taliban (which controls roughly 90 percent of the country) and the United Front for Afghanistan (also known as the Northern Alliance) committed serious human rights abuses, particularly against women and girls, in the areas they occupied and during their attempts to conquer territory.

In East Timor, paramilitary units supported by or under the control of the Indonesian military went on a rampage of violence, looting, and destruction after a United Nations-sponsored referendum saw more than 78 percent of Timorese vote for independence.

In Sri Lanka, the government's conflict with the separatist Liberation Tigers of Tamil Eelam (LTTE) continued to result in serious human rights abuses by both sides. Government security forces committed extrajudicial killings, and at least 15 individuals disappeared from their custody.

In Colombia, despite the government's efforts to negotiate an end to hostilities, widespread internal armed conflict and rampant political and criminal violence persisted. Government security forces, paramilitary groups, guerrillas, and narcotics traffickers all continued to commit numerous serious abuses, including extrajudicial killings and torture.

3. Religious Freedom.

In September the Department of State delivered to Congress the first Annual Report on International Religious Freedom. The Department carries a statutory responsibility to prepare these reports annually. The Report sought to create a comprehensive record of the state of religious freedom around the world and to highlight the most significant violations of this right. The Report demonstrates that violations of religious freedom, including religious persecution, are not confined to any one country, religion, or nationality. Throughout the world, Baha'is, Buddhists, Christians, Hindus, Jews, Muslims, and other believers continue to suffer for their faith.

Too much of the world's population still lives in countries in which religious freedom is restricted or prohibited. Totalitarian and authoritarian regimes remain determined to control religious beliefs and practice.

In October, then Secretary of State Albright informed Congress that she was designating five "countries of Particular Concern": Burma, China, Iran, Iraq, and Sudan. The Secretary also informed Congress that she was identifying as particularly severe violators the Taliban regime in Afghanistan and the government of Serbia. This last action was not taken under the auspices of the International Religious Freedom Act because the United States does not regard the Taliban as a government or Serbia as a country as envisioned by the act.

In Burma, the government arrests and imprisons Buddhist monks who promote human and political rights.

China continued to restrict freedom of religion and intensified controls on some unregistered churches. Unapproved religious groups, including Protestant and Catholic groups, continued to experience varying degrees of official interference, repression, and persecution. In Tibet, the government expanded and intensified its "patriotic education campaign" aimed at controlling monasteries and expelling supporters of the Dalai Lama, increasing pressure on Tibetan Buddhists. Controls on religious freedom in Xinjiang also remained tight. The government also launched a crackdown against the Falun Gong spiritual movement in July. Tens of thousands of Falun Gong members reportedly were detained in outdoor stadiums and forced to sign statements disavowing the Falun Gong before being released.

In Iran, the government committed numerous human rights abuses based in part on religion. Religious minorities, in particular Baha'is, continued to suffer repression by conservative elements of the judiciary and security establishment.

In Afghanistan, the ultraconservative movement known as the Taliban, which controls about 90 percent of the country, enforced their interpretation of Islamic law through punishments such as public executions for adultery or murder and amputations of one hand and one foot for theft.

Other countries also saw significant violations of religious freedom. In Saudi Arabia, neither the government nor society in general accepts the concept of separation of religion and state. The religious police enforce adherence to Islamic norms, intimidating, abusing, and detaining citizens and foreigners.

4. Press Freedom and the Information Revolution.

Attacks on independent media—whether print, broadcast, or electronic—remained commonplace. Journalists

VANTAGE POINT 12.2—*Continued*

continued to risk harassment, arrest, and even death to report the news.

In China, control and manipulation of the press by the government for political purposes increased during the year. After authorities moved at the end of 1998 to close a number of newspapers and fire several editors, the press and publishing industries were more cautious.

In Cuba, the Castro regime continued to tightly control access to information. In February the National Assembly passed the Law to Protect National Independence and the Economy, which outlaws possession and dissemination of "subversive" literature or information that could be used by U.S. authorities in the application of U.S. legislation.

In Ethiopia, fewer journalists were detained than in previous years, but at least eight remained in detention at year's end. Some 45 journalists obtained bail during the year but still are subject to trial. In Peru the government inhibits freedom of speech and of the press. Journalists faced increased government harassment and intimidation and practiced a great degree of self-censorship.

5. Women.

The plight of women in Afghanistan continues to be the most serious women's human rights crisis in the world today. Taliban discrimination against women and girls remained both systematic and institutionally sanctioned.

Elsewhere, women continue to face a wide range of human rights abuses. On a daily basis women faced violence, abuse, rape, and other forms of degradation by their spouses and by members of society at large. Women suffer domestic violence in most, if not all, countries around the world. Many governments still fail to act against "honor killings," domestic violence, and even rape. In Nigeria, for example, the law allows a husband to "chastise" his wife, as long as it does not result in "grievous harm." In China, many women contend with domestic violence. Coercive family planning practices sometimes included forced abortion and forced sterilization. Trafficking and prostitution continued. In India, Bangladesh, and Nepal, dowry-related violence remained a serious problem. In Egypt, India, Iran, Oman, Pakistan, Saudi Arabia, Sudan, Yemen, and a number of other societies where religion and tradition play a predominant role, societal and cultural constraints kept women in a subordinate position.

6. Protection of Minorities.

In some states majorities in power choose to mistreat or persecute those not like themselves. Persecution and discrimination is not confined to states, however, but also can be present in societies. Much remains to be done on the national level, and far too many governments do not grant individuals their rights because of race, sex, religion, disability, language, or social status. In many cases such repression inevitably leads to violence and separatism.

In China, for example, particularly serious human rights abuses persisted in minority areas, especially in Tibet and Xinjiang, where restrictions on religion and other fundamental freedoms intensified.

In Serbia, discrimination and violence against Kosovar Albanians, Muslims, Roma, and other religious and ethnic minorities worsened during the year.

III. Conclusion

The events of the past year have demonstrated the undisputed and growing power of transnational public-private networks in promoting democracy, human rights, and labor. Traditionally, "norm entrepreneurs" have given them the ability to influence the direction of policy. Oscar Arias Sanchez, former President Jimmy Carter, the Dalai Lama, Mahatma Gandhi, Vaclav Havel, Pope John Paul II, Martin Luther King, Nelson Mandela, and Eleanor Roosevelt are but a few of the human rights advocates who instantly come to mind. Such individuals still have an important role to play, but increasingly, public and private networks of transnational actors are becoming "norm entrepreneurs" in and of themselves. These are networks capable of mobilizing popular opinion and political support at the national and international level in order to secure international recognition and acceptance of new principles, standards, or approaches to complex human rights problems.

Source: Excerpts from: U.S. State Department. 2000. *1999 Country Reports on Human Rights Practices.* Washington: U.S. Department of State, February 25.

InfoTrac College Edition Research

Peruse the results of the search terms "United States, Department of State." What human rights concerns are revealed in some of the periodical references?

amputations, in accordance with Islamic law. The death penalty is given for acts ranging from adultery and repeated lesbianism to wine drinking (see Elias, 1986). Beginning in 1975, the Pol Pot regime in Cambodia embarked on a system of mass genocide that destroyed a large portion of that small nation's population. In Latin America right-wing governments and private government-related "death squads" kidnap and/or torture and murder individuals whom they feel threaten the state. Amnesty International estimates that ninety-eight countries practiced torture during the eighties, primarily as a tool for repression rather than to extract information (Satchell, 1988, p. 38). Amnesty International has expressed concern that, as a result of international attention focused on the plight of political prisoners, many governments may have turned to execution of dissidents (Whitaker et al., 1983, p. 52), assuming that dead people tell no tales.

In 1998 the following countries were identified by the United Nations Commission on Human Rights in Geneva as the "Most Repressive Regimes of 1998": Afghanistan, Burma, Cuba, Equatorial Guinea, Iraq, Libya, North Korea, Saudi Arabia, Somalia, Sudan, Syria, Turkmenistan, Vietnam, Kosovo, and Tibet.

Death at Tiananmen Square. Perhaps no other event in recent memory demonstrates the raw, naked power of the state to exercise its political power against popular will than the Chinese government's crackdown on the democracy movement in May 1989. While the world watched live on television, thousands took to the streets to protest authoritarian rule. Many were massacred by troops. By the time the shooting ended, more than a thousand had been killed or arrested. (Some of the latter were executed after being tried.) The Chinese government obviously had not forgotten Chairman Mao's axiom, "Power comes from the barrel of a gun."

Slavery still exists throughout the world. Britain's Anti-Slavery International estimates that there are over 100 million slaves worldwide. In some African countries, such as Mauritania and the Sudan, the Muslim elite enslave black populations. Many guest workers in Kuwait have been treated as little more than slaves. Many young women in India, Bangladesh, and Southeast Asia are sold into prostitution. When demand outstrips supply, women are simply abducted. Most are kept in debt-bondage like that of some Indian workers in Latin America where, no matter how long and hard they work, they still owe the boss. Owners of cane plantations in the Dominican Republic lure poor young Haitians into virtual servitude in which the cost of rent, food, and tools is higher than wages. Despite these and other practices, the United Nations remains reluctant to enforce its own Declaration of Human Rights (Masland et al., 1992).

Patriarchal Crime. **Patriarchal crime** refers to *crime committed against women and children as part of a system of traditional male dominance and authority.* Abuses of such a system include: industrial sweatshops, infanticide of female children, sexual mutilation, bride burning, slavery, and human rights abuses. Ideological justifications for political crime are obviously not limited to political or religious causes, but include preservation of the gender status quo.

In 2000 UNICEF (the United Nations International Children's Fund) declared a global campaign against homicidal violence against women in cultures that sanction such activity (Crossette, 2000). Their focus is on "honor killings," dowry deaths, female infanticide, and acid attacks. Areas of the Mediterranean to Pakistan, India, and Bangladesh are particular offenders.

Most of the attacks are technically legal and culturally approved in these countries. UNICEF figures showed that most of the acid attacks in Bangladesh (where men throw acid in the face of women who reject their request for dates) rose from 47 disfiguring assaults in 1996 to more than 200 in 1998. "Bride burnings" and dowry deaths take place when women are killed because the in-laws consider her dowry (money she brings with

The bones of people thrown over cliffs by the Khmer Rouge are silent witnesses to the bloodthirsty reign of Cambodia's Pol Pot.

(© John Bryson / Time Life Syndication)

her to the marriage) as inadequate or the groom was disappointed with the bride. In India in 1997 there were over 6,000 "bride burnings" (Ibid.). The U.S. State Department's Human Rights report estimates 10,000 cases of female infanticide in 1998. Male dominance, patriarchy, and power predominate in abusive cultures sometimes associated with Islamic fundamentalism, Mediterranean culture, and "machismo" in Latin America. In some Middle Eastern countries "honor killings" take place whereby female victims of rape are murdered by their own families "to preserve the honor of the family." If women stray, the dignity of men can only be restored by killing them. Marrying without the approval of parents can also provoke murder.

The U.S. State Department (2000) estimates that a million women and children, many lured by promises of legitimate employment, are smuggled to other countries and forced into prostitution and a form of slavery. This is common in India, Thailand, Brazil, the Ukraine, and Moldova. More than 100,000 people a year are forced into involuntary servitude in the United States, many of them smuggled in from Mexico and Asia. Besides being forced into prostitution, some are made to become domestic, migrant, and sweatshop workers.

About 100 million women in Muslim Africa are victims of female genital mutilation (FGM), a procedure which is culturally approved as necessary in order to preserve their virginity. The full butchery of a procedure that amounts to female castration is described by McCarthy (1996, p. 32):

> [this procedure] usually involves the complete removal of the clitoris, and often the removal of some of the inner and outer labia. In its most extreme form—infibulation—almost all the external genitalia are cut away, the remaining flesh from the outer labia is sewn together, or infibulated, and the girl's legs are bound

While Germany acknowledged its war crimes during World War II, the Japanese have been very reluctant to admit their atrocities against civilians during that war.

(© Bettmann / CORBIS)

> from ankle to waist for several weeks while scar tissue closes up the vagina almost completely. A small hole, typically about the diameter of a pencil, is left for urination and menstruation.

IN THE NEWS 12.1 describes "The Taliban War Against Women."

Genocide

Genocide, *the mass destruction or annihilation of populations,* is the ultimate violent crime by government. The term was coined by jurist Raphael Lemkin (1944), who defined *genocide* as the destruction of a nation or of an ethnic group. Genocidal conflicts have a long history, from Roman persecutions, the Crusades, Genghis Khan, and medieval pogroms against European Jews up to the horrors of the present century. In the late eighties as part of the Iran-Iraq war, Iraq used chemical weapons on civilians as well as on the Iranian military. Such a practice has been outlawed by international conventions (the 1925 Geneva Protocol) since after World War I.

Condemnation of political criminals may be compromised for other political reasons. In July 1987 the French government convicted Klaus Barbie, "the butcher of Lyons," of crimes against humanity that he had committed as a Gestapo (SS) commander during World War II. He directed the torture, death, and deportation to concentration camps of thousands of Jews, Resistance fighters, and others. Barbie had been hidden from the French after the war by the Americans, who had used him for intelligence purposes (Misner, 1987). Similar charges were levied against former UN secretary-general and Austrian president Kurt Waldheim. The charges levied were that Waldheim, while a young German lieutenant in the Balkans during World War II, knew about war crimes. Investigations of Waldheim's involvement were inconclusive. While Germany's genocide during World War II was well documented by the Nuremberg trials, Japan still has not fully acknowledged its atrocities during that war, including the "rape of Nanking," in which thousands of civilians were massacred; the Bataan death march of Allied prisoners of war; and activities of Unit 731, which involved gruesome medical experiments on Allied prisoners (Harris, 1994).

In the early nineties Brazilian business people were accused of employing "death squads" to execute poor street children. In 1989 alone 445 children were murdered as a means of eliminating street crime ("Death Squads," 1991). The implosion of the former

IN THE NEWS 12.1

THE TALIBAN WAR AGAINST WOMEN

The Taliban, an extremist Islamic sect, took control of the government of Afghanistan in 1996 and began policies that marched that country straight back into a medieval nightmare. Women were immediately ordered to wear a burqua (clothing which covers all but their eyes), or be beaten and stoned. Some have been attacked for not wearing the mesh, which should cover the front of their eyes. One woman was beaten to death for accidentally exposing her arm. Afghanistan's Taliban militias, as part of their jihad (holy war), killed wantonly, emptying communities, machine-gunning livestock, cutting down fruit trees, and blasting irrigation canals (Herbert, 1999). The most horrifying behavior by the Taliban fundamentalists has been their treatment of females, a "gender apartheid."

When the Taliban took control of the country, women were immediately forbidden to work outside the home, go to school, or even go out in public without being accompanied by a male relative. Health workers estimate that the suicide rate has soared among women who have been denied medication and treatment for severe depression. If women live in a home, the windows must be painted lest someone outside see them. Not permitted to work, those without males for support are resorting to begging and even dying. Male doctors are not allowed to examine the female body, and female doctors are forbidden to practice. Prostitution has increased, including forced prostitution. Rape and forced marriage have increased, along with mutilations and murder (Ibid.). Men have the power of life and death over females, especially their wives, children, and relatives. Women are simply sub-human creatures with no rights to the Taliban.

Source: Bob Herbert. 1999. "Fleeing the Taliban." *New York Times,* October 25, p. A27.

InfoTrac College Edition Research

Locate some recent articles on the Taliban in Afghanistan. Have their policies moderated? How has the world community reacted to their policies?

country of Yugoslavia found the new countries of Serbia and Croatia practicing "ethnic cleansing" in Bosnia-Herzegovina. This involved killing, starving, and sending to containment camps mainly Muslim residents in order to terrorize them into abandoning territory for resettlement by Croats or Serbs. In 1995 the International Criminal Tribunal for the former Yugoslavia indicted the Bosnian Serb leaders Radovan Karadzic and General Ratko Mladic as war criminals. The NATO troops enforcing a cease fire in Bosnia, however, are not under orders to arrest and pursue these and other war criminals for fear that renewed conflict would ensue. In another example, despite denials by the Reagan administration, the UN Truth Commission in 1993 concluded that the Reagan administration covered up a massacre of hundreds of innocent civilians at El Most, El Salvador, in 1981 by soldiers of that nation's select, American-trained Atlacatl Battalion (Danner, 1995).

Pol Pot's "Hell on Earth." Massive genocide did not end with Hitler's pogrom against the Jews. In the late seventies, unbelieveable horrors were practiced on Cambodia's own people by Pol Pot's Khmer Rouge regime. If one were to imagine a country ruled by the Charles Manson family, one would be close to picturing the raw terror generated by Angka (the organization of Khmer Rouge) in Cambodia. Interviews and observations showed that of all the Cambodian refugees who fled the country after its invasion by Vietnam, the most devastated were Khmer Rouge refugees ("Cambodia," 1979). The Angka, in an effort to create a radically new society overnight, had tortured, terrorized, and murdered their subjects to the point that many of them exhibited zombielike behavior devoid of many normal human emotions. By the early nineties, after the Vietnamese pullout, a new coalition government was forming in Cambodia with the Khmer Rouge as one of the parties.

In 1948 the United Nations passed a *Convention on Genocide,* in which they defined genocide as a crime (Kuper, 1981, p. 19):

> In the present Convention, genocide means any of the following acts committed with intent to destroy, in whole or in part, a national, ethnical, racial or religious group, as such:

(a) Killing members of the group;
(b) Causing serious bodily or mental harm to members of the group;
(c) Deliberately inflicting on the group conditions of life calculated to bring about its physical destruction in whole or in part;
(d) Imposing measures intended to prevent births within the group;
(e) Forcibly transferring children of the group to another group.

Despite the concerns expressed in this document, the United Nations has been less than a consistent force in condemning genocide.

Crimes by Police

In democratic societies the government is expected not only to enforce the law but also, in doing so, to obey the law itself. In the United States, the government is obliged and accountable to certain constitutional guarantees of individual rights, such as freedom of speech, due process, and the right to privacy. Despite this, federal and local law enforcement agencies, being more interested in bureaucratic efficiency than in proper law enforcement, have often ignored and violated these rights in the process of pursuing their mandate. The Skolnick (1969, p. xxv) Report to the National Commission on the Causes and Prevention of Violence, entitled *The Politics of Protest,* which analyzed U. S. violence in the sixties, indicates:

> Police response to mass protest has often resulted in an escalation of conflict, hostility, and violence. The police violence during the Democratic National Convention in Chicago (1968) was not a unique phenomenon. We have found numerous other instances where violence had been initiated or exacerbated by police actions and attitudes, although violence also has been avoided by judicious planning and supervision.

Prior to the success of the civil rights struggle, local and state officials in the southern United States systematically violated federal law in maintenance of a racist, caste system. Murders, lynchings, beatings, and institutionalized denial of constitutional guarantees were all committed in the name of "law and order." It was to the destruction of this de jure (by law) discrimination that the civil rights movement was directed; this will be discussed in detail later in this chapter.

In 1991 the nation saw televised coverage showing a bystander's videotape of the beating by Los Angeles police officers of Rodney King after a high-speed chase. The subsequent court decision that the police were not guilty led to the deadliest urban riots in the United States this century. While three or four officers had beaten King, eleven others looked on; and the first court decision—in light of the videotape—struck most of the American public and particularly blacks as unfair. Many black citizens complain of police harassment and disrespect, much of it associated with aggressive proactive patrol as part of the "war on drugs." Other abuses by government officials may include illegal surveillance of citizens, disruption of the conventional democratic process, and clandestine experiments with the public serving as unknowing subjects.

Illegal Surveillance, Disruption, and Experiments

Operation CHAOS. In 1967, during the height of dissident activity in the United States, President Johnson directed the Central Intelligence Agency (CIA) to investigate and determine the extent of foreign influence in domestic protest activity. This special operations group, **Operation CHAOS,** in surveillance activities of domestic groups, violated the CIA's initial charter, the National Security Act, which clearly excluded its activities from the domestic arena, although pressure for the expansion of activities was ordered by both President Johnson and later Nixon. Operation CHAOS and a related Project 2 placed agents in radical groups and collected 13,000 different files, over half of which were on U.S. citizens. The Rockefeller Commission (1975) investigated the impropriety of the CIA's encroaching on the domestic field of espionage, sabotage, and provocation. In activities related to these operations, the CIA and FBI in its operation Cointelpro committed 238 break-ins (black-bag jobs) and later attempted to destroy records of such activities.

Cointelpro. The misuse of power by the intelligence agencies was further illustrated in hearings conducted by the U.S. Select Committee to Study Government Operations (1979), which revealed that civil rights organizations had been investigated for over a 25-year period in order to uncover possible Communist influences.

> Dr. Martin Luther King, Jr., was harassed by anonymous letters, his telephone was tapped, his speaking engagements were disrupted by false fire alarms—all as a strategy to discredit him and his organization. In addition it is apparent that the FBI and various state police departments used agents provocateurs to infiltrate dissenting groups, radicalize the members, secure the weapons and explosives necessary for violent confrontations, and plan the target of attacks as a means to discredit dissident groups (Karmen, 1974, in Thomas and Hepburn, 1983, p. 280).

As part of **Cointelpro,** *the FBI's counterintelligence program to harass and disrupt legitimate political activity* such as the Socialist Worker's Party and various black nationalist groups, the FBI employed false letters accusing people of being informants in order to foment internal warfare (Blackstock, 1976, p. 9). The difficulty of separating ideologically motivated actions from personal corruption and vendetta is illustrated by examinations of J. Edgar Hoover's personal files, some of which were released in the 1980s under the Freedom of Information Act. In his nearly fifty years in office, Hoover kept personal files replete with gossip and defamatory information on the personal lives of public figures, particularly those whom he happened to dislike either politically or because of his racial bigotry. Eleanor Roosevelt, John and Robert Kennedy, and Martin Luther King, Jr., were just a few of the political figures about whom Hoover gathered revealing information. In addition to surveillance on Dr. King, it is alleged that the FBI sent threatening letters and a tape to Coretta King regarding her husband's sexual trysts. The opening quotation of this chapter suggests an attempt by the FBI to blackmail King into committing suicide (Garrow, 1981).

The Search for the Manchurian Candidate.

> Those whom the gods wish to destroy they first make mad.
>
> —Euripedes, *A Fragment*

In 1958 Richard Condon published a novel (later made into a movie) entitled *The Manchurian Candidate.* In Condon's very clever book, which takes place during the Korean War, a character named Raymond Shaw and a U.S. Army squad return after having been missing behind enemy lines. The other members of the squad relate Shaw's heroism in saving them from the enemy; he receives the Congressional Medal of Honor for this. In fact, Shaw and his squad were "brainwashed" or "hypnotized-programmed" by the communist Chinese. Asking Shaw to play solitaire until the queen of diamonds appeared would trigger Shaw into zombielike obedience. His own mother (a Chinese communist "mole" or spy) was his operator, and he was able to function as an assassin of the presidential nominee, thus propelling his father, the vice-presidential nominee, into the Oval Office.

Condon's theme enthralled the Western intelligence establishment, as had the "Moscow show trials" of the period, in which dissidents were paraded before cameras and, as if in a trance, admitted treasonous activities against the state (Scheflin and Opton, 1978, p. 437). How could admissions have been obtained from figures such as Hungary's Cardinal Mindszenty? Cold War propagandist Edward Hunter (1951) coined the term "brainwashing" which became a household word; however, it is very likely that Hunter popularized the concept as part of his job with the CIA (Scheflin and Opton, 1978, p. 226).

The Strange Case of Dr. Frank Olson.

> You've got to trust us. We are honorable men.
>
> —Richard Helms, former director of the Central Intelligence Agency

In the early morning of November 28, 1953, Frank Olson, a civilian employee of the U.S. Army, inexplicably jumped to his death from the tenth floor window of his New York City hotel room. The CIA stated publicly that Olson had become mentally unbalanced. Over twenty years later, during the Rockefeller Commission (1975) hearings on CIA activities, government documents revealed the actual facts of the incident, facts that had been hidden from Olson's own guilt-ridden widow and family for over two decades. As part of the secret CIA **Project Bluebird,** which involved mind-control research, the agency secretly drugged unsuspecting citizens and employees. Olson had unknowingly been slipped a very heavy dosage of LSD and literally "freaked out" (a psychotomimetic or reaction that mimics psychosis). When Olson killed himself, the agency lied, smearing Olson's reputation in the process (Marks, 1979). When the facts were revealed, the White House issued an apology to the Olson family along with $750,000. The Olson episode was just one in a series of bizarre and frightening mind-control field experiments conducted by the CIA, using unsuspecting private citizens as subjects.

The Brainwashing Myth. Scheflin and Opton (1978, p. 225) maintain that the **brainwashing** concept was a myth and that Communist methods differed little from police interrogation practices:

> That the CIA was able to take an old form of torture, dress it up with a lurid name and convince the public that a new technique for mind subversion was being practiced by the Communist nations, is a propaganda coup of stunning proportion. . . .
>
> There was absolutely no basis in fact to allege that the "communists" had started "brain warfare." It is not entirely impossible that the "brainwashing" scare was created by the CIA because it wanted to do mind-control research and considered that the safest way to get authorization was to allege that the Soviets had done it first.

With various code names "*Bluebird, Artichoke,* and *MKULTRA*" the CIA, FBI, and military in the fifties experimented with various behavioral-control devices and interrogation techniques, including ESP (extrasensory perception), drugs, polygraphs, hypnosis, shock therapy, surgery, and radiation. These projects involved secret testing on private citizens without their permission and, when death or injury took place, a cover-up. In a related example of government agencies using unknowing citizens as guinea pigs, the U.S. Army in the fifties and sixties conducted outdoor tests of poisonous bacteria (serratia), which can cause pneumonia. Due to these bacteriological warfare tests, one hospital reported twelve cases of serratia pneumonia and one death (Cousins, 1979; Simon, 1996, p. 252).

Through various fronts during this period, the CIA, apparently unknown to the recipients, also funded social psychological research by such famous names as the Sherifs, Orne, Rogers, Osgood, and Goffman (Marks, 1979, p. 121) and financed the publication of over one thousand books, pretending that they were the products of independent scholarship (Cook, 1984, p. 287).

Requiem for the Manchurian Candidate. A Canadian teenager seeking medical treatment for an arthritic leg was subjected to LSD, electroshock therapy, and forced to listen to hours of taped messages including one repeating, "You killed your mother." Such bizarre experiments, financed by the CIA with the consent of the Canadian government, were conducted by an American doctor who had been the president of the American Psychiatric Association. Over one hundred Canadians from 1957 to 1961 were unwitting brainwashing guinea pigs, causing them much psychiatric harm. In 1988 the CIA agreed to pay damages to victims of the experiment—$750,000 to be shared by eight of the victims (Witt, 1988, p. 2A).

American Nuclear Guinea Pigs. In 1986 the House Energy and Commerce Subcommittee uncovered the fact that federal agencies had conducted exposure experiments on U.S. citizens, including injecting them with plutonium, radium, and uranium over a thirty-year period beginning in the mid-1940s. The experiments included feeding elderly adults radium or thorium at MIT, inmates receiving x-rays to their testes, open-air fallout tests, and feeding people real fallout (added to their food in powder form) from a Nevada test site (Lawrence, 1988). In 1996 the U.S. government agreed to pay 12 victims $4.8 million for injecting the unwitting subjects with plutonium and uranium. Many others remain uncompensated (Dobnik, 1996). Under the shield of national security, major harm was committed by the American nuclear state (Kauzlarich and Kramer, 1998).

Scandal

English historian Edward Gibbon described history as a record of humanity's crimes, follies, and misfortunes. Nathan Miller in *The Founding Finaglers* (1976) describes corruption in various presidential administrations, which includes activities such as ordinary bribery, conflict of interest, till-tapping, and illegal and improper use of government authority for financial gain or political advantage. Presidents themselves may not always be involved in wrongdoing; but as James Madison suggested in the First Congress, a president is "responsible for the conduct of the person he has nominated and appointed" (Johnson, 1991, p. 184). Second only to Watergate as the worst public policy scandal in American history was the Iran-Contra Conspiracy.

The Iran-Contra Conspiracy. On November 4, 1986, the Lebanese magazine *Al Shiraa* revealed the existence of a secret U.S. arms sale to Iran. This would begin one of the longest (over five years) and most expensive probes in the nation's history, as of 1992 costing up to $100 million ("North Freed," 1991, p. A16). Money obtained in the sale of arms to Iran in exchange for hostages was utilized to secretly fund the Contra rebels opposing the Marxist Sandinista regime in Nicaragua (Report of the Congressional Committee, 1987).

It is difficult to succinctly present the tangled web of the privatization of foreign policy that the Iran-Contra affair represented. Marjorie Williams (1991, p. 12) describes the plot:

> Popular president sells arms to archenemy hostage-taker Iran, violating not one but two U.S. policies (against arming Iran and dealing for hostages), marking up the price of the arms and sending the profit to the Nicaraguan contras in violation of a third policy, the Congressional Boland Amendments forbidding contra aid.
>
> From there, it was all denouement, a tangled skein of money and guns, middlemen and bank accounts, dates and times and findings and channels. Polls began to show that, as the narrative fragmented, the American people, initially outraged, ceased to follow it.

The televised Iran-Contra Hearings and subsequent coverage (which was not televised) of the trial of Lt. Col. Oliver North, a National Security Council staffer, at first fascinated the American public. Draper in *A Very Thin Line: The Iran Contra Affairs* (1991, p. 580) notes:

> The Iran-Contra affairs "were made possible by an interpretation of the Constitution which Poindexter and North thought gave them a license to carry on their secret operations in the name of the president, in defiance of the law and without the knowledge of any other branch of government." Somehow the highly dubious theory of a presidential monopoly of foreign policy had filtered down to them and given them a license to act as if they could substitute themselves for the entire government.

The indictment also charged that North and retired Air Force General Richard Secord had conspired to divert millions from the sale of U.S. arms to "Enterprise," a secret organization created to privatize foreign policy. Draper (1991) estimated that the Contras may actually have received only about 20 percent of the millions raised (Bliven, 1991, p. 114). Both of these activities represented policy disputes between the executive branch and congress, with Oliver North, having lied to Congress and shredded evidence, the designated scapegoat.

North (1991) was willing to "take the rap" until it became clear that he faced criminal charges without protection from higher-ups. North's boss, General Secord, described how President Reagan was able to truthfully deny knowledge of these activities. Reagan would employ "plausible deniability" by giving general policy guidelines and letting the details be carried out by others without his specific knowledge (Bliven, 1991).

North and former National Security Advisor John Poindexter were convicted in 1989 of various charges, including altering and destroying evidence and obstructing Congress, but these charges were overturned in 1990 and 1991 on the grounds that independent counsel Lawrence Walsh had utilized immunized testimony to Congress to subsequently prosecute them. As part of the investigation, President Ronald Reagan reluctantly agreed to testify (answer prescreened questions), wherein he claimed he "could not remember" or "could not recall" 187 times (Ross, 1988, p. 279).

The Iran-Contra saga continued, with the federal grand jury in September 1991 indicting a CIA official (Clair George, former director of operations) for lying to Congress. In October 1991 Elliott Abrams, the State Department's top officer in Central America in the mid-1980s, admitted that he also lied to Congress about Contra arms. Abrams pleaded guilty. With a statute of limitations running out the end of July 1992, the grand jury subpoenaed former defense secretary Caspar Weinberger, along with his private notes regarding the Iran-Contra events.

The Constitutional questions raised by Iran-Contra were more than a partisan policy dispute. Bandow (1991, p. A19) notes:

> The diversion scheme was a direct assault on our system of constitutional liberty. A small group of men apparently bypassed the president, [perhaps] lied to Congress, and used part of the proceeds of the sale of weapons paid for by

IN THE NEWS 12.2

WHITE HOUSE CRIME AND SCANDAL FROM WASHINGTON TO CLINTON

The impeachment of President Bill Clinton in 1999 and his admission that he did, despite previous denials, have an "inappropriate relationship" with Monica Lewinsky, a then-22-year-old intern in the executive mansion, electrified Washington and the nation like nothing since Watergate; how comparable are such scandals and how do they compare with previous executive branch wrongdoing?

This author's review of presidential wrongdoing is problematic due to the fact that recent presidents are subject to more scrutiny and, thus, more reports of scandal, the creation of an independent prosecutor's office in the wake of Watergate, and difficulties in maintaining one's own political objectivity.

The first tier of presidents in terms of public policy scandals were:

Richard Nixon (Watergate)
Ronald Reagan (Iran-Contra)
Warren Harding (Teapot Dome)
U.S. Grant (Credit Mobilier)
James Buchanan (general corruption)

Of interest is the observation that, if it is a public policy or an economic scandal, it is usually a Republican (4 of the 5 in this analysis, with Buchanan the Democrat) while, if it is a sexual scandal, it is usually a Democrat (4 of 5 in this analysis, with Harding the Republican).

Watergate was, of course, the benchmark for all other political scandals in the United States. This involved the discovery of the illegal break-in of the offices of the Democratic National Committee located in the Watergate complex in Washington, D.C. Among the charges against and offenses by Nixon and associates were burglary, illegal surveillance, attempted bribery of a federal judge, selling ambassadorships in return for illegal campaign donations, having illegal "slush funds," destruction of evidence, plans of dirty tricks in political campaigns, requests for IRS audits on opponents, perjury, withholding information, altering evidence, and lying to the American public.

Between 1980 and 1988 more than 200 Reaganites came under ethical or criminal investigation, the largest number of scandals in any administration in American history (Ross, 1988, p. 1). Major scandals in the Reagan administration included corruption in the Environmental Protection Agency, the Wedtech scandal, the Pentagon procurement scandal, influence peddling at the Department of Housing and Urban Development, and the biggest one—the Iran-Contra conspiracy.

Although Reagan steadfastly refused to admit knowledge of the conspiracy, arms were secretly traded to a terrorist nation (Iran) in return for the release of U.S. hostages. These secret funds were then illegally used to supply arms to Contra rebels in Nicaragua, all against Congressional wishes. Hersh (1990, p. 47) alleges that senior members of the Congressional Iran-Contra committee agreed from the outset that specific evidence of a Presidential "act of commission" would be necessary before Reagan himself would become a target. They believed the President lacked the mental ability to fully appreciate what happened (Ibid., p. 64).

Other public policy scandals included the Credit Mobilier affair of the 1870s affecting the corrupt administration of U.S Grant. Credit Mobilier was a finance company that bribed members of Congress and inflated profits in a conspiracy of waste, crime, and corruption. Warren Harding's corrupt cabinet was involved in conspiracy, graft, fraud, bribery, and cover-ups related primarily to the "Teapot Dome scandal," the illegal sale for personal profit of U.S. naval oil reserves in Teapot Dome, Wyoming. The Buchanan administration was involved in stealing votes, fixing government contracts, and general graft and kickbacks.

taxpayers to implement their own foreign policy. That these people were well-meaning doesn't matter: the Constitution places the power of the purse in Congress, not with a handful of executive appointees. It is for the voters, not the CIA director and a Marine Corps detailee to the NSC, to decide that Congress is "on the other side."

IN THE NEWS 12.2—*Continued*

No other presidential administration has suffered the scrutiny that Bill Clinton's presidency experienced, primarily by Special Prosecutor Ken Starr, and under the rubric of "Whitewater," a land deal involving the Clintons in Arkansas. Despite over five years and $100 million dollars in investigations, Starr's office failed to pin policy scandals on Clinton. This would all change with a civil suit for sexual harassment against Clinton for an activity that took place while he was governor of Arkansas.

Sexual Scandal

In contrast with political and economic scandal, a separate list of worst presidents involved in sexual scandal finds the following as top offenders:

John Kennedy
Bill Clinton
Warren Harding
Lyndon Johnson
Grover Cleveland

Making up the remainder are a host of also-rans such as Jefferson, Garfield, Wilson, and Franklin Roosevelt.

Despite the public image of Camelot, John Kennedy was "the playboy president," the undisputed leader of presidents involved in illicit sexual escapades, having the most active extramarital sex life of any president. The press at the time followed the custom of not reporting such activity. Kennedy had affairs with movie stars such as Marilyn Monroe, shared a girlfriend with a Chicago mobster, had sex in the oval office, and had two white house "aides," dubbed "Fiddle" and "Faddle" by the secret service, who were his regular nude swimming partners in the White House pool.

Although paling in comparison with his idol, John Kennedy, Clinton's political career had been haunted by charges (usually true) from former claimed and real paramours of sexual escapades and indiscretions. Right wing enemies called him "the Caligula of the Ozarks." Due to the investigations of Special Prosecutor Kenneth Starr, Bill Clinton would become the first elected president in American history to be impeached by a partisan Republican Congress for lying under oath about a sexual affair. Congress refused, however, to remove Clinton from office.

Lyndon Johnson was a big womanizer, and even had a buzzer system installed in the oval office so he could be alerted if his wife was approaching, since Lady Bird once caught him having sex with a secretary. He once claimed, "I had more women by accident than Kennedy had on purpose" (Dalleck, 1991, p. 189). Warren Harding was alleged to have had sexual relations with his mistress (a teenager) in the White House coat closet. She had already given birth to his illegitimate daughter. Harding also visited prostitutes. Finally Grover Cleveland, called "the Beast of Buffalo" by his foes for fathering an illegitimate child, admitted to it. When his campaign opponents used the slogan, "Ma, Ma, Where's My Pa," his staff retorted, "Gone to the White House, Ha, Ha, Ha."

It appears that sexual scandal has far less to do with either public or historians' ratings of best or worst presidents. None of the worst in public policy or sexual scandal makes the historians' top list of presidents. Far more telling in the ratings are economic/political scandals, although no president making the worst list in either sexual or economic scandals was rated by historians as one of the top presidents. All of the worst for policy scandal (Reagan not rated) make the worst list by historians, but none of the worst for sexual scandal (except Harding, who was on both lists) makes historians' lists of worst presidents.

Source: Frank Hagan. 1999. "White House Crime and Scandal: From Washington to Clinton." Paper presented at the American Society of Criminology Meetings, Toronto, Ontario, Canada, November; Seymour Hersh. 1990. "The Iran-Contra Committees: Did They Protect Reagan?" *New York Times Magazine,* April 29, pp. 47–49; Shelley Ross. 1988. *Fall From Grace: Sex, Scandal and Corruption in American Politics: From 1702 to the Present.* New York: Ballantine Books; Robert Dalleck. 1991. *Lone Star Rising: Lyndon Johnson and His Times, 1908–1960.* New York: Oxford University Press.

InfoTrac College Edition Research

Choose a presidential scandal since the Carter presidency (e.g., Reagan—Wedtech, Pentagon procurement, HUD, EPA, October surprise, Debategate, or Clinton—Vince Foster suicide, Travelgate, Filegate, Whitewater, or Billingsgate) and answer the following. What were the charges? What investigation took place? What was the final resolution?

The final chapter in the Iran-Contra affair was written by former President George Bush, who shortly before leaving office issued full pardons to all who had been convicted or charged with wrongdoing in the affair.

IN THE NEWS 12.2, "White House Crime and Scandal: From Washington to Clinton," makes the point that it did not start with Clinton.

Crimes Against Government

Protest and Dissent

As previously indicated, crimes against the government may vary from illegal protests, demonstrations, and strikes to treason, sabotage, assassination, and terrorism. At various times in history, social movements that petition for change are viewed as threatening or subversive to the existing society. The American Revolution, the labor movement, the anti-Vietnam War movement, and the struggle for civil rights are examples. Demonstrators for civil rights and other causes may purposely violate laws and be arrested for disorderly conduct, breach of peace, parading without a permit, trespassing, loitering, and the like. They may also be arrested for refusing to pay income taxes to be used for military purposes, for picketing military bases, for student protests, or for refusing to register for military draft. Many student activists of the sixties viewed their universities as protecting the military, industrial, and racial status quo (Skolnick, 1969 p. xxi).

While dissent and protest activities against the government are usually perceived as "radical" (leftist) in attempting to bring about change in the existing order, they may also represent "reactionary" (rightist) activities aimed at preserving or restoring the old order, institutions, or organizational schemes that are endangered.

Groups express dissent and civil disobedience by employing sit-ins, boycotts, and freedom rides (in order to desegregate facilities) to challenge unjust laws. They consciously decide to violate certain laws to call public attention to their cause and to bring about change in the law. Civil rights leader and director of the Southern Christian Leadership Conference, Dr. Martin Luther King, Jr., a Protestant minister, came under heavy criticism from other clergy for neglecting God's work and becoming too involved in disruptive social activities.

Letter from Birmingham Jail. The Nuremberg principle or precedent supports the view that, when one is faced with the imperative of either obeying unjust laws or following a higher moral conscience, the latter takes precedence; to blindly follow orders when they violate basic human rights and dignity is unacceptable. Martin Luther King, Jr.'s

(© Andrew Lichtenstein / Cobris Sygma)

The Anti-Globalization Movement is protesting against economic policies of the World Trade Organization and International Monetary Fund, which they view as disadvantaging the poor in developing countries.

(1963) "Letter from Birmingham Jail" very movingly describes his view that immoral laws must be disobeyed:

> My Dear Fellow Clergymen:
>
> While confined here in the Birmingham city jail I came across your recent statement calling my present activities "unwise and untimely."
>
> . . . I want to try to answer your statement in what I hope will be patient and reasonable terms. . . . I am in Birmingham because injustice exists here . . . . I cannot sit idly by in Atlanta and not be concerned about what happens in Birmingham . . . . Anyone who lives inside the United States can never be considered an outsider anywhere within its bounds. You deplore the demonstrations . . . . But your statement, I am sorry to say, fails to express a similar concern for the conditions that brought about the demonstrations . . . . Birmingham is probably the most thoroughly segregated city in the United States. Its ugly record of police brutality is widely known. Its unjust treatment of Negroes in the courts is a notorious reality. There have been more unsolved bombings of Negro homes and churches in Birmingham than in any other city in the nation . . . . We had no alternative except to prepare for direct action, whereby we would present our very bodies as a means of laying our case before the conscience of the local and national community . . . . The purpose of our direct action program is to create a situation so crisis-packed that it will inevitably open the door to negotiation . . . . We know through painful experience that freedom is never voluntarily given by the oppressor; it must be demanded by the oppressed. One may well ask, "How can you advocate breaking some laws and obeying others?" The answer lies in the fact that there are two types of laws: just and unjust. I agree with St. Augustine that "an unjust law is no law at all." . . . I can urge men to disobey segregation ordinances; for such ordinances are morally wrong . . . . I submit that an individual who breaks a law that conscience tells him is unjust and who willingly accepts the penalty of imprisonment in order to arouse the conscience of the community over its injustice is in reality expressing the highest respect for the law . . . . We should never forget that everything Adolf Hitler did in Germany was "legal" and everything the Hungarian freedom fighters did in Hungary was "illegal."

Martin Luther King, Jr., and his organization, the Southern Christian Leadership Conference, advocated nonviolent, passive resistance, civil disobedience of the form that was employed so successfully by Mahatma Gandhi in overcoming British rule in India. Gandhi taught that violence on the part of those enforcing unjust laws must be met with nonviolence in order to appeal to the public's sense of justice. Incarcerated members of the Irish Republican Army in Northern Ireland also borrowed a tactic from Gandhi, the "hunger strike." Members of "H block" starved themselves to death in order to demonstrate their dedication to their cause.

Social Movements. Illegal protests, demonstrations, and strikes are often associated with social movements that advocate change in the existing order. Members and supporters of such movements are usually deeply committed to altering the status quo. The civil rights battle against racism, the feminist struggle against sexism, the labor and agrarian movements for fair wages, the antiwar movement against the escalation of the Vietnam conflict, the antinuclear, environmental, and anti- or pro-choice movements are all examples. While most such groups are intent on altering the status quo and may at times resort to violence, sabotage, and other destructive behavior, most do not resort to treason, assassination, or terrorism. Frequently, political criminals have done nothing more than exist; they suffer attack because of race, gender, ethnicity, or nationality. Expulsion, exile, curfews, confiscations, confinement, restrictions on travel, and controls over associations may all be used to subordinate, enslave, or subject to second-class citizenship subjugated groups.

In analyzing black militancy, student riots, and antiwar demonstrations of the sixties, the Skolnick Report to the National Commission on the Causes and Prevention of Violence (Skolnick; 1969, pp. xix–xx) concludes:

> . . . serious analysis of the connections between protest and violence cannot focus solely on the character or culture of those who protest the current state of the American political social order. Rather, our research finds that mass protest is an essentially political phenomenon engaged in by normal people; that demonstrations are increasingly being employed by a variety of groups, ranging from students and blacks to middle-class professionals, public employees, and policemen; that violence, when it occurs, is usually not planned, but arises out of an interaction between protesters and responding authorities; that violence has frequently accompanied the efforts of deprived groups to achieve status in American society; and that recommendations concerning the prevention of violence which do not address the issue of fundamental social and political change are fated to be largely irrelevant and frequently self-defeating.

Conscientious objectors, those who refuse to serve in the military because it violates their personal, religious, or moral principles, may also serve as an example of political offenders. In the eighties and nineties groups such as the Sanctuary Movement, pro-life and pro-choice groups on the abortion issue, and antinuclear movements participated in various forms of civil disobedience and protest activities. The **Sanctuary Movement** consisted of *church and lay workers who ran an "underground railroad" to help keep political refugees (often illegal immigrants) from being deported to their Central American homelands where they often faced political persecution.* The U.S. government claimed that such groups were in violation of the immigration laws and that the people they sought to help were economic rather than political refugees, and that the government had a right and responsibility to control the nation's borders (Crittenden, 1988; Tomsho, 1987).

Pro-life (right-to-life) forces are opposed to legalized abortion, viewing it as murder, and seek a reversal of the 1973 *Roe v. Wade* Supreme Court decision, which permits abortion on demand. Besides protests and civil disobedience, more extreme factions have bombed abortion clinics. Opponents (pro-choice) argue that such a decision is not the government's decision, but one between a woman and her physician, and that one group's morality should not become public policy in opposition to the will of the majority (Paige, 1985). With over 40,000 arrests for blocking abortion clinics, Operation Rescue, a pro-life campaign to stop abortions, may have become the largest civil disobedience campaign in U.S. history (Lawler, 1991).

Antinuclear forces are convinced that the nuclear industry is unsafe and is sapping funds from more ecologically sane energy policies such as solar energy. Such groups have violated the law in attempts to prevent startups of new reactors. An antinuclear activist ran onto a stage in 1992 while former President Reagan was speaking, broke a crystal statue Reagan had received, shoved Reagan aside, and began speaking before being arrested. "Act-uppers" are activists who wish to attract public attention and action to fight AIDS. They have interrupted meetings by blowing whistles and using other means of calling attention to their cause.

Another group that became more visible beginning in the late eighties was made up of antivivisectionists, those who oppose using animals in scientific experiments in which maiming, torture, death, or other harm is essential. Such groups have protested, raided laboratories, "liberating" animals (Regan, 1982), and photographed and released to the press some of the more grisly examples. Scientific researchers who use animals claim that such experiments are necessary for discovering medical cures and treatments. Members of the Animal Liberation Front vandalized and set fire to a mink research laboratory at Michigan State University, accusing the professor who ran the lab of killing "thousands of minks in painful and scientifically worthless experiments" ("Animal-Rights," 1991). The raid destroyed thirty years of research on the disappearance of minks in the Great Lakes area.

Sometimes crimes such as kidnapping, burglary, and robbery are committed for political purposes. For example, in 1991 in Philadelphia a $3.6 million jewelry heist was masterminded by three brothers to help fund a civil war in Yugoslavia ("Jewel Thieves," 1991). A group calling itself Earth First! with the motto "No Compromise in Defense of Mother Earth" were on trial in 1991 for ecoterrorism, such as damaging ski lifts, sawing through power poles, and plotting to sabotage three nuclear installations ("Jury Selection," 1991).

VANTAGE POINT 12.3 describes "hate crimes," a growing phenomenon in the United States. Committed for racial, gender, ethnic, or other ideological reasons, hate criminals are convinced of the rightness of their actions (see Hamm, 1994).

Beginning in 1999 and 2000, the "Anti Globalization Movement" protested at the World Bank, International Monetary Fund, and World Trade Organization meetings, as well as both the Democratic and Republican National Political conventions. The members of various groups associated with the movement charged the World Bank and other groups with imposing crushing debt on poor countries, destroying their natural resources, and exploiting their labor. An unlikely alliance of union members, environmentalists, and religious activitists, they have been using mass protests to call attention to their issues.

Assassination

In 1995, due to assassination attempts and threats against President Bill Clinton, a portion of Pennsylvania Avenue in front of the White House was closed to traffic for the foreseeable future. In 1994 a drunken crack user, Frank Corder, crashed a stolen airplane into the south facade of the presidential mansion and killed himself. Francisco Duran, an upholsterer from Colorado, opened fire on the White House with a semiautomatic rifle, claiming he was shooting aliens who were hanging as a mist over the building. On April 4, 1995,

(© Tripett / Sipa Press)

The wreck of Frank Corder's stolen plane on the south side of the White House demonstrated that security around President Clinton could be breached. Corder, who died in the crash, was able to approach the building undetected until the last few moments—so Secret Service agents had no time to act.

VANTAGE POINT 12.3

Hate Crime

Definition

A hate crime, also known as a bias crime, is a criminal offense committed against a person, property, or society, which is motivated, in whole or in part, by the offender's bias against a race, religion, disability, sexual orientation, or ethnicity/national origin.

Background

In response to a growing concern about hate crimes, Congress, on April 23, 1990, enacted the Hate Crime Statistics Act of 1990. The Attorney General designated the FBI's Uniform Crime Reporting (UCR) Program to develop a hate crime data collection system for its voluntary law enforcement agency data participants that would include data "about crimes that manifest evidence of prejudice based on race, religion, sexual orientation, or ethnicity." In September 1994 the Violent Crime Control and Law Enforcement Act amended the Hate Crime Statistics Act to add disabilities, both physical and mental, as factors that could be considered a basis for hate crimes. The disability bias data collection began in January 1997.

Hate crimes are not separate, distinct crimes, but rather traditional offenses motivated by the offender's bias; therefore, hate crime data can be collected by capturing additional information about offenses currently being reported to the UCR Program. Included are the offenses of murder and nonnegligent manslaughter; forcible rape; aggravated assault, simple assault, and intimidation; robbery; burglary; larceny-theft; motor vehicle theft; arson; and destruction, damage, or vandalism of property.

Hate crime data are submitted to the FBI on a Quarterly Hate Crime Report, which consists of a quarterly summary and an incident report for each bias incident. Agencies participating in the National Incident-Based Reporting System are able to include the hate crime data element in their submissions via magnetic tape.

The following statistics are a representation of the data received from law enforcement agencies that provided 1 to 12 months of hate crime reports during 1998. More detailed information concerning characteristics of hate crime can be found in the UCR annual publication, *Hate Crime Statistics.*

Nature

In 1998 there were 7,755 hate crime incidents reported to the FBI. Of the 7,755 reported incidents, 4,321 were motivated by racial bias; 1,390 by religious bias; 1,260 by sexual-orientation bias; 754 by ethnicity/national origin bias; 25 by disability bias; and 5 by multiple biases. The 7,755 incidents involved 9,235 separate offenses, 9,722 victims, and 7,489 known offenders. (See Table.)

Number of Incidents, Offenses, Victims, and Known Offenders By Bias Motivation, 1998

	Number of Incidents	*Offenses*	*Victims*	*Known Offenders*
Total	7,755	9,235	9,722	7,489
Single-Bias Incidents				
Race:	**4,321**	**5,360**	**5,514**	**4,626**
Anti-White	792	989	1,003	1,131
Anti-Black	2,901	3,573	3,663	2,999
Anti-Native American/ Alaskan Native	52	66	66	61
Anti-Asian/ Pacific Islander	293	359	372	245
Anti-Multi-Racial Group	283	373	410	190
Religion:	**1,390**	**1,475**	**1,720**	**536**
Anti-Jewish	1,081	1,145	1,235	394
Anti-Catholic	61	62	65	15
Anti-Protestant	59	61	62	31
Anti-Islamic	21	22	23	12
Anti-Other Religious Group	125	138	288	71
Anti-Multi-Religious Group	41	45	45	12
Anti-Atheist/ Agnostic/etc.	2	2	2	1
Sexual Orientation:	**1,260**	**1,439**	**1,488**	**1,408**
Anti-Male Homosexual	850	972	1,005	1,048
Anti-Female Homosexual	223	265	270	207
Anti-Homosexual	158	170	177	129
Anti-Heterosexual	12	13	17	7
Anti-Bisexual	17	19	19	17
Ethnicity/National Origin:	**754**	**919**	**956**	**863**
Anti-Hispanic	482	595	620	580
Anti-Other Ethnicity/ National Origin	272	324	336	283
Disability:	**25**	**27**	**27**	**42**
Anti-Physical	13	14	14	29
Anti-Mental	12	13	13	23
Multiple-Bias Incidents:	**5**	**15**	**17**	**14**

Source: Hate Crime Statistics 1998. Federal Bureau of Investigation.

InfoTrac College Edition Research

Searching "hate crimes," what are some issues raised in the periodicals on this topic?

Duran was convicted of attempted assassination. Such attacks on public figures unfortunately have a long history in American politics.

In *American Assassins: The Darker Side of Politics,* James Clarke (1982) is highly critical of the popular assumption that all or most assassins suffer from some mental pathology, that they are insane or deranged, and that this causes them to become assassins. Because sources incestuously cite each other's works and rely on inaccurate secondary literature, Clarke states that this pathological myth about assassins is continually repeated in leading works such as those by Donovan (1952), Hastings (1965), Kirkham (1969), and the Warren Commission (1964). Much observation of assassins' pathological symptoms may result from "post hoc error," the false assumption that since one variable or outcome follows another in time, it must be caused by the preceding variable. Clarke believes that most of the major works on assassins simply fail to consider the political context of assassinations (1982, p. 7).

Clarke identified five types of assassins (the examples have been provided by this writer):

1. Political assassins
2. Egocentric assassins
3. Psychopathic assassins
4. Insane assassins
5. "Atypical" assassins.

Type 1. *Political assassins* commit their acts (they believe) selflessly, for political reasons. Some examples of such assassins (successful and unsuccessful) are: John Wilkes Booth (Lincoln), Leon Czolgosz (McKinley), Oscar Collazo and Griselio Torresola (Truman), and Sirhan Sirhan (Robert Kennedy). Booth committed his crime in support of the Confederacy, Czolgosz's was in support of a class revolt, Collazo and Torresola were Puerto Rican nationalists, and Sirhan felt his act would help the Arab cause.

Type 2. *Egocentric assassins* are "persons with an overwhelming and aggressive egocentric need for acceptance, recognition and status" (Clarke, 1982, p. 7). They appreciate the consequences of their acts and do not exhibit cognitive distortion characteristic of delusion or psychoses. Some examples are: Lee Harvey Oswald (John Kennedy), Samuel Byck (Nixon), Lynette ("Squeaky") Fromme (Ford), and Sara Jane Moore (Ford). Such assassins seek attention, which they feel they have been denied, and seek to place a burden on those they feel have denied or rejected them. It would appear that John Hinckley, attempted assassin of Ronald Reagan, would fit this Type 2 description. Oswald and Byck projected their personal difficulties into political extremism. Oswald wanted to prove himself to the Cuban government and to his wife, neither of whom took him seriously. In February of 1974, Byck died in an attempt to hijack a jetliner, which he planned to crash dive into the White House in order to kill Nixon. Although "Squeaky" Fromme resembled a Type 1 assassin, her devotion was to a man (Charles Manson) and not a cause (Clarke, 1982, p. 262). Moore wished to demonstrate her commitment to radicals who had rejected her when they discovered she was an FBI informant; she also wished to obtain protective custody.

Type 3. *Psychopathic assassins,* unable to relate to others, are emotional cripples who direct their perverse rage at popular political figures. In describing Guiseppi Zangara (Franklin Roosevelt and Chicago Mayor Anton Cermak) and Arthur Bremer (George Wallace), Clarke indicates " . . . their motives were highly personal: they wanted to end their own lives in the most outrageous display of nihilistic contempt possible for a society they hated" (p. 167). Both transferred resentment for their emotional deprivation in childhood to public figures. Bremer targeted Wallace after other presidential candidates he had stalked did not offer the proper opportunity.

Type 4. *Insane assassins* have documented histories of organic psychosis, a type of mental illness caused by physiological factors either environmentally or genetically induced. They exhibit severe emotional and cognitive distortion of reality, such as paranoia, one characteristic of which might be delusions of grandeur. Such psychotic assassins include: Richard Lawrence (Jackson), Charles Guiteau (Garfield), and Joseph Schrank (Theodore Roosevelt). Guiteau and Lawrence both believed they had been selected by God to perform His will, while Schrank irrationally believed that he was avenging McKinley's assassination and that Theodore Roosevelt had been the culprit.

Type 5. *Atypical assassins* are those who defy classification, such as Carl Weiss (Huey Long) and James Earl Ray (Martin Luther King, Jr.). Weiss was a successful physician who apparently killed Long because he felt that by so doing he was protecting the lives and political jobs of his relatives. Although racism obviously was behind the King assassination, Ray, an unsuccessful career criminal, appeared to be primarily motivated by an alleged $50,000 payment for the assassination (p. 246).

Clarke concludes his analysis by indicating that, since 1963, Type 2 and 3 assassins have shared a strong desire for media notoriety and that restriction of such coverage could help discourage some assassination attempts. He also feels that there is less need for additional surveillance of suspects than for analysis of information already in the possession of organizations such as the FBI. For instance, the FBI was aware of Byck, Fromme, Hinckley, Moore, and Oswald, and even covered up information after the fact regarding the Oswald and Ray cases. (This, by the way, has led to a variety of conspiracy theories with respect to the King and John Kennedy assassinations.)

Espionage

Espionage, the *clandestine theft of information,* has been a practice since early recorded history. In the Bible, God commanded Moses to send spies to Canaan, and Joshua sent spies to Jericho. In 1987 archeologists discovered a large collection of 3,700-year-old Mesopotamian clay tablets that described, among other things, the capture and ransom of spies ("Ancient Records," 1987). Fifth century B.C. Chinese sage Sun-Tzu (1963) in his classic book, *Art of War,* provided a chapter on secret agents and types of spies. While the name Benedict Arnold, who betrayed the American colonists to the British during the Revolutionary War, lives in infamy in the United States, a statue of Nathan Hale, an American spy executed by the British, stands outside Central Intelligence Agency headquarters in Virginia (Hagan, 1987b).

Despite images of "cloaks and daggers," Mata Hari and James Bond, "black espionage" or "covert agents" ferreting out secrets, classical forms of spying have for many years ranked below "white espionage," which uses space satellites, code breaking, and collection of technical information (Marchetti and Marks, 1974, p. 186; Ranelagh, 1986). The technological revolution in espionage has replaced the "seductive, sable-coated countess traveling first class on the Orient Express" (Maclean, 1978, p. 336). "Sub rosa criminals" are spies who steal secrets. One form of spying, treason, is one of the earliest crimes punished by society and the only crime discussed in the U.S. Constitution. Despite lack of attention in the criminological literature, ***sub rosa* crime** (espionage) is more costly than traditional crime and has altered post-World War II economic and political history.

Defector and former KGB major Stanislav Levchenko was apparently the first to reveal the acronym **MICE** for describing the motives of spies (Kneece, 1986): **M**otivation, **i**deology, **c**ompromise, and **e**go. Others have expanded this acronym to SMICE, adding **s**ex as a separate motivation. There has been a major shift in the motivations of Eastern and Western spies from the ideological, Cold War fifties to the materialistic/hedonistic eighties and nineties. The ideological motivation has been replaced for the most part by mercenary considerations.

Questions have been raised as to the future of espionage, given the fact that the Cold War between the United States and the former Soviet Union has ended. Future directions appear to be in the burgeoning area of economic spying in which governments or private companies steal trade secrets from rivals. Counterespionage activities against terrorist groups or world hot spots, such as Iraq in the early nineties, are foreseen, as is a greater need for human (as opposed to electronic) intelligence gathering (Lachica, 1991; Adams, 1992).

Many previous discussions of types of spies have concentrated on specific role performance or tasks (Anderson, 1977; Sun-Tzu, 1963; Copeland, 1974; Turner, 1985). This writer proposes a **typology of spies,** which includes the following (Hagan, 1987b, 1986):

Mercenary
Ideological
Alienated/Egocentric
Buccaneer
Professional
Compromised
Deceived
Quasi-Agent
Escapee
Miscellaneous

Mercenary spies trade secrets for personal monetary reward. Andrew Daulton Lee, the "Snowman" described in Robert Lindsey's book *The Falcon and the Snowman* (1979) is an example. Lee was a highly successful drug dealer (hence the "Snowman" title) and began acting as a courier for his friend, Christopher Boyce (the "Falcon") by transporting American military secrets to the Soviets for financial reward. The majority of spy cases since 1980 have been of the mercenary variety.

The *ideological spy* is motivated by strong ideological beliefs. Such spies are political criminals and are often condemned as traitors in one country, while being heralded as heroes in the recipient nation. Julius and Ethel Rosenberg became the first and only native Americans to be executed for treason (in March 1951) for having given the Russians America's atomic secrets (Hyde, 1980). They did so out of devotion to Communism, as did the British "establishment spies," Burgess, Maclean, Philby, and Blunt. Recruited as Cambridge University students in the thirties, they rose to the highest levels as "moles" (deep cover agents) in British intelligence (Pincher, 1984; West, 1982).

The *alienated/egocentric spy* is one who betrays for personal reasons unrelated to monetary or ideological considerations. In 1985 ex-CIA employee Edward Howard Lee, having been fired by the agency, defected to the Soviets and took classified secrets with him.

The *buccaneer or sport spy* is one who obtains psychological fulfillment through spying. Turner (1985) describes them as "swashbuckling adventurers who spy for kicks." Christopher "The Falcon" Boyce and John Walker are examples, although there are many others. Boyce, the partner of Lee in *The Falcon and the Snowman* (Lindsey, 1979; 1983), was a bored 21-year-old college dropout who gave the Soviets top secret satellite information in an act of defiance against the CIA. Boyce told a federal marshal, "I guess I'm a pirate at heart. I guess I'm an adventurer" (Lindsey, 1983). John Walker, head of a spy ring that included his son, his brother, and his son's friend, was a former naval officer who passed American cryptographic codes to the Soviets from the 1960s through the mid-1980s. Walker reflected a Walter Mitty-James Bond image of spying, which included props, such as umbrella weapons and crossbows. His ring's peddling of American codes to the Soviets cost American pilots' lives in Vietnam and compromised American naval strategy (Kneece, 1986).

Professional spies are agents, careerists, or occupational employees of intelligence bureaucracies. Covert professional agents, such as Richard Sorge and Rudolf Abel, are legends in the history of espionage. Such agents usually operate under diplomatic cover and, when caught, enjoy diplomatic immunity and are dispatched out of the country. Those who lack such cover are usually swapped for other spies at a later date.

Compromised spies are at first reluctant traitors who trade secrets either for romantic purposes or because of blackmail and coercion. Many are victims of the SMICE strategy. The most celebrated case was that of U.S. Moscow Embassy Marine guards, particularly Clayton Lonetree and Arnold Bracey. The guards were allegedly victims of LeCarre's spy fiction gambit, "the honey trap." The KGB employs many "swallows" or seductive female assistants to trade sex for secrets (Kessler, 1989; Schlachter, 1986). Kessler (1989) claims that, although the U.S. government issued denials, the KGB had the run of the embassy and its secrets.

The *deceived spy* ("false flag recruit") is one who is led to believe that he or she is working for one organization when, in fact, the work is for another. Edwin Wilson, the subject of Peter Maas's book *Manhunt* (1986), was an ex-CIA employee who recruited assassins, smugglers, technicians, and spies, including high-level moonlighters from the CIA, to work for Libya. He led them to believe it was a "company" (CIA) operation (Epstein, 1983; Goulden, 1984). Industrial spies who believe they are working for a rival company may very well be working for the intelligence agency of a rival power.

The remaining types are the *quasi-agents*—dissenters, such as ex-CIA agent Philip Agee, who released classified information to the public. They resemble whistleblowers. *Escapee spies* are individuals who defect in order to avoid personal problems, while the *miscellaneous category* is for those spies who defy classification.

VANTAGE POINT 12.4 gives a brief account of the Aldrich Ames spy case. Ames constituted the highest ranking "mole" to betray his country from within the ranks of the Central Intelligence Agency.

Political "Whistleblowing"

Information is usually classified as secret to protect national security; in some instances it is to misinform the public and shroud questionable activities. It was to protest the latter that Daniel Ellsberg, an employee of the Rand Corporation (a private think-tank and research organization), violated his oath of secrecy and turned over secret government documents, *The Pentagon Papers,* to the press (Gravel, 1971). Ellsberg felt that revealing the government's deceit of the public regarding U.S. involvement in the Vietnam War outweighed his duty to keep government secrets. In an even more controversial case, former CIA agent Philip Agee (1975) wrote personal memoirs of his CIA activities in South America in which he named and, according to some, endangered CIA operatives in those countries. He disagreed ideologically with many covert policies the CIA had been carrying out in that region.

Terrorism

Viewed outside its political context, international terrorism represents some of the worst examples of mass murder in history.

- In January 1988 a bomb aboard Pan Am Flight 103 exploded over Lockerbie, Scotland, killing all 259 aboard the plane and 11 townspeople. Two Libyan intelligence officers were charged with the act of state-sponsored terrorism by Libya and Iran. The U.S. government posted a $4 million reward for their capture.
- In March 1995 poison gas attacks on five trains in Tokyo's subway system during rush hour killed 11 and injured more than 4,700. Accused was Shoko Asahara, leader of a cult

VANTAGE POINT 12.4

The Aldrich Ames Spy Case

Following a secret one-year investigation by the Federal Bureau of Investigation, espionage charges were filed against Aldrich Ames on February 23, 1994. A 32-year veteran of the Central Intelligence Agency, Ames, age 52, was the son of a career CIA officer and the highest ranking CIA official ever charged with espionage. He had been stealing secrets and selling them to the Russians (then Soviets) since 1985. That same year, while working counterintelligence in Mexico City, he recruited Maria del Rosario Casa (a Colombian native), whom he also married and who allegedly collaborated in his spying operations (Weiner, 1994a). The reader is referred to a number of books that detail the Ames case (Adams, 1995; Maas, 1995; Weiner, Johnston, and Lewis, 1995; Wise, 1995).

Aldrich Ames had been Chief of the Soviet Counterintelligence Branch of the Soviet-Eastern European Division in the mid-eighties, as well as CIA Rome Chief from 1986–1989. Although one media source describes his wife Rosario as a possible Russian "swallow" who recruited him into betrayal (Thomas et al., 1994), most sources describe him as a "walk-in" who offered his services for monetary reasons. While the full extent of the damage done by Ames may never be known, it is clear that he condemned many CIA agents to death. He sold out at least eleven Russian agents who were executed between 1985 and 1987, including America's highest Cold War double agent, the top officer of the Soviet military intelligence agency, GRU General Dimitri "Top Hat" or "Donald" Polyakov. Ames's perfidy was motivated not by passionate commitment to some ideology but, utilizing the "typology of spies," was based primarily on mercenary reasons. Similar to spy John Walker, he exhibited a "buccaneer/sport spy" orientation, an "in-your-face" profile—wanting to show how smart he was.

Because the CIA was suspicious of Ames as early as 1985, concern was expressed about why it took so long for the agency to catch its most damaging mole. On a salary that never exceeded $70,000 per year, he lived a lavish lifestyle. In addition, he had an alcohol problem that should have attracted attention. He paid $540,000 in cash for a home in Arlington, Virginia, and proceeded to spend $100,000 on improvements. He bought two new cars, including a Jaguar. He bought stock worth $165,000 and charged $455,000 on credit cards. Considering that he was the highest paid known Soviet informant (estimates range from $1.5–2.5 million), Ames could afford it. He was also able somehow to survive two lie detector tests, one in 1986 and another in 1991—although not without difficulty. While one source indicates that the FBI suspected that the Russians gave him special pills and coached him on beating the polygraphs (Wise, 1995), another claims that in addition to special tranquilizers he had been trained to lie using biofeedback techniques. Information that Ames had flunked the initial 1991 polygraph sections on personal finance and work for the Soviets was not turned over to the FBI until 1993. Case officers were permitted to retake the polygraph test until they calmed down (Walker et al., 1994). Ames begged for discovery with his ineptness, lazy work habits, excessive drinking, flaunting of money, and use of safe houses for sexual trysts. He was protected by an "old boys network" and a history of noncooperation between the CIA and the FBI. It is the duty of the latter to investigate such breaches of security. Then-CIA-Director R. James Woolsey promised a major shakeup of the CIA agency culture, which had enabled Ames to survive for so long. Ames received a life sentence for his espionage activities, and due to his cooperation gained a reduced sentence for his wife. Aldrich Ames is just one of the latest examples of spies whose changing motivations in the post-Cold War climate highlight the recent history of espionage.

Source: Frank E. Hagan, 1995, "Spies," Paper delivered at the American Society of Criminology Meetings, Boston, Massachusetts, November; Frank E. Hagan, 1997, *Political Crime: Ideology and Criminality.* Boston: Allyn and Bacon, pp. 119–120.

InfoTrac College Edition Research

Investigate the category "spies." What was the Wen Ho Lee affair and what was its final disposition?

known as Aum Shinrikyo. Other attacks in Japan were also tied to the cult when a police search of their facilities found stores of chemicals suitable for production of the gas.

- In July 1996 Islamic extremists opposing the Saudi Arabian government were believed responsible for a massive truck bomb blast at a U.S. military compound that killed 19 and wounded many others. This was the second attack against American troops in Saudi Arabia in seven months.

Definitions and Types of Terrorism. Any definition of **terrorism** is sure to arouse dispute. Definitions by the U.S. Department of Defense, FBI, State Department, Department of Justice, and Vice President's Task Force on Combatting Terrorism (1986) include:

- the unlawful use of force or violence by revolutionary organizations
- the intention of coercion or intimidation of governments for political or ideological purposes
- premeditated political violence perpetrated against noncombatant targets by subnational groups or clandestine state agents
- use of assassination or kidnapping

Terrorism may be distinguished from tragic acts of war in the willful and calculated targeting of innocents (Netanyahu, 1986, p. 8). Even during the Nazi occupation of Europe, the partisans avoided indiscriminate killing of the families of German soldiers. No such limitations on noncombatants figure into the plans of many current terrorist groups. The Federal Bureau of Investigation (Pomerantz, 1987, p. 15) defines terrorism as " . . . the unlawful use of force or violence against persons or property to intimidate or coerce a government, the civilian population, or any segment thereof, in furtherance of political or social objectives."

The *Report of the Task Force on Disorders and Terrorism* (National Advisory Committee, 1976c, pp. 3–6) provides the following **typology of terrorism:** political terrorism, nonpolitical terrorism, quasi-terrorism, limited political terrorism, and official or state terrorism. The report defines *political terrorism* as "violent criminal behavior designed primarily to generate fear in the community, or a substantial segment of it, for political purposes." *Nonpolitical terrorism* also attempts to elicit fear by means of violence, but is undertaken for either private purposes or gain. Examples of this type would include activities of organized crime, the Manson family, or Charles Whitman, "the Texas tower" sniper. *Quasiterrorism* describes "those activities incidental to the commission of crimes of violence that are similar in form and method to true terrorism but which nevertheless lack its essential ingredient." Rather than being ideologically motivated, many skyjackers and hostage takers, although employing terrorist methods, are interested in ransom. *Limited political terrorism* refers to "acts of terrorism which are committed for ideological or political motives, but which are not part of a concerted campaign to capture control of the state." Vendetta-type executions and acts of lone terrorists for essentially private motives are examples. Such terrorism is illustrated by the capture in 1996 of Theodore Kaczynski, the celebrated "Unabomber," who eluded capture for nearly two decades. An antitechnology, radical environmentalist, he killed 3 and wounded 23 before being captured.

Official or state terrorism occurs in "nations whose rule is based upon fear and oppression that reach terroristic proportions" (Simpson and Bennett, 1985). Wolf (1981) differentiates "enforcement terrorism" from "agitational terrorism," the former being used by governments to control populations.

One might add *state-sponsored terrorism,* in which countries support terrorism as "war on the cheap." For example, in 1990 Syria was the home base of the Popular Front for the Liberation of Palestine—General Command (PFLP—GC), which was believed to be involved in the bombing of the Pan-Am jumbo jet over Lockerbie, Scotland, in 1988. Syria also controls the Bekaa Valley, the terrorist training ground in Lebanon. Iran most likely commissioned the bombing of the jet in retaliation for the U. S. Navy's accidental shooting down of an Iranian civilian airliner during a crisis in the Persian Gulf (Wines, 1990). Libyan agents were blamed because the trigger to the device was similar to a type of detonator used by Libyan terrorist bombers. The device was hidden in a Toshiba radio like those used by PFLP—GC terrorists in Germany, who most likely hired the Libyans (Mossberg, 1990). The bombing turns out to have Iranian, Syrian, and Libyan connections and probably was not solely the work of isolated terrorists.

Brief History. The Assassins of the Middle East were the best known early terrorist group, although their attacks were confined to officials and authorities. The Jacobin period of the French Revolution and its "reign of terror" provided the name, while the Russian nihilists and "bomb throwers" of the late nineteenth century provided the classic vision of the terrorist. Laqueur (1987, p. 3) notes:

> . . . [T]he popular image of terrorists some 80 years ago was that of a bomb-throwing alien anarchist, disheveled, with a black beard and a satanic (or idiotic) smile, fanatic, immoral, sinister and ridiculous at the same time.

Prior to World War II, most terrorism consisted of political assassination of government officials. A second new form of terrorism was inaugurated in Algeria in the late fifties by the FLN (National Liberation Front), who popularized the random attack on enemy civilians. This is depicted well in the classic film *The Battle of Algiers.* A new third stage of terrorism has become popular since the sixties: "media terrorism"—random attacks on anyone.

Indiscriminate terrorism has become widespread only in recent times, with the invention of more effective explosives and modern mass media. Terroristic action is easier to commit than attacks against hardened targets or well-guarded leaders, and since such actions are unlikely to gain political support, they are more likely to be committed against foreigners. Most of this terrorism has been directed against democracies, with little against the more totalitarian states. Much terrorism in the eighties was "war by proxy" or *state-sponsored terrorism* by countries such as Libya, Syria, and Iran. Terrorism became an inexpensive means of waging "war on the cheap."

In the late nineteenth century the fate of captured terrorists was condemnation and execution, but few since the sixties have suffered such a fate. More likely, capture sets off a self-perpetuating cycle with new operations to effect the release of "political prisoners." Because of fears of retaliation, after World War II the punishment of terrorists became more lenient. Terrorism has become almost respectable, with a majority of the members of the United Nations opposing any action against it. The rules of international diplomacy were established by the European colonial powers and are not entirely shared by Third World countries. State terrorism, in which nation states and their officials terrorize their own populations, may be the most common form (Herman, 1982).

Terrorism: A Growing Threat? As late as 1971, terrorism throughout the world claimed fewer than two dozen lives per year. Beginning in the eighties, however, these figures escalated dramatically. Russian anarchist Peter Kropotkin (1842–1921) viewed terrorism as "propaganda by deed" (Nettler, 1982, vol. 2, p. 232). Carlos Marighella, the Latin American author of a handbook on urban guerilla warfare, felt that one purpose of terrorism was to provoke repressive responses by the state and, subsequently, public opposition to the state. While such tactics have in fact destroyed democracies and created more repressive regimes in Argentina, Uruguay, and Turkey, recent brands of terrorism have to date failed to topple any government. Terrorists often assume for themselves a higher morality in which they reject moral limitations and embrace the conviction that "righteous homicide justifies killing innocents" (Nettler, 1982, vol. 2, p. 231). While members or defenders of a status quo under siege are apt to define any revolutionary or guerilla activities as terrorism, this writer prefers to restrict the term to indiscriminate attacks on civilians and innocents. While this type of terrorism may never have toppled governments as Nettler suggests, more conventional terrorism aimed at governmental targets certainly has.

Frederick Hacker (1976, p. 69) in *Crusaders, Criminals and Crazies* points out:

> Contrary to widespread belief, terroristic violence is not always futile and ineffective in transforming reality. If it had not been for IRA terrorist activities, the Republic of Ireland never would have come into being. This is also true of independent Cyprus, Algeria, Tunisia, and possibly Israel . . . . Terrorism often is not confined to outlaws and the dregs of society (riffraff theory); it is supported by responsible citizens and organizations, either openly or in secret . . . . Terrorists are *not* all part of a Leninist-Marxist conspiracy. The IRA, particularly its activist Provisional branch, is actually conservative, patriotic, nationalistic, and rightist, and is denounced by opponents as a bunch of fascists and "crazy drunkards."

Myths Regarding Terrorism. Laqueur (1977, pp. 219–22) discusses what he claims are various **myths regarding terrorism:** (1) "Contrary to popular belief, terrorism is not a new or entirely unprecedented phenomenon." It is at least as old as the Russian Narodnaya Volya, nihilistic bomb-throwers of the last century. (2) Since one person's terrorist is another's liberator, the term is "politically loaded" and should be discarded. Most terrorism has been directed at democracies or ineffective authoritarian regimes and ignores totalitarian systems such as Nazi Germany, Fascist Italy, or the Communist regimes. (3) Although terrorism is always assumed to be "left-wing" or revolutionary, intellectual fashions change and slogans should neither be ignored nor taken too seriously. Certainly right-wing death squads in Latin America or the Ku Klux Klan illustrate terror from the right. (4) It is assumed that terrorism takes place whenever there are legitimate grievances, and that amending these conditions will bring about its cessation. The most repressive, unjust societies have been the freest of terrorism. (5) Although terrorism is viewed as highly effective, this is the case only if it is part of a larger strategy. (6) Even though terrorists are viewed as idealists, humane behavior is often sacrificed for revolutionary goals. (7) Terrorism is described as a weapon of the poor, but most terrorists come from affluent backgrounds and are often supported by outside powers such as Russia, Cuba, Libya, and Algeria (see Sederberg, 1989). Terrorism is often an act of desperate revolutionaries, those who lack effective weapons or means of obtaining redress of their grievances through other channels. During the British control of Palestine, Menachim Begin was leader of a group of terrorists, the Irgun, which blew up the King David Hotel, killing innocent victims. Later, as president of the new nation of Israel, Begin refused ever to sit across the negotiation table from PLO leader Yassir Arafat because he was a terrorist.

Some terrorists become, to use Sterling's words, "retail terrorists," a traveling circus of performers such as "Carlos the Jackal," Abu Nidal's group, or Rengo Sekigun (the Japanese Red Army). Some terrorist groups that were active internationally in the eighties and nineties include Abu Nidal's group, Basque ETA, Hamas, Hezbollah, Islamic Jihad, M–19, Palestine Liberation Front, Provisional IRA, Sikh separatists, and Tamil extremists.

Abu Nidal's group (headed by Sabri-al-Banna) is a splinter Palestinian group that had been involved in numerous terrorist attacks, often as a proxy for Iraq and later for Syria and Libya. The *Basque ETA* attack Spanish targets in their quest for a separate Basque homeland in northern Spain. **Hamas** (in Arabic, "fervor" or "zeal") is an Islamic resistance movement whose primary purpose is to prevent peace between the Israelis and Palestinians. With funds from Iran and Syria, they have made heavy use of young, suicidal bombers. Rivalling them in fanaticism is **Hezbollah** (the "Party of God") and its action arm, Islamic Jihad. It has been the principal tool by which, since 1979, the theocratic regime in Iran has pressed its jihad (holy war) against the West.

Islamic Jihad (Islamic Holy War) are Shiite fundamentalist extremists. They are responsible for bombings of the U.S. embassy and of the Marines' barracks in Lebanon and for the holding of U.S. hostages. They are backed by Iran. M–19 (April 19 Movement)

Hezbollah suicide commandos march in parade in the Bekaa Valley, Lebanon, on the last day of Ramadan.

(© Karim Daher / Gamma Liaison)

are leftist guerilla groups in Colombia. In November 1985 they seized the Justice Palace in Bogota, causing the death of 100 people. They are believed to be aligned with Cuba, as well as with "narcoterrorists." The *Palestine Liberation Front* (PLF) is a Palestinian faction headed by Abu el-Abbas, who was blamed for the 1986 Achille Lauro hijacking. The PLF is a subgroup of another breakaway group in the Palestinian movement and is aligned with Palestinian Liberation Organization (PLO) leader Yasser Arafat.

Al Qaeda (Arabic for "the Base") is a group headed by Osama bin Laden, which opposes non-Islamic governments with violence. These veterans of the Afghan war were originally trained and funded by the U.S. in opposing the Soviet Union. They consider the U.S. military's continued involvement in the Middle East as "American occupation of Islamic countries." With cells in more than sixty countries, al Qaeda was implicated in the World Trade Center bombing and the massacre of tourists in Luxor, Egypt. VANTAGE POINT 12.5 provides further description of Osama bin Laden's organization.

The *Provisional IRA* ("Provos" of the Irish Republican Army) are fighting to unite Northern Ireland (which is part of the United Kingdom) with the Republic of Ireland. They wish to drive the British from Northern Ireland and have ambushed British personnel and bombed British facilities.

Sikh Extremists seek independence for India's Sikh population in the Punjab. They are responsible for the assassination of Indian President Indira Gandhi, the bombing of civilian airlines, and booby-trap bombings throughout India. *Tamil separatists* seek independence for the northern part of the island of Sri Lanka, which is currently dominated by the Sinhalese. Both sides in this controversy have massacred civilians.

Sendero Luminoso (Shining Path) is a radical Marxist terrorist group in Peru that controls a large chunk of the rural countryside.

Domestic Terrorism, U.S.A. While incidents of international terrorism, particularly with Americans as targets, increased during the eighties, domestic terrorism in the United States in the nineties remained at a relatively low level. The 1993 bomb attack upon the World Trade Center in New York City by Islamic fundamentalists, while dramatic, was atypical. Then came the 1995 Oklahoma City bombing, and in 1996 the possibly terrorist detonation of a pipe bomb at the Atlanta Olympics. The nineties brought with it two types of groups in

VANTAGE POINT 12.5

Al Qaeda (The Base)

Al Qaeda (The Base) is the name of an umbrella group of some 20 Islamic extremist organizations headed by Osama bin Laden. Illustrating change in such terrorist groups, they are loosely organized cells with the capability of independent actions. Affiliates of Al Qaeda include Egyptian Islamic Jihad, led by Ayman al Zawahiri, and Gamaa Islamiya, led by Ahmed Refai Taha. All are under spiritual leader Omar Abdel Rahman, the blind cleric who was imprisoned in the United States for his role in a bomb plot in New York City.

The network was headquartered in Sudan until 1996 and presently is located in Afghanistan. Training camps exist in Afghanistan, Pakistan, the Sudan, Somalia, and Kenya with 2,000 to 3,000 operatives in Africa, the Mideast, Afghanistan, Pakistan, Bosnia, Kosovo, Chechnya, and Tajikistan. The "majis al shura" is the consultative council that decides on terrorist operations, while the "fativa" committee issues religious rulings. Al Qaeda is a particular problem for anti-terrorist organizations in that it consists of a large number of loosely organized, highly committed amateurs rather than a small band of highly trained operatives.

Source: Bruce Auster. 1998. "An Inside Look at Terror Inc." *U.S. News and World Report.* October 19, pp. 34–36.

InfoTrac College Edition Research

What was the USS Cole incident and do you feel that the evidence suggests that Osama bin Laden was behind it?

particular: extremist Islamic fundamentalist groups and right-wing militia or self-described "patriot groups." VANTAGE POINT 12.6 describes the World Trade Center bombing.

In the past most terrorist groups in the United States were either international or strongly identified with separatist or leftist movements. Puerto Rican Independence, anti-Castro groups, the Jewish Defense League, and similar groups were active. An explosion of right-wing KKK/Neo-Nazi hate groups—such as the Order, Posse Comitatus, American Nazi Party, the Aryan Nations, and the Covenant, Sword and Arm of the Lord (CSA)—became more prominent in the eighties. VANTAGE POINT 12.7 discusses some of these groups in detail.

Puerto Rican independence groups have historically been the most active. In 1950 one such group attempted to assassinate President Truman, and in 1954 it shot up the U.S. House of Representatives while it was in session. Such groups want a separate and independent Puerto Rico (which has been a commonwealth of the United States). The two most active groups are the FALN and the Macheteros (Puerto Rican People's Party). The FALN (Fuerzas Armadas de Liberaciòn Nacional—Armed Forces for National Liberation) has been responsible for over two hundred bombings in the United States and Puerto Rico. The Macheteros (Machete Swingers) have attacked U.S. military personnel and bases in Puerto Rico (Harris, 1987). They were also responsible for a Wells Fargo robbery in West Hartford, Connecticut, that netted $7.3 million.

While anti-Castro Cuban groups such as *Omega 7* and *Alpha 66* still exist, their activism fades as their leadership (former Cold Warriors and veterans of the Bay of Pigs invasion) ages. Their main targets have been Soviet and Cuban diplomats. The Jewish Defense League is an anti-Arab, anti-Soviet group of religious zealots who support a militant Zionism. Through bombing campaigns and harassment, they attack targets that they feel are anti-Jewish (Poland, 1988, p. 89).

"Single issue terrorists" are those who use extremist tactics in support of a single issue. Examples include: animal rights activists, pro-life and pro-choice activists, environmental activists, and others whose zealotry for their cause precipitates extreme tactics.

VANTAGE POINT 12.6

The World Trade Center Bombing

In the seventies and eighties, while Americans overseas were a major target of international terrorism, domestic terrorism was rare and even declining. The truck bomb attack on the World Trade Center in February 1993 reminded Americans of the danger of complacency, of assuming that "it cannot happen here." The World Trade Center attack and subsequent aborted scheme to simultaneously blow up the United Nations, Federal Bureau of Investigation headquarters, and the Holland and Lincoln tunnels at rush hour resembled improbable plots from some B-grade disaster movie. At the time the worst terror attack ever committed on American soil, the World Trade Center bombing involved the detonation of explosives in a Ryder van rented by Palestinian immigrant Mohammed Salameh. The mammoth explosion ripped through six underground floors, killed six people, and injured another thousand. Incredibly, the plotters had hoped to topple one giant tower into the other. While the apparent ringleader, an Iraqi using the name Ramzi Ahmed Yousef, fled the country, the four conspirators in the bombing—Salameh, Nidal Ayyad, Mahmed Abouhalima, and Ahmad Ajaj—were all convicted. Yousef had originally been permitted to come to the United States when he applied for political asylum on September 1, 1992. He fled the country but was subsequently caught and extradited to the United States. Others who were also believed to have been involved in the plot continued to be investigated.

The Trade Center bombers were described as not particularly professional in their operations. They failed to use aliases; kept incriminating evidence in their homes; and worshipped, lived, and protested together as devoted followers of an Egyptian blind Sheik, Omar Abdel Rahman. Rahman, an Islamic fundamentalist and bitter opponent of assassinated Egyptian leader Anwar Sadat and his successor Hasni Mubarek, was believed to be the inspiration for both attacks. A subsequent plan by 15 of Rahman's followers to bomb the United Nations and other targets, including the Lincoln and Holland tunnels, was aborted by FBI informer Emad Salem, who had infiltrated Rahman's organization. It is unclear as to whether these events were the work of amateurs or professionals, an example of state-sponsored terrorism. Proponents of the latter point to Yousef as an Iraqi agent and to Saddam Hussein's call for revenge for his defeat by the U.S. troops in the Persian Gulf War. On the other hand, fundamentalist Rahman, a veteran of the Afghani war against the former Soviet Union, was described as not on friendly terms with Hussein. Islamic fundamentalists after Khomeini's takeover in Iran in the late seventies were strong advocates of a crusade-like "jihad" or holy war against the secular West and infidels such as the "Great Satan" (their name at the time for the United States).

Ironically, Rahman traveled to the United States on a CIA visa, even though he was a militant on the State Department's list of undesirables. The CIA needed support for its covert war against the Soviets in Afghanistan and had unwittingly stoked Islamic fundamentalist fanaticism in the Brooklyn headquarters of Rahman. Unfortunately, the agency failed to consider that such extremists might also hate the United States and that their hostility would be strong enough to lead them to blow up the World Trade Center and plot their reign of terror on New York City. Secret CIA support and training for Afghani operations had created a "blowback," an unanticipated public policy recoil that is hard to head off (Friedman, 1995; Weiner, 1994a). They had literally "created a monster" by not weighing all the possible consequences beforehand.

On October 1, 1995, a federal jury convicted Sheik Omar Abdel Rahman and nine other defendants of seditious conspiracy for plotting assassinations and bombings related to the World Trade Center bombing of February 1993. Specifically, the group was convicted of conspiring to carry out a terrorist campaign of bombings and assassinations intended to destroy the United Nations and New York landmarks. The defendants were not accused of the World Trade Center bombing itself, but some involved in each incident were co-conspirators. At his January 1996, sentencing, the sheik received a life sentence. The others received sentences ranging from 25 years to life. On May 25, 1994, four of the men responsible for the World Trade Center bombing received "collectively" 240 years of prison time with no possibility of parole.

InfoTrac College Edition Research

Vetting the area of "terrorism," what are some recent trends in terrorist activity?

VANTAGE POINT 12.7

The Turner Diaries, ZOG, and the Silent Brotherhood—The Order

In the 1930s in beer halls in Munich, Germany, a political criminal and racist misfit, Adolf Hitler, advocated a bizarre future: a world of Wagnerian mysticism, a new order, a Third Reich.

> **But we are doing something else which is really more important than our campaign against the System. In the long run, it will be infinitely more important. We are forging the nucleus of a new society, a whole new civilization, which will rise from the ashes of the old. And it is because our new civilization will be based on an entirely different world view than the present one that it can only replace the others in a revolutionary manner. There is no way a society based on Aryan values and an Aryan outlook can evolve peacefully from a society which has succumbed to Jewish spiritual corruption (MacDonald, 1980, p. 111).**

The above statement is not an excerpt from Hitler's *Mein Kampf,* but rather from a book entitled *The Turner Diaries* by Andrew MacDonald (1980), the Nazi pen name of William Pierce, a leader of a Neo-Nazi right-wing extremist group (Wiggins, 1986a, 1986b; Holden, 1986; Sapp, 1986). Groups such as the Order, Aryan Nations, Bruder Schweigen (The Silent Brotherhood), the Covenant, Sword and Arm of the Lord, and other right-wing extremist groups are linked by "identity theology." This is an anti-Semitic ideology that views Aryans as God's chosen people and Jews as the children of Satan. Some of these groups also practice "survivalism," a belief that they must stock supplies in order to be self-sufficient as the last hold-outs in some final Armageddon.

The Turner Diaries is a thinly disguised blueprint for the Order's battle with ZOG, "Zionist Occupational Government" or "Zombies of Government." The book describes a "white revolution" launched by a terrorist group, "The Organization," to topple the U.S. government (ZOG). They support themselves through bank and armored-car robbery and counterfeiting. They assassinate key leaders and sabotage transportation and power systems. Once in power they intend to kill Jews, blacks, other minorities, and liberals (Klanwatch, 1985, p. 6). In the eighties members of these and related groups murdered Jewish talk-show host Alan Berg in Denver (1984), robbed armored cars and banks, killed and had gun battles with police and federal agents, and bombed synagogues and minority-owned businesses—the very acts outlined in the Turner diaries.

J.R.R. Tolkien's *The Lord of the Rings* trilogy is viewed by many as an allegory for the rise of Nazi Germany. Gandalf, the wizard, instructs Frodo, the Hobbit, of the nature of evil: "Always after a defeat and a respite, the Shadow takes another shape and grows again" (Howard, 1990).

By the late eighties federal authorities had concluded that the Order had been virtually wiped out as a result of FBI and local efforts, although others speculate that the Ku Klux Klan and other neo-Nazi hate groups simply regroup and reappear in new forms under new names. Skinhead white supremacists and "Identity Movement" followers continue their wars of hate.

InfoTrac College Edition Research
What role did the "Turner Diaries" play in the Oklahoma City bombing?

Radical leftist terrorist groups declined in the eighties. Groups such as the SLA (Symbionese Liberation Army), the SDS (Students for a Democratic Society), Weathermen, and Black Panthers were quite visible in the sixties and seventies. A right-wing faction of interest to law enforcement is the Sheriff's Posse Comitatus, which advocates a tax moratorium and disregard for federal and state authority. The FBI was quite effective in surveillance and deterrence of terrorist acts of such groups by means of "neutralization through preventive interviews;" that is, interviewing members and letting them know that authorities are well aware of their plans (Pomerantz, 1987). With the Oklahoma City bombing in 1995, such groups began to be taken far more seriously by

(© Robert Daemmrich / Bettmann)

The view of the north side of the Alfred Murrah Federal Building in Oklahoma City shows the extensive damage done by the car bomb that destroyed the building on April 19, 1995.

federal authorities. This required a shift in thinking. After three decades of watching possible subversion on the left, now authorities must be concerned with thunder on the right from "freemen," militias, and "patriot groups" (see Stern, 1996; Aho, 1994).

Finally, in a class by itself as the best known terrorist-hate group, is the Ku Klux Klan, whose crossburnings, arson, bombings, vandalism, intimidation, shootings, and assaults continue, although their movement may have gone underground (Klanwatch, 1985) or transformed itself into Neo-Nazi or militia groups.

VANTAGE POINT 12.8 gives an account of the annual FBI report on terrorism.

The Oklahoma City Bombing

In his *Cycles of American History* (1986), historian Arthur Schlesinger proposes that the American political mood generally undergoes an ideological shift in every generation. Terrorism in the United States may reflect these ideological cycles. Before World War II, terrorism was perpetrated largely by the right wing; after the war, it shifted to the left; and since the 1970s, it has moved back to the right. Consider the April 19, 1995, bombing of the federal building in Oklahoma City—so far the worst single act of terrorism ever committed on American soil, superseding on all levels the World Trade Center bombing of two years before. Convicted bomber Timothy McVeigh filled a rented truck with 4,800 pounds of explosives and detonated the charge at the federal building, killing 191 men, women, and children. His friend Michael Fortier assisted McVeigh, but testified against him at his trial. Another alleged accomplice, Terry Nichols, belonged to a militia group called the "Patriots," which believed in a federal government conspiracy.

The Oklahoma bombing was, in part, apparently revenge for the deaths of 79 members of David Koresh's Branch Davidian sect in Waco, Texas, who died when their compound was stormed by federal agents. The Oklahoma bombing took place exactly two

VANTAGE POINT 12.8

The FBI's Terrorism Report, 1998

Terrorism in the United States 1998

The year 1998 demonstrated the wide range of terrorist threats confronting the United States. Terrorists in Colombia continued to target private American interests, kidnapping seven U.S. citizens throughout the year and carrying out 77 bombings against multinational oil pipelines, many of which are used by U.S. oil companies. On August 7, 1998, the U.S. embassies in Nairobi, Kenya, and Dar es Salaam, Tanzania, were attacked in nearly simultaneous truck bombings that left 224 persons dead, including 12 U.S. citizens (all victims of the Nairobi attack). The bombings also wounded over 4,500 persons.

In the United States the FBI recorded five terrorist incidents in 1998. Within the same year 12 planned acts of terrorism were prevented in the United States. There were no *suspected* incidents of terrorism in the United States during 1998.

Three of the terrorist incidents recorded in the United States occurred in the U.S. Commonwealth of Puerto Rico. None of the three attacks—the bombing of a super-aqueduct project in Arecibo and separate pipe bombings at bank offices in Rio Piedras and Santa Isabel—caused any deaths. By contrast the bombing of a women's clinic in Birmingham, Alabama left an off-duty police officer dead and a clinic nurse seriously wounded. (Eric Robert Rudolph was later charged in this attack—as well as three previous bombings in Atlanta, Georgia.) The fifth incident, a large-scale arson at a ski resort in Vail, Colorado, caused an estimated 12 million dollars in damage, but resulted in no deaths or injuries. All of the terrorist incidents recorded in the United States during 1998 were attributed to domestic terrorists; there were no acts of international terrorism carried out in the United States in 1998.

Likewise, the 12 acts of terrorism prevented in the United States during the year were being planned by domestic extremists. Nine of these planned acts were prevented as a result of the arrest of several members of the white supremacist group The New Order, based in Illinois. The six men, who were arrested on weapons violations charges in February 1998, planned to conduct a crime spree that was to include bombings, assassinations, and robberies. Consistent with a steady increase in cases involving the use or threatened use of chemical and biological agents, two additional terrorist preventions involved the planned use of biological toxins. The final prevention involved a plan to detonate a bomb at an unspecified target in Washington, D.C.

The United States continued to pursue an aggressive policy toward terrorism in 1998. In January international terrorist Ramzi Ahmed Yousef received a lengthy prison sentence for masterminding the February 26, 1993 World Trade Center bombing, as well as a foiled plot to bomb U.S. commercial aircraft transiting the Far East in 1995. A Yousef accomplice in the World Trade Center bombing was also sentenced in 1998. Eyad Mahmoud Ismail Najim, who drove the bomb-laden van into the parking garage of the World Trade Center, was sentenced to 240 years in prison and ordered to pay $10 million in restitution and a $250-thousand fine. An associate of the plotters, Mohammad Abouhalima, who drove his brother (Mahmud) to Kennedy International Airport after the 1993 World Trade Center bombing, was sentenced to eight

years to the day after the Branch Davidian incident. Federal investigators concluded that, while federal agents were not without fault in managing the Waco incident, most of the casualties were caused by Koresh and his followers, who may have started the fire themselves in a mass suicide as federal agents stormed the compound. Koresh had accumulated a huge illegal arsenal of weapons, which led to confrontation with federal agents. The Waco incident, as well as a federal siege of white separatist Randy Weaver's cabin in Ruby Ridge, Idaho, in which his wife and young son were killed by snipers, became battle cries for right-wing militia movements in the United States.

Further paranoia was whipped up by militant "patriot" leaders such as "Mark from Michigan," "Mark Koernke" and other practitioners of "hate radio," such as Gordon Liddy, who advised listeners to shoot any invading ATF (Alcohol, Tobacco and Firearms) agents in the head, because they wear bulletproof vests. Paranoia has always been a factor in American political history (Hofstadter, 1965), but the Oklahoma bombing represents a

VANTAGE POINT 12.8—*Continued*

years in prison. In addition, Ibrahim Ahmad Suleiman received a 10-month sentence for providing false statements to the grand jury investigating the bombing. In May Abdul Hakim Murad, an accomplice in Ramzi Yousef's plot to bomb U.S. airliners, was sentenced to life plus 60 years in prison without parole. In June international terrorist Mohammed Rashid was rendered to the United States from overseas to stand trial on charges related to the detonation of a bomb on Pan Am flight 830 in 1982, which killed one passenger and wounded 15 others.

In addition, a number of domestic terrorists and extremists were convicted and/or sentenced for their illicit activities throughout the year. These included Terry Lynn Nichols, who was sentenced to life in prison for his role in the Oklahoma City bombing, and 21 individuals convicted of charges related to the 1996 Montana Freemen siege.

Conclusion

The nearly simultaneous bombings of the U.S. embassies in Nairobi, Kenya, and Dar es Salaam, Tanzania, on August 7, 1998, vividly underscored the continuing threats to U.S. interests around the world. Examples of terrorist violence in the United States were also all-too-evident during 1998. For the fourth consecutive year, terrorists carried out destructive attacks in the United States. Combined attacks in 1998 resulted in one death and two serious injuries.

The United States continued to take a strong stand against terrorism in 1998. Ramzi Yousef—the international rogue terrorist who masterminded the World Trade Center bombing and envisioned the deaths of thousands of innocent Americans in his foiled plot to down 12 U.S. commercial aircraft—was sentenced to consecutive sentences totalling 240 years and life in prison for the World Trade Center bombing and airliner conspiracy. Several of Yousef's accomplices also received lengthy prison sentences in 1998. Another international terrorist, Mohammed Rashid, was rendered to the United States from overseas to stand trial for a 1982 attack on a U.S. commercial aircraft. In addition, by year's end four suspects in the twin U.S. embassy bombings in East Africa were also in U.S. custody awaiting trial.

The FBI, working closely with other law enforcement agencies, also succeeded in preventing 12 planned acts of terrorism from taking place in the United States. All of these plots were being planned by domestic extremists.

The suspect in one of the five terrorist incidents to occur in the United States during the year—the January 29 bombing of a women's clinic in Birmingham, Alabama—became the 454th person to be placed on the FBI's Top Ten Most Wanted Fugitives list in May. In addition to the Birmingham bombing, Eric Robert Rudolph was also charged with the pipe bomb attack at the 1996 Atlanta Summer Olympics and two additional bombings in the Atlanta area that occurred during 1997. At year's end, a multi-agency task force continued to search for Rudolph in the remote mountains of western North Carolina.

Source: Excerpts from: FBI. 1999. *Terrorism in the United States, 1998.* Washington, D.C.: Government Printing Office.

InfoTrac College Edition Research

Searching "United States, Federal Bureau of Investigation," what is "Carnivore" and what controversies exist with respect to its usage?

critical departure—the worst terrorist incident ever committed on American soil in which large numbers of innocent persons were slaughtered by apparently remorseless fanatics and their zealous supporters who were fellow Americans. Extremist militia groups introduced another wrinkle into the "craft of terrorism" with their extensive use of the Internet, fax machines, short-wave radios, and talk radio for communicating their views.

Criminal Careers of Political Criminals

For political criminals, crime is instrumental; it is a means of achieving what they perceive as higher moral goals. As Schafer (1976, p. 139) explains:

> The convictional criminal, with his altruistic moral ideology, places less emphasis upon secrecy and even seeks publicity for his cause. Dramatic publicity,

> moreover, is almost a necessity for the convictional criminal in order to make the public understand his actions; his crime may serve as an example to would-be followers and generate further convictional crimes. His punishment is not a deterrent and may serve to interest others in the given ideal and to recruit other convictional violators of law.

The only exception to this publicity-seeking behavior are government criminals who in most instances prefer secrecy. Political criminals from the left or right tend to be convinced of the rectitude of their cause and their actions. Rather than viewing their behavior as criminal, political criminals either deny the legitimacy of existing laws or view their violation as an essential step in either preserving the existing social order (crime by government) or in bringing about change in the existing system (crime against government).

A large proportion of leftist revolutionaries are drawn from educated and middle class backgrounds rather than from the ranks of the proletariat as Marx had predicted. A similar pattern presents itself with terrorists. Laqueur (1977, p. 207) points out that in West Germany in the late sixties and early seventies there were more females than male terrorists, and the females were more fanatical than the males. Right-wing groups in the nineties appeared to draw heavily from working class white males, who often resented minorities and immigrants and blamed them for their economic slippage. Clutterbuck (1975, p. 65) indicates that "terrorist movements seldom have more than very small minority support from the people . . . [and consist of] earnest young intellectuals increasingly frustrated by their lack of response from the ordinary people."

Political criminals operate within subcultures that define their activities as appropriate or necessary. Whether it be theories of racial supremacy (the Ku Klux Klan), preservation of law and order (illegal police violence), terrorist bombing of innocent victims, the shooting down of civilian airliners (state violence), or nonviolent passive resistance, political criminals feel that they have support of immediate peers. Being convinced of the rightness of their actions, political criminals also assume that others will be impressed with their resolve, "see the light," and eventually agree with their actions. If proper subcultural support for politically deviant action is not strong, such violators may come to view their actions as illegitimate.

Although some view governmental political criminals as not ideologically committed (Allen et al., 1981, pp. 201–202), they are in fact ideologically committed to preservation of the status quo, and this convictional devotion may be distinct from the quest to preserve personal power (occupational crime). While governmental political criminals tend to be from more privileged backgrounds, many of their agents (servants of power), such as the police, are not. As previously mentioned, political criminals against the government vary considerably in background, although many leaders of the "new left" in the late sixties and early seventies in the United States and Western Europe were universally educated and drawn from the upper middle class. Even though males dominated numerically, a significant proportion of leaders of radical and terrorist groups during this period were females.

For many terrorists "the end justifies the means;" the rightness of the cause and actions are viewed as reactions to repression, injustice, or hostile acts of the enemy. It is the latter who must bear the burden of guilt for aggression.

The Doctrine of *Raison d'État*

For political crimes, government officials or their agents historically have sought justification in the doctrine of ***raison d'état*** (reason of state), usually attributed to Italian political philosopher Nicolò Machiavelli (1469–1527). This doctrine holds that some violations of the common law are necessary to serve public utility (Friedrich, 1972, pp. 21–22). This Machiavellian "end justifies the means" is a consistent rationalization of political criminals of all stripes: governmental, religious, or political. Friedrich (1972, pp. 106–107) indicates:

> The martyrs of Christianity became the saints of a triumphant Christian church; their betrayal of the Roman Empire as seen by its officers was what made them the "functionaries" of a future order. The same may be said of the "saints" of Communism and of national liberation; in the political perspective the sainthood is measured by the rightness of the cause they served, as seen by the beneficiaries of that cause.

In cases of crime committed in the act of political policing, labels of "official" secrets, "national security," and "reasons of state" shroud many incidents and evidence (Turk, 1981). Political crimes by intelligence agencies often have a "keeping up with the Joneses" quality wherein one must match the extreme measures of one's competitor in order to be successful. "To protect ourselves from the tyrannous, we have slowly built up our own tyranny" (Halperin et al., 1976, p. 236). In the Iran-Contra case discussed earlier, the conspirators invented a new word for lying—"plausible deniability," or being able to say believably that you did not know about something.

While much of the literature on terrorists plays up their intractability and uncompromising nature, one must also consider the social-structural context in which their activities occur. To take but one example, terrorism by the Provisional wing (Provos) of the Irish Republican Army is in part aimed at uniting Ireland. How much support would the Provos have, however, if a truly successful civil rights movement were to obtain equal jobs, housing, and political influence for Catholics in the North? Similarly, a Palestinian homeland in some form would remove some of the support for Palestinian terrorists.

Terrorism and Social Policy

Terrorist threats of the future promise to be more nuclear, more urban, and to involve wealthier, more skilled terrorists—often as proxy armies for sponsor countries. Terrorism is a problem to be managed rather than solved. Attempts at international cooperation are hindered by the very ideological disputes that often give rise to terrorism. A precedent does exist with respect to international cooperation. Piracy, a historically common practice, has been virtually eliminated through international agreement. At one time countries hired pirates in a form of "war by proxy;" but for centuries they have been declared *hostis humani generis* (common enemies of mankind), outlaws whose acts fall under the jurisdiction of all states. Perhaps a similar uniform international policy will evolve regarding cross-national terrorism.

Kidder (1986 and 1983) summarizes counterterrorism measures in terms of nine policies: diplomatic measures, better intelligence gathering, tighter security measures, legal and social measures, more public awareness, military and police action, arms and explosives controls, media self-regulation, and maintenance of public composure. Terrorism by "lunatic minorities" in democratic countries that provide legal recourse (for example, the ballot box) must be condemned as "crime." Sanctions must be imposed on offending regimes (state terrorism and state-sponsored terrorism). This could include withdrawal of financial aid and diplomatic recognition and invocation of strict liability (holding them legally responsible) rather than conducting business as usual (Martin and Walcott, 1988).

Societal Reaction

The *sociological nature of the concept* of political crime is illustrated by its relativity with respect to time and place. Ideologically committed spies such as the Rosenbergs, who supplied their country's atomic secrets to a foreign enemy, were traitors in the United States, but heralded as heroes in the recipient country, the Soviet Union. Even the most dastardly terrorist acts, such as the slaughter of almost the entire Israeli Olympic team in Munich, was applauded in many areas of the Arab world. This very divergence in international ideology explains the relative ineptness of world bodies such as the United Nations to act in unison in condemning global terrorism and atrocities.

Since crimes against the government threaten the status quo of society, societal reaction has been quite strong, however, until recently, public reaction to crimes by the government has been mild. This is partly because, since the government makes and enforces the law, it is hard to imagine it also violating the law. In the United States, public innocence in this regard appears to have matured since revelations of CIA and FBI wrongdoing and the events of Watergate.

Turk (1981, p. 236) indicates: "Any conception of legal deviance in political policing inevitably clashes with the fact that such organizations are invented to prevent radical political changes . . . national security . . . political and military considerations override any legal or ethical ones." While some secrecy on the part of intelligence agencies is in the public interest, the level of lying and deceit beyond the public interest is difficult to weigh, indeed the data required for such a judgment are not available until after the fact. The danger lies, of course, in the government, the servant of the people, becoming the master—Big Brother knows best.

The more complex, urban, industrial, and interrelated the world community becomes, the easier it is for a small, fanatical minority of the left or right to disrupt, destroy, or endanger not just their political targets, but all of us. At the level of collective behavior and social change, dynamic societies can continue to be expected to generate new social movements, new demands for change and, depending on the response, new political criminals either in the form of "bell-ringers" of change or of overzealous guardians at the gates.

Summary

Ideology refers to distinctive belief systems, abstract ideals that offer a design for living. *Political crime* is defined as criminal activity committed for ideological purposes. There are two types of political crime: *crimes by government* and *crimes against government.* Crimes by government exclude political corruption, which is an example of occupational crime, and refer instead to violations by secret police, abuses of human rights and constitutional privileges, and genocide, as well as crimes committed by government officials in the act of enforcing the law. Crimes against government range from protests, illegal demonstrations, and strikes to espionage, political whistleblowing, political assassination, and terrorism. The actual definition of political crime is relative to time, place, and the ideological views of those giving the definition.

All governments have criminal laws forbidding activities that threaten the state. In Anglo-American jurisprudence, political criminals are not recognized as such and are dealt with under more traditional, nonpolitical laws. The *Nuremberg principle,* established by the victorious Allies at the end of World War II, established that individuals faced with the dilemma of obeying orders that involve war crimes and crimes against humanity or following their own consciences, should disobey unjust dictates. Similar documents in the Western political tradition, as well as the UN's *Universal Declaration of Human Rights* (1948), provide customs or standards for international conduct with regard to respecting integrity of persons, basic human needs, and civil liberties. *International law,* however, is handicapped by the lack of a consensual world community as well as by the lack of power of enforcement.

Crime by government is more sociological than political. Secret police (political policing) are units of the internal security police of the state who have a mandate to suppress all serious or threatening political opposition and to control political activity. Their activities often include illegal surveillance, searches, detention, and violations of human rights. *Political prisoners* may include those who have seriously opposed the existing government, but also prisoners of conscience who are tortured, sent into exile, or murdered.

Amnesty International finds totalitarian regimes to be the greatest offenders in this area. Examples were given of Iraq's use of poison gas and of Klaus Barbie and Kurt Waldheim.

Patriarchal crime refers to crime committed against women and children in the name of traditional male dominance.

Genocide, the mass destruction or annihilation of human populations, is the ultimate violent crime by government; in the modern era, political ideologies have replaced religious justifications for genocide. In 1948 the UN *Convention on Genocide* defined it as a crime, although this same international body has been less than consistent in condemning such practices. *Political crimes by police* often involve violation of due process, freedom of speech, and invasion of privacy. These and other offenses are committed in the name of "law and order" and preservation of the existing political system.

Other abuses by government agents include illegal surveillance, disruption of democratic processes, including character assassination, and secret experiments on unsuspecting subjects. One such example was *Operation CHAOS,* which among related activities involved illegal surveillance and harassment of domestic dissidents. *Cointelpro* was the FBI's counterintelligence program to disrupt legitimate political activity such as that of the Socialist Worker's Party and black nationalist groups. Harassment of Martin Luther King, Jr., has been linked to misuse of intelligence agencies such as the FBI by J. Edgar Hoover. The case of Oliver North was also detailed. Further questionable experiments include "the search for the Manchurian Candidate," mind-control experiments conducted in search of a secret *brainwashing technique.* The latter term was coined by Edward Hunter (1951) and, according to Sheflin and Opton, was a *myth* created to justify such experiments on an unsuspecting public. Another example is the Dr. Frank Olson case. Nuclear exposure experiments were also discussed.

Crimes against government may involve activities of dissent and protest in opposition to the status quo, but may also involve reactionary opposition to changes that have taken place in the existing social or political order. Dissident activities are represented by civil rights, labor, and antiwar groups of the past; reactionary opposition can be found in right-wing "death squads," the Ku Klux Klan, and the American Nazi Party. Excerpts from Martin Luther King, Jr.'s, "Letter from Birmingham Jail" provide a very moving defense of civil disobedience and the strategy of the civil rights movement. *Social movements* advocate change in the existing order and often conflict with responding authorities. Some newer examples include the sanctuary, anti- and pro-choice, antinuclear, and antivivisectionist (animal rights) groups.

Political espionage involves stealing state secrets and is a standard international practice of intelligence agencies. "Sub rosa criminals" are spies who steal secrets. The Aldrich Ames spy case is an example.

The motivation of spies often reveals a SMICE strategy (sex, motivation, ideology, compromise, and ego). A typology of spies includes: mercenary, ideological, alienated/egocentric, buccaneer, professional, compromised, deceived, quasi-agent, escapee, and miscellaneous. *Treason* is the betrayal of one's country out of commitment to either a political ideology or a foreign power. Political "whistleblowers" such as Daniel Ellsberg violate state secrecy because they believe that the public has a right to know the truth.

Terrorism is the use of cruelty and violence in order to spread fear within a population as an instrument of gaining political power. *Types of terrorism* include: *political terrorism, nonpolitical terrorism, quasiterrorism, limited political terrorism,* and *official or state terrorism.* The last type illustrates the fact that not all terrorism involves crime against the government. While observers such as Laqueur feel the threat of terrorism in the seventies was a media event and an exaggeration, statistics from the early eighties suggest a climbing toll of victims. Examples of both international and domestic terrorist groups were detailed, including the World Trade Center and Oklahoma City bombings. *Some possible myths regarding terrorism* include beliefs that it is a new phenomenon; an inappropriate, politically loaded term; always leftist in nature due to legitimate grievances; highly effective; idealistic; and a weapon of the poor.

Examination of the *criminal careers* of political criminals indicates that they view crime as instrumental, a means to ideological ends. Most do not view their activity as criminal and tend to operate within supporting subcultures that reinforce their definitions. For government political criminals *raison d'état,* national security, and their preservation serve as justification for violations. Some government policies for dealing with terrorism were detailed. *Societal reaction* to political crime varies, with generally strong disapproval of offenders against the government and mild reaction in the past toward governmental offenders. Divergence in ideology prevents any consistent international reaction to political crime.

KEY CONCEPTS

Aldrich Ames Spy Case
Brainwashing
Brainwashing Myth
Cointelpro
Crimes Against Government
Crimes By Government
Enterprise
Espionage
Genocide
Hamas
Hate Crime
Hezbollah
Human Rights
Ideology
Myths Regarding Terrorism
Nuremberg Principle
Operation CHAOS
Patriarchal Crime
Political Crime
Project Bluebird
Raison d'Etat
Sanctuary Movement
Secret Police
SMICE
***Sub Rosa* Crime**
Terrorism
Types of Spies
Types of Terrorism
Universal Declaration of Human Rights

REVIEW QUESTIONS

1. How is the concept of political crime different from other crimes that have been examined in this course? Do you think that political crimes should be treated differently than other crimes?
2. What are secret police and their purpose? Give some examples of ways in which they can use political policing.
3. What are some basic human rights recognized by international treaty and the United Nations? Give some examples of their violation.
4. What is the meaning of the term "the search for the Manchurian Candidate"? How did this search influence U.S. intelligence agencies to become involved in wrongdoing?
5. Discuss crime and scandal during presidential administrations in the U.S. What is the impact of such scandals on a president's standing in history?
6. What were the major offenses in the Iran-Contra conspiracy? Why wasn't Reagan impeached for this affair?
7. Who wrote the "Letter from Birmingham Jail?" To whom was it addressed and what did it say?
8. What is the major issue of the "Anti-Globalization movement" and what does it wish to accomplish?
9. What is the "pathological myth of assassins?" What types of assassins were identified by Clarke? Give an example of each.
10. Discuss the various types of spies and give an example of each.

INFOTRAC COLLEGE EDITION RESEARCH

Vantage Point 12.1 InfoTrac College Edition Research Search the issue of "human rights." What are some recent human rights issues throughout the world?

Vantage Point 12.2 InfoTrac College Edition Research Peruse the results of the search terms "United States, Department of State." What human rights concerns are revealed in some of the periodical references?

Vantage Point 12.3 InfoTrac College Edition Research Searching "hate crimes," what are some issues raised in the periodicals on this topic?

Vantage Point 12.4 InfoTrac College Edition Research Investigate the category "spies." What was the Wen Ho Lee affair and what was its final disposition?

Vantage Point 12.5 InfoTrac College Edition Research What was the USS Cole incident and do you feel that the evidence suggests that Osama bin Laden was behind it?

Vantage Point 12.6 InfoTrac College Edition Research Vetting the area of "terrorism," what are some recent trends in terrorist activity?

Vantage Point 12.7 InfoTrac College Edition Research What role did the "Turner Diaries" play in the Oklahoma City bombing?

Vantage Point 12.8 InfoTrac College Edition Research Searching "United States, Federal Bureau of Investigation," what is "Carnivore" and what controversies exist with respect to its usage?

In the News 12.1 InfoTrac College Edition Research Locate some recent articles on the Taliban in Afghanistan. Have their policies moderated? How has the world community reacted to their policies?

In the News 12.2 InfoTrac College Edition Research Choose a presidential scandal since the Carter presidency (e.g., Reagan—Wedtech, Pentagon procurement, HUD, EPA, October surprise, Debategate, or Clinton—Vince Foster suicide, Travelgate, Filegate, Whitewater, or Billingsgate) and answer the following. What were the charges? What investigation took place? What was the final resolution?

SELECTED READINGS

James Clarke. 1982. *American Assassins: The Darker Side of Politics.* Princeton, NJ: Princeton University Press.
This is the best work on the subject of assassins. Clarke refutes previous myths and develops an excellent typology of spies.

Richard Condon. 1958. *The Manchurian Candidate.* New York: Random House.
This novel is a Cold War classic that scared the American intelligence community into undertaking a variety of bizarre experiments in order not to fall behind a perceived Communist mind control gap. This was later made into a movie starring Frank Sinatra and Angela Lansbury.

Congressional Research Service. 1978. *Human Rights Conditions in Selected Countries and the U.S. Response.* Washington, D. C.: Government Printing Office.
Report prepared for the House Committee on International Relations, 95th Congress, 2nd Session

Theodore Draper. 1991. *A Very Thin Line: The Iran-Contra Affairs.* New York: Hill and Wong.
An excellent account of the Iran-Contra conspiracy.

Federal Bureau of Investigation. (annually). *Terrorism.* Washington, D.C.: Government Printing Office (also available free on the World Wide Web).
This is the FBI's annual report on domestic and international terrorism.

Frank E. Hagan. 1997. *Political Crime: Ideology and Criminality.* Boston: Allyn and Bacon.
This is the author's attempt to resurrect and develop a successor to Proal's classic work. It provides comprehensive coverage of all areas of political crime from crime by government to crime against government.

Walter Laqueur. 1987. *The Age of Terrorism.* Boston: Little, Brown.
This well-written, classic text presents a very scholarly, historical account of terrorism from a European perspective.

Peter Maas. 1986. *Manhunt: The Incredible Pursuit of a CIA Agent Turned Terrorist.* New York: Random House.
A very exciting account of Edwin Wilson and his alleged "false flag" operations in support of Libya.

Nathan Miller. 1976. *The Founding Finaglers.* New York: David McKay.
A very readable, not-too-flattering account of scandal among early presidents and statesmen.

Louis Proal. 1973. *Political Crime.* Montclair, NJ: Patterson Smith. Reprint of an 1898 edition.
This is the classic on political crime. Proal's work is both eloquent and a benchmark for all other work on this topic.

Untied Nations, 1948. *Convention of Genocide.* New York: United Nations.

United States State Department. (annually). *Human Rights Report.* Washington, D.C.: Government Printing Office (available free on the World Wide Web).
This annual report to Congress evaluates how well countries throughout the world are abiding by the UN Declaration of Human Rights.

13 Organized Crime

> Cosa Nostra means Our Thing. If you use these words, it means: I belong to a Mafia family.
>
> —Court testimony by Sicilian Mafia informant Tomasso Buscetta, cited in Shana Alexander, *The Pizza Connection,* (1988, p. 43)

> "Joe, let's stop fooling around. You know I'm here because the Attorney General wants this information. I want to talk about the organization by name, rank and serial number. What's the name? Is it Mafia?"
>
> "No," Valachi said. "It's not Mafia. That's the expression the outside uses."
>
> "We know a lot more than you think. . . . Now I'll give you the first part. You give me the rest. It's Cosa."
>
> Valachi went pale. For almost a minute he said nothing. Then he rasped back hoarsely, "Cosa Nostra! So you know about it."
>
> —Peter Maas, *The Valachi Papers,* 1968, pp. 29–30

Organized Crime: A Problematic Definition

Organized crime has been variously defined and described by the general public, legislatures, law enforcement agencies, social scientists, and syndicate members themselves. Ryan (1990, p. 4) in trying to make sense of the myriad definitions notes:

> Indeed the academic community is not without conflict on the issue. Albanese observes that "there appear to be as many descriptions of organized crime as there are authors" (1989, p. 4). Some say there is no such thing as organized crime since the evidence of its formal structure is not without loopholes (Hawkins, 1969). Others, taking the lead from Ianni (1973), speak of a "social system" of organized crime that is inextricably part and parcel of American society. Others sometimes endorse the model of an organization with hierarchical authority and functional division of labor (Cressey, 1969). The idea that organized crime can be legally defined as a conspiracy (Blakey, 1967) is supported by those prosaic folk who would depict organized crime as interchangeable with mafia. The latter view seems to rely heavily on newspaper articles that shroud criminality in a mystique that suggests we can never extricate ourselves from its clutches (Smith, 1975).

Federal agencies such as the FBI and the Department of Justice use the Federal Task Force on Organized Crime's general operational definition, one that best fits the generic type, which will be described shortly:

> Organized crime includes any group of individuals whose primary activity involves violating criminal laws to seek illegal profits and power by engaging in racketeering activities and, when appropriate, engaging in intricate financial manipulations. . . .
>
> Accordingly, the *perpetrators of organized crime may include corrupt business executives, members of the professions, public officials, or any occupational group* [italics mine], in addition to the conventional racketeer element. (National Advisory Committee, 1976a, p. 213).

For the purposes of general prosecution and enforcement, most federal and state laws end up including under the definition of organized crime any group crime of a conspiratorial nature that includes types of criminal activity that we would more appropriately label as occupational, corporate, political, or even conventional crime (National Advisory Committee, 1976a, pp. 213–15).

Sources of Information on Organized Crime

> I remember when Joe was testifying before that Senate committee [McClellan] back in 1963. I was sitting in Raymond Patriarca's office [New England mob boss] . . . and we were watching Joe on television. I remember Raymond saying: "This bastard's crazy. Who the hell is he?" . . . "What the hell's the Cosa Nostra?" Henry asked [Tameleo, the underboss]. "Is he a soldier or a button man?" . . . "I'm a zipper." "I'm a flipper." . . . It was all a big joke to them. In New England we never used names like "soldiers" or "caporegimes" (Teresa, 1973a, pp. 24–25, 28).

The above account by Vincent Teresa, author with Thomas Renner of *My Life in the Mafia* (1973b), describes the reaction of a mob boss to the testimony of ex-Mafia member Joe Valachi before a Congressional committee. In *The Valachi Papers* (Maas, 1968) Valachi described the inner workings of something he called Cosa Nostra (literally, "this thing of ours"). Other such biographies and autobiographies, although of varying validity, provide rare inside glimpses of organized criminal operations. Pileggi's *Wiseguy* (1985), Pistone and Woodley's *Donnie Brasco: My Undercover Life in the Mafia* (1987), Bonanno's *A Man of Honor* (1983), and Mustain and Capeci's *Mob Star: The Story of John Gotti* (1988) serve as illustrations. Pileggi's *Wiseguy* (1985), the basis for the film *Goodfellas,* for example, details the life of Henry Hill, a career criminal who literally grew up in the mob. Hill gives an inside account of the Paul Vario organized crime family; the 1983 Lufthansa robbery at Kennedy Airport, which netted $5 million in cash; the Sindona scandal, which nearly collapsed the Vatican bank; and the Boston College basketball point-shaving scandal.

Lupsha (1982) indicates the following *sources of information on organized crime:* informers, hearings and investigations, court trial transcripts and grand jury depositions, news stories, investigative reporting, wire surveillance transcripts, memoirs/biographies, government reports and releases, law enforcement-assisted research, archives and historical documents, observation, and in-depth interviews. While any source may exhibit varying degrees of validity, far more triangulation (use of multiple methodologies in the same study) is required than has been apparent in past criminological research on organized crime (see also Bynum, 1987; Morash, 1984).

Types of Organized Crime (Generic Definitions)

Acknowledging the need for broader (or more generic) definitions of organized crime, like operational policy definitions employed by organizations such as the Federal Bureau of Investigation, Joseph Albini (1971), author of *The American Mafia: Genesis of a Legend,* offers the following:

> . . . any criminal activity involving two or more individuals, specialized or nonspecialized, encompassing some form of social structure, with some form of leadership, utilizing certain modes of operation, in which the ultimate purpose of the organization is found in the enterprises of the particular group (p. 37).

Albini then identifies **four basic types of organized crime:** political-social organized crime, mercenary (predatory) organized crime, in-group oriented organized crime, and syndicate crime (pp. 38–48).

1. *Political-Social Organized Crime:* This category best fits into the "political criminal" activity discussed earlier. These are simply guerilla and terrorist groups and various militant social movements that use violence, such as the Ku Klux Klan, the Molly Maguires, and the Palestinian Liberation Organization.

2. *Mercenary (Predatory) Organized Crime:* This category refers to crimes committed by groups for direct personal profit, crimes that prey on unwilling victims, such as juvenile and adult criminal gangs who engage in larceny, burglary, and robbery. The Mano Nera (Black Hand) is an example of the latter. These extortionist gangs (there was no one Black Hand) sent threatening notes to fellow Italian immigrants requesting money. The notes usually contained a sinister mark or sign of a black hand. Often erroneously identified as a forerunner of the Mafia, the Black Hand was more a method of crime than an organization. It provided no illicit services and could not assure immunity for its own operators through political corruption.
3. *In-Group Oriented Organized Crime:* These are groups, such as motorcycle gangs and some adolescent gangs, whose major goals are psychological gratification, "kicks," "rep," "highs," "bopping," and "trashing" rather than financial profit. Motorcycle gangs—the post-World War II prototype is Hell's Angels—have branched out since Hollywood portrayals such as Marlon Brando's in *The Wild One.* These gangs are sometimes used as "muscle" (enforcers) and for low-level jobs by larger syndicate groups (see Abadinsky, 1994, p. 282). The Pagans, begun in Prince Georges County, Maryland, in 1959, now have local chapters throughout the East Coast from Connecticut to Florida, with the heaviest membership in the Middle Atlantic states (Pennsylvania Crime Commission, 1980, p. 27). Such groups are involved in narcotics distribution, prostitution, extortion, bribery, contract murders, pornography distribution, and other activities. The Hell's Angels have also moved extensively into drug trafficking, allegedly controlling as much as 90 percent of the "speed" market in northern California ("Hell's Angels," 1979, p. 34). Hopper's (1991) field study of outlaw motorcycle gangs documented their transition from hedonistic hell-raisers to economic entrepreneurs. He also noted that females had lost status in such gangs and now play the dual roles of sex objects and money makers.

   Perhaps an apt concept to apply to such gangs is that of "semiorganized" crime, since they lack at least one of the key features of our definition of organized (syndicate) crime, to be discussed next.
4. *Syndicate Crime:* This is the category of organized crime that is the subject of this chapter and to which most writers refer when speaking of organized crime. Syndicate crime (henceforth a synonym for organized crime) may be defined as suggested by Albini (1971, pp. 47–48) as:

   a. a continuing group or *organization* that participates in illicit activity in any society by the *use of force, intimidation, or threats;*
   b. the structuring of a group or organization whose purpose is to provide *illicit services*—for which there is a strong public demand—through the use of secrecy on the part of associates;
   c. the assurance of *protection* and *immunity* necessary for its operation through political corruption or avoidance of prosecution.

In a content analysis of definitions of organized crime provided by various writers and government reports, this author (Hagan, 1983) discovered that many failed to provide any definition. The following characteristics were identified with some consensus: organized (continuing) hierarchy, rational profit through crime, use of force or threat of force, and corruption to obtain immunity. This content analysis supports a core criminological definition of organized crime that is basically consistent with Albini's (1971, p. 126) definition of syndicate crime. The *generic definition* of organized crime is not a definition of organized crime, but rather a definition of "group crime," that is, "crime committed by two or more people. . . ." Figure 13.1 summarizes the concept of "organized crime" from both a general (generic) definitional view and a more specialized (sociological/criminological) definitional view.

Organized crime is used in the most generic sense to refer to group crimes and includes many criminal behavior systems as well as "illicit enterprises" that might more appropriately

FIGURE 13.1 Generic and Specific Definitions of the Concept of Organized Crime

Organized Crime	
General Usage (Generic)	*Group Crime*
Specific Definition (Core Elements)	Violence + Illicit Demanded Services + Immunity Organized (Syndicate) Crime

be labeled professional, occupational, corporate, or even conventional criminal behavior. A more specific **criminological definition** would refer to groups that (1) utilize violence or threats of violence, (2) that provide illicit goods that are in public demand, and (3) that assure immunity for their operators through corruption and enforcement.

The Organized Crime Continuum

A continuum or ordinal model of organized crime has been suggested by others (Albini, 1971, pp. 37–38; Cressey, 1972; McIntosh, 1975, Smith, 1975, 1978, 1980). In a frequently cited "spectrum based theory of enterprises," Dwight Smith (1980) proposes that enterprises take place across a spectrum (or continuum) of possible behavior ranging from the legal to illegal, the saintly to the sinful, and that the separation of legitimate business from crime, distinguishing paragons from pariahs from pirates, is an arbitrary point on that range (Smith, 1980, p. 371).

What all of these models stress is the fact that organized criminal activity is not a simple category. Rather than viewing the concept as a matter of *kind*—i.e., is it or is it not?—it is far more useful to conceive of it as a matter of *degree*. That is, the concept "organized crime" is an "ideal type," an abstract generalization that perhaps does not exist in pure form but nevertheless represents a useful, heuristic device for purposes of analysis. Figure 13.2 outlines a continuum model of organized (syndicate) crime. Just as medicine may represent the prototype profession, the Cosa Nostra as an ideal type could similarly be a model to which to compare all other groups, but the status of which few groups can hope to attain or, in the case of the IAS, ever have attained (Hagan, 1983).

Many profit-oriented and/or violent criminal groups contain many features that may lead us to describe them as being examples of semiorganized crime. For example, organizations such as Hell's Angels or the Pagans operate on a fairly highly developed hierarchical structure that uses violence, supplies goods (particularly illicit narcotics) that are in high demand by select segments of the public, and has obtained immunity in outlying geographical areas not through corruption so much as through intimidation of local law enforcement. Thus Japanese Yakuza, Chinese Triad Societies, and other international criminal organizations to be discussed shortly can be theoretically, if not empirically, placed on the continuum—although application of the model may be limited in a non-Western context.

Types of Organized Crime (Criminological Definitions)

While a specific definition of organized crime stresses the three key dimensions of violence, provision of illicit services, and immunity, a variety of types of organized criminal groups or expressions are possible, including:

FIGURE 13.2 The Organized Crime Continuum

Nonorganized Crime	*Semiorganized Crime*	*Organized Crime*
e.g., Intrafamily assault	e.g., Some Motorcyle Gangs Narcotics Smuggling Rings	e.g., Syndicates "Cosa Nostra"
No	1. Highly Organized	Yes
Not Relevant	A. Hierarchy	Relevant
Absent	B. Restricted Membership	Present
Absent	C. Secrecy (Codes)	Present
No	2. Violence or Threats of	Yes
No	3. Provision of Illicit Goods in Public Demand	Yes
No	A. Profit-Oriented	Yes
	4. Immunity Through:	
Unconnected	A. Corruption	Connected
No	B. Enforcement	Yes

Source: An earlier version of this model appeared in: Frank E. Hagan, 1983, "The Organized Crime Continuum: A Further Specification of a New Conceptual Model," *Criminal Justice Review,* 8:52–57.

1. *Traditional Crime Syndicates:* These are comprehensive criminal organizations that definitely belong on the organized crime continuum shown in Figure 13.2. They are highly organized and characterized by hierarchy, restricted membership, secrecy, violence, provision of illicit goods, profit orientation, and the obtaining of immunity through corruption and enforcement. Yakuza, Triads, IAS (Mafia or Cosa Nostra), Camorra, Unione Corse, and other such groups serve as examples.
2. *Nontraditional Syndicates:* These are less comprehensive criminal groups that exhibit less development on the organized crime continuum. Large-scale narcotics smuggling organizations, white collar fraud groups, the so-called "Dixie Mafia" (Hunter, 1983), independent crime czars who control local vice operations, and rural organized crime networks (Potter and Gaines, 1992) are examples. Many black, Hispanic, Jamaican, Vietnamese, and other ethnic-based gangs are also examples.
3. *Semiorganized Crime Syndicates:* These groups are generally smaller and less sophisticated and exhibit a narrower range of criminal goals. Examples are some motorcycle gangs such as the Pagans and Hell's Angels, as well as organized burglary and robbery rings.
4. *Local, Politically-Controlled, Organized Crime Groups:* These are locally controlled organized criminal groups in which the local political and power structure is not simply corrupted or allied, but is an actual partner in running criminal operations; this type has been suggested by Chambliss in his study of Seattle. As previously mentioned, Block and Chambliss (1981, pp. 112–13) claim that in virtually every U.S. city, those running criminal organizations are members of business, political, or law enforcement communities and not simply "on the pad" (being paid off).
5. *National, Politically-Controlled, Organized Crime Syndicates:* In this type, organized crime operates in partnership with elements of the national power structure; national authorities actually participate in the planning and execution of criminal activities. Block and Chambliss (1981, pp. 21–25) indicate that the nineteenth-century Asian opium trade, controlled and managed by European capitalist countries, formed the capital for industrial development. France, and later the United States, in Indochina encouraged tribes to grow narcotics and traffic in them to support their resistance against communism (McCoy, 1972). Block and Chambliss (1981, pp. 153–57) claim that Swedish millionaires are the principal financiers

and organizers of illegal businesses in Sweden, with a crime cartel consisting of political figures, law enforcement officials, and drug traffickers.

Street Gangs

Goldstein (1991, pp. 30–32) indicates that the delinquent gang of yesteryear was primarily involved in acts of theft, burglary, and vandalism, with gang fighting ("gang banging") rare. The 1950s were the era of the rumble, although such skirmishes were exaggerated by the media and by the gangs themselves. Klein and Maxson (1989, p. 218) note, "In the 1950s and 1960s, gang members talked much about their fighting episodes, but [homicide] data from several projects revealed their bark to be worse than their bite." Beginning in the 1970s and continuing into the 1990s, gang violence in the United States became worse, reflecting developments on the national scene. The environmental enhancers of this violence are drugs, guns, and territory, although the latter now involves defense of selling (economic) territory and not so much physical turf (Goldstein, 1991, p. 32).

Malcolm Klein (1990) identifies four myths regarding street gangs:

1. They are highly organized, very cohesive, and have centralized leadership.
2. Street gangs are all violent.
3. Street gangs control drug distribution in our cities.
4. Los Angeles gangs franchise drug distribution to the rest of the country.

Klein and associates claim that crack distribution, for example, while involving many individual gang members, was not an organized street gang phenomenon in Los Angeles (Klein, Maxson, and Cunningham, 1991). A contrary view is suggested by Taylor (1990), who on the basis of field research in Detroit indicates that the gangs he studied transformed themselves from street punks to drug-dealing entrepreneurs worth millions (see Short, 1990, for a review of recent gang research). Sanchez-Jankowski (1991) in a ten-year participant-observation study of thirty-seven different gangs in New York, Boston, and Los Angeles was struck by the "defiant individualist character" of many gang members, as well as by their "entrepreneurial spirit." He was stabbed and shot during his research.

A gang phenomenon that emerged in the 1980s, stoner gangs are a category that the California Youth Authority describes as "generally Caucasian-based youth gangs which affiliate with Heavy Metal and punk identities and which include youth involved with satanic cults as well" (Wooden, 1989, p. 2). The term *stoner* is derived from the 1960s–1970s drug-related term *being stoned.* Some stoner groups, such as skinheads, have affiliated themselves with established racist hate groups, such as the KKK and White Aryan Resistance. Wooden's preliminary findings based on fifty-two cases conclude that racist skinheads were considered bullies in grammar school, were abused as children, and favored violence in the lyrics of their music, while teenage satanists were products of strict religious upbringing. Gang activity, particularly of a drug-related variety, will be further detailed in Chapter 12 (see Stafford, 1984; Vigil, 1988).

It is estimated that one of every ten federal prisoners is in a gang. These gangs break down on the basis of ethnic/racial ties, such as the Mexican Mafia, the Aryan Brotherhood, or the Mau Mau.

Some more organized street gangs lie somewhat near the middle of the organized crime continuum, although perhaps they are not as highly developed as some motorcycle gangs. In the 1980s many tough American street gangs were rapidly converting themselves to ghetto-based drug trafficking organizations, primarily because of the flood of low-cost cocaine (and crack or rock cocaine) from Colombia. At the onset of the nineties many of these groups were about at the same place as Italian-American groups were in the early

1920s during Prohibition (Morganthau et al., 1988, p. 22). Bloods, Crips (Los Angeles); Montego Bay, Shower, Spangler (Jamaican); Untouchables, 34th Street Players (Miami); or Cobras, Disciples, El Rukns, Latin Kings, and Vice Lords (Chicago) are often big, violent, and increasingly wealthy. In southern California the majority of street gangs are black or Latino, with Anglos normally joining motorcycle gangs. One such group, the POBOBs ("Pissed Off Bastards of Bloomington"), emerged to become the Hell's Angels, perhaps the largest and most notorious outlaw biker gang (Davis, 1982, p. 42).

Big Hawk 1987 BSVG c 187

The above illustration of gang graffiti is not a marking of gang turf—not for bragging rights, but for sales territory—and a threat to rivals. The translation is Big Hawk (a member's street name), 1987 (the year), a member of Blood Stone Villain's Gang (BSVG), which is a Bloods set (subgroup of the Bloods' gang). The lower case c, which is usually X'd out, means that Big Hawk kills Crips, and the number 187 is the section of the California criminal code for murder (Morganthau et al., 1988, p. 23).

For many gang members, self-employment in the underground drug economy provides short-term upward mobility, autonomy, a measure of dignity or self-esteem, and an opportunity to avoid low-level employment under the direction of what is perceived as hostile, outside ethnic or racial groups (Bourgois, 1988, p. 12). Street gangs, despite their penchant for what might appear to be senseless violence, sometimes represent the minor leagues or incubators for future organized criminals and syndicates.

Sanders (1994) notes that there are differences in levels of commitment of gang members (hardcore, affiliate, and fringe). Hagedorn (1994) notes that, despite high average earnings from drug sales, most gang members would prefer full-time jobs with modest wages and most move in and out of conventional labor markets. He described four types of gang members: legits, homeboys, dope fiends, and new jacks. "Legits" are those who mature out of the gang, while "homeboys" were a majority of African-American and Latino adult gang members who alternate between legitimate jobs and drug sales. While "dope fiends" stayed in the drug business in order to feed their habits, "new jacks" view illegal drug sales as their career (Hagedorn, 1994, p. 206).

International Organized Crime

Internationally, organized crime is not confined to any single political area and thrives especially in political climates such as liberal democracies and corrupt dictatorships. Because laws of liberal democracies such as the United States, Canada, post-World War II Japan, and other Western European and former British Commonwealth countries place a priority on individual civil liberties, crime control can suffer; such laws make it difficult to crack down on organized criminals and their political allies. Such nations also emphasize private enterprise, which is not restricted to the legal end of the continuum.

Robert Kelly in *Organized Crime: A Global Perspective* (1986) provides examples of organized criminal underworlds in Canada, Great Britain, the Caribbean, Italy, Poland, Israel, Africa, Japan, and Australia. "The use of street gangs by political machines in the U.S., the use of Triads by Chiang Kai Shek and the Kuomintang, the use of Corsican organized crime groups by the French government in Marseilles, and the use of Yakuza in Japan" (Lupscha 1987, p. 8) illustrate the hidden support of organized crime by governmental groups (McCoy, 1985).

Yakuza

Yakuza, the Japanese term for gangsters (literally "good-for-nothings") are organized crime syndicates of roughly 90,000 members. Also referred to as "Boryokudan" (violent ones), the power of these gangs—the most powerful is the Yamaguchigumi—can be illustrated by a recent stockmarket scandal in Japan in which top firms, such as Nomura and Nikko Securities, allowed affiliates to finance the activities of Yakuza (Kaplan, 1991). Susumi Ishii, the head of the Inagawakai syndicate, received 25 billion yen ($180 million) from these firms. One of Ishii's financial advisers in the United States was a company that employed Prescott Bush, the then-president's brother. While Prescott Bush may not have known with whom he was dealing, the Japanese security firms were aware (Kaplan, 1991).

Organized crime figures in Japan have a curious appearance: crew cuts, elaborate tattoos, and missing little fingers; they often work as "bouncers" or security guards at corporate conventions, a strategic role that enables them to gather information with which to blackmail corporate officials ("Japan," 1977, p. 40; Rome, 1975).

Representing a traditional part of Japanese society, the Yakuza were originally recruited by right-wing business leaders after World War II to intimidate left-wing opponents. In the eighties growing concern was expressed regarding Yakuza expansion into the United States (ABC, 1982). Such groups reportedly owned $100 million in Honolulu real estate, where their restaurants, clubs, and pornography shops catered to Japanese tourists. Active also in California, the groups were involved in smuggling drugs to the United States and guns to Japan as well as recruiting U.S. female "entertainers" as prostitutes in Japan.

Membership in Yakuza groups is claimed to be twenty times larger than membership in the American Mafia. There is considerable acceptance and toleration of such groups by both the public and political powers (Kaplan and Dubro, 1986). They serve a useful function for the right wing in intimidating dissenters, the free press, and free speech (CBS, 1989a). Yakuza are widely involved in sexual slavery. Thousands of mainly poor Third World women and children are forced into prostitution near military bases, to participate in the production of pornography, and to enter mail-order marriages (Kaplan and Dubro, 1986, p. 201).

One third of the members are Korean and most are from lower class backgrounds (CBS, 1988). Kaplan (1991, p. 2) explains:

> Yakuza gangs occupy a place in Japanese society hard to imagine in the West. Members sport business cards and lapel pins openly identifying their underworld affiliation. Offices proudly display the gang name and insignia, much as if one found the words "Gambino Family, Manhattan Branch" emblazoned on the door of a Mafia concern.

The success of the Japanese police in fighting Yakuza gangs is noted by Johnson (1990), who reports that their share of the prison population increased from 21 percent in 1975 to 30 percent in 1986. In the early nineties, Yakuza groups had expanded their involvement in coercive resolution of civil disputes stemming from the collection of debts, loan negotiations, bankruptcies, real estate transactions, and other matters (Johnson, 1990). In 1996 Japanese Prime Minister Ryutara Hashimoto's attempt to bail out leading banking and real estate finance companies met opposition in Parliament due to charges that many of the recipients of the bad loans were companies fronting for organized crime, and some of them had close ties to Hashimoto's party. Bankers fear seizing any real estate linked to the Yakuza for fear of being killed or beaten (WuDunn, 1996).

In 2000 shares in Yakult Honsha, a Japanese yogurt producer, fell drastically when it was revealed that for twenty years they paid gangsters to suppress criticism at shareholder meetings. The Yakuza's negative influence on the Japanese economy has been blamed to be one of the reasons for its recent decline. Japan is estimated to have spent over $3.5 trillion on public works between 1991 and 1999, and a large portion of this was wasted on useless and overpriced projects. The country's construction sector is rife with corruption, waste and Yakuza. The latter serve as protection racketeers, dispute resolvers, hiring-hall foremen, and lobbyists (Fulford, 1999). The weak economy and police crackdowns are reportedly costing Yakuza shrinking membership.

Chinese Triad Societies

Triads are secret Chinese organizations. Referred to as "black societies" by the Chinese, the British called them Triads because of their highly ritualistic use of numerology, a belief in the magical significance of numbers. The number three and multiples of three were accorded major importance by these groups. The symbol of Triad societies is an equilateral triangle with the three sides representing the three basic Chinese concepts of heaven, earth, and the human being.

Although they are of much more ancient origin and are even more cabalistic, the legends, rituals (such as initiation rites), and early history of Triads bear an uncanny resemblance to the Mafia legend in Sicily (Bresler, 1980; Morgan, 1960). The earliest Triad secret societies were founded in China two thousand years ago to oppose warlords (Robertson, 1977; Daraul, 1969). The modern Triads are traced to the latter part of the seventeenth century, when members appeared as resistance fighters against the Manchu dynasty, the "barbarian" invaders who defeated the Ming dynasty. Legend dates the founding of the first modern Triad to 128 Buddhist monks at a monastery near Foochow, Fukien province, in 1674. They were well trained in Asian martial arts, including a type they had perfected themselves—kung fu (Bresler, 1980, p. 28; Chin, 1988, p. 7). A Triad called the Fists of Harmony and Justice led the Boxer Rebellion against the European powers.

Although originating as brotherhoods for freedom (Lyman, 1974), Triads also had elements of banditry and were heavily involved in the control of vice activities. All of the Triad groups shared in common highly ritualized initiation ceremonies, blood oaths, passwords, secret signals, and hierarchical positions. Some positions in a Triad society are described by Bresler (1980, p. 28) in his *Chinese Mafia:*

489. "Shan Chu" (hill chief or head)
438. "Heung Chu" (incense master in charge of ceremonies)

Each cell (branch) had three lower-level offices:

415. the "white paper fan" (financial advisor)
426. the "red pole" (kung fu expert)
432. the "straw sandal" (messenger/liaison with other groups)
49. the ordinary member

The number "4" in all of the titles reflects the ancient Chinese belief that the world was surrounded by four seas.

> 489 and 438 are said to have been selected because the Chinese characters for 21 (the sum of 4 + 8 + 9) and for 3 and 8, when written together, form the Chinese characters for Hung, the early Ming Emperor in whose name the whole Triad organization began in the first place. 426 is constructed as 4 × 15 + 4, which equals 64. This refers to the 64 diagrams of Chinese script invented by a legendary Emperor named Fu Teh. . . . 432 becomes 4 × 32 + 4, giving us 132, which is the actual number of persons (128 monks and 4 others) supposed to have been living in the original Triad monastery near Foochow. Finally, 49 derives from 4 × 9, which equals 36. This refers to the number of oaths sworn by all new Triad members (Bresler, 1980).

Triads utilize a traditional initiation ceremony called the Hung Mun ritual, which includes the taking of thirty-six oaths, one of which says, "If I should change my mind and deny my membership of the Hung family, I will be killed by a myriad of swords" ("Hong Kong," 1986, p. 5). Triads are sometimes referred to as the Hung, named after the Ming emperor's grandson, Chiu Hung-chu (Chin, 1988, p. 8).

Chin (1988, 1990) claims that many myths, similar to early ones of an omnipotent Italian Mafia, have been created regarding Triads, and that Chinese small business owners, not Triads, are responsible for most of the drug trafficking, money laundering, and other criminal activities in U.S. Chinatowns. Care must be taken not to label all Chinese groups as Triads. For instance, one Taiwan-based crime group "the United Bamboo" clearly is not a Triad organization. Chin (1988, p. 11) tells us:

> Criminal groups in Taiwan . . . have no structural or spiritual resemblance to the Hung societies. Besides the Hung societies and the Ching societies, another major group of secret societies . . . exist[s] in Taiwan, the two societies have not been involved in the local crime scene. Since Taiwan was the colony of Japan . . . crime groups there follow the pattern of Japanese Yakuza.

With the fall of mainland China to the Communists in 1949, many Triads migrated to Hong Kong. The largest of such groups are the Green Pang (Green Gang), the Chui Chaos (Chiu Chau), and the 14K. Although the Green Pang originally controlled heroin distribution in the colony, they rely on the Chui Chaos for supplies of Thai morphine and opium (McCoy, 1972, p. 229). The Chui Chaos have important connections and even members within the Hong Kong police and control much of the drug traffic from the "Golden Triangle" (Northern Burma, Laos, and Thailand) and throughout Southeast Asia.

Triad groups are non-hierarchical and informal. Each faction is run by an independent boss and is autonomous for planning and executing criminal enterprises. They range from street gangs to sophisticated crime syndicates (Lindberg, et al., 1977).

Tongs were Chinese-American fraternal and benevolent organizations, the term meaning "town hall" or "large hall." Some of the important Tongs in the United States in the nineteenth century were Bing Kung, Hip Sing, Ying On Ton Su, and Hop Sing. Many of these fraternal organizations rely upon young street gangs to enforce their vice activities. New Tong organizations, formed in the post-World War II period, were more ferocious criminal bands made up of many felons who had fled Hong Kong and the Far East. The Flying Dragons, Ghost Shadows, Gray Shadows, and Black Ghost Shadows were some of these groups. In February 1996 federal law enforcement, after a one-year sting operation, charged leaders of several Chinese-American tongs with drug trafficking and money laundering. Indicted were members and leaders of Hip Sing Tong, the Hung Mung Association, the San Gian Tong, and the Fujien Fellowship Association. In 1994 the Tun On Association in Manhattan was found to be used by a gang for protection of its gambling operations, which later led to expanded operations resulting in ten murders. A New York Chinatown observer explains to a reporter for *The New Yorker* (Kinkead, 1991, pp. 65–66):

> Chinese invented the Mafia, and then Marco Polo took it to Italy and the Italians reinvented it. The tongs are the families—everyone knows who's a member. You don't want to cross them. Each has about fifty prominent members. Real bosses, about ten each. They post elected officers. If you're a Chan or an Eng, it's quite possible you belong to one of them. Chans or Chens are On Leong; Engs or Ongs are Hip Sing. The tongs run the gangs and the gambling houses, and they settle disputes in the old-fashioned way: you give me face, I'll give you face; if you don't listen to me, I'll break your face. Uncle 7 [Benny Eng, head of Hip sing] is the elder statesman of the underworld, but his power has been eroding for some time. . . . Also, there are the Vietnamese gangs—the tongs have no control over them.

While some observers claim that Tongs, like chop suey, were strictly an American invention, organized in the gold fields of California about 1860 (Nash, 1981, p. 337), others see them as branches of Triad societies, mainly the Chee Kung Tong, which generated many feuding rival branches (Bresler, 1980, p. 30). Since the late sixties members of Triads have emigrated and set up operations in the United States, Canada, and Europe, most notably in the Netherlands and in older established Chinatowns of San Francisco, Vancouver, and Amsterdam (Wilson, 1978).

Taking advantage of laws aimed at attracting entrepreneurial migrants, Triads have set up shop in Australia (Pincomb and Everett, 1991). In 1992 California investigators charged that many of the state's card casinos (poker clubs) were becoming fronts for "Asian Mafia groups" (Emshwiller, 1992) and that gangs such as Wo Hop To and Wah Ching were using the clubs for criminal purposes. These include money laundering, loan sharking, extortion, and the recruitment of drug couriers. Other Triads active in California currently are the Luen Kung Lok, the San Yee On, and the 14K (Poland, 1990, p. 22). The Wah Ching (Youth of China) is the most firmly entrenched Asian criminal group in the United States.

While many modern Triads are respected community organizations, others have developed criminal subgroups. Robertson (1977) claims that particularly in Western Europe nearly all Triads are engaged in prostitution, illegal gambling, extortion, and heroin trafficking. They are the major wholesale distributors and processors of opium from the Golden Triangle. "The China White Trail" is a term used by the DEA to describe the transportation of heroin from Thailand through the secret societies of Hong Kong and finally the Chinese neighborhoods of New York City (Kerr, 1987). In 1989 the FBI seized 828 pounds of heroin valued at $1 billion (the 1971 French Connection was about 220 pounds). This New York City bust was attributed to the China White Trail. Much more official attention has been paid by U.S. government officials recently than in the past to the issue of Asian organized crime. The President's Commission on Organized Crime (1984a) issued a report on Asian organized crime, as did the Department of Justice in 1988 (Baridon, 1988), as did the Hong Kong Security Forces (Fight Crime Committee, 1986; see also FBI, 1985b).

With the return of Hong Kong by the British in 1997 to the Peoples Republic of China (PRC), most had predicted that the Hong Kong Triads would migrate to the West to escape stricter law enforcement. To the contrary, preliminary signs indicate that at least some Triad groups are thriving and have even extended their operations to areas such as Huizhou, the so-called Palermo of China, where cold cash speaks louder than ideology (Viviano, 1997). Stolen cars from Hong Kong are pervasive courtesy of the 56,000 member Sun Yee On (New Discipline and Peace) Triad that also deals in narcotics, money laundering, gambling, and prostitution.

Russian Organized Crime

The most publicized of organized crime groups in the 1990s were Russian groups. Some 12 to 15 major "mafiya" groups exist, each with a federation of hundreds of smaller groups. The two largest gangs are the Moscow-based Solntsevo, which includes the U.S.-based group Organizatsiya, and the St. Petersburg group, Tambov, which is less active in the U.S. Their prime activities include health care fraud, drug and alien smuggling, prostitution, and financial fraud (Krane, 1999). With the fall of the former Soviet Union, such groups have, in some areas of Russia and the former Soviet republics, challenged the government itself as a source of power. Hundreds of gangs use extortion, fraud, and murder to operate illegal as well as legal businesses. In 1995 they controlled about 400 banks, which explains in part why Moscow, with its exploding crime rate, has few bank robberies (Hockstader, 1995, p. 6). Such groups are well armed and ruthless.

At the top of such gangs are men such as Vyacheslaw Ivankov, a *vory v zakone* ("thieves professing the code" or "thief-in-law"). The Vory had an oath of their own under the Soviet system, which shunned accepted society and defied authority. The *vory v zakone* are not members of the same gang, but an honored category of criminals empowered to resolve gang disputes. Predating the Russian revolution, this group's members were recruited in prison and branded with a tattoo of an eagle, usually on their hands (Raab, 1994). Many gangs, under increasing pressure in Russia, have migrated to Western Europe, particularly Germany, and the United States (Raab, 1994). Russian gangs have set up operations in the United

States, particularly in "Little Odessa," the Brighton Beach section of Brooklyn, where they have formed cooperative alliances with traditional mafia groups. On July 9, 1996, head of the Odessa Mafiya, Ivankov, and three co-defendants were convicted of extorting $3.5 million from owners of an investment company. They also kidnapped and then killed the father of one owner in Moscow. Ivankov's arrest was considered the outcome of growing cooperation between the FBI and Russian police to fight such groups (Kenney and Finckenauer, 1995).

In the United States, Russian groups have been involved in a large jewelry heist, as well as in insurance and Medicare fraud, heroin importation, and control of gasoline distribution in New York City. In the latter alone they evaded over $5 billion a year in taxes (Anderson, 1995, p. 43). According to one source, city police from the 60th and 61st precincts moonlight for them as bagmen, muscle, and chauffeurs; and they even participate in fake accident scams (Friedman, 1994).

Of particular concern is the fear that, among the many smuggling operations of Russian organized crime, may be nuclear weapons and materials (Hersh, 1994). Many, however, feel that these groups have other more lucrative operations that negate interest in such activities. Rosner (1995, p. 32) warns us to beware not to create an overglamorized image of the Russian mafiya in the United States:

> Lastly, the sexy Russian Mafia provides journalists and their readers with a relatively unthreatening, European model of crime—a revisited Marlon Brando world of *consiglieri, caporegima,* and soldiers. At least that is the model which is appealingly seductive, although quite inaccurate.

The Russian mafiya is a generic term for a type of criminal (black marketeer, gangster, drug trafficker, and corrupter) who arose out of social, economic, and historical forces in Russia. When all goods were owned by the state, stealing them became a necessity of life, the "Soviet way of crime" (Albini et al., 1995). Such groups often collaborated with state bureaucrats (*nomenklatura*) in what might be called the "gangster industrial complex" (Shelley, 1995). Privatization after the fall of Communism made Russia what President Boris Yeltsin calls a "superpower of crime." The Soviet Union itself resembled a criminal racket, and thoroughly corrupt officials were ill prepared for privatization (Kelly, Schatzberg, and Ryan, 1995).

There have been rising concerns over reports that Russian mobs are recruiting former KGB and former Soviet Special Forces soldiers as members. About half of the 550 Russian banks are believed to be controlled by organized crime groups. Many of the groups identified as "Russian" may include others from the former Soviet Union including Armenians, Georgians, Chechens, Ukrainians, and Lithuanians. In addition there are groups from former Eastern European satellite countries such as Slovaks, Hungarians, Poles, and Albanians. While it is easy to blame endemic corruption in Russian society for the pervasive organized crime, one must be careful not to replace the image of Russia as "the evil empire" with one of Russian gangsters. Wedel (1999) points out that in some instances U.S. policy and institutions have often been complicitous either wittingly or unwittingly in the corruption. Since 1997 the Harvard Institute for International Development has been granted a contract to assist in economic reforms in Russia. The U.S. Justice Department has been investigating the misuse of these development funds in which the privatization of Russian assets have been selectively awarded to insiders through corruption. Members of the Harvard team were criticized by the General Accounting Office for profiting from inside knowledge in these deals. During this time billions of dollars were being looted from the Russian economy and laundered through U.S. banks such as the Bank of New York (Wedel, 1999).

In 1998 it was revealed that Amy Elliott, a Citibank employee, helped Raúl Salinas, brother of the former president of Mexico, move $100 million into offshore, untraceable accounts through dummy corporations in the Cayman Islands. In the Bank of New York

(© Heriberto Rodriguez / Reuters)

Pall bearers carry the coffin of Amado Carrillo Fuentes at his funeral on July 11, 1997 at a ranch in northwestern Mexico.

(©Reuters)

Mexican military secure a large cache of cocaine for incineration in Matamoros, Mexico, in April 1977. The amount, totaling over 10 tons, was found inside a tanker truck.

scandal, some $4.2 billion was laundered in over 10,000 separate transactions. The money belonged to Semyon Yukovich Mogilevich, a top Russian boss ("Russian Mob," 1999).

Countries with corrupt dictatorships, particularly Caribbean vacation spots, became convenient gambling resort areas, especially when organized crime figures such as Meyer Lansky simply "cut in" the authorities, such as Batista in Cuba or Bahamian officials, in return for unencumbered operations.

IN THE NEWS 13.1 describes the rise and fall of Amado Carillo Fuentes, who until his death was the most powerful leader of organized crime/drug traffickers in Mexico. It also examines "Operation Casablanca," the largest sting operation in U.S. history directed at Mexican drug trafficking and money laundering.

In his *Criminal Brotherhoods,* Chandler (1976) claims that Western organized criminal groups had their beginnings with the Garduna in fifteenth-century Spain. Others, such as the Italian Camorra, the Mafia, the French or Corsican Unione Corse, and the American Cosa Nostra, at least initially, were secretive, ritualistic, and feudal in structure. The existence of

IN THE NEWS 13.1

AMADO CARILLO FUENTES AND OPERATION CASABLANCA

Amado Carillo Fuentes, who died under mysterious circumstances in July 1997, was the leader of the Juarez plaza (criminal organization), the most powerful drug trafficking-organized crime group in Mexico. In a given year his organization was believed to earn $10 billion dollars. Pem Ex, the Mexican government-owned oil company and the largest corporation in Mexico, earns $7–8 billion a year. Earnings from cocaine sales alone for all Mexican crime groups are estimated at $30–32 billion. The story is told that Carillo was considering closing down his Mexican operations in 1997, and there was fear that the country's economy would collapse.

Carillo began his apprenticeship in crime growing up in Mexico's drug-growing province of Sinaloa, working for his drug trafficking uncle. He was later a member of the Mexican secret police (DFS) for five years (Poppa, 1998). His uncle was believed to have been involved in the murder of U.S. DEA agent Enrique Camarena. The Mexican federal police were also involved. Both the Mexican army and secret police were partners with Mexican drug traffickers. Carillo would later work with Pablo Acosta, one of the top narcotrafficantes on the U.S. border. When Acosta was killed, Carillo took over his "plaza" (criminal organization). He formed relationships with the Colombian Medellin cartel that was hunting for new trafficking routes as a result of the success of crackdowns in Florida. Later, Carillo decided to skip the Colombians and began wholesaling cocaine directly from Peru and Bolivia. It was he who consolidated the other cartels and acted as the supplier.

Carillo had grown to become a legend and, without exaggeration, the single most powerful individual in Mexico. He was a hero to his home province, Sinaloa, where he built a church and assisted local charities (Bowden, 1998). His organization had encryption devices, pagers for border crossings, and spies. License plates of cars entering the DEA's El Paso Intelligence Center were recorded by his agents, and the owners' phones were tapped. The DEA moved their operations to Fort Bliss.

Carillo was not immortal, however. In July 1977 he visited doctors for plastic surgery. A nine-hour operation involving liposuction and a facelift resulted in his death due to an injection. While it was never confirmed, it was believed to be an assassination. Four months later the bodies of the surgeons involved were discovered. They had been

the Unione Corse, now headquartered in Marseilles, while rumored for years, was not accepted by the French government until the mid-sixties. It is primarily involved in narcotics, with contacts with French populations in Europe, the Middle East, Africa, Indochina, and Quebec. Organized crime in Africa is described by Opolot (1979) as involving business persons or well-placed public officials, "shady" business persons connected to criminal operations, and organizations of criminal operators involved in highway robbery, illegal immigration, smuggling, drugs, and poaching. There is, however, little evidence of tribal successions or ringleaders in African organized crime. The international operations and cooperation of these groups have made them increasingly transnational criminal enterprises involved in a variety of activities including: arms trafficking, nuclear material trafficking, automobile theft and smuggling, alien smuggling, trafficking in women and children, trafficking in body parts, and money laundering (Williams, 1995).

VANTAGE POINT 13.1 reports on the ASC Task Force on International Organized Crime.

The Nature of Organized Crime

Given our general definition of organized crime, such groups have existed in varying degrees since, or even before, the advent of modern nation states. Large, diversified syndicate crime, with control on an extraregional basis over more than a few illegal activities,

IN THE NEWS 13.1—*Continued*

brutally tortured in an attempt to discover how he had died. In the two years after his death a power vacuum existed in Juarez. Over 1,000 drug-related murders had occurred, and the believed successor was his younger brother, Vincente Carillo Fuentes. Despite the payoffs of high government officials, the police, and the military, Mexican cartels have the same problem as other illegal enterprises—how to launder the money.

Operation Casablanca

The most comprehensive undercover sting operation and criminal investigation in U.S. history was the Customs Bureau's "Operation Casablanca." This was a money laundering sting operation on the Mexican drug cartels. Posing as a U.S. financial organization, U.S. agents met with financial advisors of the Mexican drug cartels and top bankers to set up money laundering operations that they secretly videotaped. The Mexican bankers shared some of their techniques and the names of overseas and American cooperating banks.

The money laundering operation involved smuggling drug money from the U.S. and depositing it in Mexican banks. These banks issued bank drafts in U.S. dollars, which were drawn on the bank's deposits in U.S. banks. The drafts were transported to the U.S. in armored cars and deposited in cooperating U.S. banks, thus making the now "clean" funds available to be withdrawn and used for purchasing legitimate businesses. The operation ended with over 130 arrests and $100 million seized (PBS, 1999). Further investigation revealed as much as $1.5 billion in U.S. bank accounts of the Defense Secretary and "Drug Czar" of Mexico and other high officials, including the then President of Mexico. The complicity of such high officials and U.S. banks was not pursued.

The extent of the total corruption of the system can be illustrated by the fact that the Mexican "Drug Czar" lived in an apartment paid for by Carillo. This same person met with U.S. Drug Czar Barry McCaffrey to share intelligence, after which many U.S. informants in Mexico were found murdered. Despite all of the high level complicity in drug trafficking, Congress has not seen fit to decertify (decide not to share intelligence and cooperation) with Mexico.

Source: Charles Bowden. 1998. *Juarez: The Laboratory of Our Future.* New York: Aperture Foundation; Terrence Poppa. 1998. *Drug Lord: A True Story,* 2nd edition. New York: Demand Publications; PBS. 1999. "Lords of the Mafia: Mexico," (telecast); U.S. Treasury Department. 1998. "Operation Casablanca Continues Its Sweep." *Office of Public Affairs.* May 20. (www.fas.org/irp/news/1998/05/pr2467.htm).

InfoTrac College Edition Research

Do a search on drug trafficking and Mexico. What recent trends have taken place with respect to such activity in that country? What has been the response of the United States to such developments?

is primarily a phenomenon of the post-World War I period. While the focus in discussing organized crime is generally on the prototype, what has been called the "Cosa Nostra," the nature and structure of organized criminal groups are determined by the type of criminal activity they are engaged in as well as by ethnic, subcultural, and cultural values. Criminal gangs, mobs, racketeers, and organized (predatory) criminals share to a lesser degree many of the characteristics of larger syndicates.

Ethnicity and Organized Crime

Some believe that organized crime began in the United States as an import, along with mass immigration of Sicilians and Italians in the late nineteenth and early twentieth centuries. Figure 13.3 shows a random list of organized crime figures, none of whom are Italian or Sicilian. Organized crime is not simply a "Mafia transplant" or "alien conspiracy" in the United States; it obviously existed before significant Italian immigration, and it probably will exist long after Italian Americans move out of major involvement in organized crime.

Ianni (1973) proposes an ethnic succession theory of organized crime in which organized crime acts as a "queer ladder of mobility" (Bell, 1967, p. 115), an alternative means of upward mobility for ethnic minorities who, because of discrimination or lack of skills, are temporarily lodged at the bottom of the system of reward distribution in a society. Thus, while the last

VANTAGE POINT 13.1

International Organized Crime

Issues

The federal government has particular and singular responsibilities with regard to the transnational and international dimensions of organized crime (e.g., international drug trafficking, arms dealing, and murder for hire), which are unique in nature and scope. There is increasing evidence that the wealth and power of criminal organizations in various countries are growing and that international links among these organizations exist. A number of factors associated with this globalization of organized crime have implications for the United States.

A state of ungovernability, instability, and fragmentation in certain countries provides favorable conditions for the development and nurturance of organized criminal groups. This is especially true in the countries that were part of the former Soviet Union, but it also applies to Eastern Europe and countries such as Peru, Burma, Mexico, and Pakistan. These countries provide both operational bases and safe havens for international criminals.

Of continuing special concern is the problem of organized crime operating in and from the former U.S.S.R. The so-called "Russian mafia" are operating in Germany, Poland, and virtually every other state in Eastern and Central Europe. There is also a growing problem of organized criminal networks among Soviet emigrés in the United States. In the successor states of the U.S.S.R. (especially Russia), organized crime is undermining efforts to create the rule of law, as well as attacking various fledgling democratic institutions. Internationally, Russian organized crime's illegal trade in high-tech weaponry, potentially including nuclear weapons, constitutes a considerable threat.

An increasingly sophisticated use of advanced communications technology facilitates the wire transfers of money for laundering on a much greater scale than ever before. The threat to the integrity of international banking is considerable.

Coupled with the amplified scope and magnitude of international organized crime is an inadequate law enforcement response (due to the absence of international cooperation and policy), limited exchange of intelligence and mutual legal assistance, functional and bureaucratic fragmentation among the various criminal justice agencies, a dearth of specialized personnel, competition and turf battles among responsible agencies, and failure to coordinate or harmonize national and international laws.

Policy recommendations

- **Russian racketeering:** The United States should take the lead in helping Russian officials to draft effective

fifty years in the United States have witnessed the period of Sicilian-Italian domination of syndicate crime, this was preceded by Jewish (sometimes facetiously referred to as the "Kosher Nostra") and Irish domination. Prior to these groups, WASPs (White Anglo-Saxon Protestants) controlled organized crime. During these periods, many other ethnic groups—for example, Germans, Lebanese, Greeks, blacks—also participated in organized crime. At the present time, with its ethnic base largely middle class, the Italian-American Mafia might be described as in its eleventh hour, as black, Latino, Asian, and Russian groups move into positions of power in organized criminal activity with their base of operations in low-income ethnic ghettoes, long the wellspring of illegitimate careers (see Kleinknecht, 1995).

Organized crime in the 1990s was in rapid transition, and much of our image of a dominant Mafia underworld was beginning to resemble an old black-and-white gangster movie starring Edward G. Robinson or James Cagney. Former attorney general William French Smith in remarks before the President's Commission on Organized Crime (1983, pp. 124–25) indicated:

> Even as federal law enforcement agencies have worked hard to catch up on the traditional crime families found in our major cities, new forms of organized crime have emerged throughout the nation. In just the past few years, new groups have organized in pursuit of the lucrative profits that can be made in drug traf-

VANTAGE POINT 13.1—*Continued*

anti-racketeering legislation (not necessarily duplicating the RICO statute) that is appropriate to and mindful of Russia's special circumstances and legal traditions.

- **Aid tied to reforms:** American and other Western aid to Russia should be specifically targeted to combating organized crime. Steps to be taken in this effort must include: reforming the Russian judicial system; equipping law enforcement agencies with vehicles, computers, and other communications equipment; and training and providing technical assistance to law enforcement personnel in organized crime investigative techniques. Consideration should also be given to some kind of salary supplement plan. This aid must be linked to the development of aggressive methods for rooting out (and keeping out) corruption in the criminal justice system.
- **Joint data bank:** A joint Western-Russian data bank on Russian organized crime should be established. This data bank should include the names of individuals and groups known to be involved in organized crime, as well as data on their criminal histories, records of international travel, contacts in the West, criminal enterprises and legitimate businesses, etc. Interpol might do this, or at least play some role in it.
- **Financial Crimes Enforcement Network (FINCEN):** The intelligence gathering and investigative utility of FINCEN, already demonstrated in areas of international money laundering and banking schemes, and especially those involving Russians, should be expanded.
- **Criminal justice training for Russians:** A broad-based effort to improve the performance of criminal justice officials in the former Soviet Union—through recruitment, training, education, and technical assistance—should be undertaken. This effort should not be limited to include only agencies of the federal government, such as the FBI and the DEA, but also draw heavily on the resources and valuable expertise at the state and local levels. It should also involve the private sector, e.g., the Police Executive Research Forum, the Police Foundation, the National District Attorney's Association, as well as criminology/criminal justice educators and researchers in colleges and universities.

Source: "American Society of Criminology Task Force Report to Attorney General Janet Reno," *The Criminologist,* 20, 6, November/December 1995. Task Force Members: Jay Albanese and Jim Finckenauer, co-chairs.

InfoTrac College Edition Research
Examining "organized crime," what are some recent issues with respect to international organized crime?

> ficking. Although traditional organized crime is heavily involved in the drug trade also, these new groups do not have places on that family tree. They are distinguishable. They include motorcycle gangs, prison gangs, and foreign-based organizations. Some of the names of these groups will be familiar, but most are not. They are: Hell's Angels, Outlaws, Pagans, Bandidos, La Nuestra Familia, Mexican Mafia, Aryan Brotherhood, Black Guerilla Family, Japanese Yakuza, Chinese Triad Societies, Israeli Mafia, and many, many more. Of the 425 cases under investigation by the Organized Crime Drug Enforcement Task Force, which this administration established this past year, only a small number involve traditional organized crime. Most involve the new cartels.

This diversity of groups involved in organized crime is certainly well illustrated in the burgeoning international illegal drug business.

Money Laundering

Money laundering refers to making clean or washing "dirty money" (illegal funds). A classic task of organized crime syndicates has been to somehow convert large amounts of illegally gotten funds into usable money that appears to come from legitimate sources. Drug traffickers are particularly faced with the problem of laundering huge amounts of ill-gotten currency.

FIGURE 13.3 Ethnicity and Organized Crime

Irish	African-American	Asian
Dion O'Banion	Leroy "Nickey" Barnes	Chen Chung
George "Bugs" Moran	Roland Bartlett	Benny Eng
Legs Diamond (Nolan)	Jeff Fort	Johnny Kon
Danny Greene	Willie Rispers	John Chang
Jewish	**Latino**	**WASP**
Mo Dalitz	Amado Carillo Fuentes	Owen Madden
Arnold Rothstein	Pablo Escobar	William Skidmore
"Bugsy" Siegel	Ramon Arellano Felix	Bill Thompson
Meyer Lansky	Caro Quintero	Joe Hall
Arthur "Dutch Schultz" Flegenheimer	Frank Matthews	Henry Cotton
	French	Sherlock Hillman
		Mike MacDonald
	Georges Jean de Mange	Murray Humphreys

Various countries, most notably Switzerland, the Bahamas, Panama, and other "tax havens," have created bank secrecy laws that generally forbid the disclosure of the financial affairs of accountholders. This practice apparently began in Switzerland with numbered accounts to protect the finances of those whose holdings were being confiscated in Nazi Germany (Clark and Tigue, 1975). Recognizing the seriousness of such activity, the U.S. Congress passed the Money Laundering Act of 1986, which made money laundering a federal crime carrying substantial penalties (Weinstein, 1988). A growing number of countries are passing such laws (Gramckow, 1992).

The easiest way to launder money is to take a suitcase full of it to an unscrupulous bank. This bank may recycle the currency to other countries such as Argentina, where the dollar is used because the local currency is subject to hyperinflation. Other methods may include purchasing luxury goods at inflated prices from a coconspirator who transfers the excess proceeds to the purchaser's account. Proceeds from legitimate businesses such as restaurants can be augmented with illegal funds (Melloan, 1991). The U.S. Department of Justice estimates that drug traffickers launder an estimated $100 billion each year in the United States (Webster and McCampbell, 1992).

Money laundering is a three-step process:

1. Illegal money is obtained.
2. A money launderer transfers it, usually out of the country.
3. The money is moved in international channels through wire transfers, conversion, or smuggling (Florez and Boyce, 1990, p. 24).

Bank personnel are often bribed to accept large deposits without reporting them. These are then wired (transferred) to overseas accounts. The money can also be converted to cashier's checks and money orders or hidden in export items such as cars or televisions. The large-scale interconnections between drug traffickers and money launderers are illustrated by the BCCI (Bank of Credit and Commerce International) scandal, which first unravelled in 1989 (Lohr, 1992). BCCI, which operated in over seventy countries, was controlled by Middle Eastern investors and was heavily involved in the laundering of drug money, worldwide fraud and bribery, and the secret ownership of American banks including First American, whose director was Clark Clifford. Former Panamanian strongman

Manuel Noriega, terrorist Abu Nidal, and even the CIA regularly did business with BCCI. Passas (1995, p. 382) reports:

> BCCI had engaged in a huge Ponzi scheme, defrauding about a million innocent clients around the world. According to the liquidators, $9.5 billion are still unaccounted for but no one knows the precise extent of the loss. Huge amounts disappeared into the Grand Cayman portion of the BCCI Group. Series of complex manipulations and falsification of accounts (e.g., unrecorded deposits and false loans or transactions) hid BCCI's poor financial health and made it virtually impossible to reconstruct the true history of the bank. As investigations intensified and multiplied, revelations were made almost daily, over a long period, about BCCI's banking services to money launderers, drug traffickers, arms dealers, coffee smugglers, tax evaders, political offenders, dictators, and intelligence agencies around the globe. BCCI also conducted some interbank transactions and had a director in common with Banca Nazionale del Lavoro (BNL) whose Atlanta branch extended billions of dollars in illegal loans to Iraq.

Casinos can be an excellent place to launder ill-gotten funds, especially with the cooperation of insiders. In 1998 two employees of the Showboat Casino in Atlantic City were charged with helping an alleged drug dealer launder $100,000 by depositing it in the casino under a phony name. They could exchange the dirty money for checks and avoid a cash transaction report filed with the Internal Revenue Service. The "drug dealer" turned out to be an undercover IRS agent. Ill-gotten cash was converted to lucky winnings. In a typical scenario, a money launderer buys chips with dirty money, gambles, and then cashes out obtaining clean money.

Over $500 billion is laundered annually by various global institutions, making money laundering the third largest industry in the world. U.S. law requires that cash deposits of $10,000 or more must be reported to the Internal Revenue Service, but much of the laundered money ends up in secret bank accounts overseas where it can be freely moved.

Williams (1997, p. 18) reports:

> Money laundering provides one of the most important junctures between what Alex Schmid has termed the "upperworld and the underworld." Money laundering is one of the major ways in which criminal organizations penetrate the licit economy and often involves the co-option of supposedly reputable members of society such as bankers and lawyers. Allowing money laundering to go unchallenged, therefore, would have a corrosive impact on the integrity of financial institutions.

FINCEN (The Financial Crimes Enforcement Network of the U.S. Treasury Department) has uncovered a new twist to money laundering by Colombian drug traffickers in which they use peso brokers and unsuspecting U.S. companies to launder dirty money:

1. Secret stash houses in the U.S. store large amounts of dollars from street sales. This money is bought from the drug cartels at a 15–25 percent discount by a peso broker with "clean" pesos.
2. Using operatives or "smurfs" in the U.S., they deposit the cash in small increments in U.S. banks.
3. The peso broker finds Colombian businesspersons who need U.S. dollars in order to import goods.
4. In return for the businesspersons' clean money, the broker writes checks from the smurf checking accounts often exchanging the dollars for pesos at a discount.
5. The orders are welcome as new sales and the goods shipped to Colombia (France and Burnett, 1992).

Illustrating the relationships with legitimate society as well as the transnational nature of money laundering operations, a joint international sting operation involving police agencies from Canada, Italy, Spain, the United Kingdom, and the United States called "Operation Dinero" was aimed against the Cali Cartel. The Drug Enforcement Agency set up an offshore bank in Anguilla, which became a favorite money laundering site for the cartel. At one point they asked the bank to sell art masterpieces (a favorite money laundering investment) for them. Also involved was the Severa crime organization of Italy. The operation netted 88 arrests and seizure of 9 tons of cocaine and $50 million in cash and property (Williams, 1997). Peterson (1998) sees a continuum of money management sophistication from the use of profits to acquire criminal products to influencing governments. A summary of this continuum includes:

- Criminal profits are used to buy luxury items.
- Criminal profits are moved through non-bank financial institutions for use offshore.
- Smurfs using multiple accounts place criminal profits into traditional banking.
- Criminal profits are used for investments in business and financial interests including other geographic locations.
- Financial professionals and lawyers act as facilitators and "criminal" becomes "legitimate."
- Investments are made in financial institutions that can be hidden and/or invested.
- Criminal profits can be used to influence government policies.

Drug Trafficking

Gerber and Jensen (2000, p. 1) indicate:

> The United States of America has experienced periodic wars on drugs for most of its existence. During the late 19th Century, an anti-opiate campaign was initiated that targeted Chinese immigrants in general, and Chinese railroad workers in particular. The 20th Century witnessed the criminalization of marijuana, and the concomitant persecution of Mexican and other Hispanic immigrants (and to a lesser extent African Americans) in the Southwest. This effort, in turn, was followed by a revival of the criminalization of narcotics, a war on drugs during the Nixon Administration, and eventually by the most recent assault, the continuing 1986 War on Drugs. This last war targeted cocaine, crack in particular, and was thus focused to a large extent on Blacks in the United States.

While the Italian-American Syndicate has been involved in drug trafficking, the business is so large that no one group can hope to control it. Although there are many international sources of illegal drugs, the three primary centers of supply are: the Golden Triangle, the Golden Crescent, and Latin America.

The Golden Triangle is the northern border areas of Thailand, Burma, and Laos, which are major heroin-growing areas. Part of this area, called the Shan States, is controlled by an Opium Army made up of the descendants of former Chinese Nationalist troops. The Golden Crescent includes areas of Iran, Afghanistan, Pakistan, and Turkey, which made up the old "French Connection." The latter, which was the basis of a classic movie, involved the smuggling of raw opium to Marseilles, France, for processing into heroin, after which it was sent to the United States to be sold. The third source, Latin America, involves primarily cocaine and marijuana, mainly from Colombia (Abadinsky, 1994; Inciardi, 1992).

Trebach (1984, p. 132) has come up with the notion of the "Iron Law of Opium Trade" to describe a situation in which, if one source of supply is closed, another replaces it. In a six-year observational study of drug smugglers and dealers Adler and Adler (1983) found that because of the danger and legal penalties, there were "shifts and oscillations" in drug trafficking careers. Involvement was temporary, but due to the large rewards involved, many successful retirees move in and out of smuggling organizations.

Colombian Cartels

Probably the most powerful international drug trafficking organization in the world was the Medellin Cartel of Colombia, an organization that used M–19 (the April 19 Movement, a revolutionary group) as protection for their operation (Gugliotta and Leen, 1989). It was the latter terrorist group that gave birth to the cartel. In 1981, M–19 kidnapped the daughter of Fabio Ochoa, the most powerful cocaine boss. In response the Ochoas formed a cartel of two hundred other narcotics trafficking organizations in the city of Medellin and prepared to wage war with M–19. The latter group wisely released Ochoa's daughter and began a hands-off-the-cartel policy in return for a cut of the profits. The cartel used M–19 to storm the country's Palace of Justice in 1985, killing twelve of the 24 supreme court justices (Anderson and Van Atta, 1988b; Eddy, Sabogal, and Walden, 1988). Narco-terrorist groups also traffic in weapons, launder money, offer mutual assistance, smuggle contraband, and share intelligence. The Medellin Cartel was later succeeded by the Cali Cartel and other Colombian groups or baby cartels. By the 1990s Mexican drug traffickers began to supersede their previous partners, the Colombians, as a base for drug smuggling.

The Underground Empire

In an investigation of "narcotraficantes" (narcotics traffickers), James Mills in *The Underground Empire: Where Crime and Governments Embrace* (1986) makes some serious charges. " . . . [T]he largest narcotics conspirator in the world is the government of the United States whose intelligence agencies conspire with or ignore the complicity of officials at the highest levels in at least 33 countries" (p. 1160). As soon as the Drug Enforcement Administration (DEA) closed in on drug domos (bosses), the State Department or CIA sabotaged their investigations in the name of foreign policy (Hagan, 1987a). "The underground empire" is a "fourth world" of nations of institutionalized, state-supported crime.

In the early 1990s convictions of Mexican drug lords and trials of others promised to ease tension between the United States and Mexico (Branigin, 1990, p. 31):

> The trial in Los Angeles of four men accused of involvement in the 1985 murder of a U.S. narcotics agent has brought to the surface years of resentment by Drug Enforcement Administration officials of the Central Intelligence Agency's long collaboration with a former Mexican secret police unit that was heavily involved in drug trafficking.
>
> According to Drug Enforcement Administration (DEA) sources and documents, the Mexican drug-trafficking cartel that kidnapped, tortured, and murdered DEA agent Enrique Camarena in the central city of Guadalajara in February 1985 operated until then with virtual impunity—not only because it was in league with Mexico's powerful Federal Security Directorate (DSF), but because it believed its activities were secretly sanctioned by the CIA.

The arrest and conviction for former Panamanian strongman Manuel Noriega, who was also a paid CIA informant, also serves as an example. By 2000 law enforcement officials began to seize larger and larger shipments of ecstasy pills, a synthetic "psychedelic amphetamine" also known as MDMA. U.S. Customs estimates that it seized 3.5 million pills in fiscal 1999 compared with 750,000 the year before. A pill produced for less than a dollar in Europe sells for up to $40 apiece in the U.S. (Apbnews, 2000b). Once confined to dance parties called "raves," the drug has spread enormously.

VANTAGE POINT 13.2

The Origin of "The Mafia"

In an opening quotation for this chapter, informer and former mobster Joseph Valachi, during his testimony before the McClellan Commission, denies that "Mafia" is the name of the organization to which he belonged. As early as 1890 a grand jury investigating the murder of New Orleans police chief David Hennessey concluded that a secret criminal group, the Mafia, was responsible (Albini, 1971, p. 167); the existence of an organization by that name was assumed rather than proven.

Origin of Mafia

The origin of the term *Mafia* is often assumed but undocumented (that is, without sources referenced). Joseph Albini in his *American Mafia: Genesis of a Legend* (1971, pp. 83–106) notes some of the more commonly cited origins:

Maffia (Tuscan for *misery*)
Mauvias (French for *bad*)
Ma-afir (Arab tribe that settled in Sicily)
MAFIA (***M**azzini **A**utorizza **F**urti **I**ncendi **A**uvelenamenti*—Mazzini Authorizes Arson, Thefts, and Poisons)
Mu'afy (Arabic for *protect from death in the night*)
MAFIA (Battle cry during the Legend of Sicilian Vespers—a revolt against the French in 1282—***M**orte **A**lla **F**rancia **I**talia **A**nela*—"Death to all French is Italy's cry.")
Mafia (The name of a stone quarry in Sicily)
I Mafiusi di la Vicaria (A popular play by Guiseppe Rizzotto in 1860, *The Heroes of the Penitentiary*)

Of interest, but not mentioned by Albini, is Ma Fia (my daughter) (cited in Talese, 1971, p. 184). On the basis of extensive research on the subject, Albini concludes that the 1860 Rizzotto play is the most likely explanation. The play, which dealt with life among Cammorristi (organized and professional criminals) in a Palermo prison, was very popular; it was later released simply with the title, *I Mafiusi,* by then a very well-known term. This might explain the fact that the term was not popularly known before 1860, while after this period it became almost a synonym for organized crime. Thus rather than being the name of an organization, Mafia refers to a method—syndicate-type organized crime. It is a type of crime, not an organization like the Elks or Moose.

InfoTrac College Edition Research

Read Donald Tricarico's "Beyond the Mafia, Italian Americans and the Development of Las Vegas." What role did the mob have in developing the city? What influence does it have today?

Theories of the Nature of Syndicate Crime in the United States

Jay Albanese (1989, p. 101) describes three models or paradigms of organized crime that exist in the literature in the field:

1. Conspiracy theory—organized crime as a nationwide conspiracy.
2. Organized crime as local, ethnic groups.
3. Organized crime as enterprise.

The conspiracy theory is what this writer calls "cosa nostra theory," while the local ethnic groups theory is what this writer calls "patron theory." Enterprise theory as first proposed by Dwight Smith (1975, 1978) argues that organized crime and normal business are similar activities on different ends of a "spectrum of legitimacy." Organized crime represents an extension of the principles of legitimate business into illicit areas (Albanese, 1989, p. 97). VANTAGE POINT 13.2 examines the legend of the mafia.

The Cosa Nostra Theory (The Cressey Model)

The Cosa Nostra Theory is a theory of the organizational structure of syndicate crime that has as its main proponents:

1. Interpretations of the testimony of informant Joseph Valachi before the McClellan Commission in the sixties, in which the term "La Cosa Nostra" was first officially introduced.
2. The organized crime section of the President's Crime Commission Report of 1967 (President's Commission, 1967b; pp. 437–86) and theoretical interpretations of its principal consultant, sociologist Donald Cressey.
3. Official although belated policies of federal agencies such as the Federal Bureau of Investigation.

The major elements of "Cosa Nostra theory," as described by Cressey and the Organized Crime Task Force, included:

1. A nationwide alliance of at least twenty-four tightly knit "families" in the United States.
2. Membership is exclusively of Sicilian or Italian descent, and the organization is referred to as Cosa Nostra particularly by East Coast members. A title of a book by Nicholas Gage (1971) reflects the ethnic exclusivity: *The Mafia Is Not an Equal Opportunity Employer.*
3. The names and criminal activities of approximately five thousand participants have been assembled and the formal structure (see Figure 13.4) has been pieced together based on Valachi's testimony.
4. Overseeing the Cosa Nostra is a National Commission made up of the dons (heads) of the most powerful families in the United States. (Originally consisting of ten to twelve members, according to Fratianno [DeMaris, 1981, p. 294], the commission in 1981 consisted of the heads of the five New York families plus the Chicago boss.) The existence of the Commission was corroborated by means of an electronic bug placed in the dashboard of Anthony "Tony Ducks" Corallo's Jaguar (Powell et al., 1986, p. 25).

In September of 1963 mobster Joe Valachi testified before the Senate Investigations subcommittee. By implicating his former Cosa Nostra *bosses, Valachi broke his blood oath and the code of omérta—silence.*

5. LCN controls all but a small portion of illegal gambling in the United States and contains the principal loan sharks and importers and wholesalers of narcotics.
6. Much of this information is the result of detailed reports of a variety of police observers, informants, wiretaps, and electronic bugs (President's Commission, 1967b, pp. 6–8; Cressey, 1969, pp. 99–107, 241–42).

The description of the internal structure of the LCN in the President's Crime Commission Report was based primarily on Valachi's testimony. Each of the twenty-four families was described as varying in size from as many as seven hundred to one thousand men to as few as twenty. Only New York City had more than one family, and it had five. Family organization was described as being rationally designed with sets of positions similar to those in any large corporation. Figure 13.4 presents an LCN chain of command headed by a boss (*don*), with an advisor (*consigliere*) and underboss (sort of vice president). Answering to the underboss are *caporegimes* (literally, heads of regiments or lieutenants or captains). They are chiefs of operating units or soldiers (*soldati,* "buttons"). "From a business standpoint, the *caporegime* is analogous to plant supervisor or sales manager" (President's Commission, 1967b, p. 451). Soldiers may run various illicit operations on a commission basis or "own" their own operations within which a portion goes to the boss. All of these individuals are "made members" of the organization.

Below and allied with these families are various nonmember associates and employees, individuals who cooperate in and aid organizational operations. Insulation of the boss and other LCN activity is preserved supposedly according to the "oath of omerta"—a pledge of loyalty, honor, respect, absolute obedience, manliness, and silence. In the old days, accompanying the initiation was an elaborate ritual in which the novice was inducted into the LCN.

An earlier variation of the Cosa Nostra theory spoke of a crime confederation. The leading proponent of confederation theory is journalist Hank Messick in books such as *Lansky* (1973) and with Burt Goldblatt, *The Mobs and the Mafia* (1972). In this theory syndicate crime in the United States is viewed as controlled by a "crime confederation" or "combination," consisting of primarily Jewish and Italian gangsters, with the LCN only a part of the operation. Even if such a theory were historically accurate, it describes an organization long since buried (Tyler, 1962).

The Patron Theory (The Albini Model)

The "Patron theory" views organized crime as consisting of a series of patron-client relationships as advocated by Albini (1971 and 1988). According to this approach, organized crime groups and their leaders resemble a medieval system of shifting warlords in which whoever has the most power and is able to render the greatest services controls support. The occupation of specific positions within a structure is less important than a developmental-association system of peer relations that are informal, flexible, and constantly immersed in conflict. Feudalism rather than the corporate bureaucracy is the appropriate analogy for describing organized crime families, a series of shifting alliances. (See Albanese, 1989, and Kelly, 1992 for other models of organized crime.)

The Mafia Myth?

The "Mafia myth" refers to the belief that U.S. organized crime is the result of an imported alien conspiracy that controls all organized crime in the United States. The "Mafia myth" really has two models: the *conspiracy model* and the *moderate model.* While critics tend to lump these models together, separating them will assist in clarifying exactly what is in dispute. The *conspiracy model* suggests that the Mafia is an international organization that controls organized crime, particularly in the United States. Adherents of this view are

FIGURE 13.4 Internal Structure of *Las Cosa Nostra* Families

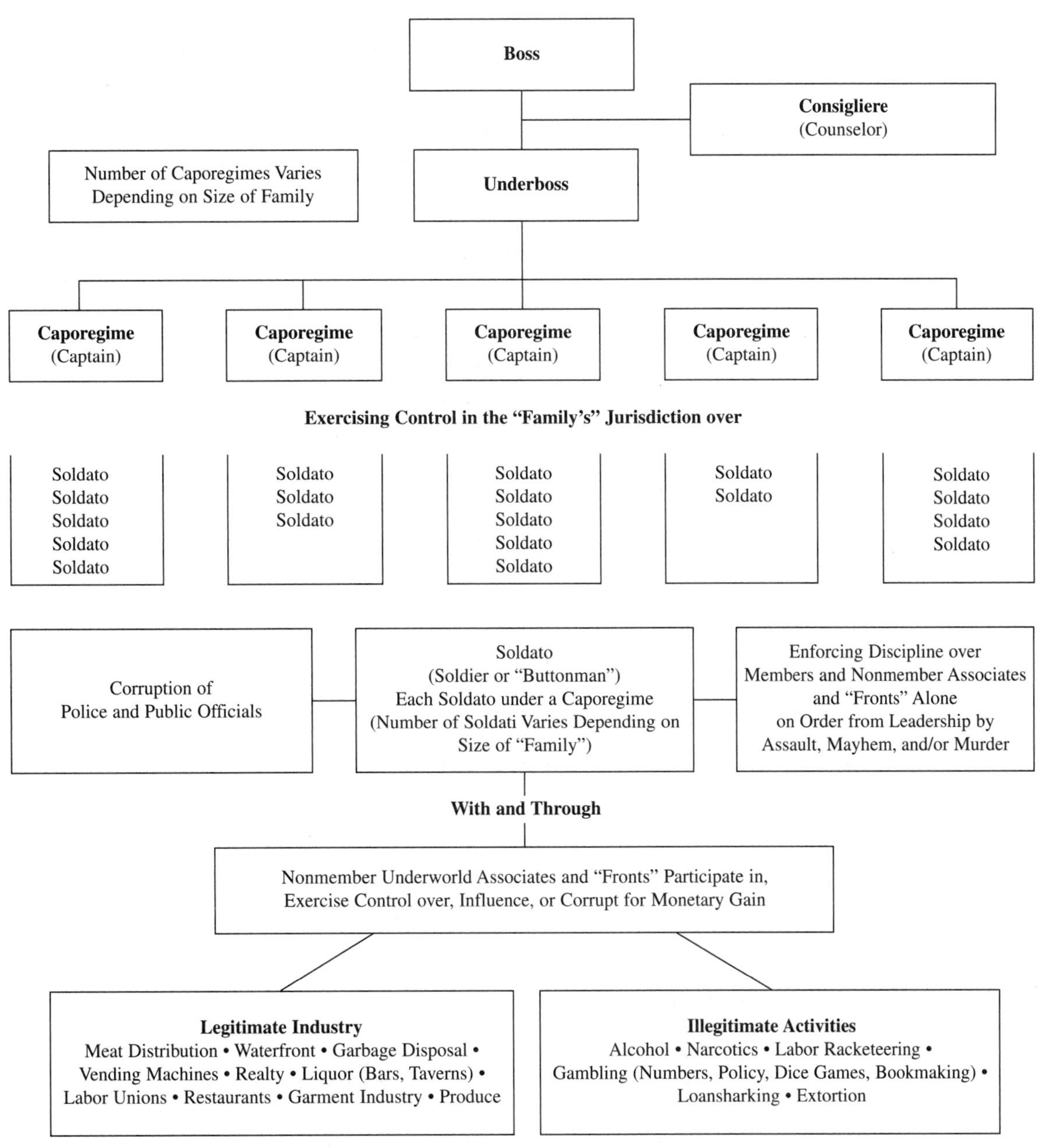

Source: U.S. Senate Permanent Subcommittee on Investigations, Committee on Governmental Affairs, *Hearings on Organized Crime and Use of Violence,* 96th Cong., 2d Sess., April 1980, p. 117.

Harry Anslinger, the former crusading director of the Federal Bureau of Narcotics; as well as Edward Allen (1962), Ed Reid (1970), and Frederic Sondern (1959). The *moderate model*—represented by Donald Cressey (1967), Robert Anderson (1965), and Ralph Salerno and John Tompkins (1969), and reflected in the President's Crime Commission Report—views the Italian-American Syndicate (IAS), which the Commission calls Cosa Nostra, as the most powerful of organized crime groups, but not as an "alien conspiracy."

The Italian-American Syndicate (IAS)

Much of what has been written about organized crime has restricted itself to an analysis of the Italian-American Syndicate (IAS), variously referred to as the Mafia or Cosa Nostra. Critics of this approach (Bell, 1967; Ianni, 1972, 1974; Morris and Hawkins, 1970; Smith, 1975) have largely made their points, among others, that organized crime in the United States is home grown and is not the product of an imported, alien conspiracy; that no one ethnic group has a monopoly on organized crime; that the picture drawn by the Organized Crime Task Force Report (1967) as presented by Donald Cressey (1969) and based largely on Joseph Valachi's testimony is overdrawn; and that it is doubtful that organized crime, or the IAS, which was the most powerful of such syndicates, ever exhibited the extreme bureaucratic, monolithic structure depicted. These critics do not, however, dispute the existence of organized crime and criminal syndicates as distinct phenomena, nor dispute that an IAS (Mafia, Cosa Nostra) is more than a creation of moral entrepreneurs or Hollywood.

While many of the descriptions of organization and structure of the IAS are dated, the vision is "skewed, not false" (Lupsha, 1981, p. 5); the initial description of the Mafia was overdone, but the reaction is perhaps equally overdone. Perhaps there has been a tendency "to throw out the baby of organized crime with the bath water of 'alien conspiracy' theory" (Lupsha, 1981, p. 4). Some critics of the "alien conspiracy" seem to suggest at times that, since the Mafia does not exist, organized crime does not exist. Saying there is no Mafia is quite different from saying there is no organized crime, and some critics seem to border dangerously on this assumption despite disclaimers that, of course, they do not mean to say there is no organized crime.

While writers such as Albini (1988, p. 350) maintain that "most research has not lent support to the Cressey model [Cosa Nostra theory]," Rogovin and Martens (1989, p. 11) note that evidence produced in recent years, as well as research and informants, have corroborated Cressey over and over again. They (Rogovin and Martens, 1992, p. 70) note:

> The volumes of evidence produced over the past eight years, as well as the books that have been published by researchers, journalists, investigative reporters, private citizens, and members of La Cosa Nostra have corroborated Cressey over and over again. Why ignore Bonanno's (1983) autobiography of his life in LCN? There is a great chapter on the "Commission" and its model of operation. Read Fratianno's account of his life in the LCN (DeMaris and Fratianno, 1981). Seek out the wiretap product which was made public in the Commission trial in New York . . . . Read the transcripts of the Scarfo trials in Philadelphia and critically evaluate the testimony of two LCN members who became state's witnesses (Cooney, 1987; Mallowe, 1988). Obtain the transcripts of the trial of Nick Civella in Kansas City (Turner, 1983, p. 30); the testimony of Cleveland LCN underboss Angelo Lonardo before the Permanent Sub-Committee on Investigations (P.S.I., 1988); or the trial testimony of Gennaro Anguilo in Boston. Surely, the infamous "Pizza Connection I" trial (Alexander, 1988; Blumenthal, 1988); the reporting of Jimmy "the Weasel" Fratianno (DeMaris and Fratianno, 1981) or Joseph Bonanno (1983), Paul Meskil (1976), and Thomas Renner (Teresa and Renner, 1973; Renner and Giancana, 1984) are relevant pieces of research literature . . . . Testimony in these trials admitted the existence of a Mafia [Albanese (1989, p. 66)].

The Classic Pattern of Organized Crime

In their book, *The Crime Confederation* (1969), Ralph Salerno and John S. Tompkins describe the "classic pattern of organized crime" as a gradual movement from "strategic and tactical crimes" such as assault, bribery, and extortion to "illegal businesses and activities" to "legitimate businesses" to "big business." Due to their willingness to commit and employ *strategic and tactical crimes,* organized gangs are thereby able to acquire both the funds and the power to be fairly successful at *illegal businesses and activities.* They are, of course, not the only types of criminals engaged in these activities but are more organized, more persistent in their efforts, and simply better at it. The types of crimes committed under strategic and tactical crimes are for the most part disapproved of by the general public, while the illegal businesses and operations often serve public demand for vices and other illicit activities. Unwittingly the government, by branding much of this activity—such as narcotics and gambling—illegal, creates a monopoly for criminal groups that are organized well enough to supply these goods and services.

A major problem of some "unconnected" or nonorganized criminals is "laundering" (making "dirty" money appear "clean") of funds obtained in illegal operations. Who brought down Al Capone? Not Elliot Ness with a Tommy gun, but Frank Wilson of the Internal Revenue Service with pencils, ledgers, and a green eyeshade (Marbin, 1989, p. Al). In the earlier history of U.S. organized crime, even "connected" figures such as Al Capone were convicted of income tax violations, and this lesson was not lost on other organized criminals as many began trading in their black shirts and white ties for Brooks Brothers suits. With funds obtained in illegal operations, organized criminals can *infiltrate legitimate businesses,* an even more fertile field for their activities. Finally, experience in such operations enables movement into even *bigger businesses.* Figure 13.5 details businesses that have been cited by appropriate sources as either presently or formerly mob influenced. (Caution must be used in interpreting this list because the original cited sources of the allegation may be dated.)

A detailed account of organized crime activities is beyond the scope of this treatment. Readers interested in such detail can consult the latest newspaper or media accounts, though reading some of the references cited in this chapter will provide a more systematic starting point.

Strategic and Tactical Crimes

The strength of organized criminal groups is based on their willingness and ability to use force or threats of force to assure discipline within and outside the organization. Although

FIGURE 13.5 Organized Crime Is Bullish on America: Businesses and Activities Alleged to Have Had, or Currently Having Some Organized Crime Influence

Tucson Printing Company[a]
Chrysler Office Building[a]
Moravian Acres Subdivision[a]
Erie Coin and Vending Company[b]
Keystone Music Company[b]
Scotto Pizza[b]
Italian Delight[b]
City Bank of Philadelphia[b]
Forte Oil Company[b]
Bonnie Stewart Dresses[b]
Medico Industries[b]
Northeastern Pa. TV Cable Co.[b]
Blue Coal Corporation[b]
Pocono Downs Racetrack[b]
Old Forge Bank (Pa.)[b]
Caesar's World, Inc.[b]
Caesar's Palace[b]
Teamster Union Pension Fund[c]
Many Las Vegas Casinos[c]
La Costa Country Club[c]
Miami Beach Hotels[c]
Bally Pinball Machines[c]
International Longshoreman's Association[d]

a. Ed Reid, *The Grim Reapers* (1970).

b. Pennsylvania Crime Commission (1980).

c. Ovid Demaris, *The Last Mafioso* (1981).

d. NBC News, 1979, "NBC Follow-Up: A Follow-Up on the 1977 Documentary on 'Racketeering and the International Longshoreman's Association,' " broadcast April 21.

activities such as assault, coercion, extortion, and murder are not the exclusive property of organized criminals, they seem to be used more frequently by this group than by most other types of criminals.

Some strategic and tactical crimes committed by organized criminals include: arson, assault, coercion, extortion, murder, blackmail, bribery, and corruption. Vincent Teresa describes an arson-related **bustout** scam in which, through intermediaries who lacked criminal records, he would open a bank account under a corporate name, lease a building, order goods, pay half the bill to build a credit line, place large orders prior to Christmas, remove unsold items from the building and sell them to a fence, then burn the place down, collect the insurance, and declare bankruptcy (Teresa, 1973b, pp. 108–109). Organized criminals also may control the insurance firm that holds the policy on the torched property.

Assault, coercion, extortion, and *murder* are bottom-line tools employed by organized crime, weapons of last resort to assure the "rational" pursuit of profit. "Make him an offer he can't refuse" is black humor, but it is an all-too-apt phrase to describe methods used by organized criminals to accomplish their will. Violence and threats of violence, demands for protection money (extortion), and, when necessary as a last resort, murder ("making your bones") is part of the repertoire. Decades of internal wars and assassinations within the ranks of organized crime attest to the fact that not only outsiders are the victims of mob discipline.

Blackmail, bribery, and *corruption* are essential strategic tools of organized crime. The American Bar Association (1952) in its *Report on Organized Crime* (p. 16) concluded: "The largest single factor in the breakdown of law enforcement dealing with organized crime is the corruption and connivance of many public officials." Blackmail is more easily achieved by organized crime figures because of their involvement in gambling casinos, pornography, and servicing of vice-related activities. Bribery and corruption of public officials make up the largest operating cost of organized criminal groups, a sort of "underground" tax or license to steal. Organized crime has been so successful in corrupting public officials that cities, counties, and entire states have been "in the bag." Success in strategic and tactical crimes provides the money, "muscle," and "respect" for success at principal illegal businesses and activities. The strategic and tactical crimes are for the most part "rackets," services that lack or do not require public demand. Organized criminal involvement in illicit enterprises or illegal businesses satisfies public demand for services or vice activities that either cannot be or are not met by legal businesses. Thus the loan shark is a banker of last resort and the fence a less expensive shopping center.

Illegal Businesses and Activities

From the end of the Prohibition era until recently, gambling has been viewed as the number-one moneymaker for organized crime. Although often described as a Depression and/or ghetto invention, lotteries flourished in the United States as far back as colonial times, used during that period to pay for public works (National Institute of Law Enforcement, 1977). In addition to lotteries, syndicates are involved in other gambling activities, such as bookmaking (taking bets on sporting events), illegal gambling devices (slot machines, punchboards, sports polls), and the running of illegal gambling establishments. The **numbers game** is by far the most popular of these activities. In this game, sometimes called policy or "bolita" in the southern United States, the basic strategy is similar to that of legalized state lotteries: the bettor tries to choose a winning three-digit number. Traditionally, number-selection methods differed from those of lotteries: numbers were chosen that matched the numbers of win-place-show horses at a track or Dow Jones averages. State lotteries choose numbers by spinning a wheel or by some other "honest" means.

The advent of legal state lotteries may not have made the dent in the illegal numbers business that many had hoped. Many numbers writers simply use the legal daily number as their own, increasing the nontaxed odds and sometimes even laying off bets with the state. Illegal casino gambling still exists in many American communities. Dice or "crap" games, wheels, and "high stakes" card games can often be found by simply asking local cabbies, "Where's the action?" Reuter, in his book *Disorganized Crime* (1984b), is quick to point out that "the Mafia" control of illegal markets is exaggerated and that the numbers, loan-sharking, and bookmaking are very disorganized businesses.

Related to gambling operations is the **loan shark** or shylock (the latter name is derived from Shakespeare's character Shylock, a money lender who demands his "pound of flesh"). Loan sharks provide quick loans on the spot to borrowers who are either high-risk or in a spot. These loans are given at usurious (illegal and exorbitant) rates. Although rates vary, a typical loan might be a "six for five" arrangement. That is, for every five dollars borrowed, six dollars must be repaid (20 percent interest) per week. Sharks are more interested in collecting periodic interest payments (called "juice," "vigorish," or "vig") than in having the loan paid off. Often borrowers give their bodies as collateral since, if they were good risks or could share their problem, they could have gone elsewhere. Gambling is the usual manner in which the successful business person, but poor gambler, is introduced to loan sharks and, if his or her luck does not improve, he or she may have some new business partners.

The Pennsylvania Crime Commission (1992) reports on organized crime infiltration of legitimate, charitable, and Indian reservation bingo games. Racketeers and mobsters were described as practicing fraud, misrepresentation, and diversion of monies from such games and using charitable organizations as fronts for skimming millions of dollars. Ironically the Pennsylvania Crime Commission itself was dissolved when it began to investigate illegal campaign contributions by gambling operators to the Pennsylvania Attorney General Ernie Preate. Preate served time in jail for his activities.

Other successful illegitimate activities of organized criminals involve labor racketeering; narcotics trafficking; prostitution; pornography (although now much of this is legal); stolen property (such as cars, stocks, and bonds); videotape, film, and record piracy; and even illegal sale of alcohol. Organized criminals will involve themselves in any scam (illegal activity) so long as it is relatively safe and profitable (Kwitny, 1979). In 1997 in Russia and Georgia (the country) it is estimated that one of five dwellings produce illegal alcohol. Organized criminal groups, sometimes protected by customs personnel, deliver the products in small ships under "Sultan," a criminal emissary of the Chechen Republic (Konstantinova, 1997). Death from the illegal consumption of alcohol in the former Soviet Union is very high.

VANTAGE POINT 13.3 describes organized crime's growing involvement with software piracy.

The growing popularity of legalized casino gambling may be slowed by research such as that done by Farrell and Case (1995), which documents corruption, deceit, and even prejudice in Las Vegas casinos. The regulatory commissions focused public attention on "the Mob" while ignoring many other criminal interests in the gaming industry.

Labor **racketeering** is infiltration of unions to use their influence for personal profit. Such operations—which may take the form of bribes, kickbacks, and extortionary threats—permit mobsters to use pension funds and to offer "no-strike insurance" (the guarantee that workers will not strike) and sweetheart contracts (collusion between employer and union officials at the expense of workers), as well as other operations.

In one federal sting operation, "Operation UNIRAC" (Union Racketeering), the FBI reported on collusion among shipping companies, the International Longshoreman's Association, and organized criminals (NBC News, 1979). According to NBC News accounts, the operation found that the Genovese, Gambino, and Marcello organized crime families controlled the International Longshoremen's Association (ILA). Hijackings were set up by ILA officials; kickbacks and pay to "phantom workers" were common. In 1990, a decade after UNIRAC, the federal government filed civil racketeering suits asking that trustees

VANTAGE POINT 13.3

"Snakeheads" and Software Mobsters

"Snakeheads" (human traffickers), a group of Asian mobsters affiliated with Chinese organized crime groups, have traditionally specialized in illegal immigrant smuggling. They routinely torture and kill their clients. Counterfeit software has moved beyond small-time hackers and has become more dangerous with the entry of Asian organized crime. The Business Software Alliance estimates that the U.S. economy loses 130,000 jobs annually to software theft. The international piracy trade is described as (Panattieri, 1999):

> **First, an organized-crime operation makes millions of dollars pushing drugs and prostitution in Asia. Next, the money is diverted to California, where it is used to purchase hardware, software, and paper goods to produce pirated CDs and user manuals. Third, the counterfeit software is distributed at computer "swap meets" held regularly on college campuses across the nation; shipped abroad; or offered for sale on the Internet. Finally, the proceeds from the pirated software are laundered through real estate purchases in California or illegally wired back to Asia.**

Snakeheads, for a $30,000 fee, smuggle illegal aliens into the U.S. Some clients become indentured servants, producing illegal software in sweatshops in order to pay off their debt. The multi-national nature of such operations produces a real challenge for law enforcement.

In investigating what they call "the software sopranos" or the "digital dons" in California, the Justice Department reports that besides the Snakeheads, the Black Dragons and Wah Ching ("Chinese Youth") gangs are also involved in product counterfeiting. Also operating are Russian groups, as well as a Vietnamese group called "The Company" that was involved in thirty armed robberies of electronic firms (Glasser, 2000b).

Source: Joseph C. Panattieri. 1999. "The Software Mobsters." *Interactive Week Online.* September 15 (www.zdnet.com); Jeff Glasser. 2000. "The Software Sopranos." *U.S. News and World Report.* February 7.

InfoTrac College Edition Research

What has been the controversy related to FAST (The Federation Against Software Theft)?

oversee elections and that Genovese operatives be permanently barred from the waterfront (Behar, 1990, p. 57). In addition, in "Operation Brilab," which disclosed official corruption in Louisiana and Texas among high state officials, the FBI concentrated on Carlos Marcello (reputed boss of New Orleans organized crime), who told two undercover agents, "We own the Teamsters" and bragged of accessibility to the union's pension fund ("Abscam," 1980).

Four unions with substantial organized crime control and influence are the International Longshoremen's Association, the Hotel and Restaurant Employees Union, the Laborers International Union of North America, and the International Brotherhood of Teamsters. Construction costs in New York City are estimated to be 25 percent higher because of the need for organized crime payoffs, and garbage collection $50 million per year more because of mob control (Powell et al., 1986, p. 28). Mob-controlled Teamster locals 295 and 851 enabled Anthony "Tony Ducks" Corallo to shake down air transport service companies for $1.1 million between 1978 and 1985 (Rowan, 1986, p. 34). In 1990 the federal government charged that for twenty years Nicodemo Scarfo, head of the Philadelphia Mafia, had been running the 22,000-member Local 54 of the Hotel and Restaurant Employees International Union from his cell in prison. The local included Atlantic City casinos (Hagedorn and Lambert, 1990, p. B6). "The Outfit" in Chicago charges a "street tax" on all illegal activities. Gamblers, vice operators, even owners of parking lots and legitimate businesses must pay 10 to 50 percent of their gross revenues to the Chicago mob.

The largest illegal business of organized criminals is now drugs. In 1986 the President's Commission on Organized Crime (1986a) estimated that organized crime took in as much as $106.2 billion, and by far the biggest money maker was illegal drug trafficking. Success and money from illegal operations, although welcome, present organized criminals with potential tax problems, further encouraging them to move into legitimate businesses. Such businesses *provide many opportunities for organized crime.* They provide a source of legal income that can help explain gangsters' high lifestyles. Because of their methods, criminals can monopolize markets and make more money than competitors. Such businesses also yield a "cover," or respectable occupation, as well as provide a base of operation and a meeting place, particularly for dealing with public officials. They enable the "washing" or "laundering" of funds and provide a diversification of operations.

Favorite businesses of organized criminals include: auto sales, bakeries, clothing manufacturing, construction and demolition, import/export, garages, hotels, vending machines, produce, trucking, bars and restaurants, garbage collection, and the like. Businesses such as vending and bars are fertile for "skimming" (hiding or not counting money earned for tax purposes). One hundred dollars skimmed every day from a busy bar would amount to over $30,000 a year, tax free, from just one business. Extortion and monopolization in vending businesses enable organized criminals to force out competitors.

Ianni in *A Family Business* (1972) suggests that the seeds of many American fortunes began with "dirty business" and progressed in a couple of generations to "respectable" business, a natural **ethnic succession** and progression. In discussing federal enforcement, Ianni is concerned that this progression not be entirely blunted. In the main, however, organized criminals in such enterprises often carry over all the same illegal techniques.

Although the integrity of legitimate owners such as Metropolitan Edison and its handling of the Three Mile Island nuclear accident is questionable, imagine if organized crime controlled your friendly local utility. In April 1980, sixty thousand 55-gallon drums of lethal waste stockpiled in the Chemical Control Corporation's Elizabeth, N.J., warehouse exploded. Fortunately, prevailing winds prevented the toxic fumes from blowing into New York City (see Szasz, 1986). The mob has owned garbage disposal firms for years and has discovered big money in illegal disposal of toxic wastes. An alleged member of the Tieri crime family, after threatening the previous owner with a gun, effectively took over the company prior to the incident ("The New Mafia," 1981, p. 39; Kelly, 1988).

With major crackdowns on traditional organized crime activities such as extortion or bid-rigging rackets, Mafia crime groups in New York were shifting some of their focus to health frauds, prepaid phone cards, and Wall Street scams. Raab (1997) indicates:

> The authorities in New Jersey said they uncovered what might be the prototype of the mob's medical care strategy in August, when they arrested 12 men accused of being members of a Genovese crew, or unit. The crew's leaders were charged with siphoning payments from Tri-Con Associates, a New Jersey company that arranged medical, dental, and optical care for more than one million patients in group plans throughout the county. Investigators said that the mobsters set up Tri-Con, investing their own money and using employees as managers, and intimidated some health plan administrators into approving excessive payments to the company. New Jersey authorities said Tri-Con in effect became a broker, linking networks of health-care providers, including physicians, hospitals and dentists, with group plans for companies and unions.

Prepaid phone cards were grossing $1 billion in the U.S. in 1996 and provided a new target for organized crime. The Gambino crime family stole over $50 million from companies and phone callers by selling $20 cards that became worthless after only $2 or $3 in calls (Bastone, 1997). Other New York City crime families have infiltrated Wall Street, particularly over-the-counter stocks handled by small brokerage firms. Brokers who are in debt or wish to expand their businesses borrow money from the mob. They are then forced to sell most of the low-priced shares in a company before they are available as initial public offerings. The value is artificially inflated by fake transactions and trading among themselves. At the same time, brokers push the stock on unsuspecting investors. The mobsters then sell, making high profits before the overvalued stock collapses (Ibid.).

Salzanno (1994) reports on organized crime infiltration of "the sludge running" business in New York and New Jersey. A sludge runner is a trucker who collects and illegally dumps hazardous "cocktailed" chemical mixtures at the expense of taxpayers and the environment.

Of major concern to law enforcement officials is the burgeoning growth in transnational smuggling of illegal aliens from underdeveloped to developed countries. Tens of thousands from the former Soviet Union, Asia, and Eastern Europe are trafficked each year, often unknowingly into forced prostitution in developed countries. They work as indentured slaves in the global sex industry in bars, massage parlors, and brothels. Most are attracted through deceit and coercion and find themselves without visas or passports in foreign lands. Human rights groups estimate millions of women and children are forced into such lives of criminal exploitation. The U.S. State Department estimates that 50,000 to 100,000 women and children are forced into the United States each year against their will. In Europe, Albanian clans are middlemen for Russian and Chinese organized-crime human smuggling operations. The lack of strict laws in some countries reflects a patriarchal culture that denigrates women (Fleishmann, 2000).

Incredibly, in something that sounds like a James Bond movie, in 1997 police investigations revealed that Russian organized crime figures in Miami Beach had claimed to Colombian drug cartel members that they could supply them with tactical nuclear weapons, as well as a submarine. Many of the Russian organized crime figures are believed to be ex-KGB members.

Big Business and Government

Success at small business permits mob infiltration of *big business,* the heartline of our nation's economy. We have already suggested the impact of mob influence on big labor unions such as the Teamsters and the Longshoremen. Banking, construction, entertainment, insurance, real estate, and even Wall Street are not immune. In the 1990s the mob has moved from shaking down indebted stockbrokers to stock price manipulation. In a classic "pump and dump" operation, brokers used high pressure sales tactics to pump up the price of a stock they owned and then the shares were dumped before their worth plummeted.

Given the classic pattern of organized crime we must ask the question "What remains?" Only government. Can or does organized crime have the capability of compromising the government itself? In "Operation Mongoose" (Ashman, 1975), the Central Intelligence Agency used syndicate criminals to put a "hit" on Cuban premier Fidel Castro in 1963. Although apparently a scam on the part of the mob in that no serious attempts took place (DeMaris, 1981, p. 267), the deal apparently called for cooperation by the CIA in smuggling prostitutes from Marseilles to staff mob brothels in Las Vegas ("Gangland Enforcer," 1977). One principal figure, John Roselli, who hinted at tie-ins with the Kennedy assassination before the House Assassination Committee, was killed by the Mafia before he could testify further (Anderson and Whitten, 1977). The U.S. House of Representatives Select Committee on Assassinations (1979) concluded that there was a conspiracy in the assassination of John Kennedy as well as possible conspiracies in the assassinations of Robert Kennedy and Martin Luther King, Jr. Chief counsels to the committee G. Robert Blakey and Richard Billing (1981), more specifically point the finger, as the title of their book indicates: *The Plot to Kill the President: Organized Crime Assassinated JFK* (see also Scheim, 1988).

Although it is not proven, it is alleged that the Mafia felt betrayed by John Kennedy. They claimed that they were responsible for getting him elected by stuffing ballot boxes in

Illinois. When the new President Kennedy appointed his mob-busting brother, Robert, to the post of Attorney General, a crusade against the mob began particularly on associates such as Teamster leader Jimmy Hoffa. This campaign did not sit well with his "subordinate," FBI Director J. Edgar Hoover. Although not proven, it has been charged that Hoover avoided any efforts against organized crime because he had been compromised, having received favors from gamblers, and perhaps blackmailed regarding an alleged secret sex life. Columnist Jack Anderson and others (Anderson and Whitten, 1977) claimed that JFK was assassinated for two reasons: first, in retaliation for assassination attempts on Castro (Santo Trafficante, one of the would-be assassins, may have defected); and second, as a way of eliminating Robert Kennedy from power. This is, of course, all speculative; but the day after the assassination of President Kennedy, Hoover, the nation's top law enforcement officer, spent the day at the racetrack.

In 1954 the U.S. Justice Department had begun deportation hearings against John LaRocca (alleged boss of the Pittsburgh mob). The Pennsylvania governor, John Fine, sabotaged the federal government's case by first issuing a pardon to LaRocca for previous lottery and larceny convictions. Even though the pardon was issued at the close of the hearings, it was scheduled to fall before the close of the hearings. Having the grounds for deportation eliminated, the federal government had no choice but to drop the proceedings (Pennsylvania Crime Commission, 1970, p. 19).

Concerns have risen regarding organized crime and drug dealers' infiltration of the Medicare system, a $250 billion-a-year business already rife with rip-offs by other crooked operators. Many moved out of the drug trade into the safer and more lucrative medical swindle business. They have set up thousands of fake clinics, medical equipment stores, and laboratories and use a maze of bank accounts and offshore accounts to move their money. It is a particular favorite of Russian organized crime groups (Hedges, 1998).

As a testimony to the power of organized crime groups, the President of Colombia, Ernesto Samper (1995, A16), shortly after the arrest of Gilberto Rodrigues Orejuela, leader of the Cali cartel, stated:

> In the past decade, Colombia has lost countless lives, including more than 3,000 police officers and soldiers, 23 judges, 63 journalists, and four presidential candidates.

The infiltration of organized criminal groups into large business enterprises is also assisted by activities of legitimate organizations themselves, some operations of which resemble those of organized crime. Bribery and corruption of national and international public officials, violence either indirectly through sale of unsafe products or directly in deposing foreign leaders such as Allende in Chile, and pushing of drugs far in excess of the medicinal needs of consumers, are just a few of such examples. A detailing of criminal activities of organized crime syndicates, and particularly the IAS, is not intended to ignore their corporate counterparts, but to recognize the former as having distinct characteristics of their own. Similarly, while the IAS did not invent and does not control all of organized criminal operations, it has been the most powerful of such groups in the United States since the 1930s.

A Brief History of Organized Crime in the United States

A detailed account of the history of U.S. organized criminal activity is beyond the scope of this text. Readers are advised to consult sources cited in the reference list, particularly Abadinsky (1994), Talese (1971), Hammer (1975), MacLean (1974), and Gage (1972). However, a brief account will familiarize the reader with some key events in the history of organized crime. Figure 13.6 contains a brief chronological list.

FIGURE 13.6 Chronology of Selected Events in the History of Organized Crime in the United States

1700s	Colonial Pirates
1800s	WASP, Irish, Jewish gangs
1890	The New Orleans Incident
1920	The Volstead Act (Prohibition)
1930–31	Castellammarese wars in New York City
1931	Would-be "Capo di Tutti Capi" Maranzano murdered
by 1934	Cosa Nostra and/or Confederation established
Post-WWII	Mob moves into Las Vegas
1950	Kefauver Committee Hearings
1957	The Apalachin "Gangland" convention
1963	McClellan Commission Hearing, featuring star witness Joseph Valachi
1970	Organized Crime Control Act of 1970
1971	Mob boss Joe Colombo shot at Columbus Day rally
1976	Carlo Gambino dies
1979–80	Mob wars continue (Galante, Bruno, Testa)
1980–81	FBI round-up of top "Cosa Nostra" bosses begins
1983–86	President's Commission on Organized Crime
1983–87	"The Commission Trials"
1985	Paul Castellano assassinated
1985–86	"The Pizza Connection"
1985–86	"The Great Mafia Trial" in Sicily
1992	Sicilian Mafia kill Falcone and Borsellino
1992	John Gotti convicted
1993–97	Federal prosecutors cripple Cosa Nostra leadership. New ethnic organized crime groups move into power
2000	Remnants of Mafia survive in New York, Chicago, Philadelphia
2001	New mobs become dominant

Before 1930

Organized crime had its beginnings in the New World with colonial pirates, former naval mercenaries working for England in her war against Spain. By the end of the seventeenth century they were an institutionalized component of international trade, intimately tied up with the business and governmental systems of the time. "The pirates, it is clear, were the racketeers of their day, bribing officials, corrupting entire governments and looting to maintain a vast underworld market in forbidden goods" (Browning and Gerassi, 1980, pp. 71–72). Organized crime appeared to be an intimate component of American cities from their beginnings, with "robber barons" or "industrial pirates" looting the landscape in early capitalism (Myers, 1936) and criminals, police, and politicians cooperatively running illicit enterprises in order to satisfy public demand for vice activity. The Irish and Anglo-Saxon street gangs in nineteenth-century New York formed organized criminal groups, just as a later generation of mostly American-born street hoodlums of Italian descent would form the most successful prototype of American syndicates, the IAS.

The view has already been espoused in this chapter that organized crime in the United States existed long before major Italian immigration, being dominated in its early history by small local mobs of WASP origin. Also described was the 1890 "New Orleans Incident" in which one of rival Italian-American criminal brotherhoods killed the city's police chief. The aftermath of that incident was a grand jury report naming a secret criminal group, "Mafia," as responsible. Due to a believed fix in the case, angered citizens stormed the parish prison, executing a number of the gang leaders and almost precipitating a war between the United States and Italy (Albini, 1971, p. 167).

Up until 1920, most organized crime was confined to relatively small, local mobs whose operations were not particularly sophisticated. Most were controlled by Irish and Jewish gangsters, although a number began to include as "muscle" a growing number of hoodlums of Italian and Sicilian descent. Prohibition was an absolute bonanza for organized crime, the one factor that made it possible for fledgling gangs to become financially successful syndicates. Frank Costello was one of the first Italian-American gangsters to make it big.

George Wolf (1975, pp. 27–29), Costello's lawyer and advisor, described the Prohibition period before 1924 as one in which bootleggers such as Costello organized a virtual naval flotilla with which to smuggle liquor into the United States. The few Coast Guard boats were unable to compete with the much faster skiffs, which raced their contraband from freighters anchored beyond the three-mile U.S. territorial limit. When the Coast Guard interdicted supplies, newspapers and the public berated them as "pirates." An $8 case of Scotch from the British Isles was sold for $65 on the freighters, $120 at dockside, and, once doctored with three times as much grain alcohol and water, brought around $400. Since many ships carried twenty thousand cases, Costello's wealth eclipsed that of his former mentor, Arnold Rothstein. "And along with his ships and yachts Frank introduced a new element into bootlegging, one that was to bring gasps of surprise in the courtroom in 1926: seaplanes for air coverage . . . the air wing of Frank's defense department" (Wolf, 1975, p. 29).

Costello, who lived in the Waldorf Astoria in Manhattan, would dine daily with city bigwigs and had so compromised and corrupted city officials that he claimed to possess an authentic, handwritten resignation letter penned by then-Mayor Paul O'Dwyer, a document that could be turned in any time the later-discredited mayor did not keep his end of the bargain. Naval and air operations by organized crime in the twenties bear an uncanny resemblance to the Colombia runs in Florida that were begun in the late seventies by drug smugglers in what has been called "The Colombian Connection," "the Cocaine Cowboys" (1980), and "Air Ganja" (Plate, 1975, p. 119).

It was Chicago in the twenties, the person of Al "Scarface" Capone, and operations like the St. Valentine's Day Massacre that caused a stereotyped picture of the mob to be drawn in the public media. Meanwhile in New York, two old "moustache petes" or "greasers" (names given to old-time, Italian-born Mafiosi) were involved in a power struggle. The lineup of contending factions reads like a Who's Who of figures who would dominate La Cosa Nostra for decades to come. Initially aligned with the Joe "The Boss" Masseria faction were Luciano, Genovese, Adonis, Anastasia, Costello, Gambino, and, through financial assistance, Capone. The rival faction, **Castellammarese** (named after the home town of most of the members, Castellammare del Golfo, Sicily), was headed by Salvatore Maranzano and included Bonanno, Profaci, Lucchese, Magliocco, Gagliano, and Magaddino. Although the Castellammarese Wars were far from the bloodbath erroneously described by chroniclers (Block, 1978), they were important in that the aftermath gave birth to the modern syndicate. Basically Luciano, Genovese, and others doublecrossed Masseria and had him killed.

The victor, Maranzano, often described as the "father of the modern LCN syndicate," was a big fan of Julius Caesar and supposedly modeled his organizational structure after the Roman legions. Unfortunately, Maranzano himself was a victim of overweening ambition, picturing himself as "capo di tutti capi" (boss of all bosses). Six months after taking power he also was killed by Meyer Lansky and "Bugsy" Siegel, who had been hired by Luciano, Genovese, and company.

The Luciano Period

Charles "Lucky" Luciano took power over the new organization, one that would have continual alliance (sometimes called the confederation) with other ethnic gangs but which itself would remain exclusively Italian. Avoiding the top boss role, Luciano supported the autonomy of bosses with a commission for settling disputes. This alliance was apparently further consolidated in the thirties, and a special "hit squad"—Murder, Inc.—was set up by Louis "Lepke" Buchalter; this group's existence would be later revealed by informant Abe "Kid Twist" Reles. Murder Incorporated's first victim in 1935 was "Dutch" Schultz, who had unwisely been advertising his plan to kill district attorney Thomas Dewey. In 1934 Genovese fled the country in order to escape a murder charge, and in 1937 Luciano himself was sentenced to a thirty- to fifty-year term for his prostitution business (so much for insulation from prosecution). It was during this period that Frank Costello acted as boss for the imprisoned Luciano. With the repeal of Prohibition, bookmaking and the numbers racket were now the chief operations.

In 1946, in part for cooperation of *Operation Underworld,* a program in which the U.S. Navy enlisted the cooperation of mobsters to prevent sabotage on the docks during the war (Gosch and Hammer, 1974; Gage, 1974). Luciano was paroled into permanent exile and, although Costello was still acting boss, the Genovese era was about to begin.

The Genovese Period

In a curious series of events, Vito Genovese, who had voluntarily exiled himself in 1934 in order to escape a murder indictment, was not only decorated with Italy's highest citizen award by Mussolini during World War II, but was also involved in other intrigue. In 1943 he hired Carmine Galante to murder the U. S. editor of an Italian language newspaper that was critical of Mussolini. Picked up for blackmarketing stolen Allied supplies and extradited to the United States for the 1934 murder charge, he was miraculously a free man when the chief corroborative witness against him was poisoned in a Brooklyn jail.

The postwar period found the mob moving into casino-building in Las Vegas and also the subject of live, televised *Kefauver Commission Hearings.* Only the later Watergate hearings would so captivate the public imagination. After testifying before the Kefauver Committee, Costello was a marked man and, barely escaping an assassination attempt, decided to retire. Behind this attempt and other murders—for example, the well-publicized murder by Joey Gallo of Albert Anastasia in the Park Sheraton barber shop in Manhattan—was Genovese, who was now consolidating his power—power that would elude him in what was to have been the "coronation," a mob convention planned for Chicago three weeks later.

The Appalachian Meetings

Although a major mob meeting was planned for Chicago, Steve Magaddino (the Buffalo boss), whose ill health prevented long travel, offered the Appalachian, New York, estate of one of his members. Besides the recognition of Genovese as top boss and assurances of peace to Costello, the meeting agenda included confirmation of the mob's antidrug policy and the need for new memberships (Talese, 1971, p. 213; Bonanno, 1983). The last was a sore point because, due to the lack of new blood, the vitality of the syndicate was in peril. Suspicions regarding informers and the lack of discipline among American-born recruits led some families to recruit "greenies" from Sicily's latifondi or farming areas (Reid, 1970, p. 72).

Before the session ended, there was a police raid, during which many were temporarily held so that their names could be obtained. This spoiled the anonymity the syndicate valued. Even more catastrophic than the Kefauver hearings, this evidence of the existence of some type of coordinated, national syndicate was now hard to deny (Bonanno, 1983). In 1958 an informant, Nelson Cantellops, assisted in convicting 24 people, including Genovese, Galante, and Joseph Valachi. Having received "the kiss of death" from Genovese in prison, and feeling that he was marked for execution, Valachi murdered by mistake a fellow prisoner and became the first public "made member" informant from the ranks of organized crime and the star witness at the McClellan Commission Hearings on Organized Crime.

The Gambino Period

From the mid-sixties and into the nineties the IAS, rather than operating as an IBM-type corporation as described in Cosa Nostra theory, resembled instead the "patron model." "The Gallo-Profaci Wars," the attempted Colombo assassination, "the Banana Split," and the "Gallo-Colombo Wars" (Diapoulos and Linakis, 1976; Talese, 1971) suggested continuing internal strife. Perhaps a small, coup-plagued, unstable, Latin-American country would be a better model than a large corporation in describing the IAS. While Carlo Gambino was consolidating his power during this period, a commentary on the 1969 truce in the Banana Wars (a rift in the Joseph Bonanno family) may have best described the dilemma faced by the IAS: "What the Mafia needed in New York in 1969 was a health clinic, not a gang war" (MacLean, 1974, pp. 341–42). Most of the leaders were dying or sick. Many were in their seventies, and their middle-level executives, due to membership moratoriums, were not much younger. Gambino controlled four of the five New York mobs with only the Bonanno family not in the fold. Although forced into involuntary exile in Arizona by the commission, Bonanno still controlled his New York organization through various loyalists. In 1974 his long-time underboss Carmine "the Cigar" Galante was released from a 12-year stretch in federal penitentiaries. Galante announced his return by blasting off the bronze doors on Frank Costello's mausoleum, warring against blacks and Latinos for the control of narcotics in the South Bronx and Harlem, and finally, according to unnamed mob sources, arranging for the death of Gambino himself by persuading the elderly, coronary-prone man to get a swine flu shot ("After the Don," 1976, p. 32).

With the death of Gambino in 1976, speculation was rife as to who was likely to emerge as the most influential boss. In 1984 Boss Paul Castellano of the Gambino family and two of his top lieutenants were indicted for extortion, pattern of racketeering, and conspiracies to commit murder. Castellano had emerged as the most powerful of the dons and appeared to be in a position to claim the "national crown" when he was gunned down outside a Manhattan restaurant on December 16, 1985. Some members were apparently disenchanted with his leadership, criticizing his favoring and rewarding members who had not "made their bones" (killed others) (Kelly, 1990, p. 18). The FBI believes that the person responsible for this assassination was an ambitious younger man, John Gotti, who then seized control of the Gambino family.

The Commission Trials

Undoubtedly, the biggest blow ever dealt to the Italian-American Syndicate was a series of prosecutions of organized crime figures by the federal government from 1983 to 1987. Indictments in 1985 alone reached almost five thousand, and alleged leaders of sixteen of the twenty-four Mafia families were indicted. Albanese (1989, p. 3), in recounting the impact of the trials, pointed out that the existence of both a Mafia and Commission was admitted.

The outcome of the trials crippled the aging upper echelons of the Mafia families. The bosses of the Colombo, Genovese, and Lucchese organized crime families were convicted of being members of "the Commission" established by Luciano in 1931, which settled underworld disputes and authorized gangland killings (Doyle, 1987). The only major survivor of the "Commission Trials" was John Gotti, who emerged as the most powerful boss of an organization that had now been weakened by criminal justice and media attention, creating a vacuum to be filled by rival ethnic gangs (Mustain and Capeci, 1988). In referring to Gotti's emergence to head a decimated Mafia, one magazine article was entitled "The Last Godfather?" (McKillop, 1989).

Gotti was a "media darling" reminiscent of a Costello or Capone. At his headquarters in Queens, the Bergen Hunt and Fish Club, Gotti operated, dapper but ruthless. He was called the "Teflon don" because of his ability to escape conviction. Finally convicted in 1992, Gotti was dubbed by the press the "Velcro don." He was convicted, in part, on the basis of the testimony of his former underboss. The American Mafia in the nineties represented a dwindling empire with some remaining strongholds, such as New York and the Chicago suburbs. The death of the American Mafia was clear in the late 1990s when the bosses of organized crime families became informants to the federal government. Angelo Lonardo (Cleveland) and Ralph Natale (Philadelphia) both broke the code of omerta and cooperated with government investigations.

Some of the Mafia's competition has included the six-thousand-member Herrera family from Mexico, triple the size of the Mafia and developing ties with Colombian groups, particularly in Chicago. Kleinknecht in *The New Ethic Mobs* (1996) claims that the most important new organized crime gangs are the Chinese, who concentrate on gambling, extortion, alien smuggling, credit card fraud, drug smuggling, and loansharking. The new Russian mobs are into white collar and financial crime, confidence games, and black market activities. The Arab mob (Christian Iraqis known as Chaldeans) commit grocery coupon fraud. Vietnamese groups in Silicon Valley have staged armed robberies of high tech firms (Sanoff, 1996). The new "Mafia" is more likely to be multiethnic and global. U.S. drug czar in the Clinton administration, Barry McCaffrey, indicated that he believed the Russians and Nigerians were the most threatening criminal organizations based in the U.S. (Farah, 1997). The Russians offer other drug syndicates weaponry previously beyond their reach and have increasingly moved into drug trafficking and money laundering. Nigerian groups have been primarily involved in confidence games and fraud. Outlaw motorcycle gangs, Colombian cocaine crime families, black criminal gangs, and Asian gangs are among the many new mobs contending for this vacated territory.

Other Developments

Jamaican organized crime groups, "posses," operate not only in Jamaica, but increasingly in the United States and Canada and are involved in narcotics trafficking, firearms smuggling, money laundering, fraud, kidnapping, robbery, and murder. A bizarre relationship exists between rival political parties in Jamaica and rival posses. Many of the latter send some of the proceeds from U.S. drug operations back home to finance political campaigns (Pincomb, 1989).

Black organized crime groups are not examples of emerging groups; they have existed for decades (Messick, 1979; Abadinsky, 1994; and Pennsylvania Crime Commission, 1986; Schatzberg and Kelly, 1995). Some of the better-known organizations were those run by Frank Matthews, Charles Lucas, Leroy Barnes, and Jeff Fort (El Rukns), but a variety of other groups are involved in such things as drug trafficking, the numbers racket, extortion, and murder. In Philadelphia in the nineties a tightly knit criminal organization calling itself "the Family" specialized in drug distribution and murder, as did "the Junior Black Mafia" (Pennsylvania Crime Commission, 1991).

Organized crime remains a "queer ladder of mobility" (Bell, 1953) for black mobs in Philadelphia and New York, Colombian and Cuban mobs in Florida, and Chinese and Chicano mobs on the West Coast. Although many of these mobs are not fully developed and structured syndicates—as in the organized crime model—they certainly represent an evolving force to be reckoned with. In a dissenting view, Lupsha (1981) argues that Italian organized crime groups still retain predominant power in many key areas of underworld crime, while Reuter (1984a) sees them as paper tigers living on their reputation.

(© Yvonne Hemsey / Gamma - Liaison)

Caught here in a casual moment, media-savvy John Gotti enjoyed his interplay with the press. Some observes speculated that Gotti's 1992 conviction heralded the demise of old-style organized crime.

"The Pizza Connection." In late 1985 to early 1986, twenty-two defendants went to trial in New York City on charges that they ran a $1.7 billion drug trafficking organization in the United States, using pizza restaurants as fronts. This group was a "Sicilian mafia," supposedly separate from and with few links to the existing "American Mafia," according to Tommaso Buscetta, who revealed their operations to U.S. authorities (Reuters, 1984a). Federal authorities did, however, find some links with "American Mafia" groups as well as cooperation in money laundering by Swiss and Italian banks and by U.S. brokerage firms E. F. Hutton and Merrill Lynch. Sicilian immigrants, called "zips" because of their rapid speech, staffed these pizza parlors (Potter, 1989; Blumenthal, 1988; Alexander, 1988).

The Sicilian Mafia. Journalist Claire Sterling in her book *Octopus: The Long Reach of the International Sicilian Mafia* (1990) mixes fact with a little fiction to describe the crossnational reach of the post-World War II Italian Mafia. With the closing of the Corsican "French Connection" in the seventies, organized crime figures in Sicily began to supply large amounts of heroin to the United States and in the early eighties began a "civil war" over control of this lucrative trade. Their violence spilled over into the murder of the head of the Italian antimob squad, General Carlo Chiesa, and his pregnant wife, as well as the murder of Judge Caesar Terranova. This enraged the Sicilian public, the church, and public officials, and spelled the doom of Sicilian Mafia groups. In February 1986 over 456 members and associates of organized crime groups were put on trial, including Michele "Pope" Greco, held by some to be the "boss of bosses." The trial took place in a specially constructed courtroom guarded by two hundred crack troops and ended in December 1987 with 338, including Greco, convicted. The key witness in the trial was a former boss, Tommaso Buscetta, who also testified in the "Pizza Connection" trials in the United States (Gage, 1988, pp. 36–37).

By 1988 only 112 of those convicted were still in jail, and in April 1991, 28 Sicilian Mafia leaders including Greco were released on a technicality. In March 1992 the Mafia killed a Christian Democratic politician, Salvatore Lima, and in May 1992 assassinated Judge Giovanni Falcone, his wife, and three bodyguards. Falcone was to enforce stronger anti Mafia laws. In July 1992 the Mafia killed his successor, Judge Paolo Borsellino (Stille and Robinson, 1992). While the Mafia was sending a message, the Italian government responded by sending the Italian army to Sicily and proposed very strong, perhaps draconian, laws with which to attack the criminal organization (Cowell, 1992).

Criminal Careers of Organized Criminals

Similar to professional crime, but unlike most other types of crime, organized criminal activity is an example of career crime, in which crime is pursued as a livelihood. Organized criminals exhibit varying degrees of the following characteristics, with those who are members of established syndicates expressing these qualities to a greater degree: they identify with crime and criminal activity, possess strong organizational identity, and tend to belong to structured groups that maintain continuance of operation.

Based on our previous description of organized crime, such criminals tend to be bred in low-income, high-crime areas of large central cities, where illegitimate opportunity structures appear more available than legitimate ones. Most begin as conventional criminals, but, rather than retiring as most do in their early twenties, they continue to progress in criminality and in association with organized criminals (Clinard and Quinney, 1973, p. 229).

To varying degrees, organized criminal groups subscribe to a code of secrecy, whether it be the "cosa de hombre" (code of manliness) of the "Nuestra Cosa" (Mexican Mafia), rules of conduct of gangs such as Hell's Angels and the Pagans, or the prototype code of "omerta" described by people like Valachi. Omerta is a Cosa Nostra code of intense loyalty, honor, secrecy, obedience, and "manly" silence—a code that renders loyalty to the organization above loyalty to country, God, or family and whose violation means death.

Secrecy, discipline, corruption, planned violence, and public demand for illicit goods in either compromised or inept political climates provide a continuing good occupational outlook for the next generation of Valachis, whatever their ethnicity. The continuing public demand for illicit goods and services and corrupt relationship with government officials may be more important factors in the persistence of organized groups than the imperviousness of their organizations.

Public and Legal Reaction

In Chapter 14 we will explore the issue of drug abuse from the standpoint of users, but our concern in this chapter has been drug trafficking in which international drug "kingpins" such as Jorge Ochoa, Pablo Escobar, and Gonzalo Rodriguez are the new Al Capones and Meyer Lanskys. In the late eighties the United States began to go after major drug "kingpins." In May 1988 Carlos Lehder-Rivas, who had been extradited from Colombia, was convicted of being responsible for up to 80 percent of the cocaine smuggled into the United States. In 1989 leaders of Colombia's Medellin Cartel were indicted on charges of cocaine trafficking, and the slayings of the Colombian justice minister as well as of a U.S. drug informant ("U.S. Indicts," 1989). Attempts to put pressure on the "Underground Empire" of drug launderers and officials were illustrated by the capture and imprisonment of Panamanian strongman Manuel Noriega. VANTAGE POINT 13.4 presents the ASC Organized Crime Task Force policy recommendations.

Drug Control Strategies

Some drug control strategies or options include: legalization, use of diplomacy, interdiction, targeting traffickers, coordination of rival departments, and prevention (Adler et al., 1988; Moore, 1988). *Legalization* is viewed as a last resort, an unnecessary risk, and a questionable moral decision. It would appear to be unwise to overreact to a crack epidemic by legalizing drugs as it might create more demand for drugs at a time when overall drug use is declining. *The use of diplomacy* or economic and political pressure to halt the drug war being waged against the United States by Colombia, Bolivia, Peru, and Mexico in particular is a supply-side strategy that is not without risk. "Anti-Yanqui" feelings may be fueled, and many countries are dependent on drug money. *Interdiction* involves stopping the transport and smuggling of drugs into the United States. With many ports of entry and endless borders, some deterrence is possible; but complete interdiction is impossible.

Targeting major traffickers such as the Medellin Cartel, while enhancing street-level enforcement to totally disrupt street traffic in drugs (Hayeslip, 1989) has possibilities. *Departmental coordination* and elimination of rivalry are claimed to be aided by the creation of a federal "drug czar" in 1989 (William Bennett) to oversee and coordinate agencies involved in the drug war. Despite the highly symbolic rhetoric of "a war on drugs" announced by President Bush in 1989, two years later many rehabilitation programs were closing down because of the loss of funding. Finally, a "demand-side" strategy of prevention offers the ultimate hope. Education and rehabilitation programs as well as policy experiments to discover programs that work are greatly needed.

Investigative Procedures

Law enforcement in the eighties and nineties finally became as organized as organized crime and began to effectively apply *a variety of investigative procedures* including: financial analysis, electronic surveillance, use of informants and undercover agents, citizens' commissions (Albanese, 1989, pp. 105–20), and computer assistance. *Financial analysis* involves following paper trails (records of transaction) in order to see if expenditures match earnings. Classic Internal Revenue Service procedures in enforcing tax codes such as analyzing net worth, expenditures, and bank deposits are utilized.

Electronic surveillance (the use of "bugs" and wiretapping in covert eavesdropping) is viewed by many authorities as one of the most effective weapons against organized crime. The use of 150 audio- and videotapes at the "Commission Trials" was very successful. The *use of informants* (insiders who provide information) as well as *undercover agents* has also been indispensable. Informants such as Jackie Presser (former Teamster President), Angelo Lonardo (former Cleveland don), and Tommaso Buscetta (Sicilian "Mafia" don) have been devastating to the syndicate. *Citizens commissions* such as the Chicago Crime Commission are essential in providing an independent watchdog function in examining organized criminal activity (Albanese, 1989, p. 116).

Finally, *computer-assisted investigation* has great potential for unraveling complicated transactions and network interrelationships. The FBI uses a sophisticated computer data base, the Organized Crime Information System, and is experimenting with artificial intelligence using a supercomputer called Big Floyd.

Laws and Organized Crime

Some specific laws that have been used against organized crime include: special laws such as the Hobbs Act; features of the Organized Crime Control Act of 1970, especially RICO

VANTAGE POINT 13.4

Domestic Organized Crime

Issues

Although seriously weakened in the past 25 years, the traditional Cosa Nostra form of organized crime has not been eliminated; instead, it has been joined by a variety of increasingly powerful domestic and international organized criminal networks operating in this country. Criminal organizations (particularly those from China and Latin America) are exploiting the increases in U.S. immigration for cover and concealment of criminal activities, as well as for recruitment. Aliens, smuggled by boat, pay exorbitant passage fees and cannot work at regular jobs; thus, they are exploited by unscrupulous employers or become active in prostitution, the drug trade, or other aspects of the illegal economy. In this way, victims become criminals themselves.

One problem in combating these groups is that citizens have not been mobilized as allies in the effort. Despite a series of significant prosecutions for racketeering conspiracies during the last decade, vast numbers of Americans continue to gamble illegally, use banned drugs, buy stolen property, and otherwise contribute to the very same conspiracies that the government is fighting to defeat.

Policy recommendations

- **Citizen mobilization:** Special grand jury provisions of the Organized Crime Control Act, calling for an investigative grand jury to be called at least every 18 months to examine organized crime and corruption in districts of more than one million citizens, should finally be implemented. Significantly, the law provides for the special grand jury to issue a report on those conditions at the end of its term. Implementation would provide a tremendous opportunity for citizens on the grand jury to help educate other citizens, through follow-up town meetings and other mechanisms, about the less obvious evils of organized crime.
- **Surveillance:** Specific policy and judicial authorization guidelines should be developed as a way to make installations of eavesdropping and monitoring devices uniform and the expectations of investigators, their supervisors, and the judiciary identical. There is no way to eliminate the danger of these installations, but law and policy must more specifically circumscribe this issue to protect those in law enforcement and negate the possibility of agency embarrassment, should an incident occur.
- **Criminal informants:** DOJ should establish a technical assistance program designed to train State and local authorities in the proper development, use, and management of criminal informants, because the misuse of informants has not only misled police but undermined public support for the use of informants. Technical assistance might consist of the development of police courses (required for those handling informants) or inservice training on this issue.
- **Uniform training standards:** DOJ should develop minimum standards and curriculum for police training

(Racketeer-Influenced and Corrupt Organizations), the Bank Secrecy Act (1970), as well as assets seizure (forfeiture).

Hobbs Act. One effective piece of legislation on the books since the mid-forties is the **Hobbs Act,** an antiracketeering act that can basically be interpreted to mean that any interference with interstate commerce to any degree whatsoever is in violation of the act. This statute has been applied, for example, against politicians in Newark, New Jersey, in accepting kickbacks from contractors who had obtained supplies from out of state.

Organized Crime Control Act. The single most effective piece of federal legislation ever passed in the United States to fight organized crime activity is the controversial **Organized Crime Control Act** of 1970, a principal feature of which is the RICO statute. **RICO** prohibits proceeds from a pattern of racketeering activity from being used in acquiring legitimate businesses that are involved in interstate commerce. Generally, a "pattern of racketeering" involves participation in any two specified crimes, such as murder or extortion, within a ten-year period.

VANTAGE POINT 13.4—*Continued*

nationwide, with special emphasis on the training of local police. Inconsistency in training hurts professionalism, lateral career mobility of officers, and interagency cooperation in combating organized crime.

- **Seizure of assets:** DOJ should develop specific guidelines for the seizure of assets to set a national standard. Public confidence erodes when seizures are made that appear questionable. Several lawsuits against police are pending on this issue. The incidence or appearance of unprofessional behavior on the part of police in organized crime control efforts must be removed.
- **Tracking illicit drugs:** DOJ should provide incentives and guidelines for states, as well as other nations, to track identified illicit drugs and to prohibit their misuse under penalty of law. Only 18 states have enacted legislation similar to the Chemical Diversion and Trafficking Act (establishing federal recordkeeping, reporting, and transaction requirements for essential chemicals), and these laws differ widely in their scope and requirements. Other jurisdictions must also be kept abreast of new synthetic chemicals that should be added each year to the list of essential chemicals.
- **Court-imposed trusteeships:** Court-imposed trusteeships should be utilized against nonunion businesses found to be controlled by organized crime. Such intervention enables the government to "restart" the business with completely new personnel and supervisory and auditing procedures to prevent the return of organized crime. This kind of intercession in nonunion businesses has occurred in few instances thus far, but its potential as a tool for long-term prevention is enormous.
- **Investigative screening:** DOJ should sponsor one or more "teams" of interested researchers and organized crime investigators to work for a period of months, since there has been too little interaction among these professionals. Together, they should test investigative screening models of businesses at high risk of infiltration by organized crime and translate their findings into usable form for investigators at the federal, state, and local levels. A proven case-screening (or business-screening) model could do much to reduce time spent on proactive investigations that lead to dead ends.
- **Shared perspectives:** DOJ should sponsor "long-term prevention" forums periodically for the specific purpose of integrating law enforcement and criminological perspectives on the problem of organized crime. Expertise and insight on both sides could be profitably shared to develop effective organized crime control innovations.

Source: "American Society of Criminology Task Force Report to Attorney General Janet Reno," *The Criminologist* (Special Issue), 20, 6, November/December 1995. Task Force members: Jay Albanese and James Finckenauer, co-chairs.

InfoTrac College Edition Research
Locate the article: "The Russki Files." What is the current threat of Russian organized crime in North America?

Some of the principal features of the act are: the creation of *special grand juries* to investigate organized criminal activity, and the provision of *general immunity for witnesses* appearing before the grand jury, in which the privilege against self-incrimination is abrogated in return for protection against the use of such compelled information in a criminal proceeding. It provides for the *incarceration of witnesses* who refuse to testify (recalcitrant witnesses), authorizes a *conviction based on irreconcilably inconsistent declarations* under oath (perjury), and provides for *protected facilities for housing government witnesses* and their families. It also authorizes the government to *preserve testimony* by the *use of a deposition* (testimony given under oath but outside the courtroom) in a criminal proceeding, a right that previously existed only for the defendant, and *prohibits any challenge to the admissibility of evidence* based on its being the fruit of an unlawful government act, if such act occurred five years or more before the event sought to be proved. The act makes it *unlawful to engage in the "illegal gambling business"* itself and contains the RICO statute.

The Bank Secrecy Act (1970) is directed at controlling money laundering. It includes features requiring banks to report transactions over ten thousand dollars or file a report if ten thousand dollars or more leaves or enters the country, and citizens to report foreign bank accounts on tax returns (Abadinsky, 1994, p. 430). *Assets seizure* (forfeiture) has emerged as one of the most powerful tools to break the back of criminal enterprises—"kick them in the assets," so to speak.

> Forfeiture, the ancient legal practice of government seizure of property used in criminal activity, may prove a particularly useful weapon against illicit narcotics trafficking (Stellwagen, 1985, p. 1).

Imprisonment and fines have been found inadequate in deterring capital organizations, while seizure of assets curtails the financial ability of such groups to continue criminal operations (Bureau of Justice Statistics, 1988b, p. 93). Assets may include money, property, businesses, cars, boats, or any item that may have been involved in or is the product of a criminal enterprise (Lombardo, 1990; Jacoby, Gramckow, and Rutledge, 1992).

The RICO Statute. The *RICO statute* authorizes the federal government to seize legitimate operations if they have been purchased with illegally gained funds (laundering) or if they are used for criminal purposes. In addition, defendants can be subject to up to twenty years' imprisonment. The law permits prosecutors greater latitude in presenting to the jury a broader picture of patterns of racketeering; this enables them to trace the pattern back to formerly insulated bosses. Because of the broad sweep of the law, lawyers and others are fearful of the application of the law to nonsyndicate crime, such as crimes by legitimate business.

At the time of the law's passage many criticized RICO as an exceptional measure (moral entrepreneurship, if you wish) that was passed/engineered in order to grant unusual powers to the government and to capitalize on public fear of crime, a ploy for the "erosion of justice and equity in America" (Smith, 1980, p. 331). However, RICO had broadened the classification of "organized lawbreaking" to include political corruption and white collar crime. In 1979 in U.S. District Court, a case was dismissed against five men accused of a Texas oil swindle. The presiding judge was quoted as stating, "RICO was designed to take racketeers out of business, not to make racketeers out of businessmen" (Mitchell, 1981, p. 41). RICO held that criminal associations need not be wholly corrupt; that is, they could be partly legitimate, thus permitting the law's application to private business, labor unions, law enforcement, judicial, and government offices. If the illegal income is derived from, or is used to acquire interest in or to conduct, an enterprise, then it is eligible for RICO. The following individuals or organizations have been RICO-ed: a hospital equipment business, the Macon County (Georgia) Sheriff's Department, a Florida state judge (his judicial district was named as the enterprise), a pornography operation, bailbondsmen, an oil platform construction company, a Michigan mayor (for shaking down real estate developers), and crooked pharmacists and nursing home operators (Press, Shannon, and Simons, 1979, pp. 82–83).

RICO charges offer a unique advantage in targeting an entire enterprise, and civil RICO laws can be used to seize cash and assets. Application of RICO charges to white collar violations, such as insider trading by brokerage firm Drexel Burnham Lambert, raises controversy. Civil RICO permits victims of fraud to bring private civil suits whether or not the Justice Department files charges ("RICO," 1989, p. 18). Threatened companies, it is claimed, are forced to settle or be branded racketeers. While some critics see it as a "statute run amok" (Boucher, 1989), others see it as a powerful tool to control white collar crime in addition to organized crime (Waldman and Gilbert, 1989; see also Safire, 1989). Greek (1990, p. 1) indicates, "RICO represents a major expansion of the federalization of crime and which for now appears to be quite acceptable, despite those protesting its widespread use, to both the courts and a large segment of the American public as well."

Until 1981 many features of RICO had lain dormant. In a case against IAS boss Frank Tieri the government alleged that Mafia families themselves constituted illegal enterprises. Los Angeles mobsters were also convicted of racketeering and conspiracy charges (Mitchell, 1981, p. 43).

The civil provisions of RICO permit U.S. attorneys and private citizens to sue for treble damages and the cost of the suit if it can be demonstrated that the plaintiff or his or her business/property was injured as a result of a pattern of racketeering. A *Continuing Criminal Enterprise* statute is similar to RICO, but targets only illegal drug activity. The statute considers it a crime to commit or conspire to commit a series of felony violations of the 1970 Drug Abuse Prevention and Control Act in concert with five or more other persons (Carlson and Finn, 1993). By the mid-nineties the growth in violent street crime perpetrated by gangs finally received serious federal attention. Federal agencies such as the FBI, DEA, and ATF began to team up with local police to target such groups. RICO charges, for instance, were successfully employed against Chicago's Latin Kings, Atlantic City's Abdullahs gang, and Shreveport's Bottoms Boys.

As an exercise in what this author would call "creative law enforcement," prior to his assassination, gangster Carmine Galante's parole was revoked on the basis of his knowingly associating with criminal elements. Mention should be once again made of yet another area of "creative law enforcement," which was made most famous with the ABSCAM operation, the undercover sting where police agents pretended to be involved in criminal operations themselves. "Operation Miporn," "Unirac," and "Brilab" all exemplify the types of aggressive operations necessary to root out aggressive and insulated syndicates.

Summary

The subject of much public interest, organized crime has been defined in a variety of ways. In the United States most federal agency and state statutes use generic definitions, which indicate that organized crime is any criminal activity involving two or more individuals. Utilizing a similar *generic (broad or general) definition,* Albini identifies four types of organized crime: political-social, mercenary (predatory), in-group, and syndicate. With the exception of the last type, syndicate crime, all of the former refer to other types of criminal activity, such as political, conventional, and professional criminal behavior.

The field of criminology defines organized crime (henceforth synonymous with syndicate crime) as a continuing group or *organization:*

1. that participates in illicit activity in any society by the *use of force, intimidation, or threats;*
2. that provides *illicit services* that are in strong public demand; and
3. that assures protection and *immunity* through corruption.

An *organized crime model* is proposed as a useful device for avoiding confusion in the process of deciding whether a group's activities represent an example of organized crime. Organized crime as a concept is *not a matter of kind,* but is rather a *matter of degree;* that is, to what extent does this type of crime possess the characteristics identified in our criminological definition of organized crime? Types of crime may be viewed as distributed along a *continuum* ranging from nonorganized to organized (syndicate) crime, depending on the degree to which they exhibit organization, the use or threat of violence, the provision of illicit goods in public demand, and the ability to obtain immunity through corruption and enforcement. *Types of organized (syndicate) crime include:* traditional crime syndicates, nontraditional syndicates, semiorganized crime, local politically controlled organized crime, and national politically controlled organized crime.

In addition to definitional problems, another problem in the study of organized crime is the poor scientific nature of much of the literature, which forces the social scientist to rely on many journalistic and autobiographical accounts. A variety of street gangs were described, and some were noted to be undergoing transition into ghetto-based drug trafficking organizations.

Internationally, organized crime thrives in two types of political environments: liberal democracies and corrupt dictatorships. *Chinese Triad societies,* highly ritualized Chinese secret organizations that are often involved in organized crime, were described.

Mafiya is a term used to refer to various Russian organized crime groups, which have grown in power since the collapse of the former Soviet Union. Organized crime, although dominated since the thirties by the Italian-American syndicate, has participation from a variety of ethnic groups. According to the "theory of ethnic succession," mobs have represented a "queer ladder of mobility" for a variety of minorities.

Money laundering involves making clean or washing "dirty money" (illegal funds). Such operations make use of unscrupulous banks that ask no questions in accepting large deposits of cash primary drug smuggling routes—the Golden Triangle, the Golden Crescent, and Latin America—were discussed, as were the Colombian Cartels and the Underground Empire.

Various theories regarding the origin of the term *Mafia* were traced, with the author agreeing with Albini that the most likely source is Risotto's 1860 play, *I Mafiusi de la Vicaria* (The Heroes of the Penitentiary). Three *theories* of the nature of syndicate crime in the United States were discussed: (1) Cosa Nostra theory, (2) confederation theory, and (3) patron theory. While the first theory, which has been accepted by federal commissions and agencies, views organized crime as centrally controlled by a formally structured Italian-American syndicate, confederation theory views it as controlled by a "combination" of ethnic groups, principally Jewish and Italian. The patron theory views organized crime as a set of shifting alliances, a "client-patron" relationship.

The "Mafia myth" is the belief that organized crime is the product of an alien conspiracy. More moderate expressions of this theme view the IAS (Italian-American Syndicate) as the most powerful of organized crime groups, but not the product of an alien conspiracy. Critics of the Mafia or Cosa Nostra (LCN, La Cosa Nostra) model argue that the terms and descriptions of these organizations are fictitious, the creations of federal law enforcement agencies. A more moderate view admits many of their criticisms, but still argues that the IAS exists, the vision being "skewed, not false."

The *classic pattern of organized crime* involves a gradual evolutionary development from strategic and tactical crimes, to illegal businesses and activities, to legitimate businesses, to an infiltration of big business and government itself. Some typical operations of organized criminal groups are arson, assault, coercion, extortion, murder, blackmail, bribery, and corruption. Typical illegal businesses include gambling operations, loan sharking, labor racketeering, record and tape piracy, and any number of other activities detailed in the chapter. Infiltration of legitimate businesses such as trucking, construction, and the hotel and restaurant industry provides cover for organized crime operations. Although it is hazardous to guess, estimated gross revenues and untaxed net profits appear to make organized crime wealthier than the nation's largest industrial corporation.

Organized crime infiltration of legitimate business may be viewed on one hand as a natural "ethnic succession" of organized crime, and on the other hand as yet another setting for illegitimate operations. Involvement of organized crime at the highest levels of government is revealed by a "CIA-Mafia link" to an attempt to assassinate Fidel Castro.

A *brief history* of organized crime traces its origins back to colonial times. The New Orleans Grand Jury report of 1890 was the first official recognition of the existence of the Mafia in this country. Other important events in the history of organized crime were traced, such as the Prohibition period, the Castellammarese Wars, the Luciano era, the Genovese era, the Kefauver and McClellan commission hearings, the Apalachin meetings, the Gambino era, and other, more recent developments in organized crime such as the Commission Trials, the Pizza Connection, and the Great Mafia Trial in Sicily.

Criminal careers of organized criminals were briefly examined. Highlighted was their strong identification with criminal careers, their recruitment, and their relationship with the public. Finally, public and legal reaction to organized crime was discussed. While public reaction to organized crime in the past was characterized as a fascinated apathy and sporadic and unorganized legal reaction, recent events suggest major inroads in the war on organized crime. Application of laws such as the Hobbs Act and the Organized Crime Control Act (1970) represent potent tools. The RICO statutes and "sting" operations by federal agencies represent creative law enforcement efforts in this regard. However, these more aggressive law enforcement efforts have been criticized for threatening civil liberties and for covering up corporate criminality.

KEY CONCEPTS

Activities of Organized Criminals
Apalachin Meetings
Assets Forfeiture
"Bust Out"
"Castellammarese Wars"
CIA-Mafia Link
Classic Pattern of Organized Crime
Commission Trials
Continuum Model of Organized Crime
Ethnic Succession Theory
Four Basic Types of Organized Crime (Generic Definitions)
Hobbs Act
Internal Structure of LCN Families
International Political Climates and Organized Crime
Iron Law of Opium Trade
Kefauver Commission
Loan Sharking
Mafiya
Major Elements of La Cosa Nostra (LCN) Theory
Medellin Cartel
"Moustache Petes"
Numbers Game
Organized Crime Control Act
"Pizza Connection"
Racketeering
RICO
Strike Forces
Theories of the Nature of U.S. Syndicate Crime
Theories Regarding Origin of Mafia
Three Elements of the Definition of Organized (Syndicate) Crime
Triads
Yakuza

REVIEW QUESTIONS

1. Discuss the various attempts to define organized crime. How does the "organized crime continuum" approach this issue?
2. What are some important sources of information on organized crime?
3. Discuss some features of Triads. Where do they operate and what are their major operations?
4. Discuss the history and present status of Russian organized crime. What are its major criminal operations, and why is it regarded as such an enormous threat?
5. Who was Amado Carillo Fuentes, and of what importance was he in the history of Mexican organized crime?
6. What is money laundering? How was "Operation Casablanca" successful in investigating and busting a money laundering operation?
7. Why was Joe Valachi so important in the history of the American Mafia?
8. What is the RICO statute? How effective has it been in the war on organized crime?
9. What are some investigative procedures and legal weapons that have been used in the war on organized crime in the United States?
10. Discuss some of the major features of the Organized Crime Control Act of 1970.

INFOTRAC COLLEGE EDITION RESEARCH

Vantage Point 13.1 InfoTrac College Edition Research
Examining "organized crime," what are some recent issues with respect to international organized crime?

Vantage Point 13.2 InfoTrac College Edition Research
Read Donald Tricarico's "Beyond the Mafia, Italian Americans and the Development of Las Vegas." What role did the mob have in developing the city? What influence does it have today?

Vantage Point 13.3 InfoTrac College Edition Research
What has been the controversy related to FAST (The Federation Against Software Theft)?

Vantage Point 13.4 InfoTrac College Edition Research
Locate the article: "The Russki Files." What is the current threat of Russian organized crime in North America?

In the News 13.1 InfoTrac College Edition Research
Do a search on drug trafficking and Mexico. What recent trends have taken place with respect to such activity in that country? What has been the response of the United States to such developments?

SELECTED READINGS

Howard Abadinsky. 2000. *Organized Crime.* 6th edition. Belmont, California: Wadsworth.
This is the bible on organized crime. It is particularly useful and interesting for its historical coverage of the Chicago and New York mobs.

Jay Albanese. 1998. *Organized Crime in America.* 3rd edition. Cincinnati: Anderson.
This is one of the best written books on the subject. It has excellent coverage of illegal activities as well as the investigation and prosecution of such activities.

Joseph Albini. 1971. *The American Mafia: Genesis of a Legend.* New York: Irvington Press.
This is a classic in the field. Albini uses a variety of sources to trace the legend, myths, and history of the American Mafia.

G. Robert Blakey and Richard Billing. 1981. *The Plot to Kill the President: Organized Crime Assassinated JFK.* New York: New York Times Books.
This controversial book by the chief counsel to the House Assassinations Committee concludes major involvement of organized crime in the assassination of President John Kennedy.

Charles Bowden. 1998. *Juarez: The Laboratory of Our Future.* New York: Aperture Foundation.
This is a biographical account of the life and times of Amado Carillo Fuentes, who until his death in 1997 was the biggest of the Mexican drug dons.

Robert J. Kelly, editor. 1986. *Organized Crime: A Global Perspective.* Totowa, N.J.: Rowman and Littlefield.
Kelly presents a very good selection of readings on transnational organized crime.

Dennis J. Kenney and James O. Finckenauer. 1995. *Organized Crime in America.* Belmont, California: Wadsworth.
This is an excellent text on organized crime and particularly on new groups such as Russian mafiya groups.

Michael D. Lyman and Gary W. Potter. 1997. *Organized Crime.* Upper Saddle River, N.J.: Prentice Hall.
This is a very good, fresh approach to examining organized crime. It is presented in a very lucid, readable format for undergraduates.

Pennsylvania Crime Commission. 1990. *Organized Crime in Pennsylvania: A Decade of Change.* Conshohocken, PA: Commonwealth of Pennsylvania.
Until its demise for political reasons by later jailed Attorney General Ernie Preate, who was a subject of its investigation, this organization consistently presented very readable investigations complete with photographs.

Vincent Teresa and Thomas Renner. 1973. *My Life in the Mafia.* Greenwich, Connecticut: Fawcett Publications.
This autobiographical account of a New England Mafia associate provides an inside look at the wold of organized crime.

PUBLIC ORDER CRIME AND THE FUTURE OF CRIME

VANTAGE POINTS

IN THE NEWS

Do It Now Before They Pass a Law Against It

—Bumper Sticker

As a result of the fascination with 'nuts, sluts, and preverts' [sic], and their identities and subcultures, little attention has been paid to the unethical, illegal, and destructive actions of powerful individuals, groups, and institutions in our society.

—Alexander Liazos (1972), "The Poverty of the Sociology of Deviance: Nuts, Sluts and 'Preverts'," *Social Problems*

It all starts on the streets. What do you see when you walk down a downtown street? Do you see the hooker conning a john? The pool hustler with his permanent pale taking a break between games? The pimp hustling a new woman? The transvestite prostitute with his head in the car window of a potential customer? Do you notice the man on the corner passing baggies to customers or the drunk in the doorway with his brown bag clutched in his hand? When you looked down the alley, did you see the people by the dumpster shooting up? Did you notice the slips of paper being passed between the news vendor and his clients? Were you surprised to see two men having sex when you stepped into the public restroom? . . . These are the players of the deviant street network at work.

—John H. Lindquist (1988). *Misdemeanor Crime: Trivial Criminal Pursuit*

Introduction

Is vice-related behavior a matter of civil liberties and individual choice in a free society? What is the role of the criminal justice system in enforcing a semblance of public morality and a sense of civic decency? Laws against **public-order criminal behavior,** sometimes referred to as "**crimes without victims**" (Schur, 1965) or "legislated morality," refer to a number of activities that are illegal because they offend public morality. Such nonpredatory crime generally includes activities such as prostitution, acts related to homosexuality, alcohol and narcotics abuse, gambling offenses, disorderly conduct, vagrancy, and minor forms of "sexual deviance." These crimes outnumber other recorded crimes and have traditionally represented the bulk of police work.

A number of other concepts have been used to refer to certain categories of public order criminal activity. Laurence Ross (1961) coined the term **folk crime** to refer to relatively common violations that occur in part because of the complexity of modern society. Traffic offenses, fish and game law violations, tax offenses, gambling and sexual deviations all can serve as illustrations. Many, but not all, of the activities to be discussed in this section are examples of crimes that are *mala prohibita,* bad because they have been prohibited by law. They violate various conceptions in society as to appropriate moral conduct, but lack the quality of acts *mala in se,* such as murder or rape, in which there is clear and abhorrent victimization of others. Offenses related to prostitution, homosexuality, gambling, and the like serve as examples of "consensual crimes" in that there is free consent on the part of participants. In many "victimless" crimes, the offenders have customers rather than victims (Silberman, 1978, p. 265).

Nuts, Guts, Sluts, and "Preverts"

Alexander Liazos (1972) published what has now become a classic sociological work, an article entitled "The Poverty of the Sociology of Deviance: Nuts, Sluts and 'Preverts'." Liazos makes the point that sociologists have concentrated too much on the "dramatic" nature of deviance, such as prostitution, homosexuality, and the like, to the neglect of more serious or harmful forms of deviance such as racism, inequitable taxation, and sexism. He states (Liazos, 1972, p. 26):

> As a result of the fascination with "nuts, sluts, and preverts [sic]," and their identities and subcultures, little attention has been paid to the unethical, illegal, and destructive actions of powerful individuals, groups, and institutions in our society. Because these actions are carried out quietly in the normal course of events, the sociology of deviance does not consider them as part of its subject matter.

This chapter will concentrate on behavior that has been labeled criminal or deviant because it is viewed either as different or as immoral or harmful to the individual. Societal attempts to regulate deviance (nuts), sex (sluts), drug and alcohol consumption (guts), and perversion (other activity, "preverts") will be explored.

Broken Windows

In their classic article "Broken Windows," Wilson and Kelling (1982) give a different view of the need to regulate such conduct. Kelling explains:

> Just as unrepaired broken windows can signal to people that nobody cares about a building and lead to more serious vandalism, untended disorderly behavior can also signal that nobody cares about the community and lead to more serious disorder and crime. Such signals—untended property, disorderly persons, drunks, obstreperous youth, etc.—both create fear in citizens and attract predators (Kelling, 1988b, p. 2).

Deinstitutionalization of the mentally ill without adequate followup or community treatment facilities has added yet another population to an already existing homeless problem. The public wants the police to assist the mentally ill, the public inebriate, and the homeless (Finn and Sullivan, 1988, p. 1). Neighborhood disorder, drunks, panhandlers, youth gangs, and other incivilities unsettle a community, produce fear, and disrupt social, commercial, and political life.

A large decrease in crime in New York City in the nineties was attributed in part to a new policing policy of zero tolerance for previously ignored squeegee men, aggressive panhandlers, subway turnstile hoppers, vagrants, and disorderly conduct. By enforcing small things the police claim to have gotten a better handle on crime in general.

While much of the reduction in crime in the 1990s was attributed to application of **broken windows theory** by its advocates, critics point out that other cities without broken windows policy also experienced similar decreases during this period.

Prostitution

Prostitution can be defined as the practice of having sexual relations with emotional indifference on a promiscuous and mercenary basis. In some countries and most U.S. states, prostitution itself is not a criminal offense; it is the act of soliciting, selling, or seeking paying customers that is prohibited. Sometimes referred to in jest as the "world's oldest profession," prostitution certainly has been widespread in societies both ancient and modern.

Until the Protestant Reformation in Western society, prostitution was pervasive and tolerated as a "necessary evil." It was often taxed by the church and was a major source of community revenue in the Middle Ages. Public health concerns that arose with the discovery of syphilis and the emergence of the Protestant ethic with its strong emphasis on individual morality were instrumental in its prohibition. Essentially, concepts of sin were translated into legal notions of crime. Despite its prohibition, prostitution exists internationally, with the exception of some preliterate societies where it would be in little demand. While prostitution is generally regarded as a low-status occupation in societies in which it is approved, in different cultures in the past certain prostitutes have enjoyed high status, such as the *hetaerae* of early Greece, the *lupanaria* in the Roman Empire, the *devadasis* in India, and the *geishas* of Japan (Davis, 1961). Such courtesans were often well-educated and trained entertainers or religious performers.

In most states, prostitution is considered a misdemeanor, and laws prohibiting it are generally enforced only when the public insists on it. Typically prostitutes are rounded up, booked, made to pay a small bail or fine, and then are put back on the streets. In order to control the undesirable activities often associated with prostitution and to avoid public complaint, many cities create vice zones or "combat zones," adult entertainment areas. Most public order offenders do not regard their behavior as criminal, perhaps in part because of general societal ambivalence toward much of it (Clinard and Quinney, 1973, p. 84). Some of the behavior may reflect personal psychological disability, but much of it reflects either adult consensual relations that are agreeable to both parties and harmful to neither or personal choice to participate in activity that the individual desires even though it may be illegal or societally disapproved.

This discussion will concentrate primarily on female prostitution, which appears to persist despite wide variations in economic, political, and social systems. One explanation is that prostitution serves a function in society: it services otherwise unmet sexual needs. There is a strong demand in many societies for no-strings-attached sexual release, particularly in relatively isolated male environments. City leaders—particularly in seaport cities such as Hamburg, Marseilles, and Baltimore—would argue that toleration of prostitution enabled the servicing of armies, the rejected, strangers, and the perverted, thus protecting "decent" females of the community. In addition to the strong demand for such services, prostitution can offer relatively lucrative rewards for females, depending, of course, on the status of customers.

Eleanor Miller, in *Street Woman* (1986) interviewed 64 prostitutes and, like Sullivan (1988), found that economic and social problems propelled young women into "hustling" as an alternative to boring, dead-end jobs. For others, it was an escape from abusive or disorganized families. Money and survival became key motivations for street hookers (Ritter, 1988).

Armstrong (1983) points out that the role of pimps (procurers) in recruiting women to prostitution is actually minimal. James (1978) notes that this is a direct challenge to the view of prostitutes as victims. James (1977) sees the view of pimps as active panderers (drumming up business and recruits) as based on past behavior of pimps, sensational journalism, and protectionist policy toward women. Lemert (1968, p. 84) describes the "white slave myth," indicating that "the trauma of forced entry into prostitution inspires sympathy and provides a way to discount responsibility for one's actions" (Armstrong, 1983, p. 214). While American explanations of recruitment point to disaffection with family, child abuse, drug use, and the like, McCaghy and Hou (1988) tell us that in Taiwan there is a historical tradition of prostitution that is sanctioned by a patrilineal system that devalues female children. Prostitution often occurs with the families' approval as a means of securing economic well-being during times of family stress.

Types of Prostitution

Prostitution involves a number of types and settings including: brothel prostitutes, bar girls, streetwalkers, massage parlor prostitutes, call girls, and other variations. Like any other occupation, prostitution is stratified, the lowest status and remuneration assigned to brothel or house prostitutes and streetwalkers and the highest prestige and reward attached to expensive call girls, who are able to command higher prices from more exclusive clientele (MacNamara and Sagarin, 1977, p. 99; Perkins and Bennett, 1985).

(© Michael Newman / PhotoEdit)

(© Michael Newman / PhotoEdit)

Left: A female prostitute hitchhikes along a road at night.
Right: A transvestite or "drag hooker" waits on a bench for a likely "John." Without the caption, would you know which was which?

Brothels—sometimes called whorehouses, cathouses, or bordellos—were widespread in the United States until the post-World War II period. Often clustered together in "red-light districts," brothels were managed by madams with whom prostitutes shared the proceeds from their tricks (sexual transactions). The term "red-light district" supposedly had its origin when railroad construction workers in the American West hung their red signal lanterns outside whorehouses they were frequenting in order to keep in contact with their dispatchers (Winick and Kinsie, 1971, p. 132). While some illegal brothels still exist, most have disappeared, although legal brothels exist in some counties in Nevada.

The following description of a red-light district in Erie, Pennsylvania, in 1907 is illustrative:

> In the three blocks of French Street mentioned, there are roughly sixteen immoral houses. Within these resorts a conservative total of 75 girls have been leading a life of shame. None of these resorts hold a liquor license, but at all of them, drinks of any description can be obtained at any hour of the day . . . by a visitor of almost any age.
>
> Seventy-five percent of the girls of the tenderloin are under 21 years of age. Ninety percent of the visitors are young men under 20. Fully thirty percent are boys of 16 and 17 ("Erie Red Light," 1907).

Streetwalkers or "hookers" parade and negotiate the sale of their wares on the public streets. The term *hooker* was apparently derived from camp or circuit traveling prostitutes who followed and serviced the Union troops of General Joseph Hooker during the Civil War (Winick and Kinsie, 1971, p. 58). Such "working girls" earn the lowest fees of all prostitutes and are most vulnerable to police interference. Streetwalkers also are most likely to have arrangements with pimps, who play the combined roles of managers, protectors, and pseudofathers. In the United States since the sixties, the majority of street pimps are black; recent research suggests that pimping is held in less regard than in the past and may be of less importance in the world of prostitution than it was at one time (Winick, and Kinsie, 1971, p. 120). While relationships between pimps and their stables of prostitutes vary, many hookers are required by their pimps to earn a certain amount per day or suffer physical harm (Milner and Milner, 1972; Slim, 1969; Sheehy, 1973).

Bar girls, or B-girls, are common in seaport cities and areas serving military populations, such as in combat zones, or adult entertainment sections of some large cities. Such hookers entice customers to buy them drinks, usually nonalcoholic ones, for ridiculous prices, while also arranging for tricks, which may occur on the premises or at nearby "hot sheet" hotels.

Call girls represent the top of the prostitution profession. Such "hookers" generally are very selective in their clientele and are highly rewarded. Most are from more educated and middle class backgrounds than streetwalkers or house girls and usually operate on referrals. "Escort services" generally are fronts for prostitution in which clients may pay per hour for the company and "services" of usually attractive young women.

According to Rosen (1983), the early twentieth-century campaign against prostitution and the banning of "red-light districts" have made it the lucrative profession it is today. Previously prostitutes, although exploited, had a certain amount of control over their earnings and working conditions. Their profiteers, madams, landlords, saloon keepers, and other intermediaries were more benign than modern pimps, and the brothel was a rational economic alternative to a sweatshop job at starvation wages.

Massage Parlors

Breslaw Executive Health Spa! 15 Lovely Girls Upstairs and 15 Lovely Girls Downstairs To Serve You! (Advertisement). Advertisements such as that quoted above appeared on Canadian commercial television (CKCO-TV, Kitchener, Ontario, September 1, 1983, 12:45 a.m. EST). The massage parlor, in which forms of commercial sex are sold under the guise of a health spa or massage service, became quite common in North America in the seventies. Journalist Gay Talese (1979), who recorded extensive participant observation studies of such operations in *Thy Neighbor's Wife,* concluded that for all practical purposes under existing laws such operations constitute legalized prostitution. Since "extras" (prohibited sexual services) must be negotiated and requested by the customer, parlor girls can avoid actual solicitation, and law enforcement agencies must be careful of entrapment or causing illegal activities to occur that would not otherwise have taken place.

A very clever means of rationalizing prostitution surfaced in Los Angeles ("Couple Call," 1989) when a couple offered sexual intercourse to members of their Church of the Most High Goddess. The woman and her husband were arrested on charges of solicitation, but insisted the state was violating their freedom of religion. The priestess absolved the sins of the male followers through sex acts, which they claimed was the revival of ancient Egyptian religious rites. The woman said, "Anything God wants from me, I will give HIM. . . . If he wants me to be monogamous, I'll be monogamous. If he says go have sex with 20,000 men, I'll do it."

Johns

While an extensive literature exists on prostitution, there has been a paucity of information regarding "**johns**" or customers, except from interviews with prostitutes. Holzman and Pines (1979) note that much of the literature on johns portrays them as socially, psychologically, or physically inadequate, having to pay for that which others can obtain free as a matter of course (Morris and Hawkins, 1970; Laner, 1974; Benjamin and Masters, 1964; Gibbens and Silberman, 1960; Ellis, 1959). The term "trick" is derisively used to refer to the fact that the hooker tricks the john into paying for what he should be able to obtain free (Milner and Milner, 1972, p. 38). Holzman and Pines (1979) indicate that much of this negative evaluation of johns has come from prostitutes and mental health practitioners and that field studies of such customers by social service researchers present a different picture (Winick, 1962; Armstrong, 1978; Simpson and Schill, 1977; Stein, 1974).

Stein, employing one-way mirrors in order to observe and record hundreds of sessions between prostitutes and clients, was struck by the normal or "straight" quality of the customers. Employing in-depth interviews of a snowball sample of thirty primarily white, middle class johns (a snowball sample asks the initial interviewee to suggest other subjects), Holzman and Pines (1979) were also unable to support the "pathology-ridden depictions of the clients of prostitutes." All of the subjects indicated current involvements in relationships that involved sex and that they experienced little problem in obtaining sex from nonprostitutes. Some prevailing motivations for visiting prostitutes mentioned by their sample included: expectations of mystery and excitement; special "professional" services; and guaranteed, easy, nonentangled sex, which excluded possible rejection. A controversial, although apparently relatively effective, means of cracking down on open solicitation by prostitutes in given urban areas is to prosecute and embarrass johns by publishing their names and addresses in the local newspaper.

Despite the increased visibility of prostitution beginning in the seventies in the United States, most studies suggest that prostitution has experienced a decline since the pre-World War II period. There appears to be an inverse or negative relationship between sexual permissiveness in a society and the strength of organized prostitution. Prostitution is strongest in countries with traditional concepts of marriage and the double standard. Countries such as France and Italy, for example, discourage divorce and tolerate different expectations of sexual conduct for males and females. Since female sexual expression is discouraged outside marriage, a small proportion of females serve the illicit, erotic desires of the male population. The decline in prostitution can be noted by comparing Kinsey's 1948 and 1952 surveys with more recent ones (Hunt, 1974, p. 144). These show that, while prior to World War II roughly 50 percent of white males had visited prostitutes, in the seventies only 25 percent of college-educated men had visited prostitutes. The erosion of the double standard has eliminated some of the demand for prostitutes' services.

Modeled after drunk driving and shoplifting programs for first-time offenders, some jurisdictions are experimenting with schools for johns. These remedial classes are designed to make such former customers of prostitutes aware of the seriousness of their offense. After completing the school, their arrest for soliciting sex is erased from their record. The eight-hour class typically deals with the following topics (Nieves, 1999, p. A1):

- A prosecutor discusses legal and practical consequences.
- A health educator discusses sexually-transmitted disease and HIV.
- Former prostitutes talk about their lives and drugs.
- Police officers talk about pimps and the recruitment and exploitation of prostitutes.
- Neighborhood and business groups discuss the degradation of their neighborhoods.
- Sexual addiction is discussed.
- Domestic violence and family relationships are discussed.

The program, which was begun in San Francisco, has shown some very positive results.

Underaged Prostitutes

Since the seventies, concern has been expressed regarding what appears to be growing participation in prostitution by youths, both male and female, under the age of eighteen. While accurate statistics are difficult to come by, journalistic reports suggest a large recent increase in the sexual exploitation of children, due in part to the youth orientation of society, to growing sexual permissiveness, and to eroding family structures (Booth, 1978, p. 23A). New York City police authorities claim that there are as many as ten thousand "chicken hawks," male prostitutes under eighteen; another estimate indicates that half of Portland, Oregon's, hookers are girls under eighteen. The so-called "Boy Scout sex ring" in New Orleans involved eighteen Boy Scouts aged eight to fifteen; in some cases, the youngsters' mothers were aware of their activities (Booth, 1978).

A large proportion of teenage prostitutes come from "damaged families" and often represent "throw-away children." Many had been raped or sexually abused by surrogate fathers. A Boston ring of homosexual boys was run by the school bus driver, who peddled the bodies of eight- and nine-year-olds and advertised them through photographs throughout the East Coast. When the ring was broken, police arrested a child psychiatrist, a clinical psychologist, a former assistant headmaster, and a teacher at a boys' prep school. The sexual exploitation of children will remain a matter of serious concern, particularly with respect to the long-term psychological impact of such victimizations on the young people involved (Sullivan, 1988; Ritter, 1988; Burgess, 1984; Weisberg, 1985).

One of the biggest trends in prostitution has been a movement from the streets to the Internet. The Internet, pagers, cellular phones, and escort services have all made prostitution less noticeable. Advertisements for sexual services flourish on Web sites.

Homosexual Behavior

Homosexuality is the desire for sexual relationships with members of one's own sex. While homosexuality itself is not a crime, certain homosexual activities may be considered criminal, depending on various state or national laws. In certain states, homosexual activity, like some heterosexual activity, may be included under various laws prohibiting adultery, fornication, sodomy, crimes against nature, or lewd and lascivious conduct. *Adultery* is sexual relations of a married person with someone other than her or his spouse. Fornication refers to sexual intercourse between unmarried persons. **Sodomy** or "crimes against nature" may cover anal intercourse, mouth-genital contact, and even mutual masturbation. The term *sodomy* is derived from the biblical city of Sodom, which (together with Gomorrah) was destroyed by God's wrath because of its rampant eroticism.

Following Judeo-Christian precepts, homosexuality was forbidden and punished in European countries until the French Revolution, after which the laws became more tolerant. Although puritanical America was slower in liberalizing its laws, sodomy statutes generally are not enforced or are selectively enforced for extortion or blackmail purposes.

From the standpoint of law enforcement, there is some criminal activity associated with the homosexual community, primarily on the part of those preying on homosexuals; entrapment, swindling, robbery, blackmail, and sometimes murder may take place. Of primary concern to the criminal justice system are cases in which the behavior is nonconsensual or involves underage minors. Also warranting attention are activities that take place in association with pickups or solicitations in public places, often involving male prostitutes who serve an almost exclusively homosexual clientele.

In 1973 the American Psychiatric Association voted at its national convention that homosexuality no longer be considered a mental illness, although a later survey of members found that a majority still regarded homosexuality as immature and abnormal behavior (Rathus, 1983, p. 395). Up until the sixties, all states forbade such conduct.

In 1986 the U.S. Supreme court upheld a Georgia law that prohibits sodomy (oral or anal sexual relations) between consenting adults. The law carried a punishment of twenty years in prison. That year twenty-six states, mostly in the South and West, had existing sodomy anti-laws; and in only five states did this refer solely to homosexual activity (Press et al., 1986).

Despite decriminalization, homosexual activity is still regulated in most states under sodomy statutes. Attempts to estimate the extent of homosexuality have produced varying figures. An Alfred Kinsey and associates (1948 and 1952) survey indicated that 10 percent of their male sample had been exclusively homosexual for at least a three-year period and 4 percent for their lifetimes. Between 2 and 6 percent of unmarried females were exclusively lesbian. A later survey by Morton Hunt (1974) placed the figures at 3 percent for males and 1 to 3 percent for females. Both of these studies have been limited by inadequate sampling procedures, however.

Although many variations could be distinguished, those participating in homosexual activity may be simply divided into two types: situational homosexuals and preferential homosexuals. *Situational homosexuals* are those who may prefer heterosexual activity but participate in homosexual activity as a temporary or substitute means of erotic gratification or a means of monetary reward. *Preferential homosexuals* seek sexual gratification predominantly and continually with members of the same sex. Such individuals tend to develop a homosexual self-concept and to join a gay or homosexual subculture. In actuality, a variety of homosexual roles can be distinguished, including overt or secret, adjusted or maladjusted, true homosexual or situational turnout, as well as primary or secondary (Clinard and Quinney, 1973, p. 87).

Many individuals participate in homosexual activity but do not identify themselves as homosexuals. Much situational homosexuality occurs in isolated sexual environments such as prisons, unisex boarding schools, and military environments. In prisons, for instance, "wolves" exert their masculinity by having fellatio (oral stimulation) performed on them or sodomizing "queens," avowed homosexuals, or "punks," weak males who are forced to perform sexual services (Sykes, 1958, pp. 95–97). Sexual behavior may reflect opportunity and circumstance in addition to preference. In many traditional Islamic countries a high premium is placed on virgin brides and there are strong prohibitions against wifely infidelity and even premarital dating. In such a system, heterosexual males use other males for sexual outlets. Sexual assaults on boys are more prevalent than attacks on women in such countries (West, 1988, p. 183).

Male prostitutes primarily serve the needs of a clientele interested in homosexual activity. In San Francisco these consist of "face-to-face" public prostitutes and "call men." Waldorf et al., (1988, p. 6) identify the subtypes of face-to-face prostitutes as trade hustlers (bisexual or homosexual men who exchange sex for money, hence, the term "trade"), drag hookers (transvestites and transsexuals), and young hustlers (very young, gay, or bisexual men who openly solicit customers). Call men are less open in obtaining customers and tend to advertise in newspapers and operate by telephone. These include erotic masseurs, call book men (who have books with names of regular clients), models/escorts, and "stars" of erotic magazines (Waldorf et al., 1988, p. 7). VANTAGE POINT 14.1 provides a description of impersonal homosexual activity in public places.

Sexual Offenses

While sexual assault, rape, and adult sexual relations with minors are taken very seriously by the criminal justice system, other acts have been given less attention by authorities in the past two decades and attract a response only when they involve other criminal activity (see Lowman, 1986; Sullivan, 1988). In addition to prostitution and homosexual offenses, some other sexual offenses that have criminal implications include exhibitionism, voyeurism, fetishism, incest, and pedophilia. Related "deviant" sexual activity that may attract criminal predators includes sadism and masochism. **Exhibitionism** usually involves the purposive and unsolicited indecent exposure of sexual parts, usually of the male penis to an unsuspecting female. **Voyeurism** consists of invading the privacy of another by viewing him or her either unclad or in a sexual situation. **Fetishism** involves obtaining erotic excitement through the perception and often collection of objects associated with the opposite sex.

VANTAGE POINT 14.1

Laud Humphreys' *Tearoom Trade*

The following is a brief account of Laud Humphreys' (1970) controversial and important study of "tearooms," public restrooms where homosexual activity is common. Such solicitations and activities cause most law enforcement attention and arrests for homosexual activity. Despite public fears of child molesters lurking in wait in such places, surprisingly little information existed prior to Humphreys' study of such localities. Using the controversial method of disguised observation, Humphreys posed as a "watch queen," a voyeur who obtains erotic excitement by observing such activities, but also serves the crucial role of lookout for police and other unfriendly strangers who may wander onto the scene and interrupt the homosexual tryst. Humphreys traced the automobile license numbers of participants and showed up at their homes, sometime later under the guise of performing a mental health survey.

According to Humphreys, tearooms are popular because they provide instant, "no-strings-attached" sex, inexpensive erotic kicks without commitment. They are not gathering places for preferential homosexuals. Such individuals have "come out of the closet," have admitted their sexual preference, and would far more likely be found in gay bars. Tearooms attract a variety of men, only a few of whom are members of the homosexual subculture. The majority have no homosexual self-concept. In fact, over half were married and currently living with their wives.

Humphreys' typology of tearoom participants included: trade, ambisexuals, gay guys, and closet queens. The predominant activity in tearooms is fellatio. Individuals classified as *trade* made up 38 percent of the subjects and were described by Humphreys as "insertors," "fellators," or those who have fellatio performed on them. Most were married, but there was little sex in their marriages. Other sexual outlets, such as affairs, were viewed as too complicated and expensive. Such individuals at the turn of the century would most likely have visited inexpensive red-light districts.

Ambisexuals are more likely to be "insertees"; that is, they perform the oral function. Representing 24 percent of Humphreys' sample, most of these men also were married and indicated that their home sex life was satisfactory. Many enjoyed the adventure, excitement, and risk of such illicit activity. *Gay guys* constituted 14 percent of the participants. Such individuals openly associate in the gay subculture. Humphreys claims that most prefer more permanent, "married" homosexual relationships, which are not to be found in the transitory atmosphere of the tearoom. *Closet queens,* hidden or unavowed homosexuals, made up the remaining 24 percent. Such persons were usually unmarried and fearful of involvement in other areas of the sexual marketplace. Many were particularly interested in young boys, although few of these are to be found in tearooms. Humphreys feels that the unwillingness of "closet queens" to come to terms with their sexual preference and participate in the homosexual subculture makes such individuals potentially dangerous. For most homosexuals the civil consequences of revelation of their activities are a greater personal concern than the threat of criminal penalties.

While most police departments do not make an active business of pursuing those involved in homosexual activity, an account from Olympia, Washington ("More Arrests," 1980), illustrates a tearoom bust. Police investigated and arrested a brewery president, a state legislator, a state official, and others at a lakefront park restroom. During a two-week period, police observed twenty-to-thirty regular visitors as well as their participation in homosexual activity. An undercover officer was solicited and also observed acts being performed in his presence.

InfoTrac College Edition Research
Review the topic of "research ethics." Do any of the articles provide guidance in deciding the ethical status of Humphreys' research?

Nonvictimless Sexual Offenses

Of more serious concern are incest and pedophilia. **Incest** is sexual intercourse between individuals who are legally defined as too closely related to marry. **Pedophilia,** or child molesting, refers to sexual relations between an adult and a child, the latter usually defined as a person under the age of 12 or one who has not yet reached the age of puberty. These two types of offenses clearly are not "victimless" and, as will be described in greater detail shortly, are the most widely condemned and seriously punished of sexual depravations.

Sadism involves the attainment of sexual gratification by means of inflicting cruelty on others, while *masochism,* sadism's mirror image, involves sexual gratification through suffering physical pain. Unless both parties consent, sadomasochistic activity, sometimes called "S and M," may entail harm or violent victimization.

While many states still have laws prohibiting certain sexual acts between consenting adults, regulations against homosexuality, cohabitation, fornication, adultery, and the like are usually ignored. Societal attempts to regulate obscenity and pornography continue to stir debate in the 1980s. VANTAGE POINT 14.2 provides a brief sketch of the pornography controversy.

In addition to relatively institutionalized forms of "sexual deviance," such as prostitution and homosexuality, and seriously regarded activities, such as child molesting and incest, there are a variety of activities that might generally be regarded as either nuisance forms of deviation or relatively rare preferences for sexual activities that may, on occasion, be harmful to one or the other or both parties.

Nuisance Sexual Offenses

Exhibitionism generally involves the purposive public exposure, usually by males, of private sexual parts, in order to elicit shock in unsuspecting victims. While laws prohibiting indecent exposure are equally applicable to both sexes and are usually enforced by public complaint, most "flashers" are male (Forgac and Michaels, 1982). Illustrated by the "dirty old man in a raincoat" who exposes his genitals, exhibitionism may also take the form of adolescent pranksterism by "mooning" (displaying one's bare buttocks to an unsuspecting audience) and "streaking" (running naked through a public gathering). While mooning and streaking are performed for kicks, there appears to be little erotic motivation on the part of the participants. The following annual tradition at one university is illustrative (Landers, 1991):

> Hundreds of Princeton University sophomores shed jeans and down jackets for a traditional event dubbed the "Nude Olympics," held to celebrate the area's first snowfall of the year. About 1,500 spectators cheered them on last week as the students, clad only in boots and hats, lit the torch before doing sit-ups and push-ups in a campus courtyard and ran up and down Nassau Street in Princeton, N.J., reported United Press International.

"Flashers," on the other hand, participate in such activity as a means of sexual arousal and gratification. Most are described as the least harmful of sexual offenders; such exhibitionists are generally immature in their sexual development, wish to evoke fear or shock, and actually would be fearful if the victim acted interested or wanted further contact (Gebhard et al., 1965).

Voyeurs attain sexual gratification by viewing others in an unclad state. While legal voyeurism can be practiced in establishments catering to such trade—for example, "topless bars" or adult entertainment districts—illegal voyeurism involves uninvited "peeping" into private homes, parked cars in "lovers' lanes," or other areas. Voyeurs are often called "peeping Toms," a name derived from the fable of the man who stole a peep at Lady Godiva on her naked ride through Coventry. While some patterns of burglary may be associated with voyeurism, in most instances it appears to be pursued as an end in itself. Voyeurism is primarily practiced by juveniles as a means of achieving erotic excitement. Most persistent voyeurs are also at a relatively immature level of psychosexual development and, contrary to the fears of many female victims, do not employ voyeurism as a prelude to sexual attack. In this sense, voyeurs are much like obscene phone callers in that they often fear contact with the opposite sex; otherwise they would avail themselves of readily obtainable erotic outlets in the adult sexual marketplace.

VANTAGE POINT 14.2

Pornography

Shortly before his execution in Florida in 1989, serial murderer Ted Bundy blamed pornography for his violent compulsion, and though many questioned Bundy's sincerity, his statements provided further fuel to the pornography debate. *Pornography* refers to erotic or sexually stimulating literature or materials; the term is derived from the Greek, meaning to write about prostitutes. Proponents of liberalized rules regulating pornography point to First Amendment freedom of speech guarantees and argue that in a democracy the state has no right to morally judge what is or is not suitable for reading or viewing. Opponents of pornography argue that such material is grossly repugnant to public morals, is degrading, may inspire sexual attacks against women, and often portrays activities, such as child pornography, that are clearly beyond freedom of speech guarantees.

The *National Commission on Obscenity and Pornography* (1970) in a review of previous as well as commissioned studies on the subject concluded that no necessarily harmful behavior resulted from individuals' viewing pornographic material. They found the predominant customers of adult bookstores to be white, middle class, married businessmen. Goldstein et al. (1973) found that rapist, homosexuals, child molesters, and transsexuals had actually experienced less than normal exposure to pornographic materials during adolescence.

Despite these findings, many women's groups and others oppose the content of pornographic material as encouraging the mythical belief among some males that females secretly desire to be raped (McCarthy, 1982), a frequent theme in pornographic literature. McCarthy (p. 219) indicates that the findings of the 1970 pornography commission are no longer valid in describing the types of more violent pornography that has emerged since 1970. In "snuff" films, for instance, females are depicted as being tortured and murdered, and sometimes the murder is the real thing. The commission has been criticized for failing to distinguish between erotic, sexually explicit material and pornographic material that exploits women (see Hawkins and Zimring, 1988).

The Attorney General's Commission on Pornography (Attorney General's Office, 1986) concluded that some forms of sexually explicit material bear a causal relationship to sexual violence and urged that police give a much higher priority to pornography cases. Most critics of the report feel that the commission had arrived at its conclusions even before conducting investigations and that the literature it cites fails to conclusively prove harmful effects of pornography (Lynn, 1986; Nobile and Nadler, 1986; Scott, 1988). By way of example, Japan has an extensive amount of pornography, but a comparatively low incidence of rape (Impoco, 1987).

A study by Seymour Fishbach and Neal Malamuth (1978) found that exposure to erotic materials had little association with violent crime, but that a link did exist between viewing violent sexual materials and a greater propensity to view such actions in a favorable light. These findings were supported by others (Goode, 1984, p. 162; Malamuth and Donnerstein, 1982). While the pornography debate continues to rage, a compromise of sorts has been struck in the direction of regulation rather than either banning or further liberalization. The Supreme Court in various rulings has recognized the right of local communities to use zoning, to ban child pornography, and in other ways to control some of the more distasteful aspects of pornography. The current state of affairs is perhaps best summed up by McConahay (1988, p. 67), who reports:

> **The new wider audience for X-rated videos means that there are too many pornography consumers, even if they do not think of it as pornography, with too much economic clout to achieve complete suppression and there is too much antipornography sentiment to tolerate complete freedom (read license). Thus, we will have to find a way to muddle through. (See Donnerstein, Linz, and Penrod, 1987.)**

InfoTrac College Edition Research
Review the issue of "pornography." Are there any regulations at all regarding this phenomenon? What regulations do you think should exist?

Fetishism involves sexual arousal from the perception of inanimate objects or articles of clothing usually associated with the opposite sex. While some level of fetishism is normal, it becomes abnormal when an individual acquires such items, often through theft, and venerates such articles as a displaced sexual object. There are, for instance, some episodes of shoplifting associated with fetishistic behavior in which the objects are sought because they have significant value for the erotic feelings they arouse.

William Cabell standing in front of his church in State College, PA, was arrested in 1991 for allegedly crossing state lines to have sex with a teenage boy he had met on the Internet.

(© Associated Press CENTRE DAILY TIMES)

Of possible concern to law enforcement are sexual practices involving sadism and/or masochism. *Sadism* involves the attainment of sexual gratification by means of inflicting pain on others. Often unable to achieve sexual arousal and/or orgasm through any other means, such individuals may harm nonconsenting partners. *Masochism* refers to the attainment of erotic satisfaction through suffering pain. The masochistic individual must be physically punished in order to gain sexual fulfillment. The leather, whips, and chains school of kinky sex is often serviced by prostitutes who specialize in catering to the even more bizarre needs of their clients.

Not every sexual deviation yields a predictable mode of behavior. While only a very small minority are potentially dangerous, any type may be associated with more serious criminality in the individual case. The vast majority of persistent offenders exhibit immature psychosexual development and, if their behavior elicits a police response, such offenders are usually treated under civil commitment proceedings. Since most research on sexual offenders relies on official statistics and the majority never come to official attention, far more reliable research is required in this area (Toch, 1979, p. 413).

Sexual Predators

One of the more shocking cases of "serial" child sexual abuse was revealed in an ABC News investigation (ABC, 1992b) of former Roman Catholic priest James Porter, who was accused by over one hundred former victims of molesting, sodomizing, and raping them when he was their parish priest in the sixties and seventies. A mass silence repressed such memories until one person came forward and organized an investigation into why the Church hierarchy ignored such activity and moved the offender from one parish to another in Massachusetts, New Mexico, and Wisconsin without warning the new parishes. On December 6, 1993, Porter was sentenced to 18 to 20 years in prison.

Child battering, which can be defined as child abuse primarily involving physical assault on children, was discussed in the chapter on violent crime. While it is difficult to draw clear distinctions between abuse and molestation, this discussion will focus on child molesting, which primarily involves the sexual abuse of children or minors past puberty. A child is defined in most states as one who has not yet reached puberty or age twelve or fourteen.

Pedophiliacs or *child molesters* are those who have sexual relations with children. For every rape in the United States in a given year it is estimated that twenty children are molested—roughly 500,000, according to official estimates in 1982 (ABC, 1983a). Many myths exist about child molesters. Some common myths are: molesters are usually strangers, molesters will be caught and jailed, and children quickly get over the emotional harm of having been molested. Most molesters, 85 percent, are known to the child and his or her family. Most are not caught and, when apprehended, are likely to be treated leniently. Fewer than 10 percent of convicted felon child molesters go to prison. One offender claims that psychiatrists will generally release them as long as they do not appear to be "mad dogs" (ABC, 1983a). Since such offenders are assumed to be mentally ill, and they are permitted to plead to lesser offenses, even though victims of child molesters report long-term psychological damage as a result of such incidents. Pressure groups such as SLAM, Society for Laws Against Molesters, are lobbying for stricter laws, insisting that repeat offenders receive mandatory prison sentences consisting of a minimum of four to eight years.

The typical act of child molesting involves an adult male and a female victim, usually 11–14 years of age. McCaghy (1976a, p. 87) identified six types of child molesters:

- High interaction molesters, who have known the children for some time and usually perform or have performed genital fondling
- Incestuous molesters, who take advantage of a child living in their household
- Asocial molesters, who are involved in illegal careers
- Senile molesters, who are older, poorly educated offenders
- Career molesters, who have persistent offense patterns involving child molestation
- Spontaneous-aggressive molesters, who have had little previous contact with their victims and tend to commit their offenses on a very physical and unplanned basis

While high interaction offenders represented only 10 percent of McCaghy's sample, it is likely that they represent the majority of molesters. Since most are well known to the family and do not employ physical force, they are less likely to be charged with the offense. Given the very sensitive nature of the subject matter, research has been scarce regarding this subject (Mohr, Turner, and Jerry, 1964; Ellis and Brancale, 1965; Gebhard et al., 1965). Although statistics are unreliable, in many cases of sexual child abuse the offenders are family members.

One overlooked aspect of the rising rate of teen pregnancy is the fact that it is often an outcome of child abuse. One study by the Alan Guttmacher Institute found that 66 percent of teen mothers had children by men who were 20 or older. A 1992 Washington study found 62 percent had been raped or molested before they became pregnant; the offenders' mean age was 27.4 years. "[G]irls who become pregnant aren't just amoral, premature tarts—they are prey" (Klein, 1996). Enforcement of statutory rape laws would be a significant start.

There have been other attempts to classify child molesters. Groth et al., (1978) describe two types: the "regressed" abuser and the "fixated" abuser. The regressed abuser is one who, having led a fairly normal sexual life, regresses to a sexual interest in children. A previously normal father who suddenly develops such sexual interest in children would be an example. Fixated abusers have an early and strongly focused interest in children as sexual objects. often to the exclusion of any other type of adult sexual activity (Crewdson, 1988). While there has been an increase in literature on the topics of sexual molestation, incest, and pedophilia, more such research is needed (Finkelhor, 1986; Holmes, 1983; O'Brien, 1986; Vander and Neff, 1986).

In 1990 the "McMartin preschool molestation trial" ended with the acquittal of all the accused. Beginning with accusations that child molesting had taken place in 1983 and continuing through three years in court, it was one of the longest and costliest criminal proceedings in U.S. history. The trial may also have represented a "moral panic" and "witch hunt." The jury finally concluded that the state's child therapist put the child abuse charges into the children's mouths through the therapist's method of questioning the children (Rabinowitz, 1991). The children were believed to be vulnerable to leading questions and wishing to please adults with their answers (Hagedorn, 1991). Care must be taken lest we railroad the wrong people in our attempts to fight such abuse. One suggestion that has been made in light of all the charges associated with child care centers is for a national registry for background checks of child-care providers that could be consulted in order to avoid hiring known child abusers.

On-line pedophiles represent an electronic version of letting perverted bogeymen into a child's bedroom. The bedrooms in this case are hooked up to the Internet and chat rooms and Web sites that entice naïve youngsters. One example was the "Wonderland Club," an international pedophile and pornography network. Members had to be approved by at least three other club members, and prospects had to demonstrate that they had access to 10,000 images of child pornography. The images they traded were of children as young as two being raped, tied up, having sex with animals, adults, or other children. Police in 12 countries synchronized simultaneous raids and arrested 100 suspects. In the operation, police were unsuccessful in infiltrating the group but traced about 200 members through wiretaps, on-line transmissions, and agents in chat rooms (Goodspeed, 1998).

In 1999 the FBI put on-line its National Sex Offender Registry, a computerized database of convicted pedophiles. This provides instantaneous background checks to law enforcement agencies. The assumption of such a registry is that, once predatory pedophiles are convicted, they lose forever their right to hide.

Finally, mention should be made of one more case that, in the era of AIDS, is hair-raising. In 1992 in Philadelphia, police arrested Edward "Fast Eddie" Savitz, a successful businessman with AIDS, who is believed to have been involved with hundreds of adolescent boys over a decade or more. Savitz invited such boys to his downtown apartment, paid them for oral/anal sex and for articles of their clothing, such as socks and underwear, and took pornographic photographs (Landsberg, 1992, pp. lA, 9A). A particularly disturbing new twist to pornography and sexual molestation has been the explosion of erotic themes on the Internet and the use of such electronic media by sexual predators to recruit and set up liaisons with underaged users. Software is being developed to help parents police the Net.

Incest. Claims of childhood sexual abuse and incest by Roseanne Barr, Oprah Winfrey, La Toya Jackson, and former Miss America Marilyn Van Derbur Atler have opened the door for others to confront long-repressed, painful memories of such abuse.

Incest is related to child molestation, which, although varyingly defined by state or national laws, refers to the universal taboo prohibiting sexual relations or marriage between those who are defined as being too closely related either by blood or marriage. At issue in this discussion is not adult relations, but forms of incest that represent a type of child molesting or sexual victimization in which an adult who is closely related to a child has sexual relations with the child.

The incidence of child sexual abuse by a natural parent is difficult to document, even though the American Humane Association has shown a sharp escalation in such statistics since the mid-seventies. Russell (1986) reports that sexual abuse by uncles is more prevalent than father-daughter incest and that incest by stepfathers is seven times more likely than that by biological fathers. "The more 'personal' the relationship between the victim and the offender, the less likely a case of sexual abuse will be reported" (Cardarelli, 1988, p. 9). While a considerable literature has accumulated on this subject, there is still a need for more empirical research (Russell, 1986; and Ekpenyong, 1988).

Since mother-son incest is rare and brother-sister incest is unlikely to involve as gross an age disparity, father-daughter and father-son incestual relationships are the primary subject of this brief presentation. One study found the average age of female victims to be 10.2 years (Finkelhor, 1979, p. 60). Incestual victimizations may be heterosexual or homosexual. Finkelhor (1979, p. 87) found that, although brother-sister incest was by far the most common, father-daughter incest was most likely to come to the attention of authorities, perhaps because of its more traumatic impact on the family and the child (Janeway, 1981; Goodwin et al., 1982). Some factors associated with incest include high proportions of stepparent, foster, or adoptive parent relationships; family disorganization (Herman, 1981); low intelligence; alcoholism; and other personality disorganization. While official reports of child battering tend to be more prevalent among low-income families, the American Humane Association Children's Division (1984) reported that sexual abuse and incest are more evenly distributed among social classes. Gordon and O'Keefe (1984), in an analysis of historical records of family violence in the Boston area from 1800 to 1960, did not find that incest offenders were poorer, more alcoholic, or sicker than other assailants. In addition, they questioned the assumption that such violators exhibited pathology or were under external socioeconomic stress.

Characteristics of Sex Offenders

Hans Toch (1979, p. 414) summarizes much of the research that has been conducted on characteristics of sex offenders:

- Most, far from being "sex fiends," are rather harmless minor offenders.
- Only about 20 percent use force on their victims.
- Untreated, convicted offenders tend to be recidivists in both sexual and nonsexual offenses, but in no greater proportions that nonsexual offenders.
- While few offenders are psychopaths, many are suffering severe neurosis, borderline psychosis, or brain impairment, but most do not fit legal definitions of mental illness.
- Most are emotionally immature and sexually constricted and inhibited, although those involved in rape and incest are more likely to be overimpulsive and oversexed.
- Convicted statutory rapists and those involved in bestiality and incest are more likely to exhibit subnormal intelligence.
- The majority of offenders are young, unmarried, and from poor educational and social-class backgrounds (see also Holmes, 1983 and 1991).

Drug Abuse

Drugs, chemical substances that alter psychological and/or physiological functioning, have been used for centuries in various cultures as stimulants or depressants for medical, social, and often religious reasons. Even today in many Middle Eastern countries alcohol is strictly forbidden for religious reasons, while the use of other highly addictive substances is tolerated. The fact that drug abuse has moved into the U.S. mainstream can be illustrated by reports of widespread abuse, particularly by professional athletes, entertainers, and prominent figures.

The types of common drugs of abuse include:

Cannabis: marijuana, THC, hashish
Depressants: barbiturates, methaqualone, tranquilizers
Stimulants: amphetamines, nicotine, caffeine
Hallucinogens: LSD, mescaline, peyote, PCP, psilocybin
Inhalants: nitrous oxide, butyl nitrite, amyl nitrite, and aerosols
Narcotics: opium, morphine, codeine, heroin, and methadone

In the examination of the legal status of drugs and their known harmful effects, the surprising fact that comes to light is that there is often little relationship between the known harmful effects of a particular drug and its legal status in many societies. Substances such as alcohol or nicotine, while possessing mild, short-term, harmful impact, have lethal, long-term effects and enjoy a legal, sometimes subsidized status. Drugs such as heroin, which may be lethal in the short run because of overdoses, are not known to be lethal in the long term, but nevertheless are strongly forbidden. The changing legal status of drugs will be discussed in detail as part of drugs and history.

Drugs and History

Opium is believed to have been discovered as early as the Neolithic Age and was used by early physicians such as Hippocrates and Galen (McCoy, 1972, p. 3). Opium, the raw base of other derivatives such as morphine and heroin, was first introduced on a wide scale to the rest of the world by Turkish traders around the eighth or ninth century (Block and Chambliss, 1981, p. 20) and was a trade commodity of European mercantilists as early as the sixteenth century, providing at one point almost half of the revenue of colonial governments. Opium dens controlled by European governments could be found in most Asian cities. When one Chinese emperor objected to such trade, the Opium Wars (1839–1842) were fought, in which the Europeans (the pushers) were the victors. American "China clipper" ships, known in the trade as "opium" clippers, had a major piece of this trade (Nash, 1981, p. 166).

While all of us are familiar with Prohibition and the attempt to enforce the outlawing of alcohol consumption in the United States, many forget the dim view taken of tobacco and caffeine in earlier Western history (Lesieur and Welch, 1991, p. 192). In the seventeenth century, Pope Urban VIII issued an edict excommunicating anyone using tobacco, European countries outlawed it, and the Ottoman Empire decreed the death penalty for smokers. In the sixteenth century, Egypt made the sale of coffee a crime and burned coffee crops. None of these laws was effective.

In 1805 morphine was derived from opium, but widespread medicinal use of morphine and other derivatives such as codeine brought the onset of serious addiction problems. By 1874 heroin, another opium derivative, was developed and was at first believed to be a nonaddicting miracle drug. Cocaine, which was isolated from coca in 1858, was first thought to be a cure for morphinism and was a popular ingredient of tonics such as Coca-Cola when the first soda fountains were introduced in the 1890s (Inciardi and McElrath, 1995). Its inclusion was outlawed by the Pure Food and Drug Laws of 1906. Backwater patent-medicine peddlers of the late nineteenth century American frontier provided highly addictive remedies such as Dover's Powders, Sydenham's Syrup, and Godfrey's Cordial, which were so widely used that by 1900 an estimated one million Americans, mostly women, were opiate users (Brecher, 1972). Brecher (p. 4) described the turn-of-the-century United States as a "dope fiend's paradise."

This relatively unregulated distribution of narcotics by physicians and pharmaceutical companies was creating a tremendous drug abuse problem. By 1924 federal authorities estimated that there were 200,000 addicts (McCoy, 1972, p. 5). International concern over growing drug trafficking led to the Hague Convention of 1912, which called for participating nations to crack down on drug distribution. The U.S. response was the **Harrison Act of 1914,** which required a doctor's prescription for narcotics and cocaine. The act required the registration of all legitimate drug handlers, but was not intended to interfere with the legitimate medical treatment of addicts. A vague clause in the law to the effect that physicians could dispense such drugs "only for legitimate medical reasons" led some overzealous federal agents to crack down on offending physicians. By the mid-twenties an estimated 25,000 physicians had been arrested, with 3,000 serving jail or prison sentences (Goode, 1984, p. 109). The net result of the Harrison Act was that physicians abandoned the treatment of addicts, and the addict as "patient" was replaced by the addict as "criminal," "dope fiend," or outside menace (Lindesmith, 1965; Duster, 1970; Goode, 1972).

Howard Becker (1963) coined the term **moral entrepreneurs** to refer to individuals who personally benefit from convincing the public to label the behavior of others as deviant or criminal. VANTAGE POINT 14.3 describes two classic moral entrepreneurs: Richard Hobson, "the hero of Santiago Bay," and Harry Anslinger, "the Carrie Nation of marijuana." Thomas Szasz in *Ceremonial Chemistry* (1974), perhaps with some exaggeration, compares the drug war with the war on witches and heretics in Europe from 1430 to 1730. The latter cost 300,000 lives and was a reflection of ignorance and superstition. Successive federal legislation from the time of the Harrison Act until the 1970s, such as the Marijuana Tax Act (1937), the Boggs Act (1951), and Narcotics Control Act (1956), were all aimed at controlling drug abuse by means of criminalization and harsher penalties.

The Phantom Army of Addicts. The history of drug statistics has been a precarious one with multiple wars on drugs declared and often little progress realized. In 1969 the Bureau of Narcotics and Dangerous Drugs (BNDD), using data from police and medical authorities, estimated the number of heroin addicts at 68,088. By 1970 an apparent heroin epidemic took place with the number of addicts set at 315,000 and for 1971, 559,000, roughly an eightfold increase in just two years. Edward Epstein (1977, p. 174) in Agency of Fear states: "A tenfold increase in the number of heroin addicts would certainly be a cause for national concern; the magnitude of the 1971 epidemic was, however, more a product of government statisticians than of heroin traffickers."

As Epstein explains it, until 1970 the official estimates of heroin addicts were arrived at by BNDD on the basis of police and medical reports. The 68,088 (1969) figure was based on the official register, while the increases in 1970 and 1971 were brought about largely because of a new estimating formula, a statistical artifact that in effect created a "phantom army of addicts." This new estimating procedure—the **mark-recapture technique**—was one widely used in the field of ecology. For example, in the tagged-fish-in-a-pond procedure (see, for instance Burnham, 1980), the number of fish in a pond is estimated by catching a sample of fish, marking or tagging them, and then releasing them. Then a second sample is caught. If, for instance, one in ten of the second sample have tags, then the entire fish population of the pond would be assumed to be ten times the number of the originally tagged sample. Suppose fifty fish were tagged in the first sample and released, then fifty more caught, of which five bore tags. The estimate of fish population would be ten times fifty or five hundred. Following this same procedure the BNDD compared the number of names on the 1970 addicts' register that had previously appeared (been tagged) on the 1969 register. Finding one-in-five to be rereports (tagged addicts) on the 1969 estimate of 68,088, it was multiplied by the calculated ratio of 4,626, providing the 315,000 figure for 1970. This is a classic example of instrumentation—changes in the instrument of measurement being responsible for changes in what is being measured. While the "mark-recapture" procedure may be useful for estimating fish, it is doubtful that drug addicts follow similar random patterns (Epstein, 1977, p. 175). While the estimates

VANTAGE POINT 14.3

Moral Panics and the Strange Career of Captain Richmond Hobson—Moral Entrepreneur

"Moral panics" refer to periods in which a previously peripheral issue is pushed onto the social agenda and perceived as a major social menace. Myths associated with such panics may lead to wasteful and dangerous diversion of scarce resources (Jenkins and Katkin, 1990; Jenkins, 1992b). Such panics may be "symbolic crusades" (Gusfield, 1963) in which "moral entrepreneurs" attempt to place their social, moral, or political views at the top of the social agenda or in the forefront of the moral landscape. Even if unenforceable, new laws may make symbolic statements that benefit particular groups (Ben Yehuda, 1990). Many laws aimed at regulating public morality, though nearly unenforceable, reinforce the values of moral guardians and agencies of social control.

On June 3, 1898, Captain Richmond Hobson, a recent Annapolis graduate and skipper of the *U.S.S. Merrimac,* piloted his vessel into the mouth of Santiago Bay, Cuba. His mission was to sink his ship in the channel, and thus block the Spanish fleet. Premature charges sank the ship before the mission could be accomplished, and Hobson not only failed in his mission but was captured by the Spanish (Epstein, 1977, p. 24).

Ironically, Hobson became the first hero of that short war when the Navy chose to decorate rather than court-martial him, and upon his release sent him on a cross-country lecture tour. Elected to Congress in 1906, Hobson campaigned first against the "Yellow Peril" and later was an organizer of the Women's Christian Temperance Union. A campaigner against the evils of alcohol, he was the highest-paid speaker on the U.S. lecture circuit in 1915. With the demise of the anti-alcohol campaign in the thirties, the undaunted Hobson shifted his crusade to an anti-heroin jihad, describing heroin as a vampiric, demonic drug that created the "living dead" and desperadoes. Heroin was viewed as an "enslavement substance" that caused addicts to become criminals.

Hobson's propaganda campaign usefully served the moral entrepreneurship of Harry Anslinger and his efforts to expand the Federal Bureau of Narcotics, which he headed. Anslinger influenced public opinion against marijuana by means of his writing and speeches. One of his articles was entitled, "Marijuana: Assassin of Youth." In it he portrays a marijuana "addict" who axe-murders his family (Anslinger and Cooper, 1937). Another propaganda feat of the period was a film entitled *Reefer Madness,* which similarly displayed marijuana users as rampaging, raving maniacs. Primarily as the result of Anslinger's efforts, the U.S. Congress passed the Marijuana Tax Act of 1937, making marijuana use a criminal matter.

InfoTrac College Edition Research
Examine the issue of "moral panics." In what ways may moral panics be used to marginalize minorities?

prior to 1970 most likely underestimated the number of addicts, the figures in 1970–1971 probably overestimated it. In a validity check, U.S. Army draftees' records at the time indicated no change, while treatment centers at the time actually showed a decrease in new addicts for several years (Epstein, 1977, p. 177). The politics of these statistics is fascinating, as well as frightening, particularly when they became the basis of an extraordinary war on an "indomitable enemy" that may not exist.

Agency of Fear. Using drug statistics such as those we have just discussed, Epstein maintains that the Nixon administration and G. Gordon Liddy, in a classic example of "moral entrepreneurship," used public fear of addiction and crime in order to create ODALE, the Office of Drug Abuse and Law Enforcement, a group that Epstein (1977) referred to as the "agency of fear." In January 1972, by executive order of President Nixon and without congressional approval, the agency was created as an extraordinary investigative agency that was run by the White House and that bypassed usual federal agencies such as the FBI and the CIA. Epstein (1977, p. 189) claims that "under the cloak of a crusade against an epidemic drug menace" the Nixon administration created this agency to conduct carte blanche investigations of political opponents, dissenters, the media, and the like.

The Nixon statistical strategy almost backfired. After having encouraged a statistical epidemic, the administration realized that an election year (1972) estimate of 559,000 would reflect badly on the incumbent Nixon administration. So the figure was arbitrarily reduced to 150,000. Actually, estimates of the number of heroin users and heroin addicts in the United States are difficult to make and, depending on the measuring instrument employed, can differ. Estimates of all who have ever tried heroin can reach as high as 2 to 3 million (Fishburne, Abelson, and Cisin, 1980).

Drug Use in the United States: The Drug Dip?

Surveys of student drug use had shown declines since the late seventies. Beginning in 1991 there was a disturbing reversal of this trend. In the annual Michigan survey of teenagers for the National Institute of Drug Abuse, illicit drug use by eighth graders nearly doubled from 11 to 21 percent, tenth graders increased from 20 to 33 percent, and seniors grew by about half to about 33 percent. This increase still left the level well below that of peak periods of the 1970s and 1980s (Thomas, 1995) and finally peaked and began to show declines in 1999.

Crack Cocaine. Coke—snow, blow, nose candy, Bolivian marching powder—the drug of Hollywood, of Wall Street, of "sex, drugs, and rock 'n' roll." Cocaine had become the "hip" drug of the last decade of the twentieth century. While at first believed to be nonaddictive, it has emerged as very dangerous; and what was at first thought to be a scare film, *Cocaine Fiends,* actually bore a close resemblance to reality (Maranto, 1985). A variation of cocaine, "crack" has considerably raised the level of violence associated with drug trafficking in inner city ghettos. Images of 12- and -13 year-olds carrying Uzi submachine guns and earning more than their parents and teachers are no exaggeration ("Drug Rings," 1988). Beginning in 1986, the crack cocaine epidemic peaked by 1992 and was reflected in declining crime rates.

Another emergent drug is related in part to the fitness craze. "Steroid abuse" came to international attention during the 1988 Olympics when Canadian gold medalist, Ben Johnson, was asked to give up his medals because of such a drug violation. Bodybuilders and athletes utilize steroids to promote tissue growth and to gain weight and muscle. While outlawed in most athletic organizations, it is used despite increasing research that shows tremendous potential harm. This may include injury to organs, early death, and possible increases in aggressive and psychotic behavior (Weaver, 1988).

Drug Abuse and Crime

As part of the war on the "phantom army of addicts," some government figures estimating the amount of street crime due to addicts amounted to statistical overkill. Estimates in the early seventies, such as $18 billion, were several times greater than the total sum of property stolen but unrecovered throughout the entire country using UCR data for the same year (Epstein, 1977, p. 177; Singer, 1971). Despite the attention called to the danger of these "mythical numbers" (Singer, 1971), Reuter (1984b, p. 136) indicates that in the thirteen years since Singer's article, "there is a strong interest in keeping the number high and none in keeping it correct." Estimates both of crime by addicts (Chaiken and Chaiken, 1982; Ball et al., 1982) and of the estimated size of the illegal drug market remain problematic. Programs such as Arrestee Drug Abuse Monitoring (ADAM), however, have improved the ability to estimate the role of drugs in crime.

The concept of **addiction** is used primarily to describe those who have become dependent on opium and opium derivatives such as morphine, heroin, and various medicines that contain opiates. Addiction involves a *physiological dependence* commonly referred to as *tolerance,* in which the body requires larger and larger dosages of the substance in order to experience the desired effect. Once this dependence is developed, absence of the required dosage produces the **withdrawal or abstinence syndrome,** physical discomfort experienced by an addict when deprived of the drug on which he or she has become dependent. Finally, *psychological dependence* involves mentally connecting the withdrawal syndrome with one's physiological dependence and the decision thereafter to continue to use the substance. The fact that addiction is less a permanent condition than it was once believed to be is illustrated by the fact that there are few heroin addicts over the age of 35. In addition, a survey of Vietnam veterans found that while about one-third used opiates in Vietnam and one-fifth were addicted, only 1 percent continued using the drugs on returning stateside (Robins, 1974).

Much of the crime associated with drug addiction is due to the high cost addicts must pay for illegal sources of supply in order to support their need for a "fix." While costs of heroin vary, assuming a hypothetical $50 per day habit, addicts would have to come up with over $18,000 a year for heroin alone. Unless addicts have occupations that provide either high income or easy access to drugs (such as the medical field), most must steal to support their habit; the major means of support for many is dealing in drugs themselves (Inciardi, 1979, 1981; Stephens and Ellis, 1975). For others, crime is the source of funds. Research has suggested that the majority of crimes committed by heroin addicts are crimes against property, such as burglary and shoplifting or prostitution for females, although 47 percent of the males had committed robbery. Gropper (1985) indicates that, contrary to what has been found in past research, heroin-using criminals are as likely as nonusing criminals to kill and rape and are more likely to commit robbery and weapons offenses. In addition there are a wide variety of different types of drug-involved offenders requiring different types of responses by the criminal justice system (Chaiken and Johnson, 1988).

In an ethnographic study of "Hustletown," a neighborhood in northern Manhattan, Strug et al. (1984) describe individuals who are equally addicted to both drugs and alcohol and who "hustle" in order to support these habits. "Hustling" includes a wide variety of illegal and quasilegal moneymaking schemes including burglary, shoplifting, prostitution, "con" games, and service roles within drug dealing. Such low-level crime becomes "the career" of street hustlers, who despair of finding adequate employment opportunities. Most of their crimes are low-level and nonviolent in nature.

In *Taking Care of Business,* Johnson et al. (1985) did a related in-depth study of 201 New York City heroin abusers. They found most of their subjects were polysubstance abusers. None used only heroin and almost all also used cocaine, alcohol, and other drugs. While most were involved in criminal activity such as shoplifting and burglary, they also supported their habits through being "user-dealers." Nurco et al.'s (1988) study of criminal activity by drug addicts found that, for those previously involved in crime, addiction simply increases an already established criminal lifestyle while ". . . for those not involved in preaddiction crime, addiction status is associated with a much sharper exacerbation in criminal behavior" (p. 418). In 1988 two-thirds of those arrested in New York City, Washington, Chicago, and Los Angeles tested positive for drugs (Kurtz, 1989, p. A14; Anglin and Speckart, 1988). Inciardi (1979) in a study of 356 Miami addicts found that they had committed 118,134 crimes during a one-year period.

In examining the relationship between addiction and crime, it is also important to recognize that many addicts were involved in criminal activity prior to their addictions and that many support their habits through funds earned in legitimate occupations. The relationship between addiction and crime is not a necessary one, as is illustrated by the British program of prescribing legal maintenance doses to heroin addicts; in that case, there is little incidental crime associated with addiction. Growth in addiction problems in the United Kingdom has led to some changes (Bennett, 1988; "British Clinics," 1985). Much of the crime related to addiction is due to the high price of drugs owing to their prohibition. Erich Goode (1981, pp. 255–56) indicates that there was little crime associated with addiction in the nineteenth century.

Drunkenness

Under English common law, drunkenness itself was not a crime; only when a disturbance of the peace or disorderly conduct occurred was it punished. *Public drunkenness* is covered by a variety of laws in different jurisdictions, such as drunk in a public place, breach of peace, disorderly conduct, and inability to care for one's own personal safety. Problem drinking was identified in Chapter 7 as a primary ingredient in other criminal activity, particularly interpersonal violence. The majority of homicides, aggravated assaults, a large proportion of rapes, and about half of all vehicular deaths are believed to be alcohol-related. Alcoholism or problem drinking remains the number one drug abuse problem in the United States, despite official concern with more esoteric drugs.

The Prohibition Experiment

In a period of missionary zeal, the temperance movement, spearheaded by the WCTU (the Women's Christian Temperance Union) pressured the U.S. Congress to pass a Prohibition amendment. This was ratified in 1919 and would, until 1933, constitute what some called "the noble experiment" and others "the great illusion." Asbury (1969, p. 58) describes this period:

> They [the temperance forces] had expected to be greeted . . . by a covey of angels bearing gifts of peace, happiness, prosperity, and salvation, which they had been assured would be theirs when the rum demon had been scotched. Instead they were met by a horde of bootleggers, moonshiners, rumrunners, hijackers, gangsters, racketeers, trigger men, venal judges, corrupt police . . . and almost total intemperance.

Prohibition did not eliminate the alcohol problem. Bootlegging became a national pastime and one of America's largest industries—circumvention of the Volstead Act, the enforcement law of Prohibition—spawned corruption, organized crime, and public cynicism. As a result of its own failure as a social control policy, as well as of counterpressure from rival urban forces. Prohibition was repealed in 1933. Although alcohol use was decriminalized, it is still regulated by state laws. Just as Brecher (1972, p. 39) had described the turn-of-the-century United States as a "dope fiend's paradise." Rorabaugh (1979) indicates that U.S. consumption of alcohol was much higher during the eighteenth and nineteenth centuries than it is presently. Even today, examination of the problem of drug abuse in the United States finds alcohol abuse still constituting the nation's number one drug problem. "**Problem drinking,**" the current preferred term for what is called alcoholism, has already been described as a major lethal ingredient in crimes of violence as well as in vehicular homicide (Collins, 1981). The other major alcohol-related problematic area in criminal justice relates to the chronic inebriates, who make up over half of U.S. misdemeanor arrestees and county jail inmates.

Problem drinkers consume alcoholic beverages in excess of dietary or social custom to an extent that affects their health and social relationships. Immersed in a drinking culture, some cross the line into problem drinking or alcoholism. In our previous discussion of "driving under the influence" we touched on the tragic repercussions of driving while experiencing the distorting effects of alcohol or drugs.

While there is no universally accepted medical or psychological model of alcoholism, many accept a "medical model," which describes it as a disease. A useful descriptive model that illustrates this approach is Jellinek's (1960) profile of the stages of alcohol addiction. These are: the prealcoholic phase, the intermediate stage, the crucial phase, and the final or bottom phase. The prealcoholic phase involves occasional relief drinking as a means of alleviating tension. After a time, greater amounts of alcohol are needed to generate the desired effect. The intermediate stage occurs when drinking is no longer simply a source of relief, but is sought as a drug. Secretive drinking, occasional blackouts or amnesia, alibis, and a compulsion to drink are accompanied by a loss of control. In the crucial phase, the loss of control becomes more complete; the drinker is no longer able to maintain a resolution not to drink. Isolation from others, including family, increases as life becomes alcohol-centered. The final or bottom phase is characterized by the drinker's extensive emotional disorganization. Ethical deterioration, impaired thinking, and obsessive drinking characterize the bottomed-out, chronic alcoholic.

Such chronic inebriates are often handled under what is called the "golden rule disposition" in which, for their own protection, they are picked up by police without formal arrest, jailed overnight, then released in the morning (see Bittner, 1967). Despite frequent arrests or processing, most such individuals do not view themselves as criminals. Arrests for such drunkenness have in fact decreased in many jurisdictions since the early seventies: more police forces have begun to employ strategies of cooperation with local social service agencies that treat such problem drinkers. Typically local police, when they come across a consistent public inebriate, call such a center. The center's personnel transport the subject to a treatment center where he or she is bathed, dried out, fed, counseled, and provided the opportunity to break the alcohol-obsessive cycle. In addition to providing more meaningful treatment, such programs relieve the police and jails of an improper burden, freeing up law enforcement resources for more appropriate tasks. The advent of promising drugs such as naltrexone (the "sobriety pill") holds hope for future treatment.

A particularly thorny problem facing campus police has been the problem of binge drinking and alcohol-related arrests on college campuses. These arrests surged 24 percent in 1998, the largest in seven years (Associated Press, 2000). In addition to heavier drinking among college students, the upsurge may also reflect greater reporting and enforcement. Alcohol abuse remains a bigger problem on campuses than other drugs. Such reporting of figures is now required by federal law. A survey by the Harvard School of Public Health found about 23 percent of the college student population reporting binge drinking in 1999. This is defined as drinking at least five (men) or four (women) drinks in a row at least three or more times in the two weeks before the survey (Ibid.).

Special Populations

A conservative political climate in the United States in the eighties led to cuts in social programs and a burgeoning homeless population, as well as a deinstitutionalized mentally ill population. The police force, although also diminished, became by default social workers of last resort. "They do so because peace officers are unique in providing free, around the-clock service, mobility, a legal obligation to respond, and legal authority to detain" (Finn and Sullivan, 1988, p. 2).

Isaac and Armat (1990) in *Madness in the Streets* note that the homeless and neglected mentally ill sometimes create the perception of "craziness" on our streets, which is destructive of the social order. The neglectful deinstitutionalization of the mentally ill brings them into oftentimes unpleasant contact with ordinary people who then have a sense of public disrepair (Johnson, 1990). A number of these contribute to the overcrowding problem in prisons. IN THE NEWS 14.1 reports on an innovative program for dealing with deinstitutionalized mentally ill populations.

Laws related to curfew violations for juveniles also serve as an example of an attempt to regulate public disorder. More kids are arrested in the U.S. for curfew violations than

IN THE NEWS 14.1

OUTPATIENT COMMITMENT PROGRAMS FOR THE MENTALLY ILL

When schizophrenic Andrew Goldstein pushed Kendra Webdale to her death under a Manhattan subway train, the issue of dumping mentally disturbed persons onto the nation's streets once again was raised. Many severely mentally ill persons function quite well as long as they remain on their medication. When they do not, they may become violent, homeless, or mad.

One solution that has been used in some states has been "outpatient commitment" programs. These programs are specifically designed for those who have a history of moving from hospitals, halfway houses, and clinics and falling off their prescribed medicinal regimens. A court orders individuals to follow their anti-psychotic medical treatment while in the community. The carefully supervised individuals can be hospitalized against their will if they fail to comply. Patients in the program spent less than half as much time in the hospital than a comparison group. The threat of recommitment was the key. While civil liberties advocates decried involuntary hospitalization, proponents of the program point out that about half of all such patients have no insight (rational choice) into their conditions nor understanding of their need for medication. The freedom to be psychotic does not appear to be a proper argument for free will.

Source: Sally L. Satel. 1999. "Real Help for the Mentally Ill." *New York Times*. January 7, p. B12.

InfoTrac College Edition Research

Searching "mentally ill offenders," what problems have been noted with Canada's "dangerous offender legislation"?

for any other single category of crime ("Curfew Violations," 1999). Research has so far shown no correlation between such laws and decreases in juvenile crime.

Societal Reactions

The rapid pace of social change and the subsequent cultural lag that it creates have been endemic in the United States in the post-World War II period. We tend to forget that early in this century cigarette smoking was considered deviant. Similarly, the consumption of alcohol was so dimly viewed that it resulted in a constitutional amendment to forbid its usage.

As previously indicated, Edwin Schur's (1965) concept of "crimes without victims" refers specifically to consensual, adult activities usually conducted in private in which there is no apparent harm to others. The criminalization of such activities, as illustrated by the Prohibition experiment, often involves ineffective **overcriminalization,** an inappropriate extension of the criminal law into areas of personal conduct and morality. Most public order crime constitutes violations of legislated morality. Prohibition of such crimes represents an effort to control or regulate moral and personal behavior through formal laws, often without attempts to mold public opinion, which is necessary in order to support the legislative and police activity. Since much of the activity is consensual and private, law enforcement efforts often involve invasion of privacy and the use of extraordinary efforts that threaten civil liberties, leading some observers to describe such efforts as not only expensive and ineffective, but also criminogenic (Morris and Hawkins, 1970, p. 2). Sumner's notion, discussed in Chapter 1, that if laws fail to obtain the support of the mores they will tend to be ineffective, suggests that criminalization of these offenses has not markedly decreased their activity. Only a small proportion of offenders are reached by the criminal justice system or deterred by the criminal status of the offense.

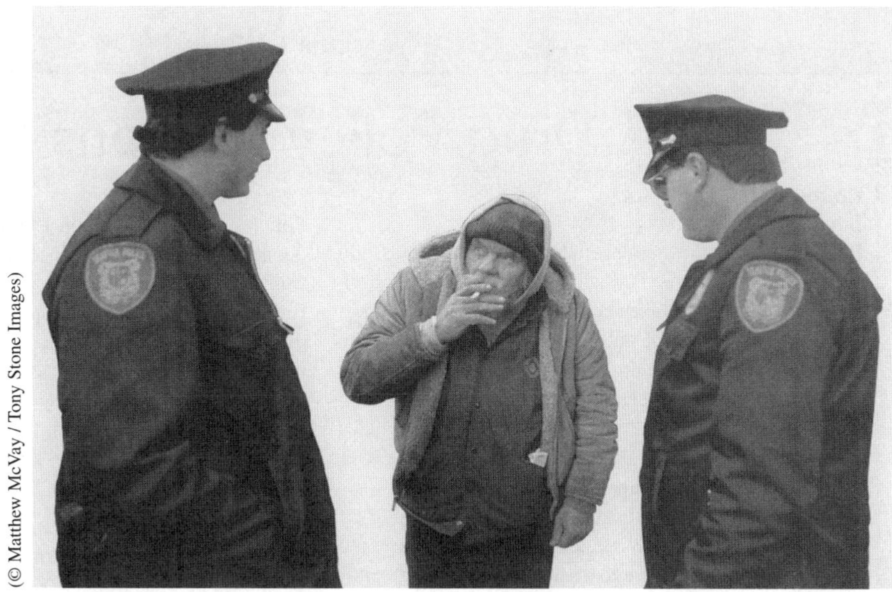

(© Matthew McVay / Tony Stone Images)

Police officers talk to a homeless man in downtown Seattle. Is this an example of the police functioning as social workers? Or—since the "homeless problem" contributes to a sense of public disorders—is it in fact police business?

In harmful, nonconsensual areas the criminal justice system can have an impact in reducing prohibited activity. In 1988 a U.S. Customs Bureau sting, "Operation Borderline," set up a phony child pornography mail-order house in Toronto and then rounded up many pedophiles who ordered such materials. They were charged under a 1984 Child Protection Act, which outlawed the distribution of all sexually explicit material involving children. Such programs are believed to have reduced considerably the child pornography trade (Cohn, 1988; Anderson and Van Atta, 1986). In consensual vice activities, however, Cook (1988, p. 1) points out: "The criminal law is a cumbersome, costly tool to wield against the harms associated with vice."

In April 1992 the Supreme Court overturned a conviction and ruled that a Nebraska farmer had been entrapped by postal agents who coaxed him for two years to buy mail-order child pornography. "Project Looking Glass" resulted in 147 convictions, of which 35 cases showed ongoing or past child abuse, although it had also resulted in four suicides (Marcus, 1991).

The history of the regulation of vice has been one of constant symbolic political posturing with little relationship between what is said and what is done. In 1987 President Ronald Reagan not only declared war on drugs but also declared victory, claiming his administration's drug jihad was "an untold American success story." Two years later national news magazines were sensationally declaring that sections of large cities were so overrun by drug gangs they were "dead zones" or "Beirut, U.S.A.," and that "the drug problem and its accompanying violence has clearly outstripped the resources and capability of local governments, police departments, courts, and prisons to cope with them" (Moore et al., 1988, p. 28). While phony wars on drugs were declared, the criminal justice and social service resources to fight the war were cut. For example, in 1973 Washington, D.C., had 5,100 police, but only 3,950 in 1989 (Kurtz, 1989). The DEA had 2,400 agents in 1986, the same number as in 1976 ("Ex-Agents Say," 1986). By 1986 the number of public facilities for treating drug abusers had been cut by one-third from their levels in the seventies (Gest, 1986). VANTAGE POINT 14.4 presents a portion of the ASC Task Force Report on Drug Policy Options.

VANTAGE POINT 14.4

Drug Policy Options

Lessons from Epidemics

Issues

Beginning with the heroin epidemic of the 1960s and continuing through the devastating crack epidemic, drug crises have regularly taken center stage in American politics and crime control policy. Through the 1980s, the central doctrine in U.S. drug policy has been "legalism." In this view, drug use challenges the established social order and moral foundations of authority. Drug policies have emphasized criminal penalties and deterrence over prevention and treatment as control mechanisms.

These drug policies have had a push-down-pop-up effect; the more pressure applied in one place, the more likely new problems were to arise in another. For example, criminal sanctions for low-level crack users have focused resources away from treatment of such users, whose behaviors are vectors for HIV transmission through high-risk sexual activity.

The lessons from decades of legalistic drug policies suggest that deterrence strategies have not been successful in reducing drug use. Enforcement strategies have consumed resources, aggravated the health risks associated with drugs, and increased the levels of violence surrounding drug markets. Drug policy has also increased profits for drug sellers and attracted other young people into selling, as the exaggerated symbols of conspicuous consumption by dealers act as a siren for younger people. Severe sentencing laws applied broadly and indiscriminately have undermined, rather than reinforced, the moral authority of the law.

Policy recommendations

Policies need to focus on reducing the harmful consequences of drug use and place criminal penalties within a framework recognizing the scale of drug problems. Enforcement and prosecution should be used to disrupt mid- and upper-level trafficking, while treatment or alternative sanctions should be used to reduce drug demand among offenders whose drug use has propelled them into the criminal justice system. The cornerstone of a new drug policy is to increase alcohol and drug treatment opportunities at all stages of the criminal justice system.

- **Treatment-oriented drug courts:** Continued experimentation with treatment-oriented drug courts should be encouraged. A potentially powerful model for linking the treatment/public health system to the criminal justice process, these courts should continue to be developed and evaluated for their long-term effectiveness. The risk of unnecessarily widening the net of social control can 1be minimized through the use of appropriate eligibility and screening criteria and comprehensive, clinically based assessment.
- **Alcohol and other drug (AOD) treatment:** Access to (AOD) treatment and public health services should be encouraged at all stages of the criminal justice process. Accordingly, opportunities for effective treatment interventions during the pretrial period, probation-supervised treatment, treatment under a community corrections model, and prison- or jail-based treatment should be studied and encouraged.

Overcriminalization

Overcriminalization or extension of the criminal law into inappropriate areas of moral conduct results in a number of outcomes:

- Many such laws are virtually unenforceable.
- They often lead to corruption of criminal justice personnel and politicians.
- They undermine public respect for the law.
- They create illicit monopolies for organized crime groups.
- They criminalize activities and stigmatize their participants.
- They reflect no consistent, defensible theory of harm (Richards, 1982, p. 194).
- They isolate and embitter offenders.
- Penalties are often ineffective and/or inappropriate. In the past, for instance, tough drug laws netted many marijuana users and few big drug pushers.
- Such laws tie up law enforcement agencies in thankless tasks that could more appropriately be performed by other social agencies.

VANTAGE POINT 14.4—*Continued*

All criminal justice-based treatment services should consider the provision of aftercare services to provide a treatment continuum.

- **Community mobilization:** Communities can effectively mobilize to disrupt drug markets and deter drug users. Many case studies have depicted the benefits of community policing with respect to reducing the size and scope of drug markets, but few systematic studies have appeared that could corroborate this effect. This approach, however, seems more likely to support the linkage of treatment and public health services to law enforcement than traditional anti-drug enforcement approaches.
- **Disaggregated prevention strategies:** Prevention strategies should be disaggregated for specific drugs and populations. They should be built from an understanding of the mechanisms through which individuals acquire information about drugs and make decisions about their use. The lessons of drug epidemics are that information about drug use rules and dangers is spread informally from credible sources and learned from social experiences; normative changes in drug use patterns are influenced weakly by legal threats.
- **Target drug treatment:** The concentration of high-rate and high-risk drug use among a small segment of the population suggests that treatment efforts should be targeted to them. Many of these individuals are in prison, and their criminality is closely (and perhaps causally) linked to drug problems. Cost arguments alone make in-prison treatment a necessary part of an overall strategy for drug control, but the opportunity to reduce criminality, together with drug problems, is a compelling reason for funding inmates' treatment.
- **Alternatives to incarceration:** Citing the need to alleviate overcrowding and prioritize prison space for violent offenders, several governors and state legislatures have recommended that penal statutes permit the sentencing of nonviolent drug offenders to nonincarcerative punishments. Expansion of viable alternatives to incarceration, however, have been stifled by fiscal restraints. Incentives must be created to sustain states' efforts to create alternatives, such as supervision programs involving urinalysis, outpatient and residential drug treatment, or health and employment programs.
- **Harm-reduction model:** Treating drug addiction as the chronic disease that it is enables legal institutions to achieve realistic and attainable goals. From this perspective, a harm reduction model becomes the framework for policy. Myriad forms of harm can be addressed by selective application of criminal "pressure" to divert users into treatment that may eventually return them to families and/or employment.
- **Buyer-seller interactions:** Supply-side strategies should focus on interactions between buyers and sellers, making drug purchases more difficult by increasing search time for buyers and decreasing revenues for sellers. International interventions and interdictions at the top of the domestic distribution system should have low priority compared to point-of-sale efforts to reduce available supplies.
- **Local concerns:** Enforcement, treatment, and health care are local matters, and responsibility for

Decriminalization

Decriminalization refers to the process of lessening the penalties attached to particular offenses. Some arguments in support of decriminalizing many public order crimes include:

- Such activities should not be the concern of the state and formal agents of social control, but are more appropriately handled by informal modes of control such as the family, community, church, and the like.
- State interference with much of this behavior often makes matters worse. The criminalization of drug users and view of them as criminals rather than people with medical problems has cut off the legal supply of drugs, created illegal monopolies, and forced many into criminal activity in order to support their habits.
- Such laws tend to accomplish little with those already favorably disposed to such activity. Homosexuality, prostitution, gambling, and the like have been and will continue to be persistent activities in modern society.

VANTAGE POINT 14.4—*Continued*

enforcement and funding of drug policy should be shifted downward to the states.

- **Federal concerns:** The development of knowledge, technology, data, and information should be organized within a policy infrastructure at the federal level.

Drugs and the Urban Community

Issues

Involvement in the illicit drug underclass has a wide-ranging negative impact on inner-city neighborhoods. The subculture demonstrates a set of values, beliefs, lifestyles, and behavioral norms that devalue legitimate means of earning money and embrace self-serving manipulation, the "fast life," and the use of violence. With the emergence of crack, the more stable organized crime groups that had been responsible for the distribution of heroin and cocaine gave way to independent, low-level crack sellers. Driven by high profits, crack distribution escalated in neighborhoods that experienced social and economic deprivation. Within these inner-city neighborhoods, crack distribution networks operate in a fluid market economy that allows freelance crack distributors to sell crack with minimal investment capital, street sellers to switch suppliers easily and control their own work schedules, and violence to flourish as a growing army of young urban crack sellers compete to protect their economic interests.

Law enforcement efforts to reduce drug use have been directed at identifying and convicting those individuals at the top of the vertical hierarchy of major drug distribution groups, in the belief that such a strategy would make it more difficult for consumers to locate drugs of choice. Thus, prices would increase, and consumption would be driven downward. Police crackdowns, whether sweeping or focused, are an alternative strategy aimed at making it more difficult to carry out drug transactions and frustrating participants at all levels of the drug distribution system. However, available research shows that the extent of drug trafficking and the crime, violence, and lawlessness associated with drugs in the inner cities have not diminished despite increasingly punitive local, state, and federal government interventions and social control. On the contrary, these social troubles have increased, in the midst of an ever-escalating and costly "war on drugs."

For the most part, inner-city communities house many African-American and Hispanic residents whose populations have been replenished (since the flight of middle class professional and working class blacks from ghetto communities) by poorer, younger newcomers from rural areas. These late arrivals were born at a time when structural shifts in the economy resulted in the relocation of manufacturing industries outside the central city, a division into high- and low-wage income sectors, and dramatic technological innovation. These shifts, coupled with the exodus of those who provided stability and helped to reinforce societal values and norms, have caused inner-city communities to experience increased joblessness and a decline in basic institutions that have led to social disorganization.

Policy recommendations

- **Economic and social context:** Drug research, and the policy stemming from it, should account for the connection between the economic and social environments into which many drug users are born. Drug use and drug addiction are tied to structural conditions that help to create a self-perpetuating cycle of pathology, which must be viewed and addressed holistically.
- **Community-based programs:** Drug and crime intervention should concentrate on chronic heroin, cocaine, and injection drug users. Arrest brings many users into contact with the criminal justice system; this contact should be used to detect and assess drug

---

- Law enforcement officers' focus on such public-order crimes overburdens the criminal justice system with inappropriate tasks, preventing the deployment of resources in combating more serious crimes.

The issue of decriminalization is a matter of degrees of regulation/deregulation rather than of categorical legalization-illegalization. Proposals for decriminalization entail lessening of penalties, but not total abandonment of public or official concern with maintaining some degree of control over such activities. Fears have been raised that decriminalization of such activities constitutes societal approval.

In 1957 the English Wolfenden Report, in examining laws related to homosexuality and prostitution, concluded that private, consensual, adult sexual relations were not the

VANTAGE POINT 14.4—*Continued*

use and present treatment options. Arrestees who test positive for substance abuse should be placed in treatment while detained. Therefore, community-based sentencing and intervention programs should be considered, rather than jail or prison, for drug abuse/possession charges.

- **Mandatory treatment:** Chronic abusers who are sentence to jail or prison should be compelled to enroll in treatment programs. Once these offenders have been released on probation or parole, legal supervision should be lengthy to reduce the likelihood of recidivism, and community-based treatment should be required.
- **Treatment evaluation:** To determine treatment needs, an evaluation of the extent of criminal involvement should be made; research indicates that the longer an individual remains in a treatment program, the greater the continuity of care, and the greater the likelihood of successful employment and reduced drug- and crime-related activities.
- **Media and school strategies:** Although gains have been made through the use of mass media campaigns, informational lectures, and denouncements made by celebrity role models, drug prevention programs must recognize that young people are impulsive, have undeveloped self-esteem, have peer-centered lives, and are easily seduced by the streets and the promise of quick and easy money. In some inner-city school settings, "resistance skills training" teaches students how to recognize and cope with peer pressure, thereby improving their social competency. Additional evaluated experimental projects should be conducted to determine the effectiveness of this psychosocial strategy designed to discourage drug use.
- **Geographically focused enforcement:** Community-based surveys of drug locations should be conducted to identify the nature of drug markets and the way that abusers utilize them. Once identified, the activity of drug markets can be investigated in terms of the convergence of consumers and sellers in space and time. In this way, it would be possible to realistically depict the drug distribution patterns in urban areas and identify specific places of ongoing drug activity for intervention.
- **Root cause strategy:** Consideration should be given to a drug strategy aimed at ameliorating those conditions that give rise to drug use in the inner city, via, a strategy that emphasizes education, job training, psychological support systems, and drug prevention. Joblessness is a fundamental problem that must be addressed, and assistance with child support programs, child care strategies, family allowance programs, and parenting skills training is needed to improve the overall life chances of children.

Source: "American Society of Criminology Task Force Report to Attorney General Janet Reno," *The Criminologist* (Special Issue), 20, 6, November/December 1995. (Excluded in the interest of space was the section on "Drugs and the Rural Community"). Task Force members: (Drug Policy Options) Steven Belenko and Jeffrey Fagan, co-chairs: (Drugs and the Community) Coramae Richey Mann, chair. Leon Pettiway, and Ralph Weisheit.

InfoTrac College Edition Research

What are some of the arguments presented by those who favor "drug legalization"? Do you agree or disagree with these arguments?

law's business. With respect to homosexuality one could ask whether individuals really have much choice in or power to change their sexual orientations. Those who oppose decriminalization of homosexual activities fear proselytizing and seduction of the young. Such a "**floodgate theory**" (the assumption that decriminalization of homosexuality will increase such behavior) has not been borne out in England (West, 1988, pp. 181, 186). While the menace of AIDS has curtailed some more promiscuous homosexual activity, for example, as in bath houses, it is probably impossible to suppress all homosexuality.

The degree of decriminalization, of course, varies with the type of offense. Few propose decriminalization of predatory or harmful practices such as child molesting or incest, as few would urge that acts that violate privacy, such as exhibitionism and voyeurism, simply be ignored. Civil commitment proceedings by which psychological treatment is prescribed are an important tool for the protection of society. In public inebriate programs, the police remain involved but maximize the use of community social service agencies. Combined with decriminalization, public media programs can play a role in discouraging undesirable activity. There has been some recent rethinking of the wisdom of decriminalizing public drunkenness. As our earlier discussion of "broken windows" (Wilson and Kelling, 1982) suggested: "The presence on the streets of boisterous, obstreperous, and sometimes belligerent drunks contributes to a sense of social disorder" (Jacobs, 1987, p. 2). A field experiment in Lynn, Massachusetts, demonstrated the efficacy of street level enforcement (making it difficult for drug dealers to make a sale and for buyers to "score" or purchase) in improving the quality of life in a community (Kleiman et al., 1988).

The declining number of Americans who smoke tobacco, from 42 percent of adults in 1956 to 33 percent in 1980 shows the effectiveness of a more moderate approach to discouraging the use of harmful substances. Arnold Trebach (1984, pp. 136–37) in "Peace without Surrender in the Perpetual Drug War" indicates:

> We did not declare a war on tobacco. We did not make it illegal we did not say that tobacco addicts . . . were evil. We did not seek to disrupt foreign or domestic tobacco supplies. Indeed, we still subsidize the production of the most dangerous psychoactive drug known to our people. We did not seek to convince our citizens not to smoke through persuasion, objective, information and education . . . . Laws do not prohibit smoking entirely, only where and when an addict can take a "fix." In other words, the law did not confront the user head on by absolutely prohibiting this deadly practice. But the law did have a role: it discouraged, it controlled, it curbed, it coaxed.

Erickson (1990) proposed an alternative to the criminalization/decriminalization debate, arguing that a public health approach to demand reduction using social disapproval; informal family, community, and peer group controls; and beefed-up educational efforts could reduce drug usage.

Evidence related to the criminalization/decriminalization debate is uncertain, as can be illustrated by attempts to control heroin or opium abuse (Inciardi, 1990). The pre-1972 British program that medically administered legal doses of heroin to addicts may have meant both a smaller addict population and little crime associated with such addiction (Trebach, 1982). On the other hand, the British Crown Colony of Hong Kong, with the same program but a different culture, has an addiction problem much greater than that in the United States. The current British program is much more similar to U.S. programs. Others report that international pressure for a consistent drug policy is forcing the Dutch government to change its practical and successful drug policy (Marshall, Anjewierden, and Van Atteveld, 1990). A five-year experiment in decriminalization of drug use was canceled in Zurich, Switzerland, as the number of addicts and dealers attracted from all over Europe overwhelmed the system (Lynch and Blotner, 1991). Similarly, in the early nineties the Netherlands decided to permit the sale of soft drugs (hashish and marijuana) in order to diminish crime and enable the police to concentrate on hard drug trafficking. Possession of even small amounts of cocaine, heroin, and other hard drugs was tolerated and viewed as a public health problem to be addressed by treatment centers. What began as a successful experiment was flooded by "drug tourists" as European unity collapsed borders. Nevertheless, Dutch policy remains one of rejecting a "war on drugs" model in favor of a harm reduction model (Leuw and Marshall, 1994).

Arguments for more zealous law enforcement efforts can point to the People's Republic of China, which, through totalitarian policing appears to have nearly eliminated the problem. Such police powers would be culturally unacceptable in Western democracies and have not been particularly successful in brutal authoritarian regimes such as contemporary Iran, where Trebach (1984, p. 137) claims heroin addiction has exploded to include the improbable estimate of one of every twelve Iranians, despite public executions of users and traffickers (see also Trebach, 1987).

Many of the issues that we have examined in this chapter are complex and laden with heavy moral implications. We have, of course, only scratched the surface of some intense debates on these subjects.

> Along with the civil right to vote, go to school and have a job is the right not to be mugged, robbed or assaulted.
>
> —Senator Edward Kennedy

> Now that the liberation of Kuwait has been accomplished, my colleagues and I propose that the federal government immediately undertake the liberation of millions of Americans trapped by the tyranny of poverty, illiteracy, hunger, unemployment, crime and hopelessness.
>
> —Ruth Messinger, Manhattan borough president, proposing on behalf of the National League of Cities an "Operation Urban Storm," 1991

Throughout this text, descriptions of the operation of the criminal justice system have been only incidental to accounts of criminals and crime. Much of the future of crime and criminal activity will be influenced by various social policies that are shaped to direct the police, the courts, and corrections.

The Ill-Fated War on Crime

A major "war on crime" in the United States was launched as a social policy with much fanfare in 1967 and, after the expenditure of approximately $8 billion, was all but abandoned in 1981. Begun as a result of rising crime rates in the sixties, it represented the first time in U.S. history that the federal government took it upon itself to fight crime. The rise and fall of the national war on crime is described by Thomas and Tania Cronin and Michael Milakovich in *U.S. v. Crime in the Streets* (1981, p. 11) as originating at a time when "America . . . did not yet doubt its pragmatic genius. Everything was possible if you just spent enough money!" Despite the fact that the federal executive office could exercise little impact in crime control—primarily a state and local responsibility as well as one of the judicial branch—political candidates for national office seized the issue. This national involvement commenced with the Safe Streets Act and the election of a law-and-order president, Richard Nixon, in 1968. Presidential counselor John Dean (1977, pp. 389–90) explains: "I was cranking out that bullshit on Nixon's crime policy before he was elected. And it was bullshit too. We knew it. The Nixon campaign didn't call for anything about crime problems that Ramsey Clark [Johnson's Attorney General] wasn't already doing under LBJ. We just made more noise."

The Cronins and Milakovich (1981, p. 78) explain that crime was largely viewed as street crime and particularly a problem of unemployed urban black male juveniles. Under the Law Enforcement Assistance Administration, large amounts of money were spent on many existing criminal justice programs that were simply relabeled in order to meet funding guidelines. By 1972 "LEAA became the unwanted child of the national government. It had become apparent even to politicians that no president could make a promise to end crime and keep that promise. . . . As lowered expectations became policy, LEAA's funding was sharply reduced until the agency was killed off" (Cronin, Cronin, and Milakovich, 1981, p. 106). It was perhaps a fitting irony that the national administration leaders who most exploited the law-and-order campaign issue were forced to prematurely resign in disgrace because of their own criminal activity.

The short-lived "war on crime" was primarily an attack on street crimes and lower class criminals, the "dangerous classes." Hardly mentioned were the most expensive areas of criminality, occupational and organizational crimes—suite crimes. While the issue of crime remained, other items, particularly environmental and economic, became preeminent on the social agenda.

The War on Drugs

Ever since the Goldwater campaign of 1964, being or sounding tough on crime has made for good sound bites, campaign ads, and "symbolic politics." In the 1988 presidential election the Bush campaign managers capitalized on the public's fear of crime and used the Willie Horton incident (a rape committed by a murderer while on weekend parole) to generate an emotional reaction and voter support (Benekos, 1991). By 1995, the "three strikes and you're out" slogan offered yet another in a long list of panaceas (Benekos and Merlo, 1995). When the Bush administration in 1989 declared yet another "war on drugs" and even appointed a drug czar, William Bennett, to head up the attack, few would argue that an assault on the U.S. drug problem was not in order. However, the strategy of the attack was disputable. The federal government talked tough about drugs but still did not provide enough resources to local criminal justice and social service systems to enable them to turn the words into actions. Gordon in *The Justice Juggernaut* (1990) feels that relying on formal controls (the police, courts, corrections) without also addressing poverty, unemployment, and urban despair has not worked. Such a get-tough policy alone reinforces a permanent underclass and is racist in that it is directed primarily against blacks and Latinos.

Fyfe (1991) argues:

> The unhappy fact is that although concentrated attacks on crime are sometimes necessary—like "wars" on dictators and disease—they can offer nothing more than temporary relief.
>
> I was a cop for 16 years and would be the last to say that strategies of deterrence, law enforcement and incarceration are not necessary. My point, though, is that they are not *sufficient,* and that any crime control agenda that relies on them without isolating and ameliorating the conditions that cause most crime is doomed to failure . . . .The lesson is plain. If people have nothing to lose by committing violent crime, some are likely to prey upon their neighbors and, occasionally, upon the rest of us. Acting on this lesson is far more difficult: If we are to deal with crime in the long term, we must ensure that the people in our inner cities have a stake in this society, that they have too much to lose to make crime a worthwhile proposition.

Dirty Secrets

The relatively conservative view that the crime problem can be solved solely by increasing the technical efficiency of the existing criminal justice system ignores what was described as "**the dirty secrets**" of crime (Gross, 1980, p. 110). The "dirty little secret" is that most violent street crime is prevalent in structural criminogenic conditions associated with poverty, unemployment, inadequate education, substance abuse, and other economic ills about which the criminal justice system can do little. The "dirty big secret" (Gross, 1980, p. 113) is that the criminal justice system is soft on corporate crime. The war on crime was war on *some* crime, reflecting a distinctive world view or ideology regarding the nature of the crime problem.

Ideology and Social Policy

Causal vs. Policy Analysis

Ideology was defined previously as a distinctive belief system about what *should* occur, consisting of an aggregate of doctrines, ideas, assumptions, attitudes, and beliefs. Theory and research provide explanations and facts regarding crime and criminal behavior; ideological viewpoints provide the political direction for guiding social policy. Historian Arthur Schlesinger, Jr., in his *Cycles of American History* (1986), argues that American history and public policy have been punctuated by pendular shifts in which a dominant liberal era runs its course, to be succeeded by a conservative era that also runs its course, to be followed once again by a liberal era. Both Wilson and Herrnstein (1985) and Hirschi (1983) expressed the point of view that the field of the family severed its connections with criminological theory in the fifties and sixties for ideological reasons that favored the examination of larger institutions. Currie (1985, pp. 183–84) also feels that directions in crime and delinquency theory often reflect broader ideological trends in society rather than reflecting new breakthroughs in research. Conservative political scientist James Q. Wilson (1983a; 1975, pp. 50–53) draws a distinction between *causal analysis* and *policy analysis* that parallels distinctions made earlier in this text between pure research/theory and applied research/theory. He calls the assumption that "no problem is adequately addressed unless its causes are eliminated" (Wilson, 1975, p. 51) the causal fallacy, claiming that ultimate causes cannot be the subject of social policy since they are not subject to change. Advocates of this view tend to consider much causal analysis as an impractical, ivory tower exercise in futility.

Policy Analysis

Policy analysis is practical, applied research and:

> begins with a very different perspective. It asks not what is the "cause" of a problem, but what is the condition one wants to bring into being . . . what policy tools does a government (in our case, a democratic and libertarian government) possess that might when applied, produce at reasonable cost a desired alteration in the present condition or progress toward the required condition? (Wilson, 1975, p. 53)

Wilson's causal vs. policy analysis distinction is simply the resurrection of the pure vs. applied research issue discussed in the first chapter. While he is correct in his insistence that something practical must be done about street crime and that policy prescriptions cannot wait until final cause is established, he is incorrect in assuming that his policy approach is atheoretical and not concerned with ultimate cause.

The Social Policy Fallacy

Any policy approach contains inherent theoretical assumptions, acknowledged or not, as can be demonstrated in an analysis of approaches to social policy. In fact, to coin a term, Wilson and others have been guilty of the **social policy fallacy,** the erroneous belief that in a democratic society applied social policy can be effective even though it ignores causal roots. Such solutions in nonauthoritarian societies represent only limited, temporary solutions so long as social policy fails to address the critical structural factors that generate the problems it is attempting to resolve.

In the definitive work on public policy, Randall Clemons and Mark McBeth (2001, p. 323) advise:

> Rather than positing rational decision making and makers, policy analysts need to recognize limitations, subjectivity, ambiguity, and public interests.

> Rather than playing the role of the expert, analysts need to be educators and facilitators. Rather than trying to take the politics out of policy and letting power hide in fancy words and carefully scripted numbers, let's bring politics out into the open.

Ideological Approaches to Criminal Justice Policy

A variety of ideological approaches could be identified, ranging from conservative to radical approaches (Miller, 1973). Herbert Packer (1968) has developed often-cited *models of the criminal justice process:* the crime control and the due process models. The **crime control model** emphasizes law and order, bureaucratic efficiency in law enforcement, and the prosecution of criminals. Packer compares this model to assembly-line justice in which the criminal justice system is judged on the basis of maximization of apprehensions and convictions. The **due process model** is viewed analogously as an obstacle course in which justice and rights of the accused are held paramount. This emphasis slows down bureaucratic efficiency, but is appropriate to a democratic society whose ideal is law, order, and justice, with justice interpreted to include protection of legal guarantees of the accused.

Conservative, Liberal, and Radical Approaches

Many ideological stances exist, but this presentation will examine two *ideological approaches to criminal justice policy:* the conservative and liberal. Each of these is viewed as an "ideal type" in that distinctions between the types are exaggerated and are unlikely to exist in pure form.

The **conservative approach** to crime control policy is represented by writers such as James Q. Wilson (1975 and 1983a) and Ernest Van den Haag (1975). Though they deny a commitment to any causal theory, most advocates of this approach reflect the classical school of criminological theory. Crime is viewed as the product of the free will of the individual actors, who can be deterred by means of more sure, swift, and certain punishment and better application of the crime control model. Such writers tend to concentrate on crime in the streets as committed by the "dangerous classes," and are oriented toward incapacitation (deterrence through incarceration) and the just-deserts doctrine (retribution).

Allen and Latessa (1982, p. 6) indicate a number of elements of the conservative position for criminal justice policy. Conservatives tend to view crime as an exercise in free will and punishment a matter of just deserts and hold that liberal Supreme Court decisions have handcuffed the police and pampered offenders. Offenders are presumed to be guilty and punishment a certain deterrence. Policies advocated by conservatives include an emphasis on electronic surveillance and wiretapping, preventive detention, capital punishment, "no-knock" searches, opposition to gun control, abolition of parole, restriction of community-based corrections and probation, and emphasis on mandatory minimum sentences. This emphasis doubled the number of incarcerated Americans in the eighties and caused the United States to beat out South Africa and the former Soviet Union in having the largest incarcerated population in the world.

In his Presidential Address before the Academy of Criminal Justice Sciences, Harry Allen (1995) noted the declining opportunities for those at the bottom of the socio-economic ladder due to social, economic, cultural, and political changes in the last quarter of the twentieth century. At risk, inner-city youth in particular are disadvantaged by these trends as are other undereducated, underemployed, and unemployed "underclass," many of whom will be unable to escape becoming the "permanent underclass." Without a major investment in social and human capital, crime and delinquency among this group is likely to continue to escalate.

The **liberal approach,** represented by such writers as Currie (1985) and Reiman (1995), as well as many others, insists that society, in addition to developing crime control measures to contain crime in the streets, must address root causes of crime such as inequality, racism, unemployment, urban blight, and the like. Most liberals also insist that inquiry be directed, not only at street crimes, but also at occupational, organizational, political, and other more elite criminal activity. They also tend to be supportive of the due process model, which views crime control as subordinate to upholding the rights of individuals, and to advocate rehabilitation as a correctional measure.

Allen and Latessa (1982) detail a number of characteristics of the liberal position for criminal justice policy, which emphasizes justice as much as law and order, rehabilitation, and social programs to address the root causes of crime. Some assumptions of the liberal position are that the government can ameliorate social circumstances that cause crime, such as poverty, racism, lack of education and the like. Crime is viewed as a symptom of these underlying problems. Slums and ghettos of the inner city must be eradicated, and the government should provide jobs and opportunities. Liberals tend to support gun control, community-based corrections, work release, parole contracts, and rehabilitation.

The Future of Crime

Criminologists lack a crystal ball with which to peer into the future and forecast its likely direction. Along with other social scientists and futurists, they can demarcate some likely directions; however, even these are affected by a myriad variables whose trends may not be fully anticipated (see Stephens, 1982; Tafoya, 1992). For example, in examining Canadian crime rates, Daniel Koenig et al. (1983, p. 98) claim:

> Very simply, Canadian crime rates whether of violence, property crime, or other offenses, do not appear to bear any consistent relationship to economic inequality, rates of unemployment or inflation, or changes in per capita income expressed either in current or constant dollars. Nor, for that matter, is there any consistent relationship between Canadian crime rates and either urbanization or the age structure of the population.

The big U.S. crime wave that began in the mid-sixties apparently stabilized in the decade of the seventies, official statistics to the contrary. Utilizing broad demographic and cultural trends, criminologists were accurate in predicting the crime dip that began in the eighties. Crime, being a socially defined behavior, can increase or decrease with legislative activity that broadens or lessens the categories included and is responsive to Ferri's "saturation law of criminology" in that it expands to fit the amount of social control activity. Donald Black (1976) has also observed that crime increases with growth in the criminal law.

The orientation of this text is one in which the reader responds to the question "What causes crime?" with the question "What type of crime?" In the same light, predictions of the future of crime will vary with the type of criminal activity that is the subject of prognosis.

Public opinion surveys suggest that the public and the media consider upper level occupational crime very serious. Whether this will be reflected in treating prominent offenders in the same manner as lower class offenders depends on ideological directions in politics. The Reagan administration tended to regard federal enforcement in corporate criminal areas and regulatory agency activity as "unnecessary red tape and government interference," while the Bush administration took federal regulatory activity a bit more seriously. The cost, quantity, and international scope of such criminality are likely to increase with the growth of multinational business enterprises. The Clinton administration sponsored the largest crime bill ($30.2 billion) since the "war on crime" of the sixties, but also for deficit reduction purposes reduced the number of federal employees, including regulators. Some features of the original Clinton crime bill (elements of which were modified by a Congressional bipartisan committee or did not survive Congressional debate) included:

- Grants to communities to hire 100,000 police officers
- Scholarships for police officers and students agreeing to serve as law enforcement officers
- Grants for rural anti-crime and drug efforts
- Byrne law-enforcement grants to states and local communities for various crime and anti-drug programs
- Incarceration and probation alternatives for young offenders
- Grants to states to build and operate prisons and incarceration alternatives
- Grants to high crime communities for crime prevention experiments
- Grants to fight crimes against women
- Drug court programs
- Local Partnership Act giving local governments quicker access to federal anti-crime funds
- After-school, weekend, and summer programs for children
- In-school programs targeting at risk youth
- Drug treatment for state and federal prisoners
- Local crime prevention block grant programs
- Expansion of the death penalty to cover more than 50 federal crimes
- A ban on the sale and possession of 19 assault weapons, copycat models, and gun clips with over 10 bullets
- Life in prison for criminals convicted of three violent felonies or drug offenses if the third conviction is a federal crime
- A requirement that sexual offenders must be registered for 10 years, and some permanently. Communities must be notified that a sexual offender lives in, or is moving into, the area
- Admission of prior sex offenses as evidence at trial
- Adult treatment of 13-year-olds charged with such violent crimes as murder, armed robbery, and rape

Gresham Sykes (1972, 1980) predicts that urban poverty associated with criminality is likely to grow and will continue to play a major role in future street crimes. The future of violent crime in the United States is uncertain; however, the United States is likely to continue to lead developed nations in criminal homicide, since it will continue to have the largest armed civilian population in the world. Urban robbery rates are likely to remain high, depending on a number of factors, including employment opportunities for young minority males. Plate (1975, p. 181) suggests that younger criminals have displaced professionals on the streets, and this is unlikely to change as long as national policies use central cities as the dumping ground for national problems, such as racism and inequality. Official statistics on violence in the family, spouse and child abuse, and rape are likely to remain high in response to better reporting and more supportive social programs for such victims.

Most areas of public order criminality are likely to continue to experience decriminalization combined with better regulation and social, psychiatric, and medical support systems. Common property crimes are likely to decrease, being most responsive to the aging demographic profile. Also continuing to decline in importance are many areas of professional criminal behavior, although frauds related to securities, credit, and computer records, as well as "knock-offs" or counterfeit products will remain problematic.

In July 1987 United Parcel Service workers in Louisville, Kentucky, opened a leaking package and, to their surprise, discovered five human heads being shipped to a medical laboratory. The heads had been stolen by Philadelphia morgue employees, who had shipped a variety of body parts to physicians and researchers. Perhaps the illegal marketing of human body parts will emerge as a major crime of the future, an updated version of grave robbing ("Charges Dropped," 1987).

Organized criminal activity will persist, although dominance by Italian-American syndicates will continue to wane while a multitude of groups capitalize on the new Prohibition era's criminal seed money—supplying illicit drugs. Political criminality will continue, particularly in the international arena, with terrorism employed as a tool of cheap "diplomatic leverage" as authoritarian and democratic regimes resort to ideological justifications in their efforts to maintain power. It is hazardous to make even these very general predictions, however; criminologists and others do not agree in their forecasts.

Georgette Bennett in *Crimewarps* (1987) made a number of interesting predictions for the future of crime, including:

- The computer will be the single greatest crime generator in the future.
- The concentration of crime in the United States will continue to shift to the Sunbelt and West.
- Low birth rates and high work rates will leave a plethora of unguarded homes ripe for daytime burglary.
- The growing service economy will create many part-time jobs that, combined with fewer student dropouts, will mean less crime.
- More abusive families will emerge as the number of single, poor, young, and undereducated mothers grows.
- Industries with older workers will experience less theft.
- The growth in the elderly population will increase medical quackery and insurance fraud.
- Fear of AIDS will reduce the demand for streetwalkers.

Felson (1987, p. 911) argues that:

> Routine activities deliver easy crime opportunities to the offender. Astute planners and managers can interfere with this delivery, diverting flows of likely offenders (such as adolescents) . . . . They can engineer traffic to provide "natural surveillance." Past trends encouraged the crime rate increases, but the developing metropolitan facility could reverse this, privatizing substantial portions of the metropolitan turf.

Gendreau and Ross (1987) indicate that the "nothing works doctrine" regarding rehabilitation simply does not match the available evidence, perhaps presaging a revivification of rehabilitation programs. Other likely directions include greater use of community policing and problem-solving strategies aimed at mobilizing communities and citizens in crime prevention (Moore, Trojanowicz, and Kelling, 1988) and greater attention to "broken windows" (Wilson and Kelling, 1982) in which the police express concern with enforcing the daily civilities without which disorder reigns (Kelling, 1988b).

Policy Experiments

A very promising development in the field of criminology and criminal justice has been the use of "**policy experiments,**" applied field experiments that address themselves to immediate, practical policy questions. In March of 1987 the National Research Council's

Committee on Research on Law Enforcement and the Administration of Justice summarized the following steps in designing policy experiments (Garner and Visher, 1988, pp. 7–8):

1. Choose an interesting problem—a policy question that people really care about or an existing procedure that clearly needs improvement.
2. Do some creative thinking to solve legal and ethical issues that may arise.
3. Rigorously maintain the random assignment of persons, cases, or other units into treatment and control groups throughout the experiment.
4. Choose a design and methods of investigation that are appropriate both to the questions to be answered and to the available data.
5. Adopt a team approach between researchers and practitioners and keep working in close cooperation.
6. Put as much into your experiment as you want to get out of it.
7. Use an experiment to inform policy, not to make policy.
8. Understand and confront the political risks an experiment may involve.
9. Insofar as possible, see that the experiment is replicated in a variety of settings before encouraging widespread adoption of experimentally successful treatments.

Policy Options

The Riot Commission

The year 1968 in the United States has been described by some historians as the year of "a national nervous breakdown," when frustration and anger over the Vietnam War, racism, and inequality spilled into the nation's streets. In April 1968, in the wake of the assassination of civil rights leader Martin Luther King, Jr., cities across the country exploded in mob fury and, for the first time since the Civil War, the U.S. military set up machine gun batteries on Capitol Hill in order to protect the center of government from its own citizens. A month prior to this, President Johnson's riot commission, the Kerner Commission (1968), called *The National Advisory Commission on Civil Disorders,* issued its report. It indicated that prejudice and discrimination reflected in white racism had plagued this nation's history and now threatened its very survival as a democracy and that racial divisions or polarization between blacks and whites, expressed in black concentration in central cities and white flight to suburbia, menaced the very future of U.S. society. More to the point, the commission indicated that unless major commitments to change were undertaken immediately, in twenty years—by 1988—this chasm would most likely become permanent—a divided society violating the very essence of American democracy.

The **Kerner Commission proposed three policy options:** the present policies option, a garrison-state option, and a commitment to change option. The *present policies option* proposed that nothing be done. The commission indicated that such a policy would produce a divided society characterized by increasing levels of intergroup violence, fear, and disorder. The *garrison-state option* resembles the conservative approach toward crime control. Without addressing root conditions of discrimination in housing, jobs, education, and the like, better policing would merely represent a temporary or stopgap approach that flirted with creating a "garrison or police state," an American version of the South African apartheid system. The third and preferred option was that of a *commitment to change,* a federal policy of encouraging open housing, affirmative action, and desegregation combined with attempts to erase income, educational, and other social deficits experienced by black Americans because of previous institutionalized racism. In short, although many specific recommendations were made by the commission, it was the belief of the members that nothing major could be accomplished without significant structural changes in the economic, social, and political systems.

Criminal Justice Policy Options

Policy options for criminal justice cannot be separated from policies for other social problems. (This statement, of course, places the author in the liberal social policy school of thought and reflects his own views.) **At least three policy options exist for future criminal justice policy:** the present policy option, the conservative option, and the liberal option. The radical-Marxist option, another version of the conservative option, is rejected because it achieves a minimal level of social justice at the expense of democratic freedoms and provides an unacceptable authoritarian political structure. In the *present policy option* the issue of criminal justice is approached from the individualistic, nineteenth-century philosophical viewpoint of the legal profession. Pendular shifts from the crime control to the due process model may or may not assure "legal justice" but do little to address "social justice." Even if the legal rights of the accused are assured under the due process model, this accomplishes little if inequitable conditions continue the criminogenic environments that guarantee future clients. The debate over nondiscriminatory provision of legal justice in our local and state courts is important but moot: under the crime control model, injustice presents itself in nonenforcement or in weak enforcement of crime in the suites; in the due process model, injustice presents itself in the continued toleration of structural conditions that breed street crime. A narrow interpretation of due process can produce the ultimate injustice—the toleration of crimes against the poor in the name of individual rights.

The *conservative option* has been described as an approach to social policy that emphasizes policy analysis, incapacitation, just deserts, and the crime control model; and as one that eschews causal analysis as ultimately impractical, viewing policies directed at resolving causal roots of crime as intractable. At an extreme level, crime control in an authoritarian state can be accomplished through sheer repression and state terrorism. Nazi Germany had law and order but little social justice. Even in a democratic state, the policies of incapacitating career criminals may be a wise, essential policy in order to address some street crime in the short term. Such policies, if they work, are aimed at protecting potential victims, particularly against stranger-precipitated violent predations. However, addressing street crimes while ignoring suite crimes institutionalizes a dual system of justice, robbing a democratic society of the legitimation and fairness necessary for political authority. While radical criminologists may be incorrect in charging discrimination in the specific legal processing of conventional offenders, they are absolutely correct in charging discrimination when legal sanctions fall upon the dangerous classes while ignoring the glamorous classes.

The *liberal option,* while calling for control of street crime, seeks also to ameliorate root causes of criminality. Besides being committed to the due process model of crime control, the liberal option tends also to be committed to the ideals of social justice, insisting that cries for law and order will be ineffective without a concomitant commitment to eradicating inequality, injustice, and underlying structural criminogenic conditions. Crime is intimately tied to the social structure of society. The relative blindness to upper-level crimes furthers inequalities and exacerbates criminogenic environments that foster street crime. VANTAGE POINT 14.5 presents three ASC Task Force Reports on Police, Corrections, and Sentencing.

In the 1990s in the United States the richest 20 percent of families controlled about 52 percent of national income and 79 percent of national wealth (stocks, bonds, real estate, and so on). Indeed, the top 5 percent owned over half the nation's wealth. The poorest 20 percent of families had less than 5 percent of national income and less than 1 percent of national wealth. In 2000 the United States had the largest gap between rich and poor of any major industrial country, and this rate had accelerated since 1980. As tax cuts have

VANTAGE POINT 14.5

ASC Task Force Reports on Police, Corrections, and Sentencing

The State of the Police

Issues

The most visible trend in policing today is the move to community- and problem-oriented models of policing (COP/POP). One thing is already clear as local police forces adopt COP/POP, care must be taken to ensure that both police responsiveness and police accountability are enhanced. Responsiveness demands sensitivity to the concerns of local communities, while accountability demands police adherence to an overriding ethic of Constitutionality and law. Unfortunately, public anxiety about crime and disorder can shift the balance. In times of great social change, responsiveness often overrides accountability, as long-term Constitutional guarantees and due process safeguards are abandoned or watered down in ill-advised attempts to provide quick fixes. It is important to avoid any methods that could permanently reduce police accountability when responding to public concerns about crime, violence, and drugs.

Traditional professions such as law and medicine have struck a balance between responsiveness and accountability that the police should emulate. What the police lack is a meaningful standard of care for police operations. For example, police manuals rarely tell officers how to respond to a crime in progress. In many departments, an officer's discretion in arrests, except for those involving domestic abuse, is not subject to official guidelines. Few agencies have meaningful guidelines on how to handle mentally or emotionally disturbed people, and police vehicle pursuit standards vary from one jurisdiction to another. Given the gravity, urgency, and potentially catastrophic results of many police field decisions, the absence of a standard is an omission of major import. It is comparable to a situation in which medical researchers, scholars, and practitioners had concentrated on hospital administration issues and neglected to develop and disseminate information about treatment techniques and strategies.

The consequences of being without an operational standard include incomplete recruiting and training of police officers, inadequate or nonexistent post-employment training, and insufficient or unrealistic criteria on which to assess the quality of police performance. Resentment can grow between police, who feel they have been unfairly criticized, and the community, which feels its members have been poorly treated.

Policy recommendations

- **Endorse COP/POP initiatives:** To the extent that COP/POP involves a partnership between the police and community, the initiatives should be vigorously supported and periodically refined.
- **Support hiring new officers:** Hiring 100,000 new officers under the 1994 Crime Law strongly supports COP/POP initiatives; there is no way to increase police visibility and interaction with the community without a significant number of additional officers. However, while the police can be active in attempting to build community, this task requires great work at all levels of government and society.
- **Develop standard of care:** A standard of care for police operations, which includes devising means of providing citizen input into both formulation and implementation of policy, should be systematically developed and disseminated. The first step is developing a methodology to help police, the public, and government officials identify desirable, realistic outcomes of police work, the means most likely to attain these outcomes, and techniques for evaluating performance in terms of these goals.
- **Increase the use of civilian advisory boards:** The trend toward civilian police advisory boards and review panels appears to be completely in line with the philosophies and logic underlying COP/POP. The boards need to be rigorously evaluated to determine what effect they have on policing and police-community relations and which of the boards' methods succeed or fail.
- **Oppose exceptions to the exclusionary rule:** "Good faith" exceptions or other modifications that would weaken the exclusionary rule in evaluating a police officer's actions should be eliminated. "Good faith" clauses tend to encourage and even reward police incompetence and failure to learn fundamental Constitutional principles. They wrongly assume that courts can identify officers who act in bad faith. Experience teaches that people who act in bad faith rarely testify in good faith about their misconduct. In every field of human endeavor, the major purpose of education, training, and discipline is to replace good faith mistakes with adherence to professional standards.

VANTAGE POINT 14.5—*Continued*

- **Combat police abuse:** The "custom and practice" authority granted to the Justice Department in the 1994 Crime Law is an invaluable means of combating police abuse. The provision eliminates the requirement that the Civil Rights Division of the Justice Department have "standing" as an injured party initiate civil litigation against police for brutality or other unconstitutional misconduct.
- **Perform analyses of causes of crime:** Meaningful analysis of the social and economic causes of crime and disorder should be conducted to develop a comprehensive approach to dealing with them. In many instances, new officers, who were hired to enhance community relations, may find no community exists. The police cannot rebuild communities by themselves.
- **Expand evaluation research:** The federal government should continue and expand support for evaluation research of policing and dissemination of its findings, with emphasis on: implementation of community- and problem-oriented policing, crime causation and prevention, development of a standard of care, accountability issues discussed here, gun detection, and police leadership.

A Crime Control Rationale for Reinvesting in Community Corrections

Issues

Last year Congress passed the most ambitious crime bill in the nation's history, the Violent Crime Control and Law Enforcement Act of 1994. It allocated $22 billion to expand prisons, impose longer sentences, hire more police, and, to a lesser extent, fund prevention programs. The bill was later amended, and nearly all of the $5 billion targeted for prevention programs was diverted into prison construction and law enforcement. Although such tough-on-crime legislation has political appeal, it finds almost no support among criminal justice practitioners and scholars.

Recently, organizations as diverse as the International Association of Chiefs of Police, the U.S. Conference of Mayors, the American Bar Association, the National Governors Association, the League of Cities, The Rand Corporation, the National Council on Crime and Delinquency, the Campaign for an Effective Crime Policy, and the National Research Council have all voiced opposition to the approach. In addition, 85 percent of nationally surveyed prison wardens—who stand to benefit by this legislation—said that elected officials are not offering effective solutions to America's crime problem.

Some people argue that the current proposals are racist or that they cost too much; however, nearly everyone agrees that they fail to prevent young people from entering and continuing a life of crime, and they leave the vast majority of criminals, who are serving sentences on probation and parole, unaffected.

Criminologists have long observed that age 18 is the year of peak criminality. Analysis recently completed by Alfred Blumstein at Carnegie-Mellon showed that today's cohort of 18-year-olds is the smallest it will be for at least the next 15 years. Next year, the number is going to start climbing, and the biggest growth will occur in the number of African-American children who are now 4-to-9 years old. As more young people are recruited into and retained in a criminal lifestyle, the ability of back-end responses (such as imprisonment) to increase public safety is severely limited because of the replenishing supply of young people who are entering criminal careers.

The second, and equally important, reason why current federal efforts will fail is that they focus exclusively on prisons as a corrections strategy, ignoring the fact that most criminals are serving probation and parole sentences. In 1991, about 16 percent of all adult probationers were convicted of violent crimes, as were 26 percent of parolees. This means that on any given day in 1991, there were resident in U.S. communities an estimated 435,000 probationers and 155,000 parolees, who had been convicted of violent crimes. In contrast to these 590,000 probationers and parolees in the community, only 372,500 violent offenders resided in prison. And in 1993, 72 percent of all identified criminals were serving sentences in the community, on probation or parole. Even though the number of prisons has quadrupled in the past decade, prisoners are still less than one fifth of the convict population, and the vast majority of offenders remain in the community. If effectively controlling crime—as opposed to exacting retribution and justice—is the goal, efforts must be focused on the community, where offenders are reporting to probation and parole officers.

Probationers represent a serious continued risk to public safety. The majority of probationers are convicted felons, have prior criminal records, and are likely to be substance and alcohol abusers with few marketable skills. Continued indifference to their behavior means missing the opportunity to intervene positively—and promises their eventual imprisonment. In addition, by not focusing on providing probationers with an appropriate level and type of supervision, crime in the community will not be abated. Current policy simply waits until their criminality escalates to a point requiring incarceration, which has been proven to be costly and ineffective in reducing crime.

VANTAGE POINT 14.5—*Continued*

Policy recommendations

- **Surveillance plus treatment programs:** Such programs should be developed for drug-involved probationers, including offenders who are convicted of drug possession and use. Program models now exist that are effective at reducing recidivism rates, and the public supports rehabilitation over incarceration for such offenders (but not for drug traffickers). The cost-benefit tradeoff between prison and community corrections is among the highest for this subpopulation.
- **Convincing the public:** The public's trust that probation and parole can be meaningful, credible sanctions must be regained. During the past decade, many jurisdictions developed intermediate sanctions as a response to prison crowding. These programs (e.g., house arrest, electronic monitoring, intensive supervision) were designed to be community-based sanctions that were tougher than regular probation but less stringent and expensive than prison. In the few instances where the organizational capacity was created to ensure compliance with court-ordered conditions, these programs reduced recidivism by between 20 and 30 percent.
- **Funding:** Sufficient financial resources must be provided so that the designed programs, combining both treatment and surveillance, can be implemented. Adequate monetary resources are essential to obtaining and sustaining judicial support and achieving program success. The resources needed will be forthcoming only if the public believes the programs are both effective and punishing.

"Three Strikes and You're Out" Legislation

Issues

Efforts to reduce violent crime and deal more effectively with repeat offenders have led to a wide range of legislative initiatives across the nation. Among the many sentence enhancement options available for dealing with habitual offenders, the "three strikes" initiative has found much resonance with the public and legislators alike. Proponents view "three strikes" sentencing legislation as the solution for dealing with the persistent, serious, and violent offender. Advocates promise that these types of sentences will both reduce crime and, ultimately, save taxpayers money. This is because they believe that "three strikes" would not only decrease the cost of victimization through incapacitation, but would also reduce the not insubstantial costs of rearrest and reprocessing of repeat offenders by the criminal justice system.

A recent RAND assessment of California's "three strikes" legislation points to its potential for reducing serious and violent crime, but at an estimated cost of about $5.5 billion over the next 25 years. A second long-term effect on costs will be the unprecedented growth of the elderly in prisons, which will contribute to higher costs because of their health needs (expected to be double or triple that of inmates from the general population).

Although more research is required on the relationship between age and crime, it is clear that categorical sentencing schemes, such as "three strikes," seem counter to existing knowledge:

- Statistically speaking, recidivism is known to decline with age.
- Offending at an early age is highly predictive of long criminal careers. Attention should be focused on crime prevention and early intervention among youths, before they become ensnared in criminal careers.
- Mandatory sentencing cannot take into account all the circumstances affecting individual cases or their various factual permutations.

Short-term effects of this legislation include a clogged court system causing rising court costs and intolerable delays in civil cases; early release of sentenced felons to make room for "three strike" detainees; and increased discretionary power for prosecutors.

Policy recommendations

- **Impact analysis:** The Attorney General should initiate a careful study of how the federal "three strikes" law is impacting the federal courts and corrections system. Beyond that, further expansions of the fed-

eroded progressive taxation (where the wealthier would have paid a much higher percentage), the percentage of national income going to the top 5 percent of households rose from 21 percent to 26 percent. For the upper fifth of households it rose from 47 percent to 52 percent, while the share fell for the rest of the population. Perhaps the most foreboding sign for the future is the present state of children. This theme was examined earlier (see Currie, 1985; Moynihan, 1986). *Fortune* magazine ("How We Can Win," 1989) indicates:

VANTAGE POINT 14.5—*Continued*

eral statute should be resisted until the analysis has been completed.

- **Informing the public:** Since the current punitive atmosphere permeates the public and body politic, the public needs to be informed of the true cost and consequences of categorical sentencing schemes. As the nation's first law enforcement officer, the Attorney General (along with the National Institute of Justice) is in the best position for getting the correct information out to the citizenry objectively and fairly.
- **Criminal justice dialogue:** The Attorney General and the National Institute of Justice should consider the development of appropriate mechanisms for beginning a dialog with prosecutors and victim advocates who are fueling the public debate on "three strikes laws." Similar mechanisms are needed to tap the abilities and experiences of judges for developing the kind of sentencing legislation that optimizes discretion to allow consideration of individual differences among offenders, while checking the abuses of the current mandatory systems.
- **Research needs:** The National Institute of Justice should encourage and assist federal and state legislative bureaus in the development of appropriate research tools and studies to estimate the impact of mandatory sentencing bills on both costs and crime rates. Legislators and the public must understand the likely impact of such laws, not only in terms of costs and consequences for prison crowding, but also in terms of related processes and issues, such as the negative effects on the civil court system and the diversion of scarce resources from education, health and welfare, the infrastructure, and other vital public services.
- **Alternative sentencing:** The National Institute of Justice should encourage the development of alternative sentencing policies that may achieve the same crime reduction benefits as "three strikes" laws at considerably less cost and assist in their evaluation, in terms of crime reduction and costs. Other "lifetime sanctions," such as intensive supervision, community service, etc. should be pursued. However, research should accompany these programs to document their effect on public safety.
- **Early intervention and prevention:** Given the likelihood that investment in youth crime prevention and early intervention programs may well be more effective than "three strikes" legislation, the Attorney General should direct the allocation of federal funding toward such programs. The collateral benefits of "front end" investments are likely to consist of improved scholastic and economic performance of those involved in the programs.
- **Regional conference:** The Attorney General should consider convening a series of regional conferences to explore the findings of existing research on the public safety impact and cost implications of various "three strikes" laws. The relative costs and benefits of early childhood crime prevention efforts, early intervention, and alternative sentencing programs should also be examined.

Source: "American Society of Criminology Task Force Report to Attorney General Janet Reno," *The Criminologist* (Special Issue), 20, 6, November/December 1995. Task force members included: Police Task Force Members: James Fyfe, Jack Greene, Harvey McMurray, Jerome Skolnick, Samuel Walker, and Ralph Weisheit; Community Corrections Task Force: Joan Petersilia, chair; "Three Strikes Legislation" Task Force: Edith Flynn, Timothy Flanagan, Peter Greenwood and Barry Krisberg.

InfoTrac College Edition Research
What do some current articles say about "Three Strikes and You're Out" legislation and policy?

There is some national embarrassment—if not shame—involved here, beginning with the state of American childhood. Consider a few more statistics remembering that this is no depression, these are "good times": Almost 40,000 of the 3.8 million American children born in 1986 died before their first birthday. Today, we rank 20th in the world, behind Spain and Singapore, in infant mortality; our black infant mortality rate would place us 28th, behind Cuba and Bulgaria . . . . Roughly half of the black children live in poverty.

While a commitment to protecting the rights of individuals in the courtroom assures legal justice, only a concomitant commitment to jobs, housing, equal opportunity, and a fair share in society will assure social justice in the streets and suites. In examining the increased racial segregation and reduction of job possibilities in U.S. central cities and the profound impact this had on family arrangements, Chilton (1991, p. 9) indicates: "Increasing the chances for more stable families, and thus the chances for basic socialization, is dependent on the provision of stable employment."

The future of crime will very much depend on which social policy options are chosen to deal with the issue. The present option promises only to condemn American society to continuing unacceptable levels of street crime while tolerating a dual system of justice that is soft on elite crime. The conservative option, while providing minimal expected protection of innocent victims from street predators, serves only as temporary first aid and offers few long-range solutions to ameliorating social forces that assure high crime rates; it also ignores much corporate and occupational criminality. The liberal option, in this writer's opinion, offers the best hope for a long-range amelioration of criminogenic forces. Repression alone is intolerable in a nation that espouses democratic doctrines.

Summary

Public order crime refers to a number of activities that are illegal because they offend public morality. Being primarily nonpredatory, *mala prohibita* acts such as behavior related to prostitution, homosexuality, drug and alcohol abuse, and sexual deviance are sometimes called "crimes without victims," consensual crimes, or folk crimes. Liazos's title "nuts, sluts and preverts" is an attempt to call attention to the fact that studies of deviance have overconcentrated on the bizarre and kinky at the expense of more serious predatory and elite criminality. The concept of "broken windows" suggests that neglect of public peacekeeping functions encourages disorder.

Prostitution involves sexual relations with emotional indifference on a promiscuous and mercenary basis; the act of soliciting or seeking paying customers is prohibited, not prostitution itself. With the exception of some preliterate societies, prostitution exists internationally and was in fact tolerated throughout most of Western history. *Homosexuality,* sexual relations with members of one's own sex, may be prosecuted under sodomy statutes that prohibit "crimes against nature," often including mouth-genital and anal intercourse and the like. These same laws, which are generally not enforced, also apply to heterosexual activity. The wide variety of *sexual offenses* includes *exhibitionism* (indecent exposure), *voyeurism* (peeping), and *fetishism* (unusual veneration of sexual attire or objects). *Nonvictimless sexual offenses* include *incest* (intrafamilial sexual intercourse) and *pedophilia* (child molesting); these two are the most seriously regarded deviations. *Sadism* (inflicting pain for sexual gratification) and *masochism* (experiencing pain for sexual gratification) also may entail nonconsensual harm. The legal status of pornography (sexually stimulating media) continues to raise controversy, as does that of gambling and abortion. *Drunkenness-related offenses* are covered under a variety of state laws such as those prohibiting public drunkenness, breach of peace, disorderly conduct, and the like. The Prohibition experiment, complete criminalization of alcohol usage, was abandoned as a failure. Efforts to control drug abuse, the misuse of chemical substances, has followed much the same pattern as those aimed at controlling alcohol abuse; that is, primary control has been attempted until recently through criminal laws and penalties. There is an inconsistent relationship between drugs' known harmful effects and illegality.

Examination of the *criminal careers of most public order offenders* finds that most do not view themselves as criminals. Most are participating in either consensual adult relations or—in the case of activities such as exhibitionism—are suffering from some psychological disorder. *Prostitution* takes a variety of forms, including brothels, bar girls, streetwalkers, massage parlors, and call girls. *Johns,* prostitutes' customers, do not necessarily fit a pathology-ridden characterization. Underaged prostitution, the sexual exploitation of children, is believed to be becoming more prevalent in part because of the erosion of family structure. *Homosexuality* may be learned as part of the process of socialization; it consists of many types, including preferential and situational patterns. Humphreys' *tearoom* study of homosexual relations in public restrooms identified several types: ambisexuals, gay guys, closet queens, and trade. Sexual offenders include the more serious *child molesters or pedophiliacs.* The latter type is illustrated by cases in which young children have been molested by teachers or other caretakers, showing that many offenders are known and trusted by the victim and his or her family. *Incest* is another intimate type of victimization. General characteristics of sex offenders were presented.

The history of drugs and drug abuse portrays increased criminalization of drug usage beginning with the Harrison Act of 1914, which resulted in the concept of addiction as a sickness being replaced with that of addiction as criminal. Much of this legal approach to drug policy was viewed as being brought about in part by *moral entrepreneurs* such as Anslinger and Hobson. Other information was given of the "phantom army of addicts" (statistical shenanigans) and the agency of fear (Nixon's ODALE). Patterns in drug use demonstrate a virtual explosion since the sixties; however, some recent data may signal the first sign of a coming drug dip.

Drug trafficking is highly lucrative and practiced by a large number of groups. While statistics regarding the association between drug abuse and crime have been subject to exaggeration, a tremendous amount of primarily nonviolent property crime is committed by addicts because of the high cost of illegal drugs. *Addiction*—which includes physiological dependence (tolerance), psychological dependence, and the abstinence syndrome—is less a permanent condition than is often suggested. Little crime is associated with addiction, however, if legal supplies are available. *Problem drinking,* alcoholism, is associated with violent crime as well as with the chronic inebriate problem. The law enforcement burden imposed by the latter has been alleviated, in part, by means of greater utilization of social service agencies.

Societal reaction to public order criminality varies between the extremes of overcriminalization and decriminalization. Totalitarian societies simply forbid such activities, while democratic societies must constantly balance the tensions between civil liberties and social morality. Various problems raised by overcriminalization were described, while arguments for decriminalization were also discussed.

Ideology guides social policy. Wilson's distinctions of *causal analysis vs. policy analysis* in fact parallel the discussion in Chapters 1, 4, and 5 regarding pure research/theory versus applied research/theory. The *social policy fallacy* refers to the erroneous belief that in a democratic society applied social policy can be effective even though it ignores causal roots. The *ill-fated war on crime* describes the period from 1967 to 1981 when the federal government for the first time in U.S. history launched a major battle against street crime. With new laws and agencies—the Safe Streets Act and LEAA—and increased funds, the federal government made a commitment to fight crimes that were largely a state and local matter. Much of this effort concentrated exclusively on conventional and violent predatory offenses, ignoring upper level crimes such as those by the Nixon administration, many members of which resigned in disgrace. The *dirty secrets* of crime represent Bertram Gross's notions that violent crimes are due to protracted structural conditions and that the criminal justice system is too lenient with elite economic criminals. Herbert Packer's crime control model, which emphasizes law and order and bureaucratic efficiency, was contrasted with his *due process model,* which emphasizes justice or the protection of individual rights.

Three ideological approaches to criminal justice policy were discussed: the conservative, liberal, and radical approaches. The *conservative approach* is based on classical theory and advocates incapacitation, just deserts, and the crime control model, whereas the *liberal approach* emphasizes reformation of social structural conditions, more equitable operation of the criminal justice system, and rehabilitation. The *radical approach* calls for revolution against capitalism, which it sees as the cause of crime.

Various *trends in future criminality* were cautiously presented, since criminologists disagree regarding such forecasts, and predictions are highly dependent on the ideological direction of social policy choices. Policy options proposed by the 1968 Kerner (Riot) Commission were discussed; these included the present policies option, the garrison state choice, and the commitment to change alternative. Similarly, *criminal justice policy options* were described as consisting of the present policy, conservative, and liberal options. The author expressed an ideological preference for the last direction.

KEY CONCEPTS

Addiction
Broken Windows
Closet Queens
Conservative, Liberal, Radical Approaches
Crime Control Model
Crimes without Victims
Criminal Justice Policy Options
Decriminalization
Dirty Secrets
Due Process Model
Exhibitionism
Fetishism
Floodgate Theory
Folk Crime
Harrison Act
Incest
Johns
Kerner Commission Policy Options
Mark-Recapture Technique
Moral Entrepreneurs
Overcriminalization
Pedophilia
Policy Analysis
Policy Experiments
Problem Drinking
Public Order Crime
Social Policy Fallacy
Sodomy
Tearoom
Types of Prostitution
Voyeurism
Withdrawal Syndrome

REVIEW QUESTIONS

1. What are "public order crimes"? How do they and their offenders differ from other types of offenders?
2. What is the notion of "broken windows"? How has this been applied in modern policing?
3. Why is prostitution such a persistent crime? What have been some recent trends in prostitution?
4. What do you feel should be the role of society in regulating pornography? Defend your views.
5. Discuss the history of attempts to regulate drug abuse. Do you feel that greater criminalization or decriminalization is required to properly deal with this problem?
6. What is a "moral panic" and what are "moral entrepreneurs"? Give some examples.
7. What were some drug policy options presented to former Attorney General Janet Reno by the American Society of Criminology task force?
8. Discuss the differences between conservative, liberal, and radical approaches to criminal justice policy.
9. Discuss some of the predictions regarding the future of crime. Do you have any additional predictions that you would like to make?
10. What are "policy experiments"? How might these be useful in enabling us to predict "what works" in criminology and criminal justice?

INFOTRAC COLLEGE EDITION RESEARCH

Vantage Point 14.1 InfoTrac College Edition Research
Review the topic of "research ethics." Do any of the articles provide guidance in deciding the ethical status of Humphreys' research?

Vantage Point 14.2 InfoTrac College Edition Research
Review the issue of "pornography." Are there any regulations at all regarding this phenomenon? What regulations do you think should exist?

Vantage Point 14.3 InfoTrac College Edition Research
Examine the issue of "moral panics." In what ways may moral panics be used to marginalize minorities?

Vantage Point 14.4 InfoTrac College Edition Research
What are some of the arguments presented by those who favor "drug legalization"? Do you agree or disagree with these arguments?

Vantage Point 14.5 InfoTrac College Edition Research
What do some current articles say about "Three Strikes and You're Out" legislation and policy?

In the News 14.1 InfoTrac College Edition Research
Searching "mentally ill offenders," what problems have been noted with Canada's "dangerous offender legislation"?

SELECTED READINGS

Howard Becker. 1963. *Outsiders: Studies in the Sociology of Deviance.* New York: The Free Press.
Becker, a major proponent of labeling theory, explores the role of moral entrepreneurs in making deviants into criminals and outsiders.

Georgette Bennett. 1987. *Crimewarps: The Future of Crime in America.* Garden City, NY: Anchor Books, Doubleday.
Bennett makes a series of predictions regarding future trends in crime as they are affected by technology, population distribution, and crime prevention strategies.

Elliott Currie. 1985. *Controlling Crime.* New York: Pantheon.
Currie has been a consistent liberal voice in an era of conservative crime control policy who objects to the latter's view of the causes of crime being intractable results of biology, psychology, and personal choice.

Diane Gordon. 1990. *The Justice Juggernaut.* New Brunswick, NJ: Rutgers University Press.
Gordon argues that reliance on formal modes of control, such as the police, courts, and corrections, while ignoring poverty, unemployment, and urban decay has not worked.

Bertram Gross. 1980. *Friendly Fascism: The New Face of Power in America.* New York: M. Evans and Company.
Gross claims that the public is not being told the "dirty big secret of crime": that the criminal justice system is soft on white collar crime.

James Inciardi and Karen McElrath, editors. 2001. *The American Drug Scene.* 2nd edition. Los Angeles: Roxbury.
In perhaps the definitive work on the subject, the authors provide an excellent selection of current and classic articles on the ever changing drug scene.

Rael J. Isaac and Virginia Armat. 1990. *Madness in the Streets.* New York: The Free Press.
The subtitle of this book explains its focus—"How Psychiatry and the Law Abandoned the Mentally Ill."

Phillip Jenkins. 1992. *Intimate Enemies: Moral Panics in Contemporary Great Britain.* Hawthorne, NY: Aldine de Gruyter.
One of the most lucid writers in the field tackles conventional wisdom regarding emergent crime problems asking whether instead they are examples of moral panics.

Alfred W. McCoy. 1972. *The Politics of Heroin in Southeast Asia.* New York: Harper and Row.
This controversial work accuses the CIA of encouraging drug trafficking in order to fight the North Vietnamese.

Eleanor Miller. 1986. *Street Woman.* Philadelphia, PA: Temple University Press.
This is Miller's ethnographic study and interviews with 64 prostitutes. It examines their motivations and escape from abusive domestic settings.

References

Abadinsky, Howard. 1983a. *The Criminal Elite: Professional and Organized Crime.* Westport, CT: Greenwood.

———. 1983b. "Professional and Organized Crime: A Symbiosis." Paper presented at the Academy of Criminal Justice Sciences Meetings, San Antonio, TX. March.

———. 1988. *Drug Abuse: An Introduction.* Chicago: Nelson-Hall.

———. 1994. *Organized Crime.* 4th edition. Chicago: Nelson-Hall.

Abadinsky, Howard. 2000. *Organized Crime.* 6th ed. Belmont, CA: Wadsworth.

ABC (American Broadcasting Company). 1982. "Yakuza." *20/20.* Broadcast May 27.

———. 1983a. "Child Molesters." *20/20.* Broadcast February 3.

———. 1983b. "The Media and Violence." Broadcast February 24.

———. 1987. "Nightly News," Broadcast August 17.

———. 1992a. "Crashers." *PrimeTime Live.* Broadcast May 23.

———. 1992b. "Child Molesting." *PrimeTime Live.* Broadcast July 19. abcnews.com. 1999. Abcnews.go.com/sections/us/killers725/index. html. March 3.

Abrahamsen, David. 1960. *The Psychology of Crime.* New York: Columbia University Press.

Abram, Susan. 1998. "Insurer Sues 45 People in Auto-Accident Scam." *LA Times,* February 24, p. A-1.

"Abscam (Cont'd): Mafiosi Call off a Summit." 1980. *Time,* February 25, p. 18.

ACJS (Academy of Criminal Justice Sciences). 1998. "Code of Ethics." Arlington, VA: Academy of Criminal Justice Sciences.

Adams, James. 1992. "Calling All Cloaks and Daggers." *Washington Post National Weekly Edition,* February 17–23, p. 25.

———. 1995. *Sellout: Aldrich Ames and the Corruption of the CIA.* New York: Viking.

Adams, Virginia. 1976. *Crime.* New York: Time-Life.

Adler, Freda. 1975. *Sisters in Crime.* New York: McGraw-Hill.

———. 1983. *Nations Not Obsessed by Crime.* Littleton, CO: Fred B. Rothman.

Adler, Freda, and Simon, Rita James, eds. 1979. *The Criminology of Deviant Women.* Boston: Houghton Mifflin.

Adler, Jerry, et al. 1988. "Getting Tough on Cocaine." *Newsweek,* November 28, pp. 76–79.

Adler, Patricia A., and Adler, Peter. 1983. "Shifts and Oscillations in Deviant Careers: The Case of Upper-Level Drug Dealers and Smugglers." *Social Problems* 31: 195–207.

"After the Don: A Donnybrook." 1976. *Newsweek,* November 1, p. 32.

Agee, Philip. 1975. *Inside the Company: CIA Diary.* New York: Stonehill.

Agnew, Robert. 1985. "Social Control Theory and Delinquency: A Longitudinal Test." *Criminology* 23: 47–61.

———. 1992. "Foundation for a General Strain Theory of Crime and Delinquency." *Criminology* 30: 47–87.

———. 1995. "Strain and Subcultural Theories of Criminality." In *Criminology: A Contemporary Handbook,* edited by Joseph F. Sheley, 2nd ed., pp. 305–327. Belmont, CA: Wadsworth.

———. 1997. "The Nature and Determinants of Strain: Another Look at Durkheim and Merton." In *The Future of Anomie Theory,* edited by Nikos Passas and Robert Agnew, pp. 27–51. Boston: Northeastern University Press.

Agnew, Robert et al. 1996. "A New Test of Classic Strain Theory." *Justice Quarterly* 13: 681–704.

Agnew, Robert, and White, Helene R. 1992. "An Empirical Test of General Strain Theory." *Criminology* 30: 475–499.

Agran, Larry. 1982. "Getting Cancer on the Job." In *Crisis in American Institutions,* edited by Jerome H. Skolnick and Elliott Currie, 5th ed. pp. 408–19. Boston: Little, Brown.

Aho, James. 1994. *This Thing of Darkness: A Sociology of the Enemy.* Seattle: University of Washington Press.

Akers, Ronald L. 1967. "Problems in the Sociology of Deviance: Social Definitions and Behavior." *Social Forces* 46: 455–65.

———. 1980. "Further Critical Thoughts on Marxist Criminology: Comments on Turk, Toby and Klockars." In *Radical Criminology: The Coming Crisis,* edited by James A. Inciardi, pp. 133–38. Beverly Hills: Sage.

———. 1994. *Criminological Theories: Introduction and Evaluation.* Los Angeles: Roxbury Press.

Albanese, Jay S. 1985. *Organized Crime in America.* Cincinnati: Anderson.

———. 1988. "The Impact of the Mob Trials on Organized Crime: Some Observations." *Criminal Organizations* 4: 3–4.

———. 1989. *Organized Crime in America.* 2nd edition. Cincinnati, OH: Anderson.

———. 1995. *White-Collar Crime in America.* New York: Prentice-Hall.

Albanese, Jay. 1998. *Organized Crime in America.* 3rd ed. Cincinnati: Anderson.

Albini, Joseph. 1971. *The American Mafia: Genesis of a Legend.* New York: Appleton-Century-Crofts.

———. 1986. "The Guardian Angels: Vigilantes or Protectors of the Community?" Paper presented at the Academy of Criminal Justice Sciences Meeting, Orlando, FL, March.

———. 1988. "Donald Cressey's Contribution to the Study of Organized Crime: An Evaluation." *Crime and Delinquency* 34: 338–54.

Albini, Joseph L., et al. 1995. "Russian Organized Crime: Its History, Structure and Function." *Journal of Contemporary Criminal Justice* 11: 213–43.

Alexander, Shana. 1988. *The Pizza Connection.* New York: Weidenfeld and Nicholson.

Allen, Edward J. 1962. *Merchants of Menace: the Mafia.* Springfield, IL: Charles C. Thomas.

Allen, Harry E. 1995. "Presidential Address." *Justice Quarterly* 12: 427–46.

Allen, Harry E., et al. 1981. *Crime and Punishment: An Introduction to Criminology.* New York: The Free Press.

Allen, Harry E., and Latessa, Edward J. 1982. "The Conservative Coup in Crime Policy and Corrections." Paper presented at the Academy of Criminal Justice Sciences Meetings, Louisville, KY, March.

Allen, John. 1977. *Assault with a Deadly Weapon: The Autobiography of a Street Criminal.* Edited by Diane Hall Kelly and Philip Heymann. New York: McGraw-Hill.

"America Next Target for Terrorism?" 1984. *U.S. News and World Report,* January 9, pp. 24–30.

American Bar Association. 1952. *Report on Organized Crime.* New York: American Bar Association.

———. 1976. *Final Report of the Committee on Economic Offenses.* Washington, DC: American Bar Association.

American Humane Association Children's Division. 1984. *Trends in Officially Reported Child Neglect and Abuse in the United States.* Denver: American Humane Association.

"American Society of Criminology Task Force Report to Attorney General Janet Reno." 1995. *The Criminologist* (Special Issue) 20:6, November/December.

Amir, Menachem. 1971. *Patterns in Forcible Rape.* Chicago: University of Chicago Press.

"Ancient Records Discovered." 1987. *Erie Morning News,* December 29, p. 4A.

Anderson, David A. 1999. "The Aggregate Burden of Crime." *Journal of Law and Economics:* 42(2)(October).

Anderson, Edward J. 1977. "A Study of Industrial Espionage, Parts I and II." *Security Management,* January and March.

Anderson, Elijah. 1981. *A Place on the Corner: Identity and Rank Among Black Streetcorner Men.* Chicago: University of Chicago Press.

———. 1990. *Streetwise: Race, Class and Change in an Urban Community.* Chicago: University of Chicago Press.

Anderson, Jack. 1983. "What's Wrong with Bribes?" *Erie Times News,* July 3, p. 7A.

Anderson, Jack, and Van Atta, Dale. 1986. "The Amount of Child Pornography Declines." *Erie Times News,* July 13, p. 5B.

———. 1987. "Danger Lurks in Counterfeit Bolts." *Erie Times News,* July 19, p. 3B.

———. 1988a. "Medical Waste Poses Health Threat." *Erie Times News,* October 16, p. 3B.

———. 1988b. "Terrorists Act as Hired Guns for Drug Cartel." *Erie Times News,* August 28, p. 3B.

———. 1990. "Human Rights—Iranian Prisons Remain a Horror." *Erie Times News,* January 14, p. 3E.

Anderson, Jack, and Whitten, Les. 1977. "Mafia Chieftain." *Erie Times News,* March 24, p. 3B.

Anderson, Robert T. 1965. "From Mafia to Cosa Nostra." *American Journal of Sociology* 71: 302–10.

Anderson, Scott. 1995. "Looking for Mr. Yaponchik: The Rise and Fall of a Russian Mobster in America." *Harper's,* December, pp. 40–51.

Anglin, M. Douglas, and Speckart, George. 1988. "Narcotics Use and Crime: A Multisample Multimethod Analysis." *Criminology* 16: 197–233.

"Animal-Rights Group Destroys Mink Research." 1991. *The Chronicle of Higher Education,* March 11, p. A5.

Annin, Peter, and Rhine, Jon B. 1999. "The Gang that Loves Glitter." *Newsweek,* September 6, p. 32.

Anslinger, Harry, and Cooper, C. R. 1937. "Marijuana: Assassin of Youth." *American Magazine* 74: 19, 50.

Anspach, Donald F. 1990. "Door to Door Mutual Funds: The Legal Taking of Other People's Money." Paper presented at the American Society of Criminology Meetings, Baltimore, MD. November.

APBnews.com. 1999a. "Workplace Violence." November 3.

———. 1999b. "New Crime Study Identifies the 25 College Communities with the Greatest Risk of Violent Crime." November 12.

———. 2000a. "Dialysis Chain Agrees to $500 Million Fraud Settlement."APBnews.com:80/safetyce. . .safety/2000/01/19/fraud0119 01.html. May 6.

———. 2000b. "Ecstasy Trade, Seizures Skyrocket." April 3.

Archer, Dane, and Gartner, Rosemary. 1980. "Homicide in 110 Nations: The Development of the Comparative Crime Data File." In *Criminology Review Yearbook,* edited by Egon Bittner and Sheldon Messinger, volume 2, pp. 433–63. Beverly Hills, CA: Sage.

———. 1984. *Violence and Crime in Cross-National Perspective.* New Haven: Yale University Press.

Ardrey, Robert. 1963. *African Genesis.* New York: Atheneum.

Armstrong, Edward G. 1978. "Massage Parlors and Their Customers." *Archives of Social Behavior* 7: 117.

———. 1983. "Pondering Pandering." *Deviant Behavior* 40: 203–17.

———. 1991. "Music and Violence." Paper presented at the Academy of Criminal Justice Sciences Meetings, Nashville, TN, March.

"Arson for Hate and Profit." 1977. *Time,* October 31, pp. 22–25.

Asbury, Herbert. 1969. *The Great Illusion.* New York: Greenwood Press.

ASC (American Society of Criminology). 1998. "Code of Ethics." http://www.asc41.com/ethics98.htm.

Ashman, Charles. 1975. *The CIA-Mafia Link.* New York: Manor Books.

Associated Press. 1994. "Criminologists' File Found." October 23.

———. 1998. "Philadelphia Crime Statistics Questioned." November 2.

———. 2000. "Surge in Campus Alcohol Arrests." News.Excite. Com. June 4.

Atkinson, A. B. 1975. *The Economics of Inequality.* Oxford: Claredon.

Attorney General's Office. 1986. *Attorney General's Commission Report on Pornography.* Washington, DC: Attorney General's Office.

Attorney General's Task Force on Violent Crime. 1981a. *Phase I Recommendations,* June 17; *Phase II Recommendations,* August. Washington, DC: U.S. Department of Justice.

Attorney General's Task Force on Violent Crime. 1981b. *Final Report,* August 17. Washington, DC: U.S. Department of Justice.

Auerbach, Ann H. 1998. *Ransom: The Untold Story of International Kidnapping.* New York: Henry Holt and Company.

August, Oliver. 1997. "Car Theft Rivals Drugs in World Crime Earnings." *The Times,* February 17.

Auster, Bruce. 1998. "An Inside Look at Terror Inc." *U.S. News and World Report,* October 19, pp. 34–36.

Austin, Tim. 1986. "Book Review of James Q. Wilson and Richard J. Herrnstein Crime and Human Nature." *Criminal Justice Policy Review* 1: 241–42.

"Auto Thieves." 1992. *PrimeTime Live.* ABC television broadcast, June 13.

Babbie, Earl R. 1975. *The Practice of Social Research.* Belmont, CA: Wadsworth.

Babcock, Charles R. 1989. "In the Matter of Lincoln Savings and Loan." *Washington Post National Weekly Edition,* November 27–December 3, p. 10.

Badillo, Herman, and Haynes, Milton. 1972. *A Bill of No Rights: Attica and the American Prison System.* New York: Outerbridge and Lazard.

Bailey, Kenneth. 1978. *Methods of Social Research.* New York: Free Press.

Bailey, William C. 1971. "Correctional Outcome: An Evaluation of 100 Reports." In *Crime and Justice,* edited by Leon Radzinowicz and Marvin E. Wolfgang, vol. 3. New York: Basic Books.

Bakan, David. 1975. *The Slaughter of the Innocents.* San Francisco: Jossey-Bass.

Balkan, S., Berger R. J., and Schmidt, J. 1980. *Crime and Deviance in America.* Belmont, CA: Wadsworth.

Ball, John C., et al. 1982. "Lifetime Criminality of Heroin Addicts in the United States." *Journal of Drug Issues* 1: 1–2.

Ball, Karen. 1990. "USX Corp. to Pay OSHA Record $3.25 Million Fine." *Erie Morning News,* December 21, p. A1.

Ball, Robert. 1980. "An Empirical Evaluation of Neutralization Theory." *Criminologica* 4: 22–32.

Balrig, Flemming. 1988. *The Snow-White Image: The Hidden Reality of Crime in Switzerland.* Oslo: Norwegian University Press.

Banas, Dennis W., and Trojanowicz, Robert C. 1985. *Uniform Crime Reporting and Community Policing: An Historical Perspective.* East Lansing, MI: National Neighborhood Foot Patrol Center, School of Criminal Justice, Michigan State University.

Bandow, Doug. 1991. "Robert Gates: A Case Worth Investigating." *Wall Street Journal,* September 12, p. A19.

Bandura, Albert. 1973. *Aggression: A Social Learning Approach.* Englewood Cliffs, NJ: Prentice-Hall.

Barak, Gregg. 1991. *Crimes by the Capitalist State: An Introduction to State Criminality.* Albany, NY: SUNY Press.

Baridon, Phil. 1988. *Report on Asian Organized Crime.* Department of Justice, Criminal Division, Washington, DC: Government Printing Office.

Barker, Thomas, and Carter, David L. 1986. *Police Deviance.* Cincinnati: Anderson.

Barlay, Stephen. 1973. *The Secrets Business.* New York: Thomas Y. Crowell.

Barovick, Harriet. 1999. "Bad to the Bone." *Time,* December 27, pp. 130–131.

Barrett, Paul M. 1991. "FTCs Hard Line on Price Fixing May Foster Discounts." *Wall Street Journal,* January 11, p. B1.

Barry, Vincent. 1983. *Philosophy: A Text with Readings.* Belmont, CA: Wadsworth.

Bartol, Curt H., and Bartol, Anne M. 1986. *Criminal Behavior: A Psychosocial Approach.* 2nd edition. Englewood Cliffs, NJ: Prentice-Hall.

Bastone, William. 1997. "Mob Bell, They're All Connected at Gotti Jr.s' Telephone Card Company." *Village Voice,* www.villagevoice.com, 80/ink/bastone.html.

Baumrind, Diana. 1978. "Parental Disciplinary Patterns and Social Competence in Children." *Youth and Society* 9: 239–76.

Bayer, Ronald. 1981. "Crime, Punishment and the Decline of Liberal Optimism." *Crime and Delinquency* 27: 169–90.

Bayley, David H. 1978. "Comment: Perspectives on Criminal Justice Research." Speech delivered to the Academy of Criminal Justice Sciences, March, New Orleans, LA. Reprinted in *Journal of Criminal Justice* 6: 287–89.

Baylor, Timothy. 1990. "Informants/Agent Provocateurs—Violators of Trust: One Element in the Tactical Repertoire of Social Control Agents." Paper presented at the American Sociological Association Meetings, Washington, DC, August.

Bearak. Barry. 1999. "A Tale of 2 Lovers, and a Taboo Recklessly Flouted." *The New York Times,* April 9, p. A7.

Beauchamp, Thomas L., ed. 1983. *Case Studies in Business, Society and Ethics.* Englewood Cliffs, NJ: Prentice-Hall.

Beauchamp, Thomas L., and Bowie, Norman E. 1983. *Ethical Theory and Business.* 2nd ed. Englewood Cliffs, NJ: Prentice-Hall.

Beccaria, Cesare. 1963. *On Crimes and Punishments.* Translated by Henry Paolucci. Indianapolis: Bobbs-Merrill.

Beck, Melinda, and Cowley, Geoffrey. 1990. "Beyond Lobotomies." *Newsweek,* March 26, p. 44.

Becker, Gary. 1968. "Crime and Punishment: An Economic Approach." *Journal of Political Economy* 76: 169–217.

Becker, Howard S. 1950. *Through Values to Social Interpretations.* Durham: Duke University Press.

———. 1954. "Anthropology and Sociology." In *For a Science of Man,* edited by John Gillin. New York: Macmillan.

———. 1963. *Outsiders: Studies in the Sociology of Deviance.* New York: The Free Press.

———. ed. 1964. *The Other Side: Perspectives on Deviance.* New York: The Free Press.

Beekman, Mary Ellen, and Daly, Michael R. 1990. "Motor Vehicle Theft Investigations." *FBI Law Enforcement Bulletin,* September, pp. 14–17.

Behar, Richard. 1990. "The Underworld Is Their Oyster." *Time,* September 3, pp. 54–57.

———. 1991. "The Thriving Cult of Greed and Power." *Time,* May 6, pp. 50–57.

Beirne, Piers, 1987. "Adolphe Quetelet and the Origins of Positivist Criminology." *American Journal of Sociology* 92: 1140–69.

———. 1991. "Inventing Criminology: The 'Science of Man' in Cesare Beccaria's *Dei Delitti e Delle Pene* (1764)." *Criminology* 29 (November): 777–820.

Beirne, Piers, and Messerschmidt, James. 2000. *Criminology.* 3rd edition. Boulder, CO: Westview.

Belknap, Joanne. 1990. "Review of 'Fraternity Gang Rape: Sex, Brotherhood and Privilege on Campus' by Peggy Reeves Sanday." *Criminal Justice Policy Review* 4 (October): 285–87.

———. 1996. *The Invisible Woman: Gender, Crime and Justice.* Belmont, CA: Wadsworth.

Bell, Daniel. 1953. "Crime as an American Way of Life." *Antioch Review 13:* 131–154.

———. 1967. *The End of Ideology.* Glencoe, IL: The Free Press.

Belson, W. A. 1978. *Television Violence and the Adolescent Boy.* Farnborough, Eng.: Saxon House.

Benekos, Peter J. 1991. "Public Policy and Correctional Reform: Politics of Overcrowding." Paper presented at the American Society of Criminology Meetings, San Francisco, CA, November.

———. 1995. "Women as Victims and Perpetrators of Murder." In *Women, Law, and Social Control,* edited by Alida V. Merlo and Joycelyn Pollock. Boston: Allyn and Bacon, pp. 219–237.

Benekos, Peter J., and Hagan, Frank E. 1991. "Fixing the Thrifts." *Journal of Security Administration* 14 (July): 65–104.

Benekos, Peter, and Merlo, Alida. 1995. "Three Strikes and You're Out: The Political Sentencing Game." *Federal Probation* 59 (March): 3–9.

Benjamin, Harry, and Masters, R. E. L. 1964. *Prostitution and Morality.* New York: Julian Press.

Bennett, Georgette. 1987. *Crimewarps: The Future of Crime in America.* Garden City, NY: Anchor Books, Doubleday.

Bennett, James. 1981. *Oral History and Delinquency: The Rhetoric of Criminology.* Chicago: University of Chicago Press.

———. 1994. "Cost of Saving Lives." *New York Times,* December 5, p. A16.

Bennett, Richard R., and Lynch, James P. 1990. "Does a Difference Make a Difference? Comparing Cross-

National Crime Indicators." *Criminology* 28 (February): 153–81.

Bennett, Trevor. 1988. "The British Experience with Heroin Regulation." *Law and Contemporary Problems* 51: 299–314.

Bennett, Vivo, and Clagett, Cricket. 1977. *1001 Ways to Avoid Getting Mugged, Murdered, Robbed, Raped or Ripped Off.* New York: Mason-Charter Publishers.

Bennett, William J., DiIulio, John J., and Walters, John P. 1996. *Body Count: Moral Poverty and How to Win America's War Against Crime and Drugs.* New York: Simon and Schuster.

Bensinger, Gad. 1987. "Operation Greylord and Its Aftermath." Paper presented at the American Society of Criminology Meetings, Montreal, November 14.

Bentham, Jeremy. 1823. *Introduction to the Principles of Morals and Legislation.* Oxford: Oxford University Press, originally published in 1789.

Ben Yehuda, Nachman. 1990. *The Politics and Morality of Deviance: Moral Panics, Drug Abuse, Deviant Science and Reversed Stigmatization.* Albany, NY: SUNY Press.

Bequai, August. 1978. *Computer Crime.* Lexington, MA: Lexington Books.

———. 1979. *Organized Crime: The Fifth Estate.* Lexington, MA: D. C. Heath.

———. 1987. *Technocrimes.* Lexington, MA: Lexington Books.

Berdie, Ralph. 1947. "Playing the Dozens." *Journal of Abnormal and Social Psychology* 42 (January): 102–21.

Berg, Eric N. 1989. "FBI Commodities 'Sting': Fast Money, Secret Lives." *New York Times,* January 30, p. A1.

Berger, Vivian. 1988. "Review Essay: Not So Simple Rape." *Criminal Justice Ethics* 7: 69–81.

Bergier, Jacques. 1975. *Secret Armies: The Growth of Corporate and Industrial Espionage.* Translated by Harold J. Salemson. Indianapolis: Bobbs-Merrill.

Berk, Richard A., and Newton, Phyllis J. 1985. "Does Arrest Really Deter Wife Battery? An Effort to Replicate the Findings of the Minneapolis Spouse Abuse Experiment." *American Sociological Review* 50: 253–62.

Bernard, Thomas J. 1987. "Structure and Control: Reconsidering Hirschi's Concept of Commitment." *Justice Quarterly* 4: 409–24.

Bertaux, Daniel, ed. 1981. *Biography and Society: The Life History Approach in the Social Sciences.* Beverly Hills, CA: Sage.

Berton, Lee. 1991. "Malleable Money Men." *Wall Street Journal,* May 15, p. A12.

Best, J., and Luckenbill, David F. 1982. *Organizing Deviance.* Englewood Cliffs, NJ: Prentice-Hall.

Biderman, Albert D., et al. 1967. "Report on a Pilot Study in the District of Columbia on Victimization and Attitudes Toward Law Enforcement," Field Surveys I, Commission on Law Enforcement and Administration of Justice. Washington, DC: Government Printing Office.

Binder, Arnold, and Meeker, James W. 1988. "Experiments as Reforms." *Journal of Criminal Justice* 16: 347–58.

Bishop, Eric, and Slowikowski, Jeff. 1995. "Hate Crime." Office of Juvenile Justice and Delinquency Prevention. Fact Sheet #29, August 1–2.

Bittner, Egon. 1967. "The Police on Skid Row: A Study of Peace Keeping." *American Sociological Review* 32: 699–715.

Black, Donald J. 1970. "Production of Crime Rates." *American Sociological Review* 35: 733–48.

———. 1976. *The Behavior of Law.* New York: Academic Press.

———. 1999. *Bad Boys, Bad Men: Confronting Antisocial Personality.* New York: Oxford University Press.

Blackman, Ann, and Simmons, Ann. 1995. "Bury My Heart in Committee." *Time,* September 18, pp. 48–51.

Blackstock, Nelson. 1976. *Cointelpro: The FBI's Secret War on Political Freedom.* New York: Random House.

Blakeslee, Sandra. 1994. "Lawyers Say Dow Study Saw Implant Danger." *New York Times,* April 7, pp. A1, A11.

Blakey, G. Robert, 1967. "Aspects of the Evidence Gathering Process in Organized Crime Cases: A Preliminary Analysis." Appendix C. Presidential Commission on Law Enforcement and the Administration of Justice, Task Force Report on Organized Crime, Washington, DC: Government Printing Office, pp. 81–83.

Blakey, G. Robert, and Billing, Richard. 1981. *The Plot to Kill the President: Organized Crime Assassinated JFK.* New York: New York Times Books.

Blakey, G. Robert, and Goldsmith, Michael. 1976. "Criminal Redistribution of Stolen Property: The Need for Law Reform." *Michigan Law Review* 74: 1518–45.

Blankenship, Michael, ed. 1995. *Understanding Corporate Criminality.* New York: Garland.

Blankenship, Michael B., and Brown, Stephen E. 1993. "Paradigm or Perspective: A Note to the Discourse Community." *Journal of Crime and Justice* 16, 1: 167–75.

Blaum, Paul A. 1991. "Crime Is a Male Domain: Researchers Explain Why Women Are Less Likely to Commit Crimes." *Intercom: Focus on Research.* Pennsylvania State University, October 17, p. 1.

Bliven, Naomi. 1991. "Books: All the President's Men II." *The New Yorker,* June 17, pp. 113–16.

Bloch, Herbert A., and Geis, Gilbert. 1970. *Man, Crime and Society.* 2nd edition. New York: Random House.

Block, Alan A. 1978. "The History and Study of Organized Crime." *Urban Life* 6: 455–74.

Block, Alan A., and Chambliss, William J. 1981. *Organizing Crime.* New York: Elsevier.

Block, Carolyn R., and Block, Richard. 1988. "Is Violent Crime Seasonal? Victimization and Visibility." Paper presented at the American Society of Criminology Meetings, Chicago, IL, November.

Bloom, Murray T. 1957. *Money of Their Own: the Great Counterfeiters.* New York: Charles Scribner's.

Blumberg, Abraham S. 1967. "The Practice of Law as a Confidence Game: Organizational Cooptation of a Profession." *Law and Society Review* 1: 15–39.

Blume, Marshall E., et al. 1974. "Stock Ownership in the United States: Characteristics and Trends." *Survey of Current Business* (U.S. Department of Commerce) 54: 16–40.

Blumenthal, Daniel, ed. 1988. *The Last Days of the Sicilians.* New York: Times Books.

Blumenthal, Ralph. 1994. "The Maddening Mysteries of the Greatest Art Theft Ever." *New York Times,* December 15, pp. B1, B6.

Blumstein, Alfred. 1994. *Youth, Violence, Guns, and the Illicit-Drug Industry.* Pittsburgh, PA: Carnegie Mellon University.

———. 1995. "Violence by Young People: Why the Deadly Nexus." *National Institute of Justice Journal.* August: 2–9.

Blumstein, Alfred, and Cohen, Jacqueline. 1987. "Characterizing Criminal Careers." *Science* 237, August 28: 985–91.

Blumstein, Alfred, Cohen, Jacqueline, and Farrington, David P. 1988a. "Criminal Career Research: Its Value for Criminology." *Criminology* 26: 1–35.

———. 1988b. "Longitudinal and Criminal Career Research: Further Clarifications." *Criminology* 26: 57–74.

Blumstein, Alfred, and Rosenfeld, Richard. 1998. "Assessing the Recent Ups and Downs in U.S. Homicide Rates." *National Institute of Justice Journal,* October: 9–11.

Blundell, William E. 1978. "I Did It for Jollies." In *Crime at the Top,* edited by John M. Johnson and Jack Douglas, pp. 153–85. Philadelphia: Lippincott.

Boccella, Kathy. 1994. "Grocery Store Workers Steal More Food, Money Than Customers Do, Survey Finds." *Your Money* (*Erie Times News*), May 31, p. 9S.

Bock, Gordon, and McWhirter, William. 1988. " 'The Chairman' and His Board." *Time,* May 30, p. 45.

Bogert, Carroll. 1990. "On Reform: Prime Time for Crime." *Newsweek,* June 4, p. 25.

Bohm, Robert M. 1982. "Radical Criminology: An Explication." *Criminology* 19: 565–89.

———. 1987. "Myths about Criminology and Criminal Justice: A Review Essay." *Justice Quarterly* 4: 631–42.

———. 1990. "In Defense of the ASC Policy: A Rejoinder to Schmalleger." *The Criminologist* 15 (January--February): 3–4.

———. 1997. *A Primer on Crime and Delinquency.* Belmont, CA: Wadsworth.

Bonanno, Joseph. 1983. *A Man of Honor: The Autobiography of Joseph Bonanno.* New York: Simon and Schuster.

Bonger, Willem A. 1969. *Criminality and Economic Conditions.* Bloomington, IN: Indiana University Press.

Bonn, Robert L. 1987. "Review of: James D. Wright and Peter H. Rossi Armed and Considered Dangerous." *Justice Quarterly* 4: 133–36.

Booth, Cathy. 1978. "Prostitutes in America: Teens, Chicken Hawks, Networks Abound." *Erie Times News,* March 12, p. 23A.

Bordua, David J. 1961. "Delinquent Subcultures: Sociological Interpretations of Gang Delinquency." *Annals of the American Academy of Political and Social Science* 338: 119–36.

———. 1962. "Delinquency and Opportunity: Analysis of a Theory." *Sociology and Social Research* 46: 167–75.

Bottom, Norman. 1989. *Industrial Espionage Intelligence Techniques.* Toronto: Butterworth.

Bottomley, A. Keith. 1979. *Criminology in Focus: Past Trends and Future Prospects.* New York: Barnes and Noble.

Boucher, Rick. 1989. "Trying to Fix a Statute Run Amok." *New York Times,* March 12, p. 4E.

Boudreau, John F., et al. 1977. *Arson and Arson Investigations: Survey and Assessment.* Washington, DC: U.S. Department of Justice.

Bourgois, Philippe, 1988. "Fear and Loathing in El Barrio: Ideology and Upward Mobility in the Underground Economy of the Inner City." Paper presented at the American Anthropological Meetings, Phoenix, Arizona, November.

———. 1995. *In Search of Respect: Selling Crack in El Barrio.* New York: Cambridge University Press.

Bowden, Charles. 1998. *Juarez: The Laboratory of Our Future.* New York: Aperture Foundation.

Bowers, William B. 1974. *Executions in America.* Lexington, MA: Lexington Books.

Bowers, William B., and Pierce, Glenn. 1975. "The Illusion of Deterrence in Isaac Ehrlich's Research on Capital Punishment." *Yale Law Journal* 85: 164–227.

Bowker, Lee, editor. 1998. *Masculinities and Violence.* Thousand Oaks, CA: Sage.

Braithwaite, John. 1981. "Paradoxes of Class Bias in Criminal Justice." Unpublished paper, Australian Institute of Criminology. Cited in Francis T. Cullen et al., 1982, "Dissecting White-Collar Crime: Offense Type and Punitiveness." Paper presented at the Academy of Criminal Justice Sciences Meetings, Louisville, KY.

———. 1989a. *Crime, Shame and Reintegration.* Cambridge, England: Cambridge University Press.

———. 1989b. "Criminological Theory and Organizational Crime." *Justice Quarterly* 6: 333–358.

Branigin, William. 1990. "With Friends Like These, Who Needs Enemies?" *Washington Post National Weekly Edition,* July 23–29, p. 31.

Brantingham, Paul, and Brantingham, Patricia. 1984. *Patterns in Crime.* New York: Macmillan.

Bratton, William J. 1996. "How to Win the War Against Crime." *New York Times,* April 5, p. A15.

Brecher, Edward. 1972. *Licit and Illicit Drugs.* Boston: Little, Brown.

Bremer, R. 1980. "Implementing a Three-Part Inventory Shrinkage Control Program." *Retail Control,* June, pp. 36–41.

Brenner, M. Harvey. 1978. "Economic Crises and Crime." In *Crime and Society,* edited by Leonard Savitz and Norman Johnston, pp. 555–72. 2nd edition. New York: Wiley.

Bresler, Fenton. 1980. *The Chinese Mafia.* New York: Stein and Day.

Briar, Scott, and Piliavin, Irving. 1965. "Delinquency, Situational Inducements and Commitment to Conformity." *Social Problems* 13: 35–45.

"British Clinics Are Struggling as Heroin Addiction Climbs." 1985. *New York Times,* April 11, p. 15A.

Brodeur, Paul. 1974. *Expendable Americans.* New York: Viking.

———. 1985. *Outrageous Misconduct: The Asbestos Industry on Trial.* New York: Pantheon Books.

Brooke, James. 1995. "Kidnappings Soar in Latin America Threatening Region's Stability." *New York Times,* April 7, p. A7.

Brown, Bertram S., et al. 1973. *Psychosurgery: Perspectives on a Current Problem.* Washington, DC: Government Printing Office.

Brown, Claude. 1964. *Manchild in the Promised Land.* New York: Macmillan.

Brown, Michael H. 1982. "Love Canal and the Poisoning of America." In *Crisis in American Institutions,* edited by Jerome H. Skolnick and Elliott Currie, pp. 297–316. 5th edition. Boston: Little, Brown.

Brown, Richard M. 1969. "Historical Patterns of Violence in America." In *Violence in America, a Staff Report to the National Commission on the Causes and Prevention of Violence,* edited by Hugh D. Graham and Ted R. Gurr, pp. 43–80. New York: New American Library.

Browning, Frank, and Gerassi, John. 1980. *The American Way of Crime.* New York: G. P. Putnam's Sons.

Brownmiller, Susan. 1975. *Against Our Will: Men, Women and Rape.* New York: Simon and Schuster.

Brunner, John. 1976. *The Shockwave Rider.* New York: Ballantine Books.

Brush, Pete. 1999. "Honor Student, Teachers Charged in Shoplift Ring." APBnews.com, May 9.

Bryson, Chris. 1998. "The Donora Fluoride Fog: A Secret History of America's Worst Air Pollution Disaster." *Earth Island Journal* Fall, www.fluoridation.com/donora.htm.

Bureau of Justice Statistics. 1981a. "Measuring Crime." *Bureau of Justice Statistics Bulletin,* February.

———. 1981b. "The Prevalence of Crime." *Bureau of Justice Statistics Bulletin,* March.

———. 1982. "Households Touched by Crime, 1981." *Bureau of Justice Statistics Bulletin,* September.

———. 1983a. "Criminal Victimization in the U.S.: 1980–81 Changes Based on New Estimates." *Bureau of Justice Statistics Technical Report,* March.

———. 1983b. *Report to the Nation on Crime and Justice: The Data.* Washington, DC: Government Printing Office, October.

———. 1984a. "Criminal Victimization 1983." *Bureau of Justice Statistics Technical Bulletin,* June.

———. 1984b. "Households Touched by Crime, 1983." *Bureau of Justice Statistics Bulletin,* May.

———. 1988a. "Criminal Victimization 1987." *Bureau of Justice Statistics Bulletin,* October.

———. 1988b. *Report to the Nation on Crime and Justice.* 2nd edition. Washington, DC: Government Printing Office, March.

———. 1994. "National Crime Victimization Survey Redesign." *Bureau of Justice Statistics Fact Sheet,* October.

———. 1996. "Criminal Victimization 1994: National Crime Victimization Survey." *Bureau of Justice Statistics Bulletin,* April.

Burgess, Ann W. 1984. *Child Pornography and Sex Rings.* Lexington, MA: D. C. Heath.

Burgess, Ann W., and Holmstrom, Lynda Lytle. 1974. *Rape: Victims of Crisis.* Bowie, MD: Robert J. Brady.

Burgess, Ann W., et al. 1987. "Serial Rapists and Their Victims: Reenactment and Repetition." In *Practical Aspects of Rape Investigation,* edited by Robert R. Hazelwood and Ann W. Burgess, New York: Elsevier.

Burgess, Ernest W. 1925. "The Growth of the City." In *The City,* edited by Robert E. Park, Ernest W. Burgess, and Robert D. McKenzie, pp. 47–62. Chicago: University of Chicago Press.

Burgess, Robert L., and Akers, Ronald L. 1966. "A Differential Association-Reinforcement Theory of Criminal Behavior." *Social Problems* 14: 128–47.

Burnett, Cathleen, 1986. "Review Essay." Criminology 24: 203–11.

Burnham, Kenneth P. 1980. "Mark-Recapture Techniques for Estimating Animal Populations: What Has Been Done in Ecology." Paper presented at the National Workshop on Research Methodology and Criminal Justice Program Evaluation, Baltimore, MD, March.

Bursik, Robert J., Jr. 1988. "Social Disorganizartion and Theories of Crime and Delinquency: Problems and Prospects." *Criminology* 26: 519–51.

Burton, Thomas M. 1991. "Cardiac Case: Sale of Medical Devices Draws New Scrutiny After Pacemaker Flap." *Wall Street Journal,* September 20, p. A1.

———. 1995. "Caremark Paid Physicians to Obtain Patients, Government Documents Say." *Wall Street Journal,* June 19, p. B8.

Butterfield, Fox. 1995. "Brady Law, in Its First Year, Halts Gun Permits for 45,000." *New York Times,* March 12, p. A13.

Buzawa, Eve S., and Buzawa, Carl G. 1990. *Domestic Violence: The Criminal Justice Response.* Newbury Park, CA: Sage.

Bynum, Timothy S., ed. 1987. *Organized Crime in America: Concepts and Controversies.* Monsey, NY: Criminal Justice Press.

Byrne, James, and Sampson, Robert. 1986. "Cities and Crime: The Ecological/Non-ecological Debate Reconsidered." In *The Social Ecology of Crime,* edited by James Byrne and Robert Sampson. New York: Springer-Verlag.

"Cambodia: Pol Pot's Lifeless Zombies." 1979. *Time,* December 3, pp. 55–56.

Cameron, Mary Owen. 1964. *The Booster and the Snitch: Department Store Shoplifting.* New York: The Free Press.

Campbell, Donald T., and Stanley, Julian C. 1963. *Experimental and Quasi-Experimental Designs for Research.* Chicago: Rand McNally.

Cantor, David, and Land, Kenneth C. 1985. "Unemployment and Crime Rate in the Post-World War II United States: A Theoretical and Empirical Analysis." *American Sociological Review* 50: 317–32.

Cardarelli, Albert P. 1988. "Child Sexual Abuse: Factors in Family Reporting." *NIJ Reports* 209, May/June: 9–12.

Carey, James T. 1972. "Problems of Access and Risk in Observing Drug Scenes." In *Research on Deviance,* edited by Jack D. Douglas, pp. 71–92. New York: Random House.

———. 1975. *Sociology and Public Affairs: The Chicago School.* Beverly Hills, CA: Sage.

———. 1978. *Introduction to Criminology.* Englewood Cliffs, NJ: Prentice-Hall.

Carey, Joseph. 1988. "From Revival Tent to Mainstream." *U.S. News and World Report,* December, pp. 52–61.

Carley, William M. 1991. "Glory of Rome: An Ancient Treasure Leads to Dark Intrigue in the World of Art." *Wall Street Journal,* March 19, pp. A1, A4.

Carlin, Jerome E. 1962. *Lawyers on Their Own.* New Brunswick, NJ: Rutgers University Press.

Carlisle, Cristina. 1998. "As Latin American Art Prices Rise, So Do Forgeries." *New York Times,* October 6, p. C1.

Carlson, Kenneth W. 1979. Statement before the Congressional Committee on Education and Labor, Subcommittee on Compensation, Health, and Safety, "Hearings on Asbestos-Related Occupational Diseases," 95th Congress, Second Session. Washington, DC: Government Printing Office, pp. 25–52.

Carlson, Kenneth, and Finn, Peter. 1993. "Prosecuting Criminal Enterprises." *Bureau of Justice Statistics Special Report,* November.

Carson, Rachel. 1962. *Silent Spring.* New York: Houghton Mifflin.

Cary, Peter. 1987. "Dial-a-dupe on Con Man's Coast." *U.S. News and World Report,* December 21, pp. 62–63.

Cater, Douglass, and Strickland, Stephen. 1975. *TV Violence and the Child: The Evolution and Fate of the Surgeon General's Report.* New York: Russell Sage.

Caudill, William A. 1958. *The Psychiatric Hospital as a Small Society.* Cambridge, MA: Harvard University Press.

CBS 1988. "Godfathers of the Ginza." *60 Minutes.* Telecast November 20.

———. 1989a. "Japan." *48 Hours.* Telecast February 23.

———. 1989b. *West 57th.* Telecast March 25.

"Cendant to Pay $2.8 Billion Fraud Settlement." 1999. APBnews.com, December 8.

Chaiken, Jan M., and Chaiken, Marcia R. 1982. *Varieties of Criminal Behavior.* Report prepared for the National Institute of Justice, U.S. Department of Justice. Santa Monica, CA: The Rand Corporation.

Chaiken, Marcia R., and Johnson, Bruce D. 1988. *Characteristics of Different Types of Drug-Involved Offenders. Issues and Practices in Criminal Justice.* Washington, DC: National Institute of Justice, February.

Chambliss, William J. 1975a. *Box Man: A Professional Thief's Journal, by Harry King.* New York: Harper.

———. 1975b. "Toward a Political Economy of Crime." *Theory and Society* 2: 152–53.

———. 1976. "Functional and Conflict Theories of Crime." In *Whose Law, What Order?* edited by William J. Chambliss and Milton Mankoff. New York: Wiley.

———. 1988a. *On the Take: From Petty Crooks to Presidents.* 2nd edition. Bloomington, IN: Indiana University Press.

———. 1988b. "State-Organized Crime." *Criminology* 27: 183–208.

Chambliss, William J., and Seidman, Robert B. 1971. *Law and Order and Power.* Reading, MA: Addison-Wesley.

Chamlin, Mitchell B., and Cochran, John K. 1995. "Assessing Messner and Rosenfeld's Institutional Anomie Theory: A Partial Test." *Criminology* 33 (August): 411–29.

Chandler, David L. 1976. *Criminal Brotherhoods.* London: Constable and Company.

Chappell, Duncan, and Fogarty, Faith. 1978. *Forcible Rape: A Literature Review and Annotated Bibliography.* Washington, DC: National Institute on Law Enforcement and Criminal Justice, May.

"Charges Dropped Against Man Selling Heads." 1987. *Erie Morning News,* January 19, p. 3B.

Cheatwood, Derral. 1988. "Is There a Season for Homicide?" *Criminology* 26: 287–306.

Cheesman, Bruce. 1999. "The Thai Dying You Won't Find in a Brochure." *World Financial Review,* December 30: 1–4.

Cherrington, David J., and Cherrington, J. Owen. 1982. "The Climate of Honesty in Retail Stores." *Journal of Security Administration* 5(2): 37–52.

Chesney-Lind, Meda. 1989. "Girls' Crime and Woman's Place: Toward a Feminist Model of Female Delinquency." *Crime and Delinquency* 35: 5–30.

Chesney-Lind, Meda, and Shelden, Randall G. 1998. *Girls, Delinquency and Juvenile Justice.* 2nd edition. Belmont, CA: Wadsworth.

Chesterton, G. K. 1935. *Avowals and Denials: A Book of Essays.* London: Methuen.

Chilton, Roland. 1991. "Urban Crime Trends and Criminological Theory." *Criminal Justice Research Bulletin* 6 (3): 1–10.

Chin, Ko-Lin. 1988. "Chinese Organized Crime: Myth and Fact." Paper presented at the American Society of Criminology Meetings, Chicago, IL, November.

———. 1990. *Chinese Subculture and Criminality.* Westport, CT: Greenwood.

Christensen, Harold T., and Gregg, Christina F. 1970. "Changing Sex Norms in America and Scandinavia." *Journal of Marriage and the Family* 32: 616–27.

Christiansen, Karl. 1968. "Threshold of Tolerance in Various Population Groups Illustrated by Results from a Danish Criminological Twin Study." In *The Mentally Abnormal Offender,* edited by A. V. S. de Reuck. Boston: Little, Brown.

"Chrysler Fined for Violations." 1990. *Erie Morning News,* August 11, p. 2A.

"City Inspectors Extorted Hundreds of Thousands from N.Y. Restaurants." 1988. *Erie Morning News,* March 25, p. 3A.

Clark, Alexander L., and Gibbs, Jack P. 1965. "Social Control: A Reformation." *Social Problems* 13: 399–415.

Clark, John P., and Tifft, Larry L. 1966. "Polygraph and Interview Validation of Self Reported Deviant Behavior." *American Sociological Review* 31: 516–23.

Clark, Thurston, and Tigue, John J., Jr. 1975. *Dirty Money: Swiss Banks, the Mafia, Money Laundering and White-Collar Crime.* New York: Simon and Schuster.

Clarke, James W. 1982. *American Assassins: The Darker Side of Politics.* Princeton, NJ: Princeton University Press.

Clarke, Stevens H. 1974. "Getting 'Em Out of Circulation: Does Incarceration of Juvenile Offenders Reduce Crime?" *Journal of Law and Criminology* 65: 528–35.

Cleckley, Hervey. 1976. *The Mask of Insanity.* 5th edition. St. Louis: Mosby.

Clemons, Randall S., and McBeth, Mark K. 2001. *Public Policy Praxis: Theory and Pragmatism: A Case Approach.* Upper Saddle River, NJ: Prentice-Hall.

Clinard, Marshall B. 1946. "Criminological Theories of Violation of Wartime Regulations." *American Sociological Review* 11 (June): 258–70.

———. 1969. *The Black Market: A Study of White-Collar Crime.* Montclair, NJ: Patterson Smith (First edition, 1952. New York: Holt).

———. 1978. *Cities with Little Crime: The Case of Switzerland.* Cambridge, England: Cambridge University Press.

Clinard, Marshall B., and Abbott, D.J. 1973. *Crime in Developing Countries:* A Comparative Perspective. New York: John Wiley.

Clinard, Marshall B. and Quinney, Richard. 1973. *Criminal Behavior Systems: A Typology.* New York: Holt, Rinehart and Winston.

Clinard, Marshall B., and Quinney, Richard. 1986. *Criminal Behavior Systems: A Typology.* 2nd edition. New York: Holt, Rinehart, and Winston.

Clinard, Marshal B. and Quinney, Richard. 1994. *Criminal Behavior Systems: A Typology.* 3rd edition. Cincinnati: Anderson.

Clinard, Marshall B., Quinney, Richard, and Wildeman, John. 1994. *Criminal Behavior Systems: A Typology.* 3rd edition. Cincinnati, OH: Anderson.

Clinard, Marshall B., and Yeager, Peter C. 1978. "Corporate Crime: Issues in Research." *Criminology* 16: 255–72.

———. 1979. *Illegal Corporate Behavior.* Washington, DC: Law Enforcement Assistance Administration.

———. 1980. *Corporate Crime.* New York: Macmillan.

Cloward, Richard, and Ohlin, Lloyd. 1960. *Delinquency and Opportunity: A Theory of Delinquent Gangs.* New York: The Free Press.

Clutterbuck, Richard. 1975. *Living with Terrorism.* New Rochelle, NY: Arlington House.

" 'Cocaine Cowboys' Running Rampant in Florida." 1980. Associated Press, *Erie Morning News,* May 6.

Cohen, Albert K. 1951. *Juvenile Delinquency and the Social Structure.* Doctoral dissertation, Harvard University.

———. 1955. *Delinquent Boys.* New York: The Free Press.

Cohen, Daniel. 1979. *Mysteries of the World.* Garden City, NY: Doubleday.

Cohen, Lawrence E., and Felson, Marcus. 1979. "Social Change and Crime Rate Trends: A Routine Activities Approach." *American Sociological Review* 44: 588–608.

Cohen, Lawrence, E., and Land, Kenneth. 1987. "Age and Crime: Symmetry vs. Asymmetry and the Projection of Crime Rates Through the 1990s." *American Sociological Review* 52: 170–83.

Cohen, Lawrence E., and Stark, Rodney. 1974. "Discriminatory Labeling and the Five-Finger Discount: An Empirical Analysis of Differential Shoplifting Dispositions." *Journal of Research on Crime and Delinquency* 11: 25–35.

Cohen, Warren. 1998. "A Couch-Potato Factor." *U.S. News and World Report,* May 25, pp. 39–40.

Cohn, Bob. 1988. "A Fresh Assault on an Ugly Crime." *Newsweek,* March 14, pp. 64–65.

Cohn, Ellen G. 1990. "Weather and Crime." *British Journal of Criminology* 30 (Winter): 51–63.

Colburn, Theo. 1996. *Our Stolen Future.* New York: Dutton.

Cole, David. 1999. *No Equal Justice: Race and Class in the American Criminal Justice System.* New York: New Press.

Coleman, Fred. 1988. "The Mobsters of Moscow." *Newsweek,* October 31, p. 44.

Coleman, James W. 1985. *The Criminal Elite.* New York: St. Martin's Press.

———. 1994. *The Criminal Elite.* 3rd edition. New York: St. Martin's Press.

Coleman, James. 1998. *The Criminal Elite.* 4th edition. New York: St. Martin's Press.

Collins, James J., Jr., ed., 1981. *Drinking and Crime: Perspectives on the Relationships between Alcohol Consumption and Criminal Behavior.* New York: Guilford Press.

Colvin, Mark, and Pauly, John. 1983. "A Critique of Criminology." *American Journal of Sociology* 89: 513–551.

Committee on the Judiciary, 1986. S. Rep., No. 433, 99th Congress, 2nd Session, 2.

"Companies Fined for Rigging School Milk Contracts." 1990. *Erie Morning News,* March 2, p. A1.

Comstock, George A. 1975. "The Effects of Television on Children and Adolescents: The Evidence So Far." *Journal of Communication* 25: 25–34.

Comte, Auguste. 1877. *A System of Positive Polity.* London: Longmans.

Condon, Richard. 1958. *The Manchurian Candidate.* New York: Random House.

"A Confession Ends Career of Robbery: 56-Bank Toll." 1994. *New York Times,* July 14, p. A8.

"Con Game Nets $3600 From Widow." 1972. *Erie Morning News.* November 7, p. 11A.

Congressional Research Service. 1978. *Human Rights Conditions in Selected Countries and the U.S. Response.* Reports prepared for the House Committee on International Relations, 95th Congress, 2nd Session. Washington, DC: Government Printing Office, July 25.

Conklin, John E. 1972. *Robbery and the Criminal Justice System.* Philadelphia: Lippincott.

———. 1977. *Illegal but Not Criminal: Business Crime in America.* Englewood Cliffs, NJ: Prentice-Hall.

———. 1981. *Criminology.* New York: Macmillan.

"Conning by Computer." 1973. *Newsweek,* April 23, p. 26.

Cook, Fred J. 1982. *The Great Energy Scam: Private Billions vs. Public Good.* New York: Macmillan.

———. 1984. *Maverick: Fifty Years of Investigative Reporting.* New York: G. P. Putnam's Sons.

Cook, Philip J. 1983. "Robbery." *Research in Brief.* Washington, DC: National Institute of Justice, June.

———, ed. 1988. "Vice." *Law and Contemporary Problems* 51 (Entire issue).

Cooley, Charles Horton. 1902. *Human Nature and Social Order.* 1964 edition. New York: Schocken Books.

Cooney, T. 1987. "The Mob Chronicles." *Philadelphia Daily News.* April 23, pp. 3, 26–27; April 24, pp. 3, 36–38.

Copeland, Miles. 1974. *Beyond Cloak and Dagger: Inside the CIA.* New York: Pinnacle Books.

Cornish, Derek B., and Clarke, Ronald V. 1987. "Understanding Crime Displacement: An Application of Rational Choice Theory." *Criminology* 25: 933–47.

Cornish, Derek B., and Clarke, Ronald V., eds. 1986. *The Reasoning Criminal: Rational Choice Perspectives on Offending.* New York: Springer-Verlag.

Cortés, Juan, with Gatti, Florence M. 1972. *Delinquency and Crime.* New York: Seminar Press.

Coser, Lewis. 1956. *The Functions of Social Conflict.* New York: Free Press.

"Cost of Crime: $674 Billion." 1994. *U.S. News and World Report.* January 17, p. 40–41.

"Couple Call Sex Cult Sacred (Police Call It Prostitution)." 1989. *New York Times,* April 18, p. 1B.

Courtright, Kevin E., and Mutchnick, Robert J. 1999. "The Cartographic School of Criminology." Unpublished paper.

Cousins, Norman. 1979. "How the U.S. Used Its Citizens as Guinea Pigs." *Saturday Review,* November 10, p. 10.

Cowell, Alan. 1992. "Inquiry into Sicilian Slaying Looks for Mafia Link to Colombia Drug Cartel." New York Times, June 21, p. 3.

———. 1994. "Where Juliet Pined, Youths Now Kill." *New York Times,* March 22, p. A4.

Cowley, Geoffrey. 1992. "Fueling the Fire Over Halcion." *Newsweek,* May 25, p. 84.

Cox, Edward R., Fellmuth, Robert C., and Schulz, John E. 1969. *Nader's Raiders: Report on the Federal Trade Commission.* New York: Grove Press.

Cranford, John Jr. 1989. "Congress OKs Sweeping Bill to Save Thrift Industry." *Congressional Quarterly* 47: 32, August 12: 2113–51.

Craven, Diane. 1996. "Female Victims of Violent Crime." *Bureau of Justice Statistics Selected Findings.* December. NCJ 162602.

Cressey, Donald. 1953. *Other People's Money.* New York: The Free Press.

———. 1960. "Epidemiology and Individual Conduct: A Case from Criminology." *Pacific Sociological Review* 3: 47–58.

———. 1967. "The Functions and Structure of Criminal Syndicates." In *Organized Crime Task Force Report.* Washington, DC: Government Printing Office.

———. 1969. *The Theft of the Nation: The Structure and Operations of Organized Crime in America.* New York: Harper and Row.

———. 1972. *Criminal Organization.* New York: Harper and Row.

Crewdson, John. 1988. *By Silence Betrayed: Sexual Abuse of Children in America.* Boston: Little, Brown.

Crichton, Robert. 1959. *The Great Imposter.* New York: Permabooks.

Crittenden, Ann. 1988. *Sanctuary: A Story of American Conscience and Law in Collision.* New York: Weidenfeld and Nicolson.

Crittenden, Kathleen S., and Hill, Richard J. 1971. "Coding Reliability and Validity of Interview Data." *American Sociological Review* 36: 1073–80.

Crockett, Art, ed. 1991. *Spree Killers.* New York: Pinnacle.

Cromwell, Paul, ed. 1996. *In Their Own Words: Field Research on Crime and Criminals—An Anthology.* Los Angeles: Roxbury Press.

Cronin, Thomas E., Cronin, Tania Z., and Milakovich, Michael E. 1981. *U.S. v. Crime in the Streets.* Bloomington, IN: Indiana University Press.

Crossette, Barbara. 2000. "Unicef Opens a Global Drive on Violence Against Women." *New York Times,* March 9, p. A6.

Crovitz, L. Gordon. 1991. "The More Lawsuits the Better and Other American Notions." *Wall Street Journal,* April 17, p. A17.

Crowe, Raymond R. 1974. "An Adoption Study of Antisocial Personality." *Archives of General Psychiatry* 31: 785–91.

Cullen, Francis T. 1983. "Public Support for Punishing White-Collar Crime: Blaming the Victim Revisited?" *Journal of Criminal Justice* 11 (6): 481–93.

———. 1984. "The Ford Pinto Case and Beyond." In *Corporations as Criminals,* edited by Ellen C. Hochstedler. Beverly Hills, CA: Sage.

Cullen, Francis T., and Agnew, Robert, editors. 1999. *Criminological Theory: Past to Present: Essential Readings.* Los Angeles: Roxbury Press.

Cullen, Francis T., and Gilbert, Karen E. 1982. *Reaffirming Rehabilitation.* Cincinnati: Anderson.

Cullen, Francis T., Makestad, William, and Cavender, G. 1987. *Corporate Crime Under Attack: The Ford Pinto Case and Beyond.* Cincinnati: Anderson.

Cullen, Francis T., et al. 1982a. "Dissecting White-Collar Crime: Offense Type and Punitiveness." Paper delivered at the Academy of Criminal Justice Sciences Meetings, Louisville, KY.

———. 1982b. "The Seriousness of Crimes Revisited: Have Attitudes toward White-Collar Crime Changed?" *Criminology* 20: 83–102.

———. 1991. "Testing the General Theory of Crime: Self-Control, Age and Lawbreaking." Paper presented at the American Society of Criminology Meetings, San Francisco, CA, November.

"Curfew Violations—A Useless Statutory Crime." 1999. *Washington Post,* September 15, p. A24.

Curran, Daniel J. 1991. "Gearing Down the Regulatory Effort: The Legacy of the Reagan Era and Coal Mine Health and Safety." Paper presented at the American Society of Criminology, San Francisco, CA, November.

Curran, Daniel J., and Renzetti, Claire M. 1994. *Theories of Crime.* Boston: Allyn and Bacon.

Currie, Elliott. 1985. *Confronting Crime: Why There Is So Much Crime in America and What We Can Do about It.* New York: Pantheon.

Dabney, Dean. 2000. "Prescription Drug Use Among Pharmacists: Do They Import the Problem or Does It Begin After They Enter the Profession." Paper presented at the National White-Collar Crime Center Conference, Austin, TX, May.

Dahrendorf, Ralf. 1959. *Class and Class Conflict in Industrial Society.* Stanford: Stanford University Press.

Dalgard, Odd Steffen, and Kringlen, Einer. 1975. "A Norwegian Twin Study of Criminality." *British Journal of Criminology* 16: 213–32.

Dalleck, Robert. 1991. *Lone Star Rising: Lyndon Johnson and His Times, 1908–1960.* New York: Oxford University Press.

Dalton, Katharina. 1961. "Menstruation and Crime." *British Medical Journal* 2: 1752–53.

Daly, Kathleen. 1989. "Gender Varieties of White-Collar Crime." *Criminology* 27 (November): 769–93.

Daly, Kathleen, and Chesney-Lind, Meda. 1988. "Feminism and Criminology." *Justice Quarterly* 5: 497–533.

Daly, Kathleen, and Tonry, Michael. 1997. "Gender, Race and Sentencing." In *Crime and Justice: A Review of Research,* vol. 22, edited by Michael Tonry. pp. 201–252. Chicago: University of Chicago Press.

Danner, Mark. 1995. *The Massacre at El Mozote: A Parable of the Cold War.* New York: Random House.

Danner, Mona. 1989. "Socialist Feminism: A Brief Introduction." *Critical Criminologist* 1: 1–2.

Daraul, Arkon. 1969. *A History of Secret Societies.* New York: Pocket Books.

Davis, Hugh, and Gurr, Ted. 1969. *Violence in America: Historical and Comparative Perspectives.* New York: The New American Library.

Davis, James. 1982. *Street Gangs: Youth, Biker and Prison Gangs.* Dubuque, IA: Kendall/Hunt Publishing Co.

Davis, Kingsley. 1961. "Prostitution." In *Contemporary Social Problems,* edited by Robert K. Merton and Robert A. Nisbet, pp. 275–76. New York: Harcourt, Brace and World.

Davis, L. J. 1995. "Medscam, A Mother Jones Investigation." *Mother Jones,* May.

Dean, John. 1977. *Blind Ambition.* New York: Pocket Books.

"Death Squads Prey on Rio Street Children." 1991. *CJ the Americas* 4 (April–May): 12.

"Declaration of the Rights of Man and of the Citizen," Article VIII, 1789. Revolutionary National Assembly of France. In *Classics of Criminology,* edited by Joseph E. Jacoby, 1979, p. 215. Oak Park, IL: Moore Publishing.

DeFleur, Melvin, L., and Quinney, Richard. 1966. "A Reformulation of Sutherland's Differential Association Theory and a Strategy for Empirical Verification." *The Journal of Research in Crime and Delinquency* 3 (January): 1–22.

DeKeseredy, Walter. 1988. "The Left Realist Approach to Law and Order." *Justice Quarterly* 5: 635–40.

DeKeseredy, Walter, et al. 1998. "The Meanings and Motives for Women's Use of Violence in Canadian College Dating Relationships: Results from a National Survey." *Sociological Spectrum* 17: 199–222.

DeKeseredy, Walter, and MacLean, Brian D. 1993. "Critical Criminological Pedagogy in Canada: Strengths, Limitations, and Recommendations for Improvements." *Journal of Criminal Justice Education* 4 (Fall): 361–76.

Del Piano, A.J. 1993. "The Fine Art of Forgery, Theft and Fraud." *Criminal Justice* 8,2 (Summer): 16–20, 56–57.

DeMaris, Ovid. 1981. *The Last Mafioso: The Treacherous World of Jimmy Fratianno.* New York: Times Books.

Denfield, Duane. 1974. *Streetwise Criminology.* Cambridge, MA: Schenkman.

Denno, Deborah. 1985. "Sociological and Human Developmental Explanations of Crime: Conflict and Consensus?" *Criminology* 23: 711–42.

———. 1990. *Biology and Violence: From Birth to Adulthood.* New York: Cambridge University Press.

Dentler, Robert A., and Monroe, Lawrence J. 1961. "Social Correlates of Early Adolescent Theft." *American Sociological Review* 26 (October): 733–43.

Department of Corporations. 1999. "Department of Corporations Issues Warning on 'Affinity Fraud.' " news.excite.com, September 7.

Department of Health and Human Services. 1981. *For Parents Only: What You Need to Know about Marijuana.* Washington, DC: Government Printing Office.

———. 1982. *Television and Behavior.* Washington, DC: Government Printing Office.

Dershowitz, Alan. 1994. *Abuse Excuse: Cop-Outs, Sob Stories and Other Evasions of Responsibility.* Boston: Little, Brown.

Detlinger, Chet, with Jeff Prugh. 1983. *The List.* Atlanta: Philmay Enterprises.

"Detroit's Former Chief Convicted." 1992. *Erie Morning News,* May 8, p. 16B.

Diapoulos, Peter, and Linakis, Steven. 1976. *The Sixth Family: The True Inside Story of the Execution of a Mafia Chief.* New York: Bantam.

Dickey, Christopher. 1989. "Missing Masterpieces." *Newsweek,* May 29, pp. 65–68.

Dionne, E. J., Jr. 1990. "The Death Penalty: Getting Mad and Getting Even." *Washington Post National Weekly Edition,* May 21–27, p. 37.

Dobash, R. Emerson, Dobash, Russell P., and Noaks, Lesley. 1995. *Gender and Crime.* Cardiff: University of Wales Press.

Dobnik, Verena. 1996. "Never Again! U.S. Government to Pay $4.8 Million." *Erie Morning News,* November 20, pp. 1A, 2A.

Doerner, William. 1988. "The Impact of Medical Resources on Criminally Induced Lethality: A Further Examination." *Criminology* 26: 171–79.

Doerner, William G., and Speir, John C. 1986. "Stitch and Sew: The Impact of Medical Resources upon Criminally Induced Lethality." *Criminology* 24: 319–30.

Dolive, Linda L. 1999. "When Criminals Rule: Corruption and Politics." Paper presented at the American Society of Criminology Meetings, Toronto, Ontario, Canada, November.

Donnerstein, Edward, Linz, Daniel, and Penrod, Steven. 1987. *The Question of Pornography.* New York: The Free Press.

Donovan, Robert. 1952. *The Assassins.* New York: Harper Brothers.

Dornfeld, Maude, and Kruttschnitt, Candace. 1991. "Is There a Weaker Sex: Mapping Gender-Specific Outcomes and Their Risk Factors." Paper presented at the American Society of Criminology Meetings, San Francisco, CA. November.

Douglas, John, and Olshaker, Mark. 1995. *Mindhunter.* New York: Pocket Star Books.

———. 1997. *Journey Into Darkness.* New York: Scribner.

Dowie, Mark. 1977. "Pinto Madness." *Mother Jones* 2 (September): 18–32. Reprinted in *Crisis in American Institutions,* edited by Jerome H. Skolnick and Elliott Currie. 1982. Boston: Little, Brown.

———. 1987. "The Dumping of Hazardous Products on Foreign Markets." In *Corporate Violence,* edited by Stuart L. Hills, Totowa, NJ: Rowman and Littlefield, pp. 47–58.

Doyle, John M. 1987. "Aging Mafia Bosses Get Century in Jail." *Erie Morning News,* January 14, p. 2A.

Draper, Theodore. 1991. *A Very Thin Line: The Iran-Contra Affairs.* New York: Hill and Wang.

"Drug Raid Conducted at Pa. Prison." 1995. *Erie Morning News,* October 24, p. 2A.

"Drug Rings Hire Gun-Toting Kids." 1988. *Erie Times News,* June 5, p. 4A.

DuBois, W.E.B. 1899 [1973]. *The Philadelphia Negro: A Social Study.* Millwood, New York: Kraus-Thomson Organization Limited.

———. 1901. "The Spawn of Slavery: The Convict-Lease System in the South." *The Missionary View of the World* 14: 737–745.

Duckworth, Michael. 1991. "Counterfeiting Credit Cards Is a Science Only One Step Behind Bona Fide Plastic." *Wall Street Journal,* October 28, p. B5D.

Duffy, Brian, et al. 1988. "The Enemy Within." *U.S. News and World Report,* July 4, pp. 16–22.

Dugan, Laura, Nagin, Daniel, and Rosenfeld, Richard. 2000. "The Declining Rate of Intimate Partner Homicide." National Criminal Justice Reference Service, NIJ Videotape (NCJ 180212).

Dugdale, Robert. 1877. *The Jukes: A Study in Crime, Pauperism and Heredity.* New York: Putnam.

Dunn, Christopher S. 1976. *Patterns of Robbery Characteristics.* Analytic Report 15. Washington, DC: National Criminal Justice Information and Statistics Service.

Durkheim, Émile. 1950. *The Rules of Sociological Method.* Glencoe, IL: The Free Press.

———. 1951. *Suicide.* New York: The Free Press.

———. 1964. *The Division of Labor in Society.* New York: The Free Press.

Duster, Troy. 1970. *The Legislation of Morality: Laws, Drugs and Moral Judgment.* New York: The Free Press.

Dutton, Denis, ed. 1983. *The Forger's Art: Forgery and the Philosophy of Art.* Berkeley: University of California Press.

Eddy, Paul, Sabogal, Hugo, and Walden, Sara. 1988. *The Cocaine Wars.* New York: W. W. Norton.

Edelhertz, Herbert. 1970. *The Nature, Impact and Prosecution of White-Collar Crime.* National Institute of Law

Enforcement and Criminal Justice. Washington, DC: Government Printing Office.

Edwards, Allen. 1957. *Techniques of Attitudes Scale Construction.* New York: Appleton.

Egger, Steven A. 1984. "A Working Definition of Serial Murder." *Journal of Police Science.* 12: 348–57.

Ehrhart, Julie K., and Sandler, Bernice R. 1985. *Campus Gang Rape: Party Games?* Project on the Status and Education of Women, Washington, DC: Association of American Colleges.

Ehrlich, Paul R., and Feldman, S. Shirley. 1977. *The Race Bomb.* New York: Quadrangle.

Eichenwald, Kurt. 1994. "Prudential's Fraud Costs to Exceed $1.1 Billion." *New York Times,* July 13, pp. C1, C13.

Ekpenyong, Rosy A. 1988. "Reviews of O'Brien and Goldstein." *The Journal of Criminal Law and Criminology* 79: 569–72.

Elias, Robert. 1986. *The Politics of Victimization: Victims, Victimology and Human Rights.* New York: Oxford University Press.

"Eli Lilly Drug Targeted." 1990. *ABA Journal,* November: 24–25.

Elliott, Delbert S. 1985. "The assumption that theories can be combined with increased explanatory power." In *Theoretical Methods in Criminology,* edited by Robert F. Meier. pp. 123–149. Beverly Hills, CA: Sage.

Elliott, Delbert S., and Ageton, Suzanne S. 1980. "Reconciling Race and Class Differences in Self-Reported and Official Estimates of Delinquency." *American Sociological Review* 45 (February): 95–110.

Elliott, Delbert S., Ageton, Suzanne S. and Cantor, Rachelle J. 1979. "An Integrated Theoretical Perspective on Delinquent Behavior." *Journal of Research on Crime and Delinquency.* 16: 3–27.

Ellis, Albert. 1959. "Why Married Men Visit Prostitutes." *Sexology* 25: 344.

Ellis, Albert, and Brancale, R. 1965. *Psychology of Sex Offenders.* Springfield, IL: Charles C. Thomas.

Ellis, Lee. 1982. "Genetics and Criminal Behavior." *Criminology* 20 (May): 43–56.

———. 1985. "Religiosity and Criminality: Evidence and Explanation Surrounding Complex Relationships." *Sociological Perspective* 28: 501–520.

———. 1991. "Monoamine Oxidase and Criminality: Identifying an Apparent Biological Marker for Antisocial Behavior." *Journal of Research in Crime and Delinquency* 28(2), May: 227–251.

———. 1996. "Arousal Theory and the Religiosity-Criminality Relationship." In *Readings in Contemporary Criminological Theory,* edited by Peter Cordello and Larry Siegel. pp. 65–83. Boston: Northeastern University Press.

Ellis, Lee, and Walsh, Anthony. 1997. "Gene-Based Evolutionary Theories in Criminology." *Criminology* 36(2): 229–276.

———. 2000. *Criminology: A Global Perspective.* Boston: Allyn and Bacon.

Empey, Lamar T., and Erickson, Maynard L. 1966. "Hidden Delinquency and Social Status." *Social Forces* 44: 546–54.

Emshwiller, John R. 1992. "Shady Dealings: California Casinos Suspected of Ties to Asian Mafia." *Wall Street Journal,* June 1, pp. A1, A6.

Engberg, E. 1967. *The Spy in the Corporate Structure.* Cleveland: World Publishing.

Ennis, P. H. 1967. *Criminal Victimization in the United States: A Report of a National Survey.* Field Surveys II, The President's Commission on Law Enforcement and Administration of Justice, Washington, DC: Government Printing Office.

Epstein, Edward J. 1977. *Agency of Fear.* New York: G. P. Putnam.

———. 1983. "Edwin Wilson and the CIA: How Badly One Man Hurt Our Nation." *Parade.* September 18, pp. 22–24.

Erickson, Maynard L., and Empey, LaMar T. 1963. "Court Records, Undetected Delinquency and Decision-Making." *Journal of Criminal Law, Criminology and Police Science* 54: 456–69.

Erickson, Patricia G. 1990. "A Public Health Approach to Demand Reduction." *The Journal of Drug Issues* 20(4): 563–75.

"Erie Red Light Resorts Pay More Than $50,000 Annually in Rentals." 1907. *Erie Morning News.* Highlights of 1907 issue, 1988, January 22, p 6A.

Erikson, Erik H. 1950. *Childhood and Society.* New York: Norton.

Erlanger, Howard S. 1974. "The Empirical Status of the Subculture of Violence Thesis." *Social Problems* 22 (March): 280–92.

Ermann, M. David, and Lundman, Richard J. 1982. *Corporate Deviance.* New York: Holt, Rinehart, Winston.

Esposito, John C., and Silverman, Larry J. 1970. *Vanishing Air: Ralph Nader's Study Group Report on Air Pollution.* New York: Grossman.

Estill, Jerry. 1988. "Feds Start 'Rapsheet' for Doctors." *Erie Morning News,* December 31, p. 1A.

Estrich, Susan. 1987. *Real Rape: How the Legal System Victimizes Women Who Say No.* Cambridge, MA: Harvard University Press.

"Ex-Agents Say Drug War Never Adequately Funded." 1986. *Erie Times News,* October 5, p. 2A.

Executive Officer of Public Safety. 1992. *Hate Crime/Hate Incidents in Massachusetts,* 1991 Annual Report. Boston: Department of Public Safety.

Eysenck, Hans. 1977. *Crime and Personality.* 3rd edition. London: Routledge and Kegan Paul.

———. 1980. "The Biosocial Model of Man and the Unification of Psychology." In *Models of Man,* edited by A. J. Chapman and D. Jones. Leicester, England: British Psychological Society.

Fagan, Jeffrey. 1990. "Intoxication and Aggression." In *Drugs and Crime,* edited by Michael Tonry and James Q. Wilson, pp. 241–320. Chicago: University of Chicago Press.

Fagan, Jeffrey, Piper, Elizabeth, and Moore, Melinda. 1986. "Violent Delinquents and Urban Youths." *Criminology* 24: 439–71.

Fagan, Jeffrey, and Wexler, Sandra. 1987. "Family Origins of Violent Delinquents." *Criminology* 25: 643–69.

Faiola, Anthony. 1999. "Bogota's 'Street of the Damned' Loses Daughters to Kidnappers." *Erie Morning News,* May 3, p. 11A.

Fairchild, Erika, and Dammer, Harry. 2000. *Comparative Criminal Justice Systems.* Belmont, CA: Wadsworth.

Fancher, Raymond E. 1985. *The Intelligence Men.* New York: W. W. Norton.

Farah, Douglas. 1997. "A Red Alert on Drugs." *Washington Post National Weekly Edition,* October 6, p. 17.

Farnworth, Margaret, and Leiber, Michael J. 1989. "Strain Theory Revisited." *American Sociological Review* 54: 263–74.

Farrell, Ronald A., and Case, Carole. 1995. *The Black Book and the Mob: The Untold Story of the Control of Nevada's Casinos.* Madison: University of Wisconsin Press.

Farrington, David P. 1973. "Self-Reports of Deviant Behavior: Predictive and Stable?" *Journal of Criminal Law and Criminology* 64: 99–110.

———. 1975. "Age and Crime." Paper presented at the American Society of Criminology Meetings, Cincinnati, OH, November.

———. 1986. "Age and Crime" in *Crime and Justice,* volume 7, edited by Michael Tonry and David Farrington. Chicago: University of Chicago Press, pp. 189–250.

———. 1990. "Implications of Criminal Career Research for the Prevention of Offending." *Journal of Adolescence* 13: 93–113.

Farrington, David, et al. 1988. "Are There Any Successful Men from Criminogenic Backgrounds?" *Psychiatry* 51 (May): 116–130.

Farrington, David P., Ohlin, Lloyd E. and Wilson, James Q., eds. 1986. *Understanding and Controlling Crime.* New York: Springer-Verlag.

FBI. 1984. *Crime in the United States,* 1983. Washington, DC: Government Printing Office.

———. 1985a. *Crime in the United States, 1985.* Washington, DC: Government Printing Office.

———. 1985b. *Oriental Organized Crime.* Washington, DC: Government Printing Office.

———. 1988. *Crime in the United States, 1987.* Washington, DC: Government Printing Office.

———. 1992. *Crime in the United States, 1991.* Washington, DC: Government Printing Office.

———. 1995. *Crime in the United States, 1994, Uniform Crime Reports.* Washington, DC: Government Printing Office.

———. 1999. *Crime in the United States, 1998, Uniform Crime Reports.* Washington, DC: Government Printing Office.

"FBI Gambling Sting Nets 23 Cleveland Police Officers." 1991. *Erie Morning News,* May 31, p. 1A.

"Feds Indict TMI Operator Over Reports." 1983. *Erie Morning News,* November 8, p. 1.

Feeney, Floyd, and Weir, Adrianne. 1975. "The Prevention and Control of Robbery." *Criminology* 13 (May): 102–105.

Feldman, Roy E. 1968. "Response to Compatriot and Foreigner Who Seeks Assistance." *Journal of Personality and Social Psychology* 10: 202–14.

Felson, Marcus, 1983. "Ecology of Crime." In *The Encyclopedia of Crime and Justice.* New York: Macmillan.

———. 1987. "Routine Activities and Crime Prevention in the Developing Metropolis." *Criminology* 25: 911–31.

Ferdinand, Theodore N. 1987. "The Methods of Delinquency Theory." *Criminology* 25 (4): 841–62.

———. 1991. "The Theft/Violence Ratio in Antebellum Boston." *Criminal Justice Review* 16 (Spring): 42–58.

Ferracuti, Franco. 1968. "European Migration and Crime." In *Crime and Culture: Essays in Honor of Thorsten Sellin,* edited by Marvin E. Wolfgang. New York: Wiley.

Ferrell, Jeff, Hamm, Mark S., and Adler, Peter. 1998. *Ethnography at the Edge: Crime Deviance and Field Research.* Boston: Northeastern University Press.

Ferri, Enrico. 1917. *Criminal Sociology.* Translated by Joseph I. Kelley and John Lisle. Boston: Little, Brown.

Fight Crime Committee. 1986. *A Discussion Document on Options for Changes in the Law and in the Administration of the Law to Counter the Triad Problem.* Hong Kong: Government Security Office, April.

Final Report of the Select Committee to Study Governmental Operations with Respect to Intelligence Activities. 1976. U.S. Senate, *Intelligence Activities and the Rights of Americans,* Book II. Washington, DC: Government Printing Office.

Finckenauer, James. 1982. *Scared Straight and the Panacea Phenomenon.* Englewood Cliffs, NJ: Prentice-Hall.

Finestone, Harold. 1976. *Victims of Change.* Westport, CN: Greenwood.

Fingerhut, L., Ingram, D., and Feldman, J. 1992. "Firearm and Nonfirearm Homicide among Persons 15 through 19 years of age: Differences by Level of Urbanization, United States, 1979 through 1989." *Journal of the American Medical Association* 267(22): 3048–3053.

Finkelhor, David. 1979. *Sexually Victimized Children.* New York: The Free Press.

———. 1986. *A Sourcebook on Child Sexual Abuse.* Beverly Hills, CA: Sage.

Finn, Peter E., and Sullivan, Monique. 1988. "Police Respond to Special Populations: Handling the Mentally Ill, Public Inebriate, and the Homeless." *NIJ Reports,* 209: 2–8.

Firestone, David. 1994. "22 Are Arrested in Burglaries of Kennedy Airport Cargo." *New York Times,* August 3, p. A1.

Fishbach, Seymour, and Malamuth, Neal. 1978. "Sex and Aggression: Proving the Link." *Psychology Today* 12: 111–22.

Fishbein, Diana H. 1990. "Biological Perspectives in Criminology." *Criminology* 28 (February): 27–72.

Fishburne, Patricia, Abelson, Herbert, and Cisin, Ira. 1980. *National Survey on Drug Abuse: Main Findings, 1979.* Washington, DC: Government Printing Office.

Fleishmann, Jeffrey. 2000. "Fleeing Poverty, Finding Slavery." *Philadelphia Inquirer,* May 12, p. A1.

Florez, Carl P., and Boyce, Bernadette. 1990. "Laundering Drug Money." *FBI Law Enforcement Bulletin,* April 22–25.

Flowers, Ronald B. 1988. *Minorities and Crime.* Westport, CT: Greenwood Press.

Fontana, Vincent J. 1973. *Somewhere a Child Is Crying.* New York: Macmillan.

Forgac, Gregory E., and Michaels, Edward J. 1982. "Personality Characteristics of Two Types of Male Exhibitionists." *Journal of Abnormal Psychology* 91 (4): 287–95.

Forsthoffer, Diana. 1999. "Robbery Suspect Wants Cultural Insanity Defense." *Erie Morning News,* December 24, p. 8B.

"42 People Indicted for Smuggling Cocaine." 1984. *Erie Times News,* May 3, p. 1A.

"4 Indicted Over Pacemaker Scam." 1988. *Erie Morning News,* September 1, p. 1A.

Fox, James A. 2000. "Homicide Trends in the United States: 1998 Update." *Bureau of Justice Statistics Crime Data Brief,* March, NCJ 179767.

Fox, James A., and Levin, Jack. 1985. *Mass Murder: America's Growing Menace.* New York: Plenum.

Fox, Richard G. 1971. "The XYY Offender: A Modern Myth?" *Journal of Criminal Law, Criminology and Police Science* 62: 59–73.

Fox, Vernon. 1976. *Introduction to Criminology.* Englewood Cliffs, NJ: Prentice-Hall.

———. 1985. *Introduction to Criminology.* 2nd edition. Englewood Cliffs, NJ: Prentice-Hall.

France, Mike, and Burnett, Victoria. 1992. "Corporate America's Colombian Connection." *Business Week,* December 1, pp. 168–170.

Frank, Nancy. 1985. *Crimes against Health and Safety.* New York: Harrow and Heston.

———. 1987. "Murder in the Workplace." In *Corporate Violence,* edited by Stuart L. Hills. Totowa, NJ: Rowman and Littlefield.

Frank, Nancy, and Lombness, Michael. 1988. *Controlling Corporate Illegality.* Cincinnati: Anderson.

Frantz, Douglas, Blumenthal, Ralph, and Vogel, Carol. 2000. "Ex-Leaders of 2 Auction Grants are Said to Initiate Price-Fixing." *New York Times;* October 8, p. A1.

Frantz, Douglas, and Nasar, Sylvia. 1994. "FBI Inquiry on Jet Engines New Jolt to Company Image." *New York Times,* July 18, p. A1.

Freedman, Monroe H. 1976. "Advertising and Soliciting: The Case of Ambulance Chasing." In *Verdicts on Lawyers,* edited by Ralph Nader and Mark Green. New York: Thomas Y. Crowell.

Freedman, Warren. 1989. *The Privilege to Keep and Bear Arms.* Westport, CT: Greenwood Press.

French, Lawrence. 1989. "Post-Traumatic Stress Disorder and Violence: Three Forensic Cases." Paper presented at the American Society of Criminology Meetings, Reno, NV, November.

Freud, Sigmund. 1930. *Civilization and Its Discontents.* Translated by Joan Riviere. Garden City, NJ: Doubleday.

Friedlander, Kate. 1947. *The Psychoanalytic Approach to Juvenile Delinquency.* New York: International Universities Press.

Friedman, Albert B. 1968. "The Scatological Rites of Burglars." *Western Folklore* 27 (July): 171–79.

Friedman, Robert. 1994. "The Organizatsiya." *New York Magazine,* November 7, pp. 52–58.

———. 1995. "The CIA's Jihad." *New York Magazine,* March 27, pp. 39–47.

Friedrich, Carl J. 1972. *The Pathology of Politics.* New York: Harper and Row.

Friedrichs, David O. 1980a. "Carl Klockars vs. the 'Heavy Hitters': A Preliminary Critique." In *Radical Criminology: The Coming Crisis,* edited by James A. Inciardi, pp. 149–60. Beverly Hills, CA: Sage.

———. 1980b. "Radical Criminology in the United States: An Interpretive Understanding?" In *Radical Criminology: The Coming Crisis,* edited by James A. Inciardi, pp. 35–60. Beverly Hills, CA: Sage.

———. 1992. "Governmental Crime: Making Sense of the Conceptual Confusion." Paper presented at the Academy of Criminal Justice Sciences Meetings, Pittsburgh, PA., March.

———. 1995. *Trusted Criminals: White-Collar Crime in Contemporary Society.* Belmont, CA: Wadsworth.

———. 2000. "Crime in High Places: A Perspective on the Clinton Case." In *Crime, Law and Deviance,* vol. 2, edited by Jeffrey T. Ulmer. pp. 281–300. Amsterdam: Elsevier Science.

Friedson, Elliot. 1970. *The Profession of Medicine.* New York: Dodd-Mead.

Fulford, Benjamin. 1999. "Japan's Cement Shoes." *Forbes Magazine (International),* February 8.

Fry, Fran, Jr. 1986. "Consumer Bag: Airport Theft." *Erie Times News,* September 21, p. 7B.

Fyfe, James F. 1991. "Some Hard Facts about Wars on Crime." *Washington Post National Weekly Edition,* April 8–14, p. 25.

Gabbidon, Shaun L. 1999. "W.E.B. DuBois on Crime: American Conflict Criminologist." *The Criminologist* 24 (January): 1,3,20.

Gabor, Thomas, and Normandeau, Andre. 1989. "Armed Robbery: Highlights of a Canadian Study." *Canadian Police College Journal* 13 (4): 273–82.

Gage, Nicholas. 1971. *The Mafia Is Not an Equal Opportunity Employer.* New York: McGraw-Hill.

———. 1972. *Mafia, U.S.A.* Chicago: Playboy Press.

———. 1974. "Questions Are Raised on the Lucky Luciano Book." *New York Times,* December 17, pp. 1, 28.

———. 1988. "A Tale of Two Mafias." *U.S. News and World Report,* January 18, pp. 36–37.

"Gangland Enforcer Paid with Life for Rifts with Mob Over C.I.A." 1977. *United Press International,* March 31.

Garner, Joel, and Visher, Christy A. 1988. "Policy Experiments Come of Age." *NIJ Reports* 201, September/October: 2–8.

Garofalo, Raffaelo. 1914. *Criminology.* Translated by Robert W. Millar. Boston: Little, Brown.

Garrow, David. 1981. *The F.B.I. and Martin Luther King.* New York: Norton.

Gebhard, Paul, et al. 1965. *Sex Offenders: An Analysis of Types.* New York: Harper and Row.

Geis, Gilbert. 1962. "Toward a Delineation of White-Collar Offenses." *Sociological Inquiry* 32 (Spring): 160–71.

———. 1974a. "Avocational Crime." In *Handbook of Criminology,* edited by Daniel Glaser, pp. 273–98. Chicago: Rand McNally.

———. 1974b. "Upperworld Crime." In *Current Perspectives on Criminal Behavior: Original Essays on Criminology,* edited by Abraham S. Blumberg, pp. 114–37. New York: Alfred A. Knopf.

Geis, Gilbert, and Bienen, Leigh B. 1998. *Crimes of the Century.* Boston: Northeastern University Press.

Geis, Gilbert, and Meier, Robert F., eds. 1977. *White-Collar Crime: Offenses in Business, Politics and the Professions.* Revised edition. New York: The Free Press.

———. 1979. "Looking Backward and Forward: Criminologists on Criminology as a Career." In *Criminology: New Concerns,* edited by Edward Sagarin, pp. 173–88. Beverly Hills, CA: Sage.

Gelles, Richard J. 1977. "Etiology of Violence: Overcoming Fallacious Reasoning in Understanding Family Violence and Child Abuse." Manuscript available through the National Criminal Justice Reference Service, Rockville, MD.

———. 1978. "Violence toward Children in the United States." *American Journal of Orthopsychiatry* 48 (October): 580–92.

Gelles, Richard J., and Straus, Murray. 1979. "Violence in the American Family." *Journal of Social Issues* 35 (March): 15–39.

Gendreau, Paul, and Ross, Robert R. 1987. "Revivification of Rehabilitation: Evidence from the 1980s." *Justice Quarterly* 4: 349–407.

Georges-Abeyie, Daniel, ed. 1984. *The Criminal Justice System and Blacks.* New York: Clark Boardman.

———. 1989. "Review of William Wilbanks: The Myth of a Racist Criminal Justice System." *The Critical Criminologist* 1 (Summer): 5–6.

"GE Pleads Guilty to Fraud Charges." 1992. *Erie Morning News,* July 23, p. 2A.

Gerber, Jurg. 1991. "Heidi and Imelda: The Changing Image of Crime in Switzerland." *Criminology* 8 (March): 121–28.

Gerber, Jurg, and Jensen, Eric. 2000. "The Internationalization of U.S. Illicit Drug Control Policy." In *Drug War, American Style,* edited by Jurg Gerber and Eric Jensen. pp. 1–22. New York: Garland Publishing.

Gerlin, Andrea. 1999. "Cure or Curse." *Erie Morning News,* October 21, p. 1A.

"Germany's 'Punks' Descend on Hanover for Repeat Performance of 'Chaos Days.' " 1995. *Erie Morning News,* August 5, p. 3B.

Gest, Ted. 1986. "The Latest Antidrug War: Better Luck This Time?" *U.S. News and World Report,* August 25, p. 18.

Gibbens, T. C. N., and Silberman, M. 1960. "The Clients of Prostitutes." *British Journal of Venereal Disease* 36: 113.

Gibbons, Don C. 1977. *Society, Crime and Criminal Careers.* 3rd edition. Englewood Cliffs, NJ: Prentice-Hall.

———. 1979. *The Criminological Enterprise: Theories and Perspectives.* Englewood Cliffs, NJ: Prentice-Hall.

———. 1982. *Society, Crime, and Criminal Behavior.* Englewood Cliffs, NJ: Prentice-Hall. (4th edition of 1977 book).

———. 1992. "Talking About Crime: Observations on the Prospects for Causal Theory in Criminology." *Criminal Justice Research Bulletin* 7: entire issue.

Gibbons, Don C., and Garabedian, Peter. 1974. "Conservative, Liberal and Radical Criminology: Some Trends and Observations." In *The Criminologist: Crime and the Criminal,* edited by Charles E. Reasons, pp. 51–56. Pacific Palisades: Goodyear.

Gibbs, Jack B. 1985. "Review Essay of Crime and Human Nature by James Q. Wilson and Richard J. Herrnstein." *Criminology* 23: 381–88.

Gil, David. 1971. Violence against Children. Cambridge, MA: Harvard University Press.

Gilham, James R. 1992. *Preventing Residential Burglary: Toward More Effective Community Programs.* New York: Springer-Verlag.

Gladwell, Malcolm. 1990. "Hot Time, Bummer in the City." *Washington Post National Weekly Edition,* July 9–15, p. 39.

Glaser, Barney, and Strauss, Anselm. 1967. *The Discovery of Grounded Theory.* Chicago: Aldine.

Glaser, Daniel. 1978. *Crime in Our Changing Society.* New York: Holt, Rinehart, and Winston.

———. 1990. "Science and Politics as Criminologists' Vocations." *Criminal Justice Research Bulletin* 5(6): 1–6.

———. 1994. "What Works and Why It Is Important: A Response to Logan and Gaes." *Justice Quarterly* 11: 711–24.

Glasser, Jeff. 2000a. "In Demand for 50 Years: The FBI's 'Most Wanted' List: Good Publicity, and a History of Success." *U.S. News and World Report,* March 20, p. 60.

———. 2000b. "The Software Sopranos." *U.S. News and World Report,* February 7.

Glasser, William. 1965. *Reality Therapy.* New York: Harper and Row.

Glick, Susan. 1994. "Good News, Bad News about FBI Crime Data." *Erie Morning News,* December 30, p. 7A.

Glueck, Sheldon, and Glueck, Eleanor. 1950. *Unraveling Juvenile Delinquency.* Cambridge, MA: Harvard University Press.

———. 1956. *Physique and Delinquency.* New York: Harper and Row.

Goddard, Henry H. 1912. *The Kallikak Family.* New York: Macmillan.

Goff, Colin, and Reasons, Charles. 1986. "Organizational Crimes against Employees, Consumers, and the Public." In *The Political Economy of Crime,* edited by B. MacLean. Toronto: Prentice-Hall of Canada, pp. 204–31.

Gold, Martin. 1966. "Undetected Delinquent Behavior." *Journal of Research in Crime and Delinquency* 3 (January): 27–46.

Goldkamp, John S. 1987. "Rational Choice and Determinism." In *Positive Criminology,* edited by Michael B. Gottfredson and Travis Hirschi, pp. 125–37. Beverly Hills, CA: Sage.

Goldstein, Arnold P. 1991. *Delinquent Gangs: A Psychological Perspective.* Champaign, IL: Research Press.

Goldstein, Michael J., et al., 1973. *Pornography and Sexual Deviance.* Berkeley: University of California Press.

Goode, Erica. 2000. "Human Behavior: Born or Made?" *New York Times,* March 14, pp. D1, D9.

Goode, Erich. 1972. *Drugs in American Society.* New York: Alfred A. Knopf.

———. 1981. "Drugs and Crime." In *Current Perspectives on Criminal Behavior,* edited by Abraham Blumberg, pp. 227–72. New York: Alfred A. Knopf.

———. 1984. *Deviant Behavior.* 2nd edition. Englewood Cliffs, NJ: Prentice-Hall.

Goodspeed, Peter. 1998. "Cracking Secret Code of an Elite Porn 'Club'." *Toronto Sunday Star,* September 6, p. A1.

Goodwin, Jean, et al. 1982. *Sexual Abuse: Incest Victims and Their Families.* Boston: John Wright.

Gordon, David M. 1973. "Capitalism, Class and Crime in America." *Crime and Delinquency* 19 (April): 163–86.

Gordon, Diane R. 1990. *The Justice Juggernaut: Fighting Street Crime, Controlling Citizens.* New Brunswick, NJ: Rutgers University Press.

Gordon, Gary R. 1991. "Economic Crime: An International Perspective." Paper presented at the American Society of Criminology Meetings, San Francisco, CA, November.

Gordon, Robert A. 1987. "SES versus IQ in the Race-IQ-Delinquency Model." *International Journal of Sociology and Social Policy.* 7 30–96.

Gordon, Linda, and O'Keefe, Paul. 1984. "Incest as a Form of Family Violence: Evidence from Historical Case Records." *Journal of Marriage and the Family* 46 (February): 27–34.

Goring, Charles. 1913. *The English Convict.* London: His Majesty's Stationery Office.

Gosch, Martin A., and Hammer, Richard. 1974. *The Last Legacy of Lucky Luciano.* New York: Dell.

Gottfredson, Michael R., and Hindelang, Michael J. 1977. "A Consideration of Telescoping and Memory Decay Biases in Victimization Surveys." *Journal of Criminal Justice* 5 (Fall): 205–16.

Gottfredson, Michael, and Hirschi, Travis. 1986. "The True Value of Lambda Would Appear to Be Zero: An Essay on Career Criminals, Criminal Careers, Selective Incapacitation, Cohort Studies and Related Topics." *Criminology* 24: 213–34.

———. 1987. "The Methodological Adequacy of Longitudinal Research on Crime." *Criminology* 25: 581–614.

———. 1988. "Science, Public Policy and the Career Paradigm." *Criminology* 26: 37–55.

———. 1990. *A General Theory of Crime.* Stanford, Calif.: Stanford University Press.

Gould, Larry C. 1969. "The Changing Structure of Property Crime in an Affluent Society." *Social Forces* 48 (September): 50–59.

Gould, Stephen J. 1981. *The Mismeasure of Man.* New York: Norton.

Goulden, J. C. 1984. *The Death Merchant: The Rise and Fall of Edwin P. Wilson.* New York: Simon and Schuster.

Gramckow, Heike. 1992. "New Money Laundering Law." *German American Legal Journal* 2 (October): 12–13.

Gravel, Senator Mike, ed. 1971. *The Pentagon Papers.* 4 vols. Boston: Beacon Press.

Greek, Cecil. 1990. "Is this the end of RICO?" Paper presented at the Academy of Criminal Justice Sciences meeting, Denver, CO, March 17.

Green, Gary. 1990. *Occupational Crime.* Chicago: Nelson-Hall.

Green, Helen T. 1979. *A Comprehensive Bibliography of Criminology and Criminal Justice Literature by Black Authors from 1895–1978.* Hyattsville, MD: Ummah Publications.

Green, Mark J., et al., eds. 1973. *The Monopoly Makers: Ralph Nader's Study Group Report on Regulation and Competition.* New York: Grossman.

Green, Wayne E., and Geyelin, Milo. 1990. "Asbestos Case Jury Awards $26.3 Million." *Wall Street Journal,* November 27, p. B6.

Greenberg, David. 1975. "The Incapacitative Effects of Imprisonment: Some Estimates." *Law and Society Review* 9 (Summer): 541–80.

———. 1981. *Crime and Capitalism.* Palo Alto, CA: Mayfield.

———, ed. 1993. *Crime and Capitalism: Readings in Marxist Criminology.* Philadelphia: Temple University Press.

Greenfeld, Lawrence A. 1988. *Drunk Driving.* Bureau of Justice Statistics Special Report. Washington, DC: U.S. Department of Justice, February.

———. 1996. "Child Victimizers: Violent Offenders and Their Victims." *Bureau of Justice Statistics Executive Summary.* March, NCJ 158625.

Greenfeld, Lawrence A., and Smith, Steven K. 1999. *American Indians and Crime.* Washington, DC: Bureau of Justice Statistics, February, NCJ 173386.

Greenfield, Lawrence A., and Snell, Tracy L. 1999. "Women Offenders," *Bureau of Justice Statistics, Special Report.* December NCJ175-688.

Greenhouse, Steven. 1999. "18 Major Retailers and Apparel Makers are Accused of Using Sweatshops." *New York Times,* January 14, p. A9.

Griffin, Katie. 1989. "Nestle Defends Its Third World Policies." *National Catholic Reporter,* February 24, p. 5.

Grimsley, Kristin D. 1996. "Cover Me—I'm Headed for Work." *Washington Post National Weekly Edition,* July 15–21, p. 34.

Gropper, Bernard A. 1985. "Probing the Links between Drugs and Crime." *Research in Brief.* National Institute of Justice, February.

Gross, Bertram. 1980. *Friendly Fascism: The New Face of Power in America.* New York: M. Evans and Co.

Groth, Nicholas, and Birnbaum, H. Jean. 1979. *Men Who Rape: The Psychology of the Offender.* New York: Plenum Press.

Groth, Nicholas, Burgess, Ann W., and Holmstrom, Lynda L. 1977. "Rape: Power, Anger and Sexuality." *American Journal of Psychiatriy* 134 (November): 1239–43.

Groth, Nicholas, et al. 1978. "A Study of the Child Molester: Myths and Realities." *LAE (Journal of the American Criminal Justice Association)* 41: 17–22.

Guerry, Andre M. 1833. *An Essay on Moral Statistics.* Paris: Crochard.

Gugliotta, Guy, and Leen, Jeff. 1989. *Kings of Cocaine.* New York: Simon and Schuster.

Gusfield, Joseph R. 1963. *Symbolic Crusades.* Urbana, IL: University of Illinois Press.

Haar, Robin N. 1992. "Examining Police Drug Corruption: Where to Go from Here." Paper presented at the Academy of Criminal Justice Sciences Meetings, Pittsburgh, PA, March.

Haas, Scott, 1985. "Bad Seeds and Social Policy: Two Histories." *Psychology Today,* December, pp. 73–74.

Hacker, Frederick J. 1976. *Crusaders, Criminals and Crazies, Terror and Terrorism in Our Time.* New York: W. W. Norton.

"Hacker Traced to Argentina." 1996. *Erie Morning News,* March 30, pp. A1–A2.

Hagan, Frank E. 1975. *Comparative Professionalism in an Occupational Arena: The Case of Rehabilitation.* Unpublished doctoral dissertation, Case Western Reserve University.

———. 1982. *Research Methods in Criminal Justice and Criminology.* New York: Macmillan.

———. 1983. "The Organized Crime Continuum: A Further Specification of a New Conceptual Model." *Criminal Justice Review* 8 (Fall): 52–57.

———. 1985. "Theoretical Range in Criminological Theory." Paper presented at the Academy of Criminal Justice Sciences Meetings, Las Vegas, NV, April.

———. 1986. "Sub Rosa Criminals: Spies as Neglected Criminal Types." *Clandestine Tactics and Technology* (A Technical and Background Data Service, International Chiefs of Police) 11: entire issue.

———. 1987a. "Book Review: James Mills' The Underground Empire: Where Crime and Government Embrace." *American Journal of Criminal Justice* 11: 128–30.

———. 1987b. "Espionage as Political Crime? A Typology of Spies." Paper presented at the American Society of Criminology Meetings, Montreal, November. Also published in *Journal of Security Administration,* 1989, 12 (1): 19–36.

———. 1987c. "The Global Fallacy and Theoretical Range in Criminological Theory." *Journal of Justice Issues* 2: 19–31.

———. 1988. "Varieties of Treason: Ideology and Criminality." Paper presented at the Academy of Criminal Justice Sciences Meetings, San Francisco, April.

———. 1989. "Single Subject Designs: Quantitative Case Studies." Paper presented at the Academy of Criminal Justice Sciences Meetings, Washington, DC, April.

———. 1991. "The Professional Criminal in the Nineties." Paper presented at the Academy of Criminal Justice Sciences Meetings, Nashville, TN, March.

———. 1992a. "Crimes of the Reagan Era." Paper presented at the Academy of Criminal Justice Sciences Meetings, Pittsburgh, PA, March.

———. 1992b. "From HUD to Iran-Contra: Crimes of the Reagan Administration." Paper presented at the American Society of Criminology Meetings, New Orleans, LA, November.

———. 1993. *Research Methods in Criminal Justice and Criminology,* 3rd edition. New York: Macmillan.

———. 1995. "Spies." Paper delivered at the American Society of Criminology Meetings. Boston, MA, November.

———. 1996a. "Panopticon." In *Encyclopedia of American Prisons,* edited by Marilyn D. McShane and Frank P. Williams, pp. 341–42. New York: Garland.

———. 1996b. "Varieties of White-CollarCrime: Corporate, Organizational, Occupational, Organized, Political and Professional." Paper presented at the National White-Collar Crime Center Symposium, Morgantown, WV, June.

———. 1997a. *Political Crime: Ideology and Criminality.* Boston: Allyn and Bacon.

———. 1997b. *Research Methods in Criminal Justice and Criminology.* 4th edition. Boston: Allyn and Bacon.

———. 1999. "White House Crime and Scandal: From Washington to Clinton." Paper presented at the American Society of Criminology Meetings, Toronto, Ontario, Canada, November.

———. 2000. "The Ghost of Chic Conwell: Professional Crime and Fraud in the Twenty-first Century." Paper presented at the National White-Collar Crime Summit, Austin, TX, May.

Hagan, Frank E., and Benekos, Peter J. 1991. "The Great Savings and Loan Scandal." *Journal of Security Administration* 14 (July): 41–64.

———. 1992. "What Charles Keating and 'Murph the Surf' Have in Common: A Symbiosis of Professional and Occupational and Corporate Crime." *Criminal Organizations* 7 (Spring): 3–27.

———. 1999. "The Nacirema Undergraduate as Criminal: Theoretical Analogies." Paper presented at the Academy of Criminal Justice Sciences Meetings, New Orleans, LA, March, 2000.

Hagan, Frank E., and Sussman, Marvin B., eds. 1988a. *Deviance and the Family.* New York: Haworth Press.

———. 1988b. "Deviance and the Family: Where Have We Been and Where Are We Going?" In *Deviance and the Family,* edited by Frank E. Hagan and Marvin B. Sussman, pp. 1–22. New York: Haworth Press.

Hagan, John. 1974. "Extra-Legal Attributes and Criminal Sentencing: An Assessment of a Sociological Viewpoint." *Law and Society Review* 8: 357–83.

———. 1987. "Review Essay: A Great Truth in the Study of Crime." *Criminology* 25: 421–28.

———. 1989. *Structural Criminology.* New Brunswick, NJ: Rutgers University Press.

———. 1993. "The Social Embeddedness of Crime and Unemployment." *Criminology* 31 (November): 465–91.

———. 1994. *Crime and Disrepute.* Thousand Oaks, CA: Pine Forge Press.

Hagan, John, Gillis, A.R., and Simpson, John. 1985. "The Class Structure of Gender and Delinquency: Toward a Power-Control Theory of Common Delinquent Behavior." *American Journal of Sociology* 90: 1151–78.

———. 1987. "Class in the Household: A Power-Control Theory of Gender and Delinquency." *American Journal of Sociology* 92: 788–816.

Hagan, John, and Palloni, Alberto. 1986. " 'Club Fed' and the Sentencing of White-Collar Offenders Before and After Watergate." *Criminology* 4: 603–21.

Hagan, John L., et al. 1980. "The Differential Sentencing of White-Collar Offenders in Ten Federal District Courts." *American Sociological Review* 45 (September): 802–20.

Hagedorn, Ann. 1991. "Prosecution of Child-Molestation Cases Grows More Wary in Wake of Acquittals." *Wall Street Journal,* April 15, p. B1.

Hagedorn, Ann, and Barrett, Paul M. 1991. "Securities Panel's Decisions Is Overturned." *Wall Street Journal,* April 22, p. B5.

Hagedorn, Ann, and Lambert, Wade. 1990. "U.S. Alleges Mob Runs Big Casino Union." *Wall Street Journal,* December 20, p. B6.

Hagedorn, John M. 1994. "Homeboys, Dope Fiends, Legits, and New Jacks." *Criminology* 32 (May): 197–219.

Hall, Jerome. 1952. *Theft, Law and Society.* Revised edition. Indianapolis, IN: Bobbs-Merrill.

Hall, Kevin G. 1992. "Truckers Set Up for Wrecks in Deadly Insurance Scam." *Erie Times News,* July 19, p. 7E.

Halperin, Morton H., et al. 1976. *The Lawless State: The Crimes of the U.S. Intelligence Agencies.* New York: Penguin.

Hamilton, Andrea. 1987. "Gang Leader's Manual Gave Youths Pointers on Shoplifting at Malls." *Erie Morning News,* April 17, p. 4A.

Hamilton, Peter. 1967. *Espionage and Subversion in an Industrial Society.* London: Hutchinson.

Hamit, Francis. 1991. "Taking on Corporate Counterintelligence." *Security Management,* October: 35–38.

Hamlin, John E. 1988. "The Misplaced Role of Rational Choice in Neutralization Theory." *Criminology* 26: 425–38.

Hamm, Mark. 1993. *American Skinheads: The Criminology and Control of Hate Crime.* Westport, CT: Praeger.

———, ed. 1994. *Hate Crime: International Perspectives on Causes and Control.* Cincinnati, OH: Anderson.

Hamm, Mark S., and Ferrell, Jeff. 1994. "Raps, Cops and Crime: Clarifying the 'Cop Killer' Controversy." *ACJS Today,* May/June: 1, 3, 29.

Hammer, Richard, ed. 1975. *Playboy's Illustrated History of Organized Crime.* Chicago: Playboy Press.

Haney, Charles, Banks, Curtis, and Zimbardo, Philip. 1973. "Interpersonal Dynamics in a Simulated Prison." *International Journal of Criminology and Penology* 1:69–97.

Haran, James F. 1982. *The Loser's Game: A Sociological Profile of 500 Armed Robbers.* Unpublished doctoral dissertation, Fordham University.

Hardt, Robert H., and Hardt, Sandra P. 1977. "On Determining the Quality of the Delinquency Self-Report Method." *Journal of Research in Crime and Delinquency* 14 (July): 247–61.

Harmer, Ruth Mulvey. 1975. *American Medical Avarice.* New York: Abelard-Schuman.

Harrington, Alan. 1972. *Psychopaths.* New York: Simon and Schuster.

Harris, John W., Jr. 1987. "Domestic Terrorism in the 1980s." *FBI Law Enforcement Bulletin.* October: 5–13.

Harris, Patricia, and Clarke, Ronald V. 1991. "Car Chopping, Parts Making and the Motor Vehicle Theft Law Enforcement Act of 1984." *Social Science Review* 75 (July): 228–37.

Harris, Sheldon H. 1994. *Factories of Death: Japanese Biological Warfare 1932–1945, and the American Cover Up.* New York: Routledge.

Harrist, Ron. 1995. "Notorious Bank Robber Met His Match in Mississippi." *Erie Morning News,* August 28, pp. A1–A2.

Hartung, Frank E. 1950. "White-Collar Offenses in the Wholesale Meat Industry in Detroit." *American Journal of Sociology* 56 (July): 25–32.

Haskell, Martin R., and Yablonsky, Lewis. 1978. *Criminology: Crime and Criminality.* 2nd edition. Chicago: Rand McNally.

———. 1983. *Crime and Delinquency.* 3rd edition. Chicago: Rand McNally.

Hastings, Donald W. 1965. "The Psychiatry of Presidential Assassination." *The Journal Lancet* 85 (March): 93–100, (April): 157–62, (May): 189–92, and (July): 294–301.

Hawkins, Darnell F., ed. 1986a. *Homicide Among Black Americans.* Lanham, MD.: University Press of America.

———. 1986b. "Race, Crime Type and Imprisonment." *Justice Quarterly* 3: 253–69.

———. 1987. "Beyond Anomalies: Rethinking the Conflict Perspective on Race and Punishment." *Social Forces* 65: 719–45.

Hawkins, Darnell F., et al. 2000. "Race, Ethnicity, and Serious and Violent Juvenile Offending." *OJJDP Juvenile Justice Bulletin,* June.

Hawkins, Gordon. 1969. "God and the Mafia." *The Public Interest* 14 (Winter): 24–51.

Hawkins, Gordon, and Zimring, Frank E. 1988. *Pornography in a Free Society.* New York: Cambridge University Press.

Hawkins, J. D., and Lishner, D. M. 1987. "Schooling and Delinquency." In *Handbook of Crime and Delinquency Prevention,* edited by Elmer H. Johnson, pp. 179–221. Westport, CT: Greenwood.

Hayeslip, David W., Jr. 1989. "Local-level Drug Enforcement: New Strategies." *NIJ Reports* March/April 2–7.

Haywood, Ian. 1987. *Faking It: Art and the Politics of Forgery.* New York: St. Martin's Press.

Hazelwood, Robert R., and Burgess, Ann W. 1987. "An Introduction to the Serial Rapist: Research by the FBI." *FBI Law Enforcement Bulletin* 58: 16–24.

Hazelwood, Robert R., and Warren, Janet. 1989. "The Serial Rapist: His Characteristics and Victim (Part I)." *FBI Law Enforcement Bulletin* 60: 10–17.

Healy, William. 1915. *The Individual Delinquent: A Textbook and Prognosis for All Concerned in Understanding Offenders.* Boston: Little, Brown.

Heath, James. 1963. *Eighteenth Century Penal Theory.* New York: Oxford University Press.

Hedges, Stephen J. 1998. "The New Face of Medicare." *U.S. News and World Report,* February 2, pp. 46–53.

Heilbroner, Robert L., et al. 1973. *In the Name of Profit: Profiles in Corporate Irresponsibility.* New York: Warner Paperback Library.

Heise, Lori. 1991. "Assaulted First by the Rapist. Then by Societal Response." *Washington Post National Weekly Edition,* December 16–22, p. 23.

Hellman, Peter. 1970. "One in Ten Shoppers Is a Shoplifter." *The New York Magazine,* March 15, p. 34.

"Hell's Angel's: Some Wheelers May Be Dealers." 1979. *Time,* July 2, p. 34.

Henderson, Joel H., and Simon, David R. 1994. *Crimes of the Criminal Justice System.* Cincinnati, OH: Anderson.

Henriques, Diana. 1995. "Hoffenberger Confesses to Ponzi Scheme." *New York Times,* April 21, p. C3.

Henry, Stuart, and Milanovic, Dragan. 1993. "Back to Basics: A Postmodern Redefinition of Crime." *The Critical Criminologist* 5: 1–2, 12.

———. 1996. *Constitutive Criminology: Beyond Postmodernism.* London: Sage.

Hepburn, John R. 1984. "Occasional Property Crime." In *Major Forms of Crime,* edited by Robert F. Meier, pp. 73–94. Beverly Hills, CA: Sage.

Herbert, Bob. 1999. "Fleeing the Taliban." *New York Times,* October 25, p. A27.

Herling, John. 1962. *The Great Price Conspiracy: The Story of the Antitrust Violations in the Electrical Industry.* Washington, DC: Luce.

Herman, Edward S. 1982. *The Real Terror Network: Terrorism in Fact and Propaganda.* Boston: South End Press.

Herman, Judith Lewis. 1981. *Father-Daugher Incest.* Cambridge, MA: Harvard University Press.

Hermann, Donald H. J. 1983. *The Insanity Defense.* Springfield, IL: Charles C. Thomas.

Herrnstein, Richard J. 1983. "Some Criminogenic Traits of Offenders." In *Crime and Public Policy,* edited by James Q. Wilson, pp. 31–49. San Francisco: Institute for Contemporary Studies.

Herrnstein, Richard J., and Murray, Charles. 1994. *The Bell Curve: The Reshaping of American Life by Differences in Intelligence.* New York: The Free Press.

Hersh, Seymour. 1990. "The Iran-Contra Committees: Did They Protect Reagan." *New York Times Magazine,* April 29, pp. 47–49.

———. 1994. "The Wild East." *Atlantic Monthly,* July, pp. 61–86.

Herskovits, Melville J. 1930. *The Anthropometry of the American Negro.* New York: Columbia University Press.

"Hertz Admits to Driving Over the Line." 1988. *Newsweek,* February 8, p. 48.

Heussenstamm, F. K. 1971. "Bumper Stickers and the Cops." *Trans-Action* 8: 32–33.

Hevesi, Dennis. 1990. "8 at Law Firm Accused of Bribing Witnesses and Faking Evidence." *New York Times,* January 12, p. 28.

Hickey, Eric W. 1986. "The Etiology of Victimization in Serial Crime." Paper presented at the American Society of Criminology, Atlanta, November.

"Hidden Cameras Project, Seattle, Washington," 1978. Exemplary Projects, A Program of the National Institute of Law Enforcement and Criminal Justice. Washington, DC: Government Printing Office. August.

Higham, Charles. 1982. *Trading with the Enemy: An Exposé of the Nazi-American Money Plot, 1933–1949.* New York: Delacorte Press.

"Highway Safety: Kentucky's Textbook Case in Drunk Driving." 1988. *U.S. News and World Report,* May 30, p. 7.

Hills, Stuart L. 1971. *Crime, Power and Morality.* Scranton, PA: Chandler.

———, ed. 1987. *Corporate Violence: Injury and Death for Profit.* Totowa, NJ: Rowman and Littlefield.

Hilts, Philip J. 1995. "U.S. Turning to Grand Juries to Scrutinize Tobacco Industry." *New York Times,* July 26, pp. A1, C19.

Hindelang, Michael. 1970. "The Commitment of Delinquents to Their Misdeeds: Do Delinquents Drift." *Social Problems* 17 (Spring): 509.

———. 1971. "Extroversion, Neuroticism and Self-Reported Delinquent Involvement." *Journal of Research in Crime and Delinquency* 8 (January): 23–31.

———. 1973. "Causes of Delinquency: A Partial Replication and Extension." *Social Problems* 21 (Spring): 471–87.

———. 1974. "The Uniform Crime Reports Revisited." *Journal of Criminal Justice* 2 (Spring): 1–17.

———. 1979. "Age, Sex, and the Versatility of Delinquent Involvements." *Social Problems* 18: 522–35.

Hindelang, Michael, Hirschi, Travis, and Weis, Joseph. 1979. "Correlates of Delinquency: The Illusion of Discrepancy between Self-Report and Official Data." *American Sociological Review* 44: 95–110.

Hindelang, Michael, Gottfredson, Michael, and Flanagan, T. 1981. *Sourcebook of Criminal Justice Statistics, 1980.* "Washington, DC: Government Printing Office.

Hindelang, Michael J., et al. 1977. "Correlates of Self-Reported Victimization and Perceptions of Neighbourhood Safety." In *Selected Papers from the Social Indicators Conference, 1975,* edited by Lynn Hewitt and David Brusegard. Edmonton: Alberta Bureau of Statistics.

Hirschi, Travis. 1969. *Causes of Delinquency.* Berkeley: University of California Press.

———. 1983. "Crime and the Family." In *Crime and Public Policy,* edited by James Q. Wilson, pp. 53–68. San Francisco: Institute for Contemporary Social Studies.

Hirschi, Travis, and Gottfredson, Michael R. 1987. "Causes of White-Collar Crime." *Criminology* 25 (4): 949–74.

———. 1989. "The Significance of White-Collar Crime for a General Theory of Crime." *Criminology* 27(2): 359–71.

———. 1990. "Substantive Positivism and the Idea of Crime." *Rationality and Society* 2 (October): 412–28.

Hirschi, Travis, and Hindelang, Michael J. 1977. "Intelligence and Delinquency: A Revisionist Review." *American Sociological Review* 42 (August): 571–87.

Hirsh, Michael. 1998. "The Hunt Hits Home." *Newsweek,* December 14, p. 48.

Hochstedler, Ellen, ed. 1984. *Corporations as Criminals.* Beverly Hills, CA: Sage.

Hockstader, Lee. 1995. "Crime Atop Chaos: In Post-Communist Russia, the Strong Arm of the Mafiya Is Everywhere." *Washington Post National Weekly Edition,* March 20–26, pp. 6–7.

Hofstadter, Richard. 1965. *The Paranoid Style in American Politics.* New York: Alfred A. Knopf.

Holden, Richard. 1986. "The Road to Fundamentalist and Identity Movements." Paper presented at the Academy of Criminal Justice Sciences meetings, St. Louis, March.

Hollin, Clive. 1989. *Psychology and Crime: An Introduction to Criminological Psychology.* London: Routledge.

Hollinger, Richard C., and Lanza-Kaduce, Lonn. 1990. "The Process of Criminalization: The Case of Computer Crime Laws." In *Criminal Behavior,* edited by Delos H. Kelly, pp. 29–43. New York: St. Martin's Press.

Holmes, Ronald M. 1983. *The Sex Offender and the Criminal Justice System.* Springfield, IL: Charles C. Thomas.

———. 1989. *Profiling Violent Crimes: An Investigative Tool.* Newbury Park, CA: Sage.

———. 1991. *Sex Crimes.* Newbury Park, CA: Sage.

Holmes, Ronald M., and DeBurger, James. 1988. *Serial Murder.* Beverly Hills, CA: Sage.

Holt, Jim. 1994. "Anti-Social Science?" *New York Times,* October 19, p. A15.

Holzman, Harold R., and Pines, Sharon. 1979. "Buying Sex: The Phenomenology of Being a 'John.' " Paper presented at the American Society of Criminology Meetings, Philadelphia, PA, November.

"Home Repair Scam Draws Jail Term." 1986. *Erie Morning News,* May 1, p. 22A.

"Hong Kong: Battling the Triads." 1986. *C. J. International* 2, September/October: 5.

Hood, Roger, and Sparks, Richard. 1971. *Key Issues in Criminology.* New York: McGraw-Hill.

Hooton, Earnest. 1939. *Crime and the Man.* Westport, CT: Greenwood.

Hopper, Columbus B. 1991. "The Changing Role of Women in Outlaw Motorcycle Gangs: From Partner to Sexual

Property." Paper presented at the American Society of Criminology Meetings, San Francisco, CA, November.

Howard, Pat. 1990. "The Shadow Grows Again." *Erie Morning News.* January 6, p. 2B.

Howe, Kenneth. 1997. "Blue Shield Pays Fine for Fraud." *San Francisco Chronicle,* May 3, p. B1.

Howlett, James B., Hanfland, Kenneth A., and Ressler, Robert K. 1986. "The Violent Criminal Apprehension Program: VICAP: A Progress Report." *FBI Law Enforcement Bulletin,* December: 14–18.

"How We Can Win the War on Poverty." 1989. *Fortune,* April, p. 10.

Huang, Carol. 1999. "Study: Shoplifters Prefer Small and Expensive." APBNews.com, November 24.

———. 2000. "Merrill Lynch Probes $40 Million Theft." APBnews.com, January 7.

Hubbard, L. Ron. 1963. *Dianetics.* New York: Paperback Library. Huff, C. Ronald.

"Historical Explanations of Crime: From Demons to Politics." In *Criminal Behavior: Text and Readings in Criminology,* pp. 161–76. New York: St. Martin's Press.

Huff, Darrell. 1966. *How to Lie with Statistics,* New York: Wiley.

Humphrey, John A., and Fogarty, Timothy J. 1987. "Race and Plea Bargained Outcomes: A Research Note." *Social Forces* 66: 176–82.

Humphreys, Laud. 1970. *Tearoom Trade: Impersonal Sex in Public Places.* Chicago: Aldine.

Hunt, Morton. 1974. *Sexual Behavior in the 1970s.* New York: Dell Books.

Hunter, Edward. 1951. *Brain-Washing in Red China.* New York: Vanguard Press.

Hunter, J. Michael. 1983. "All Organized Crime Isn't Mafia: A Case Study of a Non-traditional Criminal Organization." Paper presented at the Academy of Criminal Justice Sciences meetings, San Antonio, TX, March.

Hutchings, Barry, and Mednick, Sarnoff A. 1977. "Criminality in Adoptees and Their Adoptive and Biological Parents: A Pilot Study." In *Biosocial Bases in Criminal Behavior,* edited by Sarnoff A. Mednick and Karl Christiansen, pp. 127–42. New York: Gardner Press.

Hyde, H. Montgomery. 1980. *The Atom Bomb Spies.* New York: Ballantine.

Ianni, Francis A J. 1972. *A Family Business: Kinship and Social Control in Organized Crime.* New York: Russell Sage.

———. 1973. *Ethnic Succession in Organized Crime.* Washington, DC: Government Printing Office.

———. 1974. *Black Mafia: Ethnic Succession in Organized Crime.* New York: Simon and Schuster.

Icove, David, Seger, Karl, and VonStorch, William. 1995. *Computer Crime: A Crimefighter's Handbook.* Sebastopol, CA: O'Reilly and Associates.

Ignatius, David. 2000. "Buccaneers of the 21st Century." *Washington Post,* January 5, p. A21.

Impoco, Jim. 1987. "Porn Flourishes in Japan." *Erie Daily Times,* March 11, p. 10B.

Inciardi, James A. 1970. "The Adult Firesetter: A Typology." *Criminology* 8 (August): 145–55.

———. 1975. *Careers in Crime.* Chicago: Rand McNally.

———. 1977. "In Search of the Class Cannon: A Field Study of Professional Pickpockets." In *Street Ethnography,* edited by Robert S. Weppner, pp. 55–78. Beverly Hills, CA: Sage.

———. 1979. "Heroin Use and Street Crime." *Crime and Delinquency* 25: 335–46.

———, ed. 1980. *Radical Criminology: The Coming Crisis.* Beverly Hills, CA.: Sage.

———, ed. 1981. *The Drugs-Crime Connection.* Beverly Hills, CA: Sage.

———. 1983. "On Grift at the Superbowl: Professional Pickpockets and the NFL." In *Career Criminals,* edited by Gordon Waldo, pp. 31–41. Beverly Hills, CA: Sage.

———. 1984. "Professional Theft." In *Major Forms of Crime,* edited by Robert F. Meier, pp. 221–43. Beverly Hills, CA: Sage.

———. 1990. *The Drug Legalization Debate.* Newbury Park, CA: Sage.

———. 1992. *The War on Drugs II.* Mountain View, CA: Mayfield.

Inciardi, James A., and McElrath, Karen, eds. 2001. *The American Drug Scene.* 2nd edition Los Angeles: Roxbury.

Ingersoll, Bruce. 1991. "FDA Panel Charges Pfizer Unit Sought to Prolong Sale of Flawed Heart Valve." *Wall Street Journal.* September 13, p. A2.

Ingraham, Barton L. 1979. *Political Crime in Europe: A Comparative Study of France, Germany and England.* Berkeley: University of California Press.

Interpol. 1999. *International Crime Statistics.* Lyons, France: Interpol Secretariat.

Irvine, Martha. 2000. "Governor Orders Execution Moratorium." *Erie Morning News,* February 1, p. 5A.

Irwin, Jim. 2000. "Three Defendants Convicted in Date-Rape Drug Death." *Associated Press,* March 15.

Isaac, Rael J., and Armat, Virginia C. 1990. *Madness in the Streets: How Psychiatry and the Law Abandoned the Mentally Ill.* New York: The Free Press.

Isikoff, Michael, 1990. "Has Thornburgh Gone Soft on 'Crime in the Suites'?" *Erie Morning News,* April 28, p. 2B.

Jacks, Irving, and Cox, Steven G. eds. 1984. *Psychological Approaches to Crime and Its Correction: Theory, Research, Practice.* Chicago: Nelson-Hall.

Jackson, Bruce. 1972. *In the Life: Versions of the Criminal Experience.* New York: New American Library.

Jackson, Jerome. 1994. "Fraud Masters: Professional Credit Card Offenders and Crime." *Criminal Justice Review.* 19, January, 34–58.

Jacobs, James R. 1987. "Drinking and Crime." *Crime File.* National Institute of Justice.

———. 1988. "The Law and Criminology of Drunk Driving." In *Crime and Justice: A Review of Research,* vol.

10, edited by Michael Tonry and Norval Morris, pp. 171–230. Chicago: University of Chicago Press.

Jacobs, Patricia A., et al. 1965. "Aggressive Behavior, Mental Subnormality, and the XYY Male." *Nature* 208 (December): 1351–52.

Jacoby, Joan E., Gramckow, Heike P., and Ratledge, Edward C. 1992. *Asset Forfeiture Programs.* Washington, DC: Jefferson Institute for Justice Studies, February.

Jacoby, Joseph E., ed. 1979. *Classics of Criminology,* Oak Park, IL: Moore Publishing.

Jacoby, Tamar. 1988. "A Web of Crime behind Bars." *Newsweek,* October 24, pp. 76–81.

Jacoby, Tamar, Sandza, Richard, and Parry, Robert. 1988. "Going After Dissidents." *Newsweek,* February 8, p. 29.

James, Jennifer. 1977. "Prostitutes and Prostitution." In *Deviants: Voluntary Actors in a Hostile World,* edited by Edward Sagarin and Fred Montanino, pp. 365–429. New York: General Learning.

———. 1978. "The Prostitute as Victim." In *The Victimization of Women,* edited by Jane R. Chapman and Margaret Gates, pp. 175–201. Beverly Hills, CA: Sage.

Jamieson, Katherine M. 1995. *The Organization of Corporate Crime: An Inquiry into the Dynamics of Antitrust Violation.* Beverly Hills, CA: Sage.

Janeway, Elizabeth. 1981. "Incest: A Rational Look at the Oldest Taboo." *Ms.,* November, pp. 61–64, 78, 81, 109.

"Japan: Putting the Mafia to Shame." 1977. *Time,* October 17, pp. 40, 46.

"Japanese TV: Prime-Time Violence and Mayhem." 1992. *Erie Times News,* June 20, p. 3–A.

Japan Yearbook. 1944. "Tokyo: Foreign Affairs Association of Japan." Cited in *Japan's Imperial Conspiracy,* by David Bergamini, 1971. New York: William Morrow and Company.

Jaroff, Leon. 1988. "Fighting Against Flimflam." *Time,* June 13, p. 72.

———. 1996. "Assembly-Line Sexism." *Time,* May 6, pp. 56–57.

Jeffrey, C. Ray. 1978. "Criminology as an Interdisciplinary Behavioral Science." *Criminology* 16 (August): 153–56.

Jellinek, E. M. 1960. *The Disease Concept of Alcoholism.* New Brunswick, NJ: College and University Press.

Jenkins, Philip. 1982. "The Long Resistance: The Enemies of Positivism 1890–1945." Paper presented at the Academy of Criminal Justice Sciences Meetings, Louisville, KY, March.

———. 1984. *Crime and Justice: Issues and Ideas.* Monterey, CA: Brooks/Cole.

———. 1988. "Myth and Murder: The Serial Killer Panic of 1983–5." *Criminal Justice Research Bulletin* 3: 1–7.

———. 1989. "Book Review: Update on Organized Crime Down Under." *Criminal Organizations* 1: 12.

———. 1992a. "African-American and Serial Homicide." Paper presented at the Northeastern Academy of Criminal Justice Sciences Meetings, Newport, RI, June.

———. 1992b. *Intimate Enemies: Moral Panics in Contemporary Britain.* Hawthorne, NY: Aldine de Gruyter.

Jenkins, Philip, and Katkin, Daniel M. 1990. "Occult Criminality: Myth and Reality in a Contemporary Moral Panic." Paper presented at the American Society of Criminology Meetings, Baltimore, MD, November.

Jensen, Gary, and Eve, Raymond. 1976. "Sex Differences in Delinquency: An Examination of Popular Sociological Explanations." *Criminology* 13: 427–48.

Jesilow, Paul D., Pontell, Henry N., and Geis, Gilbert. 1985. "Medical Criminals: Physicians and White-Collar Offenses." *Justice Quarterly* 2: 151–65.

"Jewel Thieves Linked to Yugoslav Civil War." 1991. *Erie Morning News,* December 23, p. 5A.

Johnson, Ann B. 1990. *Out of Bedlam: The Truth about Deinstitutionalization.* New York: Basic Books.

Johnson, Bruce D., et al. 1983. "Economic Behavior of Street Opiate Users." New York, NY: Narcotic and Drug Research, Inc.

———. 1985. *Taking Care of Business.* Lexington, MA: Lexington Books.

Johnson, Dirk. 2000. "Cheaters' Final Response: So What?" *New York Times,* May 16, p. A6.

Johnson, Elmer H. 1978. *Crime, Correction and Society.* 4th edition. Homewood, IL: Dorsey.

———. 1990. "Yakuza (Criminal Gangs) in Japan: Characteristics and Management in Prison." Paper presented at the Academy of Criminal Justice Sciences Meetings, Denver, CO, March.

Johnson, Eric A., and Monkkonen, Eric H. 1996. *The Civilization of Crime: Violence in Town and Country Sinice the Middle Ages.* Champaign, IL: University of Illinois Press.

Johnson, Haynes. 1991. *Sleepwalking Through History: America in the Reagan Years.* New York: W. M. Norton.

Johnson, M. P. 1995. "Patriarchal Terrorism and Common Couple Violence: Two Forms of Violence Against Women." *Journal of Marriage and the Family* 57: 283–294.

Johnson, Richard E. 1979. *Juvenile Delinquency and Its Origins.* Cambridge, MA: Cambridge University Press.

———. 1986. "Family Structure and Delinquency: General Patterns and Gender Differences." *Criminology* 24: 65–84.

Johnson, Terry. 1987. "A Little House of Horrors: Murder in Philadelphia." *Newsweek,* April 6, p. 29.

Jones, Del. 1997. "48% of Workers Admit to Unethical or Illegal Acts." *USA Today,* April 3, pp. 1–4.

"Judge Agrees to TMI Plea Bargain." 1984. *Erie Morning News,* March 1, p. 3A.

Judge, Arthur V. 1930. *The Elizabethan Underworld.* London: George Routledge.

"Jury Selection Begins in 'Eco-Terrorism' Trial." 1991. *Erie Morning News,* June 11, p. 5A.

Kalish, Carol B. 1988. *International Crime Rates.* Bureau of Justice Statistics Special Report. Washington, DC: Government Printing Office, May.

Kalven, Harry, Jr., and Zeisel, Hans. 1966. *The American Jury.* Boston: Little, Brown.

Kandel, Elizabeth, and Mednick, Sarnoff A. 1991. "Perinatal Complications Predict Violent Offending." *Criminology* 29 (August): 519–29.

Kane, Edward J. 1989. *The S&L Insurance Mess: How Did It Happen?* Washington, DC: The Urban Institute Press.

Kaplan, David E. 1991. "Japanese Mob." *Criminal Organizations* 6 (Fall): 1–3.

Kaplan, David E., and Dubro, Alec. 1986. *Yakuza: The Explosive Account of Japan's Criminal Underworld.* Reading, MA: Addison-Wesley.

Kappeler, Victor E., Sluder, Richard D., and Alpert, Geoffrey P. 1994. *Forces of Deviance: Understanding the Darker Side of Policing.* Prospect Heights, IL: Waveland Press.

Karchmer, Clifford. 1977. "The Underworld Turns Fire into Profit." *Firehouse Magazine.* Read into the *Congressional Record,* U.S. Senate, October 4, 1977, p. S 16263.

Karmen, Andrew. 1974. "Agents Provocateurs in the Contemporary U.S. Leftist Movement." In *The Criminologist: Crime and the Criminal,* edited by Charles Reasons, pp. 209–25. Pacific Palisades, CA: Goodyear Publishing Company.

Katkin, Daniel. 1982. *The Nature of Criminal Law.* Monterey, CA: Brooks/Cole.

Katz, Jack. 1988. *Seductions of Crime: Moral and Sensual Attractions in Doing Evil.* New York: Basic Books.

Kauzlarich, David, and Kramer, Ronald C. 1998. *Crimes of the American Nuclear State.* Boston: Northeastern University Press.

Keil, Thomas J., and Vito, Gennaro F. 1989. "Race, Homicide Severity, and Application of the Death Penalty: A Consideration of the Barnett Scale." *Criminology* 27 (August): 511–31.

Keller, John J. 1991. "Dialing for Free: Thanks to Hackers Cellular Phone Firms Now Face a Crime Wave." *Wall Street Journal,* June 14, pp. A1, A7.

Kelling, George. 1988a. "Eliminating Graffiti from New York Subway Trains." Paper presented at the American Society of Criminology Meetings, Chicago, November.

———. 1988b. "Police and Communities: The Quiet Revolution." *Perspectives in Policing.* National Institute of Justice, June.

———. 1988c. "What Works: Research and the Police." *Crime File.* National Institute of Justice.

Kelly, Katy. 1999. "A New York Shell Game: Cheating 101." *U.S. News and World Report,* December, p. 57.

Kelly, Robert J., ed. 1986. *Organized Crime: A Global Perspective.* Totowa, NJ: Rowman and Littlefield.

———. 1988. "Review Essay/Dirty Dollars: Organized Crime and Its Illicit Partnership in the Waste Industry." *Criminal Justice Ethics* 7: 46–68.

———. 1990. "Succession by Murder: Reflections on Paul Castellano's Funeral and the Rise of John Gotti." *Criminal Organizations* 5 (1): 16–18.

———. 1992. "Trapped in the Folds of Discourse: Theorizing About the Underworld." *Journal of Contemporary Criminal Justice* 8 (February): 11–35.

Kelly, Robert J., Schatzberg, Rufus, and Ryan, Patrick J. 1995. "Primitive Capitalist Accumulation: Russia as a Racket." *Journal of Contemporary Criminal Justice* 11: 257–75.

Kelman, Herbert C., and Hamilton, V. Lee. 1988. *Crimes of Obedience: Toward a Social Psychology of Authority and Responsibility.* New Haven: Yale University Press.

Kempe, Ruth S., and Kempe, C. Henry. 1978. *Child Abuse.* Cambridge, MA: Harvard University Press.

Kenney, Dennis J., and Finckenauer, James O. 1995. *Organized Crime in America.* Belmont, CA: Wadsworth.

Kerner, Otto. 1968. *The Report of the National Advisory Commission on Civil Disorders: The Riot Commission Report.* New York: Bantam Books.

Kerner, Otto. 1968. *U.S. Riot Commission Report.* Washington, DC: Government Printing Office.

Kerr, Peter. 1987. "Chasing the Heroin from Plush Hotel to Mean Streets." *New York Times,* August 11, p. 1B.

———. 1993. "National Medical to Pay $125 Million in Accord." *New York Times,* September 30, p. D2.

Kessler, Ronald. 1989. *Moscow Station: How the KGB Penetrated the American Embassy.* New York: Charles Scribner's Sons.

Kidder, Rushworth L. 1983. *Connecting Law and Society.* Englewood Cliffs, NJ: Prentice-Hall.

———. 1986. "Unmasking Terrorism." *Christian Science Monitor Special Report,* May, pp. 17–20.

King, Harry, and Chambliss, William J. 1984. *Harry King: A Professional Thief's Journal.* New York: Wiley.

King, Martin Luther, Jr. 1963. "Letter from Birmingham Jail." In *Why We Can't Wait.* New York: Harper and Row.

Kingsworth, Rodney, and Jungsten, Michael. 1988. "Driving Under the Influence: The Impact of Legislative Reform on Court Sentencing Practices." *Crime and Delinquency* 34: 3–28.

Kinkead, Gwen. 1991. "Chinatown I" and "Chinatown II." *The New Yorker,* June 10, pp. 45–83; June 17, pp. 56–84.

Kinney, David. 1998. "Fourteen Students Charged in Riot No Longer Attend Penn State." *Erie Morning News,* December 1, p. 6C.

Kinney, Joseph A. 1990. "Why Did Paul Die?" *Newsweek,* September 10, p. 11.

Kinsey, Alfred, et al. 1948. *Sexual Behavior in the Human Male.* Philadelphia: W. B. Saunders.

———. 1952. *Sexual Behavior in the Human Female.* Philadelphia: W. B. Saunders.

Kinsey, Richard, Lea, John, and Young, Jock. 1986. *Losing the Fight Against Crime.* London: Blackwell.

Kirkham, James F. 1969. *Assassination and Political Violence.* Washington, DC: Government Printing Office.

Kirkpatrick, Clifford, and Kanin, Eugene J. 1957. "Male Sex Aggression on a University Campus." *American Sociological Review* 22 (February): 52–58.

Kitsuse, John L., and Cicourel, A. V. 1963. "A Note on the Use of Official Statistics." *Social Problems* 11 (Fall): 131–38.

Kitsuse, John L., and Dietrick, David C. 1970. "Delinquent Boys: A Critique." In *Society, Delinquency, and Delinquent Behavior,* edited by Harwin L. Voss, pp. 238–45. Boston: Little, Brown.

Kittrie, Nicholas, N., and Wedlock, Eldon D., Jr., eds. 1986. *The Tree of Liberty: A Documentary History of Rebellion and Political Crime in America.* Baltimore, MD: Johns Hopkins University Press.

Klanwatch. 1985. "Domestic Terrorists: The KKK in the 'Fifth Era.' " *Klanwatch Intelligence Report* (The Southern Poverty Law Center, Montgomery, Alabama), February, pp. 5–10.

Klaus, Patsy. 1999. "Carjackings in the United States, 1992–96." *Bureau of Justice Statistics Special Report,* March, NCJ 171145.

Kleck, Gary C. 1981. "Racial Discrimination in Sentencing: A Critical Evaluation of the Evidence with Additional Evidence on the Death Penalty." *American Sociological Review* 48: 783–805.

———. 1984. "The Assumptions of Gun Control." In *Firearms and Violence,* edited by D. B. Kates. San Francisco, CA: Pacific Institute for Public Policy Research.

———. 1992. "Handgun Violence: The Other Story." *Research in Review* (Florida State University), Spring/Summer: 3–5.

Kleiman, Mark A. R., et al. 1988. *Street-Level Drug Enforcement: Examining the Issues.* National Institute of Justice, August.

Klein, Joe. 1996. "The Predator Problem." *Newsweek,* April 29, p. 32.

Klein, John F. 1974. "Professional Theft: The Utility of a Concept." *Canadian Journal of Criminology and Corrections* 16 (April): 133–43.

Klein, John F., and Montague, A. F. 1977. *Check Forgers.* Lexington, MA: Lexington Books.

Klein, Malcolm W. 1990. "Having an Investment in Violence: Some Thoughts about the American Street Gang." Presentation upon receiving the Edwin H. Sutherland Award, American Society of Criminology Meetings, Baltimore, MD, November.

Klein, Malcolm W., and Maxson, Cheryl L. 1989. "Street Gang Violence." In *Violent Crime, Violent Criminals,* edited by Neil A. Weiner and Marvin W. Wolfgang, pp. 198–234. Newbury Park, CA: Sage.

Klein, Malcolm W., Maxson, Cheryl L., and Cunningham, Lea C. 1991. " 'Crack' Street Gangs and Violence." *Criminology* 29 (November): 623–50.

Klein, Stephen P., Turner, Susan, and Petersilia, Joan. 1988. *Does Race Make a Difference in Sentencing?* Santa Monica, CA: Rand Corporation.

Kleiner, Carolyn, and Lord, Mary. 1999. "The Cheating Game." *U.S. News and World Report,* November 22, pp. 55–66.

Kleinknecht, William. 1995. *The New Ethnic Mobs.* New York: Simon and Schuster.

———. 1996. *The New Ethic Mobs.* New York: The Free Press.

Klemke, Lloyd W. 1992. *The Sociology of Shoplifting: Boosters and Snitches Today.* Westport, CT: Praeger.

Klepper, Steven, Nagin, Daniel, and Tierney, Luke-Jon. 1983. "Discrimination in the Criminal Justice System: A Critical Appraisal of the Literature." In *Research in Sentencing: A Search for Reform,* volume 2, edited by Alfred Blumstein, Jacqueline Cohen, Susan E. Martin, and Michael H. Tonry, pp. 55–128. Washington, DC: National Academy Press.

Klockars, Carl. 1974. *The Professional Fence.* New York: The Free Press.

———. 1979. "The Contemporary Crisis of Marxist Criminology." *Criminology* 16 (Fall): 477–515.

Knapp Commission Report on Police Corruption. 1972. New York: Braziller.

Kneece, Jack. 1986. *Family Treason: The Walker Spy Ring Case.* New York: Stein and Day.

Kobrin, Solomon. 1982. "The Use of Life History Documents for the Development of Delinquency Theory." In *The Jack-Roller at Seventy: A Fifty-Year Follow-Up,* edited by Jon D. Snodgrass, pp. 153–65. Lexington, MA: D. C. Heath.

Koenig, Daniel J. 1991. "Conventional Crime." In *Criminology: A Canadian Perspective,* 2nd edition, edited by Rick Linden.. Toronto: Holt, Rinehart, Winston.

Koenig, Daniel J., et al. 1983. "Routine Activities, Impending Social Change, and Policing." *Canadian Police College Journal* 7 (2): 96–136.

Kohn, George C. 1989. *Encyclopedia of American Scandal.* New York: Facts on File.

Kohut, John. 1997. "Kidnap Corp." Asia-Inc.Online.com.

Kolata, Gina. 1994. "Bodies of Patients Newly Dead Used for Practice by Hospitals." *New York Times,* December 15, p. A14.

Kolbert, Elizabeth. 1994. "Television Gets Closer Look as a Factor in Real Violence." *New York Times,* December 14, pp. A1, A13.

Konstantinova, Natalia. 1997. "South of Russia May Become the Centre of Illegal Import." *The Independent* (Moscow), 8, p. 16.

Kornhauser, Ruth. 1978. *Social Sources of Delinquency and Its Origins.* Chicago: University of Chicago Press.

Koski, Patricia R. 1988. "Family Violence and Nonfamily Deviance: Taking Stock of the Literature." In *Deviance and the Family,* edited by Frank E. Hagan and Marvin B. Sussman, pp. 23–46. New York: Haworth Press.

Krahn, Harvey, Hartnagel, Timothy, and Gartrell, John. 1986. "Income Inequality, and Homicide Rates: Cross-National Data and Criminological Theories." *Criminology* 24: 269–95.

Krane, Jim. 1999. "Russian Mobsters Kick Down World Doors." APBnews.com, March 7.

———. 2000. "Databases Revolutionize Pawnshop Policing." APBnews.com, February 7.

Kraska, Peter B. 1989. "The Sophistication of Hans Jurgen Eysenck: An Analysis and Critique of Contemporary Biological Criminology." *Criminal Justice Research Bulletin* 4 (5): 1–7.

Kratcoski, Peter C. 1988. "Families Who Kill." In *Deviance and the Family,* edited by Frank E. Hagan and Marvin B. Sussman, pp. 47–70. New York: Haworth.

Krauss, Clifford. 1995. "Burglaries Show Big Decline in New York and Its Suburbs." *New York Times,* March 15, p. A12.

Kretschmer, Ernst. 1926. *Physique and Character.* Translated by W. J. H. Sprott. New York: Harcourt, Brace.

Krisberg, Barry. 1975. *Crime and Privilege: Toward a New Criminology.* Englewood Cliffs, NJ: Prentice-Hall.

Kruttschnitt, Candace, et al. 1987. "Abuse-Resistant Youth: Some Factors That May Inhibit Violent Criminal Behavior." *Social Forces* 66: 501–19.

Krzycki, Lenny. 1994. "It's Not That Simple." *ACJS Today,* September/October: 1, 3, 28.

Kuhl, Anna F. 1985. "Battered Women Who Murder: Victims or Offenders?" In *The Changing Roles of Women in the Criminal Justice System,* edited by Imogene L. Moyer, pp. 197–216. Prospect Heights, IL: Waveland Press.

Kuhn, Thomas S. 1962. *The Structures of Scientific Revolutions.* Chicago: University of Chicago Press.

Kuper, Leo. 1981. *Genocide: Its Political Use in the Twentieth Century.* New Haven: Yale University Press.

Kurki, Leena. 1999. "Incorporating Restorative and Community Justice into American Sentencing and Corrections." (Sentencing and Corrections Issues for the 21st Century) National Institute of Justice, *Research in Brief.* Papers for the Executive Sessions on Sentencing and Corrections No. 3, September.

Kurtz, Howard. 1989. "Across the Nation, Rising Outrage." *Washington Post,* April 4, pp. 1A, 14A, 16A.

Kutchins, Herb. 1988. "Making Criminals Crazy: The Impact of New Psychiatric Diagnosis on the Criminal Justice System." Paper presented at the American Society of Criminology, Chicago, November.

Kwitny, Jonathan. 1979. *Vicious Circles: The Mafia in the Marketplace.* New York: W. W. Norton.

Lab, Steven P., and Hirschel, J. David. 1988a. "Climatological Conditions and Crime: The Forecast is . . . ?" *Justice Quarterly* 5: 281–99.

———. 1988b. " 'Clouding the Issues': The Failure to Recognize Methodological Problems." *Justice Quarterly* 5: 311–17.

Lachica, Eduardo. 1991. "Businesses Try to Get Smart with Ex-Spies." *Wall Street Journal,* August 8, p. B1.

Ladinsky, Jack. 1963. "Careers of Lawyers, Law Practice and Legal Institutions." *American Sociological Review* 28 (February): 47–54.

Lafave, Wayne R. 1964. *Arrest: The Decision to Take a Suspect into Custody.* Boston: Little, Brown.

LaFraniere, Sharon. 1999. "A Money Trail That Leads to Yeltsin." *Washington Post,* September 13, p. 16.

Landers, Ann. 1991. "Bare Facts Shocking to Mother of Son Bound for Princeton." *Erie Times News,* October 6, p. C8.

Landsberg, Mitchell. 1992. "Eddie's Kids." *Erie Morning News,* April 5, pp. 1A, 9A.

Laner, Mary R. 1974. "Prostitution as an Illegal Vocation: A Sociological Overview." In *Deviant Behavior: Occupational and Organizational Bases,* edited by Clifton Bryant, pp. 406–18. Chicago: Rand McNally.

Langan, Patrick A., and Farrington, David P. 1998. "Crime and Justice in the United States and in England and Wales, 1981–96." *Bureau of Justice Statistics Executive Summary,* October, NCJ 173402.

Lange, Johannes. 1931. *Crime as Destiny: A Study of Criminal Twins.* Translated by Charlotte Haldane. London: George Allen and Unwin.

Langway, Lynn, and Smith, Sunde. 1975. "Warning! Someone May Try to Steal Your Money." *Newsweek,* October 6, p. 67.

Lappé, Frances M., and Collins, Joseph. 1977. *Food First: Beyond the Myth of Scarcity.* New York: Ballantine Books.

Laqueur, Walter. 1977. *Terrorism.* Boston: Little, Brown.

———. 1987. *The Age of Terrorism.* Boston: Little, Brown.

Larimer, Tim. 1996. "A Freer Vietnam Brings Rise in Violent Crime." *New York Times,* March 8, p. A7.

Larzelere, Robert E., and Patterson, Gerald R. 1990. "Parental Management: Mediator of the Effect of Socioeconomic Status on Early Delinquency." *Criminology* 28 (May): 301–23.

Lasley, James. 1998. " 'Designing Out' Gang Homicides and Street Assaults." *National Institute of Justice Research in Brief,* November.

Laub, John H. 1983. *Criminology in the Making: An Oral History.* Boston: Northeastern University Press.

Laub, John H., and Sampson, Robert J. 1988. "Unraveling Families and Delinquency: A Reanalysis of the Gluecks' Data." *Criminology* 26: 355–80.

Launer, Harold M., and Palenski, Joseph E., eds. 1988. *Crime and the New Immigrants.* Springfield, IL: Charles C. Thomas.

Lauter, David. 1988. "Children Must Testify Face-to-Face in Abuse Cases." *Erie Morning News,* June 30, p. 6A.

"Lavelle Indicted on Five Felony Counts." 1983. *Erie Times News,* August 5, p. 1.

Lawler, Philip F. 1991. "An Issue This Paper Can't Side-step." *Wall Street Journal,* August 29, p. A11.

Lawrence, Jill. 1988. "Feds Used Human Subjects in Radiation Exposure Experiments." *Erie Times News,* October 25, pp. 1A, 12A.

Lawrence, Richard. 1998. *School Crime and Juvenile Justice.* New York: Oxford University Press.

———. 2000. "School Violence, the Media, and the ACJS." *ACJS Today* 20, 2, May/June.

Lea, John and Young, Jack. 1984. *What is to be Done about Law and Order.* Harmondsworth, England: Penguin.

LeBeau, James L. 1988. "Comment—Weather and Crime: Trying to Make Social Sense of a Physical Process." *Justice Quarterly* 5: 301–309.

LeBeau, James L., and Langworthy, Robert H. 1986. "The Linkages between Routine Activities, Weather, and Calls for Police Service." *Journal of Police Science and Administration* 14: 137–45.

Ledeen, Michael A. 1988. *Perilous Statecraft: An Insider's Account of the Iran-Contra Affair.* New York: Charles Scribner's Sons.

Lefer, David. 1999. "Pyramids of the Greedy: Worldwide Bank Note Scam Bilks Investors of Millions." *New York Daily News,* March 14.

Leftkowitz, N. M., et al. 1977. *Growing Up to Be Violent: A Longitudinal Study of the Development of Aggression.* New York: Pergamon.

Leitenberg, Harold. 1987. "Primary Prevention of Delinquency" in *Prevention of Delinquent Behavior* edited by John D. Burchard and Sara N. Burchard. Newbury, 312–331. NJ: Sage.

Lemert, Edwin M. 1951. *Social Pathology.* New York: McGraw-Hill.

———. 1953. "An Isolation and Closure Theory of Naive Check Forgery." *Journal of Criminal Law, Criminology and Police Science* 44 (September): 296–307.

———. 1958. "The Behavior of the Systematic Check Forger." *Social Problems* 6 (Fall): 141–49.

———. 1967. *Human Deviance, Social Problems and Social Control.* New York: Prentice-Hall.

———. 1968. "Prostitution." In *Problems in Sex Behavior,* edited by Edward Sagarin and Donal E. J. MacNamara. New York: Crowell.

Lemkin, Raphael. 1944. *Axis Rule in Occupied Europe.* Washington, DC: Carnegie Endowment for International Peace.

Leonard, William N., and Weber, Marvin G. 1970. "Automakers and Dealers: A Study of Criminogenic Market Forces." *Law and Society Review* 4 (February): 407–24.

Lesieur, Henry R., and Welch, Michael. 1991. "Vice, Public Order and Social Control." In *Criminology,* edited by Joseph F. Sheley, pp. 175–98. Belmont, CA: Wadsworth.

Letkemann, Peter. 1973. *Crime as Work.* Englewood Cliffs, NJ: Prentice-Hall.

Leuw, Ed, and Marshall, Ineke H. 1994. *Between Prohibition and Legalization: The Dutch Experiment in Drug Policy.* Amsterdam: Kulgler.

Levathes, Louise E. 1985. "The Land Where the Murray Flows." *National Geographic,* August, pp. 252–78.

Levine, James P. 1976. "The Potential for Overreporting in Criminal Victimization Surveys." *Criminology* 14 (November): 307–30.

Levitt, Steven, and Donohue, John. 1999 "Legalized Abortion and Crime." *Chicago Tribune,* August 8.

Levy, Clifford J. 1995. "A Bulletin Board Is Virtual but Hacker Arrests Are Real." *New York Times,* September 12, pp. A1, A14.

Lewin, Tamar. 1995. "Parents Poll Finds Child Abuse to Be More Common." *New York Times,* December 7, p. A17.

Leyton, Elliott. 1986. *Compulsive Killers: The Story of Modern Multiple Murders.* New York: Washington News Book.

Liazos, Alexander. 1972. "The Poverty of the Sociology of Deviance: Nuts, Sluts and 'Preverts'." *Social Problems 20* (Summer): 103–20. Reprinted in Readings in *Social Problems* 79/80, pp. 22–31. Guilford, CT: Dushkin.

Lieber, Arnold L., and Sherin, Carolyn R. 1972. "Homicides and the Lunar Influence in Human Emotional Disturbance." *American Journal of Psychiatry* 129 (July): 69–74.

Liebert, R. M., and Baron, R. A. 1972. "Some Immediate Effects of Televised Violence on Children's Behavior." *Developmental Psychology* 6: 469–75.

Liebow, Elliott. 1967. *Tally's Corner: A Study of Negro Streetcorner Men.* Boston: Little, Brown.

Light, Ivan, and Bonacich, Edna. 1988. *Immigrant Entrepreneurs: Koreans in Los Angeles, 1965–1982.* Berkeley: University of California Press.

Lilly, J. Robert, Cullen, Francis T., and Ball, Richard A. 1995. *Criminological Theory: Context and Consequences.* 2nd edition. Beverly Hills, CA: Sage.

Lindberg, Kristen, et al. 1997. "The Changing Faces of Organized Crime." *Crime and Justice International* 13, November: 5–6, 20–33. Reproduced from The Chicago Crime Commission Report. 1997. *The New Faces of Organized Crime.*

Lindesmith, Alfred R. 1965. *The Addict and the Law.* Bloomington, IN: Indiana University Press.

Lindesmith, Alfred R., and Levin, Yale. 1937. "The Lombrosian Myth in Criminology." *American Journal of Sociology* 42 (March): 653–71.

Lindquist, John H. 1988. *Misdemeanor Crime: Trivial Criminal Pursuit.* Newbury Park, CA: Sage.

Lindsey, Robert. 1979. *The Falcon and the Snowman.* New York: Simon and Schuster.

———. 1983. *The Flight of the Falcon.* New York: Simon and Schuster.

Lippman, Matthew. 1987. "Iran: A Question of Justice?" *C. J. International* 3: 5–6.

Lippman, Thomas W. 1991. "At Hanford's Nuclear Graveyard, A Nightmare of Endless Potential." *Washington Post National Weekly Edition,* December 9–15, p. 33.

Litton, Roger A. 1990. *Crime and Crime Prevention for Insurance Practice.* Aldershot, England: Gower.

"Lockheed Ordered to Pay $45 Million." 1990. *Erie Morning News,* November 16, p. 12A.

Loeber, Rolf, and Stouthamer-Loeber, Magda. 1986. "Models and Meta-Analysis of the Relationship between Family Variables and Juvenile Conduct Problems and Delinquency." In *Crime and Justice: An Annual Review of Research,* volume 7, edited by Norval Morris and Michael Tonry, pp. 29–149. Chicago: University of Chicago Press.

Lofquist, William S. 1992. "Corporate Sentencing and the United States Sentencing Commission: The Development of Organizational Probation." Paper presented at the Academy of Criminal Justice Sciences, Pittsburgh, PA, March.

Lohr, Steve. 1992. "Trial of a Bank Scandal Leads On and On." *New York Times,* August 8, pp. E1, E18.

Lombardo, Robert M. 1990. "Civil Forfeiture: A Powerful Tool against Commercial Gambling." *Criminal Organizations* 5: 3–5.

Lombroso, Cesare. 1911. "Introduction." In *Criminal Man according to the Classification of Cesare Lombroso,* edited by Gina Lombroso-Ferrero. New York: Putnam.

Lombroso-Ferrero, Gina, ed. 1972. *Criminal Man according to the Classification of Cesare Lombroso.* Montclair, NJ: Patterson Smith [reissue of 1911 work].

Londer, Randi. 1987. "Can Bad Air Make Bad Things Happen?" *Parade,* August 3, pp. 6–7.

Longmire, Dennis R. 1988. "Crimes of Power and Opulence: Criminological Researcher's Experience with Taboos." Paper presented at the American Society of Criminology Meetings, Chicago, November.

Lorenz, Konrad. 1966. *On Aggression.* New York: Harcourt, Brace, Jovanovich.

Lowenthal, Max. 1950. *The Federal Bureau of Investigation.* New York: William Sloane Associates.

Lowman, J., et al., eds. 1986. *Regulating Sex: An Anthology of Commentaries on the Badgley and Fraser Reports.* Burnaby, B.C.: Simon Fraser University.

Luckenbill, David F. 1991. "Criminal Homicide as a Situated Transaction." *Social Problems* 25: 176–86.

Luckenbill, David F., and Doyle, Daniel P. 1989. "Structural Position and Violence: Developing a Cultural Explanation." *Criminology* 27 (August): 419–36.

Lupsha, Peter A. 1981. "Individual Choice, Material Culture and Organized Crime." *Criminology* 19 (May): 3–24.

———. 1982. "Networks vs. Networking: An Analysis of Organized Criminal Groups." Paper presented at the American Society of Criminology Meetings, Toronto, November.

———. 1987. "Predicting Organized Crime: Some Variables." *Update* (International Organization for the Study of Organized Crime) 3: 7–8.

Lyman, Michael D. and Potter, Gary W. 1997. *Organized Crime.* Upper Saddle River, NJ: Prentice Hall.

Lyman, Stanford M. 1974. *Chinese Americans.* New York: Random House.

Lynch, Gerald W., and Blotner, Roberta. 1991. "Failed Zurich Test a Fatal Blow to Case for Decriminalization." *Law Enforcement News,* April 15, p. 8.

Lynch, Michael J., and Patterson, E. Britt, eds. 1992. *Race and Criminal Justice.* Fairfax, VA: Harrow and Heston.

Lynn, Barry W. 1986. *Polluting the Censorship Debate: A Summary and Critique of the Final Report of the Attorney General's Commission on Pornography.* Washington, DC: ACLU.

Lyons, Richard. 1980. "Reports on U.S. Oil Companies." *Erie Morning News,* June 23, p. 4.

Lytton, H. 1990. "Child and Parent Effects in Boys' Conduct Disorder: A Reinterpretation." *Developmental Psychology* 26: 683–97.

Maas, Peter. 1968. *The Valachi Papers.* New York: Bantam Books.

———. 1975. *King of the Gypsies.* New York: Bantam.

———. 1986. *Manhunt: The Incredible Pursuit of a CIA Agent Turned Terrorist.* New York: Random House.

———. 1995. *Killer Spy: The Inside Story of the FBI's Pursuit and Capture of Aldrich Ames, America's Deadliest Spy.* New York: Warner Books.

MacDonald, Andrew. 1980. *The Turner Diaries.* Arlington, VA: National Vanguard Books.

MacDonald, John M. 1971. *Rapists and Their Victims.* Springfield, IL: Charles C. Thomas.

Mack, John A. 1972. "The Able Criminal." *British Journal of Criminology.* 12 (January): 44–54.

———. 1974. *The Crime Industry.* Westmead, England: Saxon House.

MacLean, Brian D., and Milovanovic, Dragan. 1998. *Thinking Critically About Crime.* Vancouver, B.C., Canada: Collective Press.

MacLean, Don. 1974. *Pictorial History of the Mafia.* New York: Pyramid Books.

Maclean, Fitzroy. 1978. *Take Nine Spies.* New York: Atheneum.

MacNamara, Donal, and Sagarin, Edward. 1977. *Sex Crime and the Law.* New York: The Free Press.

Malamuth, Neil M., and Donnerstein, Ed. 1982. "The Effects of Aggressive-Pornographic Mass Media Stimuli." *Advances in Experimental Psychology* 15: 103–56.

Mallowe, M. 1988. "Arrivederci, Nicky." *Philadelphia Magazine,* May, p. 106.

"The Man behind Abscam." 1980. *Erie Morning News,* February 12, p. 1A.

Mankoff, Milton. 1980. "A Tower of Babel: Marxist Criminologists and Their Critics." In *Radical Criminology: The Coming Crisis,* edited by James A. Inciardi, pp. 139–48. Beverly Hills, CA: Sage.

Mann, Coramae Richey. 1984. *Female Crime and Delinquency.* University, AL: University of Alabama Press.

———. 1989. "Random Thoughts on the Ongoing Wilbanks-Mann Discourse." *The Critical Criminologist* 1 (Summer): 3–4.

———. 1993. *Unequal Justice: A Creation of Color.* Bloomington, IN: Indiana University Press.

Mann, Kenneth J., et al. 1980. "Sentencing the White-Collar Offender." *American Criminal Law Review,* 17: 479–500.

Mannheim, Herman. 1965. *Comparative Criminology.* Boston: Houghton Mifflin.

———, ed. 1969. *Pioneers in Criminology.* Chicago: Quadrangle Books.

Manning, Peter K. 1975. "Deviance and Dogma." *British Journal of Sociology* 15 (January): 1–20.

Mansnerus, Laura. 1989. "As Racketeering Law Expands, So Does Pressure to Rein It In." *New York Times,* March 12, p. 4E.

Maranto, Gina. 1985. "Coke: The Random Killer." *Discover,* March.

Marbach, William D., Conant, Jennet, and Rogers, Michael. 1983. "New Wave Computer Crime." *Newsweek,* August 29, p. 45.

Marbin, Carol. 1989. "IRS 'Giant Killers' Fighting Drug War." *Palm Beach Post,* April 17, pp. 1A, 6A.

Marchetti, Victor, and Marks, John D. 1974. *The CIA and the Cult of Intelligence.* New York: Dell.

Marcus, Amy D. 1990. "Thievery by Lawyers Is on the Increase, with Duped Clients Losing Bigger Sums." *Wall Street Journal,* November 26, p. B1.

———. 1991. "Murder Trials Introduce Prozac Defense." *Wall Street Journal,* February 7, p. B1.

Marcus, Ruth. 1991. "When Does the Government Make Criminals Out of Honest Citizens?" *Washington Post National Weekly Edition,* December 16–22, p. 34.

Mark, Vernon, and Ervin, Frank. 1970. *Violence and the Brain.* New York: Harper and Row.

Markhoff, John. 1988. " 'Virus' in Military Computers Disrupts Systems Nationwide." *New York Times,* September 4, p. 1.

———. 2000. "An Online Extortion Plot Results in Release of Credit Card Data." *New York Times,* January 10, pp. A1, A16.

Marks, John. 1979. *The Search for the Manchurian Candidate: The CIA and Mind Control.* New York: Times Books.

Marquart, James W. 1986. "Doing Research in Prison: The Strengths and Weaknesses of Full Participation as a Guard." *Justice Quarterly* 3 (March): 15–32.

Marsh, Frank H., and Katz, Janet, eds. 1985. *Biology, Crime and Ethics: A Study of Biological Explanations for Criminal Behavior.* Cincinnati, Ohio: Anderson.

Marshall, Ineke H., Anjewierden, Oscar, and Van Atteveld, Hans. 1990. "Toward an 'Americanization' of Dutch Drug Policy?" *Justice Quarterly* 7 (June): 393–420.

Marshall, Jonathan. 1992. "Targeting the Drugs, Wounding the Cities." *Washington Post National Weekly Edition,* May 25–31, p. 23.

Martin, David W., and Walcott, John. 1988. *Best Laid Plans: The Inside Story of America's War against Terrorism.* New York: Harper and Row.

Martin, John M., Haran, James F., and Romano, Anne T. 1988. "Espionage: A Challenge to Criminology and Criminal Justice." Paper presented at the Academy of Criminal Justice Sciences meetings, San Francisco, CA: April.

Martin, Randy, Mutchnick, Robert J., and Austin, W. Timothy. 1990. *Criminological Thought: Pioneers Past and Present.* New York: Macmillan.

Martinson, Robert. 1974. "What Works?: Questions and Answers about Prison Reform." *The Public Interest* 35 (Spring): 22–54.

———. 1979. "New Findings, New Views: A Note of Caution Regarding Sentencing Reform." *Hofstra Law Review* 7: 242–58.

"Martinson Attacks His Own Earlier Work." 1978. *Criminal Justice Newsletter* 9 (December): 4.

Maruschak, Laura M. 1999. "DWI Offenders Under Correctional Supervision." *Bureau of Justice Statistics Special Report.* June, NCJ 172212.

Marx, Gary. 1979. "External Efforts to Damage or Facilitate Social Movements: Some Patterns, Explanations, Outcomes and Complications." In *The Dynamics of Social Movements,* edited by Mayer N. Zald and John D. McCarthy. Cambridge, MA: Winthrop Publishers.

———. 1990. *Undercover: Police Surveillance in America.* Berkeley, CA: University of California Press.

Maser, Werner. 1979. *Nuremberg: A Nation on Trial.* Translated by Richard Barry. New York: Scribners.

Masland, Tom. 1992. "Slavery." *Newsweek,* May 4, pp. 30–39.

Matsueda, Rose L. 1988. "The Current State of Differential Association Theory." *Crime and Delinquency* 34: 277–306.

Matthews, Roger, and Young, Jock. 1986. *Confronting Crime.* Beverly Hills: Sage.

Matza, David. 1964. *Delinquency and Drift.* New York: Wiley.

Maurer, David W. 1940. *The Big Con.* Indianapolis, IN: Bobbs-Merrill.

———. 1964. *Whiz Mob.* New Haven: College and University Press.

Mayer, Martin. 1990. *The Greatest Ever Bank Robbery: The Collapse of the Savings and Loan Industry.* New York: Charles Scribner's.

Mayhew, Henry. 1862a. *London Labour and the London Poor.* 2 vols. London: Griffin.

———. 1862b. *London's Underworld.* London: Spring Books.

McCaghy, Charles. 1976a. "Child Molesters: A Study of Their Careers as Deviants." In *Criminal Behavior Systems,* edited by Marshall B. Clinard and Richard Quinney, pp. 75–88. New York: Holt, Rinehart and Winston.

———. 1976b. *Deviant Behavior.* New York: Macmillan.

———. 1980. *Crime in American Society.* New York: Macmillan.

McCaghy, Charles, and Hou, Charles. 1988. "Cultural Factors and Career Contingencies of Prostitution: The Case of Taiwan." Paper presented at the American Society of Criminology Meetings, Chicago, November.

McCaghy, Charles, Giordano, Peggy, and Henson, Trudy Knicely. 1977. "Auto Theft." *Criminology* 15 (3): 367–81.

McCall, Nathan. 1994. *Makes Me Wanna Holler: A Young Black Man in America.* New York: Random House.

McCandless, Boyd R., Persons, W. Scott, and Roberts, Albert. 1972. "Perceived Opportunity, Delinquency, Race and Body Build among Delinquent Youth." *Journal of Consulting and Clinical Psychology* 38 (April): 281–87.

McCarthy, Bill. 1995. "Not Just 'For the Thrill of It:' An Instrumentalist Elaboration of Katz's Explanation of Sneaky Thrill Property Crimes." *Criminology* 33 (November): 519–38.

McCarthy, E. D., et al. 1975. "The Effects of Television on Children and Adolescents: Violence and Behavior Disorders." *Journal of Communications* 25: 71–85.

McCarthy, Sarah J. 1982. "Pornography, Rape, and the Cult of Macho." In *Crisis in American Institutions,* edited by Jerome H. Skolnick and Elliott Currie, pp. 218–32. Boston: Little, Brown.

McCarthy, Sheryl. 1996. "Fleeing Mutilation, Fighting for Asylum." *Ms.* July-August.

McConahay, John B. 1988. "Pornography: The Symbolic Politics of Fantasy." *Law and Contemporary Problems* 51: 31–69.

McCord, Joan. 1990. "Crime in Moral and Social Contexts" The American Society of Criminology, 1989 Presidential Address." *Criminology* 28: 1–26.

McCord, William, and McCord, Joan. 1958. "The Effects of Parental Role Model on Criminality." *Journal of Social Issues* 14: 66–75.

McCormick, Albert E., Jr. 1977. "Rule Enforcement and Moral Indignation: Some Observations on the Effects of Criminal Antitrust Convictions upon Societal Reaction Process." *Social Problems* 25 (January): 30–39.

McCoy, Alfred W. 1972. *The Politics of Heroin in Southeast Asia.* New York: Harper and Row.

———. 1976. Report from the Golden Triangle. Unpublished paper. Cited in *Organizing Crime,* by Alan A. Block and William J. Chambliss, 1981, p. 36. New York: Elsevier.

———. 1985. *Drug Traffic, Narcotics, and Organized Crime in Australia.* New South Wales: Harper and Row Australasia.

McDermott, M. Joan. 1979. *Rape Victimization in 26 American Cities.* Washington, DC: Government Printing Office.

———. 1992. "The Personal is Empirical: Feminism, Research Methods and Criminal Justice Education." *Journal of Criminal Justice Education* 3 (Fall): 237–49.

McFadden, Robert D. 1994. "The Sting, FBI Gets Hot Cars, Great Deals and 30 Suspects." *New York Times,* September 9, p. A13.

McGrory, Mary. 1988. "Owning Up to Atomic Injustice." *Washington Post,* March 27, p. 1.

———. 1999. "An Overdue Apology: President Clinton has finally expressed the nation's regret for its role in Guatemala." *Washington Post National Weekly Edition,* March 22, p. 23.

McIntosh, Mary. 1975. *The Organization of Crime.* London: Macmillan.

McKillop, Peter. 1989. "The Last Godfather? Going After Gotti." *Newsweek,* February 6, p. 25.

McKinney, John C. 1966. *Constructive Typology and Social Theory.* New York: Appleton-Century-Crofts.

McMullan, John L. 1984. *The Canting Crew: London's Criminal Underworld, 1550–1700.* New Brunswick, NJ: Rutgers University Press.

McNamara, Robert P., ed. 1995. *Sex, Scams and Street Life: The Sociology of New York City's Times Square.* Westport, CT: Praeger.

Mead, George H. 1934. *Mind, Self and Society.* Chicago: University of Chicago Press.

"Meatpackers Hit with Record OSHA Fine." 1988. *Erie Morning News,* October 29, p. 2A.

Mednick, Sarnoff, and Volavka, Jan. 1980. "Biology and Crime." In *Crime and Justice: An Annual Review of Research,* edited by Norval Morris and Michael Tonry, vol. 1, pp. 85–159. Chicago: University of Chicago Press.

Mellgren, Doug. 1994. "Norwegian Girl's Slaying Spurs TV Violence Debate." *Erie Morning News,* October 19, p. 1A.

Melloan, George. 1991. "It's Hard to Make Money Laundries Come Clean." *Wall Street Journal,* April 29, p. A11.

Mellow, Jeff. 1996. "Measuring Race: Historical and Contemporary Issues." *The Criminologist,* March/April: 6–7.

Melusky, Joseph. 2000. *The American Political System: An Owner's Manual.* New York: McGraw-Hill.

Menard, Scott. 1987. "Short-term Trends in Crime and Delinquency: A Comparison of the UCR, NCS and Self-Report Data." *Justice Quarterly* 4: 455–74.

Mendelson, Benjamin. 1963. "The Origin and Doctrine of Victimology." *Excerpta Criminologica* 3 (June): 239–44.

Mendelson, Mary A. 1975. *Tender Loving Greed.* New York: Vintage.

"Men of God." 1991. *Prime Time Live.* ABC television broadcast, November 21.

Merlo, Alida. 1995. "Female Criminality in the 1990s." In *Women, Law, and Social Control,* edited by Alida V. Merlo and Joycelyn M. Pollock, pp. 119–34. Boston: Allyn and Bacon.

Merry, Robert W. 1975. "The Law Is on Trial." *The National Observer,* November 1, pp. 1–3.

Merton, Robert K. 1938. "Social Structure and Anomie." *American Sociological Review* 3 (October): 672–82.

———. 1957, 1968. *Social Theory and Social Structure.* Revised edition. New York: The Free Press.

———. 1961. "Social Problems and Sociological Theory." In *Contemporary Social Problems,* edited by Robert K. Merton and Robert M. Nisbet, pp. 702–23. New York: Harcourt, Brace and World.

Meskil, Philip S. 1976. *The Luparelli Tapes.* Chicago: Playboy Press.

Messerschmidt, James. 1997. *Crime as Structured Action.* Thousand Oaks, CA: Sage.

Messerschmidt, James W. 1986. *Capitalism, Patriarchy, and Crime: Toward a Socialist Feminist Criminology.* Totowa, NJ: Rowman and Littlefield.

Messerschmidt, James W. 1993. *Masculinities and Crime.* Lanham, MD: Rowman and Littlefield.

Messick, Hank. 1973. *Lansky.* New York: Berkley Publishing Company.

———. 1979. *Of Grass and Snow: The Secret Criminal Elite.* Englewood Cliffs, NJ: Prentice-Hall.

Messick, Hank, and Goldblatt, Burt. 1972. *The Mobs and the Mafia.* New York: Ballantine.

Messner, S. F. 1980. "Income Inequality and Murder Rates: Some Cross-National Findings." *Comparative Social Research* 3 (January): 185–98.

Messner, Steven F., Krohn, Marvin D., and Liska, Allen E., eds. 1989. *Theoretical Integration in the Study of Deviance and Crime: Problems and Prospects.* Albany: State University of New York Press.

Messner, Steven F., and Rosenfeld, Richard. 1994. *Crime and the American Dream.* Belmont, CA: Wadsworth.

Messner, Steven F., and Tardiff, Kenneth. 1985. "The Social Ecology of Urban Homicide: An Application of the 'Routine Activities' Approach." *Criminology* 23: 241–67.

"Miami Police Scandal Called Worst in U.S. Since Prohibition." 1987. *Erie Times News,* November 8, p. 1C.

Michalowski, Raymond J. 1993. "(De)construction, Postmodernism, and Social Problems: Facts, Fiction and Fantasies at the 'End of History.' " In *Reconsidering Social Constructionism: Debates in Social Problems Theory,* edited by James A. Holstein and Gale Miller. New York: Aldine De Gruyter.

Milbank, Dana, and Allen, Michael. 1991. "Alcoa Pleads Guilty in Toxic Waste Case." *Wall Street Journal,* July 12, p. B2.

Milgram, Stanley. 1974. *Obedience to Authority: An Experimental View.* New York: Harper.

Miller, Eleanor. 1986. *Street Woman.* Philadelphia, PA: Temple University Press.

Miller, Jerome. 1989. "The Relationship between Child Abuse and the Commission of Violent Crime by Adolescents and Adults: An Overview." Paper presented at the American Society of Criminology Meetings, Reno, NV, November.

Miller, J. Mitchell, and Tewksbury, Richard. 2000. *Extreme Methods: Innovative Approaches to Social Science Research.* Needham: Allyn and Bacon.

Miller, Susan L., ed. 1998. *Crime Control and Women.* Thousand Oaks, CA: Sage.

Miller, Walter. 1958. "Lower Class Culture as a Generating Milieu of Gang Delinquency." *Journal of Social Issues* 14 (May): 5–19.

———. 1973. "Ideology and Criminal Justice Policy: Some Current Issues." *Journal of Criminal Law and Criminology* 64 (May): 141–73.

———. 1975. *Violence by Youth Gangs and Youth Groups as a Crime Problem in Major American Cities.* Washington, DC: Government Printing Office.

———. 1980. "Gangs, Groups, and Serious Youth Crime." In *Critical Issues in Juvenile Delinquency,* edited by David Schichor and Delos Kelly. Lexington, MA: Lexington Books.

Mills, C. Wright. 1952. "A Diagnosis of Moral Uneasiness." In *Power, Politics and People,* edited by Irving L. Horowitz, pp. 330–39. New York: Ballantine.

Mills, James. 1986. *The Underground Empire: Where Crime and Governments Embrace.* New York: Doubleday.

Milner, Christina, and Milner, Richard. 1972. *Black Players: The Secret World of Black Pimps.* Boston: Little, Brown.

Milanovic, Dragan. 1992. *Postmodern Law and Disorder: Psychoanalytic Semiotics, Chaos, and Juridic Exegeses.* Liverpool: Deborah Charles.

Milovaniovic, Dragan. 1996. "Postmodern Criminology." *Justice Quarterly,* 13: 567–610.

Minor, Horace. 1956. "The Body Ritual of the Nacirema." *American Anthropologist* 58(3): 503–507.

Minor, W. William. 1981. "Techniques of Neutralization: A Reconceptualization and Empirical Examination." *Journal of Research in Crime and Delinquency* 18: 295–318.

———. 1984. "Neutralization as a Hardening Process." *Social Forces* 62: 995–1019.

Minty, Brian. 1988. "Public Care or Distorted Family Relationships: The Antecedents of Violent Crime." *Howard Journal* 27: 172–87.

Mintz, Morton. 1987. "At Any Cost: Corporate Greed, Women, and the Dalkon Shield." In *Corporate Violence,* edited by Stuart L. Hill, pp. 30–40. Totowa, NJ: Rowman and Littlefield.

Misner, Gordon E. 1987. "Proces Barbie: Lyons, and the Nazi Trial." *C. J. International* 3: 3–4, 28–32.

Mitchell, G. 1981. "The Trouble with RICO." *Police Magazine,* May, pp. 39–44.

Mitford, Jessica. 1963. *The American Way of Death.* New York: Paperback Library.

Mock, Lois Felson, and Rosenbaum, Dennis. 1988. *A Study of Trade Secret Theft in High-Technology Industries.* Washington, DC: National Institute of Justice, May.

Moffett, Matt, and Friedland, Jonathan. 1996. "Larcenous Legacy: A New Latin America Faces a Devil of Old: Rampant Corruption." *New York Times,* July 1, pp. A1, A46.

Mohr, J. W., Turner, R. E., and Jerry, M. B. 1964. *Pedophilia and Exhibitionism.* Toronto: University of Toronto Press.

Mokhiber, Russell. 1988. *Corporate Crime and Violence.* San Francisco: Sierra Club Books.

Monahan, John, and Splane, Stephanie. 1980. "Psychological Approaches to Criminal Behavior." In *Criminology Review Yearbook,* edited by Egon Bittner and Sheldon L. Messenger, vol. 2, pp. 17–47. San Francisco: Sage.

Monmaney, Terence, and Robins, Kate. 1988. "The Insanity of Steroid Abuse." *Newsweek,* May 23, p. 75.

Monroe, Russel R. 1978. *Brain Dysfunction in Aggressive Criminals.* Lexington, MA: D. C. Heath.

Moore, Mark. 1988. "Drug Trafficking." *Crime File* (National Institute of Justice).

Moore, Mark, Trojanowicz, Robert C., and Kelling, George L. 1988. "Crime and Policing." *Perspectives on Policing* 3, June.

Moore, Thomas, et al. 1988. "Dead Zones." *U.S. News and World Report,* April 10, pp. 20–33.

Moran, Richard, ed. 1985. *The Insanity Defense.* Beverly Hills, CA: Sage.

Morash, Merry. 1984. "Organized Crime." In *Major Forms of Crime,* edited by Robert F. Meier, pp. 191–220. Beverly Hills, CA: Sage.

Morash, Merry, and Chesney-Lind, Meda. 1991. "A Reformulation and Partial Test of the Power Control Theory of Delinquency." *Justice Quarterly* 8 (September): 347–77.

"More Arrests Seen for Lewd Conduct." 1980. *Erie Times News,* February 17, p. 4A.

Morgan, W. P. 1960. *Triad Societies in Hong Kong.* Hong Kong: Government Press.

Morganthau, Tom. 1988. "The Drug Gangs." *Newsweek,* March 28, pp. 20–29.

Morganthau, Tom, et al. 1988. "Nuclear Danger and Deceit." *Newsweek,* October 31, pp. 26–29.

Morley, Jefferson. 1995. "Crack in Black in White." *Washington Post National Weekly Edition,* December 4–10, pp. 21–22.

Morris, Norval. 1987. "Insanity Defense." *Crime File.* National Institute of Justice.

Morris, Norval, and Hawkins, Gordon. 1970. *The Honest Politician's Guide to Crime Control.* Chicago: University of Chicago Press.

Mossberg, Walter S. 1990. "Pan Am Bombing Probe Takes New Turn as Device Points to Libyan-Based Agents." *Wall Street Journal,* October 11, p. A11.

"Mounties, U.S. Agents Nab Canada Counterfeiters." 1998. *Reuters,* December 11.

Moushey, Bill. 1998. "Win at all Costs." *Pittsburgh Post Gazette.* 10-part series beginning November 22.

Moyer, Imogene L., ed. 1990. *The Changing Roles of Women in the Criminal Justice System.* 2nd edition. Prospect Heights, IL: Waveland Press.

Moyer, Kenneth E. 1976. *The Psychology of Aggression.* New York: Harper and Row.

Moynihan, Daniel P. 1986. *Family and Nation.* New York: Harcourt, Brace, Jovanovich.

Muraskin, Roslyn. 2000. *It's a Crime: Women and Justice.* Upper Saddle River, NJ: Prentice Hall.

Murr, Andrew, and Rogers, Adam. 1995. "Violence, Reel to Real." *Newsweek,* December 11, pp. 45–47.

Murray, Charles A. 1976. *The Link between Learning Disability and Juvenile Delinquency.* Washington, DC: National Institute of Juvenile Justice and Delinquency Prevention.

"Museum Jewel Robbery." 1964. *Time,* November 6, p. 23.

Mustain, Gene, and Capeci, Jerry. 1988. *Mob Star: The Story of John Gotti.* New York: Dell.

Myers, Gustavus. 1936. *The History of Great American Fortunes.* New York: Modern American Library.

Myers, Martha, and Talarico, Susette. 1986. "The Social Contexts of Racial Discrimination in Sentencing." *Social Problems* 33: 236–51.

———. 1987. *The Social Contexts of Criminal Sentencing.* New York: Springer-Verlag.

Nader, Ralph. 1965. *Unsafe at Any Speed.* New York: Grossman.

———. 1970. Foreword to *The Vanishing Air,* by John C. Esposito. New York: Grossman.

———. 1973. *The Consumer and Corporate Accountability.* New York: Harcourt, Brace, Jovanovich.

Nader, Ralph, and Green, Mark J., eds. 1973. *Corporate Power in America.* New York: Grossman.

Nader, Ralph, Green, Mark J., and Seligman, Joel. 1976. *Taming the Giant Corporation.* New York: Norton.

Nader, Ralph, Petkas, Peter J., and Blackwell, Kate. eds. 1972. *Whistle Blowing: The Report of the Conference on Professional Responsibility.* New York: Viking Penguin.

Nagel, Ilene H., and Hagan, John. 1983. "Gender and Crime: Offense Patterns and Criminal Court Sanctions."

In *Crime and Justice: An Annual Review of Research,* vol. 4, edited by Michael Tonry and Norval Morris, pp. 91–144. Chicago: University of Chicago Press.

"Naked Vandalism Replaced Nude Run." 1994. *Erie Morning News,* May 5, p. 3A.

Nash, Jay Robert. 1975. *Bloodletters and Badmen.* 3 volumes. New York: Warner.

———. 1976. *Hustlers and Con Men.* New York: M. Evans and Co.

———. 1981. *Almanac of World Crime.* Garden City, NY: Doubleday.

Nasheri, Hedieh, and O'Hearn, Timothy J. 1998. "Crime and Technology: New Rules in a New World." *Information and Communications Technology Law* 7,2: 145–157.

National Advisory Committee on Criminal Justice Standards and Goals. 1976a. *Organized Crime: Report of the Task Force on Organized Crime.* Washington, DC: Law Enforcement Assistance Administration.

———. 1976b. *Criminal Justice Research and Development.* Report of the Task Force on Criminal Justice Research and Development. Washington, DC: National Institute of Law Enforcement and Criminal Justice.

———. 1976c. *Report of the Task Force on Disorders and Terrorism.* Washington, DC: Government Printing Office.

National Association of Elementary School Principals. 1980. *The Most Significant Minority: One-Parent Children in the Schools.* New York: Charles F. Kettering Foundation.

National Commission on the Causes and Prevention of Violence. 1969. *To Establish Justice, to Insure Domestic Tranquility.* New York: Award Books.

National Commission on Obscenity and Pornography, 1970. *Commission on Obscenity and Pornography Report.* New York: Bantam Books.

National Council on Crime and Delinquency. 2000. *And Justice for Some.* San Francisco: National Council on Crime and Delinquency.

National Crime Survey. 1977. "Basic Screen Questions." Form NCJ–1. Washington, DC: U.S. Bureau of Census, April 19.

National Crime Survey. 1981. *Criminal Victimization in the United States, 1979.* Washington, DC: Government Printing Office.

National Criminal Justice Reference Service. 1979. *We Are All Victims of Arson.* Washington, DC: Government Printing Office.

National Institute of Justice. 1991. *Drug Use Forecasting: Drugs and Crime, 1990 Annual Report.* Washington, DC: National Institute of Justice, August.

———. 1998. *ADAM: 1997 Annual Report on Adult and Juvenile Arrestees.* Washington, DC: National Institute of Justice.

National Institute on Drug Abuse. 1982. *National Household Survey on Drug Abuse.* Washington, DC: Government Printing Office.

National Institute on Law Enforcement and Criminal Justice. 1977. *The Development of the Law of Gambling 1776–1976.* Washington, DC: Law Enforcement Assistance Administration.

National White-Collar Crime Center. 1996. *Symposium on White-Collar Crime.* Morgantown, WV, June.

———. 2000. *The Internet as an Investigative Tool.* Morgantown, WV: National White-Collar Crime Center, C.D.

NBC News. 1979. "NBC Follow-Up: A Follow-Up on the 1977 Documentary on 'Racketeering and the International Longshoreman's Association'." NBC television broadcast, April 12.

NBC Whitepaper. 1983. "Crime and Insanity." Broadcast April 26.

Neergaard, Lauran. 1991. "Study Shows Alcohol-Related Traffic Deaths Decreasing." *Erie Morning News,* December 6, p. 1A.

———. 1994. "Consumer Group Claims U.S. Doctors Performing Unnecessary C-Sections." *Erie Morning News,* May 14, p. 8C.

Neff, Joseph. 1991. "Recession 'Prime Market' for Con Artists." *Erie Morning News,* June 1, p. 11A.

Nelan, Bruce W. 1997. "The Ponzi Revolution." *Time,* March 17, p. 32.

Nelkin, Dorothy. 1995. "Biology Is Not Destiny." *New York Times,* September 28, p. A1.

Netanyahu, Benjamin, ed. 1986. *Terrorism: How the West Can Win.* New York: Farrar, Straus and Geroux.

Nettler, Gwynn. 1974. "Embezzlement without Problems." *British Journal of Criminology* 14 (January): 70–77.

———. 1978. *Explaining Crime.* 2nd edition. New York: McGraw-Hill.

———. 1982. *Criminal Careers.* 4 vols. Cincinnati, OH: Anderson.

———. 1989. *Criminology Lessons.* Cincinnati, OH: Anderson.

"The New Mafia: How the Mob Really Works." 1981. *Newsweek,* January 5, pp. 34–43.

Newman, Anne. 1990. "Sensormate Electronics' Investors Expect Anti-Theft Devices to Be a Hit in Recession." *Wall Street Journal,* November 12, p. C6.

Newman, Graeme. 1978. *The Punishment Response.* Philadelphia, PA: Lippincott.

———. 1979. *Understanding Violence.* New York: Lippincott.

Newman, Graeme, and Marongiu, Pietro. 1990. "Penological Reform and the Myth of Beccaria." *Criminology* 28 (May): 325–46.

Newman, Graeme, ed. 1999. *Global Report on Crime and Justice.* New York: Oxford University Press,

Nicolova, Rossitsa. 1999. "Global Crime Puts Business People at Risk." *Kansas City Business Journal,* January 25: 1–4.

Nielson, Marianne. 1998. "A Comparison of Canadian Youth Justice Commission and Navajo Peacemakers." *Journal of Contemporary Criminal Justice* 14, January: 6–25.

Nielson, Marianne, Fulton, Dorothy, and Tsosie, Ivan. 2000. "Recent Trends in Community-Based Strategies for Dealing with Juvenile Crime on the Navajo Nation." Paper presented at the Academy of Criminal Justice Sciences Annual Meeting, New Orleans, LA, March 21–25.

Nieves, Evelyn. 1999. "For Patrons of Prostitutes, Remedial Instruction." *New York Times,* March 18, pp. A1, A19.

Noack, David. 2000. "Employees, Not Hackers, Greatest Computer Threat." APBnews.com:80/newscent.

Nobile, Phillip, and Nadler, Eric. 1986. *United States of America vs. Sex: How the Meese Commission Lied about Pornography.* New York: Minotaur Press.

North, Oliver, with William Novak. 1991. *Under Fire: An American Story.* New York: Harper Collins.

"North Freed." 1991. *Wall Street Journal,* September 17, p. A16.

Nurco, David N., et al. 1988. "Differential Criminal Patterns of Narcotic Addicts Over an Addiction Career." *Criminology* 26: 407–23.

"Nuremberg Principle." 1970. *The Nation,* January 26, p. 78.

"NYC's Mollen Commission Paints Grim Corruption Picture." 1993. *Law Enforcement News* 19 (November 30): 11.

Nye, F. Ivan, and Short, Jr., James F. 1956. "Scaling Delinquent Behavior." *American Sociological Review* 22: 326–31.

Nye, F. Ivan, Short, Jr., James F., and Olson, Virgil J. 1958. "Socioeconomic Status and Delinquent Behavior." *American Journal of Sociology* 63 (January): 381–89.

O'Brien, Shirley. 1986. *Why They Did It: Stories of Eight Convicted Child Molesters.* Springfield, IL: Charles C. Thomas.

O'Connor, Tim. 1987. "The Misfortune Tellers." *Woman's World,* February 2, p. 41.

Office of Management and Budget. 1973. *Social Indicators.* Washington, DC: Government Printing Office.

Ohmar, Kenichi. 1991. "The Scandal behind Japan's Financial Scandals." *Wall Street Journal,* August 6, p. B1.

"OJJDP (Office of Juvenile Justice and Delinquency Prevention) Announces Guidelines Aimed at Juvenile Gangs and Repeat Offenders." 1983. *Juvenile Research* (Bureau of Justice Statistics), November/December.

Olson, Walter K. 1991. *The Litigation Explosion: What Happened When America Unleashed the Lawsuit.* New York: Dutton.

Opolot, J. S. E. 1979. "Organized Crime in Africa." *International Journal of Comparative and Applied Criminal Justice* 3 (Fall): 177–83.

"Options Scam in Boston." 1978. *Time,* January 30, pp. 49–50.

"An Option to Run." 1978. *Newsweek,* January 30, pp. 64–66.

Orcutt, James D. 1987. "Differential Association and Marijuana Use: A Closer Look at Sutherland (With a Little Help from Becker)." *Criminology* 25: 341–58.

Organized Crime Control Act of 1970, Public Law 91–452. 1970. *Crime Law Reporter,* 8 (5); October 21, 1–32.

Organized Crime Task Force Report. 1967. Washington, DC: Government Printing Office.

Orland, Leonard. 1980. "Reflections on Corporate Crime: Law in Search of Theory and Scholarship." *American Criminal Law Review* 17 (Spring): 501–20.

Packer, Herbert L. 1968. *The Limits of Criminal Sanction.* Stanford: Stanford University Press.

Page, Joseph, and O'Brien, Mary Win. 1973. *Bitter Wages: Ralph Nader's Study Group Report on Disease and Injury on the Job.* New York: Grossman.

Paige, C. 1985. *The Right to Lifers: Who They Are, How They Operate, Where They Get Their Money.* New York: Summit Books.

Palmer, Laura. 1990. "Coming Home from Nam." *Erie Morning News,* July 16, p. 4A.

"Panasonic Gets Zapped, Too." 1989. *Newsweek,* January 30, p. 54.

Panattieri, Joseph C. 1999. "The Software Mobsters." *Interactive Week Online.* September.

Panel for the Evaluation of Crime Surveys. 1976. *Surveying Crime.* Washington, DC: National Academy of Sciences.

Parenti, Michael. 1980. *Democracy for the Few.* 3rd edition. New York: St. Martin's Press.

Park, Robert E. 1952. *Human Communities.* Glencoe, IL: The Free Press.

Parker, Donn. 1976. *Crime by Computer.* New York: Charles Scribner's Sons.

———. 1979. *Computer Crime: Criminal Justice Resource Manual.* Washington, DC: Government Printing Office.

———. 1983. *Fighting Computer Crime.* New York: Charles Scribner's Sons.

Partridge, Ben. 1999. "EU Commissioner Worried by Corruption in Candidate States." www.rferl.org:80/nca/features/1999/03/ F.RU.990322131614.html.

Passas, Nikos. 1995. "The Mirror of Global Evils: A Review Essay on the BCCI Affair." *Justice Quarterly* 12 (June): 377–406.

Pasztor, Andy. 1991. "U.S. to Use Paisley's Bribery Admission to Find How High Corruption Reached." *Wall Street Journal,* July 17, p. C10.

Patterson, Gerald R. 1982. *Coercive Family Process.* Eugene, OR: Castalia.

Patterson, Gerald R., and Dishion, Thomas J. 1985. "Contributions of Families and Peers to Delinquency." *Criminology* 23: 63–79.

Pauly, David, Friday, Carolyn, and Foote, Jennifer. 1987. "A Scourge of Video Pirates." *Newsweek,* July 27, pp. 40–41.

PBS. 1999. *Lords of the Mafia: Mexico.* (telecast)

Pearson, Geoffrey. 1982. *Hooligans: A History of Respectable Fears.* New York: Schocken.

Pelfrey, William V. 1980. *The Evolution of Criminology.* Cincinnati, OH: Anderson.

Pennsylvania Crime Commission. 1970. *Report on Organized Crime.* Harrisburg, PA: Commonwealth of Pennsylvania.

———. 1974. Report on Police Corruption and the Quality of Law Enforcement in Philadelphia. St. Davids, PA: Pennsylvania Crime Commission.

———. 1980. *A Decade of Organized Crime: 1980 Report.* St. Davids, PA: Pennsylvania Crime Commission.

———. 1986. *The Changing Face of Organized Crime: 1986 Report.* Conshohocken, PA: Pennsylvania Crime Commission.

———. 1991. *Organized Crime in Pennsylvania: A Decade of Change, 1990 Report.* Conshohocken, PA: Pennsylvania Crime Commission.

Pennsylvania Crime Commission. 1990. *Organized Crime in Pennsylvania: A Decade of Change.* Conshohocken, PA: Commonwealth of Pennsylvania.

———. 1992. *Racketeering and Organized Crime in the Bingo Industry.* Conshohocken, PA: Pennsylvania Crime Commission.

Pennsylvania Securities Commission. 1983a. "Oil and Gas Lease Lottery Investments." *Investor Alert,* April.

———. 1983b. "Tax Shelters." *Investor Alert,* November.

———. 1984a. "Business Opportunity and Franchise Fraud." *Investor Alert,* November.

———. 1984b. "Commodity Investments." *Investor Alert,* April.

———. 1984c. "Penny Stock Frauds." *Investor Alert,* August.

———. 1984d. "Vacation Timesharing." *Investor Alert,* January.

———. 1987. "Precious Metal Bank Financing Programs." *Investor Alert,* August.

———. 1988. " 'Dirt Pile' Gold Swindles." *Investor Alert,* September.

Pepinsky, Harold E., and Jesilow, Paul. 1984. *Myths That Cause Crime.* Cabin John, MD: Seven Locks Press.

Pepinsky, Harold E., and Quinney, Richard, eds. 1991. *Criminology as Peacemaking.* Bloomington, IN: Indiana University Press.

Perin, Monica. 1997. "Auto Theft: Costs are High for Both Insurers, Victims." *Houston Business Journal,* February 17.

Perkins, Roberta, and Bennett, Garry. 1985. *Being a Prostitute: Prostitute Women and Prostitute Men.* Sydney, Australia; George Allen and Unwin.

Perls, Frederick. 1970. "Four Lectures." In *Gestalt Therapy Now,* edited by John Fagan and Irma Lee Shepherd, pp. 14–38. New York: Harper and Row.

Permanent Subcommittee on Investigations of the Committee on Governmental Affairs. 1979. *Illegal Narcotics Profits Hearing.* Testimony of Jack Key, Staffperson to the Subcommittee, 96th Congress, 1st Session, December 7, 11, 12, 13, 14.

———. 1980. *Hearings on Organized Crime and Use of Violence.* 96th Congress, 2nd session, April.

Peter, Laurence J., ed. 1977. *Peter's Quotations.* New York: William Morrow.

Petersilia, Joan. 1983. *Racial Disparities in the Criminal Justice System.* Santa Monica, CA: Rand Corporation.

Petersilia, Joan, Greenwood, Peter W., and Lavin, Marvin. 1977. *Criminal Careers of Habitual Felons.* Santa Monica: Rand Corporation.

Peterson, Marilyn. 1998a. "Assessing Criminal Organizations Through their Management of Profits." New Jersey Division of Criminal Justice (unpublished paper).

Peterson, Melody. 1998b. "Lawsuits by Rivals Accuse Textile Maker of Corporate Espionage." *New York Times,* October 13, p. C7.

Pfohl, Stephen J. 1985. *Images of Deviance and Social Control.* New York: McGraw-Hill.

———. 1993. "Twilight of the Parasites: Ultramodern Capital and the New World Order." *Social Problems* 40: 125–51.

"Phar-Mor Discloses `Financial Swindle' of $350 Million." 1992. *Erie Morning News,* August 5, pp. 1A, 2A.

Pileggi, Nicholas. 1985. *Wiseguy: Life in a Mafia Family.* New York: Simon and Schuster.

Piliavin, Irving, et al. 1986. "Crime, Deterrence, and Rational Choice." *American Sociological Review* 51: 101–119.

Pilzer, Paul Z., and Deitz, Robert. 1989. *Other People's Money: The Inside Story of the S&L Mess.* New York: Simon and Schuster.

Pincher, Chapman. 1984. *Too Secret, Too Long.* New York: St. Martin's Press.

Pincomb, Ronald A. 1989. "Jamaican Gangs: A Summary." *Criminal Organizations* 2: 7–10.

Pincomb, Ronald A., and Everett, Ernest M. 1991. "Hong Kong's Triads Move into Australia." *Criminal Organizations* 6 (Fall): 15.

Pinkerton Inc. 1999. "Top Security Threats Facing Corporate America." http://nt.excite.com/news/bw/990317/ca-pinkerton.

Pinter, Rudolph. 1923. *Intelligence Testing: Methods and Results.* New York: Holt.

Pistone, Joseph, and Woodley, Richard. 1987. *Donnie Brasco: My Undercover Life in the Mafia.* New York: New American Library.

Piven, Frances Fox. 1981. "Deviant Behavior and the Remaking of the World." *Social Problems* 28 (June): 489–508.

Pizzo, Stephen, Fricker, Mary, and Muolo, Paul. 1989. *Inside Job: The Looting of America's Savings and Loans.* New York: McGraw-Hill.

Plagens, Peter, Starr, Mark, and Robins, Kate. 1990. "To Catch an Art Thief." *Newsweek,* April 2, pp. 52–53.

Plate, Thomas. 1975. *Crime Pays: An Inside Look at Burglars, Car Thieves, Loan Sharks, Hit Men, Fences and Other Professional Criminals.* New York: Ballantine.

Plate, Thomas, and Darvi, Andrea. 1981. *Secret Police: The Inside Story of a Network of Terror.* Garden City, NY: Doubleday.

Platt, Anthony. 1974. "Prospects for a Radical Criminology in the United States." *Crime and Social Justice* 1 (Spring): 2–10.

Platt, Tony. 1985. "Criminology in the 1980s: Progressive Alternatives to Law and Order." *Crime and Social Justice* 21–22: 191–199.

Poggio, Eugene C., et al. 1985. *Blueprint for the Future of the Uniform Crime Reporting Program: Final Report of the UCR Study.* Washington, DC: Department of Justice.

Pokorny, Alex D. 1964. "Moon Phases, Suicide and Homicide." *American Journal of Psychiatry.* 121 (January): 66–67.

Pokorny, Alex D., and Jachimczyk, John. 1974. "The Questionable Relationship between Homicides and Lunar Cycle." *American Journal of Psychiatry* 131 (June): 827–29.

Poland, James M. 1988. *Understanding Terrorism.* Englewood Cliffs, NJ: Prentice-Hall.

———. 1990. "Asian Crime Groups in the United States." *Criminal Organizations* 5 (1): 19–24.

Police Foundation. 1977. *Domestic Violence and the Police: Studies in Detroit and Kansas City.* Washington, DC: Police Foundation.

"Police Lobbying Fails to Save 'Brady' Gun Control Amendment." 1988. *Criminal Justice Newsletter* 19: 1.

Polsby, Daniel. 1994. "The False Promise of Gun Control." *The Atlantic Monthly,* March, pp. 1–7.

Polsky, Ned. 1967. *Hustlers, Beats and Others.* Chicago: Aldine.

Pomerantz, Steven L. 1987. "The FBI and Terrorism." *FBI Law Enforcement Bulletin,* October: 14–17.

Pontell, Henry, Calavita, Kitty, and Tillman, Robert. 1994. *Fraud in the Savings and Loan Industry: White-Collar Crime and Government Response.* Washington, DC: National Institute of Justice.

Pope, Carl. 1980. "Patterns in Burglary: An Empirical Examination of Offense and Offender Characteristics." *Journal of Criminal Justice* 8 (1): 39–51.

Poppa, Terrence. 1998. *Drug Lord: A True Story.* 2nd ed. New York: Demand Publications.

Port, Bob. 1999. "America's 25 Highest-Risk Shopping Center Neighborhoods." APBnews.com:80/safetyce. . .ity/mallcrime/ mallrisk1214 01.html.

Post, Tom, and Field, Catherine. 1992. "The Strict Rules of Revenge." *Newsweek,* April 13, p. 45.

Potter, Gary W. 1989. "Book Review: Zips, Pizza and Smack." *Criminal Organizations* 4: 17–18.

Potter, Gary W., and Gaines, Larry K. 1992. "Country Comfort: Vice and Corruption in Rural Settings." *Journal of Contemporary Criminal Justice* 8 (February): 36–61.

Pound, Edward T. 1990. "House Government Operations Panel Assails Former HUD Secretary Pierce." *Wall Street Journal,* November 2, p. 8B.

Powell, Stewart, et al. 1986. "Busting the Mob." *U.S. News and World Report,* February 3, pp. 24–32.

Power, William. 1991. "Broker's Case Shows Justice Can Be Slow." *Wall Street Journal,* April 12, pp. C1, C17.

President's Commission on Law Enforcement and the Administration of Justice. 1967a. *The Challenge of Crime in a Free Society.* Washington, DC: Government Printing Office.

———. 1967b. *Task Force Report: Organized Crime.* Washington, DC: Government Printing Office.

President's Commission on Organized Crime. 1983. *Organized Crime: Federal Law Enforcement Perspective.* Record of Hearings I. Washington, DC: Government Printing Office.

———. 1984a. *Organized Crime of Asian Origin.* Washington, DC: Government Printing Office.

———. 1984b. *Organized Crime and Money Laundering.* Record of Hearing II. Washington, DC: Government Printing Office.

———. 1985. *Organized Crime and Gambling.* Record of Hearing VII. Washington, DC: Government Printing Office.

———. 1986a. *America's Habit: Drug Abuse, Drug Trafficking and Organized Crime.* Interim Report. Washington, DC: Government Printing Office.

———. 1986b. *The Edge: Organized Crime, Business and Labor Unions.* Interim Report. Washington, DC: Government Printing Office.

President's Task Force on Victims of Crime. 1982. *Final Report.* Washington, DC: Government Printing Office.

Press, Aric. 1983. "Mapping the Streets of Crime." *Newsweek,* December 19, p. 68.

Press, Aric, Shannon, Elaine, and Simons, Pamela Ellis. 1979. "Rico the Enforcer." *Newsweek,* August 20, pp. 82–83.

Press, Aric, et al. 1986. "A Government in the Bedroom." *Newsweek,* July 14, pp. 36–38.

Pressley, Sue Anne. 1998. "Spiderman Scaling Condos to Rob from Rich." *Erie Times News,* December 9, p. A1.

Preston, Douglas J. 1986. *Dinosaurs in the Attic: An Excursion into the American Museum of Natural History.* New York: St. Martin's Press.

Price, Betsey. 1994. "The Criminologist and the Indian." *The Criminologist,* November/December: 1, 415, 24

Proal, Louis. 1973. *Political Crime.* Montclair, NJ: Patterson Smith. Reprint of an 1898 edition. New York: D. Appleton.

"Prudential Fined Millions." 1996. *Erie Morning News,* July 6, p. A1.

Prus, Robert, and Sharper, C. R. D. 1977. *Road Hustler.* Toronto: Gage.

Quetelet, Adolphe. 1984. *Research on the Propensity for Crime at Different Ages.* Translated with an introduction by Sawyer F. Sylvester. Cincinnati, OH: Anderson.

Quetelet, L. A. J. 1869. *Physique Sociale,* volume 2. Brussels, Belgium. Cited in *The Growth of Crime,* edited by Leon Radzinowicz and Joan King, 1977, pp. 64–65. New York: Basic Books.

———. 1969. *A Treatise on Man and the Development of His Faculties.* Gainesville, FL: Scholar's Facsimiles and Reprints.

Quinney, Richard C. 1963. "Occupational Structure and Criminal Behavior: Prescription Violations by Retail Pharmacists." *Social Problems* 11 (Fall): 179–85.

———. 1964. "The Study of White-Collar Crime: Toward a Re-Orientation in Theory and Research." *Journal of Criminal Law, Criminology, and Police Science,* 55. Reproduced in *White-Collar Crime: Offenses in Business, Politics, and the Professions,* edited by Gilbert Geis and Robert F. Meier, 1977, pp. 283–95. New York: Free Press.

———. 1970. *The Social Reality of Crime.* Boston: Little, Brown.

———. 1974a. *Criminal Justice in America: A Critical Understanding.* Boston: Little, Brown.

———. 1974b. *Critique of Legal Order: Crime Control in Capitalist Society.* Boston: Little, Brown.

———. 1974c. *Criminology: Analysis and Critique of Crime in the United States.* Boston: Little, Brown.

———. 1977. *Class, State and Crime: On the Theory and Practice of Criminal Justice.* New York: David McKay.

———. 1979. *Criminology.* 2nd edition. New York: McGraw-Hill.

———. 1980. *Providence.* New York: Longman.

———. 1988. "Crime, Suffering, Service: Toward a Criminology of Peacemaking." *The Quest,* Winter: 102–16.

———. 1991. "The Way of Peace: On Crime, Suffering, and Service." In *Criminology as Peacemaking,* edited by Harold E. Pepinsky and Richard Quinney. pp. 3–13. Bloomington: University of Indiana Press.

Quinney, Richard C., and Wildeman, John. 1977. *The Problem of Crime.* 2nd edition. New York: Harper and Row.

Quittner, Joshua. 1995. "Cracks in the Net." *Time,* February 27, pp. 34–45.

Raab, Selwyn. 1994. "Top Echelon of Mobsters Pose Threat." *New York Times,* August 23, p. A7.

———. 1997. "Officials Say Mob is Shifting Crimes to New Industries." *New York Times,* February 10, p. A1.

Rabinowitz, Dorothy. 1991. "Parents and Children on Trial." *Wall Street Journal,* May 6, p. A14.

Rabow, Jerome. 1964. "Research and Rehabilitation: The Conflict of Scientific and Treatment Roles in Corrections." *The Journal of Research in Crime and Delinquency* 1 (January): 67–79.

Radzinowicz, Leon. 1966. *Ideology and Crime.* New York: Columbia University Press.

Radzinowicz, Leon, and King, Joan. 1977. *The Growth of Crime: The International Experience.* New York: Basic Books.

Raffali, Henri C. 1970. "The Battered Child." *Crime and Delinquency* 16: 139–50.

Rafter, Nicole Hahn, ed. 1988. *White Trash: The Eugenic Family Studies 1877–1919.* Boston, MA: Northeastern University Press.

Rafter, Nicole Hahn, and Maher, Lisa, eds. 1995. *International Feminist Perspectives in Criminology.* New York: Open University Press.

Ragavan, Chitra, and Kaplan, David E. 1999. "Why Auto Theft is Going Global." *U.S. News and World Report,* June 14, pp. 16–20.

Rand, Michael R. 1994. "Carjacking." *Crime Data Brief.* National Crime Victimization Survey. Washington, DC: Bureau of Justice Statistics, March.

Randi, James. 1988. *The Faith Healers.* New York: Prometheus.

Ranelagh, John. 1986. *The Agency: The Rise and Decline of the CIA: From Wild Bill Donovan to William Casey.* New York: Simon and Schuster.

Rashke, Richard. 1981. *The Killing of Karen Silkwood.* Boston: Houghton Mifflin.

Rathus, Spencer. 1983. *Human Sexuality.* New York: Holt, Rinehart and Winston.

Rebovich, Don, and Layne, Jenny. 1999. "The 1999 National Public Survey of White-Collar Crime Completed." *NCWCCRFocus* (National Consortium for White-Collar Crime Research) 3, 1, Spring, p. 1.

Reckless, Walter C., 1961. *The Crime Problem.* 3rd edition. New York: Appleton-Century-Crofts.

———. 1967. *The Crime Problem.* New York: Appleton-Century-Crofts.

Reckless, Walter C., and Dinitz, Simon. 1967. "Pioneering with Self-Concept as a Vulnerability Factor in Delinquency." *Journal of Criminal Law, Criminology and Police Science* 58 (December): 515–23.

Reckless, Walter C., Dinitz, Simon, and Kay, Barbara. 1957. "The Self-Component in Potential Delinquency and Potential Nondelinquency." *American Sociological Review* 22 (October): 566–70.

Reckless, Walter, C., Dinitz, Simon, and Murray, Ellen. 1956. "Self-Concept as an Insulator against Delinquency." *American Sociological Review* 21 (December): 744–56.

———. 1957. "The 'Good Boy' in a High Deliquency Area." *Journal of Criminal Law, Criminology and Police Science* 48 (May): 18–25.

Reed, Gary E., and Yeager, Peter C. 1991. "Organizational Offending and Neoclassical Criminology: A Challenge to Gottfredson and Hirschi's General Theory of Crime." Paper presented at the American Society of Criminology Meetings, San Francisco, CA, November.

———. 1996. "Organizational Offending and Neoclassical Criminology: Challenging the Reach of a General Theory of Crime." *Criminology* 34 (August): 357–82.

Regan, Tom. 1982. *All That Dwell Therein: Animal Rights and Environmental Ethics.* Berkeley: University of California Press.

———. 1999. "Logging on to Cyber-crime." *Christian Science Monitor,* July 8, p. 1.

Regenstein, Lewis. 1982. *America the Poisoned.* Washington, DC: Acropolis Books.

Regoli, Robert, and Poole, Eric. 1978. "The Commitment of Delinquents to Their Misdeeds: A Reexamination." *Journal of Criminal Justice* 6: 261–69.

Reibstein, Larry, and Drew, Lisa. 1988. "Clean Credit for Sale." *Newsweek,* September 12, p. 49.

Reichstein, Kenneth J. 1965. "Ambulance Chasing: A Case Study of Deviation and Control within the Legal Profession." *Social Problems* 13 (Summer): 3–17.

Reid, Ed. 1970. *The Grim Reapers: The Anatomy of Organized Crime in America, City by City.* New York: Bantam Books.

Reid, Susan Titus. 1982. *Crime and Criminology.* 3rd edition. New York: Holt, Rinehart, and Winston.

Reidel, Marc, and Zahn, Margaret. 1985. *The Nature and Pattern of American Homicide.* Washington, DC: Government Printing Office.

Reiman, Jeffrey. 1984. *The Rich Get Richer and the Poor Get Prison.* 4th edition. New York: Wiley.

Reiman, Jeffrey H. 1995. *The Rich Get Richer and the Poor Get Prison.* 4th edition. New York: Macmillan.

Reiss, Albert J., Jr. 1967. "Studies in Crime and Law Enforcement in Major Metropolitan Areas." Field Surveys III, President's Commission on Law Enforcement and the Administration of Justice. Washington, DC: Government Printing Office.

Rengert, George, and Wasilchick, John. 1985. *Suburban Burglary: A Time and Place for Everything.* Springfield, IL: Thomas.

Renner, Thomas, and Giancana, A. 1984. *Mafia Princess.* New York: William Morrow.

Rennison, Callie M., and Welchans, Sarah. 2000. "Intimate Partner Violence." *Bureau of Justice Statistics Special Report,* May, NCJ 178247.

Renzetti, Claire M. 1993. "On the Margins of the Malestream (Or, They Still Don't Get It, Do They?): Feminist Analyses in Criminal Justice Education." *Journal of Criminal Justice Education* 4 (Fall): 219–34.

Repetto, Thomas A. 1974. *Residential Crime.* Cambridge, MA: Ballinger Press.

Report of the Congressional Committee Investigating the Iran-Contra Affair, with Supplemental, Minority and Additional Views. 1987. Washington, DC: U.S. Government Printing Office.

Report of the National Advisory Commission on Health Manpower. 1968. Quoted in *Crisis in American Institutions,* edited by Jerome H. Skolnick and Elliot Currie, 5th edition, 1982, p. 390. Boston: Little, Brown.

Ressler, Robert K., and Shachtman, Tom. 1992. *Whoever Fights Monsters.* New York: St. Martin's Press.

Reuter, Peter. 1984a. "The (Continued) Vitality of Mythical Numbers." *The Public Interest* 75 (Spring): 135–47.

———. 1984b. *Disorganized Crime.* Cambridge, Mass.: MIT Press.

Revell, Oliver B. 1988. *Terrorism: A Law Enforcement Perspective.* Federal Bureau of Investigation, January.

Rhodes, Robert P. 1977. *The Insoluble Problem of Crime.* New York: Wiley.

Richards, David. 1982. *Sex, Drugs and the Law: An Essay on Human Rights and Overcriminalization.* Totowa, NJ: Rowman and Littlefield.

"RICO: Assault with a Deadly Weapon." 1989. *New York Times,* January 30, p. 18.

Rittenhouse, C. Amanda. 1991. "The Emergence of Premenstrual Syndrome as a Social Problem." *Social Problems* 38 (August): 412–23.

Ritter, Bruce. 1988. *Sometimes God Has a Kid's Face: The Story of America's Exploited Street Kids.* New York: Covenant House.

Roberts, Steven V., Shapiro, Joseph P., and Taylor, Ronald A. 1989. "The Undoing of Sam Pierce." *U.S. News and World Report,* September 18, pp. 29–32.

Robertson, Frank. 1977. *Triangle of Death: The Inside Story of the Triads.* London: Routledge and Kegan Paul.

Robin, Gerald D. 1991. *Violent Crime and Gun Control.* Cincinnati: Anderson.

Robins, Lee N. 1974. *The Vietnam Drug User Returns.* Monograph, Series A, Number 2. Rockville, MD: National Institute on Drug Abuse.

Robinson, William S. 1950. "Ecological Correlations and the Behavior of Individuals." *American Sociological Review* 15 (June): 351–57.

Rockefeller Commission. 1975. *The Rockefeller Report to the President by the Commission on CIA Activities.* Washington, DC: Government Printing Office.

Roebuck, Julian, and Weeber, Stanley G. 1978. *Political Crime in the United States: Analyzing Crime by and against the Government.* New York: Praeger.

Roebuck, Julian, and Windham, Gerald O. 1983. "Professional Theft." In *Career Criminals,* edited by Gordon B. Waldo, pp. 13–29. Beverly Hills, CA: Sage.

Rogers, Tony. 1992. "Outgunned 'Computer Posse' Tracks High-Tech Criminals." *Erie Morning News,* June 8, p. A4.

Rogovin, Charles H., and Martens, Frederick T. 1989. "Albini on Cressey." *Criminal Organizations* 4, 4: 11–14.

———. 1992. "The Evil That Men Do." *Journal of Contemporary Criminal Justice* 8 (February): 62–79.

Rome, Florence. 1975. *The Tattooed Men: An American Woman Reports on the Japanese Criminal Underworld.* New York: Delacorte Press.

Rorabaugh, W. J. 1979. *The Alcoholic Republic: An American Tradition.* New York: Oxford University Press.

Rosanoff, A. J., Handy, L. M., and Plesset, I. R. 1934. "Criminality and Delinquency in Twins." *Journal of Criminal Law and Criminology* 24 (May): 923–34.

Rosberg, Robert R. 1980. *Game of Thieves.* New York: Everest House.

Rose, Peter I., Glazer, Myron, and Glazer, Penina Migdal. 1982. *Sociology: Inquiry into Society.* 2nd edition. New York: St. Martin's Press.

Rosen, Lawrence, and Neilson, Kathleen. 1978. "The Broken Home and Delinquency." In *Crime in Society,* edited by Leonard Savitz and Norman Johnston, 2nd edition, pp. 406–15. New York: Wiley.

Rosen, Ruth. 1983. *The Lost Sisterhood: Prostitution in America, 1900–1918.* Baltimore, MD: Johns Hopkins University Press.

Rosenbaum, Jill. 1987. "Social Control, Gender and Delinquency: An Analysis of Drug, Property and Violent Offenders." *Justice Quarterly* 4: 117–32.

———. 1989a. "Family Dysfunction and Female Delinquency." *Crime and Delinquency* (January): 31–44.

———. 1989b. "Women and Crime." Special Issue. *Crime and Delinquency* 35 (January): entire issue.

Rosenberg, Tina. 1991. *Children of Cain: Violence and the Violent in Latin America.* New York: Morrow.

Rosenthal, Robert. 1966. *Experimenter Effects in Research.* New York: Appleton.

Rosner, Lydia S. 1995. "The Sexy Russian Mafia." *Criminal Organizations,* Fall: 28–32.

Ross, Edward. 1907. "The Criminaloid." *The Atlantic Monthly* 99 (January): 44–50. Reprinted in *White-Collar Crime,* edited by Gilbert Geis and Robert F. Meier, 1977, pp. 29–37. New York: The Free Press.

Ross, H. Laurence. 1961. "Traffic Law Violation: A Folk Crime." *Social Problems* 9 (Winter): 231–41.

Ross, Lee, and Edwards, Willie. 1998. "Publishing Among African American Criminologists: A Devaluing Experience." *Journal of Criminal Justice* 26 (1): 29–40.

Ross, Lee A., and McMurray, Harvey L. 1996. "Dual Realities and Structural Challenges of African-American Criminologists." *ACJS Today* 15 (May/June): 1, 3, 9.

Ross, Shelley. 1988. *Fall from Grace: Sex, Scandal, and Corruption in American Politics from 1702 to the Present.* New York: Ballantine.

Rossi, Peter, Waite, E., Bose, C.E., and Berk, R.E. 1974. "The Seriousness of Crimes: Normative Structure and Individual Differences." *American Sociological Review* 39 (April): 224–37.

Rounds, Delbert, ed. 2000. *International Criminal Justice: Issues in a Global Perspective.* Boston: Allyn and Bacon.

Rovetch, Emily L., Poggio, Eugene C., and Rossman, Henry H. 1984. *A Listing and Classification of Identified Issues Regarding the Uniform Crime Reporting Program of the FBI.* Cambridge, MA: Abt Associates.

Rowan, Roy. 1986. "The Biggest Mafia Bosses." *Fortune,* November 10, pp. 24–38.

Rupe, R. A. 1980. "Formula for Loss Prevention." *Retail Control.* March, pp. 2–15.

Russell, Diane. 1986. *The Secret Trauma: Incest in the Lives of Girls and Women.* New York: Basic Books.

Russell, Kathryn K. 1998. *The Color of Crime.* New York: New York University Press.

———. 1999. "Is There a Witness" (Book review of David Cole's *No Equal Justice*). *Washington Post National Weekly Edition,* February 22, p. 32.

———. 1992. "Development of a Black Criminology and the Role of the Black Criminologist." *Justice Quarterly* 9 (4): 667–683.

"Russian Mob May Have Laundered Billions at Bank of New York." 1999. *Russia Today,* August 23. (www.russiatoday.com: 80/news).

Ryan, Patrick J. 1990. "RICO, OCCA, and Defining Organized Crime [Organized Crime Is What Organized Crime Does]." *Criminal Organizations* 5 (2): 2–8.

Ryan, William. 1971. *Blaming the Victim.* New York: Random House.

Safire, William. 1989. "The End of RICO." *New York Times,* January 30, p. 19.

Sagarin, Edward. 1973. "Introduction." to *Political Crime,* by Louis Proal. Montclair, NJ: Patterson Smith.

———, ed. 1980. *Taboos in Criminology.* Beverly Hills, CA.: Sage.

Salerno, Ralph, and Tompkins, John S. 1969. *The Crime Confederation.* Garden City, NY: Doubleday.

Salwen, Kevin G. 1991. "SEC Charges Firm with Defrauding 40,000 Investors." *Wall Street Journal,* May 17, p. B8.

Salzanno, Julienne. 1994. "It's a Dirty Business: Organized Crime in Deep Sludge." *Criminal Organizations* 8, 3: 17–20.

Samper, Ernesto. 1995. "Colombia's War on Drugs." *Wall Street Journal,* June 30, p. A16.

Sampson, Robert J. 1985. "Structural Sources of Variation in Race-Age Specific Rates of Offending Across Major U.S. Cities." *Criminology* 23: 647–73.

Sanchez-Jankowski, Martin. 1991. *Islands in the Street: Gangs and American Urban Society.* Berkeley, CA.: University of California Press.

Sanday, Peggy R. 1990. *Fraternity Gang Rape: Sex, Brotherhood, and Privilege on Campus.* New York: New York University Press.

Sanders, William B., ed. 1976. *The Sociologist as Detective.* 2nd edition. New York: Praeger.

———. 1994. *Gangbangs and Drivebys: Grounded Culture and Juvenile Gang Violence.* New York: Aldine De Gruyter.

Sanoff, Alvin P. 1996. "The Hottest Import Crime." *U.S. News and World Report.* September 30, pg. 4.

Sapp, Allen. 1986. "Organized Linkages of Right Wing Extremist Groups." Paper presented at the Academy of Criminal Justice Sciences meetings, St. Louis, March.

Sarbin, Theodore R., and Miller, Jeffrey E. 1970. "Demonism Revisited: The XYY Chromosome Anomaly." *Issues in Criminology* 5 (Summer): 195–207.

Satchell, Michael. 1988. "The Just War That Never Ends." *U.S. News and World Report,* December 19, pp. 31–38.

Satchell, Michael, et al. 1987. "Narcotics: Terror's New Ally." *U.S. News and World Report,* May 4, pp. 30–37.

Satel, Sally L. 1999. "Real Help for the Mentally Ill." *New York Times,* January 7, p. B12.

"Satisfied Workers Don't Steal." 1983. *Criminal Justice Newsletter* 14 (July): 6–7.

Savage, George. 1976. *Forgeries, Fakes and Reproductions.* London: White Lion Publishing.

Savitz, D. 1959. "Automobile Theft." *Journal of Criminal Law, Criminology and Police Science* 50 (July): 132–43.

Savitz, Leonard D. 1978. "Official Police Statistics and their Limitations." In *Crime and Society,* edited by Leonard D. Savitz and Norman Johnston, pp. 69–81. New York: Wiley.

Savitz, Leonard, Kumar, Korni S., and Zahn, Margaret. 1991. "Quantifying Luckenbill." *Deviant Behavior* 12: 19–29.

Savonna, Ernesto U. 1998. *European Money Trails.* New York: Harwood Press.

"Scared Straight Found Ineffective Again." 1979. *Criminal Justice Newsletter* 10 (September): 7.

Scarpitti, Frank, Murray, Ellen, Dinitz, Simon, and Reckless, Walter. 1960. "The Good Boy in a High Delinquency Area: Four Years Later." *American Sociological Review* 23 (August): 555–58.

Scarpitti, Frank, and Nielsen, Amie L., eds. 1999. *Crime and Criminals.* Los Angeles: Roxbury.

Scarr, Harry A. 1973. *Patterns of Burglary.* Washington, DC: Government Printing Office.

Schafer, Stephen. 1969. *Theories in Criminology: Past and Present Philosophies of the Crime Problem.* New York: Random House.

———. 1971. "The Concept of the Political Criminal." *Journal of Criminal Law, Criminology and Police Science* 62 (Spring): 380–87.

———. 1974. *The Political Criminal.* New York: The Free Press.

———. 1976. *Introduction to Criminology.* Reston, VA: Reston Publishing Company.

Schatzberg, Rufus, and Kelly, Robert J. 1995. *African-American Organized Crime.* New York: Garland.

Schauss, Alexander. 1980. *Diet, Crime and Delinquency.* Berkeley, CA.: Parker House.

Scheflin, Alan W., and Opton, Edward M., Jr. 1978. *The Mind Manipulators.* New York: Paddington Press.

Scheim, David E. 1988. *Contract on America: The Mafia Murder of President John F. Kennedy.* New York: Shapolski Publishers.

Schellhardt, Timothy D. 1990. "Anti-Shoplifting Statutes." *Wall Street Journal,* October 15, p. B2.

Schichor, David. 1982. "An Analysis of Citations in Introductory Criminology Textbooks." *Journal of Criminal Justice* 10 (March): 231–37.

Schlachter, Barry. 1986. "Women Find Success in Espionage." *Buffalo News,* June 15, p. A–14.

Schlegel, Kip, and Weisburd, David, eds. 1994. *White-Collar Crime Reconsidered.* Boston: Northeastern University Press.

Schlesinger, Arthur M., Jr. 1986. *The Cycles of American History.* Boston: Houghton Mifflin.

Schloss, B., and Giesbrecht, N. A. 1972. *Murder in Canada: A Report on Capital and Non-Capital Murder Statistics 1961–1970.* Toronto: Centre of Criminology, University of Toronto.

Schmalleger, Frank. 1990. "A Call for Caution on Capital Punishment Policy." *The Criminologist* 15 (January-February): 4.

Schmitt, Richard B. 1992. "An Insurer's Sleuth Sniffs Out Lawyers Inflating Their Bills." *Wall Street Journal,* July 21, pp. A1, A5.

Schorr, Daniel. 1996. "Violence on TV: So, What's New?" *USA Today,* February 13, p. 9A.

Schrag, Clarence. 1962. "Delinquency and Opportunity: Analysis of a Theory." *Sociology and Social Research* 46 (January): 165–75.

———. 1971. *Crime and Justice: American Style.* Washington, DC: Government Printing Office.

Schrager, Laura Shill, and Short, Jr. James F. 1978. "Toward a Sociology of Organized Crime." *Social Problems* 25 (April): 407–19.

———. 1980. "How Serious a Crime? Perceptions of Organizational and Common Crimes." In *White-Collar Crime: Theory and Research,* edited by Gilbert Geis and Ezra Stotland, pp. 14–31. Beverly Hills, CA.: Sage.

Schuerman, Leo A., and Kobrin, Solomon. 1986. "Community Careers in Crime." In *Communities and Crime,* edited by Albert J. Reiss, Jr., and Michael Tonry. Chicago: University of Chicago Press.

Schuessler, Karl. 1952. "The Deterrent Influence of the Death Penalty." *Annals of the Academy of Political and Social Sciences* 284: 54–62.

———. 1954. "Review." *American Journal of Sociology* 49: 604.

Schuessler, Karl F., and Cressey, Donald R. 1953. "Personality Characteristics of Criminals." *American Journal of Sociology,* 55: 166–76.

Schulsinger, Fini. 1972. "Psychopathy, Heredity and Environment." *International Journal of Mental Health* 1 (January): 190–206.

Schur, Edwin M. 1965. *Crimes without Victims: Deviant Behavior and Public Policy.* Englewood Cliffs, NJ: Prentice-Hall.

———. 1969. "Reactions to Deviance: A Critical Assessment." *American Journal of Sociology* 75 (November): 309–22.

———. 1971. *Labeling Deviant Behavior.* New York: Harper and Row.

———. 1980. *The Politics of Deviance.* Englewood Cliffs, NJ: Prentice-Hall.

Schwartz, John. 1990a. "The Hacker Dragnet." *Newsweek,* April 30, p. 50.

———. 1990b. "Hackers of the World, Unite!" *Newsweek,* July 2, pp. 36–37.

Schwartz, Martin D., and Friedrichs, David O. 1994. "Postmodern Thought and Criminological Discontent: New Metaphors for Understanding Violence." *Criminology* 32 (May): 221–46.

Schwartz, Michael, and Tangri, Sandra. 1965. "A Note on Self-Concept as an Insulator against Delinquency." *American Sociological Review* 30: 922–26.

Schweinhart, L. J., and Weikart, D. P. 1980. *Young Children Grow Up: The Effects of the Perry Preschool Program on Youths through Age 15.* Ypsilanti, Mich.: High/Scope.

"Scientology Fraud." 1983. *20/20.* ABC television broadcast, January 6.

Scott, Donald W. 1989. "Policing Corporate Collusion." *Criminology* 27 (August): 559–88.

Scott, Joseph E. 1988. "Book Reviews of Attorney General's Commission on Pornography and Related Works." *Journal of Criminal Law and Criminology* 78: 1145–165.

"The Secret of South Africa's Hit Squad." 1989. *Newsweek,* November 25, p. 56.

Sederberg, Peter C. 1989. *Terrorist Myths: Illusion, Rhetoric and Reality.* Englewood Cliffs, NJ: Prentice-Hall.

Seidman, David, and Couzens, Michael. 1974. "Getting the Crime Rate Down: Political Pressure and Crime Reporting." *Law and Society Review* 8 (Spring): 457–93.

Sellin, Thorsten. 1938. "Culture Conflict and Crime." *Social Science Research Council Bulletin* 41: 1–7.

———. 1957. "Crime in the United States." *Life,* September 9, p. 48.

———. 1959. *The Death Penalty.* Philadelphia: American Law Institute.

Sellin, Thorsten, and Wolfgang, Marvin E. 1964. *The Measurement of Delinquency.* New York: Wiley.

Senate Permanent Subcommittee on Investigations. Committee on Governmental Affairs. 1979. 96th Congress, First Session, December 7, 11, 12, 13, and 14.

———. 1983. 98th Congress, First Session, August 3.

"700 Million Ponzi Schemer Draws Record Prison Term." 2000. *Bloomberg News,* April 29.

Shah, Saleem A., and Roth, Loren H. 1974. "Biological and Psychophysiological Factors in Criminality." In *Handbook of Criminology,* edited by Daniel Glaser, pp. 101–73. Chicago: Rand McNally.

Shapiro, Joseph, and Wright, Andrea R. 1995. "Sins of the Father." *U.S. News and World Report,* August 14, pp. 52–53.

Shaw, Clifford R. 1929. *Delinquency Areas: A Study of the Geographic Distribution of School Truants, Juvenile Delinquents and Adult Offenders in Chicago.* Chicago: University of Chicago Press.

———. 1930. *The Jack Roller.* Chicago: University of Chicago Press.

Shaw, Clifford R., and McKay, Henry D. 1942. *Juvenile Delinquency and Urban Areas.* Chicago: University of Chicago Press.

Shaw, Clifford R., McKay, Henry D., and MacDonald, James F. 1938. *Brothers in Crime.* Chicago: University of Chicago Press.

Shaw, George Bernard. 1941. "Preface to The Doctor's Dilemma" in *The Doctor's Dilemma,* edited by George Bernard Shaw. New York: Dodd, Mead and Company.

Sheehy, Gail. 1973. *Hustling: Prostitution in Our Wide Open Society.* New York: Delacorte Press.

Sheldon, William H. 1940. *The Varieties of Human Physique.* New York: Harper and Row.

———. 1949. *Varieties of Delinquent Youth.* New York: Harpers.

Sheley, J. F. 1979. *Understanding Crime: Concepts, Issues, Decisions.* Belmont, CA: Wadsworth.

Sheley, Joseph F., and Wright, James D. 1995. *In the Line of Fire: Youth, Guns, and Violence in Urban America.* Hawthorne, NY: Aldine de Gruyter.

Shelley, Louise I. 1981. *Crimes and Modernization.* Carbondale, IL: Southern Illinois University.

———. 1995. "Privatization and Crime: The Post-Soviet Experience." *Journal of Contemporary Criminal Justice* 11 (December): 244–56.

Sherif, Muzafer, and Sherif, Carolyn. 1966. *Groups in Harmony and Tension.* New York: Octagon.

Sherman, Larry, and Berk, Richard. 1984. "The Specific Deterrent Effects of Arrest for Domestic Assault." *American Sociological Review* 49: 261–72.

Sherman, Lawrence W. 1992. *Policing Domestic Violence: Experiments and Dilemmas.* New York: The Free Press.

Sherman, Lawrence W., et al. 1997. *Preventing Crime: What Works, What Doesn't, What's Promising: A Report to the United States Congress.* Washington, DC: National Institute of Justice, February, NCJ 165366

Sherman, Lawrence W., Shaw, James W., and Rogan, Dennis P. 1995. "The Kansas City Gun Experiment." *National Institute of Justice Research in Brief,* January.

Shoemaker, Donald L., and Williams, J. Sherwood. 1987. "The Subculture of Violence and Ethnicity." *Journal of Criminal Justice* 15: 461–72.

Short, James F., Jr., 1990. "Gangs, Neighborhoods and Youth Crime." *Criminal Justice Research Bulletin* 5 (4): 1–11.

Short, James F., Jr., and Nye, F. Ivan. 1958. "Extent of Unrecorded Delinquency: Tentatitve Conclusions." *Journal of Criminal Law, Criminology and Police Science* 49 (December): 296–302.

Short, James F., Jr., and Strodtbeck, Fred L. 1965. *Group Process and Gang Delinquency.* Chicago: University of Chicago Press.

Shover, Neal. 1973. "The Social Organization of Burglary." *Social Problems* 20 (Spring): 499–514.

———. 1983. "The Later Stages of Ordinary Property Offender Careers." *Social Problems* 31 (December): 208–18.

Siconolfi, Michael, and Johnson, Robert. 1991. "Broker Grandmother Accused of Losing Clients' Cash at Baccarat." *Wall Street Journal,* August 29, pp. C1, C11.

Sigler, Robert T., and Haygood, Donna. 1988. "The Criminalization of Forced Marital Intercourse." In *Deviance and the Family,* edited by Frank E. Hagan and Marvin B. Sussman, pp. 71–85. New York: Haworth Press.

Silberman, Charles E. 1978. *Criminal Violence, Criminal Justice.* New York: Random House.

Silk, L. Howard, and Vogel, David. 1976. *Ethics and Profits: The Crisis of Confidence in American Business.* New York: Simon and Schuster.

"Silkwood Vindicated." 1979. *Newsweek,* May 28, p. 40.

Simcha-Fagan, Ora, and Schwartz, Joseph E. 1986. "Neighborhood and Delinquency: An Assessment of Contextual Effects." *Criminology* 24: 667–703.

Simmel, Georg. 1955. *Conflict and the Web of Group Affiliations.* Translated by Kurt H. Wolff and Reinhard Bendix. New York: Free Press.

Simmons, Jerry L. 1969. *Deviants.* Berkeley, CA: Glendessary Press.

Simon, David R. 1996. *Elite Deviance.* 5th edition. Boston: Allyn and Bacon.

Simon, David. 1999. *Elite Deviance.* 6th edition. Boston: Allyn and Bacon.

Simon, David R., and Hagan, Frank E. 1999. *White-Collar Deviance.* Boston: Allyn and Bacon.

Simon, David R., and Swart, Stanley L. 1984. "The Justice Department Focuses on White-Collar Crime: Promises and Pitfalls." *Crime and Delinquency* 30 (January).

Simon, Rita J. 1975. *Women and Crime.* Lexington, MA: Lexington Books.

———. 1990. "Women and Crime Revisited." *Criminal Justice Research Bulletin* 5 (5): 1–8.

Simon, Rita J., and Aaronson, David E. 1988. *The Insanity Defense: A Critical Assessment of Law and Policy in the Post-Hinckley Era.* New York: Praeger.

Simpson, John, and Bennett, Jana. 1985. *The Disappeared and the Mothers of the Plaza.* New York: St. Martin's Press.

Simpson, M., and Schill, T. 1977. "Patrons of Massage Parlors: Some Facts and Figures." *Archives of Sexual Behavior* 6: 521.

Simpson, Sally S. 1989. "Feminist Theory, Crime, and Justice." *Criminology* 27: 605–32.

Simpson, Sally S., and Elis, Lori. 1995. "Doing Gender: Sorting Out the Caste and Crime Conundrum." *Criminology* 33: 47–81.

Simpson, Sally S., and Koper, Christopher S. 1991. "Deterring Corporate Crime." Paper presented at the American Society of Criminology Meetings, San Francisco, CA, November.

Sinclair, Upton. 1906. *The Jungle.* New York: Doubleday and Page.

Sinden, P. G. 1980. "Perceptions of Crime in Capitalist America: The Question of Consciousness Manipulation." *Sociological Focus* 13: 75–85.

Singer, Max. 1971. "The Vitality of Mythical Numbers." *The Public Interest* 23 (Spring): 3–9.

Singer, Max, and Levine, Murray. 1988. "Power Control Theory, Gender, and Delinquency: A Partial Replication with Additional Evidence on the Effects of Peers." *Criminology* 26: 627–47.

Singer, Simon I. 1978. "Comments on Alleged Overreporting." *Criminology* 16 (May): 99–103.

Skinner, B.F. 1953. *Science and Human Behavior.* New York: Macmillan.

———. 1971. *Beyond Freedom and Dignity.* New York: Knopf.

Skogan, Wesley G. 1987. *Victimization Surveys and Criminal Justice Planning.* Monograph. Washington, DC: National Institute of Law Enforcement and Criminal Justice, July.

Skolnick, Jerome. 1997. "Tough Guys." *The American Prospect* 30 (January): 86–91.

Skolnick, Jerome H. 1969. *The Politics of Protest: The Skolnick Report to the National Commission on the Causes and Prevention of Violence.* New York: Ballantine Books.

Skolnick, Jerome H., and Currie, Elliot, eds. 1988. *Crisis in American Institutions.* Boston: Little, Brown.

Skorneck, Carolyn. 1991. "Former Air Force Official Pleads Guilty to Taking Bribe." *Erie Morning News,* August 23, p. 3A.

Skrzycki, Cindy. 1996. "Deregulation by Default." *Washington Post National Weekly Edition,* March 4–10, pp. 6–8.

Slade, Margot. 1994. "At the Bar." *New York Times,* May 26, p. B12.

Slim, Iceberg. 1969. *Pimp: The Story of My Life.* Los Angeles: Holloway House.

Smigel, Erwin O. 1970. "Public Attitudes toward Stealing as Related to the Size of the Victim Organization." In *Crimes against Bureaucracy,* edited by Erwin O.

Smigel and H. Laurence Ross, pp. 15–28. New York: Van Nostrand Reinhold.

Smigel, Erwin O., and Ross, H. Laurence, eds. 1970. *Crimes against Bureaucracy.* New York: Van Nostrand Reinhold.

Smith, Adam. 1953. *The Wealth of Nations.* Cambridge, MA: Harvard University Press.

Smith, Bradley F. 1977. *Reaching Judgment at Nuremberg.* New York: Basic Books.

Smith, Dwight C., Jr. 1975. *The Mafia Mystique.* New York: Basic Books.

———. 1978. "Organized Crime and Entrepreneurship." *International Journal of Criminology and Penology* 6 (May): 161–77.

———. 1980. "Paragons, Pariahs and Pirates: A Spectrum-Based Theory of Enterprise." *Crime and Delinquency* 26 (July): 358–86.

Smith, Hedrick. 1989. *The Power Game.* PBS television broadcast, February 6.

Smith, J. David. 1985. *Minds Made Feeble: The Myth and Legacy of the Kallikaks.* Aspen, CO: Aspen.

Smith, Mary S. 1996. "Crime Prevention Through Environmental Design in Parking Facilities." *National Institute of Justice Research in Brief.* April.

Snider, Donald L. 1978. "Corporate Crime in Canada." *Canadian Journal of Criminology* 20 (April): 142–68.

Snider, L. 1982. "Traditional and Corporate Theft: A Comparison of Sanctions." In *White-Collar and Economic Crime,* edited by Peter Wickman and Timothy Dailey, pp. 235–58. Lexington, MA: Lexington.

Snodgrass, Jon D. 1972. *The American Criminological Tradition: Portraits of the Men and Ideology in a Discipline.* Unpublished doctoral dissertation, University of Pennsylvania.

———. 1982. *The Jack Roller at Seventy: A Fifty-Year Follow Up.* Lexington, MA: D. C. Heath.

Snyder, Howard N., and Sickmund, Melissa. 1999. *Juvenile Offenders and Victims, 1999 National Report.* Washington: Office of Juvenile Justice and Delinquency Prevention.

Snyder, Lynn Page. 1994. "The Death-Dealing Smog Over Donora, Pennsylvania: Industrial Air Pollution, Public Health Policy and the Politics of Expertise, 1948–1949." Doctoral dissertation, University of Pennsylvania.

Solzhenitsyn, Alexander I. 1975. "The Gulag Archipelago." New York: Harper and Row.

Somers, Christina H. 1994. *Who Stole Feminism?* New York: Simon and Schuster.

Sondern, Frederic J. 1959. *Brotherhood of Evil: The Mafia.* New York: Straus and Giroux.

Southerland, Daniel. 1991. "A Witness against China's Export Practices." *Washington Post National Weekly Edition,* October 7–13, p. 20.

"Soviet Crime Rate Up." 1989. *Los Angeles Times,* February 14, p. 1A.

Sparks, Richard F. 1980. "A Critique of Marxist Criminology." In *Crime and Justice,* edited by Norval Morris and Michael Tonry, volume 2, pp. 159–208. Chicago: University of Chicago Press.

Sparrow, Malcolm. 1998. "Fraud Control in the Health Care Industry." *National Institute of Justice Research in Brief,* December.

Spencer, C. 1966. "A Typology of Violent Offenders." *Administrative Abstracts* No. 23, California Department of Corrections, September. Cited in *The Nature of Crime,* by Harold J. Vetter and Ira J. Silverman, 1978. Philadelphia, PA: W. B. Saunders.

Spernow, Bill. 1995. Videoconference presented by the National White-Collar Crime Center. Morgantown, WV: November.

Spitzer, Robert J. 1995. *The Politics of Gun Control.* Chatham, NJ: Chatham House Publishers.

Spitzer, Steven. 1975. "Toward a Marxian Theory of Deviance." *Social Problems* 22 (September): 638–51.

Spohn, Cassia, and Cederblom, Jerry. 1991. "Race and Disparities in Sentencing: A Test of the Liberation Hypothesis." *Justice Quarterly* 8 (September): 305–27.

Springer, Karen. 1991. "A Slippery Pyramid: To Some Nu Skin May Be Nu Scam." *Newsweek,* July 22, p. 39.

Staats, Gregory R. 1977. "Changing Conceptualizations of Professional Criminals: Implications for Criminology Theory." *Criminology* 15 (May): 53–63.

Stafford, Mark. 1984. "Gang Delinquency." In *Major Forms of Crime,* edited by John F. Meier, pp. 167–90. Beverly Hills, CA: Sage.

Stark, Rodney. 1987. "Deviant Places: A Theory of the Ecology of Crime." *Criminology* 25: 893–909.

Stecklow, Steve. 1996. "Trustee for New Era is Suing Prudential." *Wall Street Journal,* June 27, p. A3.

Steffens, Lincoln. 1904. *The Shame of the Cities.* New York: McClure, Phillips.

Steffensmeier, Darrell. 1978. "Crime and the Contemporary Woman: Analysis of Changing Levels of Female Property Crime, 1960–1975." *Social Forces* 57: 566–84.

———. 1986. *The Fence: In the Shadow of Two Worlds.* Totowa, NJ: Rowman and Littlefield.

———. 1989a. "Age and the Distribution of Crime." *American Journal of Sociology* 94: 803–31.

———. 1989b. "On the Causes of 'White-Collar' Crime: An Assessment of Hirschi and Gottfredson's Claims." *Criminology* 27 (May): 345–58.

Steffensmeier, Darrell, and Allan, Emilie A. 1988. "Sex Disparities in Arrests by Residence, Race and Age: An Assessment of the Gender Convergence/Crime Hypothesis." *Justice Quarterly* 5: 53–80.

———. 1990. "Physical Fitness, Age, and Crime: The Significance of Biological Aging vs. Social Aging in Explaining the Rapid Decline in Offending in the Late Teens." Paper presented at the American Sociological Association Meetings, Washington, DC, August.

Steffensmeier, Darrell, and Kramer, John F. 1990. "Race Differences in Sentencing: Research Continuities and Further Developments." Paper presented at the American Society of Criminology Meetings, Baltimore, MD, November.

Stein, Martha L. 1974. *Lovers, Friends, Slaves . . . : The Nine Male Sexual Types.* Berkeley, CA: Berkeley Publishing Corporation.

Stein, Maurice R. 1964. *The Eclipse of Community: An Interpretation of American Studies.* New York: Harper and Row.

Steinmetz, Suzanne K., and Straus, Murray. 1978. "The Family as a Cradle of Violence." In *Readings in Criminology,* edited by Peter Wickman and Philip Whitten, pp. 59–65. Lexington, MA: D. C. Heath.

Stellwagen, Lindsey D. 1985. "The Use of Forfeiture Sanctions in Drug Cases." *Research in Brief.* National Institute of Justice, July.

Stephens, Gene, ed. 1982. *The Future of Criminal Justice.* Cincinnati: Anderson.

Stephens, Richard C., and Ellis, Rosalind D. 1975. "Narcotics Addiction and Crime: An Analysis of Recent Trends." *Criminology* 12: 474–87.

Sterling, Claire. 1981. *The Terror Network: The Secret War of International Terrorism.* New York: Holt, Rinehart and Winston.

———. 1990. *Octopus: The Long Reach of the International Sicilian Mafia.* New York: W. W. Norton Inc.

Stern, Kenneth S. 1996. *A Force Upon the Plain: The American Militia Movement and the Politics of Hate.* New York: Simon and Schuster.

Stevens, Mark. 1991. *The Big Six: The Selling Out of America's Top Accounting Firms.* New York: Simon and Schuster.

Steward, David W., and Spille, Henry A. 1988. Diploma Mills: *Degrees of Fraud.* New York: Macmillan.

Stewart, James B. 1991a. *Den of Thieves.* New York: Simon and Schuster.

———. 1991b. "Scenes from a Scandal." *Wall Street Journal,* October 2, pp. B1, B6.

Stewart, James K. 1988. "Foreword." *Research Program Plan, Fiscal Year 1988.* Washington, DC: National Institute of Justice.

Stewart, John E., and Cannon, Daniel A. 1977. "Effects of Perpetrator Status and Bystander Commitment on Response to a Simulated Crime." *Journal of Police Science and Administration* 5: 318–23.

Stieg, Bill. 1990a. "Judge Fines GE $10 Million; Sentences 2 Employees to Prison." *Erie Morning News,* July 27, p. 2A.

———. 1990b. "A Philly Favorite: Faking Injuries." *Erie Times News,* November 4, p. 16A.

Stille, Alexander, and Robinson, Linda. 1992. "Guns Drawn, the Mafia Turns Against the Rest of Italy." *U.S. News and World Report,* August 3, p. 42.

"The Sting." 1976. *Newsweek,* March 15, p. 35.

Stirling, Nora. 1974. *Your Money or Your Life.* Indianapolis, IN: Bobbs-Merrill.

Stout, Hilary. 1991. "Stanford Accused of Overcharging U.S. for Research." *Wall Street Journal,* March 14, p. C15.

———. 1992. "Dozens of Pharmacists, Doctor Charged with Billing-Fraud Insurance Schemes." *Wall Street Journal,* July 1, p. A3.

Straus, Murray A. 1994. *Beating the Devil Out of Them: Corporal Punishment in American Families.* San Francisco: Lexington Books.

———. 1999. "The Benefits of Avoiding Corporal Punishment: New and More Definitive Evidence." Unpublished paper. University of New Hampshire, December 15.

Straus, Murray A., and Gelles, Richard J. 1986. "Societal Change and Change in Family Violence from 1975 to 1985 as Revealed by Two National Surveys." *Journal of Marriage and the Family* 48: 465–79.

Straus, Murray A., Gelles, Richard, and Steinmetz, Susan. 1982. "The Marriage License as a Hitting License." In *Crisis in American Institutions,* edited by Jerome H. Skolnick and Elliott Currie, 5th edition, pp. 273–87. Boston: Little, Brown.

Straus, Murray, Gelles, Richard J., and Steinmetz, Susan. 1980. *Behind Closed Doors: Violence in the American Family.* New York: Doubleday.

Streitfeld, David. 1992. "Stealing from the Stacks." *Washington Post National Weekly Edition,* April 6–12, p. 10.

Strug, D., et al. 1984. "Hustling to Survive: The Role of Drugs, Alcohol and Crime in the Life of Street Hustlers." Paper presented at the Academy of Criminal Justice Sciences Meetings, Chicago, March.

Sullivan, Terence. 1988. "Juvenile Prostitution: A Critical Perspective." In *Deviance and the Family,* edited by Frank E. Hagan and Marvin B. Sussman, pp. 113–34. New York: Haworth Press.

Sumner, William G. 1906. *Folkways.* New York: Dover.

Sun-Tzu. 1963. *The Art of War.* Translated by Samuel B. Griffith. New York: Oxford University Press.

"Super Sleuths." 1991. *In Sync.* Erie Insurance Group, Summer, pp. 2–5.

Surgeon General's Scientific Advisory Committee on Television and Social Behavior. 1972. *Television and Growing Up: The Impact of Televised Violence.* Washington, DC: Government Printing Office.

Survey of Inmates of State Correctional Facilities—Advance Report. 1976. March. Washington, DC: Government Printing Office.

Suskind, Ron. 1991. "Bank Robbers Find Automated Tellers a Real Convenience." *Wall Street Journal,* May 17, pp. A1, A6.

Sussman, Marvin B., and Haug, Marie R. 1967. "Human and Mechanical Error: An Unknown Quantity in

Research." *American Behavioral Scientist* 2 (November): 55–56.

Sutherland, Edwin H. 1937. *The Professional Thief.* Chicago: University of Chicago Press. Reissued 1956. Chicago: Phoenix.

———. 1940. "White-Collar Criminality." *American Sociological Review* 5 (February): 1–12.

———. 1941. "Crime and Business." *Annals of the American Academy of Political and Social Science* 217 (September): 112–18.

———. 1945. "Is 'White-Collar Crime' Crime?" *American Sociological Review* 10 (April): 132–139.

———. 1947. *Principles of Criminology.* 4th edition. Philadelphia, PA: Lippincott.

———. 1949. *White-Collar Crime.* New York: Holt, Rinehart and Winston.

———. 1956a. "Crime of Corporations." In *The Sutherland Papers,* edited by Albert Cohen, Alfred Lindesmith, and Karl Schuessler, pp. 78–96. Bloomington, IN: Indiana University Press. Also in *White-Collar Crime,* edited by Gilbert Geis and Robert F. Meier, 1977, pp. 71–84. New York: Free Press.

———. 1956b. "The Development of the Theory." In *The Sutherland Papers,* edited by Albert Cohen, Alfred Lindesmith, and Karl Schuessler, pp. 13–29. Bloomington, IN: Indiana University Press.

Sutherland, Edwin H., and Cressey, Donald C. 1960. *Criminology.* Philadelphia: Lippincott.

———. 1974. *Criminology.* 9th edition. Philadelphia: Lippincott.

———. 1978. *Criminology.* 10th edition. Philadelphia: Lippincott.

Swigert, Victoria, and Farrell, Ronald. 1980. "Corporate Homicide: Definitional Processes in the Creation of Deviance." *Law and Society Review* 15 (Autumn): 161–82.

Swisher, Kara. 1994. "Office Violence is on the Rise, and Firms Aren't Ready." *Your Money (Erie Times),* May 31, p. 11S.

Sykes, Gresham M. 1958. *The Society of Captives: A Study of Maximum Security Prison.* Princeton, NJ: Princeton University Press.

———. 1972. "The Future of Criminality." *American Behavioral Scientists* 15 (January): 403–19.

———. 1978. *Criminology.* New York: Harcourt, Brace, Jovanovich.

———. 1980. *The Future of Crime.* Rockville, MD: National Institute of Mental Health.

Sykes, Gresham, and Matza, David. 1957. "Techniques of Neutralization: A Theory of Delinquency." *American Sociological Review* 22 (December): 664–70.

Szasz, Andrew. 1986. "Corporations, Organized Crime, and the Disposal of Hazardous Waste: An Examination of the Making of a Criminogenic Regulatory Structure." *Criminology* 24: 1–28.

Szasz, Thomas. 1974. *Ceremonial Chemistry: The Ritual Persecution of Drugs, Addicts and Pushers.* New York: Anchor Books.

Tafoya, William. 1992. "Law Enforcement in the Year 2010." Paper presented at the Academy of Criminal Justice Sciences Meetings, Pittsburgh, PA, March.

"Taking a Byte Out of Crime." 1990. *Lotus Quarterly,* Winter, pp. 27–28.

Talese, Gay. 1971. *Honor Thy Father.* Greenwich, CT: Fawcett.

———. 1979. *Thy Neighbor's Wife.* Greenwich, CT: Fawcett Crest Books.

Tannenbaum, Frank. 1938. *Crime and the Community.* Boston: Ginn.

Tappan, Paul. 1960. *Crime, Justice and Correction.* New York: McGraw-Hill.

Tarde, Gabriel. 1912. *Penal Philosophy.* Boston: Little, Brown. Reissued 1968. Montclair, NJ: Patterson Smith.

Taylor, Bruce M. 1989. "New Definitions for the National Crime Survey." Bureau of Justice Statistics Special Report, March.

Taylor, Carl S. 1990. *Dangerous Society.* East Lansing, MI: Michigan State University.

Taylor, Ian, et al. 1973. *The New Criminology: For a Social Theory of Deviance.* New York: Harper and Row.

———, ed. 1975. *Critical Criminology.* London: Routledge and Kegan Paul.

Taylor, Laurie. 1984. *In the Underworld.* Oxford, England: Basil Blackwell.

Taylor, Ralph B., and Harrell, Adele V. 1996. *Physical Environment and Crime.* Washington, DC: National Institute of Justice, May.

Taylor, Stuart, Jr. 1985. "U.S. Defends Disputed Hutton Decision." *New York Times,* May 16, p. D5.

Tennebaum, David. 1977. "Research Studies of Personality and Criminality." *Journal of Criminal Justice* 5 (January): 1–19.

Teresa, Vincent. 1973a. "A Mafioso Cases the Mafia Craze." *Saturday Review,* February, pp. 23–29.

Teresa, Vincent, with Renner, Thomas. 1973b. *My Life in the Mafia.* Greenwich, CT: Fawcett Publications.

Terrill, Richard. 1999. *World Criminal Justice Systems: A Survey.* 4th edition. Cincinnati: Anderson.

Tesla, Paul G. 1990. *Crime and Mental Disease in the Hand: A Proven Guide for the Identification and Pre-Identification of Criminality, Psychosis and Mental Defectiveness.* Lakeland, FL: Osiris Press.

"There's a New Sheriff in Town." 1995. *New York Times,* November 10, pp. C1, C7.

Thibault, Edward A. 1992. "The Violent Woman at Home." Paper presented at the Northwestern Academy of Criminal Justice Sciences Meetings, Newport, RI, June.

"13th Victim of Cult Discovered." 1989. *Erie Morning News,* April 14, p. 1A.

Thomas, Charles W., and Hepburn, John R. 1983. *Crime, Criminal Law and Criminology.* Dubuque, IA: William C. Brown.

Thomas, Edward, et al. 1994. "Deadly Male." *Newsweek,* March 7: 20–31.

Thomas, Pierre. 1995. "Using More, Worrying Less." *Washington Post National Weekly Edition,* December 25–31, p. 32.

Thomas, William I., and Swaine, Dorothy. 1928. *The Child in America.* New York: Knopf.

Thompson, Marilyn W. 1990. *Feeding the Beast: How Wedtech Became the Most Corrupt Little Company in America.* New York: Charles Scribner's.

Thompson, Terri, Hage, David, and Black, Robert F. 1992. "Crime and the Bottom Line." *U.S. News and World Report,* April 13, pp. 55–58.

Thornberry, Terrence P., et al. 1999. *Family Disruption and Delinquency. OJJP Juvenile Justice Bulletin,* September.

Thornberry, Terrence, et al. 1991. "Testing Interactional Theory." *Journal of Criminal Law and Criminology.* 82: 3–35.

Tittle, Charles R. 1988. "Two Empirical Regularities (Maybe) In Search of an Explanation: Commentary on the Age/Crime Debate." *Criminology* 26: 75–85.

Tittle, Charles, Villemez, W., and Smith, D. 1978. "The Myth of Social Class and Criminality: An Empirical Assessment of the Empirical Evidence." *American Sociological Review* 43: 643–56.

Tjaden, Patricia. 1997. Summary of a presentation entitled "The Crime of Stalking: How Big is the Problem?" *National Institute of Justice Research Preview,* November.

Toby, Jackson. 1980. "The New Criminology Is the Old Baloney." In *Radical Criminology: The Coming Crisis,* edited by James A. Inciardi, pp. 124–32. Beverly Hills, CA: Sage.

Toch, Hans. 1979. *Psychology of Crime and Criminal Justice.* New York: Holt, Rinehart and Winston.

Toch, Hans, and Adams, Kenneth. 1991. *The Disturbed Violent Offender.* New Haven: Yale University Press.

Toennies, Ferdinand. 1957. *Community and Society.* Translated by Charles Loomis. East Lansing, MI: Michigan State University.

Tomsho, Robert. 1987. *The American Sanctuary Movement.* Austin: TX: Monthly Press.

Trasler, Gordon. 1962. *The Explanation of Criminality.* London: Routledge and Kegan Paul.

Traub, James. 1990. *Too Good to Be True: The Outlandish Story of Wedtech.* New York: Doubleday.

Travis, Lawrence F. 1983. "The Case Study in Criminal Justice." *Criminal Justice Review* 8 (Fall): 46–51.

Trebach, Arnold S. 1982. *The Heroin Solution.* New Haven: Yale University Press.

———. 1984. "Peace without Surrender in the Perpetual Drug War." *Justice Quarterly* 1 (March): 125–44.

———. 1987. *The Great Drug War.* New York: Macmillan.

Truzzi, Marcello. 1976. "Sherlock Holmes: Applied Social Psychologist." In *The Sociologist as Detective,* edited by William B. Sanders, 2nd edition, pp. 50–86. New York: Praeger.

Tunnell, Kenneth. 1991. *Choosing Crime: The Criminal Calculus of Property Offenders.* Chicago: Nelson-Hall.

Tunnell, Kenneth. 2000. *Living Off Crime.* Chicago: Burnham.

Turk, Austin T. 1969a. *Criminality and the Legal Order.* Chicago: Rand McNally.

———. 1969b. "Introduction." In *Criminality and Economic Conditions,* edited by Willem Bonger. Bloomington, IN: Indiana University Press.

———. 1972. *Legal Sanctioning and Social Control.* Washington, DC: Government Printing Office.

———. 1980. "Analyzing Official Deviance: For Nonpartisan Conflict Analyses in Criminology." In *Radical Criminology: The Coming Crisis,* edited by James A. Inciardi, pp. 78–91. Beverly Hills, CA: Sage.

———. 1981. "Organization Deviance and Political Policing." *Criminology* 19 (August): 231–50.

———. 1982. *Political Criminality: The Defiance and Defense of Authority.* Beverly Hills, CA: Sage.

———. 1984. "Political Crime." In *Major Forms of Crime,* edited by Robert F. Meier, pp. 119–35. Beverly Hills, CA: Sage.

Turner, Frederick Jackson. 1975. *The Frontier in American History.* Huntington, NY: R. B. Krieger.

Turner, James S. 1970. *The Chemical Feast: Nader's Raiders Study Group Report on the Food and Drug Administration.* New York: Grossman.

Turner, Jonathan H. 1974. *The Structure of Sociological Theory.* Homewood, IL: Dorsey.

Turner, Stansfield. 1985. *Secrecy and Democracy: The CIA in Transition.* New York: Houghton Mifflin.

Turner, W. 1983. "Testimony Details City Underworld's Control of a Las Vegas Casino." *New York Times,* June 12, p. 30.

Twain, Mark. 1899. *Following the Equator: A Journey around the World.* New York: Harper.

"21 Brokers Charged in Price-Rigging Scheme." 1991. *Erie Morning News,* January 24, p. 5A.

Tyler, Gus, ed. 1962. *Organized Crime in America.* Ann Arbor, MI: University of Michigan Press.

United Nations. 1974. *Demographic Yearbook.* New York: United Nations, Publishing Service.

United Press International. 1969. "Text of Terrorist Letter," March 12.

"U.S. Begins Price-Fixing Prosecution." 1975. *Erie Times News,* September 9, p. 10.

U.S. Bureau of Census. 1970. "Victim Recall Pretest." *Household Surveys of Victims of Crime.* Washington, DC: Bureau of Demographic Surveys Division. Mimeograph.

———. 1983. *Statistical Abstracts of the United States, 1982.* Washington, DC: Government Printing Office.

———. 1987. *Statistical Abstracts of the United States, 1986.* Washington, DC: Government Printing Office.

———. 1989. *Money Income and Poverty Status of Persons in the United States: 1988.* Washington, DC: Government Printing Office.

U.S. Congress. 1976. *Hearings before the Subcommittee on Energy and Environment of the Committee on Small Business,* 94th Congress, 2nd Session, April 26, May 20.

———. 1981. *Hearings before the Subcommittee on Oversight and Investigations of the Committee on Energy and Commerce.* 97th Congress, 1st Session, March 12, April 2, 3.

U.S. Department of Justice. 1974. *Crime in Eight American Cities.* National Criminal Justice Information and Statistics Service. Washington, DC: Government Printing Office.

———. 1975a. *Criminal Victimization Surveys in the Nation's Five Largest Cities.* National Criminal Justice Information and Statistics Service. Washington, DC: Government Printing Office.

———. 1975b. *Criminal Victimization in Thirteen American Cities.* National Criminal Justice Information and Statistics Service. Washington, DC: Government Printing Office.

———. 1976. *Criminal Victimization in the United States.* National Criminal Justice Information and Statistics Service. Washington, DC: Government Printing Office.

———. 1978. *Myths and Realities about Crime.* National Criminal Justice Information and Statistics Service. Washington, DC: Government Printing Office.

———. 1979. *Criminal Victimization in the United States. 1977.* National Criminal Justice Information and Statistics Service. Washington, DC: Government Printing Office.

———. 1980. *Profile of Jail Inmates: Sociodemographic Findings from the 1978 Survey of Inmates of Local Jails.* Washington, DC: Government Printing Office.

———. 1983. "An Overview of the Criminal Justice System: The American Response to Crime." *Bureau of Justice Statistics Bulletin,* December.

———. 1988. *Bureau of Justice Statistics Annual Report, Fiscal 1987.* Washington, DC: Government Printing Office, April.

U.S. House of Representatives. 1979. *Select Committee on Assassinations Hearings.* 95th Congress, 2nd Session.

"U.S. Indicts Colombian Drug Cartel." 1989. *Erie Morning News,* May 23, p. 1A.

U.S. Select Committee to Study Government Operations. 1979. Cited in *Crime, Criminal Law and Criminology,* edited by Charles W. Thomas and John R. Hepburn, 1983. pp. 279–80. Dubuque, IA: William C. Brown.

U.S. Senate Permanent Subcommittee on Investigations, Committee on Governmental Affairs. 1980. *Hearings on Organized Crime and the Use of Violence.* 96th Congress, 2d Session, April.

U.S. State Department. 2000. *Human Rights Report, 1999.* Washington, DC: Government Printing Office.

Universal Declaration of Human Rights. 1948. United Nations, General Assembly Official Records, Resolutions, 3, Part 1.

Valachi, Joseph. 1969. Testimony cited in "The Conglomerate of Crime." *Time,* August 22, 17–27.

"Vandals Inspired by Movie 'Home Alone.' " 1991. *Erie Morning News.* September 25, p. 14B.

Van den Berghe, Pierre. 1974. "Bringing Beasts Back In: Toward A Biosocial Theory of Aggression." *American Sociological Review* 39 (December): 777–88.

Van den Haag, Ernest. 1966. "No Excuse for Crime." *Annals of the American Academy of Political and Social Sciences* 423 (January): 133–41.

———. 1975. *Punishing Criminals.* New York: Basic Books.

Van den Haag, Ernest, and Conrad, John P. 1983. *The Death Penalty: A Debate.* New York: Plenum.

Verhovek, Sam H. 1994. "2 Ohioans Arrested in Series of Slayings." *New York Times,* September 7, p. A8.

Vander, Brenda J., and Neff, Ronald J. 1986. *Incest as Child Abuse: Research and Applications.* New York: Praeger.

Van Dijk, Frans, and de Waard, Jaap. 2000. *Legal Infrastructure of the Netherlands in International Perspective: Crime Control.* Amsterdam: Ministry of Justice, the Netherlands.

Van Dijk, Jan J., Mayhew, Pat, and Killias, Martin. 1990. *Experiences of Crime Across the World; Key Findings of the 1989 International Crime Survey.* 2nd edition. Cambridge, MA: Kluwer.

Van Dijk, Jan, and Kangaspunta, Kristina. 2000. "Comparing Crime Across Countries," *National Institute of Justice Journal,* January: 35–41.

Van Voorhis, Patricia, et al. 1988. "The Impact of Family Structure and Quality on Delinquency: A Comparative Assessment of Structural and Functional Factors." *Criminology* 26: 235–61.

Vetter, Harold J., and Silverman, Ira J. 1978. *The Nature of Crime.* Philadelphia, PA: W. B. Saunders.

Vice President's Task Force. 1986. *Report on the Vice President's Task Force on Combatting Terrorism.* Washington, DC: Government Printing Office.

Vigil, James Diego. 1988. *Barrio Gangs: Street Life and Identity in Southern California.* Austin: University of Texas Press.

Vilhelm, Aubert. 1968. "White-Collar Crime and Social Structure." In *White-Collar Criminal: The Offender in Business and the Professions,* edited by Gilbert Geis, pp. 173–84. New York: Atherton.

"Violence in Canadian Society." 1987. *Juristat.* Ottawa, Statistics Canada, vol. 7, June.

Viviano, Frank. 1997. "Hong Kong Triad's New Frontier." *San Francisco Chronicle,* May 28, p. A1.

Vold, George B. 1958. *Theoretical Criminology.* New York: Oxford University Press.

———. 1979. *Theoretical Criminology.* With Thomas J. Bernard, 2nd edition. New York: Oxford University Press.

———. 1986. *Theoretical Criminology.* With Thomas J. Bernard, 3rd edition. New York: Oxford University Press.

Volk, Klaus. 1977. "Criminological Problems of White-Collar Crime." In *International Summaries,* volume 4, pp. 13–21. Rockville, MD: National Criminal Justice Reference Service.

Von Hentig, Hans. 1948. *The Criminal and His Victim.* New Haven: Yale University Press.

Voss, Harwin. 1963. "Ethnic Differentials in Delinquency in Honolulu." *Journal of Criminal Law, Criminology and Police Science* 54 (September): 322–27.

Wade, Andrew L. 1967. "Social Processes in the Act of Juvenile Vandalism." In *Criminal Behavior Systems: A Typology,* edited by Marshall B. Clinard and Richard Quinney, pp. 94–109. New York: Holt, Rinehart and Winston.

Wade, Wyn Craig. 1987. *The Fiery Cross: The Ku Klux Klan in America.* New York: Simon and Schuster.

Waldman, Michael, and Gilbert, Pamela. 1989. "RICO Goes to Congress." *New York Times,* March 12, p. 4E.

Waldman, Steven. 1989. "The Revolving Door." *Newsweek,* February 6, pp. 16–19.

Waldo, Gordon, and Dinitz, Simon. 1967. "Personality Attributes of the Criminal: An Analysis of Research Studies, 1950–1965." *Journal of Research in Crime and Delinquency* 4 (July): 185–201.

Waldorf, Dan, et al. 1988. *Needle Sharing Among Male Prostitutes: Preliminary Findings of the Prospero Project.* Alameda, CA: Institute for Scientific Analysis.

Walker, Douglas. 1992. "The Open Barn Door." *Newsweek,* May 4, pp. 58–60.

Walker, Douglas, et al. 1994. "How Ames Fooled the CIA." *Newsweek,* May 9, pp. 25–26.

Walker, Samuel. 1989. *Sense and Nonsense About Crime: A Policy Guide.* 2nd edition. Monterey, CA: Brooks/Cole.

Walker, Samuel, Spohn, Cassia, and DeLone, Miriam. 1995. *The Color of Justice: Race and Crime in America.* Belmont, CA: Wadsworth.

Wallace, Bill. 1998. "Credit and Counterfeiting on the Rise." *SFGate News,* September 16.

Wallerstein, James S., and Wyle, Clement J. 1947. "Our Law-Abiding Law Breakers." *Probation,* April, pp. 107–18.

Walsh, Marilyn E. 1977. *The Fence.* Westport, CT: Greenwood Press.

Walters, Glenn, D., and White, Thomas W. 1989. "Heredity and Crime: Bad Genes or Bad Research?" *Criminology* 27 (August): 455–86.

Warchol, Greg. 1998. "Workplace Violence 1992–1996." *Bureau of Justice Statistics Special Report,* July, NCJ 168634.

Warner, Barbara D., and Pierce, Glenn L. 1991. "Testing Social Disorganization Theory Using Calls to Police." Paper presented at the American Society of Criminology Meetings, San Francisco, CA, November.

"War without Boundaries." 1977. *Time,* October 31, pp. 28–41.

Warr, Mark, and Stafford, Mark. 1991. "The Influence of Delinquent Peers: What They Think and What They Do?" *Criminology* 29 (November): 851–66.

Warren Commission. 1964. *Report of the President's Commission on the Assassination of President Kennedy.* Washington, DC: Government Printing Office.

Wartzman, Rick. 1992. "Counterfeit Bills Confound Detectors at the Fed, Sleuths at the Secret Service." *Wall Street Journal,* July 2, p. A8.

"Washington vs. GM: Duel over X-Cars." 1983. *U.S. News and World Report,* August 15, p. 9.

Wayne, Leslie. 1999. "Grand Jury Indicts Fugitive Financier on Fraud and Other Charges." *New York Times,* October 8, p. C1.

Weaver, Warren, Jr. 1988. "Justice Department Detects a Gain in Drive on Steroid Abuse." *New York Times,* December 11, p. 2A.

Webb, Eugene J., et al. 1981. *Nonreactive Measures in the Social Sciences.* New York: Houghton Mifflin.

Weber, Max. 1949. *The Methodology of Social Sciences.* Translated by Edward A. Shils and Henry A. Finch. New York: The Free Press.

Webster, Barbara, and McCampbell, Michael S. 1992. "International Money Laundering: Research and Investigation Join Forces." *National Institute of Justice Research in Brief,* September.

Wedel, Janine R. 1999. "Harvard's Complicity in Laundering Billions in Western Aid for Russia." *Erie Times News,* September 14, p. 11A

Weiner, Tim. 1994a. "Blowback: From the Afghan Battlefield." *New York Times Magazine,* March 13, pp. 52–55.

———. 1994b. "Agency Chief Pledges to Overhaul Fraternity Atmosphere at the CIA." *New York Times,* July 19, pp. A1, A10.

Weiner, Tim, Johnston, David, and Lewis, Neil A. 1995. *Betrayal: The Story of Aldrich Ames, an American Spy.* New York: Random House.

Weinstein, Adam K. 1988. "Prosecuting Attorneys for Money Laundering: A New and Questionable Weapon in the War on Crime." *Crime and Contemporary Problems* 51: 369–86.

Weisberg, D. Kelly. 1985. *Children of the Night: A Study of Adolescent Prostitution.* Lexington, MA: Lexington Books.

Weisburg, David, et al. 1990. *Crimes of the Middle Class: White- Collar Offenders in the Federal Courts.* New Haven, CT: Yale University Press.

———. 1991. "Class, Status and Punishment of White-Collar Criminals." *Law and Social Inquiry* 4: 223–43.

Weiser, Benjamin. 1999. "U.S. Charges 8 Inspectors in Kickback Scheme at Bronx Produce Market." *New York Times,* October 28, p. A21.

Wellford, Charles. 1975. "Labelling Theory and Criminology: An Assessment." *Social Problems* 22 (February): 332–45.

Wellford, Harrison. 1972. *Sowing and Wind: A Report from Ralph Nader's Center for Study of Responsive Law.* New York: Grossman.

"Wells Fargo Guard Dopes Boss, Robs Armored Car." 1983. *Erie Morning News,* September 14, p. 5A.

Werthman, Carl. 1967. "The Function of Social Definitions in the Development of Delinquency Career." The President's Commission on Law Enforcement and Administration of Justice. *Task Force Report: Juvenile Delinquency and Youth Crime.* Washington, DC: Government Printing Office.

West, Donald J. 1988. "Homosexuality and Social Policy: The Case for a More Informal Approach." *Law and Contemporary Problems* 51: 181–99.

West, Donald J., and Farrington, David P. 1977. *The Delinquent Way of Life.* London: Heinemann.

West, Nigel. 1982. *The Circus: MI 5 Operations, 1945–1972.* New York: Stein and Day.

Westin, Alan L. 1981. *Whistle-Blowing! Loyalty and Dissent in the Corporation.* New York: McGraw-Hill.

Wheeler, David L. 1995. "Protesters Disrupt Meeting On Possible Genetic Basis of Criminal Behavior." *Chronicle of Higher Education,* October 6, p. 1.

Wheeler, Gerald R., and Hissong, Rodney V. 1988. "Effects of Criminal Sanctions on Drunk Drivers: Beyond Incarceration." *Crime and Delinquency* 34: 29–42.

"When Is an Assault Not an Assault." 1995. *Law Enforcement News,* November 30: 5.

Whitaker, Mark, et al. 1983. "The Forgotten: The Prisoners of Conscience." *Newsweek,* February 14, pp. 40–55.

White, Garland. 1990. "Neighborhood Permeability and Burglary Rates." *Justice Quarterly* 7 (March): 59–67.

White, Jennifer L., et al. 1991. "Preliminary Results from a Study of the Relationship Between Impulsivity and Delinquency." Paper presented at the American Society of Criminology Meetings, San Francisco, CA, November.

"White-Collar Crime: Second Annual Survey of Laws." 1981. *American Criminal Law Review* 19: 173–520.

Whitelaw, Kevin. 1999. "Your Money or Your Life." *U.S. News and World Report,* March 22, pp. 34–41.

Whitman, David. 1987. "The Numbers Game: When More Is Less." *U.S. News and World Report,* April 27, pp. 39–40.

"Why So Few Drunk Drivers Go to Jail." 1983. *U.S. News and World Report.* September 12, p. 14.

Whyte, William F. 1955. *Streetcorner Society.* Chicago: University of Chicago Press.

Widom, Cathy S. 1989. "Child Abuse, Neglect and Violent Criminal Behavior." *Criminology* 27 (May): 251–71.

———. 1992. "The Cycle of Violence." *National Institute of Justice Research in Brief,* October.

Wiggins, Michael E. 1986a. "An Extremist Right-Wing Group and Domestic Terrorism." Paper presented at the Academy of Criminal Justice Sciences meetings. St. Louis, March.

———. 1986b. "The Turner Diaries: Blueprint for Right-Wing Extremist Violence." Paper presented at the Academy of Criminal Justice Sciences meetings, St. Louis, March.

Wilbanks, William. 1987. *The Myth of a Racist Criminal Justice System.* Monterey, CA: Brooks/Cole.

Wilbanks, William, and Kim, K. H. 1984. *Elderly Criminals.* Lanham, MD: University Press of America.

Will, George F. 1991. "Unburied Past." *Erie Morning News,* December 30, p. 5A.

Williams, Frank. 1984. "The Demise of Criminological Imagination: A Critique of Recent Criminology." *Justice Quarterly* 1 (March): 91–106.

Williams, Frank, and McShane, Marilyn. 1988. *Criminological Theory.* Englewood Cliffs, NJ: Prentice-Hall.

———. 1994. *Criminological Theory.* 2nd edition. Englewood Cliffs, NJ: Prentice-Hall.

Williams, Jay, and Gold, Martin. 1972. "From Delinquent Behavior to Official Delinquency." *Social Problems* 20: 209–29.

Williams, Juan. 1991. "Japan: The Price of Safe Streets." *Washington Post,* October 13, pp. C1, C4.

Williams, Marjorie. 1991. "Getting a Grip (or Losing It) on Iran-Contra." *Washington Post National Weekly Edition,* September 30-October 6, pp. 11–12.

Williams, Phil. 1995. "The New Threat: Transnational Criminal Organizations and International Security." *Criminal Organizations,* Summer: 3–19.

———. 1997. "Money Laundering." *Criminal Organizations* 10 (Spring): 18–27.

Wilson, Edward O. 1975. *Sociobiology.* Cambridge, MA: Harvard University Press.

Wilson, James Q. 1975. *Thinking about Crime.* New York: Basic Books.

———, ed. 1983a. *Crime and Public Policy.* San Francisco: Institute for Contemporary Studies.

———. 1983b. *Thinking about Crime.* Revised edition. New York: Basic Books.

Wilson, James Q., and Herrnstein, Richard J. 1985. *Crime and Human Nature.* New York: Simon and Schuster.

Wilson, James Q., and Kelling, George L. 1982. "Broken Windows: The Police and Neighborhood Safety." *The Atlantic,* March, pp. 27–38.

Wilson, James Q., and Lowry, Glenn C., eds. 1987. *From Children to Citizens: Volume III, Families, Schools and Delinquency Prevention.* New York: Springer-Verlag.

Wilson, Robert. 1978. "Chinatown: No Longer a Cozy Assignment." *Police Magazine* 1 (July): 19–29.

Wilson, William J. 1987. *The Truly Disadvantaged: The Inner City, the Underclass, and Public Policy.* Chicago: University of Chicago Press.

Windrem, Robert. 2000. "U.S. Spying Paying Off for Business." MSNBC.com, April 19.

Wines, Michael. 1990. "Ex-C.I.A. Official Says U.S. Ignores Syrian Terror." *New York Times,* December 21, p. A7.

Winick, Charles. 1962. "Prostitutes' Clients Perceptions of Prostitutes and of Themselves." *International Journal of Psychiatry* 8: 289.

Winick, Charles, and Kinsie, Paul M. 1971. *The Lively Commerce: Prostitution in the United States.* Chicago: Quadrangle Books.

Winslow, Robert. 1970. *Society in Transition: A Social Approach to Deviancy.* New York: Free Press.

Wirth, Louis. 1938. "Urbanism as a Way of Life." *American Journal of Sociology* 44 (July): 8–20.

Wise, David. 1995. *How Aldrich Ames Sold the CIA to the KGB for $4.6 Million.* New York: Harper Collins.

Wise, David, and Ross, Thomas B. 1967. *The Espionage Establishment.* New York: Bantam Books.

Witkin, Gordon. 1994. "Should you Own a Gun?" *U.S. News and World Report,* August 15, pp. 24–31.

———. 1995. "When the Bad Guys Are Cops." *U.S. News and World Report,* September 11, pp. 20–22.

———. 1998a. "The Crime Bust: What's Behind the Dramatic Drug Bust?" *U.S. News and World Report,* May 25, pp. 28–37.

———. 1998b. "Making War on Handguns." *U.S. News and World Report,* November 23, p. 28.

Witkin, Gordon, Friedman, Dorian, and Guttman, Monika. 1992. "Health Care Fraud." *U.S. News and World Report,* February 24, pp. 34–43.

Witkin, Herman A., et al. 1976. "XYY and Criminality." *Science* 193 (August 13): 547–55.

Witt, Howard. 1988. "CIA Sued for Attempts at Brainwashing." *Erie Daily Times,* October 3, p. 2A.

Wolf, George. 1975. *Frank Costello: Prime Minister of the Underworld.* New York: Bantam Books.

Wolf, J. B. 1981. "Enforcement Terrorism." *Police Studies* 3: 45–54.

Wolfgang, Marvin E. 1958. *Patterns in Criminal Homicide.* Philadelphia: University of Pennsylvania Press.

———. 1960. "Cesare Lombroso." In *Pioneers in Criminology,* edited by Hermann Mannheim, pp. 168–227. Chicago: Quadrangle Books.

———. 1963. "Criminology and Criminologists." *Journal of Criminal Law, Criminology and Police Science* 54 (June): 155–162.

———. 1980a. "Crime and Punishment." *New York Times,* March 2, p. E21.

———. 1980b. "On an Evaluation of Criminology." In *Handbook in Criminal Justice Evaluation,* edited by Malcolm W. Klein and Katherine S. Teilman, pp. 19–52. Beverly Hills, CA: Sage.

———. 1987. *From Boy to Man, From Delinquency to Crime.* Chicago: University of Chicago Press.

Wolfgang, Marvin E., and Ferracuti, Franco. 1967. *The Subculture of Violence: Towards an Integrated Theory in Criminology.* London: Tavistock Publications.

Wolfgang, Marvin E., Figlio, Robert M., and Sellin, Thorsten. 1978. *Delinquency in a Birth Cohort.* Chicago: University of Chicago Press.

Wolfgang, Marvin E., Figlio, Robert M., and Thornberry, Terence B. 1978. *Evaluating Criminology.* New York: Elsevier.

Wood, Arthur L. 1967. *Criminal Lawyer.* New Haven, CT: College and University Press.

Wooden, Wayne S. 1989. "Profile of Stoner Gang Members in the California Youth Authority." Paper presented at the American Society of Criminology Meetings, Reno, NV, November.

Wright, James D., and Rossi, Peter H. 1986. *Armed and Considered Dangerous: A Survey of Felons and Their Firearms.* Hawthorne, NY: Aldine.

Wright, Kevin N. 1985. *The Great American Crime Myth.* Westport, CT: Greenwood Press.

Wright, Kevin, and Wright, Karen E. 1995. *Family Life, Delinquency, and Crime: A Policymaker's Guide: Research Summary.* Washington, DC: Office of Juvenile Justice and Delinquency Prevention, August.

Wright, Richard T., and Decker, Scott H. 1994. *Burglars on the Job: Streetlife and Residential Break-ins.* Boston: Northeastern University Press.

———. 1996. *Burglars on the Job.* Boston: Northeastern University Press.

———. 1997. *Armed Robbers in Action: Stickups and Street Culture.* Boston: Northeastern University Press.

WuDunn, Sheryl. 1996. "Uproar Over a Debt Crisis." *New York Times,* February 14, p. C1.

Wunderlich, Ray. 1978. "Neuroallergy as a Contributing Factor to Social Misfits." In *Ecologic-Biochemical Approaches to Treatment of Delinquents and Criminals,* edited by Leonard Hippchen, pp. 229–53. New York: Van Nostrand Reinhold.

Yablonsky, Lewis. 1962. *The Violent Gang.* Baltimore, MD: Penguin Press.

———. 1965a. "Experiences with the Criminal Community." In *Applied Criminology,* edited by Alvin Gouldner and S. M. Miller. New York: The Free Press.

———. 1965b. *Synanon: The Tunnel Back.* Baltimore, MD: Penguin.

Yin, Tung. 1992. "Sears Is Accused of Billing Fraud at Auto Centers." *Wall Street Journal,* June 12, p. B1.

Yochelson, Samuel, and Samenow, Stanton E. 1976. *The Criminal Personality,* volumes 1 and 2. New York: Jason Aronson.

Young, Vernetta, and Sulton, Anne T. 1991. "Excluded: The Current Status of African-American Scholars in the Field of Criminology and Criminal Justice." *Journal of Research in Crime and Delinquency* 28(1): 101–116.

Zalba, Serapio R. 1971. "Battered Children." *Transaction* 8 (July): 58–61.

Zatz, Marjorie. 1987. "The Changing Forms of Racial/Ethnic Biases in Sentencing." *Journal of Research in Crime and Delinquency* 24: 69–92.

Zeisel, Hans. 1957. *Say It with Figures.* 4th edition. New York: Harper.

Zeitz, Dorothy. 1991. *Women Who Embezzle orx Defraud: A Study of Convicted Felons.* New York: Praeger.

Zimring, Frank E. 1987. "Gun Control." *Crime File* (National Institute of Justice).

Zimring, Franklin, and Hawkins, Gordon. 1973. *Deterrence: The Legal Threat to Crime Control.* Chicago: University of Chicago Press.

Name Index

Subject Index